THE
ECONOMISTS'
VOICE

THE ECONOMISTS' VOICE

TOP ECONOMISTS
TAKE ON
TODAY'S PROBLEMS

Joseph E. Stiglitz
Aaron S. Edlin
J. Bradford DeLong

EDITORS

Columbia University Press
New York

Columbia University Press
Publishers Since 1893
New York   Chichester, West Sussex
Copyright © 2008 Columbia University Press

A Caravan book. For more information,
visit www.caravanbooks.org

Library of Congress Cataloging-in-Publication Data
The Economists' voice : top economists take on today's problems / Joseph E.
Stiglitz, Aaron S. Edlin, and J. Bradford DeLong, editors.
      p. cm.
  Includes bibliographical references and index.
  ISBN 978-0-231-14364-6 (cloth : alk. paper)
    1. United States—Economic conditions—21st century.   2. United States—
Economic policy—21st century.   3. United States—Social conditions—21st
century.   4. United States—Social policy—21st century.   5. Environmental
policy—United States—History—21st century.   I. Stiglitz, Joseph E.
II. Edlin, Aaron S.   III. De Long, J. Bradford.   IV. Title: Economists take
on today's problems.

HC106.83.E26 2007
330.9'0511—dc22

                                                                    2007034372

Columbia University Press books are printed on permanent
and durable acid-free paper.

This book is printed on paper with recycled content.

Printed in the United States of America

c 10 9 8 7 6 5 4 3 2 1

References to Internet Web sites (URLs) were accurate at the time of writing.
Neither author nor Columbia University Press is responsible for URLs
that may have expired or changed since the manuscript was prepared.

Contents

THE
ECONOMISTS'
VOICE

PART I

GLOBAL WARMING

THE SUBJECT OF global warming makes people hot under the collar. Is it happening? Almost surely, according to the scientific consensus. Is it man made? Again, almost surely. Yet people who don't argue about other scientific consensuses do argue about this one.

Even whether to call it "global warming" or "global climate change" generates agitated debate. Some people say "global climate change" is more accurate because some regions will cool and others warm. Others argue that such a neutral term is less likely to generate action and that "warming" is more apt because on average, the climate is expected to warm.

The essays here ask whether action is merited, what action is merited, and how nations can credibly commit to act.

Nobel Laureate Thomas Schelling distinguishes what is certain from what is uncertain and argues that the uncertainties do not justify inaction and the certainties justify urgent action to develop technologies to combat and limit warming.

Nobel Laureate Kenneth Arrow takes a critical look at the recent Stern report and the question of whether the benefits of serious action justify the costs. Many have criticized the Stern report because it doesn't discount the future benefits of acting *now* to limit global warming *later*. In this essay, however, Arrow argues that the call to action in the Stern report does not depend on that controversial assumption. Unless one unreasonably discounts the future, it makes sense to act.

Saying that the world must act is easier of course than getting it to happen. How can the free rider problem be overcome and nations be made to undertake costly action today for the sake of future generations in other nations tomorrow?

In the next essay, another Nobel Laureate, one of the editors of this volume and the journal *The Economists' Voice,* suggests that the way to get nations, and particularly the United States, to reduce CO_2 emissions significantly is to use trade sanctions. Joseph Stiglitz argues that the United States, and implicitly other nations who are doing little to curb emissions, are unfairly subsidizing their exports by not forcing manufacturers to pay the full cost of emissions. To avoid trade sanctions, nations should tax carbon emissions to reflect the long-term social cost of emissions. If trade sanctions could be used this way, one nation might force another to tax its emissions, not necessarily because it cares about the environment, but for the myriad reasons that a nation seeks to raise the cost of other nations' exports.

In the final essay, Sheila Olmstead of Yale and Robert Stavins of Harvard provide a detailed blueprint of what they think is a sensible and possible way forward. They propose in the second commitment period for Kyoto to expand participation to include all key countries. Step two is to use an extended time path for reductions so that the largest reductions occur after the current capital stock is exhausted and lower emissions technologies emerge. The key is to credibly commit today to future reductions so that these technologies do, in fact, emerge.

CHAPTER 1

Climate Change: The Uncertainties, the Certainties, and What They Imply About Action

Thomas C. Schelling

FIRST THE UNCERTAINTIES; then the certainties; then the urgencies; and finally, what do uncertainties imply about waiting for their resolution before acting?

The uncertainties are many and great. How much carbon dioxide may join the atmosphere if nothing is done about it? That depends on projections of population, economic growth, energy technology, and possible feedbacks from warming that reduce albedo—ice and snow cover, for example.

Next, how much average warming globally is to be expected from some specified increase in the concentration of carbon dioxide

Winner of the 2005 Nobel Prize in Economics, Thomas C. Schelling has published widely on military strategy and arms control, energy and environmental policy, climate change, nuclear proliferation, terrorism, organized crime, foreign aid and international trade, conflict and bargaining theory, racial segregation and integration, the military draft, health policy, tobacco and drugs policy, and ethical issues in public policy and in business.

and other "greenhouse" gases? For a quarter century the range of uncertainty has been about a factor of three. (As more becomes known, more uncertainties emerge. Clouds and oceans are active participants in ways unappreciated two decades ago.)

How will the average warming translate into changing climates everywhere: precipitation, evaporation, sunlight and cloud cover, temperature and humidity (daytime/nighttime, summer/winter) over oceans and plains and mountains, and the frequency and severity of storms and of protracted droughts? Will rain replace snow in mountains and the melting of snow cover occur before irrigation can benefit?

What will be the impacts of such changes in climate on productivity, especially in agriculture, fisheries, and forests, and on comfort and health? Both the vectors and the pathogens of disease, especially in the tropics, will be affected, almost certainly for the worst. (Here productivity enters again: will malaria, river blindness, etc., have been overcome by advances in public health technology?) What will happen to ecological systems, to vulnerable species?

How well can people, businesses, governments, and communities adapt to the climate changes, especially in countries heavily dependent on food production, in countries with poor educational and technological attainment, poor fiscal or legal systems?

And of course, what are the likely costs of various mitigation strategies, mainly shifting to renewable energy sources and conserving energy with technologies mostly not yet ready?

Finally, what will the world be like in fifty, seventy-five, or a hundred years when climate change may become acute? Think back seventy-five years: what was the world like compared with now? Will the world be as different from now in seventy-five years as it is now from seventy-five years ago? How would we, seventy-five years ago, have predicted the consequences of climate change in today's world, and who are "we" who might have predicted those consequences?

The uncertainties are immense, and I'll draw some conclusions shortly. But what are the certainties?

It has been known for a century that the planet Venus is so bathed in "greenhouse gases" that its surface temperature, hundreds of degrees above Earth's, does not allow water to exist in liquid form, and that Mars is so deficient in greenhouse gases that its temperature is too cold to allow water to exist in liquid form on its surface. Earth has been blessed with such a concentration of gases in the atmosphere that it has a climate consistent with liquid water and terrestrial life.

It has been known for a century that if a glassed chamber of carbon dioxide is subjected to infrared radiation—the radiation by which Earth's heat, perpetually renewed by sunlight, is returned to space to keep our temperature even—the energy output is less than the energy input in direct proportion to the rise in temperature of the gas in the chamber. The greenhouse "theory," as it is sometimes disparagingly referred to, is established beyond responsible doubt.

So the basics of global warming are not in scientific dispute. There is serious uncertainty about the quantitative parameters, and there can be doubt whether the experienced warming of recent decades is entirely due to the "greenhouse effect," there being other conjectured possible solar influences. But the "theory" is not in doubt. (Incidentally, actual greenhouses don't work by the "greenhouse effect," but it is too late to change the terminology.)

If we know that Earth is ineluctably warming, with possible drastic effects on climates around the world, but not how fast or how far, what are the most urgent things to do about it? One, of course, is to keep studying the phenomena; huge advances in understanding the climate phenomena and their ecological impact are occurring. It is a happy coincidence that concern for climate-affected greenhouse gases arose just as Earth-reconnaissance satellites became available to study glaciers, forests, sea level, atmospheric and ocean temperatures, snow and ice albedo, sunlight-reflecting aerosols of sulfur, cloud reflectance, and all manner of things we need to understand.

Under "urgencies," I put energy research and development, especially government-sponsored research and development (R&D) and, most important, multi-government R&D. We need, urgently, better to understand what alternatives to fossil fuels there will be, how much energy can be conserved, how to extract carbon dioxide from the atmosphere, and if necessary how to increase Earth's albedo, its reflectance of incoming sunlight.

There are two important ways to induce or provide the necessary research and development. One is to use the price system, the "market," letting private initiative finance and direct the work, through appropriate taxes, subsidies, rationing, and—most important—through convincing the private sector, firms and consumers, that fossil fuels are going to become progressively and, probably, drastically more costly as the decades go by.

The other is for R&D to be financed and directed, cooperatively with business, by governments. Some essential R&D will not be undertaken by private interests; the "market" will not induce the necessary outlays; the benefits cannot be "captured" by the investors. Examples are multitudinous, but one or two may suffice.

It has long been understood that carbon dioxide produced in large stationary plants such as electric-power stations can be "captured" and piped to where it can be injected into underground caverns (or possibly ocean beds). In fact, carbon dioxide from such sources has been used for decades to stimulate the flow of oil from exhausting oil wells. Twenty-five years ago it was estimated that capturing the CO_2 output from power plants and injecting it underground would double the cost of electricity; it now appears that costs may be more modest. There are experiments underway, only a few, that should help to determine what technologies may prove most economical, not necessarily a single technology but alternatives for different regions.

If it proves economical to "capture" and "sequester" carbon dioxide from stationary plants, and if adequate underground repositories

can be found all over the world, a huge reduction of emissions into the atmosphere may make less drastic the need to curtail the use of coal. China, with huge coal deposits it plans to exploit, could greatly reduce its carbon emissions by using this technology.

But the research and development that will be required, not only in the technology of capture, transport, injection, and sealing but also in geologic exploration all over the world for sites suitable for permanent storage, will be beyond the purview of any private interest. This is one example of R&D that depends on government involvement, preferably multinational.

Another area of research that deserves attention, which will not receive it from the private sector, goes currently under the name of "geoengineering." (The subject requires an article of its own, but a few words can be offered here.) Some of the sunlight reaching Earth is absorbed by the ocean, the forests, the plains, the urban areas; some is reflected away. Forests absorb more than plains and deserts; Arctic ice reflects more away than bare oceans. Some is reflected away by aerosols, particles in the atmosphere that often form the basis for droplets that are reflective.

It has long been known that some volcanic eruptions, namely those that produce lots of sulfur, can cool Earth significantly. Pinatubo, in the Philippines in the 1990s, had a noticeable effect. It is estimated that sulfur currently in the atmosphere, mainly from combustion of coal and oil, may be masking a significant part of the expected greenhouse effect—perhaps a significant fraction of a degree. The question arises naturally, could some of the greenhouse effect, or all of it, be offset by putting something in the stratosphere that could reflect incoming energy?

It has been estimated that to offset a doubling of the concentration of greenhouse gases would require reflecting away something like 1½–2 percent of incoming sunlight. (Not all the adverse effects of CO_2 would be offset: ocean acidity would be affected by continuing injections of CO_2.) Sulfur is not an attractive substance; when it

comes down it is not healthful for people or fish. But the amount of sulfur that might be required, in annual injection into the stratosphere, is quite small because it stays up there longer compared with what is already being put into the lower atmosphere. It would make sense to do small, reversible, experiments to ascertain what substances might, with what lifting technology, be put at what altitude, and to include the results in the global climate models to ascertain where—what latitudes and longitudes—would be most effective and most benign. Needless to say, this is not a task for the private sector, and some international sponsorship might be appropriate.

Now the critical question: what does uncertainty have to do with the question whether to proceed with costly efforts to reduce CO_2 abatement in a hurry or wait until we know more?

In some public discourse, and in sentiments emanating from the Bush administration, it appears to be accepted that uncertainty regarding global warming is a legitimate basis for postponement of any action until more is known. The action to be postponed is usually identified as "costly." (Little attention is paid to actions that have been identified as of little or no serious cost.) It is interesting that this idea that costly actions are unwarranted if the dangers are uncertain is almost unique to climate. In other areas of policy, such as terrorism, nuclear proliferation, inflation, or vaccination, some "insurance" principle seems to prevail: if there is a sufficient likelihood of sufficient damage we take some measured anticipatory action.

At the opposite extreme is the notion, often called the "precautionary principle" now popular in the European Union, that until something is guaranteed safe it must be indefinitely postponed despite substantial expected benefits. Genetically modified foods and feedstuffs are current targets. (One critic has expressed it as, "never do anything for the first time.") In this country the principle says that until a drug has proven absolutely safe, it must be deferred indefinitely.

Neither of the two extreme principles—doing nothing until we are absolutely sure it's safe; doing nothing until we are absolutely

sure the alternative is dangerous—makes economic sense, or any other kind of sense. Weigh the costs, the benefits, and the probabilities as best all three are known, and don't be obsessed with either extreme tail of the distribution.

There are a few actions that the uncertainties make infeasible for now, and probably for a long time, and thus not worth attempting. Deciding now, through some multinational diplomatic process, what the ultimate ceiling on greenhouse gas concentrations must be to prevent, in the immortal words of the Framework Agreement, "dangerous anthropogenic interference with the climate system," as a basis for allotting quotas to participating nations, is in contradiction to the acknowledged uncertainty about the "climate sensitivity" parameter, with its factor of three in the range of uncertainty. Individual commentators have strong opinions, often quite low, but any nation's representatives can adduce substantial evidence in favor of twice that level.

The most terrifying possible consequence of global warming that has been identified is the possible "collapse" of the West Antarctic Ice Sheet. This is a body of ice that rests on the bottom of the sea and protrudes a kilometer or two above sea level. It is not floating ice; floating ice, when it melts, does nothing to sea level. This ice sheet is essentially an iceberg that has grown so large it rests on the bottom: there is enough of it above sea level that, if it glaciated into the ocean, it could raise sea level by something like twenty feet.

That would truly be a disaster. We might save Manhattan (expensively!) with dikes, as the Dutch have done for centuries, or Los Angeles or Copenhagen or Stockholm, or Boston or Baltimore. But dikes can't save Bangladesh: not only is there too much coastline, but also dikes would produce freshwater floods. (Rivers cannot rise up over a dike to reach the sea.) And tens of millions of Bangladeshi would have to migrate or die.

Estimates of the likelihood of collapse, or the likely time of collapse, of the West Antarctic Ice Sheet have varied for three decades.

Recent studies of the effect of ocean temperature on the movement of ground-based ice sheets are not reassuring. It has occasionally been proposed that the collapse might become irreversible before the world has taken action to mitigate warming. In my reading—this is not my profession; I just try to keep up with the latest research—the likelihood of collapse in this century is small. But it is uncertain!

How should we respond to that kind of uncertainty? Wait until the uncertainty has been resolved completely before we do anything, or act as if it's certain until we have assurance that there's no such danger?

Those two extremes are not the only alternatives!

CHAPTER 2

Global Climate Change:
A Challenge to Policy

Kenneth J. Arrow

LAST FALL, THE United Kingdom issued a major government report on global climate change directed by Sir Nicholas Stern, a top-flight economist. The Stern report amounts to a call to action: it argues that huge future costs of global warming can be avoided by incurring relatively modest costs today.

Critics of the Stern report don't think serious action to limit carbon dioxide (CO_2) emissions is justified because there remains substantial uncertainty about the extent of the costs of global climate change and because these costs will be incurred far in the future. They think that Stern improperly fails to discount for either uncertainty or futurity.

I agree that both futurity and uncertainty require significant discounting. However, even with that, I believe the fundamental

Kenneth J. Arrow won the Nobel Memorial Prize in Economics in 1972. He is the professor of economics emeritus and professor of management science and engineering emeritus at Stanford University. He thanks the Hewlett Foundation for research support.

conclusion of Stern is justified: we are much better to act to reduce CO_2 emissions substantially than to suffer and risk the consequences of failing to meet this challenge. As I explain here, this conclusion holds true even if, unlike Stern, one heavily discounts the future.

A PERSONAL INTRODUCTION TO GLOBAL WARMING

I first heard of the effect of industrialization on global temperatures long before the present concerns became significant: in the fall of 1942, to be precise. I was being trained as a weather officer. One course, called "dynamic meteorology," taught by Dr. Hans Panofsky at New York University, dealt with the basic physics of weather systems (pressure variations, the laws determining the strength of winds, the causes and effects of precipitation, and similar matters). One of the first things to understand was what determines the general level of temperature. The source of terrestrial temperature is of course solar radiation. But heating of the earth from the sun's rays causes the earth to emit radiation at frequencies appropriate to its temperature, that is, in the infrared low-frequency portion of the electromagnetic spectrum. Since the earth radiates into empty space, where the temperature approximates absolute zero, it would appear that in equilibrium the earth should come to that temperature also, as is indeed the case with the moon.

What makes the difference is the earth's atmosphere. The vast bulk of the atmosphere is made up of nitrogen and oxygen, transparent to both the visible radiation coming from the sun and the infrared radiation emitted by the earth and hence without effect on the equilibrium temperature. However, the atmosphere also contains, we learned, a considerable variety of other gases in small quantities. These "trace gases" include most notably water vapor, carbon dioxide, and methane, though there are many others. These trace gases have the property of being transparent to radiation in the visible part of the spectrum but absorbent at lower frequencies, such as infrared. Hence, the effect of these gases is to retain the outgoing radiation and so raise the temperature of the earth to the point in which life can flourish. The effect is strictly parallel to the use of glass in greenhouses, also transparent to visible radiation but not to infrared; hence, the widespread term, "greenhouse effect."

Where do these trace gases come from? The water vapor comes from the passage of air over the large expanses of water in the earth's surface, particularly when the water is warmer than the air. The carbon dioxide and methane come from some nonbiological sources, such as volcanic eruptions, but also from the respiration of animals and from organic wastes. (Vegetation, on the contrary, absorbs CO_2.)

Our instructor then added one more observation. CO_2 is a by-product of combustion. There are fires due to volcanoes and lightning, and mankind has lit fires for 500,000 years, but the pace of combustion has vastly increased since the Industrial Revolution. So, concluded Dr. Panofsky, we can expect the world temperature to rise steadily as CO_2 continues to accumulate and at an increasing rate with the growth of industry. This was not presented as a jeremiad or as controversial. Indeed, we were clearly being told this to vivify the quite arid set of facts we had to learn rather than to move us to action.

As any economist accustomed to general equilibrium theory might guess, the implications of a given increase in greenhouse gases for the weather are mediated through a very complex interactive system with both positive and negative feedbacks. Elaborate climate models have been developed, each admittedly falling short of catching some significant aspect. (Economists will understand.) Nevertheless, serious studies have lead to a considerable consensus, although with a wide range of uncertainty. I draw upon the most recent report, prepared by a team directed by Sir Nicholas Stern for the United Kingdom prime minister and chancellor of the exchequer

(Stern 2006). The mean levels of different magnitudes in this report are comparable to those in earlier work, but the Stern report is more explicit about ranges of uncertainty.

The current level of CO_2 (plus other greenhouse gases, in CO_2 equivalents) is today about 430 parts per million (ppm), compared with 280 ppm before the Industrial Revolution. With the present and growing rate of emissions, the level could reach 550 ppm by 2035. This is almost twice the preindustrial level and a level that has not been reached for several million years.

POTENTIAL CLIMATE CHANGE AND ITS IMPACTS

Most climate change models predict that a concentration of 550 ppm would be associated with a rise in temperature of at least two degrees Centigrade. A continuation of "business-as-usual" trends will likely lead to a trebling of CO_2 by the end of the century, with a 50 percent chance of exceeding a rise of five degrees Centigrade, about the same as the increase from the last ice age to the present.

The full consequences of such rises are not well known. Some of the direct effects are obvious: implications for agriculture (not all bad; productivity in Canada and northern Russia will rise, but negative effects predominate where moisture is the limiting factor and especially in the heavily populated tropical regions) and a rise in sea level, which will wipe out the small island countries (e.g., the Maldives or Tonga) and encroach considerably on all countries. Bangladesh will lose much of its land area; Manhattan could be under water. This rise might be catastrophic rather than gradual if the Greenland and West Antarctic ice sheets melt and collapse. In addition, temperature changes can change the nature of the world's weather system. A reversing of the Gulf Stream, which could cause climate in Europe to resemble that of Greenland, is a distinct possibility. There is good reason to believe that tropical storms will become more severe, since the energy that fuels them comes from the rising temperature of the oceans. Glaciers will disappear, indeed have been disappearing, rapidly, and with them, valuable water supplies.

ARE THE BENEFITS FROM REDUCING CLIMATE CHANGE WORTH THE COSTS?

The available policies essentially are ways of preventing the greenhouse gases from entering the atmosphere or at least reducing their magnitude. Today the source of 65 percent of the gases is the use of energy; the remainder arises from waste, agriculture, and land use. A number of behavioral changes would mitigate this problem: (1) shifting to fuels that have higher ratio of useful energy to CO_2 emissions (e.g., from coal to oil or oil to natural gas); (2) developing technologies that use less energy per unit output; (3) shifting demand to products with lower energy intensity; (4) planting trees and reducing deforestation, since trees absorb CO_2; and (5) pursuing an unproven but apparently feasible policy of sequestering the CO_2 by pumping it directly into underground reservoirs. We can go further and simply restrict output.

Two factors deserve emphasis, factors that differentiate global climate change from other environmental problems. First, emissions of CO_2 and other trace gases are almost irreversible; more precisely, their residence time in the atmosphere is measured in centuries. Most environmental insults are mitigated promptly or in fairly short order when the source is cleaned up, as with water pollution, acid rain, or sulfur dioxide emissions. Here, reducing emissions today is very valuable to humanity in the distant future. Second, the scale of the externality is truly global; greenhouse gases travel around the world in a few days. This means that the nation-state and its subsidiaries, the typical loci for internalization of externalities, are limited in their remedial ability. (To be sure, there are other transboundary environmental externalities, as with water pollution in the Rhine Valley or acid rain, but none is nearly so far-flung as climate change.) However, because the United States contributes about 25 percent of the world's CO_2 emissions, its own policy could make a large difference.

Thus, global climate change is a public good (bad) par excellence. Benefit-cost analysis is a principal tool for deciding whether altering this public good through mitigation policy is warranted. Economic analysis can also help identify the most efficient policy instruments for mitigation, but I leave that to other essays in this issue.

Two aspects of the benefit-cost calculation are critical. One is allowance for uncertainty (and related behavioral effects reflecting risk aversion). To explain economic choices such as insurance or the holding of inventories, it has to be assumed that individuals prefer to avoid risk. That is, an uncertain outcome is worth less than the average of the outcomes. As has already been indicated, the possible outcomes of global warming in the absence of mitigation are very uncertain, though surely they are bad. The uncertain losses should be evaluated as being equivalent to a single loss that is greater than the expected loss.

The other critical aspect is how one treats future outcomes relative to current ones. The issue of futurity has aroused much attention among philosophers as well as economists. At what rate should future impacts—in particular, losses of future consumption—be discounted to the present? The consumption discount rate, δ, can be expressed by the following simple formula:

$$\delta = \rho + g\eta$$

where ρ is the social rate of time preference, g is the projected growth rate of average consumption, and η is the elasticity of the social weight attributed to a change in consumption.

The parameter η in the second term accounts for the possibility that, as consumption grows, the marginal unit of consumption may be considered as having less social value. It is analogous to the idea of diminishing marginal private utility of private consumption. This component of the consumption rate of discount is relatively uncontroversial, although researchers disagree on its magnitude. The appropriate value to assign to η is disputed, but a value of 2 or 3 seems reasonable (the Stern report uses 1, but this level does not seem compatible with other evidence).

Greater disagreement surrounds the appropriate value for ρ, the social rate of time preference. This parameter allows for discounting the future simply because it is the future, even if future generations were to be no better off than we are. The Stern report follows a considerable tradition among British economists and many philosophers against discounting for pure futurity. Most economists take pure time preference as obvious. Tjalling Koopmans pointed out in effect that the savings rates implied by zero time preference are very much higher than those we observe. (I am myself convinced by this argument.)

Many have complained about the Stern report adopting a value of zero for ρ, the social rate of time preference. However, I find that the case for intervention to keep CO_2 levels within bounds (say, aiming to stabilize them at about 550 ppm) is sufficiently strong as to be insensitive to the arguments about ρ. To establish this point, I draw on some numbers from the Stern report concerning future benefits from keeping greenhouse gas concentrations from exceeding 550 ppm, as well as the costs of accomplishing this.

The benefits from mitigation of greenhouse gases are the avoided damages. The report provides a comprehensive view of these damages, including both market damages as well as nonmarket damages that account for health impacts and various ecological impacts. The damages are presented in several scenarios, but I consider the so-called high-climate scenario to be the best-based. Figure 6-5c of the report shows the increasing damages of climate change on a business-as-usual policy. By the year 2200, the losses in gross national product

(GNP) have an expected value of 13.8 percent of what GNP would be otherwise, with a .05 percentile of about 3 percent and a .95 percentile of about 34 percent. With this degree of uncertainty, the loss should be equivalent to a certain loss of about 20 percent. The base rate of growth of the economy (before calculating the climate change effect) was taken to be 1.3 percent per year; a loss of 20 percent in the year 2200 amounts to reducing the growth rate to 1.2 percent per year. In other words, the benefit from mitigating greenhouse gas emissions can be represented as the increase in the growth rate from today to 2200 from 1.2 percent per year to 1.3 percent per year.

We have to compare this benefit with the cost of stabilization. Estimates given in table 10.1 of the Stern report range from 3.4 percent down to 3.9 percent of GNP. (Since energy saving reduces energy costs, this last estimate is not as startling as it sounds.) Let me assume then that costs to prevent additional accumulation of CO_2 (and equivalents) come to 1 percent of GNP every year forever.

Finally, I assume, in accordance with a fair amount of empirical evidence, that η, the component of the discount rate attributable to the declining marginal utility of consumption, is equal to 2. I then examine whether the present value of benefits (from the increase in the GDP growth rate from 1.2 percent to 1.3 percent) exceeds the present value of the costs (from the 1 percent permanent reduction in the level of the GDP time profile). A straightforward calculation shows that mitigation is better than business as usual—that is, the present value of the benefits exceeds the present value of the costs—for any social rate of time preference (ρ) less than 8.5 percent. No estimate for the pure rate of time preference, even by those who believe in relatively strong discounting of the future, has ever approached 8.5 percent.

These calculations indicate that, even with higher discounting, the Stern report's estimates of future benefits and costs imply that current mitigation passes a benefit-cost test. Note that these calculations rely on the Stern report's projected time profiles for benefits and its estimate of annual costs. Much disagreement surrounds these estimates, and further sensitivity analysis is called for. Still, I believe there can be little serious argument over the importance of a policy of avoiding major further increases in combustion by-products.

REFERENCES AND FURTHER READING

Stern, Nicholas. 2006. *The Economics of Climate Change.* http://www.hm-treasury.gov.uk/Independent_Reviews/stern_review_economics_climate_change/sternreview_index.cfm.

CHAPTER 3

A New Agenda for Global Warming

Joseph E. Stiglitz

GLOBALIZATION HAS MADE the world increasingly interdependent and has increased the need to work together to solve common problems. But as I point out in my recent book, *Making Globalization Work,* it will do us little good to solve our common global economic problems if we do not do something about the most pressing common environmental problem: global warming.

In Kyoto, nine years ago, the world took an important first step to curtail the greenhouse gas emissions that cause global warming. But in spite of Kyoto's achievements, the United States, the world's largest polluter (contributor to greenhouse gas emissions), refuses to join in and continues to pollute more and more, while the developing countries, which in the not-too-distant future will be contributing 50 percent or more of global emissions, have been left without firm

Joseph E. Stiglitz is the editor of *The Economists' Voice* and University Professor at Columbia University. He served on the 1995 IPCC Assessment Panel, chaired President Clinton's Council of Economic Advisers and was chief economist of the World Bank. He won the Nobel Memorial Prize in Economics in 2001. He is the author of the global best seller, *Globalization and Its Discontents.* His latest book, *Making Globalization Work,* was published by W.W. Norton.

commitments to do anything. It is now clear that something else is needed. I propose here an agenda to deal first with the United States' pollution and second with that of developing countries.

REDUCING UNITED STATES' EMISSIONS

The first step is to create an enforcement mechanism to prevent the United States, or any country that refuses to agree to or to implement emission reductions, from inflicting harm on the rest of the world. It was, perhaps, predictable that the United States, the largest polluter, would refuse to recognize the existence of the problem. If the United States could go its own merry way—keeping the carbon dioxide it emits over its own territory, warming up its own atmosphere, bearing itself whatever costs (including hurricanes) that result, that would be one thing. But that is not so. The energy-profligate lifestyle of the United States inflicts global damage immensely greater than any war it might wage. Under current projections, unless drastic measures are taken, the Maldives will within fifty or seventy five years be our own twenty-first-century Atlantis, disappearing beneath the ocean; a third of Bangladesh will be submerged, and with that country's poor people crowded closer together, incomes already close to subsistence level will be even further depressed.

At first, President George W. Bush effectively denied global warming. Then when his own National Academy confirmed what every other scientific body had said, he promised to do something—but did little. Some American politicians whine that emissions reduction will compromise America's living standards, but America's emissions per dollar of gross domestic product are twice that of Japan. America not only can afford to conserve more, it also would enhance its energy security by doing so. It would be good for its environment and for its economy—though not, perhaps, for the oil companies that have prospered so well under the current administration.

Fortunately, we have an international trade framework that can be used to force states that inflict harm on others to behave better. Except in certain limited situations (like agriculture), the World Trade Organization (WTO) does not allow subsidies—obviously, if some country subsidizes its firms, there is not a level playing field. A subsidy means that a firm does not pay the full costs of production. Not paying the cost of damage to the environment is a subsidy, just as not paying the full costs of workers is. In most of the developed countries of the world today, firms are paying the cost of pollution to the global environment in the form of taxes imposed on coal, oil, and gas. But American firms are being subsidized—and massively so.

There is a simple remedy: other countries should prohibit the importation of American goods produced using energy-intensive technologies or, at the very least, impose a high tax on them to offset the subsidy that those goods currently are receiving. Actually, the United States itself has recognized this principle. It prohibited the importation of Thai shrimp that had been caught in "turtle unfriendly" nets—nets that caused the unnecessary death of large numbers of these endangered species. Though the manner in which the United States had imposed the restriction was criticized, the WTO sustained the important principle that global environmental concerns trump narrow commercial interests, as well they should. But if one can justify restricting importation of shrimp in order to protect turtles, certainly one can justify restricting importation of goods produced by technologies that unnecessarily pollute the precious global atmosphere upon which we all depend for our very well-being in order to protect it.

Japan, Europe, and the other signatories of Kyoto should immediately bring a WTO case against the United States charging unfair subsidization. Of course, the Bush administration and the oil companies to which it is beholden will be upset. They may even suggest that this is the beginning of a global trade war. It is not. It is simply pointing out the obvious: American firms have long had an unfair trade advantage because of their cheap energy, but while they get the benefit, the world is paying the price through global warming. This situation is, or at least should be, totally unacceptable. Energy tariffs would simply restore balance—and at the same time provide strong incentives for the United States to do what it should have been doing all along.

In some ways, the United States should welcome this initiative. It has often complained that one of the problems with the Kyoto Protocol is the lack of an enforcement mechanism. It claims that if it were to sign, it would feel obliged to meet its commitments while other countries would not, and this would put the United States in a disadvantageous position. With a strong international sanction mechanism in place, all could rest assured that there was, at last, a level playing field.

GETTING THE DEVELOPING WORLD TO ADDRESS THE PROBLEM

There is a second problem with Kyoto: how to bring the developing countries within the fold. The Kyoto Protocol is based on national emission reductions relative to each nation's level in 1990. The developing countries ask, why should the developed countries be allowed to pollute more now simply because they polluted more in the past? In fact, because the developed countries have already contributed so much, they should be forced to reduce more. The world seems at an impasse: the United States refuses to go along unless developing countries are brought into the fold, and the developing countries see no reason why they should not be allowed to pollute as much per capita as the United States or Europe. Indeed, given their poverty and the costs associated with reducing emissions, one might give them even more leeway. But, because of their low levels of income, such reasoning would imply that no restraints would be imposed on them for decades.

There is a way out, and that is through a common (global) environmental tax on emissions. There is a social cost to emissions, and the common environmental tax would simply make everyone pay the social cost. This is in accord with the most basic of economic principles, that individuals and firms should pay their full (marginal) costs. The world would, of course, have to agree on assessing the magnitude of the social cost of emissions; the tax could, for instance, be set so that the level of (global) reductions is the same as that set by the Kyoto targets. As technologies evolve, and the nature of the threat of global warming becomes clearer, the tax rate could adjust, perhaps up, perhaps down.

It would be good if the world could agree to use the proceeds to finance the range of global public goods that are so important for making globalization work better—for instance, for promoting health, research, and development. But that may be too ambitious. Alternatively, each country could keep its own revenues and use them to replace taxes on capital and labor: it makes much more sense to tax "bads," such as pollution and greenhouse gas emissions, than to tax "goods," such as work and saving. (Economists refer to these taxes as corrective taxes.) Hence, overall economic efficiency would be increased by this proposal. The big advantage of taxation over the Kyoto approach is that it avoids most of the distributional debate. Under Kyoto, getting the right to pollute more is, in effect, receiving an enormous gift. (Now that pollution rights are tradable, we can even put a market value on them.) The United States might claim that because it is a larger country, it "needs" more pollution rights. Norway might claim that because it uses hydroelectric power, the scope for reducing emissions is lower. France might claim that because it has already made the effort to go into nuclear energy, it should not be forced to reduce more. Under the common tax approach, these debates are sidestepped. All that is asked is that everyone pay the social cost of their emissions, and that the tax be set high enough that the reductions in emissions are large enough to meet the required targets.

The economic cost to each country is small—in some cases, actually negative. The cost is simply the difference in the "deadweight loss" of the emission tax and the tax for which it substitutes, and it is only these differences that determine the differential effects on each country.

CONCLUDING THOUGHTS

The world has invested enormously in the Kyoto approach, and the success achieved is impressive. But no one has suggested a way out of the current impasse, and it is time to start exploring alternatives. Global warming is too important to simply rely on the hope that somehow a solution will emerge, and it is also too important to rely simply on the goodwill of the United States, especially given its flawed political system where campaign contributions from oil companies and others who benefit from emissions play such a key role. The well-being of our entire planet is at stake. We know what needs to be done. We have the tools at hand. We only need the political resolve.

CHAPTER 4

A Meaningful Second Commitment Period for the Kyoto Protocol

Sheila M. Olmstead and Robert N. Stavins

IN 1997, MORE than 160 nations agreed on the text of the Kyoto Protocol to the United Nations Framework Convention on Climate Change. Shortly afterward, many economists—particularly American economists—began to condemn the protocol as excessively costly, environmentally ineffective, or politically. Indeed, we have written such critiques ourselves. Today, however, even if we have not come to praise the Kyoto Protocol, neither have we come to bury it. Rather, we ask how it can be modified for its second commitment period (2012–2016) so that it will provide a way forward that is scientifically sound, economically rational, and politically pragmatic. We seek to be responsive to two pressing questions that are now being asked: How can the United States be brought on board? And how can meaningful participation by developing countries be financed?

Sheila M. Olmstead is an assistant professor of environmental economics at the School of Forestry and Environmental Studies, Yale University; Robert N. Stavins is the Albert Pratt Professor of Business and Government at the John F. Kennedy School of Government, Harvard University, and a University Fellow of Resources for the Future.

Our answer includes three elements: a means to ensure that key nations are involved; an emphasis on an extended time path of action; and the inclusion of firm-level market-based policy instruments.

WHO—EXPAND PARTICIPATION TO INCLUDE ALL KEY COUNTRIES

Broad participation, by major industrialized nations and key developing countries, is essential to address this global commons problem effectively and efficiently in the second commitment period and beyond. China will surpass the United States as the world's leading producer of greenhouse gas emissions by 2009 (International Energy Agency 2006). Developing countries are likely to account for more than one-half of global emissions well before 2020 (Nakicenovic and Swart 2000).

Many argue that the industrialized countries should take the first steps to combat climate change, because they are responsible for the bulk of man-made current greenhouse gas concentrations. But developing countries currently provide the greatest opportunities for low-cost emissions reductions. Furthermore, if developing countries are not included, comparative advantage in the production of carbon-intensive goods and services will shift outside the coalition of participating countries.

The shift of production of carbon-intensive goods and services to developing countries will counter the impacts of emissions reductions among participating countries (a phenomenon called "leakage"). Moreover, this shift will push nonparticipating nations onto more carbon-intensive growth paths, increasing their costs of joining the coalition later.

So, on the one hand, for purposes of environmental effectiveness and economic efficiency, key developing countries should participate. On the other hand, for purposes of distributional equity (and international political pragmatism), they cannot be expected to incur the consequent costs.

It turns out that the two issues can be reconciled. Our answer is a set of growth-indexed emissions limits that are set initially at business-as-usual (BAU) levels for respective developing countries but become more stringent as those countries become wealthier. Harvard economist Jeffrey Frankel, who participated in the Kyoto meetings in the United States delegation, has noted that this would be a natural extension of the allocation pattern in the Kyoto Protocol's first commitment period (2008–2012), where targets for industrialized countries become, on average, 1 percent more stringent for every 10 percent increase in a country's per-capita gross domestic product (GDP) (Frankel 1999).

Joining the international market for emissions trading could make developing countries better off—even in immediate income terms. The reason is tied to the fact that reductions or reduced increases in emissions for these countries often will be cheaper than for the developed world. As a result, the developing world can sell its "right to pollute" to firms in the developed world in a system that allows trade of emissions permits. Such sales could increase the income of developing countries even if the system requires that they reduce their emissions.

Hence, cost-effectiveness and distributional equity could both be addressed. In fact, tradable permits, which make reductions cost-effective, can be used to achieve distributional equity because the allocation of permits determines the distribution of burdens and benefits.

WHEN—USE AN EXTENDED TIME PATH, AND "RAMP UP"

The Kyoto Protocol's targets are "too little, too fast." Global climate change is a long-term problem, because greenhouse gases remain in the atmosphere for decades to centuries. In this setting, economics would suggest that emissions targets to address the problem of green-house gas concentrations ought to begin at BAU levels, and then depart gradually, so that emissions increase at first but at rates below BAU. These targets should reach a maximum level and then decrease—eventually becoming much more severe than the constraints implied by the Kyoto Protocol's first commitment period targets, which translate to an average 5 percent reduction from 1990 levels by 2008–2012. Let's take each of these arguments in turn.

Why should targets begin at or close to BAU levels? Moderate targets in the short term will avoid rendering large parts of the capital stock prematurely obsolete. Investment in the capital equipment used in the burning of fossil fuels, such as the boilers on electric power plants, have been made in a world of free carbon emissions. Thus, significant emissions reductions today would require the retirement of much of this equipment (how much will depend on the stringency of emissions targets). This equipment, and similar investments by households in automobiles and major appliances, would typically only be replaced every several years, or several decades.

The protocol's initial targets may sound modest, but they translate into severe 25–30 percent cuts for the United States from its BAU path, because of the rapid economic growth the country experienced during the 1990s. The same is true for other nations that have experienced significant economic growth post-1990, raising the costs of 1990-based emissions targets and making them politically infeasible as well as economically unreasonable. It is not surprising that many signatories to the protocol are not on track to meet their emissions targets.

Our second argument is that targets should "ramp up" over time, eventually reaching levels much more stringent than the protocol's targets. This approach, if made clear at the outset, will alter firms' (and households') capital investment decisions, setting countries on a carbon-intensity path that will allow the achievement of long-run targets. Most important, stringent long-run targets known today will spur current and future technological change, bringing down costs over time. Of course, the long-term targets should be flexible, because there is great uncertainty throughout the policy-economics-biophysical system, some of which will be resolved over time.

Our proposal is also consistent with a time path of "price" targets—for example, a time-profile of carbon prices (taxes on the carbon content of fossil fuels). In any event, such a long-term time path of targets involving increasingly aggressive action is the most cost-effective and fair approach. It is also a politically pragmatic approach. Politicians in representative democracies are frequently condemned when they yield to incentives to place greater costs on future rather than current voters. This is typically a politically pragmatic strategy, one that is often denigrated as "politics as usual." In the case of global climate policy, however, this may also be the scientifically correct and economically rational approach.

HOW—EMPLOY MARKET-BASED POLICY INSTRUMENTS

Most economists agree that conventional regulatory approaches cannot do the job, certainly not at acceptable costs. To keep costs down in the short term and bring them down even lower in the long term through technological change, it is essential to embrace market-based instruments.

On a domestic level, systems of tradable permits might be used to achieve national targets. This approach was used in the United States to phase out leaded gasoline in the 1980s at a savings of more than $250 million per year over an equivalent traditional regulatory approach (Stavins 2003), and it is now used to cut sulfur dioxide (SO_2) emissions from power plants by half, at an annual cost savings of $1 billion compared to a command-and-control approach (Ellerman et al. 2000). The better policy model for climate change is the upstream lead-rights system in which trading occurred at the refinery level (analogous to trading on the carbon content of fossil fuels) rather than the downstream SO_2 emissions-trading system.

For some countries, systems of domestic carbon taxes (as opposed to permits) may be more attractive. A particularly promising approach is a hybrid of tax and tradable permit systems—an ordinary tradable permit system, plus a government promise to sell additional permits at a stated price (the "tax" component). This "safety-valve" approach addresses cost uncertainty by creating a price (and thereby cost) ceiling so that if reductions prove more costly than expected there will be a known and limited increase in the cost of carbon emissions.

International policy instruments are also required, and the Kyoto Protocol already includes a system whereby the parties to the agreement can trade their "assigned amounts"—their national reduction targets—translated into emissions terms. In theory, such a system of international tradable permits—if implemented only for the industrialized countries—could reduce costs by 50 percent. If such a system were to include major developing countries as well, costs could be lowered by half again (Edmonds et al. 1997). To be effective, however, trading must ultimately be among sources (firms), not among nations per se. Nations are not simple cost-minimizers, and they do not have the information needed to make cost-effective trades. Therefore, an international trading system must be designed to facilitate integration with a set of domestic trading systems.

International carbon trading markets are of course subject to the same problems as any other market and may not work well if transaction costs are high or some nations or firms have a sufficient concentration of permits (or excess permits). The latter concern is a real one in the climate policy context. If, for example, the majority of excess permits (allowable emissions in excess of BAU emissions) are found in a relatively small number of nations, then the possibility increases of collusion among sellers (Manne and Richels 2004).

In any event, the initial allocation of permits among nations can imply exceptionally large international wealth transfers. Several analysts have identified this as a major objection to an international carbon trading regime and have endorsed international tax approaches for this and other reasons. However, taxes will also have distributional effects through the recycling of revenues; moreover if tax rates are equalized across countries as efficiency requires, they do not provide control over the wealth transfers. Wealth transfers can be broadly controlled to achieve distributional equity with particular permit allocations. And it is precisely this feature of the permit allocation that allows cost-effectiveness and distributional equity to be addressed simultaneously.

THE WAY FORWARD

The three-part global climate policy architecture we propose can form the foundation for the second commitment period (and beyond) for the Kyoto Protocol. But can countries credibly commit to the long-term program that is part of this proposed architecture? Our answer is that once nations have ratified the agreement, implementing legislation within respective nations would translate the agreed long-term targets into domestic policy commitments. Such commitments would send signals to private industry and create incentives to take action. Ultimately, such domestic actions provide the signals that other countries need to see. This represents a logical and ultimately feasible chain of credible commitment.

This overall approach is scientifically sound, economically rational, and politically pragmatic. Without doubt, the challenges facing adoption and successful implementation of this architecture for the Kyoto Protocol's second commitment period and beyond are significant, but they are no greater than the challenges facing other approaches to the threat of global climate change.

REFERENCES AND FURTHER READING

Aldy, Joseph E., Scott Barrett, and Robert N. Stavins. 2003. "Thirteen Plus One: A Comparison of Global Climate Policy Architectures." *Climate Policy* 3 (4): 373–397.

Cooper, Richard N. 1998. "Toward a Real Treaty on Global Warming." *Foreign Affairs* (March/April), 77 (2): 66–79.

Edmonds, J. A., S. H. Kim, C. N. MacCracken, R. D. Sands, and M. A. Wise. 1997. *Return to 1990: The Cost of Mitigating United States Carbon Emissions in the Post-2000 Period*. Washington, DC: Pacific Northwest National Laboratory, operated by Battelle Memorial Institute.

Ellerman, A. Denny, Paul L. Joskow, Richard Schmalensee, Juan-Pablo Montero, and Elizabeth M. Bailey. 2000. *Markets for Clean Air: The U.S. Acid Rain Program*. New York: Cambridge University Press.

Frankel, Jeffrey A. 1999. "Greenhouse Gas Emissions." Policy brief no. 52. Washington, DC: Brookings Institution.

Hahn, Robert W. and Robert N. Stavins. 1999. *What Has the Kyoto Protocol Wrought? The Real Architecture of International Tradable Permit Markets*. Washington, DC: American Enterprise Institute Press.

International Energy Agency. 2006. *World Energy Outlook 2006*. Paris: International Energy Agency.

Manne, Alan S. and Richard G. Richels. 1997. "On Stabilizing CO_2 Concentrations—Cost-Effective Emission Reduction Strategies." *Environmental Modeling and Assessment* (December), 2 (4): 251–265.

———. 2004. "U.S. Rejection of the Kyoto Protocol: The Impact on Compliance Costs and CO_2 Emissions." *Energy Policy* (March), 32 (4): 447–454.

McKibbin, Warwick J. and Peter J. Wilcoxen. 2002. "The Role of Economics in Climate Change Policy." *Journal of Economic Perspectives* (Spring), 16 (2): 107–129.

Nakicenovic, Nebojsa and Robert Swart, eds. 2000. *Intergovernmental Panel on Climate Change Special Report on Emissions Scenarios*. Cambridge: Cambridge University Press.

Newell, Richard G. and William A. Pizer. 2003. "Regulating Stock Externalities Under Uncertainty." *Journal of Environmental Economics and Management* (March), 45 (2S): 416–432.

Nordhaus, William D. 2005. "Economic Analyses of the Kyoto Protocol: Is There Life After Kyoto?" (October 21–22). Conference paper presented at "Global Warming: Looking Beyond Kyoto," Yale University, New Haven, CT.

Olmstead, Sheila M. and Robert N. Stavins. 2006. "An International Policy Architecture for the Post-Kyoto Era." *American Economic Review Papers and Proceedings* (May), 96 (2): 35–38.

Pizer, William A. 2002. "Combining Price and Quantity Controls to Mitigate Global Climate Change." *Journal of Public Economics* (September), 85 (3): 409–434.

Richels, Richard G., Alan S. Manne, and Thomas M. L. Wigley. 2004. "Moving Beyond Concentrations—The Challenge of Limiting Temperature Change." Working paper no. 04–11. Washington, DC: AEI-Brookings Joint Center for Regulatory Studies.

Stavins, Robert N. 2003, "Experience with Market-Based Environmental Policy Instruments." In *Handbook of Environmental Economics, Volume I*, eds. Karl Goran Mäler and Jeffrey Vincent, pp. 355–435. Amsterdam: Elsevier Science.

———. 2004. "Forging a More Effective Global Climate Treaty." *Environment* (December), 46 (10): 23–30.

Watson, Robert T., ed. 2001. *Climate Change 2001: Synthesis Report. Contributions of Working Group I, II, and III to the Third Assessment Report of the Intergovernmental Panel on Climate Change.* Cambridge: Cambridge University Press.

Wigley, Thomas M. L., Richard G. Richels, and Jae Edmonds. 1996. "Economic and Environmental Choices in the Stabilization of Atmospheric CO_2 Concentrations." *Nature* (January), 379 (6562): 240–243.

II

THE INTERNATIONAL
ECONOMY

THERE ARE SOME questions in international economics that divide economists into opposing camps and others on which the profession is near-unanimous, disagreeing only on the details. This section offers examples of both types of questions.

In the first essay, J. Bradford DeLong sets out the two contrasting views among economists on the implications of the huge U.S. current account deficit. Macroeconomists who tend to focus on domestic markets, on the one hand, tend to believe that the trade deficit will correct itself without great consequence: a falling dollar will be a boon for exporters, which will stimulate growth and correct the current account deficit. International economists, on the other hand, are not so sanguine: they see a potentially dramatic decline in the U.S. currency, which could trigger financial market turmoil.

The second essay, by Diana Farrell, turns to offshoring. Worries about offshoring have moved from shipping manufacturing jobs abroad in the 1980s to shipping service jobs to India today. Two questions arise: how large an issue is offshoring of services, and is it good or bad? Although most U.S. workers regard offshoring as an unambiguously damaging phenomenon, most economists would disagree, provided policies are implemented to help Americans make the transition to the new jobs created in the domestic economy as a result of the productivity gains from offshoring. Economists for the most part believe voluntary trade is mutually beneficial, provided those individuals who lose out as a result can be assisted. Farrell does two things. First, she lays out a case that offshoring of services is likely to be relatively limited; second, she sets out the kind of adjustment measures needed.

Turning to a more global perspective, the authors of the third essay in this section turn economics into a deal to fight disease. Creating vaccines is a scientific and medical problem, but creating the proper incentives to fund that creation is an economic one. Owen Barder, Michael Kremer, and Heidi Williams explain why the kinds of disease that mainly affect very poor countries have been poor investments for pharmaceutical companies. They make an innovative proposal that has been gaining traction in the international and charitable communities to create commitments to buy vaccines that prevent tropical diseases at attractive prices.

The final essay in this section brings us back to consider capital flows and a growing controversy among economists. Bradford DeLong again describes his own shift away from the traditional view by economists in favor of capital market liberalization by developing countries. DeLong's worries about the traditional laissez faire view echo those of many economists who have come to doubt the mantra that free trade is always good, whether it is in goods, services, or currencies.

CHAPTER 5

Divergent Views on the Coming Dollar Crisis

J. Bradford DeLong

AMERICA'S INTERNATIONAL FINANCE economists and its domestically oriented macroeconomists have very different—indeed, opposed—views of the likely consequences of America's huge current-account deficit. International finance economists see a financial crisis as likely, followed by a painful and perhaps prolonged recession in the United States. Domestically oriented macroeconomists, by contrast, see a forthcoming fall in the value of the dollar not as a crisis but as an opportunity to accelerate growth. Why the difference?

J. Bradford DeLong is a professor of economics at the University of California at Berkeley, a research associate of the National Bureau of Economic Research, and former deputy assistant secretary for economic policy in the United States Treasury. He tries to maintain an uneasy balance in his interests among economic history, macroeconomics, and other topics. He received his Ph.D. from Harvard in 1987 and his B.A. from Harvard in 1982.

THE DOMESTIC-MACRO VIEW

Domestically oriented macroeconomists look at the situation roughly like this: at some point in the future, foreign central banks will become less willing to continue buying massive amounts of dollar-denominated securities. It looks like in 2005 China, Japan, and other Asian central banks will buy $500 billion of dollar-denominated assets in order to prop up the greenback so that their exports to the United States continue to flow and grow. Eventually, this massive flow of foreign funds must stop (Quiggin 2004). When they cease their large-scale dollar-purchase programs, the value of the dollar will fall—and it will probably fall hard.

But, according to the domestically oriented macroeconomists, this devaluation is not a large problem for the United States. (However, it is a very big problem for economies that export to the United States.) As the dollar's value declines, U.S. exports will become more attractive to foreigners and American employment will rise, with labor reallocated to the newly vibrant export sector. It will be like what happened in Britain after it abandoned its exchange-rate peg and allowed the pound to depreciate relative to the Deutschmark, or what happened in the United States in the late 1980s when the dollar depreciated against the pound, the Deutschmark, and—most important—the Japanese yen.

THE INTERNATIONAL FINANCE VIEW

International finance economists see a far bleaker future. They see the end of large-scale dollar-purchase programs by central banks leading not only to a decline in the dollar but also to a spike in U.S. long-term interest rates, both nominal and real, which will curb consumption spending immediately and throttle investment spending after only a short lag.

To be sure, international finance economists also see U.S. exports benefiting as the value of the dollar declines, but the lags in demand are such that the export boost will come a year or two after the decline in consumption and investment spending. Eight million to 10 million workers in America will have to shift employment from services and construction into exports and import-competing goods. This cannot happen overnight. And during the time needed for this labor-market adjustment, structural unemployment will rise.

Moreover, there may be a financial panic: large financial institutions with short-term liabilities and long-term assets will have a difficult time weathering a large rise in long-term dollar-denominated interest rates. This mismatch can cause financial stress and bankruptcy just as easily as banks' local-currency assets and dollar liabilities caused stress and bankruptcy in the Mexican and East Asian crises of the 1990s and in the Argentinean crisis of this decade.

CAN THE FED AVERT A CRISIS?

When international finance economists sketch this scenario, domestically oriented macroeconomists respond that it sounds like a case of incompetent monetary policy. Why should the Federal Reserve allow long-term interest rates to spike just because other central banks have ceased their dollar-purchase programs? Should not the Fed step in and replace them with its own purchases of long-term U.S. Treasury bonds, thereby keeping long-term interest rates at a level conducive to full employment?

To this, international finance economists respond that the Fed will not wish to do so. When forced to choose between full employment and price stability, the international finance economists say that the Fed will choose price stability, because its institutional memory of the 1970s, when inflation ran rampant, remains very strong. A fall in the value of the dollar raises import prices, and thus is as an inflationary shock to the supply side of the economy just as the oil shocks of the 1970s were. The Fed today puts preserving its inflation-fighting credibility as priority one. The Fed will want to raise, not lower, interest rates; to sell, not buy, bonds; and thus to reinforce rather than damp the interest rate rise coming from the shift in the exchange rate.

Moreover, the international economists say, the Fed can only influence and not control long-term real interest rates. If Asian central banks stop buying $500 billion of U.S. long-term bonds each year, real interest rates will rise because the Fed cannot step in to replace them without consequence. The only way the Fed could finance large-scale purchases of U.S. Treasury bonds on a $500-billion-a-year scale would be to increase America's monetary base by 60 percent per year. That would mean inflation on a scale not seen in this or the last century. Because the Fed cannot risk such inflation, it simply does not have the power to keep U.S. interest rates from rising.

I find this distressing.

Serious economists whom I respect enormously find themselves taking strong positions on opposite sides of this debate. I'm not wise enough to say which side is right, but I certainly know which side I hope is wrong.

REFERENCES AND FURTHER READING

Quiggin, John. 2004. "The Unsustainability of U.S. Trade Deficits." *The Economists' Voice* 1 (3), art. 2. http://www.bepress.com/ev/vol1/iss3/art2.

Setser, Brad. 2005. "$709 Billion in Reserve Accumulation in 2004." http://www.rgemonitor.com/blog/setser/91467.

CHAPTER 6

U.S. Offshoring: Small Steps to Make It Win-Win

Diana Farrell

COMPANIES FROM THE United States lead the world in offshoring white-collar jobs to low-wage countries. Today they employ more than 900,000 service workers overseas. But widespread concern about the effects on the U.S. job market has prompted policymakers to call for curbs on offshoring, and some states have already adopted such policies.

Trying to protect jobs this way is a mistake. For one thing, fears of job losses caused by offshoring are greatly exaggerated. New research by the McKinsey Global Institute (MGI) shows the United States will likely lose to offshoring no more than 300,000 jobs each year, an insignificant number when set against normal job turnover in the economy: some 4.7 million Americans started jobs with a new employer in the single month of May 2005. Offshoring will also have a negligible impact on U.S. wage levels because of its limited scale.

Diana Farrell is the director of the McKinsey Global Institute, the economics research arm of the global consulting firm McKinsey & Company.

In addition, curbs on offshoring would deprive the United States of its many benefits and impose new costs instead. Savings from offshoring allow companies to invest in next-generation technologies, creating jobs at home as well as abroad. Global competition also sharpens companies' skills. Conversely, refusing to buy services from overseas will invite retaliation. The United States runs a trade surplus in services and attracts more foreign direct investment than any other country, so it has most to lose from a services trade war.

Policymakers should let offshoring continue. But that doesn't mean they should ignore its consequences. None of the benefits of offshoring currently flow directly to those who suffer most directly, namely U.S. workers whose jobs move overseas. Companies can and should therefore use some of their gains from offshoring to help their displaced employees cope. Wage loss insurance, for example, would cost only a fraction of the savings that offshoring will bring. Governments too, must work with companies to increase retraining, provide lifelong learning programs, and ensure portable health and pension benefits. Indeed, all workers need more help in preparing for the faster rate of job change that goes with globalization.

JOB LOSS WILL BE LIMITED

According to MGI research, the maximum number of U.S. service jobs that could in theory be performed offshore is 11 percent of total service employment. And, keep in mind that this is a *maximum*. In reality, MGI estimates that less than 2 percent of all U.S. service jobs actually will be done offshore by 2008, and U.S. companies will create some 200,000 to 300,000 offshore jobs per year over the next thirty years.

Why will so few service jobs go overseas?

Only a small fraction of service jobs could ever go offshore mostly because a much larger percentage require face-to-face customer interactions or a worker's physical presence, for example, to stock shelves, provide nursing care, or install networks. In two of the largest service sectors—health care and retail—only 8 percent and 3 percent of jobs, respectively, could be performed remotely for this reason. And the industries in which the highest percentage of jobs could be performed remotely—packaged software (49 percent) and IT services (44 percent)—represent only 1–2 percent of overall employment.

Even fewer jobs actually will migrate for several reasons. About one-third of U.S. workers work for companies too small to justify the costs of offshoring. Even larger companies sometimes find the major changes to processes and information systems that offshoring requires to be a significant deterrent. Insurance firms, for example, would need to integrate their legacy computer systems with those of overseas service providers, a massive task. For other companies, a lack of global experience discourages them.

Furthermore, the rational location for many jobs that could in theory be done anywhere will *still* be the United States. Companies consider a host of factors beyond labor cost when deciding where to place an activity, including each potential location's risk profile, infrastructure, domestic market, nonlabor costs, business and living environment, and the availability of vendors. Against these criteria, the United States remains a logical choice for the many companies that do not rank labor cost far above other factors. That is why the United States continues to attract so many global jobs from foreign companies.

A new offshore job does not always represent a job lost at home, because many offshore jobs would not be viable at higher wage levels. E-Telecare, a call center vendor in the Philippines, employs one manager to eight customer service agents, compared with a ratio of 1:20 or more in similar U.S. call centers.

Mounting evidence confirms that offshoring is not what lies behind mass layoffs. The U.S. Bureau of Labor Statistics confirms that only 1 percent of service layoffs involving more than fifty employees in the first quarter of 2004 was associated with offshoring (Bureau of Labor Statistics 2004).

IMPERCEPTIBLE IMPACT ON WAGES

Because offshoring has such a limited impact on the U.S. jobs market, its effect on U.S. wages will also be negligible, even in the computer and data-processing industry where offshoring is commonplace. In the United States, overall employment in that industry has been growing at over 2 percent per year since 2000, compared to 0.4 percent in the rest economy. Although many programming jobs have moved offshore, more positions for systems analysts and software engineers have been created in the United States. Average wages have actually grown at a faster pace than elsewhere in the economy, because the new jobs have higher productivity and create more value.

These findings confirm what other research has found. A new study by Mary Amiti and Shang-Jin Wei (2004), two economists at the International Monetary Fund (IMF), confirms that U.S. and UK service sectors subject to offshoring are creating as many—or more—new jobs than the ones that move offshore. Another study by Brad Jensen and Lori Kletzer (2005) reports that service sectors facing international trade competition, such as software publishing and the securities industry, have fared better in terms of employment and wages than sectors that do not, such as newspapers and waste management.

OFFSHORING BENEFITS THE UNITED STATES

Past MGI research found that for every $1 of cost on services that U.S. companies move offshore, the U.S. economy gains at least $1.14.

The companies doing the offshoring reap 58 cents of these gains. This gives companies scope to invest in new opportunities that create jobs both at home and abroad, to raise shareholder dividends, and to lower prices to consumers.

Offshoring also gives companies access to distinctive skills abroad, making them more competitive. By moving its operations to China, home to some of the world's most sophisticated wireless chip and software designers, one U.S. electronics maker has tripled its manufacturing productivity and, at the same time, cut product development cycle times and defects. In an era of global competition, companies cannot afford to pass up on such opportunities.

The U.S. also benefits as a *destination* for offshoring companies. In 2004, it received $121 billion of direct investment from foreign companies, more than any other country. Foreign subsidiaries provided jobs for 5.4 million U.S. workers in 2002. They also accounted for 14 percent of U.S. private sector research and development expenditures in 2002, the last year for which data is available, and 20 percent of U.S. exports.

With the world's most developed and competitive service industries, the United States stands to benefit more than any other nation from free trade in services. In 2003, the United States exported $15 billion more business services than it imported. U.S. trade negotiators are arguing for freer trade in services precisely because so many companies in financial services, accounting, law, consulting, and IT services would gain.

HELPING DISPLACED WORKERS IS
BETTER THAN PROTECTIONISM

Continuing to allow offshoring and free trade in services will benefit the United States as a whole. But one undeniable corollary is less job security: there will be more jobs but a higher level of job turnover.

Workers need help coping with the accelerated pace of job change that accompanies openness to trade in services. So rather than trying to prevent offshoring, governments and companies should ease the transition for those workers it displaces and prepare all workers for more frequent job changes.

EASE THE TRANSITION

Not all workers who lose their jobs find new ones quickly, and many that do suffer pay cuts. More than 75 percent of U.S. service workers who lose their jobs due to trade find new jobs within six months; however, the median wage of those re-employed is 11 percent below the level of their previous jobs.

The United States already has two welfare programs targeting workers displaced by trade, the Trade Adjustment Assistance and the Alternative Trade Adjustment Assistance, but neither has been particularly effective. U.S. spending on policies to assist displaced workers, at 0.5 percent of gross domestic product, is low compared with other developed nations—the United Kingdom spends 0.9 percent, Germany 3.1 percent, and Denmark 3.7 percent—even though the United States has the highest job churn rate.

U.S. policymakers should invest in additional measures to help workers move between jobs, especially job retraining credits for employers to encourage them to hire displaced workers and provide on-the-job training, demonstrably the most effective kind. Continuing education grants will help workers to build skills in demand, particularly from growing areas of the economy such as health care, education, and social services. Portable medical insurance plans and pension benefits are also essential to a workforce changing jobs more frequently.

Companies benefiting from offshoring can ease the plight of displaced workers too. More generous severance packages would help. Companies could also fund wage insurance programs to help fill the gap between workers' previous wages and their new ones, thus encouraging them to avoid long-term unemployment. MGI has calculated that if U.S. companies spent just 4–5 percent of their cost savings from their first two years of offshoring, they could make up 70 percent of lost wages for all full-time employees displaced by offshoring, as well as give them health-care subsidies for up to two years. Companies may not volunteer to do this on their own, suggesting that some kind of public policy intervention may be warranted.

Indeed, policymakers might consider extending wage insurance to all displaced workers, not just those whose jobs were lost to trade. Globalization and advances in technology require a more flexible and fluid workforce than ever before. But there is no reason that individual workers should bear the full cost of that flexibility. Robert Litan and his colleagues (Brainard, Litan, and Warren 2005) found that a wage insurance program that insures 30–70 percent of wage loss for two years for all involuntarily displaced full-time workers with two years or more of tenure would cost only $1.5 billion to $7 billion (depending on the program design), or $12 to $50 per worker per year.

Forward-looking labor unions are beginning to push for similar approaches, rather than trying to protect jobs. For instance, the U.S. IT firm Computer Sciences Corporation (CSC) has agreed with the UK union Amicus that it will retrain 10,000 UK staff when it moves their work offshore. Similar deals have been struck between unions and UK banks. This kind of response to offshoring gives union members a better chance of long-term future employment than struggling to preserve existing jobs.

PREPARE PEOPLE FOR MORE JOB CHANGES

Changes to the U.S. educational system are also needed to prepare future workers for more job changes in their working lives. As well as technical skills, which may become obsolete, students will need business knowledge, and teamwork and communication skills, to be more broadly employable. Engineering, computer science, and other science programs at U.S. universities should adapt their curriculums accordingly and combine teaching IT skills with other, less narrowly focused disciplines, among them business knowledge, psychology, and anthropology. Lifelong learning should be an aspiration for all workers in the economy.

At the same time, industry associations, unions, and companies can collaborate to help workers anticipate job changes. They could, for example, monitor occupations where employment demand is rising—in health care, business services, communications, and leisure—and plot potential career paths for workers switching into them. Software programmers may need to become systems analysts; information specialists may need to move into analysis. But companies and unions can identify future employment opportunities and help workers prepare for them.

Fears about job losses and wage cuts in the United States due to offshoring are vastly overstated. Protectionism may save a few jobs for a while, but it will stifle innovation and job creation in the longer term. Rather than trying to stop globalization, the goal must be to let it happen, while easing the transition for workers who lose out.

REFERENCES AND FURTHER READING

Amiti, Mary and Shang-Jin Wei. 2004. "Demystifying Outsourcing: The Numbers Do Not Support the Hype Over Job Losses." *Finance and Development* (December): 23–27.

Baily, Martin N. and Diana Farrell. July 2004. "Exploding the Myths of Offshoring." *The McKinsey Quarterly.* http://www.mckinseyquarterly.com.

Brainard, Lael, Robert Litan, and Nicholas Warren. July 2005. "Insuring America's Workers in a New Era of Offshoring." Policy brief no. 143. Washington, DC: Brookings Institution.

Bureau of Labor Statistics. First Quarter 2004. "Extended Mass Layoffs Associated with Domestic and Overseas Relocations."

Farrell, Diana, et al. 2005. *The Emerging Global Labor Market.* McKinsey Global Institute (July). http://www.mckinsey.com/mgi.

Farrell, Diana, Martha Laboissiere, and Jaeson Rosenfeld. 2005. "Sizing the Emerging Global Labor Market." *The McKinsey Quarterly* 3: 92–104.

Jensen, J. Bradford and Lori G. Kletzer. 2005. "Tradable Services: Understanding the Scope and Impact of Services Offshoring." Working paper. Institute for International Economics, Washington, DC.

Kletzer, Lori and Robert Litan. February 2001. "A Prescription to Relieve Worker Anxiety." Policy brief no. 01–2. Institute for International Economics, Washington, DC.

CHAPTER 7

Advance Market Commitments: How to Stimulate Investment in Vaccines for Neglected Diseases

Owen Barder, Michael Kremer, and Heidi Williams

MALARIA, TUBERCULOSIS, AND strains of HIV common in Africa kill 5 million people each year, almost all of them in poor countries. Vaccines arguably offer the best hope for tackling these and other so-called neglected diseases concentrated in poor countries, yet, relative to the social need, there is a dearth of research and development (R&D) on such vaccines.

In this article, we outline the economic rationale for the "Advance Market Commitment" proposal, which the G8 finance ministers decided to pilot in 2006. Under the proposal, donors commit to help finance the purchase of vaccines against neglected diseases, if and

Owen Barder is the director of global development effectiveness in the UK Department for International Development, the government department that leads the United Kingdom's fight against global poverty. Michael Kremer is the Gates Professor of Developing Societies in the Department of Economics at Harvard University and senior fellow at the Brookings Institution. Heidi Williams is a doctoral student in economics at Harvard University.

when such vaccines are developed. In 2007, the first such commitment was put in place: a group of rich country governments, together with the Bill & Melinda Gates Foundation, committed $1.5 billion for a vaccine against pneumococcus, a major source of child mortality in poor countries.

We first summarize the value of vaccines in addressing diseases in poor countries and then outline two market failures that limit private sector investment in vaccines against neglected diseases. We argue that advance market commitments could accelerate the development of new vaccines for neglected diseases by addressing each of these market failures, and we describe how such commitments can be designed to facilitate widespread access to these vaccines if they are developed. Finally, we discuss evidence suggesting that advance market commitments would be a cost-effective way for donors to save more lives than would be saved by virtually any comparable health expenditure.

THE VALUE OF VACCINES IN POOR COUNTRIES

Vaccines are perhaps the quintessential example of a cheap, easy-to-use technology that can have tremendous health impacts even in very poor countries with weak health-care infrastructures. Compared with drug treatments, vaccines require little training or expensive equipment for delivery, do not require diagnosis, can be taken in a few doses instead of needing longer-term regimens, and rarely have major side effects.

Despite the challenges facing health systems in many poor countries, three-quarters of the world's children already receive a standard package of childhood vaccines through the Expanded Programme on Immunization (EPI). The EPI vaccines save an estimated 3 million lives annually—almost ten thousand lives a day—and protect millions more from illness and permanent disability (Kim-Farley and the Expanded Programme on Immunization Team 1992).

An expanded version of the standard EPI vaccine package is among the most cost-effective health interventions for poor countries—costing an estimated \$16 to \$22 per life-year gained in poor countries (World Bank 1993a, adjusted to 2005 prices).[1]

At this cost per life-year saved, immunization is an extremely cost-effective intervention by any measure. In the United States (Neumann et al. 2000) and the United Kingdom (Towse 2002), medical interventions are considered cost-effective at \$50,000 or \$100,000 per life-year saved. In poor countries, health interventions are generally considered extremely cost-effective if the cost per life-year saved is either less than \$100 (World Bank 1993b) or less than a country's annual per capita income (GAVI 2004). Vaccination is also highly cost-effective compared with other health interventions for poor countries; for example, anti-retroviral drug treatments for HIV cost a great deal more than \$100 per life-year saved (Creese et al. 2002). As we shall see, vaccines purchased under an advance market commitment are estimated to cost as little as \$15–\$30 per life-year saved.

MARKET FAILURES FOR VACCINES FOR NEGLECTED DISEASES

Poor countries have benefited enormously from the EPI vaccines, but these vaccines were developed largely in response to the prospect of valuable sales in rich-country markets. In the case of neglected diseases, there are no such market incentives, and so, as argued by Michael Kremer and Rachel Glennerster in their recent book *Strong Medicine* (2004), private firms lack incentives to undertake R&D on these diseases. One indicator of this lack of investment is that of the 1,233 drugs licensed worldwide between 1975 and 1997, only four were developed by commercial pharmaceutical firms specifically for tropical diseases of humans (Pécoul et al. 1999).

One reason for the lack of incentives for R&D on vaccines for neglected diseases is that the potential consumers of these vaccines (that is, individuals and their governments) are poor. In a technical sense, this is not a market failure. But there are two key market failures that limit R&D on vaccines needed primarily in poor countries.

First, governments and other purchasers of vaccines face *time-inconsistent incentives.* Before a vaccine is developed, governments want vaccine producers to invest in R&D and to establish large-scale production facilities. But once a vaccine has been developed, governments want the vaccine to be sold at the lowest possible price, to allow limited budgets to purchase the vaccine for as many individuals as possible. Governments are the main purchasers of vaccines, and vaccines used in poor countries are purchased through a small number of international agencies (such as UNICEF). These institutions can use their dominant purchasing power and regulatory control (as well as the power of public opinion) to drive prices down once vaccines have been developed—thus making it difficult for firms to recoup their R&D investments. Private firms anticipate this time-inconsistent behavior, which thus reduces incentives for firms to make the necessary R&D investments in the first place.

Second, R&D in new medicines is a *global public good.* Because the benefits of scientific advances on (for example) an HIV vaccine would spill over to many countries, none of the many small countries that would benefit from such a vaccine has an incentive to unilaterally encourage the development of a vaccine. Whereas intellectual property rights create incentives for innovation, granting private firms temporary market exclusivity increases dynamic benefits (that is, creates incentives for innovation) at the cost of static welfare (in the form of reduced access to medicines).

The goals of creating incentives for R&D on new medicines (which requires high prices) and ensuring wide access to medicines once developed (where low prices enable limited budgets to go further) are often pitted against each other. However, as we explain, advance market commitments can decouple these goals and promote both effectively.

ADVANCE MARKET COMMITMENTS: ADDRESSING MARKET
FAILURES AND FACILITATING ACCESS TO NEW VACCINES

One proposal that seeks to address both of these market failures is an advance market commitment. A working group convened by the Center for Global Development, with financial support from the Bill & Melinda Gates Foundation, explored the details of how this proposal could be implemented (Barder et al. 2005).

Under an advance market commitment, sponsors make a legally binding commitment to fully or partially finance the purchase of qualifying vaccines for poor countries, at a prespecified price and for up to a fixed number of individuals immunized. Poor countries decide whether to purchase a vaccine, and they (or donors, on their behalf) pay a low price (say, $1) per person immunized. Sponsors then top up this low price to a higher, subsidized price (say, $15 per person immunized), which provides market returns to the vaccine developer comparable to those of other, average-revenue pharmaceutical products. Once the predetermined number of treatments (say, 200 million persons immunized) is purchased at the high price, manufacturers are then contractually obliged either to sell further treatments at a low, affordable price in the long-term, or to license their technology to other manufacturers. If no vaccine were to be developed, no donor funds would be spent.

This Advance Market Commitment approach addresses the two market failures identified above:

- First, it addresses the time inconsistency market failure by precommitting governments and other vaccine purchasers not to negotiate down the price once a vaccine has been developed and productive capacity has been built.
- Second, it addresses the public good market failure by remunerating investment in R&D without restricting access to the product. The producer receives a high price that enables

recovery of its R&D investment, and the purchaser pays an affordable price that reflects the low marginal cost of producing vaccines.

In rich countries, public and philanthropic resources fund basic scientific and clinical research on new medicines for diseases prevalent in those countries, and the prospect of profits in rich-country markets provides incentives for private sector firms to transfer basic research into useable products. In the case of neglected diseases, the second half of this pipeline is currently missing. Advance market commitments, complementing public investment in R&D, replicate, for neglected diseases, the mixture of public and private financing that exists for diseases prevalent in rich countries.

A key issue from the perspective of improving public health in developing countries is that policies should not only provide incentives for innovation but also link these incentives to access to products once they are developed. In recent years, there have been long delays in introducing new vaccines on a broad scale in poor countries; for example, even as much as fourteen years after the introduction of the *Haemophilus influenzae B* (Hib) vaccine in the United States and Europe, fewer than 10 percent of infants in the world's poorest seventy-five countries were routinely receiving this vaccine (Levine et al. 2004). As a result of these delays, more than 2 million individuals in poor countries die annually from vaccine-preventable diseases (GAVI 2006).

A key advantage of advance purchase commitments is that they can be structured to ensure that vaccines—once developed—are made available quickly and affordably to individuals in poor countries. In the short term, access to the vaccine in countries that need it most is facilitated through donor purchasers at the higher, prespecified purchase price per person immunized. In the long term, financially sustainable access to these technologies is facilitated by a contractual requirement on developers to drop the price to a low level (close to marginal cost) after the high-price purchases have been made.

COST-EFFECTIVENESS OF AN
ADVANCE MARKET COMMITMENT

Under an advance market commitment, donor funds are spent *only* if desired products are developed. In this section we discuss how, if desired vaccines are indeed developed, an advance market commitment is an extremely cost-effective expenditure from a public health perspective.

The specified price and quantity of vaccine that will be purchased at the higher, subsidized price together determine what size of market will be generated under an advance market commitment. One reasonable way of setting this market size is to examine the realized revenues of drugs and vaccines that have, in the past, been developed by private firms—under the rationale that the expected market sizes of these medicines must have been sufficient, in the past, to spur private sector innovation.

A recent study by Ernst Berndt and colleagues (2007) calculates that the mean revenues for a sample of new drugs developed during the 1990s, adjusted down for lower marketing expenditures, had a net present value of approximately $3.1 billion in 2004 prices. Berndt and colleagues outline how this estimate can be combined with estimates of likely revenues from private markets—such as travelers, the military, and middle-income countries—to determine the size of the donor commitment that would provide an overall market size comparable to the realized revenues of existing medicines.

Based on the cost per life-year saved as a result of vaccines purchased under an advance marked commitment, the commitment would be extremely cost-effective. Berndt and colleagues estimate that creating a $3.1 billion market for a malaria, HIV, or tuberculosis vaccine would cost approximately $15, $17, or $30 per life-year saved, respectively.[2] These expenditures would be among the most cost-effective development interventions, and Berndt and colleagues document that advance market commitments would be cost-effective within a wide range of possible commitment sizes. Smaller commitments could also be used to scale up the supply of vaccines for which the R&D is already largely complete—such as pneumococcal or rotavirus.

CONCLUSION

Though vaccines for diseases concentrated in poor countries hold enormous potential social benefits, two key market failures reduce incentives for R&D on such vaccines. Advance market commitments, such as the pneumococcal vaccine commitment announced in 2007, could accelerate the development of new vaccines for neglected diseases by addressing both market failures, and they can be designed so as to facilitate widespread access to these vaccines, if they are developed. Such commitments could provide a highly cost-effective, market-led, results-based way for donors to save more lives than would be possible with virtually any comparable health expenditure.

NOTES

1. "Life-years," throughout this paper, refer to disability-adjusted life-years (DALYs).

2. These calculations were done prior to the recent announcement by the Bill & Melinda Gates Foundation of the partnership between the Malaria Vaccines Initiative and GlaxoSmithKline, which will enable further progress to be made on a leading malaria vaccine candidate; this development should be taken into account in the design of an advance market commitment for malaria.

REFERENCES AND FURTHER READING

Acemoglu, Daron and Joshua Linn. 2004. "Market Size in Innovation: Theory and Evidence from the Pharmaceutical Industry." *Quarterly Journal of Economics* 119 (3): 1049–1090.

Barder, Owen, Michael Kremer, Ruth Levine, and the Advanced Market Commitment Working Group. 2005. *Making Markets for Vaccines.* Washington, DC: Center for Global Development.

Berndt, Ernst, Rachel Glennerster, Michael Kremer, Jean Lee, Ruth Levine, Georg Weisäcker, and Heidi Williams. 2007. "Advance Market Commitments for Vaccines Against Neglected Diseases: Estimating Costs and Effectiveness." *Health Economics* 16 (5): 491–511.

Berndt, Ernst and John Hurvitz. 2005. "Vaccine Advance-Purchase Agreements for Low-Income Countries: Practical Issues." *Health Affairs* 24 (3): 653–665.

Creese, Andrew, Katherine Floyd, Anita Alban, and Lorna Guinness. 2002. "Cost-Effectiveness of HIV/AIDS Interventions in Africa: A Systematic Review of the Evidence." *Lancet* 359: 1635–1642.

Global Alliance for Vaccines and Immunization (GAVI). 2004. "Health, Immunization, and Economic Growth, Research Briefing #2, Vaccines Are Cost-Effective: A Summary of Recent Research." http://www.gavialliance.org/General Information/Immunization informa/ Economic Impact/vacc cost.php (accessed May 30, 2006).

———. 2006. "Immunization." http://www.gavialliance.org/resources/ FS_Immunisation_Aug06_en.pdf (accessed August 14, 2007).

Kim-Farley, Robert and the Expanded Programme on Immunization Team. 1992. "Global Immunization." *Annual Review of Public Health* 13: 223–237.

Kremer, Michael and Rachel Glennerster. 2004. *Strong Medicine: Creating Incentives for Pharmaceutical Research on Neglected Diseases.* Princeton, NJ: Princeton University Press.

Levine, Orin, Thomas Cherian, Raj Shah, and Amie Batson. 2004. "PneumoADIP: An Example of Translational Research to Accelerate Pneumococcal Vaccination in Developing Countries." *Journal of Health, Population, and Nutrition* 22 (3): 268–274.

Neumann, Peter, Eileen Sandberg, Chaim Bell, Patricia Stone, and Richard Chapman. 2000. "Are Pharmaceuticals Cost-Effective? A Review of the Evidence." *Health Affairs* 19 (2): 92–109.

Pécoul, Bernard, Pierre Chirac, Patrice Trouiller, and Jacques Pinel. 1999. "Access to Essential Drugs in Poor Countries: A Lost Battle?" *Journal of the American Medical Association* 281 (4): 361–367.

Towse, Adrian. 2002. "What Is NICE's Threshold? An External View." In *Cost Effectiveness Thresholds: Economic and Ethical Issues*, eds. Nancy Devlin and Adrian Towse, chap. 2. London: Kings Fund/Office of Health Economics.

World Bank. 1993a. *Investing in Health: The World Development Report 1993*. Washington, DC: World Bank.

———. 1993b. *Disease Control Priorities in Developing Countries*. New York: Oxford Medical Publications, Oxford University Press for the World Bank.

CHAPTER 8

Should We Still Support Untrammeled International Capital Mobility? Or Are Capital Controls Less Evil Than We Once Believed?

J. Bradford DeLong

FIFTEEN YEARS AGO, I found it easy to be in favor of international capital mobility—the free flow of investment financing from one country to another. Then, it was easy to preach for an end to the systems of controls on capital that hindered this flow.

"Why not free up capital flows to encourage large-scale lending from the world's rich countries to the world's poor countries?" I and others asked. Such lending, we hoped, might cut a generation off the time it otherwise would have taken developing countries' economies to catch up to the industrial structures and living standards of wealthier countries.

More than a century ago, large-scale borrowing and lending had played a key role in the economic development of the late nineteenth-century temperate periphery of Canada, the western United States, Australia, New Zealand, Chile, Argentina, Uruguay, and South

Africa. Why shouldn't it similarly benefit twentieth-century developing countries?

This reasoning seemed compelling then. Today, however, it is much harder for me to support untrammeled international capital mobility. I am no longer as sure that capital flows are efficient. Too many external costs associated with financial crises and the fact that capital seems to want to flow not from but to where it is already abundant make me fear that my standard economist's model is simply not working.

Worse yet, even if capital flows *are* efficient, it seems increasingly likely that these flows could benefit rich people from poor countries at the expense of the countries themselves—including their poor.

Thus, lifting capital controls—far from helping the world's poor, as many had hoped—may actually hurt them.

THE DREAM OF INTERNATIONAL CAPITAL MOBILITY

To see why capital mobility has not lived up to our earlier dreams, it is important first to describe exactly what those dreams were in the first place. Neoliberals like me saw three important ways that removing capital controls could potentially improve life in poor countries. But history showed that, in practice, these improvements did not happen as we had hoped.

First, the resulting capital inflows, we thought, would directly boost production and productivity. Capital controls had kept the level of investment in peripheral developing countries down, or so we believed. This seemed to have a very negative economic impact. Higher investment boosts a country's capital stock, and thus directly raises labor productivity and wages.

Second, we thought that with capital controls removed, developing countries' industries and people would enjoy the benefits that flow from technological advances and from learning by doing using modern machinery. After all, such benefits had been at the heart of so much of the productivity growth of the past two centuries.

Third, capital controls created large-scale opportunities for corruption, and we hoped that the removal of capital controls would reduce corruption and improve the quality of government in these countries. In highly corrupt societies, tax rates and the regulatory barriers to starting businesses are idiosyncratically and randomly high. Such societies cannot be productive or equitable.

Whoever got the scarce permissions to borrow abroad had a good chance of becoming rich, and somehow those who got them often turned out to be married to the niece of the vice minister of finance. When capital controls are in place, people who badly want to move their capital across borders cannot—unless they can find some complaisant bureaucrat. A well-functioning market economy needs to minimize the incentives and opportunities for corruption or it will begin to decline.

Together, these three reasons seemed to make up an overwhelming case for lifting capital controls. The world's system of relative prices is tilted against the poor: the products they export are cheap, yet the capital goods they must import in order to industrialize and develop are expensive. The hope was that this inequity could be at least partially remedied by open capital flow.

PROOF THAT THE DREAM DIDN'T COME TRUE: MEXICO'S EXAMPLE

Working at the U.S. Treasury in 1993, I naively projected that after NAFTA (North American Free Trade Agreement) there would be a net capital flow of some $10 billion to $20 billion a year to Mexico for decades to come. I predicted that investors around the world would now build factories in Mexico, where they not only could pay low wages to workers but also could enjoy guaranteed tariff-free access to the largest consumer market in the world. Sadly, however, it did not turn out that way.

Here is what's really happening. The good part is that Mexican workers and entrepreneurs are gaining experience in export manufactures, and they are exporting enough to the United States to run a trade surplus. But the flip side of the trade surplus is a capital outflow—from Mexico to the United States, rather than from the United States to Mexico. Should capital-poor Mexico really be financing a further jump in the capital intensity of the U.S. economy?

Why didn't this dream come to fruition? There are several basic explanations for the disparity between dream and reality.

ONE PROBLEM WITH THE DREAM: CASH FLOW INTO, NOT OUT OF, RICH COUNTRIES

One basic problem for the dream was that capital did not, in practice, flow from rich to poor, as we'd hoped. Instead, it flowed from poor to rich—and overwhelmingly, in recent years, into the United States.

The United States' rate of capital inflow is now the largest of any country, anytime, anywhere. The U.S. economy became, and remains, a giant vacuum cleaner, soaking up all of the world's spare investable cash.

How much money, exactly, are we talking about? As best we can calculate, the United States has run current-account deficits averaging 2.5 percent of gross domestic product (GDP) over the past two decades—that's $270 billion a year at today's level of GDP.

It is true that at most only one-third of this—about $90 billion—can be attributed to inflows from the developing world. But from the perspective of the developing world, that is an overwhelming, crushing amount of money. Consider, for example, that $90 billion a year is the (current exchange rate) income of the poorest 500 million people in India.

At this point, we must concede that the hope for a repetition of the late nineteenth-century experience—in which core investors' money gave peripheral economies the priceless gift of quick economic development—has so far proved vain.

WHY CAPITAL FLOWED INTO, NOT OUT OF, RICH COUNTRIES

This fact is clear: Capital is flowing into the United States and other wealthy countries but not into poorer countries. But what are the reasons?

Some may say the inflow of capital into America was and is justified because of the high quality of American investments. But if these investment opportunities are truly so great, why aren't Americans themselves saving more—both privately and publicly—to take advantage of them?

In fact, it seems that the reasons capital flowed into America and other countries were largely *not* based on the supposed superiority of these countries' investments. International capital mobility was supposed to add to, not drain, the pool of funds financing development in peripheral countries. Why didn't it happen that way? Which investors and banks, in particular, chose to send capital to the United States and other wealthy countries rather than to developing countries?

First, there were first-world investors who feared investing in developing countries. They worried about sending their money down the income and productivity gap after the crises of Mexico in 1995, East Asia in 1997, and Russia in 1998. U.S. investments, although potentially less lucrative, seemed much more stable. In particular, techno-enthusiasts were prone to chase the returns of the American technology boom.

Second, there were investors, governments, and banks from developing countries themselves. Central banks sought to keep the values of their home currencies down so that their workers could gain valuable experience in exporting manufactured goods to the post-industrial core.

Third, the third-world rich often thought a large Deutsche Bank account would be a good thing to have in case something went wrong and they suddenly had to flee the country in the rubber boat (or the Learjet). Again, stability in investment—as opposed to potential future returns—was the key.

Many billions of dollars of capital has fled Russia in the past decade. These capital exports were presumably in the interest of the Russian oligarchs who moved their wealth to Finland and Cyprus. The example of Yukos baron Mikhail Khodorkovsky—who now sits in jail for displeasing President Vladimir Putin—suggests that they were personally very wise to do so. But did their actions benefit Russia as a whole?

ANOTHER PROBLEM WITH THE DREAM: INCREASED SYSTEMIC RISK

Even more worrisome than the fact that money seemed to be flowing in the wrong direction was the increased vulnerability to financial crises of peripheral countries with open capital flows.

Currency mismatch, duration mismatch, and risk mismatch left Mexico, East Asia, Brazil, Turkey, and others desperately vulnerable when first-world investors' perceptions turned against them.

I and other advocates of mobility suggested that these risks could be dramatically lessened. We suggested that before controls were lifted, it was important to first establish an effective system of financial regulation. Such a system, we hoped, would ensure that financial firms' bets would not create large amounts of systemic risk.

This hope, however, was too optimistic. Consider that the United States does not have an easy time regulating its financial system when the salary differential between the bureaucratic regulators and those they regulate is five to one. Then ask yourself: What chance does an Indonesia, a Thailand, or a Brazil have when the salary differential between the bureaucratic regulators and those they regulate is ten to one?

With a disparity like this, the regulators are nearly powerless— unable to enforce the regulations they opt for—and those who are regulated are immensely powerful in comparison. It's no surprise that regulation is ineffective.

COMPARING THEORIES OF INTERNATIONAL LENDING: TWO ERAS, TWO APPROACHES

1960–1985 was the era in which development was to be financed by *public* lending by institutions like the World Bank. The idea was that market failures and distrust of governments had made it very hard for poor countries to borrow on the private market. But public lending would fill the breach. This era was hardly an unqualified success. But neither was the era that followed—the era we are living in now.

1985–2004 was the era in which development was to be financed by *private* lending, from first-world investors to those countries that had adopted the free-market policies that were supposed to produce high returns and rapid growth. But again, it didn't happen that way: First-world investors didn't invest in developing countries, and indeed, to the contrary, developing countries often invested in the first world—especially the United States.

It's hard, then, to say that the second era was better than the first. The anti-corruption effect of opening up capital flows still remains. But the other hoped-for effects—capital flow to poorer countries and corresponding technological advances—did not occur as planned.

CAN THE REVERSE CAPITAL FLOW, FROM POOR
TO RICH COUNTRIES, BE DEFENDED?

Can the flow of capital from poor to rich countries be defended? Perhaps it can from an efficiency standpoint—but not from any standpoint that considers even modest hopes for income equality.

It seems plausible that this reverse capital flow is economically efficient. Rich Mexicans certainly have the choice between investing in their own country and investing in America, and they are deciding to do the second. They may be seeking high expected returns in the United States—the United States is, indeed, an immensely productive, technologically inventive, and potentially fast-growing economy. They may also be diversifying against economic and political risks: they want to have something in America in case the rubber boat scenario comes to pass. (What better way is there to give your grandchildren the option of moving to the United States than by having large investments there?)

A standard economic analysis might stop here: It might say that although it is surprising that the net flow of capital is from poor to rich and not from rich to poor, the market knows best. The market is efficient, and voluntary acts of economic exchange are mutually beneficial. Never mind that they do not achieve the increased parity of rich and poor that we dreamed of—and indeed, that they may have just the opposite effect.

A FLAWED SITUATION THAT MAY STILL BE
THE BEST WE CAN DO

For anyone who cares at all about income equality, the current situation is disturbing. Already dramatic inequalities may only be exacerbated by reverse capital flow from poor to rich countries.

Nevertheless, a card-carrying neoliberal like me still cannot wish for any but the most minor of controls to curb the most speculative of capital flows. Capital markets can get the allocation of investment badly wrong. But governments are likely to get it even worse. In addition, the incentives for bureaucrats to become corrupt must be kept as low as possible. In the end, we may have to tolerate the equality-lessening reverse flow of capital in order to promote the equality-increasing and wealth-increasing diminution of corruption in less-developed countries.

REFERENCES AND FURTHER READING

Goldstein, Morris. 1998. *The Asian Financial Crisis: Causes, Cures, and Systemic Implications.* Washington, DC: Institute for International Economics.

Mussa, Michael. 2002. *Argentina and the Fund: From Triumph to Tragedy.* Washington, DC: Institute for International Economics.

Roubini, Nouriel. Roubini Global Economics (RGE) Monitor. http://www.stern.nyu.edu/globalmacro/.

PART **III**

ECONOMICS OF
THE IRAQ WAR

WHAT HAS BEEN the cost of the Iraq war? In its early days, the Bush administration focused on estimated budgetary costs of $100 billion to $200 billion. At the time, some thought these were overestimates. They are large enough numbers, but they have, in any case, turned out to be underestimates—especially when the wider costs to the economy on top of the burden of additional government spending are factored in.

The following two essays take this wider economic perspective on the costs of the war, although each has a somewhat different focus. In the first essay, Scott Wallsten takes into account the missing productivity contribution and earnings of reserve troops, and the economic costs of the loss of life and injuries due to the war, in addition to the direct impact of the war in increasing current federal spending. Altogether, this takes the estimated cost to the United States to about $500 billion through mid-2005, with about another $200 billion in costs for coalition partners and Iraq itself.

The second article, by Joseph Stiglitz, goes wider still, incorporating the future burden on the government's budget of additional military pensions and adding the impact of higher oil prices on the economy as well as the opportunity cost of government spending diverted from other areas to fighting the war. It estimates the figure could be one to two *trillion* dollars. Needless to say, all of the types of costs considered have continued to rise since the estimates here were prepared.

Why do the precise figures matter? The answer is that all policy decisions imply costs and benefits. Choosing policies wisely depends on the balance between the two. If more economists had engaged actively in the debate about the likely costs of the Iraq war—all of the costs, not just the direct impact on the budget—right from the start, perhaps the choice would then have looked rather different to the American people. Was the war the best use of these resources? Could they have been better spent on fighting global climate change, on providing vaccine commitments to fight tropical diseases, on brokering Israeli-Palestinian peace, or on giving ten million children in the United States or abroad each a $100,000 college scholarship?

CHAPTER 9

The Economic Cost of the Iraq War

Scott Wallsten

IN 2002, LAWRENCE Lindsey, then director of the White House National Economic Council, surprised the Bush administration by saying that a war in Iraq could cost $100 billion to $200 billion. His estimate, considered by some to be exaggerated, has turned out to be too low.

Since the war in Iraq began, economists haven't been heavily involved in the public debate regarding the conflict. That absence is a mistake.

Choosing to go to war reflects a belief that the expected benefits of the conflict exceed the expected costs and that society's scarce resources could not be better deployed elsewhere. Although justification for war is rarely couched in purely economic terms, the tools of cost-benefit analysis can be applied there, just as they can be to any policy decision.

Scott Wallsten is a senior fellow and director of communications policy studies at the Progress and Freedom Foundation and also a lecturer in Stanford University's public policy program. Before joining PFF, he was a senior fellow at the AEI-Brookings Joint Center for Regulatory Studies and a resident scholar at the American Enterprise Institute. He has also served as an economist at The World Bank, a scholar at the Stanford Institute for Economic Policy Research, and a staff economist at the U.S. President's Council of Economic Advisers.

Granted, some of the tools may be too crude, and the data too spotty, to allow us to reach firm conclusions. And we may dispute how to monetize some benefits and costs. Nonetheless, the debate about the war should be informed by estimates—even if imprecise— of its actual economic costs.

I estimate that through the summer of 2005, the direct economic costs of the war in Iraq to the United States were about $300 billion. Including costs to Iraq and coalition partners, the global cost comes closer to $500 billion. Looking forward, the total net present value of the costs could double before this war is done.

The conflict, however, has also led to some savings. I estimate that the avoided costs of no longer enforcing U.N. sanctions and of Saddam Hussein no longer murdering people are about $120 billion to date, and they could total around $430 billion by 2015.

IT'S A MISTAKE TO EQUATE BUDGET ALLOCATIONS WITH ECONOMIC COSTS

Before the war, several economists weighed in on its likely costs. In 2002, David Nordhaus noted that politicians throughout history have underestimated the costs of war, and he estimated that the economic costs could be anywhere from $100 billion to $2 trillion. Then, in 2003, Steven Davis, Kevin Murphy, and Robert Topel compared the costs of continuing with the then-status quo of sanctions and inspections with the costs and benefits of a war. Their estimates of the economic and other devastation caused by Saddam Hussein suggested that a war would eventually yield net welfare gains.

Since the war began, though, most of the discussion regarding the costs has focused on the federal budget alone. To some extent, that focus is understandable. After all, the government's resources, like anyone else's, are limited. And although taxes themselves are just transfer payments, the act of raising taxes and borrowing funds has real economic costs.

But as Warwick McKibbin and Andrew Stoeckel noted in 2003, "merely presenting the cost to the fiscal position as the cost of a war is a significant underestimate of the overall cost of conflict just as changes in fiscal balances are an inappropriate measure of the possible gains from war."

In the next section I present a framework for estimating the direct costs that are *not* reflected in the budget.

HOW SHOULD WE ESTIMATE THE DIRECT
ECONOMIC COSTS OF THE WAR?

Alongside the budget debate is anxiety about the war's other impacts, including deaths, injuries, and the mobilization of National Guard and reserve troops for extended tours of duty. Those are all real costs. Monetizing them provides a coherent way for policymakers to compare the costs and cost-effectiveness of the war with those of other policies and thus use our scarce resources in the most efficient manner possible.[1]

Consider the use of the Guard and Reserves. About 40 percent of the 140,000 American troops in Iraq belong to the Guard or Reserves, and an additional 63,000 have been mobilized to replace active-duty troops now in Iraq. These erstwhile "weekend warriors" can't do their civilian jobs while they're on active military duty. The cost to the economy is their lost civilian productivity, or about $4 billion per year.[2]

Measuring lost productivity is relatively straightforward. Monetizing lives, however, is more controversial—how can a dollar figure reflect the death of a child, spouse, or parent? Indeed, economic analyses do not attempt to value any particular individual's life. Instead, they assess how much individuals are willing to pay to reduce their risks of death and use that information to calculate a "value of a statistical life"

(VSL). In policy analysis, these assessments are crucial for evaluating whether benefits outweigh costs and whether society's limited resources are being deployed effectively.

By the end of October 2005, more than 2,000 American soldiers had died in Iraq. Economists estimate VSL to be between $4 million and $9 million (in 2000 dollars).[3] An estimate in the middle of that range suggests that the cost of American dead is around $15 billion (in 2005 dollars).

We can monetize injuries similarly, assuming two major costs: (1) lifetime care and treatment and (2) welfare loss to the wounded person. We can then estimate these costs using data from the Defense Department on injury types and calibrating injuries to VSL by their severity. This approach suggests that injuries have cost another $20 billion.

Including budget allocations specifically for Iraq, these estimates yield a total cost to date to the United States of around $300 billion.

What about other direct global costs? The VSL estimate used here is based on studies in the United States and may not be applicable to other countries. In a 2003 survey of the research around the world, Viscusi finds that for each 1 percent change in per capita income, estimated VSL changes by about one-half of a percent.

It is possible to monetize non-American lives using that result, the American VSL, and estimates of countries' per capita income. Nobody knows the Iraqi death toll for certain, but according to one commonly cited source, more than 35,000 Iraqis have died.[4] That represents a human cost to Iraq of around $120 billion.

Similar costs to non-American coalition countries and the costs of physical damage caused during the war add another $70 billion or so to the global tab, which comes to around $500 billion to date.

The war has also led to some direct cost savings, too. In particular, we are no longer enforcing U.N. sanctions and Saddam Hussein is no longer killing people. Davis, Murphy, and Topel (2003) estimated that enforcing the sanctions cost about $13 billion per year and that

Hussein was responsible for an average of 10,000 deaths a year. Those avoided costs top $300 billion so far.

All of those costs, though, are sunk. What about the future?

Nobody knows how long the war will last. But by making several assumptions we can apply this framework and estimate the net present value of expected future costs. Using Congressional Budget Office projections of troop strength and military expenditures through 2015; assuming that future trends in the death and injury rates and Guard and Reserve use remain constant; and using a 5 percent discount rate, the expected net present value of the incremental cost of the war could be $300 billion to the United States, $50 billion to non-U.S. coalition partners, and $200 billion to Iraq.

In other words, the war could still cost the world another half trillion dollars.

THE LESSONS OF THE ANALYSIS: IT'S VALUABLE,
BUT MORE RESEARCH IS NEEDED

These calculations are not exhaustive. They do not, for example, take into account the war's impact on oil prices or other parts of the macroeconomy.

They also exclude the possibility of certain benefits. By some measures, for example, the Iraqi economy is recovering from its total devastation under Saddam Hussein and U.N. sanctions. The wetlands of southern Iraq, drained by Hussein in his campaign against the "marsh Arabs," may return to their natural state, yielding environmental benefits. And maybe a robust democracy will emerge.

Despite its shortcomings, this analysis offers several lessons.

First, the tools of cost-benefit analysis can be used as a framework for estimating the costs of war, facilitating comparisons with the costs of other government policies.

Second, additional research is needed to fine-tune these tools for use in analyzing the expected cost of war. The value of a statistical life I used in this analysis, for example, is based primarily on studies of the civilian labor force. That's fine for evaluating, say, proposed environmental regulations that affect broad swaths of the population. But in 2004, Viscusi found that these values vary over industries and occupations. Is a military VSL different from a civilian VSL? Is the nature of military service different in ways that require us to rethink the concept of VSL for soldiers?

Third, war involves tremendous uncertainty. We need to incorporate mechanisms to better analyze these questions. Information markets, for example, which are already used to aggregate information for better prediction of business, finance, and politics, might be useful here, too. Information markets might have shed light, for instance, on how likely it was that Iraq had weapons of mass destruction, or whether a war with Iraq would affect the probability of another major terrorist attack and by how much. This information could then be incorporated into a rigorous cost-benefit analysis.

So this analysis can't conclude, as President George W. Bush did recently, that the war is "worth it"—nor can it conclude, as his critics have, that it is not. But it can begin to frame the question of whether it is a good use of our resources: Is bringing democracy to Iraq, for example, worth another half trillion dollars?

Perhaps more important, as we search for an endgame to the war, we need an objective, rigorous, and transparent framework to choose a policy expected to make the best use of our resources. Maybe economics can help provide one.

NOTES

1. For complete details on methodology and data sources, see Wallsten and Kosec (2005).

2. Here, I'm assuming an average annual income of about $33,000 based on data from the Defense Department on Reservists' occupations and from the Bureau of Labor statistics on wages by occupation and industry. Congressional appropriations for military operations in Iraq include funds to pay Guard and Reserve troops and are subtracted from our total to avoid double-counting the cost of those troops.

3. See Viscusi (2004) for a thorough review of the literature.

4. http://www.iraqbodycount.net/.

REFERENCES AND FURTHER READING

Davis, Steven J., Kevin M. Murphy, and Robert H. Topel. 2003. "War in Iraq versus Containment: Weighing the Costs." Working paper, University of Chicago Graduate School of Business. Available at http://faculty.chicagogsb.edu/steven.davis/research/.

Iraq Body Count, 2003–2007. http://www.iraqbodycount.net/.

McKibbon, Warwick J. and Andrew Stoeckel. 2003. "The Economic Costs of a War in Iraq." Washington, DC: Brookings Institution. www.brookings.edu/views/papers/mckibbin/20030307.htm.

Nordhaus, William D. 2002. *The Economic Consequences of a War with Iraq*. Working paper no. 9361. Cambridge, MA: National Bureau of Economic Research.

Viscusi, W. Kip. 2004. "The Value of Life: Estimates with Risks by Occupation and Industry." *WEF* 42 (1): 29–48.

Viscusi, W. Kip and Joseph E. Aldy. 2003. "The Value of a Statistical Life: A Critical Review of Market Estimates Throughout the World." *The Journal of Risk and Uncertainty* 21 (1): 5–76.

Wallsten, Scott and Katrina Kosec. 2005. "The Economic Costs of the War in Iraq." Working paper. Available at http://aei-brookings.org/publications/php?pid=988 (accessed January 11, 2006).

10

The High Cost of the Iraq War

Joseph E. Stiglitz

THE MOST IMPORTANT things in life, and life itself, are priceless. But that does not mean that issues involving the preservation of life (or a way of life), such as defense, should escape cool, hard economic analysis. They should not.

Shortly before the current Iraq war, when Bush administration economist Larry Lindsey suggested that the costs might range between $100 billion and $200 billion, other officials quickly demurred. For example, Office of Management and Budget Director Mitch Daniels put the number at $60 billion. It is now clear that Lindsey's numbers were a gross underestimate (Bumiller 2002).

Concerned that the Bush administration might be misleading everyone about the Iraq war's costs, just as it had about Iraq's weapons of mass destruction and connection with al-Qaida, I teamed up with Linda Bilmes, a budget expert at Harvard, to examine the issue. Even as opponents of the war, we were staggered by what we found. Our estimates range from slightly less than a trillion dollars (our conservative estimate) to more than $2 trillion (our moderate estimate). These and all subsequent figures can be found in Stiglitz and Bilmes (2006).

HOW THE COSTS ADD UP

Our analysis starts with the $500 billion that the Congressional Budget Office (CBO) openly talks about, which is already ten times higher than what the administration said the war would cost. This estimate, though, falls far short of the full costs of the war because the reported numbers do not even include the full budgetary costs to the government, which are but a fraction of the costs to the economy as a whole.

For example, the Bush administration has been doing everything it can to hide the huge number of returning veterans who are severely wounded—over 12,000 so far, including roughly 20 percent with serious brain and head injuries. So it is no surprise that the CBO's figure of $500 billion ignores the lifetime disability and health-care costs that the government will have to pay for years to come.

Nor does the administration want to face up to the military's recruiting and retention problems. The result is large reenlistment bonuses, improved benefits, and higher recruiting costs—up 20 percent just from 2003 to 2005. Moreover, the war causes extreme wear on equipment, some of which will have to be replaced.

These budgetary costs (exclusive of interest) amount to $652 billion in our conservative estimate and $799 billion in our moderate estimate. Arguably, since the government has not reined in other expenditures or increased taxes, the expenditures have been debt financed, and the interest costs on this debt add another $98 billion (conservative) to $385 billion (moderate) to the budgetary costs.

Of course, the brunt of the costs of injury and death is borne by soldiers and their families. But the military pays disability benefits that are markedly lower than the value of lost earnings. Similarly, payments for those who are killed amount to only $500,000, which is far less than standard estimates of the lifetime economic cost of a death, sometimes referred to as the statistical value of a life ($6.1 million to $6.5 million).

But the costs don't stop there. The Bush administration once claimed that the Iraq war would be good for the economy, with one spokesperson even suggesting that it was the best way to ensure low oil prices. As in so many other ways, things have turned out differently: the oil companies are the big winners, while the American and global economies are losers. Being extremely conservative, we estimate the overall effect on the economy if only $5 or $10 of the increase in the price of oil per barrel is attributed to the war. Combined with assumptions about the length of price increases, assumed to be between five and ten years, this implies a cost to the American economy of $125–300 billion.

At the same time, money spent on the war could have been spent elsewhere. We estimate that if a portion of that money had been allocated to domestic investment in roads, schools, and research, the American economy would have been stimulated more in the short run, and its growth would have been enhanced in the long run.

There are a number of other costs, some potentially quite large, although quantifying them is problematic. For instance, Americans pay some $300 billion annually for the "option value" of military preparedness—being able to fight wherever needed. That Americans are willing to pay this suggests that the option value exceeds the costs. But there is little doubt that the option value has been greatly impaired and will likely remain so for several years.

In short, even our moderate estimate may significantly underestimate the cost of America's involvement in Iraq. And our estimate does not include any of the costs implied by the enormous loss of life and property in Iraq itself.

THE IMPLICATIONS

We do not attempt to explain whether the American people were deliberately misled regarding the war's costs or whether the Bush administration's gross underestimate should be attributed to incompetence, as it vehemently argues is true in the case of weapons of mass destruction.

Nor do we attempt to assess whether there were more cost-effective ways of waging the war. Recent evidence that deaths and injuries would have been greatly reduced had better body armor been provided to troops suggests how short-run frugality can lead to long-run costs. Certainly, when a war's timing is a matter of choice, as in this case, inadequate preparation is even less justifiable.

But such considerations appear to be beyond the Bush administration's reckoning. Elaborate cost-benefit analyses of major projects have been standard practice in the Department of Defense and elsewhere in government for almost a half-century. During the planning stages, the Iraq war was expected to be an immense "project," yet it now appears that the initial analysis of its benefits was greatly flawed and that of its costs virtually absent.

One cannot help but wonder: were there alternative ways of spending a fraction of the war's $1–2 trillion in costs that would have better strengthened security, boosted prosperity, and promoted democracy?

REFERENCES AND FURTHER READING

Bumiller, Elisabeth. 2002. "Threats and Responses: The Cost: White House Cuts Estimate of Cost of War with Iraq." *New York Times*, December 31, A1.

Stiglitz, Joseph E. and Linda Bilmes. 2006. *The Economic Costs of the Iraq War*. Working paper no. 12054. Cambridge, MA: National Bureau of Economic Research. http://www2.gsb.columbia.edu/faculty/jstiglitz/ (accessed August 17, 2007).

Wallston, Scott. 2006. "The Economic Cost of the Iraq War." *The Economists' Voice* 3 (2), art. 1. http://www.bepress.com/ev/vol3/iss2/art1 (accessed August 17, 2007).

PART IV

FISCAL POLICY

THE CLAIMS AND counterclaims about fiscal policy during the 2004 presidential election campaign offered Michael Boskin the chance, in the first of the two essays in this section, to clarify the terms of the debate. How much does it matter to the economy that the federal government moved from a large surplus to a large deficit in the years after 2000? Boskin sets out the different concepts of the budget balance and discusses how much deficits matter in the short, medium, and long terms.

Large federal government deficits can be appropriate in some circumstances—such as in a recession, or indeed in the case of a temporary spending need such as fighting a war—and have adverse effects on the economy in other cases. When the economy is strong, the budget should be in a surplus. Although it is impossible to be precise about the exact length of the short term, a period over which a deficit does not matter if it is cushioning the economy against the worst effects of a business cycle downturn, it is clear that large deficits year after year are a matter for concern. They imply an ever-growing tax burden on future generations of taxpayers. Boskin argues that we should not just look at the absolute size of the deficit itself, and he provides a framework that he contends enables us to ascertain more clearly whether we should or should not be worried about the size of the deficit.

In the second essay, Ronald McKinnon offers a different perspective. He blames the deindustrialization of America on the soaring federal deficit. The reason: the need for large infusions of foreign savings to finance government borrowing sent the dollar higher and made it much harder for U.S. manufacturers to export their goods overseas. He calls the United States government the world's champion borrower in international capital markets and argues that foreigners are buying Treasury bonds in place of exports of American goods and services. Does this matter? His answer is yes, not least because of the damaging effects on employment and the political consequences. His conclusion, too, is that the federal budget deficit has been too big for too long and now urgently needs correcting.

CHAPTER 11

Sense and Nonsense About Federal Deficits and Debt

Michael J. Boskin

RENEWED ATTENTION IS focusing on the federal government's taxes and spending, deficit and debt. President George W. Bush credits his tax cuts with strengthening the recovery and wants to make them permanent. Senator John Kerry condemns the deficit and proposes to raise taxes on "the wealthy" (which includes many small businesses). Former Treasury secretary Robert Rubin frets over a fiscally induced economic collapse. However, Wall Street yawned when the deficit projections soared. Both Bush and Kerry pledge to cut the deficit in half over the next few years. Kerry would increase health-care and other spending, requiring still higher taxes to meet his deficit target,

Michael J. Boskin is a Hoover Institution senior fellow, Friedman Professor of Economics at Stanford University, and a research associate at the National Bureau of Economic Research. He chaired the President's Council of Economic Advisers, 1989–1993, and later the highly influential Commission on the Consumer Price Index (CPI). Boskin is internationally recognized for authoring over 100 books and articles on economic growth and public finance. He received his B.A. and Chancellor's Award as outstanding undergraduate in 1967, M.A. in 1968, and Ph.D. in 1971 from University of California–Berkeley.

which he says will be his top priority. Bush's budget sharply curtails spending growth, which requires a marked change from his first term. Are large (relative to the size of the economy) federal government deficits good, bad, or irrelevant? In fact, they can be each, depending upon circumstances.

THE SHORT RUN

Government deficits, more accurately increases in deficits, are not only natural but desirable in recessions and early in recoveries. In a downturn, receipts collapse and spending automatically increases; these so-called automatic stabilizers help cushion the decline in after-tax income and mitigate the swings in economic activity. The impact of the economy on the budget balance is swifter, surer, and larger than the impact of the budget balance on the economy. In the severe recession of 1982, these automatic stabilizers accounted for more than half of the then-record deficit. All economists agree we should allow the automatic stabilizers to work. Most, myself included, believe that monetary policy should be the main countercyclical tool. Fiscal policy is too clumsy to use to fine-tune the economy, given usual lags in legislative implementation. The major exception occurs when the Fed lowers short-run interest rates close to zero in a potentially severe downturn. The Fed reduced the federal funds rate to 1 percent in the recent downturn amid serious concern over even the small risk of a Japanese-style deflation and lost decade. Hence, additional fiscal policy insurance was necessary. From 2001 to 2003, the standard measure of short-run fiscal stimulus, the change in the cyclically adjusted budget deficit went from a surplus of 1.1 percent of gross domestic product (GDP) to a deficit of 3.1 percent of GDP, over a 4 percent of GDP swing. This was one of the largest and best-timed uses of fiscal policy in history, helping to prevent a much worse downturn; but it would have been better still if the tax rate cuts had been immediate and real spending controls enacted simultaneously to take effect well into the economic expansion.

It is appropriate, but not necessary, to finance (some) long-lived investment by government borrowing, because the benefits will accrue for many years and future taxpayers might equitably bear part of the burden. This is done routinely by state and local governments. Further, the economic harm caused by taxes rises with the square of tax rates; thus, doubling tax rates quadruples the "deadweight loss" caused because taxes distort economic decisions. It is thus more efficient to keep tax rates stable over time and to debt-finance temporary large spending needs such as military buildups during, or to prevent, war. Indeed, in every year of World War II, government borrowing exceeded tax revenues. Debt finance in this case is both equitable and efficient.

The usual measures of the deficit and debt can be extremely misleading. The deficit is heavily affected by the business cycle. Inflation erodes the value of the previously issued national debt, that is, the real debt declines with inflation (and conversely increases with deflation). More than half of the debt is held in government accounts or by the Fed (see figure 11.1). The federal government has many assets

FIGURE 11.1

Holding of the National Debt as of June 30, 2004

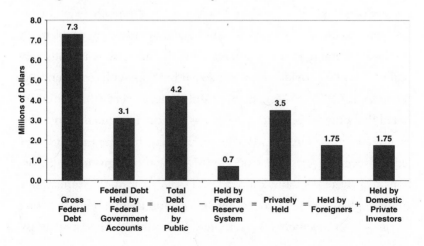

as well as debts. These include tangible capital such as buildings, computers, and planes; land and mineral rights; inventories; and financial assets. These currently total about $3 trillion, a large fraction of the national debt held outside the government. The federal government has other liabilities in addition to the debt, for example, for federal employees' health and retirement. Further, the government has potential large future unfunded liabilities in Social Security and Medicare (discussed briefly below).

The deficit measures how much the government borrows but does not distinguish whether the borrowing is financing consumption or investment. Unlike private business accounting, there is no capital budget, little accrual accounting, and no widely used balance sheet. In short, the budget says nothing about why and for what the added debt is incurred. Only if there were zero inflation, no capital spending, no need for temporary military buildups, no business cycles, and no previously issued debt or government assets would a balanced budget mean that current taxes are paying for current real government consumption.

Finally, the deficit is the difference between spending and taxes, the level, composition, and growth of which are the more fundamental fiscal indicators. Surely the United States is better off with our current size government and a small deficit than a European-size government and a balanced budget. Further, even if the U.S. federal budget were balanced, there would still be a large spending problem, as very few federal programs are target effective and cost conscious; virtually all could provide larger net social benefits with less spending. Indeed, the Office of Management and Budget's performance review noted that only 30 percent of programs had demonstrated even modest effectiveness. This is especially unfortunate because each dollar of federal revenue costs the economy $1.40 or more, given the distortions to private decisions caused by the taxes and the administrative and compliance cost of collecting and paying them. There is a long way to go to implement even remotely rigorous cost-benefit analysis.

TABLE 11.1

Alternative Budget Surplus/Deficit Concepts

1. *Unified* nominal surplus/deficit = nominal revenues – nominal outlays; "headline" numbers

2. *Operating* surplus/deficit = unified deficit – net investment (public capital investment – depreciation of public capital)

3. *Primary* surplus/deficit = unified deficit – interest outlays on inherited debt

4. *Cyclically adjusted* surplus/deficit: unified deficit adjusted to "high employment," that is, removes effect (+ and –) of business cycle on revenues and outlays (i.e., removes effect of "automatic stabilizers")

5. *Standardized* surplus/deficit: adjusts unified deficit for business cycle and some other transitory items, for example, the inflation component of interest, receipts from allies for Desert Storm, and deposit insurance outlays for failed S&Ls, that are unlikely to affect real income

To make sense of these issues, economists employ several related measures in addition to the traditional nominal cash budget balance (see table 11.1). The standardized budget surplus or deficit subtracts some transitory items such as deposit insurance outlays and receipts from allies for Desert Storm, the inflation component of interest outlays, and the cyclical factor. The primary budget deficit nets out interest, the cost of servicing the previously issued debt. The primary budget balance determines the evolution of the national debt (the present value of future primary surpluses must equal the national debt, net of assets). A balanced primary budget means that current outlays are paid by current revenues, and the inherited debt burden is neither rising nor falling, as the debt grows at about the same rate as the economy.

An operating budget balance nets out public capital investment,[1] from computers to planes, net of depreciation (of course, not all public investment is productive), which is commonly debt-financed by state and local governments. Finally, an expanded operating budget nets out a rough estimate of our most important investment: any systematic national security buildup or drawdown. Rough balance of a real standardized operating budget implies that, on average over time, additions to the debt burden are only for investment purposes, not to finance current consumption at the expense of future taxpayers, a much more precise measure than the headline nominal budget deficit of what the late senator Pat Moynihan called "throwing a party."

For the upcoming 2005 fiscal year, the deficit projected in the president's budget is roughly $350 billion, or 2.8 percent of GDP. Current inflation estimates and the interest and maturity structure of the $4 trillion of publicly held debt imply a decline by about $75 billion in real value. So the first $75 billion of the deficit is not a real deficit at all. Another $135 billion is President Bush's real homeland security and military buildups. Other federally financed investment outlays net of depreciation are roughly $70 billion. Thus, netting gets us to a deficit of $75 billion or so, a few tenths of a percent of GDP. If there were still some modest cyclical component to the deficit, a real cyclical operating budget would be almost balanced. Given that interest payments are projected to be $180 billion, roughly half real, half inflation, this means that, net of the investment components of the budget, and adjusting for inflation, President Bush's budget (FY2005) would actually slightly reduce the real burden of the net (of assets) debt. Of course, some might argue that the investments, including the military investments, are not worth it, that their dollar value greatly exaggerates the benefits the investment is leaving to future generations along with any debt, but that is the basis on which the argument ought to occur. Although in the long run the economy would be better served with low taxes and less spending, running modest deficits was a reasonable response to war and recession.

If desirable in war and recession, when and how do large deficits become a problem? Large deficits potentially cause two separate but related problems: shifting the bill for financing the current generation's consumption to future generations and crowding out private investment. Thus, deficits are more problematic well into a solid economic expansion. They are more of a problem if their impact is to reduce domestic investment and hence future income rather than to raise foreign capital imports or private saving:[2] They are more likely to be a problem if the level of the national debt, the accumulation of all previous deficits, is high or rapidly rising toward high levels relative to GDP. They are more problematic if they finance consumption, not productive public investment.

Turning to political economy, they are more problematic if they do not constrain future spending or if they lead to inflationary monetary policy. None of these conditions appears operative at the moment. If President Bush's budget plan, including both a sharp curtailment of spending growth and making the tax cuts permanent, is implemented, none is likely to occur in the next decade. Of course, this would require President Bush to be much tougher on spending than in the first term. Likewise, if Senator Kerry's proposal to reduce the deficit were put in place, which would require abandonment of most of his plans for federal health care and other spending, none of these conditions would occur either. If Bush got his tax cuts but no spending control, or Kerry his spending plans without even larger tax hikes, the deficits and debt would grow substantially relative to GDP, unless the deficits constrained future spending and hence enabled lower taxes which could increase future income and partially offset the initial deficit increase.

It is likewise instructive to probe deeper into the oversimplified budget myths surrounding previous administrations. For example, in 1999, the seventh year of the Clinton administration, the nominal budget was in a surplus to the tune of $126 billion or 1.4 percent of GDP, but the Congressional Budget Office (CBO) estimates that cyclical and temporary items virtually eliminate the surplus. The headline surplus was an artifact of the bubble. A primary surplus indicates progress was being made in reducing the debt burden, but partly by massive military spending cuts (38 percent relative to GDP). In 1992, the last year of the George H.W. Bush administration, the nominal budget deficit was $290 billion or 4.5 percent of GDP, but, net of cyclical and temporary items like deposit insurance outlays to finally clean up the S&Ls, the primary budget was roughly balanced. Finally, in 1984, the fourth year of the Reagan administration, the nominal deficit was $185 billion, about 4.7 percent of GDP; but netting cyclical factors, temporary items, the inflation component, net investment, and the military buildup, the deficit was just $8 billion, or 0.2 percent of GDP. The real borrowing financed net investment and the military buildup that helped win the cold war, not mostly current consumption expenditures, not a "party."

My point here is not to defend or criticize these particular budget outcomes but rather to demonstrate that it is necessary to dig down below the headline deficit numbers to appreciate the real economics of the budget and to demonstrate there is sometimes valid economic justification for large swings in the budget balance.

THE MEDIUM RUN

The CBO projects gradually declining deficits to almost balance over the next decade and a stable, then declining debt-GDP ratio. For the president's budget, it projects $2.7 trillion in cumulative additional debt over the next decade. This reflects a debt-GDP ratio that rises slightly to peak at about 40 percent in two or three years, below the post–World War II historical average and far below Euroland and Japan. It then stabilizes for the rest of the decade through 2014 even as the tax cuts are made permanent, so long as the post-1998 splurge in nondefense discretionary spending is slowed substantially. With interest outlays projected at 2 percent of GDP, the president's end-of-decade deficit of 1.6 percent of GDP would actually be a primary surplus of 0.4 percent of GDP (see figure 11.2). This is hardly a debt spiraling out of control, leading to inflation fears fueling a financial crisis and economic calamity. The resulting net deficit will cause a small increase in interest rates. Evidence here is weak, but the best

FIGURE 11.2

Debt Held by the Public as Percentage of GDP

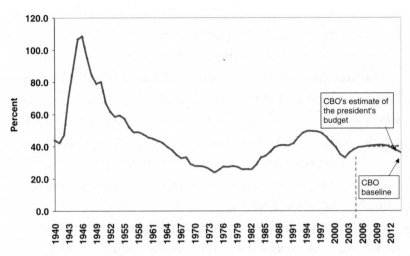

estimate is that interest rates would increase 25bp per 1 percent of GDP, or 40bp, or less, once any additional feedback effects of rate cuts on revenue and deficits on future spending are included.[3] This in turn will reduce domestic investment, but less than dollar for dollar, as the deficit will partly be financed from abroad.[4] The effect is important, but hardly a cause for hysteria.[5] Of course, President Bush's tax cuts and Senator Kerry's spending increases would likely have ramifications well beyond the next decade, when fiscal pressures will become even more pronounced.

THE LONG RUN

In several decades, the deficits in Social Security and Medicare are expected to be much larger than those projected in the unified budget for the next decade. The long-run deficit projections exceed $50 trillion in net present value. These projections may overstate the problem, for several reasons. They assume quite modest long-run annual growth. They project increases in health-care outlays far in excess of GDP growth for the better part of a century (the only way that would happen is if the health benefits were sufficient for citizens to want to spend that much). They assume large real benefit increases per beneficiary in Social Security will continue. They assume continuous tax cuts to offset real bracket creep, the AMT (Alternative Minimum Tax), and other factors that, under current law, are projected to raise taxes relative to GDP by one-third (compare the four panels in figure 11.3). But even with less stark projections, there would still be large deficits and large tax increases looming, which need to be addressed by reducing the growth of spending and by future tax reduction and reform.

Although it would be wise to control spending further and actually reduce the debt-GDP ratio over the coming decade, the far more important issue is to put in place, sooner rather than later, some of the common-sense Social Security and Medicare reforms that would gradually and cumulatively address their problems. Such reforms would have little impact on the budget in the next decade. Every year, the potential unfunded accrued liabilities grow, and the fraction of the voters receiving benefits rises relative to those paying taxes, thus making it increasingly difficult to enact the necessary reforms. I will discuss these issues in more detail in a future article.

Finally, economic policy should focus on the denominator as well as the numerator of the debt-GDP ratio. Maximizing noninflationary growth will require: (1) the lowest possible tax rates, (2) serious spending control, (3) sensible Social Security and Medicare reform, (4) regulatory and litigation reform, (5) trade liberalization, and (6) sound monetary policy.

Properly implemented, such a set of policies would stabilize the debt-GDP ratio at a modest level, except in economic downturns or periods of temporarily large or, conversely, small military spending or other vital public investment. The nominal dollar headline unified

FIGURE 11.3

Total Federal Spending and Revenues Under Different Long-Term Budget Scenarios

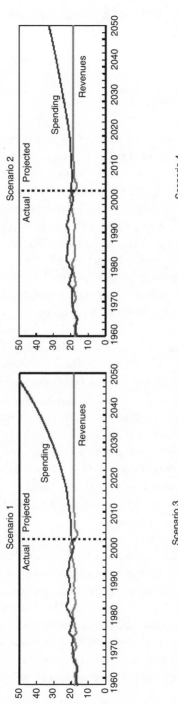

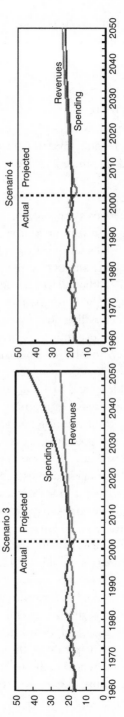

Source: CBO, Long-Term Budget Outlook, December 2003

The main driving assumptions: differentiating the scenarios are as follows:

Scenario 1: revenues flat at 18.4 percent of GDP; health spending grows 2.5 percent per year more rapidly than GDP

Scenario 2: revenues flat at 18.4 percent of GDP; "excess" health spending 1 percent per year more than GDP

Scenario 3: revenues as under current law; real bracket creep and AMT increase to 24.7 percent of GDP; health spending is 2.5 percent over GDP growth

Scenario 4: current law revenues grow to 24.7 percent of GDP; excess health spending is 1 percent over GDP growth budget might still run a "deficit" much of the time, but the true "burden of the debt" would not be rising.

NOTES

1. The federal government does not produce regular operating and capital budgets; these have to be derived from underlying data, as I have done below.

2. Some economists argue that, given the level of spending, it is irrelevant whether taxes or debt are used to finance it. The argument is that debt implies an equivalent present value of future taxes and forward-looking consumers will anticipate these higher future taxes and adjust their saving a corresponding amount, so there will be no net wealth effect of government bonds. Although most economists, myself included, do not fully accept this view, there may be some private saving offset, and this is another reason why crowding out may be less than dollar for dollar.

3. Deficits eventually exert some restraint on the course of subsequent government spending, although less than the dollar for dollar some imply. The gross historical experience in the late 1990s–2001 at the federal level and in California suggests that running a surplus leads to great pressure for legislatures to spend. Hence, it is unclear that a systematic policy of running budget surpluses, for example, in anticipation of future fiscal pressures, is even feasible.

4. External debt does not cause a substitution of government bonds for tangible capital in domestic portfolios and hence does not crowd out private investment. There is a concern that foreign holdings of U.S. government securities may be more mobile than domestic holdings and thus pose more risk of an abrupt dislocation.

5. The deficits causing serious inflation or financial and economic collapse scenarios would theoretically occur when bond holders reach, or anticipate reaching, an upper limit to the share of their wealth they are willing to hold in government bonds, as might be the case with the debt ratios projected in several decades. There would then be intense pressure on the central bank to monetize the deficit by buying up the bonds. The anticipation of the inflation (alternatively, strong depreciation of the currency) could then lead to a rise in interest rates, reduced capital formation, slower growth, and even recession if abrupt enough.

CHAPTER 12

Government Deficits and the Deindustrialization of America

Ronald I. McKinnon

DEINDUSTRIALIZATION IN THE United States is being accelerated by large federal fiscal deficits. Should we care? Absolutely.

Manufacturing and manufacturing-associated education, in the form of learning by doing,[1] are most likely powerful sources of external benefits that accelerate economy-wide productivity growth. In addition, the loss of manufacturing jobs is a powerful source of anger against free trade—and the more free trade is restricted, the more the American economy is hurt.

If current trends continue, Americans should not be surprised to find U.S. productivity growth slowing. As America becomes less productive, it will also predictably become more protectionist: a development that will further impoverish the country by destroying some of the gains from international trade.

Ronald I. McKinnon is the William D. Eberle Professor of International Economics at Stanford University. His latest book, *Exchange Rates Under the East Asian Dollar Standard: Living with Conflicted Virtue,* was published by the MIT Press in 2005.

THE DEINDUSTRIALIZATION OF AMERICA:
FOUR DECADES OF SHRINKAGE

For four decades, employment in U.S. manufacturing as a share of the labor force has fallen farther and faster than in other industrial countries. In the mid-1960s, manufacturing output was 27 percent of gross national product (GNP), and manufacturing's share of total employment was 24 percent. By 2003, these numbers had precipitously fallen, to about 13.8 percent and 10.5 percent, respectively.

Employment in manufacturing remains particularly weak in 2004. The Labor Department's September payroll survey, for example, showed an absolute decline of 18,000 jobs.

GROWING DEFICITS HAVE ACCOMPANIED
SHRINKING INDUSTRY

At the same time, the orgy of U.S. tax cutting with major revenue losses continues unabated—and has been coupled with excessive debt, resulting in a huge deficit. On October 6, 2004, for example, House and Senate negotiators approved an expansive tax bill that showers corporations and farmers with about 145 billion dollars' worth of rate cuts and new loopholes in the tax code—on top of what were already unprecedented fiscal deficits.

Ironically, the net result of this new bill, called the *American Jobs Creation Act of 2004*, is likely to be further declines in manufacturing employment—for, as I explain, deficits and deindustrialization are linked.

The United States is the world's champion borrower in international markets. Foreign central banks, which hold more than half the outstanding stock of U.S. Treasury bonds, have become the principal source of finance for the federal government's bourgeoning fiscal deficits—about 4 percent of gross domestic product (GDP) in 2004.

Besides this massive government dissaving, meager saving by American households forces U.S. corporations also to borrow abroad to supplement finance for domestic investment.

Thus dollar earnings by foreigners selling exports to the United States that would normally be used to buy American goods and services are being diverted and used to buy Treasury bonds instead. The upshot is today's current account deficit of more than $600 billion per year, a measure of overall net borrowing from foreigners amounting to almost 5.5 percent of U.S. GDP. Heavy foreign borrowing and associated trade deficits began in earnest in the 1980s, and so today America's cumulative net foreign indebtedness is 30 percent of GDP and rising fast.

HOW DEFICITS AND DEINDUSTRIALIZATION ARE CONNECTED

In the long run, America's heavy foreign borrowing impinges on the size of its manufacturing sector—meaning that deficits and deindustrialization go hand in hand.

The transfer of foreign saving to the United States is embodied more in goods than in services. Outsourcing to India aside, most services are not so easily traded internationally. Thus, when American spending rises above output (income), the net absorption of foreign goods—largely raw materials and manufacturers—increases.

True, in 2003 and 2004, the unusually high price of oil also significantly increased the U.S. current account deficit. However, since the early 1980s, the trade deficit in manufactures alone has been about as big as the current account deficit, that is, as big as America's saving shortfall—as shown below in figure 12.1.

If American households' and firms' spending for manufactured goods is more or less independent of whether the goods are produced at home or abroad, then domestic production shrinks by the amount of the trade deficit in manufactures.

FIGURE 12.1

U.S. Current Account Balance and Manufacturing Sector Trade
Balance (Percent of GDP)

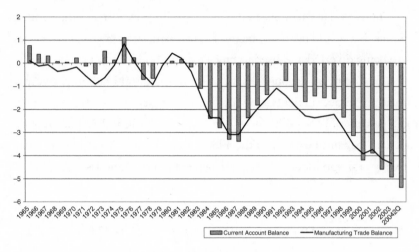

Source: Bureau of Economic Analysis

The consequent job loss depends inversely on labor productivity
in manufacturing, which rises strongly through time. If the trade
deficit in manufactured goods is added back to domestic production
to get "adjusted manufactured output," and labor productivity (output per person) in manufacturing remains the same, we get projected
employment in manufacturing.

In figure 12.2, below, the unbroken dark line traces the actual
share of manufacturing in total employment from 1965 to 2003.
The dashed line is the projected share of manufacturing employment if there had been no current account deficit (or trade deficit
in manufacturing)—that is, no saving deficiency in the American
economy.

For example, in 2003, actual employment in manufacturing was
just 10.5 percent of the American labor force, but it would have been

FIGURE 12.2

Projection of Labor Growth in Manufacturing Under Balanced
Manufacturing Trade

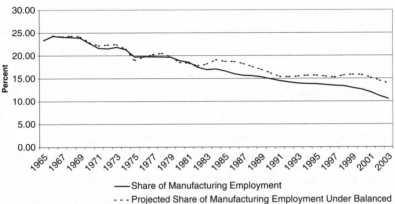

——Share of Manufacturing Employment

- - - Projected Share of Manufacturing Employment Under Balanced
Manufacturing Trade

Source: Bureau of Economic Analysis, Survey of Current Business

13.9 percent without a trade deficit in manufactures: this difference is
4.7 million lost jobs in manufacturing.

In the 1980s, employment in manufacturing began to shrink
substantially because of the then large current-account deficit (see
figure 12.1) attributed to the then large fiscal deficit: the infamous
twin deficits of Ronald Reagan's presidency.

In the 1990s, with fiscal consolidation under President Bill Clinton, the saving gap narrowed, but it wasn't closed, for American
household saving weakened.

Now, under President George W. Bush, the fiscal deficit has exploded again, while household saving remains weak. The result is
extremely heavy net borrowing from foreigners, leading to all-time
highs in the U.S. current account deficit in 2003 and 2004—also
shown in figure 12.1. The main component remains the trade deficit
in manufactured goods, leading to intensified shrinkage in American manufacturing employment.

THE ANSWER IS MORE SAVING, NOT MORE PROTECTIONISM

Is there cause for concern? Note that I do not suggest that overall employment has decreased but only that its composition has been tilted away from tradable goods—which are largely manufactured goods. In the long run, the U.S economy remains a very efficient job-creating machine, with growth in service-sector employment largely offsetting the decline in manufacturing.

However, the rate of technical change in manufacturing is much higher than in other sectors. And it is hard to imagine the United States sustaining its technological leadership with no manufacturing sector at all. As noted above, it is very probable that manufacturing and its associated learning by doing serve as a strong engine for the creation of the external benefits that accelerate economy-wide productivity growth. That means that the loss of manufacturing will inevitably be accompanied by a decrease in productivity growth.

A continuing loss of manufacturing jobs will also have noxious political consequences. More congressmen, pundits, and voters will feel justified in claiming that foreigners use unfair trade practices to steal American jobs, particularly in manufacturing.

Meanwhile, protectionists will find more and more voters persuaded by their proposal to impose tariffs or other restraints on manufactured imports into the United States. Plenty of pretexts are available to rationalize such tariffs: the concern with outsourcing, the claim that East Asian countries (particularly China) undervalue their exchange rates, the existence of poor working conditions in countries that are naturally poor, and so on.

Ironically, though, if imports from foreigners were somehow greatly reduced, the result could be exactly the opposite of the one protectionists say they seek: job preservation. The result would be to prevent the transfer of foreign saving to the United States, which would lead to a credit crunch.

If foreigners could not sell their goods in the United States to get dollars, who would purchase the government bonds that are issued every month? Interest rates might skyrocket to finance the deficit. And the credit crunch, in turn, would lead to an even greater loss of American jobs. Workers in import-competing manufacturing industries would gain, but workers in construction and capital goods-producing industries would lose big time.

What is to be done? The answer is not tariffs, or quotas, or exchange rate changes, or tax and other subsidies to American manufacturing that further increase the U.S. fiscal deficit. Rather, the proper way to reduce protectionist pressure and relieve anxiety about American manufacturing is for the federal government to consolidate its finances and move deliberately toward running surpluses. Put another way, the answer is, through these measures, to eliminate the saving deficiency in the American economy.

NOTE

1. "Learning by doing" is the process by which individuals, firms, or nations as a whole get better and more efficient at doing things by doing them. It is the economists' name for "practice makes perfect."

PART V

SOCIAL SECURITY

SOCIAL SECURITY IS without question a hot political issue, but the heat of the debate often exceeds the light shed. Economists are as partisan as anyone else on many aspects of the debate. But in this section, the first two contributions focus on setting out some of the key economic issues. Paul Krugman describes the key questions: What is the status of the Social Security trust fund? What is the potential impact of private Social Security accounts? And how should we think about the liabilities today's Social Security payments leave for future generations of taxpayers?

In the following essay, Don Fullerton and Michael Geruso explore the many possible meanings of the concept of privatization of Social Security. As they note, the debate is often muddied by the fact that participants are using different definitions of the term. Debate about the potential benefits and costs needs to make clear what definition is intended: fully private accounts, equivalent in all ways to a private pension? Or something less than this, such as a move from defined benefit to defined contributions or a move from mandatory to voluntary contributions?

Edward Lazear is an advocate of private accounts—closely in line with the first of the above definitions, albeit with a government-guaranteed minimum return on investment to guard against extreme poverty in old age. The government promise to pay the return due on Treasury bonds in which private accounts would be invested is more secure, in his view, than the politically vulnerable government promise to pay Social Security at any given level of benefits and eligibility.

In the final essay in this section, however, Barbara Bergmann attacks the notion met from time to time in the political debate that Social Security could go broke. Because this claim is often used to make the case for privatization, it is important to understand its limits.

None of these essays offers the definitive verdict in the debate about Social Security, as political judgments play a part along with economic analysis. However, together the economists allow readers to clarify in their own minds what the key issues are and how to choose among Social Security reform proposals.

CHAPTER 13

Confusions About Social Security

Paul Krugman

SINCE THE BUSH administration has put Social Security privatization at the top of the agenda, I'll be writing a lot about the subject in my *New York Times* column over the next few months. But it's hard to do the subject justice in a series of 700-word snippets. So I thought it might be helpful to lay out the situation as I see it in an integrated piece.

There are three main points of confusion in the Social Security debate (confusion that is deliberately created, for the most part, but never mind that for now). These are:

- *The meaning of the trust fund*: In order to create a sense of crisis, proponents of privatization consider the trust fund either real or fictional, depending on what is convenient.

Paul Krugman won the John Bates Clark medal in 1991—awarded every second year to a single economist—for his work on imperfect competition and international trade. He is now a professor of economics and international affairs at Princeton University, and a regular op-ed columnist for the *New York Times*. He received his Ph.D. from Massachusetts Institute of Technology in 1977.

- *The rate of return that can be expected on private accounts*: Privatizers claim that there is a huge free lunch from the creation of these accounts, a free lunch that is based on very dubious claims about future stock returns.
- *How to think about implicit liabilities in the far future*: Privatizers brush aside the huge negative fiscal consequences of their plans in the short run, claiming that reductions in promised payments many decades in the future are an adequate offset.

Without further ado, let me address each confusion in turn.

THE TRUST FUND

Social Security is a government program supported by a dedicated tax, like the one for highway maintenance. Now you can say that assigning a particular tax to a particular program is merely a fiction, but in fact such assignments have both legal and political force. If Ronald Reagan had said, back in the 1980s, "Let's increase a regressive tax that falls mainly on the working class, while cutting taxes that fall mainly on much richer people," he would have faced a political firestorm. But because the increase in the regressive payroll tax was recommended by the Greenspan Commission to support Social Security, it was politically in a different box—you might even call it a lockbox—from Reagan's tax cuts.

The purpose of that tax increase was to maintain the dedicated tax system into the future, by having Social Security's assigned tax take in more money than the system paid out while the baby boomers were still working, and then use the trust fund built up by those surpluses to pay future bills. Viewed in its own terms, that strategy was highly successful.

The date at which the trust fund will run out, according to Social Security Administration (SSA) projections, has receded steadily into the future: ten years ago it was 2029, now it's 2042. As Kevin Drum, Brad DeLong, and others have pointed out, the SSA estimates are very conservative, and quite moderate projections of economic growth push the exhaustion date into the indefinite future.

But the privatizers won't take yes for an answer when it comes to the sustainability of Social Security. Their answer to the pretty good numbers is to say that the trust fund is meaningless because it's invested in U.S. government bonds. They aren't really saying that government bonds are worthless; their point is that the whole notion of a separate budget for Social Security is a fiction. And if that's true, the idea that one part of the government can have a positive trust fund while the government as a whole is in debt does become strange.

But there are two problems with their position.

The lesser problem is that if you say that there is no link between the payroll tax and future Social Security benefits—which is what denying the reality of the trust fund amounts to—then Greenspan and company pulled a fast one back in the 1980s: they sold a regressive tax switch, raising taxes on workers while cutting them on the wealthy, on false pretenses. More broadly, we're breaking a major promise if we now, after twenty years of high payroll taxes to pay for Social Security's future, declare that it was all a little joke on the public.

The bigger problem for those who want to see a crisis in Social Security's future is this: if Social Security is just part of the federal budget, with no budget or trust fund of its own, then, well, it's just part of the federal budget: *there can't be a Social Security crisis*. All you can have is a general budget crisis. Rising Social Security benefit payments might be one reason for that crisis, but it's hard to make the case that it will be central.

But those who insist that we face a Social Security crisis want to have it both ways. Having invoked the concept of a unified budget to reject the existence of a trust fund, they refuse to accept the implications of that unified budget going forward. Instead, having changed the rules to make the trust fund meaningless, they want to change the rules back around fifteen years from now: today, when the payroll tax takes in more revenue than Social Security benefits, they say that's meaningless, but when—in 2018 or later—benefits start to exceed the payroll tax, why, that's a crisis. Huh?

I don't know why this contradiction is so hard to understand, except to echo Upton Sinclair: it's hard to get a man to understand something when his salary (or, in the current situation, his membership in the political club) depends on his not understanding it. But let me try this one more time, by asking the following: What happens in 2018 or whenever, when benefits payments exceed payroll tax revenues?

The answer, very clearly, is nothing.

The Social Security system won't be in trouble: it will, in fact, still have a growing trust fund because of the interest that the trust earns on its accumulated surplus. The only way Social Security could get in trouble is if Congress were to vote not to honor U.S. government bonds held by Social Security. That's not going to happen. So legally, mechanically, 2018 has no meaning.

Now it's true that rising benefit costs will be a drag on the federal budget. So will rising Medicare costs. So will the ongoing drain from tax cuts. So will whatever wars we get into. I can't find a story under which Social Security payments, as opposed to other things, become a crucial budgetary problem in 2018.

What we really have is a looming crisis in the General Fund. Social Security, with its own dedicated tax, has been run responsibly; the rest of the government has not. So why are we talking about a Social Security crisis?

It's interesting to ask what would have happened if the General Fund actually had been run responsibly—which is to say, if Social

Security surpluses had been kept in a "lockbox" and the General Fund had been balanced on average. In that case, the accumulating trust fund would have been a very real contribution to the government as a whole's ability to pay future benefits. As long as Social Security surpluses were being invested in government bonds, they would have reduced the government's debt to the public, and hence its interest bill.

We would, it's true, eventually have reached a point at which there was no more debt to buy, that is, a point at which the government's debt to the public had been more or less paid off. At that point, it would have been necessary to invest the growing trust fund in private-sector assets. This would have raised some management issues: to protect the investments from political influence, the trust fund would have had to be placed in a broad index. But the point is that the trust fund would have continued to make a real contribution to the government's ability to pay future benefits.

And if we are now much less optimistic about the government's ability to honor future obligations than we were four years ago, when Alan Greenspan urged Congress to cut taxes to avoid excessive surpluses, it's not because Social Security's finances have deteriorated— they have actually improved (the projected exhaustion date of the trust fund has moved back five years since that testimony). It's because the General Fund has plunged into huge deficit, with Bush's tax cuts the biggest single cause.

I'm not a Pollyanna; I think that we may well be facing a fiscal crisis. But it's deeply misleading, and in fact an evasion of the real issues, to call it a Social Security crisis.

RATES OF RETURN ON PRIVATE ACCOUNTS

Privatizers believe that privatization can improve the government's long-term finances without requiring any sacrifice by anyone—no new taxes, no net benefit cuts (guaranteed benefits will be cut, but people will make it up with the returns on their accounts). How is this possible?

The answer is that they assume that stocks, which will make up part of those private accounts, will yield a much higher return than bonds, with minimal long-term risk.

Now it's true that in the past stocks have yielded a very good return, around 7 percent in real terms—more than enough to compensate for additional risk. But a weird thing has happened in the debate: proposals by erstwhile serious economists such as Martin Feldstein appear to be based on the assertion that it's a sort of economic law that stocks will always yield a much higher rate of return than bonds. They seem to treat that 7 percent rate of return as if it were a natural constant, like the speed of light.

What ordinary economics tells us is just the opposite: if there is a natural law here, it's that easy returns get competed away, and there's no such thing as a free lunch. If, as Jeremy Siegel tells us, stocks have yielded a high rate of return with relatively little risk for long-run investors, that doesn't tell us that they will always do so in the future. It tells us that in the past *stocks were underpriced.* And we can expect the market to correct that.

In fact, a major correction has already taken place. Historically, the price-earnings ratio averaged about fourteen. Now, it's about twenty. Siegel tells us that the real rate of return tends to be equal to the inverse of the price-earnings ratio, which makes a lot of sense.[1] More generally, if people are paying more for an asset, the rate of return is lower. So now that a typical price-earnings ratio is twenty, a good estimate of the real rate of return on stocks in the future is 5 percent, not 7 percent.

Here's another way to arrive at the same result. Suppose that dividends are 3 percent of stock prices and that the economy grows at 3 percent (enough, by the way, to make the trust fund more or less perpetual). Not all of that 3 percent growth accrues to existing firms; the Dow of today is a very different set of firms than the Dow of fifty years ago. So at best, 3 percent economic growth is 2 percent growth for the set of existing firms; add to dividend yield, and we've got 5 percent again.

That's still not bad, you may say. But now let's do the arithmetic of private accounts.

These accounts won't be 100 percent in stocks; more likely, 60 percent will be in stocks. With a 2 percent real rate on bonds, we're down to 3.8 percent.

Then there are management fees. In Britain, they're about 1.1 percent. So now we're down to 2.7 percent on personal accounts—barely above the implicit return on Social Security right now but with lots of added risk. This is a formula to make everyone, except for Wall Street firms collecting fees, worse off.

Privatizers say that they'll keep fees very low by restricting choice to a few index funds. But let me make two points.

First, I don't believe it. In the December 21 *New York Times* story on the subject, there was a crucial giveaway: *"At first,* individuals would be offered a limited range of investment vehicles, mostly low-cost indexed funds. After a time, account holders would be given the option to upgrade to actively managed funds, which would invest in a more diverse range of assets with higher risk and potentially larger fees" (emphasis added).

At first? Hmm. So the low-fee thing wouldn't be a permanent commitment. Within months, not years, the agitation to allow "choice" would begin. And the British experience shows that this would quickly lead to substantial dissipation on management fees.

Second point: if you're requiring that private accounts be invested in index funds chosen by government officials, what's the point of calling them private accounts? We're back where we were above, with the trust fund investing in the market via an index.

Now I know that the privatizers have one more trick up their sleeve: they claim that because these are called private accounts, the mass of account holders will rise up and cry foul if the government tries to politicize investments. Just like large numbers of small stock-holders police governance problems at corporations, right? (That's a joke, by the way.)

If we are going to invest Social Security funds in stocks, keeping those investments as part of a government-run trust fund protects against a much clearer political economy danger than politicization of investments: the risk that Wall Street lobbyists will turn this into a giant fee-generating scheme.

To sum up: Claims that stocks will always yield high, low-risk returns are just bad economics. And tens of millions of small private accounts are a bad way to take advantage of whatever the stock market does have to offer. There is no free lunch, and certainly not from private accounts.

THE DISTANT FUTURE

The distant future plays a strangely large role in the current discussion. To convince us of the direness of our plight, privatizers invoke the vast combined infinite-horizon unfunded liabilities of Social Security and Medicare. Their answer to that supposed danger is to borrow trillions of dollars to pay for private accounts, which supposedly will solve the problem through the magic of high stock returns (a supposition I've just debunked.) And all that borrowing will be harmless, say the privatizers, because the long-run budget position of the federal government won't be affected: payments thirty, forty, fifty years from now will be reduced, and in present value terms that will offset the borrowing over the nearer term.

I'm all for looking ahead. But most of this is just wrong-headed, on multiple levels.

Let me start with the easiest piece: why the distant future of Medicare is something we really should ignore. And bear in mind that most of those huge numbers you hear about implicit liabilities come from Medicare, not Social Security; more to the point, they mostly come from projected increases in medical costs, not demography.

Now the main reason medical costs keep rising is that the range of things medicine can do keeps increasing. In the last few years my father and mother-in-law have both had life-saving and life-enhancing medical procedures that didn't exist a decade or two ago; it's procedures like those that account for the rising cost of Medicare.

Long-run projections assume, perhaps correctly, that this trend will continue. In 2100 Medicare may be paying for rejuvenation techniques or prosthetic brain replacements, and that will cost a lot of money.

But does it make any sense to worry now about how to pay for all that? Intergenerational responsibility is a fine thing, but I can't see why the cost of medical treatments that have not yet been invented and apply to people who have not yet been born should play any role in shaping today's policy.

Social Security's distant future isn't quite as speculative, but it's still pretty uncertain. What do you think the world will look like in 2105? My guess is that by then the computers will be smarter than we are, and we can let them deal with things; but the truth is that we haven't the faintest idea. I doubt that anyone really believes that it's important to look beyond the traditional seventy-five-year window. It has only become fashionable lately because it's a way to make the situation look direr.

Now let's return slightly more to the world outside science fiction and ask the question: can we really count purported savings several decades out as an offset to huge borrowing today?

The answer should be a clear no, for one simple reason: a bond issue is a true commitment to repay, whereas a purported change in future benefits is just a suggestion to whoever is running the country decades from now.

If the Bush plan cuts guaranteed benefits thirty years out, what does that mean? Maybe benefits will actually be cut on schedule, but then again maybe they won't—remember, the over–sixty-five voting bloc will be even bigger then than it is now. Or maybe, under budgetary pressure, benefits will be cut regardless of what Bush does now, in which case his plan doesn't really save money in the out years.

Financial markets, we can be sure, will pay very little attention to projections about how today's policies will affect the budget thirty years ahead. In fact, we've just had a demonstration of how little attention they will pay: the prescription drug plan.

As has been widely noted, 2004's prescription drug law worsens the long-run federal budget by much more than the entire accounting deficit of Social Security. If markets really looked far ahead, the passage of that law should have caused a sharp rise in interest rates, maybe even a crisis of confidence in federal solvency. In fact, everyone pretty much ignored the thing—just as they'll ignore the putative future savings in the Bush plan.

What markets will pay attention to, just as they did in Argentina, is the surge in good old-fashioned debt.

PRIVATIZATION IS A SOLUTION IN
SEARCH OF A PROBLEM

As I've described it, the case for privatization is a mix of strange and inconsistent budget doctrines, bad economics, dubious political economy, and science fiction. What's wrong with these people?

The answer is definitely *not* that they are stupid. In fact, the case made by the privatizers is fiendishly ingenious in its Jesuitical logic, its persuasiveness to the unprepared mind.

But many of the people supporting privatization have to know better. Why, then, don't they say so? Because Social Security privatization is a solution in search of a problem. The right has always disliked Social Security; it has always been looking for some reason to dismantle it. Now, with a window of opportunity created by the public's rally-around-the-flag response after 9/11, the Republican leadership is making a full-court press for privatization, using any arguments at hand.

There are both crude and subtle reasons why economists who know better don't take a stand against the illogic of many of the privatizers' positions. The crude reason is that a conservative economist who doesn't support every twist and turn of the push for privatization faces political exile. Any hint of intellectual unease would, for example, kill the chances of anyone hoping to be appointed as Greenspan's successor. The subtle reason is that many economists hold the defensible position that a pay-as-you-go system is bad for savings and long-run growth. And they hope that a bad privatization plan may nonetheless be the start of a reform that eventually creates a better system.

But those hopes are surely misplaced. So far, everyone—and I mean everyone—who has signed on to Bush administration plans in the hope that they can be converted into something better has ended up used, abused, and discarded. It happened to John DiIulio, it happened to Colin Powell, it happened to Greg Mankiw, and it's a safe prediction that those who think they can turn the Bush drive to dismantle Social Security into something good will suffer the same fate.

NOTE

1. For those who want to know: suppose that the economy is in steady-state growth, with both the rental rate on capital and Tobin's q constant. Then the rate of return on stocks is equal to the earnings-price ratio. Obviously that's an oversimplification, but it looks pretty good as a rule of thumb.

CHAPTER **14**

The Many Definitions of Social Security Privatization

Don Fullerton and Michael Geruso

IN THE PAST decade, debate over Social Security privatization has exploded in the United States. The Bush administration, think tanks, and academic economists have all pushed cases for privatizing the U.S. public pension system.

When you look under the hood, though, "privatization" can mean a different thing to almost every advocate. Privatization usually means that workers get individual retirement accounts in their own names, as with a private defined contribution (DC) pension. But, does privatization necessarily entail all aspects of a private pension? Must contributions be voluntary and accounts privately managed? Must pensioners have choice over investments and receive

Don Fullerton is the Addison Baker Duncan Centennial Professor of Economics at the University of Texas at Austin and director of the NBER Working Group on Environmental Economics. He has served in the U.S. Treasury Department as deputy assistant secretary for tax analysis (1985–1987). Michael Geruso is an engineering manager at National Instruments, a Truman Scholar, and a research assistant with the Department of Economics at the University of Texas at Austin. The authors are grateful for suggestions from Jeff Brown, Aaron Edlin, and Kent Smetters.

payouts that are actuarially fair? Or can privatization include plans where the government retains control over some of those decisions? In current usage of the term, privatization may mean any of those things.

This ambiguity of the term "privatization" muddles the public and scholarly debate over changes to Social Security. Some proponents of privatizing Social Security desire a strengthening of our public old-age insurance system, whereas other proponents of privatization desire the end of it.

Probably worse, it is common for an advocate of reform to bundle together several aspects of privatization and then justify the package by pointing to benefits that could be achieved with much less radical changes.

DECOMPOSING PRIVATIZATION

Seven vectors capture the salient features of most privatization plans. As shown in table 14.1, the current system is pay-as-you-go (PAYGO), meaning that funds from current workers are used to pay the benefits of current retirees. It is a defined benefit (DB) plan, which means that each retiree's benefits are prescribed in a way that does not depend on funds in a personal account. Workers and employers are required to make contributions to the system through Old Age Insurance payroll taxes, and any receipts in excess of expenditures are held in an aggregate fund managed and invested by the federal government. Benefits are paid only as an annuity (on a monthly basis throughout retirement with no lump-sum payout option). The design of tax and benefit schedules and other rules mean that the system redistributes across demographic groups.

In contrast, looking down the right column of table 14.1, a *purely* private pension would be characterized by full funding and by personal accounts of a DC plan.[1] It would have voluntary levels

TABLE 14.1

Direct Comparison of Seven Attributes

Current Social Security	Typical Private Pension
PAYGO Funding	Full Funding
Defined Benefit	Personal Defined Contribution Accounts
Mandatory Contributions	Voluntary Contributions
Government Management	Private-Sector Management
No Investment Choice	Investment Choice
Annuity Only	Lump-Sum Payout Option
Redistribution	Actuarial Fairness

of contribution, private-sector management, individual investment choice, a lump-sum payout option, and actuarial fairness.

A reform to privatize Social Security might change any one of these seven rows, or attributes, without necessarily affecting any of the others. Complete repeal of Social Security would include all seven. Ignoring potential dependencies, 127 possible plans could be formed from this list (by including at least one attribute and possibly all seven attributes)!

For example, a fully funded Social Security trust fund could be invested in equities without changing the prescribed benefits formula or introducing personal accounts. Conversely, a reform could introduce purely notional personal accounts without funding them. And each of those reforms must decide about other options, such as whether to have private-sector management or individual choice of investments. In the last row of the table, the current Social Security system could shift toward actuarial fairness without added funding, personal accounts, or any other feature listed.

Most actual privatization proposals would reform more than one but not all of the seven attributes. One plan proposed by Laurence Kotlikoff (2000) and endorsed by a long list of academicians entails a fully funded system under which workers make mandatory contributions into personal accounts managed by the private sector. These accounts would offer only a single investment portfolio, and contributions would be matched on a progressive basis to add redistribution. Upon retirement, account holders would have to annuitize their benefits. That plan includes only three of the seven possible attributes of privatization.

Of course, describing privatization as a list of seven binary choices is a massive simplification. Because each attribute is actually a vector, we mean to allow for degrees of adoption. For example, workers may not have full freedom in choosing investments, but they may be able to choose among a constrained set of funds managed by competing private-sector entities, as is done in Chilé.

THE PROBLEM WITH AMBIGUITY

By now it should be clear that the definition of privatization matters. The problem with the term's ambiguity is that it has led to imprecise analysis and commentary on changes to Social Security. The most striking problems occur when the analysis of just one attribute of privatization is used to justify a much broader schedule of changes. Consider a *Washington Post* article by José Piñera (1998), Chilé's former minister of labor and social security who presided over that country's transition to a private pension system. He proposes a plan to transform the U.S. Social Security system along the lines of Chilé's system of personal accounts. In this article, Piñera invokes Martin Feldstein's analysis of the benefits of funding to argue that the U.S. should follow Chilé's example. But in doing so, he twists together several attributes of privatization that are completely separable. The benefits of prefunding do not require a system of privately managed pension investments in mutual funds. Nor do those benefits necessitate a lump-sum payout option or any other particulars of Chilé's plan. The desire to achieve benefits derived from just one feature of privatization is thus conflated with the need to adopt a whole array of changes.

Definitions also differ among academic economists. In his 1996 analysis, Kotlikoff considers a privatization plan that sounds like repeal of Social Security, and he measures efficiency gains from improved labor supply and saving incentives. Yet these gains do not require repeal. His results depend on funding, but they do not require changes in any other row of table 14.1, even that assets be held in personal accounts! Feldstein's (1998) definition of privatization also calls for funding, but he would have mandatory contributions to individually managed accounts. In contrast, Geanakoplos, Mitchell, and Zeldes (1998) characterize privatization as the creation of a system of individual accounts, but this definition does not require funding nor that individuals choose investments. Thus, even though each author has a consistent definition of privatization, the same term is used to denote incompatible concepts.

Justifying a privatization plan on the basis of expected benefits requires that we make explicit the source from which those benefits are expected to flow. In general, anyone who aims to show gains to economic efficiency from privatization should specify which attributes of table 14.1 are key to the results. In many economic models, Social Security's full privatization will increase national savings. But the gains to national savings might have nothing to do with putting investment decisions in the hands of individuals and everything to do with fully funding the system. In other words, repeal in such a case is not necessary to achieve the desired benefits.

We may have good reasons for funding our nation's Social Security system. And we may have good reasons for keeping contributions to the system mandatory, or keeping investments under government management, or keeping benefits redistributive. Fortunately, the choice to fund Social Security does not constrain our choices along any of these other vectors.[2]

Likewise, if we fear the prospect of retired Americans ending up penniless and desperate in old age, then perhaps giving workers full control over their retirement savings presents a risk too great to bear.

But the desire to preserve this form of social insurance no more rules out Social Security's privatization than full funding requires Social Security's repeal. Like Singapore's Central Provident Fund, a privatized U.S. pension system could restrict retirement investments to relatively safe options, such as government bonds and government-managed savings accounts.[3] Thus, before Wall Street brokerage firms become too enamored of the idea of privatization, it is a valid question whether Wall Street should be directly involved in a privatized system at all.

CONCLUSION

All of this is to say that describing a plan to change Social Security as *privatization* gives precious little information. In order to distinguish clearly among the many possible formulations of privatization, research papers and policy briefs that mention privatization must define what specific subset of the seven attributes is intended.

Deliberately specifying these attributes will make explicit the connection between proposed changes and supposed benefits. This protects against having some desirable effect of privatization become the hostage of a broader set of changes that are not necessary to achieve it. The alternative to this type of deliberate exposition is an increasingly muddled debate in which one analysis of Social Security's privatization is incommensurable with the next.

NOTES

1. A private pension need not be a defined contribution plan, just as a social security system need not be a defined benefit plan. Still, the dichotomy in the second row of table 14.1 best highlights a key aspect of the current debate: the switch from our current DB system to "personal accounts" of a DC plan. Most important, such a reform could shift

investment risk to retirees who would then gain from extraordinary returns but suffer from unusually low returns.

2. If putting Social Security surpluses into a government-held trust fund leads to larger deficits in other government spending, then Social Security is not truly funded. If personal accounts are necessary to achieve true funding, then the two issues are not practically separable.

3. See http://www.cpf.gov.sg. Singapore's fund also shows how a government can exercise considerable control in a privatized system. In particular, it is invested largely in public housing.

REFERENCES AND FURTHER READING

Feldstein, Martin. 1998. "Preface." In *Privatizing Social Security,* ed. Martin Feldstein, pp. ix–x. Chicago: University of Chicago Press for NBER.

Geanakoplos, J., O. S. Mitchell, and S. P. Zeldes. 1998. "Would a Privatized Social Security System Really Pay a Higher Rate of Return?" In *Framing the Social Security Debate: Values, Politics, and Economics,* eds. R. D. Arnold, M. J. Graetz, and A. H. Munnell, pp. 137–157. Washington, DC: Brookings Institution.

Kotlikoff, Laurence. 1996. "Privatization of Social Security: How It Works and Why It Matters." In *Tax Policy and the Economy,* vol. 10, pp. 1–32. Cambridge, MA: MIT Press for NBER.

———. 2000. "Privatizing Social Security the Right Way." *The Independent Review* (Summer), 5 (1): 55–63.

Piñera, José. 1998. "In Chilé, They Went Private 16 Years Ago." *Washington Post,* March 22.

CHAPTER 15

The Virtues of Personal Accounts for Social Security

Edward P. Lazear

MUCH OF THE rhetoric regarding the establishment of private accounts for retirement benefits has missed the main issues. Some proponents argue that recipients will earn higher returns from private accounts—likely true. Opponents counter that the higher returns come at the cost of greater risk—also likely true. Further, opponents argue that the current system is not too much worse than the market alternative and that transaction costs will eat up much of the additions—questionable and not especially relevant.

Many of these arguments miss the mark. The Social Security system is not a mere intermediary as is a stock broker. The current

Edward P. Lazear is the Morris Arnold Cox Senior Fellow at the Hoover Institution, the Jack Steele Parker Professor of Human Resources, Management and Economics at Stanford University's Graduate School of Business, and chairman of the President's Council of Economic Advisers since 2006. He was formerly a member of President Bush's advisory Tax Reform Panel. One of the world's eminent labor economists, he was recently awarded the prestigious 2004 IZA prize for labor economics by the Institute for Labor in Bonn, Germany. He is the 2006 recipient of the Jacob Mincer Prize for lifetime achievement in the field of labor economics.

system has goals and functions that go beyond those of a fund manager's. So to determine the desirability of private accounts, we must look at all of the fundamentals of the current system.

The real issues should be: What does the current system do? What should be the goals of the system? Would private accounts achieve the desired goals more efficiently?

The answer is that the current system has some desirable features, but it also creates undesirable consequences. Private accounts accomplish the desired goals, but they eliminate most of the undesired consequences. Thus, private accounts are the right solution—but not necessarily because they offer account holders potentially greater returns.

Private accounts allow consumer sovereignty, provide additional security for recipients, and reduce the excessive government spending that is inherent in the current system. Additionally, none of the advantages of the government-administered program would be lost with a properly run system of private accounts.

THE CURRENT SOCIAL SECURITY SYSTEM:
ITS THREE FUNCTIONS

To begin, consider the functions of the current Social Security system. At base, it does three things.

First, the Social Security system forces saving. Some individuals might be inclined to save less than the amount set aside through payroll taxes.

Second, the current system provides insurance. It does so in a number of ways. One example is that individuals who work ten years are entitled to the same benefits as those who work much longer. As a result, someone who becomes ill during middle age receives the same benefits as someone who is able to work until sixty-five, provided they have the same income for calculating benefits. The system thereby pools risk across individuals. Insurance is also provided by making the benefits received independent of variations in returns to securities in which an individual might otherwise invest.

Third, Social Security redistributes income. The structure of floors and ceilings on benefits and contributions results in redistribution from some sets of individuals to others. For example, life expectancies differ across groups in well-known ways. Women live longer than men, whites live longer than African Americans, nonsmokers live longer than smokers. Other things equal, groups with short life expectancies transfer income to groups with long life expectancies through the Social Security system. Additionally, caps on benefits provide redistribution from the rich to the poor, but caps on contributions imply redistribution from the middle to the rich. The net redistributive flows depend on the actual history of contributions and benefit payments, but many of these transfers are secondary consequences of the system and some are adverse from a social equity point of view.

THE GOALS OF THE SOCIAL SECURITY SYSTEM: WHICH FUNCTIONS ARE PROPER?

What should the system do?

To begin, the legitimate goal of Social Security is to ensure that everyone has sufficient income to support some basic standard of living throughout retirement. Thus, forced saving is at the heart of the system.

Were individuals not forced to save, some would engage in moral hazard, overconsuming when young and allowing themselves to be destitute when old, knowing that they could then count on relatives, churches, or communities to care for them. Others would be less strategic, but they might end up in the same situation simply for lack of foresight.

The current system accomplishes forced saving, but it is unnecessary to have the government administer the system to accomplish forced saving. The government need only require that individuals save the desired amount. Nothing says that the saving must occur through a government-run fund.

Implicit in the notion that there should be some basic level of income is a desire to provide insurance, by putting a floor on the amount of benefits. The provision of some insurance, at least in terms of providing minimum benefits, is appropriate.

Critics of private accounts worry about the insurance role of the Social Security system. But private accounts, properly administered, can provide adequate minimum income to recipients, as I discuss below.

Government-administered Social Security redistributes income and this is more problematic. The Social Security system was not designed to tackle the major issue of optimal income distribution. As a result, its redistribution can lack rhyme or reason: Do we really intend low-income African Americans who die young to redistribute income to affluent whites who live long lives?

SOME INITIAL ADVANTAGES OF PRIVATE ACCOUNTS

Can a Social Security system incorporating private accounts address the legitimate goals of the Social Security system as well—or better—than the current system? There are three main advantages that private accounts have over a government-run system.

First, private accounts are more consistent than the government program with fundamental economic principles—namely, the principle that we ought to honor consumer sovereignty and keep the market free of significant distortions.

Second, private accounts enhance, rather than reduce, the likelihood that contributors will receive what they expect. Benefits are more, not less, secure with private accounts.

Third, private accounts reduce government moral hazard and do not sacrifice any of the benefits associated with the government-run Social Security program. Moving pension funds to the private sector removes another source of revenues that government officials have not been able to resist spending.

John Cogan (1998) has shown that for every dollar of unanticipated increase in government funds through the payroll tax, there is a corresponding increase of one dollar in government expenditures. When the economy is good and payroll taxes rise as a consequence of increased employment and rising incomes, the government collects more money. At the same time, it spends it. (Similar work by Gary Becker and Casey Mulligan [2003] finds that state governments do the same thing. Increases in state revenues associated with changes in the economy are met by increases in state expenditures.)

Moving money from the payroll tax to the private sector will allocate resources more in line with market principles. Granted, some increased expenditure by the government that follows unanticipated increases in revenues may be worthwhile. But most economists believe that the market does a better job than politicians of allocating resources in an efficient manner.

CAN PRIVATE ACCOUNTS SERVE THE PROPER GOALS OF THE SOCIAL SECURITY SYSTEM?

These advantages of private accounts are attractive, but do private accounts achieve Social Security's legitimate goals? Yes, they do.

The primary goal of Social Security is to force individuals to save. Private accounts not only accomplish this goal but also have the additional advantage of allowing consumer sovereignty, especially for the majority of individuals. Most economists have a deep appreciation for individual choice, as long as there are no obvious externalities. Choice is important only for those who, if left on their own, would not choose to save enough in the form of an asset with the same pay-off properties as Social Security. For individuals who would save significantly more in a Social-Security–like asset than the amount forced through the payroll tax, choice is not an issue. An individual who, in the absence of government programs, would save $5,000 per year, investing $2,000 in a diversified stock portfolio and $3,000 in a Social-Security–like asset is unaffected by a $2,500 payroll tax that pays out in accordance with returns on government bonds. He simply reduces his private investment in that asset to $500, maintains the investment in stocks at the $2,500 level, and allows the government to provide $2,500 worth of Social Security.

The difference comes for individuals who would not voluntarily choose to invest more than the mandated amount in a Social-Security–like asset. These individuals are forced to distort their investment decisions and to accept the risk-return profile that the government chooses for them. Given the large fraction of individuals who have very few retirement assets other than Social Security and some home equity, the constraint is binding for a large part of the population.

A complication of this analysis is that there is no true Social-Security–like asset. An obvious candidate is a U.S. Treasury bond, but the comparison does not hold. Individuals who buy Treasuries privately can be virtually assured that the return they receive is that promised: the bonds' face value. But there is no guarantee in a pay-as-you-go Social Security system that the benefits, even on average, will reflect the market rate of interest on Treasuries. After all, benefits and contributions are politically determined and Congress has the power to change benefits.

How about Social Security's second goal, namely, the provision of a certain amount of income insurance? At first glance, private accounts might seem to conflict with this goal. Individuals who do not have the vision to provide for themselves in old age cannot be expected to hedge future income risks appropriately. As a result, the government might be forced to bail out those who make bad investments or to bail out a large segment of society if even safe investments turn out to yield very low returns. But there are at least two solutions to this problem—solutions that would allow the system to both incorporate private accounts and achieve its insurance goal.

The first solution is the one currently being discussed, which is to provide a base level of benefits from government-run pension programs, namely Social Security. As long as that is sufficient to provide some base level standard of living, nothing else may be required.

An alternative solution is to insure the private accounts, whereby the government guarantees a minimum return or minimum annuity. To do this, it is necessary to regulate the kinds of investments that can be part of the private accounts, lest we see a repeat of the S&L crisis, as individuals take on high risk, high return investments knowing that they have a government bailout.

Another advantage of private accounts is that they provide a more secure flow of benefits than does a government-run system. Investments made privately provide a stronger lockbox than any offered by the government. To see why, suppose that the government promises to provide a specified return on the payroll tax that individuals have contributed throughout their lifetimes. Pressure on the government to reduce spending or eliminate deficits could, at any point in time, induce legislators to reduce benefits, change the age of eligibility, or make any variety of changes that would force legislators to break the promise and to reduce the actual return. In contrast, U.S. Treasury bonds' nominal value will be paid with virtual certainty: That promise is far less likely to be broken. Individuals who invest their retained payroll taxes in U.S. Treasuries are not subject to the whims of future legislators.

THE TRANSITION TO PRIVATE ACCOUNTS

What about transition costs? The worry about the transition has been overstated. In reality, there will be few costs of transition.

Granted, if the current working generation is permitted to take, say, one-half of its payroll tax and divert it to the private sector, then the current generation of retirees must receive some of their support from other funds. And those funds will have to come from a current or future working generation.

The next generation, however, receives its own benefit. Because one-half of the payroll tax has gone into private saving, now only one-half of the total benefits received by pensioners must be paid through government funds. So the next generation would pay less than the current one to support the retirement of their parents.

To make the overall impact on each generation fairly neutral, the current working generation could pass on to the next generation the one-half obligation to support current retirees (that part of Social Security that is no longer paid through the payroll tax). Deficit spending that is paid for by floating Treasuries would leave each generation's wealth unchanged to a first approximation.

The alternative of taxing the current working population to pay the bill would put tax policy at odds with itself: The point is to lower government intermediation, and raising taxes (say, through the income tax) to pay the bill would just offset the reduction in the payroll tax. Indeed, when the Social Security fund is in surplus, we are already overtaxing ourselves to cover the future. Deficit spending is consistent with the original notion of pay-as-you-go, leaving the situation of the previous, current, and future generations unchanged.

In conclusion, the popular debate about private Social Security accounts—arguing that they would improve return but increase risk—is off the target. The important point is that private accounts would serve Social Security's legitimate purposes—encouraging saving and effectively providing insurance—just as well, if not better than, the current system. Private accounts, correctly structured, will actually be safer than the current system: a more credible and trustworthy form of insurance. And the transition can be easily handled.

At the same time, private accounts would eliminate the perverse redistributive effects of the current Social Security system and eliminate the moral hazard that the government will break benefits promises and quickly spend whatever revenue it receives.

REFERENCES AND FURTHER READING

Becker, Gary S. and Casey Mulligan. 2003. "Deadweight Costs and the Size of Government." *Journal of Law and Economics* (October): 293–340.

Cogan, John. 1998. "The Congressional Response to Social Security Surpluses, 1935–94." *Essays in Public Policy*. Stanford, CA: Hoover Institution, Stanford University.

CHAPTER 16

Could Social Security Go Broke?

Barbara R. Bergmann

THE PUBLIC WANTS Social Security to be fixed and the sooner the better. The public is anxious because it has been told that Social Security will run out of money around 2042, that it won't be there for our young people, and that it will go bankrupt.

This scare talk is profoundly misleading. The Social Security system cannot go bankrupt. Businesses or individuals can go bankrupt when they are legally obligated to make payments, do not have enough money coming in to cover those payments, and have no way to increase their inflow of money. A U.S. government program like Social Security will never be in such a situation. Social Security gets the money it needs to make benefit payments from taxes. If Social Security taxes and benefits get out of balance, either or both can be adjusted by our democratic processes.

The need to make such adjustments from time to time does not mean the program is unsound, or dishonest, or can go bankrupt. In

Barbara R. Bergmann is professor emerita at the University of Maryland and American University. She is the author of *Is Social Security Broke? A Cartoon Guide to the Issues* and coauthor of *America's Child Care Problem*.

fact, the ability of the government to make these adjustments is one of the great strengths of the system. It allows Social Security to continue as long as the American people want it to. In the past, Congress has changed Social Security taxes and benefits whenever adjustments were needed or desired.

America will certainly have the capacity to pay the higher taxes projected to be needed in the rather distant future to finance current-formula Social Security benefits. President George W. Bush's economists project that by 2080 the payroll tax will have to rise, raising the total tax burden on the American public by 4 percent of gross domestic product (GDP) to about 31 percent. That is a significant rise, but it is far from impossible as a matter of economics or politics. Consider that France currently takes about 45 percent of its GDP in taxes, and Sweden takes 60 percent. Both countries have economic growth about as fast as ours.

We could raise taxes over the next seventy-five years to that extent, and we could do so without materially slowing economic growth. But does America wish to bear that extra burden on behalf of the nation's old people? In the past, Americans have always chosen to shore up the Social Security system by increasing taxes when they were told it was necessary to preserve benefits. Working Americans don't want their parents and grandparents to be forced to move in with them. Nor do they want to see large numbers of old people descend into poverty or even become homeless. That's why it is easy to make them anxious with talk of Social Security's demise.

Would it be a good idea to reduce benefits or increase Social Security taxes starting right now? I believe not. If the public prefers, after an honest debate on the subject, to avoid some of the tax increases by cutting Social Security benefits in the future or increasing the retirement age, we should give lots of advance notice so that people can plan. But we shouldn't increase Social Security taxes ahead of the time we will need the extra money for pensions. Doing so does not make it easier to pay for pensions in the future. Here is why:

Whenever Social Security collects more in taxes than it is paying out in benefits, it passes those funds on to the Treasury. The Treasury prints up bonds and sends them to Social Security, and they end up in a drawer marked "Social Security Trust Fund." The money the Treasury gets from Social Security is used to pay for regular federal government expenditures. That does not increase the real resources available to pay future pensions. When the wheel turns and Social Security is collecting less in taxes than it is paying out in benefits, Social Security can ask the Treasury to redeem those bonds. The Treasury would get the money to do so by raising the income tax, reducing expenditures, or selling bonds to the public. But it could raise the money for Social Security pensions by doing that whether there are bonds in the trust fund drawer or not.

Raising Social Security taxes in advance of higher spending on benefits increases the share of federal spending financed by the regressive payroll tax. A big premature raise in the Social Security tax took place during the Reagan administration, at the behest of Alan Greenspan (who is now telling us we have to reduce benefits). As a result, 20 percent of regular government spending that used to be financed by income taxes is now being financed by money from the regressive Social Security tax. Raising the Social Security tax again would be just a sneaky way of making the tax system less progressive.

Politicians have not stressed that the Social Security system can be very easily shored up and that there is no danger that it will stop paying pensions. Politicians who want to replace our present publicly run pension system with private accounts want the public to think that radical surgery is necessary. And some of those who might favor keeping the present system intact hunger for credit for "saving Social Security." So the public has been pummeled with misinformation from all sides on Social Security. But the program will probably survive in its present form: it is needed, and it is popular.

VI

TAX REFORM

THE PUBLICATION OF the 2005 report of the President's Advisory Panel on Tax Reform prompted many economists to think about the problems of the U.S. tax system. In the first essay in this section, Michael Boskin takes a broad-ranging look at the consequences of the tax system for economic growth. He argues that, looking across the industrialized countries of the Organization for Economic Co-operation and Development (OECD), a high burden of taxation and government spending is clearly bad for growth (although many citizens of France and Germany would disagree with his contention that their countries are "economic and social disasters"). The two key plans set out by the panel—a Simplified Income Tax (SIT) and a Growth and Investment Tax (GIT)—both include as key elements the broadening of the tax base and lower rates of taxation, satisfying one item in Boskin's checklist for assessing reform proposals.

In the second essay, Michael Graetz agrees with the underlying principles of simplification in the SIT and GIT, but he argues that each has fatal political drawbacks and that there is a more realistic way of achieving the broader tax base and lower tax rates. That would be to replace part of the revenue raised by taxes on personal and corporate income with a value-added tax, widely used in OECD countries.

The remaining two essays address the problem of America's very low savings and ask how tax reform might increase savings and investment. Their answers come from opposite ends of the political spectrum. Martin Feldstein argues that taxes on saving and investment, through the capital gains tax and corporation tax, are too high. This discourages saving for the future overall, and, what's more, it distorts the saving and investment that do occur. Too much capital is directed to noncorporate rather than wealth-creating corporate investment, and corporations are discouraged from paying dividends to their investors.

Robert Frank, however, thinks the problem is that taxes on consumption spending are too low. People spend too much now and save too little for the future. The reason lies less perhaps in the tax on interest that Feldstein and others emphasize but more in human psychology: we lack willpower to save for the future and find it hard to jump off the rat race. Frank advocates a progressive tax on consumer spending to discourage conspicuous consumption and reduce inequality in society.

CHAPTER 17

A Broader Perspective on the Tax Reform Debate

Michael J. Boskin

WITH THE RECENT release of the report of the President's Advisory Panel on Federal Tax Reform, one might have expected a vigorous national debate on the level, structure, and growth of taxes and their effect on our economy and society. Unfortunately, the meager post-report discussion thus far has focused on narrow issues of limiting this deduction or that credit. So much more than that is at stake. The evolution of taxes and spending will be a primary determinant of whether America remains a successful dynamic economy, providing rising standards of living, low unemployment, and upward economic mobility or slides into complacent economic stagnation and socio-economic ossification.

We don't need an academic treatise to demonstrate what is at stake (although see, for example, Engen and Skinner 1996). History has performed that experiment. Daily we witness economies, such as the French and German, staggering under bloated welfare spending and oppressive tax burdens, with standards of living 30 percent below American levels. The economies of Western Europe set their taxes and government spending at about half of gross domestic product (GDP). In the United States, the figure is about one-third (including state and local government). Although that is still too high, we have demonstrated we can make the current level of government in the economy consistent with solid economic growth and rising standards of living. A substantially higher tax and spending burden does not appear consistent with such performance. To see why, consider figure 17.1, which portrays the negative correlation between economic growth rates and government tax and spending burdens in the OECD countries. There are many other factors that influence growth rate and per capita income differentials, which explain why, of course, all countries don't lie exactly on the line. But moving from U.S. tax levels to Western European levels might cut the growth rate by up to a full percentage point. Over a generation, that cumulates to huge differences in standards of living (as demonstrated by Prescott 2002).

Under current law, the federal government tax burden is projected to rise by more than one-third as a share of GDP in coming decades, because of the combined effects of the alternative minimum

FIGURE 17.1

Economic Growth Rates and Government Tax and Spending Burdens in OECD Countries

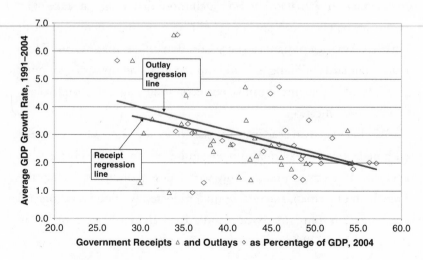

tax, real bracket creep, and other factors. Back in the Kennedy years, Democrats as well as Republicans used to worry about such "fiscal drag." Surely any sensible strategic management of our economic affairs starts with preventing that giant step toward a European-style social welfare state. To do that, we will have to continuously "cut" taxes and spending relative to their projected growth.

Whereas deductions and/or credits are theoretically desirable under some circumstances in an optimal tax system, as Joseph Stiglitz and I (1977) and Martin Feldstein (1980) have demonstrated, a broad tax base and low rate or rates are highly desirable. The nine distinguished members of the panel outline two such reform plans: The Simplified Income Tax Plan (SIT) and the Growth and Investment Tax Plan (GIT). The SIT would reduce the number of tax brackets from six to four (with a top rate of 33 percent); limit or eliminate popular deductions for mortgage interest, charitable contributions, employer-provided health care, and state and local income and property taxes; abolish both private and corporate alternative minimum tax (AMT); consolidate the many tax-deferred saving vehicles into three simple plans; exclude 75 percent of capital gains and 100 percent of dividends paid from domestic profits; simplify accelerated depreciation; limit the anticompetitive double taxation of foreign source income of American companies; and reduce the corporate rate to 31.5 percent. It would also clean up definitions and numerous other provisions.

The more desirable GIT has much in common with the SIT, but it moves the system closer to a progressive tax on consumed income, an ideal favored by economists for many decades. It would have three rates (with a top of 30 percent); tax dividends, capital gains, and interest at 15 percent; replace the corporate income tax with a 30 percent business cash flow tax; and allow expensing of investment but eliminate interest deductions. The plans include transition rules, for example to grandfather existing mortgages, so the adjustment for the economy and individual taxpayers will be less wrenching.

The SIT and GIT, in essence, swap capping or eliminating the popular deductions for abolition of the alternative minimum tax (which would eventually prevent a growing fraction of Americans from fully realizing the value of these deductions in any event). They also make the Bush tax rate cuts (plus a little more) permanent. Both plans stabilize federal taxes at the 18 percent of GDP historical average. This is by far the most important aspect of the proposals. The current 2005 17.6 percent tax share of GDP is projected to rise to just under 20 percent over the next decade (and to about 25 percent thereafter), including the expiration of the Bush rate reductions and continuing AMT and bracket creep. But, between the uproar from those who would lose popular deductions and the fact that most Americans are unaware of the AMT, even these incremental reform plans—which should be the starting, not the end, point of reform—may be a very tough sell until many more voters are trapped by the AMT.

The panel discusses, but does not recommend, replacing the corporate and personal income taxes with any of four more fundamental tax reforms: a progressive consumed income tax, a flat-rate (consumption) tax, a value-added tax (VAT), and a retail sales tax. The pure, some would say theoretical, versions of each would be more pro-growth than either the SIT or GIT. The panel summarizes most of the pros and cons of these more fundamental reforms. For example, the VAT and retail sales taxes are viewed as risking becoming additional rather than replacement taxes, as potentially financing a big expansion of government (some commission members opposed them on this ground; others thought they were a good way to finance growth in entitlement costs), and as becoming potential infringements on federalism. The flat tax and progressive consumed income tax were ruled out on (static) distributional grounds. Perhaps that is where Congress will eventually wind up, but wouldn't it be better to have a serious national debate on whether we are willing to trade potentially stronger growth and higher future living standards for relaxing narrow, and static at that, distributional constraints—especially when the main driver of the large effects of the federal government on the distribution of economic well-being is in transfer payments, not the tax system?

FIVE BIG-PICTURE TESTS FOR TAX REFORM

I use five big-picture tests to judge tax reform proposals.

1. Will tax reform improve the performance of the economy? By far the most important aspect of economic performance is the rate of economic growth, because that growth determines future living standards. The most important way the tax system affects living standards is through the rate of saving, investment, work effort, entrepreneurship, and human capital investment.

Modern academic public economics concludes that immense harm is done by high marginal tax rates, especially on capital income. This is a major reason virtually all prominent academic economists who have studied the issue recommend taxing consumption or that part of income that is consumed. Such a tax is neutral with respect to saving and investment, (intertemporal neutrality) and also among types of investment (atemporal neutrality). Think of intertemporal neutrality as a level playing field goalpost to goalpost and atemporal neutrality as level sideline to sideline. Even a perfect income tax (which would require measuring true economic depreciation and inflation adjustment, among other difficulties) would only achieve atemporal neutrality, not the far more important intertemporal neutrality. A pure consumption tax, however levied, would guarantee both.

As I first demonstrated thirty years ago (Boskin 1975), it is the progressive rate structure that deters human capital investment. Most on-the-job training and much of higher education costs are financed by foregone earnings, which are not taxed. It is as if the foregone earnings were included in taxable income but then immediately expensed. So a flat tax rate does not affect the net returns to such human investment decisions, but a progressive rate structure would reduce the returns and impede investment because the higher earnings generated by the investment would be taxed at a higher rate than that at which the investment was expensed.

On these criteria, low flat-rate consumption taxes work best, high-rate progressive income taxes worst. A growing body of research (chronologically, Boskin 1978; Summers 1981; and Lucas 1990 are important examples) suggests that replacing the corporate and personal income taxes with a low-rate pure consumption tax is the single most potent policy reform available.

An important dimension of economic performance is administrative and compliance costs, estimated by the panel at over $140 billion per year. Here the flat tax, retail sales tax, and VAT do far better, and the SIT and GIT somewhat better, than current law if enacted as a replacement. But if a sales tax or a VAT were added without removing the income taxes, large additional administrative and compliance costs would result. And any improvement in the federal income tax would only be an improvement in this dimension for taxpayers in the few states that do not have income taxes or explicitly piggyback on the federal tax base. For most taxpayers, they would only be an improvement when and if their states adopted tax bases (nearly) identical to the new federal law.

Another dimension of economic performance is vertical equity. Is the current distribution of the tax burden, shown in table 17.1, about right? The current income tax system is very progressive (the top 1 percent pays 34 percent of the federal income taxes, double its share of income; the top 5 percent pays 54 percent; the top 50 percent pays 97 percent); if every reform has to make the tax code even more progressive, we will wind up with an even smaller minority of voters paying all the income taxes, an unhealthy political dynamic in a democracy. This is especially true when combined with

TABLE 17.1

Federal Income Tax Shares, Selected Years

	Top 1%	Top 5%	Top 25%	Top 50%	Bottom 50%
1980	19%	37%	73%	93%	7%
1988	28%	46%	78%	94%	6%
1996	32%	51%	81%	96%	4%
2003	34%	54%	84%	97%	3%

Source: IRS, Statistics of Income

Note: Data are rounded to nearest percent. Including the corporation income tax could make the distribution even more progressive on standard incidence assumptions; the net payroll tax financing of general government, less so.

For 2003, the top 1 percent had 17 percent of income, the bottom 50 percent, 14 percent. The adjusted gross income cutoffs were $295,000 and $29,000, respectively.

the aging of the population in which the fraction of the voters receiving government old-age benefits will increase 50 percent in the next twenty years and double in the next fifty. We can keep the tax distribution progressive with family exemptions and the Earned Income Tax Credit (EITC), even if we go to a single flat rate, and somewhat more progressive if there are two or three rates, as in the GIT. What is important is that the rate(s) be as low as possible, especially the top rate on the most economically productive group in the population.

2. Will tax reform affect the size of government? It is important to control spending for its effect on tax burdens and economic performance. The economic harm done by taxes distorting private decisions to save, invest, work, and so forth goes up with the square of tax rates. Doubling tax rates quadruples the cost. The marginal cost is proportional to tax rates. Hence, each dollar of additional revenues costs the economy about $1.40. When it is spent—as legislated by Congress, adjudicated in the courts, and administered by human beings—some of it is wasted, some not narrowly targeted on the intended purpose. Perhaps 80 or 90 cents contributes to the intended outcome in a well-run program; only 30 or 40 cents contributes in a poorly designed and administered program. Furthermore, some of that government spending crowds out private spending on the targeted activity. So the net government-financed increase in spending on the activity is even less. Thus, rigorous cost-benefit tests would reveal many spending programs badly in need of reform and retrenchment.

Tax reforms that more closely tie the payment of taxes to expenditures will promote a more effective and efficient government. A new tax—a broad-based consumption tax, like a European VAT, for example—may just be piled on top of the existing taxes and used to raise revenue to grow government. This is what has happened in many European countries and is now a major detriment to their economic performance.

If everybody pays at a common rate, it will be harder to expand government and raise the rate, because a larger fraction of potential voters will have a stake in limiting the spending. The more progressive the tax system becomes and the more concentrated among the few taxes become, the easier it is to expand government at the expense of a minority paying the bulk of costs. This was Milton Friedman's (1962) most important insight when he first proposed a flat tax in *Capitalism and Freedom*. This aspect of the case for a flat tax has unfortunately almost been lost in recent decades, as attention has focused on the important goal of simplicity, as in the postcard filing in the Hall-Rabushka (1983) flat tax.

Highly progressive rates also create an unhealthy dynamic in which revenues surge disproportionately in booms, the legislature spends it all (or more), and in the next downturn it is impossible to cut spending, leaving a growing fiscal gap and pressure to raise taxes to allow spending to ratchet up in the next boom. This is precisely what happened in California in 1999–2001 when revenues surged far more than rapidly rising income during the tech bubble, and state spending went up faster still. The inevitable correction led to a crisis, with the state's credit rating below Puerto Rico's and the governor recalled.

Some proponents of the retail sales tax believe it would help control the growth of government spending by forcing an explicit transparent payment in support of spending on all consumers at the point of transaction, thereby greatly expanding the fraction of voters paying something to finance general government. Others believe a broad-based retail sales tax or VAT would collect so much revenue per percentage point that it would too easily finance government growth.

3. Will a new tax structure affect federalism? Some federal tax reforms risk crowding out state and local activity, for example, a retail sales tax (or a VAT) might make it harder for state and local governments to raise revenue. Likewise, limiting or abolishing the deductibility of state and local income and property taxes as in the SIT, GIT, and flat tax will increase the net cost of revenue raised by state and local governments. Although we should favor those that strengthen federalism and devolve authority and resources to state and local governments, the current system in effect subsidizes state and local spending relative to private or federal spending.

4. Will a new tax structure likely endure? We have had more than a dozen major tax law changes in the last quarter-century, about one every Congress. We should be concerned that we might move to a better tax system only to undo it shortly thereafter. In 1986, the trade-off was lower rates for a broader base. That was slightly undone in 1990, and dramatically so in 1993, whereas in the past four years, rates have been reduced. A more stable tax system would both reduce uncertainty and be less complex, as taxpayers would not have to learn and adjust to new laws every year or two.

All tax systems are subject to intense economic and political pressure to change. The current system has many temporary features that need to be extended episodically; low-rate taxes on a broader base could raise much more revenue per percentage point increase. So which system is most likely to endure in some relatively pure form for a significant period? Here, simplicity, transparency, and common low-to-modest rates are more promising than complexity and high rates. Spending control is also vital to minimize pressure for more revenue.

5. Over time, will tax reform contribute to a prosperous, stable democracy? Are we likely to see a change in the ratio of taxpayers to people receiving income from government? We now have a much higher ratio of people who are net income recipients to people who are taxpayers than in any time in our recent history, reflecting not only traditional transfers but the rapid growth of the EITC and other features of the income tax itself. Do we really want to continue an income tax system in which almost half the population pays virtually no taxes (see table 17.1)? If the median voter has no "skin in the game," not even a tiny pro-rata share of the financing of general government, the constituency for limiting government spending will be weak, and the economy, which ultimately will have to finance the growing government spending by either current or future taxes, will eventually be severely damaged.

As the baby boom generation approaches retirement, the fraction of the population in any given year who are receiving more than they are paying will grow. We must deal with this both on the tax side (smaller underground economy, decreased proportion of population off the income tax rolls) and, especially, on the transfer payment side (slower benefit growth for the well off in entitlements programs) and do so soon, or we risk sliding into a spiral of higher benefits, higher tax rates, a weaker economy, and ever-greater political conflict between taxpayers and transfer recipients.

This suggests we should be combining the best of recent tax and budget policies: the tax "reductions" and reforms of President Ronald Reagan and President George W. Bush with the spending controls of President George H. W. Bush, extended by the Congress and President Bill Clinton, which worked quite well to control spending until the budget went into surplus in the late 1990s.

CONCLUSION

We have a rapidly closing window within which to have this great national strategic debate about the role of government in our economy, about the level and structure of spending and taxes. In a few years, the demographics may drive an unstable political economy with an ever-larger fraction of voters demanding higher spending financed by higher taxes on a dwindling fraction of the population. Witness how difficult it is for the Europeans—with their larger ratios of benefit recipients to taxpayers—to make reforms that we would consider trivial, even from much higher levels of spending and taxes.

Our collective interest is in keeping the hand of government in the economy light; in keeping tax rates as low as possible; And in preventing spending and tax decisions from gradually turning our society into the economic equivalent of a France or Germany, for that would surely portend economic and social disaster. Replacing the corporate and personal income taxes with the GIT or something still closer to a pure flat-rate consumption tax would be an important step in doing so.

REFERENCES AND FURTHER READING

Boskin, Michael. 1975. "Notes on the Tax Treatment of Human Capital." In *Proceedings of the Treasury Conference on Tax Policy*. U.S. Department of the Treasury. (Explaining how progressive rates impede human capital investment.)

———. 1978. "Taxation, Saving and the Rate of Interest." *Journal of Political Economy* (April). (Estimating the reduction in saving from lower interest rates and higher capital income taxes)

Engen, E. and J. Skinner 1996. "Taxation and Economic Growth." *National Tax Journal* (December).

Feldstein, M. 1980. "The Theory of Tax Expenditures." In *The Economics of Taxation*, eds. H. Aaron and M. Boskin. Washington, DC: Brookings Institution. (Showing that deductions can be efficient.)

Friedman, M. 1962. *Capitalism and Freedom*. Chicago: University of Chicago Press. (Presenting proposal and case for a flat tax.)

Hall, R. and A. Rabushka. 1983. *Low Tax, Simple Tax, Flat Tax*. Stanford, CA: Hoover Press. (Providing a detailed analysis and description of a simple two-part flat-rate consumption tax composed of a personal wage tax and business value added less wages paid tax.)

Lucas, R. 1990. "Analytical Foundations of Supply-Side Economics." *Oxford Economic Papers*. (Discussing the history of thought and developing a model of benefits of reducing capital income taxes.)

Prescott, E. 2002. "Prosperity and Depression." *American Economic Review*. (Arguing that high French taxes are the primary reason for French depression relative to U.S. prosperity.)

Stiglitz, J. and M. Boskin. 1977. "Some Lessons from the New Public Finance." *American Economic Review*. (Deriving criteria under which deductions or credits might be desirable.)

Summers, L. 1981. "Capital Taxation and Accumulation in a Life-Cycle Growth Model." *American Economic Review*. (Showing the gains from reducing capital income taxation.)

U.S. Congressional Budget Office. December 2003. "The Long-Term Budget Outlook." (Estimating that unless changes are made to the U.S. tax code the tax share of GDP will climb to 25 percent in coming decades.)

———. August 2005. "The Economic and Budget Outlook, An Update." (Estimating the rising ratio of taxes to GDP over the next decade.)

18

Tax Reform: Time for a Plan C?

Michael J. Graetz

ON NOVEMBER 1, 2005, the President's Advisory Panel on Tax Reform unanimously recommended two alternative plans: a simplified income tax (SIT) and a growth and investment tax (GIT). The panel considered plan C—a partial replacement of individual and corporate income taxes with a value-added tax (VAT), but although the panel found the VAT possibility worthwhile, it could not reach unanimity. The panel rejected a fourth alternative: substitution of a retail sales tax for the corporate and individual income taxes.

Fundamental tax reform to make the tax system genuinely better should be along the lines of the VAT proposal. In fact, I have long favored limiting the income tax to income over $100,000 and making up the revenue lost with a VAT. This would eliminate the need for 100 million tax returns each year, producing real simplification.

Once people realize the shortcomings of the panel's two unanimous proposals, I hope that they will begin to focus on a plan C: using a VAT to replace much of the income tax. The VAT has been

Michael J. Graetz is the Justus S. Hotchkiss Professor of Law at Yale Law School and was formerly deputy assistant secretary for tax policy, U.S. Treasury, 1990–1992.

successful throughout the world, often operating alongside an income tax. Why not use it here to replace the income tax for 150 million Americans?

THE PANEL'S PROPOSALS

Both of the panel's two recommended plans propose to do the following: (1) reduce the top marginal tax rates—to 33 and 30 percent, respectively; (2) eliminate the alternative minimum tax (AMT) and phaseouts of tax benefits; (3) replace the earned income tax credit and refundable child credits with a work credit; (4) replace personal exemptions, the standard deduction, and child tax credits with a family credit; (5) eliminate all deductions for state and local taxes; (6) extend deductions for interest on home mortgages and charities to non-itemizers but reduce deductible amounts; (7) cap the exclusion for employer-provided health insurance; and (8) expand and simplify tax-favored savings opportunities. Both plans also eliminate many deductions and credits. In addition, the SIT eliminates tax on dividends distributed by U.S. corporations from U.S. earnings and exempts 75 percent of capital gains on the sale of corporate stock; other dividends and capital gains would be taxed at the standard rates.

Once the panel decided to eliminate the AMT, which costs more than $1 trillion over the ten-year budget period, it struggled to find offsetting revenues to achieve revenue neutrality. This required attacking political sacred cows, such as the mortgage interest deduction.

As a result of taking on these sacred cows, neither of the panel's plans has been endorsed by congressional Republicans or Democrats. Both have criticized the elimination of deductions for state and local taxes and the reduction of home mortgage interest deductions. Republicans complain that the panel did not recommend a greater reduction in tax rates, and Democrats criticize the panel for favoring capital over labor income.

Although the SIT is in the tradition of the base-broadening, rate-reducing 1986 Tax Reform Act and contains many income tax improvements, its base-broadening is too politically painful and its rate cuts too trivial for it to make it through Congress—or the White House—without major changes. The principal benefit of the plan—repeal of the AMT—avoids only future potential pain and is not likely to motivate its potential beneficiaries.

The GIT, the so-called Growth and Investment Tax, is a variation on David Bradford's (2005) "X" tax, which is itself a progressive-rate variation on Robert Hall and Alvin Rabushka's (1995) flat tax.

At the individual level, the GIT taxes wages at progressive rates up to 30 percent and all dividends, capital gains, and interest income at 15 percent. The panel describes this tax as "equivalent to a credit-method value added tax at a 30 percent rate, coupled with a progressive system of wage subsidies and a separate single rate tax on capital income" (President's Advisory Panel 2005, 171). This suggests that the GIT is a higher rate VAT than those of Europe or elsewhere in the OECD. The GIT denies deductions for interest paid. It excludes the financial income of nonfinancial corporations from tax. It allows businesses to expense investments. Financial institutions are taxed on a cash-flow basis.

Unfortunately, although the GIT will appeal to academics, it is not a practical alternative. First, many U.S. businesses will not relish giving up their interest deductions in trade for immediate expensing of investments and exclusion of financial income. Second, as the panel recognized, special rules are needed for financial institutions, raising line-drawing difficulties that may prove insuperable (245). Third, the panel tacked a 15 percent individual investment income tax onto a consumption tax, creating significant incentives to shift investment income to a business and offending consumption tax advocates. (I agree, however, with the panel's judgment that taxing people only on wages will never fly politically.) Fourth, the panel used a gimmick to push costs outside the budget window in order to get the GIT rate down to 30 percent; this gimmick has not gone unnoticed. Finally, and most important, the panel recognized that the GIT violates our major trade treaty (the General Agreement on Trade and Tariffs [GATT]) and all eighty-six of our existing bilateral income tax treaties. A tax proposal so out of sync with international trade and tax arrangements would be unrealistic, even if it did not have the domestic failings I just listed.

All of which brings us to plan C.

PLAN C

For a serious alternative, we must look to the panel's third suggestion: the partial replacement of both corporate and individual income taxes with a credit-method VAT, like that used in every other OECD country and by nearly 150 countries worldwide.

The panel failed to reach consensus for this plan but describes it as "worthy of further consideration." The panel was unable to "develop an approximately distributionally neutral" plan because the "Treasury Department did not develop a modified credit and rate structure that would make the Partial Replacement VAT structure approximately as progressive as current law" (President's Advisory Panel 2005, 194).

The Treasury instead gave the panel a revenue-neutral plan illustrating a 15 percent rate for the VAT, the corporate income tax, and the top bracket of the income tax.[1] For the income tax, the Treasury modified the SIT proposal by suggesting only two rates of 5 percent and 15 percent and increasing family and work credits to prevent any tax increase for the lowest two quintiles of the population. With this structure, there would be a tax increase in the third and fourth quintiles and a cut for the highest quintile (President's Advisory Panel

2005, 195). The panel points out, however, that adjusting the individual income tax rates and the family credit amounts, could produce a revenue and distributionally neutral plan.

Indeed, a VAT-income tax hybrid that is roughly as progressive as current law and also revenue neutral is quite possible. In a *Yale Law Journal* essay (2002) and a book, *100 Million Unnecessary Returns* (2008), I have proposed a plan that is both. My plan would return the income tax to its pre–World War II status—a much simpler low-rate tax on a relatively thin slice of higher-income Americans—and replace the lost revenue with a VAT. A 10 percent to 14 percent VAT would finance an income tax exemption for families with $100,000 of income or less and allow a simpler income tax at a no more than a 25 percent rate applied to individual incomes over $100,000 and a 15 to 20 percent rate on corporations. (The broader income and VAT bases of the panel's plan would allow even lower tax rates than in my plan.) Yes, you read correctly: Those with under $100,000 of income would pay no income tax and file no income tax form!

The earned income tax credit would be replaced by a refundable payroll tax offset or a smart card, rather than by increasing income tax credits as the panel suggests. A smart card or payroll tax offsets would also be used to protect low- and moderate-income families from any tax increase. Providing relief this way would allow for the elimination of low- and middle-income tax returns and free about 150 million people from the task of filing income tax returns.

Both the panel's VAT plan and mine would broaden the income tax base but in different ways. Both retain deductions for charitable contributions and home mortgage interest (but the panel's plan reduces deductible amounts). Under both plans, employers would have incentives to provide tax-favored retirement savings and health insurance. Both attack the marriage penalties. Both greatly simplify the taxation of small businesses, and my plan allows small businesses to qualify for the $100,000 exemption.

A credit-method VAT works well. It facilitates exemptions for small businesses (and for specified goods or services if such exemptions become politically necessary). A broad VAT tax base with a single rate minimizes economic distortions. Both my VAT and the panel's VAT exempt small businesses from collecting VAT or filing returns unless they elect to come into the system. This exemption would relieve small businesses from the costs of compliance, greatly reduce the number of VAT returns, and free the tax collector from chasing after small amounts. Although their rules vary significantly, European VATs tend to impose compliance costs about one-fifth to one-third as large as our income tax, according to Joel Slemrod (2005), a tax expert at the University of Michigan.

Many countries allow retailers to bury the amount of VAT imposed on the goods they sell in the prices of those goods. Both the panel and I recommend addressing this weakness by having Congress require that the total amount of VAT be separately stated whenever goods or services are sold.

CONCLUSION

Using a VAT to replace much of the income tax has many advantages. It combines two of the world's most common tax mechanisms to exploit our nation's advantages as a low-tax country. A combined VAT and income tax system would make the United States quite similar to the average OECD country with regard to consumption taxes relative to GDP and tax rates on consumption. Our income tax, however, would be much smaller than what people generally face abroad. In 2002, the U.S. individual and corporate income taxes were about 12 percent of GDP, compared to an OECD average of about 13 percent and a European average of about 14 percent. My plan would reduce the U.S. income tax to just over 4 percent of GDP, and eliminate 100 million of the 135 million income tax returns that are now filed. For most Americans, April 15 would just be another day.

The tax system would then be far more favorable for savings and economic growth. Most Americans would owe no tax on savings. Taxes on savings and investment would be lower for everyone. The United States would be an extremely attractive place for corporate investments. Thus this plan should stimulate economic growth and create additional jobs for American workers.

Moreover, this plan avoids the difficult issues of transition to an entirely new system that have haunted other proposals to move away the income tax, and it fits well within existing international tax and trade agreements.

NOTE

1. Because the VAT rate, like the income tax rates, is shown on a tax-inclusive basis, this 15 percent VAT should be compared to a 17.6 percent tax exclusive rate typically used to describe VAT rates.

REFERENCES AND FURTHER READING

Bradford, David. 2005. "A Tax System for the Twenty-First Century." In *Fundamental Tax Reform*, eds. Alan J. Auerbach and Kevin A. Hassett, pp. 11–33. Washington, DC: AEI Press.

Ebrill, Liam P., Michael Keen, John-Paul Bodn, and Victoria Summers. 2001. *The Modern VAT*. Washington, DC: International Monetary Fund.

Graetz, Michael J. 1999. *The U.S. Income Tax: What It Is, How It Got That Way, and Where We Go From Here*. New York: Norton.

———. 2002. "100 Million Unnecessary Returns: A Fresh Start for the U.S. Tax System." *Yale Law Journal* 112: 261–310.

———. 2005a. "A Fair and Balanced Tax System for the Twenty-First Century." In *Fundamental Tax Reform*, eds. Alan J. Auerback and Kevin A. Hassett, pp. 48–69. Washington, DC: AEI Press.

————. 2005b. Testimony before the President's Advisory Panel on Tax Reform.   http://www.tax.reformpanel.gov/meetings/docs/graetz_ 052005.ppt (accessed August 30, 2007).

————. 2008. *100 Million Unnecessary Returns: A Simple, Fair, and Competitive Tax Plan for the United States.* New Haven, CT and London: Yale University Press.

Hall, Robert E. and Alvin Rubushka. 1995. *The Flat Tax,* 2nd ed. Stanford, CA: Hoover Institution Press.

President's Advisory Panel on Tax Reform. 2005. *Simple, Fair and Pro-Growth: Proposals to Fix America's Tax System.* Washington, DC: Government Printing Office.

Slemrod, Joel. 2005. Testimony before the President's Advisory Panel on Tax Reform. http://www.taxreformpanel.gov/meetings/docs/ slemrod_03032005.ppt (accessed August 30, 2007).

CHAPTER 19

Taxes on Investment Income Remain Too High and Lead to Multiple Distortions

Martin Feldstein

THANKS TO RECENT tax reforms, the marginal tax rates on saving in the United States today are significantly lower than in the past, which correspondingly reduces society's losses from the drag that our tax system puts on saving and investment. That's the good news. But there is bad news.

The first piece of bad news is that tax rates on saving and investment remain much higher than they would be in any rational system of taxation. The second piece of bad news is that these taxes continue to seriously distort the economy: they cost us a lot. The third piece of bad news is that many economists grossly underestimate the efficiency

Martin Feldstein is the George F. Baker Professor of Economics at Harvard University and president and CEO of the National Bureau of Economic Research. From 1982 through 1984, he was chairman of the Council of Economic Advisers and President Ronald Reagan's chief economic adviser. He served as president of the American Economic Association in 2004.

cost of our system of taxing capital income: they think that if the taxation of capital income does not cause a big reduction in saving, it is not a problem. They are wrong, as I explain.

A LITTLE TAX HISTORY

Back in 1963, the highest marginal rate of personal income tax was 93 percent: a taxpayer in the top bracket got to keep only seven cents out of every extra dollar that he earned. I used to work for one of those taxpayers: Ronald Reagan. His experience of the adverse effects of such high tax rates on his decision making and those of his Hollywood peers is an important reason that we have much lower marginal tax rates today.

Even as recently as 1980 the top income tax rate was 70 percent on interest and dividends and 50 percent on wages and other personal services income. Today the top statutory federal marginal income tax rate is 35 percent (however, the effective marginal tax rate on earned income for many well-off taxpayers is about 50 percent when the Medicare payroll tax, the phaseout of deductions, and state tax systems are taken into account). In many well-off two-earner families, at least one of the two faces a marginal Social Security payroll tax as well, bringing their total marginal tax rate as high as 60 percent.

Today's statutory tax rates on capital income consists of a corporate tax rate down from 46 percent in 1980 to 35 percent now, a maximum tax rate on capital gains (which in 1980 could reach more than 40 percent as a result of tax add-ons and offsets) of 15 percent (which could revert to 25 percent if Congress remains deadlocked), and a current 15 percent tax rate on dividend income (which could revert to 35-plus percent if Congress remains deadlocked). The decline in the rate of inflation has also lowered the effective tax rate on investment income. When inflation was at double-digit levels in the late 1970s, the taxation of nominal interest and capital gains and the use of historic cost depreciation raised the effective tax rate substantially, to more than 100 percent in some years and cases.

But it would be wrong to conclude from the recently reduced rates on dividends and capital gains and today's much more modest rate of inflation that the tax on capital income is now low. The full tax on capital income includes not only the taxes paid by the individual investors but also the corporate income tax. When these taxes are combined, the result is still a marginal tax rate that is high—albeit not as high as in the 1960s and 1970s—and that is thus capable of doing a great deal of economic harm.

Two kinds of efficiency losses result from our current taxation of capital income. First, the tax wedge that reduces the return to saving means that we consume too much now and in the near future and too little in the distant future. The nature of this distortion and the magnitude of the resulting deadweight loss are still very badly understood.

Second, specific distortions are generated because of the structure of capital income taxation. We allocate too little capital to corporations and too much capital to noncorporate forms of business. Companies pay too little in dividends and retain too much in earnings. Corporations take on too much debt and issue too little equity. Capital gains realizations are postponed too late. Businesses that should be located in the United States place themselves abroad instead. The tax structure distorts each of these decisions in ways that cause deadweight losses.

THE TAX ON THE RETURN TO SAVING AND THE TIMING OF CONSUMPTION

Let's look first at the effects of our capital income taxes that drive a wedge between the social return to saving and the net return to savers—the corporate income tax; the taxes paid by individuals on dividends, interest, and capital gains; and the estate tax. Despite the recent reductions in the tax rates on dividends and capital gains, the cumulative corporate and individual taxes still typically take one-third or more of the real pretax return to capital.

Even saving that takes place in tax-favored IRAs, 401(k) accounts, and other vehicles is subject to a large tax wedge because of the combination of the corporate tax and the ultimate taxation of distributions at ordinary income tax rates. For those whose saving exceeds the maximum amount that can be deposited in IRAs and 401(k) accounts, the marginal distortion in the return to saving is as large as it would be without access to those tax-preferred accounts.

How much damage does the tax wedge that reduces the rate of return to savers do? It does much more damage than is generally understood.

THE LARGE LOSSES FROM DIMINISHED
FUTURE CONSUMPTION

It is natural (but wrong) to think about the deadweight efficiency cost of taxing the return to saving by asking how much that tax reduces the amount of saving. We think about the deadweight efficiency cost of a tax on apples by asking how much that tax reduces the quantity of apples consumed. We think about the deadweight efficiency cost of a tax on labor income by asking how much that tax decreases people's willingness to work.

Many economists still think—incorrectly in my judgment—that savings are not very responsive to the net after-tax rate of return. They combine this empirical view with the belief that you measure the efficiency loss by looking at how the tax affects the volume of saving. They conclude that taxes that lower the return to saving create little deadweight loss. In their view, the tax on capital income is thus from an efficiency point of view a "good tax," like the standard textbook case of a tax on a commodity with inelastic demand: little change in the amount of saving, little deadweight efficiency cost.

But that is wrong.

The deadweight loss of a tax on the return to saving depends not on how the tax affects current saving but on how the tax affects future consumption. Why? Because deadweight losses depend on how taxes affect the things that people care *directly* about. We don't really care directly about how much we save (though we may care about it as an indirect indicator of future consumption). We do care about how much we consume, both now and in the future.

The right way to think about saving is that it is the amount that we "spend" today to buy future consumption. When we think about a tax on apples, we measure the deadweight loss by looking at the impact of the tax on the number of apples that are consumed. We don't conclude that the deadweight efficiency loss from a tax on apples is zero if total consumer spending on apples is unchanged. For example, a tax that raises the price of apples by 10 percent and causes a 10 percent reduction in the number of apples consumed means that there will be no change in spending on apples. But we still recognize that the reduction in apple consumption causes a net loss. Similarly, a tax on capital income should be evaluated by looking at how it affects the level of future consumption bought by saving, not what happens to the amount of saving by itself.

A capital income tax that does not change saving at all can still cause a very large deadweight efficiency loss.

Consider this illustrative example: Assume that in the absence of all capital taxes, 10 percent is the real rate of return that individual savers would receive. If capital income taxes take half this return, the net return to the saver is 5 percent. Think about someone who saves at age forty-five and dissaves thirty years later at age seventy-five. With a 10 percent real rate of return, each dollar saved at age forty-five grows to $17.45. In contrast with a 5 percent rate of return, a dollar saved at age forty-five grows to only $4.32—a decline of 75 percent.

This example has two implications. First, the individual would be better off if the government collected the same amount of revenue by a lump-sum tax or a tax on labor income at age forty-five and allowed the individual to invest the remainder at the higher rate of return: the deadweight loss depends on the distortion of consumption, not on the change in saving. The large magnitude of the difference in future consumption means that this deadweight loss could be very large.

Second, the example reminds us that a tax on investment income is also a tax on extra work, because some of the income from that work would be saved and consumed during retirement years. If each extra dollar of earnings at age forty-five buys $17.45 of age-seventy-five retirement income, the individual has much more incentive to earn income than if those extra dollars each buys only $4.32. So the tax that reduces the return to saving reduces labor supply broadly defined.

This effect occurs even if the tax on the return to saving does not alter the amount of saving. But my reading of the evidence on saving is that taxes that lower the return to saving do reduce saving. The most convincing evidence on this point are the studies of 401(k) plans by David Wise and his coauthors that show that individuals who have access to 401(k) plans save substantially more than those who do not.

I will not pursue these issues further but turn instead to four ways in which our complex system of taxing capital income distorts the use of capital in the economy.

DISTORTING THE USE OF CAPITAL

The differential taxation of profits in the corporate sector—by the corporate income tax and then by the taxes on dividends and capital gains—drives capital out of the corporate sector and into other activities, particularly into foreign investment and real estate. Shifting capital abroad causes a real loss of income in the United States as tax revenue shifts from the U.S. Treasury to foreign governments. The shift of capital from corporate businesses to real estate creates a loss of efficiency: there is a gap between the higher pretax return to capital in the corporate sector and the lower return to capital in the more lightly taxed real estate sector.

The reduction of the corporate tax rate from 46 percent to 35 percent in 1986 reduced this deadweight loss. By keeping more of the capital in the corporate sector, it caused the revenue loss to be less than static estimates. The lower tax rates on dividends and capital gains has also helped to keep capital in the corporate sector and so reduced the revenue cost of those lower tax rates. Should the Congress fail to extend the current tax rates on capital gains and dividends, the higher rates would exacerbate the sectoral misallocation of capital and would produce less revenue than static revenue estimates predict.

The recent reduction in the tax rate on dividends has led many corporations to start paying dividends and many others to increase their dividend payout rates. This increase in dividends improves economic efficiency by making funds available to new and growing businesses and by imposing greater discipline on corporate managements that must now seek outside funding more often. And, of course, the rise in dividend payouts means that the government collects more revenue than predicted by static analysis.

Also, the current tax system encourages firms to use debt finance rather than equity finance: interest payments are deductible by borrowing firms, whereas dividend payouts are not. This makes firms more vulnerable to adverse business cycle conditions. It also causes firms to be more cautious in their investments, foregoing projects with more uncertain payoffs or with longer-term payoffs even if those would be more productive. In both of these ways, the tax system-generated bias toward debt finance is a source of economic inefficiency. Another of the advantages of the recent reduction in the tax on dividends is that it reduces this bias in favor of debt.

Consider the realization of capital gains. The capital gains tax is essentially a voluntary tax: individuals can postpone the realization of the capital gain and the payment of the resulting tax liability. They can even avoid the tax liability completely by using the appreciated property to make a charitable contribution or by holding it until they bequeath it at death. The extent to which the tax is voluntary can be seen by comparing the relatively small amount of taxable capital gains realized in each year with the full amount of the accrued gain in the same year.

An individual investor's decision not to sell appreciated property reduces the funds available for new and growing businesses. It also causes the investor to have a riskier portfolio because he retains appreciated stock rather than rebalancing. It discourages investors from shifting funds to companies in which they wish to invest by locking them into their old positions. Each of these causes a deadweight loss and also reduces tax revenue. Lowering the capital gains tax rate to 15 percent thus reduces efficiency losses and reduces revenue by less than a static forecast would predict.

CONCLUDING THOUGHTS

The tax system today is more efficient than it was in the past. Tax rates are lower on all forms of income. But marginal tax rates on capital income are still relatively high. And the efficiency costs of the resulting distortions are much greater than is generally understood. Taxes on capital income produce large deadweight losses even when the saving rate itself is not very sensitive to the net rate of return. Analysts who believe otherwise do so because they fail to understand that the right quantity measure to use in their calculations of the deadweight losses from taxation is not the amount saved but rather the amount of future consumption purchased by current saving.

Taxes that reduce the net rate of return to saving also reduce the reward for working when the individual is young because each dollar earned translates into less consumption when old. The lower reward for working reduces labor supply broadly defined to include not only the number of hours worked but also the accumulation of human capital, the amount of effort, the choice of education, and so on.

Moreover, the combination of taxes on corporate profits, dividends, and capital gains introduce further efficiency costs and depress tax revenue in a variety of ways.

It is thus important to retain the gains that have been made by reducing tax rates in general and the taxes on dividends and capital gains in particular. The corporate tax system itself deserves a serious reexamination. Much can be done to improve the tax policy process. The revenue estimators need to recognize and report the extent to which taxes change behavior in both the short run and the longer term. And the measurement of economic efficiency and deadweight losses deserves to be a focus of the analysis alongside estimates of the effects on tax revenue.

My sense is that the need for these improvements is now better understood in both the academic world and here in Washington. And that makes me optimistic about the future path of tax policy.

20

Progressive Consumption Taxation as a Remedy for the U.S. Savings Shortfall

Robert H. Frank

THE AMERICAN SAVINGS rate, always low by international standards, has fallen sharply in recent decades. One in five American adults now has net worth of zero or less, and more than half of all retirees experience significantly reduced living standards when they stop working.

Why do we save so little, and is there anything we can or should do about it? I argue here that low U.S. savings rates are in large part a result of pressures to keep pace with community spending standards, pressures that have been exacerbated by rising income and wealth inequality. Replacing the income tax with a progressive consumption tax would stimulate additional savings

Robert H. Frank is the Henrietta Johnson Louis Professor of Management and Professor of Economics, Johnson School of Management, Cornell University. He thanks Aaron Edlin and Brad DeLong for helpful comments on an earlier draft.

by reducing the price of future consumption relative to current consumption as compared to its price under the current income tax. Perhaps more important, a progressive consumption tax would stimulate savings by altering the social context that shapes spending decisions.

WHY DO AMERICANS SAVE SO LITTLE?

Although numerous factors contribute to our savings deficit, I mention only two and focus on one. First, we often find it difficult to summon the willpower to save. And second, we often confront pressures to keep pace with community spending standards. The self-control problem can be remedied by individual action. But the problem of keeping pace requires collective action.

THE SELF-CONTROL PROBLEM

Although the pain from reducing current consumption is experienced directly, the pain from diminished future consumption can only be imagined (Pigou 1929, and more recently, Ainslie 1992; Laibson 1998; and O'Donoghue and Rabin 1999). So the act of saving requires self-control. If the temptation of current consumption were the only important source of our savings shortfall, individuals could solve the problem unilaterally—for example, by signing a contract to divert some portion of future income growth into savings until a target savings rate were to be reached (Thaler and Ben-artzi 2004).

Thus, if a family's income were to grow by 3 percent each year, it could commit itself to divert, say, one-third of that amount—starting the *next* year—into savings.

THE COLLECTIVE-ACTION PROBLEM

Our savings shortfall also stems from a second source, one that is much harder to address by unilateral individual action. The following thought experiment illustrates the basic problem: If you were society's median earner, which of these two worlds would you prefer?

A. You save enough to support a comfortable standard of living in retirement, but your children attend a school whose students score in the twentieth percentile on standardized tests in reading and math; or

B. You save too little to support a comfortable standard of living in retirement, but your children attend a school whose students score in the fiftieth percentile on those tests.

Because the concept of a "good" school is inescapably relative, this thought experiment captures an essential element of the savings decision confronting most middle-income families. If others bid for houses in better school districts, failure to do likewise will often consign one's children to inferior schools. Yet no matter how much each family spends, half of all children must attend schools in the bottom half. The choice posed by the thought experiment is one that most parents would prefer to avoid. But when forced to choose, most say they would pick the second option.

Context influences our evaluations of not just schools but virtually every other good or service we consume. To look good in a job interview, for example, means simply to dress better than the other candidates. It is the same with gifts: "In a poor country, a man proves to his wife that he loves her by giving her a rose but in a rich country, he must give a dozen roses" (Layard 1980, 741).

The savings decision thus resembles the collective-action problem inherent in a military arms race. Each nation knows that it would be better if all spent less on arms. Yet if others keep spending, it is simply too dangerous not to follow suit. Therefore, curtailing an arms race requires an enforceable agreement. Similarly, unless all families can bind themselves to save more, those who do so unilaterally will pay a price. They risk having to send their children to inferior schools. Or they may be unable to dress advantageously for job interviews. Or they may be unable to buy gifts that meet social expectations.

Temptation and collective-action problems may explain why Americans save too little, but why do we save less than other nations that face similar problems?

HOW INCOME INEQUALITY EXACERBATES
THE SAVINGS SHORTFALL

Inequality in income and wealth has always been more pronounced in the United States than in other industrial nations. That fact helps explain why our savings rate was lower to begin with. And the fact that inequality has increased in recent decades helps explain why the savings gap has grown.

Inequality is linked to savings because of its effect on community consumption standards. This is a controversial claim because, according to the reigning economic theories of consumption, the distribution of income has no effect on individual spending decisions (Friedman 1957; Modigliani and Brumberg 1955).

These theories predict that consumption in the various income categories will rise in proportion to the corresponding changes in income. Given observed income growth rates in the United States, the top 1 percent of earners should thus be spending about three times as much now as in 1979, the median earner only about 15 percent more.[1]

In contrast, models that incorporate positional concerns predict that sharply increased spending by top earners will exert indirect upward pressure on spending by the median earner. When top earners build larger houses, for example, they shift the frame of reference that defines the aspirations of others slightly below them. And when those slightly below the top earners build bigger houses, they in turn shift the frame of reference for others just below them, and so on. This explains why the median size of a newly constructed house, which stood at less than 1,600 square feet in 1980, had risen more than 30 percent to over 2,100 square feet by 2001—roughly twice the increase predicted by traditional theories based on the observed 15 percent growth in median income.[2]

Additional evidence supports the view that expenditure cascades in housing and other areas, and the implied reductions in savings rates, are at least in part a consequence of increased income inequality. For example, U.S. counties with higher earnings inequality have significantly higher median house prices, personal bankruptcy rates, divorce rates, and average commute times (Frank et al. 2005). Total hours worked, both across countries and over time within countries, are also positively associated with higher earnings inequality (Bowles and Park 2002). Models that incorporate positional concerns predict these links.[3] Traditional models do not.

STIMULATING ADDITIONAL SAVINGS

A law requiring that each family save a portion of its income growth each year would attack the self-control and collective-action problems simultaneously. A less intrusive approach would be to make consumption less attractive by taxing it. Shifting to a progressive consumption tax would change our incentives in just this way.[4] Because the amount a family consumes each year is just the difference between the amount it earns and the amount it saves, a system of progressive consumption taxation could be achieved by making savings exempt from tax. A family would report its income to the IRS just as it does now but would then deduct the amount it had saved during the year. Annual savings would be documented in much the same way that families now report annual contributions to 401(k) accounts.

Because most middle- and low-income families currently save very little, a large standard deduction would be required to maintain revenue neutrality across income classes. Thus, if the standard deduction were, say, $7,500 per person, a family of four would be taxed on only that portion of its annual expenditures in excess of $30,000 plus the amount it saved. The marginal tax rate on low levels of taxable consumption would start low—say, at 20 percent. Maintaining the current tax burden across income levels would also require that marginal tax rates rise steadily with taxable consumption, ultimately reaching levels considerably higher than the current top marginal rates on income.

The objection that higher marginal tax rates on income discourage investment does not apply to higher marginal tax rates on consumption. Indeed, because a progressive consumption tax exempts income from taxation until it is spent, the tax would shift incentives in favor of savings and investment.[5]

It might seem that steep marginal tax rates at the highest consumption levels would severely compromise the ability of many wealthy Americans to support the standard of living to which they have grown accustomed. But what sorts of sacrifices, exactly, would this tax entail? Many top earners currently spend their marginal dollars in ways that could be curtailed with little real sacrifice.

Consider, for example, Patek Philippe's Calibre '89, considered to be the most remarkably elaborate and accurate mechanical watch ever built. With its $2.7 million price tag, it is purchased only by persons of extreme wealth. Among its features is a "tourbillon"—a gyroscope that turns about once each minute, whose purpose is to offset the distortionary effects of the earth's gravitational field. (Even with this, the Calibre '89 is actually less accurate than a battery-powered quartz watch costing less than $20, the precision of whose works are unaffected by gravity.)

Men who purchase mechanical Patek Philippe watches priced at $45,000 and more (women almost never buy them) often own several, which confronts them with a special problem: Although the watches are self-winding, they will stop if put aside for a few days. So people who own several watches must often reset each one before wearing it.

One could hardly expect men of means to tolerate such a problem. And sure enough, there is now a ready solution. On display in the Asprey & Garrard showrooms in Manhattan on Fifth Avenue, discerning buyers will find a finely tooled calfskin-leather–covered box with a golden clasp, whose doors open to reveal six mechanical wrists that rotate just often enough to keep the mechanical wristwatches they hold running smoothly. Its price? At $5,700, it is a bargain compared with the price of the equipment it holds.

If, as appears, the demand for expensive mechanical wristwatches is driven largely by social context, an across-the-board reduction in expenditure would entail no hardship. If the affluent reduced their spending on such wristwatches by half, a $20,000 watch would serve every purpose that a $40,000 watch currently does.

Similarly, an American CEO "needs" a 30,000-square-foot mansion only because others of similar means have houses that large. To have a lesser dwelling would risk social embarrassment or raise questions about the health of his business. Yet if all CEOs were to build smaller houses, no one would be embarrassed in the least. Indeed, many CEOs might even prefer to have smaller houses. It is a nuisance, after all, to recruit and supervise the staff needed to maintain a large mansion.

Whereas expenditures on many forms of consumption could be reduced at little sacrifice, the additional funds thereby diverted into savings would generate real benefits. For example, additional savings would provide extra security in the event of catastrophic medical expenses or an unexpected loss of earning power.

A progressive consumption tax would increase savings not only by reducing the price of future consumption relative to its price under the current income tax system but also by changing the frame of reference that shapes spending. Each individual's spending, after all, constitutes part of the frame of reference that influences what others spend. If people at the top built smaller mansions, those just below the top would be influenced to spend less as well, quite apart from any change in relative prices. Their cutbacks, in turn, would influence others just below them, and so on, all the way down the income ladder. Given the importance of context, the indirect effects of a progressive consumption tax promise to be considerably larger than the direct effects.

HOW A PROGRESSIVE CONSUMPTION TAX WOULD AFFECT GROWTH AND STABILITY

It might seem natural to worry that a tax that limits consumption could lead to recession and unemployment. However, money that is not spent on consumption would be saved and invested. Many who are now employed to produce consumption goods would instead be employed to produce capital goods. This would increase the economy's productive capacity and growth rate in the long run.

Should a recession occur in the short run, a more powerful fiscal remedy would be available under a consumption tax than is currently available under the income tax. A standard textbook remedy for recession is a temporary income tax cut. One problem, however, is that those who remain employed have a strong incentive to save their tax cuts as a hedge against the possibility of becoming unemployed. A temporary consumption tax cut would sidestep this difficulty, because the only way consumers could benefit from it would be to spend more money now. Transition problems could be minimized by phasing the program in gradually—with phased increases in the amount of savings a family could exempt and phased increases in the highest marginal tax rates.

CONCLUDING REMARKS

With unpaid credit card balances currently averaging about $9,000 for families that have at least one card, there is little question that Americans save too little. Evidence suggests that we do so in part because we face pressure to keep pace with escalating community consumption standards. To solve this collective-action problem, we must change incentives. A progressive consumption tax would directly increase the incentive to save for individual families at all income levels. And the resulting changes in spending would alter social frames of reference in ways that would further increase savings.

Is there any prospect that a progressive consumption tax might actually be adopted? Many conservatives have long advocated that we move from income taxation to consumption taxation. Their preferred form of consumption tax, the flat tax, has drawn fire on distributional grounds. The low marginal tax rate characteristic of the flat tax would also do very little to curb the high-end spending that shapes community consumption standards, because the advantages of ceasing to tax the returns to capital would be offset by the increased after-tax wealth that the affluent would realize from lower tax rates. If the flat tax fails to attract political support, pro-growth conservatives might be willing to consider a progressive consumption tax in its place. Indeed, just such a tax—the so-called Unlimited Savings Allowance Tax—was introduced in the Senate in 1995 with bipartisan sponsorship.[6] This proposal is ripe for another look.

NOTES

1. http://www.inequality.org.

2. http://www.census.gov/prod/2003pubs/02statab/construct.pdf; http://www.census.gov/hhes/income/histinc/f03.html.

3. These models also predict the observed negative relationship between income inequality and average happiness levels. See Alesina et al. 2001.

4. Consumption taxation has been proposed before. See Hall and Rabushka 1995 for a discussion of the so-called flat tax, a form of consumption tax. For earlier proposals of a progressive consumption tax, see Fisher and Fisher 1942; Friedman 1943; Bradford 1980; Courant and Gramlich 1984; and Seidman 1997. Others have defended income taxes with reference to concerns about relative position.

5. To illustrate, consider a taxpayer whose marginal rate under the current income tax is 0.33 and whose marginal rate under a progressive consumption tax would be 0.70. Under each tax regime, suppose that this taxpayer foregoes an extra dollar of consumption for the length of time it takes for money in a savings account to double in value. How much extra future consumption will his sacrifice support in each case? Under the current income tax, his dollar of foregone consumption generates a bank deposit of $1, which becomes $2 on the date in question. When he withdraws the $2, he must pay 33 cents in income tax on his $1 of interest income. So $1 of foregone consumption today translates into $1.67 of future consumption under the current income tax. Under the consumption tax, by contrast, foregoing $1 of consumption today would result in a 70 cents reduction in current tax liability, and so would support a current bank deposit of $1.70. At withdrawal time, this deposit will have grown to $3.40. To find C_F, the amount of future consumption this deposit will support, we solve $C_F + 0.7C_F = \$3.40$ for $C_F = \$2$. Giving up $1 of current consumption thus supports only $1.67 of future consumption under the current income tax, but $2 under the progressive consumption tax.

6. The USA Tax was proposed by Senators Sam Nunn (D-GA) and Pete Domeneci (R-NM). For a detailed analysis of their proposal, see Seidman 1997.

REFERENCES AND FURTHER READING

Ainslie, George. 1992. *Picoeconomics*. New York: Cambridge University Press.

Alesina, Alberto, Rafael Di Tella, and Robert McCulloch. July 2001. "Inequality and Happiness: Are Europeans and Americans Different?" Discussion paper no. 2877. Washington, DC: CEPR.

Bowles, Samuel and Yongjin Park. 2002. "Emulation, Inequality, and Work Hours: Was Thorstein Veblen Right?" Santa Fe Institute mimeograph.

Bradford, David F. 1980. "The Case for a Personal Consumption Tax." In *What Should Be Taxed?* ed. Joseph Pechman, pp. 75–113. Washington, DC: Brookings Institution.

Carroll, Christopher D. 1998. "Why Do the Rich Save So Much?" In *Does Atlas Shrug: The Economic Consequences of Taxing the Rich*, ed. Joel Slemrod, pp. 465–484. New York: Oxford University Press.

Courant, Paul and Edward M. Gramlich. 1984. "The Expenditure Tax: Has the Idea's Time Finally Come?" In *Tax Policy: New Directions and Possibilities*. Washington, DC: Center for National Policy.

Duesenberry, James. 1949. *Income, Saving, and the Theory of Consumer Behavior*. Cambridge, MA: Harvard University Press.

Fisher, Irving and Herbert W. Fisher. 1942. *Constructive Income Taxation*. New York: Harper and Brothers.

Frank, Robert H. 1999. *Luxury Fever*. New York: The Free Press.

Frank, Robert H., Bjornulf Ostvik-White, and Adam Levine. 2005. "Expenditure Cascades." Cornell University mimeograph.

Friedman, Milton. 1943. "The Tax as a Wartime Measure." *American Economic Review* (March), 33: 50–62.

———. 1957. *A Theory of the Consumption Function*. Princeton, NJ: Princeton University Press.

Hall, Robert E. and Alvin Rabushka. 1995. *The Flat Tax*, 2nd ed. Stanford, CA: Hoover Institution.

Laibson, David. 1998. "Life Cycle Consumption and Hyperbolic Discounting Functions." *European Economic Review Papers and Proceedings* 42: 861–871.

Layard, Richard. 1980. "Human Satisfactions and Public Policy." *Economic Journal* 90: 737–750.

Modigliani, Franco and R. Brumberg. 1955. "Utility Analysis and the Consumption Function: An Interpretation of Cross-Section Data."

In *Post-Keynesian Economics*, ed. K. Kurihara, pp. 388–436. London: Allen and Unwin.

O'Donoghue, Ted and Matthew Rabin. 1999. "Doing It Now or Later." *American Economic Review* (March), 89: 103–124.

Pigou, A. C. 1929. *The Economics of Welfare*. London: Macmillan.

Seidman, Laurence. 1997. *The USA Tax: A Progressive Consumption Tax*. Cambridge, MA: MIT Press.

Thaler, Richard, and Shlomo Benartzi. 2004. "Save More Tomorrow: Using Behavioral Economics to Increase Employee Savings." *Journal of Political Economy* (February), 112.1, part 2: S164–S187.

VII

SOCIAL POLICY

THE ESSAYS IN this section offer economists' perspectives on a range of social issues. One central question is the effectiveness of government policy in tackling poverty. The welfare reform signed by President Bill Clinton in 1996 was a major policy initiative targeted at the situation of unemployed single mothers dependent on welfare. The reform was controversial and many critics—including Rebecca Blank, author of the first essay—were skeptical about the ability of states to get women into work and feared they would be left in dire poverty with their welfare checks cut off. Their fears proved unfounded in one sense: welfare case loads plummeted between 1996 and 2000. But Blank points out that the contribution of welfare reform, higher minimum wages, the Earned Income Tax Credit, and the booming economy are hard to separate. What's more, unemployment among single mothers declined sharply, but poverty fell by far less.

In a second contribution on welfare, Janet Currie attacks four myths that she believes make Congress less inclined to reauthorize welfare programs than it ought to be. Contrary to the general perception, most welfare payments are received in kind (food stamps, in-school nutritional programs, child-care subsidies) rather than in cash; welfare programs *do* cut poverty; programs are typically not rife with fraud and waste; and state provision would not be more effective than the federal safety net because only the federal budget can insure programs against economic downturns.

The remaining essays address a range of themes. Aaron Edlin proposes a scheme to coordinate the level of charitable giving through a tax credit system but decentralize individual decisions about who gets the money. Edward Glaeser asks whether it would have been better, after Hurricane Katrina, to give residents of New Orleans individual checks rather than spending federal money on rebuilding the city, a place of high unemployment and low incomes, which has been in economic decline since its heyday in 1840. One hundred billion dollars of federal spending would have amounted to a life-changing $200,000 for each resident of a city where the average yearly income pre-hurricane was $20,000. Lisa Barrow and Cecilia Elena Rouse ask whether college still pays after steep increases in tuition in recent years, and answer with a firm yes. Tuition is only a minor part of the cost of education compared with the lost earnings while in school. Those lost earnings have risen very little, and there is still a large wage premium to college-educated workers. Finally, Bruno Frey asks what policies will help tackle terrorism and says they are threefold: ensure the economy, government, and society are decentralized to reduce the number of central targets; create incentives for young men to leave terrorism and engage in society; and divert media attention from individual terrorist groups.

21

Was Welfare Reform Successful?

Rebecca M. Blank

WELFARE REFORM WAS passed by Congress and signed by President Bill Clinton in August 1996. Back then there were many skeptics: several senior members of President Clinton's administration resigned in protest. Now, it is ten years and many research articles later. What do we know about the success or failure of these policy changes?

The Clinton administration and state governors both pointed to the legions of people who went off the welfare rolls as a sign of success. But, what happened to these women and children once they left welfare? Did they find employment? Was their economic well-being higher or lower?

It turns out that those who left welfare did well enough to surprise the skeptics, myself included, but it remains hard to identify all the reasons.

Rebecca M. Blank is the Henry Carter Adams Professor of Policy, professor of economics, and co-director of the National Poverty Center at the University of Michigan. During the Clinton administration, she was a member of the President's Council of Economic Advisers.

THE REFORMS

The 1996 law (1) abolished the Federal Cash Assistance program, Aid to Families with Dependent Children (AFDC); (2) turned program design authority for cash welfare assistance over to the states; and (3) replaced the AFDC program with a federal funding stream to the states, the Temporary Assistance to Needy Families (TANF) block grant. By giving the states primary authority for program design, the law eliminated the federal entitlement to cash assistance for low-income families with children. The new law gave the states strong incentives to push more welfare recipients into jobs or job placement programs. Furthermore, concerned about long-term welfare use, it mandated time limits on access to federally funded programs, limiting eligibility to sixty months over the recipient's lifetime.

Most people who supported the legislation believed that it would reduce welfare usage and move more women more quickly into employment, increasing their earnings and leaving them better off in the long run. (Although a small share of welfare-recipient families is married couples, 90 percent is single mothers. I refer mostly to single mothers in this article, as they compose the group of most concern.)

Critics of the new law worried whether the states would help women find employment and feared the states would cut off people from cash assistance without enabling them to find alternative income sources. The time limits were particularly criticized. Moreover, those who found employment in unstable low-wage and/or part-time jobs might not be able to fully replace welfare benefits with earnings and could end up worse off.

I was one of those wary about welfare reform. Although substantial evidence in the mid-1990s indicated that the states could increase work and reduce welfare usage with well-run welfare-to-work programs, there was less evidence that family incomes would increase. I feared the effects of time limits and get-tough welfare-to-work programs that pushed women into the labor market without providing resources to find reliable child care or that pushed them into short-term unstable jobs that quickly ended, leaving them with neither earned income nor welfare benefits.

THE AFTERMATH

In the years following 1996, welfare reform became one of the most studied public policy changes in recent history. Researchers used administrative data to track welfare recipients over time; new data collection efforts were launched to provide additional information on the circumstances of ex-welfare recipients; and existing national databases were used to extensively study changes among single-mother families post-1996.

Welfare caseloads, which started to fall in 1994, plummeted from 1996 through 2000. By 2001, they were at their lowest level in thirty years, despite a vastly larger single-mother population. The caseload decline stopped and caseload numbers became flat after the early 2000s, as unemployment started to rise and jobs became scarcer. However, there was no caseload increase. Even the strongest supporters of welfare reform in 1996 would not have dared forecast the steep declines and continued low levels of welfare caseloads a decade later.

At the same time as welfare usage fell, work increased. Among single mothers, labor force participation rose from 44 percent to 66 percent between 1994 and 2001—a much faster labor force participation growth than among any other group of women over this time period. Labor force participation tapered off somewhat in the slower economy of the early 2000s and was down to 61 percent by 2004. Yet, it remains well above where it was in the early 1990s.

Finally, incomes rose, and earnings increases were larger than welfare benefit declines. The average income for single moms was around $18,000 from the mid-1980s through the mid-1990s. Between 1995 and 2001, it rose to nearly $23,000. Poverty rates among single-mother households fell to historically low levels by the late 1990s. Although they have ticked up slightly in the past four years, they still remain well below where they were in the early 1990s.

It is worth noting that increases in employment were greater than declines in poverty. More women went to work, but only some earned enough to escape poverty. As a result, the share of working poor rose in the late 1990s and has remained higher than the early 1990s.

Some critics of welfare reform suggest that we are not adequately measuring the pain associated with these changes. Our measures of income do not take into account increased work expenses that these women bear, nor do they measure changes in stress as mothers of young children juggle day care and jobs. There is at least some evidence that cohabitation has increased post-1996 and that a slightly higher share of children are living with adults who are not their parents.

The well-being of children following welfare reform is hard to study with existing data. In general, most research suggests that there do not appear to be large positive or negative effects on children as a result of welfare reform. Income increases in low-income families are generally associated with improved school performance and lower levels of behavioral problems among children, which suggest welfare reform has had positive effects on children. The increase in the use of center-based child care, due to the growing availability of child care subsidies, seems to be associated with some positive behavioral and achievement effects for younger children. However, a few studies have found that more time spent at work by mothers seems to have had some small negative effects on adolescent school performance.

One of the most troubling statistics is the rising number of single-mother families who report themselves as not being on welfare and not working; and their reported income appears inadequate. From our available data, it is simply hard to say how they are actually surviving. The research does suggest one group that seems clearly worse off following welfare reform: those women who are involuntarily terminated from welfare benefits due to time limits or sanctions appear to have lower incomes and worse outcomes than others.

These are serious concerns, and they suggest that some women have become worse off following welfare reform. However, the overall rise in incomes among single mothers and the decline in poverty suggest that many women did gain following welfare reform.

HOW MUCH WAS DUE TO WELFARE REFORM?

With low and stable welfare caseloads, increased numbers of single mothers at work, and higher incomes for single mothers, many politicians (particularly state governors) have declared welfare reform a major success.

The research on welfare reform's effects is somewhat more ambiguous. Welfare reform did not occur in a vacuum. In the mid-1990s, several other major policies changed and increased the rewards to work: substantial expansions in the Earned Income Tax Credit (EITC), increases in the minimum wage, expansions in child care subsidies, and ongoing efforts to broaden Medicaid to cover all children in low-income families. The economy boomed—1996 to 2000 saw low unemployment and rising wages among all skill groups and in all regions.

Only some of the major behavioral changes in the mid-1990s were due to welfare reform per se. Increases in EITC benefits and the ready availability of jobs in a booming economy were also important.

From a statistical viewpoint, it is hard to fully explain the major declines in caseloads and increases in employment. Most regressions explain—at best—one-third of the caseload and labor force changes. My own interpretation is that we don't know how to adequately specify the synergies that happened when all of these policy and economic changes pushed in one direction and were matched with a strong public message that welfare was going to be much less available in the future and that work was going to be the only choice for the long term.

Nevertheless, it is clear that more welfare recipients were able and willing to enter the labor force than most of us would have predicted. The U.S. labor market, with a large number of lower-wage and lower-skilled jobs, does provide work opportunities—anybody who has watched either welfare reform or the growth in new immigrants over the past decade is very skeptical about claims that the United States is losing its low-wage jobs overseas. And, a high share of single mothers with younger children, when given some support for job searches, seem able to find and retain some employment. The rate for welfare leaving and job finding was much higher than I would have predicted, with real gains in income. The supporters of welfare reform a decade ago were right in claiming that more low-skilled single mothers could find work. Furthermore, these behavioral changes seem to have been maintained, even in the slower-growing and less job-rich economy of the early 2000s.

OPEN QUESTIONS

I am struck at how much we still don't know about these mid-1990s changes in behavior and well-being among single-mother families. Let me note three major issues that remain unresolved—and perhaps are irresolvable, at least given the data we currently have available.

First, we really don't know what combination of positive and negative incentives reduced welfare caseloads so dramatically. Was it the greater rewards to work (higher EITC payments, higher minimum wages, lower benefit disregard rates, etc.), the greater availability of work due to lower unemployment rates, or the greater effort within the welfare system to push people out (sanctions, time limits, and messages that welfare was no longer available or desirable)?

Second, most observers (myself included) are puzzled not only by the rapid magnitude of these changes in the late 1990s but also by their persistence in the 2000s when the labor market was no longer so hospitable. The economic problems of the early 2000s were focused in the manufacturing and traded-goods sectors. Strong consumer spending throughout the 2000s may have protected many welfare leavers' jobs, typically located in the retail-trade or health-care sectors of the economy, but even women who lost jobs appear to have worked hard to find new jobs or made do (perhaps with income from boyfriends or off-the-books work) rather than return to welfare.

I continue to believe that a deeper economic downturn that reduces jobs in the sectors where low-skilled women are employed would produce a renewed demand for cash support, but so far we haven't experienced that downturn. It is also possible that welfare offices in some states have become hostile enough to new applicants that increased applications will not produce increased caseloads. Other programs may have picked up some of the worst off who left welfare; for instance, many states actively worked to reduce their welfare rolls by moving some persons into the federally funded Supplemental Security Income (SSI) program for disabled adults and children.

Third, the question that most people asked following welfare reform was: Are the women and children better or worse off? Although there is a lot of evidence that work has increased and that earnings on average rose more than benefits fell, the translation of these facts into a definitive statement about well-being is hard to make. More women are now working and poor rather than nonworking and poor. More women are now paying for child care out of their earnings. More women appear to be sharing more income with other adults in their lives. Some of you who read this will immediately think that these results are good news; some of you will believe that these are problematic. The interpretation of these behavioral changes remains unsettled. We do not have the nuanced data on well-being nor do we have enough data on the long-term effects of these behavioral changes on children or families to yet make definitive pronouncements on the long-term successes and failures of welfare reform.

A decade ago, the United States took a major step in moving from a cash-support-oriented welfare system to a work-support-oriented system. Some of the primary public subsidies available to low-income families are now conditional upon employment. Although there is broad consensus about demanding employment among those able to work, there remain large gaps in the system. Child care subsidies remain inadequate, particularly if we want women to utilize center-based care (and a growing amount of evidence suggests that good center-based care improves child outcomes relative to other child care options). The lack of health insurance coverage for low-wage working adults (even as we've covered their children) continues to create problems. I worry that we have cut the availability of traditional welfare payments in ways that makes them inadequate for the ongoing groups in the population for whom employment (much less economic self-sufficiency) is just not possible. Particularly in the face of a major economic shock (such as we saw in the early 1980s), the current system of public assistance may not provide adequate support for many of our poorest families if high job losses suddenly occurred in this population.

But, the supporters of welfare reform tell me that I'm just too used to being a critic and can't acknowledge good news when I see it.

REFERENCES AND FURTHER READING

Blank, Rebecca M. 2002. "Evaluating Welfare Reform in the U.S." *Journal of Economic Literature* (December), 40 (4): 1105–1166.

————. 2006. "What Did the 1990s Welfare Reforms Accomplish?" In *Poverty, the Distribution of Income and Public Policy*, eds. Alan J. Auerbach, David Card, and John M. Quigley, pp. 33–79. New York: Russell Sage Foundation.

Grogger, Jeffrey and Lynn A. Karoly. 2005. *Welfare Reform: Effects of a Decade of Change*. Cambridge, MA: Harvard University Press.

Smolensky, Eugene and Jennifer Appleton Gootman, eds. 2003. *Working Families and Growing Kids: Caring for Children and Adolescents*, Chap. 7. Washington, DC: National Academies Press.

Weaver, R. Kent. 2000. *Ending Welfare As We Knew It*. Washington, DC: Brookings Institution.

22

Cutting the Safety Net One Strand at a Time

Janet Currie

BALLOONING FEDERAL DEFICITS threaten all social spending in this country, but programs for vulnerable women and children may be most at risk. Unlike Social Security, many of these programs must be periodically reauthorized in order to continue to exist. Yet—as I explain—a number of pernicious myths may make Congress less inclined to reauthorize them than it should be.

A MYTH ABOUT AID TO POOR FAMILIES: IT'S MOSTLY CASH WELFARE PAYMENTS

The first myth is that poor women and their children benefit from generous cash welfare payments. That is entirely wrong, for a number

Janet Currie is the Charles E. Davidson Professor of Economics at UCLA. Her work focuses on the evaluation of a broad array of public policies affecting children, including early intervention, health, and nutrition programs. She was one of the first directors of the National Bureau of Economic Research's Program on Children and Families, and is a research associate of the NBER, a research fellow at Instituts zur Zukunft der Arbeit (IZA), and an affiliate of the University of Michigan's National Poverty Center.

of reasons. First, even prior to welfare reform in 1996, most states set welfare benefits at levels far below the poverty line. Moreover, women who worked would see their benefits reduced a dollar for every dollar that they earned. This system created obvious incentives to cheat, because women had to supplement their welfare payments in order to survive and quickly learned not to report additional under-the-table earnings.

The enactment of welfare reform (and economic growth in the late 1990s) led to dramatic declines in the fraction of poor, single women who were receiving cash welfare payments. The cuts in welfare were accompanied by predictions of disaster. For example, Marian Wright Edelman (1995) of the Children's Defense Fund wrote an open letter to President Bill Clinton protesting that "it would be a great moral and practical wrong for you to sign any welfare 'reform' bill that will push millions of already poor children and families deeper into poverty."

But the predicted increase in poverty never happened. One reason is that, as noted above, most women on welfare were already working to make ends meet, even if they were not reporting these earnings. A second reason is that although most Americans do not realize it, an increasing fraction of the aid delivered to poor families over the past thirty years has been in kind, which means that it comes in the form of specific goods or services, not cash. These in-kind programs were largely unaffected by welfare reform.

In 2002, only a small fraction of aid to families (that is, to the non-elderly poor), less than 10 percent, was in the form of cash welfare payments. Only 5 million people received cash welfare under TANF (the Temporary Assistance for Needy Families, which replaced the old Aid to Families with Dependent Children program in 1996) at a cost of about $21.5 billion.

In contrast, more than 30 million women and children participated in in-kind safety-net programs, at a cost of approximately $120 billion. These programs include Medicaid, food stamps, public housing, school nutrition programs (the National School Lunch and the School

Breakfast programs), WIC (Supplemental Nutrition for Women, Infants, and Children), Head Start, and child care subsidy programs.

The bulk of cash assistance—under the Earned Income Tax Credit (EITC)—now goes not to welfare but to assist the working poor. Indeed, the EITC has eclipsed welfare as a source of cash support to poor families, providing benefits worth $27.8 billion in 2002. Together EITC money and in-kind supports, such as public health insurance, are essential to families making the welfare-to-work transition. Even conservative commentators agree with Douglas Besharov (2003) of the American Enterprise Institute, who notes that "only the expanded aid now available to low-income, working families . . . makes it worthwhile for them to leave welfare."

The in-kind programs have already been subject to the 0.8 percent across-the-board cut in domestic spending that was enacted as part of the fiscal year 2005 omnibus appropriations bill. They may well be subject to more drastic cuts in the future.

The result could be great cruelty—taking away in-kind payments means taking away medicine and children's food—and additional barriers to families' making the welfare-to-work transition.

A SECOND MYTH: THE CLAIM THAT ANTI-POVERTY PROGRAMS SIMPLY DON'T WORK

Why has there been so little controversy about these cuts? One reason, I believe, is the widespread perception that anti-poverty programs do not actually fight poverty.

This perception is based in part on misleading statistics: Official poverty statistics do not include in-kind benefits. So these statistics make it seem that, no matter how much aid is given to a family, it will never raise them above the poverty line. In fact, families do effectively rise above the poverty line—or at least, linger less far below it—as the result of in-kind programs.

More substantively, the idea that government programs don't work is deeply engrained in the American psyche. Part of the reason is that when we evaluate these programs' success, we make unrealistic comparisons—wrongly comparing deeply disadvantaged children with average children rather than properly comparing the lives of deeply disadvantaged children with and without a given program.

So suppose we see, for example, that children who attended Head Start are still more likely to drop out of school than the average child. This tends to confirm our worst suspicions about the futility of government intervention to break the cycle of poverty. The comparison of the Head Start child with the average child tells us that Head Start did not, by itself, solve the problem of poverty. But this comparison tells us nothing about whether the program benefited the target child. To answer this question, we need to ask: Are children less likely to drop out than they would have been without Head Start? When the question is posed this way, the answer begins to look much more hopeful.

Put another way, a sensible analysis of the effects of government anti-poverty programs has to take account of the fact that these programs typically serve the most disadvantaged families. Reports on the programs' effectiveness must take as a given that participants are not "average children."

When estimates of program effects do take proper account of selection (which is the technical term for the difference between the average child and the child actually in the programs), they typically find that in-kind anti-poverty programs are—contrary to popular opinion—quite effective. Expansions of Medicaid to low-income children and pregnant women have reduced infant mortality and improved access to medical care for millions of children. Head Start has lasting effects on the prospects of many children, increasing their probability of graduating from high school as much as a quarter. School nutrition programs generally provide healthier meals than students otherwise would receive, and WIC improves the health of newborns and reduces hospital costs. For example, WIC participation has been estimated to reduce the risk of low birth weight by 10 percent to 43 percent.

Even public housing, which may have the worst reputation of any large government program, has been shown to have some positive effects on children. The reputation of all housing projects may have been unjustly tarred by the hellish conditions in the worst large-scale projects. Again, to see if there have been positive effects the question to ask is not: How is public housing compared to the housing the average child enjoys? It is: Is public housing better than the alternative— which might be homelessness—for the children it affects?

A THIRD MYTH: IN-KIND ASSISTANCE PROGRAMS ARE RIFE WITH FRAUD, WASTE, AND ABUSE

Some critics do grudgingly agree that federal programs have positive effects, at least in some cases. But if they make this concession, they often also allege that these benefits are offset by large-scale fraud, waste, and abuse. These types of allegations have a long history— remember Ronald Reagan's Cadillac-driving welfare queen? He alleged that the woman in question had used eighty aliases, thirty addresses, a dozen Social Security cards, and four fictional dead husbands to defraud the government of $150,000. According to the *Washington Monthly* (2003), the woman he was referring to had used two aliases to collect $8,000 in overpayments, but the truth did not matter. The public was outraged because the story fit negative perceptions about gross fraud in welfare programs.

Virtually every program that has come up for reauthorization in recent years has been attacked in this way. In 2000, Congress was incensed by the fact that the number of people enrolled in WIC exceeded the number the Department of Agriculture thought were eligible. A National Academy of Sciences panel was convened to investigate the problem. It turned out that whole classes of eligible women and children were excluded from the government's calculations and that, in fact, many eligible women and, especially, children were *not* being served.

In 2003 and 2004, the Agriculture Department conducted a number of studies to investigate alleged widespread fraud in the school nutrition programs. Again, these studies showed that most participants were actually eligible and that nonparticipation by eligible children was a larger issue than fraudulent participation by children whose incomes were slightly above the program thresholds.

In the end, the Child Nutrition and WIC Reauthorization Act of 2004 took measures to increase legitimate participation rather than focus on weeding out supposed fraud. It adopted changes, such as certifying children for the entire academic year and making participants in other programs automatically eligible, thus simplifying the application process and making it easier for children to receive benefits.

The cases of fraud that do occur make headlines and are ceaselessly referenced, creating the impression that abuse is typical. For example, in 2003, an expose in the *Kansas City Star* reported that one Head Start executive had a $300,000 salary and a leased Mercedes sport-utility vehicle paid for by Head Start funds. This case led Congress to request a General Accounting Office study of the more than 3,500 local agencies that administer Head Start. The study disclosed only three cases in which Head Start executives were earning more than $230,000 (and in those cases, 30 percent of that compensation came from sources other than Head Start). Indeed, the average salary for a Head Start director was only $36,876, suggesting that the pay might actually be too *low* to attract the most qualified applicants.

These examples suggest that the perception that government programs are riddled with fraud is generally inaccurate, and that nonparticipation by those who are eligible is likely to be a larger problem than fraudulent participation by those who are not eligible.

It is heartening that in the case of WIC and the school nutrition programs Congress was swayed by the evidence and took action to address the real problem: Many poor children are not receiving benefits. But the fate of Head Start is still in the balance, because Head Start reauthorization stalled in 2004. When Congress does decide on Head Start, it shouldn't let the few highly paid directors take center stage; it should remember to look at the typical director who, despite impressive credentials and excellent service, pulls in less than $37,000 per year.

A FINAL MYTH: IT WOULD BE BETTER TO PUT THE STATES IN CHARGE OF AID

A final line of attack on the federal safety net is to argue that responsibility for anti-poverty programs should devolve to the states. Thus, an alternative vision of the safety net would take the money set aside for federal programs, give each state a "block grant," and allow considerable flexibility in the spending of that grant.

A major practical difficulty with this proposal, however, is that—unlike the federal government—most states cannot run budget deficits. Under the current system, with federal control, more people are eligible and entitled to assistance when times are bad—which is as it should be; aid should match need.

But suppose the states take over more programs. If state revenues fall as need grows, then there will be cutbacks in state-financed services during recessions. This is exactly what we are currently seeing with respect to the SCHIP (the State Child Health Insurance Program). Thousands of children have been dropped from state rolls in recent years, whereas others have seen increases in co-payments and/or reductions in covered services. It is grotesque if aid becomes cyclical—increasing in booms, when it may not be as urgently needed, and shrinking in recessions, when times are especially desperate for the poor.

Proponents of shifting responsibility to the states argue that states are better able to match the aid they do give out to local needs. But such matching is already occurring: Many "federal" programs are in fact already administered at the state or local level. For example, public housing is run by local housing authorities, and Head Start is run by many small local agencies. In these cases, eliminating the federal program might, ironically, further centralize rather than decentralize control over local programs—meaning any such matching will be lessened, not increased.

In the end, though, the most fundamental objection to the block-grant-to-each-state approach is simply this: It would abandon any pretext of a uniform national safety net for low-income children. And that is unacceptable.

We say that no American child should be malnourished, that all children should have access to necessary medical care, and that every child should have good quality child care. If we truly believe this, then it makes sense for the federal government to specify minimum standards for these services and to make sure that even the poorest states have the resources to provide them.

Congress ought to reauthorize current aid programs at the federal level. And when it does so, it ought to ensure that its aid matches the true need that exists: the poor, especially poor children, should not bear the brunt of national belt-tightening.

REFERENCES AND FURTHER READING

Besharov, Douglas J. 2003. "The Past and Future of Welfare Reform." *The Public Interest* (Winter), pp. 4–21.

Burghardt, John, Philip Gleason, Michael Sinclair, Rhoda Cohen, Lara Hulsey, and Julita Milliner-Waddell. 2004. "Evaluation of the National School Lunch Program Application/Verification Pilot Projects: Volume 1: Impacts on Deterrence, Barriers, and Accuracy." Report # CN-04-AV1. Alexandria, VA: U.S. Department of Agriculture Food and Nutrition Service.

Burghardt, John, Tim Silva, and Lara Hulsey. 2004. "Case Study of National School Lunch Program Verification Outcomes in Large Metropolitan School Districts." Report no. CN-04-AV3. Alexandria, VA: U.S. Dept. of Agriculture Food and Nutrition Service.

Currie, Janet. 2003. "U.S. Food and Nutrition Programs." In *Means-Tested Transfer Programs in the United States*, ed. Robert Moffitt. Chicago: University of Chicago Press for NBER.

———. 2005. *The Invisible Safety Net: Protecting Poor Women and Families.* Princeton NJ: Princeton University Press.

Edelman, Marian Wright. 1995. ". . . Protect Children from Unjust Policies." *Washington Post*, November 3, p. A23.

National Research Council Committee on National Statistics. 2001. *Estimating Eligibility and Participation for the WIC Program: Phase I Report*, eds. Michelle Ver Ploeg and David Betson. Washington, DC: National Academy Press.

Smith, DeAnn and Dan Margolies. 2003. "Head Start Fallout Spreads, Congress Notices KC Director's Salary." *Kansas City Star*, October 18.

U.S. House of Representatives, U.S. Committee on Education and the Workforce. May 13, 2004. "New HHS Report Offers Mixed Results on Accountability in Head Start, Raises New Questions." http://www.policyalmanac.org/education/archive/Head_Start_Criticism_2004.shtml.

Washington Monthly Staff. 2003. "The Mendacity Index: Which President Told the Biggest Whoppers." *The Washington Monthly* (September). http://www.washingtonmonthly.com/features/2003/0309.mendacity-experts.html.

CHAPTER 23

The Choose-Your-Charity Tax: A Way to Incentivize Greater Giving

Aaron S. Edlin

WHY DON'T I—and others—give more to charity? And, how can that be changed?

One reason that many people, such as me, do not give as much as they can afford is the seeming irrelevance of a single contribution. The problem with good causes is that the very thing that makes a charity a good cause is the enormity of the problem it is fighting. Yet because the problem is so vast, my gift is a drop in the bucket. The problem will still be there when I am done giving. The problem will be there if I do not give. So, what difference would my gift make?

Charities, of course, understand this problem, and they have developed tactics to deal with it. One is to shrink the problem by

Aaron S. Edlin is the Richard Jennings professor of economics and law at the University of California at Berkeley and a research associate at the National Bureau of Economic Research. He is co-author with P. Areeda and L. Kaplow of the leading antitrust casebook. He was formerly the senior economist covering regulation, antitrust, and industrial organization at the President's Council of Economic Advisers, and he has taught or held research positions at Yale, Stanford, and Columbia. He received his Ph.D. and J.D. from Stanford in 1993 and his A.B. from Princeton in 1988.

personalizing it: You can "adopt" a particular child in Africa and feed him or her.

Another tactic is the matching grant. If my grant is matched by another donor, I am more apt to give because I can give twice as much at the same price. The "price" of a $1 gift is only 50 cents when my gift is matched.

These tactics are clever and effective. But we must be more ambitious if we seek to solve truly vast problems. In this chapter, I propose a more aggressive tactic, expanding upon the idea and power of a matching grant: the Choose-Your-Charity Tax.

A TAX CREDIT TO BOOST CHARITABLE GIVING

Under our current tax system, contributions to eligible charities are tax-deductible. But this proposal would replace that rule—and go much further.

The new rule would be this: People would get a tax credit of $1 for each dollar they spend, up to a certain limit, on a charitable contribution. To make the plan revenue-neutral for the government, that limit would be equivalent to a tax increase.

How would this work in practice? Suppose the limit is 10 percent of income. And suppose a given taxpayer has $75,000 in taxable income. That taxpayer has a choice: to either pay a $7,500 increase in taxes or give $7,500 to the charity of his or her choice and receive a $7,500 tax credit.

From the taxpayer's point of view, these two alternatives are financially equivalent. But the charitable gift provides an option the tax payment does not: it allows the giver to specifically choose the recipient of the payment.

Those who believe in giving money to the poor can opt to give to charities that directly help them. In contrast, those who believe in self-reliance—opposing the Great Society programs on the ground that they create a culture of dependency and preferring to teach a man to fish rather than giving him a fish—can direct their dollars elsewhere. For instance, they may want to contribute to domestic training programs or infrastructure programs in the developing world.

Finally, those who continue to have a faith in government transfer programs, or who worry about the U.S. budget deficit, could choose not to take the credit at all. They could thus pay their extra tithe to the government and consider that their gift.

SUPPORTING THE TAX IS LIKE CHOOSING TO GIVE WITH A 100-MILLION-TO-ONE MATCHING GRANT

The reader might object that this kind of tax credit will never come to be. It is tantamount to requiring taxpayers to give 10 percent of their income to charity (or the government, if they don't claim the credit). If taxpayers don't give that much now, why would they support a policy that forces them to do it?

The answer is matching. The Choose-Your-Charity Tax would be, in effect, the ultimate matching grant.

Matching is a central feature of taxation, though it is one that most voters don't think about. If they did, taxation might be more popular than it is.

Consider a person who—like me and, probably, like you—is not currently giving 10 percent of her income to charity. She might feel her individual decision to tithe to charity would involve great personal sacrifice, yet it would not go very far toward curing any of the world's or the nation's great ills. If she thinks about it, though, she might feel very differently about the tax increase, combined with the offsetting Choose-Your-Charity Tax credit.

A decision to vote for the Choose-Your-Charity Tax expresses a willingness to endure significant personal sacrifice, but *a willingness to do so only if others match that willingness.*

And, if others match, then the result is not a drop in the bucket but a great wave of change—and the taxpayer knows that. By matching contributions with over 100 million U.S. taxpayers, it would be possible to solve vast problems. Roughly speaking, supporting such a policy is equivalent to being willing to give $1 when the personal price of giving that dollar is one-hundred-millionth of a dollar. This is the ultimate expansion of the proven "matching" tactic that has already helped increase donations to charities.

And here's the extra added attraction of the Choose-Your-Charity Tax, which makes it more palatable than an ordinary tax increase: The taxpayer gets to direct exactly where his or her own contribution goes and can make sure it is well spent (for instance, by a charity with far lower administrative costs than, say, the U.S. government). The rest of the money will, of course, be spent by other taxpayers, but their choices may not be so different from your own.

THE TAXPAYER'S CHOICE: DIFFERENT FOR INDIVIDUAL GIVING THAN A TAX AND CREDIT

If you were to call me and ask me to give a charity 10 percent of my taxable income (let's say $4,000 if I am the average taxpayer), I would ask myself whether I would rather have this $4,000 in my pocket or the charity's. Sadly, my answer—like that of so many other Americans—is that I would rather have it in my own. And this is true even though I've read philosopher Peter Singer—who convinces my higher self of the essential injustice of my selfishness.

But consider calling me and asking me, instead, if I support the Choose-Your-Charity Tax. Like an individual donation to charity, this tax would also take $4,000 out of my pocket. But it could produce $400 billion per year in extra charity in the United States, assuming all taxpayers decide to exhaust their credits.

Now, when I ask myself whether I would prefer having this $4,000 in my pocket or $400 billion in extra charity, I may just give. The matching grant, after all, is whopping: it's 100 million to one. (For a richer taxpayer the match might be somewhat less, and for a poorer taxpayer the match would be even more.)

HUGE PROBLEMS COULD BE SOLVED WITH
A 100-MILLION-TO-ONE MATCH

With $400 billion per year, think what could be done: There could be no homelessness in America. Job retraining could be available for all.

And that's only on the domestic side. If half of this charity went abroad, U.S. foreign aid would increase by a factor of fifteen. Instead of fast becoming one of the most hated nations in the world, the United States could quickly become the most loved.

A SOLUTION THAT OUGHT TO APPEAL
TO CONSERVATIVES AND LIBERALS ALIKE

The Choose-Your-Charity Tax ought to garner bipartisan support. Liberals should like the tax, because it will route more money to their favorite causes. And conservatives should like it because it moots the problem they often raise: big government bureaucracies are often ineffective and inefficient at dealing with problems.

Conservatives favor private, not public, solutions—and they have long said that private charity is more efficient than higher taxes. In this case, they get the best of both worlds: the matching advantage of the tax system that I described above and the ability to greatly amplify the "thousand points of light" that they see in private charities.

The program will also harness the power of competition among charities: those that do the best works will attract the most charitable giving. Such competition already exists in the current system, but with the Choose-Your-Charity Tax it would be greatly amplified.

Perhaps 10 percent is too ambitious, or perhaps lower-income taxpayers should be excluded. Even a 1 percent Choose-Your-Charity Tax could generate $40 billion in extra charitable giving. The point is that the Choose-Your-Charity Tax, however calculated, could convince individuals to listen to their higher selves—not their innate selfishness—with the assurance, through matching, that they are not alone in doing so.

REFERENCES AND FURTHER READING

Balkovic, Brian. 2003. "Individual Income Tax Returns, Preliminary Data, 2002." *Statistics of Income Bulletin*, Winter 2003–2004. http://www.irs.gov/pub/irs-soi/02inplim.pdf.

Cooter, Robert and Brian Broughman. 2005. "Charity, Publicity and the Donation Registry." *The Economists' Voice* 2 (3), art. 4. http://www.bepress.com/ev/vol2/iss3/art4.

Singer, Peter. 1999. "The Singer Solution to World Poverty." *New York Times Sunday Magazine*, September 5. http://people.brandeis.edu/~teuber/singermag.html.

CHAPTER 24

Should the Government Rebuild New Orleans or Just Give Residents Checks?

Edward L. Glaeser

IN THE WAKE of Hurricane Katrina, President George W. Bush declared that a "great city will rise again." He promised, "Throughout the area hit by the hurricane, we will do what it takes—we will stay as long as it takes—to help citizens rebuild their communities and their lives" (2005).

Lawmakers have stumbled over each other to suggest greater and greater public spending to rebuild New Orleans. While details remain to be settled, the current estimates are that federal spending will be close to $200 billion.

Edward L. Glaeser is the Fred and Eleanor Glimp Professor of Economics in the Faculty of Arts and Sciences at Harvard University, where he has taught since 1992. He is the director of the Taubman Center for State and Local Government and director of the Rappaport Institute of Greater Boston.

Senator Edward Kennedy has proposed a $150 billion agency specifically dedicated to Gulf-area infrastructure. This spending is being justified as federal insurance against disaster.

But the concept of insurance hardly leads inexorably to the conclusion that the government must spend money directly to rebuild New Orleans. To the contrary, if there is disaster insurance, then it is, presumably, the people of New Orleans who are insured, not the place itself. After all, people (or corporations) hold insurance; places don't.

IT SEEMS CLEAR THE GOVERNMENT WILL PAY
TO REBUILD. BUT HOW, EXACTLY?

Economists emphasize the moral hazard problems in providing free disaster insurance to high-risk areas. Gary Becker (2005) has argued, for example, that free insurance creates a "Good Samaritan" problem that encourages bad location decisions.

As a matter of economic principle, Becker is surely right. Going forward, residents of high-risk areas should—from an economic efficiency perspective—be charged for the implicit federal insurance that they receive. But politically, given Florida's status as a battleground state, this isn't likely.

Moreover, even if we agree that in the future we should not distort location decisions by providing free insurance, we should presumably still fulfill the current obligations to the residents of New Orleans. And politicians have promised to do just that.

So for the moment, let's accept the principle that the federal government has—wisely or not—insured against disasters. That principle still tells us little about how, exactly, these insurance claims should be paid out.

SHOULD THE GOVERNMENT REBUILD, OR SHOULD
RESIDENTS GET CHECKS OR VOUCHERS?

We could try to make good on the idea that the government provides insurance by rebuilding the city. Alternatively, we could provide residents with checks or vouchers, and let them make their own decisions about how to spend that money—including the decision about where to locate, or relocate, themselves.

When your car is damaged you can often "cash out" and receive cash to do with as you wish instead of having your car repaired. And, when your car is "totaled," the insurance company generally won't fix your car at all; it will only provide cash compensation, and then you decide how to spend it.

In the context of the president's comments, there is a big difference between rebuilding lives and rebuilding communities. Given limited funds, the two objectives may well conflict, and the usual lesson from economics is that people are better off if they are given money and allowed to make their own decisions, much as they are with car insurance.

The case for rebuilding New Orleans, then, depends on whether the residents of New Orleans will be made better off by this spending than by being given checks or vouchers.

VOUCHERS OR CHECKS WOULD BE LIFE-CHANGING
FOR POOR NEW ORLEANS RESIDENTS

To put the numbers in context, imagine that we were to spend $100 billion on infrastructure for the residents of the city. An alternative to this spending is to give each one of the city of New Orleans's residents a check for more than $200,000.

Annual per capita income in that city is less than $20,000, so this check would amount to ten years' income, on average—a hefty, and potentially life-changing sum. That is enough to send several children to college, to buy a modest home, and/or to relocate and start a dreamed-of business.

If this money were spread over the 1.33 million residents in the New Orleans metropolitan area, each resident would still receive $75,000, still enough to pay for a home in many areas of the country.

Can the benefits to the residents' use of local infrastructure possibly equal the benefits for receiving three or ten years' income as a lump sum? One has to wonder.

COULD PUBLIC SPENDING POSSIBLY BENEFIT RESIDENTS MORE THAN CHECKS OR VOUCHERS COULD?

Indeed, there are many reasons to suspect that spending vast sums to rebuild the city may not make sense. New Orleans is like many great American cities that were built during previous eras and have become somewhat obsolete.

Before 1900, moving goods by water was much cheaper than moving goods by land. As a result, all of the great American cities were built on rivers or where an important river meets the sea. From that perspective, the location of New Orleans was unbeatable: it is the port at the mouth of America's greatest river system.

New Orleans reached its peak of economic importance relative to the United States in 1840. But the Civil War and the decline of water-based transportation relative to rail caused the city to lose ground, relative to northern cities, through much of the nineteenth century.

In 1840, New Orleans was America's third-largest city (after New York and Baltimore); by 1920, it had dropped to being only its seventeenth-largest city. Still, the city's edge as a port continued to ensure that its population increased until the 1950s.

New Orleans began to decline, in absolute terms, in 1960. The port remains important, but increasing mechanization and containerization together meant that fewer and fewer people were needed to work in that port. Today, according to the 2003 County Business Patterns, less than one-twentieth of the employees in Orleans County are in transportation industries, and more than a quarter of these aren't even working in the port or pipelines (U.S. Census).

Even the vaunted energy industry employs a remarkably small number of people. County Business Patterns reports that there are fewer than 2,000 people in the county working in oil and gas extraction, and fewer than 100 people working on pipeline transportation.

Whereas there are fewer than 7,500 people working in the port, there are 32,000 employees in health care and social assistance. New Orleans's biggest industry is tourism, and there are 37,000 employees working in food services and accommodation.

New Orleans remains an important port, but this port doesn't need a large city, and over time, the city has contracted. New Orleans's population has declined steadily—from 627,000 residents in 1960 to 485,000 residents in 2000.

If the American Community Survey is to be believed (this is based on a smallish sample), New Orleans has lost another 40,000 inhabitants between 2000 and 2004. The 4.1 percent growth of the New Orleans metropolitan area in the 1990s put it far below the average U.S. population growth. It is hard to find a Sun Belt city that is doing as badly as New Orleans.

All of this information cuts strongly against any claim that the rebuilding of New Orleans would be more beneficial for its residents than their receiving a large check or voucher that would enable them not only to rebuild but also to transform their lives.

COULD NEW ORLEANS, WITH SPENDING, SOMEHOW
RETURN TO ITS LONG-PAST GLORY?

Granted, some previously great ports have managed to rebuild themselves around new industries. New York is now devoted to finance. San Francisco is the center for information technology.

But New Orleans has never been able to reinvent itself, perhaps because it lacks the human capital that has been so heavily correlated with urban success over the past fifty years. Moreover, New Orleans's port locale raises construction costs, relative to, say, the flat, featureless plains of Las Vegas. And New Orleans's climate is problematic relative to California. My own guess is that the city would have declined by more than it has if it were not for the durability of its housing stock and other infrastructure. And now, thanks to Hurricane Katrina, that last asset has been decimated.

Furthermore, New Orleans's housing stock was not very valuable, in the market, to begin with. The decline in New Orleans's population has been accompanied by economic distress and by low housing prices.

The 2000 Census reported that more than 27 percent of New Orleans residents were in poverty (relative to 12 percent for the United States as a whole). Median family income was only 64 percent of the median family income in the United States.

In 2004, according to the American Community Survey, the unemployment rate for the city was over 11 percent. And New Orleans's housing prices, pre-hurricane, remained far below those of the nation as a whole, providing further evidence of weak preexisting demand for living in the city.

By most objective measures, the city, pre-hurricane, was not doing a good job of taking care of its poorer residents. For most students of urban distress, New Orleans was a problem, not an ideal. Poverty and continuing economic decline fed upon each other, delivering despair to many of the city's residents.

MORE LIMITED REBUILDING, COMBINED WITH
AID TO RESIDENTS, MAY BE WISER

New Orleans's decline suggests that spending huge sums betting on the future of the city makes little sense. Perhaps there are externalities or coordination failures that argue for rebuilding, but they do not immediately come to mind.

Most sensible theories about externalities suggest that giving checks to impacted residents, who then will move to Houston or Atlanta or Las Vegas, will actually reduce the negative spillovers from dysfunctional neighborhoods—not increase them.

None of this means, of course, that we shouldn't rebuild New Orleans's port or its pipelines. But rebuilding this basic infrastructure doesn't mean rebuilding the entire city, and it doesn't necessarily require federal funding.

The port and the energy sector are thriving economic entities. Their users can be charged for the costs of this infrastructure. We will all eventually pay those costs in the form of higher prices, but this is surely more efficient than funding reconstruction with tax dollars.

Rebuilding New Orleans requires a cost-benefit analysis that is far beyond the scope of this chapter. At this point, the only thing that I strongly endorse is having an open-minded national debate about costs and benefits. However, I suspect that for much of the proposed rebuilding, the costs will greatly outweigh the benefits.

One of the biggest problems of urban decline is how to help those residents caught in a declining city. Perhaps, if significant funds are given to New Orleans residents to help them start life anew in a more vibrant city, then there will be a silver lining to Katrina after all.

REFERENCES AND FURTHER READING

Becker, Gary. 2005. The Becker-Posner Blog. http://www.becker-posner-blog.com/archives/2005/09/major_disasters.html.

Bush, George W. 2005. September 15 speech, New Orleans, Louisiana. http://www.whitehouse.gov/news/releases/2005/09/20050915-8.html.

Glaeser, Edward and Joseph Gyourko. 2005. "Urban Decline and Durable Housing." *Journal of Political Economy* 113 (2): 345–375.

Glaeser, Edward and Janet Kohlbase. 2004. "Cities, Regions and the Decline of Transport Costs." *Papers in Regional Science* 83 (1): 197–228.

U.S. Census. http://factfinder.census.gov/servlet/SAFFFacts?_event=Search&geo_id=&_geoContext=&_street=&_county=new+orleans&_cityTown=new+orleans&_state=04000US22&_zip=&_lang=en&_sse=on&pctxt=fph&pgsl=010. (Giving demographic facts.)

——. http://www.census.gov/population/www/documentation/twps0027.html. (Giving historical facts on city sizes.)

——. County Business Patterns. http://censtats.census.gov/cgi-bin/cbpnaic/cbpsect.pl.

CHAPTER 25

Does College Still Pay?

Lisa Barrow and Cecilia Elena Rouse

IN THE 1980S the value of a college education grew significantly. According to U.S. Census data, in 1979 those with a bachelor's degree or higher earned roughly 45 percent more per hour than workers with only a high school diploma. By 1989 wages of college graduates were more than 70 percent higher than those of high school graduates.[1] This dramatic change revived arguments over the cause-and-effect relationship between education and higher income. In other words, was education driving income levels or was the education trend a byproduct of rising income levels? This debate spawned a very large literature tying increasing income inequality to a decrease in demand for workers without marketable skills. A key reason for the increasing value of a college education was the increasing cost of

Lisa Barrow is an economist at the Federal Reserve Bank of Chicago and Cecilia Elena Rouse is Theodore A. Wells '29 Professor of Economics and Public Affairs at Princeton University. We thank Gadi Barlevy, Jonas Fisher, and Alan Krueger for useful conversations and Kyung-Hong Park for expert research assistance. All errors in fact or interpretation are ours. The opinions in this chapter do not reflect those of the Federal Reserve Bank of Chicago or the Federal Reserve System.

not having one: real earnings of workers without some college education fell during the 1980s, as earnings of the more highly educated increased. Politicians and policymakers tried to enact policies to improve educational attainment, for as President Bill Clinton stated: "Today, more than ever before in our history, education is the fault line between those who will prosper in the new economy and those who will not."[2]

But the labor market changed in the mid-1990s. The hourly wage gap between those with a college education and those without, which had grown by 25 percentage points in the 1980s, grew by only 10 percentage points in the 1990s. At the same time, college tuition rates increased extremely rapidly. The wage-gap slowdown has led some to wonder: Has college ceased being the better deal over the past few years? Do rising tuition levels mean that the value of a college education has peaked? And even, is attending college still worth the costs?

Our answer to the final question is yes. College is definitely still worth the investment. In fact, there are no signs that the value of a college education has peaked or is on a downward trend. Also, the rapid annual percentage rise in the cost of tuition has had little effect on the value of a college education, largely because tuition is a relatively small part of the true total economic cost of attending college. Most of the true economic cost of college is the wages students forego while they attend—and those have not risen by very much at all.

THE CHANGING VALUE OF EDUCATION

To make sense of trends in the economic value of education, one must first understand what economists see as the "return to education." The return to education is the capitalized present value of the extra income an individual would earn with additional schooling, after taking into account all of the costs of obtaining the additional schooling.[3] This return to education may change because of a shift in the income for individuals who obtain more schooling or a shift in the income of those who do not. Also, a change in the economic costs of education can affect the return to education.

Figure 25.1 shows the average hourly real wages (relative to hourly wages in 1980) for four sets of workers between 1980 and 2004. The four categories include: those who did not complete high school; those who earned only a high school diploma; those who have some college education but did not earn a bachelor's degree; and those who earned at least a bachelor's degree. Through the mid-1990s, average hourly

FIGURE 25.1

Hourly Wages by Education Group Relative to 1980 Hourly Wages

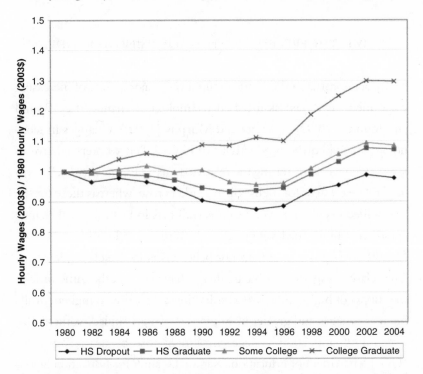

Source: Authors' calculations from the 1980–2004 (even years only) Current Population Survey Outgoing Rotation Group files available from Unicon. We limit the sample to individuals between ages of twenty-five and sixty-five years, and drop observations with wages less than half of the minimum wage or above the 99th percentile of the distribution.

wages increase fairly steadily among those with at least a bachelor's degree, whereas the real wages of high school dropouts and of those with only a high school diploma decline. These trends account for the large increases in the return to schooling through the mid-1990s.

Since the mid-1990s the average wages of college graduates have skyrocketed, increasing by 18 percent by 2004. However, the wages of high school dropouts have also risen, climbing by 10 percent in the second half of the 1990s from their lowest levels in 1994. Because of this turnaround in the wages of high school dropouts, the college wage premium has risen at a much slower rate of increase than before. And rapidly rising tuition costs must be set against this slower rate of increase.

WHY IS THE PREMIUM NO LONGER RISING AS RAPIDLY?

Many economists in the 1990s thought the major source of increasing wage inequality was "skill-biased technological change" (see Bound and Johnson [1992] and Katz and Murphy [1992]). Changes in technology increased the productivity of high-skilled workers relative to low-skilled workers, raising the relative demand for the former. Therefore, relative wages for high-skilled workers rose, whereas those for the less-skilled declined. An end to this skill bias in technological change could account for the leveling off of the return to education.

Although possible, we do not believe this is a likely explanation. The relative wages of college graduates have risen at the same time as the supply of high-skilled workers has increased, due to higher enrollment at colleges and greater immigration of high-skilled workers. Between 1996 and 2000, college enrollment rose by nearly 7 percent (U.S. Department of Education, National Center for Education Statistics 2005). Since 1999, 36 percent of immigrants entering the United States had at least a bachelor's degree compared with 24 percent of immigrants arriving in the 1980s (U.S. Census Bureau 2003). The share of the population aged twenty-five to sixty-five years old with at least a bachelor's degree rose from 26 percent in 1996 to 30 percent in 2004.[4] Despite the growth in the relative supply of college graduates, the wages of college graduates have continued to rise dramatically, which indicates an increasing—not a decreasing—demand for their skills. Moreover, average wages of workers with lower levels of education have also increased since 1995; it is this turnaround in the trend that accounts for the slowing growth in the return to schooling.

Thus the relevant question is: Why have the wages of these lower-skilled workers increased in the past decade?

Minimum wage increases in the late 1990s helped increase the wages of the lowest-skilled workers, but it is unlikely to account fully for the turnaround. First, the last increase in the federal minimum wage came in late 1997, two years after average wages of the lowest-skilled workers began to increase. It cannot account for subsequent increases in the wages of low-skilled workers. The states that have raised their minimum wages since 1997 make up only about one-third of U.S. payroll employment: it is unlikely that state minimum wages can fully account for changes in average wages across the entire country.[5] Moreover, there is an anomaly in the time-series relationship between minimum wages and inequality: in the data, the level of the minimum wage is correlated with inequality at both the bottom (where it should be) and the top (where it shouldn't be, if a low minimum wage is a cause and not a consequence of high inequality) of the wage distribution.[6] The booming economy of the late 1990s is the most likely explanation for the turnaround, as it raised the average wages of all workers, including those with the lowest skills.[7]

WHY COLLEGE EDUCATION IS STILL WORTH IT

How good an investment finishing college is depends on both earnings and costs—the earnings of college graduates relative to high school graduates and the costs of attending college (both tuition and foregone earnings). Tuition and fees for a four-year college for the 2003–2004 academic year averaged $7,091; the average net price—tuition and fees net of grants—was $5,558 (both amounts in 2003 dollars).[8] If we assume that tuition and fees continue to rise as they did between the 1999–2000 and 2003–2004 school years and conservatively look at sticker rather than net prices, the average full-time student entering a program in the fall of 2003 who completes a bachelor's degree in four years will pay $30,325 in tuition and fees. If we assume an opportunity cost equal to the average annual earnings of a high school graduate (from the March 2004 Current Population Survey) and a 5 percent discount rate for time preference, the total cost of attending college rises to $107,277. In other words, college is worthwhile for an average student if getting a bachelor's degree boosts the present value of his or her lifetime earnings by at least $107,277.

What is the boost to the present value of wages? At a 5 percent annual discount rate, it is $402,959. The net present value of a four-year degree to an average student entering college in the fall of 2003 is roughly $295,682—the difference between $402,959 in earnings and $107,277 in total costs.[9] A student entering college today can expect to recoup her investment within ten years of graduation.

It still pays to go to college—very much so, at least as much as ever before.[10]

NOTES

1. All levels of education have become more valuable since the late 1970s. The return on each year of schooling was 6.6 percent (in terms of hourly wages) in 1979, compared with 9.8 percent in 1989 and 10.9 percent in 2000. We focus on college education here due to space limitations.

2. "Opening Wide the Doors of College: President Clinton's Call to Action for American Education in the 21st Century." February 1997.

http://www.ed.gov/updates/PresEDPlan/part9.html (accessed April 4, 2005).

3. Ideally, one would observe a worker's income were he or she to obtain the additional schooling and then compare this with the worker's income were he or she to obtain no further schooling. Because an individual either obtains more schooling or does not, this ideal is impossible to measure. Therefore, economists typically compute the return to schooling by comparing the average income of workers who have obtained the additional schooling with those who have not. The main conceptual issue with this observed return to schooling is a concern that workers who obtain the additional schooling may also differ from those that do not along unobserved dimensions (such as they are more motivated or hard working). Further discussion of these issues is beyond the scope of this paper; however, we refer the interested reader to Card (1999).

4. The authors' calculations are based on March CPS data. Autor, Katz, and Kearney (forthcoming) also find that the relative supply of college-equivalent labor continued to increase throughout the late 1990s and early 2000s.

5. States that raised their minimum wages include Alaska, California, Connecticut, Delaware, Hawaii, Illinois, Massachusetts, Maine, New York, Oregon, Rhode Island, Vermont, and Washington. The District of Columbia also raised its minimum wage.

6. Lee (1999) finds that in the 1980s the fall in the real value of the minimum wage can account for increasing inequality at the bottom of the wage distribution, suggesting that minimum wage increases of the mid-1990s also propped up wages at the bottom of the wage distribution, although Autor, Katz, and Kearney (forthcoming) raise some caution about this interpretation. Namely, they highlight that much of the decline in the real value of the minimum wage during the 1980s occurred during an economic downturn, whereas the minimum wage increases in the 1990s were legislated during economic expansions.

7. Studies of labor market cyclicality, such as, Hoynes (2000) and Hines, Hoynes, and Krueger (2001), show that earnings and (especially) employment are procyclical and that less-educated individuals experience greater cyclical variation than more-educated individuals.

8. Figures are based on data from the National Postsecondary Student Aid Study (U.S. Department of Education 2005).

9. Assuming that the college graduate–high school graduate earnings gap is constant over the life cycle and equals the difference in average annual earnings for these two education groups as measured in the 2004

March Current Population Survey, a college graduate earns $27,800 more in inflation-adjusted dollars per year. Alternatively, if we assume annual earnings will follow average earnings by age, the net present value to a first-year student in the fall of 2003 is roughly $246,923 ($354,200 in earnings minus $107,277 in tuition, fees, and lost wages). Note that by using annual earnings we take into account the higher rates of unemployment among high school graduates. This may not be correct, to the extent that lower unemployment is not the result of completing the bachelor's degree; rather, it may be result of having the personal factors that made it likely that an individual would complete the degree in the first place.

10. Note, however, that future changes in the U.S. labor market might affect relative compensation. If many more people who otherwise would not have attended college decide to do so, a dramatically increased supply of college graduates would compete in the labor market, and hence, the net benefits of college might be significantly smaller than we calculate.

REFERENCES AND FURTHER READING

Autor, David H., Lawrence F. Katz, and Melissa S. Kearney. "Trends in U.S. Wage Inequality: Re-Assessing the Revisionists." *The Review of Economics and Statistics* (forthcoming).

Bound, John and George Johnson. 1992. "Changes in the Structure of Wages in the 1980s: An Evaluation of Alternative Explanations." *The American Economic Review* 82 (3): 371–392.

Card, David. 1999. "The Causal Effect of Education on Earnings." In *Handbook of Labor Economics*, vol. 3A, eds. Orley C. Ashenfelter and David Card, pp. 1801–1863. Amsterdam: Elsevier.

Hines Jr., James R., Hilary W. Hoynes, and Alan B. Krueger. 2001. "Another Look at Whether a Rising Tide Lifts All Boats." In *The Roaring Nineties: Can Full Employment Be Sustained?* eds. Alan B. Krueger and Robert M. Solow, pp. 493–537. New York: Russell Sage Foundation.

Hoynes, Hilary W. 2000. "The Employment and Earnings of Less Skilled Workers Over the Business Cycle." In *Finding Jobs: Work and Welfare Reform*, eds. Rebecca Blank and David Card, pp. 23–71. New York: Russell Sage Foundation.

Katz, Lawrence F. and Kevin M. Murphy. 1992. "Changes in Relative Wages, 1963–1987: Supply and Demand Factors." *The Quarterly Journal of Economics* (February), 107 (1): 35–78.

Lee, David S. 1999. "Wage Inequality in the United States During the 1980s: Rising Dispersion or Falling Minimum Wage?" *The Quarterly Journal of Economics* (August), 114 (3): 977–1023.

Pierce, Brooks. 2001. "Compensation Inequality." *The Quarterly Journal of Economics* (November), 116 (4): 1493–1525.

Snyder, T. D., A. G. Tan, and C. M. Hoffman. 2004. "Table 174: Total Fall Enrollment in Degree-Granting Institutions, by Attendance Status, Sex of Student, and Control of Institution: 1947 to 2001." *Digest of Education Statistics, 2003* (NCES-2005–025). U.S. Department of Education, National Center for Education Statistics. Washington, DC: Government Printing Office. http://www.nces.ed.gov/programs/digest/d03/tables/xls/tab174.xls (accessed April 1, 2005).

U.S. Census Bureau, Current Population Survey. 2003. "Table 2.5: Educational Attainment of the Foreign-Born Population 25 Years and Over by Sex and Year of Entry: 2003." The Foreign-Born Population in the United States: March 2003 (P20–551). http://www.census.gov/population/socdemo/foreign/ppl-174/tab02–05.xls (accessed April 1, 2005).

U.S. Department of Education, National Center for Education Statistics. 2005. National Postsecondary Student Aid Study: Undergraduate Online Data Analysis System.

26

How to Deal with Terrorism

Bruno S. Frey

DETERRENCE AND PREEMPTIVE strikes are currently being used to fight terrorism, but they work badly, if at all, and in some cases are even counterproductive. As viable positive alternatives, the following three strategies are proposed:

1. Reduce vulnerability by decentralizing society.
2. Strengthen positive incentives to leave the terrorist camp.
3. Divert media attention from terrorist groups.

INEFFECTIVENESS OF DETERRENCE

After the attacks of 9/11, the American president declared a "crusade" against terrorists. This crusade was, after some thinking,

Bruno S. Frey is a professor of economics at the University of Zurich, Switzerland. His research team has pioneered using economics to study people's happiness, intrinsic motivation, procedural utility, pro-social behavior, and direct democracy. He is author of more than a dozen books and many articles in academic journals in economics and other social sciences. He received his Ph.D. from the University of Basel in 1965 and honorary doctorates from the University of Goeteborg and University of St. Gallen.

changed into a "war against terrorism." This war on terrorism is totally based on deterrence and preemptive strikes. Actual and prospective terrorists must be wiped out by killing or at least capturing them, holding them prisoner, or (perhaps) putting them on trial and sentencing them to imprisonment for long periods or indefinitely. Such treatment is expected to make the penalty for the crime so harsh that no individual will engage in terrorist activities in the future.

History and recent experience suggest, however, that deterrence is ineffective and may even be counterproductive in dealing with terrorism. Moreover, the extent of terrorist acts may well increase rather than decrease. A policy based on deterrence has a second disadvantage: it threatens civil and human rights in the countries engaged in fighting terrorism. Deterrence thus tends to undermine exactly those values it claims to protect.

Many people share this concern but see no alternative to deterrence. I want to show that such alternatives do exist and are viable, specifically, the three strategies listed above.

DECENTRALIZATION REDUCES VULNERABILITY AGAINST TERRORIST ATTACKS

Any system with many different centers is more stable due to the ability of the various centers to substitute for each other. When one part of the system is negatively affected, another part or parts can take over. This basic insight also applies to terrorism. A target's vulnerability is lower in a decentralized society than in a centralized society. The more centers of power there are in a country, the less terrorists are able to hurt it. In a decentralized system, terrorists do not know where to strike because they are aware that each part can substitute for the other so that a strike will not achieve much. In contrast, in a centralized system most decision making takes place in one location. This power center is an ideal target for terrorists and therefore is in great danger of being attacked.

As a means of reducing vulnerability, decentralization can be achieved in various ways:

- Decentralize the *economy* by relying on the market as the major form of resource allocation.
- Decentralize the *polity* by resorting to the classical division of power among the government, the parliament, and the courts. Decentralization over space is achieved by a federalist structure with decision-making power attributed to lower levels of the polity (states, provinces, regions, and communes).
- Decentralize the *society* by allowing for many different actors, such as churches, nongovernmental organizations, clubs, and families.

POSITIVE INCENTIVES TO ACTUAL AND PROSPECTIVE TERRORISTS NOT TO ENGAGE IN VIOLENT ACTS

Positive incentives consist in providing people with previously nonexistent or unattainable opportunities, thus increasing their utility. The opportunity costs of remaining or becoming a terrorist are raised because other valued possibilities are now available. Various approaches are possible.

Terrorists can be reintegrated. One of the most fundamental human motivations is the need to belong, and this also applies to terrorists. The isolation from other social entities gives strength to the terrorist group because it has become the only place where a sense of belonging is nurtured. An effective way to overcome terrorism is to break up this isolation. The (potential) terrorists must experience that there are other social bodies able to care for their need to belong. Interaction between groups tends to reduce extremist views, which are more likely to flourish in isolated groups of like-minded people. Segregation reinforces extremism and vice versa. Therefore, breaking up this vicious circle of segregation and extremism should lower terrorists' inclination to participate in violent activities.

There are various methods of motivating terrorists to interact more closely with other members of society, thus overcoming their isolation. The terrorists can be involved in a discussion process, which takes their goals and grievances seriously. Moreover, terrorists can be granted access to the normal political process. This lowers the costs of pursuing the political goal by legal means and hence raises the opportunity costs of terrorism.

The same principle of antiterrorist policy can be applied to nations supporting or harboring terrorists. When such countries are internationally isolated and identified as "rogue states," they tend to become more extreme and ideological. A more fruitful strategy is to help them to reenter the international community and to adopt its rules.

Repentants can be welcomed. Persons engaged in terrorist movements can be offered incentives, most importantly reduced punishment and a secure future life if they are prepared to leave the organization they are involved with and are prepared to talk about it and its projects. Terrorists who credibly show that they wish to renounce terrorist activities should be supported and not penalized (principal witness programs). A member's opportunity costs of remaining a terrorist are therewith increased.

Valued opportunities can be offered. Persons inclined to follow terrorist ideas and undertake terrorist actions can be invited to visit foreign countries. Universities and research institutes, for example, can offer such persons the opportunity of discussing their ideology with academics and other intellectuals. Liberalism is based on the conviction that the atmosphere of discourse existing in such places of learning tends to mellow terrorist inclinations. If prospective terrorists do not change their views, the situation is not worse than before. The very least to be achieved is that the (potential) terrorists have access to new and radically different ideas compared with the situation in which they live within a closed circle of other extremists.

Providing terrorists positive incentives to no longer engage in violent actions represents a completely different approach from the conventional antiterrorist policy of deterrence based on coercion. An effort is made to break the organizational and mental dependence of persons on the terrorist organizations by offering them more favorable alternatives.

ATTENTION TO BE DIVERTED FROM
THE TERRORIST GROUPS

The relationship between terrorists and the media can be described as symbiotic. The interests of the terrorists are similar or even identical to those of the media: both want to make news, and both want the terrorist act to remain in the news as long and as prominently as possible.

Terrorists have become very skilled in using the media to achieve a maximum effect. They have learned to exploit the media to propagate their political demands to millions and even billions of people. Terrorists have fully adjusted their tactics in order to accommodate media needs.

Terrorists can be prevented from committing violent acts by reducing the utility gained from such behavior. A specific way for terrorists to derive lower benefits from terrorism consists in the government ascertaining that a particular terrorist act is not attributed to a particular terrorist group. This prevents terrorists from receiving credit for the act and from gaining the public's attention associated with committing the act. The government must see to it that a particular terrorist group does not monopolize media attention.

This does not mean that the government should suppress information. This is not possible in an open society. The government can divert attention from terrorist organizations and their goals by supplying more information to the public than desired by the terrorist group responsible for a particular violent act. It must be made known that several terrorist groups could be responsible for a particular terrorist act. Experience shows indeed that in the case of most terrorist attacks several groups of terrorists have claimed to be responsible. The authorities have to reveal that they never know with certainty which terrorist group may have committed a violent act. Rather the government must publicly discuss various reasonable hypotheses.

The strategy of refusing to attribute a terrorist attack to one particular group systematically affects the behavior of terrorists. The benefits derived from having committed a terrorist act decreases for the group having undertaken it because the group does not reap the public attention hoped for. The political goals it wants to publicize are not propagated as much as desired. This reduction in publicity makes the terrorist act (to a certain degree) senseless, as modern terrorism essentially depends on publicity. Terrorists who are ready to take a high risk, even the risk of death, in order to put forth their political beliefs feel deeply dissatisfied. Their frustration is intensified by the feeling that other, not equally as "brave" political groups are given a free publicity ride. This frustration is often intense because terrorist groups tend to be in a state of strong competition even when they have similar political beliefs.

CONCLUSIONS

The proposed antiterrorist policy based on a positive approach has two important advantages over a coercive policy:

- The whole interaction between terrorists and the government takes the character of a positive sum game: All sides benefit. The effort of the government is no longer directed solely toward destruction. Rather, the government makes an effort to raise the utility of those terrorists who choose to enter the programs offered. It provides alternatives to persons considering becoming terrorists. In contrast, deterrence policy by necessity produces a worse position for both sides. The terrorists are punished (incarcerated, killed, or mutilated), and the deterrence strategy is very costly in terms of resources and civil rights.

- The strategy undermines the cohesiveness of the terrorist organization. The incentive to leave is a strong threat to the organization. The terrorist leaders no longer know whom to trust because, after all, most persons can succumb to temptation. An effort to counteract these temptations by prohibiting members from taking up the attractive offers leads to conflicts between the leaders and the rank and file. With good outside offers available to the members of a terrorist group, its leaders tend to lose control. The terrorist organization's effectiveness is thereby reduced.

The application of the economic approach to terrorism offers a range of superior antiterrorism policies to deterrence. They are effective in dissuading potential terrorists from attacking. All of these policies are based on the notion that a positive approach is preferable to one based on the use of force. The policies are positive as they do not seek to harm or kill potential and actual terrorists, but rather they seek to reduce terrorist activities. The policies are not retributive but antiterrorist. The positive approach here championed is not the only effective strategy and it does not work in every case; but, compared to the now dominant deterrence and preemption policy, the favorable features by far prevail. There is no need to restrict policies to deterrence; the positive approaches presented are in many respects superior alternatives.

A crucial question is why deterrence policy is so often undertaken though it is far from successful and why the positive policies are disregarded. The reason is that government politicians derive additional private benefits from using force. The same holds for the military, the police, and the secret service. In contrast, the proponents of positive antiterrorist policies are weak, at least in the short run. However, the outcome of the political struggle can be influenced by political persuasion, giving the positive approach a better chance.

PART VIII

THE DEATH PENALTY

WHAT CAN ECONOMISTS contribute to the debate on capital punishment? There has been a lively controversy among economists about its pros and cons, informed by the fact that the United States is alone among OECD countries in its frequent use of the death penalty.

The economic assessment of capital punishment consists of several elements. First is its effectiveness as a deterrent—does the prospect of execution deter a murderer? Other questions are: How often are the innocent executed? How much does capital punishment cost in budgetary terms compared with the alternative of life imprisonment? And—although in practice this question is unanswerable—how does the utility that the victim's family and friends gain from an execution compare with the loss of utility to the family and friends of the prisoner?

In the first essay here, Richard Posner comes down in favor of the United States continuing the practice of capital punishment, on the basis of its effectiveness as a deterrent. His co-blogger, the Nobel Laureate Gary Becker, considers the evidence and comes down with Posner. In the remaining essays, John Donohue and Justin Wolfers engage Paul Rubin in a spirited debate about the statistical evidence for deterrence, contending that, put simply, there is no such evidence. Read on and draw your own conclusions.

CHAPTER 27

The Economics of Capital Punishment

Richard A. Posner

THE RECENT EXECUTION by the State of California of the multiple murderer Stanley "Tookie" Williams has brought renewed controversy to the practice of capital punishment, a practice that has been abolished in about a third of the states and in most of the nations that the United States considers its peers; the European Union will not admit to membership a nation that retains capital punishment.

From an economic standpoint, the principal considerations in evaluating the issue of retaining capital punishment are the incremental deterrent effect of executing murderers; the rate of false positives (that is, execution of the innocent); the cost of capital punishment relative to life imprisonment without parole (the usual alternative

Richard A. Posner is a founder of law and economics. Since 1981, he has served as a judge of the U.S. Court of Appeals for the Seventh Circuit. He is also a senior lecturer in law at the University of Chicago and the author of numerous leading academic articles and books, including *Economic Analysis of Law,* now in its seventh edition. He received his LL.B. from Harvard in 1962 and B.A. from Yale in 1959. This chapter was originally published as a column at Becker-Posner-blog.com, December 18, 2005.

nowadays); the utility that retributivists and the friends and family members of the murderer's victim (or, as in Williams's case, victims) derive from execution; and the disutility that fervent opponents of capital punishment, along with relatives and friends of the defendant, experience. The utility comparison seems a standoff, and I will ignore it, although the fact that almost two-thirds of the U.S. population supports the death penalty is some, albeit weak (because it does not measure intensity of preference), evidence bearing on the comparison.

Early empirical analysis by Isaac Ehrlich (1975) found a substantial incremental deterrent effect of capital punishment, a finding that coincides with the common sense of the situation: it is exceedingly rare for a defendant who has a choice to prefer being executed to being imprisoned for life. Ehrlich's work was criticized by some economists, but more recent work by economists Hashem Dezhbakhsh, Paul Rubin, and Joanna Shepherd (2003) provides strong support for Ehrlich's thesis; these authors found, in a careful econometric analysis, that one execution deters eighteen murders. Although this ratio may seem implausible given that the probability in the United States today of being executed for committing a murder is less than 1 percent (most executions are in southern states—fifty of the fifty-nine in 2004—which that year had a total of almost 7,000 murders), the probability is misleading because only a subset of murderers are eligible for execution. Moreover, even a 1 percent or one-half of 1 percent probability of death is hardly trivial; most people would pay a substantial amount of money to eliminate such a probability.

As for the risk of executing an innocent person, this is exceedingly slight, especially when a distinction is made between legal and factual innocence. Some murderers are executed by mistake in the sense that they might have a good legal defense to being sentenced to death, such as having been prevented from offering evidence in mitigation of their crime, such as evidence of having grown up in terrible circumstances that made it difficult for them to resist the temptations of a life of crime. But they are not innocent of murder. The number of people who are executed for a murder they did not commit appears to be vanishingly small.

It is so small, however, in part because of the enormous protraction of capital litigation. The average amount of time that a defendant spends on death row before being executed is about ten years. If the defendant is innocent, the error is highly likely to be discovered within that period. It would be different if execution followed the appeal of the defendant's sentence by a week. But the delay in execution not only reduces the deterrent effect of execution (though probably only slightly) but also makes capital punishment quite costly, since there is a substantial imprisonment cost on top of the heavy litigation costs of capital cases, with their endless rounds of appellate and post-conviction proceedings.

Although it may seem heartless to say so, the concern with mistaken execution seems exaggerated. The number of people executed in all of 2004 was, as I noted, only fifty-nine. (The annual number has not exceeded ninety-eight since 1951.) Suppose that were it not for the enormous delays in execution, the number would have been sixty, and the additional person executed would have been factually innocent. The number of Americans who die each year in accidents exceeds one hundred thousand; many of these deaths are more painful than death by lethal injection, though they are not as humiliating and usually they are not anticipated, which adds a particular dread to execution. Moreover, for what appears to be a psychological reason (the "availability heuristic"), the death of a single, identified person tends to have greater salience than the death of a much larger number of anonymous persons. As Joseph Stalin is reported to have quipped, "A single death is a tragedy, a million deaths is a statistic."

But that's psychology; there is an economic argument for speeding up the imposition of the death penalty on convicted murderers eligible for the penalty; the gain in deterrence and reduction in cost would be likely to exceed the increase in the very slight probability of executing a factually innocent person. What is more, by allocating more resources to the litigation of capital cases, the error rate could be kept at its present very low level even though delay in execution would be reduced.

However, even with the existing excessive delay, the recent evidence concerning the deterrent effect of capital punishment provides strong support for resisting the abolition movement.

A final consideration returns me to the case of "Tookie" Williams. The major argument made for clemency was that he had reformed in prison and, more important, had become an influential critic of the type of gang violence in which he had engaged. Should the argument have prevailed? On the one hand, if murderers know that by "reforming" on death row they will have a good shot at clemency, the deterrent effect of the death penalty will be reduced. On the other hand, the type of advocacy in which Williams engaged probably had some social value, and the more likely the advocacy is to earn clemency, the more such advocacy there will be; clemency is the currency in which such activities are compensated and therefore encouraged. Presumably grants of clemency on such a basis should be rare, because there probably are rapidly diminishing social returns to death-row advocacy, along with diminished deterrence as a result of fewer executions. For the more murderers under sentence of death there are who publicly denounce murder and other criminality, the less credibility the denunciations have.

REFERENCES AND FURTHER READING

Dezhbakhsh, Hashem, Paul Rubin, and Joanna Mehlop Shepherd. 2003. "Does Capital Punishment Have a Deterrent Effect? New Evidence from Postmoratorium Panel Data." *American Law and Economics Review* 5: 344–376.

Ehrlich, Isaac. 1975. "The Deterrent Effect of Capital Punishment: A Question of Life and Death." *American Economic Review* 65 (3): 397–417.

CHAPTER 28

On the Economics of
Capital Punishment

Gary S. Becker

RICHARD POSNER PROVIDES a good discussion of the various issues related to capital punishment. I will concentrate my comments on deterrence, which is really the crucial issue in the acrimonious debate over capital punishment. I support the use of capital punishment for persons convicted of murder because, and only because, I believe it deters murders. If I did not believe that, I would be opposed, because revenge and the other possible motives that are mentioned and discussed by Posner should not be a basis for public policy.

As Posner indicates, serious empirical research on capital punishment began with Isaac Ehrlich's (1975) pioneering paper. Subsequent studies have sometimes found much weaker effects than he found,

Gary S. Becker won the Nobel Prize in 1992 and is a senior fellow at the Hoover Institution and a professor of economics and sociology at the University of Chicago. He is internationally recognized for pioneering work on human capital, discrimination, the economic analysis of crime, and the economics of the family. He received his A.B. from Princeton University in 1951 and his A.M. in 1952 and Ph.D. in 1955 from the University of Chicago.

whereas others, including the study by Dezhbakhsh, Rubin, and Shepherd cited by Posner (2006), found a much larger effect than even that found by Ehrlich. The available data are quite limited, however, so one should not base any conclusions solely on the econometric evidence. Still, I believe the preponderance of evidence does indicate that capital punishment deters, although a recent article by John J. Donohue and Justin Wolfers (2005) in the *Stanford Law Review* reaches the opposite conclusion after a review of many studies on the subject. In correspondence I gave them some reasons why I believe they understate the evidence that capital punishment deters.

Of course, public policy on punishments cannot wait until the evidence is perfect. Even with the limited quantitative evidence available, there are good reasons to believe that capital punishment deters murders. Most people, murderers in particular, fear death, especially when it follows swiftly and with considerable certainty following the commission of a murder. David Hume said in discussing suicide that "no man ever threw away life, while it was worth living. *For such is our natural horror of death*" (2004, 8). Arthur Schopenhauer added also in discussing suicide, "As soon as the terrors of life reach a point at which they outweigh the terrors of death, a man will put an end to his life. *But the terrors of death offer considerable resistance*" (1970, 78).

As Posner indicates, the deterrent effect of capital punishment would be greater if the delays on its implementation were much shortened and if this punishment were more certain to be used in the appropriate cases. But I agree with Posner that capital punishment has an important deterrent effect even with the way the present system actually operates.

TRADING OFF LIVES IS INEVITABLE

Opponents of capital punishment frequently proclaim that the state has no moral right to take the life of anyone, including that of a most reprehensible murderer, even if we assume that the deterrent effect on murders is sizeable. Yet that is absolutely the wrong conclusion for anyone who believes that capital punishment deters. To show why, suppose that for each murderer executed (instead of, say, receiving life imprisonment), the number of murders is reduced by three, which is a much lower number than Ehrlich's and some other estimates of the deterrent effect. This implies that for each murderer not given capital punishment, three generally innocent victims would die. This argument means that the government would indirectly be taking many lives if it did not use capital punishment. The lives so taken are usually much more worthwhile than that of the murderers who would be spared execution. For this reason, the state has a moral obligation to use capital punishment if such punishment significantly reduces the number of murders and saves lives of innocent victims.

Saving three other lives for every person executed seems like a very attractive trade-off. Even saving two lives per execution seems like a persuasive benefit-cost ratio for capital punishment. But let us go further and suppose only one life is saved for each murderer executed. Wouldn't the trade-off still be desirable if the life saved is much better than the life taken, which would usually be the case? As the deterrent effect of capital punishment is made smaller, at some point even I would shift to the anti-capital punishment camp.

Admittedly, the argument becomes less clear-cut as the number of lives saved per execution falls from two to lower values, say, for example, to one life saved per execution. Many readers of the Posner-Becker blog have objected to this comparison of the qualities of the life saved and the life taken. Yet I do not see how to avoid making such a comparison. Consider a person with a long criminal record who holds up and kills a victim who led a decent life and left several children and a spouse behind. Suppose it would be possible to save the life of an innocent victim by executing such a criminal. To me it is obvious that saving the life of such a victim has to count for more than taking the life of such a criminal. To be sure, not all cases are so clear-cut, but I am just trying to establish the principle that a comparison of the qualities of individual lives has to be part of any reasonable social policy.

WHY CAPITAL PUNISHMENT IS NOT APPROPRIATE
FOR LESSER CRIMES

The above argument helps explain why capital punishment should be used only for some murders and not for theft, robbery, and other lesser crimes. For then the trade-off is between taking lives and reducing property theft, and the case in favor of milder punishments is strong. However, severe assaults, including some gruesome rapes, may approach in severity some murders and might conceivably at times call for capital punishment, although I do not support its use in these cases.

A powerful argument for reserving capital punishment for murders is related to what is called marginal deterrence in the crime and punishment literature. If perpetrators of assaults were punished with execution, an assaulter would have an incentive to kill the victims in order to reduce the likelihood that he would be discovered. That is a major reason why more generally the severity of punishments should be matched to the severity of crimes. One complication is that capital punishment may make a murderer fight harder to avoid being captured, which could lead to more deaths. That argument has to be weighed in judging the case for capital punishment. Although marginal deterrence is important, I believe the resistance of murderers to being captured, possibly at the expense of their own lives, is really indirect evidence that criminals do fear capital punishment.

THE PROBLEM OF EXECUTING THE INNOCENT

Of course I am worried about the risk of executing innocent persons for murders committed by others. In any policy toward crime, including capital punishment, one has to compare errors of wrongful conviction with errors of failing to convict guilty persons. My support for capital punishment would weaken greatly if the rate of killing innocent persons were as large as that claimed by many. However, I believe along with Posner that the appeal process offers enormous protection not so much against wrongful conviction as against wrongful execution, so that there are very few, if any, documented cases of wrongful execution. And this process has been strengthened enormously with the development of DNA identification. However, lengthy appeals delay the execution of guilty murderers, and that can only lower the deterrent effect of capital punishment.

FINAL COMMENTS

European governments are adamantly opposed to capital punishment, and some Europeans consider the American use of this punishment to be barbaric. But Europeans have generally been "soft" on most crimes during the past half-century. For a long time they could be smug because their crime rates were well below American rates. But during the past twenty years, European crime has increased sharply whereas American rates have fallen—in part because American apprehension and conviction rates have increased considerably. Now some European countries have higher per capita property crime rates than the United States does, although violent crimes are still more common in the United States. At the same time that America was reducing crime significantly in part by greater use of punishments, many European intellectuals continued to argue that not just capital punishments but also punishments in general do not deter.

To repeat, the capital punishment debate comes down in essentials to a debate over deterrence. I can understand that some people are skeptical about the evidence, although I believe they are wrong both on the evidence and on the common sense of the issue. It is very disturbing to take someone's life, even a murderer's life, but sometimes highly unpleasant actions are necessary to deter even worse behavior that takes the lives of innocent victims.

REFERENCES AND FURTHER READING

Becker, Gary. 2005. "Further Comments on Capital Punishment." December 25. http://www.becker-posner-blog.com/archives/2005/12/.

Donohue, John J. and Justin Wolfers. 2005. "Uses and Abuses of the Evidence in the Death Penalty Debate." *Stanford Law Review* 58: 791.

Ehrlich, Isaac. 1975. "The Deterrent Effect of Capital Punishment: A Question of Life and Death." *American Economic Review* 65 (3): 397–417.

Hume, David. 2004. *Essays on Suicide and the Immortality of the Soul.* Whitefish, MT: Kessinger Publishing.

Posner, Richard. 2005. "The Economics of Capital Punishment." http://www.becker-posner-blog.com/archives/2005/12/25.

———. 2006. "The Economics of Capital Punishment." *The Economists' Voice* (March). http://www.bepress.com/ev.

Schopenhauer, Arthur. 1970. *On Suicide, Essays, and Aphorisms.* London: Penguin Books.

CHAPTER 29

The Death Penalty: No Evidence for Deterrence

John Donohue and Justin J. Wolfers

DESPITE CONTINUING CONTROVERSY, executions continue apace in the United States. Late last year, we witnessed the thousandth U.S. execution since the Supreme Court reinstated capital punishment in 1977. The United States trails only China, Iran, and Vietnam in the number of executions, according to Amnesty International (2006).

The debate over the death penalty has hung on several major issues. Here, we'll concentrate on one: Does it act as a deterrent?

The claim that it does, is for many people the main reason to support it. George W. Bush stated in the 2000 presidential debates, "I think the reason to support the death penalty is because it saves other people's lives," and further that "it's the only reason to be for it." By contrast, earlier that year, Attorney General Janet Reno stated, "I have inquired for most of my adult life about studies that might show

John Donohue is the Leighton Homer Surbeck Professor of Law at the Yale Law School. Justin J. Wolfers is a professor at the Wharton School of Business and a faculty research fellow at the National Bureau of Economic Research.

that the death penalty is a deterrent, and I have not seen any research that would substantiate that point" (2000).

Gary Becker (2006) and Richard Posner (2006) have recently taken George Bush's side, but our own comprehensive evaluation of the econometric evidence supports Reno.

THE ACADEMIC CASE FOR THE DEATH PENALTY

Over the last few years, a number of highly technical papers have purported to show that the death penalty is indeed a deterrent. Cass Sunstein and Adrian Vermeule (2005a) initially argued, based on studies like these, that "capital punishment is morally required" given the "significant body of recent evidence that capital punishment may well have a deterrent effect, possibly a quite powerful one." In a reply paper subsequent to our review of the evidence, they have adopted a more agnostic tone, however, stating that "we do not know whether deterrence has been shown. . . . Nor do we conclude that the evidence of deterrence has reached some threshold of reliability that permits or requires government action" (2005b).

More recently, in *The Economists' Voice*, Posner and Becker have adopted the position vacated by Sunstein and Vermeule. Posner (2006) claims that "the recent evidence concerning the deterrent effect of capital punishment provides strong support for resisting the abolition movement." Becker (2006) adds, "I support the use of capital punishment for persons convicted of murder because, and only because, I believe it deters murders."

The empirical research relied on by both Becker and Posner, however, is a skewed sample of available evidence: early research by Isaac Ehrlich (1975) and more recent research by Hashem Dezhbakhsh, Paul Rubin, and Joanna Shepherd (2003).

As we show in a recent *Stanford Law Review* article (2005) and describe below, when one considers all the evidence the empirical support for the proposition that the death penalty deters is at best weak and inconclusive.

THE FLAWED STATISTICAL EVIDENCE IN SUPPORT OF DETERRENCE FROM EXECUTIONS

Isaac Ehrlich's 1975 *American Economic Review* paper analyzed U.S. time series data on homicides and execution from 1933 to 1969, finding that each execution yielded eight fewer homicides. This result was somewhat puzzling in light of the fact that an 80 percent drop in the execution rate from the late 1930s until 1960 had been accompanied by falling murder rates. A subsequent reanalysis by Peter Passell and John Taylor (1977) showed that Ehrlich's estimates were entirely driven by attributing a sharp jump in murders from 1963 to 1969 to the post-1962 drop in executions.

But the mid-1960s decline in homicide occurred across all states—including those that had never had the death penalty. Moreover, Ehrlich's own model showed no correlation between executions and murder if one simply lopped off the last seven years of his data.

No wonder, then, that a National Academy panel savaged Ehrlich's analysis. Its modern-day impact beyond the University of Chicago campus is extremely limited.

But Posner does cite one recent study (by Dezhbakhsh, Rubin, and Shepherd [2003], hereafter DRS) that finds that each execution saves on balance eighteen lives. As we show in our recently published piece in the *Stanford Law Review*, however, these estimates are simply not credible.

An immediate problem is that DRS do not actually run the regression that they claim to run—the regression they claim to run actually yields the opposite result: each execution is associated with eighteen more executions! (The different results turn on how they measure the key variable defined as "the percent Republican vote in the most recent presidential election.") We do not suggest, though, that this specific result should be seriously entertained either, as the paper is far more fundamentally flawed.

Like Ehrlich's early work, the DRS study misuses a sophisticated econometric technique—instrumental variables estimation. Statistically, the cleanest way to estimate the effect of the death penalty would be to run an (unethical and impossible) experiment, executing convicts more vigorously in randomly selected states, and then comparing the changes in homicide rates across states. DRS attempt to create econometrically a quasi-experiment by identifying a set of variables, "instruments," that might cause changes in the execution rate but not otherwise affect the homicide rate.

Unfortunately, small misspecifications in this technique can yield extremely misleading results. Instrumental variables estimation requires a valid instrument. And the instruments that DRS use are not valid, and it stretches plausibility to believe that they generate quasi-experiments in capital punishment policy rather than simply reflect changes in crime markets or social trends.

These instruments are: (1) the statewide aggregate number of prison admissions, (2) the total statewide aggregate police payrolls, (3) the judicial expenditures (albeit not adjusted for inflation or state size), and (4) the statewide percent Republican vote in the most recent presidential election. To be valid, they would have to influence executions, and there would have to be no other link between these variables and the homicide rate.

This is not the case. For example, DRS tell us that Republicans tend to be tougher on crime. If true, that would imply that not only does the percent Republican vote correspond with executions (as DRS posit) but it is likely also related to other get-tough measures that might cause crime to fall (say, tougher sentencing laws or more vigilant policing).

Indeed, all three authors of the DRS study have used these very same instruments in assessing the impact of other anticrime measures, indicating that their own work is premised on the belief that there are other pathways from these instruments to the crime rate. If these alternative pathways are important, then their estimates of the deterrent effects of capital punishment are severely overstated.

We show that with the most minor tweaking of the DRS instruments, one can get estimates ranging from 429 lives saved per execution to 86 lives lost. These numbers are outside the bounds of credibility. With 1,000 executions over the last twenty-five years, if we had saved 429,000 lives (against an actual murder toll of roughly 500,000 over that period), the impact of the death penalty would leap out of the data. Murders would have plummeted in death penalty states compared with non-death penalty states, or in the United States compared with non-executing Canada. In fact, when we make precisely these comparisons, the murder rates across the controls and treatments seem to follow virtually identical paths.

A further important problem with the DRS study is that it analyzes county-level panel data, making no adjustment for either the correlation of the relevant variables through time or the correlation across counties within a state.[1] Following standard adjustments (clustering the standard errors by state to take account of these correlations) yields vastly higher standard errors and a confidence interval around their preferred point estimate that extends from 119 lives saved per execution to 82 lives lost! We are prepared to believe that this interval captures the true effect of each execution, but this provides little guidance to policymakers.

WHY PRICE THEORY DOESN'T FILL THE GAPS
IN THE STATISTICAL EVIDENCE

Other studies also claim to draw strong conclusions from noisy data. But they are also rife with coding errors and overstatements of statistical significance, or they are not robust to small changes in sample, functional form, or control variables. The problem is simply that execution rates have varied too little over the last thirty years to admit any robust inference from data collected over this period.

Becker (2006) thus rightly admits that "the evidence is decidedly mixed," and that "the weight of the positive evidence should not be overstated," and hence he founds his presumption in favor of deterrence on a belief "that most people have a powerful fear of death." Thus, Becker suggests that price theory can fill in where empirical evidence is lacking: capital punishment is akin to a rise in the price of murder and hence might be expected to lessen the number of murders.

But if the price rises, by how much does it rise? Is capital punishment a poor bargain, from a consequentialist's viewpoint? After all, the cost of capital trials often runs into several millions of dollars.

That can only be determined empirically, and the issue is complex: one needs to evaluate both how much the "price" rises when capital punishment is used instead of other punishments and the marginal response of potential murderers to this increase.

The penalty for committing a capital murder (if one is caught) is already extraordinarily high—being locked in a cage for the rest of one's life without possibility of parole. So what is the marginal deterrence of an infrequently administered additional sanction of death, many years later? Indeed, executions are so rare and appeals so lengthy that it is not even clear that being sentenced to death reduces the life expectancy of a criminal (especially given the high risks of death on the street). For instance, in 2004 there were 16,137 homicides, and only 125 death sentences were handed out; of the 3,314 prisoners on death row, only 59 were executed.

Finally, other factors (some of which Becker and Posner mention) may weaken or even entirely undercut any deterrent effect. For instance, state-sanctioned executions may lower the social sanctions regarding taking the lives of others, thereby reducing the price of murder.

MODEL DEPENDENCE IN ESTIMATING THE DETERRENT
EFFECT OF EXECUTIONS

Posner (2006) omits to mention a key paper by Lawrence Katz, Steven Levitt, and Ellen Shustorovich (2003; hereafter, KLS), which appeared in the same issue as DRS. KLS analyzed annual state homicide execution data from 1950 to 1990, publishing four models with a full set of controls. These models yielded the following alternative estimates of net lives saved per execution: 0.6, 0.4, −0.8, and −0.5 (with the negative numbers suggesting net lives lost per execution).

We have updated KLS's data to include a longer time period, extending it to cover 1934–2000. (Reliance on the death penalty was far greater seventy years ago than it has been in the past two decades, and this greater variation is necessary to obtain reasonably precise estimates.) The resulting four estimates for the longer data period, −1.5, −1.5, −1.7, and −1.0, now uniformly suggest no benefit from executions (an estimate of −1 implies that no murders were deterred and one life was lost by virtue of the execution). These results are shown in figure 29.1 as the solid triangles.

We also tried two further specifications, coding the execution variable as executions per capita (shown as squares) and executions per (lagged) homicide (shown with circles). In other respects, we followed the KLS specifications and include a rich set of controls, including the (non-execution) prison death rate, prisoners per crime, prisoners per capita, real income per capita, and the proportion of the state population that is black, living in urban areas, and ages 0–24 and 25–44. In each case, we converted the estimated coefficients into the implied number of lives saved per execution.

Across each of these quite reasonable specifications, we find considerable variation in the estimated relationship between executions and the murder rate. Our reading of these results suggests (weakly) that the preponderance of the evidence supports the view that increases in executions are associated with increases in lives

FIGURE 29.1

Estimated Lives Saved per Execution Katz-Levitt-Shustorich
Specification Plus Robustness Tests, 1934–2000

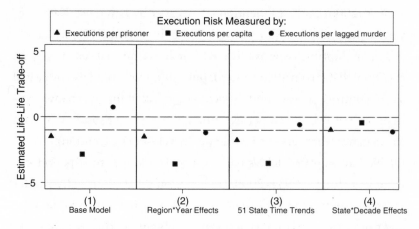

All models include state and year fixed effects and control for state economic and demographic variables.

lost, although further permutations of the full array of plausible
models would be needed before strong conclusions could be
reached.

One reason to believe that the KLS methodology yields unbi-
ased estimates is that the focus of the authors' paper is not on the
deterrence effect: for them, capital punishment is only a control
variable. Why is this better? Because it makes it less likely that they
would be tempted to tailor their specification to generate a particular result concerning the impact of the death penalty. Our reanalysis of the existing literature suggests a tendency of many authors to
only report results that were favorable to a particular political
position.

Our guess is also that estimating more models will only reinforce
the lack of robustness of any particular finding, confirming the high
degree of model dependence in the estimated effects of the death penalty. Moreover, we should emphasize that these regressions merely

highlight an association between executions and homicides, and the direction of the causal arrow remains an open question.

THE BOTTOM LINE

The view that the death penalty deters is still the product of belief, not evidence. The reason for this is simple: the United States has not experimented enough with capital punishment policy to permit strong conclusions. Even complex econometrics cannot sidestep this basic fact. The data are simply too noisy, and the conclusions from any study are too fragile. On balance, the evidence suggests the death penalty is as likely to increase the murder rate as to decrease it; and if it does decrease the murder rate, any decrease is likely small. In light of this evidence, is it wise to spend millions on a process with no demonstrated value that creates at least some risk of executing innocents when other proven crime-fighting measures exist? Even consequentialists ought to balk.

NOTE

1. Recall that DRS (2003) are trying to estimate the effect of executions on county murder rates, but they only have data on executions by state, which is less than ideal.

REFERENCES AND FURTHER READING

Amnesty International. 2006. *Facts and Figures on the Death Penalty*. http://web.amnesty.org/pages/deathpenalty-facts-eng.

Becker, Gary. 2006. "On the Economics of Capital Punishment." *The Economists' Voice* 3 (3), art. 4. http://www.bepress.com/ev/vol3/iss3/art4.

Bush, George W. 2000. "The Third Presidential Debate, 2000." Center for Presidential Debates Transcripts. http://www.debates.org/pages/trans2000c.html.

Dezhbakhsh, H., P. Rubin, and J. Shepherd. 2003. "Does Capital Punishment Have a Deterrent Effect? New Evidence from Postmoratorium Panel Data." *American Law and Economics Review* 5: 344.

Donohue J. and J. Wolfers. 2005. "Uses and Abuses of Statistical Evidence in the Death Penalty Debate." *Stanford Law Review* 58: 787.

Ehrlich, Isaac. 1975. "The Deterrent Effect of Capital Punishment: A Question of Life and Death." *American Economic Review* 65 (3): 397–417.

Katz L., S. Levitt, and E. Shustorovich. 2003. "Prison Conditions, Capital Punishment, and Deterrence." *American Law and Economics Review* 5: 318.

Liebman, J. S., J. Fagan, and V. West. 2000. "Capital Attrition: Error Rates in Capital Cases, 1973–1995." *Texas Law Review* 78: 1839–1861.

Passell, Peter and John B. Taylor. 1977. "The Deterrent Effect of Capital Punishment: Another View." *American Economic Review* 67: 445–451.

Posner, Richard. 2006. "The Economics of Capital Punishment." *The Economists' Voice*, 3 (3), art. 3. http://www.bepress.com/ev/vol3/iss3/art3.

Reno, Janet. January 20, 2000. Weekly media briefing. U.S. Justice Department.

Sunstein, C. and A. Vermeule. 2005a. "Is Capital Punishment Morally Required?" *Stanford Law Review* 58: 706.

———. 2005b. "Deterring Murder: A Reply." *Stanford Law Review* 58: 848.

CHAPTER 30

Reply to Donohue and Wolfers on the Death Penalty and Deterrence

Paul H. Rubin

WHILE JOHN DONOHUE and Justin Wolfers are mainly concerned with criticizing Richard Posner and Gary Becker (who can take care of themselves), they also comment unfavorably on a paper of which I was a co-author (Dezhbakhsh, Rubin, and Shepherd 2003). Their comments are in some instances unfair or incorrect, and I want to briefly correct some of their misstatements. (It should be noted that Hashem Dezhbakhsh and I have prepared a lengthy reply to Donohue and Wolfers which is available online and which will be submitted to a peer-reviewed journal in the near future.)

As they point out, an important issue is the specification of the measure of Republican voting in the most recent election; we used separate variables for each presidential election whereas Donohue and Wolfers (2005) use one variable to measure voting in all presidential

Paul H. Rubin is Samuel Candler Dobbs Professor of Economics and Law at Emory University and has been senior staff economist at President Reagan's Council of Economic Advisers, chief economist at the U.S. Consumer Product Safety Commission, and director of advertising economics at the Federal Trade Commission.

elections. It is true that we state the measure ambiguously in our paper. We originally received the data and the presidential voting variables from John Lott and David Mustard, and we measure this variable in the same way that they did. The theory behind Lott and Mustard's choice of separate election variables seemed also to apply in our case: because candidates and issues vary among elections, the correlation between support for Republican candidates and capital punishment will also vary among elections. Indeed, Wolfers and Donohue do not claim that their Republican voting variable is better than our variables; it is simply measuring the relationship differently.

As readers of our paper can see, we tried numerous (about forty-eight) specifications in the paper (many suggested by referees and by commentators from numerous presentations at several universities and academic conferences). Following other empirical and theoretical papers examining capital punishment's deterrent effect, we used different measures of the probability of execution that were based on different ways that criminals might form perceptions.

As any empiricist knows, it is difficult to ever find perfect instrumental variables that are completely uncorrelated with crime rates. Most of our instrumental variables have been used in numerous empirical papers because previous researchers believed (often based on empirical testing) that the instruments were as uncorrelated with crime rates as one was likely to find. Indeed, numerous referees and commentators also believed that the instrumental variables were sound. Unfortunately, we did not try Donohue and Wolfers's instrumental variables; if we had we would have recognized that our results were fragile to some choices of instruments and refined or expanded our analysis.

However, it seems disingenuous to argue that our paper does not meet "even a minimal quality threshold" when no readers prior to Wolfers and Donohue noticed the difficulty. Indeed, we presented our paper at the American Economic Association Meetings in a session with Donohue (when the Levitt-Donohue abortion paper was also presented) and Professor Donohue did not comment at that time on our "error." We have examined this issue and provide further analysis in the paper mentioned above.

Finally, let me state categorically that their comment that "the authors of these papers started with strong beliefs in the deterrent effect of the death penalty and chose to emphasize the evidence supporting these prior beliefs" is simply incorrect. My co-authors and I had no strong prior beliefs; one of us was actually opposed to the death penalty. In fact, one of my co-authors has recently written a paper that claims that the deterrent effect may be limited to a few states and that in most states, capital punishment likely has no effect, or even a positive effect, on murders (Shepherd 2005). The econometric specification we used gave us strong results (which Donohue and Wolfers [2005] were able to exactly replicate) and the numerous robustness tests (albeit using the same instruments) gave us confidence in these results. Moreover, unlike Donohue and Wolfers (2005), we made every effort to elicit comments before we published our paper. For example, as mentioned above, we presented it numerous times at professional meetings and universities. We originally posted the paper on SSRN in 2001, and we posted a revision in 2003. We sent our paper to a refereed journal for publication rather than to a law review. None of these guarantee that a paper will be error free, but we made every effort to obtain professional criticism of the paper and to respond to such criticisms before publication.

Thanks to Joanna Shepherd for comments on this note.

REFERENCES AND FURTHER READING

Dezhbakhsh, Hashem and Paul H. Rubin. "From the 'Econometrics of Capital Punishment' to the 'Capital Punishment of Econometrics': On the Use and Abuse of Sensitivity Analysis." Available at SSRN .com and at BEPress.com.

Dezhbakhsh, Hashem, Paul H. Rubin, and Joanna M. Shepherd. 2003. "Does Capital Punishment Have a Deterrent Effect? New Evidence from Postmoratorium Panel Data." *American Law and Economics Review* 5: 344.

Donohue, J. and J. Wolfers. 2005. "Uses and Abuses of Statistical Evidence in the Death Penalty Debate." *Stanford Law Review* 58: 787.

Shepherd, Joanna M. 2005. "Deterrence versus Brutalization: Capital Punishment's Differing Impacts Among States." *Michigan Law Review* 104: 203.

CHAPTER 31

Letter: A Reply to Rubin on the Death Penalty

John Donohue and Justin J. Wolfers

WE WOULD LIKE to respond to the previous chapter, Paul Rubin's "Reply to Donohue and Wolfers on the Death Penalty and Deterrence." There, he defended the analysis he did with his co-authors (Dezhbakhsh, Rubin, and Shepherd 2003) that estimated that each execution deters eighteen homicides. His work is widely cited and is the basis for his recent congressional testimony about the deterrence value of capital punishment (Rubin 2006). We have critiqued this estimation and found it wanting in a number of respects. Rubin's response to our critique suggests that it might be helpful to emphasize three points.

First, in their original article, Rubin and his co-authors described their key instrument for executions as "the Republican presidential candidate's percentage of the statewide vote in the most recent election" (Dezhbakhsh, Rubin, and Shepherd 2003). But using that precise instrument leads to the exact opposite finding that they reached: each execution causes eighteen more homicides.

Second, the instrumental variables regressions employed by Rubin and his co-authors require one to believe that spending on police,

261

the courts, prison admissions, and partisan shifts affect homicide through execution policy but not through other pathways. To us, this claim is simply not credible, and our intuition is supported by a Hausman test for overidentification, which easily rejects the validity of the instruments.

Rubin responds as follows: "Most of our instrumental variables have been used in numerous empirical papers because previous researchers believed (often based on empirical testing) that the instruments were as uncorrelated with crime rates as one was likely to find" (2006).

But, as we pointed out, the previous use of these instruments is one of the things that suggests they cannot be validly used in this context. In separate papers, Rubin and his co-authors have used the same instruments (or subsets of them) as providing variation in truth-in-sentencing legislation, firearms right-to-carry laws, sentencing guidelines, and California's three-strikes law. It cannot be the case that these previous papers were correct in positing that these instruments affect homicides only through that array of channels *and* that Rubin is correct that these instruments influence homicides through their effect on execution policy to the exclusion of other pathways. Yet without valid instruments, one cannot generate reliable results nor offer useful policy recommendations from an instrumental variables estimation. Their results turn out to be extremely fragile to the inclusion or exclusion of particular instruments.

Third, even if we believed that their instruments were valid, we find that by failing to account for spatial and intertemporal correlation in their data, Rubin and his co-authors substantially overstate the precision of their estimates. With appropriate corrections, the 95 percent confidence interval surrounding their key estimate ranges from massive increases in homicide to massive decreases, instead of a relatively tight band around eighteen lives saved as they claim.

REFERENCES AND FURTHER READING

Dezhbakhsh, H., P. Rubin, and J. Shepherd. 2003. "Does Capital Punishment Have a Deterrent Effect? New Evidence from Postmoratorium Panel Data." *American Law and Economics Review* 5: 344.

Donohue, J. and J. Wolfers. 2005. "Uses and Abuses of Statistical Evidence in the Death Penalty Debate." *Stanford Law Review* 58: 787.

Rubin, Paul. 2006. "Statistical Evidence on Capital Punishment and the Deterrence of Homicide." Testifying in hearings on "An Examination of the Death Penalty in the United States," Senate Judiciary Committee, February 1. http://judiciary.senate.gov/testimony.cfm?id=1745&wit_id=4991.

32

Reply: The Death Penalty
Once More

Paul H. Rubin

I WOULD LIKE to clear up the important misimpression that John
Donohue and Justin Wolfers create in their earlier article implying
that they have been unable to reproduce our results. To the contrary,
and as they concede in their article in the *Stanford Law Review:* "Dezhbakhsh, Rubin, and Shepherd generously shared their data and
code, and Joanna Shepherd assisted our efforts, enabling us to perfectly replicate all of their results" (Donohue and Wolfers 2005).
Only when they misinterpreted our admittedly ambiguous description of our instrument did they get different results. However, we
cleared up this ambiguity with them long ago, allowing complete
replication.

Instead, they show that some different specifications find no deterrence. They concede in their paper that the specifications they
report are not necessarily superior: "Our point is not that one specification is preferable to the other. Indeed, sorting that out would be
a difficult task." They simply found different models and data that
yielded different results.

Moreover, in my congressional testimony (2006), I cited not only my own article but also a total of twelve studies by fifteen different authors that find a deterrent effect. (Steven Levitt has claimed that I mischaracterized his results; some of his specifications found deterrence, but others did not. Even ignoring his article, there are still eleven published articles that have found deterrence.) Although Donohue and Wolfers's (2005) *Stanford Law Review* article criticizes some of these, the vast majority of studies, not just our paper, find deterrence. Nevertheless, in my congressional testimony I discussed briefly the Donohue and Wolfers *Stanford Law Review* piece and indicated that the issue was still open.

As I indicated in my previous article in Chapter 30, Hashem Dezhbakhsh and I have prepared a detailed reply to their comments in which we explore the econometric and other issues in detail. This will further our understanding of the issues under discussion.

REFERENCES AND FURTHER READING

Dezhbakhsh, Hashem and Paul H. Rubin. "From the 'Econometrics of Capital Punishment' to the 'Capital Punishment of Econometrics': On the Use and Abuse of Sensitivity Analysis, available at SSRN .com and at BEPress.com.

Dezhbakhsh, H., P. Rubin, and J. Shepherd. 2003. "Does Capital Punishment Have a Deterrent Effect? New Evidence from Postmoratorium Panel Data." *American Law and Economics Review* 5: 344.

Donohue, J. and J. Wolfers. 2005. "Uses and Abuses of Statistical Evidence in the Death Penalty Debate." *Stanford Law Review* 58: 787.

Rubin, Paul. 2006. "Statistical Evidence on Capital Punishment and the Deterrence of Homicide." Testifying in hearings on "An Examination of the Death Penalty in the United States," Senate Judiciary Committee, February 1. http://judiciary.senate.gov/testimony.cfm?id= 1745&wit_id=4991.

PART IX

REAL ESTATE

THE HEALTH OF the housing market is a matter of pressing interest to homeowners. Their homes are important investments and the places they live, and most have borrowed large sums of money to finance their purchase. Moreover, a serious downturn in the housing market could spill over to the whole economy and cause a recession. The increases in house prices in recent years led many economists to question the sustainability of the housing boom and to ask what might happen when it comes to an end. Robert Shiller opens this section by considering very long-term data in home prices in various countries. He finds that there is no long-term upward trend in real (inflation-adjusted) home prices. The recent run-up in prices is a bubble, and the only question for him is whether it will end with a soft landing or, on the contrary, with a sharp correction. With such a large degree of irrational overpricing, he believes a sharp fall in prices is more likely. Dean Baker, author of the second essay, agrees: there has been no change in long-term fundamentals to warrant the level of house prices today, he argues. What's more, the sooner the bubble is burst the better: delaying the economic pain will only make it worse. He believes the Federal Reserve should ensure housing bubbles do not get out of hand. In most parts of the country, housing prices have fallen from their peaks—how far they fall remains to be seen.

In the final essay in this section, Edward Glaeser and Dwight Jaffee turn to another housing problem, namely, the difficulties of the two government-backed bodies, Fannie Mae and Freddie Mac. Both securitize mortgages—they buy lenders' mortgage books and package them up into securities, which spread the risks of the individual loans, to sell on to investors. They do so with an implicit government guarantee. But both have used that government guarantee to borrow cheaply themselves and make a higher return by investing in riskier assets. If either fails, the bill will fall to taxpayers. The authors argue the government should charge the agencies in the form of a tax for the risks they are imposing on taxpayers. The subprime mortgage crisis in the summer of 2007 may add weight to this view.

Taken together, these three essays paint a worrisome picture.

CHAPTER 33

Long-Term Perspectives on the Current Boom in Home Prices

Robert J. Shiller

HOMEOWNERS WANT TO KNOW: Is the current boom in home prices temporary? Is a crash possible? And if prices do fall, will they come back up fairly soon, or will they stay down for many years?

Some have written reassuringly, downplaying concerns about possible price falls. Examples are Cynthia Angell and Norman Williams; Ben Bernanke; Charles Himmelberg, Christopher Mayer, and Todd Sinai; the Joint Center for Urban Studies; David Lereah; Frank Nothaft; and Jonathan McCarthy and Richard Peach. The general tone of reassurance in many of their articles appears unwarranted.

Angell and Williams (2005), for example, concluded that "in over 80 percent of the metro-area price booms we examined between 1978 and 1998 the boom ended in a period of stagnation. . . . The ex-

Robert J. Shiller is the Stanley B. Resor Professor of Economics, Department of Economics and Cowles Foundation for Research in Economics, Yale University, and fellow at the International Center for Finance, Yale School of Management. In addition to being the author of numerous academic articles, he is the author of the acclaimed book *Irrational Exuberance*.

269

pectation would be that metro-area home price busts will continue to be relatively rare." But they reach their conclusion based only on a twenty-year period of United States data.

Indeed, all these studies confined themselves to no more than a few decades' recent data. Such data simply cannot provide useful insights to homeowners planning to occupy homes for thirty or forty years and wondering whether a general uptrend in home prices will inevitably carry them over any possible price declines.

To answer the important questions, we first need to find out if there have been other booms similar to this one and what happened after such booms ended. Until now long-term price indexes have not been generally available to allow us to do this. I have constructed one, based in part on the S&P/Case-Shiller repeat-sales indexes that Karl Case and I pioneered and that are now produced by Fiserv Inc. with Standard & Poor's, and also, for earlier years, on other indexes as well.

The news is not good for homeowners. According to our data, homeowners face substantial risk of much lower prices that could stay low for a long time after they drop. Luckily, though, derivative products, notably a futures market, are being developed that they will soon be able to use to insure against this risk.

THE DATA SHOW NO LONG-TERM UPTREND IN REAL HOME PRICES

Figure 33.1 shows three long-term series of real home prices. All attempt to control for changing size and quality of homes; all are corrected for inflation in consumer prices.

I constructed the United States series 1890–2007 by linking together the Grebler Blank and Winnick index for twenty-two U.S. cities 1890–1934; a median asking price of homes advertised in newspapers for Boston, Washington, DC, Chicago, New Orleans, and Los Angeles 1934–1953; the U.S. Bureau of Labor Statistics

(BLS) January Consumer Price Index home purchase component 1953–1975; the U.S. Home Price Index from the U.S. Office of Housing Enterprise Oversight 1975–1987 for the first quarter of each year; and the S&P/Case-Shiller U.S. National Home Price Index (CSI) for the U.S. 1987–2007, for the first quarter of each year.

Piet Eichholtz (1997) constructed the Amsterdam series 1628–1973, a repeat-sales price index based on selling prices of homes along the Herengracht Canal, a small region of Amsterdam that was originally zoned for large lots and expensive homes and for which data have been carefully maintained. Homes are thought to have remained relatively unchanged there for centuries.

Øyvind Eitrheim and Solveig Erlandsen (2004) constructed the Norway series 1819–1989, another repeat-sales price index, this time based on individual home sales data for Bergen from 1819 to 1989, Oslo from 1841 to 1989, Kristiansand from 1867 to 1989, and Trondheim from 1897 to 1989.

Note the enormous current boom in home prices in the United States since 1997, which has shown only a slight hint of reversing in 2007. The magnitude of the current boom is practically unique in history, making it difficult to predict what comes next based on historical examples. Amsterdam and Norway have also seen sharp upswings since 1997, but these price indexes terminate before 1997 and so are not visible on figure 33.1.

Do real home prices have a substantial long-term uptrend? The chart suggests not.

First, what about the United States? It's notable that until the recent explosion in home prices, real home prices in the United States were virtually unchanged from 1890 to the late 1990s.

The Amsterdam data show lots of ups and downs but only the slightest hint of an uptrend. Prices approximately doubled, but it took nearly 350 years to do so, implying an annual average price increase of only 0.2 percent a year.

FIGURE 33.1

Real Home Price Indexes for the United States 1890–2005 (Shiller 2005), Amsterdam 1628–1973 (Eichholtz 1997) and Norway 1819–1989 (Eitrheim and Erlandsen 2004)

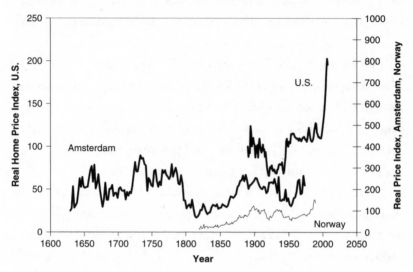

The Norway data do suggest such an uptrend, but viewed from the longer perspective of the Amsterdam data, that uptrend seems to be merely part of a long cycle from the early nineteenth century to the late nineteenth century. And even leaving the context added by Amsterdam aside, Norway's real price growth is, on average, negligible: only 1.3 percent a year.

ACCOUNTING FOR THE CURRENT BOOM:
A HISTORICAL COMPARISON

If the current boom doesn't reflect a long-term uptrend in real home prices, when will the market correct for this short-term discrepancy? And will the correction be smooth or drastic?

The only other time the United States has experienced a large home price boom was around the end of World War II. According to these data, real home prices went up 60 percent from 1942 to 1947 and then leveled off into a "soft landing," merely restoring real prices to levels seen before World War I.

The current boom is of a similar and even greater magnitude. From the first quarter of 1997 to the first quarter of 2005, real home prices went up 71 percent according to the Case-Shiller Index and by 52 percent according to the OFHEO repeat-sales index.

Will this boom end in a soft landing as the prior boom did? Possibly, but just as that boom had a different history—it followed the tumult of the interwar period of low construction and declining prices—today's boom may well have a different result.

RECESSION: THE ONLY WAY THE CURRENT BOOM
CAN END? NOT NECESSARILY

Many think that only a recession can end a home price boom, and no recession is on the horizon: therefore, a soft landing is most likely. But this comforting syllogism is an overextrapolation from the last two real estate cycles. The magnitude of the current boom is much greater than past booms, and so the way the boom ends may be more unpredictable and dramatic.

Figure 33.2 shows a longer view, giving unemployment rates and home prices since 1890. Two things stand out: first, the current boom is far more dramatic than its predecessors, and second, even prior booms do not necessarily track the unemployment rate such that their ends are signaled by recessions.

Granted, the real estate boom-bust in the late 1970s and early 1980s does match up roughly with fluctuations in the unemployment rate. And so does the boom-bust of the late 1980s and early 1990s. But that is not true if we look at a longer time span.

The huge depressions of the 1890s and the 1930s had no discernable effect on home prices. The recession of 1950–1951 had no

FIGURE 33.2

U.S. Real Home Price Index 1890–2005 (Shiller 2005, updated) and
U.S. Unemployment Rate 1890–1930

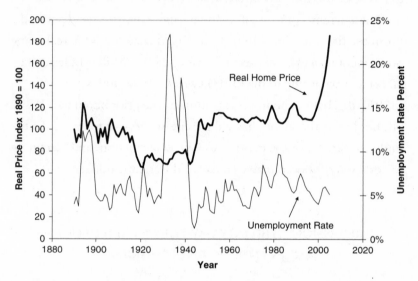

Source: Bureau of Labor Statistics, Current Population Survey, and, before 1930, Romer
(1986).

effect on the then-current boom in home prices, and the recessions
of 1953–1954, 1957–1958, 1960–1961, 1967–1968, and 1974–1975 had
no important effect on home prices. Similarly, the recession of 2001
had no obvious effect on the boom in home prices then underway.

Although the last two real estate boom cycles did end in recession, that is not the rule historically.

REAL RENTS, THE RENT-PRICE RATIO, AND
REAL INTEREST RATES

It is striking that, although there does not seem to be a genuine long-
term uptrend in real house prices, there does seem to be a genuine
long-term downtrend in real rents.

Indeed, according to BLS data, real housing rents have been in decline—falling about 50 percent in total—ever since the Consumer Price Index was created in 1913. See figure 33.3. (The CPI rent series is quality controlled, that is, adjusted for changes in the number of bedrooms, bathrooms, utilities, and facilities provided or changes in services expected of the renter, though there have been criticisms of the adequacy of this quality control, Gordon and van Goethem [2004].)

It is thus surprising that the real price of American housing, also shown in figure 33.3, has had an uptrend since 1913—although, as noted above, there is no long-term uptrend if pre-1913 years are taken into account. It is perhaps more accurate to say the real price of housing has been flat since 1913 except for two episodes: the home price boom that followed World War II (which essentially restored home prices to their 1913 level) and the current home price boom.

FIGURE 33.3

U.S. Real Rent of Primary Residence, January, 1913–2005 (Bureau of Labor Statistics) and Real Home Price, 1913–2005 (Shiller 2005)

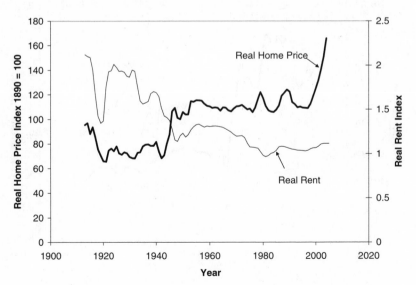

IN THEORY, REAL RENTS AND REAL HOME PRICES MIGHT
BE EXPECTED TO TRACK EACH OTHER

In theory, one might expect real home prices to represent the present discounted value of future rents. After all, people can move from renting to owning with relative ease. And although there's an obvious tax advantage to owning—including to owning a second home—in the form of the home mortgage deduction, that advantage could be easily valued and taken into account in the calculations. If we accept the approximation that rents are a random walk, then prices should closely track rents. If rents are close to a random walk but mean reverting, we might expect price to track rents but to be less volatile than rents.

FIGURE 33.4

Real interest rate is defined as long-term government bond yield described in Shiller (2005), minus the rate of change of the consumer price index for the preceding year. The index of the rent/price ratio is defined as the U.S. consumer price index for rent of primary residence, 1982–4=100, divided by the Shiller (2005) U.S. home price index, and the result rescaled to 1980=1.

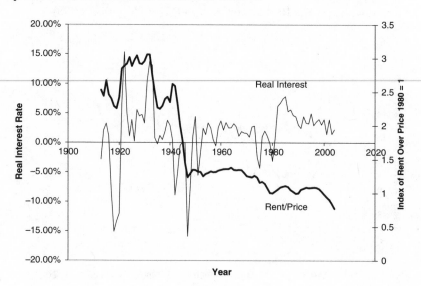

In practice, however, the situation is very different: not only do real home and rent prices fail to track each other, but also the rent-price ratio has shown a remarkable downtrend since 1913 (see figure 33.4). But why?

Interest rates are not the explanation, as some have suggested (notably Himmelberg, Mayer, and Sinai 2005). The rent-to-price-ratio downtrend is not matched by a downtrend in real long-term interest rates, here measured as a long-term U.S. government bond yield minus the previous year's CPI inflation rate (see Shiller 2005). Also, real rates today, though much lower than in 1980, do not appear low by historical standards.

The recent divergence between real interest rates and real rental-price ratios suggests the possibility of an irrational overpricing today and a huge fall in home prices in coming years. However, more study of these series in association with present value models and other data would be warranted before drawing strong conclusions just from this comparison.

THE CHARACTER OF THE CURRENT BOOM: A GLAMOUR CITY BOOM MORE THAN A LAND BOOM

Nationwide, there is something of a land price boom going on too. Using data from the United States Department of Agriculture, the U.S. real (CPI inflation-corrected) estimated market value of cropland per acre rose a total of 29 percent between 1997 and 2005. Over the same period, real average cash rents per acre for cropland were virtually constant, so the agricultural land boom shows up in the price-rent ratio as well.

But, the 29 percent increase in real agricultural land prices is a lot less than the 71 percent increase we saw in figure 33.1 in real home prices. Moreover, some of this land price boom is from acreage that is in the immediate vicinity of urban areas, and so some of this boom is just the same urban real estate boom that we have already seen.

The cause of the home price boom does not seem to be an unsatisfied hunger for land services or housing services above other goods and services: We saw in the preceding section that rents have not been increasing as much as consumer prices. Expenditure on housing services in the United States as a share of gross domestic product has been relatively constant at about 15 percent since 1929. Expenditures have kept up with rising incomes not because rents or prices have been increasing but because we have increased the amount of real housing services that we buy. U.S. Census data reveal that the average size of new houses increased from 1,100 square feet in the 1940s to 2,150 square feet in 1997 as the number of people per household dropped from 3.67 in 1940 to 2.64 in 1997. There were about 800 square feet per family member in 1997 compared with 300 square feet per family member in the 1940s.

We appear to be seeing growth in a different kind of hunger: a hunger for investments in real estate that can be expected to do extremely well. The home price boom is in large measure a boom in investments in glamorous urban areas and vacation spots that appear to investors to have sharp appreciation potential.

According to the National Association of Realtors, 36 percent of all homes purchased in 2004 were second homes: investment properties or vacation homes. Mortgage data at Freddie Mac from Frank Nothaft (2005) suggest that since 1999, in the United States, mortgages for purchases of second homes have doubled as a percent of all mortgages. (Data are limited to the market conforming to Freddie Mac's mortgage securitization requirements.)

Particular examples bear out the general thesis that the boom is very strong in desirable cities and vacation spots. Consider that the Case-Shiller Indexes show that from the first quarter of 1997 to the first quarter of 2005, when nationwide real home prices went up 71 percent, real home prices rose 93 percent in Boston, the home of universities and intellectuals, and 151 percent in Los Angeles, the home of movie stars. Over this same interval, real home prices went up 137 percent in Barnstable County, Massachusetts—the elite area of Cape Cod summer homes, and 114 percent in Collier County, Florida, one of the most exquisite vacation areas in the United States and with the beautiful Ten Thousand Islands.

A "SOFT LANDING" AFTER ALL?
THE SAFETY-VALVE HYPOTHESIS

The variance across regions of home prices, relative to construction costs, has increased over this interval in the United States and is very high by world standards.

Goldman-Sachs chief economist Jan Hatzius believes this variance creates a greater safety valve in the United States: homeowners can move to lower-priced land to build their houses. Congested centers still command high prices, but the equilibrium prices in these centers tend to be lower because there is the possibility of moving elsewhere. The process takes time: businesses have to move with people, and new urban areas have to be planned and built. If he is right, then the housing boom, if it cools, may have a "slow crash" instead of a "soft landing."

Figure 33.5 shows that residential investment has tended to be high when the home price index that I constructed for 1890–2005 has been high. That conclusion makes sense: When houses seem to be a good investment, more is spent on them. This investment is essential to the process that brings home prices back down when they are high.

High prices in some cities appear to be related to local zoning restrictions that inhibit construction in those cities. Glaeser and Gyourko (2002) found that in 1990 there was virtually no correlation across metropolitan areas in land area per household and the percent of homes selling above construction costs. If deviations of home

FIGURE 33.5

Residential Investment as a Share of GDP 1929–2004 from National
Income and Product Accounts, Table 1.1.10, and Real Home Price
Index for the United States, Shiller (2005)

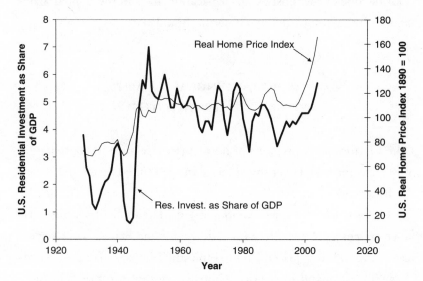

prices from construction costs across cities were due simply to scarcity of land, then cities with high deviations would economize on
land, build taller buildings, and use smaller lots.

Zoning changes can be intentionally used by local governments
to slow a potential bust in the housing market. However, zoning
changes could inadvertently accelerate the bust: if such changes make
big cities less desirable—owing, for instance, to more of the type of
high-rise apartment buildings disliked by wealthy residents—then
we may see price declines in the boom cities.

It seems likely that some neighborhoods of unique value will see
their value protected by zoning laws, even into the distant future.
The neighborhoods of Georgetown in Washington, DC, of Beacon
Hill in Boston, and of Beverly Hills in Los Angeles have great historic value, proximity to important economic centers, and absence of
vacant land. The beautiful cities of Aspen, Colorado, and Santa Fe,

New Mexico, have unique ambience that would be disrupted by high-density housing or high-rises, and voters there know that. It appears unlikely that significant numbers of homes in these choice regions will be demolished to make way for higher density housing for the foreseeable future, and perhaps not for centuries (as indeed, some centuries-old choice neighborhoods can still be found today).

But, these are rare places. Most neighborhoods are not so unique or special that they will necessarily encounter resistance from residents if an economically advantageous offer is made. Studies of zoning laws, such as that by Fischel (2004), show that we have only imperfect understanding of the political forces that shape zoning laws, and we cannot make a case that there is any fundamental force that will keep zoning very tight in the future.

Zoning laws do appear to have become gradually more effective over the course of the twentieth century, according to the research of Edward Glaeser and Joseph Gyourko (2005). But still they are local, and still there is an incentive for communities somewhere to welcome economic development. Even if the rare places can't be built up more, upward pressure on their prices can be relieved by new construction elsewhere, even far away.

When Walt Disney felt hemmed in by expensive land around his 170 acres of Disneyland in Anaheim, California, he announced in 1965 that he would build a new Disney World complex of entertainment, hotels, industrial parks, research centers, and residential communities on 27,000 acres on the other side of the country, in Orlando, Florida. The land was cheap then in this mosquito-ridden town of cowboys and citrus farmers, and it was far away from either the Atlantic Ocean or the Gulf of Mexico where tourists then flocked. Today, the glamorous Orlando area is dotted with expensive homes and commercial buildings. Luxury hotels and communities have created their own glamour and their own artificial bodies of water for swimmers and sunbathers. For the future, Florida awaits countless more development projects: in Florida there are still vast tracts of land in agricultural or other low-intensity use or just lying vacant.

When the Yale & Towne lock company decided in 1959 to shut down forever its manufacturing operations in Stamford, Connecticut (an already-declining industrial town then called "lock city," thirty-five miles from New York City), the Stamford city planners, fearing the consequences of the loss of jobs, made an effort to redesign and rezone the city to attract businesses. Their success was phenomenal, and starting in 1973 with GTE, many corporate headquarters have moved to Stamford. The exodus from New York helped take the pressure off New York real estate prices. Today, Stamford's concerns have been transformed totally: the city leaders are worried that real estate prices have risen so high that the traditional inhabitants of that city can no longer afford to live there. The next step will likely be urban renewals in cities yet farther out from New York and business parks and planned communities in what are today either declining cities or quaint New England countryside, taking the pressure off of Stamford real estate prices and further taking pressure off of New York real estate prices.

The history of world real estate has been like this for centuries. Zoning laws have not stopped new construction, and newly valuable urban areas keep appearing. We still see the glamour areas persist indefinitely (just as the Herengracht in Amsterdam remains a glamour area today), but we will see more and more of such places appearing (just as the Herengracht is now among multitudes of new glamour places of similar value). The glamour areas are likely to be like ever-expanding and replicating mesas of value rather than ever-rising mountains of value as the conventional urban land model is often taken to suggest.

At some point, with prices high relative to construction costs in big cites, and construction proceeding quickly outside the cities, a decline seems likely to follow. Whether the landing will be hard or soft remains to be seen.

FADS CAN FADE FAST

The preceding discussion did not touch upon behavioral economics. I argued in *Irrational Exuberance* (2005) that there is substantial evidence that there is a strong psychological element to the current housing boom. Whereas the boom may continue for some time, the psychological element is likely to die away as thinking changes and current folk expectations for further price increases are lost. I argued that the current home price boom is best thought of as a social epidemic: a fad of sorts. And yet social epidemics are not even mentioned by most of those who say reassuringly that there is no reason to worry about home prices. Social epidemics can unwind sharply as psychology changes, suggesting the worrisome possibility of a rather hard landing.

WITH THE HOUSING MARKET RISKIER THAN IT SEEMS, HEDGING INSTRUMENTS ARE INVALUABLE

The outlook for home prices is not as certain as many of those reassuring economists cited at the beginning of this paper imply. The "fundamentals" that they cite in support of their confident assessments are surprisingly weak at explaining historical prices. The market for homes is a very risky place.

The recent tremendous boom in home prices shows that there are risks on the upside: people who are underexposed to real estate may miss out on a rising market. And, the historical tendency for booms to be reversed eventually shows that there are risks on the downside: people who are overexposed to real estate may suffer when prices collapse.

It is vitally important that vehicles be created to hedge these risks and to allow people to manage their exposure to the real estate market. Creating hedging vehicles that protect agents from such major risks enables them to act without the hindrance of idiosyncratic risk, and creating liquid international markets for real estate price risk achieves price discovery that allows economic decisions to be made much better.

There have been a number of efforts over the years to create hedging instruments for real estate price risk, but none of these has really caught on to date. Notably, the London Futures and Options Exchange in 1991 created UK property futures markets that were cash settled based on the Halifax hedonic home price index. There was very little trade in the market when it was created, and unfortunately exchange members reacted by fraudulently padding the volume of trade numbers to create the appearance of success. The market was shut down in scandal in a matter of months, before it had a chance to develop, and this debacle has tainted the idea of real estate futures ever since.

But one failure, and other failures or half successes, does not disprove the concept of real estate risk management. The Chicago Mercantile Exchange, under the guidance of Felix Carabello, John Labuszewski, and Sayee Srinivasan and in collaboration with the firm that Allan Weiss, Samuel Masucci, and I founded, MacroMarkets LLC, has announced plans to create futures markets for home prices in ten U.S. metropolitan areas. The price indexes will be the Case-Shiller Indexes that Karl Case and I originally developed, now produced by a team headed by David Stiff and Linda Ladner at Fiserv, Inc. The contracts will be launched April 26, 2006, and will be traded on the Globex electronic market. Futures markets have come a long way since 1991, and although past experience suggests that trading may get off to a slow start, there is a real expectation that the CME can make these markets work.

This chapter has argued that price declines are more likely than most people seem to think, but it has not pinned down exactly how likely such declines are, when such declines might occur, or how far prices might fall. A futures market will generate price discovery for this: market expectations. If the futures market in effect concludes that real estate price declines are likely, then we might see backwardation in the futures market: futures prices lower than today's cash market prices and futures prices declining with horizon. In this case, speculators who expect prices to fall less than the market expects will tend to be long the futures market. Speculators who expect prices to fall more than the market expects will tend to be short the futures market. Hedgers will take sides depending on their preexisting exposure to the real estate market. The big unknown today is just where these futures prices will be to clear the market. We will learn a lot when we see these futures-market-clearing expectations at an array of horizons, and that knowledge ought to have fundamental effects, helping to rationalize the real estate markets and the economy at large.

Expanded risk markets may lead the way to other innovations in real estate risk management. Investment banks may offer real estate index-linked notes and hedge the risk that they incur in offering them by taking a position in the futures markets. Insurance companies may expand their homeowners insurance offerings into home equity insurance, which will insure the values of homes, and then hedge the risks they incur by writing such policies using the futures market. Mortgage lenders may create new mortgage products that will protect the borrower against the possible effects of a decline in home values, and they can hedge their resulting risks using the futures market.

The presence of a futures market may further facilitate increasing the supply of homes by reducing their risk. It may weaken the impact of zoning laws, for, as Fischel (2004) argues, the ability to hedge the value of homes will reduce the incentive for urban dwellers to vote for strict zoning to reduce risks to the value of their homes.

There is a basic principle here: there really are substantial risks to the market value of homes, and so major risk management tools will be central mechanisms of our future economy. When home value risk management is finally made possible, we will see some fundamental economic transformations as a result.

REFERENCES AND FURTHER READING

Angell, Cynthia and Norman Williams. 2005. "U.S. Home Prices: Does Bust Always Follow Boom?" Washington, DC: Federal Deposit Insurance Corporation.

Bernanke, Ben S. October 20, 2005. "The Economic Outlook." Testimony before the U.S. Joint Economic Committee. http://www .whitehouse.gov/cea/econ-outlook20051020.html (accessed November 25, 2005).

Case, Karl E., Robert J. Shiller, and Allan N. Weiss. 1993. "Index-Based Futures and Options Markets in Real Estate." *Journal of Portfolio Management* (Winter): 83–92.

Eichholtz, Piet. 1997. "A Long Run House Price Index: The Herengracht Index, 1628–1973." *Real Estate Economics* 25: 175–192.

Eitrheim, Øyvind and Solveig K. Erlandsen. 2004. "House Prices in Norway 1819–1989." Norges Bank working paper no. 2004-21. *Scandinavian Economic History Review.*

Ellickson, Robert C. 1977. "Suburban Growth Controls: An Economic and Legal Analysis." *Yale Law Journal* 86 (3): 385–511.

Fischel, William, 2004. "An Economic History of Zoning and a Cure for Its Exclusionary Effects." *Urban Studies* 41 (2): 317–340.

Glaeser, Edward L. and Joseph Gyourko. March 2002. "The Impact of Zoning on Housing Affordability." Working paper no. 8835. Cambridge, MA: National Bureau of Economic Research.

———. February 2005. "Why Have Housing Prices Gone Up?" Working paper no. 11129. Cambridge, MA: National Bureau of Economic Research.

Gordon, Robert J. and Todd van Goethem. 2004. "A Century of Housing Shelter Prices: How Big Is the CPI Bias?" Unpublished paper, Northwestern University.

Grebler, Leo, David M. Blank, and Louis Winnick. 1956. *Capital Formation in Residential Real Estate.* Princeton NJ: Princeton University Press.

Himmelberg, Charles, Christopher Mayer, and Todd Sinai. September 2005. "Assessing High House Prices: Bubbles, Fundamentals and

Misperceptions." Unpublished paper, Federal Reserve Bank of New York.

Joint Center for Urban Studies of Harvard University. 2005. *The State of the Nation's Housing: 2005*. Cambridge MA: Joint Center for Urban Studies.

Lereah, David. 2005. *Are You Missing the Real Estate Boom? Why Home Values and Other Real Estate Investments Will Climb Through the End of the Decade—And How to Profit from Them*. New York: Currency-Doubleday.

McCarthy, Jonathan and Richard W. Peach. 2004. "Are Home Prices the Next Bubble?" *Federal Reserve Bank of New York Policy Review* (December), 10 (3): 1–17.

Nothaft, Frank E. 2005. "Investing in a Second . . . The Rise of Investor and Second Home Purchases." Special Commentary from the Office of the Chief Economist. Freddie Mac. http://www.freddiemac .com/news/finance/commentary/sp-comm_080105.html   (accessed November 25, 2005).

Romer, Christina. 1986. "Spurious Volatility in Historical Unemployment Data." *Journal of Political Economy* 94 (1): 1–37.

Shiller, Robert J. 2005. *Irrational Exuberance*, 2nd ed. Princeton, NJ: Princeton University Press.

34

The Menace of an Unchecked Housing Bubble

Dean Baker

AN UNPRECEDENTED RUN-UP in the stock market propelled the U.S. economy in the late nineties, and now an unprecedented run-up in house prices is propelling the current recovery. Like the stock bubble, the housing bubble will burst. Eventually, it must. When it does, the economy will be thrown into a severe recession, and tens of millions of homeowners, who never imagined that house prices could fall, likely will face serious hardships.

THE INCREDIBLE INCREASE IN HOUSE PRICES

The basic facts on the housing market are straightforward: Quality-adjusted house prices ordinarily follow the overall rate of inflation.

Dean Baker is the co-director of the Center for Economic and Policy Research. Dr. Baker put his money where his mouth is by selling his downtown Washington, DC, condominium in May of 2004.

FIGURE 34.1

Home Sale Prices and Rents (Inflation Adjusted)

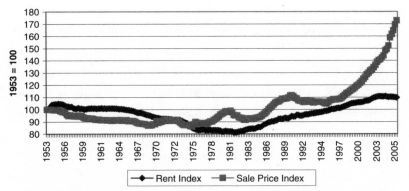

Source: BLS, BEA, and OFHEO.★

However, in the last eight years house prices have risen by almost 50 percent in real terms, as shown in figure 34.1. The run-up has not been even. In large parts of the country (most of the South and Midwest) there has been little real appreciation in house prices. In contrast, the run-ups in the bubble areas (the West Coast, the East Coast north of Washington, DC, and Florida) have been close to 80 percent in real terms.

The housing bubble spurs the economy directly by increasing home construction, renovation, and sales and indirectly by supporting consumption. The run-up in house prices has created more than $5 trillion in real estate wealth compared with a scenario where prices follow their normal trend growth path. The wealth effect from house prices is conventionally estimated at five cents on the dollar, which means that annual consumption is approximately $250 billion (2 percent of gross domestic product [GDP]) higher than it would be in the absence of the housing bubble.

★The series use the CPI rent index from 1953 to 1982 and the owner's equivalent rent index (which excludes utilities) since 1982 for the rent index. The sales price index uses the BLS CPI home price index until 1975, averages the change in the CPI index and the OFHEO House Price Index (HPI) from 1975 to 1982, and the HPI since 1982. All numbers are deflated by the GDP deflator.

FUNDAMENTALS OR A SPECULATIVE BUBBLE?

Nobody doubts that there has been a sharp increase in house prices. The question is why: is it because of fundamentals or a speculative bubble?

A quick examination of the fundamentals should remove any doubts on this issue. On the demand side, neither income nor population growth has been especially rapid. Real per capita income has grown at a respectable rate of 2 percent annually since 1997, but this is considerably slower than the 2.8 percent annual rate from 1953 to 1973, a period that saw no run-up in house prices.[1] Furthermore, the median family income has actually been falling since 2000.

Population trends also would not suggest a surge in demand for housing. The number of households grew by an average of 1.4 million a year from 1995 to 2004. This is far slower than the 2.8 million annual growth rate in the 1970s when the baby boomers were first forming their households.[2] The age distribution is also not consistent with a surge in demand for housing. The rapidly rising house prices come at a time when the baby boomers are moving out of their years of peak housing demand.[3]

There also is no obvious supply-side story. Although there are environmental restrictions on building, this is not a new phenomenon, and there is no reason to believe that these have become more restrictive in a period of Republican ascendancy. Moreover, the near record pace of housing construction the last few years indicates that these restrictions have not been an impediment to construction.

The best evidence that fundamentals are not the cause of the run-up in housing prices is the fact that there has been no comparable increase in rental prices. Although rental prices did rise somewhat more rapidly than the overall rate of inflation during the first part of the house price run-up (see figure 34.1), in the last couple of years they have been falling behind inflation. If the run-up in home sale prices were being driven by fundamentals in the supply and demand for housing, then there should be substantial price increases in both the rental and ownership markets. The fact that only the ownership market shows an unusual run-up in prices strongly supports the view that this price increase is being driven by speculation rather than fundamentals.

THE BUBBLE WILL BREAK EVENTUALLY

If housing prices are a speculative bubble, then eventually, prices will return to normal levels reflecting the value of housing services. The country has been building houses at a near record pace for the last few years, and this pace will continue as long as prices remain near their bubble peaks. At the moment, this oversupply has been absorbed by speculators and by a record vacancy rate in the rental market, but eventually excess supply will put downward pressure on sale prices (part of this story is the conversion of rental property to ownership units), which will cause speculative demand to evaporate.

Just as the supply of shares of worthless Internet companies eventually outstripped demand, the supply of housing will eventually place enough downward pressure on housing prices that the bubble levels will prove unsustainable. How fast this happens depends on how quickly mortgage interest rates rise from what are still extraordinarily low levels.

The adjustment process will not be pretty. Residential construction accounts for more than 6 percent of GDP, and construction drops off tremendously during times of recession. For example, in the mid-seventies construction dropped almost 40 percent, and in the early eighties it fell by almost 30 percent. Given the unprecedented burst of construction over the last five years, downturns of this magnitude are certainly plausible. In addition, with a correction in housing prices, the loss of bubble wealth will lead to a sharp decline in consumption. If the full $5 trillion in bubble wealth were to disappear, the implied drop in consumption would be $250 billion annually, or 2 percent of GDP.

Another consequence of the collapse of the housing bubble will be the financial fallout from an unprecedented wave of defaults. Nationwide, homeowners' ratio of debt to equity is at a near record high. This is itself a startling fact given all the equity created by recent appreciation. People have been borrowing against their homes as they have increased in value and many new homebuyers are buying homes with smaller than normal down payments. When the downturn in house prices occurs, many homeowners will have mortgages that exceed the value of their homes, a situation that is virtually certain to send default rates soaring. This will put lenders that hold large amounts of mortgage debt at risk, and possibly jeopardize the solvency of Fannie Mae and Freddie Mac, because they guarantee much of this debt. If these mortgage giants faced collapse, a government bailout (similar to the S&L bailout), involving hundreds of billions of dollars, would be virtually inevitable.

BREAKING THE BUBBLE SOONER IS BETTER THAN LATER

Given the prospect for a collapse of the housing bubble and its impact on the economy and the financial system, there is a strong case for a preemptive strike. The government cannot prevent the market from collapsing and sustaining the bubble just leads to more overbuilding, which will make the eventual collapse even worse. The government should have taken steps to prevent the bubble from ever getting this large. Having failed thus far, the best it can do at this point is to burst the bubble before it gets even larger, creating the conditions for an even bigger disaster down the road.

The best and simplest way to burst a bubble is talk. If the Fed and top Treasury officials simply made the basic data available and explained to the public about the inconsistency of current housing prices with long-term trends (as they have done with budget deficits), their warnings would almost certainly be widely reported in the media. Every real estate pusher in the country would have to deal with buyers armed with this information. Although the typical home-buyer may never understand these economic arguments, the fact that people in positions of authority are issuing warnings about future house prices would almost certainly dampen their enthusiasm for home ownership.

Whether talk would be sufficient to burst a financial bubble is an open question—it has never been tried—but since talk is cheap, there seems little reason not to use the power of information as the first weapon against a bubble. If this fails, the Fed has a second weapon: higher interest rates. Low mortgage rates have been the essential fuel for this run-up in home prices. If mortgage rates were pushed back to more normal levels (e.g., 7–8 percent), then it would almost certainly lead to a sharp reduction in housing prices.

Deliberately destroying trillions of dollars of wealth may seem like perverse policy, but it is important to recognize the context. If there is in fact an unsustainable run-up in housing prices, then the question is not *whether* prices will fall, but rather *when* prices will fall. The wealth is not really there. It is an illusion.

The economy, and tens of millions of homeowners, will certainly be better off if the fall occurs sooner rather than later. The longer the bubble persists, the more overbuilding takes place, and the more resources will eventually have to be diverted from homebuilding to some other sector of the economy. Similarly, the amount of bubble-induced debt, and subsequent defaults, will also grow larger as long as the bubble persists. The recession following a housing collapse will likely be more severe the longer the bubble persists.

Similarly, the number of homeowners who are adversely affected grows greater each month that the bubble persists. A homeowner who bought a house fifteen years ago and sees the price triple and then decrease by 40 percent will no doubt be upset over not having sold at the peak price, but he is not directly harmed by this fall. However, a family that buys its home at the bubble peak and then the value of its major financial asset falls by one-third will be badly hurt. Every year, more than 8 million people are buying new or existing homes, most at bubble-inflated prices.

In addition, tens of millions of baby boomers are approaching retirement with plans based on the assumption that the value of their home will hold steady, or even continue to rise. As a result, they are saving very little. The decision not to save because of the wealth created by the housing bubble (and previously the stock bubble) will leave this huge cohort ill-prepared for retirement, a problem that worsens each month the bubble persists.

THE FED NEEDS TO STEP UP TO THE PLATE

The Fed has taken the view that bubbles come and go and that this is not their business—a view that seems difficult to justify given the enormous consequences from the growth and collapse of financial bubbles. These consequences certainly seem much larger than the impact of modest upticks in the inflation rate, which has been the Fed's driving concern over the last two decades.

The decision to ignore financial bubbles also seems inconsistent with the Fed's past decisions, where it has made the stability of the financial system a central concern. This was its justification in stemming the 1987 stock crash and more recently when it intervened in the unraveling of the Long-Term Capital hedge fund. Because the Fed recognizes the need to act to preserve the stability of the financial system, there seems little justification for sitting on the sideline when financial bubbles that pose enormous threats dominate the economy. It is unfortunate that it might require the collapse of the housing bubble, and the enormous damage it will entail, to finally prompt some new thinking on this issue among the nation's policymakers.

NOTES

1. NIPA table 2.1, line 37.

2. Data on the number of households for 1995 to 2004 is from statistical abstract table 53, for 1970 to 1980, from U.S. Census Bureau, Mini Historical Statistics No. HS-12. Available at http://www.census.gov/statab/hist/HS-12.pdf.

3. The 35–44 age grouping spends 15.8 percent of its income on shelter, compared with 13.6 percent for the 45–54 grouping and 12.1 percent for the 55–64 grouping. (See BLS, Consumer Expenditure in 2003, table 4. Available at http://www.bls.gov/cex/csxann03.pdf.)

REFERENCES AND FURTHER READING

Baker, D. 2002. "The Run-Up in Home Prices: Is It Real or Is It Another Bubble?" Washington, DC: Center for Economic and Policy Research. http://cepr.net/publications/housing_2002_08.htm.

Baker, D. and D. Rosnick. 2005. "Will a Bursting Bubble Trouble Bernacke? The Evidence for a Housing Bubble." Washington, DC: Center for Economic and Policy Research. http://www.cepr.net/publications/housing_bubble_2005_11.pdf.

Shiller, R. 2005. *Irrational Exuberance*, 2nd ed. Princeton, NJ: Princeton University Press.

CHAPTER **35**

What to Do About Fannie and Freddie?

Edward L. Glaeser and Dwight M. Jaffee

IN MAY 2006, the Office of Federal Housing Enterprise Oversight issued a blistering report on Fannie Mae (the Federal National Mortgage Association). The opening two bullet points in the executive summary are:

- Fannie Mae senior management promoted an image of the Enterprise as one of the lowest-risk financial institutions in the world and as "best in class" in terms of risk management, financial reporting, internal control, and corporate governance. The findings in this report show that risks at Fannie Mae were greatly understated and that the image was false.

Dwight M. Jaffee is the Willis Booth Professor of Banking, Finance, and Real Estate at the Haas School of Business, University of California at Berkeley, where he serves as co-chair of the Fisher Center for Real Estate and Urban Economics. His main areas of current research include real estate finance and catastrophe insurance (terrorism and earthquakes).

- During the period covered by this report—1998 to mid-2004—Fannie Mae reported extremely smooth profit growth and hit announced targets for earnings per share precisely each quarter. Those achievements were illusions deliberately and systematically created by the Enterprise's senior management with the aid of inappropriate accounting and improper earnings management.

Perhaps a steady stream of corporate scandals has made us blasé about earnings misstatements, lavish executive compensation, and understatement of risk. In most cases, economists can at least argue that private scandals require no government intervention because their costs are born mainly by asset holders, who earned a risk premium ex ante to compensate them for just such adverse outcomes.

However, Fannie Mae and Freddie Mac (the Federal Home Loan Mortgage Corporation), hereafter F&F, are different. In this case, there is an implicit government guarantee that backs up their debt. Because the guarantee allows F&F to borrow at artificially low rates, they have borrowed and invested in retained mortgage portfolios now totaling $1.5 trillion. If they go bankrupt, it seems likely that U.S. taxpayers, not F&F bondholders, will pay the costs. The guarantee creates an externality, where the actions of F&F impose potential costs on the broader population, and this externality provides a strong rationale for government intervention.

If the externality can't be eliminated by ending the implicit guarantee, the government has two options: a quota that limits the size of F&F portfolios and a tax that charges F&F for the risks they impose on taxpayers. In this case, economics favors a quantity control over a tax, because we are surer that the optimal size of the F&F portfolio is zero than we are about the exact size of the externality, but political factors strongly favor a tax. To increase political support, the funds from a tax can be targeted toward particular forms of spending that might generate more interest group enthusiasm.

THE BASIC ECONOMICS OF FANNIE AND FREDDIE

The core business of F&F is securitizing mortgages, but over the past fifteen years both firms have created a second business line that now provides the bulk of their profits: an on-balance sheet portfolio invested in mortgage-backed and related securities. F&F borrow money at close to risk-free rates and purchase these risky securities enjoying the risk premium they pay. This is certainly good business for F&F, but the ultimate source of value is that the implicit U.S. government guarantee keeps F&F's borrowing costs artificially low.

The risk associated with mortgage portfolios comes from interest rate swings and the imperfect dynamic strategy used by F&F to hedge some of this risk. The Office of Federal Housing Enterprise Oversight (OFHEO) report claims, "Fannie Mae consistently took a significant amount of interest rate risk and, when interest rates fell in 2002, incurred billions of dollars in economic losses" (2006). Results from the OFHEO stress tests and papers by Dwight Jaffee in 2003 and 2006 confirm that F&F are systematically exposed to potentially large losses from interest rate fluctuations in either direction.

This risk imposes costs on the U.S. public through the implicit guarantee of F&F debt. Despite the attempts of the U.S. government to deny that such a guarantee exists, reasonable observers are not buying it. The Congressional Budget Office stated in 1996: "On the strength of that implied guarantee, investors continued to lend money to Fannie Mae and Freddie Mac at relatively low interest rates even during the early 1980s, when Fannie Mae was economically insolvent." The belief in an implicit guarantee is supported by both history and forward induction. In the past, the government did bail out Fannie Mae with tax breaks when it got into trouble in the early 1980s. Looking forward, a run on F&F securities could be so catastrophic that the government would feel compelled to intervene.

The market's belief in an implicit guarantee is best seen in the low interest rates paid by F&F. A standard estimate is that F&F pay forty basis points less than comparable private borrowers on their debt. Furthermore, the spread between F&F securities and Treasury bills often seems immune to the financial troubles at these institutions. In an American Enterprise Institute report, Peter Wallison (2005) notes that "despite all Fannie's troubles, the spread of its debt over treasuries . . . narrowed considerably." Financial irregularities usually cause an increase in the yields associated with debt but not in the debt of F&F, presumably because the market trusted in the implicit guarantee.

TWO APPROACHES TO THE EXTERNALITY

The existence of an implicit guarantee means that F&F's borrowing creates an externality on U.S. taxpayers. Ideally, perhaps the government could just eliminate the guarantee, but changing the guarantee means committing not to bail out F&F, and this seems impossible, at least for now. If the guarantee continues to exist, then an externality continues to exist, and there are two natural approaches to the externality. First, the government could adopt a quantity control and limit either the amount of debt that F&F can issue or the size of their retained portfolios. Second, the government could impose a Pigouvian tax on F&F based on the estimated size of the externality. To be effective the tax would need to be tied to F&F interest rate risk, for which the amount of F&F debt is a good proxy.

Following Weitzman's classic analysis of quantity controls and taxes, we think that this represents an almost ideal case for quantity controls. We are far more confident about the optimal quantity than we are about the optimal tax. As we discuss later, it is difficult to accurately assess the externality, and there is a good case that the optimal retained mortgage portfolios for F&F are close to zero. Any social gains from having this portfolio presumably come from the ability of F&F to act like a hedge fund allocating mortgage risk and funding efficiently. The OFHEO report casts doubt on the ability of

F&F to run a world-class hedge fund, and there is no lack of private competition in this area.

This approach is at least more politically realistic than ending the subsidy altogether. During the past two years, OFHEO has capped the retained portfolios of F&F in response to accounting irregularities, and there is a bill in the Senate (the Shelby bill) proposing the elimination of discretionary portfolios. However, the fact that the bill has been discussed for the last two years without significant progress illustrates the difficulties of fighting a complex, probabilistic externality. The complexity of this problem means that F&F are quite capable of muddying the waters so that many may truly believe that there is little real cause for government action. Perhaps even more important, no interest groups stand to benefit from reducing the size of the F&F portfolios, so any action pits a highly organized political lobby against diffuse consumer interests.

The second course of action is to impose a classic Pigouvian tax where F&F would be charged for the costs they impose on taxpayers. From an economic perspective, this course is complicated by the fact that measuring the externality perfectly is difficult. Politically, though, this course offers greater possibilities. Because a tax on F&F offers the possibility of large revenues—a forty basis point annual charge on the portfolios would produce over $6 billion per year—these revenues can be targeted to generate support. This may be the only politically feasible course of action, but, as we discuss next, its implementation is far from trivial.

IMPLEMENTING A PIGOUVIAN TAX

The two key issues surrounding a Pigouvian tax on F&F borrowing are the size of the tax and the ways that the money will be spent. A bill passed by the House suggests a tax of between 3.5 percent and 5 percent on F&F profits, which will be used to create an affordable housing fund. This approach is off in three ways: the dollar amounts are too small, the tax is on profits not borrowing, and the affordable housing fund seems like an invitation for egregious waste. F&F have already shown themselves to be adept in manipulating profits, and a modest tax on profits is hardly targeted in a way that will change behavior. A better policy is to target the tax directly on the externality creating behavior: F&F borrowing with an implicit guarantee.

How big should the tax on F&F debt actually be? In principle, F&F should face a tax equal to expected losses from a government bailout. Because calculating those numbers is quite difficult, an alternative approach (which should conceptually be equivalent) is to charge F&F based on the gap between their borrowing costs and the borrowing costs for comparable private sector firms. Many analysts use this borrowing cost differential, which is usually estimated at forty basis points, as the basis for their estimate of the subsidy to F&F.

Using this borrowing cost differential, the Congressional Budget Office in 2004 estimated a total subsidy to F&F of $23 billion, based on the new debt that F&F issued during that year. There is a debate about how much is passed through to borrowers and how much to shareholders, but that does not affect the appropriate Pigouvian tax. The appropriate Pigouvian tax must match the subsidy.

A reasonable Pigouvian tax might therefore be a charge of forty basis points per year on all F&F debt or just the debt that was used to fund the retained mortgage portfolio. In principle, the Pigouvian tax might be best applied to the amount of F&F's interest rate risk, but rate risk is very hard to measure directly, whereas debt provides a very good and accessible proxy measure. The tax could be either a yearly tax on all debt outstanding or imposed at the time of the debt's issuance as a function of the net present value of the subsidy over the life of the loan. In any case, the tax could raise revenue of about $6 billion (0.4 percent of $1.5 trillion) if there is no behavioral response. This quantity also almost exactly corresponds to current estimates of F&F's excess profits for 2003, that is, profits above 11 percent return on equity; Fannie Mae has not issued any earnings reports since 2003.

The congruence of numbers is reassuring. Of course, if the tax works properly, then it will raise far less than $6 billion annually because it will cause the portfolios of F&F to shrink. Even so, a tax geared toward the subsidy is likely to be much larger and better targeted than the House bill's small tax on profits.

WHAT IS TO BE DONE WITH THE MONEY?

In standard Pigouvian problems, economists don't worry about the uses of the tax revenues, but in this case the central appeal of the Pigouvian tax is that the revenues can be used to support housing programs. Housing support, after all, is why F&F were created in the first place. The relative ease with which the House passed its bill, because of support from affordable housing advocates eager for F&F dollars, can be compared with the difficulties facing the Shelby bill in the Senate.

Imposing the Pigouvian tax should generate pure welfare gains by changing F&F's behavior (a classic welfare triangle), but it will also represent a transfer from F&F shareholders and management to some other group (a classic welfare rectangle), and if the losses involved with the transfer are sufficiently large, this could overwhelm the gains from changing behavior. The key is to balance the political gains from appealing to particular interest groups with the waste involved in spending that is attractive to interest groups.

The House bill favors a fund that can be dispersed for general affordable housing causes. This seems like an approach that maximizes political support, at least among housing advocates, but places few checks against rampant waste. The history of wasteful government construction suggests that there is great scope from truly monumental waste with this sort of fund.

A better approach might target the dollars specifically toward Section VIII vouchers. The vouchers program has been relatively successful, relatively free of waste and scandal, and relatively effective at actually reaching the less advantaged. A slight twist on this proposal might use F&F dollars to create vouchers that could be used either for rental payments (like Section VIII vouchers) or for interest payments on homes. In either case, a tight income requirement would apply.

REFERENCES AND FURTHER READING

Congressional Budget Office. May 1996. "Accessing the Public Costs and Benefits of Fannie Mae and Freddie Mac." http://www.cbo.gov/ftpdocs/0xx/doc13/Franfred.pdf.

———. April 8, 2004. "Updated Estimates of Subsidies to Housing GSEs." http://www.cbo.gov/ftpdoc.cfm?index=5368&type=0&sequence=0.

Jaffee, Dwight. 2003. "The Interest Rate Risk of Fannie Mae and Freddie Mac." *Journal of Financial Services Research* 24 (1): 5–29.

———. April 2006. "Controlling the Interest Rate Risk of Fannie Mae and Freddie Mac." Policy brief no. 04. Indianapolis: Networks Financial Institute, Indiana State University. http://www.networks financialinstitute.org/pdfs/profiles/2006-PB-04_Jaffee.pdf.

Office of Federal Housing Enterprise Oversight. 2006. "Report of the Special Examination of Fannie Mae." http://www.ofheo.gov/media/pdf/FNMSPECIALEXAM.PDF.

———. "Stress Test Results, History." http://www.ofheo.gov/media/pdf/CritCapHistory63006.pdf (accessed June 30, 2006).

Passmore, Wayne. 2003. "The GSE Implicit Subsidy and the Value of Government Ambiguity." Finance and Economic Discussion Series No. 2003–64. Board of Governors of the Federal Reserve System. http://www.federalreserve.gov/pubs/feds/2003/200364/200364pap.pdf.

Wallison, Peter. 2005. "Regulating Fannie Mae and Freddie Mac: Now It Gets Serious." American Enterprise Institute. http://www.aei.org/publications/pubID.23187/pub_detail.asp.

Weitzman, M. L. 1974. "Prices vs. Quantities." *Review of Economic Studies* 41 (4): 477–491.

———. 1978. "Optimal Rewards for Economic Regulation." *American Economic Review* 68 (4): 683–691.

Index

305

ALONG THE INFINITE SEA

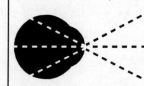

This Large Print Book carries the
Seal of Approval of N.A.V.H.

ALONG THE INFINITE SEA

BEATRIZ WILLIAMS

THORNDIKE PRESS

A part of Gale, Cengage Learning

GALE
CENGAGE Learning·

Farmington Hills, Mich • San Francisco • New York • Waterville, Maine
Meriden, Conn • Mason, Ohio • Chicago

GALE
CENGAGE Learning®

LIBRARY OF CONGRESS CATALOGING-IN-PUBLICATION DATA

Names: Williams, Beatriz.
Title: Along the infinite sea / by Beatriz Williams.
Description: Large print edition. | Waterville, Maine : Thorndike Press, 2016. | ©2015 | Series: Thorndike Press large print core
Identifiers: LCCN 2015040072| ISBN 9781410481894 (hardcover) | ISBN 1410481891 (hardcover)
Subjects: LCSH: Large type books. | GSAFD: Romantic suspense fiction.
Classification: LCC PS3623.I55643 A79 2016 | DDC 813/.6—dc23
LC record available at http://lccn.loc.gov/2015040072

Published in 2016 by arrangement with G. P. Putnam's Sons, an imprint of Penguin Publishing Group, a division of Penguin Random House LLC

Printed in Mexico
1 2 3 4 5 6 7 20 19 18 17 16

To those who escaped in time
and those who did not
and those who risked their lives to help

■ ■ ■ ■

OVERTURE

■ ■ ■ ■

"To see all without looking; to hear all without listening."

CÉSAR RITZ
King of Hoteliers, Hotelier of Kings

ANNABELLE

PARIS 1937

All you really need to know about the Paris Ritz is this: by the middle of 1937, Coco Chanel was living in a handsome suite on the third floor, and the bartender — an intuitive mixologist named Frank Meier — had invented the Bloody Mary sixteen summers earlier to cure a Hemingway hangover.

Mind you, when I arrived at Nick Greenwald's farewell party on that hot July night, I wasn't altogether aware of this history. I didn't run with the Ritz crowd. Mosquitoes, my husband called them. And maybe I should have listened to my husband. Maybe no good could come from visiting the bar at the Paris Ritz; maybe you were doomed to commit some frivolous and irresponsible act, maybe you were doomed to hover around dangerously until you had drawn the blood from another human being or else had your own blood drawn instead.

But Johann — my husband — wasn't around that night. I tiptoed in through the unfashionable Place Vendôme entrance on

9

my brother's arm instead, since Johann had been recalled to Berlin for an assignment of a few months that had stretched into several. In those days, you couldn't just flit back and forth between Paris and Berlin, any more than you could flit between heaven and hell; and furthermore, why would you want to? Paris had everything I needed, everything I loved, and Berlin in 1937 was no place for a liberal-minded woman nurturing a young child and an impossible rift in her marriage. I stayed defiantly in France, where you could still attend a party for a man named Greenwald, where anyone could dine where he pleased and shop and bank where he pleased, where you could sleep with anyone who suited you, and it wasn't a crime.

For the sake of everyone's good time, I suppose it was just as well that my husband remained in Berlin, since Nick Greenwald and Johann von Kleist weren't what you'd call bosom friends, for all the obvious reasons. But Nick and I were a different story. Nick and I understood each other: first, because we were both Americans living in Paris, and second, because we shared a little secret together, the kind of secret you could never, ever share with anyone else. Of all my brother's friends, Nick was the only one who didn't resent me for marrying a general in the German army. Good old Nick. He knew I'd had my reasons.

The salon was hot, and Nick was in his shirtsleeves, though he still retained his waistcoat and a neat white bow tie, the kind you needed a valet to arrange properly. He turned at the sound of my voice. "Annabelle! Here at last."

"Not so very late, am I?" I said.

We kissed, and he and Charles shook hands. Not that Charles paid the transaction much attention; he was transfixed by the black-haired beauty who lounged at Nick's side in a shimmering silver-blue dress that matched her eyes. A long cigarette dangled from her fingers. Nick turned to her and placed his hand at the small of her back. "Annabelle, Charlie. I don't think you've met Budgie Byrne. An old college friend."

We said *enchantée.* Miss Byrne took little notice. Her handshake was slender and lacked conviction. She slipped her arm through Nick's and whispered in his ear, and they shimmered off together to the bar inside a haze of expensive perfume. The back of Miss Byrne's dress swooped down almost to the point of no return, and her naked skin was like a spill of milk, kept from running over the edge by Nick's large palm.

Charles covered his cheek with his right hand — the same hand that Miss Byrne had just touched with her limp and slender fingers — and said that bastard always got the best-looking women.

I watched Nick's back disappear into the crowd, and I was about to tell Charles that he didn't need to worry, that Nick didn't really look all that happy with his companion and Charles might want to give the delectably disinterested Miss Byrne another try in an hour, but at that exact instant a voice came over my shoulder, the last voice I expected to hear at the Paris Ritz on this night in the smoldering middle of July.

"My God," it said, a little slurry. "If it isn't the baroness herself."

I thought perhaps I was hallucinating, or mistaken. It wouldn't be the first time. For the past two years, I'd heard this voice everywhere: department stores and elevators and street corners. I'd seen its owner in every possible nook, in every conceivable disguise, only to discover that the supposed encounter was only a false alarm, a collision of deluded molecules inside my own head, and the proximate cause of the leap in my blood proved to be an ordinary citizen after all. Just an everyday fellow who happened to have dark hair or a deep voice or a certain shape to the back of his neck. In the instant of revelation, I never knew whether to be relieved or disappointed. Whether to lament or hallelujah. Either way, the experience wasn't a pleasant one, at least not in the way we ordinarily experience pleasure, as a benevolent thing that massages the nerves into a

12

sensation of well-being.

Either way, I had committed a kind of adultery of the heart, hadn't I, and since I couldn't bear the thought of adultery in any form, I learned to ignore the false alarm when it rang and rang and rang. Like the good wife I was, I learned to maintain my poise during these moments of intense delusion.

So there. Instead of bolting at the slurry word *baroness,* I took my deluded molecules in hand and said: *Surely not.*

Instead of spinning like a top, I turned like a figurine on a music box, in such a way that you could almost hear the tinkling Tchaikovsky in my gears.

A man came into view, quite lifelike, quite familiar, tall and just so in his formal blacks and white points, dark hair curling into his forehead the way your lover's hair does in your wilder dreams. He was holding a lowball glass and a brown Turkish cigarette in his right hand, and he took in everything at a glance: my jewels, my extravagant dress, the exact state of my circulation.

In short, he seemed an awful lot like the genuine article.

"There you are, you old bastard," said Charles happily, and *sacré bleu,* I realized then what I already knew, that the man before me was no delusion. That the Paris Ritz was the kind of place that could conjure up anyone it wanted.

"Stefan," I said. "What a lovely surprise."

(And the big trouble was, I think I meant it.)

■ ■ ■ ■

FIRST MOVEMENT

■ ■ ■ ■

"Experience is simply the name we give
our mistakes."

OSCAR WILDE

PEPPER

1.

The Mercedes-Benz poses on the grass like a swirl of vintage black ink, like no other car in the world.

You'd never guess it to look at her, but Miss Pepper Schuyler — that woman right over there, the socialite with the golden antelope legs who's soaking up the Florida sunshine at the other end of the courtyard — knows every glamorous inch of this 1936 Special Roadster shadowing the grass. You might regard Pepper's pregnant belly protruding from her green Lilly shift (well, it's hard to ignore a belly like that, isn't it?) and the pastel Jack Rogers sandal dangling from her uppermost toe, and you think you have her pegged. Admit it! Lush young woman exudes Palm Beach class: What the hell does she know about cars?

Well, beautiful Pepper doesn't give a damn what you think about her. She never did. She's thinking about the car. She slides her gaze along the seductive S-curve of the right

17

side fender, swooping from the top of the tire to the running board below the door, like a woman's voluptuously naked leg, and her hearts beats a quarter-inch faster.

She remembers what a pain in the pert old derrière it was to repaint that glossy fender. It had been the first week of October, and the warm weather wouldn't quit. The old shed on Cape Cod stank of paint and grease, a peculiarly acrid reek that had crept right through the protective mask and into her sinuses and taken up residence, until she couldn't smell anything else, and she thought, *What the hell am I doing here? What the hell am I thinking?*

Thank God that was all over. Thank God this rare inky-black 1936 Mercedes Special Roadster is now someone else's problem, someone willing to pay Pepper three hundred thousand dollars for the privilege of keeping its body and chrome intact against the ravages of time.

The deposit has already been paid, into a special account Pepper set up in her own name. (Her own name, her own money: now, that was a glorious feeling, like setting off for Europe on an ocean liner with nothing but open blue seas ahead.) The rest will be delivered today, to the Breakers hotel where Pepper is staying, in a special-delivery envelope. Another delightful little big check made out in Pepper's name. Taken together, those

checks will solve all her problems. She'll have money for the baby, money to start everything over, money to ignore whoever needs ignoring, money to disappear if she needs to, forever and ever. She'll depend on no one. She can do whatever the hell she pleases, whatever suits Pepper Schuyler and — by corollary — Pepper Junior. She will toe nobody's line. She will fear nobody.

So the only question left in Pepper's mind, the only question that needs resolving, is the niggling Who?

Who the hell is this anonymous buyer — a woman, Pepper's auction agent said — who has the dough and the desire to lay claim to Pepper's very special Special Roadster, before it even reaches the public sales ring?

Not that Pepper cares who she is. Pepper just cares who she *isn't*. As long as this woman is a disinterested party, a person who has her own reasons for wanting this car, nothing to do with Pepper, nothing to do with the second half of the magic equation inside Pepper's belly, well, everything's just peachy keen, isn't it? Pepper will march off with her three hundred thousand dollars and never give the buyer another thought.

Pepper lifts a tanned arm and checks her watch. It's a gold Cartier, given to her by her father for her eighteenth birthday, perhaps as a subtle reminder to start arriving the hell on time, now that she was a grown-up. It didn't

19

work. The party always starts when Pepper gets there, not before, so why should she care if she arrives late or early? Still, the watch has its uses. The watch tells her it's twenty-seven minutes past twelve o'clock. They should be here any moment: Pepper's auction agent and the buyer, to inspect the car and complete the formalities. *If* they're on time, and why wouldn't they be? By all accounts, the lady's as eager to buy as Pepper is to sell.

Pepper tilts her head back and closes her eyes to the white sun. She can't get enough of it. This baby inside her must have sprung from another religion, one that worshipped the gods in the sky or gained nourishment from sunbeams. Pepper can almost feel the cells dividing in ecstasy as she points herself due upward. She can almost feel the seams strain along her green Lilly shift, the dancing monkeys stretch their arms to fit around the ambitious creature within.

Well, that makes sense, doesn't it? Like father, like child.

"Good afternoon."

Pepper bolts upright. A small and slender woman stands before her, dark-haired, dressed in navy Capri pants and a white shirt, her delicate face hidden by a pair of large dark sunglasses. It's Audrey Hepburn, or else her well-groomed Florida cousin.

"Good afternoon," Pepper says.

The woman holds out her hand. "You must

be Miss Schuyler. My name is Annabelle Dommerich. I'm the buyer. Please, don't get up."

Pepper rises anyway and takes the woman's hand. Mrs. Dommerich stands only a few inches above five feet, and Pepper is a tall girl, but for some reason they seem to meet as equals.

"I'm surprised to see you," says Pepper. "I had the impression you wanted to remain anonymous."

Mrs. Dommerich shrugs. "Oh, that's just for the newspapers. Actually, I've been hugely curious to meet you, Miss Schuyler. You're even more beautiful than your pictures. And look at you, blooming like a rose! When are you due?"

"February."

"I've always envied women like you. When I was pregnant, I looked like a beach ball with feet."

"I can't imagine that."

"It was a long time ago." Mrs. Dommerich takes off her sunglasses to reveal a pair of large and chocolaty eyes. "The car looks beautiful."

"Thank you. I had an expert helping me restore it."

"You restored it yourself?" Both eyebrows rise, so elegant. "I'm impressed."

"There was nothing else to do."

Mrs. Dommerich turns to gaze at the car,

21

shielding her brows with one hand. "And you found it in the shed on Cape Cod? Just like that, covered with dust? Untouched?"

"Yes. My sister-in-law's house. It seemed to have been abandoned there."

"Yes," says Mrs. Dommerich. "It was."

The grass prickles Pepper's feet through the gaps in her sandals. Next to her, Mrs. Dommerich stands perfectly still, like she's posing for a portrait, *Woman Transfixed in a Crisp White Shirt.* She talks like an American, in easy sentences, but there's just the slightest mysterious tilt to her accent that suggests something imported, like the Chanel perfume that colors the air next to her skin. Though that skin is remarkably fresh, lit by a kind of iridescent pearl-like substance that most women spent fruitless dollars to achieve, Pepper guesses she must be in her forties, even her late forties. It's something about her expression and her carriage, something that makes Pepper feel like an ungainly young colt, dressed like a little girl. Even considering that matronly bump that interrupts the youthful line of her figure.

At the opposite end of the courtyard, a pair of sweating men appear, dressed in businesslike wool suits above a pair of perfectly matched potbellies, neat as basketballs. One of them spots the two women and raises his hand in what Pepper's always called a golf wave.

22

"There they are," says Mrs. Dommerich. She turns back to Pepper and smiles. "I do appreciate your taking such trouble to restore her so well. How does she run?"

"Like a racehorse."

"Good. I can almost hear that roar in my ears now. There's no other sound like it, is there? Not like anything they make today."

"I wouldn't know, really. I'm not what you'd call an enthusiast."

"Really? We'll have to change that, then. I'll pick you up from your hotel at seven o'clock and we'll take her for a spin before dinner." She holds out her hand, and Pepper, astonished, can do nothing but shake it. Mrs. Dommerich's fingers are soft and strong and devoid of rings, except for a single gold band on the telling digit of her left hand, which Pepper has already noticed.

"Of course," Pepper mumbles.

Mrs. Dommerich slides her sunglasses back in place and turns away.

"Wait just a moment," says Pepper.

"Yes?"

"I'm just curious, Mrs. Dommerich. How do you already know how the engine sounds? Since it's been locked away in an old shed all these years."

"Oh, trust me, Miss Schuyler. I know everything about that car."

There's something so self-assured about her words, Pepper's skin begins to itch, and not

23

just the skin that stretches around the baby. The sensation sets off a chain reaction of alarm along the pathways of Pepper's nerves: the dingling of tiny alarm bells in her ears, the tingling in the tip of her nose.

"And just how the hell do you know that, Mrs. Dommerich? If you don't mind me asking. Why exactly would you pay all that money for this hunk of pretty metal?"

Mrs. Dommerich's face is hidden behind those sunglasses, betraying not an ounce of visible reaction to Pepper's impertinence. "Because, Miss Schuyler," she says softly, "twenty-eight years ago, I drove for my life across the German border inside that car, and I left a piece of my heart inside her. And now I think it's time to bring her home. Don't you?" She turns away again, and as she walks across the grass, she says, over her shoulder, sounding like an elegant half-European mother: "Wear a cardigan, Miss Schuyler. It's supposed to be cooler tonight, and I'd like to put the top down."

2.

At first, Pepper has no intention of obeying the summons of Annabelle Dommerich. The check is waiting for her when she calls at the front desk at the hotel, along with a handwritten telephone message that she discards after a single glance. She has the doorman call her a taxi, and she rides into town to deposit the

24

check in her account. The clerk's face is expressionless as he hands her the receipt. She withdraws a couple hundred bucks, which she tucks into her pocketbook next to her compact and her cigarettes. When she returns to the hotel, she draws herself a bubble bath and soaks for an hour, sipping from a single glass of congratulatory champagne and staring at the tiny movements disturbing the golden curve of her belly. Thank God she hasn't got any stretch marks. Coconut oil, that's what her doctor recommended, and she went out and bought five bottles.

The water turns cool. Pepper lifts her body from the tub and wraps herself in a white towel. She orders a late room-service lunch and stands on the balcony, wrapped in her towel, smoking a cigarette. She considers another glass of champagne but knows she won't go through with it. The doctor back on Cape Cod, a comely young fellow full of newfangled ideas, said to go easy on the booze. The doctor also said to go easy on the smokes, but you can't do everything your doctor says, can you? You can't give up everything, all at once, when you have already given up so much.

And for what? For a baby. *His* baby, of all things. So stupid, Pepper. You thought you were so clever and brave, you thought you had it all under control, and now look at you.

All knocked up and nowhere to go.

The beach is bright yellow and studded with sunbathers before a lazy surf. Pepper reaches to tuck in her towel and lets it fall to the tiled floor of the balcony. No one sees her. She leans against the balcony rail, naked and golden-ripe, until her cigarette burns to a tiny stump in her hand, until the bell rings with her room-service lunch.

After she eats, she sets the tray outside her door and falls into bed. She takes a long nap, over the covers, and when she wakes up she slips into a sleeveless tunic-style cocktail dress, brushes her hair, and touches up her lipstick. Before she heads for the elevator, she takes a cardigan from the drawer and slings it over her bare shoulders.

3.

But the elevator's stuck in the lobby. That was the trouble with hotels like the Breakers; there was always some Greek tycoon moving in, some sausage king from Chicago, and the whole place ground to a halt to accommodate his wife and kids and help and eighty-eight pieces of luggage. Afterward, he would tell his friends back home that the place wasn't what it was cracked up to be, and the natives sure were unfriendly.

Pepper taps her foot and checks her watch, but the elevator is having none of it. She heads for the stairs.

On the one hand, you have the luxurious appointments of the Breakers, plush carpets and mirrors designed to show you off to your best advantage. On the other hand, you have the stairwell, like an escape from Alcatraz. Pepper's spindly shoes rattle on the concrete floors; the bare incandescent bulbs appear at intervals as if to interrogate her. She has just turned the last landing, lobby escape hatch in sight, when a man comes into view, leaning against the door. He's wearing a seersucker suit — a genuine blue-striped seersucker suit, as if men actually wore them anymore — and his arms are crossed.

For an instant, Pepper thinks of a platinum starlet, sprawled naked on her bedroom floor a few years back. *Killed herself, poor bimbo,* everyone said, shaking the sorrowful old head. *Drugs, of course. A cautionary Hollywood tale.*

"Nice suit," says Pepper. "Are they making a movie out there?"

He straightens from the door and shoots his cuffs. "Miss Schuyler? Do you have a moment?"

"I don't think so. Certainly not for strangers who lurk in stairwells."

"I'm afraid I must insist."

"I'm afraid you're in my way. Do you mind stepping aside?"

In response, Captain Seersucker stretches his thick candy-stripe arm across the passage

and places a hand against the opposite wall.

"Well, well," says Pepper. "A nice beefy fellow, aren't you? How much do they hire you out for? Or do you do it just for the love of sport?"

"I'm just a friend, Miss Schuyler. A friend of a friend who wants to talk to you, that's all, nice and friendly. So you're going to have to come with me."

Pepper laughs. "You see, that's the trouble with you musclemen. Not too much in the noggin, is there?"

"Miss Schuyler —"

"Call me Pepper, Captain Seersucker. Everyone else does." She holds out her hand, and when he doesn't take it, she pats his cheek. "A big old lug, aren't you? Tell me, what do you do when the quiz shows come on the TV? Do you just stare all blank at the screen, or do you try to learn something?"

"Miss Schuyler —"

"And now you're getting angry with me. Your face is all pink. Look, I don't hold it against you. We can't all be Einstein, can we? The world needs brawn as well as brain. And the girls certainly don't mind, do they? I mean, what self-respecting woman wants a man hanging around who's smarter than she is?"

"Look here —"

"Now, just look at that jaw of yours, for example. So useful! Like a nice square piece

28

of granite. I'll bet you could crush gravel with it in your spare time."

He lifts his hand away from the wall and makes to grab her, but Pepper's been waiting for her chance, and she ducks neatly underneath his arm, pregnancy and all, and brings her knee up into his astonished crotch. He crumples like a tin can, lamenting his injured manhood in loud wails, but Pepper doesn't waste a second gloating. She throws open the door to the lobby and tells the bellboy to call a doctor, because some poor oaf in a seersucker suit just tripped on his shoelaces and fell down the stairs.

4.

"I thought you wouldn't come," says Mrs. Dommerich, as Pepper slides into the passenger seat of the glamorous Mercedes. Every head is turned toward the pair of them, but the lady doesn't seem to notice. She's wearing a wide-necked dress of midnight-blue jacquard, sleeves to the elbows and hem to the knees, extraordinarily elegant.

"I wasn't going to. But then I remembered what a bore it is, sitting around my hotel room, and I came around."

"I'm glad you did."

Mrs. Dommerich turns the ignition, and the engine roars with joy. *Cars like this, they like to be driven,* Pepper's almost-brother-in-law said, the first time they tried the engine,

29

and at the time Pepper thought he was crazy, talking about a machine as if it were a person. But now she listens to the pitch of the pistons and supposes he was probably right. Caspian usually was, at least when it came to cars.

"I guess you know how to drive this thing?" Pepper says.

"Oh, yes." Mrs. Dommerich puts the car into gear and releases the clutch. The car pops away from the curb like a hunter taking a fence. Pepper notices her own hands are a little shaky, and she places her fingers securely around the doorframe.

Just as the hotel entrance slides out of view, she spots a pair of men loitering near the door, staring as if to bore holes through the side of Pepper's head. Not locals; they're dressed all wrong. They're dressed like the man in the stairwell, like some outsider's notion of how you dressed in Palm Beach, like someone told them to wear pink madras and canvas deck shoes, and they'd fit right in.

And then they're gone.

Pepper ties her scarf around her head and says, in a remarkably calm voice, "Where are we going?"

"I thought we'd have dinner in town. Have a nice little chat. I'd like to hear a little more about how you found her. What it was like, bringing her back to life."

"Oh, it's a girl, is it? I never checked."

"Ships and automobiles, my dear. God

30

knows why."

"You know," says Pepper, drumming her fingers along the edge of the window glass, "don't take this the wrong way, but I can't help noticing that you two seem to be on awfully familiar terms, for a nice lady and a few scraps of old metal."

"I should be, shouldn't I? I paid an awful lot of money for her."

"For which I can't thank you enough."

"Well, I couldn't let her sit around in some museum. Not after all we've been through together." She pats the dashboard affectionately. "She belongs with someone who loves her."

Pepper shakes her head. "I don't get it. I don't see how you could love a car."

"Someone loved this car, to put it back together like this."

"It wasn't me. It was Caspian."

"Who's Caspian?"

Pepper opens her pocketbook and takes out her compact. "We'll just say he's a friend of my sister's, shall we? A very good friend. Anyway, he's the enthusiast. He couldn't stand watching me try to put it together myself."

"I'm eternally grateful. I suppose he knows a lot about German cars?"

"It turns out he was an army brat. They lived in Germany when he was young, right after the war, handing out retribution with

31

one hand and Hershey bars with the other."

Mrs. Dommerich swings the heavy Mercedes around a corner, on the edge of a nickel. Pepper realizes that the muscles of her abdomen are clenched, and it's nothing to do with the baby. But there's no question that Mrs. Dommerich knows how to drive this car. She drives it the way some people ride horses, as if the gears and the wheels are extensions of her own limbs. She may not be tall, but she sits so straight it doesn't matter. Her scarf flutters gracefully in the draft. She reaches for her pocketbook, which lies on the seat between them, and takes out a cigarette with one hand. "Do you mind lighting me?" she asks.

Pepper finds the lighter and brings Mrs. Dommerich's long, thin Gauloise to life.

"Thank you." She blows a stream of smoke into the wind and holds out the pack to Pepper. "Help yourself."

Pepper eyes the tempting little array. Her shredded nerves jingle in her ears. "Maybe just one. I'm supposed to be cutting back."

"I didn't start until later," Mrs. Dommerich says. "When my babies were older. We started going out more, to cocktail parties and things, and the air was so thick I thought I might as well play along. But it never became a habit, thank God. Maybe because I started so late." She takes a long drag. "Sometimes it takes me a week to go through

a single pack. It's just for the pure pleasure. It's like sex, you want to be able to take your time and enjoy it."

Pepper laughs. "That's a new one on me. I always thought the more, the merrier. Sex *and* cigarettes."

"My husband never understood, either. He smoked like a chimney, one after another, right up until the day he died."

"And when was that?"

"A year and a half ago." She checks the side mirror. "Lung cancer."

"I'm sorry."

They begin to mount the bridge to the mainland. Mrs. Dommerich seems to be concentrating on the road ahead, to the flashing lights that indicated the deck was going up. She rolls to a stop and drops the cigarette from the edge of the car. When she speaks, her voice has dropped an octave, to a rough-edged husk of itself.

"I used to try to make him stop," she says. "But he didn't seem to care."

5.

They eat at a small restaurant off Route 1. The owner recognizes Mrs. Dommerich and kisses both her cheeks. They chatter together in French for a moment, so rapidly and colloquially that Pepper can't quite follow. Mrs. Dommerich turns and introduces Pepper — *my dear friend Miss Schuyler,* she calls her —

33

and the man seizes Pepper's belly in rapture, as if she's his mistress and he's the guilty father.

"So beautiful!" he says.

"Isn't it, though." Pepper removes his hands. Since the beginning of the sixth month, Pepper's universe has parted into two worlds: people who regard her pregnancy as a kind of tumor, possibly contagious, and those who seem to think it's public property. "Whatever will your wife say when she finds out?"

"Ah, my wife." He shakes his head. "A very jealous woman. She will have my head on the carving platter."

"What a shame."

When they are settled at their table, supplied with water and crusty bread and a bottle of quietly expensive Burgundy, Mrs. Dommerich apologizes. The French are obsessed with babies, she says.

"I thought they were obsessed with sex."

"It's not such a stretch, is it?"

Pepper butters her bread and admits that it isn't.

The waiter arrives. Mrs. Dommerich orders turtle soup and sweetbreads; Pepper scans the menu and chooses mussels and canard à l'orange. When the waiter sweeps away the menus and melts into the atmosphere, a pause settles, the turning point. Pepper drinks a small sip of wine, folds her hands on the

edge of the table, and says, "Why did you ask me to dinner, Mrs. Dommerich?"

"I might as well ask why you agreed to come."

"Age before beauty," says Pepper, and Mrs. Dommerich laughs.

"That's it, right there. That's why I asked you."

"Because I'm so abominably rude?"

"Because you're so awfully interesting. As I said before, Miss Schuyler. Because I'm curious about you. It's not every young debutante who finds a vintage Mercedes in a shed at her sister's house and restores it to its former glory, only to put it up for auction in Palm Beach."

"I'm full of surprises."

"Yes, you are." She pauses. "To be perfectly honest, I wasn't going to introduce myself at all. I already knew who you were, at least by reputation."

"Yes, I've got one of those things, haven't I? I can't imagine why."

"You have. I like to keep current on gossip. A vice of mine." She smiles and sips her wine, marrying vices. "The sparky young aide in the new senator's office, perfectly bred and perfectly beautiful. They were right about that, goodness me."

Pepper shrugs. Her beauty is old news, no longer interesting even to her.

"Yes, exactly." Mrs. Dommerich nods. Her

hair is cut short, curling around her ears, a stylish frame for the heart-shaped, huge-eyed delicacy of her face. A few silver threads catch the light overhead, and she hasn't tried to hide them. "You caused a real stir, you know, when you started working in the senator's office last year. I suppose you know that. Not just that you're a walking fashion plate, but that you were good at your job. You made yourself essential to him. You had hustle. There are beautiful women everywhere, but they don't generally have hustle. When you're beautiful, it's ever so much easier to find a man to hustle for you."

"Yes, but then you're stuck, aren't you? It's his rules, not yours."

The skin twitches around Mrs. Dommerich's wide red mouth.

"True. That's what I thought about you, when I saw you. I saw you were expecting, pretty far along, and all of a sudden I understood why you fixed up my car and sold it to me for a nice, convenient fortune. I understood perfectly."

"Oh, you did, did you?" Pepper lifts her knife and examines her reflection. A single blue Schuyler eye stares back at her, turned up at the corner like the bow of an especially elegant yacht. "Then why the hell were you still curious enough to invite me out?"

The waiter arrives solemnly with the soup and the mussels. Mrs. Dommerich waits in a

36

pod of elegant impatience while he sets each dish exactly so, flourishes the pepper, asks if there will be anything else, and is dismissed. She lifts her spoon and smiles.

"Because, my dear. I can't wait to see what you do next."

6.

Pepper lights another cigarette after dinner, while Mrs. Dommerich drives the Mercedes north along the A1A. *For air,* she says. Pepper doesn't care much about air, one way or another, but she does care about those two men hanging around the entrance of the hotel before they left. She can handle one over-grown oaf in a stairwell, maybe, but two more was really too much.

So Pepper says okay, she could use some air. Let's take a little drive somewhere. She draws the smoke pleasantly into her lungs and breathes it out again. Air. To the right, the ocean ripples in and out of view, phosphorescent under a swollen November moon, and as the miles roll under the black wheels Pepper wonders if she's being kidnapped, and whether she cares. Whether it matters if Mrs. Dommerich acts for herself or for someone else.

He was going to track her down anyway, wasn't he? Sooner or later, the house always won.

Pepper used to think that *she* was the

house. She has it all: family, beauty, brains, moxie. You think you hold all the cards, and then you realize you don't. You have one single precious card, and he wants it back.

And suddenly three hundred thousand dollars doesn't seem like much security, after all. Suddenly there isn't enough money in the world.

Pepper stubs out the cigarette in the little chrome ashtray. "Where are we going, anyway?"

"Oh, there's a little headland up ahead, tremendous view of the ocean. I like to park there sometimes and watch the waves roll in."

"Sounds like a scream."

"You might try it, you know. It's good for the soul."

"I have it on good authority, Mrs. Dommerich — from a number of sources, actually — that I haven't got one. A soul, I mean."

Mrs. Dommerich laughs. They're speaking loudly, because of the draft and the immense roar of the engine. She bends around another curve, and then the car begins to slow, as if it already knows where it's going, as if it's fate. They pull off the road onto a dirt track, lined by reeds a yard high, and such is the Roadster's suspension that Pepper doesn't feel a thing.

"I'm usually coming from the north," says Mrs. Dommerich. "We have a little house by the coast, near Cocoa Beach. When we first

38

moved here from France, we wanted a quiet place where we could hide away from the world, and then of course the air-conditioning came in, and the world came to us in droves." She laughs. "But by then it didn't seem to matter. The kids loved it here too much, we couldn't sell up. As long as I could see the Atlantic, I didn't care."

The reeds part and the ocean opens up before them. Mrs. Dommerich keeps on driving until they reach the dunes, silver and black in the moonlight. Pepper smells the salt tide, the warm rot. The car rolls to a stop, and Mrs. Dommerich cuts the engine. The steady rush of water reaches Pepper's ears.

"Isn't it marvelous?" says Mrs. Dommerich.

"It's beautiful."

Mrs. Dommerich finds her pocketbook and takes out a cigarette. "We can share," she says.

"I've already reached my limit."

"If we share, it doesn't count. Halves don't count."

Pepper takes the cigarette from her fingers and examines it.

Mrs. Dommerich settles back and stares through the windshield. "Do you know what I love most about the ocean? The way the water's all connected. The bits and pieces have different names, but really it's all one vast body of salt water, all the way around the earth. It's as if we're touching Europe, or

39

Africa, or the Antarctic. If you close your eyes, you can feel it, like it's right there."

Pepper hands back the cigarette. "That's true. But I don't like to close my eyes."

"You've never made an act of faith?"

"No. I like to rely on myself."

"So I see. But you know, sometimes it's not such a bad thing. An act of faith."

Pepper snatches the cigarette and takes a drag. She blows the smoke back out into the night and says, "So what's your game?"

"My game?"

"Why are you here? Obviously you know a thing or two about me. Did *he* send you?"

"He?"

"You know who."

"Oh. The father of your baby, you mean."

"You tell me."

Mrs. Dommerich lifts her hands to the steering wheel and taps her fingers against the lacquer. "No. Nobody sent me."

Pepper tips the ash into the sand and hands back the cigarette.

"Do you believe me?" Mrs. Dommerich asks.

"I don't believe in anything, Mrs. Dommerich. Just myself. And my sisters, too, I guess, but they have their own problems. They don't need mine on top of it all."

Mrs. Dommerich spreads out her hands to examine her palms. "Then let me help instead."

40

Pepper laughs. "Oh, that's a good one. Very kind of you."

"I mean it. Why not?"

"Why not? Because you don't even know me."

"There's no law against helping strangers."

"Well, I certainly don't know a damned thing about you, except that you're rich and your husband died last year, and you have children and love the ocean. And you drove this car across Germany thirty years ago —"

"Twenty-eight."

"Twenty-eight. And even if that's all true, it's not much to go on."

"Isn't it? Marriages have been made on less knowledge. Happy ones."

That's an odd thing to say, Pepper thinks, and she hears the words echoing: *an act of faith.* Well, that explains it. Maybe Mrs. Dommerich is one of those sweet little fools who thinks the world is a pretty place to live, filled with nice people who love you, where everything turns out all right if you just smile and tap your heels together three times.

Or maybe it's all an act.

A little gust of salt wind comes off the ocean, and Pepper snuggles deeper into her cardigan. Mrs. Dommerich finishes the cigarette and smashes it out carefully into the ashtray, next to Pepper's stub from the ride up. She reaches into the glove compartment and draws out a small thermos container.

41

"Coffee?" she asks, unscrewing the cap.

"Where did you get coffee?"

"I had Jean-Louis fill it up for me before we left."

Pepper takes the small plastic cup. The coffee is strong and still hot. They sit quietly, sipping and gazing, sharing the smell of the wide Atlantic. The ocean heaves and rushes before them, unseen except for the long white crests of the rollers, picked out by the moon.

Mrs. Dommerich asks: "If I were to guess who the father is, would I be right?"

"Probably."

She nods. "I see."

Pepper laughs again. "Isn't it hilarious? Who'd have thought a girl like me could be so stupid? It isn't as if I didn't have my eyes open. I mean, I knew all the rumors, I knew I might just be playing with a live grenade."

"But you couldn't resist, could you?"

"The oldest story in the book."

The baby stirs beneath Pepper's heart, stretching out a long limb to test the strength of her abdomen. She puts her hand over the movement, a gesture of pregnancy that used to annoy her, when it was someone else's baby.

Mrs. Dommerich speaks softly. "Because he was irresistible, wasn't he? He made you think there was no other woman in the world, that this thing you shared was more sacred than law."

42

"Something like that."

Mrs. Dommerich pours out the dregs of her coffee and wipes out the cup with a handkerchief. "I'm serious, you know. It's the real reason I wanted to speak to you. To help you, if I can."

"You don't say."

Mrs. Dommerich pauses. "You know, there are all kinds of heroes in the world, Miss Schuyler, though I know you don't believe in that, either. And you're a fine girl, underneath all that cynical bluster of yours, and if this man wasn't what you hoped, I assure you there will be someone else who is."

Pepper looks out at the ocean and thinks about how wrong she is. There will never be someone else; how could there be? There will be men, of course. Pepper's no saint. But there won't be someone else. The thing about Pepper, she never makes the same mistake twice.

She folds her arms atop her belly and says, "Don't hold your breath."

Mrs. Dommerich laughs and gets out of the car. She stretches her arms up to the night sky, and the moon catches the glint in her wedding ring. "What a beautiful night, isn't it? Not too cool, after all. I can't bear the summers here, but it's just the thing to cheer me up in November."

"What's wrong with November?"

Mrs. Dommerich doesn't answer. She goes

43

around the front of the car and settles herself on the hood, tucking up her knees under her chin. After a moment, Pepper joins her, except that Pepper's belly sticks out too far for such a gamine little pose, so she removes her sandals, stretches her feet into the sand, and leans against the familiar warm hood instead.

"Are we just going to sit here forever?" Pepper asks.

Mrs. Dommerich wraps her arms around her legs and doesn't speak. Pepper wants to tap her head like an eggshell, to see what comes out. What's her story? Why the hell is she bothering with Pepper? Women don't usually bother with Pepper, and she doesn't blame them. Look what happens when you do. Pepper fertilizes her womb with your husband.

"Well?" Pepper says at last, because she's not the kind of girl who waits for you to pull yourself together. "What are you thinking about?"

Mrs. Dommerich starts, as if she's forgotten Pepper is there at all. "Oh, I'm sorry. Ancient history, really. Have you ever been to the Paris Ritz?"

Pepper toes the sand. "Once. We went to Europe one summer, when I was in college."

"Well, I was there in the summer of 1937, when the Ritz was the center of the universe. Everybody was there." She stands up and

44

dusts off her dress. "Anyway. Come along, my dear."

"Wait a second. What happened at the Ritz?"

"Like I said, it's ancient history. Water under the bridge."

"You were the one who brought it up."

Mrs. Dommerich folds her arms and stares at the ocean. Pepper's toe describes a square in the sand and tops it off with a triangular roof. She tries to recall the Ritz, but the grand hotels of Europe had all looked alike after a while. Wasn't that a shame? All that effort and expense, and in a week or two they all blurred together.

Still, she remembers a bit. She remembers glamour and a glorious long bar, a place where Pepper could do business. What kind of business had sweet, elegant Mrs. Dommerich done there?

Just as Pepper gives up, just as she reaches downward to thread her sandals back over her toes, Mrs. Dommerich turns away from the ocean, and you'd think the moon had stuck in her eyes, they're so bright.

"There was this party there," she says. "A going-away party at the Ritz for an American who was moving back to New York. It was the kind of night you never forget."

ANNABELLE
ANTIBES 1935

1.

But long before the Ritz, there was the Côte d'Azur.

My father had used the last of Mummy's money to lease his usual villa for the summer, perched on a picturesque cliff between Antibes and Cannes, and such was the lingering glamor of his face and his title that everybody came. There were rich American artists and poor English aristocrats; there was exiled Italian royalty and ambitious French bourgeoisie. To his credit, my father didn't discriminate. He welcomed them all. He gave them crumbling rooms and moderately fresh linens, cheap food and good wine, and they kept on coming in their stylish waves, smoking cigarettes and getting drunk and sleeping with one another. Someone regularly had to be saved from drowning.

Altogether it was a fascinating summer for a young lady just out of a strict convent school in the grimmest possible northwest corner of Brittany. The charcoal lash of

46

Biscay storms had been replaced by the azure sway of the Mediterranean; the ascetic nuns had been replaced by decadent Austrian dukes. And there was my brother, Charles. I adored Charles. He was four years older and terribly dashing, and for a time, when I was young, I actually thought I would never, ever get married because nobody could be as handsome as my brother, because all other men fell short.

He invited his own guests, my brother, and a few of them were here tonight. In the way of older brothers, he didn't quite worship me the way I worshipped him. I might have been a pet lamb, straying in my woolly innocence through his fields, to be shooed gently away in case of wolves. They held their own court (literally: they gathered in the tennis courts at half past eleven in the morning for hot black coffee and muscular Turkish cigarettes) and swam in their own corner of the beach, down the treacherous cliff path: naked, of course. There were no women. Charles's retreat was run along strictly fraternal lines. If anyone fancied sex, he came back to the house and stalked one or another of my father's crimson-lipped professional beauties, so I learned to stay away from the so-called library and the terrace (favored hunting grounds) between the hours of two o'clock in the afternoon and midnight, though I observed their comings and goings the way

other girls read gossip magazines.

Which is all a rather long way of explaining why I happened to be lying on the top of the garden wall, gazing quietly toward the lanterns and the female bodies in their shimmering dresses, the crisp drunk black-and-white gentlemen, on the moonless evening they brought the injured Jew to the house.

At half past ten, shortly before the Jew's arrival, I became aware of an immense heat taking shape in the air nearby. I waited for this body to carry on into the garden, or the scrubby sea lawn sloping toward the cliffs, but instead it lingered quietly, smelling of liquor and cigarettes. Without turning my head, I said, in English, "I'm sorry. Am I in your way?"

"I beg your pardon. I did not wish to disturb you." The English came without hesitation, a fluid intermingling of High German and British public schools, delivered in a thick bass voice.

I told him, without turning my head, that he hadn't. I knew how to kick away these unwanted advances from my father's accidental strays. (The nuns, remember.)

"Very good," he said, but he didn't leave.

He occupied a massive hole in the darkness behind me, and that — combined with the massive voice, the hint of dialect — suggested that this man was Herr von Kleist, an army general and Junker baron who had arrived

48

three days ago in a magnificent black Mercedes Roadster with a single steamer trunk and
no female companion. How he knew my
father, I couldn't say; not that prior acquaintance with the host was any requirement for
staying at the Villa Vanilla. (That was my
name for the house, in reference to the sandy-
pale stone with which it was built.) I had
spoken to him a few times, in the evenings
before dinner. He always sat alone, holding a
single small glass of liquor.

I rose to a sitting position and swung my
feet down from the wall. "I'll leave you to
yourself, then," I said, and I prepared to jump
down.

"No, please." He waved his hand. "Do not
stir yourself."

"I was about to leave anyway."

"No, you mistake me. I only came to see if
you were well. I saw you steal out here and
lie on the garden wall." He gestured again. "I
hope you are not unwell."

"I'm quite well, thank you."

"Then why are you here, alone?"

"Because I like to be alone."

He nodded. "Yes, of course. This is what I
thought about you, when you were playing
your cello for us the other night."

He was dressed in a precise white jacket
and tie, making him seem even larger than he
did by day, and unlike the other guests he
had no cigarette with him, no glass of some

cocktail or another to occupy his hands, though I smelled both in the air surrounding him. The moon was new, and I couldn't see his face, just the giant outline of him, the smudge of shadow against the night. But I detected a slight nervousness, a particle of anxiety lying between me and the sea. I'd seen many things at the Villa Vanilla, but I hadn't seen nervousness, and it made me curious.

"Really? Why did you think that?"

"Because —" He stopped and switched to French. "Because you are different from the others here. You are too young and new. You shouldn't be here."

"None of us should be here, really. It is a great scandal, isn't it?"

"But you particularly. Watching this." Another gesture, this time at the terrace on the other side of the wall, and the shimmering figures inside it.

"Oh, I'm used to that."

"I'm very sorry to hear that."

"Why should you be sorry? You're a part of it, aren't you? You came here willingly, unlike me, who simply lives here and can't help it. I expect you know what goes on, and why. I expect you're here for your share."

He hesitated. There was a flash of light from the house, or perhaps the driveway, and it lit the top of his head for an instant. He had an almost Scandinavian cast to him, this baron,

so large and fair. (I pictured a Viking longboat invading some corner of Prussia, generations ago.) His hair was short and bristling and the palest possible shade of blond; his eyes were the color of Arctic sea ice. I thought he was about forty, as old as the world. "May I sit down?" he asked politely.

"Of course."

I thought he would take the bench, but instead he placed his hands on the wall, about five feet down from me, and hoisted his big body atop as easily as if he were mounting a horse.

"How athletic of you," I said.

"Yes. I believe firmly in the importance of physical fitness."

"Of course you do. Did you have something important to tell me?"

He stared toward Africa. "No."

Someone laughed on the terrace behind us, a high and curdling giggle cut short by the delicate smash of crystal. Neither of us moved.

Herr von Kleist sat still on the brink of the wall. I didn't know a man that large could have such perfect control over his limbs. "My friend the prince, your father, I saw him quite by chance last spring, at the embassy in Paris. He told me that I must come to his villa this summer, that I am in need of sunshine and *amitié*. I thought perhaps he was right. I am afraid, in my inexperience, I did not guess

51

the meaning of his word *amitié.*"

"Your inexperience?" I said dubiously.

"I have never been to a place like this. Like the void left behind by an absence of imagination, which they are attempting, in their wretchedness and ignorance, to fill with vice."

"Yes, you're right. I've just been thinking exactly the same thing."

"My wife died eleven years ago. *That* is loss. That is a void left behind. But I try to fill that loss with something substantial, with work and the raising of our children."

What on earth did you say to a thing like that? I ventured: "How many children do you have?"

"Four," he said.

I waited for him to elaborate — age, sex, height, education, talents — but he did not. I stared down at the gossamer in my lap and said, "Where are they now?"

"With my sister. She was the one who insisted I go, and so I did. I regretted it the instant I walked through the door. There was a woman in the hall, a dark-haired woman, and she was smoking a cigarette and using the most unkempt language."

"Probably Mrs. Henderson. She's desperately rich and miserable. An American. She sleeps with everybody, even the servants."

"It grieves me to hear this."

"I'm afraid it's true."

"No, not that it's true. I do not give a damn

— pardon, Mademoiselle — about Mrs. Henderson. It grieves me that you know this about her. That your family would allow you under the same roof as such a woman as that."

"Oh, it's not as bad as that. My father doesn't allow me to mingle very much with his guests, except to entertain them with my cello after dinner. He doesn't know what to do with me at all, really, since I left Saint Cecilia's, and I'm too old for a governess."

"He ought to send you to live with a relative."

"I would run away. I'd return here."

"Why? You will pardon my curiosity. Why, when you are not like them?"

"Why not? I'm like a scientist, studying bugs. I find them fascinating, even if I don't mean to turn into a mosquito myself."

Herr von Kleist had placed his hands on his knees, and as large as his knees were, his hands dwarfed them. "Mosquitoes. Very good," he said gravely. "Yes, this is exactly what I imagined about you, when I saw you lying on the garden wall just now, observing the mosquitoes."

We had switched back into English at some point, I couldn't remember when.

I said, "Really, you shouldn't be here. You should go home to your children."

He made another one of his sighs, weary of everything. "*You* are the one who should

leave. There is not much hope for us, but you can still be saved. This is not the place for you."

I jumped down from the wall and dusted the grit from my hands. "I'd say there's plenty of hope for you. You seem like a decent man. Anyway, this is the only place I know, other than the convent."

"Then go back to your convent."

I was about to laugh, and I realized he was serious. At least his voice was serious, and his eyes, which were sad and invisible in the darkness. "But I don't want to go back."

"No, of course you do not. You want to live. You are how old?"

"Nineteen."

He made a defeated noise and slid down from the wall. "You think I am ancient."

"No, not at all," I lied.

"I'm thirty-eight. But that does not matter." He picked my hand from my side and kissed it. "It is you who matter."

He was drunk, of course. I realized it now. He was one of those lucky fellows who held it perfectly, without slurring a single word, but he was drunk nonetheless. There was the slightest waver in his titanic frame as he stood before me, engulfing my fingers between his two leathery palms, and there was that waft of liquor I'd noticed from the beginning. Who could blame him? It took such an unlikely amount of moral resolve to remain sober at

the Villa Vanilla.

When I didn't speak, he moved his heavy head in a single nod. "Yes. It is better this way. Nothing valuable is ever gained in haste."

"Quite true," someone said, but it wasn't me. It was my brother, Charles, coming up behind me like a cat in the night, and before either of us had time to reflect on the silent surprise of his appearance, he had pried my hand from the grasp of Herr von Kleist and begged the general's forgiveness.

An urgent matter had arisen, and he needed to borrow his sister for a moment.

2.

"Borrow me?" I jogged to keep up as my brother's long legs tore the scrubby grass between the garden and the cliffs. "Are you short for poker?"

"Of course not." He yanked the cigarette stub from his mouth and tossed it on the ground, into a patch of gravel. "What the hell were you doing with that Nazi?"

"Nazi? He's a Nazi?"

"They're all Nazis now, aren't they? Pay attention, it's the cliff."

I wasn't dressed for climbing. I gathered up my skirts in one hand. We started down the path, over the lip of the cliff, and the sea crashed in my ears. I followed the flash of Charles's shoes just ahead. "What's the

hurry?" I asked.

"Just be quiet."

The last of the light from the house had dissolved, and I began to stumble in the absolute blackness of the night. I had only the faint ghostliness of Charles's white shirt — he had somehow shed his dinner jacket — to guide me, as it jerked and jumped about and nearly disappeared in the space before me. The toe of my slipper found a rock, and I staggered to the ground.

"What's the matter with you?" Charles said.

"I can't see."

He swore and fumbled in his pockets, and a second later a match struck against the edge of a box and hissed to life. "My God," I said, staring at Charles's face in the tiny yellow glow. "Is that blood?"

He touched his cheek. "Probably. Look around. Get your bearings."

I looked down the slope of the cliff, the familiar path dissolving into the oily night. "Yes. All right."

The match sizzled out against his fingers, and he dropped it into the rocks and took my hand. "Let's go. Try to keep quiet, will you?"

I knew exactly where I was now. I could picture each stone, each twist in the jagged path. Inside the grip of Charles's hand, my fingers tingled. Something was up, something extraordinary — so extraordinary, my brother was actually drawing me under the snug

56

shelter of his confidence. Like when we were children, before Mummy died, before we returned to France and went our separate ways: me to the convent, my brother to the École Normale in Paris. That was when the curtain had come down. I was no longer his co-conspirator.

But I remembered how it was. My blood remembered: racing down my limbs, racing up to my brain like a cleansing bath. *Come down to the beach, I've found something,* Charles would say, and we would run hand in hand to the gritty boulder-strewn cove near the lighthouse, where he might show me an old blue glass bottle that had washed up onshore and surely contained a coded message (it never did), or a mysterious dead fish that must — equally surely — represent an undiscovered species (also never); and once, best of all, there was a bleached white skeleton, half articulated, its grinning skull exactly the size of Charles's spread head. I had thought, *We're in trouble now, someone will find out, someone will sneak into the house and kill us, too, to eliminate the witnesses;* at the same time, I had cast about for the glimpse of wood that must be lying half hidden in the nearby sand, the treasure chest that this skeleton had guarded with his life.

Now, as I stumbled faithfully down the cliff path in Charles's wake, and my eyes so

adjusted to the darkness that I began to pick out the white tips of the waves crashing on the beach, the rocks returning the starlight, I wondered what bleached white skeleton he had found for me tonight.

And then the path fell into the sand, and Charles was tugging me through the dunes with such strength that my slippers were sucked away from my feet. We made for the point on the eastern end of the beach, where the sea curled around a finger of cliff and formed a slight cove on the other side. There was just enough shelter from the current for a small boathouse and a launch, which the guests sometimes used to ferry back and forth to the yachts in Cannes or Antibes. I saw the roof now, a gray smear in the starlight. Charles plunged straight toward it, running now. The sand flew from his feet. Just before he ducked through the doorway, he stopped and turned to me.

"You *did* say you nursed in a hospital, right? At the convent? I'm not imagining things?"

"What? Yes, every day, after —"

"Good." He took my hand and pulled me inside.

There were four of them there, Charles's friends, two of them still in their dinner jackets and waistcoats. An oil lantern sat on the warped old planks of the deck, next to the nervously bobbing launch, spreading just enough light to illuminate the fifth man in

the boathouse.

He sat slumped against the wall, and his bare chest was covered in blood. He lifted his head as I came in — the chin had been tucked into the hollow of his clavicle — and he said, in deep German-accented English, much like the voice of Herr von Kleist, only more slurred and amused: "*Thi*s is your great plan, Créouville?"

3.

But his chest wasn't injured. As I cried out and fell to my knees at his side, I saw that he was holding a thick white wad to his thigh, around which a makeshift tourniquet had already been applied, and that the white wad — a shirt, I determined — was rapidly filling with blood, like the discarded red shirts next to his knee.

"Actually, it seems to be getting better," he said.

I adjusted the tourniquet — it was too loose — and lifted away the shirt. A round wound welled instantly with blood. I said, incredulous: "But it's a —"

"Gunshot," he said.

I pressed the shirt back into the wound and called for whisky.

"I like the way you think," said the wounded man.

"It's not to drink. It's to clean the wound. How long ago did this happen?"

"About twenty minutes. Right, boys?"

There was a general murmur of agreement, and a bottle appeared next to my hand. Gin, not whisky. I lifted away the shirt. The flow of blood had already slowed. "This will sting," I said, and I tilted the bottle to allow a stream of gin on the torn flesh.

I was expecting a howl, but the man only grunted and gripped the side of the leg. "He needs a doctor, as quickly as possible," I said to the men. "Has someone telephoned Dr. Duchamps?"

There was no reply. I put my fingers under the injured man's chin and peered into his eyes. His pupils were dilated, but not severely; he met my gaze and followed me as I turned my face from one side to the other. I glanced back at Charles. "Well? Doctor? Is he on his way?"

Charles crouched next to me. "No."

"Why not?"

"Too much fuss. There's someone meeting you on the ship."

"Ship? What ship?"

The injured man said, "My ship."

"You're going with him," said Charles. "You can still drive the launch, can't you?"

"What?"

"You're the only one who can do it. The rest of us have to stay here."

"What? Why?"

"Cover," said the injured man, though his

60

gritted teeth.

I looked back down at the wound, which was now only seeping. Probably the bullet had only nicked the femoral artery, otherwise he would have been dead by now. He was a large man — not as large as Herr von Kleist, but larger than my brother — and he had plenty of blood to spare. Still, it was a close thing. My brain was sharp, but my fingers were trembling as I pressed the shirt back down. Another fraction of an inch. My God. "I don't have the slightest idea what you mean," I said, "and why not one of you perfectly able-bodied men can help me get this man to safety, but we don't have a minute to waste arguing. Give him a fresh shirt. If he can hold it to his leg himself, I can take him to his damned yacht. It *is* a yacht, isn't it?"

"Yes, Mademoiselle," the man said humbly.

"Of course it is. And if the police catch up with us, what am I to say?"

"That you know nothing about it, of course."

I took the fresh shirt from Charles's hand and replaced the old; I took the man's large limp hand and pressed it to the makeshift bandage. "I'll take the gin. Charles, you put him in the launch."

"You see?" said Charles. "I told you she was a sport."

61

4.

On the launch, I took pity on the man and gave him the bottle of gin, while I steered us around the tip of the Cap d'Antibes and west toward Cannes, where his yacht was apparently moored. He took a grateful swig and tilted his head to the stars. The lantern sat at the bottom of the boat, so as not to be visible from shore.

"You are very beautiful," he said.

"Stop. You're *not* flirting with me, please. You came three millimeters away from death just now." The draft was cool and salty; it stung my cheeks, or maybe I was only blushing.

"No, I am not flirting. But you *are* beautiful. A statement of fact."

I peered into the dark sea, seeking out the distant harbor lights, smaller than stars on the horizon. The water was calm tonight, only a hint of chop. As if God himself were watching over this man.

"Am I allowed to ask your name?" I said.

He hesitated. "Stefan."

"Stefan. Is that your real name?"

"If you call me Stefan, Mademoiselle, I will answer you."

"I see. And what sort of trouble gets a nice man shot in the middle of a night like this, so he can't see a doctor onshore? Argument at the casino? Is the other man perhaps dead?"

"No, it was not an argument in the casino."

He tilted the bottle back to his lips. I thought, I must keep him talking. He has to keep talking, to stay conscious. "And the other man?"

"Hmm. Do you really wish to know this, Mademoiselle?"

"Oh, priceless. I'm harboring a criminal fugitive."

"Do not worry about that. You will be handsomely rewarded."

"I don't want to be *rewarded*. I want you to live."

He didn't reply, and I glanced back to make sure he hadn't fainted. I wouldn't have blamed him, lighter as he was of a pint or two of good red blood. But his eyes were open, each one containing a slim gold reflection of the lantern, and they were trained on me with an expression of profound . . . something.

I was about to ask him another question, but he spoke first.

"Where did you learn to treat a wound from a gun, Mademoiselle de Créouville?"

"I've never even seen a wound from a gun. But the sisters ran a charity hospital, and the men from the village got in regular brawls. Sometimes with knives."

"The sisters? You are a nun?"

"No. I was at a convent school. I've only just escaped. Anyway, they made us all work in the charity hospital, because of Christ

tending the feet of the poor. Hold on!" We hit a series of brisk chops, the wake of some unseen vessel plowing through the night sea nearby. Stefan grunted, and when the water calmed and I could relax my attention to the wheel, I glanced back again to see that his face was quite pale.

He spoke, however, without inflection. "You have a knack for it, I think. You did not scream at the blood, as most girls would. As I think most men might."

"I have a brother. I've seen blood before."

"Ah, the dashing mademoiselle. You tend wounds. You drive a boat fearlessly through the dark. What sort of sister is this for my friend Créouville? He said nothing about you before."

"He has successfully ignored me for the past half decade, since we were sent back to France after our mother died."

"I am sorry to hear about this."

I tightened my hands on the wheel and stared ahead. The pinpricks were growing larger now, more recognizably human. I hardly ever ventured into Cannes, and certainly not by myself, but I'd passed the harbor enough to know its geography. "Where is your ship moored?" I asked.

He muttered something, and I looked back over my shoulder. His eyes were half closed, his back slumped.

"Stefan!" I said sharply.

He made a rolling motion and braced his hand on the side of the launch. His head snapped up. "So sorry. You were saying?"

I couldn't leave the wheel; I couldn't check his pulse, his skin, the state of his wound. A sliver of panic penetrated my chest: the unreality of this moment, of the warm salt wind on my face, of the starlight and the man bleeding in the stern of my father's old wooden launch. Half an hour ago, I had been lying on a garden wall. "Stefan, you've got to concentrate," I said, but I really meant myself. Annabelle, you've got to concentrate. "Stefan. Listen to me. You've got to stay awake."

His gaze came to a stop on mine. "Yes. Right you are."

"How are you feeling?"

"I am bloody miserable, Mademoiselle. My leg hurts like the devil and my head is a little sick. But at least I am bloody miserable with *you.*"

I faced the water again and turned up the throttle. "Very good. You're flirting again, that's a good sign. Now, tell me. Where is your ship moored? This side of the harbor, or the other?"

"Not the harbor. The Ile Sainte-Marguerite. The Plateau du Milieu, on the south side, between the islands."

I looked to the left, where a few lights clustered atop the thin line between black

water and blacker sky. There wasn't much on Sainte-Marguerite, only forest and the old Fort Royal. But a ship moored in the protected channel between Sainte-Marguerite and the Île Saint-Honorat — and many did moor there; it was a popular spot in the summer — would not be visible from the mainland.

"Hold on," I said, and I began a sweeping turn to the left, to round the eastern point of the island. The launch angled obediently, and Stefan caught himself on the edge. The lantern slid across the deck. He stuck out his foot to stop its progress just as the boat hit a chop and heeled. Stefan swore.

"All right?" I said.

"Yes, damn it."

I could tell from the bite in his words — or rather the lack of bite, the dissonance of the words themselves from the tone in which he said them — that he was slipping again, that he was fighting the black curtain. We had to reach this ship of his, the faster the better, and yet the faster we went the harder we hit the current. And I could not see properly. I was guided only by the pinprick lights and my own instinct for this stretch of coast.

"Just hurry," said Stefan, blurry now, and I curled around the point and straightened out, so that the Plateau de Milieu lay before me, studded with perhaps a dozen boats tugging softly at their moorings. I glanced back at

Stefan to see how he had weathered the turn.

"The western end," he told me, gripping the side of the boat hard with his left hand while his right held the wadded-up white shirt against his wound. Someone had sacrificed his dinner jacket over Stefan's shoulders, to protect that bare and bloody chest from the salt draft and the possibility of shock, and I thought I saw a few dark specks on the sleek white wool. But that was always the problem about blood. It traveled easily, like a germ, infecting its surroundings with messy promiscuity. I turned to face the sleeping vessels ahead, an impossible obstacle course of boats and mooring lines, and I thought, We have got to get that tourniquet off soon, or they will have to remove the leg.

But at least I could see a little better now, in the glow of the boat lights, and I pushed the throttle higher. The old engine opened its throat and roared. A curse floated out across the water behind us, as I zigzagged delicately around the mooring lines.

"I see you are an expert," said Stefan. "This is reassuring."

"Which one is yours?"

"You can't see it yet. Just a moment." We rounded another boat, a pretty sloop of perhaps fifty feet, and the rest of the passage opened out before us, nearly empty. Stefan said, with effort: "To the right, the last one."

"What, the great big one?" I pointed.

"Yes, Mademoiselle. The great big one."

I opened the throttle as far as it could go. We skipped across the water like a smooth, round stone, like when Charles and I were children and left to ourselves, and we would take the boat as fast as it could go and scream with joy in the briny wind, because when you were a child you didn't know that boats sometimes crashed and people sometimes drowned. That vital young men were shot and sometimes bled to death.

Stefan's yacht rose up rapidly before us, lit by a series of lights along the bow and the glow of a few portholes. It was long and elegant, a sweet beauty of a ship. The sides were painted black as far as the final row of portholes, where the white took over, like a wide neat collar around the rim, like a nun's wimple. I saw the name *Isolde* painted on the bow. "Ahoy!" I called out, when we were fifty feet away. "*Isolde* ahoy!"

"They are likely asleep," said Stefan.

I pulled back the throttle and brought the boat around. We bobbed on the water, sawing in our own wake, while I rummaged in the compartment under the wheel and brought out a small revolver.

"God in heaven," said Stefan.

"I hope it's loaded," I said, and I pointed the barrel out to sea and fired.

The sound echoed off the water and the metal side of the boat. A light flashed on in

68

one of the portholes, and a voice called out something outraged in German.

I cupped my hands around my mouth. "*Isolde* ahoy!"

"*Ja, ja!*"

"I have your owner! I have — oh, damn."

The boat pitched. I grabbed the wheel. Behind me, Stefan was moving, and I hissed at him to sit down, he was going to kill himself.

But he ignored me and waved the blood-stained white shirt above his head. He brought the other hand to his mouth and yelled out a few choice German words, words I didn't understand but comprehended perfectly, and then he crashed back down in his seat as if the final drops of life had been wrung out of him.

"Stefan!" I exclaimed. The boat was driving against the side of the ship; I steered frantically and let out the throttle a notch.

A figure appeared at the railing above, and an instant later a rope ladder unfurled down the curving side of the ship. I glanced at the slumping Stefan, whose eyes were closed, whose knee rested in a puddle of dark blood, and then back at the impossible swinging ladder, and I yelled frantically upward that someone had better get down here on the fucking double, because Stefan was about to die.

PEPPER

1.

Mrs. Dommerich leans back on her palms and stares at the moon. "Isn't it funny? The same old moon that stood above the sky when I was your age. It hasn't changed a bit."

"I don't do moons," says Pepper. "Who was this American of yours? The one having the party?"

"He was a friend. He was living in Paris at the time. A very good friend."

"What kind of friend?"

Mrs. Dommerich laughs. "Not *that* kind, I assure you. He might have been, if I hadn't already fallen in love with a friend of his." Without warning, she slides off the hood of the car to stand in the sand, staring out into the ocean. "We should be going."

"Going where?"

She doesn't answer. Unlike Pepper, she didn't follow her own advice and wear a cardigan, and her forearms are bare to the November night. She crosses them against her chest, just beneath her breasts. The mate-

70

rial falls gently from her body, and Pepper decides she isn't quite like Audrey Hepburn after all. She's slender, but she isn't skinny. There is a soft roundness to her, an inviting fullness about her breasts and hips and bottom, which she carries so gracefully on her light frame that you almost don't notice, unless you're looking for it. Unless you're a man.

She turns to Pepper. "I have an idea. Why don't you come back with me to Cocoa Beach? We have a little guest cottage in the back. You can stay there until you're ready to make some decisions. A little more private than the Breakers, don't you think?"

"Are you serious?"

"Of course. I'd love the company. To tell the truth, it's a bit lonely, now that my husband's gone and the children are grown. And you need me."

Pepper opens her mouth to say that she doesn't need anyone.

"Yes, you do," says Mrs. Dommerich, before the words come out.

"You're just nuts, do you know that?"

"No, you're nuts. You think — what? That I'm involved in some vast conspiracy to keep all this out of the public notice?" She waves her hand at Pepper's belly. "That I'm in cahoots with the great man himself?"

"I'd be crazy not to consider it."

Mrs. Dommerich narrows her eyes to

71

consider Pepper's point of view. "I suppose that's fair enough," she says. "But you're already here. You've trusted me this far."

"I haven't trusted you a bit. I'm just trying to figure out your game."

"Figure it out at my place, then." Mrs. Dommerich walks around the left fender and opens the door. "It's a hell of a lot more comfortable, for one thing. What have you got to lose?"

"My luggage. For one thing."

Mrs. Dommerich swings into her seat and starts the engine. She calls out, over the throaty roar: "We'll ring up the Breakers in the morning and have it sent over."

Pepper stands there in the beam of the headlights, arms still crossed, trying to find Mrs. Dommerich's heart-shaped face in the middle of all that glare. Mrs. Dommerich gives the horn an impatient little toot.

"All right," Pepper says at last, walking back to her door and climbing inside. The leather seat takes her in like an old friend. "After all, I don't suppose I have any choice."

Mrs. Dommerich turns the car around and starts back down the dirt track to the highway, chased by the moon.

"Honey, you always have a choice," she says. "The trick is making the right one."

2.

"I suppose you can call me Pepper now," she says, as they bounce elegantly back down through the parting in the reeds, "since I'm going to be your houseguest, and not a very good one."

Mrs. Dommerich changes gears and accelerates down the dirt track.

"You'll be a wonderful houseguest, Pepper. Better than you think. And you can call me Annabelle."

3.

They are back on the highway, roaring north under the moon. The landscape passes by, dark and anonymous. Pepper yawns in the passenger seat. "Tell me about this lover of yours."

"I thought you weren't interested in romance."

"I'm just being polite. And I don't like silence."

Annabelle shakes her head. "Tell me something. What *do* you believe in, Miss Pepper Schuyler?"

"Me? I believe in independence. I believe in calling the shots and keeping your eyes wide open. Because in the end, you know, he just wants to get into bed with you. That's what they're after. They'll kiss you in the sunset, they'll carry you upstairs, they'll gaze into your eyes like you might disappear if they

stop. They might even tell you they're in love. But the point is to seduce you."

Annabelle taps her thumbs on the steering wheel and considers this. "Do you know, though, I think I was the one who seduced him, in the end."

"Well, that's how they do it, the best of them. They make you think it was your idea."

The draft whistles around them. Pepper checks her watch. It's half past eleven o'clock, and she's getting sleepy, except that the baby is pressing on a nerve that tracks all the way down her foot and turns her toes numb. She shifts her weight from one leg to the other.

"Do you know what I think, Miss Schuyler?"

"Call me Pepper, I said."

"Is that your real name?"

"Pepper will do. But really. Tell me what you think about me, Annabelle. I'm dying to know."

"I think you really *are* a romantic. You're longing for true love with all your tough little heart. It's just that you're too beautiful, and it's made you cynical."

"That doesn't make any sense."

"Yes, it does. Any unearned gift makes you cynical, unless you're a psychopath."

"Beauty hasn't made *you* cynical."

"But I'm not beautiful. I suppose I'm attractive, and I have a few nice features. My eyes and skin. My figure, if you like your

women petite. But I was never beautiful, certainly not compared to someone like you."

"Don't sell yourself short. Look at those cheekbones of yours."

"Not like *yours*. I could hang my hat on yours. No, there were just two men in my life who thought I was beautiful, and I think they thought I was beautiful because they loved me, because they were attracted to something inside me, and not the other way around."

Pepper laughs. "Trust me, it was the other way around."

"How can you say that? You don't know either man."

"I know men."

"You think you know men, but you only know cads, because the cads are the only ones brash enough to take you on. You don't know the first thing about a man capable of a great love."

"Because there's no such thing. It's just the sex instinct, the need for reproduction, and the more attractive the man, the more women he wants to reproduce with."

"All right, Miss Schuyler. That's quite enough. You just shut that steely old mouth of yours and hear me out."

"So you're feisty, after all!"

"When I have to be. So be quiet and listen up, and you might actually learn something, my so-wise friend with the prize-winning cheekbones and the knocked-up belly." Anna-

belle taps her long fingers against the steering wheel. "In fact, I'll make you a bet."

A bet. Pepper's heart does the old flutter.

"I don't know," she says, poker-faced. "What're the stakes?"

"Stakes?"

Pepper shrugs. "It's got to be interesting, that's what my mother says. The only true crime is boredom."

Annabelle laughs. "My, my. The apple doesn't fall far. Well, then. Let's see. You're an unwed mother on the run, in need of a little extra insurance. I'll bet my black pearl necklace to your gold Cartier watch that I'll have you believing in true love by the time that baby of yours sees daylight."

"I don't know." Pepper brushes her lap. "I haven't seen this pearl necklace of yours."

"My husband gave me that necklace as a Christmas present in 1937, from the Cartier shop on rue de la Paix, because he could not find another jeweler in Paris who was skilled enough to satisfy him."

Pepper makes a few rapid calculations, carries the eight, adds a zero or two. The old heart flutters again.

"True love, you said?"

"True blue, faithful and everlasting."

"In that case," Pepper says, "you're on."

4.

Annabelle asks if there is any more coffee. Pepper reaches for the thermos and gives it a jiggle.

"Not much." She pours what's left into the plastic cup and hands it to Annabelle.

"Thank you."

"You're not getting sleepy, are you? I can always take a turn at the wheel."

"Not on your life." Annabelle hands back the empty cup. "Not that you're not perfectly capable, I'm sure. But I'd like to drive her myself."

Pepper tucks the thermos back into the glove compartment and latches the polished wooden door. "Because you have history, don't you?"

"Yes, we do." Annabelle pats the dashboard.

"I'd ask how it happened, but I'd rather stay awake."

"I can't really tell you, anyway. Too many lives involved."

"My God, what a relief. I bore so easily, you understand."

Annabelle laughs. "Do you, now? Have you ever been in love, Miss Schuyler?"

"It's Pepper, remember?"

"Pepper, then. Tell me the truth. I'm taking you home with me, so you've got to be honest." She pauses, and when Pepper doesn't speak, she adds: "Besides, it's one o'clock in the morning. No secrets after midnight."

"I don't know." Pepper looks out the side, at the shadows blurring past. "Maybe."

"Were you in love with the father of your baby, or someone else?"

"I was very deeply in lust with him, if that's what you mean."

"That's not at all what I mean, but it can be very hard to tell the difference. Do you still want him?"

Pepper's hand finds the neck of her cardigan. She thinks of the last time she saw the father of her baby, the day before she left Washington. "No. Not anymore. I'm cured."

"If you say so. We're very good at pretending, we women. And the heart is such a complicated little organ."

A light flashes in the rearview mirror, and Pepper jumps in her seat. Annabelle glances into the mirror and slows the car a fraction. The light grows larger and brighter, resolving into two headlamps, and the drone of an engine undercuts the noise of their own car, their own draft. Annabelle glances again into the mirror and says something under her breath.

Pepper's fingernails dig into the leather seat next to her leg. "What is it?" she says.

There is a flash of bright blue, followed instantly by red, and the shriek of a siren sails above their heads. Annabelle swears again — loudly enough that Pepper recognizes the curse as French — and slows the car.

"What are you doing?"

"What else can I do?"

The car drifts to the shoulder, and the siren reaches a new pitch behind them. The red and blue lights fill the air, throwing a lurid pattern on Annabelle's cheeks and neck. She brakes gently, until the car comes to a stop. The siren screams in Pepper's ears. She clenches her hands into balls of resistance against the authority of the roaring engine drawing up behind them, the unstoppable force that has found them here, of all places, in the middle of the night, on a deserted Florida highway next to the restless Atlantic. Two well-dressed women inside a car of rigid German steel.

The steel vibrates faintly. The lights and the roar increase to gigantic proportion, drenching the entire world, and then everything hurtles on to their left. The siren begins its Doppler descent, and the world goes black again, except for the flashing lights that narrow and narrow and finally disappear around a curve in the road, and the moon that replaces them.

"Holy God," says Pepper, and she opens the car door and vomits into the sand.

ANNABELLE

ISOLDE 1935

1.

The doctor arrived over the side of the boat just after I laid Stefan out on the deck and loosened the tourniquet.

"Why did you loosen this?" he demanded, dropping his bag on the deck and stripping his jacket.

"Because it had been on for well over half an hour. I wanted to save the leg."

"There is no use saving the leg if the patient bleeds to death."

At which point Stefan opened one eye and told the esteemed doctor he wanted to keep his fucking leg, and if the esteemed doctor couldn't speak with respect to the woman who had saved Stefan's life, the esteemed doctor could walk the fucking plank with a bucket of dead fish hanging around his neck to attract the sharks.

The doctor said nothing, and I assisted him right there on the deck as he dug into the hole and extracted the bullet, as he cleaned and stitched up the wound and Stefan drifted

in and out of consciousness, always waking up with a faint start and a mumbled apology, as if he had somehow betrayed us by not remaining alert while the forceps dug into his raw flesh and the antiseptic was poured over afterward.

"You are a lucky man, Silverman," said the doctor, dropping the small metal bullet into a towel, and I thought, Silverman, Stefan Silverman, that's his name, and wiped away the gathering perspiration on his broad forehead.

The doctor asked for the sutures, and I rooted through the bag and laid everything out on the towel next to Stefan's arm: sutures, needle, antiseptic. "What's your blood type, nurse?" the doctor asked as he worked, as I silently handed him each suture, and I said I was O negative, and he replied: "Good, what I hoped you would say. Can you spare a pint, do you think?" and I said I could, of course, of course. I was glowing a little, in my heart, because he had called me *nurse,* and no one had ever called me anything useful before. And because I had brought Stefan Silverman safely to his ship through the dark and the salt wind, and the doctor was efficiently fixing him, putting his leg back together again, and the ball of terror was beginning to drop away from my belly at last.

The doctor stood at last and told me that he was finished, and I should dress the wound. "Not too tight; you nurses are always

81

dressing a wound too tight. I will have to come back with the transfusion equipment. It may take an hour or two. Can you stay awake with him?"

Yes, I could.

"Then we will put him in his bed." He signaled for one of the crew, who were hovering anxiously nearby, and somehow made himself clear with gestures and a few scant words of German. Two of the men hoisted Stefan up — he was out cold by now, his dark head turned to one side — and the doctor yelled at them to be careful. He turned to me. "Don't leave his side for a second. You know what to look for, I think? Signs of shock?"

"Yes. I will watch him like a child, I promise."

2.

He *did* look like a child, lying there on his clean white bed, when I had tucked the sheets around his bare chest, and his face was so pale and peaceful I checked his pulse and his breathing every minute or so to make certain he hadn't died. I turned off the electric light overhead and kept only the small lamp burning next to his bed, just enough to see him by. His skin was smooth, only a few faint lines about the eyes, and his hair was quite dark, curling wetly around his ears and forehead. He was about my brother's age, I thought, twenty-three or -four. His lashes were long

and dark, lying against his cheek, and I wondered what color his eyes were. Stefan Silverman's eyes. When I touched his shoulder, his lids fluttered.

"Shh," I said. "Go to sleep."

He opened those eyes just long enough for me to decide that they were probably brown, but a very light brown, like a salt caramel. He tried to focus and I thought he failed, because his lids dropped again and his head turned an inch or two to the side, away from me.

But then he said, almost without moving his lips: "Stay, Mademoiselle."

I smoothed the sheets against his chest, an excuse to touch him. He smelled of gin and antiseptic. I thought, It's like waiting forever for the film to start, and then it does.

"As long as you need me," I told him.

3.

At half past eight o'clock in the morning, Stefan's mistress arrived.

Or so I assumed. I could hear a woman on the other side of the cabin door, shrill and furious like a mistress. She was remonstrating with someone in French (of course), and her opponent was speaking back to her in German. Stefan opened his eyes and stared, frowning, at the ceiling.

"I think you have a visitor," I said.

He sighed. "Can you give us a minute or two, Mademoiselle?"

"You shouldn't see anyone. You have lost so much blood. You need to rest."

"Yes, but I'm feeling better now."

I wanted to remind him that he was feeling better only because he had a pint of Annabelle de Créouville coursing through his veins. I rose to my feet — a little carefully, because a pint of blood meant a great deal more to me than it did to him — and went to the door.

The woman stopped shrilling when she saw me. She was dressed in a long and shimmering evening gown, and her hair was a little disordered. There was a diamond clip holding back a handful of once-sleek curls at her temple, and a circle of matching diamonds around her neck. Her lipstick was long gone. Her eyes flicked up and down, taking me in, exposing the line of smudged kohl on her upper lid. "And who are you?" she asked, in haughty French, though I could tell from her accent that she was English.

"His nurse."

"I must see him."

I stood back from the door. "Five minutes," I said, in my sternest ward sister voice, "and if you upset him even the smallest amount, if I hear so much as a single *word* through this door, I will open your veins and bathe in your blood."

I must have looked as if I meant it, for she ducked through the door like a frightened

rabbit, and when six minutes had passed without a single sound, I knocked briefly on the door and opened it.

Stefan lay quite still on the bed. His eyes were closed, and the woman's hand rested in his palm. She was curled in the armchair — *my* armchair, I thought fiercely — and she didn't look up when I entered. "He is so pale," she said, and her voice was rough. "I have never seen him like this. He is always so vital."

"As I said, he has lost a great deal of blood."

"May I sit with him a little longer?"

She said it humbly, the haughtiness dissolved, and when she tilted her head in my direction and accepted my gaze, I saw a track of gray kohl running down from the corner of her eye to the curve of her cheekbone. She had dark blond hair the color of honey, and it gleamed dully in the lamplight. Her gown was cut into a V so low, I could count the ribs below her breasts. I looked at Stefan's hand holding hers, and I said, "Yes, a little longer," and went back out the door and down the narrow corridor to the stern of the ship, which was pointed toward the exposed turrets of the Fort Royal on the Île Sainte-Marguerite, where the Man in the Iron Mask had spent a decade of his life in a special isolated cell, though no one ever knew who he was or why he was there. Whether he had a family who mourned him.

4.

I had sent a note for Charles with the departing doctor, in the small hours of the morning, and I expected my brother any moment to arrive on the yacht, to assure himself of Stefan's survival and to bring me home.

But lunchtime came and went, the disheveled blonde departed, and though someone brought me a tray of food, and a bowl of hot broth for Stefan, Charles never appeared.

Stefan slept. At six o'clock, a boat hailed the deck and the doctor's head popped over the side, followed by his bag. The day had been warm, and the air was still hot and laden with moisture. "How is our patient this evening?" he asked.

"Much better." I turned and led him down the hallway to Stefan's commodious stateroom. "He's slept most of the day and had a little broth." I didn't mention the woman.

"Excellent, excellent. Sleep is the best thing for him. Pulse? Temperature?"

"All normal. The pulse is slow, but not alarmingly so."

"To be expected. He is an active man. Well, well," he said, ducking through the door, "how is our intrepid hero, eh?"

Stefan was awake, propped up on his pillows. He shot the doctor the kind of look that parents send each other when children are present, and listening too closely. The doctor glanced at me, cleared his throat, and set his

bag on the end of the bed.

"Now, then," he said, "let us take a look at this little scratch of yours."

On the way back to the boat, the doctor gave me a list of instructions: sleep, food, signs of trouble. "He is quite strong, however, and I should not be surprised if he is up and about in a matter of days. I shall send over a pair of crutches. You will see that he does not overexert himself, please."

"I don't understand. I had no expectation of staying longer than a day."

The doctor stopped in his tracks and turned to me. "What's this?"

"I gave you a message, to give to my brother. Wasn't there a reply? Isn't he coming for me?"

He pushed his spectacles up his nose and blinked slowly. The sun was beginning to touch the cliffs to the west, and the orange light surrounded his hair. The deck around us was neat and shining, bleached to the color of bone, smelling of tar and sunshine. "Coming for you? Of course not. You are to care for the patient. Who else is to do it?"

"But I'll be missed," I said helplessly. "My father — You must know who I am. I can't just disappear."

The doctor turned and resumed his journey across the deck to the ladder, where his tender lay bobbing in the *Isolde*'s lee. "My dear girl, this is nothing that young Créou-

ville cannot explain. He is a clever fellow. No doubt he has already put about a suitable story."

"But I don't understand. What's going on? What sort of trouble is this?"

"I don't know what you mean," he said virtuously.

"Yes, you do. What sort of trouble gets a man shot in the night like that, everything a big secret, and what . . . what does my *brother* have to do with any of it? And why the devil are you smiling that way, like a cat?"

"Because I am astonished, Mademoiselle, and not a little filled with admiration, that you have undertaken this little adventure with no knowledge whatever of its meaning."

We had reached the ladder. I grabbed him by the arm and turned him around. "Then perhaps you might begin by explaining it to me."

He shook his head and patted my cheek. His eyes were kind, and the smile had disappeared. "I cannot, of course. But when the patient is a little more recovered, it's my professional opinion that you have every right to ask him yourself."

5.

The next day, Stefan roared for his crutches, an excellent sign, but I wouldn't let him have them. I made him eat two eggs for breakfast and a little more beef broth, and he grumbled

and ate. I told him that if he were very good and rested quietly, I would let him try out the crutches tomorrow. He glared with his salt caramel eyes and directed me to go to the *Isolde*'s library and bring him some books. He wrote down their titles on a piece of paper.

The weather was hot again today, the sun like a blister in the fierce blue sky, and every porthole was open to the cooling breeze off the water. I passed along the silent corridor to the grand staircase, a sleek modern fusion of chrome and white marble, filled with seething Mediterranean light, and the library was exactly where Stefan said it should be: the other side of the main salon.

It was locked, but Stefan had given me the key. I opened the door expecting the usual half-stocked library of the yachting class: the shelves occupied by a few token volumes and a great many valuable *objets* of a maritime theme, the furniture arranged for style instead of a comfortable hours-long submersion between a pair of cloth covers.

But the *Isolde*'s library wasn't like the rest of the ship. There was nothing sleek about it, nothing constructed out of shiny material. The walnut shelves wrapped around the walls, stuffed with books, newer ones and older ones, held in place by slim wooden rails in case of stormy seas. A sofa and a pair of armchairs dozed near the portholes, and a

small walnut desk sat on the other side, next to a cabinet that briefly interrupted the flow of shelving. I thought, Now, here is a room I might like to live in.

I looked down at the paper in my hand. Goethe, *Die Leiden des jungen Werthers;* Locke, *Some Thoughts Concerning Education.* Dumas *père, Le vicomte de Bragelonne, ou Dix ans plus tard.*

When I returned to Stefan's cabin a half hour later, he was sitting up against the pillows and staring at the porthole opposite, which was open to the breeze. The rooftops of the fort shifted in and out of the frame, nearly white in the sunshine. It was too hot for blankets, and he lay in his pajamas on the bed I had made expertly underneath him that morning, tight as a drum. "Here are your books," I said.

"Thank you."

"How are you feeling?"

"Like a bear in a cage."

"You are certainly *acting* like a bear."

He looked up from the books. "I'm sorry."

"I've had worse patients. It's good that you're a bear. Better a bear than a sick little worm."

"Poor Mademoiselle de Créouville. I understand your brother has ordered you to stay with me and nurse me back to health."

"Not in so many words." I paused. "Not in any words at all, really. He sent over a few

clothes and a toothbrush yesterday, with the doctor, but there was no note of any kind. I still haven't the faintest idea who you are, or what I'm doing here."

He frowned. "Do you need one?"

I folded my arms and sank into the armchair next to the bed. His pajamas were fine silky cotton and striped in blue, and one lapel was still folded endearingly on the inside, as if belonging to a little boy who had dressed himself too hastily. The blueness brought out the bright caramel of his eyes and, by some elusive trick, made his chest seem even sturdier than before. His color had returned, pink and new; his hair was brushed; his thick jaw was smooth and smelled of shaving soap. You would hardly have known he was hurt, except for the bulky dressing that distended one blue-striped pajama leg. "What do you think?" I said.

He reached for the pack of cigarettes on the nightstand. "You are a nurse. You see before you an injured man. You have a cabin, a change of clothes, a dozen men to serve you. What more is necessary for an obedient young lady who knows it is impertinent to ask questions?"

I opened my mouth to say something indignant, and then I saw the expression on his face as he lit the cigarette between his lips with a sharp-edged gold lighter and tossed the lighter back on the nightstand. The end

of the cigarette flared orange. I said, "You *do* realize you're at my mercy, don't you?"

"I have known that for some time, yes. Since you first walked into that miserable boathouse in your white dress and stained it with my blood."

"Oh, you're flirting again. Anyway, I returned the favor, didn't I?"

"Yes. We are now bound at the most elemental level, aren't we? I believe the ancients would say we have taken a sacred oath, and are bound together for eternity." He reached for the ashtray and placed it on the bed, next to his leg, and his eyes danced.

"If that's your strategy for conquering my virtue, you'll have to try much harder."

Stefan's face turned more serious. He placed his hand with the cigarette on the topmost book, the Goethe, nearly covering it, and said, "What I mean by all that, of course, is *thank you,* Mademoiselle. Because there are really no proper words to describe my gratitude."

I leaned forward and turned the lapel of his pajamas right side out. "Since we are now bound together for eternity," I said, "you may call me Annabelle."

6.

Of course, my full name was much longer.

I was christened Annabelle Marie-Elisabeth, Princesse de Créouville, a title

bought for me by my mother, who married Prince Edouard de Créouville with her share of the colossal fortune left to her and her sister by their father, a New England industrialist. Textiles, I believe. I never met the man who was my grandfather. My father was impoverished, as European nobility generally was, and generously happy to make the necessary bargain.

At least my mother was beautiful. Not beautiful like a film star — on a woman with less money, her beauty would be labeled *handsome* — but striking enough to set her apart from most of the debutantes that year. So she married her prince, she gave birth to Charles nine months later and me another four years after that, and then, *ooh la la,* caught her husband in bed with Peggy Guggenheim and asked for a divorce. (*But everybody's doing it,* my father protested, and my mother said, *Adultery or Peggy Guggenheim?* and my father replied, *Both.*) So that was the end of that, though in order to secure my father's cooperation in the divorce (he was Catholic and so was the marriage) my mother had to leave behind what remained of her fortune. *C'est la vie.* We moved back to America and lived in a modest house in Brookline, Massachusetts, summering with relatives in Cape Cod, until Mummy's appendix burst and it was back to France and

Saint Cecilia's on the storm-dashed Brittany coast.

"But that is medieval," said Stefan, to whom I was relating this story a week later, on a pair of deck chairs overlooking a fascinating sunset. He was still in pajamas, smoking a cigarette and drinking a dry martini; I wore a lavender sundress and sipped lemonade.

"My father's Paris apartment was hardly the place for an eleven-year-old girl," I pointed out.

"True. And I suppose I have no right to complain, having reaped the benefit of your convent education. But I hate to think of my Annabelle being imprisoned in such a bitter climate, when she is so clearly meant for sunshine and freedom. And then to have lost such a mother at such an age, and your father so clearly unworthy of this gift with which he was entrusted. It enrages me. Are you sure you won't have a drink?"

"I *have* a drink."

"I mean a real one, Annabelle. A grown-up drink."

"I don't drink when I'm on duty."

"Are you still on duty, then?" He crushed the spent cigarette into an ashtray and plucked the olive out of his martini. He handed it to me.

I popped the gin-soaked olive into my mouth. "Yes, very much."

"I am sorry to hear that. I had hoped, by now, you were staying of your own accord. Do you not enjoy these long hours on the deck of my beautiful ship, when you read to me in your charming voice, and then I return the favor by teaching you German and telling you stories until the sun sets?"

"Of course I do. But until you're wearing a dinner jacket instead of pajamas, and your crutches have been put away, you're still my patient. And then you won't need me anymore, so I'll go back home."

He finished the martini and reached for another cigarette. "Ah, Annabelle. You crush me. But you know already I have no need of a nurse. Dr. Duchamps told me so yesterday, when he removed the stitches." He tapped his leg with his cigarette. "I am nearly healed."

"He didn't tell *me* that."

"Perhaps he is a romantic fellow and wants you to stay right here with me, tending to my many needs."

Suddenly I was tired of all the flirting, all the charming innuendo that meant nothing at all. I braced my hands on the arms of the deck chair and lifted myself away.

"Where are you going?" asked Stefan.

"To get some air."

The air at the *Isolde*'s prow was no fresher than the air twenty feet away in the center of the deck — and we both knew it — but I

spread my hands out anyway and drew in a deep and briny breath. The breeze was picking up with the setting of the sun. My dress wound softly around my legs. I wasn't wearing shoes; shoes seemed pointless on the well-scrubbed deck of a yacht like this. The bow pointed west, toward the dying red sun, and to my left the water washed against the shore of the Île Saint-Honorat, a few hundred yards away.

I thought, It's time to go, Annabelle. You're falling in love.

Because how could you not fall in love with Stefan, when he was so handsome and dark-haired, so well read and well spoken and ridden with mysterious midnight bullets — the highwayman, and you the landlord's dark-eyed daughter! — and you were nursing him back to health on a yacht moored off the southern coast of France? When you had spent so many long hours on the deck of his beautiful ship, in a perfect exchange of amity, while the sun glowed above you and then fell lazily away. And it was August, and you were nineteen and had never been kissed. This thing was inevitable, it was impossible that I *shouldn't* fall in love with him.

For God's sake, what had my brother been thinking? Did he imagine I still wore pigtails? I thought of the woman who had visited Stefan that first day, who had held Stefan's hand in hers, tall and lithe and glittering. She

hadn't returned — women like her had little to do with sickrooms — but she would. How could you not return to a man like Stefan?

Time to go home, Annabelle. Wherever that was.

I closed my eyes to the last of the sun. When I turned around, Stefan's deck chair was empty.

7.

I didn't have much to pack, and when I finished it was time to bring Stefan his dinner, which I had formed the habit of doing myself. He wasn't in his room, however. After several minutes of fruitless searching, I found him in the library, with his leg propped up on the sofa.

He waved to the desk. "You can put it there."

"Oh, yes, my lord and master." I set the tray down with a little more crash than necessary.

Stefan looked up. "What was that?"

I put my hands behind my back. "I'm leaving tomorrow morning. The wound is healing well, and you're well out of danger of infection. You don't need me."

He placed his finger in the crease of the book and closed it. "What makes you think that?"

"Because the flesh has knit well, there's no sign of redness or suppuration —"

97

"No, I mean thinking that I don't need you."

I screwed my hands together. "I'm going to miss this flirting of yours."

"I am not flirting, Annabelle."

His face was serious. A Stefan without a smile could look very severe indeed; there was a spare quality to all those bones and angles, a minimum of fuss. My hands were damp; I wiped them carefully on the back of my dress, so he wouldn't see. "I've already packed," I said. "It's for the best."

He went on looking at me in his steady way, as if he were waiting for me to change my mind. Or maybe not: Maybe he was eager for me to leave, so his mistress could return. Nurse out; mistress in. The patient's progress. For everyone's good health and serenity, really.

"Well," I said. "Good night, then."

"Good night, Mademoiselle de Créouville," he said softly, and I turned and left the room before I could cry.

8.

I woke up suddenly at three o'clock in the morning and couldn't go back to sleep. The wind had changed direction, drawing the yacht around on her mooring; you started to notice these things when you'd been living on a ship for a week and a half, the subtle tugs and pulls on the architecture around

you, the various qualities of the air. My legs twitched restlessly. I rose from my bed and went out on deck.

The night was clear and dry and unnaturally warm. I had been right about the change in wind: the familiar shape of the Île Sainte-Marguerite now rose up to port, lit by a buoyant white moon. I made my way down the deck, and I had nearly reached the railing when I realized that Stefan's deck chair was still out, and Stefan was in it.

I spun around, expecting his voice to reach me, some comment rich with *entendre.* But he lay still, overflowing the chair, and in the pale glow of the moon it seemed as if his eyes were closed. I thought, I should go back to my cabin right now.

But my cabin was hot and stuffy, and while it was hot outside, here in the still Mediterranean night, at least there was moving air. I stepped carefully to the rail, making as little noise as possible, and stared down at the inviting ripples of cool water, the narrow silver path of moonlight daring me toward the jagged shore of the island.

If I were still a girl on Cape Cod, I thought, I would take that dare. If I hadn't spent seven years at a convent, learning to subdue myself, I would dive right off this ship and swim two hundred yards around the rocks and cliffs and the treacherous Pointe du Dragon to stagger ashore on the Île Sainte-Marguerite,

where France's most notorious prisoner spent a decade of his life, dreaming over the sea. I had been like that, once; I had taken dares. I had swum fearlessly into the surf. When had I evaporated into this sapless young lady, observing life, living wholly on the inside, waiting for everything to happen to me? When had I decided the risk wasn't worth the effort?

I looked back over my shoulder, at Stefan's quiet body. He wasn't wearing his pajamas, I realized. He was wearing something else, a suit, a dinner jacket. As if he were waiting to meet someone, at three o'clock in the morning, on the deck of his yacht; as if he had a glamorous appointment of some kind, and the lady was late. The blood splintered down my veins, making me dizzy, the kind of drunkenness that comes from a succession of dry martinis swallowed too quickly.

You should wake him, I thought. You should do it. You have to be kissed by someone, sometime. Why not him? Why not here and now, in the moonlight, by somebody familiar with the practice of kissing?

"Good evening," he said.

I nearly flipped over the railing, backward into the sea. "I didn't realize you were here."

"I'm here most nights. The cabin's too stuffy for me." He sat up and swung his left foot down to the deck, next to a silver bucket, glinting in the moonlight. "Join me. I have

champagne."

"At this hour?"

"Can you think of a better one?"

"I don't drink on duty."

"But you're not on duty, are you? You have tendered your resignation to me, and rather coldly at that, considering what we have shared." He rested his elbow on his left knee and considered me. I was wearing my nightgown and my dressing gown belted over it, like a Victorian maiden afraid of ravishment. My hair was loose and just touched my shoulders. "Is something the matter?" he said.

"No."

"There must be something the matter. It's not even dawn yet, and here you are, out on deck, looking as if you mean to do something dramatic."

I laughed. "Do I? I can't imagine what. I don't do dramatic things."

"Oh, no. You only wrap tourniquets around the legs of dying men —"

"You weren't dying, not quite, and anyway, I wasn't the one who put the tourniquet on you."

He waved his hand. "You carry him in a boat across the sea —"

"Across a *harbor,* a very still and familiar harbor."

"Toward an unknown destination, a yacht, and you nurse him back to health. All without

101

knowing who he is, and why he's there, and why he's been shot through the leg and nearly killed. Whether you've just committed an illegal act and are now wanted by a dozen different branches of the police."

"Am I?"

"I doubt it. Not in France, in any case."

"Well, that's a relief."

He reached into his inside jacket pocket and drew out his cigarette case. "So I've been lying here, day after day, and wondering why. Why you would do such a thing."

"You might just have asked me."

"I was afraid of your answer."

I watched him light the cigarette and replace the case and the lighter in his pocket. The smoke hovered in the still air. Stefan waved it away, observing me, waiting for me to reply.

"There's nothing to be afraid of," I said. "It's simple. My brother asked me to."

"You trust your brother like that?"

"Yes. He would never ask me to do something dishonorable."

He muttered something in German and swung himself upright.

"You should use your crutches," I said.

"I am sick of fucking crutches," he said, and then, quickly, "I beg your pardon. I find I am out of sorts tonight."

I gripped the rail as he limped toward me. "I suppose I am, too."

"Ah. Now, this is a curious thing, a very interesting thing. Why, Annabelle? Tell me."

"Surely you know already."

"I know very well why *I* am out of sorts. I am desperate to know why *you* are out of sorts."

The water slapped against the side of the ship. I counted the glittering waves, the seconds that passed. I pressed my thumbs together and said: "I don't know. Just restless, I suppose. I've been cooped up for so long. I'm used to exercise."

He leaned his elbow on the railing, a foot or so from mine. I felt his breath as he spoke. "You are bored."

"Not bored."

"Yes, you are. Admit it. You have had nothing to do except fetch and carry for a grumpy patient who does not even thank you as you deserve."

I laughed. "Yes, that's it exactly."

"There is an easy cure for your boredom. Do something unexpected."

"Such as?"

"Anything. You must have some special talent, besides nursing. Show it to me." He transferred his cigarette to his other hand and reached into his pocket. "Do you draw? I have a pen."

"I don't have any paper."

"Draw on the deck, if you like."

"I'm not going to ruin your deck. Anyway,

I'm hopeless at drawing."

"A poem, then. Write me a poem."

I was laughing, "I don't write, either. I play the cello, quite well actually, but my cello is back at the Villa Vanilla."

"The Villa Vanilla?"

"My father's house."

Stefan began to laugh, too, a handsome and hearty laugh that shivered his chest beneath his dinner jacket. "Annabelle. Am I just supposed to let you slip away?"

"Yes, you are." His hand, broad and familiar, had worked close to mine on the railing, until our fingers were almost touching. I drew my arm to my side and said, "I do have one talent."

"Then do it. Show me, Annabelle."

I reached for the sash of my dressing gown. Stefan's astonished eyes slid downward.

The bow untied easily. I let the gown slip from my shoulders and bent down to grasp the hem of my nightgown.

"Annabelle —"

I knotted the nightgown between my legs and turned to brace my hands on the railing. "Watch," I said, and I hoisted myself upward to balance the balls of my feet on the slim metal rod while the moonlight washed my skin.

"My God," Stefan said, reaching for my legs, but I was already launching myself into the free air, tucking myself into a single

104

perfect roll, uncurling myself just in time to slice into the water beneath a silent splash.

9.

"You are quite right," called Stefan, when my head bobbed at last above the surface. "That is an immense talent."

"I was club champion four years running." The water slid against my limbs, sleek and delicious.

He pointed to the side of the ship. "The ladder is over there, Mademoiselle."

"So it is."

But I didn't swim toward the ladder. I turned around and kicked my strong legs and stroked my strong arms, toward the shore of the Île Sainte-Marguerite, waiting quietly in the moonlight.

10.

I lay in the rough sand without moving, soaking up the faint warmth of yesterday's sun into my bones. I thought I had never felt so magnificent, so utterly exhausted and filled with the intense pleasurable relief that follows exhaustion. The water dried slowly on my legs and arms; my nightgown stiffened against my back. I inhaled the green briny scent of the beach, the trace of metal, the hint of eucalyptus from the island forest, and I thought, Someone should bottle this, it's too good to be true.

I didn't count the passing of minutes. I had no idea how much time had passed before I heard the rhythmic splash of oars in the water behind me.

"There you are, Mademoiselle," said Stefan. "I had some trouble to find you in the darkness."

I sat up. "You haven't rowed all the way over here!"

"Of course. What else am I to do, when Annabelle dives off my ship and swims away into the night?"

I rose to my unsteady feet and took the rope from his hand. "Let me do that."

"I assure you, I can manage."

"If your wound opens —"

"Don't be stupid." He pulled on the rope and the boat slid up the sand. I took a few steps away and sat down again. My legs were still a little wobbly, my skin still cool after the long submersion in the sea. Stefan reached into the boat and drew out the silver bucket and a pair of glasses.

"You've brought champagne?"

"What's this? Did you think I would forget the refreshment?" He sank into the gravelly sand next to me and braced the bottle between his hands. His thumbs worked expertly at the cork until it slid out with a whisper of a pop.

"You are quite mad."

"No, only a little. A little mad, especially

when I saw Annabelle's body lying there like a ghost in the moonlight, without moving." He handed me a foaming glass. "And then I thought, No, my Annabelle would never swim so far through the water and then give up when she had reached the shore. But here." He set down his own glass in the sand and shrugged his dinner jacket from his arms. "You must take this."

"I'm not that cold, really. Nearly dry."

"And how would I answer to God if Annabelle caught a chill while I still wore my jacket?" He placed it over my shoulders, picked up his glass, and clinked it against mine. "Now drink. Champagne should always be drunk ice-cold on a beach at dawn."

"Is it dawn already?"

"We are close enough."

I bent my head and sipped the champagne, and it was perfect, just as Stefan said, falling like snow into my belly. Next to me, Stefan tilted back his head and drank thirstily, and the beach was so still and flawless that I thought I could feel his throat move, his eyelids close in bliss.

"That woman," I said. "The blond woman, the one who came to visit you. Is she your mistress?"

"Yes," he said simply, readily, as if there couldn't possibly exist any prevarication between us.

"She's very beautiful."

107

"That is the way of it, I'm afraid. Only the rich deserve the fair."

I laughed. "I thought it was the brave. Only the brave deserve the fair."

"A silly romantic notion. When have you ever seen a beautiful woman with a poor man? An ugly man perhaps, or a timid one, or a stupid one, or even an unpleasant one. But never a poor one."

"Do you love her?"

"Only so much as is absolutely necessary."

I swallowed the rest of my champagne and set the glass in the sand between us. My vision swam. "I don't quite know what you mean."

"No," he said. "Of course you don't."

He lay back in the sand, and after a moment I lay back, too, a few inches away, listening to the sound of his breath. The beach was coarse, not like the sand on my father's beach; the little rocks poked into my back. Stefan's jacket brushed my jaw, enclosing me in an intimate atmosphere of tobacco and shaving soap. The moon had slipped below the horizon, and we were lit only by the stars, just as we had on the first night as we rushed through the water toward the safety of Stefan's yacht. I had known almost nothing about him then, and ten days later, having lived next to him, having spent hours at his side, having talked at endless length about an endless variety of subjects, I didn't know

108

much more.

"I love your library," I said. "You have so many lovely books."

"Yes, it is the family library, collected over many generations."

"Your *family* library? Don't you think that's risky? Keeping it all on a ship?"

"No more risky than keeping it in our house in Germany, in times like this. When a Jew is no longer even really a citizen."

I lifted my head. "You're a Jew?"

"Yes. You didn't know that?"

"I never thought about it." I laid my head back down and studied the stars. Stefan's fingers brushed my hand, and I brushed them back, and a complex and breathless moment later we were holding hands, studying the stars together.

"Tell me, Annabelle," he said. "Why have you never asked me how I came to be shot in the leg, one fine summer night on the peaceful coast of France?"

"I thought you'd tell me when you trusted me. I didn't want to ask and have you tell me it was none of my business."

"Of course it is your business. I will tell you now. The men who shot me, they were agents of the Gestapo. You know what this is?"

"Yes, I think so. A sort of secret police, isn't it? The Nazi police."

"Yes. They rather resent me, you see, because instead of waiting quietly for the next

law to be passed, the next column to be kicked out from under me, I am seeking to defend the country that I love, the real Germany, the one for which my father lost his eye and his jaw twenty years ago."

"I see."

"I will not bore you with the details of what I was doing that night. But you are in no danger from the French authorities. I want you to know that, that I have not made you some sort of fugitive. But it was necessary, you see, that the man who shot me didn't know what became of me, or who had helped me to safety."

"My brother."

"Yes, de Créouville and his friends. And you." He lifted my hand and brought it to his lips, which were warm and soft and damp with champagne.

My heart was jumping from my chest. I felt my ribs strain, trying to contain it. I opened my mouth to say something, and my tongue was so dry I could hardly shape the words.

"I'm glad," I said, "I am *proud* of my brother, that he was helping you."

"Yes, he is a good man."

"I suppose" — I swallowed — "I suppose you'll go on doing these things, whatever they are. You will go on putting yourself in this danger."

He didn't speak. We lay there in darkness, shoulders touching, hips touching, hand

110

wound around hand. I might have drifted to sleep for a moment, because I opened my eyes to find that the stars had disappeared, and the sky had turned a shade of violet so deep it was almost charcoal. Next to me, Stefan lay so still I thought he must be asleep. I didn't move. I was afraid to wake him.

I thought, I will remember this always, the smell of him, cigarettes and champagne and salt warmth; the strength of his hand around mine, the rhythm of his breath, the rough texture of sand beneath my head.

"It's almost dawn," he said softly.

"I thought you were asleep."

"I was."

The water slapped against the sand. A perimeter of color grew around the horizon, and Stefan sat up, still holding my hand. "The sun will be up soon," he said. "We can't see it yet, because of the cliffs to the east. In Venice, it is fully light."

"I haven't been to Venice."

"It is beautiful, a kind of dreamy beauty, like a painting of someone's memory. Except it smells like the devil, sometimes." He nodded at the faint violet outline of the Fort Royal, just visible above the trees. "I have been staring at that building through my porthole, every day. Thinking about the men who were imprisoned there."

"Yes, I noticed that book, when I brought it from the library. The Dumas, the one about

the Man in the Iron Mask."

"Except it wasn't really an iron mask. It was velvet black, according to those who saw him. Voltaire was the one who turned it into iron, for dramatic purposes, or so one supposes."

"Have you ever been inside?"

"No." He paused and smiled. "Would you like to go now?"

"What, now? But it isn't open yet."

"Even better. We will have the place to ourselves." He swung to his feet, a little awkwardly, and pulled me up with him. "A good thing, since you are only wearing a nightgown and my dinner jacket."

"What about your leg?" I said breathlessly.

He shrugged. "Don't worry about my leg anymore, Nurse. You are off duty, remember?"

11.

We walked slowly, because of my bare feet and Stefan's leg, and because the world around us seemed so sacred and primeval, like Eden, filling with pale new light, fragrant with pine and eucalyptus. There was a long straight *allée* leading directly to the fort, and we saw nobody else the entire way. "There are fisherman in the village," Stefan said. "They are probably setting out in their boats. And there will be a lot of tourists later in the morning and the afternoon."

"I'd rather wake up early and spend time

with the fishermen. I'd rather see the place as it really is, as it used to be lived."

"Yes, the tourists are a nuisance. Have you been to Pompeii?"

"No. I've never been to Italy at all."

"We must go there someday. You would like it very much. It is as if you have walked into an ordinary old village, except you begin to walk down the street and you see how ancient it is. There are shards of old pottery littering the ground. You can pick one up and take it with you."

"Don't they mind?"

"They only really care about the frescoes. The frescoes are astonishing, though they are not for the faint of heart."

"Are they violent?" I asked, thinking of the gladiators and the casual Roman lust for blood.

"No, they are profoundly erotic."

A bird sang at us from within a tree somewhere, a melancholy whistle. The low crunch of our footsteps echoed from the woods.

"There are also casts," Stefan said. "They found these hollows in the ash, the hardened ash, and so they had the good idea to pour plaster of Paris into these hollows, and when it dried and they chipped away the molds, there remained these exact perfect casts of the people who had died, who had been buried alive in the ash. You can see the terror in their faces. And *that,* my Annabelle, is

when you realize that this thing was real, that it actually happened, this unthinkable thing. Each cast was a living person, two thousand years ago. These casts, they are proof. They are photographs of a precise moment, the moment of expiration. They are like the resurrection of the dead."

"How awful."

"It's awful and beautiful at once. The worst was the dog, however. I could bear the sight of the people, but the dog made me weep."

"You don't mind the people dying, but you mind the animals?"

"Because the people knew what was happening to them. They knew Vesuvius was erupting, that the town was doomed. They couldn't escape, but at least they knew. The dog, he had no idea. He must have thought he was being punished."

"The people thought they were being punished, too. That the gods were punishing them."

"Yes, but we humans are all full of sin, aren't we? We know our mortal failings. We know our own culpability. This poor dog never knew what he had done wrong. Here we are."

A wall appeared to our right, behind the trees. I looked up, and the dawn had broken free at last, gilding the peaks of the fort, which had somehow, in the course of our conversation, grown into a forbidding size

and complexity. Ahead, the trees cleared to reveal a paved terrace.

"Can we go in?" I asked.

"We can try."

The sun had not quite scaled the rooftops yet, and the terrace was in full shade. We walked up the path until an entrance came into view, interrupting the rough stone of the fort walls: a wide archway beneath a modest turret. There was no door, no impediment of any kind. A patch of white sun beckoned on the other side.

"Are there any soldiers about, do you think?"

"No, the garrison was disbanded some years ago, I believe. It is now a — I don't know if there is some particular term in English — a *monument historique.* I suppose it belongs to the people of France."

"Then it's mine, because I am a person of France, after all," I said, and I walked under the archway and up the stairs to the patch of light that squeezed between the corners of two buildings.

"But you are not simply a person of France, are you?" said Stefan, coming up behind me. "You are a princess of France."

"That doesn't mean anything anymore. We're a republic. We shouldn't even have titles at all. Anyway, I'm half American. It's impossible to be a princess and speak like a Yankee."

115

"It suits you, however. Especially now, when the sun is touching your hair."

I stopped walking and turned to Stefan, who stopped, too, and returned my gaze. He was almost a foot taller than I was, and the sun had already found his hair and eyes and most of his face, and while he could sometimes look almost plain, because his bones were arranged so simply, in the full light of morning sunshine he was beautiful.

"Don't look at me like that," he said.

"Like what?"

"Like you want me to kiss you."

"But I do want you to kiss me."

Stefan shook his head. "How can you be like this? No one in the world is like you."

"I was going to say the same about you."

He lifted his hand and touched the ends of my hair, and such was the extraordinary sensitivity of my nerves that I felt the stir of each individual root. "I don't know how I am going to bear this, Annabelle," he whispered. "How am I going to survive any more?"

I didn't say anything. I didn't want to disturb the delicate balance, one way or another. I took a step back, so I was standing against the barracks wall, which was already warm with sunshine, and Stefan followed me and raised his other hand to burrow into my hair, around the curve of my skull. His gaze dropped to my lips.

"Alles ist seinen Preis wert," he said, and he

116

lowered his face and kissed me.

I held myself still as his lips touched mine, lightly at first and then deeper, until he had opened me gently to taste the skin of my mouth. I didn't know you could do that, I didn't know you could kiss on the inside. I thought it was all on the surface. He tasted like he smelled, of champagne and cigarettes, only richer and wetter, alive, and I lifted my hands, which had been pressed against the barracks wall, and curled them around his waist, because I might never have the chance to do that again, to hold Stefan's warm waist under my palms while his mouth caressed mine. He cradled the back of my head with one hand and the side of my face with the other, and he ended the kiss in a series of nibbles that trailed off somewhere on my cheekbone, and pressed his forehead against mine. I relaxed against the barracks wall and took his weight. A bird chattered from the ridgepole.

"All right," he said. "Okay. Still alive."

"I'm sorry. I don't really know how to kiss."

"Don't ever learn."

I laughed softly and held him close against my thin nightgown. The new sun burned the side of my face. I said, "I suppose your mistress wouldn't be happy to see us now."

Stefan lifted his head from mine. "As it happens, I do not give a damn what this woman thinks at the moment, and neither

should you. But come. The groundskeepers will be coming soon, and then the tourists. It will be a great scandal if we are seen."

"I don't care."

"But I do. I will not have Annabelle de Créouville caught here in her nightgown with her lover, for all the world to stare." He gave my hair a final stroke and picked up my hand. "Can you walk all the way back in your bare feet, do you think?"

"Must we? I wanted to see the rest of the fort."

"We will come back someday, if you like."

His voice was warm in my chest. I wanted him to kiss me again, but instead I followed him around the corner of the barracks to the stairs. *Your poor feet,* he said, looking down, and I said, *Your poor leg,* and he kissed my hand and said, *The lame leading the lame.*

I said, *I thought it was the blind, the blind leading the lame,* and he said, *I am not blind at all. Are you?*

No, I told him. *Not blind at all.*

There were two weather-faced men smoking on the terrace when we passed under the arch. They looked up at us and nearly dropped their cigarettes.

"Bonjour, mes amis," said Stefan cheerfully, and he bent down and lifted me into his arms and carried me the rest of the way, to hell with the wounded leg.

12.

An hour later, we were standing inside the *Isolde*'s tender, a sleek little boat with a racehorse engine, motoring across the sea to my father's villa on the other side of the Cap d'Antibes. The wind whipped Stefan's hair as he sat at the wheel, and the sun lit his skin. Against the side of the boat, the waves beat a forward rhythm, and the breeze came thick and briny.

We hardly spoke. How could you speak, after a morning like that? And yet it was only seven o'clock. The whole day still lay ahead. We rounded the point, and the Villa Vanilla came into view, white against the morning glare. Stefan brought us in expertly to the boathouse, closing the throttle so we wouldn't make too much noise.

"I will walk you up the cliff," he said. "I do not trust that path."

"But I've climbed it hundreds of times. I walked down it in the dark, the night we met."

"This I do not wish to think about."

The house was silent when we reached the top. No one would be up for hours. There was a single guilty champagne bottle sitting on the garden wall, overlooked by the servants. Stefan picked it up as we passed and then looked over at the driveway, which was just visible from the side as we approached the terrace. "My God," he said, stopping in his tracks. "Whose car is that?"

I followed his gaze and saw Herr von Kleist's swooping black Mercedes, oily-fast in the sun. "Oh, that's the general, Baron von Kleist. I'm surprised he's still here. He didn't seem to be enjoying himself."

"Von Kleist," he said.

"Do you know him?"

"A little."

We resumed walking, and when we had climbed the steps and stood by the terrace door Stefan handed me the empty champagne bottle and the small brown valise that contained my few clothes. "You see? You may tell your brother I have returned you properly dressed, with your virtue intact. I believe I deserve a knighthood, at least. The Chevalier Silverman."

"What about me? I was the one who nursed you back to health, from the brink of death."

"But you are already a princess, Mademoiselle. What further honor can be given to you?"

All at once, I was out of words. I was empty of the ability to flirt with him. I parted my lips dumbly and stood there, next to the door, staring at Stefan's chin.

His voice fell to a very low pitch, discernible only by dogs and lovers. "Listen to me, Annabelle. I will tell you something, the absolute truth. I have never in my life felt such terror as I did when I saw you lying on that beach this morning in your white night-

120

gown, surrounded by the rocks and that damned treacherous Pointe du Dragon."

"Don't be stupid," I whispered.

"I *am* stupid. I am stupid for you. I am filled with folly. But stop. I see I am alarming you. I will go back to my ship now. It is best for us both, don't you think?" He kissed my hand. I hadn't even realized he was holding it. He kissed it again and turned away.

"Wait, Stefan," I said, but he was already hurrying down the stones of the terrace, and the sound of his footsteps was so faint, I didn't even notice when it faded into the morning silence.

13.

I passed through the dining room on the way to the stairs, and instead of finding it empty, I saw Herr von Kleist sitting quietly in a chair, eating his breakfast. He looked up at me without the slightest sign of surprise.

"Good morning, Mademoiselle de Créouville," he said, pushing back his chair and unfolding his body to an enormous height.

"Good morning, Herr von Kleist." I was blushing furiously. The champagne bottle hung scandalously from one hand, the valise from the other. "I didn't expect anyone up so early."

"I am always up at this hour. May I call some breakfast for you?"

"No, thank you. I think I'll take a tray in

my room."

"We have missed you these past ten days."

"I've been staying with a friend."

"So I was told." He remained standing politely, holding his napkin in one hand, a man of the old manners. The kitchen maid walked in, heavy-eyed, holding a coffeepot, and stopped at the sight of me.

"*Bonjour,* Marie-Louise," I said.

"*Bonjour,* Mademoiselle," she whispered.

I looked back at Herr von Kleist, whose eyes were exceptionally blue in the light that flooded from the eastern windows, whose hair glinted gold like a nimbus. He was gazing at me without expression, although I had the impression of great grief hanging from his shoulders. I shifted my feet.

"Please return to your breakfast," I said, and I walked across the corner of the dining room and broke into a run, racing up the stairs to my room, hoping I would reach my window in time to see the *Isolde*'s tender cross the sea before me.

But it did not.

PEPPER

1.

Annabelle waits for her to finish, like a woman who's done this before: waited patiently for someone else to finish vomiting. When Pepper lifts her head, she hands her a crisp white handkerchief, glowing in the moon.

"Thank you," says Pepper.

"All better? Can we move on?"

"Yes."

The engine launches them back down the road. Pepper leans her head back and allows the draft to cool her face. Annabelle bends forward and switches on the radio. "That was too late for morning sickness," she observes.

"I don't get morning sickness."

"Lucky duck. Nerves, then?"

"I don't get nerves, either." She pauses. "Not without reason."

The static resolves into music. The Beatles. "Yesterday." So far away. Annabelle pauses, hand on the dial, and then lets it be. She sits back against the leather and says, "Are you

123

saying the bastard's been threatening you?"

"He's been trying to find me, and I've been making myself scarce, that's all."

"Why? He *is* the father, after all."

"Because I know what he wants." Pepper examines her fingernails. She thinks, You're an idiot, Pepper Schuyler, you're going to spill it, aren't you? You're just going to lose it right here. Her throat still burns. She says, "I didn't even tell him. He found out, I don't know how. He called me up at the hotel and yelled at me. Why couldn't I get it taken care of, he wanted to know."

"What a gentleman."

Pepper gives up on her fingernails and looks out the side. They're passing close to the ocean right now, that grand old Atlantic, toiling away faithfully under the moon. "He was very good at the chase, I'll say that. I always swore I'd never sleep with a married man. I know what everyone says about me, lock up your husbands, but the truth is I just flirt. Like a sport, like some women play bridge. And silly me, I thought he knew that. I thought we weren't taking it past first base, until we did, one night. Big victory, big glasses of champagne, big beautiful hotel suite, and before you know it, the all-star hits himself a home run right out of the park, a grand goddamned salami. Oopsy-daisy, as my sister Vivian would say."

Annabelle drives silently. She keeps one

hand on the wheel and one elbow propped on the doorframe beside her. Pepper steals a glance. Her head is tilted slightly to one side, showing off her long neck. The skin is still taut, still iridescent in the moonlight. What bargain did she make with the devil for skin like that? Whatever it is, Pepper would happily take that bargain. What was the point of an eternal soul, anyway? It just meant you spent eternity in fleecy boredom, strumming your harp. Pepper would rather have twenty good years on earth, flaunting her iridescent skin, and then oblivion.

"What are you thinking?" asks Pepper.

Annabelle raises her head and laughs, making the car swerve slightly. "Do you really want to know?"

"It beats the Beatles."

"I was thinking about when I fell in love, actually. How grateful I am for that. We were in the South of France, in the middle of August, and I was nineteen and just crazy about him. We were right by the sea. I thought I was in heaven."

"What was his name?"

She pauses. "Stefan."

The radio plays between them, the instrumentals, a low and mournful string. Someone believes in yesterday. Pepper stares at her thumbs in her lap and thinks about the night she lost her virginity. There was no sunshine, no Mediterranean, no mysterious Stefan.

There was a friend of her mother's, after a party. She had flirted with him, because flirting gave you such a rush of delicious power. Such confidence in this newfound seventeen-year-old beauty of yours, that a man twenty years older hung on your every banal word, your every swooping eyelash. That he would tell you how you'd grown, how you were the most beautiful girl he'd ever seen. That he would lead you dangerously into a shady corner of the terrace, overlooking Central Park, and feed you a forbidden martini or two and kiss you — you'd been kissed before, you could handle this — and then do something to your dress and your underpants, and a few blurry moments later you weren't handling this at all, you were bang smack on your back on the lounge chair with no way to get up, and maybe it was a good thing he'd fed you those martinis, maybe it was a good thing you couldn't remember exactly how it happened.

The song changes, some new band that Pepper doesn't recognize. She reaches forward and shuts off the radio.

2.

They reach Cocoa Beach at half past one o'clock in the morning. A bank of clouds has rolled in, obscuring the moon, and Pepper can't see a thing beyond the headlights. She's too tired to care, anyway.

126

"Here we are," Annabelle says cheerfully. "The housekeeper is in bed, but the cottage should be ready."

"You do this kind of thing often?"

"No. I just had a hunch I'd have company."

Pepper stumbles out of the car and follows Annabelle across a driveway and up a pair of stone steps. A little house by the beach, she said, but this is more like a villa, plain and rough-walled, like something you might find in Spain or Italy, somewhere old and hot. The smell of eucalyptus hangs in the air.

Annabelle holds open the door. "I expect you're tired. I couldn't keep my eyes open when I was pregnant. I'll save the tour for tomorrow and take you straight to bed."

"I've heard that one before."

Annabelle laughs. "I expect you have, you naughty girl."

Pepper is just awake enough to appreciate the lack of censure in Annabelle's voice. Well, she is European, isn't she? She has that welcome dollop of joie-de-whatever, that je ne sais no evil. She's not one to judge. Maybe that's why Pepper spilled her guts back there, in the middle of the road, like a cadaver under dissection. Or maybe it was the moon, or the goddamned ocean, or the baby and the hormones and the nicotine starvation. Whatever it was, Pepper hopes to God she won't regret all this over breakfast.

"We bought the place in 1941," Annabelle

127

was saying, as they passed through the darkened rooms. "It was built in the twenties, during the big land rush. We got it for a song. It was in total disrepair, not even properly finished, but the bones were good, and there was plenty of room for the children, and it was all by itself, no nosy neighbors. There was something rather authentic about it, which is a difficult thing to find in Florida."

"I'll say."

"I mean, except me, of course!" Annabelle's midnight exuberance is almost certifiable. Pepper wants to throttle her. Of course, six months ago, Pepper could midnight with the best of them. Six months ago, midnight was just the beginning. That was how she got into this mess, wasn't it? Too much goddamned midnight, and now here she was, stumbling through an old house in the middle of Florida, knocked up and knocked out.

A latch clicks, a door swooshes open, and now they're in a courtyard, full of fresh air and lemon trees. Annabelle turns to the wall and switches on a light. Pepper squints.

"Just over here, honey," says Annabelle.

Pepper follows. "I don't mean to be pushy, but does this guest cottage of yours happen to have a working lavatory?"

Annabelle claps a hand to her cheek. "Oh, my goodness! What an idiot I am! It's been so long since I had babies. Come along. My dear, you should have said something. I

didn't realize you were so polite."

"I'm not, I assure you. I just didn't happen to spot any flowerpots along the way."

The grass is short and damp. They've moved beyond the circle of light from the house. Pepper sees a rectangular shadow ahead and hopes to God it's the cottage, and nobody's waiting inside. Peace and quiet, that's all she needs. Peace and quiet and a toilet.

A step ahead, Annabelle opens the door and steps aside for Pepper to enter first. The smell of soap and fresh linen rushes around her.

"Home sweet home. The bathroom's on the right."

3.

When Pepper emerges from the bathroom ten minutes later, Annabelle is standing by the window, looking into the night. From the side, her face looks a little more fragile than Pepper remembers, and she thinks that maybe Annabelle is right, that she isn't really beautiful. The nose is too long. The chin too sharp. The head itself is out of proportion, too large on her skinny long neck, like a Tootsie Pop.

Then she turns, and Pepper forgets her faults.

"All set?"

"Yes. Thanks for the nightgown and toothpaste. I'm beginning to think you had this all

planned out."

"Maybe I did." Annabelle smiles. "Does that make you nervous?"

Pepper yawns. "Nothing's going to make me nervous right now."

"All right. Sleep in as long as you like. I'll have coffee and breakfast waiting in the main house, whenever you're up. Is there anything you need?"

"No, thanks." Pepper hesitates. Gratitude isn't her natural attitude, but then you didn't spend your life dangling elegantly from the pages of the Social Register without learning how to keep your legs crossed and your hostess well buttered. "Thanks awfully for your hospitality," she adds, all Fifth Avenue drawl, emphasis on the *awful.*

"Oh, not at all. I'm happy I could help."

Pepper's radar ears detect a note of wistfulness. She sinks on the bed, bracing her arms on either side of her heavy belly, and says, "Helped me? Kidnapped is more like it."

"Miss Pepper Schuyler," Annabelle says, shaking her head, "why on this great good earth are you so suspicious? What have they done to you?"

"A better question, Mrs. Annabelle Dommerich, is why you care."

An exasperated line appears between Annabelle's eyebrows. She marches to the bed, drops down next to Pepper, and snatches her hand. Her hand! As if Annabelle is the

130

mother bear and Pepper is Goldilocks or something. "Now, look here," she actually says, just like a mother bear, "you are *safe* here, do you hear me? Nobody's going to call you or make demands on you or — God knows, whatever it is you're afraid of."

"I'm not afraid —"

"You're just going to sit here and grow your baby and think about what you want to do with yourself, is that clear? You're going to relax, for God's sake."

"Hide, you mean."

"Yes, hide. If that's what you want to call it. There's a doctor in town, if you need to keep up with any appointments. The house-keeper can drive you. You can telephone your parents and your sisters. You can telephone that horse's ass who put you in this condition, and tell him he can go to the devil."

Pepper cracks out a whiplash of laughter. "Go to the devil! That's a good one. I can just picture him, hanging up the phone and trotting off obediently into the fire and brimstone, just because Pepper Schuyler told him to. Do you have any idea who his friends are? Do you have any idea who owes him a favor or two?"

"He's no match for *you.* Trust me. You hold the cards, darling. You hold the ace. Don't let those bastards convince you otherwise."

Pepper stares at the mama-bear hand covering her own. The nails are short and well

trimmed, the skin smooth and ribbed gently with veins the color of the ocean. Annabelle doesn't use lacquer.

"You still haven't answered my question," Pepper says. "Why do you care?"

Annabelle sighs and heads for the door. She pauses with her hand right there on the knob. Dramatic effect. Who knew she had it in her?

"All right, Pepper. Why do I care? I care because I stood in your shoes twenty-nine years ago, and God knows I could have used a little decent advice. Someone to keep me from making so many goddamned mistakes."

ANNABELLE

ANTIBES 1935

1.

A week passed. Charles had left with his friends before I returned; I was now wise enough to suspect why. Herr von Kleist packed up his few trunks and roared away in his beautiful Mercedes Roadster later that afternoon. My father — as always — rose late, retired late, and reserved nearly all of his time for his remaining guests. I had little to do except wander the garden and the beaches, to practice my cello for hours, to walk sometimes into the village, to examine the contents of my memory for signposts to my future.

On the seventh day of my isolation, I woke up under the settled conviction that I would move to Paris, to Montparnasse, and teach the cello while I found a master under whom to study. It seemed a natural place for me. I was both French and American, and I had read about how the streets and cafés around the boulevard du Montparnasse rattled with Americans seeking art and life and meaning and a cheap accommodation. If a certain

handsome young German Jew were then to turn up on my stoop one day, perhaps requiring immediate medical assistance, why, I would take him in with cheerful surprise. I would find a way to weave him into the hectic fabric of my happiness.

I was not going to wait any longer for my life to start. I was going to start my life on my own.

I repeated this to myself — a very nice tidy maxim, suitable for cross-stitch into a tapestry, a decorative pillow perhaps — as I walked down the stairs on my way to the breakfast room, where I expected the usual hours of peace until the rest of the household woke up. Instead, it was chaos. The hall was full of expensive leather trunks and portmanteaus, the rugs were being rolled up, the servants were running about as if an army were on the march. In the middle of it all stood my father, dressed immaculately in a pale linen suit, speaking on the telephone in rapid French, the cord wound around him and stretched to its limit.

"Papa?" I said. "What's going on?"

He held up one finger, said a few more urgent words, and set the receiver in its cradle with an exhausted sigh. He closed his eyes, collecting his thoughts, and then stepped to the hall table and set down the telephone. *"Mignonne,"* he said in French, opening his

arms, "it is eight o'clock already. You are not ready?"

I took his hands and kissed his cheeks. He smelled of oranges, the particular scent of his shaving soap, which he purchased exclusively from a tiny apothecary in the Troisième, on the rue Charles-François-Dupuis. "Ready for what, Papa?"

"You did not see my message last night?" His eyes were heavy and bruised.

"What message? Papa, what's wrong?"

"I slipped it under your door. Perhaps you were already asleep." He released my hands and pulled out a cigarette case from his jacket pocket. His fingers fumbled with the clasp. "It is a bit of a change of plans. We are leaving this morning, returning to Paris."

"But we were to stay another week!"

"I'm afraid there is some business to which I must attend." He managed to fit a cigarette between his lips. I took the slim gold lighter from his fingers and lit the end for him. I concentrated on the movements of my fingers, this ordinary activity, to keep the panic from rising in my chest.

"But what about our guests?" I said.

"I have left messages. They will understand, don't you think?" He pulled the cigarette away and kissed my cheek. "Now run upstairs, *ma chérie,* and pack your things. Come, now. It is for the best. One should always leave the party before the bitter end,

isn't it so?"

"Yes," I said numbly, "of course," and I turned and ran up the steps, two at a time, and burst without breath into my room, where I stayed only long enough to snatch the pair of slim black binoculars from my desk and bolt down the hall in the opposite direction, to the back stairs.

It was now the third week of August, and the sea washed restlessly against the rocks and beaches below as I stumbled along the clifftops, sucking air into my stricken lungs. I inhaled the warm scent of the dying summer, the weeks that would not return. I thought, I don't care, I don't care if we leave now and return to Paris, I have my own plans, I will live in Montparnasse, I will be sophisticated and insouciant, and he can find me or not find me, he can love me or not love me, I don't care, I don't care.

I skidded to a stop at the familiar rock, the rock where I had sat every day and watched the traffic in the giant mammary curves of the bay, in the delicate cleavage of which perched the village of Cannes. From here, you could see the boats zagging lazily, the ferries looping back and forth to the isles Lérins, to Sainte-Marguerite, where the fort nestled into the cliffs. I climbed to the top of the boulder and lifted the binoculars to my eyes and thought, I don't care, I don't care, please God, please God, I don't care.

From this angle, to the east of the islands, it was impossible to see where the *Isolde* lay moored — if she still lay moored at all — behind the Pointe du Dragon. I had tried — no, I hadn't *tried,* of course not, I had only dragged my gaze about as a matter of idle curiosity, but there was no glimpse of the beautiful black-and-white ship, longer and sleeker than all the others moored there in the gentle channel between the two islands. I had taken her continued presence there as an article of faith. I had watched the boats ply the water, the stylish motorboats and the ferries and the serviceable tenders, and refused to think about the honey-haired woman who had come to see Stefan that first morning, and whether she was making another trip. Whether an unglamorous nineteen-year-old virgin was easily forgotten in the face of those kohl-lined eyes, that slender and practiced figure.

My legs wobbled, and the vision through the binoculars skidded crazily about. I planted my feet more firmly, each one in a separate hollow, and set my shoulders. The sea steadied before me, blue and ancient under the cloudless sky, and as I stared to the southeast, counting the tiny white waves, as if in obedience to a miraculous summons, I saw a long yacht come into view, around the edge of the point, black on the bottom and gleaming white in a rim about the top of

the hull, steaming eastward toward Nice or Monaco, perhaps, or even farther south toward Italy.

The Cinque Ports were supposed to be beautiful at this time of year, and Portofino.

My heart grew and grew, splitting my chest apart, lodging somewhere in my throat so I couldn't breathe.

"She is a beautiful ship, don't you think?" said a voice behind me.

I closed my eyes and allowed my arms to fall, with the binoculars, into my thighs. I thought, I must breathe now, and I forced my throat to open. "Yes, very beautiful."

"But you know, ships are so transient and so sterile. Nothing grows in them. So I have been thinking to myself, I must really find myself a villa of some kind, somewhere in the sunshine where I can raise olives and wine and children, with the assistance of perhaps a housekeeper to keep things tidy and make a nice hot breakfast in the morning, and a gardener to tend the flowers."

My chest was moving in little spasms now, taking in shallow bursts of air. I said, or rather sobbed, "And what — will you do — in the winter?"

"Ah, a good question. Perhaps an apartment in Paris? One can follow the sun, of course, but I have always thought that it is best to know some winter, too, so that the summer, when it arrives, is the more grate-

fully received."

I turned to face him. A tear ran down from each of my eyes and dripped along my jaw. Stefan stood with his hands in his pockets, right next to the rock, staring up at me gravely. His hair had grown a little, a tiny fraction of an inch, perhaps. I leaned down and put my hands on his shoulders.

"How strange," I whispered. "I have just been thinking the same thing."

He reached up and hooked me by the waist and swung me down from the top of the rock.

"Hush, now," he said, between kisses. "Annabelle, it is all right, I am here. *Liebling*, stop, you are frantic, you must stop and think."

"I don't want to think. I don't want to stop." I kissed his lips and jaw and neck, I kissed him everywhere I could, wetting us both with my tears. "I have been stopping all my life. I want to live."

"Ah, Annabelle. And I would have said you were the most *alive* girl I've ever met."

"That's you. You have brought me to life."

Stefan paused in his kisses, holding my face to the sunlight, as if I were a new species brought in for classification and he had no idea where to begin, my nose or my hair or my teeth. "Tell me what you want, Annabelle," he said.

"But you know what I want."

He took my hand and led me up the slope,

where a cluster of olive trees formed an irregular circle of privacy. He urged me carefully down and I put my arms around his
neck and dragged him into the grass with me.
"I thought you had gone off with her," I said,
unbuttoning his shirt.

"What? Gone off with whom?"

"The honey-haired woman, the one you
used to make love to."

He drew back and stared at me. "My God.
How stupid. What do I want with her?"

"I don't know. What you had before."

"What I had before." He lowered his head
into the grass, next to mine. His body lay
across me, warm and heavy, supported by his
elbows. "You are the death of me," he said
softly. "I have no right to you."

"You have every right. I'm giving you the
right."

He turned his mouth to my ear. "Don't say
that. Tell me to stop, tell me to take you
home."

"No. That's not why you came for me, to
take me home."

He lifted his head again, and his eyes were
heavy and full of smoke. "No. God forgive
me. That is not why I came for you."

I touched his cheek with my thumb and
began to unbutton my blouse, and he put his
fingers on mine and said, "No, let me. Let
me do it."

He uncovered my breasts and kissed me,

140

and his hands were gentle on my skin. "So new and pure," he said. "I don't think I can bear it."

I spread out my arms in the warm grass.

"God will curse me for this," he said.

"No, he won't."

He kissed me again and lifted my skirt to my waist. I hadn't worn stockings or a girdle. He worked my underpants down my legs and leaned over my belly to touch me with his gentle fingers, in such an unexpected and unbearably tender way that my legs shook and my lungs starved, and at last I made a little cry and grabbed his waist, because I couldn't imagine what else to hold on to. His shirt was unbuttoned and came away in my hands. "Tell me to stop, Annabelle," he said.

"Please don't stop. I'll die if you stop."

He muttered something in German and fumbled with his trousers and lowered himself over me, so that his forearms touched my shoulders and he arched above my ribs. I felt his legs settle between mine, pushing me apart while the grass prickled my spine. I loved his breath, the tobacco smell of him.

"Put your arms around me, Annabelle," he said, and I pressed my palms against the back of his sunburned neck. He reached down with one hand and bent my knee upward, and I thought, My God, what have I done? He said, with his hand still on my raised knee, *Are you sure, Annabelle, are you sure you want*

141

this? and I nodded my head once, because even when you looked down from the heights to measure the distance to the surface, and the terror turned your limbs to water, you knew you had to dive, you had no choice except to jump. And as I nodded, I lifted my other knee because I thought I'd be damned if I didn't jump in with both feet. Stefan's eyes went opaque. He sank his belly down to mine and said my name as he pushed into me, just my name — twice, a cry that was more like a groan, *Annabelle, Annabelle* — but I, Annabelle, had no air in my lungs to say anything at all, no way of telling him what I felt, the splitting apart, the roar of panic smothered by the gargantuan joy of possession.

He lay buried and still, breathing hard, and I thought, so dizzy I was almost sick, So that's it, it's over, we've made love, but then he moved again and I cried out, and he stopped and kissed me and said my name again, stroking my hair. *Open your eyes,* he said, but I couldn't. He moved again, kissing me as he went, and the sickness undulated into something else, a collusion between us, his skin on my hands, the roughness of his breath. I opened my eyes and thought, My God, this is it, now we are making love.

2.

We lay submerged for ages, while the morning went on without us. I had no will to move, no idea what movement was. At some point I opened my eyes and found the slow crump of my heartbeat against Stefan's ribs. He was beautifully heavy, pinning us to the earth, and in my bemusement I thought he had fallen asleep. The tiny green leaves rustled above us, as if nothing had happened, nothing had changed at all. I watched them move, watched the patient blue sky beyond them, the wisps of dark hair near my eyes. Stefan's neck was smooth and damp beneath my fingers. Between my legs, I was shocked and stretched and aching, and I did not want it to stop, I wanted this abundance to continue forever.

When he spoke, the softness of his voice stunned me.

"*Gott im Himmel.* Annabelle. I did not expect that."

"It was unexpected and beautiful."

"Everything about you has been unexpected and beautiful." He pushed back my hair, which had come loose across my face. "Look at you. What a brute I am."

"I didn't give you a choice."

"A man has always the choice. Did I hurt you?"

"No, no."

"Yes, I did. I hurt you. I tried to be gentle,

but I have never done that before, been with an innocent."

"Never? Really?"

"Never. And I can't seem to regret it. A cad as well as a brute." He kissed my lips, rose up on his hands, and lifted himself carefully away. He gazed back at me and his face was deep with remorse. I sat up and laid my bold palms against his cheeks. "Don't look at me like that."

"Like what?"

"Like you want to take it all back."

"No, never. It's done now. We're in God's hands."

"Listen to you. A moment ago you were offering me a villa by the sea and a shameless apartment in Paris."

"Because I did not think you would be so foolish as to accept. I thought you would slap me as I deserved and stalk back to your father's house."

"But I'm unexpected."

"Unexpected and beautiful." He pulled my hands from his face and kissed each one, and he drew me into his chest and settled us in the grass. I lay bare and marveling in the curve of his body, thinking, My God, we are lovers now, we have actually made love together.

The silence stretched out lazily. I said, "I've shocked you, haven't I?"

He laughed. "You have shocked and de-

lighted me beyond words. But I must think a little. I must think what is to be done now."

"You mentioned a villa."

"Yes, I did. But this villa is something of a dream, and there is a reality to be considered first." He shifted me on his chest and reached for his jacket, and this time he drew out his cigarettes and lit one briskly with his gold lighter. "Do you know what I have been thinking about, this past week?"

"I know I've spent the past week wishing that I did."

"I have been thinking how I have arranged my life in a certain way, according to certain principles, and a rather arrogant belief that this was what God intended of me, and he would therefore overlook any little sins I might commit. And I have been wondering whether perhaps God has intended some-thing entirely different, or if he has merely decided he should punish me after all."

"Is this one of those little sins?"

"Yes, I suppose it is, according to the covenant. But I don't regret it, I will never regret this moment. I am only pondering the path now before us." He lay there, smoking quietly with one hand and holding me to his chest with the other. "You are a great compli-cation, you know," he said solemnly, after a moment.

"Am I?"

"A tremendous complication. So I suppose,

before I ponder this matter any longer, I should humble myself to ask you what *you* want. What path you imagine for us. Since I find myself bound to you, by the pint of your blood that communicates in my veins, and now by honor, so therefore I am your servant on earth."

This time, it was my turn to laugh. "I love your chivalry. You talk like a man from a hundred years ago."

"Hmm. Yes. And what is your plan for this ancient servant you have brought under your command?"

"Well. I like the sound of this villa of yours, with the olives and the grapes." I paused, because I had left something out, and I wanted to see if he would supply the word for me. But he said nothing, and I went on: "And then there's that talk about Paris, and by a strange coincidence, I was just thinking this morning that an apartment in Montparnasse might be the very thing for me."

"Montparnasse! Annabelle in Montparnasse?"

"Yes. Why not? It's crammed with Americans and art. It's the most interesting place in the world right now. I could live in some grubby little room above a café and teach the cello to the daughters of the bourgeoisie."

"You realize that in Montparnasse, you will be expected to take a new lover every night, as a matter of course?"

146

"Ah, but I'm unexpected, remember? I think I'll be happy with just the one."

"I see. I suppose, so long as this lover is me, I cannot object."

"Yes, this lover would be you." I rolled over and propped my chin on my hands, atop his chest, between the white sides of his unbuttoned shirt. Stefan stubbed out his cigarette in the grass and cupped his hands around the backs of my bare shoulders. I felt suddenly daring and desirable, like somebody's mistress. I said, "What do you think of my path, Herr Silverman? Would you like to travel it with me?"

He kissed me. The smoke was returning to his eyes. He kissed me again, a little harder. "This is your path. This is what you want of me."

"Only if you want it, too."

He studied me, kissed me, and then studied me again, as if the kiss might have made a difference. "All right, then. All right, Mademoiselle de Créouville. I will see what I can arrange. I will take care of everything for us. But come. The tide will be turning soon. I must be off." He reached for my blouse and helped me into it.

"The tide?"

"Yes, the tide. I have left the tender at the Hôtel du Cap."

"But where are you going?"

He was standing up, fastening his trousers,

147

buttoning his shirt. "To my ship, of course. She is off to her winter mooring in Monte Carlo, which I must oversee. You will stay with your father for a few more days, and then I will return and take you —"

My hands froze on my buttons.

"What is it?" he asked.

"My father. My God, I forgot all about it."

"Forgot about what? Why are you laughing?"

"I can't stay here with my father. He's leaving this morning for Paris. That's why I ran out here, to see if I could find you somehow, because he's already packed, we're to leave right away. Poor Papa, he's probably mad with impatience by now."

"Ah, yes. So it is true. I heard a rumor that a certain impoverished prince was experiencing some new difficulties in his poverty, which is why I woke up this morning and thought perhaps it was time to act. Well, then. It seems God, in his wisdom, has arranged things in a very satisfactory manner. You will come with me, of course. We cannot have you going off to Paris with your father and forgetting me altogether."

"I don't think there's much chance of my forgetting you."

He kissed my hand. "Then come. We will telephone your father from the hotel."

"What on earth am I going to tell him?"

"The truth, of course. That you're not yet

148

ready to leave the seaside, and will spend the last few days of summer with your very dear friend, with whom you were staying before."

"And then?"

He picked up his jacket, slung it over his shoulder, and leaned down to place a soft kiss on my lips. "And then we will see what comes next."

3.

When we caught up with the *Isolde* in Monte Carlo, she was already moored in the harbor, surrounded by a few dozen yachts of similar proportion, but without her elegance. Stefan pulled me to the tender's wheel. "Wait here just a moment," he said. "I have a few instructions for the crew."

I kept the tender close, no easy feat in the constant chop of the busy harbor. The sun beat on my head; I hadn't worn a hat. I looked up the familiar sides of the ship and remembered how I had arrived with Stefan at this exact spot in the middle of the night three weeks ago, on the brink of adventure, and now here I was again and the adventure had grown into dazzling dimensions, an infinity of adventure.

I looked at my hands: one on the wheel, one on the throttle. There was still a soft ache between my legs. My skin felt as if it had been rubbed all over by a very fine grade of sandpaper. An hour ago, I had been lying on

149

the grass with Stefan, and now I was running away with him, we were lovers running away together.

True to his word, Stefan climbed back down the ladder a few minutes later and jumped nimbly into the boat. I smiled up at him and he took my shoulders and said, "My God, you're here. It wasn't a dream."

I laughed, because I'd been thinking the same thing. "No, of course not."

There was a hum of energy surrounding him, crackling the air. I wanted to fling my arms about his neck and kiss him, but instead I stepped back from the wheel so he could grab it. He took the wheel in one hand and the throttle in the other. "Let's go, *Liebling*," he said.

"Where are we going?" I shouted, over the engine and the salt breeze.

"I have a friend who keeps a place here, just outside of town. He lets me use it when the ship is in port for repairs and so on. It's very nice, though the staff is all gone. I hope these nuns of yours have taught you to cook in addition to applying tourniquets."

"I guess I can boil an egg or two, in a pinch."

"Good. There is plenty of wine and a bakery in the fishing village, a kilometer away. I will bring us our daily bread, how does that sound?"

I leaned into his ear and said, "I don't have

150

any things with me."

"Ah, don't worry. Did I not say I would take care of everything for us?" He brought his arm around my shoulder, drawing me close as we edged westward out of the harbor, toward Stefan's little place, just outside of town.

4.

The house was small and beautiful, a miniature villa tucked into the cliffs, made of crumbling yellow bricks and crumbling red tile on the roof. There was a tiny dock and boathouse and a stairway cut into the rocks, leading up to the house.

Inside, the house smelled like the sea and the eucalyptus that grew near the windows for shade. "First of all, I must draw you a bath," said Stefan. "I am a terrible blackguard for taking you on a forced march like this, instead of making sure you are comfortable."

"I'm perfectly comfortable," I said, and he laughed.

"You are such an eager little liar, Annabelle, *Liebling*. Come. Let us see if the old boiler is working."

Stefan got the boiler working, and in half an hour the taps ran hot. He showed me the rooms, the kitchen and the living room, and the beautiful terrace overlooking the sea, planted with lemons. The bedroom upstairs had a balcony that opened out into the lemon

branches, so that the scent of lemons mingled with the brine and the eucalyptus. Stefan stood behind me and stretched out his hand. "See there, to the east? You can just find the *Isolde,* if you look hard."

I peered past his pointing finger. "Oh, yes! I see her."

"I have always loved coming here. It is the most peaceful place I know, and yet Monte Carlo is a half hour's walk away. I come here to be alone and think."

"Then I'm interrupting your solitude."

"No, you are improving it beyond measure. I have never wanted to bring another human being here until now." He kissed my temple. "Let's get you in your bath."

He made the strangest chambermaid I'd ever known, moving about the marble bathroom with his cigarette stuck at the corner of his mouth, sniffing a bottle of bath oil while the faucet poured forth with hot water. He added a few drops to the tub and replaced the lid. "That will do, I believe," he said, and turned to me. His hair curled with the steam. He smiled, the kind of too-wide smile that made me think he was nervous. "I will walk into the village and get us a little lunch while you are soaking, Mademoiselle. But there is no hurry. Is there anything else I can do for you? How are you feeling?"

I thought, I love you.

He frowned. "Annabelle?"

I took the cigarette from his fingers and crushed it into the tray on the windowsill. "I'm very well, Stefan, thank you. I guess losing your virginity isn't a mortal illness after all, whatever those old nuns used to tell us. Now, will you help me with this dress?"

5.

When Stefan returned, an hour or so later, he found me standing on the balcony, wrapped in a dressing gown that was several sizes too large. I held up my flopping arms. "The best I could do. But at least I'm all freshened up."

He dropped the net bag on the floor. There was a soft thump of a bottle hitting wood. "Oh, God," he said.

"Is something wrong?"

"No."

I pushed my loose hair over my ear. The sun flooded Stefan's face, turning his eyes to caramel, touching the tiny bristles of his beard. He looked stricken and beautiful. I nodded at the bag on the floor. "Did you find lunch?"

He stepped toward me and laid his hand along my cheek. "I don't remember," he said.

6.

"So, then, Mademoiselle. You enjoy this sort of activity," said Stefan.

"Shouldn't I?"

We were sitting together on a chair on the balcony, perfectly still. I was on Stefan's lap, wrapped in a single white sheet and glowing like a forge. The sea glittered before us, crossed by lazy boats. I smelled the lemon and the eucalyptus and thought, I will always remember this, the scent of lemon will always remind me of this moment.

"Not every woman does," he said, and then added hastily, "or so I am told."

"Well, I do. I enjoy it very much indeed."

He kissed my hair. "For this, I am most profoundly glad."

"But you know," I said, after a moment, "I think I like this even more. The afterward."

"This?"

"Yes. Sitting together like this, still humming. Close your eyes." I passed my hand over his eyelids. "Do you feel it?"

"Hmm. Yes. I see what you mean."

"It's as if I'm inside your skin, and you're inside mine at the same time. Like we can say things to each other, without speaking."

"And what am I saying to you now, *Liebling*?"

I listened carefully to his heartbeat. "That you have fallen in love with me. That you love the way my skin smells, and the way my belly feels under your hand."

"Ah, very good. But you didn't mention the rest. How I love your hair and your soft, round breasts and your enormous brown

eyes, and your crooked toes and your legs, and the hollows of your arms, and your wide American mouth, and the way you look at me when I am inside you."

"How do I look at you?"

"As if I could do anything. As if I am invincible."

"But you are. You *are* invincible." I stretched out my leg and wiggled the foot. "Are my toes really crooked?"

"Yes, they are beautifully crooked. I want to kiss every one of them."

I laughed. "You see what I mean? This is the best part of all."

"No, love. You are the best part of all. Because this has never been the best part for me, until you were in it."

"Why? What did you do before?"

He yawned. "Left, if I could. Now don't talk anymore. Close your eyes and listen to my heart instead."

I closed my eyes and counted the beats of his heart. When I reached infinity, the faint drone of an engine interrupted the quiet. I lifted my head and saw a motorboat breaking away from the harbor traffic, in a straight line toward us. "Someone's coming," I said.

Stefan opened his eyes and lifted his head from the chair. "Ah. I believe that will be my coxswain, bringing your cello."

"What cello?"

"The cello I found for you this past week,

from a very reputable dealer in Monte Carlo who assures me it is an Amati. I am hoping you will try it out and tell me I have not been taken for a fool."

7.

I played for nearly an hour, while the tears swam from my eyes: The first Bach cello suite, which I knew from memory, restless and hopeful, each note emerging from inside the miraculous wood like the revelation of a mystery. And then Chopin, because there are certain things that only Chopin knows how to say.

When at last I laid the beautiful curves back in their case and wiped the strings clean, I kissed Stefan on the lips and told him he was not a fool.

8.

Later that afternoon, we climbed back down the cliff to walk on the stone beach. Stefan held my hand as we scrambled over a stand of slippery rocks, exposed by the tide. "About our villa," I said. "Can it be by the sea?"

"Wherever you like."

"I want it to be just like this. I want to look out in the morning and see the water, and think about the Romans and the Etruscans crossing the harbors, and Hannibal with his elephants, and Dido waiting for Aeneas. And Napoleon's ships sneaking across to Alex-

andria, and Nelson coming after him."

Stefan's eyes narrowed into the sun. His skin was darker now, a smooth golden tan, as if he'd spent the past week entirely outdoors. Doing what? I wondered. He said, "I love that, too. How ancient it is. How we are all mere specks in time, perched on the shore, watching each other pass in turn."

He was holding the last end of a cigarette in his other hand. I pried it loose and tossed it on the rocks and put my arms around his neck. I kissed him and he kissed me back until we fell on the rocks together, laughing, and he put my hands away. "No, we must stop," he said. "It's too soon. I am not such a brute as that. It is tempting fate, making love so much."

"I can't stop. I have to touch you, to remind myself that it's real."

He held me against him while the sun grew heavy across the water. A seagull cried furiously nearby, the only movement in the world, except for the quiet beat of Stefan's heart against my back. I loved his smell, his warm arms secure around me. I thought I had nothing to fear now.

"Yes," he said at last. "I know what you mean."

9.

After a dinner of cold chicken and bread and cheese, I played the Boccherini in B-flat

157

major, one of my favorites, in the lemon-scented courtyard, until the sky was black and full of stars, and Stefan drew the cello from my hands. His face was so tender it hurt my throat. "Time for sleep, Annabelle. You have had a long day, haven't you?" he said, and I told him I wasn't ready to sleep yet, and he carried me to bed anyway, where we made love for the third time. Stefan thought we shouldn't, not just because of tempting fate but because he was afraid of hurting me. I said it hurt only a little, just at the beginning, and I didn't mind that because of what came after.

He was worried and careful and thoroughly aroused. I loved that: how I could make him want me, against his own premonitions, even against his own conscience. I loved the skillful way he moved inside me, the way he turned me on my stomach and asked how I liked this, if it gave me more pleasure or less, more relief or less from the tender abrasion. I never imagined you could mate like that, like beasts, feverish and deep, and I cried out that yes, yes, I liked it very much.

When we finished, there was nothing left on the bed but the two of us, panting softly against each other. *I have been very selfish today, Mademoiselle,* Stefan whispered, and I wanted to tell him that it was the opposite, that he had given me everything, but I was too tired even to move my lips.

158

10.

The strangest part, stranger even than having made love to begin with, was sleeping next to him. He was hot and large by my side, his arm heavy over my ribs. I didn't know if he was sleeping or keeping watch. I kept waking up, though I was exhausted, just to make sure he was still there, that he hadn't left, that his smell — smoke and after-dinner cognac and a kind of warm, sweet sweatiness — still surrounded me.

Once, it didn't. I sat up and saw his shadow against the bedroom window. I called his name and he came back to the bed, and I told him I was afraid he'd gone away.

No, he said, never that.

Then what were you doing? I asked.

I have been thinking about the two of us, that's all. Now go to sleep.

Only if you sleep too.

I will, *Liebling.* I will now.

11.

I first heard about Peggy Guggenheim from one of the other girls at Saint Cecilia's. Until then, I hadn't quite understood what my father had done that was so awful. I thought my mother was to blame somehow, that she had been hard and unforgiving over some simple human crime, and she should have been kinder to him.

But one night, while we were saying our

159

prayers, Camille Montmorency had leaned over to me and whispered that *Peggy Guggenheim a sucé la bite de ton père.* I was only thirteen, and I had never heard of such a thing, either in English or in French (in which, like most things, the concept was rendered more elegantly). I denied it fiercely, of course, but the seed was planted. So that summer, at the Villa Vanilla, I asked my brother about it. He had looked at me speculatively and said he guessed I was old enough to know by now. He explained what had happened, how mother had returned home early with a headache from some party, and found the two of them locked in what the French (again, more elegantly) call *le soixante-neuf,* right there in the ancient marital bed of the de Créouvilles. Upon investigation, it seemed they had been carrying on an affair for some time, and in fact Papa had been carrying on such affairs with multiple women over a great deal of time, and did not see why he should desist from such innocent pleasures, simply because his so-Puritan wife disapproved of them.

From that instant, my sympathies had switched sides. I couldn't hate my Papa, of course, who was always kind in those few moments he could spare for me. But this Peggy Guggenheim. How I hated her. I read about her in the newspapers, and the more I read the more I hated her. She would sleep with

anybody, she had no morals at all. No man was safe from her talons.

For a long time, I lived in despair. I thought there was no escape from being either a Peggy Guggenheim or a victim of such women, unless you didn't marry at all, unless you never allowed yourself to fall in love. Like most adolescent obsessions, this had faded over time, but I'd never quite lost the dread entirely. It had hovered like a ghost in the back of my heart, sometimes howling and rattling its chains, and sometimes quiet. On the first night I slept in Stefan's bed, an image woke me with a jolt in the hour before dawn: Stefan standing half dressed before a window, like a man I had glimpsed once at the Villa Vanilla, holding the head of a glossy-haired woman who knelt between his legs.

"What's the matter?" said Stefan, waking, too.

The dream was so vivid, I thought it had actually occurred. My heart was pounding; my stomach felt as if it had been turned the wrong way. "How do I know you're not going to sleep with Peggy Guggenheim?" I demanded.

Stefan was still half asleep, and understandably confused. He propped himself up on his elbows. "Peggy Guggenheim? Why the devil would I want to sleep with her? She is as old as my mother."

"With anyone. How do I know you're not

161

going to sleep with someone else?"

He stared at me with his morning eyes. His hair spilled recklessly into his forehead. He was not ignorant; he must have known the scandal of my parents' marriage. "You don't," he said gently.

Stefan's face looked exactly as it had in my dream, except his eyes were open now, instead of closed in rapture. I rolled over into the pillow, away from him, and he laid his palm on the small of my back.

"You don't know that, Annabelle. You simply have to trust me."

"How do I trust you?" I whispered.

"Do you want me to make a promise to you? I will, if you want, but everyone can make a promise."

"No. I don't want you to promise me."

His hand was warm and still on my back. "So I will tell you this, Annabelle. I am not one of your Christian saints, but I am a fair man. It seems to me that since I am the first man you have ever had in your bed, it is only justice that you are the last woman I will have in mine."

I stared at the dark wall and reflected.

"I don't know. That sounds an awful lot like a promise."

"No, it is not. A promise is like the law, it can be broken. Not without consequence, but it can be broken. This is more like your American constitution. It is the terms by

which I have allowed myself to form this union with you."

I turned over and found his face close to mine, too close and too shadowed to make him out. "But why? Why me?"

He shrugged. "Because you are Annabelle. I can either be the man who deserves the love of Annabelle de Créouville, for whose happiness this fidelity is essential, or I will have to do without her. And since it seems I cannot do without you . . . well . . ." He shrugged again. "So there it is."

"Well," I said, when I could speak, "you seem to have given this some thought."

"Yes. Now stop looking at me in this manner, or I will be forced to make love to you again, and you will not be able to walk."

I slid my arms around his neck. "But why would I need to walk anywhere?"

12.

We stayed at the little villa by the sea for three days and four nights. The skies were blue and hot, the evenings full of stars. We didn't see another soul, except when we went into town for food, and we shed our modesty and our clothes in the luminous August air and bound ourselves together, sometimes only talking and sometimes making love, sometimes silent and sometimes clamorous, sometimes slow and gentle and sometimes feverish, sometimes in bed and sometimes on the balcony

163

or in the courtyard or the bath.

And once — because after all we were young, and this was the ancient sun-drenched coast of Europe — on the beach after dark, in the company of a bottle of ice-cold champagne and a thick blanket to soften the ground.

The sun had been exceptionally hot that day, and by evening the temperature in the house was almost unbearable. After a late dinner, we had swum in the sea to cool off and dragged ourselves onto the blanket, still dripping. The moon hadn't risen yet, and I could hardly see Stefan's body against mine. His skin tasted like salt. He lifted himself on his elbows and eased slowly inside me, and as he did, he said something in German, under his breath.

"What does that mean?"

"Nothing, love."

I wrapped my legs around him and said that wasn't fair, we couldn't keep our thoughts from each other after all we had done.

He went still inside me. The rocks rubbed my back through the blanket. Stefan touched my hair with his fingers and moved again, a slow rhythm. "I will tell you if it comes true, Annabelle, but not before."

"A wish?"

"Yes, Annabelle. Now let us put you on top of me instead, so we do not injure your beautiful back on these damned rocks."

He rolled over and positioned me above him. I came first, in a cry that ricocheted gently from the cliffs, until Stefan gripped my hips and followed me. Afterward, we slept on the beach until the air began to cool, and Stefan carried me up the path to the house, and into a bed that had never felt so soft.

13.

On the morning of the fourth day, I woke to find Stefan already awake and dressed, smoking on the balcony while the sun crept up from behind Italy.

"You're up early," I said.

"Yes." He nodded to the harbor. "The ship is ready, as you see."

I lifted my hand to my brow. I couldn't see anything; the glare of the rising sun found my eyeballs at a crucifying angle. "What a pity. Can't we stay a little longer?"

"No, my love. We cannot. We have already ignored the world too long."

His voice was stern and melancholy. I came around in front of him and knelt between his outstretched legs. The new pink sunshine coated his face. I laid my hands on his thighs and said, "So do we leave for Paris now? Or do we search for our villa with the olive groves and the vineyards?"

He took the cigarette from his mouth and stubbed it out in the ashtray on the floor. "Ah, yes. This path we will travel together."

"Yes. Our path. Or have you changed your mind?"

I was naked between his legs, and the breeze touched my skin, cool with the early sea. Stefan's eyes were wholly absorbed in me. He touched the tiny bumps on my arms. "I have not changed my mind, Annabelle. You know that. But listen to me. This thing you want, this path, it is a complication for me. It is a path I did not imagine until now, and there are some family affairs I must arrange. On my own, love, back home in Germany. Do you understand?"

"Of course."

He leaned forward, until his face was inches away from mine. "No, don't look at me like that. I am *happy* to do this. I am so happy, I will make these arrangements of mine with the utmost haste, so I can return to you, and we can plant our olives and our vineyards before the winter sets in. But in the meantime, you must stay here a little longer, Annabelle, just until I can arrange for —"

"Stay here without you?"

"Yes." He hesitated. "Just for a short while. Just until I can return to you."

"But I can't stay here, all alone. I'll have to go to Paris, to my father —"

"No! No, not to your father. Listen to me. This is why I have been thinking, on my ship last week and late at night when you are asleep. I have an idea. Do this for me, Anna-

belle. You know that right near your father's villa is the Hôtel du Cap."

"Of course I know it."

"If I take a room there for you, if I leave you some money, can you stay there quietly until I can return for you?"

His hands were curled around my arms, and his eyes had lost their smoke and grown sharp and intent, like a general planning a campaign. I hardly recognized him. I said, a little bewildered, "But how long will that be?"

He hesitated. "I don't know. As soon as I can, is that fair? And I will write to you faithfully, whenever possible, though you must not try to reply. We will find you a quiet room, and in a week or two when the summer is over this circus will be tranquil, the crowds will have left. Say you will do it, Annabelle, you will wait there for me."

Wait for Stefan, while he went off without me. To Germany, to his friends and old mistresses, the life he had without me. I felt the old panic rise up in my chest.

"But — I don't know, I haven't thought — what will my brother say?" I said helplessly.

"Don't tell him. God, don't tell him about us, not until I return and I can come to him properly. Can you promise me?" He took my face in his hands and kissed me so passionately, I couldn't breathe. "Promise me. You will wait quietly, you will tell no one about us. I must make things safe for you

167

first, Annabelle, safe for us both, and then we will have no more secrets from the world. We will be together before God and man."

I wanted to protest. But how could you say *no* to words like that? When you are so young, and he is so urgent. When the blood thrills down your fresh new limbs at the idea of waiting in a room at the Hôtel du Cap, overlooking the autumn sea, for your lover to return to your arms.

I was so young, and we had just made love. My heart was turned over, my body remade. In three days and four nights, I had come to think that everything was possible, that you could live by love alone. I had come to think that my mother had made a terrible mistake, that she had chosen a title over love, decadence over purity, but I in my extravagant wisdom had chosen so much better than she had. I had chosen Stefan, and things would be different for me.

So I kissed him and said *Yes, yes,* and he helped me dress, and I helped him pack up the house. We climbed back down the cliff to where his motorboat bobbed by the little jetty, waiting to whisk us away to paradise. To the Hôtel du Cap.

14.

We drove without speaking around the curves of the Antibes road, straight to the hotel, where Stefan with careless arrogance ar-

168

ranged a room under the name of Mr. and Mrs. Silverman. The clerk didn't raise a single eyebrow. My cheeks were bright with shame. I scribbled out a note and addressed the envelope to my father in Paris. Stefan tipped the clerk generously.

"There, you see?" he said, tossing his hat on the chair, when we had arrived in the room and dispatched the bellhop, who had led us to our room and pretended to carry our nonexistent luggage, with a ten-franc note. "Nothing could be easier."

I turned around in a slow circle. "You said something about a discreet room?"

"This? This is nothing. Besides, if we had asked for a cheap room, the clerk would have thought it suspicious."

I glanced down at my dusty and rumpled skirt, my bare legs. "I'm not exactly dressed like a lady, am I?"

Stefan lit a cigarette. "You are perfect. A perfectly respectable woman who has been out walking all morning. If you were a prostitute, you would be wearing stockings and a silk dress."

"And how would you know that?"

He smiled and shrugged. "Common knowledge."

I came to stand against the French door to the balcony, as far away as I could from the open entryway to the bedroom. The walls and furniture were dressed abundantly in blue

toile. Our house by the sea was so simple, I had almost forgotten what decoration was like. My cheeks were still pink; I felt the heat simmering just under my skin. Across the room, Stefan leaned against a too-delicate chair and watched me.

"So, my *Liebling*," he said. "Why don't you take a nice bath, and I will order us a room-service lunch to make up for all the humble meals I offered you in Monte Carlo."

"I loved those meals. I loved eating them with you."

"This is very kind. But there is something to be said for fine cuisine, too, don't you think?"

"Very well," I said. "But no mushrooms."

He smiled and picked up the curving receiver of the telephone. "No mushrooms."

15.

When I emerged from the bath, a table had materialized in the middle of the room, covered with white linen and silver domes. Stefan stood by the open French door, smoking and watching the sea crash into the cliffs beyond. He had poured himself a drink, which sat half empty on the console near his elbow, next to an ashtray already half full of stubs. His hands were crammed in his pockets. Without looking at me, he removed the cigarette from his mouth and asked me how I enjoyed my bath. I said very much, and it

was true. The miracle of water.

"Good." He placed his fist on the door-frame, and his knuckles were white. He asked me how I was feeling.

I thought, I love you.

He turned his head. His eyebrows were worried. "Annabelle?"

"I'm feeling famished, Stefan, after that thing you did to me this morning, when we were supposed to be packing."

Stefan picked up his drink and finished it off. He looked into the glass, as if he could somehow conjure more. "Are you, now?" he said.

"Famished."

"Then I suppose it is fortunate I ordered such an immense quantity of food."

Under the silver domes, there was roasted chicken and delicate new potatoes, haricots verts and a fragrant red Burgundy. We ate without saying much. Afterward we had chocolates and coffee, and Stefan sat back in his chair and smoked a cigarette while I tucked my feet up under the robe and sipped from a delicate demitasse cup. The coffee was hot and strong and expensive. "When do you leave?" I asked.

"I ought to have left already."

"But that would hardly have been polite."

"No." He let out a paper-thin stream of smoke and smiled vaguely at me. He had taken off his jacket and his tie; the day was

171

growing warm, and even the sea breeze from the balcony couldn't budge the heat from the noontime sun, which streamed directly through the south-facing window. I spotted a bowl of gardenias sitting on the console next to the doors, the source of the perfume.

"I'm going to miss you," I said.

"Yes." He stubbed out the cigarette and rose. I watched him walk to the balcony doors and open them to the widest possible extent. The breeze moved his white shirt. I set down my cup and went to him.

"What's wrong?" I whispered, touching his back.

He raised his arm and pointed. "Look. You can see Sainte-Marguerite from here. There is the fort where I kissed you."

"Stefan, for God's sake. Tell me."

He sighed deeply. "You are ruthless, Mademoiselle. You are like the damned bloodhound on the scent sometimes."

"Yes, when I have to."

His hand, which was braced on the doorframe, dropped away and slipped into his pocket. "I have been pondering my own selfishness, I suppose."

"You weren't being selfish. I was. I threw myself at you, I wanted whatever you had to give me."

"No, I mean my whole life. I have been very thoughtless, without even realizing it. I have simply taken pleasure and tried, on occasion,

to return it. And now there is you, Mademoiselle."

"A complication."

"Yes, a complication. But something else. I have been trying to think of the English word. A reckoning? I am forced to consider my own sins, for the first time in my life, and it is a sober task."

"I don't know why making love to me should make you consider your sins."

He touched my cheek. "Because you are an innocent, Annabelle, and for all my crimes I had never yet corrupted the innocent."

"You didn't corrupt me. That was the opposite of corruption. Those were the most beautiful days of my life."

Stefan let out a sigh and turned away to light another cigarette. "Can there be any more proof than *that*?" he murmured, and he walked through the French doors to the balcony and leaned his elbows on the railing. I followed him. He plied the cigarette between his fingers and said quietly, "I have had the feeling, since we drove away from the house, that I was leaving behind my own happiness. That when I made love to you there this morning, it was the last time I ever would."

The sun lit the curling tips of Stefan's hair. I laid my elbow on the railing and faced his gaunt profile. "Oh, so is that what's brought on all this moping? A premonition?"

He turned. "You are a silly blithe American

gentile, Annabelle de Créouville, with no respect at all for the perversity of the universe."

"Because the universe is not perverse. The universe is beautiful. Look at us here, the two of us, finding each other among billions."

"Yes," he said, "that's what is so perverse."

"I don't understand."

He smoked quietly for a moment, staring into the trees below us. "Do you want to know how I imagined my life ten years ago, Annabelle? This is how my life was supposed to go. I go to university, I join my father's firm, I manage our businesses without, I hope, disgracing myself. I enlarge the family fortune. I find a nice lovely Jewish girl, as a good Jewish son is supposed to do, and we settle down together and grow old and everybody is happy, me and my family and my nice Jewish wife, and whatever else God chooses to bless us with."

"And now there is me," I whispered.

"Now there is you."

"I don't want to upset your family."

He looked up. "My family, Annabelle? My family?"

"Because I'm not a Jew."

Without warning, Stefan whirled around and slammed his fist against the paved wall behind us. I heard the sick sound of his flesh connecting with the pale stone. He said, into the wall, "No, Annabelle. You are not a Jew."

From the gravel path below came the sound of female laughter, as bright and unexpected as sleigh bells in the hot afternoon. A hundred yards away, the Mediterranean glittered and heaved, speckled with shipping, yachts and fishing boats and ferries and tenders, all of them absorbing the last hours of summer in perfect contentment and lazily unaware of the perverse universe contained atop this small hotel balcony. I picked up Stefan's hand and kissed the torn and bleeding knuckles, one by one. I said, "Stay with me here, then. Stay a few days, away from everything else, your family and obligations and these stupid rules we're supposed to follow."

"I have already done that, as long as I could. I cannot just pretend it isn't there, Annabelle. I cannot just hide with you forever. I have to find some way for us to live."

"It doesn't matter how we live, as long as we're together."

He shook his head. "You are so *young*, Annabelle. What am I going to do with you?"

"You're going to come inside and take me to bed. You're going to let me show you how wonderful the universe can be."

Stefan studied my mouth. His face remained still, while his eyes filled with smoke. The laughter grew louder and then ended abruptly, as a door closed below us. He took his hand from mine, folded his arms, and looked at me gravely. "You do not understand

a word I have said, Mademoiselle. Nothing could be worse than such audacity. The universe would then be ten times against us."

I untied the sash of my robe, right there on the open balcony while the woman laughed below us, and it occurred to me that we had done this before: me parting a dressing gown, Stefan gazing at me with astonished rapacity, as I prepared to commit an act of unexpected daring.

"On the other hand, the universe might just be forced to surrender and join us," I said, and I opened up the robe.

16.

You see? You were wrong, after all. No thunderbolts from above. We survived.

Speak for yourself, Mademoiselle.

So you're not worried about the universe anymore?

Liebling, if you think I am capable of any rational thought at this moment, then I fear you have still much more to learn about this business of making love.

(I laid my head against his bare shoulder.)

You know, I'm not asking you to leave your family. I would never do that.

Of course you would not, Mademoiselle. Which is why these delicate matters are left to me.

17.

I wanted to go walking that afternoon, but Stefan insisted we stay in our room. He would leave in the morning, he said, and he didn't want to share me with another living creature. He didn't want to have to nod and smile at other guests when he could be filling his eyes with me.

I slipped from his arms and took out my beautiful new cello from its case. I tuned each string and played the entirety of the first Bach cello suite in G major — prelude, allemande, courante — while Stefan lay on his back in the bed behind me and smoked in silence. When I finished, he asked me to play something else, and I did. For an hour I played for him, until he got up to pour himself another drink and came up behind me to kiss my neck. I put down my bow in mid-measure. No, he said. Don't stop. I want you to play everything you have ever played for me, one more time.

That will take a while, I said.

We have all night.

18.

The afternoon fled, and I had to stop before my fingers bled. Stefan made me put on a dressing gown and ordered dinner. What about the restaurant? I asked, and he said no, we would have dinner here on the balcony, just the two of us, while the sun sank and the

pungent Mediterranean colors faded to indigo.

When the table was cleared away, I told Stefan we had to go outside now, because the rooms were so full of smoke that I couldn't breathe. All right, he said, I suppose it's dark enough.

We walked along the gardens and cliffs without saying much. The air was cooler now and gentle and smelled of newly caught fish. I took the breeze deep into my lungs. Stefan held my hand. When we came to the Eden-Roc, he led me down the stairs to the little stone beach and put his arms around me as we looked out to sea.

"What do you think of Capri?" he said.

"I don't know. I've never been there."

"It is beautiful. We will have the sea and our privacy. We can raise our olives and our children. I will have my agent look into some villas there."

A wave washed up, higher than the rest, and wet my toes.

"What about the wine?" I whispered.

"I am not certain if the soil is suitable for vineyards. I will investigate this for us. But if we cannot make wine?"

I covered his hands with mine, around my waist.

"Then I suppose we'll have to be content with what we have."

19.

We returned to our room smelling of the sea. The smoke had left through the open windows and the balcony doors, and I made Stefan promise not to light any more cigarettes. We undressed and got into bed, me on the left and Stefan on the right, the way we had arranged it from the first night. Let's just sleep, Stefan said, facing me in the darkness. I want to see if I can resist you.

You can't resist me, I said, and I was right. You will wake up tomorrow and you won't be able to walk, Stefan said sadly afterward, cradling me against him, and I told him I was at the Hôtel du Cap, I didn't need to lift a finger if I didn't want to. The windows were all open, and the room was cool and new. We lay quietly entangled, inhaling the gardenias, inhaling the salty marine scent of each other, and I thought, This is the last time, I will wake up tomorrow and he'll be gone. And I won't be able to walk.

20.

Once, during the night, I sat up and saw Stefan's shadow against the bedroom window. I called his name and he came back to the bed, and I told him I was afraid he'd gone already.

"No," he said, "not yet. In a few hours, before the sun comes up. Go back to sleep, Annabelle, *Liebling.*"

"What were you doing?"

He took me back against his chest, in the way we had been lying before. "I put some money in the desk drawer for you. There is also the name of my banker in Paris, who will help you if you need anything else while I am gone."

"What else would I need? You won't be gone that long, will you?"

"I mean in case there is an emergency, or you perhaps need to tell me something."

In my innocence, I couldn't imagine what I would need to tell him, other than everything. I lay there quietly, matching my breathing to his, paying attention to each respiration so I would remember them all.

Stefan said, "Also, I have been thinking a little, about this constitution that governs our union."

"You wish to add an amendment or two? An escape clause?"

"No. I have been thinking that perhaps *constitution* is the wrong word. It is maybe more like a covenant."

"Stefan," I said in French, "I think I'm falling in love with you."

He lifted my hair and kissed me in the tender sliver of skin above my ear. *"Oui, Mademoiselle de Créouville. C'est la même chose avec moi."*

21.

When I woke up, the sun was just rising, and Stefan was gone.

I rolled onto my stomach and went back to sleep, with his pillow pressed across my breast.

PEPPER

COCOA BEACH 1966

1.

The shower in Annabelle Dommerich's guest cottage runs hot as blazes, the way Pepper likes it. She closes her eyes while the water burns down her back, turning her skin red, raising blisters almost. Like a disinfectant.

The baby stirs. Pepper looks down at her belly, the curious round ball of it, and pushes her finger against a protruding wet lump. The lump shifts and pushes back, and Pepper, transfixed, says the only thing that comes to mind.

Hello.

How crazy, being pregnant. You said to yourself casually, "I'm pregnant," like you might say you were bored or sunburned, and in the beginning that's what it was, a theoretical condition, manifest in inconvenient little symptoms that had no obvious link to the biological reality, the peculiar fact that a new and separate human being was growing inside the center of you. You didn't notice the human being until much later, and you still

couldn't quite picture it in your head, a baby. A real one. A tiny fat red little person.

I'm sorry about all this, Pepper adds. (Not aloud, for God's sake.)

But that's the trouble. Sorry isn't enough, is it? You could never be sorry enough.

2.

Because she hadn't set out to sleep with another woman's husband, had she? She had her scruples, believe it or not. Everyone always said, *It's Pepper Schuyler, lock up your husbands,* but it wasn't true. This was the first husband she'd ever slept with.

She'd taken the job after Vivian got married, because a girl had to do something with her life; she couldn't just sit around waiting for her own Dr. Charming to show up, and anyway Pepper wasn't really interested in marrying Dr. Charming. Too much fun to be had, too many adventures to record in the precious few years of excitement your youth and beauty — they did run together, youth and beauty, didn't they? — allowed you. New York was getting old, and she looked down the New Jersey Turnpike toward Washington and said *I'll have that.* Of course, Dad wouldn't even consider law school — *I've wasted enough money educating daughters* — so she made a few phone calls, called in a few favors, and what do you know, the new

183

junior senator from New York needed a Girl Friday.

So that part was all on the up and up. Pepper needed a job in Washington, Pepper found the best job going for a sparky young woman with an English degree, grades not to be ashamed of, manner polished, face and figure top-drawer. She never imagined she would fall in love.

She's always scorned that phrase, *falling in love.* It implies a certain lack of conviction, a lily-livered helplessness that Pepper despises. How could you just *fall* in love? You stepped into love willingly, didn't you, and if it wasn't convenient, you found someone else to step into: *Voilà.* So maybe that was why it happened. Her guard was down. The hours were long, the quarters close, the job intense, the man himself so . . . well. Let's pick an example. One night, working late, everyone else gone, the old story. He offered her a ride home. She accepted. The convertible, the warm breeze, the Lincoln Memorial passing in a noble floodlit blur. They got to talking. His thick hair rustled, his eyes gleamed. She thought, alive and sleepy at the same time, What would it be like to kiss him? And then he did. Kiss her. Pulled over on the deserted street next to the Potomac and kissed her, and he tasted of the bottle of Scotch they'd been sharing, and cigarettes, and warm human mouth. She had wrapped her hand

around the nape of his neck and kissed him back, an act of instinct, because at two o'clock in the morning after a long day's Washington work you clean forgot about a wife you'd never met, tending a litter of unknown children. He pulled away, looking adorably confused. *I'm sorry, I didn't mean that. The Scotch, I guess.* And Pepper patted her hair and agreed that it must have been the Scotch, and they didn't say another word, and that was when it started. That was when she fell in love with him, tumbled right off the branch and never hit bottom, and maybe she should have quit there. Yes, that was her mistake, that she didn't quit right there. Because once she started falling, the sex was inevitable, one way or another. Yes, she had gone home and scrubbed herself all over, thought, What have I done? And then, I will never, ever do that again. But when a man liked sex as much as he did, and a woman was as beautiful and besotted as Pepper, they had better get the hell away from each other, or one day at least one of them will have too much to drink, will be working too hard and feeling sorry for herself and let her guard down. One day they will end up drunk in a hotel bed somewhere, making love three times in one night, and at least one of them will come to repent it.

And that's exactly what happened.

3.

So there it is, the ticking face of her gold
Cartier watch, and it says *Eleven o'clock, you
lazy bitch,* and it can't be wrong, can it?
Pepper pushes open the French door to the
main house and calls out *Hello?* like a question, because the only two sounds are the
fountain tinkling in the courtyard and the
relentless songbirds in the lemon trees, who
seem to have taken a wrong turn looking for
Sleeping Beauty.

In the dining room, calls out Annabelle.

Pepper might well ask *Where's the dining
room?* but instead she follows her nose to the
coffee and the bacon, and her nose — another
valuable Schuyler inheritance — doesn't lead
her astray. The dining room has high ceilings
and a pair of French doors open to the
sunshine and the songbirds, and, more important, a heavy wooden sideboard loaded with
breakfast in chafing dishes. Annabelle sets
down her newspaper and waves to the chair
opposite, which is set with cutlery and an
empty coffee cup. The pot stands to the right.

"Good morning," says Annabelle. "Please
help yourself."

Pepper is already snatching a plate and
sinking a silver serving spoon into an impossibly creamy batch of scrambled eggs. Bacon.
Link sausage. Porridge (ignored). Pitchers of
orange and tomato juice. Pepper picks the

tomato, even though she's in Florida. "Clara will bring your toast," says Annabelle.

Pepper sits and pours the coffee. "Thank you."

"You're welcome. Feeling better?"

"Divine. Do you always have a spread like this at breakfast?"

Annabelle laughs. "Poor Clara. I told her I had a guest, and she's so used to a houseful, she doesn't know how to do it differently. Luckily, I'm a good eater."

"How many is a houseful?"

"Oh, my goodness. Including the older ones and their spouses and kids?" Annabelle ticks on her fingers, frowns, and ticks again.

"You're a grandmother?"

"Oh, yes. Several times over."

The coffee is hot and dark as oil. Pepper adds a pinch of sugar but no cream. "You don't look it."

"I was a young bride."

"Where are all these teeming hordes now?"

"My youngest are in college. The older ones settled in New York, the Washington suburbs. But everyone meets here at Christmas and in the spring. The din is atrocious."

"You make it sound so alluring."

Annabelle folds up her newspaper and finishes her coffee. Pepper gazes at the slim blue pack of cigarettes resting at her one o'clock position, next to the saucer, a blue-and-white pattern: Wedgwood, maybe. As a

187

young debutante, Pepper never paid much attention to china; that was her older sister Tiny's expertise. Tiny's one of those girls who picked out her wedding pattern when she was eight years old.

Annabelle stands up and hands her the newspaper across the table. Her eyes are as warm and sympathetic as chocolate. "You might want to take a look at the headlines," she says. "Something about one of your sisters."

4.

Pepper considers calling her mother first. She taps her fingernails against the telephone receiver, *click click click,* and stares out the mullioned window to the deserted beach across the road.

Mums doesn't know about the baby. That's why Pepper buried herself at Tiny's house in Cape Cod at the beginning of summer, because she couldn't face Mums and Daddy. She couldn't even face Vivian. Strange that she should go running to Tiny in her time of trouble, to perfect Tiny, who never set a well-turned toe in the wrong place. Maybe she knew all along that Tiny had a juicy little secret of her own. Maybe she sensed the unhappiness churning behind Tiny's immaculate shell, as opposed to the happiness that beams right out of Vivian's eye sockets these days. Maybe she knew Tiny would

188

prove a better companion in misery, during the slow, hot summer in Cape Cod.

Or maybe Annabelle was right. Maybe she was just trying to punish herself.

When Pepper was thirteen or fourteen, out in East Hampton for the summer, she wore her first bikini. She'd bought it in town with her careful hoard of spending money, and the following day, a Wednesday, she made her debut on the beach atop a colorful beach blanket, stretching her golden limbs toward the sun. No umbrella. A pair of older boys had wandered over within five minutes, the neighbor boys, sixteen and eighteen. *If it isn't little Pepper, all grown up,* the eighteen-year-old said, toeing a friendly sprinkle of sand onto her bare abdomen. They had played a little volleyball, they had splashed in the surf. Billy (the older one) had put his hands around her naked waist and tossed her into a wave or two. Later, when she walked away to change, he had followed her and kissed her behind the weathered gray boards of the bathhouse, and while he was kissing her he slipped his hand inside the wet triangle covering her right breast and rubbed her nipple. *I have to go now,* she said, breaking away, and she had run up the steps and into the house before he could catch her — she could sprint, Pepper, when she had to — and there was Mums on the back porch, reading a news-

paper, drinking something clear with a slice of lime and plenty of ice. Pepper never forgot the look on her mother's face when she burst up the final step, panting, a little blurry. The sad shake of her head. *You're like me, aren't you?* she said. *You just can't help yourself.* And Pepper said, *Don't be a square, we were just having fun,* and Mums said, *Sure, fun for him,* and Pepper said, *You don't understand anything,* just exactly like every teenager since the beginning of time.

Mums hadn't gotten mad. Mums kept her cool. She just laughed and finished her drink and said, *Well, for God's sake, whatever you do, don't let them get you pregnant.* Those exact words. Pepper recalls them like yesterday's breakfast.

Click click click.

Pepper lifts the receiver and dials up her sister Vivian in Gramercy Park.

"PEPPER! MY GOD! WHERE ARE YOU?"

"I'm in Florida, love, keeping up my suntan. How's things?"

"MY GOD! HAVEN'T YOU HEARD?"

"What, that Tiny's getting a divorce? Old news."

"YOU KNEW ABOUT IT ALREADY?"

"Of course I knew about it." Pepper examines her fingernails. "I was on the Cape all summer, wasn't I? I had a ringside seat."

"AND YOU DIDN'T SAY ANYTHING?"

"For God's sake, stop shouting like that. It was a private little matter, wasn't it, and anyway, it's not the kind of thing you can talk about over the telephone, in-laws lurking in every corner. Especially when your sister writes the nosiest gossip column in New York."

"It is *not* a gossip column." With dignity. "It's a witty and elegant disquisition of social customs in our magnificent little town. And it's the most-read page in the entire *Metropolitan* magazine."

"I rest my case," says Pepper.

The line goes quiet.

"Vivian?"

"I'm here."

Pepper winds the cord around her fingers. "Have you talked to Tiny about it?"

"No, as a matter of fact. She's nowhere to be found. Mums got a letter from her yesterday. She's not saying what's in it. Poor Mums, she had her heart set on Tiny being First Lady. Now she's stuck with a divorcée and a doctor's wife. Her dreams crumbled in the dust. I guess it's all up to you now, Pepper, sweetheart. Any promising young senators up your sleeve?"

"Actually, I'm pregnant," says Pepper.

Again with the silent receiver.

"Vivian?"

"Say that again, Pepper. I'm not sure I

191

heard you properly."

"I'm pregnant."

"That's what I thought."

"Don't fall all over yourself with congratulations."

Vivian draws in a long breath that crackles against Pepper's ear. "Well, well. My God. Knocked up, the middle child. You're sure?"

Pepper looks down at her stomach. "Pretty sure."

"Does Mums know?"

"Of course not."

"When are you due?"

"February."

"FEBRUARY! But that's — that's —"

"Soon. I know."

"Holy moley. How the hell did you hide it from Tiny?"

"I didn't. She knows. That's why she let me stay on the Cape into the autumn. Fixing up that old car of hers."

Vivian snorts. "Oh, *now* I get it. I should have smelled a rat, Pepper Schuyler rattling around in a greasy old garage for months on end. And I thought there must be a man involved."

"Oh, there was. A delicious one. Regretfully, he wasn't mine. He was Tiny's."

"TINY!"

"Indeedy. The ex–Mrs. Hardcastle. Not so virtuous as one might think."

There is a groan, as of stones being laid

192

atop an already heavy burden. "Stop. You're hurting my ears. I'm going to have to sit down."

"Sit down? You, Vivian?"

"Well, I'm in a delicate condition, too, if you'll recall. By my legitimate husband, I feel compelled to add."

"That's a first."

"No sass from you, young lady. I was respectably married for *several* months before Junior arrived."

"Do you want a medal for that?"

A creak of springs sounds faintly in the distance. Pepper props herself on the edge of the sofa table and waits for Vivian's familiar voice to reappear in her ear. The knot in her belly is beginning to unwind, under the tug of Vivian's familiar banter. Why didn't she call up Vivian before? They were born only eleven disgraceful months apart, after all, and it might as well be none. The snappy, happy Schuyler girls, tearing apart Manhattan and putting it back together again. Two and a half years ago, when Vivian moved into her own apartment after college, a dismal grubby fifth-floor walkup (it's always the fifth floor of a five-floor walkup, isn't it?), they had gone out to six different nightclubs before dawn, had smoked and drank and laughed and kissed all kinds of unsuitable men. And then they had gone back to Vivian's grubby apartment, holding each other up as they mounted

193

the vomit-scented stairs, and collapsed to-gether on Vivian's bed. Not another man in sight, at the end of the night: just two sisters, holding each other up.

"So. How are the hemorrhoids?" Vivian asks.

"Speak for yourself."

"You're feeling good, then?"

"Tip-top. I never tossed a single cookie."

"Ah, the luck of the wicked," says Vivian. "Have you been seeing a doctor?"

"I guess that depends on what you mean by *seeing*."

"Not in the biblical sense."

"Then yes. At reasonably regular intervals. Everything seems to be shipshape." The telephone cord crosses Pepper's belly in elongated squiggles. It's the same dress as last night, the blue tunic that matches her eyes. Pepper watches the fabric move, the cord shift. Baby's restless. "Any more ques-tions?" she adds, though of course there is one last question, the obvious question, the biggie, the question even Vivian is almost too tactful to ask.

"So. Who's the father?" asks Vivian.

"No one you know," says Pepper.

"Not at present, maybe, but I can guarantee he's going to know me shortly." Vivian's tone is that of a cumulonimbus, towering on the horizon.

Pepper's already shaking her head, almost

as if her sister can see her. "Down, Vivian."

"If this little man-swine thinks he can get my sister in trouble and walk away scot-free —"

"I don't want to have anything to do with him, do you hear me? Not a single god-damned thing." The words hurt her throat; she actually places her hand against the cords of her neck as she says them. The last word, *thing,* is just a whisper, stripped of conviction. Pepper shuts her eyes and squeezes her throat, squeezes hard, until her windpipe lies flat against the hard muscle. If she can't breathe, she can't speak, can she? She can't tell Vivian about the telephone call and the notes, the messages to the hotel, Captain Seersucker, the men outside who might be tourists and might not.

"That bad, is it?" Vivian says.

"Yeah."

"So come home."

Pepper shakes her head. "Can't."

"Why not?"

"Because I like the weather down here, that's why."

"At least tell me where you are."

Pepper hesitates. "Cocoa Beach."

Vivian sighs again, and for some reason Pepper thinks of her father, who was also there that day when she was fourteen, the day she wore her first bikini and found out what the older kids got up to during the sum-

mer, and who looked up from his newspaper when she ran in from the porch, clutching Mums's words to her half-naked bosom. He was sitting in the chair next to the window, and he looked as if he'd swallowed a peach pit. *Had a good time?* he asked, in such a way that Pepper knew he'd seen every little thing from his perch up there above the beach, where he liked to spend his summer days watching the pretty girls go by. She said *Go to hell,* like every other teenager since after the war, while inside her head she thought, *My God, you old drunk, why don't you go out and tell Billy he can't just cop a feel like that, I mean, go out and thrash the sonofabitch for grabbing your fourteen-year-old daughter's tits behind the bathhouse.* Care, *for God's sake.*

But he hadn't, had he? He hadn't heard what was pounding inside her head. He turned to the ashtray and made busy with the cigarette, and somewhere in the middle of all that stubbing he said, *Put something on, will you, before you start a riot.*

Pepper was on her own, he meant. In these matters, Pepper would have to take care of Pepper.

Vivian speaks carefully into her ear. "You're sure you're all right, honey?"

Oh, Vivian. You with the nice doctor husband and the nice little cherub, the pretty sun-filled apartment in Gramercy and the

glamorous job writing about glamorous people. Vivian, whose pregnant belly is perfectly legitimate, created in mutual love with her nice doctor husband. No more reckless nights out for Vivian, no more commiseration between Vivian and Pepper. How could you commiserate with someone who had no misery to share with you?

"I'm sure," says Pepper, and before either of them can say anything else, she hangs up the receiver in its handsome ivory cradle, and for a long while afterward that rattle is the last sound in the room.

5.

But you can't keep Pepper cooped up indoors all day. Sooner or later she finds her way to the beach across the road, where the weather is mild and the surf gentle. The tide reaches a few feet below the line of seaweed that serves as a high-water mark, and after a quarter-hour of walking, Pepper decides it's on its way out.

The comely young doctor in Chatham said that a long, brisk walk every morning was good for the baby and good for her. So Pepper walks briskly, a mile or so up the beach, and the sun is so warm she sits down on the deserted sand and stretches her toes toward the ocean. No curious eyes on her belly, no men grabbing her arm in a stairwell and telling her they had something important

197

to discuss. No messages. No urgent notes. *Pepper, I don't know what kind of game you're playing, but we have to come to some kind of agreement here. A man in my position . . .*

A man in his position. A man in his position could do whatever the hell he wanted, couldn't he? He could call on any resources he needed to track her down.

Three hundred thousand dollars was supposed to buy her safety. But where could she go that he couldn't find her? Her family, maybe. Her family would protect her, if they had to. The Schuylers might snipe among themselves, but they banded together effectively against outside attack. That was how they'd survived, while other families rose and fell around them: they stuck together. They held the line.

Except that this was no ordinary attack. And *attack* in any case meant casualties, and who knew what kind of casualties might be inflicted on innocent bystanders, as a result of Pepper having accidentally fallen in love and broken a commandment or two?

Pepper sits up. The sand falls away from her hair. She stares at the plumb horizon and thinks, My God, I made love to this man, we shared a hotel bed. We shared drinks and cigarettes and sex, we shared our bodies, the rummage of our souls.

And now this. Wondering whether her family is even safe. Whether her family would be

safer if she goes to them, or safer if she does not. A doozy of a decision for Pepper to make, at a time like this.

6.

As Pepper crosses the road and starts along the circular drive toward the house, a pair of dogs lopes out to greet her. Weimaraners. She allows herself to be sniffed and inspected, and apparently she passes muster, because the dogs fall back to her heels and escort her inside like a visiting dignitary.

The rooms are still and sepulchral. Pepper was too distracted to pay much attention earlier — maybe she's still too distracted, but the long walk and the long ocean have settled her nerves just enough to make room for curiosity — and now she recognizes the quiet elegance of the house, the villa-like proportions, the simple furnishings. Annabelle Dommerich has taste. Pepper tosses her hat on the dining room table and wanders into the living room, from which she placed her telephone call to Vivian a few hours ago.

"Annabelle?" she calls out. "Mrs. Dommerich?"

One of the dogs nudges her hand. Dogs are marvelous, aren't they? No matter what your sins, if a dog can stand you, there must be some hope left for your soul. Pepper takes in the square proportions, the blue-and-white décor — Greece, she thinks, or some other

lovely spot perched on the Adriatic, washed by a pale, hot sun — and she thinks, I could just about like this place.

The dog nudges her hand again, and Pepper, turning away from a large abstract painting, realizes that no one answered her call. The air is overgrown with silence. She casts a final glance along the four walls, the neat furniture, and as she fondles the dog's ears and prepares to leave, she thinks, That's strange, something's missing from this charming blue-and-white room overlooking the ocean, home in certain seasons to a large and fruitful family. Something no happy home ever lacks, something even the Schuylers display in silvery abundance, crowding every possible surface.

There aren't any photographs.

7.

Pepper crosses the hall, calling Annabelle's name. She sticks her head inside the next room, which seems to be a music room of some kind: there is a handsome ebony piano next to the window, and a straight-backed chair placed before a wooden music stand. A cello case is propped against the wall.

Pepper prepares to withdraw her head, but something on the opposite wall catches her eye. She steps closer and sees a large black-and-white photograph — yes, a photograph at last — depicting a dainty dark-haired

woman on a stage somewhere, holding a cello between her knees. Her face is rapturously crinkled, a kind of ecstasy of concentration, and her arms have been caught in the very act of creation. She's wearing a dress that might be any color from black to scarlet, but you didn't really notice the dress, did you? You noticed that rapturous face, those poised and graceful arms, the curving cello between her legs.

Annabelle Dommerich, in the act of ecstatic creation.

Annabelle Dommerich. Wasn't there something familiar about that name, after all?

Pepper begins to breathe again, and that's when she notices that she had, in fact, stopped. Breathing, that is. That her chest had frozen a little, at the sight of that photograph. How old is that black-and-white image? How long ago did Annabelle Dommerich play the cello on a stage like that? Impossible to tell by the dress or even the hairstyle. Annabelle is so perfectly ageless.

So. Annabelle Dommerich's got a history of her own — not an everyday, trials-and-tribulations history, births and deaths and whatever else, but the kind of breathless and brilliant history that gives Vivian her *Metropolitan* magazine fodder. Fame and fortune and forbidden passion. But more than that. A rare black Mercedes, fleeing into the German night and then disappearing into a shed on

Cape Cod.

A cello.

Pepper runs her curious finger along the curve of the top of the cello case, which is old and leathery and somewhat battered, not the kind of case you'd expect from a world-class musician. On the other hand, why not? Pepper doesn't do symphonies, at least not since the entire junior class at Nightingale-Bamford went to a matinee at Carnegie Hall, a compulsory exercise. It was the end of autumn, and a famous pianist was performing, but Pepper had spent the first half of the concert in the ladies' room with Edie Brooks-Huntington, whose boyfriend had just jilted her. Edie was a weepy kind of girl, went through a box of tissues at least, so Pepper took her seat only after the intermission, and even then, for the first ten minutes, her brain was occupied with plots for revenge against the Faithless Michael, until at last the music stole over her, note by note, and she realized that the piano was in some mysterious way expressing the exact same emotion. That the piano lamented, too; the piano wanted revenge.

Pepper never returned to Carnegie Hall. But she hadn't forgotten that moment of companionship with the grand piano. When, several years later, she was passing by Daddy's study and heard that same piece of music floating through the doorway, she had

actually paused in the hallway outside and pressed her quiet hand against her ribs, until the last note bled away and the needle scratched to the end of the record, and Daddy had risen from his chair, lifted the arm, and changed the record to something else, a violin concerto, never knowing that Pepper stood there in the hallway, hidden by the door, sharing the music with him.

Pepper looks back at the photograph — one single photograph in the whole entire pad, and this would be it — and calls out softly, maybe not even meaning to be heard.

Annabelle?

8.

When she reaches the dining room, the French doors stand open to the courtyard, channeling a tide of ripe lemon and spicy eucalyptus. Pepper opens her throat and breathes it in. "Annabelle?" she calls again.

The dogs start off down the opposite corridor. Pepper follows them. Beautiful, athletic things. Their coats are a healthy silver-taupe, their tails undocked and wagging briskly. The hindquarters disappear around a corner, and for the first time Pepper hears a human voice, fondly scolding the dogs, *Oh, you wicked things, there you are, stay down now.* But it's not Annabelle Dommerich; it's the woman who brought in Pepper's toast and refilled her coffee.

"Oh, hello, Clara," Pepper says. "I don't suppose you know where I might find my hostess?"

Clara says, "I was just coming to find you, Miss Schuyler. Mrs. Dommerich left an hour ago."

"Left? Where to? Errands?"

"Oh, no. Gone off on one of her trips again." Clara offers an apologetic smile and sticks a hand into her apron pocket. She pulls out a sheet of thick ecru writing paper, folded in half. "She told me to tell you she was sorry not to say good-bye in person."

Pepper takes the paper. The dogs have run on ahead, to the kitchen, probably. The note weighs heavily between her fingers, and for some reason she doesn't want to open it here, in front of Clara. Just in case. "Good-bye? That sounds rather dramatic. Did she say when she'd be back?"

"No, ma'am. She usually doesn't. But she did say you're to make yourself right at home while she's gone."

ANNABELLE

ANTIBES 1935

After a day or two, I could walk again. I was ready to see the world, the good earth I would shortly inherit with Stefan, or at least that little corner of it occupied by the Hôtel du Cap. My trunks appeared, and a note from Papa: *Enjoy yourself, mignonne, and remember my home is always open to you. Kisses, Papa.* I fingered the paper and thought, What a strange thing for a father to write. But then, what else could I have expected?

In the desk drawer, I found an envelope containing ten thousand francs and a scrap of notepaper bearing a name and a Paris address I didn't recognize. I put them both away. I didn't want to look at them; I didn't want to think about what they represented. I put on my sandals and my hat and slipped down the stairs and along the graveled drive to the Eden-Roc pavilion overlooking the bay.

The hotel beach was small and rocky and not much used — most guests preferred the

saltwater pool nestled into the basalt — and I had no company when I stripped away my dress and arched across the gathering waves into the sea. I swam for an hour, until my limbs were limp, until my head was heavy, and then I crawled shivering to the shore and lay there on the stones while the last of the August sun warmed my back.

When Stefan comes back, I thought, we'll lie here together, except the air will be much cooler. We'll put on our robes and curl up together in the shelter of the cliff, and Stefan will bring out a bottle of champagne, and we will laugh about that night on the tiny beach on Sainte-Marguerite, and how we kissed for the first time in the fort while the sun rose over the rooftops.

My skin dried, and then my swimming costume. I stopped shivering. I realized the emptiness in my belly wasn't loneliness but hunger, and I put on my dress and climbed the stairs to the tearoom. I ordered coffee and a small plate of sandwiches. As I waited, I heard a laugh like sleigh bells from the table behind me, and there was something so familiar about the noise and the throat from which it came that I feigned interest in the architecture around me and glanced over my shoulder.

Isn't it funny, the way we know when someone's watching? At the exact instant my eyes found the laughing woman's face, her

206

eyes slid directly to mine, and though she was wearing a beautiful curved hat and an afternoon dress, I recognized her lips and her eyes and the shape of her chin before I turned back to my white tablecloth and my view across the bay, while my breath tripped up in my chest.

Stefan's mistress. She was wearing less kohl, and her lipstick this afternoon was fresh and berry-red, but you couldn't mistake a face like that. The waiter arrived with my coffee and sandwiches, and I drank the coffee without thinking and scalded my tongue.

She hadn't recognized me. Surely she hadn't recognized me.

"I beg your pardon," said a drawling English voice behind me, "but you're the nurse from the yacht, aren't you? You're Stefan's nurse."

I set down the cup and looked up into her face, which was less beautiful and more riveting than I remembered. She had languorous green eyes: that was the trick. The rest didn't matter, when you had eyes like that, but the rest of her was still marvelous. Her hair was honey-dark and glossy beneath the crown of her hat, and she wore the kind of dress that film stars wore, the kind of dress that actually anticipated what everybody would be wearing next year, without really trying. It was navy blue and absolutely snug around a carved miniature waist, and the color made

her berry mouth pop out from that silky tanned face.

I rolled my own unvarnished lips together and nodded. "You have an excellent memory."

"Yes, rather. So do you. You recognized me straightaway, didn't you? How is he?"

"All better."

"Of course he is. He's such a feral thing. Do you mind if I join you?"

"If you like."

She turned her head to the table where she'd been sitting. "Peter, darling. I'm going to be a few minutes. Do run up to the room and fetch my bathing costume, there's a good chap."

Her companion, a middle-aged man in a white jacket, looked us both over and stubbed out his cigarette. "I thought we weren't swimming today," he said petulantly.

"I've changed my mind. Run along, now, and for heaven's sake stop sulking."

Peter rose from the table. He had thinning blond hair and a very slight belly interrupting a frame that was otherwise lean. "Your servant, ma'am." He sighed, and picked up his hat and left the room.

Stefan's mistress turned back to me and smiled. "He's a good sort of egg, really, but awfully dull. Do you mind if I sit?"

"Please." I gestured.

"My name is Alice. Lady Alice Penhallow."

She sat down and held out a slender hand, weighed down with rings.

I hesitated for an instant and then took her hand. Her grip was soft and uninterested. "Annabelle de Créouville."

At that, her eyebrows lifted. "Gracious me. Are you really? We all thought you were just a rumor, the prince's cloistered daughter. Well, that's trumped me, for certain. I don't suppose I stand a chance now."

"Haven't you moved on already?"

"Peter? He's lovely, at least when he's not sulking, but really just an expedient. I won't say I've been hanging about for any particular reason, but perhaps I have. I suppose you've slept with him, however."

I flinched.

"Yes, of course you have. He's irresistible that way, isn't he?" She plucked a sandwich from my plate and nibbled at the end. "And so fearsomely rich, like all good Jews. I don't blame you a second. I rather thought I was in trouble, when I first saw you on the yacht. And then he didn't invite me back. Did he mention me at all?"

"Not very much, I'm afraid."

"No, of course not. He's always observed a certain code of courtesy, even when he's juggling us about like ninepins. I've never heard him say a cross word about any woman." She swallowed and nibbled again, like a glamorous rabbit. "Even his wife."

You never do see it coming, do you? A shock like that. I suppose that's why it's a shock. Like an automobile collision, like the time I was eight years old and my nanny was taking me to a children's party, not far from this very spot. We were late, and she was driving fast. There had been a calamitous afternoon thunderstorm, and I suppose my nanny was too young and experienced to know that if you were driving fast enough, your automobile (however heavy) would skim like a seaplane across the surface of a good-sized puddle. I sat in the back, watching the landscape go by, thinking about one of the older girls who would be at the party and how she liked to pull my braids and call me the Princess of Crybabies, the Princess of Crayfish (she was American, too, the daughter of one of the rich expatiates who flooded this particular stretch of coast in the twenties), when I heard a sharp noise and I was flying, and then there came a horrific smash of metal and I thought, Someone's had an accident, and the very next instant my head hit the front seat and I realized it was us. I don't know how I survived. I had cuts and bruises and a broken finger; the nanny spent the next two months in the hospital with her leg in traction, contemplating the folly of speeding through the rain on your way to a children's party. Her head was never quite the same.

Even when he's juggling us about like nine-

pins, said Lady Alice, nibbling my sandwich, and I was flying through the air.

Even his wife, she said, and I heard a crash and thought, Someone's had an accident, and I realized it was me.

"His wife," I said, after a pause. "Of course."

But Lady Alice was an old hand. "What, didn't you know he was married?"

"I . . . He never mentioned . . ."

"Oh, you poor darling." She set down her sandwich, and she really did look concerned. Up close, she was younger than I imagined. The sleek glow of her skin was genuine, not manufactured, and the bosom beneath her swinging neckline had that springy quality you couldn't bring back, once it was lost. "Now I really *am* upset with him. That's the sort of secret a man shouldn't keep to himself. Though perhaps he assumed you already knew. I thought everyone knew."

I hardly heard her. I certainly didn't comprehend her, not until later. The room was falling in pieces around me. My stomach was sick, rejecting the alien morsels of sandwich and coffee. I put my hand to my mouth.

Lady Alice reached across the table and touched my forearm. "Does it matter so much to you?"

I couldn't speak. *Wife.* The word turned in my brain. My mother had been a wife, until another woman slept with her husband. A

very bad woman, a woman I hated, who was now me.

"Where is he now?" she asked gently.

"Germany," I said. I was too stunned to say anything but the truth, and Lady Alice was so improbably sympathetic, as if we had somehow found ourselves fighting on the same side in a long and muddy war. "He went back to Germany two days ago to . . . he said . . . to settle some affairs. He was going to come back for me."

Some family affairs, he had said. Some arrangements, which I was not to mention to anyone. I was not to mention anything about us to anyone, and especially not to his good friend Charles.

Lady Alice was replying, in a soothing voice, "Of course he was. You mustn't doubt that. I'm quite sure he cares for you very much. You're the kind of girl he *would* care for, now that I think about it. You're nothing like his usual sort. I'm sure he'll come back for you. He always keeps his word." She snapped her fingers. "Perhaps he was going to see her, to tell her he had found someone serious this time . . ."

"She knows?"

Lady Alice laughed. "She's the greatest fool alive if she doesn't."

A small black fly had found its way to the edge of my plate. The hairlike legs climbed in the direction of the sandwiches, delicately

uncertain, hardly daring to hope. I didn't have the heart to brush it away. I listened to the gentle clink of china around me, the patter of conversation, and thought, I am the greatest fool alive.

"My dear girl," said Lady Alice, "are you quite all right? You look as if you might be sick."

I said that I was all right, thank you.

She continued. "When he comes back, you mustn't let him off the hook. You've got to ask him very specific questions. I know it's terribly romantic to have a love affair — it's your first, isn't it? I was the same way — but they're like worms, you know, they'll try to find a way to wiggle off, any way they can. What has he told you about himself?"

What, indeed? "Not a great deal," I said, and I realized how true it was. We had talked for hours, we had spent long days together, and in my newfound wisdom I thought I knew him. I knew the shape of his face and the color of his eyes. I knew that his skin tanned easily. I knew that he was handsome in pajamas and dinner jackets and especially nothing at all, except when he was in a grim mood; I knew that he was about six feet tall and quite lean, that he was made of neat, well-packed muscle, though he wasn't bulky by nature. I knew that he could sail, that he preferred tennis to golf; that he had gone to boarding school in England and university in

213

Berlin, though I didn't know which ones he attended and I couldn't have said what he studied. I knew that he disliked excessive displays of emotion, though he felt deeply. I knew that he preferred martinis before dinner and brandy after it, that he tolerated whisky only if it was served neat at room temperature. I knew he smoked strong Turkish cigarettes that he had delivered from a tobacconist in Paris. I knew that he spoke German, English, and French with great fluency, that he had a smattering of Spanish and Italian, that he read Virgil in the original Latin. I knew that he had a high tolerance for pain and a low tolerance for nonsense. I knew that he liked women. I knew that women liked him. I knew the way his face grew heavy when he wanted me, the way his eyes filled with smoke. I knew the way his body shuddered when he achieved his *petite mort.* I knew the way he sank upon me afterward, the sensation of his weight, the distribution of his limbs. I knew the smell of his skin.

But I didn't know his father's name. I didn't know the town where he lived. I didn't know what business his family was in, shipping or textiles or banking. I didn't know what, exactly, he was doing the night he fell bleeding into my life; I didn't know if his parents were alive, or if he had any siblings, or if he had any close friends other than my brother. I didn't know his age. I knew exactly

where he existed in my heart; I had no idea where he existed in the universe.

I didn't know he had a wife.

"The truth is, they're all beasts," Lady Alice was saying. "Every man alive, even dear old Peter, would happily get his leg up on another woman if he could, and if he thought he could get away with it. You mustn't let it destroy you, darling. Enjoy him, by all means. Fall in love with him, if you like. I suppose you already have. But for heaven's sake, enjoy him with your eyes open."

I looked up. "Do they have children together?"

She frowned thoughtfully. "I think there's a son. He doesn't say a word about him, however. I've always thought he isn't fond of children; you know how careful he is."

"Careful?"

"Yes, always." She paused and leaned forward. Her beautiful green eyes turned round under the pencil-thin lines of her eyebrows. "My dear girl. You don't know what I'm talking about, do you?"

"Of course I know."

"No, you don't. Oh, the rat. The dirty little rat. I say, he really *had* better come up to scratch, or he'll hear from me about it. You're how old?"

"Nearly twenty."

"Nineteen. The horror. It doesn't bear thinking about. Well, we'll cross our fingers,

won't we? Peter! There you are. I'm afraid there's been another change of plans."

I swiped my thumbs at the corners of my stunned eyes and looked up at Peter's weary face. He was holding a straw basket in one hand and a bottle in the other.

"Another one?" he said.

Lady Alice took the bottle from Peter's limp hand and examined the label. "Yes. Poor Annabelle here has had a dreadful shock. This will do for a start. Would you mind fetching us a pair of glasses? There's a dear chap."

Peter slunk obediently off to the bar. Lady Alice returned her attention to me. Her smile was bright and large and white-toothed, almost American.

"Don't worry about a single little thing, my dear. Alice knows exactly what to do."

■ ■ ■ ■

SECOND MOVEMENT

■ ■ ■ ■

"Paris is always a good idea."
AUDREY HEPBURN

Annabelle

PARIS 1935

1.

I hadn't planned on marrying anyone, let alone the Baron von Kleist. I didn't want to sleep with anyone, ever again, though Lady Alice said it was like falling off a horse: you should climb back on right away, or you would develop a complex. Lady Alice was big on complexes. She was devoted to modern psychoanalysis. She had explained everything to me on the night train to Paris: I had gone to bed with Stefan because my father was a philanderer, and my mother was dead, and my brother paid no attention to me. I had all sorts of unresolved desires that I had gathered up and transferred onto Stefan's person, like the decorations on a Christmas tree. All quite natural, she had said breezily, and nothing to be ashamed of. There were worse ways to lose your virginity. One day, she would tell me how she lost hers, but not yet. The story was not for the young at heart.

By then we were already bosom friends. I had told her my history over that first bottle

219

of wine, and I don't remember what I said over the second. We had left for Paris that night, without even composing the customary note of vicious explanation. I wanted the break to be quick and clean; I wanted to flummox Stefan as thoroughly as he had flummoxed me. I wanted to leave no sign that our connection had even taken place, except for the precious Amati cello and the ten thousand francs, both of which I had left behind in the room Stefan had paid for in advance — *two months' accommodation, Madame Silverman. Are you* quite *sure you wish to depart so soon?* asked the astonished clerk — along with the scribbled name and the address in Paris.

I hadn't wanted the temptation. I hadn't wanted a single thread to dangle near my hand, asking to be pulled.

At dawn, the wagon-lit from Nice had deposited us like so much refuse into the greasy morning stink of the Gare de Lyon, and we shared a taxi to the rue de Berri and the shabbily grand apartment of my astonished father. It was the last day of August, and Paris was rubbing its eyes and waking up to the rising autumn. And that is how I came to become intimate with Johann von Kleist.

2.

It wasn't Carnegie Hall, or the Paris Opéra. But the music room in my father's apartment

220

was large and beautiful, and the end of it contained only me; in the rest of the space crammed my father's friends, cheek by jowl with Lady Alice's companions in debauchery. An atmosphere of hushed reverence coated the furniture. The lights were hot on my skin. At the front of the threadbare orchestra, the conductor's baton angled in the air, and the conductor's eyes found mine.

In that instant of anticipation — as my mind skimmed across the bars of music ahead, encompassing thousands of notes into a single three-dimensional model, a living thing built of sound — I almost forgot Stefan.

3.

We held a party afterward in the drawing room. The long balcony doors were thrown open to the syrupy air of early October. Papa brought out champagne and Lady Alice brought out her friends. "You were smashing!" she shouted in my ear, and she handed me a glass of champagne and stood on a chair. She was wearing a ravishing violet dress, a glittering V neckline that ended just above her navel. Nobody but Lady Alice could have pulled it off so elegantly. She raised her glass and her voice. *"Bonsoir, mesdames et messieurs!"* she called out, and everybody hushed, because it was Lady Alice.

221

"Thank you all for joining us tonight, to celebrate the musical debut of my precious talented friend, Annabelle de Créouville." She held out her hand to me and hauled me up on the neighboring chair. There was a roar. I wore black, because I was a Serious Musician, and my neckline was actually that: a line halfway up my neck, separating black from porcelain white. But the material was a lovely lithe satin that clung to my breasts and waist and hips, all the way down to a magnificent fishtail below, wide enough to accommodate a cello between my knees — like a tiny beautiful black mermaid, Lady Alice said, except for the scales — and I knew I was just as *ravissement* as she was. She went on, enjoying herself thoroughly: "I plucked this flower from the dry soil of the Mediterranean a month ago, ladies and gentleman, and just look how the darling thing has bloomed. Drink your champagne, love." (I drank.) "And I hope *all* of you drink loads of champagne and get terribly drunk, so the real fun can begin." Another roar. "Now enjoy yourselves, darlings, and remember to thank Annabelle's father for all the marvelous bubbles."

She jumped down and I jumped after her, and someone took me by the neck and kissed my cheek. I pulled away, laughing, and set my empty champagne glass on the table. A full one was placed in my hand. Charles came

up and embraced me and told me I was wonderful. He had brought several friends with him, and they all lined up and explained how moved they had been by my performance. One of them was American, extremely tall, wearing the kind of canine open grin that was all over the States and so rare over here, though his eyes were serious and European. He was holding a glass of champagne in one hand and a newly lit cigarette in the other. He transferred the champagne skillfully into the grip of his cigarette fingers and held out his hand.

"That was wonderful, Mademoiselle de Créouville," he said, in an endearing American accent that made me want to fall on his chest.

"It's Annabelle," I said, taking his hand.

"I especially enjoyed the Dvořák. My mother used to play that one on her old Victrola when I was a kid. Really took me back, and it's a lovely piece of music to begin with. I won't exactly *admit* you brought a tear to my eye, but that doesn't mean you didn't." He winked.

"Well, thank you very much, Mr. . . . ?" I lifted the last word inquisitively.

"Greenwald," he said. "Nick Greenwald."

"Mr. Greenwald. Thank you for coming, and especially for your very extravagant praise."

"It's Nick, and I don't think I was being

223

extravagant at all." He leaned forward. His eyes had softened a bit, and though I couldn't see their color beneath Papa's aging chandeliers, I liked their shape, and the trustworthy way the skin crinkled around them when he smiled, which he was doing now. "Actually, we've met already. I guess you don't remember. In a certain boathouse, at the beginning of August? I lost my dinner jacket that night."

The champagne caught in my throat. He waited patiently while I coughed. When I raised my head again, he was still smiling. "I'm a little insulted you didn't recognize me, actually," he said, "but I guess you had plenty of distraction."

"Yes."

"I hear you stitched the old man right up, though, and sent him happily on his way."

"I wasn't the one who stitched him up."

He shrugged a pair of wide American shoulders. "Close enough. Did he ever tell you anything about what happened that night?"

"No, as a matter of fact. He didn't tell me much at all."

"I see." He swirled the champagne in his glass, as if he wanted to say something else and didn't know how.

My throat hurt. I needed to take Nick Greenwald by the arm and ask him a thousand questions: how he knew Stefan, and what Stefan was doing now, and did he know

224

Stefan's wife, and what was she like? Had Stefan returned to the Hôtel du Cap to find me, and what had he done when I wasn't there? But I had spent the last several weeks ignoring those questions when they scored along my brain, on the street and in the café and in my bed at night, and I wasn't going to start reopening the wound now, when it had finally begun to knit.

"Well," I said, tilting my glass toward him, "all's well that ends well."

Nick Greenwald touched his glass to mine, but his face wasn't in it. He bent his head a little closer to me, and his lower eyelids squinted upward in concentration. "Yes. All's well that ends well, right?"

"As far as I know. The last I heard, Stefan Silverman was heading back to his wife and son in Germany."

"Daughter," said Nick.

I smiled. "Daughter. I must have misheard. But I haven't heard from him since. Your information is much better than mine."

"Actually, I haven't heard from him since the end of August."

"Well, then. He must be very happy indeed," I said.

Nick lifted his cigarette thoughtfully. "So you haven't heard anything at all?"

"No. Should I have?"

Maybe I said it too eagerly, because Nick Greenwald removed the cigarette from his

225

lips and leaned so close, I could smell the champagne on his breath. "Because I got a note from him, just before he left, that there was a girl who might need help. And I had a hunch just now, watching you play . . ." He trailed off expectantly, and I thought, *It's him, my God, the friend in Paris.*

I knit my other hand around my glass, so it wouldn't shake. "I have no idea what you're talking about. I don't need any help."

"Listen, I'm not going to tell your brother, if that's what —"

A hand fell on my shoulder, and I turned gratefully into the glowing face of my papa — *C' était magnifique, ma chérie, magnifique!* — and by the time I turned around Nick Greenwald was gone.

Thank God.

So I pushed Nick and Stefan out of my mind, and we laughed and drank and smoked for hours and hours, until Paris drained the last guest away just before dawn, and I fell asleep on a cherry Empire sofa with one hand resting on my cello case, still wearing my marvelous black dress, like a dark mermaid beached on a red shore.

4.

I had a lesson the next morning in Neuilly, not a long walk, but impossible while carrying a cello. I rang up Charles and asked if he would mind driving me there in his car, a

wretched Renault from the previous decade. His voice on the other end was not pleased.

"Charles," I said, "when you dragged me from my nice comfortable garden wall to the boathouse last August, did I hesitate for even a second? Or did I scramble down the cliff path in my slippers and sacrifice ten days of my life to the service of your friend?"

"That's not the same thing." He paused. "What time is the lesson?"

"Eleven o'clock. But the traffic will be immense. You'd better come now, dressed or not."

5.

"Is everything all right?" Charles said, as we spun around the Étoile, dodging a lumbrous delivery truck in a display of expert metropolitan reflexes.

"Everything's wonderful."

"Because you seem different."

"In what way?"

"I don't know. I was thinking about it last night, while you were sawing away up there in your black dress. I wouldn't have recognized you."

"Thank you."

He changed gears noisily and swerved down the avenue de la Grande Armée, toward Neuilly. A flower seller looked up from his daffodils and tulips and thrust his hand into the air. "And then on the telephone this

227

morning. I hung up the phone and thought, You know, I'll bet she'd never do that now."

"Do what?"

"Drop everything and run down the cliff and spend half of August nursing a gunshot wound, without asking any questions."

"Yes, I've learned to ask questions now," I said.

The buildings slid by, cafés and shopfronts, Paris in the reckless enthusiasm of spring-time. The sidewalk tables were already out, and the patrons smoked languorously and drank small cups of coffee. Charles had the top down, so I could smell the unmistakable city air: the bread ovens, the cigarettes, the sultry stench of automobile exhaust. I could hear the accordion lilt of a street musician, somewhere nearby. I had always loved Paris, the little I knew of it, and I loved it even more now. I loved the hustle-bustle, the knowledge that I played a small but essential note in this glorious symphony.

"But you're quieter, too," said Charles.

"Am I? I don't think so."

"That's why I asked if something was wrong. I can't put my finger on it. There used to be this light inside you, this spark of life, and it's gone out. Even last night, when you were laughing, you didn't seem happy. And you're pale."

"I've always been pale."

He sighed. "All right. If you don't want to

talk about it."

We stopped in midstream, waiting for the traffic ahead to clear. My cello sat on the seat between us, its black rounded end sticking up like a third head. I placed my hand around the edge, near the metal fastening, and as I did I heard my own voice echo back from an Antibes cliff: *That's you. You have brought me to life.*

The car jerked forward, and I pushed the thought away.

6.

The lesson lasted an hour, and I emerged into the open air to find a steady spring rain soaking the pavement, and not a taxi in sight. I trudged to the Métro. By one o'clock in the afternoon I was thrusting open the door to the apartment on the rue de Berri, bellowing for lunch.

Alice had just arisen. "But what about breakfast?" she asked innocently, lighting a cigarette. She was dressed in an emerald-green kaftan and managed to look expensive, even creased with sleep.

"Breakfast is long past. But you can have eggs and coffee if you like. What are these?"

"Flowers for you, *ma petite*. Lovely, aren't they?"

"For me?" I dropped my cello case against one of the chairs and stared at the vase on the round center table, which overflowed with

229

close-packed blooms, all of them conspicu-
ously out of season. I realized I had smelled
the stargazer lilies all the way from the
entrance hall.

"Rather a humbling moment for your
obedient servant." Lady Alice joined me at
the table, bringing an air of reverence with
her. "One's used to having worshipful flowers
all to oneself."

"What's this?" asked my father, from the
doorway. He looked even more exhausted
than Alice, though he was already washed
and dressed, his dark hair damp against his
neck.

"Flowers for your daughter," said Alice.

He walked across the room to join us and
placed a kiss on Alice's shoulder, where the
kaftan had slipped down. (What, this shocks
you? I assure you, it took them all of two
weeks.) "From whom?" he asked.

"Not Charles," I said.

"No, Charles hasn't two francs to rub
together," Alice said confidently. "But I took
the liberty of opening the card myself." She
plucked it from the table and handed it to
me. "Some German chap."

"German!"

"Don't be silly, darling. A nobleman, with
terribly elegant handwriting. See for yourself."

I opened the card.

With great Esteem on the Occasion of your musical Debut.

Across the top, the name *Johann von Kleist* was engraved in discreet black letters.

"Mon Dieu," said my father. "What a very great surprise. I didn't know the fellow had it in him."

7.

In the beginning, Lady Alice had loved the idea of Paris. *We'll make you into a goddess,* she had said on the train. *We'll be the queens of Montparnasse.* She could use a change herself, something more interesting than luxury. She was tired of sleeping with rich men; she would try poor artists now, and see if that saved her soul.

As I said, that resolution lasted all of two weeks, not that my father was all that rich anymore. But he wasn't poor in the ordinary sense of the word, and the apartment was grand and littered with treasures, and the two of them actually seemed to be in love. Like to like, I supposed. Alice now wafted an air of delicate self-satisfaction like the most precious French perfume, and naturally her attention turned to my own affairs.

"Of course you should see him," she said to me, over lunch. "That's what would complete things for you — your rehabilitation, I mean. A love affair."

"I don't want to have a love affair."

"Of course you do. They're great fun, for one thing, and for another, I think you need it. I was talking to an analyst the other day, and he said that you need to go to bed with someone else soon, before you develop a sexual complex."

"You and your complexes."

"They're not *my* complexes, darling. They're yours."

"I suppose your analyst proposed himself to do the honors."

She tipped her cigarette into the ashtray. "He did, in fact. But that doesn't mean he's not right."

"You do realize it's all nonsense, this psychoanalysis business. This modern obsession with sex."

"No, it's true. The sexual instinct is perfectly natural, it's our life force, and when we suppress it the way you do —"

"Herr von Kleist is twice my age," I said.

"Generally speaking, when it comes to lovers, the older the better," said Lady Alice. "I daresay you haven't looked at him properly. I did, at the concert. He was sitting at the back, looking aloof and powerful. That's what age does to a man, the lucky chaps."

I thought of what Charles had said, on the pathway down to the boathouse. "Also, he's probably a Nazi."

She blinked. "But why should that matter?

You're just going to bed with him; it isn't as if you're discussing politics and the Rhineland. I slept with a committed Communist once, the son of a filthy-rich banker. It was quite nice. We saw each other for a month or two, and he gave me the loveliest presents. I heard he later tried to bomb the Bourse."

The waiter arrived with lunch. We were sitting in the café around the corner, a sidewalk table that Lady Alice had obtained for us with a single silky gaze from her green eyes. She liked sitting outdoors, being on display. She would fold one gamine leg over the other and drape her hand with its cigarette around the curve of her knee; the other hand would caress a cup of coffee or a cocktail of some sort, depending on the hour (or not). Her honey hair would glint in the old autumn sunshine. Cafés were expensive, and cash was never all that plentiful in my father's household, but somehow Alice always scraped together enough francs for a coffee and a sandwich at the Maginot.

"Besides," she said, when the waiter had left, "that's part of the old frisson, isn't it? Knowing you really shouldn't sleep with him, and then you do." She winked at me over the crust of her sandwich.

Well, I couldn't argue with that, could I? I thought about the horrifying inevitability with which I'd fallen into bed with Stefan. Yes, he

was forbidden and dangerous. He was older and German and Jewish; he had just been mysteriously shot in the leg. What man could have been more perfectly unsuitable for me?

So maybe Alice and her analyst were right, and I had a deep psychological appetite for unsuitable men. That was it, that was all it was. I hadn't been in love at all, I was simply acting out a kind of script, like an actress playing herself. And now the play was over, and everyone had left the stage and gone home.

Well, not quite everyone. Nick Greenwald. Stefan had sent a note to Nick Greenwald before he left France, asking him to look after this girl he'd fucked over the summer, in case she was pregnant.

I lifted my knife and fork to the omelet before me. "It's just a vase of flowers," I said. "There's no address. He was just being kind. He's a friend of my father's."

"*Kindness* is a dozen tulips, not a bouquet worth a thousand francs."

"A thousand francs! How do you know that?"

"Because I'm an expert, my dear. I can look at a thing and know its worth in a second. It's my particular talent. And what they say about love and money, that high-minded philosophy, it's rubbish. You can always tell how much a man values you by the presents he gives you."

"Heartwarming."

"Isn't it?" She put down her sandwich and lit another cigarette. "So I can assure you, Annabelle, darling," she said, smiling, blowing smoke into the sidewalk, "we haven't heard the last from this baron of yours."

Of course, she was right. The afternoon post brought a letter, addressed to me, on snowy thick stock, begging Mademoiselle de Créouville for the honor of accepting Fraulein Frieda von Kleist, age eleven, to her list of students.

8.

Eight days later, a few minutes before eleven o'clock in the morning, I arrived at the von Kleists' apartment, a magnificent fifteen-room residence occupying three floors of a monumental Haussmann building on the avenue Marceau, for Fraulein von Kleist's first lesson on the cello.

Alice drove me there in Charles's battered Renault. He had departed Paris abruptly a few days earlier, leaving behind the usual brief note, without any clue regarding his destination. But he had written a postscript, entirely atypical: *Cheer up, Sprout,* which was his childhood nickname for me.

"I can't tell you how thrilled I am," said Alice. "This is exactly what you need."

"Yes, another fifty francs a week."

"You should hold out for a hundred. I'm

235

sure he'll pay whatever you ask."

The car rolled to a stop at the curb. I looked up at the monumental entrance and remembered that last scene at the Villa Vanilla, the look of terrible grief in von Kleist's blue eyes, and the feeling that he had lived many decades longer than I had. There was something frightening about that, the knowledge of his experience and his misfortune. As if misfortune were somehow contagious, like a disease.

Alice watched me pull my cello through the door. "Shall I pick you up afterward?"

I rested the cello on the pavement and closed the door. "No, thank you. I'll take a taxi."

I was ushered into the entrance hall promptly by a housekeeper in a neat black-and-white uniform, who called me *votre altesse* and asked me if I needed refreshment. I declined politely and sat down in a chair next to an empty Second Empire fireplace while my pulse knocked in my throat.

I am here to teach music, I thought. That is all.

The clock chimed, the door opened promptly, and a servant announced that Fraulein von Kleist was ready for her lesson.

She was a lovely girl. She had her father's icy coloring, except that on her the effect was bright and ethereal rather than arctic. She

actually rose to her feet and curtsied when I entered, and her face was full of reverence. "Mademoiselle de Créouville," she said, in perfect French, "I am so gratified that you have agreed to take me on. When I listened to you play at His Highness's apartment last week —"

"Were you there?" I asked, surprised.

"Oh, yes! It was wonderful. My father had spoken so highly of your talent, and I have always wanted to learn the cello. I adore the voice, don't you? Oh, of course you do! How silly of me. But really, it's so rich and melancholy and delicious. Papa told me you were giving a concert, and I begged him to let me go." She spoke sunnily, not at all like a girl who had lost her mother; in fact, her entire body — she was quite tall and slender, so that she looked older than eleven — radiated sunshine, from her pale blond hair to her luminous young skin. She'd said the word *melancholy* with the kind of relish only a girl of her age and innocence could muster.

"I'm very flattered," I said.

"Of course, he hurried me away when the concert was over. He said the party afterward was just for the grown-ups." Frieda might have let her eyes roll a fraction of an inch, and I nearly laughed because she reminded me of myself, and here I was, not twenty years old, feeling ancient by comparison.

"Your father is very wise. Is this your instrument?"

She turned to the cello, which was propped against a sturdy armchair, bow resting gently on the cushion. "Yes. Is it acceptable?"

"It looks very fine."

"Papa's very serious about music. He said there was no point in getting an inferior instrument."

I ran my fingers along the strings. "I understand you play the piano?"

"Yes, and the harp."

"So you can read music already, and have some musical theory."

"Yes, Mademoiselle. I could read music almost before I could read books."

She was so eager and happy. I smiled at her and settled on the piano bench next to the armchair.

"Very good, Fraulein," I said. "Now sit down, pick up your bow like so, and we will begin with the A string."

9.

The lesson was an hour, and when the elegant ormolu clock on the mantel read five minutes to eleven, the door of the music room opened and Herr von Kleist walked inside, wearing a plain military jacket of field gray and a pair of riding breeches.

I looked up from the music, but he motioned for us to continue and sat down on

the sofa by the window, one leg crossed over the other. He was wearing leather riding boots the color of cognac, polished to an oily gleam. He sat absolutely still against the blue damask, while the sunlight fell on his pale hair and his daughter concentrated ferociously on her bowing. At one minute to twelve, he rose to his feet.

"Very good, Mademoiselle de Créouville. I appreciate your patience, teaching a novice."

"Not at all. I wish all my students were so eager to learn."

He turned to his daughter. "Frieda, my dear. Thank Mademoiselle for her time and trouble."

"Thank you, Mademoiselle!" She rose to her feet, bow in hand.

"You're welcome, Fraulein. You are an excellent student."

I showed her how to loosen her bow and put away the instrument in its case. When she finished, von Kleist told her to go upstairs to Fraulein Schmidt for her lunch, and as soon as the door closed behind her, he turned back to me with an expression I might almost have called sheepish.

"She is my youngest," he said, "so I indulge us both with a governess, instead of sending her away to school."

"She's a lovely girl. Whatever you're doing, it seems to be the right thing."

"Thank you, Mademoiselle. Luncheon is

239

now being served. Would you care to stay?"

I had been expecting something from him — an invitation to meet later and more discreetly, or perhaps a note of some kind — but not this, abrupt and formal and respectable. My fingers froze on the fastening of the cello case. "I don't wish to impose," I said.

"Nonsense. I have already made the arrangements with my housekeeper. Frieda will eat upstairs with Fraulein Schmidt."

I could have refused. I thought, If I am going to refuse him, if I'm not going to go through with this, I should do it now. But as I straightened from the cello, and my mouth, panicked and guilty, opened to make the excuses, I caught a glimpse of von Kleist's stiff face, and the vulnerability of his eyes, and I felt a surge of perverse power.

The clock chimed noon. I smiled. "In that case, I should be delighted."

10.

Von Kleist's silent housekeeper ushered us into a small but elegant dining room — the family dining room, he assured me — which was already set intimately for two. The spring sun burst through the pair of large windows, overlooking what must be the garden below, or perhaps a courtyard. I glimpsed the nearby buildings, the multitude of windows and balconies, and felt the unbearable visibility of the city. A bowl of delicate new white roses

240

nestled in the middle of the silver and crystal, and a bottle of champagne in a bucket next to one of the chairs. Von Kleist held out the other one for me.

Lady Alice had dressed me in sky-blue silk that morning, because it suited my eyes, she said. My dark hair and my large brown eyes, my round little French figure and my large red American smile. *He can't resist you in a dress like that,* she said, and I told her I wasn't sure if I wanted him to resist me or not, and she laughed and said, *You'll make up your mind after he pours the champagne,* and as von Kleist eased the cork softly out of the bottle — the familiar pop made me flinch — and drizzled it into my glass, I wondered how she had known. The champagne was Laurent-Perrier, and the worn label suggested something vintage. I remembered what Lady Alice had said over lunch, about the value of a man's presents. Or perhaps he simply liked vintage champagne.

Von Kleist filled his own glass and said, "I hope you are comfortable, Mademoiselle."

"Quite comfortable. This is a lovely room."

"Thank you. I have leased the apartment for some time, since I first came to Paris." He sat down and lifted his glass. The sunlight entered his eyes. "I am very glad to see you are well, Mademoiselle."

I touched my glass to his. "It's Annabelle.

241

And I'm glad to see you're well, too."

When we had finished lunch, the sun had tipped over the roof and the room had turned blue and almost dusky. Herr von Kleist asked if I would like to see the other principal chambers of the apartment and I said I would. He stood and helped me from my chair, and his hand was dry and large in contrast to mine. When I stood, dizzy with champagne, he seemed enormous.

"How tall are you, really?" I asked.

"A hundred and ninety-six centimeters."

"It's very intimidating."

"Is it? I hope not."

"Yes, it is. You have almost thirty-two centimeters over me. More than a foot." I didn't know why I was saying these things. I had had too much champagne. I stared at the buttons of von Kleist's uniform, holding the field gray forcibly closed over his warlike chest, and I thought it was impossible that someone so big could covet someone so little.

"But why should that frighten you?" he said. "It is the natural duty of the large to protect the small."

I had to tilt back my head to see his face, which was shadowed and quizzical in the absence of the sun. "I'd like to see the library first," I said.

11.

We made a circuit, and ended in the library again, where the housekeeper had laid out coffee. It was now two o'clock. "I'm afraid I've kept you from your work," I said.

"Not at all. What do you think of the place?" He accepted a cup and saucer. Men poured wine, women poured coffee and tea. There was something in there, an important reflection, but I was still a little too dull from the champagne to capture it.

"It's magnificent and beautiful and terribly orderly," I said.

He laughed for the first time, and it was richer than I imagined. "You were perhaps expecting chaos from me?"

"No." I laughed, too. "But it's very different from my father's apartment. Of course, they'd cleaned it all up for the concert, but you must have noticed the dilapidation."

He shrugged politely. "I like the peace, you see. If there is disorder, it is hard for the spirit to be peaceful."

I nodded to the silver-framed photographs clustered on the round table by my side. "Is that your wife?"

"Yes."

I set down my cup and lifted one of them, of a blond woman who held a giggling flaxen-haired child in her arms. They were outdoors, in a field of some kind, with a tree in the background to the left. The woman was smil-

ing hugely. "She looks happy. And quite young."

"She was. She was seventeen when we married. We knew each other as children. When I returned home from the front on convalescent leave, I discovered she had grown rather abruptly into a young lady, as girls do. I fell in love with her at once. By the end of summer we were engaged, and the wedding took place in October, before I left for the front again. I had just turned twenty."

"Then you had many happy years together."

"Yes. We were very happy. She is holding our second child in that photograph. Marthe. She was four then; she is now fourteen and at school."

"And the others?"

He was sitting in the armchair, several feet away. The coffee cup rested in his lap, and a single index finger curled around the handle. He looked not at the photograph, but at me. "Frederick, our oldest. He is fifteen. Then after Marthe came Klaus, who will be thirteen next month. And Frieda." He paused. "My wife's name was Frieda. We had not yet christened the baby when she died."

"I'm very sorry."

"Yes," he said. "So was I. At the time, I thought I had accepted her death as God's will, but looking back, I see how bitter I was, and how melancholy."

"Of course you were. You loved her very much."

His gaze shifted at last to the photograph. "It is impossible to describe how much."

The room was protected from the sunlight, as libraries are, and the glow that came from the half-shaded windows fell softly on his face. I had thought last summer that thirty-eight was a vast age, but as I looked at him now I thought thirty-eight was terribly young.

I rose from my seat and went to the corner of the sofa, next to the chair in which he was sitting. His knee nearly touched my dress. It was massive and thick next to mine, the knee of a giant. I couldn't quite comprehend his size; it was so out of scale to what I was used to. He was still wearing his boots and riding breeches. He had apologized earlier for not changing. I laid my hand on his knee, and the patella alone was so huge, my palm couldn't quite cover it.

"You must have been very lonely," I said.

He didn't move, but his eyes met mine, quite steady. "No. It is impossible to be lonely when there are children about."

"Is that why Frieda still has her governess?"

He removed the cup and saucer from his lap and set them down on the rug next to the chair, which seemed to me a reckless act of disorder. "You are very perceptive, Mademoiselle," he said.

"Please, it's Annabelle. And it doesn't take much perception to see that you're lonely."

"If I am to call you Annabelle, then you must call me Johann."

I smiled. "I can't. It's far too casual a name to be flinging about in front of that uniform."

"We are at an impasse, then, Mademoiselle."

"So it would seem."

He lifted my hand from his knee and kissed the ends of my fingers. "My intentions are not dishonorable, you know."

"I didn't think they were."

"Yes, you did, or you would not have taken so long to reply to my note."

I smiled. "All right. I did."

"Then why did you accept my offer?"

His expression was grave and impermeable before me, as if he had staked his all on my reply. His hand still enclosed my fingers. "I suppose I was grateful for the flowers," I said. "And I need the work."

"If you are short of money, Mademoiselle —"

"No, no. I have exactly what I need. I will gladly accept payment for today's lesson, however."

"Of course. But I am afraid I have forgotten to ask the fee."

"A hundred francs an hour. I hope you can afford it."

He studied me without speaking. His

thumb moved slightly, sliding against the knuckle of my index finger. I thought, Here it is, this is the moment. Time to make good. But my limbs were like molasses, too thick to move. I imagined him kissing me, pushing me back on the sofa, pulling up my dress. I imagined his bristling hair under my fingers, his weight on my limbs, and the bristling hair turned dark and curling, and the body moving on mine belonged to Stefan.

I said boldly, seeking out his gaze, "Lady Alice thinks you want me to be your mistress."

"Lady Alice should know that I don't keep mistresses."

"And I don't allow myself to be kept." I lifted his hand and drew the warm fingers against the side of my breast, atop the sky-blue silk that Lady Alice had chosen for me. His bones were heavy and stiff. "But I don't want to be lonely, either."

"Annabelle," he said, without moving his hand, "this is not necessary."

"I think it is."

He looked utterly unmoved. But my thumb, pressed against his wrist, detected a bounding radial pulse, and his pupils were like drops of oil inside his pale irises. I thought, when his lips parted, that he would lean forward and kiss me, but instead he said gently, "Why, Annabelle? So that you can become a mosquito, like the others?"

"A mosquito?"

"Don't you remember what you said to me on your garden wall, last summer? You could study the bugs without becoming a mosquito."

I couldn't breathe. Before I even realized that my eyes had blurred, a tear dropped onto von Kleist's hand, sliding between the knuckles, and then another. And I had never cried once since August; I had prided myself that I hadn't shed a single tear.

His hand moved from my breast to my chin, and his thumb wiped my cheek. "You don't need to be a mosquito for me, Annabelle. I would rather prefer that you were not."

"I'm sorry. I've made a fool of myself, haven't I?"

"No." He drew out a handkerchief from his pocket and put it in my hand. "Annabelle, if you want me to make love to you, I will make love to you. I don't think I can resist you if you ask me. But let it not be because you are wishing I was another man."

"No." I folded the handkerchief and gave it back to him. "You are far better than that."

"No, keep it. A souvenir of this first meeting." He sat back in his chair and lowered his hand to retrieve his coffee cup, while I wrestled with my composure. "Do you ride, Mademoiselle?"

"I used to, before we moved back to

America."

"I ride every morning in the Bois de Boulogne. Perhaps you will allow me to mount you there, from time to time." He finished the coffee in a final gulp, rose to his feet, and held out his hand to me. "But come. You must go now, Annabelle. I will drive you home myself."

12.

When I burst through the doorway of my father's apartment half an hour later, my hair was full of wind and sunshine and my arms were full of cello. I dropped the instrument in its place next to the sofa and looked about for Lady Alice.

She wasn't there, but the afternoon post lay on the table, a few notes only. One of them was postmarked in Paris and addressed to me. I opened it and read that Nick Greenwald had something important to communicate to me about a mutual friend, and would I meet him at my earliest convenience?

I tore the notecard into small pieces and threw it in the wastebasket.

13.

Two days later, I went riding in the Bois de Boulogne with Johann von Kleist.

We met at six o'clock outside my apartment, where Johann was waiting in his rumbling black Mercedes roadster. My eyes were

hooded and sleepy, my hair bound back in a clumsy chignon. I had unearthed a set of my mother's old riding clothes in a back closet of the apartment, but Mummy had been tall and they were too large. Yesterday in the market, I had found a pair of secondhand boots that nearly fit.

"I will take those to my valet afterward," said Johann, as we drove through the chill morning air, "and he will polish them properly for you."

Already my nerves were coming alive. Maybe it was the vibration of that enormous engine, the energy in the car's swooping curves. I glanced at Johann, who sat rigidly in his seat, polished bright, as if he'd been up for hours. He wore his officer's cap over his blond hair, and his eyes were fixed on the half-dark streets ahead. I had no idea how he packed those legs under the dash. He was so tall, he looked over the rim of the windshield rather than through it.

We were met at the avenue Foch by Johann's groom, who held two gleaming horses by the reins, one a large bay and the other a smaller chestnut mare with a wide and irregular white blaze down the length of her head. Around the rim of the trees ahead, the sky was a pale and expectant blue. The entire city of Paris lay between us and the sunrise. The groom stepped aside and Johann helped me mount. "Just like old times," I said,

gathering up the reins.

"Like the bicycle, isn't it?" said Johann, and when I looked down I saw that the sunrise was touching the top of his cap, and he was smiling.

He was right about bicycles. My muscles remembered how to ride, though my legs didn't appreciate the activity. We entered through the empty Porte Dauphine and angled left to the lakes, and Johann asked me how I felt and if I thought I should like to go faster. I said I would. When I nudged her, the chestnut moved willingly into a gentle trot, and I found the rhythm at once, the slight and steady up-down that still lingered in my bones, like a waltz I had danced long ago. Around us, the grass and trees were wet with dew, and a yellow-pink haze floated in the air. "It's easier than I thought," I said to Johann. "And the park is beautiful at this hour."

"Yes," he said, looking at me.

He wasn't smiling, but his face was softer. He rode like a centaur, like he had come into the world on top of a horse. In the primeval mist, he might have been a thousand years old, dressed in leather and blue paint, riding across the steppes with an army of barbarians, except that he was manifestly not a barbarian. You could not imagine Johann von Kleist without his pressed uniform and his polished boots.

251

We went off the gravel path and into a meadow, damp and fragrant with new grass, and as the ground opened up I realized how perfectly alone we were, how obviously he was courting me. He didn't want to have an affair; he wanted more from me, and the possibility was too huge, the length and breadth of the opportunity too impossible to imagine. For an instant, I pictured myself a baroness at twenty, with a rich estate in Prussia and four stepchildren, with an apartment in Paris and a fine upstanding husband who would keep me in silks and jewels and never, ever stray.

"You love riding, don't you?" I said stupidly, because I had to say something.

"Yes."

I thought of his expression a moment ago. I said in French, "You seem different somehow. A little softer, perhaps?"

He chuckled, a relaxed sound. "Maybe so. It is the rhythm, I believe, and maybe the freedom, too. And the horse, naturally. The horse has none of the vices of humanity." He reached down and patted the bay's neck.

"I see what you mean. You can be yourself with a horse, can't you? You don't have to pretend anything, like with people." I had switched back to English.

"Yes, exactly. And then one dismounts and goes home and to work, and puts the mask back on. So it goes."

"I suppose you wear a very stern mask at work. I shudder to think about it," I said. "What does a military attaché do, exactly?"

"Nothing very interesting, I'm afraid. A great deal of paperwork."

"But you must meet loads of important people."

"Annabelle," he said, "unless you want me to put on my very stern mask again, we must change the subject."

"I'm sorry. I didn't mean to pry."

"It is not you who should be sorry," he said.

"That's a cryptic thing to say."

He nudged the bay faster. "Come along. Let us see how well you sit a canter."

14.

At the lower lake we dismounted and watched the last of the mist float off the water. The horses stretched their necks to the grass and I sat on a rock, while Johann braced his booted foot next to me and took out a cigarette case. "I didn't know you smoked," I said.

"On occasion."

"Is that even possible?"

"If one is disciplined." He leaned down and offered me the open case. I shook my head. He took one, a long white brand with which I was not familiar. He lit himself up with a gleaming silver lighter and smoked silently, watching the water. A bird cried softly from

253

the trees. I felt his boot near my leg, the unending heat of his body.

I broke the silence first. "Where did you learn to speak English so well?"

"In England. My father died of peritonitis when I was six. My mother married an Englishman a few years later, and I lived at home with them until I was old enough for boarding school."

"But what happened during the war?"

He put his hand in his pocket, fingering something there. His lighter, I thought. "I fought for Germany, of course. I was wounded twice but somehow escaped being killed. A miracle, I think. My stepfather was not so lucky. He was killed on the third day of the Somme."

"How horrible for your mother."

"She died not long after. I'm afraid I never saw her again, once the war began." He lifted the cigarette, which was nearly finished, and inhaled slowly. "They had two children. My sister Margaret, who is nine years younger, and my brother Benedict, who was born a month after my stepfather died." He dropped the cigarette in the grass and crushed it under his heel. "In another hour the lake will be full of boats. Would you like to go boating some-day?"

"Yes, but not here. It's too public."

He took my hand to lift me to my feet. "I agree."

15.

We finished where we started, near the Porte Dauphine, now crowded with people and morning light. The groom was waiting next to the black Mercedes. He jumped to attention when he saw us, like a marionette.

"I will drive you home, of course," said Johann.

"Only if it won't make you late for your work."

"Do not concern yourself with that."

"The lateness or the work?"

"Either one."

It took much longer to drive home, because of the traffic. Paris was in full flow. The streets stank of fish and garbage and exhaust. "I would stop for breakfast," said Johann, "but I'm afraid I do have an appointment."

We wound our way down the crowded avenues and narrow streets to my father's apartment, in a massive silence met by the roaring undertone of the engine. Johann looked up dubiously to the building. "I hope it is safe, at least. Not so licentious as that damned villa last summer."

"Oh, very safe. Not all that warm in winter, but safe."

He dropped his gaze to my face and frowned. "I don't like this for you, Annabelle."

"Do you have a better suggestion?"

"Not at present." He climbed out of the car

and walked around to my side, next to the sidewalk, where he opened the door and grasped my hand to draw me out of the low-slung seat. He straightened my hat and tucked a piece of loosened hair behind my ear. "You are windblown and beautiful, Mademoiselle," he said, kissing my hand. "I will come for you again on Saturday morning."

16.

I lay for an hour afterward in a warm bath, staring at the ceiling and wondering what to do with him. Whether I wanted him for myself, or just to banish the memory of Stefan. Whether it was possible to inoculate yourself against future heartbreak. Whether one man could keep you safe from wanting another.

PEPPER

COCOA BEACH 1966

1.

On the ninth day after Annabelle's departure, Pepper takes the Ford Thunderbird out of the garage and drives herself into town.

Well, maybe "day" isn't quite the right word for it, when you consider that the sun has already fallen and the sky is purple-black. Back home in New York City, there will be a hard frost overnight, and the last tenacious leaf will shiver to the ground. But here in Florida, the daytime temperature touched eighty degrees, and Pepper wandered up and down the beach in a too-short sundress borrowed from Annabelle's closet (she has decided not to trust the Breakers with her current address) while the dogs chased each other in large circles across the empty sand, until the shadows lengthened and the horizon turned pink, and Pepper thought, I've got to get out of here, I've got to do something.

Itchy feet. They've gotten Pepper into trouble before, and they'll do it again. Tonight she's painted them both a fresh, crisp red at

the tips and slipped them back into her sandals, and the one on the right is pressed against the accelerator, the faster the better. A tiny toe beats a tattoo into the wall of her abdomen, as if in sympathy, or maybe protest. Or else warning?

Well, too late for that.

Now her hair flutters in the draft, her lipstick is warm and sticky-red on her lips. She glances in the rearview mirror, and her skin glows back at her, reckless and pregnant. She's not out to find a man, of course not. She just needs to know that she's still beautiful. That her face, which has gotten her into so much trouble before, is yet capable of more.

2.

As usual, the trick is finding the right spot. There's always a spot, and Pepper has a nose for them. She parks the car and reaches for her pocketbook on the empty passenger seat. She checks her lipstick in the mirror and slings her cardigan over her shoulders.

Inside, the air is polished and classy and not too old. Pepper pauses in the doorway, just long enough for someone to catch sight of her, and then it passes in a familiar ripple through the room. Awareness. The electric pause, the drinks set down, the sidelong stares. There is the usual narrowed hostility from one of the women, the quick look away

from the man who pretends he doesn't give a damn, the shy glance into the whisky from the one who thinks he doesn't stand a chance, the bold stare of the one who's confident he does. The same old chain reaction, the same old Pepper.

The thing about Pepper she hasn't actually slept with that many men, if you line them up end to end. There was the father of her baby, of course. Oopsy-daisy. There was a supremely eligible young man in New York, before she left, a friend of her cousin Nick Greenwald: a lawyer who wanted to marry her, a man she probably should have married if she knew what was good for her. Before that, a photographer who enchanted her, who was her lover for a year and a half, who called her his muse and took thousands of pictures of her; a man whom she actually thought she might marry, until he moved to Paris one afternoon with a seventeen-year-old fashion model, a change of heart she discovered two weeks later from a mutual friend. An older man, one summer on Long Island, on the sly. A boy in college who worshipped her. The man on the terrace, who sent her bouquet after bouquet, note after note, begging her to see him again, until even her parents took notice and registered disapproval.

But mostly, Pepper loves to flirt. She loves the joy of the hunt, though she stops short of the kill. Like any Thoroughbred, she was born

to run. That's what matters, after all: the knowledge that you were the fleetest animal in the pack, and who cares if you get to stand in the winner's circle with the flashbulbs popping and the garland looped around your neck? All you need, all you really feed on, is the knowledge that you're the most desirable woman in the room.

Until it doesn't matter anymore.

Because she's not the same old Pepper, is she? Because at this very second, her right hand, obeying a primeval impulse, lies across the apex of her belly. She couldn't have stopped it if she tried, if she actually held it down with her left hand. She, the predatory Pepper, is now on the defensive. She's got something worth protecting.

She can't win. She can't go back. Somewhere around the fourth or fifth month of pregnancy, she crossed an invisible line, a Rubicon of biology, and became a mother. She doesn't belong here anymore. She may never belong here anymore.

The reflection breaks over her like one of the more vigorous waves washing up on the beach this afternoon — the surf was brisk, the weather was on the move — and for an instant she hesitates, there in the doorway with all eyes on her.

The instant passes and so does Pepper, right back into the Thunderbird, right back to the old house by the sea, though she

maybe makes a wrong turn or two along the way.

3.

By the time Pepper undresses and crawls into bed, her limbs are done for the night. Her brain, on the other hand, doesn't know when to quit.

The room is peacefully dark, not a drop of light. She lies on her side, gazing at the space where the opposite wall should stand — if she could see it — and forces her eyes shut, except that they keep pinging open again, like a child's pop-up toy, indefatigable. The baby kicks around in sympathy.

After half an hour or so, she sits up and turns on the light. What's happening to her, that her body is so weary and her brain can't stop jumping? She wants to sleep. She wants to finish something first, and she doesn't know what it is.

Pepper used to sleep naked. It's a sensual thing, a freedom thing, but since coming to Annabelle's house, since jumping awake at every little whisper in the night, wondering if they've tracked her down already, she's taken to wearing underwear and a long shirt. She still resents them for it. She swings her legs over the side of the bed and reaches for the linen robe draped across the nearby chair. She slings her arms inside and belts the sash high, above her bump. She leaves the slippers

behind and makes her way softly across the midnight courtyard to the main house, which is unlocked, and pauses in the doorway, because she doesn't know what she's doing here.

In the absence of purpose, she wanders to the kitchen and pours herself a drink of water from the tap. The house is so silent, she wants to scream.

She stares through the kitchen window into the black courtyard. This silence, my God, this void. This itchy absence of sound. She would talk to anybody right now, just to get rid of the quiet. But mostly, she thinks, gazing at the corner of the courtyard where the lemon trees grow side by side with the bougainvillea, she wants to talk to Annabelle. Gentle, frank Annabelle, who disappeared nine days ago.

She sets the empty glass in the sink and turns off the light. There is no Annabelle; even her dogs sleep elsewhere, in Clara's quarters, down a corridor somewhere. She wanders back into the hall, bumping into corners, feeling her way along until her fingers strike air where the study should be. A pretty room; Pepper's seen it from the outside. Though the furniture is sturdy and wholesome, and the colors richly neutral, Pepper has the feeling that this was Annabelle's office and not her husband's.

She steps inside and flips on the light.

The switch illuminates not an overhead fixture but the lamp on the desk, an old-fashioned number that looks like a retrofit from the days of kerosene. The rest of the desk is mostly empty. A telephone sits at the corner. Pepper's heard it ring once or twice. It seems to have its own line; the one in the living room doesn't ring in tandem. At the top of the desk is a small clock. Pepper walks around the corner and reads it. Half past one.

If she picked up that telephone right now, at half past one in the morning, and she called her mother and said *I'm pregnant, Mums, I want to come home,* what would her mother say in return?

She pulls out the chair and sinks down to stare at the telephone.

She could call Vivian again. She *should* call Vivian again.

She should call her mother.

She puts out her hand and rests it on the smooth bakelite curve of the receiver, just centimeters away from the round dial, the little black numbers and letters. *Hello, Mums, you'll never guess. Pepper's in trouble. Big, big trouble. Maybe even a little bit scared. Maybe, for once in her life, not quite sure what to do next.*

The hand falls away.

Also, at the top of the desk, there is a pair of handsome pens in a small marble stand.

263

Right next to the clock, right next to half past one in the morning.

Pepper doesn't write letters. She writes the occasional thank-you note, when she has to, but the humility and patience of letter writing don't exactly flow like milk and honey in her veins. She'd rather talk to you in person, face-to-face, so she can put all her talents to use.

But maybe this is one of those things you wrote down on paper, instead of telling them live and unrehearsed. Pepper takes one of the pens out of its holder and fingers the tip. Dear Mums and Dadums, It's the craziest thing. Dear Mums and Dadums, I'll bet you're surprised to see a letter from me, your own daughter. Dear Mums and Dadums, I think it's time I told you something.

Yes, that was it.

Pepper leans down and rummages through the desk drawers until she finds a box of stationery, thick and expensive and anonymous, no monogram or heading of any kind. She selects a few sheets and squares them on the blotter. She picks up the pen and writes the date and *Dear Mums and Dadums,* and that's when she hears the front door opening and closing, so softly you'd have to be paranoid to notice it.

4.

For an instant, Pepper freezes. She grips her pen and thinks, It's Annabelle, of course it's Annabelle, but that doesn't stop her heart from smashing against the wall of her chest. Doesn't stop the adrenaline from hurtling through her veins.

The lamp.

Pepper pushes back the chair and launches herself to the switch on the wall. She turns off the light and flattens herself in the lee of the half-open door.

The house has gone still again. No footsteps, not the slightest sound. But there should be footsteps, shouldn't there? If someone's just entered the house. Annabelle's heels should be clattering happily along the flagstones of the entry. She should be rattling her car keys, setting down her suitcase, tossing her pocketbook on the table, going through the mail. But there's nothing, a distinct void of noise, as pregnant as Pepper's belly. She puts a hand on top, just to be sure, and tries to stop breathing.

And then. A voice. Deep but soft, a male voice that wants to be heard by one person alone.

"Who's there?"

If she could, Pepper would dissolve into the wall, become one with the paint and the plaster. Wouldn't that just fix everything? Pepper Schuyler, dazzling socialite, shimmer-

265

ing Girl Friday, now a wall in a seaside Florida villa.

The baby turns around and slugs her in the kidneys.

Pepper releases a tiny gasp, just a tiny one, but it's enough.

"Who's there?" This time, it's a demand.

Precious little light filters through the window and the half-open door. Pepper looks around slowly, keeping her cool, trying to remember what lay where. From the hallway outside comes the sound of footsteps, heavy, muffled by the rug.

The bookshelf along the wall. Pepper reaches out her arm and fingers her way along the top, something, anything. A metal shape finds her palm, too small, but that's all there is. She can feel the footsteps now, vibrating the floorboards beneath her slippers. The object is slender but heavy, a small statue of some kind. Pepper slips back behind the door, just as it begins to move, just as a hand appears around the edge.

She swings.

But the hand, the damned hand actually knows she's coming. Before she can snap her elbow forward, the fingers enclose her wrist, stopping the arc of the blow, and the next thing she knows, she's tucked in a headlock against a too-solid chest, the metal object drops on her right foot, and as she opens her mouth to scream, the voice from the hallway

growls in her ear.

"What the hell have you done with my mother?"

ANNABELLE
PARIS 1935

1.

At first, I refused to believe that I was pregnant. It didn't seem possible; August was like another lifetime, an Annabelle who no longer existed. The antiseptic language of reproduction — *The average emission of the human male contains some three to four hundred million individual gametes* — had nothing to do with the breathless and beautiful act of intercourse with Stefan, the long heat-soaked hours in his arms.

I ignored the signs staunchly, inventing every possible excuse, until I could not. Until Alice caught me vomiting in the bathroom at the end of October and brought me a worn white washcloth from the linen cupboard, which she ran under the faucet and handed to me with a sigh of resignation. "I suppose it was inevitable, the two of you so young and virile," she said. "Really, he ought to have known better. I'll ask around for a doctor. You will have to get it taken care of at once,

of course, before poor von Kleist suspects anything."

I straightened. "What do you mean?"

"My dear, he's not going to want to have an affair with a pregnant woman. He's certainly not going to want to wait around until the child's born. And unless you've slept with him already, he won't possibly believe it's his."

"No." I sank down on the stool and put my face in my hands. The washcloth was cool and damp against my cheek. "I haven't slept with him."

I hadn't even kissed him. I arrived every Tuesday morning for Frieda's lesson, and had lunch with Johann afterward, though we took no more tours of the apartment and he hurried back to the embassy after driving me home in the black Mercedes.

On Thursdays and Saturdays we went riding in the park. Johann called for me promptly at six, and I was back in my father's apartment by nine-thirty, soaking my worn muscles in a hot bath. The pattern had become so regular, I arranged my week around it. Twice a week, on Tuesdays and Fridays, a large bouquet of flowers arrived from a fine Parisian florist. The blooms varied, but they were always fragrant and expensive. Alice and I would sit around the table and admire them as we drank our morning coffee. "I do hope he's getting his

269

money's worth, then," Alice said, a week ago, and when I told her that he wasn't, not even a sou, she laughed. "Trust you to find the only man in Paris who doesn't make his mistress earn her keep," she said, shaking her head, and I didn't bother to argue that he wasn't keeping me at all. He sent flowers and gave me lunch and paid me a hundred francs a week for Frieda's lesson: that was all.

On the other hand, he demanded nothing of me except my conversation, and not very much of that. It wasn't that we didn't talk; he was just economical with words and ideas. We spent most of our time in a kind of easy and understanding silence, a relief after the frenetic energy of Alice.

"Well, then," she said. "I'll see what I can do. You'll burn in hell, of course, but then won't we all?"

2.

A month before my mother died, we had an enormous row. I was eleven and old enough to know things. There had been a father-daughter tea at my school, and of course I had no father to go with me, and so I went with my uncle, the husband of my mother's sister, and sat awkwardly with him, drinking watery tea and eating stale cake, while the other girls laughed and talked with their genuine fathers, basking in their warm baths of paternal adoration. I came home and threw

my hat against the wall in the parlor that smelled of lemon polish and damp wool. "It's *your* fault, *you* left him! Why did you leave my father? You were cruel to him so he found another woman."

She had slipped her index finger in her book and closed the pages over it. Her face had gone a little pale. "You mustn't speak about things you don't understand, Annabelle."

"I understand more than you think. You drove him to someone else, and then you left him, and now I don't have a father. I could be in France, I could be a princess, and instead I'm stuck *here*!" I pointed to the faded wallpaper, the shabby furniture, the tired knickknacks on the shelves, the battered radiator that banged in the corner. "And it's your fault!"

"You'll understand when you're older. It's not that simple."

"When I'm grown up, I'm going to be a *good* wife. I'm going to lavish my husband with love so he'll never go to another woman. I'm going to make sure my children have a father."

She replied in a quiet monotone that — at the time, so young — I had wrongly imagined was emotionless. "Darling, sometimes it doesn't matter how good you are, and how much you love your husband. There are some men who need more than that, who will never

271

be happy with just one woman. I did what I thought was right for you."

I had stamped my foot on the threadbare rug and told her she was wrong, that it was her fault. I would never do such an awful thing to my children. I would make sure they had a father who loved them.

Oh, Annabelle, she said.

I hate you, I shouted.

Then I had run up the stairs to my room and shut the door and put my head under the pillow, so I wouldn't hear her crying.

3.

The day after Alice discovered me in the bathroom, I went to the doctor, though not the one she recommended. I had no intention of seeing Alice's doctor. I had seen the women in the convent hospital who had tried to get rid of their babies. Some of them had died. Others had been so ravaged inside that it was a wonder they had lived. We had treated them, of course, but the nuns had told us afterward that these were the wages of sin, that God might forgive a woman for some things, but not for this. Stefan's child was my punishment for having loved Stefan without repenting, for having shared sexual passion with a married man.

I went instead to my father's doctor, a man named Périgault who looked nearly sixty and had gentle hands. He told me what I already

knew, that I was going to have a baby at the end of May.

"Very well," I said. "What do you recommend?"

Dr. Périgault drummed his fingers against the edge of the desk. His eyebrows made a ragged line along the top of his spectacles. "I recommend you find a husband, Mademoiselle de Créouville, with preference to the man who is the father of your baby."

I stared at his gray hair, at the bushiness of his brows above the round wire frames of his eyeglasses, and I wondered if he had known my mother at all.

"What very helpful advice, Doctor," I said. "But I'm afraid that isn't possible. The man is already married."

4.

Lady Alice was waiting outside in Charles's old Renault. When she saw me, she dropped her cigarette on the pavement and reached across the seat to open the door. "Well? All sorted out?" she said.

"I'm pregnant, if that's what you mean."

"And didn't the good doctor give you lots of lovely advice?"

I turned my head to the blur of striped awnings and said, after a moment, "I swore, when I was a child, that I would never raise my children without a father. I would never do what my mother did."

"Darling, everyone's doing it these days. Well, not everybody. But it's not like thirty years ago, when your life would be ruined. Actually, it might make you a divine novelty, if you play your hand properly."

"I don't want to be a divine novelty."

"What do you want, then? To be some stupid respectable housewife in the *banlieues,* tending her flowers and her fat old husband?"

"It doesn't have to be so extreme."

"Yes, it does. Nobody stays in love forever, and then you're just stuck together out of habit and inertia and bloody sniveling children. If you simply go on having passionate affairs, you never have to give it up. It's like being in love constantly, for ever and ever, only with different people."

"Until you're old and nobody wants to sleep with you."

She laughed and leaned her elbow on the doorframe. A delivery van reared up before us, and she wound around it, grinding what was left of the gears. "That will never happen to me," she said. "I'll kill myself before I get old."

"What a rosy picture you've painted for me. I can't wait to get started."

"All I'm saying is that you're looking at this all wrong. There's no law that says you have to get married. So you're convinced you have a propensity to sleep with philanders, because of your mother and father and all that. I'm

274

sure my analyst would agree with you there. But don't weep about it. Every girl wants to, if she admits it. If she would let herself. They're heaps more fun, for one thing."

"But then they leave you, or they sleep with someone else."

"What's the matter with that? You simply find yourself a new one. They're not rare, I assure you."

"Because it hurts," I said. "It hurts like the devil."

The signal changed again, and we charged forward. I clutched the side of the door until my knuckles turned white.

Lady Alice glanced at my face and nearly drove the Renault into a lamppost. She straightened the wheels and set the brake, oblivious to the horns sounding around us. "Why, you poor thing. Is it that bad?"

"Yes, by God. It *is* that bad. It is for me. It's horrible."

She reached for my shoulders and drew me down into her scented lap, there by the curb, next to a shabby bar tabac and a florist putting out the last hardy blooms of the season. My tears stained her silk dress in large patches, but she never said a word about it, then or since.

5.

The next day was Saturday, and Johann picked me up as usual at six o'clock. By now,

it was still quite dark at that hour, and chilly enough that I wore a thick scarf over my riding coat. The wind froze my cheeks. I stared silently ahead as the street unfolded in the glare of Johann's headlamps, and I thought, I'll have to tell him today. I can't go on pretending.

I would tell him when we stopped for his cigarette at the lower lake, and that would be that. This was the last time we would drive together like this, through the Paris dawn in his beautiful oil-black Mercedes, to the horses waiting at the Porte Dauphine.

We stopped at our usual spot, near the lower lake. The sky was just beginning to lighten. Johann lit his usual cigarette and said, "Is something wrong, my dear? You are quiet this morning."

"I'm always quiet." I watched him suck on the cigarette for a moment. His lips were thin, and when he smoked, they seemed to disappear altogether. I wondered what it would have been like if I had kissed him, if I had asked him to make love to me. I found myself regretting that I hadn't. I turned my head, until he existed only in the corner of my eye, and said, "I'm going to have a baby."

He didn't reply at first. I don't think he even moved. He stared at the lapping water and flicked some ash into the grass, and after a moment he said, "I see."

"It happened at the end of August, when

276

everyone had left. I was lonely and innocent. A very stupid little affair. I never saw him afterward."

He said, "Do you *want* to see this man again?"

"No. Never." On the lake before me, a pair of swans glided free from the mist, white against the black shore. "I found out he was married."

"I see," he said again. He finished the cigarette and turned to me. His face was pale and stern. "You are in no condition to finish our usual ride, I think. Let us return to the car."

We rode miserably back to the Porte Dauphine. Johann kept his mighty bay to a walk, a half length ahead of me, and I watched his upright back, the reddened plane of his jaw, and wondered if I would see them again. The trees thinned and the darkness lifted, revealing a heavy layer of autumn cloud that obscured the chimney pots of the emerging buildings. The air was damp and cold and smelled of smoke. When we reached the groom, Johann jumped off his horse and helped me dismount.

We had driven several minutes before I realized we were heading in the wrong direction. "I thought you were taking me home," I said.

"I thought we might go to my apartment instead, where we can have breakfast and

discuss what is to be done."

"There is nothing to be done. I'm having a baby in the spring. I suppose my father won't turn me out; it's not as if he has any ground to stand on."

Johann said nothing. The smell of exhaust, the movement of traffic was turning me a little sick. We arrived at the avenue Marceau, and Johann helped me out of the car and up the stairs to the louvered double doors on the second floor. We went to the study, and Johann asked the housekeeper for breakfast to be brought on a tray. He led me to the sofa and made me sit; he sat down next to me and picked up my hand and asked how I was feeling.

Numb, I thought.

"Well enough," I said.

"You must take good care of yourself," he said. "It is an important business, having a baby. There is a new life to be considered."

"Yes." I said the word without really meaning it, because I still hadn't translated this state of being — pregnancy — with a living baby. The one didn't seem to have anything to do with the other. I couldn't conceive that there was a human being growing inside me: my child, Stefan's child.

Johann patted my hand. "Good, good."

"You're being very kind," I said, looking down at our linked hands. "I don't deserve your kindness. The father —"

"Shhtt," he said sharply. "You are not to speak this blackguard's name. You are not even to think it. From now on, as far as I am concerned, as far as you and the world are concerned, I am the father of this child."

My head snapped up. *"You?"*

"Yes, Annabelle." He kissed my hand. "You are, I think, in need of a friend, a devoted friend. A husband."

"Husband?" I said stupidly.

"Forgive me. I am not elegant with words, as some men are. I am not skilled at wooing. But I have wished for some time to marry you, Mademoiselle de Créouville, and I think perhaps the earlier this service is performed, the more convenient it will be."

His words reached me from a distance. When I tried to breathe, the air was too thin. I said, in a voice so faint it couldn't possibly have been mine, "You can't be serious. I'm carrying another man's child."

He shook his head. "If we marry, Annabelle, the child is mine. He will have my name, he will have a home and a father and four doting brothers and sisters. God willing, we will give him more of them, in time."

"But your own children. A stepmother. They will hate me."

"On the contrary, Frieda will be delighted. She adores you. She has in fact been hinting to me, and not too delicately. The others, I suspect, have long wanted me to find some-

one to cheer me a little."

"You are mad," I whispered.

"No, I am not mad. I have never been so clear in my objective. I am in love with you. I have been consumed with you since I first saw you in your father's home, playing your cello for a roomful of people who were not worthy to hear you."

"Johann, stop," I said desperately.

"I realize I am not a handsome man, nor a charming man, but you will find me a faithful and devoted husband, my Annabelle" — he kissed my hand again — "if you will allow me that honor. You are weeping."

"I don't deserve this. I don't deserve your kindness."

"It is not kindness, Annabelle. I am taking gross advantage of your situation to win the hand of a woman to whom I could not otherwise aspire. Now relieve my anxiety and tell me you will marry me."

He didn't look anxious. His large face had taken on color, and his eyes were bright, but his expression had hardly changed at all. My pulse clicked in my ears, my head rang. Marry him. Marry Johann. Safe, stern, faithful Johann, who had no hidden wife, no mistress. Johann, who loved me so much, he would take my shameful baby, too. I stared at his pale bright eyes, washed free of color, and I knew I would never catch Johann in bed with Peggy Guggenheim. I would never walk

into a party and count a dozen other women he had slept with. Imagine that, a lifetime of secure love, a houseful of children and loyalty. Between myself and the cautionary tale of my mother's life, I would have Johann standing in protection, a reliable giant.

I had spent the last few weeks half expecting him to propose, half preparing to reject him, half preparing to accept him, and now that the opportunity had arrived, at the exact moment I had thought it lost forever, I didn't know how to reply. I stammered a helpless cliché: "I don't know what to say."

"You must say yes. You must. You have no choice. I am determined, Annabelle."

"Then yes," I said recklessly, and a wave of shock passed across my stomach. Marry Johann. I pulled my hand from his grasp and reached up to snatch his face between my palms, so I wouldn't be afraid of what I had just done. Who could be afraid, when Johann von Kleist stood between you and the world? "Yes, Johann. I'll marry you."

I crashed my lips into his, and the violence of his response made me gasp into his mouth. He seized my shoulders and stood, lifting me with him, holding me against his chest while he kissed me. The blood roared so loudly in my ears, I didn't hear the knock on the door, but Johann did. He set me back on the floor and took up my hand, and he told the surprised housekeeper to congratulate him,

281

because Mademoiselle de Créouville had just agreed to become his wife.

6.

We were married the following Saturday, first at the German embassy by the ambassador and then at the Mairie de Paris, where our papers were properly stamped and the marriage made official. My reeling father attended, and a delighted Lady Alice, and all four of Johann's children, along with his sister, who had traveled from Berlin. Charles had still not returned, and nobody knew where to find him.

Afterward, we all had dinner at the Ritz, where Johann and I were to spend the night before leaving on our wedding trip to Rome. I sat between the two oldest children, Frederick and Marthe, who were perfectly friendly, if perhaps stiff. I couldn't blame them. Had their father given them any hint that he was thinking of marrying? Or had they just received telegrams at school, and the necessary train tickets to Paris? Frederick liked to play sports and ride like his father; Marthe was fond of tennis and books. They had been to Florence last summer with their father to see the art and enjoyed it very much, but their favorite part was when they woke up at dawn and drove to Siena for the Palio. One of the jockeys had fallen off, not fifteen feet away from where they were standing, and had

nearly been killed. Frederick described this scene with vigor, using the salt and pepper to illustrate the various positions. I stared at his moving hands and thought, My stepson.

My father drank a great deal to overcome his shock. He gave a splendid toast and remarked on the absent Charles: *He will now think more carefully before leaving town without a forwarding address, eh?* Everyone laughed. Johann also rose and gave a brief toast, thanking everyone for attending on such short notice, but at his age one had lost the patience for a long engagement. He thanked me, his new wife, for the favor of marrying him, and he promised to make my happiness the study of his life.

We had a small but elegant white cake. Johann's half-English sister Margaret took pictures of us cutting it. When everyone finished, she shepherded the children to taxis, though not before lining them up to kiss their father and their new mother good-bye. The scent of sugar hung behind them. My father and Alice left shortly after that.

7.

As a surprise, Johann had booked the legendary Imperial Suite for our wedding night. It was only seven o'clock, but the November sky had already been dark for hours, so the evening felt much later.

We hadn't kissed since the moment of our

engagement. There was too much planning to be done, too many logistics to be sorted out. We had not had five minutes for romance, and Johann was, after all, an orderly man, who wanted to wait until our union was properly sanctioned. Now the plans had been executed, the logistics completed. We were man and wife, and there was nothing to do but to be married.

At the door to the suite, Johann bent down and lifted me into his arms to carry me across the threshold. I gasped at the opulence of the rooms. There was a bucket of champagne on the table in the drawing room, next to an enormous vase of fresh red roses, just opening and deeply fragrant. Johann opened the bottle and poured out two glasses. We drank to each other. Johann set down his glass and lit a cigarette with quick, nervous fingers. I had never seen him nervous. The understanding of his anxiety calmed my own jumping pulse, my panicked blood. I took his hand and asked him to show me the other rooms.

We saw the dining salon, the marble bathroom, the guest bedroom. We arrived at the splendid master bedroom, gilded, hung with silk damask, where the imperial bed confronted us, as wide as the ocean. I began to shake again, because it was done, there was no turning back: I was now irrevocably the wife of Johann von Kleist, and in a moment he was going to start kissing me, he was go-

ing to start making love to me. That was his right as my husband. A man who wasn't Stefan was now my husband. A man who wasn't Stefan was going to make love to me, consummating our marriage, and without the least warning a cry of grief ripped the interior of my lungs, like a cat clawing for escape: a cry of what in French we call *agonie,* because it was November and August was gone forever.

I must put August out of my mind, as if it didn't exist.

Johann took my champagne glass from my hand (it was only half finished) and set it on the bedside table next to his. He put out his cigarette in a small gold tray shaped like a seashell. He removed his splendid dress uniform jacket and hung it carefully in the wardrobe, and then he drew me into his enormous arms and kissed me, without uttering a word, and I thought, It's better this way, it's better that we don't say anything at all.

8.

It seemed almost silly, afterward, to fall asleep in bed together at the absurdly early hour of eight-thirty in the evening, though it would have been equally silly to rise. It was our wedding night, after all.

Johann climbed out of bed to fetch his cigarettes. When he returned, the mattress

bowed to his weight, and I rolled helplessly into his side. He smoked for a while, without speaking, and finished his champagne. I fell asleep to the sound of his breathing and woke at eight to find my husband fully bathed and dressed, having already ordered breakfast, which was laid out neatly around a vase of fragrant gardenias on a table next to the bed: the start of our married life.

PEPPER
COCOA BEACH 1966

1.

Pepper screams. Not because of the headlock, but because a current of pain has just thundered up her foot like an approaching freight train, and then slammed into her brain in a cataclysmic explosion, like you see in the movies.

Without warning, the arms drop away, and Pepper staggers face-first onto the oriental rug.

"Jesus!" the man says. "You're pregnant!"

The lamp flashes back on. Pepper rises on her elbow and clutches the top of her foot, encased in its slipper. Already a bubble of numbness is forming around the pain, an ominous sign. "Holy *fuck,*" she whispers.

"Who the hell *are* you?"

"You just broke my foot."

"I didn't break your foot!" He crouches down next to her and lifts her hand away. "Oh. Jesus. Ouch."

"I'll say." An unfamiliar pricking sensation surrounds Pepper's eyeballs, like she might

287

— please, God, no! — actually cry.

"Can you wiggle your toes?"

Pepper tries. "No."

"Damn it. I guess it's the ER. What the hell did you do?"

"What did *I* do? *You* were the one who grabbed me in a headlock, sonny."

"*You* were the one lurking behind the door in my mother's study, about to clobber me! *In the dark!*"

"I thought you were a burglar!"

"Me? For all I know, *you're* the burglar."

"Oh, you've got a nerve. Do I look like a burglar to you?"

Pepper lifts her head, tosses back her hair, and gives him a gander, just to make her point. And . . . well. Not quite what she expected, is he? Big young man, broad shoulders, dark hair, strong face, cranky eyebrows. Annabelle's son? Not that she cares. Not that it matters whether she cares, because in that instant of connection, right before her eyes, the cranky expression transforms to astonishment.

"Jesus. Pepper *Schuyler*?"

She frowns, or rather deepens her frown. "I'm sorry. Do I know you?"

His hand falls away from her foot. He looks at her face, blinking a little, as if to clear his eyeballs of her image and replace it with one he likes better. "I guess not," he says. "All right. You sit here, I'll get some ice."

"I'm not just going to *sit* here and wait for *ice*."

Annabelle's son rises to his feet and stares down at her. "Well, Miss Schuyler. I don't mean to be rude, but I'd say you don't really have a choice."

2.

"So how exactly did you hurt that foot?" asks Annabelle's son, as they drive to the hospital through the dark Florida night in the same Ford Thunderbird Pepper drove earlier that evening. Except that Annabelle's son has put the top back up, and her hair is quiet about her face.

"Because you stepped on it, you big ox."

"No, I didn't."

Pepper sighs. "It was the thing I was about to hit you with."

"What thing was that?"

"I don't know. It was dark. Some sort of statue on the bookshelf. I dropped it when you grabbed me."

He starts to laugh. "You were going to hit me with Mama's *Grammy*?"

"Her what?"

"Her Grammy Award. A music award. She's a cellist. You know, plays the cello." He motions with one hand, a fair bowstroke.

"I *know* she plays the cello. Obviously." Pepper speaks with dignity, and tries to ignore the rich quality of his laughter, which

would be far more attractive if she weren't holding a bag of ice to her throbbing foot, thanks to his existence on this earth. She adds: "We're friends."

"God, I hope so, or I'll have to have you arrested for trespassing."

"Oh, wouldn't that be rich. Considering she practically kidnapped me and dragged me to her lair."

"Oh, really? Sounds like Mama, all right."

That laugh again. Pepper looks out the window, though there's nothing to see, just black shapes sliding past, houses and palm trees and telephone poles crawling with vines. There's always something a little overgrown about Florida, isn't there? As if the landscape is just waiting for its chance to take over again.

"Sure, go ahead and laugh," she says. "You're not the one with a broken foot, being held against your will."

"Nice try, but I'm not buying it. No one holds Pepper Schuyler against her will."

She turns her head and narrows her eyes at his dark profile. "You seem to know a lot about me, for a man I don't know from Adam."

"I work for a law firm in Washington. I've seen you around."

"Oh, another lawyer. I should have known."

"You've got a problem with lawyers?"

"No. I just seem to attract them, that's all."

He shrugs. "Flies to the honeypot. So how did Mama kidnap you?"

"I sold her a car."

"A car? What kind of car?"

"Didn't she tell you?"

There is a little silence. He checks the rearview mirror, slows the car, makes a left turn across an empty street, into an even emptier street. He drives competently, she'll give him that: fast and easy, clutch and gears in perfect synchronization. His hands are large and firm on the steering wheel, a detail Pepper admits reluctantly, because she's in no mood to find any man attractive, let alone this one, who just broke her foot.

"No," he says at last. "Why? Should she?"

"It's a mighty nice automobile, that's all. Cost her a fortune. Where's this hospital of yours, anyway? North Carolina?"

A nice easy chuckle. "No. Coming right up. How are you feeling?"

"Like a pregnant woman with a broken foot."

"I'm glad to hear it."

"Oh, a masochist, too. It figures."

A flurry of lights appears before them on the right-hand side of the road. He brakes carefully, and Pepper has the feeling he's grinning, the bastard.

"I'm not a masochist. I just figure you must be all right, if you can still snap like a turtle."

291

3.

"I suppose I should ask your name," Pepper says, as he's carrying her to a wheelchair inside a pair of thick arms. Her nose bobs along next to his neck, which smells absurdly of soap, sweet and clean. Soap! Who still smells like soap at two o'clock in the morning? Annabelle's son, apparently. She tilts her nose away.

"Oh, Mr. Dommerich will do."

"Not for what I have in mind."

"You're a tough customer, Miss Schuyler." He deposits her in the wheelchair and swings around to grasp the handles. "It's Florian."

"Florian?"

"Dare I hope it rings a bell?"

"It's not Tom, Dick, or Harry, anyway."

"Well, I guess you'll remember me now, at least. The ox with the oddball name who broke your foot." He pushes her confidently down an antiseptic white corridor. A nurse looks up from the station as they pass.

"Mr. Dommerich!"

"Well, hello, Nurse Smith. Long time no see. Late shift tonight?"

"Lucky me." She glances down at Pepper, and her mouth turns downward. She points her sharp finger to the right. "Labor and delivery is that way."

Florian laughs that laugh again. "Nope, not yet, Smitty. Just a broken foot. We're headed to the ER."

He must have flashed her a hell of a smile as he said it, because she brightens like a Christmas tree, right before she flushes like a beet.

"Oh! Of course! The ER is straight ahead," she sort of stammers, and Pepper rolls her eyeballs.

"I know. But thank you, Smitty. I'm just flattered you recognized me." He puts the faintest emphasis on the word *you.*

"Of course. I — I didn't realize you were married, Mr. Dommerich."

"Full of surprises," he says, over his shoulder.

Pepper says, once the nurse is behind them: "On familiar terms, I see."

"My dad was in and out of here for a while before he died. I got to know the joint pretty well. Here we are."

"Oh, God, I'm sorry. Of course. I wasn't thinking."

"What, an *apology*? Christ, what's next? You'll be thanking me, and I'll expire from shock." He addresses the orderly at the admittance desk. "Good morning. Not too busy, I hope?"

The orderly points to the door. "Labor and delivery, not ER. Don't they tell you anything?"

"No baby tonight, actually. Broken foot, if I know my metatarsals, and it's a doozy. The right one. How's the wait?"

The orderly looks down at Pepper's foot and frowns. He pulls out a clipboard from a stack, sticks in a sheet of paper, and hands it to Florian. Pepper makes a move to snatch it away, but Florian shoos her expertly. "You sit tight with the ice bag, all right? I'll take care of this."

"Are you the husband?" says the orderly.

Pepper opens her mouth to say no.

"Looks like it," says Florian.

The orderly laughs. "Name?"

"Florian Dommerich."

"I mean your wife's name."

"Oh. Pepper."

A frown. "Her real name, Mr. Dommerich."

There is an awful little silence. Pepper is still sitting in her state of shock; the casual word *wife* seems to have glued her jaw shut.

"Darling," says Florian, "what *is* your real name? I've forgotten."

Nobody knows Pepper's real name, if she can help it. She stares mutinously at the orderly, whose blue ballpoint pen stands poised over the paperwork on his desk.

"She's kind of funny about it," Florian says. "Wouldn't tell me until right before the ceremony, and even then she made me whisper the word, so only God could hear me. Just one of her adorable little foibles."

She was going to kiss him. She was going to murder him.

"I don't have all night, Mrs. Dommerich," says the orderly.

Florian coughs. "You can't just write down Mrs. Florian Dommerich? We are one flesh, after all. Joined at the hip."

"Is *your* foot broken, Mr. Dommerich?"

"Well, no."

The orderly points his pen at Pepper. "So I'll be needing *her* name, okay? And condiments don't cut it, not in the ER, not on my watch."

"With all due respect —"

"Prunella," says Pepper. "Okay? It's Prunella. Family name."

The orderly's eyebrows rise. Behind her back, Florian's chest makes a grave little shudder that travels through his arms to vibrate the wheelchair. He lifts one hand and snaps his fingers.

"Ah! That's it. How could I forget?" he says. "Prunella."

4.

On the way back to the villa, Pepper asks him why he did it.

"Did what?"

"Pretend you were my husband, back there."

"Oh, you know. Makes the paperwork easier, doesn't it? No awkward questions."

His tone is light. His tone is mostly always light, as if nothing is too serious for him to

295

handle, everything's a joke; that taking a stranger, a heavily pregnant woman, to the emergency room in the middle of the night and pretending she's your wife is . . . well, just one of life's little adventures. He's rolled up his shirtsleeves, and his forearms are sturdy, his hands strong as they hold the wheel. He is altogether dependable.

"Well, it ends now, okay?" she says. "No husbandly privileges when we get back."

"Perish the thought." Florian reaches for the radio dial and fiddles with it. Static, mostly, and then a thin stream of lonely trumpet pierces the noise. "I also figured you might need a break."

"A break, do I?"

"You know, holed up like this, no one around to rub your feet and buy you jars of pickles. Mama's got a nose for folks in trouble. I thought maybe you didn't need any more of it. Trouble, I mean."

There are all kinds of heroes, Annabelle said, on the ride up to Cocoa Beach, and as Pepper stares at the gray landscape a week and a half later, through an entirely different windshield, she hears those words again. Almost like the woman's sitting right there, like a chaperone — yes, right there delicately on the bench seat between the two of them, Florian and Pepper — and whispering in Pepper's ear.

"I can handle trouble, all right. People say it's my middle name. My first name, too, if

you think about it."

"Oh. Prunella, you mean?"

"Don't get sassy."

"I'll get sassy if I feel like it, Miss Trouble. It's the least I can do for you, get you snapping again. Back in fighting-turtle form."

"What the hell does that mean?"

Florian slows the car and turns, and Pepper realizes they're already back at the house, that the dark space washing away to her right is the ocean, and the line of pink above is the breaking dawn.

"It means I like you how I saw you in Washington, Pepper Schuyler, even if you wouldn't give me the time of day. I like you conquering the world, not sitting back and letting it conquer you."

Pepper looks through the bug-spattered glass at the approaching garage and bursts into tears.

5.

She hates the crutches, and the crutches hate her. Florian knows better than to offer help. He just opens the doors wide as she comes to them, and smiles from the corner of his mouth as she swears.

"Need anything else?" he says, when she swings herself through the doorway of the guest cottage and tosses the crutches on the floor.

"Trust me, you've done enough."

297

"All right, then. Keep the handkerchief. Take your pills. Sleep as long as you like. I'll tell Clara to keep the coffee warm."

He starts to close the door, and Pepper says *Wait.*

Florian pauses with his large hand on the doorknob, eyebrows expectantly high.

"Thanks," she says.

He places his hand to his chest and staggers backward, shutting the door as he goes.

ANNABELLE

PARIS 1936

1.

By the time I saw Nick Greenwald again, in the first week of March, the baby had grown quite large, and I had to dress carefully to disguise the size of my belly. I was glad I did. Nick took off his hat and reached for my hand, and his eyes ran up and down me as if to assess me for slaughter.

"Good morning, Frau von Kleist," Nick said formally. "Thanks for agreeing to meet me here."

"It's Annabelle, and I can't stay long. I have an appointment in half an hour."

The appointment was manufactured, but my reluctance was not. I had told Johann in the morning, before he left for the embassy — since January, he had been working day and often night, something to do with treaty obligations — that I was going shopping for baby things today, and I hadn't lied. The evidence sat on the floor next to my chair: a small assortment of wrapped packages, and many more to be delivered to the apartment

later in the afternoon. But I knew without asking that my husband wouldn't be pleased at my meeting another man alone — he trusted me without reserve, he said again and again, but he did not trust other men around me — and so I hadn't asked. I had only agreed to meet with Nick because I was afraid of the consequences if I didn't: Nick showing up at the apartment, or, worse yet, Stefan himself.

For months now, I hadn't let the thought of Stefan intrude on my happiness. I had forced him away with an iron discipline. I was happy, I told myself: I felt fit and healthy as my pregnancy progressed; I had had a luxurious honeymoon, a husband who worshipped me daily, a beautiful Paris apartment, an affectionate stepdaughter. After a month in Italy, motoring about in Johann's magnificent Mercedes, we had traveled straight to Westphalia for Christmas, where Johann had introduced me to the staff of his estate as the new baroness, and the children had arrived home to celebrate the season. We had all gotten along well, though Frieda was the only one who sought me out, to play the cello together and to take walks on the bitter winter grounds. "You must give them time, of course," said Johann. "They will learn to love you as I do."

"Not *quite* as you do, I hope," I had replied, because my new husband had spent those

weeks in Italy like a penitent who has finally emerged from a long and grueling fast, far more interested in the feast he had married than the art and monuments surrounding us. But that was what a honeymoon was for, wasn't it? To seal man and wife together, before they faced the world again. When you made constant love to someone, you drove out everything and everyone else, until you almost forgot there *was* a world outside your union, full of messiness and complication and old lovers. All that physical intimacy made you feel as if you really *were* in love, you really *were* married forever.

Just that morning, I had opened my eyes to Johann's farewell kiss, and I had thought how handsome he was, how I couldn't imagine another face bending down to mine in the morning. And, of course, he wasn't handsome, not objectively. But at that moment, while the baby kicked softly in my belly, and the sheets smelled warmly of Johann, I loved his face too much to think him otherwise.

So as I stared down Nick Greenwald's lanky form across the grubby café table, I stiffened my chest against him and thought that he deserved that little lie about the appointment.

"I'll be brief, then," said Nick, lighting a cigarette and signaling the waiter. His face was grim and his eyes, when they looked at me, were hard and resentful. "I just have a

few questions for you, on behalf of a mutual friend."

"I don't believe I owe you any answers."

He raised his eyebrows. The waiter arrived, and Nick ordered coffee. He took a long drag of his cigarette, and when the waiter had passed out of earshot, he blew out the smoke and said, "I suppose you've heard he's out of prison now."

"*What?* Who?"

"Stefan."

I couldn't breathe. The baby kicked against the wall of my stomach, and I put my hand on my side. "He's in prison?" I whispered.

"You didn't know?"

"No. I never heard a word from him, not since August."

Nick sat back in his chair, and a little of the resentment left his eyes, which, in the watery March sunshine that percolated through the window next to us, proved to be a charming shade of hazel. "I don't understand. Your brother never told you?"

"I haven't seen Charles since he left town in November. He doesn't approve of my marriage."

"It was a shock."

"It shouldn't have been. My husband is a good man. He's loyal and faithful, and I love him." I pushed hard on the word *faithful,* and my hand moved in a slow circle on my side, around the baby's protruding foot.

Nick's gaze dropped to my hand and back again. "So I see."

"If you have any questions," I said, "I wish you would ask them."

"Why did you meet with me, if you're so in love with your husband?"

"Not because I felt I owed you any explanation."

"Really? None at all? Not to *me*, I mean. I'm only here because Stefan asked me to see you."

My palms were damp. I flattened them against my dress. "Did he?"

"Yes. He rang me up a week ago, from Frankfurt. They're not letting him out of the country, you know. They're following him everywhere."

"I don't understand. Who's following him? Why was he in prison?"

His voice lowered. "The Gestapo, for God's sake. Don't tell me you don't know."

"I know a little. Not very much. Is he all right?" My throat shook a little.

"Well, he was arrested as soon as he set foot in Germany, the twenty-ninth of August. He was put in the new camp at Dachau, near Munich. Have you heard of it?"

"No."

"It took us months to figure out where he was, and then your brother went off to try to get him released. That was November. They finally let him out in February, banged up

but alive, and your brother got him settled and came home to Paris, and that's when he found out, as you know, that you were married to von Kleist and expecting a baby already. And meanwhile Stefan was going crazy over there, he wanted to jump the border and find you, and when I told him the news over the telephone I thought he was going to shoot himself. He said there had to be some mistake. I said there wasn't." Nick crushed out his cigarette in the ashtray, just as the waiter arrived with his coffee. He added a teaspoon of sugar and took a careful sip. I couldn't speak. I watched his lips. He put down the cup and said, "He seemed to think the baby might be his."

"It isn't," I said instantly. "I started meeting Johann as soon as I came to Paris. I was furious and I wanted to forget, and Johann —"

"Furious?" said Nick. "Furious with Stefan?"

"Yes, because he hadn't told me he was married. And I had always sworn I would never go to bed with a married man, I would never do that to another woman, because of my mother. It killed my mother."

Nick was staring at me, astonished. His hand lay still on his cup; his back was rigid against the chair. "Are you kidding me?" he said. "*That's* why you left?"

"Yes. And I happen to think it was a

damned good reason. I wouldn't ever knowingly betray another woman. So I married Johann, and yes, we're having a baby together, and I am certain, *certain,* that I've done the right thing this time, and I'll be damned if I let you convince me otherwise." I sat back, breathless, cradling the round ball of my belly, the fetus who was beating an irregular rhythm against my abdomen, unused to all this turmoil.

"All right," Nick said. "Keep your voice down."

I picked up my glass of water and drank it dry. Nick lit another cigarette and turned back his head to watch the smoke ebb upward into the stained ceiling. His fingers played with the sugar spoon, turning it this way and that in the cradle of his hand.

"I have to admire your principles," he said. "Most girls would carry on the affair anyway. But not Annabelle. She doesn't sit around feeling sorry for herself. She doesn't confront him and make a big stink. She just runs right off and marries the first man who asks her, a nice boring old German general who won't ever break her heart."

"He's not boring. He is the best man I know. And I make him happy. Every day, every morning I wake up and I know I've done the right thing."

Across the room, the waiter eyed us, arms crossed, resentful that we were taking up one

305

of his best tables at the window with a glass of water and a cup of coffee. The baby was pressing against a nerve, making my right toes go numb. I shifted in my seat and opened my mouth to close the conversation.

"I don't know if I should tell you this or not," Nick said.

"Tell me what?"

He set down the sugar spoon and ran his thumb around the rim of the cup. "Can I ask you a question? Who told you he was married?"

"Lady Alice Penhallow. His old mistress. I met her at the Hôtel du Cap, after Stefan left."

"Ah. Good old Lady Alice. And she didn't tell you that his wife had actually left him by then, had taken their daughter last March and gone off with some lover of hers, some neighbor, a childhood friend, as I understand it? That Stefan had gone home to give her the divorce she wanted, so that he could marry you, and that was when they caught him, crossing the border into Germany?"

The air left the room. The swallowed water rose up in my throat. I gripped the edge of the table, but it didn't help. "Excuse me," I said to Nick Greenwald, and I rushed to the dirty staff toilet in the back, where I heaved up the water and what remained of my breakfast, and then I heaved up nothing at all, just dry yellow bile and nothing else.

2.

Lady Alice wasn't at home, but my father was, still nursing his head from the night before. "Is something wrong, *mignonne*?" he asked, removing the ice pack from his head, and I said there was nothing wrong, I just had a question I needed to ask her.

He fell back on the sofa and closed his eyes. He assured me he would have her telephone me when she returned.

I went back downstairs to the waiting taxi. Nick Greenwald had offered to drive me home, but I refused. Actually, he had been quite kind. "It's a damned thing," he said, "an awful damned thing," and I remembered my brother told me that Nick had had some sort of love affair, back home in the States, that had gone badly. It was hard to imagine any girl breaking Nick Greenwald's heart, but Charles said Nick had been a wreck when they first met, drinking all night, taking women home from parties and discarding them afterward. There had been some legendary house party at a Loire chateau. Charles refused to disclose the details, and I had pieced together a few rumors that I thought could not possibly have been true. But that was the trouble about rumor, wasn't it? You never knew what to believe. You never knew for certain if a man was a hero or a villain or an ordinary human being.

But Charles had also said that Nick had

returned from the house party a changed man: had sworn off drink (mostly) and women, and had singlehandedly rescued his family firm from the brink of bankruptcy. Again, that information might or might not have been true; all I knew was that Nick Greenwald couldn't have been kinder as he found me a taxi outside the café and helped me inside with all my packages, which I would have forgotten if Nick hadn't noticed them. He had rested his elbows on the edge of the door and gazed at me with compassion.

"It's a damned thing," he said again.

"Yes."

"What the hell do I say to Stefan?"

I gripped his arm. "Please don't tell him anything at all. Don't say anything to anyone."

"Hell," said Nick Greenwald. He lifted himself away from the taxi door and we pulled away from the curb, and the sight of his face, bruised and tender, stayed with me the rest of the afternoon, until Johann came home.

3.

During our wedding trip, Johann and I had spent a week on the Amalfi Coast, driving from village to village, and one evening, over dinner, Johann announced that he wanted to visit Pompeii the next day. I told him I wasn't

interested, and he agreed we should go to Positano instead, but as I lay in bed that night, locked inside the coil of Johann's sleeping body, I thought about his disappointed face and his deep interest in military history and Roman civic organization, and when I woke up the next morning I told him that I had changed my mind, and if he wanted to visit Pompeii we should go.

It was the middle of November, and there were very few visitors. We pulled off the dusty road at nine o'clock and Johann pointed out the window and said, "There it is." I followed his finger and saw a cluster of crumbling yellow buildings, looking exactly like every other decrepit Italian village, except for an absence of the familiar red-orange roof tiles, and I thought, My God, it's just like Stefan said.

We wandered for a few hours among the buildings and monuments, the perfect amphitheater and the paved streets. At one point I bent down and picked up a shard of ochre-colored pottery and said, "Look at this. Let's take it back with us," and Johann said no, we should leave it here where it fell, like a soldier in battle. He pointed out the expert grading of the streets, the drainage, the orderly layout of the buildings. We walked for some time, and after consulting a map Johann suggested we visit the Antiquarium, where many of the frescoes and the artifacts were displayed, along with some plaster casts of the victims. I

said no, I didn't want to see that at all, and Johann frowned in disappointment and looked back down at the map.

All right, I said. *Let's go.*

The museum was crammed with shelves and displays, a superabundance of antique detritus. I walked past great glass cases in which mothers clutched their children, and merchants clutched their bags of treasure, and I averted my eyes. Johann made his way more slowly, studying the angles of death, the quality of the plaster. We turned a corner, and there before us was a case containing a dog on its back, contorted in agony, bearing a thick collar around its sternum. I put my fist to my mouth and turned away, sobbing, and Johann said, *Annabelle, what's wrong?* and I said, *It's true, the poor dog, look at his face, the poor thing, he never knew.*

Johann patted my back and said, "Ah, don't fret so, Annabelle. It's just a plaster cast, not a real dog. Nothing to cry over." After a moment, he took my hand and we moved on to inspect a collection of gold bracelets in the shape of coiled snakes.

The pottery shard had traveled quietly that day in the pocket of my skirt, and I kept it now in the bottom of my drawer, beneath my underwear, where Johann would never dream of looking.

4.

I rose from the floor of the nursery, where I was inspecting fabric samples. I had brought the phonograph into the room, and the room was full of Puccini. "You're home early," I said to my husband.

Johann walked to the phonograph and lifted the needle away. The music stopped in mid-phrase, with a tiny scratch. He caught my hands and helped me up just as I found my feet. "Yes, it was rather a trying day, and I decided that there was no point in being such an important man if I could not leave my work to others and join my bride when she is expecting our baby."

"Not for another ten weeks."

He bent down and kissed me. "It cannot be soon enough for me. Are these for the nursery?"

"Yes. The curtains. What do you think?"

"Make sure they are good and thick. A well-darkened room is necessary for good napping."

I looked again at the samples. "Oh, of course. I didn't think of that."

"That's why it's useful to marry a man who has had children already. You see what a clever girl you are?"

I sank back to my knees on the rug and picked up two swatches, one in each hand, and I hated them both. "Yes, a very clever girl."

Johann crouched next to me. "Annabelle. Look at me."

I looked up.

"You have been crying, haven't you? Are you well?"

"I'm quite well, it's just these stupid swatches the draper gives me. None of them are right, and it will still take weeks to have them made, and the baby will be here soon, and I don't know what to do —"

He drew me against his woolen chest. "Shh. Calm down. It is nothing, Annabelle. It doesn't matter, the color of the curtains. The baby will not even notice, I promise you."

The wool scratched my forehead. I heard Nick's voice: *I thought he was going to shoot himself.*

The parting began again in my ribs. I took Johann's lapels in my fists and forced Nick's voice away. I forced away the image of Stefan on the telephone, fresh from the prison where they had sent him after he crossed the border into Germany on the twenty-ninth of August, listening to Nick Greenwald explain that Annabelle de Créouville was not waiting faithfully for him in Paris, but instead had married a Prussian baron and was pregnant with his child. I pictured Stefan's shocked dark eyes, his gaunt face.

"Annabelle," Johann said gently. "You are distressed."

I looked up and thought, It's not his fault,

312

it's my fault. What had Stefan said? *We are in God's hands now.* I remembered feeling a warm glow when he said those words, because in my innocence I thought they meant that God had brought us together, that we were intended for each other, and God would solve all our difficulties and bring us together.

But, as usual, I had misunderstood. It seemed God had not intended me for Stefan, after all. He had intended me for Johann von Kleist, who had lost so much in his thirty-eight years, and needed a fresh young wife to comfort him.

The thing was done.

There was a brief knock, and the nursery door burst open. It was Frieda, telling me that Lady Alice was on the telephone for me.

5.

"Darling, I had no idea," Lady Alice said. "It's not the sort of gossip that spreads easily. If she'd been somebody important, of course, I might have heard about it."

I glanced out the tiny round window into the courtyard. Johann hated the telephone, and we had only one in the apartment, relegated to a closet off the library. I wondered if she was telling the truth, and whether it mattered.

"Anyway," she went on blithely, "the fact remains, he never told you about her, or the daughter. That's not fair play, is it?"

"No."

"So it makes no difference, really."

"Yes, it does. If I'd known she'd left him, I might have waited for an explanation, at least." I spoke in a hushed whisper.

"But he still would have been caught at the border and thrown in prison, wouldn't he? So there's no telling how everything might have worked out. And think of poor Johann. Aren't the two of you just appallingly happy these days?"

"Yes, we're very happy."

"So there's no use thinking about it, is there? What's done is done. You're far better off with your lovely loyal old hound of a Prussian, the one you're married to. Put the whole matter out of your head. I assure you, Stefan will have no trouble finding another pretty young thing to lick his wounds for him. And whatever else needs licking."

She made perfect sense. Stefan would surely be back to his old ways in no time, and I had faithful Johann and the baby, who needed me. There was only Nick Greenwald's voice at the back of my head — *I thought he was going to shoot himself,* and sometimes *He seemed to think the baby might be his* — and Nick's voice was easily silenced, if I concentrated hard enough, if I drowned it out with other things.

"All right," I said. "I suppose so, when you

put it that way. I was just feeling low, and a little guilty."

She laughed right into the receiver, crackling the hairs of my ears. "Oh, for heaven's sake, darling, don't do *that*. Life is far too short to look back."

6.

That night, Johann made respectable married love to me in our bed, turning me on my side and entering me from behind so the baby would not be crushed between us, a position we had adopted a month or two ago.

When we had both caught our breath, he cupped his hand around my heavy womb and said, "Annabelle, I will be very busy in the next few days. I may have to go away."

"Where to?"

"Perhaps to Berlin. Perhaps to a few other places." He paused. "There is nothing to worry about."

"Should I be worried?"

"I have just told you, there is nothing. But if I send word that you are to join me somewhere, to leave Paris at once, you will do so, won't you?"

"Why, Johann? What's going on?"

"You know I cannot say."

My heart thudded in its empty cavity. I thought, What if we go to Germany? Stefan is in Germany. I said, "You can't even hint? Don't you trust me?"

315

"It isn't a matter of trust, *meine Frau.* It is a matter of honor. But you will do as I ask, won't you? You will come to me at once, if I send for you?"

The baby stirred under his hand. I laid my fingers over his and said, "Can you feel him?"

"Yes, of course. The tiny foot, right there. But you have not answered my question, Annabelle, *Liebling.*"

"Yes, Johann," I said, staring at the wall. "Of course I will come to you."

He let out a sigh onto the top of my head. "Good. Because there is one thing I cannot bear, and that is the absence of my Annabelle. And of our little child, it is unthinkable."

"You should never worry about that. I'm yours now."

"Yes, I know that. I know your noble heart. It is what I prize most in you." He kissed me tenderly. "I have always loved this part, when my wife is round and beautiful, and we lie here in our bed and wonder what our child will be like when he is born."

"Yes." The tears fell silently into the pillow. "I love this, too."

7.

At dawn the next morning, nineteen German infantry battalions entered the Rhineland, on the eastern border between France and Germany, in violation of some treaty, I forget

which, made in the previous decade, which had guaranteed its permanent demilitarization.

I learned all this from the housekeeper, because Johann had already left the apartment. For the next several days, I did not see my husband, who worked and slept at the German embassy, waiting for the French response. He later told me that if the French had mobilized, if the French had offered even a hint of military opposition, they would have had to retire at once, the defeat would have been total.

But the French did not mobilize, and Johann returned home nine days later, after a further trip back to Berlin for debriefing, heavy-eyed and triumphant.

When we were alone in our bedroom, he sank to his knees before me and lifted my dress to kiss my swollen skin. "Now our child will be born into a safe, strong Fatherland," he said, "with nothing more to fear."

8.

I went into labor twelve weeks later, on the ninth of June — *first babies are always late,* said Dr. Périgault, shaking his head as if the babies were somehow willfully to blame — and gave birth early the next morning to a boy, eight pounds thirteen ounces, bearing a shock of black hair and a pair of lungs like an army sergeant.

"He has his mother's coloring," said the nurse, handing the army sergeant to his father for the first time, later that afternoon.

"Thank God for that," Johann replied. He looked into the baby's squashed red face with the same rare rapture as he had regarded me on our wedding night, and touched his cheek with a most delicate finger. The squalls faded into gasps, and then silence.

The nurse smiled beatifically. "Have you decided on a name?"

"Yes," I said, exhausted and entranced, from the nest of white pillows on my hospital bed. (His wife, Frieda, had hemorrhaged to death at home before the doctor could arrive, and Johann refused to take any chances with me.) I watched Johann straighten the swaddling into a more expert tuck. The baby looked tiny and safe and quiet in his enormous arms, and the breath fell from my lungs.

I turned my face to the nurse. "His name is Florian, for his grandfather."

■ ■ ■ ■

INTERMEZZO

■ ■ ■ ■

June suns, you cannot store them
To warm the winter's cold
                                    A. E. HOUSMAN

ANNABELLE
GERMANY 1936

1.

It was three days before Christmas, and the girls and I had motored into Berlin to shop, leaving Florian at home with his father and brothers.

We traveled not in Johann's black Mercedes, which we left in Paris, but in the massive Daimler Johann kept here in Germany, driven by a chauffeur in a field-gray uniform. The trip took two and a half hours along a highway of rich new asphalt, and Frieda did most of the talking.

"He has a new tooth coming in, the one on the right side," she said. "Did you see it?"

"I didn't need to *see* it. I've felt it the past few days," I said, and I laughed to cover the ripping sound in my chest, because I hated leaving my son even for an hour, let alone for an entire day of shopping in Berlin. *The Baroness von Kleist, she is such a devoted mother,* they said in Paris, bewildered, where mothers of a certain class happily handed off

the baby to the nursemaid after a friendly morning cuddle, but the truth was far more elemental than that, a chemical intensity of emotion that had begun its slow combustion about the third or fourth day after Florian's birth, in some tranquil hour before dawn, when he was suckling at my breast and his eyes wandered up to mine in such a perfect representation of Stefan that I felt the universe move in my marrow, as if I had fastened all my ideas of the infinite upon a single black eyelash. The sensation might possibly be described in music or in mathematical equations or in geometric designs, but not in words.

Johann had been the one to suggest, two nights ago, that I leave Florian at home and go into Berlin for the day. We had converted a box room adjacent to our bedroom into a small nursery, and I was there in my dressing gown, nursing Florian inside a pink haze of bliss. I had looked up, bewildered, and said, "Go into Berlin? But what about the baby?"

"He will be looked after well. The housekeeper knows what to do. He has a father who adores him, and brothers who tolerate him without too much complaint."

"But his milk!"

"We have some bottles. And he is eating now." He knelt down next to the chair and touched my hand. "Annabelle, *Liebling,* you are a wonderful and devoted mother, but you

must learn to leave him a little, too. He is six months old. The doctor says you should not even be nursing him still, or he will get a complex."

"That's nonsense. You and Lady Alice and your complexes. I know my son far better than old Périgault. Look at him, he's perfectly healthy."

"It is not a question of physical health. It is his attachment to you. We do not want our fine strapping son to become a mama's boy, do we?"

Yes, we do, I thought passionately. I gazed down at Florian's working mouth, his inquisitive dark eyes, and my arms ached around him.

Johann went on. "The two of you, you are like a closed link, and nobody else comes inside. But we all need you, *meine Frau.* Our girls need you, and our boys. And you know how desperately *I* need you, your poor lonely husband."

He had chosen his tactics well, like the general he was, and he knew I couldn't resist an appeal like that. So here I sat in the monumental Daimler, rushing into the center of Berlin, heart bleeding out into the seats, discussing Florian's new tooth with my stepdaughters.

"Does it hurt?" Marthe asked practically. "The tooth, I mean, when you feed him."

"Not really. He's very good."

Frieda said, "He is. He is the most darling baby. I can't wait until you have another."

I laughed again. We were just turning the corner of Leipziger Platz, and the crowds thickened at once, a mass of woolen coats and hats, the steady buzz of humanity. "One baby at a time, sweetheart. Look, we're almost there. Where shall we start?"

"Wertheim, of course!" Frieda said.

Marthe frowned and looked out the window.

Berlin's largest department store was predictably packed, from its ground floor overflowing with hats and scarves and haberdashery to its monumental staircases like the channels of an ant farm. We shouldered through the entrance into a warm draft of perfume-scented air. Frieda exclaimed with joy at every display. Though she lived in Paris, in the heart of the fashionable district, we hardly ever went shopping. I was too occupied with Florian, and Johann disliked the idea of letting her roam free among the shops and streets. *It is nothing but material excess,* he said, *nothing but decadence.*

Marthe seemed to share her father's opinion. She trailed behind us with her arms folded across the chest of her red woolen coat. She was a beautiful girl, almost a young lady, who (like Frieda) wore her spun-gold hair in a thick braid around her head like a crown, a few shades richer than her father's.

Her large blue eyes were set in a perfect oval face that Johann said was an exact replica of her mother's, down to the picturesque freckles on her nose. Her school reports were uniformly excellent; Johann was immensely proud of her. Of the two sisters, she was the more reserved, although she had a lovely singing voice and often joined me in the evenings, after dinner, when Johann encouraged his wife and children to come together and play Christmas hymns. Just now, however, her pink mouth was turned down at the corners and tight in the middle, not festive at all.

I fell back and took her arm. "Is something the matter, darling?"

She pulled the arm away. "No, Mother."

Frieda picked out a cashmere scarf for her father and leather gloves for the older boys. We went upstairs to the children's department, where she found a pretty blue woolen hat for Florian. She paid for everything herself from a carefully husbanded allowance, and watched with a radiant face as the little packages were wrapped in paper.

Marthe's arms were still folded. She tapped her toe against the floorboards and stared somewhere above us, to the tops of the polished shelves.

A woman passed by, pushing a baby in a perambulator. The baby was about Florian's age, maybe a month or two younger, propped

up against his white bedding — it was a boy, wrapped in a pale blue knitted sweater and matching cap — and his curious eyes caught mine. I put my hand against the counter to support myself and thought, Johann is right, it's healthy to be away for a bit, but I didn't feel healthy at all. My breasts hurt, my nipples smarted. I felt the milk leak eagerly into my brassiere and was glad for my thick coat, my tweed jacket beneath it, the practical cotton shirt from which such stains could easily be washed.

The packages were wrapped and bound in string for a delighted Frieda. We edged our way through the hot crowd to the stairs. "Are you all right, Mother?" asked Frieda, slipping her hand into mine, and I said of course I was all right, I just needed a bit of air; it was so warm in here with all the people.

We started down the stairs. Marthe trailed a step or two behind. Ahead of us in the crowd was a man wearing a navy blue hat above a neat navy blue suit; a line of dark curling hair showed below the brim of the hat, against a strong white neck.

There was something so familiar about that neck, that hair. The carriage of his head.

No, it's impossible, I thought. Of course it was impossible. Germany was a very large country, and Stefan was supposed to be in Frankfurt; he was in Frankfurt when he spoke to Nick Greenwald.

But I could not look away from that dark hair. I thought I could discern every strand. I stretched my neck in an effort to catch the man's profile, the line of his jaw, the shape of his nose. My heartbeat thudded in my neck and fingertips. The hat disappeared for an instant, and I sidled past a pair of women, pulling Frieda along with me, wheeling around the corner for the next flight. "Wait, Mother!" Frieda said, and I stumbled downward, running my eyes feverishly over the mass of identical hats seething before me.

"Mother!" called Marthe from behind, and at the same second her voice reached my ears, I caught sight once more of the familiar neck, the familiar dark hair, and I darted down, feet flying, fingertips thudding, like a woman holding a single ticket in a sweepstakes, who knows the odds are impossibly against her, who didn't until this moment realize that she wanted so badly to win, who knows in her heart that she *can't* win. But she still thinks, as the number is drawn among millions, that it will be hers.

I let go of Frieda's hand to take the man's navy wool elbow, and I shouted, *Stefan!*

I realized, as I turned, that the man was at least two inches too short. My cheeks already burned by the time I saw the shape of his nose (too large) and the line of his jaw (too narrow).

"Es tut mir leid, es muss ein Irrtum sein," he

327

said. There must be some mistake. The girls assembled at my elbows. Frieda had dropped her packages on the stairs. The man helped her pick them up, while the other shoppers flowed around us, grumbling, like a river parting around an unwelcome obstruction.

Marthe turned to me, still frowning. "Who is Stefan?" she said.

2.

We had lunch in a small restaurant nearby: tea and sandwiches and hot cabbage soup. I wasn't very hungry. "Mother, it is so hot in here. Why don't you take off your coat?" asked Frieda, and I opened the top two buttons and said I would be fine. My hands were still clumsy as I operated my spoon. I set my teacup carefully in its saucer so it wouldn't shake.

We talked very little. I paid the bill and walked out the door behind the girls, and as I turned to close the door behind us I noticed a sign in the window I hadn't seen on the way in:

JUDEN NICHT WILKOMMEN

3.

We visited a few more shops and found the chauffeur parked on the corner of Wilhelmstrasse, as we had arranged, at three o'clock. The light was already starting to fade. Marthe was still quiet as we started off through

the streets of Berlin. She kept her arms folded across her chest and looked out the window, at the passing buildings, while Frieda exclaimed about all the goods in the shops.

"And that hat for Florian," she said, turning to me. "Won't he look just sweet wearing that hat?"

I opened my mouth to say, Yes, of course, we would take a photograph of him wearing it on Christmas morning.

Marthe's head turned. "It's un-German," she said.

"What's that?"

"The *Warenhausen,* they're un-German. We should not have gone there, to Wertheim."

"Un-German?" I said, astonished. "How could Wertheim possibly be any *more* German?"

"They are owned by the Jews, these department stores. Good German businesses suffer because of them." Her mouth compressed in a belligerent line.

"But that's nonsense. Who told you this?"

"It's not nonsense. We have been learning it all at school. The *Warenhausen* are like great leeches set on the cities. They sell cheap goods, and all the money goes to make the Jews richer. Wertheim is the worst of all."

Frieda was quiet, her lips parted in a small round hole of astonishment. I stared at Marthe's profile, stern and blond. Through the window, I saw a few flakes of snow shooting

behind her, like distant meteors.

I said quietly, "Have you talked to your father about this?"

"He feels the same way."

"I find it difficult to believe that the man I married is a bigot," I said, "and I am disappointed beyond words to find this true of my daughter."

She turned to the window and muttered something in German. I couldn't quite pick out the words — I was still learning the language — but Frieda gasped and looked at me. I took her hand and shook my head.

Frieda leaned toward Marthe and whispered in her ear. Marthe went on staring at the shooting snowflakes, the bleak brown winter suburbs, and didn't reply.

I leaned my head back against the cloth seat. Under my skin, in the cavity around my heart, I could still feel the splinters of shock from my flight down the stairs. If I closed my eyes, I could still see that line of dark hair against a white neck, and it really did belong to Stefan, even though it hadn't; I thought I could feel him move in my head and lay a soothing hand on my splintering skin. I thought, *What should I say, Stefan? What do I say to her? What do I do?*

And he said back, *You know what to do, Annabelle.*

Frieda's body was warm and lithe next to

mine, new and untried. I drew her against me and put my arm around her shoulders. "It was lovely shopping with you today, girls, but I confess I can't wait to be back in our nice warm house with your father and the boys."

4.

Before we even entered the house, I could hear Florian's cries. "He wouldn't take the bottle," Johann said, haggard, almost tossing the baby into my arms.

"Thank God," I muttered, because I was ready to burst. I collapsed into the chair and ripped open my blouse. He nursed furiously for half an hour before falling unconscious against my skin, trailing a thin line of contented milk from the corner of his mouth, and I kissed the top of his dark head and promised him I wouldn't go away like that again.

"Perhaps we should consider weaning him," said Johann. He stood at the window, watching the lines of snow cross the glass and disappear into the black night.

I moved Florian carefully to my shoulder. "Not yet."

"But soon, perhaps," said Johann, so softly that I looked up in surprise. His face was dark against the window, and golden with lamplight on the other side. One pale eye regarded us. He let the curtain fall back and said, "I

would like to have more children."

"Of course we'll have more children. But he's still a baby, and there's plenty of time."

"I will be forty years old next month."

I smiled. "But I'm only just twenty-one. Anyway, you've got plenty of children to occupy you for now. How many does one man need, really?"

"I miss you."

"Johann, I'm right here. I sleep next to you every night."

"We have not made love since he was born."

"I didn't realize you wanted to." Florian burped against my shirt. I picked up a cloth, dabbed my shoulder, and brought him back into the cradle of my arms. His eyes were closed, and the sight of his cheeks brought the splinters back to my skin.

"Of course I want to make love to you, Annabelle. I am only a man, after all. But it is for you to decide when you're ready to have another baby."

Again I looked up in surprise. "But we don't have to make a baby. There are many ways to prevent conception."

He frowned. "What do you know of these?"

"Lady Alice."

He brought his fist against the window, making it rattle through the curtain, and pushed himself away to cross the room. "A man does not wear a sheath with his wife,

Annabelle. They are for whores and mistresses."

"Nonsense," I said crisply.

He muttered something to the carpet.

"I'm simply not ready for another baby, Johann. I want to wait until Florian is at least a year old before we try again."

"A year!"

"Johann, please. It's not unreasonable, is it? We can still make love, if you want."

"If *I* want? Don't you want to make love with me?"

I looked back down at Florian's sleeping face. "Of course I do. But we must take precautions, that's all."

He came toward us in two giant strides and knelt next to the chair. "Annabelle, I need you. Look at my two hands. They are aching to touch you again, the way we used to. Don't you ache for me?"

I looked at him helplessly. "Of course I do."

"No, you do not. Of course you do not." He closed his eyes. "But you are so good and loyal, Annabelle. That, I could not do without. I could not live without your loyalty. You don't understand, I think, how much I need you."

"Then touch me, Johann. Kiss me."

"I cannot. I cannot stop if I do."

"I'll put the baby to bed."

He rose and looked down at us both. "No. I don't wish to disturb you."

He walked to the door, and I called after him. "Johann, there's something I need to speak to you about."

He stopped with his hand on the door handle and said, over his shoulder, "So do I, with you. But it is time for dinner, *Liebling*. It can wait."

5.

At Johann's house in Westphalia, which his family had owned since the seventeenth century, we dined at a magnificent walnut table in a paneled room, attended by two servants, and we dressed in formal clothes. The wine was always German. After the main course was cleared away and the table stripped for dessert, Johann dabbed his mouth with his napkin and rose to his feet.

I sat at the other end of the table, with the girls on my right and the boys to my left. I drank the last of my wine and set down the glass. Everyone had turned to Johann, who stood there like a colossus, making even the table seem small. He looked around the room, across the tops of our heads, and I had the feeling he was hesitating.

"Johann, what's the matter?" I said.

"I have a bit of an announcement." He pressed his fingertips into the edge of the table. "I have been asked to assist the government with a project of great importance in Berlin, which will shortly require us to move

to the capital for a certain period."

"Move to Berlin?" I said stupidly.

"Yes, my love. We will live in Berlin, much closer to the children and their schools, which, among other things, will enable us to raise Florian in his own country with a proper understanding of his home and his native language."

"I don't understand," I said.

Frederick spoke up, saying something enthusiastic in German, and Johann stopped him.

"Speak in English, Frederick, so your mother can understand us."

"I'm sorry," Frederick said, glancing at me with his startling pale eyes, exactly the same shade as his father's. "It is wonderful news, that's all. We will be more like a family again."

"That is my hope," Johann said, smiling benignly across the table, as if he had not just laid the perfect ambush and executed it without mercy. "Don't you agree, my love?"

My face was hot. Johann's image blurred in front of me. I laid my napkin on the table and rose.

"Excuse me," I said. "I believe I'll go check on the baby."

6.

I had fallen in love with the Kleist family estate at the moment Johann had driven me up the road in his black Mercedes Roadster.

The top was up, because it was December, so I couldn't see the house itself until we had come around the last bend in the graveled drive, and then it appeared, yellow-walled, in perfect proportion, too sober to be called baroque and too exuberant to be classical. In the center grew a small blue dome, decorated with elegant stone scrollwork. The shrubbery outside was covered in sacking against the bitter frost.

"Oh, it's lovely!" I had exclaimed, peering forward through the windshield. "Why didn't you tell me it was so lovely?"

"Would you have married me sooner if I had?"

I had turned and kissed his cheek. "I don't think it would have been possible for me to marry you sooner."

He had taken me on a long and thorough tour — *You are the baroness now, my love, it is all yours* — which had taken most of the afternoon and evening. I had felt disoriented in the profusion of rooms and furniture and artwork, the reek of beeswax and old plaster, and held on firmly to Johann's elbow, wondering how on earth I could possibly be expected to manage all this.

The next day, while the younger ones were outside playing in a new fall of snow, and Johann had settled himself in his office to scale a mountain of neglected paperwork, I had begun to explore the house on my own.

The eastern wing was my favorite. At the other end of the library was a pair of intimate rooms, connected by a door that could be left open or shut, where I could read quietly by myself, or practice the cello. The decoration was simpler, as if the old castoff furniture had traveled here to die in peace. Johann told me that his wife, Frieda, had spent much of her time there, too, and I had often wondered how much we were alike, and whether we would have liked each other.

After Johann's grand announcement at dinner, I didn't return to the dining room, nor to the music room, where we usually spent the last of the evening. Johann found me around ten o'clock in the smaller of the two rooms, playing Schubert while the snow blew horizontally outside the window and the gusts of wind made the chimney whistle.

"It was just a surprise, that's all," I said, without looking up from the music. "You should have told me."

"There wasn't time."

"Of course there was time. But you wanted to tell me in front of the children, so I couldn't contradict you." I rested the cello against my knee and looked up.

"But why would you want to contradict me?" He appeared genuinely bewildered. "It's a great honor, this post. A tremendous advance for my career."

"Paris is my home."

"Annabelle, we are a family. You are German now."

I rose from the chair passionately. "I am not German! I won't be German. Do you know what your daughter said today, when we were leaving Berlin? She said that we shouldn't shop at Wertheim, because it's owned by a Jew. She said the department stores are like leeches, sucking Germany dry."

He blinked his eyes. "What's this?"

"It's true. That's what they're teaching her at school. And all over Berlin there are signs in the shops and restaurants, about Jews not being welcome. I don't know much German, but I understood that. It's disgusting, the bigotry. I won't live in a city like that. I won't allow my son to be poisoned like that." I knelt and laid the cello in its case and picked up a cloth to wipe the resin from the strings.

Johann stood silently in the center of the room. His hands were closed against his sides, flexing slightly. "He is *our* son," he said quietly.

"Go ahead," I said. "Go ahead and denounce it."

"Annabelle."

"Please denounce it, Johann. You can love Germany and still denounce this. If you *do* love Germany, you will."

"Of course it is distasteful," he said.

"Distasteful? Is that all?"

"What do you want me to say, Annabelle?

338

Of course I do not share this opinion."

"But you won't do anything about it, will you? You'll go on supporting these horrible men who stir up people's lowest instincts just for their own gain. You'll allow them to poison your own children instead of standing up for what's right."

"That's not fair, Annabelle. This . . . this thing, it is just a kind of sickness, a malady of spirit. It will pass. It will fade away, when times are better. It always does."

"But in the meantime, people will suffer. It isn't *right,* Johann. I won't live here. I won't do it."

"You speak as if Germany is the only place where this happens, the only place where Jews are not welcome. Look at France, the Dreyfus affair. Look at the pogroms in Russia. Even in New York and London, Jews are not received in the clubs or the drawing rooms. It is simply how things are." Johann's face was turning red, right up to the roots of his hair, so that his pale blue eyes looked like chips of ice perched in a tomato aspic.

I tilted up my chin to face his passion. "Don't be disingenuous, Johann. You know what's going on here."

"I am not. I admit it's wrong. But this is not such a great matter as you say. It is just a yearning for racial separation, which is a primeval human instinct, and therefore difficult to control. We see it in all countries. I

339

do not advocate it. I have nothing against the Jews. But I understand why these passions are stirred, and I understand there is nothing to be done. It must simply run its course."

"Run its course? Are you mad?" I stabbed my finger at his chest. "You're a powerful man, an army general, a baron! You can do something! But you won't, will you? You're too scared of that stupid man. You're scared they will call you a Jew lover, or say you're un-German. You're —"

"You know *nothing* about this, Annabelle. *Nothing.* Don't speak of things of which you are ignorant."

"Oh, of course. How stupid of me. My job is to lie on my back and spread my legs and make more babies, and to raise your children and adorn your house, not to have opinions and especially not to discuss them. I don't know why I bother with this old thing any-more." I kicked the cello case. "It's not as if you're going to let me out of the house with it, God forbid."

Johann's face was aglow, his shoulders rigid. He turned and grasped the edge of the mantel with his right hand, so forcefully I thought it might splinter. The clock ticked endlessly next to his chest. "Forgive me," he said at last. "I have made you unhappy."

"I am not unhappy. But I don't want to move to Berlin."

"It is only temporary. Six months, or

340

perhaps a year."

"I can't do it."

He picked up the poker and nudged a charred log into place. "You have become a champion of some cause, it seems."

"I'm a champion of humanity. And it's inhuman, what I saw in Berlin. What your own daughter said to me."

He went on poking needlessly at the simmering fire. He was still dressed in his dinner jacket, sharp and black against the pale blue walls and the creamy mantel. Sometimes I forgot how big he was, until his size rushed against me — like now, when I measured him and realized he took up half the wall. I wondered how we looked together, to an outsider: my delicate bones against his blunt ones. When I was wearing high evening shoes, the top of my head came to his collar. I must look like a child next to him.

"I wonder," he said, in the same soft voice, "whether it is really Berlin you object to."

"What else would it be?"

He set the poker in the stand and turned to me with his bleak face. The blood had drained away from his skin, as if he had gained conscious control of his unruly circulation. Another gust hit the chimney, and the wind whistled down the column at a furious pitch. The sound made me shiver.

"I don't know," he said. "Perhaps you would like to tell me, Annabelle."

341

"There's nothing to tell. I don't understand."

"Marthe tells me you met a man named Stefan at the department store today."

I crossed my arms. "I saw someone on the stairs, in the crowd. I thought I recognized him, but I was wrong. It wasn't him. Very silly."

"Did you want it to be this man? This Stefan?"

"Of course not! He just looked familiar, that's all. Is that what you're so mournful about this evening?"

Johann stepped away from the mantel and took my left hand in a sandwich between his. "I want to make you happy, Annabelle. I want to be a husband to you."

"You *are* my husband, Johann. I don't understand."

"I mean the husband you *want*. The husband in your heart."

There was something so melancholy in his voice, as if his own heart lay in two pieces on the floor between us. I leaned forward and touched his cheek. "You are, Johann. Of course you are. You're a wonderful husband, the most wonderful father to Florian."

"But you cannot follow me."

"I can't go against my own conscience. If you really loved me, you wouldn't want me to."

He sighed and released my hand. "Is it

342

really your own conscience? Or is this only an excuse?"

"Johann, wait. You're turning everything upside down, you're making it sound as if —"

"I must go to bed now, *meine Frau*. I will be very busy over the next few weeks." He turned and walked to the door. "I hope you will change your mind."

"Johann, stop."

But he didn't turn back. His body swallowed the door like a blotch of deep black ink.

■ ■ ■ ■

THIRD MOVEMENT

■ ■ ■ ■

"Where there is marriage without love,
there will be love without marriage."
BENJAMIN FRANKLIN

ANNABELLE
PARIS 1937

1.

When I woke up on that hot July morning, seven months later, I had not the slightest intention of betraying my husband by the end of the evening.

I had expected the usual day, the usual routine of caring for Florian and managing our small household, perhaps a walk to the park if it wasn't too sultry, a visit to the nearby shops when Florian took his nap, reading and music in the evening. There was almost always a letter from Johann in the morning post, to which I replied by afternoon; sometimes Lady Alice would stop by to visit and gossip. In a few weeks, we would pack for a month in Westphalia, until the younger children went back to school and Frederick left for university. An entire month, in which to mend together the tattered ends of my marriage.

You see? I still held out hope.

At the end of the Christmas holidays, I had returned to Paris while Johann remained in

Berlin. We had explained to our families that Johann's post was only temporary, so we hadn't wanted to upset our routine, or give up the Paris apartment, which was so desirable. Johann had arrived with me to help me with the luggage, and he had left by ten o'clock on the wagon-lit to Berlin, without staying a single night. He wrote faithfully every day, a single page describing his activities and the weather, ending each letter in a copperplate *Yours always, Johann,* and I replied faithfully to every one.

In April he had come to Paris for a few days on business. I had met him in the morning at the Gare de Lyon in the Mercedes, and he had driven us back to the apartment and taken Florian in his arms and exclaimed over how well he had grown, what a fine boy he was. His stony face had softened with love. The two of them had spent the rest of the morning on the floor of the nursery, trying out one toy after another, while the delicate spring sunshine lit the windows.

I had tried to make my husband welcome. I had kissed him and taken his arm, I had planned dinner and the theater to show him how wonderful things could be, safe in Paris with his son and his young French wife. I thought if we could just go to bed again, the way we had before Florian was born, we could find our way back. I would feel once more like Johann's wife. I would absorb

myself once again in the duties and pleasures of matrimony, and I would no longer see Stefan's face in a department store crowd, or on the train, or in the park eating ice cream on a bench. Lady Alice had helped me pick out a gown for the evening. When we arrived back home, I asked him to help me with the zipper.

He had gazed at me sadly for a moment, as if to say, *Poor Annabelle, trying that old trick.* He had walked around to my back and drawn down the zipper. Then he had excused himself and gone to the bathroom to brush his teeth.

And out of nowhere came the prayer: *Thank God.*

I suppressed it at once, of course. But the prayer couldn't be un-prayed. God had heard me and knew that for that instant, I had been grateful my husband didn't want me, after all.

On the way to the Gare de l'Est a few days later, I said, "Your back doesn't have to be so straight, Johann. You might try to understand." He had occupied himself with the manic Paris traffic and hadn't replied. Florian sat on my lap, playing with the buttons of my blouse. We pulled to the curb across from the terminus and Johann had got out of the car with his valise. I slid to the driver's seat, put my hands on the wheel, and looked up expectantly for his farewell.

Johann had gazed back down at me with his ice-chip eyes. "Frieda misses you. When she is home from school on the weekend, she hopes every time she will see you there."

I said I missed her, too.

For a moment, he seemed to soften, and he touched my hair and said we would have time this summer to be a family again. He kissed Florian's cheek, and then he turned away and picked up his valise and crossed the street. Florian stretched out his arms and started to cry.

When I came back home to the vast and empty apartment, I put Florian down for his nap and wandered back to my own room to spread myself out on the bed I shared with Johann. I stared at the canopy overhead, which was not quite so monumental as the one at Schloss Kleist. It was a happy yellow silk instead of a twilight-blue velvet, and it made me think of the sun. It made me think, for a moment, what would happen if I did not go to Westphalia in August.

If, instead, I put Florian in the Mercedes with me and drove down to the little sun-drenched villa by the sea in Monte Carlo.

2.

"It's a great shame, of course," said Lady Alice philosophically, that hot July morning, "but I suppose he's served his purpose."

"What purpose is that?"

"Why, saved you from infamy, of course. That *is* what you wanted, isn't it?"

"No. I wanted a father for my child. I wanted a partner to share my life with."

"Then I suppose the great shame is you forgot he was German."

"I don't care that he's German," I said. "But I can't live there. Not now."

She rolled her eyes and reached for the teapot. She was still living with my father, which was something of a miracle, and even more miraculously, they were quite happy together. Papa's face glowed when she came into the room. She hardly ever went out at night, at least on her own, and she had even taken to wearing dresses that displayed no more than an inch or two of her breasts. "I don't know," she said. "I think they've managed to order things rather well, haven't they? You should have seen Berlin five years ago. Absolutely ramshackle. Of course, it's heaps more fun that way, but one's got to be sensible and think about the economy from time to time."

"I don't think you've thought about the economy in your life, Alice, and what's all this about being sensible?"

She set down the teapot and the strainer and sank her spoon into the sugar. "The thing is, I'm going to have a baby."

"What?"

"Isn't it charming? A bit of an accident, I'll

351

admit, but your father can't contain his delight now that it's done. You'd think he had impregnated an entire nunnery."

"My God."

"I think you're supposed to congratulate me, darling."

I rose at once and kissed her cheek, and told her she could go through Florian's things and have whatever she wanted. *But what about your own babies?* she asked, and I said there wasn't much prospect of that at the moment, and she said, *Nonsense, you have all August ahead of you, and how could Johann possibly resist?* If that was what I wanted, of course. To have a nice conventional marriage and a belly fat with my husband's child.

At that moment, Florian wandered by — he had just begun to walk — and paused at my knee, looking up at me with his most hopeful expression, and I lifted him into my lap and buried my face in his sweet-smelling hair.

3.

When Lady Alice left, I found my hat and gloves and brought out Florian's perambulator from the corner of the entryway. "I'm taking the baby for a walk," I told the housekeeper, and just as I maneuvered the wheels into place and reached for my son, my brother Charles strolled through the door, whistling a jazz song.

352

I nearly dropped the baby.

"Charles!" I screamed.

"Well, hello, sister dear." He kissed my cheek as if we'd last seen each other a week ago. "Is this the little tyke? My God, he looks like you."

That was what everyone said, that he looked like me, because he had my darker coloring instead of Johann's. But that was the thing about coloring; it was the superficial detail that everyone noticed. If you looked more closely, you saw that Florian really had Stefan's coloring, and Stefan's eyes, and most certainly Stefan's chin and jaw.

But people saw what they expected to see.

Florian looked into Charles's face and burst into tears.

"Now, now, darling," I said. "This is your uncle Charlie."

"Jesus Christ," said Uncle Charlie. "I guess I am."

4.

We struck off toward the Jardin des Tuileries, Florian's favorite excursion. "I don't suppose this means you've forgiven me," I said.

"Forgiven you for what? Marrying that old Nazi?"

"He isn't a Nazi."

"Beg to differ. By Christ, it's hot. Do you want to get an ice cream?"

"He isn't a Nazi. He's a member of the

353

party, of course — he has to be. It doesn't mean he shares their beliefs. Here, you take him," I said, offering the handlebar to Charles.

"What do I do?"

"You push it, Charles. It's not that hard."

Charles dropped his cigarette on the pavement and took up the handlebar. "Nice little machine," he said. "Well sprung. Little guy seems to like it, at any rate."

"I wish you would tell me why you're here. It's making me nervous you're going to tell me some awful news, that you've got cancer or liver cirrhosis."

"No, it's not that. Actually, it's Nick."

"Nick! Nick Greenwald? He's got cancer?"

"Calm down. No, he's not sick. He's going back to New York. His father went toes-up a month ago, and he's got to take charge of the home office."

"I see."

We paused to cross the Place de la Concorde, a complex maneuver that absorbed our attention until we reached the high black railing around the Tuileries and the warm green scent of the trees. I heard the tinkling of the carousel above the blaring of traffic behind me. Florian, who knew what was coming, gripped the edge of his perambulator and tried to climb out.

"Anyway," said Charles, looking unspeakably out of place as he pushed the baby car-

riage along in his threadbare suit and boater hat, "there's a party tonight, a farewell bash kind of thing, and Nick asked me to bring you along to say good-bye."

"Why does he want me to come with you?"

"I don't know," Charles said innocently. "Maybe he just wanted to give us a chance to break the ice and get to know each other again."

My brother stared straight ahead, squinting, sturdy and handsome, as he pushed Florian's carriage along the fence, toward the entrance along the rue de Rivoli. His cheeks were a little pink from the sun, or maybe it wasn't the sun.

I put my hand on his and made him stop. He looked down at the pavement below the shining chrome handlebar. I put my hands on his waist and turned him toward me, and I put my head against his chest.

"I've missed you," I whispered.

His arms came around me.

"I missed you, too, little Sprout," he said, into my hair.

5.

So that was how I came to stand before Stefan Silverman on a July night in 1937 at the bar of the Hotel Ritz in Paris, married and restless, like a housecat left alone for the weekend, who has already eaten all the food in her dish.

PEPPER

COCOA BEACH 1966

1.

Maybe it's the painkillers. When Pepper wakes up, she has to blink several times at the wall to remember her own name, and several more times to recall where she is and why. The room is full of sunshine. Her stomach moans with hunger. She hasn't slept so deeply since she was a child.

She sits up, and her foot explodes with pain.

Oh, God. The study, the letter, the front door, Florian, *OUCH,* hospital.

Florian.

Florian Dommerich. Annabelle's son.

Pepper sinks back on the pillow. A few feet away, the cheerful yellow curtain represses a brilliant sunlit afternoon, just bursting to get through the window glass and fall on her naked skin. Her crutches lean against the nearby wall, in a pool of discarded nightgown. Pregnant, on the lam, and now this. A broken foot that's taken up a nice neat throb of pain, in rhythm with her heartbeat.

Florian Dommerich. She remembers the

name. She now remembers that at some point, at some Washington party, she was introduced to a man with the unusual name of Florian. But she doesn't remember that specific moment of introduction, not even if she screws her eyes shut and digs deep. She doesn't remember looking up into a handsome face, or admiring a pair of sturdy forearms as she shook a large and dependable hand. Because it was already too late, wasn't it? She was already besotted with another man. Life was like that, wasn't it? You got on the wrong train and missed your stop, and then you couldn't go back. By the time you retraced your steps, the right train had already left, gone, departed, the train not taken.

It's a depressing thought, and should keep a woman in bed for the rest of the day. But that's not Pepper, is it? Pepper shakes out her hair and thinks, Well, who needs trains, anyway? Noisy big smelly things, never on time, breaking down in all the wrong places. Better off without them.

She swings her feet to the floor and reaches for the bottle of pills on the bedside table, the ones the hospital pharmacy dispensed to her before she left. The label on the side says MRS. PRUNELLA E. DOMMERICH, and she'll be damned if she tells you what the *E* stands for.

2.

The table in the dining room is laid for one, and breakfast is still laid out on the sideboard in a series of patient silver chafing dishes. Pepper sets the crutches against the wall and helps herself. Clara wanders in with a pot of coffee, gratefully received, and after the first scorching gulp Pepper sets down her cup and asks Clara if Mr. Dommerich is around.

He's taken the dogs for a walk on the beach, Clara tells her, and from the shining look on Clara's face, she envies the dogs.

"Is he, now?" says Pepper. She eats two helpings of eggs and six slices of crisp bacon, washed down with coffee. The sun spills against her back through the French doors, warm and cheerful. A shame she can't see the beach from here, but the dining room lies against the courtyard, probably to catch the sunset. (Strawberry preserves on the toast, don't you think? The toast is always tip-top, the butter melted just so, the rich flavor complementing the sweetness of the pre-serves.) Oh, but don't misunderstand! Not because of Florian walking the dogs. Heavens, no! That's incidental. She just wants to watch the *beach,* the flat and infinite ocean, to remind her how unimportant she is, just another speck of pregnant sand under the sun. Pepper wipes her mouth on the napkin, drains the last of the coffee, and rises.

Clara's back in the kitchen. Pepper calls

out a *Thank you* anyway, because the Schuylers have their faults but they always thank the staff, whether or not they mean it. She rises, grabs her crutches, and heads for the door.

3.

The dogs find her first. Dogs love Pepper and she loves them back, because dogs never let you down. Their idolatry never dims. Toby inspects her crutches while Oliver inspects her crotch. She fondles a silky head and tells him how wicked he is, and he agrees, tongue lolling.

A whistle. The dogs swivel their ears, toss her a pair of identical apologetic glances — *Duty calls, ma'am!* — and race back up the beach.

Pepper removes the crutches from her armpits and drops them on the sand. The tide's low, exposing irregular lines of refuse that reek familiarly of rot and brine. She lowers herself into a warm hollow. When she was little, she would walk along the beach in summer with her father and sisters, and they would look for sea glass. Tiny liked the clear ones most (diamonds are a girl's best friend, don't you know), but Pepper and Vivian fought over the colorful ones, the ones that still retained bumpy traces of lettering, hinting at a past life as a bottle of tonic or a jar of preserves. Eventually they worked out an

amicable split: Vivian kept the blue glass, and Pepper the greens and browns. The shards still sit in a large glass container in her old bedroom in East Hampton, unless Mums threw it out. But then Mums doesn't throw things out, does she? So it's probably still there, sitting on the window ledge, catching the sun.

A wet nose finds Pepper's hand, and she closes her eyes and smiles.

"I'm pretty sure the nice doctor said you were to rest that foot as much as possible."

She lifts her heavy right foot, bound snugly in plaster of paris. "I'm resting it right here, aren't I?"

Florian sits down next to her, smelling like the sea. Toby climbs between his knees and licks his chin with a long, thick tongue, which Florian just manages to keep away from his lips. "Slept well?" he says.

"I did indeed. Those were lovely pills. You should break my bones more often."

"Well, you're looking better."

"What does that mean?"

He holds up his hands, palms out. "Nothing. Just, you know, a little haggard last night."

"Haggard?"

"And then your hair." Waggles his forefinger next to his ear.

"Well. My God. It's a wonder you didn't just call an ambulance and save yourself all

that trouble."

Snaps his fingers. "Damn it! Why didn't I think of that? Could've slept like a baby instead."

"Don't lay that at *my* door. You slept when you got back."

Toby lopes off with Oliver, a game of tag, and Florian settles back in a hollow and puts his hands behind his head. His feet are bare and bony, his dungarees rolled a few inches above his ankles, wet at the edges and dusted with sand. "Not really," he says.

"Oh." She wiggles her toes. "Sorry."

"There you go again with the apologies."

"Crazy, huh? Must be the dope they gave me."

"Or the baby. I hear they do things to your minds."

He brings the subject up so naturally, Pepper forgets to be awkward. She puts her hand on her stomach and says, "Tell me about it."

No reply. The water rushes in and out, stirring a crusted patch of seaweed left behind at the last tide. The dogs cross before them. Pepper stares at Florian's toes, the healthy and unbroken bones of his feet, attached to a pair of strong ankles. She wonders what the rest of him looks like, under those damp and wrinkled dungarees and that sky-blue shirt that's rolled up to each elbow. If she looks out of the bottom corner of her eye, she can

just make out the shape of a well-hewn thigh. She pictures that clean square-cut face, that dark curling hair, those chocolate-brown eyes, and God, just kill her now. It's been so long since she's kissed a man, *so long* since she's held a man in her arms, that she actually — while staring at his toes and calculating the difference in height between big toe and second toe, because wasn't that supposed to signify something? — yes, she actually contemplates what it would be like to have sex with him. What it would be like to kiss Florian. Be naked with Florian. Whom she just met yesterday.

The baby makes an inquisitive movement under her hand.

Oh, yes. The baby. The baby! Thanks ever so much, baby dear, for reminding Pepper that she might as well give this fantasy free rein, go all the way, indulge herself to the limit of her imagination, because that's all it is. Fantasy. The sex-starved fantasy of a pregnant woman, who is alluring only in memory. The formerly alluring Miss Pepper Schuyler.

"Can I ask you a personal question?" Florian says.

"That depends on whether you want it answered."

"Why are you having this baby, all by yourself?"

Pepper struggles to her feet, and in a flash

362

Florian is up beside her, steadying her elbow.

"All right," he says. "Too personal."

"I'll tell you what. I'll answer yours if you'll answer mine."

"Fine. Sock it to me."

"What are they saying in Washington?"

"About you?"

"Yes, you big lug. About me. About where I am and why I left."

He shrugs. "Just that you're another Fifth Avenue deb, can't handle a real job. Had a fight with your boss and split."

"For real?"

"What do you mean, *for real*? I don't lie, Pepper."

"No, of course you don't."

"Honest to God. You shocked the bejesus out of me last night, and not just that you turned up in my mother's study. Of all the girls in the world."

She exhales slowly. There's some meaning in that last sentence, but she's too relieved by his news to give the words the attention they deserve. Florian bends down and hands her the crutches, fitting them under each arm, just like the orderly last night.

"You really shouldn't be walking around like this. You should be slumped in a chair with your foot up on a stool."

Pepper turns her head and looks at him straight. "Get real, Dommerich. Me sitting on a chair all day?"

He laughs, just as the dogs come up behind him and knock him in the knees, sending him staggering nearly into her arms, except that her arms are caught in the crutches. At the last instant, he whirls himself safely around the edge of her. "All right, all right. Here you go, boys." He picks up a stick and catapults it down the empty beach, and they stand there together, watching the eager hindquarters pump away, the sand fly like dust beneath the paws. Toby reaches the stick first, and Oliver disputes it with him. Florian turns as if to say something, and stops with the words still in his mouth.

"What is it?" Pepper pushes her hair behind her ear.

"Damn it all, you really are beautiful, you know that? I'm sorry. I know you couldn't care less at the moment, but God almighty. When the sun's on you like that."

"You should have seen me before." She whistles.

"I did see you before, remember? And I thought you were beautiful then. But Jesus." He shakes his head and steps forward to meet the incoming dogs.

"I'm a mess," she calls after him. "You can't even see my cheekbones. Or my waist."

He hurls the stick. "My dad always said Mama looked best when she was pregnant. He said it was the greatest sight in the world."

"Yeah, well, it was *his* baby, wasn't it? His

wife and his baby."

Pepper turns and plunges her crutches into the sand, heading back to the house. Seconds later, Florian catches up with her. "Hey. Hold on."

"Look, I don't need your pity, all right? And I certainly don't need you taking advantage of the situation."

"Taking advantage? Of *you*?"

"I think I know when a man's trying his luck."

"Wait a second." He takes her arm and pivots to face her, just as they reach the edge of the empty road separating the villa from the beach. "You honestly think I would make some kind of move on my mother's house-guest? My mother's *pregnant* houseguest?"

"That's what it sounded like from my end."

"Trust me, I've got no reason to make a move on you."

"Then what was all that about? *Oh, Pepper, you're so beautiful, even when your belly's all the way out to Kansas.*"

He shrugs. "Statement of truth, and a fact you're already plenty well aware of. I also happen to think you're a bossy hoyden who thinks a little too much of her sex appeal and likes to sail way too close to the wind. *And* your toes are crooked."

"My toes aren't crooked."

"They are the hell crooked."

Pepper looks both ways and crosses the

street. Behind her, Florian whistles for the dogs. When she hears the scratch of toenails on asphalt, she says, over her shoulder, "Because I wanted it."

"Wanted what?"

"Wanted the baby. That's why I'm having it."

4.

A half hour later, Pepper sits in the blue-and-white armchair in the living room overlooking the ocean, flipping without much interest through a year-old copy of *Vogue* magazine. Her foot reposes on a matching blue-and-white ottoman, and her face, when she looks up to find Florian and a pair of root beers, should have warned him away.

Not Florian. He holds out a root beer, still frosty, cap removed. "Peace offering."

"I didn't realize we were at war."

"You sounded pretty warlike out there."

"That's just me." She takes the bottle. She hasn't drunk root beer since she was a kid, and she's surprised to find that it still tastes exactly like it used to.

Florian settles himself in the matching chair and balances the root beer in his cupped palms. "I have a few questions."

"Some men never learn."

"Not personal ones, this time. At least, not that personal. I was wondering about Mama, actually. When she split. What she said before

366

she left."

"Why's that?"

"Because I haven't heard from her in two weeks, and she usually telephones about something or other every couple of days."

Pepper shrugs. "Your guess is as good as mine. We're not exactly lifelong friends. She bought the car from me, took me to dinner, dragged me to her lair, and left the next afternoon. She never said why."

"Didn't leave a note?"

"She left a note, but it just said that something had come up, and she'd be back in a few days."

"How long ago was that?"

Pepper swallows back her root beer. "Nine, maybe ten days ago."

"And you weren't worried?"

"Well, no. Should I have been?"

"This is normal behavior in your book? Inviting a stranger to stay in your house and then disappearing for a week and a half?"

"Oh, I've seen odder, believe me."

"You didn't wonder where she'd gone?"

"Not really. I was just grateful for the hot breakfasts."

The dubious eyebrows.

"All right, I wondered a little," Pepper concedes. "But she's a big girl, wouldn't you agree? She can go where she likes. Clara said she goes on trips like this sometimes. Anyway, it would have seemed rude just to call a cab

and catch a flight home, without saying good-bye."

"For what it's worth, I'm glad you didn't."

"Thank you," she says acidly.

He smiles, almost as if he means it. "No, really. I'm just surprised you stayed on so long, that's all. Don't you have family to hurry back to?"

"No more than most people."

"Because of the holiday, I mean."

"What holiday?"

"Pepper," he says, looking at her seriously, "Thanksgiving is in three days."

Pepper chokes on her root beer. "What?"

"It's Monday. Thanksgiving is Thursday. That's why I'm here, because Mama's supposed to join us at my brother's house for turkey and pumpkin pie, and no one's heard from her in two weeks."

"Thanksgiving." Pepper dabs the corner of her mouth with her forefinger. Jesus, what's happening to her? She can't even keep track of the calendar. "How about that."

Florian's frowning at her, and the crease in his forehead mesmerizes her momentarily, so that when he asks her if everything's all right, she answers with all honesty: "Yes. Perfectly."

"So then why aren't you off on a jet plane, Miss Trouble, heading home for turkey with your folks?"

"We aren't the cuddliest family, rumor has it."

"They don't know about the baby, do they?"

"Of course they know." She finishes the root beer and sets it down on the lamp table. "Two of them do, anyway. My sisters."

"But not your parents."

"You know," she says, steepling her fingers together and leaning forward, "I think the larger problem here is Annabelle. Let's talk about her. Where the devil might she have gone to?"

He sighs and rubs the adorable furrows in his forehead. "You name it. Ever since Dad died, she's gone off on these little trips, a few days here or there, not letting anyone know where she is. Then she pops back up as if nothing happened. It's just that it's been a couple of weeks now, and Thanksgiving's coming up, and we're all kind of waiting for her to let us know she's still alive."

"Don't you ever ask her where she's been? Since you're such a cute and loving family."

"She just says she's doing research."

"For what?"

"I don't know. Genealogy or something. We were just happy she found something to keep her occupied. She stopped playing her cello when Dad was diagnosed, just stopped cold turkey."

"Really? That doesn't sound good."

Florian rose from the chair and set down

369

his bottle with a crash next to Pepper's. "Oh, thanks."

"Oh, relax. I'm sure she's fine." Pepper pauses delicately. "You know, there's another explanation, though you probably don't want to hear it."

"What's that?"

"Maybe your mother has a gentleman friend."

From the shocked expression on Florian's face, she can tell he's never considered this possibility. "What, *Mama*?"

"She's a very attractive woman."

He stares at Pepper as if she's just renounced her American citizenship and run off to join a Soviet collective. "You don't understand. She would *never.*"

"Oh, yes, she would."

"Dad and Mama . . . they were like . . . I can't explain . . . they had this connection. They never even argued. Dad was German, did you know that? They fled the Nazis together, back in 1938. They raised us all together. We had to change our names, because the Gestapo was after us. Dad and Mama, they were everything to each other."

"I'm sure that's true. But — well, I don't mean to shock you, but a woman has her needs. If you know what I mean."

He snaps back: "Look, Pepper. Not every woman is like *you.* If you know what I mean."

The words are so crisp and cruel, so unlike

370

Florian, that Pepper has to pick through them all, one by one, to assemble their meaning. She returns his stare, and when he drops his gaze to the floor, she knows she heard him right.

"I'm sorry. I didn't mean that."

"Yes, you did." Pepper swings her feet to the rug and reaches for her crutches. "No hard feelings. I mean, I can't exactly argue with you, can I?"

"What does that mean?"

She puts the crutches under her arms. "I like sex. Actually, I love sex. I think sex is fucking terrific, excuse the pun, when it's done right. If that makes me different from the girls you know, well, I am most profoundly sorry for them all. You, too, I guess. Excuse me."

She hops past his stiffened figure — she's getting a little more agile with the crutches, by now — and into the hallway, thinking she'll head to her room, maybe even pack her few things and call a taxi for God knows where, but the sharp ring of the doorbell stops her halfway.

Mama! shouts Florian, from the living room.

She turns, just in time to see Florian shoot around the corner and reach for the doorknob.

But it's not Annabelle Dommerich on the other side. It's a very, very pretty girl with

golden curls and blue eyes and a polka-dot dress (yes, actual real live polka dots, white on yellow), who flings her arms around Florian's neck and kisses his cheek like she could eat it right up. "You're back!" she says, when she's done, and then she notices the astonished pregnant woman in the hallway behind him.

It speaks volumes for her confidence that not a single trace of jealousy crosses that very, very pretty face. She blushes a little — she's a nice girl, after all, and she's just been caught throwing herself on a man's chest — and ducks around Florian's stunned shoulder to hold out her hand, the exact way a good debutante should.

"Hi! I'm so sorry, I didn't see you there!"

"Obviously."

"I'm Susan Willoughby. A friend of the family. Are you staying with Mrs. Dommerich?"

Pepper props one crutch against the wall and shakes Susan's outstretched hand. "Why, yes, Miss Willoughby," she says. "Yes, I am."

ANNABELLE

PARIS 1937

1.

Stefan held out his hand to me. "Good evening, Frau von Kleist. This is a tremendous surprise."

"Yes, a great shock." I put my hand in his palm.

He brought the gloved fingertips courteously to his lips. "You're looking exceptionally well. I think marriage suits you."

"Now, now," Charles said. "Nick and I have agreed that we're not holding the Nazi against her any longer."

"He's not a Nazi." I took my hand back, but the faint pressure of those lips remained on the beds of my fingernails.

Stefan straightened, and the light from one of the chandeliers caught his face. He looked the same, only horribly different, because there were a few lines now at the corners of his eyes and mouth, and a scar ran neatly along his left temple and underneath the cover of his hair.

"My God," I whispered.

Stefan looked a little quizzical, and then touched the scar with his finger. "Ah, of course. A souvenir, as the French say. One should never try to escape from prison without an accurate map of the premises."

Charles said, "Are you all right, Annabelle?"

"Just a bit dizzy. It's terribly hot, don't you think?"

Stefan set his drink on a nearby table and wrapped his hand around my elbow. "I will take Frau von Kleist for some air."

"No! I'm fine."

"Actually, you're awfully pale," Charles said, frowning. "Go with Stefan. I'll fetch a glass of water."

"There is no need," Stefan said. "I will find water."

2.

I followed him numbly. There didn't seem to be a choice; I didn't seem able to choose another path except to follow Stefan's smooth black back down the length of the bar, where he stopped and made an inquiry from one of the bartenders, which ended in a glass being pressed into his hand.

I had thought in the beginning that he was drunk, but his steps were steady as he led me out of the bar to the busy corridor, and down the corridor to a small plain door, which he opened to usher me inside. It was a private sitting room of some kind, empty except for

the usual elegant furniture. Stefan urged me into a chair and went to open the window. I stared at the glass of water in my hand.

"There, now," he said, turning toward me, leaning against the window. "Is that better?"

"Yes."

"I didn't mean to surprise you like that."

I sipped the water. "Did you know I would be here?"

"I thought it was possible."

I thought, This is Stefan standing before me. Stefan, real and whole, the same bone and muscle, the same brain and voice and hair I had loved, the arms that had held me, the mouth I had kissed and the ribs I had counted, one by one. It was not possible that he was here, Stefan, *Stefan,* a few yards away, Stefan, who had fathered a child with me. Florian's father. Now a stranger.

I looked into the glass. "How long have you been in Paris? I thought you were in Germany. Nick said you couldn't leave the country, it was part of the terms of your release."

"Hmm. It appears I am a fugitive, then."

I snapped up. "Are you?"

"Yes." He shrugged. "Really, it makes little difference, one way or the other. They cannot actually arrest me without consulting the French authorities first, and the French authorities are not particularly inclined to

cooperate with requests from the German ones."

I couldn't meet his gaze. My eyes stopped somewhere around his neck, which was deeply tanned next to the glowing starched white of his collar. I wanted to say how sorry I was. I wanted to say how much I had suffered, knowing he had suffered, and that it was my fault, because he had been arrested coming back into Germany for my sake. I wanted to say how I had tried to avoid ever seeing him again, and how I had been sick with wanting to see him again. I wanted to say what a mistake I had made, running off like that: how I had thought marrying Johann was the right thing, the noble thing, and now maybe it wasn't, that you couldn't just make yourself love someone when your heart had lodged somewhere else, you couldn't pretend something was love when it was not.

I wanted to tell him we had a son.

Or did he know that already?

I curled my fingers around the hard glass, in the shape of a prayer.

"Annabelle," he said gently, "don't be frightened."

"I'm not frightened."

"You look like death. Very beautiful, but deathly. Come, now. It isn't that bad, surely? I am not so fearsome as that."

"I'm not afraid of *you*," I said.

"Then why will you not look at me?"

This was the trouble with Stefan: I couldn't lie to him. How could I lie to Stefan? How could I say things to him that weren't true? It was like lying to yourself. There was no point.

"Because I'm ashamed. I made you suffer."

"But you have suffered, too, haven't you?"

"Yes."

"And you have suffered because I didn't tell you the truth, I didn't tell you about Wilhelmine, because I was bloody terrified that you would run away from me and never come back. So I have been the author of my own suffering. It is no more than I deserve, for being a faithless husband and a false lover. And if you don't look at me this moment, Annabelle, I will not forgive myself."

I looked at him.

His face was calm and golden in the lamplight. He was so beautifully proportioned, leaning there against the window, his hands braced on the wooden sill. I had forgotten that about him, the perfect arrangement of his limbs.

"Tell me about her," I said. "Tell me everything."

He sighed. "We are no longer married. She is married to her lover, a man named Matthias, who was her lover at university and — what is the word — jilt? There was a stupid argument of some kind, and he jilted her. That is why she agreed to marry me, because she was angry at him. And I married her

because our families were close, and it was the wish of my parents."

"Did you love her?"

"Yes, as one loves a dear friend. A very careless love. I had other interests, political interests, and I was often gone, and I thought nothing of seeking other company when I was gone."

"Company like me."

"Not like you."

I set down the glass of water and rose from the chair. "And your daughter?"

"Else. She lives with her mother. She is three years old and beautiful and astonishing. She breaks my heart when I think of her, because I believe I have failed her most of all." He paused. "She is very fond of Matthias. I saw her a month ago, before I left Frankfurt, and I was almost a stranger to her. Wilma is pregnant again, she will have the baby in September, and Else is over the moon to have a baby sister. She will not consider that it might be a boy."

"I'm sorry."

"It's no more than I deserve. I was away. I was trying to rescue the fucking world from itself. I fell in love with another woman. I allowed my wife to fall in love with another man." He patted the sides of his chest, as if hunting for his cigarettes in a pocket, and then he found my eyes and stopped. His hands fell back to the windowsill behind him.

378

"I will do everything I can for my daughter," he said. "I will open my veins for her if she needs it, but I have lost her for myself."

"Oh, Stefan —"

"But you. Tell me about your son."

There was no particular emphasis on the words. His expression didn't change, except to brighten a little, the way it does when you turn the conversation from something melancholy to something new.

I said, "His name is Florian. I don't think I could have lived without him."

"Yes." He hesitated. "I would like to meet him one day, unless you think it is improper."

"Why do you want to meet him?"

"Because he is yours, of course."

I stood there looking at him, because I couldn't think of anything to say. Not one word to say to him, to Stefan.

"Annabelle?" he said.

"I can't believe this. I can't believe we're talking like this."

Stefan turned away and braced his knuckles on the windowsill. The street outside was dark, except for the passing flashes of the headlights, the dull sodium glow of a nearby lamp gilding the top of his hair. "This is what I meant, Annabelle."

"The perverse universe."

"Yes."

"You seem to have accepted it without any trouble. I thought you would be drunk and

angry, if I saw you again. I thought you would hate the sight of me."

"I *am* drunk and angry, Annabelle. I am so angry I cannot breathe, sometimes. I am so consumed I cannot sleep. But I am not angry at *you*. I do not hate the sight of you." He paused and said something I couldn't hear.

"What did you say?"

He turned his head to the side. "I said, there is not one moment I have not wished you well. But maybe that is not quite the truth. There was the moment Greenwald told me the news. There are the moments I think of you with your husband."

"Don't, please."

"Don't think of you? Or don't speak of it?"

"Both."

"Does he treat you well?"

"Oh, yes. Yes, he is very kind. He loves me very much."

"He would be an even greater blackguard than I am if he did not."

I looked down at my dress, the embroidered mauve silk that slunk down my limbs and ended a fraction of an inch above the oriental rug. Alice and I had gone to one of the ateliers together, and she had made me order this one, which she said suited my figure and my coloring perfectly. I had telephoned Johann in remorse that afternoon and told him the price, expecting him to tell me to cancel the order. But he had said, gruff and

astonished and full of static, "But of course you must buy this gown. You must be dressed suitably." I had told him that it was a very decadent dress, and he said that the Baroness von Kleist was expected to wear gowns according to her station, there was nothing decadent about that. This was in March, a few weeks before his visit in April. The dress was delivered a month later.

I touched the tiny leaf of a trailing vine, embroidered delicately in pale green and silver, and said, "He's in Berlin just now. He's been there since Christmas."

"Yes, I had heard."

"Is that why you're here in Paris?"

The air in the room was warm and thick, so much that though my arms were bare, I felt the prickles of perspiration in the small of my back. Stefan leaned in to the enormous panes of the window. The gathered draperies touched his black shoulder.

"Annabelle," he said softly, gazing through the glass, "I did not come here to take you away from your family. I think I have done enough ruin to marriages already."

"But you wanted to see me."

"Yes. I needed to see you again. I needed to see that you were safe, that you were well."

"I *am* safe and well. It isn't the same, of course. Not the same as with you."

"Annabelle, I know that."

"How do you know?"

He turned, so that his shoulder held up the windowpane, and his hand played with the swoop of the silk curtains. The light from the streetlamp outlined his profile. "Because my Annabelle is not capable of loving another man in the same way she loved me. Certainly not within the space of a few months."

I sank back into the chair and buried my face in my hands.

"Shh. Don't, love."

"*Why* did you come? It was so much easier when you were a beast. When I hated you. I nearly forgot you, did you know that? I nearly pushed you out of my memory. And now I can't, I can't force you out, you're always there. Why couldn't you be a beast?"

"I am a beast."

"You should have told me in the beginning."

"I know that!"

"We were so close! All those hours and days together, those beautiful days. I slept next to you. I was inside your skin, remember? How could you hold me like that and not tell me you had a child, a *daughter*!"

"Because I was scared to death, Annabelle. I thought, She will run away; she won't understand. She will think I am like her father. And maybe I was, maybe you were right, maybe I *am* just a fucking beast and never deserved you."

"If you'd only told me she left you!"

"I didn't dare. I was so besotted, do you not understand that? Do you not comprehend that I was out of my mind for you? I loved you so much, I couldn't think or breathe or hear. I was stupid, stupid with love. I thought, If I can just keep her from knowing until the divorce is arranged. I thought, If we can just —" He turned away from the window and yanked a cigarette case from his inside pocket. "I'm sorry, I know you hate these."

"I don't hate them."

"The last day, at the hotel . . ." He lit himself up and paced along the opposite wall.

"Because you wouldn't stop. The rooms were full of smoke."

"I'm sorry." He stopped in front of an enormous portrait of a young lady, dressed in white, and gazed up at her. "I'm sorry I didn't tell you."

"You didn't trust me."

"No, I suppose I didn't. I couldn't imagine that you would still want me."

I looked down at my hands, which were damp with my tears. But I wasn't crying now. My eyes were dry. "Don't be stupid. There was nothing I wouldn't have forgiven you for, if you'd asked me. When did I ever deny you anything you asked for?"

He made a noise like an animal and kicked the thick wooden baseboard beneath the painting. The thump was catastrophic, like someone had fallen through a table.

I heard Nick Greenwald's voice: *It's a damned thing.* I wondered if Stefan's shoe had actually splintered the wood.

Stefan said, "The perverse universe, you see. Didn't I tell you? And now we are here in this room, and my hand that holds this cigarette is shaking, because I want to touch you so much, and I cannot."

"But why not?" I said, and the door banged open.

"There you are," Charles said. "What the hell was that noise?"

3.

The motor wouldn't start, so Charles went to find one of the Ritz chauffeurs to help. I stood outside on the rue Cambon, inhaling the heavy night air, the dirty, warm smell of Paris. The sky was clear, but there was too much light from the city to see the stars. I thought of the August sky above the *Isolde,* and how Stefan and I would sit in our deck chairs and count the stars together, and Stefan would drink his martinis and smoke his cigarettes and the smoke would drift like a ghost in the space between us, like another person. When he finished the first drink, some member of the crew would bring him a second, but that was all. *You don't appreciate the third,* he said, when I asked him why. *It's better to stop at two.* Later, at our little house, the stars weren't quite so plentiful because of

nearby Monte Carlo. There were no martinis in the courtyard or the garden, just a shared bottle of wine and the smell of lemon and eucalyptus, and Stefan's cigarettes, one by one, until I asked him to stop.

Then I will need something else to do with my mouth, he said, and I gave it to him. I always gave him what he wanted.

I wrinkled my nose, because I could smell someone's cigarette now, but it didn't belong to Stefan, whose cigarettes were a special Turkish variety and bore a particular odor that made my blood jump. I turned my head and saw a man leaning against the wall, in the shadow between two streetlamps. His body was long and lean, and I realized it was Nick Greenwald.

He had disappeared shortly after dinner, and the beautiful dark-haired woman, too. I realized it only now. When I hadn't been observing Stefan from the corner of my eye, I had been picking out Stefan's voice at the other end of the long table. I had been tracing his movements with some primeval part of my brain that detected such things without seeing them. I had been wholly absorbed in this man who was not my husband. I hadn't noticed Nick Greenwald at all, once the necessary toasts had been made.

I called out to him now and asked if he needed a lift home. A silly question. Nick was as rich as Croesus, Charles had once said, or

at least Croesus's banker cousin. He was never in need of anything.

No, thanks, he called back.

I walked toward him and put my hand on his arm. "Is everything all right?" I asked.

"No," he said. He lifted his arm, causing my hand to fall away, and put his cigarette to his mouth. "I just did a stupid thing, that's all."

"Is there anything I can do to help?"

He turned his head, as if he just noticed me there, and straightened from the wall. "Yes, there's something you can do," he said, and he took me by the ears and bent his head down and kissed me.

His lips were soft and tasted strongly of Scotch whisky, and I was too surprised to do anything but hold on and kiss him back. It lasted only a few seconds, five or six at most, though it seemed like forever, the way time warps in funny ways when you're in shock.

Then he lifted his head and said he was sorry.

"What was that for?" I gasped.

He dropped the cigarette on the pavement and crushed it under his shoe. "I just didn't want her to be the last girl I kissed, that's all. Good night, Annabelle. Take care of my old buddy Stefan, will you?"

I wanted to tell him that Stefan wasn't mine to take care of, but Nick Greenwald was already striding down the sidewalk to the

corner, where a long, dark automobile reclined by the curb.

I cupped my hands around my mouth. "Good luck in New York!"

He waved his hand and opened the door of the car. The engine started without a hitch, and Nick Greenwald roared away down the rue Cambon.

4.

The old Renault was hopeless, and we took a taxi home. It was now two o'clock in the morning and I had been awake since the previous dawn. I leaned my head against the window, but my eyes wouldn't close.

Charles eyeballed me from across the seat. "So, Sprout. Slap me if I'm out of line. Is there something going on with you and Stefan?"

I raised my head. "How could there be? He's been in prison."

"Well, I thought I noticed what old Papa would call a frisson in there."

"You're imagining things. I'm married, remember?"

He laughed from the bottom of his chest. "All right, all right. Whatever you like. Look, did he get around to talking about anything special?"

"Stefan? No, nothing in particular."

"Thought he wouldn't. And now I guess I know why."

387

"Oh? And what's *that* supposed to mean?"

Charles crossed one leg atop the other and wrapped one hand around his ankle. With the other hand, he reached inside his jacket pocket and produced a pack of cigarettes. He shook it open and held it out to me. I declined.

"Tell me, Sprout," he said, lighting his cigarette, "what do you know about this husband of yours?"

I was still a little reckless from the wine at dinner, from the half hour in the salon with Stefan, from Nick Greenwald's unexpected kiss. What a goddamned night, I thought, and now this. There was a distant rumble of thunder through the sultry air.

I folded my arms. "Johann? He's a devoted father and husband, an expert in military history, and an unimaginative but enthusiastic lover with an organ the size of Gibraltar."

"Christ, Annabelle!"

"You asked what I know about him."

"That's not what I meant."

"Then *tell* me what you mean, for God's sake! I am so *sick* of all your innuendos, all of you, talking in your codes."

"Innuendoes?"

I waved my hand. "All of you. Your secret club."

Charles sucked on his cigarette, glanced at the driver, and rolled down the window an inch or two. He said, in a low voice, "Here's

388

the thing. We toss around this term *Nazi,* you and I, but there are Nazis and there are Nazis."

"Tell me something I don't know."

"Well, I don't know what you don't know. That's the point. I don't know how much you know about your husband and what, exactly, he's doing in that new position he's got in Berlin."

"He's part of the Oberkommand."

"Yes, but do you know what he does?"

Another crash, louder this time, and a wave of rain crackled suddenly against the window. The taxi had stopped; the driver was swearing under his breath.

"Not exactly, no. Whatever they do in the general staff. He doesn't talk about his work."

"No, of course not." He tipped the end of the cigarette over the window's edge, releasing the ash. "We'll be printing textbooks one day about them, the Nazis, how to consolidate power. A few years ago they were the joke of Europe, and now look. Anyway, the old Prussian aristocrats hate them, have always hated them, but they've had to join the party or be shut out."

"Like Johann, you mean?"

"Well, that's the thing, you know. These Germans, they put loyalty to *Deutschland über alles,* especially after what happened in the war and after it; I mean, you can't blame them for closing ranks after Versailles. So

these Junker barons, who should be leading Germany out of this madness, they just sit on their hands and say *ja, ja,* and now Hitler's a goddamned emperor, he can do what he wants. And it's nearly impossible to say who's really behind him, or who's just afraid of him, or who's just keeping his mouth shut and hoping it all blows over. Do you know what I mean, Annabelle?" He blew an expert stream of smoke through the crack in the window and turned to stare at me. His face was lined and serious in the gloomy gray light, not at all the jaunty tennis-playing Charles I carried in my head, and I thought of the scene in the boathouse, and the blood, and the urgency, and I realized I didn't know my brother at all.

The rain drove hard against the window. The taxi lurched forward and stopped again, and the driver released a torrent of vulgar French.

"Are you asking me to spy on my husband?" I asked softly.

"That's an ugly word."

"It's an ugly thing to do."

"Well, you're the one who keeps insisting he's on the right side. That he's not a real Nazi. And if you're right, and he's not, well —" The taxi moved again, and he braced himself against the seat ahead, nearly dropping the cigarette.

"Well?" I said.

"Maybe you could help us out."

"You? You and Stefan?"

"And a few others. A band of brothers, you might say. Trying to find a way in, trying to stop this thing at the highest level. Do you know what I mean?"

I didn't say anything. The audacity of it.

"Come on, Sprout." Charles nudged me. "What do you think?"

The rain picked up speed against the window. I thought about Florian, asleep in his crib upstairs, his cheeks flushed and a little damp. I knew exactly how he looked when he slept, exactly how he felt, his puppy-sweet smell. I knew every intimate detail about my son.

"And whose idea was this?" I asked. "Stefan's?"

A slight hesitation. "Mine. Stefan was supposed to ask you about it tonight."

I looked out the window and recognized the Café Maginot, where I sometimes still met Alice for lunch, when I could get away. The apartment on avenue Marceau was just around the corner. "I'm not going to spy on my husband for you. I'll talk to him, if you like, the next time he's in Paris, but I'm not going to spy on him."

Charles straightened against the seat. "That's all we ask," he said eagerly. "Sound him out. Find out how he feels, *really* feels, not just the patriotic backwash they spit up

to strangers. Groom him, if you can. Let me know what he says about everything, anything, the Jews and Nuremberg and Hitler and Weimar and the Treaty of fucking Versailles."

"It's a long way from privately objecting to the Nuremberg laws to betraying your country," I said, full of acid.

Charles dropped the stub of his cigarette out the window. "Don't worry," he said, smiling at the corner of his full mouth. "If he bites, we'll take it from there."

"And if he doesn't?"

"Then you'd better the hell divorce the lousy Nazi bastard, or I'll never speak to you again." The taxi stopped. Charles reached forward to pay the driver. "I'm kidding you, Sprout. But think about it, will you?"

I sat back and let him pay, let him walk me swiftly across the sidewalk to the shelter of the building entrance, without once telling him that I already had. I already had thought about it.

5.

I went to see Stefan the next day. I had a hunch, based on his intimate familiarity with the Ritz, that he was staying there himself. I was right. I arrived in the lobby at half past noon, while Florian was taking his nap, and Stefan popped out of the elevator on his way to lunch at twelve forty-five.

392

I rose from the bench. "Hello, Stefan."

At least I had the satisfaction of shocking him. "I was just going to find you," he said, taking off his hat, and his face was pale beneath his tan.

"Then I've saved you the trouble, haven't I? I have a question for you. It won't take long. Is there somewhere we can be private?"

He cast an eye around the teeming lobby. "There's my room."

"I can't think of a better place. You're not in the Imperial Suite, are you?"

"God, no."

"What a pity."

In fact, the room was a standard box on the fourth floor, overlooking the Place Vendôme. The window was cracked open, but the air was still stuffy. I tossed my hat and my white cotton gloves on the writing desk. "You wanted me to spy on my husband?" I said. "That's why you came to Paris?"

He stood edgily by the door. "That was the excuse, yes."

"You *do* know how a wife gets information from her husband, don't you? You *do* know how marital intimacy is achieved?"

"Yes."

I threw my pocketbook across the room. It hit the wall with a bang, sending lipstick and compact and loose change flying in all directions.

"Annabelle —"

"To hell with you all!"

"Annabelle, calm down —"

"Don't tell me to calm down. I'm tired of being calm. I'm tired of keeping every last little lousy thought inside. I'm tired of being moved about like a pawn on a chessboard —"

He closed his hands around my upper arms and forced me to sit on the bed. "Listen to me. Just listen to me for *one moment,* Annabelle."

"I said yes." I looked up at him mutinously. "I told Charles I would do it."

His hands were warm and rigid on my arms, and his face was so close I could count the flecks of color around his black pupils. If I could have dropped my gaze to his mouth, I imagined his teeth would be bared.

"That is your choice, of course," he said, and he released my arms and straightened.

"You don't care?"

"I don't have the right to care, do I?"

"So you just went along with the idea. Oh, yes, excellent, let us turn Annabelle into a whore with her own husband —"

"Stop this," he said. "Just stop it. It wasn't my idea, all right? I certainly did not want you to agree to it. But I went along with this plan, because it gave me an excuse to see you, Annabelle, to leave fucking Frankfurt and get you in a room and talk to you and just — my God — just to *see* you. That's all. I wanted

394

to see you, just once." He turned away and went to the window, which he forced open another foot, and leaned down to take in the air.

"That's why you left Frankfurt?"

"Yes."

"But you might have been arrested again."

"What the hell do I care about that? Anyway, it is much easier to avoid these chaps if you know they're looking for you."

I rested my palms on either side of my legs and stared at my knees. My dress had ridden up a few inches, and my stockings were bare to the sunlight that crept past Stefan's body into the room. I turned around his words: "To see me, just once."

"Yes."

A horn sounded from an angry motorcar on the street below, and the sound was so distant it might have belonged to another universe.

I realized I should not have come here. Nothing could have been more foolish than this. Poor Johann, I thought, and then, I should leave.

I should leave now.

I lifted my face and saw my own reflection in the mirror above the desk: fair skin, wide American mouth, dark hair curling in the heat, dark eyes large with alarm. My red lips moved. "Well, what do you think?"

"About what?

"Do you think I could help? That Johann would help you?"

He stared quietly down at the street below. The brim of his hat curled up against the windowpane.

"I don't know," he said at last. "You could answer that better than I could, I suppose."

There was a ceiling fan above the bed, stroking the hot air in long sweeps. It wasn't much, but at least it was circulation. It was movement. I concentrated on the stirring at the back of my neck and said, "He almost never talks to me about politics, though. It's two separate compartments in his mind: family and politics. I got him to talk about it once, last Christmas, and it ended rather badly."

Stefan lifted his head from the window. "Did he hurt you?"

"No. God, no. He would never do that." I smoothed out the creases in my dress. "I think it's fair to say he believes in Germany rather than Hitler. But I don't think he sees them in opposition. He thinks the worst aspects of Nazism will simply go away when times are a little better."

"He's wrong."

"Well, I'm willing to ask him, if there's the smallest chance."

Stefan straightened and folded his arms against his white shirt. "I thought you were angry about our little plan."

"I don't mind talking to Johann, if it helps you. I just didn't want you to want me to do it."

"Did I ask you to do this, last night? Did I say one word about it?"

"No."

"No, I didn't, because it makes me sick to think of you with him, plying him for information. I don't want to give you a single reason to go back to Germany and to be his wife."

"Well, I *am* his wife."

"I know you are."

"And there must be some reason I'm his wife, instead of yours. It must have some purpose. So maybe this is it. This is why I'm married to Johann."

"Ah, yes. Your continuing belief in a logical universe, despite all indication to the contrary."

"Is it so wrong, to have faith?"

He stared at me for a moment, head tilted to the right, and then he walked across the room to the chair before the desk and sank into the seat. "All right, then. Let us suppose you were designed by God to lure the general to the just cause. What then? Let us suppose he takes your bait, and we formulate a plan to overturn Herr Hitler and his odious ideas. Let us suppose it is successful, and Germany is saved, maybe Europe itself is saved, hurrah. We are all heroes, we are all grateful to

397

Herr von Kleist and his loyal wife, who helped him to see the justice of our cause." He laid his arm on the desk and rubbed one finger against the polished wood, back and forth. His eyes held mine, narrowed and hard. "What then, my dear Frau von Kleist? Do you leave him in the lurch?"

"I — I don't know."

"Or perhaps we have already run off together, you and I. Perhaps you have left your husband and son —"

"I would never leave Florian."

"Then perhaps you have torn the boy away from his father and brought him with you to live with me, a stranger. Is that all part of this faith of yours?"

"You're being cruel."

"The *thing* is cruel, Annabelle. The whole damned thing." He reached into his jacket for his cigarettes and placed one in his mouth. "Have you heard of the fucking Nuremberg laws?"

"Yes, I — I have. It's horrible. Something to do with property and registration and —"

"I will explain. First of all, this legislation means that I am not a citizen of Germany any longer, because I am a Jew." He paused to light the cigarette. "It means also that — I speak hypothetically, of course — should you happen to divorce your honorable husband for my sake, I cannot marry you, because a Jew cannot marry a gentile, it is against the

law. And I cannot say *Aha!,* I will simply marry you here in Paris and then take you home to Germany, because the marriage is null and void the instant we cross the border."

"Since we are speaking hypothetically," I said, "I will then observe that marriage isn't necessary to me. I'm long past caring about a piece of paper."

"Ah! Well, that is what is so elegant about these laws, Annabelle, because it turns out it doesn't matter if we are man and wife, we are still breaking the law, since in Germany a Jew cannot fuck a gentile. Did you know that? He cannot fuck a gentile, he cannot make a mongrel *Mischling* baby with her. They will send him to the camps if he dares to try. Do you know about these camps, Annabelle?"

I thought of Florian and his sweet dark hair curling on his temple, his red mouth and soft tongue, and I wrapped my hands around my knees so they wouldn't shake. Stefan's face was bright with passion, a few yards away. I said softly, "Then I suppose — again, hypothetically — we would simply live elsewhere."

"Brilliant! Yes. The perfect solution to our hypothetical dilemma. Except that my daughter remains in Germany, to say nothing of my parents and siblings, which is a little problem for me, you understand. The people I love, our business. Our damned money, of which there is so much. Shoes, you know." He laughed bitterly. "The irony, eh? My fam-

ily sells the Nazis the very boots with which they seek to kick us."

"Can't you convince them to emigrate?"

He laughed again and reached for the ashtray in the corner of the desk. "Oh, yes. I can see the conversation now: *Mother, Father, listen to me. I have in mind to marry again, a dazzling woman, you'll adore her, except for a few small matters. She is a gentile, and the divorced wife of a fucking Nazi general, so unless you are prepared to leave Germany, which you have told me again and again you will never do, why, you will never see us again.*"

I whispered, "Surely not."

"And there is my daughter. My daughter, Annabelle. How do I say to my Else, *Goodbye, my dear little love, I have fallen in love, and unless your mother and stepfather kindly agree to emigrate for our sake, I cannot see you again?* I cannot do it, Annabelle. I will damn myself forever if I do. No. I am already damned. I am damned to hell for loving you, who are married to another man. And if I say, well then, to hell with right and wrong, I will break God's law and take this woman I love to my bed, married or not, then I am breaking also the law of the Nazis." He brought his fist down on the desk and pointed to the bed with his other hand, the one holding the cigarette. He was almost shouting now. "*This* is the perversity of the universe.

Do you understand now, Annabelle? Do you understand this perversity? It is so perverse that my own family is in perfect harmony with the damned Nazis on this point. So at last I have fallen in love, in the manner of the great romantics, but if I want to marry this woman, if I want to take this woman I love back to my own country and fuck her, I am breaking the law, Annabelle. I am breaking the *fucking law* in my own home!"

"But they can't do that! I'm a French citizen, I'm an American, too, and they can't tell me I can love one man and not another."

Stefan tossed the cigarette in the ashtray and leaned down on his elbows to bury his hands in his hair. "Don't you see, Annabelle? That is exactly the point. That is exactly what they are trying to do."

"Then let's not let them win," I said passionately. "Right now, let's beat them, let's love each other."

"I thought we were speaking hypothetically."

"Don't be stupid, Stefan."

He sighed, rose from the chair, and picked up my pocketbook from the floor. One by one, he added the contents: lipstick, compact, ticket stubs, coins. "They already *have* won, my love. It is already done. I am not going to ask you to divorce your husband. We are not going to fuck like a pair of fugitives, not in this room now, not in Paris or Berlin or any

401

damned place." He snapped the pocketbook shut and reached for my hat and gloves. "I am going to drive you back to your apartment now."

I stood numbly. The breeze from the window moved my dress against my legs. I held out my hands for my hat and gloves and pocketbook, and Stefan gave them to me, white-faced. Our fingers nearly touched, but not quite.

"My God, you are beautiful, though," he said softly. "The shape of your eyes. That skin. I thought my memory must have been mistaken."

When I first realized I was going to have a baby, before Johann had proposed, while I was sick with pregnancy and with the thought of what I had done with Stefan, I had spent many hours staring up at the ceiling above my bed, reconfiguring the scenes of our meeting in such a way that I could have resisted him. I could have prevented this entire disaster. I decided he wasn't really all that handsome, and his charisma was just a mirage, an image of an oasis in a desert, easily ignored. That sense of connection with him, those hours of discovery, had been proven a lie: I hadn't really known him at all.

But I had been a fool, hadn't I? Standing here before Stefan's bed, two years later, a wholly different Annabelle, a wife and mother, accepting my hat from his hands

without quite touching his fingers, I returned Stefan's gaze with equal wonder. I realized that no one could be so breathtaking, no one could be so familiar and so perfectly connected to me. His bones were like my bones. The shape of my eyes was like the shape of his.

How can we bear this? I asked.

(He took the hat from my hands and placed it gently on my head.)

Because we have to. Because you will know my heart is somewhere in the world, beating for you.

(I secured my hat and wiggled my fingers into my gloves. I asked if I would see him again.)

No, he said. It was for the best if we didn't.

6.

Eight days later, we lay side by side on Stefan's bed on the fourth floor of the Paris Ritz. The wooden fan rotated slowly above us. The heat had intensified, an almost unbearable compression of July air, ninety-nine parts automobile exhaust and one part oxygen.

"We should drive away somewhere," I said.

"Where? The heat is general across Europe, I believe."

"Anywhere. We could go to Versailles, or to Antibes. Your friend's house in Monte Carlo."

"I'm afraid he is living there himself, at present."

"What about your yacht?"

Stefan blew out a long cloud of smoke. "She is anchored in Capri. I am thinking of selling her."

I sat up, shocked. "You can't sell her!"

"Why not? There is not much point anymore. How can I sail in her again, when your darling shade haunts every last corner? Lie down, now. You are blocking the air from the fan."

I sank back into my hollow in the bedspread. I was damp with perspiration, and so was Stefan: all sheen and languor, not because we had made love three times in the past hour — we had not — but because today was the twenty-fourth of July, and all Paris was gripped with heat, and we lay together on a bed, fully clothed, down to our shoes.

That was our rule, you see. We could not possibly be having an affair if our shoes remained snug on our feet, if our clothes remained intact, if we did not touch each other's skin except by accident or necessity, such as the handing over of the gloves and the hat, or the pouring of a drink, or the lighting of a cigarette, which I sometimes liked to do for him, simply because I envied the cigarette.

"It is still a matter of sin, however," Stefan had said, the second day we had met like this. "We are indulging in the most elemental intimacy, and there is also the necessity for

404

self-abuse, without which I could not possibly lie here next to you every day with any pretense of tranquility."

I'd told him that this wasn't strictly necessary, that there were plenty of women downstairs who would be happy to perform on him whatever form of abuse he required, and he hadn't answered except to snort and reach for his drink on the bedside table. I had spent the following twenty-three hours wondering what particular meaning was contained in that snort, until Stefan opened the door to my knock the next day and took my hat and gloves, and it wasn't that I had forgotten the question: I simply ceased to care about the answer.

I came back the next day, and the next. I developed an affectionate relationship with the plasterwork of the ceiling above the bed. I imagined how we must look from above, and how the gilded borders formed a kind of picture frame around the two of us, Annabelle and Stefan, lying on our backs in the center of the bed, elegantly dressed, not quite touching. I knew each repeat, each fold and flaw, each nick in the paint and the gilding as I knew my own skin. I followed the familiar creamy progress of a scroll and said, "What are we doing here?"

"I haven't the slightest idea," said Stefan. "This is an unprecedented exercise for me."

"I don't think it's a sin. How can it be a

sin? It's so pure, existing like this with you."

"My dear, it is worse than a sin. We could commit the physical act of adultery, and we would not, in the middle of it, be so perfectly attached as we are like this."

"Then why don't we make love? Since it's the lesser of two evils."

"Because the one would not negate the other. Because if we made love, it would not make this existing together any more innocent."

The shadows of the fan blades chased themselves fruitlessly around the ceiling. They had lengthened by at least two centimeters since I had arrived. The minutes bled out, one by one, and soon there would be nothing left. I would rise from the bed and take my gloves and my hat, and I would walk out into the shimmering sidewalk as if I had not left all my blood inside.

"Then let's at least hold hands," I said.

"We should not under any circumstances hold hands, Annabelle."

My fingers touched his, and our damp hands curled together on the bedspread.

7.

My father adored Florian, and the affection was mutual. I would watch them play together on the floor next to the sofa, spreading toys and books all over the august inlaid floors of the apartment, and feel a strange combina-

tion of bemusement and betrayal.

"You weren't like this with me or Charles," I said, the day after I had held Stefan's hand on the fourth-floor bedspread of the Paris Ritz.

"Wasn't I?"

"No. You were off amusing yourself most of the time."

"I am amusing myself now," he said, demonstrating a proper rhythm on the samba drums, and I looked at Alice, who reclined on the sofa with a magazine. She smiled beatifically and shrugged her bare shoulders.

We went into lunch a half hour later, and no amount of squealing and messiness could interrupt Papa's enchantment with his grandson. "Thank God he does not have his father's coloring," Papa said, "as if someone had poured a measure of bleach over his head."

Alice suppressed a giggle.

"I happen to like Johann's coloring," I said.

"Oh, of course. It suits him perfectly, doesn't it? Like a great Teutonic iceberg."

"Papa!" said Florian, and he threw his bread on the floor.

I bent over to retrieve the bread. "He can understand more than you think, you know."

"Yes, of course. He is the cleverest boy, aren't you, *chouchou*?" Papa made a face, and Florian squealed.

I gazed at the two of them over the rim of

my wineglass. "I suppose you might as well get used to this, since you're starting over again with one of your own."

"Oh! We're getting married, by the way," said Alice. "Next month, at the Hôtel du Cap. I should very much like you to be matron of honor, if your family can spare you."

I stopped the wine on my lips. "Married?"

"Yes, of course," said Papa. "I am not such an old blackguard as that."

I set down the glass and wiped my fingers on my napkin. I thought, Poor Mummy. "Oh, I can imagine your asking. But I can't imagine a clever girl like Alice accepting you."

"I hadn't much choice, I suppose. But I believe I know how to manage him."

"You manage me extremely well," Papa said, and they exchanged a look of such happiness that I lost my breath.

Why, they're in love, I thought, and the panic rose up from my chest to choke me. Alice wasn't supposed to be happy like this; she was supposed to be restless and eternally dissatisfied, and I was supposed to be the wise matron who had chosen her partner well, who dispensed wise advice about the care and management of husbands, and the joys to be discovered in a wholesome family life.

Florian jettisoned another piece of bread. His caramel eyes grew round and wet. "Want Papa," he said, between heaving sobs, and he

stretched out his arms to me.

I lifted him from his chair and held him against my chest, and his little heartbeat pattered against mine, his little fist curled around mine. "Presumably you'll do a far better job of managing him than Mama did," I said.

"But that was my fault, *mignonne,*" said Papa.

"Oh, you're admitting it, are you? That's a step in the right direction."

"I am older and wiser, that's all," said Papa. "Is it not possible for an old dog to learn his new tricks? I have determined that sexual congress is perhaps not so essential to happiness, after all."

"But bloody important, nonetheless," said Alice.

"Better late than never, I suppose," I said.

Alice lit a cigarette. "But can you come? To the wedding, I mean. Will you be irrevocably in Germany, or does he let you out on good behavior, from time to time?"

"I'm sure he won't mind if I slip down for a few days."

I began to ask Alice about the arrangements, dress and flowers and guests, and Papa excused himself. I stroked Florian's damp hair. The storm had passed, and his breath tickled the hollow of my throat, steady and gentle. Alice watched the door, and when it had closed behind my father's neat gray-suited back, she turned to me and asked me

what was all this about my having an affair.

My hand went still on Florian's hair. "I'm not having an affair."

"Then it's all perfectly innocent, your meeting a man every day at the Ritz?"

I whispered, "Where did you hear that?"

"The usual birdie. You haven't even bothered to disguise yourself, I'm told. Such an amateur." She reached for Florian and settled him on her lap to play with her necklace. "It's Stefan, isn't it?"

I hesitated. Was there any point in lying to her? "Yes, it's Stefan, but it's not what you think."

"My dear, you don't think I disapprove, do you? Enjoy yourself, by all means. When the cat's away and all that. I'm hardly the girl to judge." She held Florian's fingertips and let him rise to his feet on her lap. He laughed and grabbed her cheeks, and her arms went around him as if she were born for it, born to cuddle a baby on her lap. "Just watch yourself, lovest. I suspect this particular cat doesn't like his little mouse to play."

8.

Can I ask you something?

Whatever you like, Annabelle.

What did you say to me, that time we made love on the beach?

(Stefan smoked his cigarette and sipped back the rest of his brandy.)

Don't say you don't remember.

Yes, I remember. I remember it well. I was praying to God that we would make a baby together in that moment, so that you would have no choice but to become mine, and vice versa.

(Around and around went the blades of the fan.)

I suppose it was a selfish thing to pray for, after all. You were not even twenty. But I could not help myself. I wanted some sign that I was not deluded, that God in his mercy had actually meant me for you.

(Around and around, making long swishing sounds like the ocean.)

Is something the matter, Annabelle?

No, Stefan. Nothing's wrong. But I think it's probably time for me to go home now.

9.

When I returned home, Florian hadn't yet woken up from his nap. He slept on his stomach, wearing only a shirt and napkin, damp and a little flushed by the heat. I stood by his crib and touched his dark hair. His fist made a twitch, a flexing of his small perfect fingers, and I remembered how I had watched Stefan sleep one afternoon in Monte Carlo, naked on the bed, in the exact center of a beam of white sunlight. The utter peace of him. I remembered thinking how beautiful he was, and how lucky I was that I would

411

spend my entire life watching him like this, as he slept off the bliss of lovemaking inside a patch of sun.

10.

I turned on my side to face Stefan's gaunt profile. "What if I don't go to Germany next month? What if we take Florian in the car with us and drive to Antibes for my father's wedding?"

Stefan's hands were folded beneath his head. He stared up at the rotating shadows on the ceiling. "You are not to ask me these things, Annabelle. You are to say to me, *Stefan, this is what I want,* and I will do it. God forgive me. I will find a way to give you what you want."

11.

"I can't do it," I said to Charles. "I can't spy on Johann for you. It's not honest."

We were walking along the Seine with Florian, poking into the bookstalls and perspiring. Charles stopped and turned to me. A book lay open in his hands. Proust.

"But it's not spying," he said. "Not really."

"That's not why it's dishonest. It's dishonest because I'll have to pretend everything is normal. That I'm still in love with him, if I ever really was."

Charles looked shocked, standing there holding his open Proust. Florian darted

around the corner of the bookstall, and I launched myself after him, losing my hat to the hot wind. He giggled and made me chase him, and when I caught him at last, I blew a raspberry into his tender throat and told him how much Mama loved him, how beautiful he was, how miraculously like his father.

"Papa!" he exclaimed, and he threw his arms around my neck.

12.

It was the twenty-ninth of July, and Stefan and I faced each other atop his bed on the fourth floor of the Paris Ritz. Our shoes were off — it was too hot, I said, and it was silly to think that shoes made any difference — and I was tracing my finger down the scar on the side of Stefan's face.

"I think I'm ready to tell you something," I said.

He put his finger across my mouth.

"Let's not talk," he said. "It is too hot to speak."

13.

When I arrived home at the avenue Marceau an hour and a half later, I put my key into the lock and realized at once that something was different. A current of energy ran from lock to key to hand, as if someone had wired the door for electricity while I was out visiting Stefan at the Ritz.

413

I turned the handle and opened the door, and there was a great peal of laughter from the drawing room, yes, a great peal of laughter from a delighted Florian, and an answering roar from deep in an enormous chest.

14.

The day my mother's appendix burst, we were on Cape Cod, staying with her sister and my multitude of cousins. Mummy had complained of a sour stomach the night before, and my aunt, always intensely practical, always a little jealous of Mummy's French title and perhaps a little smug that the expensive French marriage had ended exactly as she had predicted on their wedding day, told Mummy she had always been too soft, and to take an Alka-Seltzer and go to bed.

The next morning, I awoke to a strange quiet in the house, as if every floorboard had lost its will to live. I looked across the still air to Charles's bed, which lay empty and unmade, the sheets flung back in haste.

I sat up, and the door cracked open. It was my cousin Franklin, golden-skinned and blue-eyed and white-toothed, a perfect American teenager. He was off to Harvard in the fall, and eventually he was supposed to be president. Charles hated him. He took cheap shots at football, Charles said.

"Awake?" asked Franklin.

"Why is the house so quiet?"

He told me that the house was so quiet because everyone was at the hospital, and everyone was at the hospital because my mother had been taken there in the night, and now she was dead.

Dead, I said.

Dead, said Franklin. I'm sorry.

I said it was a stupid joke, and Franklin said he was sorry but it wasn't a joke. It was appendicitis. They had tried to operate, but it was too late.

I sank back in my pillow and drew the blanket over my head. I said four Hail Marys, and when I finished the last one I knew it was true, that Mummy was gone, that I would always hate Franklin Hardcastle for saying he was sorry when he really wasn't.

Later, when the shock had worn off, I wondered how the floorboards had known. How the house had known something was wrong before I had.

15.

In the drawing room, Florian was riding on top of Johann's back as if my husband were a horse in the Bois de Boulogne. Johann saw me first. He lifted his large head in mid-whinny and his face shed its delight.

"Johann," I whispered. "I thought you were in Germany."

He reached behind his back and grasped

415

Florian's kicking legs, and he maneuvered the two of them until he was standing before me with Florian in his arms, clinging for dear life. His eyes were a clear and somber blue.

"My wife," he said, "my darling wife, I had to come. I have missed you so much."

I opened my mouth to reply, but the door from the hallway banged open and a ball of blondness hurtled into my arms. "Mother!" exclaimed Frieda, and I burst into tears instead.

16.

Johann asked me if I had eaten, and I said I had. He gave Florian to Frieda and said she must play with her brother while Papa talked with Mother. He had given me his handkerchief, and I was still cleaning myself up while he took my hand and led me into the bedroom and closed the door. He picked up my other hand and fell to his knees and kissed my fingers. "*Mein Liebling,* my treasure. My wife. Annabelle. I am so sorry."

I thought, This can't be happening. I'm supposed to meet Stefan in an hour, I'm supposed to pack two suitcases — one for me and one for Florian — and meet Stefan on the eastern side of the Place Vendôme at four-thirty precisely, where he will be waiting in a hired automobile to drive us south to Antibes.

I tugged my husband upward. "Johann,

please. Get up. Don't say that."

He moved his hands to the small of my back and pressed his mouth into my stomach. "Ah, your smell," he said. "My God. I am holding you finally. I have been so sick, Annabelle, and I have been wrong. My son, I have missed him so much."

"He's missed you, too," I whispered. My hands went to his hair, because what else could I do? The short blond bristles were soft on my palms.

"On my knees, Annabelle, I ask you to forgive me. Forgive your old husband, who became too stiff and proud and forgot what it is like to be twenty-one."

"There's nothing to forgive, Johann. Please. Get up."

He rose and pressed me to his chest. "It was Frieda. She said to me, *Father, you are moping, I have never seen you so unhappy. You must do something.* And she said, *Annabelle is not like Mama, you cannot make her something she is not.* And I realized she was right. I have been an old fool with his young wife."

"Stop, Johann. You're not old, you're not a fool, it's just —"

"Annabelle, please."

I pushed him away. "Johann, I can't. I have to think."

He picked up my hand and kissed it. "Lis-

417

ten to me. Listen to this one fact at least. I have told the Oberkommando in Berlin that I am resigning my post there and returning to Paris, in my old role if they will have me, and as a private citizen if they will not. I have withdrawn the children from their schools. This September, the boys will start at Charterhouse, my old school in England, and the girls will move here to Paris with us. She is so delighted, she would not stop talking on the train."

"But your career. They will ruin you. They'll say you're disloyal."

"I do not give a damn what they say."

"Oh, Johann."

He kissed my hand again. "If that is what you want, Annabelle. If I am not too late to win back your esteem."

I stared at my hand inside his, at the size of Johann's fingers. I felt as if someone had attached a tube to my chest and drained away my vital fluids.

"I cannot live any longer like this," said Johann. "I cannot live without my wife and my little son. I cannot go back to that. I will do whatever you want."

Through the door came the sound of Frieda's laughter, and the scurry of Florian's feet on the sleek parquet floors that smelled of beeswax.

Johann said, "We need you, Annabelle."

In my head, I said four Hail Marys, and

418

when I finished the last one I knew he was telling the truth.

I slipped my hand from his. "I'm so hot and dusty, Johann. I need to take a bath."

17.

The cars buzzed along the middle of the Place Vendôme and around its corners, but not one of them came to a stop along the eastern side. I checked my watch at four twenty-eight, and again at four twenty-nine, and very resolutely waited until four thirty-two before checking again. The sun burned the crown of my hat. My hands grew damp inside my white cotton gloves.

At four thirty-nine I crossed to the western side of the Place Vendôme and approached the front desk of the Hotel Ritz. I inquired whether Stefan Silverman had passed through the lobby, and the clerk, who must have recognized me, said that Monsieur Silverman had checked out of his room two hours ago.

Thank you, I said. Was there any message for me?

No, there was not.

If he returns, will you please give him this note?

(I handed the clerk a sealed envelope.)

Of course, Madame, said the clerk. Would there be any reply?

No, I said, I didn't need any reply, and I

walked out of the Paris Ritz and returned to the apartment on the avenue Marceau.

18.

"Have you had a good walk?" Johann said, rising from his desk. The chair scraped painfully against the floor. His face was pale and vulnerable in the faint afternoon sunlight.

"Yes, thank you." I hid my trembling hands in the folds of my skirt.

The clock ticked behind me on the mantel. Johann gazed at my hair, eyes puckered fearfully, lips parted as if he wanted to ask me a question.

He is so tall, I thought, so large and formidable. He commands an army. And he cannot ask me a question.

"I will go and see the cook about dinner," I said, and I turned and left the room.

19.

After dinner, I played the cello with Frieda, and when I went to the nursery to put Florian to bed, I found him curled up on the floor with Johann, who was reading him a story.

"Time for bed," I said.

My husband hoisted a sleepy Florian onto his massive knee. "There we are, son. Your mama commands us to go to bed, and we must always obey Mama."

Johann carried him to his crib and laid him

in the sheets. It's too hot for blankets, I said, and Johann leaned down and kissed Florian's forehead. He brushed back the dark curls and said Papa's darling boy had grown, he was a little man now. Florian's eyelids sagged at the familiar timbre of Johann's voice.

I turned off the light.

20.

In the beginning, when I had returned to Paris after Christmas, I had kept to my own side of the bed and left Johann's side empty, the way the wives of some soldiers still laid a place at the table for the missing husband. After the disastrous April visit, however, I began to creep over the invisible line that separated his space and mine, inch by inch, until I lay sprawled every night in the center of the bed, like a defiant starfish.

Now it was July, and my husband had returned to our home and asked for my forgiveness. He had fallen to his knees and reminded me that I was, after all, his wife. He had brought his young daughter who needed a mother, his big arms in which my son fit so securely.

I slipped off my dressing gown and drew back the counterpane and raged at the white sheets. *It's a damned thing,* Nick Greenwald said, shaking his head. The bathroom door opened behind me.

"Annabelle," said Johann.

I closed my eyes.

21.

I waited while he fit a sheath awkwardly on himself. When he entered me, I held back the gasp in my throat and lay still beneath him. I will not feel this, I thought, but friction is friction and flesh is flesh, and my body was young and starved of love. We rocked together silently for long minutes, until my reluctant heels found the backs of his legs.

What he did next astounded me. He rolled onto his back and brought me with him, so that I wobbled above his mountainous chest and sank down hard. He put his thick hands on my hips and ordered me in German to use him hard — I don't think he knew the words in English — and as I rose and obediently fell he said more German words, admiring my waist and breasts and my snug little *Muschi,* lifting his hips to meet mine, and I thought in despair, closing my eyes, I'm sorry, Stefan, I'm so sorry, I can't help it, I am going to come.

Then I lay flat on the damp white mountain of Johann's sternum and stared at the wall, while his hand traced the cavity of my spine. It is done, he said, we are man and wife again.

PEPPER

COCOA BEACH 1966

1.

Susan is creasing her very, very pretty forehead. "You're saying nobody's heard from
her since last week?"

"Seems so," says Florian. "Pepper's the last
one to speak to her."

Pepper spreads her hands. "She didn't say
where she was going, I'm afraid, and I never
had the chance to ask her."

"Oh, dear." Susan gazes up at Florian's
face. "And she's been acting so oddly since
— well."

"Since Dad died."

"She seemed all right to me," says Pepper.
"She spoke of him fondly, of course, but she
wasn't exactly grief-stricken. On the other
hand, she had just dropped three hundred
large on an old car, so —"

Florian turns to her. "What did you say?"

"The car. The car I sold her."

"Three hundred *thousand dollars*?"

Pepper looks back and forth between the
two of them. They're sitting at the dining

423

room table, Florian and Susan on one side and Pepper on the other, a pitcher of lemonade and an exquisite Meissen plate between them, piled high with macaroons. The sun has just begun to tilt through the French doors, and it forms a halo over Susan's golden hair. "You didn't know?"

"What kind of car costs three hundred thousand dollars?" Susan says breathlessly. Her eyes are large and far too blue for Pepper's taste.

"A Mercedes. A 1936 Special Roadster. Only a few of them were ever built."

Florian chokes. "A *what* Mercedes?"

"A very special Mercedes," says Pepper. "In fact, the exact same one in which your mother fled Germany back in 1938. It turned up in my sister's shed on Cape Cod, and I spent the summer restoring it."

Under Florian's astounded gaze, she reaches for the pitcher of lemonade and refills her glass. The lemon slices bump lazily against the spout. No one has touched the macaroons. Pepper lifts one up and sniffs it. "Almond?" she says.

"Coconut. Clara's secret recipe. Did you just say it was the same car she and Dad drove out of Germany? The exact one?"

Susan's eyes are like a pair of awed wet cornflowers. "And you restored it? All by yourself?"

"I had a little help," Pepper says modestly.

"But how did it end up in a shed on the Cape?"

Pepper gestures with her cookie. "Now, that, you see, is the mystery. Maybe that's what your mother is trying to find out. My God, these are the macaroons they serve in heaven."

Florian leans forward. "How do you know it's the same car?"

"Because she told me."

"How did she know?"

"I think she'd recognize her own car, don't you? And trust me, this isn't the kind of car you'd mistake for another one. Every part is engineered and hand-fitted and caressed into place. It's the most beautiful thing you've ever seen."

Susan smiles at Florian's cheek. "It's so romantic, don't you think?"

Pepper and Florian turn to her in tandem. "Romantic?"

Jinx, Pepper thinks.

"Why, that she'd spend all that money to buy back the car that carried her and her husband to their new life." She aims the cornflowers at Florian, flutter flutter. "It's beautiful, really."

He bolts to his feet.

"I don't care if it's beautiful or not. My mother's driven off in a three-hundred-thousand-dollar car without telling anyone where she's gone, and I'd like to find her

425

before the coroner does!"

Susan's alarmed. "The coroner!"

"That's a little dramatic, don't you think?" says Pepper.

Florian brings his knuckles to rest on the table. "You want to see dramatic? This is my *mother* we're talking about!"

"That's true, the poor dear, but as the dead German said, what doesn't kill a girl makes her stronger. She's around somewhere, alive and kicking. Trust me."

"*Somewhere* is a damned big word, Schuyler. Considering we don't even know where to start looking."

"Cape Cod?"

"She did *not* drive to Cape Cod. Not in November."

"How do you know?"

"Trust me, all right? She can't stand the cold. She lives for sunshine."

"You see? We've narrowed it down already. Somewhere sunny in November, check."

"She had to have told you something. She had to have left *some* kind of clue."

"Well, she didn't. I'll show you the note. I've seen telegrams more verbose."

"Did she take a lot of luggage?"

"I'm afraid I didn't count, since I wasn't even there when she left. Any more questions?"

Florian sinks back in his chair and runs a hand through his hair. His eyes are puckered

with worry, poor thing. What kind of mother is Annabelle Dommerich, to inspire such illogical concern for her welfare? Because motherhood doesn't always end so well for the Schuylers. Motherhood usually goes splash headfirst into a vodka tonic, with lime. He says grimly, "We'll just have to start calling hotels, I guess."

"That will take ages."

"I know." He swears softly. "Anyone got any better ideas?"

Pepper taps her chin and examines another macaroon. Her fourth, if she allows it entrance, but then she's never tasted macaroons like melted coconuts, and what if she never has the chance again? Florian picks up his glass and stares keenly through the trickles at a refracted courtyard full of lemon trees. Behind him, the brass carriage clock on the mantel lets out a pair of delicate chimes.

Susan clears her very pretty throat. "I'm sorry, this is going to sound really dumb. But have you thought of searching her study?"

Florian is shocked. *Shocked.* "You mean ransack her private papers?"

"I'm sorry. I know. Dumb idea."

Pepper sets down the macaroon and reaches for her crutches.

"Jesus Christ, Susikins. I'm starting to like you after all."

2.

Susan bends flexibly to the rug, flashing a dangerous length of golden thigh. "What's Mrs. Dommerich's Grammy doing on the floor?"

"Breaking my foot."

Susan picks up the statuette and arranges it on the shelf with reverent hands, while Florian eases himself into Annabelle's desk chair and sets eight fingers along the edge of the polished wood, ever so gingerly. He frowns and lifts up a piece of paper. "What's this?"

"Nothing." Pepper snatches it away. "I already told you, I was writing a letter."

"On my mother's stationery?"

"Oh, please. It's not personalized."

"So you *were* writing home, after all. Commendable."

"You're not supposed to read people's personal correspondence."

"I beg your pardon." He offers a smile that comes off like a scowl. "Isn't that exactly what we're doing now?"

Susan turns from the shelf, sets her hands on her dainty hips, and beams. "Don't you just love this room? If I had a study of my own, I'd want it to look *just like this.*"

"Imagine that," murmurs Pepper. She settles herself on the edge of the desk, an inch or two away from Florian's leftmost pinkie finger, and admires the plentiful curve of his shoulder. He looks a little too large for the

428

chair, a little out of place in the room, which is distinctly feminine without being an inch pink. Something about the creaminess of the paintwork and the attractive arrangement of the furniture. Or maybe it's the cheerful yellow paisley armchair in the corner, an article no man would ever allow in his private study. "I was just thinking," she says softly.

"And?" Florian is lifting up the blotter a fraction, opening up the drawers a crack, wearing an expression that suggests he's changing diapers instead.

"About that morning. Afternoon, really. I slept in a wee bit. I had breakfast in the dining room, and Annabelle was there, and there wasn't any talk about going away. In fact, I distinctly recall her suggesting we go into town later and shop."

"Shop?" Florian's head pops up, like Sherlock sniffing a clue. "Shop for what?"

"It doesn't matter what. Clothes for me, clothes for the baby. Who cares. My point is that no earlier than half past noon on the date of her so-called disappearance, she was planning on hanging around. And then she left. So what caused her to leave?"

"A telephone call?" suggests Susan.

Florian snaps his fingers. "Or the mail."

"She did say she was going to catch up on the post while I went for a walk."

Florian looks down at the tidy desk. "No mail here."

Pepper shimmies off the desk and hops to the door. "Clara!" she calls out, into the pristine hallway, and a moment later the housekeeper arrives at a canter.

"What is it, Miss Schuyler? You need your pills? You need more macaroons?"

"No. I mean yes! *Yes, please,* to more macaroons. But can you also tell me where you stash Mrs. Dommerich's mail, when she's away?"

3.

For the record, Pepper's not the slightest bit concerned about the health and safety of Mrs. Annabelle Dommerich. The woman is no shrinking cornflower. Besides, if the Nazis couldn't thwart her, nobody could, right? But Pepper has inherited — along with her tip-tilted dark blue eyes and her penchant for choosing the wrong man — the Schuyler nose for dirt, and her talented proboscis began twitching madly right about the moment handsome Florian uttered the magic words.

Ever since Dad died.

Now, what could *that* possibly signify, except that Annabelle's hiding something under her ladylike fingertips? Something like . . . let Pepper ponder for a moment . . . *dirt.*

Not that it's any of her business. But when did Pepper ever mind her own business? Your own business is so unfruitful, so tedious, so

lacking in neat solutions and satisfactory conclusions. But the beeswax of others! It gives you a charge, doesn't it, a burst of not-too-commendable energy to plow right past your own tribulations and frolic about in the muck of someone else's. For a change.

"The trouble with your mother," Pepper says, head bent over an open manila folder, "among other things, is that she's so damned organized. Really, who pays the bills and files everything away just hours after getting home from abroad?"

"She hates loose ends." Florian doesn't look up. He's sitting in the desk chair, flipping through a file folder that rests on his lap, looking as if he'd rather poke through a garbage can.

"Or she's hiding something."

Susan says, a bit throaty, "This feels so naughty, looking through her papers."

"Oh, admit it, you're enjoying the thrill. Not that there's anything thrilling to discover, unless you're turned on to know she paid five dollars a week to have the flowers watered." Pepper tosses the folder aside and bends back over the file drawer. "Dommerich. You're awfully quiet over there. Tell me more about this genealogy research of hers."

"I don't know. She was pretty vague."

"You don't say."

"She would clip things from newspapers and magazines. There was someone she had

431

in Washington, looking up records and archives."

"Do you happen to know his name?"

"Nope."

Pepper flips past the files, which are organized alphabetically, until she comes to a tab marked in thick black letters: HARRIS.

"Was it Harris?" she asks. "The man in Washington?"

"No idea."

She pulls the file free and flips it open. A fan of typewritten letters spreads out before her, some attached to newspaper clippings with small silver paper clips. *Dear Mrs. Dommerich,* one began, dated March of 1965, *The possible lead in San Diego appears not to be significant after all. (Please see the attached report for details.) I have now begun research into the candidate in Oklahoma* [there is an angry blue margin note: *Not Oklahoma! Coast!!*] *and will shortly provide an update . . .*

Genealogy, my aunt Julie, thinks Pepper.

There is a ceiling fan overhead, twirling the air in lazy circles. The draft ruffles the thin corners of the letters — cheap typing paper, the kind they used in small and ramshackle offices — and in the lull of conversation, Pepper considers whether to hold this remarkable paper aloft right now, to wave it triumphantly underneath the steady stroke of the ceiling fan, or whether to keep it in its

place, inside the folder marked HARRIS, for the private eye tracking somebody down for Mrs. Annabelle Dommerich. Somebody she must have known well, or at least well enough to be quite certain he (or she!) would never put down roots in the nation's heartland, far from the sea.

Of course, there are other letters. Pepper skims. They have all been arranged in chronological order, oldest to youngest, beginning in January of last year (now, when, exactly, did Mr. Dommerich ascend to the great tobacco shop in the sky?) and ending — Pepper licks her thumb and shuffles to the back of the folder, hoping and praying, because she could use a little excitement here —

November 6, 1966.

4.

"I'm going with you," says Susan. Her bottom lip is fixed stubbornly beneath the upper.

Florian puts his hand on her arm. "Sue, you're much better off down here. I'll telephone and let you know how it goes."

"But I can help!"

She gazes upward, and Pepper thinks, My God, you're better at this than I am, aren't you? The three of them are standing rather intimately in Florian's bedroom, neatly made, while Florian packs his toothbrush back into

433

his overnight bag. He's already dressed for the ride, in a comfortable cotton shirt and dungarees, beaten-up loafers fitted snugly to his feet. Outside, the afternoon light is yellowing with age.

He smiles down at Susan. "That's sweet of you, kid, but Pepper's the one who knows the most about what's going on."

"Pepper's going?"

"I'm going?" Pepper says.

Florian turns to her, eyebrows raised. "Aren't you?"

"No, no, no." She gestures to her belly. "Pregnant lady. A cripple! I can't handle another all-night car ride. Take Susan instead. I'm sure she can see to your needs much better than I can."

"I don't know about that," Susan says modestly.

"Sure you can, honey. He seems like a simple enough man to me."

"Pepper," says Florian, "can we step outside for a moment?"

5.

They stop under the shade of a lemon tree, and Pepper turns to face Florian, crutches braced under her arms.

"Before you say a word, just consider for a moment. You can't possibly be thinking of keeping poor Sue-Sue at home while you whisk another woman off in your T-Bird."

The astounded look again. "But there's nothing going on with the two of us. It's strictly platonic."

"My God. Do you know nothing about women at all, Dommerich?"

"I know a lot about women."

"So you say. But don't you know that dear Susan will spend the next week imagining us pulling off the road every five miles to have screaming fog-up-the-windows sex in the backseat?"

Florian's gaze drops down to her belly and back up again. "You're kidding, right?"

"My goodness. How flattering."

"I'm not saying you're not attractive. Christ. I think I already made that clear. But — well, for one thing, the logistics —"

"Where there's a will there's a way."

A slow shade of pink rises up Florian's neck and over his cheeks.

"Not that I've actually tried it," Pepper admits. "But I do have an imagination."

"Well, that's not the point. It's none of Susan's business who I'm sleeping with or not sleeping with."

"Really? Because I get the feeling she wants it to be her business. And don't even try to tell me you're not aware of that little fact."

He had the grace to look embarrassed. "Maybe so. But she also knows me better than that."

"Does she?"

"Yes. I may be a lawyer, but I'm not a cad. Anyway, I've got other things on my mind. You're coming along because you're familiar with the car Mama's driving, you're familiar with her state of mind and all that, and you're just — well, you're just a little more — I don't know. Resourceful."

"I think you underestimate Miss Willoughby."

"She's not that kind of girl, that's all."

Pepper curls her fingers around the handles of the crutches. "Oh? And what kind of girl is that, hmm?"

Florian holds up his hands. "I'm not going to let myself fall in that trap again, believe me. You're just two different women. Not bad or good. Just different. And if I need someone back me up while I track down my mother somewhere on the Georgia coast, someone I can count on, I want *your* type of woman."

"And if you're going to get married and have pretty babies, you want her type?"

"What are you talking about? Who's getting married?"

Pepper puts her hand on Florian's arm, just above the elbow. A lemon branch, heavy with fruit, brushes her shoulder. "Look. Take my advice. Bring Susan with you, okay? She's stronger than you think. Besides, this way you really *can* pull off the road and have sex with her, if you feel the itch."

436

"Actually, the thought didn't cross my mind."

"Now it will."

6.

From the grateful look on Susan's face, Pepper knows she did a Good Thing. She hopes God is taking note, assuming He hasn't given up on her long ago.

Susan hurries home to pack a few things (she says). Her family's house is about a quarter-mile down the road. That's how they met, Florian says, as they watch her car pull away in a puff of dust. They played in the ocean together as kids. The girl next door, says Pepper. Just like the movies.

She heads back to her room to rest, tosses her crutches in the corner, lies back on her neat bed, and watches the ceiling fan rotate above her. The baby, awakened by the stillness, begins to squirm inside her. You did a Good Thing, she tells herself, though she doesn't feel particularly good. She feels as if a hollow has opened up in her chest, occupying a space she didn't know existed. It interferes with the businesslike beat of her heart.

A few minutes later, there's a knock on the door. "It's me," says Florian, through the crack.

"Haven't you left yet?"

"Are you decent?"

"I'm never decent, or so they tell me."

He opens the door. Pepper sits up.

"Are you sure you won't come?" he says, filling the doorway, framed by the growing blue twilight.

She shakes her head. "Third wheel."

"You wouldn't be a third wheel. Anyway, what are you going to do? I can't let you stay here alone."

"I won't steal anything, I promise. Throw any wild parties and drink up your liquor."

"That's not what I meant." He sits down carefully at the end of the bed, sinking the mattress, and stares down at his knitted hands. "You should go home to your folks."

"Wouldn't that be a delightful Thanksgiving surprise! Pepper waddles in on her crutches, looking unnervingly like the turkey on the table. No, I'll wait just a bit longer. Like they used to do it, you know. Sending the shameful daughter off to Switzerland for a six-month walking holiday with a trusted female relative."

"Except you don't have one of those around here."

She snaps her fingers. "Oh, damn. Well, modern times."

"This is stupid," he says. "You should be with your family."

"My family's not the same as yours, darling. We're better off without each other, in times of trial. Otherwise the arsenic bottle

gets uncorked, and the police have to get involved."

"Pepper," he says, shaking his head.

"Off you go, now. I'll be all right. I have Clara to run for the doctor, if anything goes horribly wrong." She reaches over and pushes his shoulder, because she can't resist, just once.

Florian lifts his large hand and places it over hers. "I'll telephone and let you know what we find out."

"Do that thing."

She slides her hand away. He climbs to his feet and scowls down at her. His waist is right at the level of her eyes: his trim stomach, his brown leather belt pinning the dungarees in place.

"Take care of that foot, all right? Use your crutches."

"Would I never?"

And then his hand is cupping her chin, and she has to look down at his blurry wrist, because the two of them combined — his gaze and his touch — create way too much firepower for the hollow in her chest to contain.

"Off you go," she says again, and the hand falls away.

He makes it to the door and stops. "Oh, hold on. This is for you."

She looks up. He's holding out a small envelope between his fingers.

"What's that?"

"Letter for you. Clara sent it along."

When she doesn't get up, when she doesn't even move, eyes frozen on the white rectangle in Florian's paw, heart frozen inside the black hollow, Florian shrugs and sets the envelope down on the lamp table near the door.

7.

Pepper's heart starts again, at a brisk hand gallop. But she's not the kind of girl who avoids bad news, is she? She's not the kind of girl who sits and stares for an hour at the Ominous Object, before she finally gathers up the strength to pick it up with trembling fingers.

Not Pepper.

She doesn't bother with the crutches. She hops ungracefully across the rug and snatches up the envelope. The light has faded fast, the way it does in November. She switches on the lamp and rips open the flap.

The handwriting. How could you possibly rage at the familiarity of someone's messy black handwriting? But she does. She wants to rip it to pieces. She reads it instead.

We need to talk. Forget the lawyers. I'm waiting on an airplane at the Melbourne Municipal Airport. Let's work this out together.

It was unsigned. Of course.

Lawyers. What a hoot. If Captain Seer-

440

sucker has a law degree, she's Marie Antoinette.

Pepper rips the note to pieces, and when she's done, and her heart is once more cold in her breast, shooting frozen blood all over the place, she finds her toothbrush and a clean dress and a change of underwear. She throws them in a linen laundry bag, tucks her pocketbook over her shoulders, grabs her crutches, and hobbles out the door of the guest cottage, through Annabelle's soft-scented courtyard and toward the driveway.

8.

They haven't left yet. Florian is putting Susan's bag in the trunk of the Thunderbird. Susan's in the passenger seat, touching up her lipstick.

"I've changed my mind!" Pepper says, tossing the laundry bag to Florian.

He grins, catches it handily, and closes the lid of the trunk.

■ ■ ■ ■

FOURTH MOVEMENT

■ ■ ■ ■

"The supreme art of war is to subdue the
enemy without fighting."

SUN TZU

Annabelle
GERMANY 1938

1.

In the pasture nearest the tennis court, Johann was teaching Florian how to ride a pony, using a longe line and an enormous amount of patience. I sat on a picnic cloth, with Frieda and Alice and my new baby sister, and watched them circle under the hot sun. Frieda was giving little Margot her bottle. Above the waving grass, I could hear Johann's bass voice, giving out instructions in German, though I couldn't make out the words.

"Is it perfectly safe, do you think?" said Alice.

"The younger the better, Johann says."

"Oh, yes," Frieda said. "We all started when we were two. I think Frederick is more horse than boy, sometimes."

"He looks as if he's enjoying it, at any rate." Alice drew her knees up under her chin. She wasn't wearing a hat, and her blond hair, streaked by the persistent sunshine, was gathered into a chignon. She wore a dress of

445

white eyelet and looked like a daisy. When Margot began to fuss, she turned her head and stretched out her long arm to tickle her daughter's chin. "What's the matter, darling? Are you keen to be off riding horses, too?"

Frieda laughed and put the baby to her shoulder. "She just needs to burp, I think."

Alice lay back on the cloth. "You're far better at this than I am, aren't you? Perhaps I should let you adopt her."

"I like babies, that's all," Frieda said.

I gazed across the hot meadow grass. Florian looked so grown-up in his riding clothes and leather boots. I could tell by the set of his shoulders that he was concentrating fiercely on Johann's words. He was always desperate to please his father.

His father.

And there it was, just like that: the knot of pain in my chest, which had become smaller and appeared less frequently as the months passed, but which never quite disappeared. I imagined it was a permanent condition, a chronic illness to be managed in the privacy of my own brain. It helped, perhaps, that I hadn't heard a single word from Stefan himself since we parted on that hot July day a year ago. He had walked out of the Paris Ritz and vanished. Not even Charles knew where he was, or maybe he wasn't telling me. A clean break, like an amputation. Eventually, you realized you could survive without

all your limbs, that you could function and even thrive, because human beings were designed to take a battering. And though you weren't whole, you at least had a son. And though it sometimes seemed as if your heart had stopped beating, you at least knew that somewhere in the world, another heart was beating for you.

Margot burped daintily, and I shifted my gaze to my baby sister and marveled at the difference between her and Florian. Her delicate lips, her perfect tiny fingers. If I leaned in to smell her hair, I knew she would be puppy-sweet. How was it possible that my sturdy son, rising and falling in his stirrups as the pony moved to a trot, had been nursing at my breast only a year and a half ago? My baby was gone forever. I wouldn't get him back. I had this new Florian, this walking, talking, pony-riding Florian, a swaggering miniature image of the man who had created him inside me. But my baby was gone.

"Are you all right, Mother?" asked Frieda. "You look a little ill."

I rose to my feet and shook the crumbs from my dress. "I'm fine, darling. I think I'll just take a walk."

2.

We sat down to lunch an hour or so later. The sunshine poured through the long French doors, and as I took my seat at the

end of the table and picked up a glass of water, the housekeeper came up behind me and told me that a woman had been here to see me.

"Who?" I asked in surprise. I had no friends here in Germany, only a few neighboring acquaintances who didn't approve of me at all.

"She did not leave her name, Frau von Kleist, but she gave me this note for you and explained that it was urgent."

Alice and my father were already in place, drinking their wine and talking animatedly about tennis. The smoke from their cigarettes drifted to the ceiling. The boys scraped back their chairs. Johann looked expectantly across the table, which was fragrant with a profusion of red roses I had cut just that morning

I tucked the note under my plate. "Thank you, Hilda."

3.

For a house so large, Schloss Kleist offered little privacy. Actually, it wasn't the house itself, it was the inhabitants. You could not be called to the telephone without everyone wanting innocently to know who had called; you could not play tennis without at least a pair of spectators. It was easier at night, when I could retreat to my cozy rooms at the end of the east wing without some request bouncing my way every four minutes. During the

day, I could achieve a quiet moment only in the lavatory, which is exactly where I opened the note Hilda had delivered to me at lunch.

It was written on a leaf of cheap notepaper, the kind you might pick up in a hotel or a train station. The words were English and neatly printed, as if the writer wanted to be sure I could read them properly.

I need your help. Wilhelmine. 23 Marktstrasse

I folded the paper and put it back into my pocket. Just before I opened the door, I remembered to flush the toilet and run the faucet, so I could pretend to wash my trembling hands.

4.

I found Johann upstairs in our bedroom, changing into his tennis clothes.

"Isn't it a little hot for tennis?" I said.

"Your father made me a challenge. One does not turn down a challenge from the father-in-law." He reached for his shirt. His chest was pink and enormous, like a side of beef. "Will you come to watch?"

"Thank you, no. I thought I might motor into the village for a bit of shopping," I said.

"Shopping?" He stopped and lifted his eyebrows. "But you do not like to shop."

"I need to order a hat for the festival."

"Have the milliner come to us. It is what Frieda would always do."

"I'm not Frieda, remember?"

He set the shirt aside and smiled. "No. You are my beautiful Annabelle. I almost die to look at you."

"Johann, stop."

"Come here, beautiful Annabelle." He snared me around the waist and slipped his hand inside the opening of my blouse.

"Johann! What's gotten into you?"

He kissed me, and when he lifted his face away, his eyes were soft. "The sunshine, I think. It is so good to have the sunshine again."

5.

I waited until the tennis balls had actually launched into the air before I slipped into the garage and started up the Mercedes.

The village was a few miles away, down a meandering road that glared white in the sun. I had put the top down, and the draft pulled at my hat, smelling of ripe hops and sunshine. I concentrated on keeping the car steady, on breathing just the right amount of oxygen into my lungs: not too much, not too little.

Marktstrasse was almost deserted; everyone had done her shopping early and gone home to enjoy the summer afternoon. I pulled up in front of number 23 — a small hotel I'd never noticed before — and a slim figure

stepped out of the shadow of the eaves.

"Frau von Kleist?" she said.

She was pretty, I thought, in a cold wash of jealousy. She stood taller than I did, and her curling dark hair bobbed about her ears. She looked more modern than I had imagined. She wore no makeup, except for a bit of lipstick, and she didn't need to. Her silk blouse and wide trousers were well made and a little mannish, almost like a movie star's, suiting her the way Alice's deep V-necked dresses suited Alice. I could well imagine Wilhelmine as an elegant new bride in a hotel bed, making love to Stefan, making a daughter with Stefan.

"Wilhelmine," I said. "I'm sorry, I don't know your last name."

"It's Himmelfarb," she said in perfect English. "May I get in?"

"Of course."

She got in the passenger side and shut the door. "Let's drive somewhere, if you don't mind. I have already taken enough risk."

I released the clutch and we set off down Marktstrasse in a little spurt of white gravel. She leaned her elbow on the door and turned her head to watch me, as if she was waiting for me to start the conversation.

So I did. "It's Stefan, isn't it? Something's happened to Stefan."

She went on regarding me, without speaking.

451

"Tell me, please. At least tell me he's alive, for God's sake."

"I'm sorry," she said. "I was just trying to see if you were sincere."

"What the hell does that mean? For God's sake, tell me what's happened!"

"He's alive," she said, and my shoulders slumped. The car swerved to the edge of the road, and Wilhelmine gripped the edge of the doorframe and pressed her right foot into the floorboards. When I had righted the car, she said, "All right. So you don't know anything about it."

"I haven't heard from Stefan in a year. Not since he walked out of the Paris Ritz last July."

"Ah. Then I suppose you don't know he was taken by a pair of Gestapo agents as soon as he turned the corner into the rue Cambon to fetch his automobile, and he has been held like a dog in the Dachau camp ever since."

I stuffed my hand into my mouth and swerved to the side of the road — this time deliberately — slamming the brake with my foot, until the Mercedes bumped to a stop alongside a weathered fence. The engine coughed and died. I opened the door just in time to vomit into the grass.

6.

"It was a month or two before we realized he was actually missing," Wilhelmine said, "and it was several more months before we found

out for certain where they had taken him. He is a very special prisoner, you know. They would not let me see him. I managed at last to get a message to him, and he sent a reply that he was fine, but I could hardly recognize the writing."

"Oh, God," I said, holding my fist to my mouth. I thought of my tranquil autumn and winter, settling Frieda into her school, resuming my cello studies, a recital Johann arranged at a music conservatory that was very well received. He said he was proud of me. Christmas in Paris, surrounded by my new family. A pile of decadent presents under the tree, including a breathtaking necklace of black pearls from Johann, which he fastened around my neck himself. Plenty of food and wine, plenty of music and warm fires. At night, Johann would hold me close to his chest, because a Paris apartment, however grand, is always drafty in winter; and as I drifted to sleep, safe and warm, I would say *Good night, Stefan* in my head, and wonder if he were keeping some woman warm in his own arms while she drifted to sleep.

Sometimes, when the bitterness ebbed in my heart, I even wished he were. I wished he did have a woman in his arms, because no one should lie alone in the middle of winter.

"That was in May," said Wilhelmine. "The officials refused to tell us any more, only that he was being held indefinitely for crimes

453

against the state. So I demanded to know what crimes, and after many weeks of letters and telephone calls, they at last sent me this." She handed me a piece of paper, folded twice into a square.

I stared at the paper between my fingers. "You said *us*. Whom do you mean?"

"His family, of course. His parents cannot sleep for worry."

"Of course."

"I have not told my daughter. She loves him so much. She draws pictures of him and hangs them in her room."

The tiny indentations of the typewriter were like Braille under my fingertips. The paper was crisp and thin and terribly official. I unfolded the page: not in the easy flips by which you opened the morning news, but by brute force, the individual grasping of each leaf, requiring dogged concentration.

"As you see," said Wilhelmine — I did not see, actually; I could not comprehend the German script before me — "this is an arrest order for one Stefan Silverman, for the crimes of murder and treason and various other infractions, according to evidence and sworn statements."

"Murder," I said. "Did he really commit murder?"

"Does it matter?"

"No." My back rested against a fence post. Someone was mowing a field nearby; the

drone of the engine floated along the motionless summer air. If I closed my eyes, I could
smell the wholesome brown scent of newly
cut hay. I said, "How did you know about
me?"

Wilhelmine's arms were folded across her
silk chest. Her breasts were small and lean,
like the rest of her. I thought she wasn't wearing a brassiere. She was practical and stylish
all at once; she was indomitable. "Do you
have a cigarette? I left mine in my motorcar."

I said I didn't.

She crossed one leg over the other. "I knew
he had a mistress in Paris, a married woman,
and he had gone to see her during the summer. So in May, after I got this arrest paper
at last, I went to France. I went first to the
Ritz, because he always saw his women there;
it was such a great pleasure to him, to screw
some beautiful woman in the bed of the
Imperial Suite." She paused. "I'm sorry, that
was rather cruel, wasn't it? I have always said
I would not be bitter. I did love him, you
know. I still admire him very much. It is
impossible not to admire such a man as that.
He has such qualities." She made a circle in
the dust with the toe of her elegant shoe.

"Please go on," I said.

"So I went to the Ritz, and at first Alfonse
would not tell me anything, though I could
see perfectly well that he knew all about you.
I am old hands with Alfonse, you see. He

455

prizes discretion above everything. I had gone there to murder my husband a few years ago, and Alfonse stood very firm, even though I was Stefan's lawful wife. He would not let me disturb the bastard." She laughed. "But this time I told him it was a matter of life and death, that their precious client had been arrested and thrown in a prison when he walked out of the hotel last July, and that he was now in great danger. So Alfonse gave me the note you left for Stefan."

I squeezed my eyes shut and contemplated this. "But I only signed it *Annabelle.* There was no surname."

"Oh, that was the easy part. Everyone knew that the Baron von Kleist had made a fool of himself over a young French wife named Annabelle."

Across the road, the cows were on the move, wandering slowly across a tender green pasture. "I don't understand," I said. "What does my husband have to do with any of this?"

Wilhelmine straightened her lean body away from the fence and turned to me. "Are you serious? You are this ignorant?"

I looked up at her helplessly, into the full glare of her contempt. The air around us seemed to be cracking into pieces, preparing to shatter. "Yes," I said. "I am this ignorant."

Her small dark eyes traveled over my face, taking my inventory: forehead, brows, eyes,

mouth, chin. "I suppose that is why he fell in love with you, of all of us. You are so fucking innocent. It must have been a relief." She laid her thumb against my cheekbone, like a lover's caress. "Sweet thing. Look again at the paper. Tell me if there is any other name that springs from the page."

I lifted the paper and stared at it. The gothic script had always confounded me; I had learned a great deal of German during my marriage, but I seemed to lose the meaning when I saw the words written in that dense medieval lettering. But now my eyes, as if knowing what to look for before my brain did, traveled down the page and fastened on the words *Johann von Kleist.*

"You do not know that the two of them, they are like Javert and Valjean? They are immortal enemies. It all made sense to me, when I saw that Annabelle von Kleist was Stefan's lover. Why your husband would not let him go, like the bloodhound tracking down the fox. Why there is now no possibility of Stefan's release."

I slid down the fence post and came to rest in the dusty grass. "It's not true."

"You know it is. You are ignorant but not foolish."

"But Johann's a general in the army, not Gestapo."

She snorted. "This is Hitler's Germany, Frau von Kleist. No one is what he seems.

Do you know what your husband did in Berlin last year? He oversaw the reorganization of the prisons, the prisons in which they put the people who do not agree with the Nazis, so that now they go to the rehabilitation camps, these beautifully designed camps, even bigger and better than before."

"My God."

"But it is more than that. There has always been a grudge. I believe Stefan pinched his nose a few years ago, intercepted some papers or some matter like that. And then there was this murder of a police agent, who was sent to catch him and put him in the prison. And I think you understand your husband, Frau von Kleist. I think you understand he is a man of rules and consequence. He is dogged in pursuit of his goal."

"Yes, I understand that." At the word *understand,* the shattering began at last. The fatal tap on the cracked grass. Stefan and Johann. Johann denouncing Stefan, having him arrested and thrown into Dachau to be tortured, and then going home to our Paris apartment and playing horses with Stefan's son. Taking Stefan's lover to bed, the final stroke. *We are man and wife again.*

I wanted to crawl out of my revolted skin. I wanted to vomit again, but there was nothing left in me. I took off my hat and let the sun bake into my hair.

Wilhelmine sat down next to me, Indian-

style. A wooden slat creaked as she leaned her back against it. Her knee was sharp and bony against my thigh.

I whispered, "He never said anything. Stefan never said a word."

"No, I am not surprised. Stefan has his faults, but he plays fair. He does not turn women into pawns."

I tilted my head back into the fence post and stared at the hot sky. A few small clouds sat against the blue, not moving. I waited for them to splinter and break apart with the force of my shock, but they did not. The sky stayed in place, the clouds stayed in place. The sun kept burning, white and distant. The same objects, except the world was now utterly changed, a different universe from the one in which I had existed an hour ago.

"So, then, Frau Himmelfarb," I said. "What do you propose we do to save him?"

7.

When I returned to Schloss Kleist an hour later, the house was in uproar. Frieda flew across the entrance hall and wrapped her arms around me. She was my height now, almost taller. "Oh, Mother! There you are! It's so awful!"

"What's happened?" I touched her blond hair and my ribs ached.

"It's Papa! They were playing tennis, and it was so hot, and he must have had a dizzy

spell. He fell and hit his head."

I stepped back. "Where is he now?"

"He's upstairs in bed. The doctor is coming. Oh, Mother, will he be all right?"

I was already climbing the stairs. "I certainly hope so," I muttered.

The bedroom was dark and smelled of lemon and vomit. Someone had closed the curtains. Hilda sat by the bed, holding a cloth to Johann's forehead. His eyes squinted open when I entered.

I let out a sigh. At least he was awake.

"Thank you, Hilda," I said. "I'll take care of him until the doctor arrives."

"But Frau von Kleist —"

"Don't worry, I've had some training as a nurse."

She rose from the chair and handed me the cloth, which was cool and damp and lemon-scented. I lost my breath, thinking of Monte Carlo, and dropped into the chair.

Before me, Johann tried to smile. "Hello, *mein Liebling.* Not quite so heroic a pose, I am afraid."

I picked up his hand and tried his radial pulse. A little rushed, but steady and sharp. I placed the cloth against his forehead, where a large purple bump had already risen. "You'll be all right, I think. A concussion."

The door closed behind Hilda.

Johann whispered, "You were right about tennis —"

"Never mind the tennis, Johann," I said crisply. "I am leaving you this afternoon. As soon as the doctor comes, I'm packing my things and Florian's, and I'm leaving with a friend."

Johann's eyes flared. He tried to raise his head from the pillow. I pushed him back.

"Don't. You'll hurt yourself. There's nothing you can do. Stefan's former wife came to see me today, after lunch."

"Stefan?"

"Yes, Stefan. My lover, Florian's father. But you knew that, didn't you?"

"*My* son."

"No, he's not. I spent three days with Stefan in Monte Carlo, the three happiest days of my life, and we made Florian there. And then you had Stefan arrested, and you gallantly married me while he was safe in prison, and you never said a word." I paused. "What a triumph, to take Stefan's lover and his baby, too. You must have felt so triumphant."

Johann struggled against his foggy brain. His head moved from side to side. "No. No. This is not true. I love you, I saw you first, I loved you *first,* before I even knew — before he —" He made a grunting noise.

"Don't upset yourself, Johann. You'll only make your injury worse."

"No. No. I love — love you both. Not because — Stefan —"

"Don't lie to me."

461

"True. Stefan is a criminal." He said that clearly, at least. "A murderer. Broke the *law.*"

"If you weren't hurt, I would smack you. I would bloody murder *you.* Do you know what you've done?"

"He broke the law!"

"Stop it. Just stop it. He may have broken the law, but his cause was just. At least he was *doing* something about this horrible situation, while you sat back and said, *Ja, ja, the people will come to their senses.* You had him arrested and thrown in prison, and then you went home and tucked Stefan's baby son into his crib, and then you took me to bed and you screwed me good and hard, didn't you? What a goddamned thrill that must have been for you."

He removed the cloth from his head and dropped it on the rug. He said, in his thready, stunned voice, "What is this? What are you saying? *You.* You went back to him. My heart broke."

"No, I didn't. We hardly even touched each other, did you know that? I admit, I went to see him, but we never even kissed. I loved him so, and I never so much as kissed him. And then I thought about running away with him, and I came home and you were there with Florian and darling Frieda, and I knew I couldn't do that to you. You asked me to forgive you, and I was so full of guilt and shame. I thought it wasn't your fault, and

you had tried so hard, you had given me so much when I needed you, and now you needed me. So I gave him up and went back to you. My God, what a fool, what an utter fool. I actually said to myself, *It's not his fault, he's a good man, I have to find a way to love him.* To *love* you!" I was crying now, beating my fist on the counterpane next to Johann's beefy leg. "I am such a fool."

"Annabelle. Please." He started forward and I jumped back from the bed, wiping my face.

"Don't you dare. It *is* your fault. It *was* your fault, and I'm leaving you. I'm taking Florian and going to find a way to get Stefan out of prison, and if you dare to stop me, I'll find a way to ruin you. I'll tell Frieda what you did. I will blacken your name across Europe. Florian will curse you all his life. Do you understand me?" I shouted.

Johann's head fell back. The door rattled with a loud knock, and an instant later it flung open to reveal the shocked doctor. "Frau von Kleist!" he hissed.

"I'm sorry." I swiped my cheeks. "I will leave you to your examination, Herr *Doktor*."

PEPPER
A1A 1966

1.

The backseat of a Ford Thunderbird isn't designed for a heavily pregnant woman to lie back and take a nap, plaster-wrapped foot and all, but Pepper's too pooped to care. Besides, up front are Florian and Susan, and Susan's resting against Florian's shoulder, and that's really not a sight for sore eyes, is it?

So she curls on her side, facing the slick leather back of the front seat, and enjoys the disembodied rush of the automobile as it consumes forty miles an hour of the black highway, the old faithful A1A that connects the extreme barrier coast of Florida with the rest of the Eastern seaboard. Florian looked at the map and said they should be there by morning, and Pepper believes him. He said they could pick up the interstate in Daytona Beach, save a lot of time. Pretty soon the interstate would reach all the way down to Miami, imagine that. You could drive the length of Florida in less than a day.

464

Florian's voice drifts over the seat. "How are you doing back there? Asleep?"

"I'm all right."

"Comfortable?"

"I've slept in worse places."

He laughs, nice and throaty, and Pepper just closes her eyes and enjoys the male sound. The car hums underneath, a reliable American engine, eating the open road. If only she could fall asleep.

"Is Susan awake?"

"Nope. Out like a light. My arm went numb a few miles back." He pauses. "You should try to sleep."

"Can't. You know how it is."

Another handsome chuckle. "Yeah, I guess so."

The leather sticks to her cheek. She licks her lips and thinks about telling him the whole story. Getting this fear off her chest and onto his. After all, she's concerning herself in *his* beeswax, isn't she? It's only fair.

Because it's not as if his opinion of her morals can sink any lower.

But her lips remain closed, and it's Florian who speaks into the midnight quiet, almost as if he heard her regardless.

"I've got another personal question for you, Schuyler."

She sighs. "Some men never learn."

"Is everything okay with you?"

Pepper licks her lips again. "Peachy keen."

His shoulder has apparently had enough of its tender burden. He shuffles about, adjusting Susan's weight to a more convenient location. She murmurs protest and then goes quiet. "I've been thinking," he says.

"Not that again."

"Pepper, if you're in trouble of some kind . . ."

Pepper laughs.

"I mean other than the obvious. Are you?"

Her foot hurts. She forgot to take the painkiller before they left, and now there's a dull ache that surrounds her like a bandage right at the arch, and is now starting to creep its way into her ankle. She tries to move the foot more comfortably, but the cast is too heavy, and she's too tired. "What makes you say that?"

"Oh, I don't know. The letter I gave you. The way you changed your mind about coming along with us."

"Oh, that? I just decided the two of you needed a responsible chaperone."

"So listen," says Florian quietly, so she has to strain her ears to hear him. "I'm going to make a little confession here, because I want you to trust me, all right? That's how it works, according to the shrinks. An exchange of trust. I tell you something I'd rather keep secret, and then afterward you maybe feel like you can do the same."

"What if I don't trust shrinks?"

"That's all right. I'll say it anyway." He pauses, and Pepper guesses they're passing someone, because his dark head moves and his profile appears as he checks the road behind, and then the engine roars happily and the car makes a lateral shift. He continues, when the machine returns to its ordinary purr: "I guess you could say I had a little thing going for you, this past year."

As declarations go, it's a simple one. Once, when Pepper was in college, a boy sent her a bouquet of roses attached to a love sonnet attached to a diamond bracelet. She sent back the flowers and the poem but kept the diamonds. (No, she didn't! But she was tempted.) This is no bouquet, no handwritten sonnet, no string of costly jewels. But the clean and simple lines of *I had a little thing going for you,* spoken in Florian's assured voice, achieve what no passionate paragraphs did before: they make Pepper cry. Just a little, from the corner of her left eye, dripping past the bridge of her nose and into the no-man's-land of what-might-have-been.

"Only a little one? I must be losing my touch."

"Look, considering you didn't know I even existed, you should be grateful for what you've got."

"Fair enough."

"Anyway, that was my fault. The thing is, you knocked me off the rails when I first saw

467

you. I'd heard about you before — everyone was raving about Pepper Schuyler — and to be honest, I take a little pride in not falling for the girl that everyone else is falling for. But *you.*"

"But me?"

"You. You have a way of casting a spell. I guess you know that. You're like one of those attractor beams."

"Oh, that's right. Leading all you poor helpless men to your doom."

"No, but it wasn't just that." A pause. "You know, the thing about sirens, they make you think there's this extraordinary creature behind the lights and music, but when you yank away the drapes there's nothing to see. But you were the opposite. You were at a party, holding court, and I swear I heard you quote two or three different Enlightenment philosophers in a single fucking sentence, and not one of those idiots listening to you had any idea what you just did."

"Well, you know what they say. Law is wasted on the lawyers."

"Yeah, well, that's what I thought. That you were wasted on that crowd."

Pepper doesn't reply. Susan stirs a little, maybe at the animation in Florian's voice, and then drops back off. When he speaks again, his tone is softer.

"Did you ever think about going to law school yourself?"

She lets out a sharp laugh. "Daddy wouldn't let me. Well, specifically, he wasn't going to pay for it, and I didn't want to have to earn my degree on my back."

"Neanderthal."

"Now, now. That's my father you're maligning." She props her head up on her elbow and studies the back of his head, a round silhouette in the glow of the headlamps ahead. "So if you were so crazy about me, why didn't you try your luck?"

He shrugs. "Because you were already in love with someone else. But I *was* crazy about you. I admit it. I thought, That girl is throwing herself away. She could do so much better if she just . . ."

"Just what?"

"Slowed down for a moment. Realized there's more to life than sex appeal. More to *you* than sex appeal."

"Well, you're wrong there. Not much inside."

"The hell there isn't," he snaps, and Susan grunts. He repeats it more softly. "The hell there isn't, Pepper."

The car finds a bump on the road, and Pepper's heavy body jolts against the cushion. She puts out her arm and braces it on the front seat.

"Sorry," says Florian.

"No harm."

"Anyway, I guess I'm just trying to say that

I know a little more than you think. That maybe I could help you, if you let me."

Pepper asks, "What made you stop?"

"Stop? Stop what?"

"Being crazy about me."

Florian drives silently, without replying. Pepper reaches for the crank and rolls down the window a couple inches. The breeze is chillier than she expects, but it's a small price to pay for some goddamned air. The draft ripples loudly in her ears, but she still picks out the words when Florian finally speaks, maybe because her ears are a little bit in love with the sound of his voice.

"I don't know. Maybe I didn't."

2.

At one point, they stop for gas, right about the time Pepper has finally managed to drift off to sleep. She wakes in terror, heart smacking, breath choked, and sits up to the anemic glow of a pair of streetlamps leaking through the blackness, exposing Florian as he stands underneath, leaning against the pole, watching the sleepy attendant as he pumps the gas.

There's no sign of Susan. Pepper peeks over the edge of the seat and there she is, the little darling, still sleeping, a tiny smile suspended on her rosebud mouth. Pepper crawls out on the driver's side, so as not to disturb her.

As she approaches Florian, she realizes she's dying for a cigarette. She hasn't smoked

since the third day in Cocoa Beach, when the carefully rationed pack ran dry, and she misses not so much the delirious hit of nicotine but the smell, the taste, the lazy ceremony of lighting up and drawing the smoke down your throat and into your lungs. The curls of white billowing upward, like your own thoughts traveling to heaven for inquisition.

"I don't suppose you have a smoke," she says.

His face is sallow under the lamp, his eyes deep-set and hollow, and his hands are shoved into the pockets of his dungarees. "Sorry. I quit the day my dad got diagnosed."

Damn it, Pepper thinks.

"You were pretty close?"

"Yeah. Best friends. I could tell him any-thing, things I couldn't say to Mama." He pauses. His eyes haven't shifted from the pimply young attendant, as if he's making sure the kid doesn't take off in the shiny blue T-Bird himself, sleeping Susan and all. "I have this memory of him, my earliest memory. I think it must have been when we were still in Germany. We're making paper airplanes and flying them into the fireplace, and they burst into flame. I thought it was the greatest. I thought he was the greatest."

"How old were you?"

"I guess I couldn't have been more than two." He shakes his head. "It's just a brief

memory, like a flash. But vivid, you know? I can still see that fireplace. The puffs of flame."

"Pyromaniac."

"That's what boys do. Make stuff and then destroy it." He laughs.

"You must miss him. Your father."

"Every second." He pushes away from the lamppost and digs his wallet out of his back pocket. "Looks like he's done. Is Susan awake?"

"No. I'm beginning to think that woman can sleep through an artillery bombardment."

"You can stretch your legs for a bit, if you want."

"No, I can't." She gestures to her foot.

An outraged look fills his face. "Wait a minute. Why aren't you on your crutches?"

"They're in the trunk."

He swears and reaches down to pick her up, and Pepper doesn't complain. She just holds her head virtuously away from his shoulder and thinks, This is the last time ever, scout's honor.

Hardly worth mentioning, really, but the Girl Scouts kicked Pepper out after a month. Something about sassing the scout leader.

3.

They are headed to Cumberland Island, off the southern coast of Georgia. Pepper's not quite sure what Florian expects to find there. That last letter from Harris, P.I. — the one

472

dated November 6, three days before Pepper arrived in Cocoa Beach — informed Annabelle Dommerich that she might find the contents of the enclosed newspaper article of interest as a possible lead, and he would be happy to travel to Cumberland Island to investigate in person, with her written authorization, expenses billed according to the usual arrangement.

The article itself had been removed, though the small silver paperclip remained, attaching the letter to nothing.

"It's not exactly proof," Susan said doubtfully, but Florian said it was the way the facts fit together. The only logical conclusion.

So here they are, climbing onto the brand-new interstate highway near Daytona Beach at half past two in the morning, while the Thunderbird's three hundred horses whinny in unison. Susan wakes up suddenly, lifting her head against the glow of the streetlights on the onramp. She asks where they are, and Florian says they're heading onto the interstate, they'll be in Georgia around sunrise.

All right, she says, and her head disappears again, behind the flat ledge of the front seat.

4.

When Pepper wakes up a few hours later, she's aware of two facts, and that's all: she's lying on the backseat of a car, and the car has stopped.

Her hand goes straight to her belly and finds — with relief — the strong little ball, still in place. Still there.

And then she remembers there's nothing to fear. She's escaped into the night again, just in the nick. She's headed for Georgia. A vagabond. Pepper on the run.

She sits up and looks out the window at a salmon-pink sunrise rising above the distant marsh grass. On the other side of the car lies a wide street, silent as the grave, studded with tombstone cars. Beyond, a pilloried white building glows hopefully in the dawn. The Riverview Hotel, the sign says.

"I guess we're in Georgia," she says, to no one in particular, because the front seat is empty. Which rather offends Pepper, because who leaves a pregnant woman asleep on an unknown street at dawn?

She stretches, runs her fingers through her unkempt hair, and opens the door.

Outside, it's chillier than she expected, as if they've crossed some invisible line from the endless summer of Florida into a world in which seasons existed. Pepper tucks her cardigan about her shoulders and inhales the Georgia morning. A suggestion of smoke lingers in the air, mingling with the fishiness of the nearby sea, and Pepper realizes she's standing at the edge of a glassy tidal river, that the distant marsh is actually the opposite shore, and that a modest white boat lies

474

moored to the railing, next to a sign that reads CUMBERLAND ISLAND FERRY. A figure leans back against the rightmost edge of the ferry sign, covering the last three letters. One arm crosses beneath a round bosom, while the other operates a cigarette in short and furtive strikes.

Well, well. Not so squeaky-clean after all.

Pepper reaches back in the car for her crutches and hobbles toward Susan. Her limbs are stiff and ungainly after the rocky night, and her tongue is coated in fur. Dollars to doughnuts, she looks like hell. But then Susan looks remarkably like hell, too. The skin actually sags beneath her lashes, an effect made worse by raccoonlike smears of black mascara, and her blond curls have expired. Two pretty women brought low by a night in a Ford Thunderbird.

Susan waves her cigarette. "Don't tell."

"Wouldn't dream of it."

"Want one?"

Pepper nearly says yes, and then she thinks of Florian quitting cold turkey the day his father got cancer. "I'm laying off the smokes right now. But I might just huddle around your lighter for a second to warm up."

Susan laughs. "I almost forgot what cold felt like. Florian told me to pack a jacket, but it slipped my mind. Serves me right."

"Speaking of which, where is the little devil?"

"My jacket?"

"Florian."

"Oh, he's just getting rooms, so we can rest and freshen up before the ferry leaves." The cigarette is nearly finished. She holds it between her thumb and forefinger, sucking every last drop into her pale mouth. Her skin is pink with cold, her eyes excessively blue inside their charcoal circles.

"I could use a little freshening." Pepper watches longingly as Susan drops the final crumb into the turf and crushes it under her pristine white sneaker. "And then the fun begins."

"The fun? You mean looking for Mrs. Dommerich?"

"Well, maybe *fun* isn't quite the word. Fireworks is more to the point, when Florian finds out that his dear mama is tracking down an old flame."

Susan hesitates. "Do you think so?"

"You don't agree?"

A look of wariness enters Susan's young forehead. "It could be an old school friend," she says.

"Come on, honey. We both know you're not nearly as naïve as you let on."

"Oh, I don't know." She looks down. "I guess it doesn't matter anymore, now that Mr. Dommerich is gone. I'd just hate to think she was . . . you know, that it was anything . . ."

Pepper braces the crutches under her arms and clasps her hands together. She's warmed up a little, thanks to the miniature furnace burning away inside her, but her fingers feel like numb little sausages. "You never know what's really going on in someone else's marriage."

"My mother didn't like him," Susan says. "Mr. Dommerich. She said he wasn't very pleasant. He didn't like to talk about himself. But I thought he was nice, once you got to know him. I think he was just quiet because of what happened, you know, back in Germany."

"What happened back in Germany?"

"I don't know exactly, but I always got the feeling it was something terrible. Because he wouldn't ever talk about it, wouldn't even allow any photographs in the house. Like he thought someone might, I don't know, recognize him, or something like that."

"But they got out before the war even started."

"I know. But that was just the feeling I had." She pauses. "He used to teach me German words, until my mother got upset. I think maybe they were vulgar; he had this naughty sense of humor, though you wouldn't think it at first. He seemed very proper. I called him by his first name once, Rudolf, and he looked at me like I was crazy. I was so sorry when he got sick." She eyes her pocket-

477

book, as if considering another cigarette. "He about worshipped the ground Mrs. Dommerich walked on, and you could tell she loved him back. The way they looked at each other, like they were sharing a secret. They had all these kids. Stepkids and half-siblings and full siblings. I couldn't tell half of them apart sometimes. Keep straight who was who. They were mostly older, except for the twins. They had twins after they moved to America. Margot and Lizzie. They're in college now. I only have one sister, so I loved going over there, everybody crawling over each other. She just loved taking care of them all, Mrs. Dommerich. She's one of those mother hens, you know? I don't know how she found the time for her music."

"Or anything else," murmurs Pepper.

"What's that?"

"Nothing. And you and Florian?"

"Oh, him." Her cheeks are already blushing with cold, but Pepper imagines a little more color. "Don't tell him, but I had a crush on him since I was a little kid, when he saved our beagle Molly after she got caught in the surf. He came up out of the water — it was a horrible riptide, there was a storm offshore — all dripping and handsome, and I was a goner. Isn't that the most? And he never paid the slightest bit of attention to me. I was just Margot and Lizzie's friend."

"Oh, that's just boys. Trust me, he had his

478

eye on you, a pretty thing like you."

"Well, if he did, he didn't let on for years."
She casts a hairy eyeball at the hotel entrance.
"Not until last summer. He was back for a
week or two, and he finally noticed I existed.
Asked me to dinner. I had a date with Billy
Fielder —"

"Oh, who's Billy?"

"Just a boy." She looks away. "I called Billy
up and canceled, and — well. We had a real
nice time. He kissed me good night."

"Better late than never."

"Yes, I guess so." Again with the hesitation.
Susan's such a good girl, she hates to hurt
anyone's feelings, even when they're not
around. She opens her mouth, closes it, and
discovers her pocketbook again. "It's funny,"
she says, rummaging for the cigarettes,
"nothing's ever quite what you expect, is it?
Even something you've wanted for years."

"That's life, honey."

She lights up and draws in deeply, eyes
closed. "But what am I saying? He's terrific.
He's the best. He always opens the car door
for me and gives me his jacket when it's cold
out. He said his mom made him take her out
on a date when he turned sixteen, so he
would know how to treat a lady. Don't you
love that?"

"It sounds like Annabelle, all right."

"He called me a few times when he went
back to Washington, wrote me a couple of

letters. I missed him like crazy. I thought about moving there to be with him, but Mom said no, you make them come to you. Like dogs, she said. Or was it sheep?"

"Mom is probably right. But it's easy for her to say, isn't it?"

"I'll say. Oh, shoot!" She snatches the cigarette from her mouth and drops it on the ground. "Here he comes."

"You know, he can still smell the smoke on you."

"Oh no. Do you think so?"

Pepper shrugs. "Don't worry. I'll say it was me. Just don't let him get too close until you've washed your mouth out with Listerine."

5.

But sneaky cigarettes are the last thing on Florian's mind. He strides across the parking lot like a warrior advancing over enemy territory, and from the wattage of his eyes, Pepper guesses it's news. Good or bad?

"She's here," he says. "*Was* here. Right here at this hotel."

Pepper scans the street for a vintage black Mercedes, a pearl among swine. "*Was* here? So where is she now?"

"On the island. Cumberland Island, like we guessed. She took the ferry out yesterday."

"And she's still there?" Susan's words

emerge in a cloud of guilty cinnamon Den-tyne.

"They don't know. That's the thing. She never checked out of the hotel. She didn't take a suitcase or anything. But . . ." Florian holds his hand up to his brow and turns to stare at the boat moored beside them, and he looks like he's forty years old, just like that. He looks as old as God.

"But?" Pepper says softly.

He turns not to Susan, but to Pepper, and his eyes are like two brown stones. "But when the last ferry came in, she wasn't on it."

ANNABELLE
GERMANY 1938

1.

At the top of the entrance gate to the prisoner's camp at Dachau, the iron formed into the words ARBEIT MACHT FREI.

"In English, it means, literally, *Work makes freedom*," said the man next to me, with conspicuous pride. "Though perhaps it is more usefully translated as *Work will make you free.* You will find, Frau von Kleist, that all our prisoners are kept occupied with honest and wholesome labor, for the great progress of the Reich."

"So my husband tells me."

The September sun shone white on my face. Underneath my neat suit of light blue wool, I was dripping with perspiration, though the morning was still cool. I followed the officer through the gate, past the barbed wire and the ominous empty strip of land overlooked by the tower. The officer was explaining how perfectly secure the camp was, how I had nothing to fear. There were

sharpshooters in the top of that tower, guns already cocked, eyes and muzzles trained on any movement. A prisoner had no chance of escape.

"What if he were to dig a tunnel of some sort?" I asked.

The officer shook his head and told me this was impossible, that every prisoner was required to strip naked and relinquish everything in his possession upon entry into the camp. He was then issued a striped uniform and a number. Unless this prisoner were to dig with his bare fingers — here the officer laughed — he would have no capability for such a project.

"Besides," he went on, "that is why we keep them occupied with physical labor during the day. They have no thought of anything but sleep at night."

Of course, I said. How clever.

2.

We toured the various buildings — the infirmary, the canteen, the camp offices — and saw the gray-striped prisoners shuffling about the laundry. The interiors were spotless and smelled of lye and disinfectant. Lieutenant Helmbrecht repeated at intervals what an honor it was to have the general's wife inspect the camp, and how he hoped I appreciated the genius of its design and operation, its remarkable efficiency. While the

483

SS were of course in charge, the prisoners actually ran the camp themselves, organizing into work details and operating the laundry and the library and the infirmary. Work and responsibility, sobriety and industry: these were the pathways to rehabilitation. The new complex had just been opened last month, a model for future camps. The lieutenant was young and fair and high-pitched with enthusiasm, a bit like Frieda describing the day's tennis. I complimented him on his exact knowledge of the camp, his thorough attention to his duty. He blushed and consulted his watch.

"It is nearly time for the midday prisoner muster, Frau von Kleist," he said. "May I have the honor of presenting this spectacle to you? I assure you, it is perfectly safe. The prisoners would not dare to step from line."

I said I would enjoy that very much.

3.

"Tell me more about your prisoners," I said, as we walked toward the beaten rectangle of the assembly area. Lieutenant Helmbrecht's leather boots had taken on a film of dust, dulling their shine, but they still struck impressively on the ground. He kept his hands folded behind his back as he walked.

"They are divided into two groups at present," he said. "The political prisoners, who are classified by a red badge, and the criminal

ones, who wear green. Here we have mostly the political prisoners, because that is the purpose of building these camps: a place to hold these dangerous men without overburdening the state prisons."

"Are they ever released?"

"Very rarely, I am afraid. The tendency to sedition and agitation is a chronic condition. If released, they will simply continue their criminal activities against the state." Lieutenant Helmbrecht shook his head in a way that suggested profound regret. "I have often wondered if there is some mental weakness or disorder associated with this tendency."

"A fascinating theory, Lieutenant Helmbrecht. I shouldn't be at all surprised."

We came to a halt at the edge of the assembly ground, where long lines of men in striped clothes were filing into order, a strange sort of convict army. Like soldiers, except they were not. Like trailing ants, except they were men.

I thought, He's here, Stefan is here. One of these men is Stefan.

At the outset, I had conveyed to the lieutenant and the camp authorities that my German was limited, but this was a lie. In fact, I'd spent many hours dedicating myself to the study of my husband's native language since our reconciliation last year. Johann had been so pleased. He helped me practice, pointed out the nuances of *Sie* and *Du.* He

said that he hoped I would be able to converse with his friends, to see that there was nothing to fear, that good people and good intentions prevailed in Germany. I never had that opportunity, but I could listen now as the commands rang around the muster grounds. I could understand what was happening. The prisoners stood in line, wearing identical striped uniforms and caps. The ones with the green badges stood to the right, and the ones with red badges stood to the left; the red badges far outnumbered the green. Each row lay in a precise line, separated from the others by the same distance. I gazed across the rows of gray-striped limbs, the expressionless faces beneath the caps, and I thought, in panic, I will never find him; this is impossible.

Lieutenant Helmbrecht turned to me. "There are four thousand two hundred and five prisoners in total, of which —"

"May I walk down the rows? My husband is a humanitarian, Lieutenant Helmbrecht, and he instructed me specifically to examine the condition of the prisoners."

"But Frau von Kleist, I assure you we take the strictest care of these men. The prisoners themselves are in charge of their own governance. We watch continually for signs of infection, and sickness is quarantined at the first symptom. There is an infirmary, staffed by the prisoners themselves, those who were

employed in the medical profession —"

"And I confess, I'm a little curious about these incorrigible criminals, and how thoroughly you have managed to subdue their dangerous tendencies. I'm eager to report to my husband how brilliantly Dachau fulfills its mission, and whether any of its techniques can be copied at the other camps."

Lieutenant Helmbrecht's young cheeks turned a little pink. "Of course, Frau von Kleist."

He shouted a command to one of the guards, who stepped forward and accompanied us down the first row of prisoners. The red badges were vivid against the gray and white of their uniforms, as if an artist had tinted some aspect of a monochrome photograph for visual effect. Each face was fixed with the same expression of neutral hatred, and as I walked down the row, sweeping my gaze along the procession of cheekbones and gaunt eyes, I realized that the Nazis had won: I could not tell these men apart. Everyone was thin, everyone was striped, every face matched the other. You hardly noticed who was tall and who was short. You didn't see the cropped hair hidden under the striped cap. You saw no difference in complexion between one sunburn and another.

"Excellent," I said to Lieutenant Helmbrecht, as we came to the end of the row.

"Thank you, Frau von Kleist."

I looked again across the rows and columns, which were so exactly spaced that from where I stood, at the diagonal, the men formed yet another straight line. They must have drilled them this way, all day in the hot summer, until they got it right. And Stefan had lived here for a year. All year, last summer and autumn, the bitterness of winter and spring and summer again, he had worn his striped uniform and stood out here while the sun shone and the wind blew and the snow fell.

Where was he?

Do something, I thought. Show me where you are. You must know it's me. You must know why I'm here.

And as I gazed across the motionless lines of men, doing my best to appear pleased with what I saw, I realized that he would not. Of course he would not. Stefan would open his own veins before he would allow me to risk myself for his sake.

I put my gloved hand on Lieutenant Helmbrecht's shoulder and let out a little cry.

"Frau von Kleist!"

"I'm just — oh, dear — the sun —"

I sagged to the ground, and as I did I caught the motion of one single man stepping reflexively out of line, some distance to the left, at the edge of a row about halfway down the column.

4.

I protested that I was quite all right, just a passing dizziness, but Lieutenant Helmbrecht insisted that we head to the infirmary and see the doctor. He took my elbow and led me down the center aisle, and I clutched my hat to my head and watched the faces stream by, until we had gone halfway down and I saw them, as if they were magnets: a pair of hard caramel eyes trying not to find me.

"Lieutenant Helmbrecht! Wait a moment!"

"Yes, Frau von Kleist?"

"That man there! I think — I'm not sure —"

"Is something wrong?"

"No, no." I went on, stopped, and turned again. "No, I must examine him."

"Why, what's the matter?"

"Has he been seen by a doctor recently?"

"All our prisoners are under the close supervision of the barracks government. If any symptoms of sickness are detected, they are immediately referred to the infirmary." He trailed just behind me, grasping at my elbow, but I was marching like a nurse now and would not be grasped. Stefan's neck beckoned ahead, sunburned instead of white, dark hair cropped so short it was only a shadow at the bottom of his cap, but this time it was really his. It was Stefan, really Stefan, a few yards away. In a few seconds, I would

489

be touching him.

"I am a trained nurse, Lieutenant Helmbrecht, and I am quite sure I saw symptoms of typhoid in that man."

At the word *typhoid,* the lieutenant stopped short. I went on, turning down the correct row, and then I stopped before Stefan. Or rather, an apparition who resembled Stefan: too brown and bony and empty to be the man who had faced me on a fourth-floor bed of the Paris Ritz and laid his finger across my lips. The scar shone white against his sunburn. On his chest, the red triangle-shaped badge bore a number I couldn't quite read.

"How lucky I am wearing my gloves." I touched the corner of his eye, which was pleading with me.

"Frau von Kleist!" exclaimed the lieutenant.

"Oh, dear," I said. "This is very serious. How are you feeling, prisoner?"

"Get the hell out of here," Stefan muttered in English.

"I see. Very bad indeed. Let me see your palm."

I took his hand and turned it over. His palm was scarred and blistered. I ran my finger over the lines. "Have you had any episodes of rash, prisoner? Dizziness and headache?"

"Please go."

I gave him back his hand, but not before I had slipped a capsule from the inside of my

490

glove and placed it in the center of his palm. His fingers swallowed it at once. "Take this at once," I said in English, and then I turned to the lieutenant, who stood at the end of the row, barking at the terrified prisoners to get back in line.

"Lieutenant, it is as I feared. He can hardly stand. He is almost delirious. He must go the infirmary at once for treatment, before he infects the entire camp."

"My God!" said Lieutenant Helmbrecht. He turned to the guard who hovered next to him. "Take that prisoner to the infirmary at once."

The guard, horrified, stepped down the line and took Stefan's elbow. He threw me a last look of shocked understanding and staggered forward. As he did so, his hand came up to his mouth.

"You see?" I said. "He is falling on his feet. You may need an orderly and a stretcher." I bent down to help him up and whispered in English, as we rose together: *Be ready.*

The guard took back Stefan's elbow and forced him down the row. The prisoners stepped back in horror as we went, covering their mouths. I walked a pace or two behind and watched the back of Stefan's neck as it bobbed and slumped like the neck of a man on the brink of collapse. I thought for an instant of Tosca, instructing her Mario to play his part well, to convince the guards he had

really been shot, and then I remembered that this was real, that I had actually done this, that I was actually walking down this row of prisoners at Dachau under the September sunshine, hoping I had not just given Stefan a death sentence.

"Well," I said to Lieutenant Helmbrecht, when the prisoners were dismissed and the assembly ground returned to peace, "how very fortunate for you that I am a trained nurse. Of course, these gloves should be burned at once."

5.

The rain arrived at sunset two days later, and by the time we reached the crossroads and parked the car on the grass, it rattled against the windshield as if it never meant to stop. Wilhelmine opened her window an inch or so and lit a cigarette. "Now we wait," she said.

I turned my head to glance into the back-seat, where Florian lay in a deep sleep underneath his favorite blanket. We had left the Himmelfarbs' house near Stuttgart an hour ago, when the telephone call had arrived at last, and had bundled Florian inside without even waking him. He had stirred but never opened his eyes, having spent the entire day playing outside with his half-sister, Else. At one point I had gone out to take him in for his nap, but Wilhelmine had stopped me. Let them play, she said. They may not get

another chance.

"Don't say that."

She had shrugged and leaned forward to wipe the mess from Henrik's mouth. He was sitting in his high chair, and she had been feeding him peas. "Matthias refuses to leave. He says he will not let Hitler drive him away like a dog."

"It's common sense, though. You can't keep fighting when everyone is against you."

"Not everyone in Germany is like Hitler, Annabelle. Most of my neighbors, they are disgusted."

"But they won't speak up, will they? Which is worse, I think. Look at my husband. He never believed in all the Nazi propaganda, but he went along with them, he did everything they asked, because he's afraid to do anything else."

She laughed. "Can you blame him? Did you not see what they have done to Stefan?" When I didn't reply, she went on. "Anyway, I think you are wrong about von Kleist. He is not bad. He is simply a man of duty, that is all. I mean, there is no doubt that Stefan broke the law, that he killed a Gestapo agent and all these things. He killed that agent with his bare hands, and maybe the man was a bad man, maybe he wanted to arrest Stefan and put him in prison, but he was still a man who had a wife and three children, I believe. So it was your husband's duty to hunt down

493

the man who had killed this agent, and by God he did."

"You can't possibly be excusing him."

"No, not exactly. But I think I understand him. And I will tell you this: I even think, if I were you, I would rather be married to a von Kleist than to a Stefan. I would pick the steady sun over the starburst."

"But he *is* the sun. Stefan is the sun."

She shook her head.

I put my hand on her arm. "Wilhelmine, you've got to leave. You can't stay here."

"And where would we go? Germany is our home. Everywhere it is like this, really. There is nowhere we are safe. There is no country on earth that will open its arms and shout, *Welcome, Jews!* Even in America, you cannot get a visa anymore unless you are a millionaire or a personal friend of Mr. Roosevelt, or I suppose if you are Albert fucking Einstein."

How could I answer her?

We had sat in silence, except for the sound of Henrik eating his peas, until Wilhelmine removed the bowl and lifted him out of his chair to rest on her shoulder. "So we will take our chances, as always. Like our fathers and mothers did before us."

I had muddled over her words for hours, and I muddled over them now, watching the rain track down the windshield. There was just enough moon to see the road nearby, to

see the shadows of the trees and mountains around us. Wilhelmine tucked her feet up underneath her on the seat and smoked quietly, tipping the ash out the crack in the window. She had been to university in Stuttgart — that was where she met Matthias — and studied English and history, and she carried about her an air of trouser-wearing worldliness that saturated her skin. I thought Stefan was a fool for letting her go, and that maybe he loved me because I was her opposite. I did not believe in a perverse universe. I didn't believe in fate, except for the one that bound me to Stefan.

"I think you are right," Wilhelmine replied, when I said this thought aloud, a little more delicately. "He was never in love with me. We had some attraction, but I could not satisfy something in him. And he drove me crazy. Always restless, always wanting to change things. *Why can you not stay home with your wife and your daughter?* I shouted to him. *Why do you have to go out and pinch the nose of the fucking Gestapo?* And he said that someone had to." She dropped the cigarette stub outside the window and put her arms around her legs. "I said there was no object. He was going to get killed for no object at all."

"Then why are you risking yourself for him now?"

"Because I am an idiot, Annabelle." She

picked up her cigarette case from the seat between us. "Anyway, it is the last time. He is your problem now."

"But what about Else? He'll want to see her."

"Then he should not have got himself arrested by the Gestapo, should he?"

I asked if she would let me have a cigarette, and she laughed and lit one for each of us. The smoke burned my lungs, but after a minute or two I noticed my nerves settle, one by one, as if they were being put to bed by a comforting hand. I held the cigarette in front of my eyes and examined it. "It's not so bad."

"I expect they will kill me one day, but I don't care enough to stop. Just don't have a second one, and you will be safe."

A light appeared in the darkness ahead. Wilhelmine straightened in her seat. "Okay, now. If that is not the ambulance, you let me do the talking, all right?"

I coughed, put out the cigarette, and said: "You know, your English is really very good."

"Eh. I used to watch a lot of American movies."

The light resolved through the gloom into a pair of headlamps. "It's big enough," said Wilhelmine. Her fingers tapped the steering wheel. A few more damp seconds passed, and then: "It's them."

The air inside the car was like a cigarette fog. I realized I couldn't breathe. I opened

up the door and set my foot into the soggy turf. "Wait," said Wilhelmine, but I was already walking through the rain to the approaching headlamps, waving my arms, sucking the wet October night into my lungs.

Wilhelmine caught up with me an instant later. "You fool," she said.

"You told me it was them."

The glare grew larger and hurt my eyes. I stepped back and she caught my arm. "I might be wrong."

The brakes squeaked softly through the drumming rain. A man jumped out of the gray cab almost before the truck stopped. Wilhelmine called to him: *Bellende Hunde!*

Beissen nicht, he replied.

Wilhelmine turned to me. "All right. Let's get the bastard out."

The driver set the brake and opened the door, swearing at the rain. Wilhelmine and I were already dashing to the back of the truck with the first man. He swung the doors open and I hoisted myself onto the bed, slipping and streaming, calling out Stefan's name.

"It's no use," said the driver. "He's either asleep or delirious, or both."

I flung out my arms and found a warm body on a stretcher. *Stefan,* I said.

He muttered a word.

I ran my hands up his torso until I found his hair, hot and dry, like kindling. I fell to my knees next to the stretcher and cradled

his head in my palms, brushing his shorn hair, kissing his cheeks. I whispered to him that I was here, Annabelle was here, he was safe, I would never leave him again.

6.

Stefan's fever broke two days later, right on schedule. He opened his eyes and asked first for a cigarette and then for coffee. I put the cigarette in his mouth and lighted it, and his eyes widened with pleasure.

"Where did you get these?"

"I wired my father in Paris and had him send them."

"You will go to heaven one day."

"I'm already there, Stefan." I kissed his forehead and went to make coffee.

7.

When I returned with the coffee, I led in Florian by the hand. Stefan turned his head toward us, and his face, already stark, went rigid with shock. He stubbed out the cigarette.

"I was going to wait," I said, "but he's really too young to leave alone."

Stefan took a long time putting out his cigarette. When he lifted his eyes from the ashtray, they were wet.

I set down the coffee and lifted Florian into my arms. "He's yours," I said.

"I know."

Florian held a biscuit in one hand. His hair, always unruly, spilled into his forehead. He stared curiously at Stefan and then turned to me. "Is he sick?"

"Yes, darling. Stefan is a little sick. But he'll be up and about in no time, and you two will have such fun together."

Florian turned this over in his head and looked back at Stefan. "Ride horses."

"Yes, you can ride horses if you like."

"Papa ride horses."

"Yes. Papa rides horses, too."

In the bed, Stefan held very still, watching his son's lips as he spoke. His knuckles were white around the edge of the blankets. I carried Florian with me to the chair next to the nightstand and sat down.

"I thought it was so obvious," I said, "but everyone just thinks he looks like me, because he has dark hair and brown eyes."

"Yes, I know."

"How do you know?"

"Because I would watch you two in the Tuileries, when you went for your walk and your ice cream."

"What?"

Florian struggled in my arms. I set him down and he ran to the window, zooming his toy airplane in an arc above his head. Stefan watched him go. "That was why I came to Paris, Annabelle. The real reason. I could keep myself away from you because I knew

this was the right thing, but I had to see my son. I had to know what he looked like."

"You *knew*?"

"I am not stupid, Annabelle." He was still watching Florian zoom about the room on his sturdy legs, and the expression on his battered face was so warm and tender I had to look away. "I never meant to disturb you, I swear it. But then I saw you together, and you were so beautiful, and he was so beautiful, and I thought this very dangerous thought. I thought, Please God, let me just speak to her once and set us both to rest. I swore to God I would not fall into temptation." He shook his head. "Obviously I am not to be trusted."

I took his hand. "I am so glad you did. If you hadn't, we wouldn't be together now."

"No, this is true."

"So you see? I was right after all."

"About what, Annabelle?"

"The perverse universe."

He would not stop looking at Florian, following Florian around the floor, and his eyes were still warm and tender, but a little mournful, too, turned down at the corners like a dog that doesn't hope for much. "Yes, you were right," he said softly.

8.

Stefan drank his coffee and watched Florian play, while I made some toast and brought a

few toys into the bedroom.

"I suppose I should ask where we are," he said.

"We're on Lake Konstanz, in a house owned by Matthias's family. Wilhelmine's husband, though he wasn't very happy about it."

"Ah. I suppose Wilhelmine helped you with all this."

"Yes, she did. She found men to forge papers and then find an ambulance. I came up with the plan, though."

"A very good plan. You almost had me fooled. Maybe a little risky, though."

"I'm sorry you had to suffer, but we had little choice except to trick them somehow."

"May I ask what was in that capsule you gave me?"

"It was a weakened form of the typhoid bacterium. One of Wilhelmine's university friends got it for us. He works in a medical research laboratory. I think it's an experiment of some kind, but I had to take the risk, and he assured me it wouldn't kill you."

"Ah, very clever. So you gave me this pill and waited for the symptoms to take effect, and then you waited until they made the decision to transfer me to a hospital?"

"No, that was the clever part. Charles helped me with that. He knew a doctor at the military hospital in Frankfurt. He had him call up the camp and say that they'd heard

there was this case, and could they please send you over for trial of an experimental medication? And of course the doctor in the infirmary said yes, because first of all he is a prisoner, too, and second, we had sent him a message in a shipment of aspirin, and third, he gets along very well with the camp commandant."

"My brilliant Annabelle. This must have taken a great deal of planning. How did your husband never suspect?"

I glanced at Florian and lowered my voice. "I left Johann in August, Stefan. You see, I didn't know. I had no idea he was the one who had you arrested. Wilhelmine told me, and I took Florian and left him that day."

I delivered this information like a thunderbolt, but Stefan only gazed back at me with quiet eyes, unmoved.

"And all this time, he has not tried to find you?"

"No. He had a concussion playing tennis, that same afternoon. He couldn't stop me."

"Not then, no. But he could have sent somebody. He commands an army, not just the official one but an unofficial army, too. You have no idea how much power he has. He could at least have told the officials at Dachau to be prepared for a possible escape by me."

I opened my mouth and closed it again.

Stefan leaned back into his pillow. His face

was pale beneath his sunburn. He must have lost fifty pounds since I saw him last; the bones were so prominent on his face, everything sharp and drawn. I had seen bruises and scars on his body, as I washed and dressed him, and I had cried over them. But what alarmed me most was the expression in his eyes. The hollowed-out glassiness, as if he were staring into another universe.

"So," he said. "It seems the good Johann has let us both go."

"But that's impossible."

"On the contrary. It is the only possible reason I am lying here in this bed next to you and my son. I wonder whether he has discovered a tender spot for me after all, or whether I owe all this to his love for you."

I seized Stefan's hand. "He doesn't love me, not the way you do. Not the way I love you. He loves me as an object, as an ornament. As a substitute for his first wife."

"No, he is very much in love with you for yourself, Annabelle, and I have never blamed him for that. I am guilty of the same crime."

I laid my head next to his on the pillow and stared at the white scar that trailed down the side of his face. "What have they done to you?" I whispered.

"My dear and innocent love. You do not really want to know."

9.

I brought my cot into Stefan's room and slept with Florian there, so we could be a family. By the next day, Stefan was taking a few steps out of bed. He went to the window first, and looked across the autumn trees to the distant lake. "I presume we are on the German side still," he said.

"Yes. I didn't dare cross over while you were unconscious, and anyway, Matthias said it would be better to wait a few weeks, until the alarm fades. But I have papers for you. We can cross whenever you like. Or we can take our chances with a boat on the lake, but Matthias says it's risky, there are guards everywhere these days."

"Very wise of Matthias."

For some reason, he looked taller in his new gauntness. His wide and fleshless shoulders stuck out like the arms of a clothes hanger. I hadn't shaved him, and his beard bristled from his chin. I put my arms around his waist. "We'll go to Monte Carlo and take the *Isolde* to Capri. We'll have our vineyard at last. We'll give Florian a sister and a brother and teach them how to press the grapes and the olives."

"This is a tempting picture."

"It's our picture, and it will be real. I'm going to drown you with my love, Stefan, and make you all better."

He braced one hand against the windowsill.

"I had better return to bed, then, and get my rest."

10.

The weather continued warm. Back in America, they would have called it an Indian summer, but here in the Alpine foothills it was just a pleasant warm autumn, crisp in the mornings, bright with foliage. After a few days, I brought Stefan outside, where he played with Florian on the lawn. I told Florian not to be rough, that Stefan had been very sick and needed his strength.

"What have you told him?" Stefan asked, lighting a cigarette as Florian went off to play with the croquet set he'd unearthed in the shed.

"Nothing, yet. He was very fond of Johann. I don't want to confuse him, and anyway, if we tell him you're his father instead, he might resent you. We'll know when the time is right."

"You are a good mother."

"You'll make a wonderful pair, once you get to know each other."

"I already know him. I know him like I know my own palm. Whether he will appreciate *me* is another matter." He lay back on the grass and stared at the blue sky. "It is a lovely autumn."

"Yes, it is."

I lay back next to him and took his hand.

"Thank you for my son," he said.

"You're welcome."

11.

Matthias Himmelfarb's summer house was not especially large, but it was comfortable and well loved, smelling of pine and a hint of camphor against the moths. There were four bedrooms upstairs — we slept in the largest one — and two ancient bathrooms, one of which connected to the master bedroom. Downstairs, there was a kitchen and an informal dining room, a living room, a small library, and a sunroom. A pair of small bedrooms communicated with the kitchen, for the use of the maids. They were both empty, of course, and twice a week I took the car into the village and collected groceries, which I cooked myself, not very expertly. *Eat,* I told Stefan, and he ate, but as a matter of duty, not because he was hungry.

You don't understand, he told me. I do not know what to do with a large meal anymore.

I threatened to hire a cook if he didn't eat more, and so he did eat more, mouthful after mouthful, a forced march of nutrition. His face filled out a little. One evening he asked if there was any wine, so I brought back a few bottles from the village the next day, and we drank them both together that evening, after Florian was in bed, and promptly fell

506

asleep on the sofa. When I woke up, he was gone.

I sat up in panic, but he was only standing by the window, staring at the lake, which was pregnant with a whole silver moon. *You frightened me, running off like that,* I said, and he told me not to worry; he couldn't sleep, that was all.

"Why not?"

"There is too much in my head now, love."

"Then push it out. Let me inside instead. I can make you sleep."

"Ah, Annabelle."

We stood next to the silver window, staring and staring.

"You are such a fool, Annabelle. You should have stayed with him."

"What are you talking about? I couldn't stay with him."

"You deserve better than me. I smoke and drink and fornicate, all to excess."

"Yes, but only with me. Our covenant, remember?"

"Yes, I remember. And all this time, I have been true to this covenant and its commandments. Can you believe that?" He laughed. "But then I have not had much opportunity, and we have seen how little I am to be trusted with a beautiful woman."

"Only with *me.* You can't be trusted with *me.*"

He sighed, as if acknowledging a religious

truth. "Only with you, Mademoiselle. If that is what you want from me."

I knelt before him and pulled the drawstring of his pajamas.

This is what I want from you.

Annabelle, no, he said, but his hands went to my hair and he leaned back against the window with a sigh that was more like a groan. After a moment, he whispered, *You have not ever done this thing before, have you?*

I said I hadn't, that he would have to show me what to do.

Ah, no, you will kill me, he said, but his hands were already guiding me, his bony hips were already moving in rhythm with me, and it was like the dream I had, the first night I spent in his bed, except that the adulterous woman kneeling between his legs at the window, enjoying the clutch of his fingers in her dark hair, was me. Was Annabelle von Kleist.

He lasted only a minute or two, and when he finished, he could not stop shuddering. He sank onto the hard floor with me and wept into my hair, and we didn't say anything. Not a single word. Just holding each other, until we fell asleep.

12.

I woke up the next morning in bed, nestled inside the skeletal curve of Stefan's body, and his smell and touch were so familiar, it was

as if the past three years hadn't existed. I opened my eyes in joy, expecting to find a Mediterranean sunrise.

Instead, I saw Florian's empty cot.

I bolted upright. "Florian!"

"He's all right. I gave him a little breakfast. He is reading some books in the library. I can hear him from here."

"But he can't read yet."

"He does not seem to accept this limitation."

I smiled. "Like his father."

"I would say, like his mother."

Stefan lay flat on his back, watching me from the pillow. His pajamas were buttoned primly to the neck. He had begun shaving his beard as soon as he could walk to the bathroom, and the flesh on his jaw was now a little thicker, a little more substantial. I touched it with my finger.

"We have a son."

"Yes, Mademoiselle. A wonderful son."

I lay back down on my side, pressing against him. "Don't look so somber. It's over. We're safe."

"Not quite safe. We are still in Germany."

"We can cross the border whenever you like. You should grow your beard or a mustache first, though, and maybe let your hair lengthen a bit."

"I suppose that is sensible."

He reached for his cigarettes, but I lifted

myself across his chest and stopped his hand.

"How busy is Florian?" I said softly.

"Not busy enough, I think."

"We can be very quiet."

He reached again for the cigarette case. "You are a very reckless woman, Annabelle von Kleist, and always have been."

I took the case from his hand and plucked out a cigarette. They weren't like ordinary ones you bought from a drugstore or a newsagent; they were long and wrapped in brown paper, like a cigar. I slipped one between his lips and lit him up myself. "I won't let you do this, Stefan."

"Do what?"

"I won't let you barricade me outside your skin."

"I am not barricading you."

"Yes, you are. You don't want me in. You think I'll be appalled at what I find there, and you're wrong. I already know what's inside you. I've already been inside your skin, remember?"

"You have no idea, Annabelle, no possible idea what is inside me now."

"It doesn't matter. That's the point of having this thing, this rare and perfect thing we share. Whatever is in you, it's mine. You're mine. You can't resist me, so you might as well stop fighting and let me back in."

He turned his face to one side and let out a long stream of Turkish smoke, but his eyes

didn't leave me. He was thinking about the night before — I knew he was, I could see the tiny reflection of the memory as it reeled behind his eyes — and what I had done to him before the window. The brief moment of his resurrection, the instant of hope.

I took his face in my hands. "You see?"

"Yes, Annabelle. I am yours. That was never in doubt. But you see, I am not now perfectly certain that you belong to *me.*"

I turned on my back and pulled him over me.

"Then let me convince you."

13.

We made love without speaking, almost without moving, listening for signs of Florian through the doorway. Stefan's hips ground carefully into mine. At the end, I stifled my cry into his shoulder, and he bent his face into the pillow while his body made a series of rapid convulsions and then went perfectly still, except for the tiny stroke of his thumb against my temple. The room was so quiet, I could hear the last of Stefan's cigarette sizzle to ash in the tray. I could name each individual bone of Stefan's body, each rib, each breath like a bellows, each section of brutalized skin. The scent of tobacco and sweat, the soft reek of sex. Stefan, lost and found.

For God knew how many minutes, we lay just like that, transfixed by the audacity of

511

what we had just done, by the fact of Stefan's intimate flesh inside me, as if in obedience to some natural law. The slow crash of his heartbeat against mine. Over and over. Again. And again.

Until life returned to us. Until the small sound of footsteps climbed the staircase and we broke apart, straightening our nightclothes like guilty lovers. I swung my feet to the ground just as our son appeared in the doorway, looking so much like his father that I couldn't say a word.

Florian didn't seem to notice this curiosity, that he had found me here in Stefan's bed, flushed and disheveled. He hoisted an enormous illustrated book onto the white counterpane, next to my legs, and pointed to a painting of Frederick the Great on horseback. "Papa!" he said, and his face shone with hope.

14.

November arrived suddenly, in a gust of cold new wind that made the roof shriek and left six inches of surprised wet snow across the landscape. Florian jumped on our bed at half past six with the news, and Stefan valiantly rose from beneath the covers to bundle his son in an inadequate coat and take him outside to make snowballs.

They came stomping in half an hour later, red-skinned and shivering and identical, and I directed them to the old stove and the hot

512

cocoa as if we'd been doing this for years. "To think it was sixty degrees and sunny yesterday," I said, when we were curled up together on the sofa, mugs in hand, watching the fire. "Maybe it's time to fly south."

"Like birds," said Florian.

"Yes, darling. Like birds, to Stefan's ship. He's going to sail us to a beautiful island, where the sun is always shining and warm, and we can grow grapes and olives." I turned to Stefan. "What do you think?"

"I think you are right. It is time to move on, before we are found." He disengaged from us gently and rose to put another log on the fire. He had gained weight, but he was still too thin, and he no longer moved with the fluid grace I had loved. He moved like a marionette, or rather like a man who was trying not to move like a marionette. He straightened from the fire and put one hand on the stone mantel. A cigarette dangled from the other.

"Do you think they might find us here?"

"Frankly, I am surprised they have not found us already. But then, we seem to be the children of good fortune at this moment." He turned and smiled. "Florian, how would you like to go into the library with me, and I will show you how to make a paper airplane."

Florian jumped from the sofa and took Stefan's hand, and they came back an hour later with their arms full of paper airplanes, which

they flew into the fireplace, one by one, to the screeching delight of Florian as each one burst to its spectacular end.

15.

"Are we really in danger?" I whispered to Stefan, when we crept into bed that night.

"Of course we are in danger."

"Then why haven't we left already?"

"We are in danger wherever we go, Annabelle, and this place is as good as any. Besides, I like it here. The peace, and the lake, and no people at all."

"Except me and Florian."

"Except the two of you."

"Are you happy? Would you rather be alone?"

A long pause, and then: "Annabelle, I am grateful to God for every day he allows us together."

"There will be thousands more days to be grateful for. Years and years."

Stefan was lying on his back, while I curled around him. His arm lay around my shoulders; mine crossed his concave stomach. "Yes, of course," he said.

"That wasn't very convincing."

He shifted around me and quietly kissed my neck, while his hands found the edge of my nightgown and drew it up my legs. "Then let me convince you," he whispered.

The action caught me by surprise. We had

made love often as October bled quietly away, but always it was Annabelle who first laid her hands on Stefan, always it was me who led him, inch by inch, past the possibility of resistance. He seemed to act under the conviction that God had allotted the two of us, Annabelle and Stefan, only a finite amount of sexual consummation, like coins in a purse, and he didn't want to spend them all too quickly and be left with nothing. *Ah, Annabelle,* he would whisper, the sign of his capitulation, and we would mate in silence, under the covers, slow as tar, hot as blazes, straining to maintain the perfect tranquility of the bedsprings, so that release came like the smothered hiss of a blowtorch, and we would fall asleep exactly as we were, too depleted to move, while Florian turned in his sleep and snored innocently in his cot nearby. (It was unthinkable to us that he should sleep in another room.)

But this time was different, as if a shallow but significant tide had turned between us. This time Stefan was the one who urged me along, who pulled back the covers and lifted my nightgown to my waist; Stefan who trailed his lips up my legs until I had to stuff my fist into my mouth; Stefan who then turned me on my stomach and entered me with lazy grandeur, like the unfurling of a giant canvas; until he could give no more and sank down to cover me, flush against my back, breathing

in my ear.

I am inside your skin, he whispered. I am reading your thoughts.

What am I thinking?

That you have fallen in love with me all over again. That you love my scars and my sinful habits, and my loyal heart that beats for you. That you want me to make another baby inside you, so there is no chance God will put us asunder again.

(I shut my eyes.)

Very good. But you didn't mention the rest. You forgot your beautiful eyes, and your skin, and — and —

Don't cry, Annabelle.

Let's not talk anymore.

(He lifted himself on his elbows and began to move inside me.)

If that is what you want, *mein Engel.*

16.

The next morning, my period arrived.

"Don't say it's God's will," I told him. "Don't say it's a sign of a perverse universe."

Stefan held up his hands. "I am not saying anything. I am only here to give you what you want."

"I just want *you,* and Florian, and the three of us together, and nothing to pry us away from each other, ever again!"

"Shh. Calm down." He held me close against his chest. "Then I will find a way to

hold the three of us together, Annabelle. If I have to take on the entire universe, I will do it. I will give you what you want."

I listened to his heartbeat beneath the pajama shirt.

"But what do *you* want?" I whispered. "Do you want another child?"

"I want you to be happy. That is all. That is all that is left."

17.

That night, I dreamed about Johann.

Probably it was Florian who planted the seed. The two of them had grown so exceptionally close over the past year. At times, it sickened me to remember how Johann had chased Florian around the nursery floor, pretending to be a great bear, while Stefan's son squealed in delight. Other times, I thought how peacefully they had sat together in a sunlit window, reading from a book, and I marveled that Johann could have loved this boy so profoundly, this Jewish boy sired by his great rival, and whether that love was born of perversity or generosity. I alternated between rage and pity, hate and wistfulness. I would focus my brain on his duplicity, I would recall every scar on Stefan's body, and then into my head flashed Wilhelmine's words — *He killed the agent with his bare hands; he had a wife and three sons* — or Frieda's blond head under Johann's huge and

517

gentle hand.

Mostly, I tried not to think of Johann at all.

But Florian thought of him for me. Florian played happily and affectionately with Stefan, but he hadn't forgotten the man who had once cradled his purple newborn body in a pair of thick palms. That afternoon, Stefan chopped wood while Florian and I carried the split logs across the dying grass to the woodshed, and Florian said in German, "Where is Papa?"

"He's back home, darling."

"When do we go home, too?"

We set the wood into the pile and I fingered his hair. He was bundled in his warm coat — I had found a new, thicker one in the village — and his cheeks were pink. "Aren't you happy here?"

"I want Papa," he said, and he started to cry.

Stefan paused in his chopping and turned to look at us. I gathered Florian against my chest and picked up his hand to wave at Stefan, at Stefan's jacket made of rusty wool, and asked Florian if he could count the number of logs Stefan had split with his ax. It was that easy, distracting Florian, because he was not quite two and a half years old, but when you are twenty-two years old and have lived with a certain man as your husband for three years, more or less, you cannot banish his memory so easily, even when you want

518

to, even when you now sleep heavily beside the man who owns your heart and your blood and the marrow of your eternal bones. It takes strength to hate that husband, the relic of your former life, and when you fall asleep, your brain's fortifications fall away.

You realize, in horror, that there is a small but inevitable hole in your heart, a hole you never wanted but perhaps deserve. A man who is no longer your husband, and a child who will never be born.

18.

Stefan had stopped shaving his upper lip two weeks ago, and his mustache was now a sinister thing, dark and thick: longer than Hitler's, but not by much.

"What do you think?" he asked me, turning from the mirror, waggling his eyebrows.

"I think it's monstrous, but if it helps us across the border, I'll worship it forever."

"Then let's leave tomorrow."

"Tomorrow." I went to the library and read the calendar on the wall. "That would be the ninth of November. An auspicious date?"

Stefan bent down to grasp Florian and hoist him on his shoulders. "What do you think, little man? Are you ready to sail away?"

Florian squealed with pleasure and reached for the brass arms of the chandelier. "Sail-boat!" he said.

"Not quite." I stretched to my tiptoes to

kiss the dimple in his knee. "But I think you'll like Stefan's ship even more than a sailboat."

19.

We woke up before sunrise the next morning, into a hard frost beneath a massive fall of leaves. Florian was still asleep. I washed in the bathtub while Stefan stood in a towel before the mirror and shaved carefully around his new mustache, dangling a cigarette from his lips. I parted the curtain and stepped from the tub and found my own towel, and when I glanced at the mirror I saw he was watching my reflection. I let the towel drop to the floor.

"You are so perfect." He wrapped his hands around my waist and examined the meeting of his thumbs. "You are so small and round and warm and full, all at once. Like the buns they make in England, at Easter."

"Hot cross buns."

"Yes, those. They always looked so delicious, when I saw them through the window of the bakery, making the glass fill with steam."

"Forbidden bread?"

He laughed, and the sound was magnificent. "Yes, very much."

I put my arms around his neck. "And now you have a bun of your very own."

"My own delicious hot cross Annabelle bun, to be gobbled up each morning with hot coffee and a good smoke."

520

20.

"You see?" I gasped, several minutes later. "It's beautiful. The universe is so beautiful."

"*Gott im Himmel,* Annabelle bun. At this moment, the universe is whatever you say it is."

21.

We packed up the old blue Opel Matthias had lent us and tucked a sleepy Florian between us on the front seat. I watched Stefan as he locked the door of the Himmelfarbs' house and stepped back for a last look before tucking the key beneath an empty flowerpot.

When he climbed inside the car and started the engine, I said, "We've been happy here, haven't we? In spite of everything."

"I think we have been happy here *because* of everything," he said, and he backed the car out of the drive and onto the narrow and curving road toward Lake Konstanz.

PEPPER

1.

The first ferry doesn't leave until half past nine, and the fishing fleet is long gone. Not a boat in sight, for love or money. Florian's ready to swim out to Cumberland, but Pepper convinces him he's better off eating breakfast instead.

"She's fine," Pepper says, over coffee and bacon.

"How can you possibly know she's fine? She's gone missing!"

"She's not missing. We know exactly where she is."

"With a stranger."

"A stranger to us, maybe, but not to her. Because I don't doubt for a second that she knows this person on Cumberland. In fact, I'd go so far as to say that they're probably good friends."

He sets down his coffee cup and stares at his plate. "What makes you say that?"

"An educated hunch. Putting two and two together." She taps her nose. "The old female

522

intuition."

"You don't know anything about it."

"Maybe not. But I'll bet you do, if you're willing to admit it."

He looks up. "What the hell does that mean?"

Now, Pepper's always been a breakfast kind of girl, even when breakfast falls somewhere between lunch and dinner. She likes her coffee and her sun-bright orange juice, she likes her smoky rich bacon and her scrambled eggs, she likes her toast hot hot hot with butter on top, and maybe a little strawberry jam, too, and she likes all this even more now that she's growing another human being on the strength of that feast. If she were in Pompeii, and the ash were raining down, she would still insist on wiping her yolks clean with the last of the toast before evacuating the city.

But as she takes in Florian's beleaguered face, his ravaged eyes and his jaw composed of honest right angles, she discovers that her stomach is already occupied by a pair of eager butterflies. She discovers that her heartbeat isn't in need of a further dose of the hot black stuff. All she needs is more of what's sitting across the table from her, turning to her in his hour of need, treating her not as an object of irresistible sexual allure — God knows she's no longer *that* Pepper — but as a comrade.

She sets down her fork and thinks about

laying her hand on his. Then she does. She tries not to sound too throaty as she purrs: "You said something, back in the car, about being honest with each other."

"I've been nothing but honest with you."

"Well, then maybe you're not being honest with yourself."

He frowns. She pats the hand.

"Look, I'm not going to tell you what I think your mother's doing on Cumberland Island, and why I think she's in the best of hands. I want you to tell me what *you* think she's doing. Tell me what *you* know, in your heartiest heart of hearts."

He stares at her slender hand on top of his thick brown paw, and then he finds her face. "Are you actually suggesting Mama's having an affair?"

"Not at present, maybe. But you're a lawyer. Look at the evidence." She ticks her fingers. "Mama drops a fortune on a sentimental car from her Germany days. Mama hires a gumshoe on the sly to track down a person or persons unknown. Mama gets news of said person and bolts off like a schoolgirl for a Beatles concert. It adds up to something, by anyone's math. Even yours."

He shakes off her hand. "I can't believe you're even suggesting this."

"Tell me something. Was it ever hinted at any time, by either of them, that maybe someone left something valuable behind,

524

back in Germany? Something that, once the faithful spouse is honorably buried, might possibly be reclaimed?"

"What the hell gave you that kind of crazy idea?"

Among her other skills, Pepper knows when to beat a strategic retreat. She withdraws to her coffee, which isn't quite as strong as she likes it, but coffee is like doughnuts: even a bad batch is better than no batch at all. Susan's still upstairs, fixing her hair after a long hot shower, probably finger-curling the way her mama taught her. Pepper knocked on the door fifteen minutes ago. *You go on without me,* Susan said absently. *I'm just freshening up.* Pepper shrugged and said, *Suit yourself.* Who was she to judge? A woman involved in the intricate choreography of getting her man: you didn't second-guess her choice of steps. You let her be to get on with the dance. Pepper, now, she was ready to trot downstairs for breakfast after only a two-minute shower, a slathering of Pond's, a swipe of lipstick and a ponytail, but Pepper wasn't looking for a husband.

But. This man. This Florian. Bemused and angry and worried, the more so because he knew Pepper was probably right, and this pretty story he'd constructed around his parents' marriage — true love and abiding faithfulness and unchecked adoration — was

just a pretty story, after all. It always was. Pepper knows. You have the rush of falling in love, the chemical combustion of mutual attraction, *Oh, he's The One* and *We'll never stray* and *Eternity isn't long enough for us, praise God.* And then there are babies and cracker crumbs left in the sheets, there is stomach flu and flatulence and hangovers, there is the way he always eats his peas by spearing them one by fucking one with the leftmost prong of his fork, there is the way she leaves smears of beige makeup all over the washcloths by the sink. There is the pretty young secretary at the office, there is the handsome new tennis pro at the club. And you find a way to smile and kiss and pretend everything is blissful, when in fact you've only learned the secret of mutual tolerance.

"Sweetheart," she says, as kindly as she can, "this doesn't mean your parents don't love each other. Mine do, in their way, against all odds and affairs. But your mother said something to me, while we were driving up from Palm Beach. She said — first of all — that she'd been in my position once, and everything turned out all right."

"What? *Your* position?" He looks in horror at the edge of the table, where the top of Pepper's pregnant belly forms a ski jump into the butter.

"She also said that she had left a piece of

her heart behind."

Florian's cheeks turn pale. He sets his fingers on the table and rises to his feet. "This is bullshit," he says, and he walks straight out of the empty dining room, leaving behind a plate still criminally full of breakfast.

And Pepper, who sighs and reaches across the salt to capture Florian's bacon.

2.

She gives him twenty minutes. Twenty minutes should do the trick, right? Enough time to settle the angry red blood cells back in his veins, so he could see the cold blue light of reason.

She finds him on the side of the porch facing the river. His hands are braced on the railing. She leans back next to his right forearm and crosses her hands demurely under her bump.

"Ferry leaves in an hour. Are you sure you want to be on it?"

"If only to prove you wrong."

"Frankly, you should be hoping I'm right."

"Why's that?"

"Because what's the alternative? You want her to spend the night with a total stranger, possibly not at her own request?"

He swears quietly.

"You know what?" says Pepper. "It's her life. You're all grown up. Your father's been dead for a year. Let her have some happi-

ness, if this is what makes her happy. Let her go."

A blanket of clouds has unrolled overhead, while the three of them were cleaning and dressing and eating breakfast, and now it's begun to drizzle. Pepper listens to the soft drum of the rain and tilts her head just enough that she can see the side of Florian's grim head, the tension in his jaw.

"You know, it doesn't mean their marriage was a lie," she says. "I asked Susan. She says they loved each other. It's not the world shattering around you. She left a piece of her heart behind, not the whole thing."

"All my life," he says, "I've wanted what they had. All my life. I mean, I won't lie. I dated some girls, I had some fun. But all that time, I was waiting. That's why I never asked you to dinner. I knew if I did, I was a goner. I was going to fall straight in love with you, and my odds weren't great, were they? My odds weren't great that you were going to fall in love right back. Settle down with one lucky guy."

"Don't be so sure."

Florian's body is still next to hers, and so close she can feel the flex of the tendons of his arms, the muscles of his waist. There is a competent trimness to him, as if he could change shoes and hike straight up the Appalachian Trail, all the way to Maine, and she wishes to God she could remember. Remem-

ber the moment they first met, in a Washington living room. Why can't she remember? If only she could remember, if only she could locate that critical instant, maybe she could go back and change it. Move the pieces around, so the game ended differently.

But then, poor Susan. Stuck with Billy Whatshisname.

"That's all right," she says, when he doesn't reply. "You made the right decision. Susan's a terrific girl. She's crazy about you."

"I know that."

A car edges into view around the corner, a long flat hood, newish and bluish. It rolls to a stop on the opposite side of the road, parking just behind Florian's Thunderbird. The chrome-tipped tailfins rise into the drizzle. The driver switches off the ignition but doesn't get out.

"So maybe I was an idiot," Florian says. "Maybe you don't worry about true fucking love, or a happy marriage with the nice house and the nice kids. Maybe you just ask the girl out to dinner."

"Unless it's too late." Pepper caresses the side of her belly and watches the blue car. "Unless the girl's already got herself in too much trouble."

"Pepper," he says warmly, and he lifts himself from the railing and turns to her, covering her hand, and for just the sweetest instant in the world there are no blue cars

and no Susans and no missing mothers.

But then there are.

"Florian! There you are," chirps an unnaturally cheerful Susan, beautifully coiffed and impeccably dressed for a dune-swept barrier island in November, pressed Levi's and short rubber boots and a crisp white blouse unbuttoned all the way to there.

Susan. Unmarried, unpregnant, unimpeachable.

3.

Pepper waits until the ferry is out of sight before she turns to the man on the bench. "I appreciate your patience," she says.

He puts his hands on his knees and rises slowly, as if he's had a hard night of his own. Maybe he has. His cheeks are a little ruddy, his eyes heavy. "I wasn't in the way, was I?"

"Not at all. I don't think they even knew you were there."

"Good, good." He smiles. "It's not so easy to be inconspicuous, with a face like mine."

"Don't flatter yourself. They have more important things to think about." She gestures to the front door. "Shall we go inside? They've got a cozy little sitting room off the lobby. Just the thing for clandestine shenanigans, but well within screaming distance if you try any funny business."

"All right. Lead the way."

Pepper stops by the front desk on the way

and asks for coffee. She could use a little something warm, to heat the chill in her blood at the sight of this man's familiar face, his thick waving hair and his eyes that look as if someone has tugged the ends downward.

So very like his big brother.

Only not quite. A bit fresher, a bit round-cheeked still. Give him time, Pepper thinks, leading him into the parlor. Trying not to waddle.

The room is old and charming, the fire crackling in the fireplace. Really, it's a lovely little hotel, neat as a pin, polished to a mellow gleam. The smell of woodsmoke lies pleasantly over the beeswax and the nearby tide. He waits for her to sit first; he was raised that way. She chooses the extreme end of the sofa. He finds a nearby armchair and offers her a cigarette, which she refuses. No, she doesn't mind if he smokes anyway.

When the cigarette is lit, he tells her he's glad she agreed to see him.

"I didn't have much choice, did I? You've cornered me, fair and square."

"That wasn't my intention. We just wanted to talk with you."

"Then you shouldn't have sent your goons to threaten me in a stairwell in Palm Beach."

"That was a mistake. That was the lawyer's gig; we had no idea."

Pepper leans her elbow on the sofa arm, props her head on her hand, and thinks about

this little word *we.* Two innocuous letters, so much stronger than *I.* That's the trouble with this family of his, isn't it? You're never dealing with just one of them. You take on one, you take them all. You stood no chance against a front like that.

"Well, the whole affair wasn't what I'd call gentlemanly."

"Nor would I. But we —"

But he's interrupted by the coffee, which is carried on a tray with a plate of gingersnaps. The owner doesn't seem to recognize him, or maybe she's just being polite. The hotel is family run, seeping at the seams with the spirit of southern kinship. She pours them both coffee from an old silver pot and directs them to the cream and sugar. When she's gone, Pepper reaches for the coffee and selects a gingersnap, the largest one.

"You're looking well," he says. "Seeing a doctor?"

"Of course I'm seeing a doctor. Saw one two weeks ago, right before I came down to Florida. I'm fit as a fiddle. Both of us are." She crunches her gingersnap in two. "Absolutely blooming, the doctor said."

"Well, good. That's the most important thing." He rests his cup on his knee. "We do want what's best for you, Pepper. No one's trying to evade responsibility here."

"Oh, God, no. The cost in lawyers alone must be crippling you."

"You could have avoided all of this by taking a phone call or two."

"There wasn't any point. Your brother wants me to give up the baby. I'll see him in hell first. What's there to discuss?"

"Nothing, I guess, if you're going to be stubborn and unreasonable. If you're going to get greedy and vindictive instead of doing what's right."

"What's right for *you,* you mean. You and your family."

"What's right for everyone. Including you. Including the baby." He leans forward to rest his elbows on his thighs. He's a big man, football big. The cigarette looks tiny between his meaty fingers. "I know you think we're just trying to cover up a mistake here. But we're not. This is my brother's child we're talking about."

"A child he wanted me to get rid of."

"Well, you didn't, and now he wants — we all want — for that baby to have the best possible life."

"Then we have nothing more to talk about. Stay out of my life, stay out of my baby's life, and I promise you we'll stay out of yours. I have a family of my own to make sure this baby is well taken care of."

He sighs and crushes out his cigarette into the ashtray on the coffee table. His briefcase sits upright next to the chair, just a few feet from the fire. He takes a drink of coffee and

lifts the briefcase onto his lap, unsnapping the fastenings in two loud cracks.

"Is that really true, Pepper? Is your family really prepared to take this baby into its heart and give it the love and care it needs? Do your parents even know you're pregnant? Because I don't see them here anywhere. I don't see your sisters or your aunts and uncles lavishing you with love in your time of need."

"We're not the lavishing kind of family, but we muddle through."

He withdraws a sheaf of papers from the briefcase, shaking his head as he goes. "You're a single woman, Pepper. A child needs a secure home with a mother and father."

"He has a mother. Me."

"But what about a father? Every kid needs a father. And who's going to marry you, Miss Schuyler, in your present state? Or saddled with a newborn? Who's going to take you on?"

"Plenty of men."

"That's exactly what we're afraid of. Plenty of men. Because that's who you are, right? You're not mother material. Let's be honest. You're Holly Golightly, nothing wrong with that. Everyone's different. You'll be much happier if you give this baby up and continue with your life, free and clear. And the baby, too."

He hands her the papers. She closes her

hands on her lap and stares him down, keeping her mouth shut, afraid of what the hell she might say if she opened it.

"When exactly are you due, Miss Schuyler?"

"Ask your brother. He can do the math."

"January? February?"

Pepper presses her lips together and sits back in the sofa, sipping her coffee, any old pregnant housewife entertaining a guest in her living room.

"Let's say February," he says, glancing at her belly. "Let's say you have the baby in the middle of winter. Do you know what it's like, living with a newborn? And you're on your own, you're bored and cooped up, you can't have any fun. You like to have fun, don't deny it. Newborns are no fun, honey. Trust me."

"Like I said, I'll muddle through."

He lifts the papers an inch or two from the leather surface of his briefcase. "Expensive, too."

"I have money."

"Listen to me. You don't have to do this. We've got papers all drawn up. We have a couple ready to take the baby, as soon as it's born, and care for it like it's their own."

"Have you, now? John and Jane Smith from Long Island, loyal Democrats?"

"No. Me. My wife and I. We'll take the baby."

"Like hell."

535

He holds up the papers. "See for yourself. We've discussed this at home. My brother came to us with the idea, actually. I think maybe you know my wife's had a couple of miscarriages. She'd welcome this baby with open arms."

"Sure she would. Did you tell her whose it is?" Pepper laughs. "What am I saying? She'll probably think it's yours."

The ruddiness in his cheeks spreads to the tip of his nose. "Don't be an idiot, honey. You're not a fit mother. That baby will be loved and cared for, far better than if you tried to raise it yourself. And you'd be free. No more worries, no more responsibility. You can live your life." A delicate hesitation. "We'll compensate you, of course."

Pepper knots her hands around the coffee cup so he won't see the rage inside them, shaking like a volcano on the verge of eruption. She freezes her mouth in a smile and says idly, like it's a game, like there's nothing in the world at stake: "You seem to think I'm one of your bimbos. You seem to think I'm just one of your usual girls."

He drums his fingers on the briefcase and smiles. "You know, that's the funny thing about you bimbos. You all think *you're* the one who's not the bimbo."

Pepper sets down her coffee cup. "Off you go. Discussion's over."

"I'm not leaving."

"Then I am."

She sashays . . . well, not exactly. She waddles elegantly down the line of the chintz sofa, between the chairs and to the door, and she's just about found the knob with her trembling volcanic fingers when his hand takes her by the elbow.

"You're not just walking away from this."

"Watch me."

She yanks the door open, and guess who? Black-robed and elegant.

Annabelle.

ANNABELLE
GERMANY 1938

1.

We had stayed only a month in the Himmelfarbs' house, but I felt as if we were emerging, drowsy-eyed, from a Rip van Winkle
hibernation. The world seemed to have
changed somehow: not just the fallen leaves
and the cold air, but the constitution of the
physical universe. The atoms and molecules
had realigned on a different axis.

By nine o'clock, we had reached Konstanz,
on the rim of the lake. We had our story
polished and ready: We were the Dommer-
ichs, Rudolf and Annabelle and our son, Florian, skiing enthusiasts, visiting friends in the
mountains near Verbier. Stefan was going to
do all the talking. If the guard asked me a
question, I was to answer in one word if possible, and if he questioned my accent, I was
to say I had been brought up by an aunt and
uncle in Geneva because my parents died
when I was little.

"But he won't ask you any questions, I
think," Stefan said. "You have your big, in-

nocent eyes. He will think you are nothing but a sweet little hausfrau and I am a lucky man."

"Little does he know."

The streets were quiet. Stefan parked the car outside a tobacconist and went inside for newspapers and cigarettes. "You poor thing," I said. "They don't have your favorites. That will be something to look forward to, when we get to Monte Carlo."

He lit himself up and sighed in relief. "Do you know what I am looking forward to most of all?"

"Safety? Being on your ship again? Making love to me in your splendid stateroom?"

"Yes, all these things, and especially the last one. But mostly I am looking forward to hearing you play your music again."

"But I left the Amati at the hotel in Antibes."

He shook his head and picked up the newspaper. "I had it taken back to the *Isolde*. It is waiting for you there, in my cabin."

I caught my breath and said, "Our cabin."

"Yes. Our cabin." He frowned at the headline before him.

"What's wrong?"

He swore under his breath. "They have shot vom Rath."

"Who's vom Rath?"

"He is no one, just a diplomat in Paris, at the German embassy. Your husband probably

539

crushed him under his heel on his way to work each day and never even noticed the mess. But now some stupid Jew has walked in and shot him in his office."

"Is he dead?"

"No. Not yet." He swore again and tossed the newspaper into my lap, next to Florian's sleeping head. "But you will never guess. The fucking Nazis are calling for blood."

2.

At the crossing, a long line of automobiles stretched down the road. Nobody was moving; most had shut down their engines and gotten out of their cars, smoking and talking. Stefan opened the door and said he was going to find out what was going on.

He came back half an hour later, and his face was grim. Florian was awake and eating an apple. "We're going to find a hotel," he said. "They have closed the border temporarily. No one knows if they will open it today."

"Can't we just wait and see?"

"I don't want to give them any chances."

We found a plain but comfortable hotel on the outskirts of town, overlooking the main road, so that Stefan could watch for any signs of activity. The weather was too cold for Florian to play outdoors for long. We kept to our room and ordered our lunch, while the line of cars grew along the road outside. Stefan smoked and paced the wall, glancing out the

540

window from time to time, until I asked him to stop and read Florian a story. All right, he said, stubbing out his latest cigarette, and while he was explaining about the three little pigs, room service knocked on the door.

Because he had slept so long in the car, Florian didn't want to take his usual nap after lunch. He ran around the room, firing an imaginary gun at imaginary pirates, while I chased fruitlessly after him and Stefan stood perplexed at the end of the bed.

"Go," I said at last, brushing my hair from my face. "Go downstairs and see if you can get any news."

Stefan, looking relieved, grabbed his coat and hat and cigarettes and hurried from the room.

By three o'clock, Florian had at last fallen asleep, and Stefan hadn't returned. I pulled a chair next to the window and sat there, pretending to read in the fading autumn light. The line of cars had shortened, but I couldn't tell if this was because the border had opened or because people had simply given up. A large number of men milled about on the sidewalks and streets, some of them in uniform. I felt the waves of their restlessness rippling upward through the window glass, like a field of visible energy, and for the first time my blood began to quicken. One man stopped right under the window and looked up, as if he knew I was

541

watching, and the look he sent me was so full of blank hatred I startled up from the chair. The book spilled to the floor. The man spat on the sidewalk and moved on.

When Stefan finally opened the door at half past four, I rushed to his arms. "What is this?" he said, taking me against his chest.

"What's going on out there?"

"A damned mess." He gave me a last squeeze and tossed his hat onto the writing desk in the corner. "There is no word yet on the border."

"What are all those men doing out there?"

"Waiting for a fucking riot, I think." He glanced at Florian, who was stirring on the bed, though his eyes were still closed. "We had better hope that fool vom Rath stays alive."

"A riot? Here?"

"My dear, they are waiting for it. They are waiting for a damned excuse."

"Who are 'they'?"

"Hitler, Goebbels, every man down the line. The pretext, it doesn't even matter. I went to the newsstand for a paper, and do you know what? The Jewish papers were not there. They have stopped publication, by order of the Reich, because they say there is a great Jewish conspiracy afoot, but really because they want to strip us of everything we have left, every possible means of protest and information. Meanwhile, they are expel-

ling Jews who were not born here. They are sending them to Poland by the trainload, and Poland sends them back. That is why this man Grynszpan shot vom Rath, because his family had been expelled to Poland with hardly the clothes on the back."

"My God."

"There is nothing left." He was speaking in a hushed voice, pacing, lighting a cigarette. "They are ready to strike. The Gauleiters are waiting for the signal from Goebbels, I have no doubt. Waiting to hear that vom Rath has died, or not even that. They will send the local party members to attack every fucking synagogue in Germany, every Jew they can lay their hands on. I must telephone Wilhelmine."

"Wilhelmine?"

"Because of Else, Annabelle." He turned to me, and his eyes were wide and shocked and exhausted. "They are not letting Jewish children in the schools anymore. My daughter, she is not even a human being here anymore."

"Of course, of course. Call her now."

There was a large black telephone on the writing desk. Stefan sank down in the chair and picked up the receiver. I had borrowed clothes for him from Matthias, who was an inch or two shorter and perhaps fifty pounds heavier, so that gray wool jacket hung from Stefan's shoulders and exposed his wrists. I

thought, We will have to go shopping for him in Monte Carlo and buy him several fine new suits and white shirts, and this time I'll iron them for him myself with a bit of starch, the way he likes them. Stefan flicked the ash from his cigarette and told the operator that he was making a long-distance call to Stuttgart, gave the exchange and the number, and tapped his heel against the floor while he waited for the connection.

Florian stirred and sat up on the bed. "Mama?"

"Right here, darling." I sat down next to him and cuddled him against my side.

Stefan straightened and spoke into the receiver, in German, asking for Mrs. Himmelfarb. There was a pause, and a crease opened between his eyebrows. "I see," he said "Perhaps Mr. Himmelfarb is available? No? Can you tell me when she is expected to return? I see. Then will you please tell Mrs. Himmelfarb that Rudolf Dommerich called from Konstanz, on the border, and to please return my call at once. The Nazarene Hotel" — he glanced at the paper on the writing desk — "room number 209. Thank you."

He set down the receiver and said to me in English, "They're out, it seems."

"So I gathered."

"Your German has improved, at least." His smile was forced.

Florian shook off the last of his nap and

wriggled down the bed to the floor. Stefan looked at him and his mouth softened. He held out his arms and Florian ran tipsily into them, to be swung up on his father's knee.

"She'll be fine," I said. "Else will be fine."

"Yes."

Stefan brushed his nose in Florian's hair, the way I always did, inhaling his little-boy smell, and my ribs hurt as I watched them, identical hair and identical eyes, the son giving comfort to the father in his ill-fitting suit, his gaunt Dachau frame. When I closed my eyes, I could still see every detail, and I thought, I will never forget this, I will always remember the two of them sitting on the chair in the dull November afternoon, in the hotel room that smelled of Lysol and cigarettes and dread.

3.

The telephone rang at half past ten o'clock, waking the three of us like the sting of a wasp. Stefan stumbled from the bed and grasped the telephone receiver, while I gathered Florian against me and stroked his damp hair.

"Wilhelmine! Where are you? Yes? Yes?" He cursed. "No, we can't anyway, the border's closed. No. Just stay where you are, do you hear me? Stay where you are, and I will come to get her. For God's sake. You must come, too." A pause. "Tell him he is a fucking idiot. Tell him Stefan said he is a fucking idiot. God

damn it. All right. I'm leaving now."

As he spoke, I thought I heard the distant sound of something shattering.

Stefan slammed the receiver into the cradle and turned to me. I couldn't see him very well in the darkness, but I felt the angry energy that rippled from his body.

"I have got to go to Stuttgart at once," he said. "Vom Rath has died. The Gauleiters are already at work with their minions. Wilhelmine says she can hear the smashing and screaming from her window. She wants me to take Else. She wants us to take Else with us, out of the country, to safety."

"Of course, of course. My God." I scrambled out of the covers. "Of course we'll take her. But what about Wilhelmine and poor little Henrik?"

He shook his head and turned on the lamp. "That idiot Matthias won't leave, and Wilhelmine knows he is an idiot and still she will not leave him. It is a nightmare." He was tearing off his pajamas and reaching for his suitcase.

I climbed out of bed and ran to my suitcase.

"What are you doing?"

"Getting dressed."

"What? No. You are staying here, Annabelle. You are staying here with Florian."

"And let you go off by yourself? Are you kidding me?" I lifted my nightgown over my head and reached for my blouse. "Not a

546

chance."

"Don't be stupid, Annabelle. I will be there and back by morning. You will wake up and find me, you will hardly even know I left."

"Do you think I'm a fool? I've spent the last three months trying to save you and keep you safe, and I'm not going to let you out of my sight. Tonight of all nights."

He seized my arms. "Annabelle, no. Please don't do this. You've got to stay here. You'll be safe in the hotel, you and Florian."

"I don't want to be safe if you're not."

"But Florian!"

"Don't you *dare.* Don't you *dare* blackmail me. We are a *family,* Stefan, we are not going to break apart. Do you hear me? I'm in your skin, remember? We're a *family.* I swore it when I found you again, I swore I'd never give you up. Stefan, please, you have *got* to understand, you have got to take me with you."

"You are killing me, Annabelle."

Florian began to cry.

I put my hands on Stefan's cheeks. His bones fit into my palms. "I won't let you. I won't let you walk out of this room alone. You are not allowed to do this alone any-more."

"Annabelle, please —"

Florian slithered from the bed and ran to Stefan's legs. "Don't leave. Don't leave."

"You see?" I whispered. "This is all there

is. This is all we have. The three of us."

Stefan closed his eyes. His hand dropped to Florian's head, to the sobbing face that stuck to his knees and wet the legs of his pajamas.

"Stefan. I gave you my own blood, remember?"

It was a cheap plea, and he must have known it. That pint of blood had entered his veins three years ago, and by now it was gone, churned over and converted into Stefan's own. But as I said the words, I recalled the drone of the tender's engine, the slap of waves against the hull of the *Isolde,* the briny smell of the sea and the reek of gasoline exhaust. I remembered Stefan's brave and lugubrious voice, telling me not to be stupid, and the giddy plunge in my belly as I fell in love with him. The sight of my red blood flowing through the tube and into the vein on his wrist, to bring him back to life.

Stefan said, in a defeated voice, "You will do exactly as I say, is that understood? You will hide in the boot if I tell you to hide in the boot. If there is the least trouble, I will deposit you in the nearest hotel and you will wait there quietly with our son, is that clear?"

I fell on his chest.

"Yes. Yes, that's clear."

4.

We reached the outskirts of Stuttgart just before two o'clock in the morning. A lurid

548

yellow-orange glow hung over the rooftops, like a bank of fog. "They have started burning," Stefan said.

"What are they burning?"

"Whatever they can, probably. Synagogues, businesses. Maybe houses."

"My God."

"What did you expect, Annabelle? They want to destroy us, don't you know that?"

"Destroy? You don't mean that."

"What do you think I mean? I mean destroy. I mean obliterate, I mean they want us blistered from the face of the earth."

"But how could they do that, while good people are watching? While the world is watching? They can't possibly think they can get away with it."

"That is the point. They want to see what they can get away with. The entire history of the past five years, they have been seeing what the world will let them get away with. And the world is so sick of everything, it doesn't care."

"It will have to act now."

"Just watch, Annabelle. Just watch and see what the world does and doesn't do."

I stared at the lurid sky.

"It's impossible. They just want to get rid of you. They just want you out of Germany."

"You do not understand a thing, Annabelle. Not a fucking thing."

"But you're talking about murder."

549

He tossed his cigarette out the window. "Do you want to know how many times they tried to kill me at Dachau? They called it punishment and rehabilitative labor and all kinds of nice, clean things. But they just wanted to kill me, that is all, neat and simple. Only I would not give them the satisfaction."

"Then why did they agree to let you out to go to the hospital?"

"A very good question, Annabelle. I have asked this myself many times."

I looked down at Florian's sleeping head in my lap. "You think it was Johann."

"I do not think anything anymore. I just want to get the hell out of here with my wife and my son and daughter. I want to get the fuck out of Germany while we are all still alive. What is it?"

"You called me your wife."

"And you are crying about *this*?"

"Yes, damn you. I am crying about this."

5.

Everywhere you could hear the sound of smashing glass. Stefan drove quickly, past throngs of young men whose faces were yellow under the streetlights and the glow of the fires, whose eyes were lit by something else, but you couldn't outrun that sound. It shattered the ends of your nerves; it made your heart explode and explode in your chest. *Hurry,* I said to Stefan, pressing my feet on

the floorboards, but it was a stupid thing to say. He was already driving as fast as he dared.

He knew the way, which was fortunate because I didn't recognize anything in this strange glow that had overtaken the city. The Himmelfarbs lived in a residential neighborhood, lined with trees, and as we approached the district the crowds of young men seemed to thin out. Maybe we're past the worst, I said, and Stefan didn't reply.

We turned a corner, and I recognized the street. My gaze traveled down a few houses to the right, and there it was, the familiar low iron gate, the tiny garden, the five steps leading to the stoop. The sidewalk was empty and still, except for the distant sound of shouts and breaking glass, a radio play of destruction. All the lights were out in the houses. Stefan stopped the car and jumped out. He went around the passenger side, took Florian from my arms, and grabbed my hand. We hurried up the stoop and banged on the door.

"It's me, Wilma! It's Stefan! Open the damned door!"

The door sprang open over the last two words, and Wilhelmine Himmelfarb stood gray-faced in the entry, her hair lank over her forehead, holding Henrik on her hip.

"Thank God," she said.

PEPPER

1.

Pepper stares downward at that Audrey Hepburn neck, ending in the crisp triangles of a black collar, a trench coat belted chicly at the waist.

"There you are," Annabelle says brightly, holding out a black leather hand.

"Here I am."

Annabelle turns her attention to the man at Pepper's elbow. "Good morning. I don't believe we've been introduced. My name is Annabelle Dommerich."

The hand again. He takes it, shakes it briefly, mumbles his name.

"Enchanted," says Annabelle.

"I thought you were on Cumberland Island," says Pepper.

"Yes, I expect you did. Well, I'm back now. As you see."

"But Florian and Susan are on the ferry out, the one that just left. You've just missed them." It occurs to Pepper that this remarkable failure might not necessarily be a co-

552

incidence.

"Yes."

"I'm sorry, Mrs. Dommerich, but if you don't mind, the lady and I were having a discussion —"

Annabelle turns and gives him the blinding smile. "As a matter of fact, sir, I do mind. I need to speak rather urgently to Miss Schuyler. I'm afraid your little discussion will have to wait."

He gives her an amazed look, the look of a man unaccustomed to hearing the word *wait*. The astonishment lifts his thick eyebrows almost into his hairline.

Pepper links elbows with Annabelle. "Poor dear," she says. "That's twice in one morning."

"Twice what?"

"Refused."

2.

"I don't believe that man means to leave," says Annabelle, staring down from Pepper's second-floor window to the blue Lincoln parked outside. The drizzle has let up, but the blanket of gray remains, deadening the chrome on the bumpers and the tailfins.

Pepper stretches out on the narrow single bed and props her foot on a pillow. "It's a genetic disease that runs in the family. They can't hear the word *no*."

Annabelle makes an irritated noise.

553

"Anyway," Pepper continues, hardly missing a beat, "enough about little old me. What the hell are *you* doing here?"

"Hmm." She turns from the window and leans against the sill. "What do you think of my son?"

"I think he's delicious. So does the fair Susan. They'll make you some beautiful grandkids, those two."

Annabelle frowns, but it's not the ordinary kind of frown. It's a flat-browed, purse-lipped kind of frown that says, *Not on my watch, sister.*

"If Florian marries that girl, I'll disown him," she says.

"What's this? You don't like Susan?"

"I like her enormously, but she's not marrying my son." Annabelle pauses. "She's tone-deaf. I won't have Florian living without music."

"That seems a little unfair. It's not her fault, is it?"

"And she'll let him walk all over her. Florian can be a little bossy, like his father. He needs someone who'll stand up to him." She gazes innocently at the ceiling.

"And yet you let them sail off to Cumberland Island together, without any adult supervision." Pepper holds up her hand. "Don't even try to tell me you didn't know they were on that ferry. I just want to know how you gave them the slip. And maybe why."

554

Annabelle turns back to the window. The overcast sky is flat against her face, ironing out every possible sign of age. She could be twenty years old. "He's taking something out of the trunk," she says.

"Never mind him. You said you had to speak to me."

"That was only to rescue you."

Pepper sits up. "What happened out there?"

"On the island, you mean? Nothing. I went, I came back."

"And the part in the middle? Did you find what you were looking for?"

"Yes. Oh, now he's coming back inside. There's something under his arm, a large envelope. My God, the look on his face."

"I said never mind him. I want to know what happened last night. Why you came back, looking like a chocolate éclair that's had all the cream taken out."

Annabelle walks to the fireplace and holds out her hands to the flames. Pepper admires her fingers, long and beautifully shaped. Her head is bowed a little, examining the nails. "Like I said, nothing happened. I went to see if I was right, if an old friend of mine was living there."

"An old lover."

"I suppose you could say that."

"Well, was he?"

"Yes, he was. It was him, all right." She rubs her hands together, and with her right thumb

555

she twiddles the slim gold wedding ring on the fourth finger of her left hand.

"Well? Did you say hello? Throw yourself in his arms? Spend the night in bed?"

"None of those things." She picks up the silver candlestick on the mantel and studies the base, like she's looking for the hallmark. "I managed to find out where he lived. It was a bit of a trek. I took a bicycle. I waited outside for a bit, gathering up my courage. It's a bit frightening, you know, seeing someone again after such a long time. You don't know how they've changed, or how much you've changed, or whether they forgive you for everything. So I waited."

A knock sounds on the door.

"Ignore it," says Pepper. "You waited?"

"I waited until midnight, and then I turned around and went back to the inn, and this morning I found a fisherman to take me back to the mainland. And now I'm packing up and going home."

Pepper stands up, grabbing the sofa arm for support. "What? You gave up?"

Annabelle looks at her sharply. "Why do you care?"

I have no idea.

"I just do, that's all."

The knock sounds again. A thick masculine voice: "Miss Schuyler! I need to speak with you."

Annabelle lifts her eyebrows. "We could

sneak out the back way and leave in my car, if you don't mind leaving your things behind for Florian to bring later."

"No, I'm going to settle with him, believe me. But you first. I need to know why you gave up. You of all people. You gave up on his doorstep."

"Gave up what?"

"Everything! Claiming him back."

"Claim him back? But that wasn't the point, darling. That wasn't the point, after all these years. He has his own life now. I just wanted to see if it was really him. I just wanted to make sure he was all right."

"You went to all that trouble, just to look at his house? You didn't even knock and say hello?"

"No. There was no point."

"Why not?"

Annabelle smiles and spreads out her hands. "Because he wasn't alone."

3.

Pepper plants her crutches into the rug. "This had better be good. I'm heading upstairs right now to pack up."

His face is a picture of anger, all grim and highlighted in red. He strides right past her and tosses the long manila envelope on the coffee table, next to the remains of the gingersnaps. "Come here."

"I'll stand right here, thanks."

Pepper can still hear the click of Annabelle's shoes on the stairs, making her defeated way to her room, where she will pack her things for the drive back to Florida, to the big empty villa by the ocean. Or maybe she will just go straight to her son's house in the Washington suburbs, for Thanksgiving? The widowed matriarch, presiding over her sprawling family. Someday Pepper will have to get the whole story out of her. The car, the man she left behind. The man she married.

"All right," he says. "Have it your way."

He unties the fastening on the envelope and draws out a thin stack of papers. "Please understand, we don't want to have to use these. Your family, they're an institution in New York, they've given this country some of its finest citizens. So we'd really hate to have to send this information to the press."

He spreads the papers out on the coffee table, pushing the plate with the gingersnaps into the corner. Some of them are typewritten pages; some are photographs. A nice little collection. Pepper recognizes her father in one of them. He seems to be naked.

"We did a little research," he says, in an apologetic tone, as if to say, *You left us no choice, honey, no choice but to dig up all this dirt from under the carpet.*

Well, every family has its dirt, doesn't it? But Pepper's family is so old and distinguished, so sprinkled with rebellious and ec-

558

centric characters. The dirt accumulates gradually in a family like hers, but it's a rich and fertile kind of dirt: the kind that, if you plant a seed, will grow a whole goddamned garden of scandal. And maybe that kind of thing doesn't matter anymore. Maybe it won't get you struck from the Social Register, or blackballed from the Knickerbocker Club, or (shame of shames!) ostracized from the best Fifth Avenue drawing rooms.

But maybe it will.

It all depends, doesn't it, on what's contained in that little array laid out on the coffee table, next to the gingersnaps.

Pepper hobbles across the old rug and stares down at the field of white rectangles. She picks up one of the typewritten pages and reads about Uncle Freddie, whom everybody knew had gotten his oil contracts the old-fashioned way, but really. To see the whole affair in black-and-white.

He clears his throat. "The attorney general may have to prosecute."

She looks up. "The irony here is that *your* family's done worse."

He shrugs. Because it hardly needs saying that if a man smuggles in a bottle or two of whiskey from Canada and the cops are paid not to hear him, it didn't really happen.

What a nuisance, Pepper thinks. What a damned nuisance. I'm going to have to be a hero, aren't I?

After all this, I'm going to have to take the fall.

4.

He lets her go upstairs to pack. It's not as if she's going to try any funny business, is she, not when those papers still lie in their manila folder, under his arm. He even takes the laundry bag and carries it to the blue Lincoln himself, what a gentleman, dropping it into the trunk like a sack of refuse. Then he opens the door for her.

"Thank you," she says, removing her crutches from under her arms and tossing them inside. The seats are pure virgin white, not a single smear, reeking of cigarettes. She pauses with her hand on the top of the doorframe and stares at the generous porch of the Riverview Hotel, the empty ferry landing to the side. The river, leading out to the wide blue sea.

He swings around to the driver's side and puts the key in the ignition. The engine takes a few turns to get going, but then it lets out a nice handsome roar, eager to be off, eager to drive right out of this damp and sleepy town and head back to Washington in time for Thanksgiving.

"Stop!"

A lithe black figure leaps down the front steps toward the street.

"Pepper, no! Don't get in the car with that man!"

"Get in," he says to Pepper. "Now."

Pepper braces herself on the door and swings inside, and the Lincoln lurches forward, away from the curb, racing back up the street toward the brand-new interstate.

5.

After a block or two, he glances in the rearview mirror and turns on the radio. Roy Orbison. "Who the hell was that, anyway?" he asks.

"You've never heard of Annabelle Dommerich? The cellist?"

He whistles. "No kidding. How do you know her?"

"We met in Palm Beach."

He glances again in the mirror. "She's a very attractive woman. Married?"

"I don't think you're her type."

"They all say that at first."

She looks out the window. The town still looks asleep. Each block blurs past her eyes, doors closed, sidewalks empty. Maybe it's the drizzle, which has begun again, pattering against the windshield. He turns on the wipers. *Swish, swish,* into the dull drone of the engine, the rattle of rain.

He reaches across her and unlatches the glove compartment. "Mind if I smoke?"

"Suit yourself." She rolls down the window

a pair of inches and thinks, I'll probably have to kill him. Kill him and steal the envelope and disappear somewhere, start a new life in Canada or Mexico or Australia, all by myself, assumed name, the works. Maybe they'll write a book about me one day. *Pepper: She Really Was That Bad.*

All right. Not kill him. She's not *really* that bad. But knock him out. How? Well, somehow. Knock him out and steal the envelope and . . .

But they probably have copies somewhere, don't they? This is not a family that leaves things to chance. This is a family that lays it plans with care.

Damn it. Damn it all. She's stuck.

She'll think of something.

She's stuck.

Breathe, Pepper. The baby needs oxygen. You'll think of something. You always do.

You're stuck.

He fumbles with the cigarettes. The buildings thin out, the turn in the highway approaches. Somehow he juggles it all: cigarettes, lighter, turn. Pepper puts her hand on the door handle and braces her feet against the floorboards. He's taking it a little fast, isn't he? But the blue Lincoln can handle it.

They straighten out, and a black shape appears before them, stopped in the road: a beautiful swooping Mercedes-Benz Special Roadster, stretched out like a shiny black

panther, and a woman slamming the door and turning to face them, arms crossed, eyes fierce.

"Stop!" shouts Pepper, and he looks up from his cigarette and slams the brakes.

ANNABELLE
GERMANY 1938

1.

The house was dark, except for Wilhelmine's feeble flashlight jiggling ahead. My eyes picked out the familiar details: the newel post at the bottom of the stairs, shaped like a pineapple; the worn oriental rug; the elegantly cluttered mantel of the parlor fireplace, as we flashed past the doorway. She led us downstairs to the basement. A child's whimper floated upward. Stefan pushed past us both and vaulted down the rest of the stairs. When I turned the corner, he was holding Else up to his chest. She was fully dressed in a thick wool cardigan and plaid skirt. His face was buried in her dark hair.

"Else!" cried Florian, and I shushed him, but Else was already wriggling out of her father's grasp, as Florian struggled from mine.

"They played together so happily when I was staying here," I whispered to Stefan.

"Thank God," he said, and his voice was like the crunch of fine gravel. He turned to

Wilhelmine. "Where is Matthias?"

"He is upstairs, closing all the shutters. Henrik is asleep."

"Get him. Get him dressed. You've got to come with us, the both of you."

"But Matthias —"

"Damn Matthias! He is an idiot. There is a mob three streets away. Do you hear me? A mob. They are smashing windows and taking people from their homes." He spoke in English, crisp and raging.

Wilhelmine's mouth parted.

"Go!" thundered Stefan, and she turned and raced up the stairs.

"This is unreal," I said. "I can't believe this is happening."

He was pacing along the wall, running a hand through his dark hair. "It is perfectly real. It is exactly what I have been saying for five fucking years. God damn it!" he shouted, and turned to drive his fist against the wall.

Else and Florian stopped playing and stared at him. The light from the single bare bulb cast a harsh shadow along the side of his face, making him look a little mad. "Stefan, the children," I whispered.

He lifted his eyes to me. "I need a gun. I need a gun to protect us, I need two or three. And do you think the civilized Matthias has a single gun in his civilized house? Of course not. We are left to defend ourselves with our bare hands. Because right is on our side. We

can put that on our tombstones, eh? *Right was on our side.* How — what is the English word? — how very poignant."

The sound of urgent voices drifted down the stairs, arguing in German. The soft wail of Henrik, awake now.

"Stefan, please." I knelt down and gathered the children against my legs. "It will be all right. We'll drive all night if we have to."

"And how are we going to get across the border, hmm? We will have to swim down the Rhine."

"I'm an American. We can go to the consulate."

"But I am a fugitive, remember? There is nothing your Roosevelt can do for me, even if he wanted to."

The voices were getting louder, strong and male. Stefan and I locked eyes and realized, at the same precise and horrified instant, that the sound came not from Matthias and Wilhelmine, arguing about whether to flee their home or to ride out the storm, but from outside the house. From the street outside the window.

"Stay here," Stefan said.

"Don't go up!"

Booted footsteps thundered up the front steps, just above our heads. An instant later came the crash of fists against the door, the shouted demand: *Öffnen!*

Stefan reached for the chain dangling from

the light socket and turned off the bulb. Else cried out. "Shh," he said, and in the faint light from the stairs he bent down and kissed her head and then Florian's. "Stay here with your mother," he said in German. "I will be right back."

A crash, as the door came open. A flurry of shouts. Wilhelmine screaming.

Stefan was heading for the stairs. I grabbed his arm. "Don't go up there!"

"Just stay here, all right? Listen to me. If they come down to search, if you hear them coming down, you take that back door into the garden. There is a hidden gate at the end, behind the shed. Do you know it?"

"Yes."

"Take the children out that way. Find a house somewhere, somewhere to spend the night, and then go to the consulate."

"Not without you!"

He gripped my shoulders with his hands, strong enough that the tears started in my eyes. "Take the children! Please, Annabelle. They are all there is left."

His face was lurid and anguished. The sound of his whisper was so hoarse, I could hardly understand him.

"I can't leave you here," I said.

"I'll find you. I swear to God I will find you." He leaned forward and kissed me hard, so I knew without doubt he was lying, that there was no chance I would see him again in

this life, and then he ran up the stairs and into the light, and closed the door behind him.

2.

"All right, children," I whispered in German, because Else's English was not very good. "We are going on a little adventure. We are going to sneak out through the garden and play hide-and-seek with the rest of the grown-ups."

My voice was shaking, my hands were cold. I couldn't see them, because Stefan had closed off the door at the top of the base-ment stairs, leaving us in a thorough dark-ness that was both velvety and ominous, a black paradox. I found their woolen shoul-ders, their silken heads, and herded them to the back of the basement. From upstairs came shouting. Wilhelmine screamed.

"Mama!" said Else, breaking free.

"No, darling!"

Shuffling, pounding. A gun fired, a crack of manufactured thunder unlike any sound I'd ever heard, and then the authoritative thump of a human body falling against a wooden floor.

No. Please. Not this.

Hail Mary, full of grace, the Lord is with thee . . .

"Else, come here." I scrambled after her.

Someone wailed, a voice that was neither

568

male nor female, rising up above the scuffle and the pounding.

. . . Blessed art thou among women . . .

Another shot, rattling the floorboards above us.

. . . and blessed is the fruit of thy womb, Jesus . . . Please, please, God, no, not this . . .

My hands found the shoulder of Else's woolen sweater. I dragged her from the bottom of the stairs.

. . . Holy Mary, mother of God . . .

Crack. Crack.

. . . pray for us sinners . . .

Crack.

. . . now and in the hour of our death . . .

I hauled Else back across the basement floor, kicking and wailing. I held my hand over her mouth, trying to stifle her agony so they wouldn't hear us. Wouldn't come downstairs and find the children, too.

Crack. Crack. Crack. Now I felt the sound, rather than heard it. My ears had gone as numb as my fingers.

Hail Mary, full of grace . . .

Florian flung himself against my leg as I reached the back of the basement. I fumbled for the doorknob, but my hands were so numb, and I couldn't see.

. . . full of grace . . .

The door, the door. Smooth brass. The knob. Turn.

. . . pray for us sinners . . .

Crack.

A rush of cold, clear air. Shouts drifting out from the upstairs window. Set down Else, grab her hand, grab Florian's hand.

. . . pray for us sinners . . .

Running across the damp grass, fighting the moonlight, Else sobbing. The garden wall. Where is the gate? To the right, the right. Lift the latch.

. . . pray for us sinners . . .

Push the children through the gateway, into the empty alley behind the house. Running down the pavement. Which house? The friend, the children we played with that hot August day, which house? Turn the corner. Smell the smoke. Shouting.

A group of men. Uniforms. My God. Stop. Go back.

I turned, saw more soldiers, turned back to the first group, which had rattled to a halt next to a streetlamp, five or six yards away.

Nowhere to go. I clutched the children to my skirt. "Mama?" said Florian, like a question.

Somewhere in the middle of that throng, a figure staggered downward, was hauled up again by a pair of soldiers, flailed, shouted my name.

"Stefan!" I gasped.

A man at the front of the pack stepped forward, immense and dark-coated, into the light from the streetlamp. Beneath the brim

of his cap, his eyes were such a pale shade of blue, they were almost white, and I gasped in recognition.

"Frau Silverman," he said, "you must come with me."

Pray for us sinners, now and in the hour of our death.

Amen.

3.

The butt of a rifle guided me into the back of the truck. I gripped the children's hands and helped them up and inside, onto the benches lining the sides. Stefan was thrown in right behind us. I tried to lunge toward him, but a pair of arms jerked me back. In the next instant, something warm and wriggling shoved up against my chest in a shriek of outrage: Henrik. I hadn't even heard him.

The gears ground, the truck lurched forward. There was now no sign of Johann. Perhaps he was riding up front. I was too sick to feel anger, too desperate to keep the children steady on the bench as we bounced down the road. Too drenched in relief and fear at the sight of Stefan, slumped on the opposite side, his feet a few inches from my feet, prodded upright from time to time by a rifle.

It will be all right, I thought. We will find a way out of this.

I thought, He's alive. Stefan's alive. We will live.

In a day, in a week, in a month, we will be safe and free, we will be sailing through an empty blue ocean in the *Isolde,* pointing out the dolphins to the children, making love all night in the wide white bed in Stefan's stateroom.

I closed my eyes and whispered in English: "Are you hurt?"

"A little."

I laid a hand over Florian's ear. "Where is Wilhelmine?"

"Dead, my heart. They are both dead."

The children grew magically quiet in the rhythmic bounce of the back of the truck. I wedged the four of us into a corner, to give my arms a rest, inhaling the sweat of the soldiers and the dirty mildew of the canvas top. I thought, I hope it was quick. Dear Wilma. I hope it was quick. Please, God.

Hail Mary, full of grace. The Lord is with thee.

Was that right? But it was the only prayer I could think of.

Blessed art thou among women, and blessed is the fruit of thy womb, Jesus.

I said aloud: "I'm sorry."

"The fault is mine, Annabelle. They were looking for me."

"It's not your fault. It's their fault. It's Johann's fault."

Holy Mary, mother of God, pray for us sin-

ners, now and in the hour of our death.

I asked, "Did Johann kill them himself?"

"No. He came at the end. To make sure they took me alive."

The truck squealed to a halt, and then made a sharp turn to the left. Henrik nearly fell from my arms. Henrik, the orphan baby Jew, motherless and fatherless. He began to cry again, and I cradled him up against my shoulder and hushed him softly.

Amen.

4.

The children slept, as children will. The air inside the back of the truck grew humid and stank with human occupation. I nearly fell asleep, too — my brain was so stunned — but I kept awake by pinching myself and by staring at Stefan's shadow a few feet away. Sometimes a little light came through the canvas, and I saw there was a stain of blood on the shoulder of his jacket, but I didn't know if it belonged to him or to someone else. It was a large stain, and very dark, almost black.

I didn't count the hours. How could I? But the night went on forever anyway. We had arrived in Stuttgart sometime after three, and spent no more than twenty minutes inside the Himmelfarbs' house. Let us say it was four o'clock when we left. Shouldn't the sun have risen by now? Yet the canvas remained

black, the interior of the truck filled only with shadows, the suggestions of men. No one spoke. Just grunts and shuffles, the occasional broken wind. I couldn't even see what uniforms they wore. Which particular tentacle of Germany's monster had snatched us.

The truck lurched and then staggered to a stop, in a series of squeals from the naked brakes. Stefan straightened, slumped, and straightened again. I brought the children close. Henrik was damply asleep against my shoulder; Else's head lay on my lap. Every muscle ached. I couldn't feel my arms, because of the pressure on the various nerves. My shoes hurt my feet, too tight and too hot.

Could I move, if I had to?

Florian stirred against my ribs.

A metallic bang, and the back of the truck opened up to reveal a forest clearing, trimmed faintly in the pink of a rising dawn. A white young face appeared in the gap.

Aussteigen! he shouted.

Out we stumbled from the back of the truck, blinking and bleary in the gray-pink light. Else ran to Stefan and clutched his leg, and he tried to kneel and comfort her, but the guard wouldn't let him. So she went on clinging and sobbing, *Papa, what's happening? Papa!,* while his large hand cupped the side of her head. The guard turned to me and motioned angrily. I shrugged and gave him a helpless look. I was carrying Henrik in one

arm and holding Florian's hand with the other. The guard's face compressed with anger, but he let Else stay.

I came up to Stefan and breathed in the sticky scent of his neck. "Where is Johann?" I whispered in English.

"I don't know. Not in the truck."

Ruhig! said the guard.

I thought, If I can just speak to Johann. If I can just reason with him.

But I knew, even as I hoped, that this was impossible. That I never would have stood a chance: Annabelle against Johann's rigid professional duty. I never had. Not even when we were living as man and wife.

So when he appeared through the rose-colored mist, dressed in full uniform, flanked by a lanky adjutant, even more giant than I recalled, I looked into his pale heavy face and my lips moved in prayer.

Hail Mary, full of grace, the Lord is with thee.

Johann stopped and took us in, the five of us, Stefan and me and the three children who clung to us.

"Papa?" said Florian, and I tightened my hand around his, and for some reason, perhaps Johann's splendid uniform, perhaps the faintness of the early light or the stern lines of Johann's face, my son stayed right where he was, next to my leg.

Johann's gaze flicked down to Florian, but I saw not the slightest softening of his stiff

expression. He turned to the adjutant and muttered an order, and the adjutant turned to the guards and barked in a high and crackling voice, the German words so shrill that I had to pick through them one by one to understand.

By then, the men were already scrambling to obey. One of the guards took Florian by the arm and yanked him ahead, while another prodded his rifle into the small of my back. We stumbled forward. Johann turned smartly and led the way; the adjutant stayed behind with the truck and the other guards. Stefan walked a pace or two ahead of me, limping a little, holding Else's hand. Her ribbon had come loose, and her dark hair spilled about her shoulders. She clung to Stefan's hand with both of hers.

"Johann, please," I called. "The children. For God's sake. Have mercy."

But Johann's massive legs marched on, his field-gray shoulders remained square and polished in the soft dawn. To the right, I spied the familiar lines of the black Mercedes, parked in the mist at the edge of the clearing. The sight made my stomach contract. Henrik's heavy body slipped downward on my hip. "Please, slow down," I said, and Johann stopped and, without even turning, pointed to the car and ordered the guard at my back to put the woman and the children inside.

"No!" I shouted, but I couldn't fight the

guard, not when Florian hung from one arm and Henrik lay heavily on my hip. And then I thought, Yes, why not, put the children in the car where they will be safe. Where they won't see what happens. The guard jerked the door open and pushed the small of my back. Florian crawled onto the seat and found the steering wheel. I set Henrik down with my shaking hands and turned for Else.

But Else wouldn't leave Stefan. She wrapped her arms around his leg and clung, like a sobbing burr, impossible to extract. The guard, exasperated, grabbed her small shoulder, and Stefan, without warning, swung his fist into the guard's face. The man stumbled back with a cry. The blood flooded downward from a cut under his left eye. Stefan pressed forward, hitting him again, hitting his jaw and nose, knocking the rifle from his hand, and the attack was so swift and vicious that the other guard was only just turning, only just setting his rifle to his shoulder by the time the other guard fell to the grass and Stefan swooped the dropped rifle into his hands.

The gun, at last, that he needed.

As soon as Stefan's fist had connected with the guard's jaw, I ran to Else, who stood stunned a few feet away, her red mouth open in a frozen scream. I lifted her in my arms and tossed her into the car, and when I whipped around, slamming the door behind

me, the second guard fired his rifle at Stefan.

"No!" I screamed, but it didn't matter, the bullet whistled past and hit the car instead, punching a perfect hole in the rear bumper.

In the same instant, Stefan fired back twice, *bang bang,* and the guard's head snapped back, and then his entire body staggered and flew, like a man kicked by a horse, and the pieces of his skull and his brain splattered the damp grass and the gray wool of Johann's left arm in tiny pink chunks, while a crimson flower opened over his chest. His feet twitched and then went still, and I thought, as I compressed my cheeks between my two shocked hands: Now he will kill Johann. My God, Stefan is going to kill Johann.

5.

The day after our wedding, the morning after our wedding night, Johann and I had driven down to Italy along a southern route, because the Alpine passes were already covered in snow and Johann did not want to take such a risk with his beautiful car and his new wife. We reached Nice by evening and Johann asked if I would like to stay overnight or to drive straight through, and I glanced at the glassy dark Mediterranean and the red sun dropping below it, and I said I would like to drive straight through, if he wasn't too tired. So we did.

Johann telephoned ahead to the hotel in

Florence, so they were expecting us when we arrived just before dawn. He carried me up to the room, which was old and decorated with beautiful stuccos, and the sleepy bellboys followed with our luggage. We were to stay in Florence for two weeks, and I remembered thinking, as I lay on the bed and listened to Johann's exhausted snoring, it would be lovely to stay forever.

I had slept for an hour or two before the bells of the cathedrals woke me. There was some light creeping between the slats of the shutters. I turned my head and for an instant the sight of Johann's sleeping face shocked me. Then I remembered: we were married.

I rose and went to the suitcases, which had been left unpacked because we were so tired. I opened up mine first. I hung my dresses in the wardrobe and put my underthings in the drawer; there were not many, and I thought perhaps we would do a little shopping. Italian clothes were supposed to be beautiful. When I had emptied my own bags, I turned to Johann's single brown leather-covered trunk, plain and ancient, and I hesitated. But we're married now, I remembered. He's my husband, and a wife is supposed to unpack her husband's things, to make his life more comfortable for him.

So I opened the trunk and discovered a miracle of precise and efficient packing, no more than I supposed I should have expected.

579

I put his shirts and underclothes in the drawer, and I hung his suits and his single dress uniform, which he had worn for our wedding. At the bottom of the trunk I found his pistols.

There were two of them, exactly alike, made of cold black metal and utterly forbidding. I stared at them for a moment, not quite sure what to do, and then Johann's voice came to me from the bed.

"Annabelle? What are you doing?"

"Unpacking. What would you like me to do with your pistols?" I said it casually, as if cold black service pistols made an everyday appearance in my life.

"Bring them here."

I picked up the pistols, one in each hand, and brought them to Johann, who was sitting up in the bed, a little blurry still, his bare chest dusky in the shuttered light. He took the pistols from me and explained that these were Lugers, the Pistol 08 manufactured by the Mauser works, a very fine example of German engineering and craftsmanship. He showed me the mechanisms and let me hold one and lift the safety on and off, so there would not be any tragic mistakes. A pistol like this was not a toy: it was a tool, a weapon of extreme lethality. Did I understand? Because the thought of some accident occurring to his Annabelle, of any harm at all coming to his beloved wife, was too much to bear.

I said I understood, and he placed them in the drawer of the bedside table, next to his head.

I sat on the edge of the bed, a few inches away, and nudged him playfully. "What kind of man brings pistols along on his honeymoon?"

"A man who is ready to protect his wife at all times," he said, and his face and voice were so serious that I lost my smile.

"But surely we're safe here," I said, gesturing to the dark and elegant room around us.

He shrugged and said you were never completely safe in this world, that the threat always came when you least expected it, and his words reminded me how his first beloved wife had died without warning. How a wicked invader had stolen into their bedroom and killed her, and Johann had been helpless to stop it.

I leaned down and kissed him deeply and honestly, almost passionately, and he lifted me into his arms and told me that he would take me out to the shooting range when we arrived home in Germany. He would show me how to use a pistol properly, so I could protect myself if such a thing ever became necessary, God forbid.

As it turned out, the snow had already fallen by the time we reached Schloss Kleist, covering the shooting range in a thick blanket of virgin white, and the secret of firing a

lethal black Luger pistol remained unknown to me.

But I had been assured, over and over, by those who knew my husband well, that I had nothing to worry about, because Johann was an expert.

6.

By the time Stefan had fired his rifle, by the time the guard's body had hit the ground, already dead, Johann had drawn his pistol from the belt at his waist and stood calmly, oblivious to the gore around him, pointing the barrel at Stefan's chest.

Perhaps fifteen yards of grass separated them, no more. At such a short distance, even the thick yarns of mist were no impediment. The burnt scent of saltpeter filled my nose and stayed there. I couldn't breathe it in, could not even draw the air into my lungs to scream or plead or reason. My feet stuck to the ground, planted side by side in front of the closed door of the Mercedes, where the children sat waiting. I wanted to run out, to stop them, to throw myself on Johann's pistol. But if I moved, I would distract Stefan, and Johann would fire.

Or the other way around.

I heard Wilhelmine's voice. Wilhelmine, who now lay dead in the hallway of her house in Stuttgart.

You do not know that the two of them, they

are like Javert and Valjean? They are immortal enemies.

Neither man spoke. Each mouth sent regular white plumes into the November air, but no words. There was already so much between them, a long and tangled history of which I knew almost nothing, incidents and encounters that had occurred before I met either man. Dark-haired Stefan holding his stolen rifle, fair Johann with his pistol. Like a duel, like a pair of Regency rakes, except that it was real. Except that one of them would actually kill the other.

Which one?

Holy Mary, mother of God, pray for us sinners, now and in the hour of our death.

So intent was I on the two men standing across from each other, still as volcanoes, pointing their weapons, that at first I didn't notice the other guard when he stirred from the grass behind Stefan.

I didn't see him place his hand on the ground and hoist himself up, shaky and enormous and silent. Only when he leapt toward Stefan's back did the sight of him register in my brain, and I knew, even as my mouth opened, even as I screamed *Watch out!* that I was too late, that I had failed, that Stefan was the man who would die this November morning.

Crack.

A puff of smoke drifted from the tip of

Johann's pistol, and the guard dropped from Stefan's back, leaving half of his forehead behind.

Stefan staggered sideways under the impact, and set his knee on the ground. My feet moved at last. I ran across the grass and took Stefan's weight on my chest; I wrapped my arms around Stefan's back and gasped, *Are you hurt? Are you hurt?*

No, he said.

He looked over my shoulder. I turned, too.

Johann, face impassive, put his pistol back in his holster. He walked toward the second guard, examined him for a second, and turned to the two of us, Stefan and Annabelle, sitting stunned in the bloody grass.

"Get in the car. We must leave at once, before the border closes."

■ ■ ■ ■

Fifth Movement

■ ■ ■ ■

"When a man steals your wife, there is no better revenge than to let him keep her."
SACHA GUITRY

PEPPER

1.

Bed rest, the doctor says, and Pepper's not pleased.

"But there's nothing wrong with me," she says. "I'm fine, the baby's fine."

"By the grace of God. You're lucky that lovely Mrs. Dommerich found you and brought you in, after a fall like that." He peers at her over the clipboard. He has nice blue eyes, she thinks. Maybe a little too blue. Could you trust a man with eyes that blue? He says, like it's her fault: "I still don't quite understand how it happened."

Pepper considers telling him the truth. There's no reason she shouldn't, really, except that he wouldn't believe a sitting United States senator would behave so ignobly at the scene of a traffic accident. Certainly not in a humble seaside town like Saint Mary's, Georgia. She holds up her hands helplessly. "My crutches slipped."

"Hmm." He pats her foot. "We've reset the bone, and this time there will be no more

587

walking about until it's healed. Especially not on slippery November sidewalks. Is that understood?"

"Yes, sir," Pepper says meekly. "Whatever you say, sir."

He leans forward over the bed. "It's not going to work."

"What's not going to work?"

"That pretty face of yours, darlin'." He straightens, winks, makes a note on the chart, and walks to the door.

"Doctors these days," says Pepper.

"I heard that. And you're lucky I don't tell your father."

"Tell me what?" says Dadums, walking through the open door with two steaming cups of coffee.

2.

As Thanksgiving dinners go, Pepper's had worse. You wouldn't believe how many Schuylers could fit in a single Georgia hospital room, holding plates of rubber turkey and canned gravy, just like Mums didn't used to make, ever. Pepper's little nephew Lionel listens to her stomach with a stethoscope and announces it's twins. Maybe triplets.

"Good," Pepper says. "You can adopt one of them."

Daddy avoids looking at her stomach at all, but at least he's there, blaming everything on her mother, dodging volleys of returning

blame. The water in his glass is probably vodka. Her sister Vivian's husband reads Pepper's chart and assures her that the — what had she called him? — goddamned hayseed country doctor out here really does know what he's doing, no matter how many times he drops his *G*'s and calls her darlin'.

"He's rather handsome, too," says Mums.

"Give it a rest, Mums. You've already got a dishy young doctor for a son-in-law. You don't need another."

"Just an observation, that's all. If you'd taken more of my advice, you wouldn't be in this little fix, now, would you?"

"If I'd taken more of your advice, I'd be keeping the drunks company in the church basement."

In short, another festive holiday with the Schuylers.

3.

Daddy remains behind, after an exchange of eloquent glances with her mother that ends in a resigned sigh. He drops down in the chair next to the bed and asks her what the hell happened.

"It's a long and sordid story."

He doesn't take her hand and say, *Try me.* He really, truly doesn't want to know the details. He strokes his chin a few times, and then he lights a cigarette and blows the smoke out to the side. His face is gray and heavy.

"Well," he says at last, "at least you're all right now."

"I'd say that's a matter of opinion."

He stares at her ankle. "Next time, come to us a little earlier, all right?"

"Now, why didn't I think of that?" She smacks her forehead.

Her father says to the ankle: "I just — I didn't know what to do with you. Whether to let you make your own mistakes or step in. You were always full of trouble. I was damned if I did, damned if I didn't. Maybe that's no excuse, but it was true." He turns back to her face, the seat of her trouble. "And I didn't want to hurt your spirit. I loved your spirit."

She can't say a word.

"You'll understand when you have one of your own."

She nods.

"We'll take care of you. Everything's going to be all right."

"But what if it's not?" she says. "What if you open up the newspaper tomorrow and someone's leaked out some story about Uncle Freddie, about how he bribed that senator to get his oil contracts?"

There is a small silence, during which Daddy's eyes grow small and hard, like a pair of agates.

He says quietly: "Who? Who's leaked out some story?"

She shrugs. "Someone might."

He stubs out the cigarette in the ashtray next to her bed and finishes the water in his glass. He rises from his chair, all paunchy and once-handsome, smelling familiarly of hair oil and cigarettes and just a hint of booze, and he pats the top of her head, as if she were eight years old again.

"I'd just like to see the honorable gentleman try it."

4.

Pepper's not prepared for the feeling of relief that drenches her when Florian Dommerich's dark head appears through the crack in the door.

"Am I allowed inside?" he asks.

She sets aside her book, taking time with the tasseled bookmark and laying the volume just so on the blanket next to her thigh. "I don't suppose I'm in any condition to stop you."

He smiles, and the rest of him unfolds from behind the door, just as capably handsome as she remembers. His hands are full of coffee. Pepper's chest seems to have run out of room for her vital organs, pushing them upward into her throat.

"You're looking well," he says. "May I sit down?"

She gestures to the chair.

"Mama'll be along soon. She's talking with your doctor. I understand it's bed rest for

591

you, young lady." He gives her a stern look and hands her a foam cup of coffee. The other one remains in his palm, looking small.

"That's what happens when your mother blocks the street with her three-hundred-thousand-dollar car and causes an accident." Pepper blows across the surface of the coffee. "How's the car, by the way? I almost wept when I saw the damage."

"Oh, it'll be fine. We found a good mechanic in Washington. He about lost his jaw when he saw it." Florian chuckles, and Pepper's a goner. That chuckle.

"Did you have a nice Thanksgiving?"

"Sort of. Two pregnant sisters-in-law snapping at each other, one nephew with pneumonia, one brother quit his job to become a musician and move to California. The usual. You?"

"Vodka in the aspic, arsenic in the cranberry. The usual."

He grins. "I told you so."

"Told me what?"

"Your family would take care of you, if you gave them a chance."

"Trust me, Dommerich. I liked it better when I was on my own."

"Liar, liar." He drinks his coffee and smiles at her, a little goofy. There's something relaxed about his face, something pleasant, and she wonders if it's relief, and whether her face looks the same way.

"How's Susan?" she asks.

He runs a hand through his hair. "Susan's back with her folks in Florida. Had a nice Thanksgiving, she says."

"You talked to her?"

"Called her up this morning. We talked for a bit." He swishes the coffee in long waves along the side of his cup, staring down intently, like he's calculating sine, cosine, and tangent. "She thinks Hobbes is a brand of shoe."

"No, she doesn't."

He looks up. "Yep."

Pepper puts on a grave face. "She was probably just kidding you."

"Maybe. Anyway, I'm glad you're all right. I was a little panicked when I got the message at the hotel."

"The Mercedes got the worst of it."

He was shaking his head. "I'd never have forgiven my mother if something happened."

"It wasn't her fault. It was that idiot driving the car. There was plenty of time to stop if he hadn't been trying to light a cigarette. She just wanted to stop him, that's all."

"Well, at least she did that."

"Yes. You should have seen her." Pepper looks at the ceiling and smiles. "She stripped him bare. Flayed him like he was eight years old. I couldn't get a word in edgewise. I was so mad I hopped out of the car and forgot all about the crutches."

He gestures to her foot in its outsized cast, lying in state on the pillow. "You won't forget now."

"No."

"And now he's out of your life for good. His brother, I mean. Both of them."

Pepper looks back down at the gentle mountain of her pregnancy, this foreign salient of her once-lithe body. For maybe the thousandth time, she thinks, My God, I'm going to be a mother, and for the thousandth time it doesn't quite sink in. Maybe it won't sink in until the baby's born, until it's alive and kicking in her arms, until it's nursing at her breast, further ruining her perfect curves. Maybe not even then. Maybe the sonofabitch was right, when he spoke to her there in the parlor of the Riverview Hotel; maybe Pepper isn't mother material.

"That depends," she says. "I mean, it's his baby, too. I can't just say never, can I? I'm kind of stuck with him."

"That's generous of you."

"It's not for his sake, or his family's sake. It's for the baby's sake. The baby deserves a father, if his father decides he wants to be a father."

"Or she."

Pepper looks up.

Florian's smiling. "Might be a girl."

"Might be. God help her."

Florian goes back to swishing his coffee.

"So I was thinking . . ."

"You could use a haircut? A decent necktie?"

"Probably both of those things. But mostly I was thinking we might have coffee sometime."

"Unless I'm hallucinating, that's what we're doing right now."

"So maybe we could have coffee more often. A regular thing."

"Don't you have to go back to work on Monday morning?"

"I could visit on weekends."

"That's a hell of a drive."

He leans in close, so she can smell the flavor of his shaving soap. "I could fly."

Maybe she banged her ribs in the accident. Maybe it's pneumonia. A heart attack. Whatever it is, there's definitely something wrong with Pepper's chest. She'll have to ask that nice doctor for an X ray, the next time he comes around.

"It's a dumb idea," she says. "The dumbest idea I've ever heard. I'm not much fun at the moment."

"That's okay. I happen to like you when you're not much fun."

Jesus. Now her eyes.

"I guess I'm not in any condition to stop you," she says, and then, without thinking, "even if I wanted to," and thank God the door opens right then, before she can go on

to say something even more stupid, and Annabelle Dommerich marches into the room, carrying a big bunch of fragrant pink roses.

"They're really from Florian," she says, planting a kiss on Pepper's forehead, "but he was too shy to give them to you himself."

"Mama, for chrissakes," says Florian.

5.

"Thank God you're all right," says Annabelle. "I'd never have forgiven myself."

Pepper lets out an aggrieved sigh. "You were trying to help."

"Well, I did, didn't I? All's well that ends well."

"Speak for yourself." Pepper gestures to the whole lot: belly, bed, cast. "And now I've got my family crowding half drunk around my bedside every second, thanks to your meddling."

"Yes, I was right about that, too," Annabelle says smugly. "I just had to pin you down, nice and helpless, so you could see for yourself. And the car will be fixed by the end of the week. *And* I got rid of Susan."

"How did you manage that?"

"Oh, I may have hinted that Florian was conceived out of wedlock, or something like that." She leans forward, woman to woman. "He likes you, you know."

"I know."

"So don't you go around breaking my son's heart. He's really very tender inside, though he hates to show it."

"Trust me, I wouldn't dare. I saw what you did to that sonofabitch outside."

"Good, then. You'll be very happy. I can see you're already in love with him. I'll have that Cartier watch on my wrist by Christmas." She winks. "Our bet, remember?"

Pepper rolls her eyes and reaches for the cherry Jell-O.

"By the way," Annabelle continues, examining her fingernails, "I'm taking your advice."

"I beg your pardon? When did I ever give *you* advice?"

"About my friend on Cumberland Island. I realized you were right, that I was a coward. And I suppose my pride was hurt as well. Every woman likes to dream that a man will pine for her eternally, when the reality is that the poor dears just need some company. They can't manage on their own forever." She smiles brightly. "So I'm off on the afternoon ferry. Finish off that unfinished business and brush my hands clean."

Pepper scrapes her spoon around the sides of the Jell-O cup, wondering if it would be bad form to lick it clean. "I'm glad to hear it. Tell me how everything goes. I hope you kick the bitch out."

Annabelle laughs. "I'll do no such thing. I'm just going to say hello, give him some-

thing back, and wish him well."

Pepper looks up. "But don't you want to wait until the car is all fixed?"

"The car?"

"I mean, what are you going to say? *I've bought back the Mercedes, please don't mind that crumpled mess in the rear wheel well.*"

Annabelle's face clears. "Oh, my dear. I'm not bringing him the car. Why would I?"

"But I thought it was his. His car."

"No, no. The car belonged to my dear husband, God rest his soul. And it's a beautiful car, and my husband loved it very much and was sorry to see it go, and I'm sure he's very happy, wherever he is, to know that I've found it again. No, for this man, I have something far more valuable." She looks at her watch, starts, and picks up her gloves and pocketbook, which are made of rich blue leather in contrast to her neat black trousers and cashmere turtleneck sweater. She picks up her coat, made of beautiful aubergine wool, and slings it over her shoulder. "I'm going to be late."

"But wait! I'm confused. I thought —"

But Annabelle is already slipping through the door into the bright hospital corridor, an elegant blue-tipped bird among the antiseptic white walls.

Pepper sets aside the empty Jell-O cup and says aloud, to the baby: You know, one day,

we have really got to make her sit down and tell us the whole damned story.

ANNABELLE

GERMANY 1938

1.

In the interior of the Mercedes, nobody spoke. Johann drove intently along the dirt road, glancing into the mirror every so often, while Stefan and I occupied the other seat, covered with sleeping children, staring like corpses through the windshield, too shocked to say anything at all. To ask a single question.

Until Florian woke up. Florian lifted his head from Stefan's chest and saw Johann driving keen-eyed, both hands gripping the wheel, washed clean by the morning light, and he shouted, "Papa!" and flung himself on Johann's thick arm.

Johann had already taken off his jacket that was covered in brains, and he opened up his arm and pressed Florian to his shirt, without saying a word.

Next to me, Stefan closed his eyes and stroked Else's dark hair, and a minute later his breathing relaxed, and he seemed to have fallen asleep.

2.

Johann lit a cigarette and asked if I wanted one. I said no, thank you.

"Are you well?" he said. "You are not hurt?"

"No."

He adjusted Florian in his arm, so he could smoke and drive at the same time. "Good. I had some concern, when I saw them putting you in the truck like that."

"You didn't show it."

"I couldn't."

The air was close inside the car, despite the late autumn chill. I found myself wishing we could open the top. I leaned across Henrik's sleeping body and turned off the heater. "Where are we going?"

"To the border crossing at Neuenbürg, about a hundred kilometers away, south of Freiburg. It's a smaller one, in case we have any trouble."

"I don't understand."

He maneuvered around Florian to tap his cigarette into the ashtray. "Listen to me. If we are going to get you across in safety, you must do exactly as I say, all right?"

"All right."

"We are husband and wife. These are our children. We are going south to Italy, to spend the winter there for your health. You've been sick, okay?"

"Yes. What about Stefan?"

"We will stop shortly, about a mile from

the border, and put him in the boot."

"The boot? Won't they look?"

"No," he said, "because I am a general in the German army, you understand. I am a senior official; I am a confidant of the Führer. I outrank any idiot officer at the Neuenbürg crossing, at least until they find out what I have just done."

He took in a long draft from his cigarette, which was nearly finished, and then he pulled the pack from his shirt pocket and lit another one from the end of the first, which he stubbed out in the ashtray.

"And what have you done?" I asked softly.

"I have committed an act of treason, I suppose."

"You have saved us. You saved Stefan."

He shrugged.

"Why?" I asked.

"Not for his sake, certainly. Not even wholly for yours."

"Then whose?" But I knew the answer.

He drove on silently for a moment, negotiating a series of curves in the road. There were no other cars, an eerie absence of other people, and I remembered the riots last night. The riots that had started all this, and now seemed like another age. The smoke was so thick, I couldn't breathe. I rolled down the window a couple of inches.

"I was in Munich yesterday," he said. "There was a great meeting, a celebration,

actually, a commemoration of the — oh, what is it in English? — I believe it's called the Beer Hall Putsch. When they sent Hitler to jail, many years ago, and he wrote his book. We were all expected to be there. A very nice dinner, a big dinner, and then we got word that vom Rath had died, the poor bastard. And instead of giving his speech, Hitler left, and Herr Goebbels spoke instead."

"What did he say?"

"He said that the party wouldn't instigate any demonstrations, but that they wouldn't stop them, either. If the people wanted to kill Jews in revenge, no one would stop them." He cracked open his own window and blew out the smoke. "And all I could think was Florian. This enemy, this animal they were talking about, was my boy. They want to kill my boy." His voice broke. "They will kill my dear boy because he is a Jew."

I waited while he struggled. My eyes blurred, so that I couldn't quite see the road ahead, and turned my head to the window instead, where the smudging of the passing trees was a normal optic effect.

Johann went on: "So I left, before anyone could see what was in my face, and returned to my hotel, and there was a message there that they — the Gestapo agents, these men I have worked with many times — had discovered who was involved in the escape of Stefan Silverman a month ago and that they

were planning a raid that night on the house of the Himmelfarb family in Stuttgart. Why tonight? Of course, because the demonstrations would lend them the perfect cover; they could do what they wanted this night."

"Oh, God," I whispered.

"I got in my car that instant and left. By then, I think I had gone a little mad. I thought, I have been wrong. I have been wrong about my country. I have been what I believe the Americans call a stooge . . . is that the word? Stooge?"

"Yes, I think so."

"A stooge for these men, these selfish men who will commit any crime to win themselves another gram of power. I have got to do this, I have got to stop them. I have got to do this for my boy."

He wiped his face and dropped his cigarette out the window.

"In the event, I arrived too late. They had already shot the Himmelfarbs like dogs in their own house. I saw the wife there on the rug, shot through the forehead, here, and the stomach." He gestured. "But then I saw Silverman. He was fighting like a madman. I thought, My God, what the fuck is Silverman doing here, when he should be safe in Switzerland? The goddamned bastard is more a hero than I am, he is fighting for his people instead of enjoying his new wife and his son and his freedom. And I realized in that

second what God was asking me to do."

He started another cigarette, and the sun, now fully risen, darted out from a cloud, blinding the windshield. Else stirred and groaned, and I put my hand over her brow to shield her.

"How are the girls?" I said. "How is Frieda?"

"She was distraught when you left. She is a little better now. She is with my sister."

There was a low ache in my gut, like the removal of some vital organ. I stroked Else's hair and said, "And you? How are you?"

He glanced down at Florian's head, and then he lifted his hand, the one with the cigarette, and rubbed his forehead with his thumb. "For some time, I wished I would die. Not to kill myself. But that God would take me in the night, so I would not wake up and find you both still gone. I thought He must be punishing me, and yet what had I done? I was only doing my duty. I had done what I supposed was right."

I thought, His face is so lean. His big frame, there isn't an ounce of extra weight. He hasn't been eating. He is smoking too much.

I thought staunchly, But he deserves that. He deserves not to eat, for what he did to Stefan.

"Now, of course," Johann went on, in a quiet voice, "I see why God allowed me to live."

He slowed the car, and we turned from the smaller road onto a large paved highway. A signed passed by: FREIBURG, 78 KILOMETERS. In a hundred kilometers we would be out of Germany.

A thought occurred to me. "So what will you do?" I exclaimed. "You can't go back, can you?"

"No, they would probably arrest me if I tried. I sent a telegram to my sister before I left Munich. She was to pack up everything she could and bring the girls to Paris. I hope to God she has succeeded. The boys are still at school in England."

"Thank God."

"Yes." He paused. "They will confiscate my estate, however."

"I'm sorry."

"Don't be sorry. Maybe it is what I deserve." He pulled out another cigarette. His voice was rough, as if he were choking on glass. "You must take care of Florian. You must take care of my dear boy. He will not remember me."

"He might."

"No. He is too young. If he were three or four, perhaps. But this is for the best." He lost himself a little on the last word, and covered it with the cigarette. With his thumb he rubbed the inner sockets of his eyes.

I couldn't think of anything more to say. Thank you? My limbs were tired and aching

from holding the children, from the long night without sleep, from the avalanche of fear and dread piled on my shoulders.

All at once, I couldn't hold my head up any longer. I leaned my heavy cheek against Stefan's shoulder, and as I listened to his breathing, the rhythm of his respiration that I knew more intimately than my own, I realized that he was awake.

3.

We passed Freiburg just before noon, and a few kilometers later Johann pulled over into a field by the side of the road. The children were awake by now, restless and hungry and confused.

"Let them stretch a bit," said Johann. "Then we must go into the village for a little food and to clean up, so we look like a civilized family. Silverman, it is best if you wait here, I think."

"Of course," said Stefan.

"I will need napkins for Henrik, and milk," I said.

"Yes, we will get all these things." He looked up at the sun, or the spot overhead where the sun would be, if the clouds hadn't moved in the way. "I have been thinking that we might wait until it is closer to dusk. Dusk is a good hour — harder to see details, but there is not so much suspicion as at night."

Stefan nodded. "Very well." He was watch-

607

ing the children in the field.

In the village, Johann visited a barber for a shave. I took the children into the market and bought food and milk and cigarettes. The atmosphere was deeply subdued; hardly anybody was out. There were thick black headlines on all the newspapers, but I didn't read them. In another shop I found a bottle for Henrik, and napkins. I bought five, enough to last a day or two, until I could find a way to wash them. Johann was waiting for me at the car, freshly shaven, jacket miraculously cleaned. He took the packages from me and put them in the boot.

"How did you get the jacket cleaned?" I asked.

"I had the barber do it. I explained that we had hit a deer along the road."

"Did he believe you?"

Johann shrugged. "He didn't ask any questions."

We drove back through the eerie streets to the field where we'd left Stefan. I let the children out of the car and stepped out after them to look around. There was no sign of Stefan's dark hair, his gaunt brown shoulders. I turned to Johann. "Where's Stefan?"

Johann was unwrapping the food. "He'll be back."

"But where has he gone?"

"For a walk, I think. She was his wife once."

"I've got to find him."

Johann put a hand on my arm. "Let him be, Annabelle. He'll be back. He will be back for you and the children."

There was an unsettling normalcy to it all, eating lunch with Johann and Florian and Wilhelmine's children. The air had warmed a bit, so we sat in our seats in the car and kept the doors open. Henrik insisted on sitting in the grass. Else and Florian chased each other. My brain was still so numb; I could hardly comprehend the past twenty-four hours. I had focused on the necessary details, hygiene and food and sleep. But the great truth sat behind it all, the awfulness, like a gorgon waiting for night. And this man, sitting next to me. Johann, my onetime husband, lost and found. Soon to be lost again, this time for good.

It's a damned thing.

"I don't know what to tell Else," I said. "How do I tell her?"

"Wait until she asks, and then tell her the truth. You will know what to say. She is very young still. It's much easier when they are so young. Once they have turned five or six, they understand what has happened. They know enough to grieve."

I rose and brushed the crumbs from my skirt. "Could you watch them for a moment? I'm going to find Stefan."

4.

I found Stefan on a fallen tree, in the woods at the perimeter of the field, not far away, after all. He was smoking a cigarette and drinking from a bottle of Scotch whisky.

"Where did you find that?" I asked.

"In the car, before you left."

I sat down beside him. "Are you all right?"

"No, I don't think so. Not at the moment."

I laid my hand on his thigh. "We'll raise her children. That's all any mother wants, that her children are safe."

"We left her lying there in the hallway. You did not see her face, Annabelle, but I will see it always." He looked at his hands, the one with the bottle and the other with the cigarette. "You are a good mother. It was the last thing on my mind, on the yacht, when I was going mad for you, lying awake and imagining what it would be like to have you. But now I'm grateful."

"Listen to me." I turned his face toward me. "We have each other, and the children. We'll learn to be happy again."

"Listen to you. There is no one in the world like you."

"That's what you said when you kissed me, that first time."

"Yes, I remember."

I put my hands on his cheeks and kissed him, the way he had kissed me three years ago on the Île Sainte-Marguerite, and I ended

the kiss the way he had, sliding my lips across his cheek to his ear.

"The damnedest thing about all of this," he said, "is that if I hadn't wanted to do the right thing, it would have been all right."

"What do you mean?"

"I would have taken you to Paris, instead of going to Germany to finish things with Wilma first. I would have slept by your side through the long winter, watching the baby grow. Maybe it would have been a sin, living with you like that, but it would have been better than prison, and no one would have died. God in Heaven, how happy we would have been. I would have held my son in my two hands. So where is the nice moral here? I should have been a scoundrel instead."

"Don't say that. Don't talk as if this was your fault."

"But it is. Their blood is on my hands." He dropped the cigarette into the leaves and squashed it under his heel. "Though I suppose my original sin was to seduce you in the first place, instead of leaving you for von Kleist to marry."

"No, because I seduced you. And there would have been no von Kleist if there had been no Stefan."

"Then some other worthy man, as God meant for you."

I put my arms around his neck. "God didn't mean me for some stupid worthy man."

He set the bottle on the wet ground and kissed me, because he had no choice, because when you are covered in death you crave life. He kissed me feverishly, there in the quiet woods, and tucked his hands inside my coat, covering my breasts with his hands. "In prison, I dreamed always of this, your breasts in the August sunshine. We had only a few days, didn't we, but when I dreamed, I swear it was like the whole of my life."

"Because it will be. It will be the whole of our lives, from now on."

He bent down and buried his face in my chest. His hands crept under my dress, and I felt something wet against my feet, as the bottle of whisky spilled over my shoes. We sat there quietly, while his breath warmed my breasts and his hands warmed my hips. "What are you doing?" I asked softly, even though I knew the answer.

"Listening."

"What am I saying to you this time?"

"Ah, the usual absurd things. That you love my hands on your skin. That you want me to make love to you, even here in this wretched cold November woods. That, in your stupid American optimism, you are already counting the children we will have together, and the olives we will grow, when we finally reach our island."

I nearly laughed in relief. "Yes, exactly."

He stroked my thighs with his thumbs.

"That your heart still beats for me."

"Yes, always. And yours?"

"Do you need to ask?"

I tried to lift his head and kiss him, but he wouldn't let me. "No, please, a moment more, Mademoiselle. Just another moment like this, with no more talking."

There were no birds to sing for us. The last leaf had already fallen. I stared up at the bony tops of the trees, at the gray sky above, and listened to Stefan's heartbeat against my belly. The air smelled of whisky and rotting leaves. In Capri, I thought, the sun will be shining, and it will smell like lemon and eucalyptus.

"You're shivering," he said at last.

"Not from the cold."

He lifted his head. "We should get back to the car."

5.

We stayed in the field for a few more hours. Stefan played with the children while Johann slept in the car. When it was time to go, Stefan took the passports and papers from the inside pocket of his jacket, the ones that Wilhelmine had had made for us, and he gave them to Johann. "You can use these to cross the border," he said, "in case the guards have already been alerted. It will be safer this way, if you don't wear your uniform."

Johann stared at the papers, turned them

over, and nodded. "These are good forgeries," he said, and he took off his uniform jacket and asked if he could trade with Stefan. The sleeves were too short, and the wool strained against his shoulders, but only if you looked closely. He tucked the papers into his pocket, lifted the lid of the boot, and made an apologetic gesture. "It will not be too long, I hope."

Stefan climbed obediently into the boot, a little stiff and trying not to show it. He had to bend his body to fit inside. When he was comfortable — or at least as comfortable as he could make himself — I leaned inside and kissed him, and I didn't care if Johann saw us. "Everything will be fine," I said.

"It seems your husband is a decent chap after all."

"He's not my husband anymore," I whispered, kissing him again, holding his cheek. "I'm Mrs. Annabelle Dommerich now, and I'm married to you."

"As you say."

Johann stepped in and closed the lid. He leaned against the metal and said, "Okay?"

"Okay," came Stefan's faint response.

We drove the last twenty kilometers in silence. Johann smoked cigarette after cigarette, holding each one close to the crack in the window, checking the mirror from time to time as if wary of pursuit. The children clustered on my lap, restless and bored, pok-

614

ing at the gears and the dials. Else asked for her mother. The sky had already begun to darken by the time we reached the signposts for the border, for the bridge across the Rhine into France.

"Here we go," said Johann, rolling to a stop, and I looked ahead to the striped metal pole across the white pavement, while my stomach turned sick with fear.

Johann glanced at me. "Don't worry. Smile, okay?" A face appeared in the window, and he turned. *"Guten Tag, mein Herr."*

The man's eyes took in the interior of the car, the size of the passenger inside, and his face registered surprise, which he smothered quickly. "Heil Hitler. Passports, please."

"Of course." Johann reached inside his jacket pocket and produced the papers. "Here you are."

The soldier took the passport from Johann's fingers. He cast another curious glance at the elegant Mercedes, the beautiful polished wood inside, and then he looked down at the first passport and fumbled through the pages. "Mr. Dommerich?" he said.

"Yes, sir. My family and I are heading to Italy before the snow falls. My wife is in poor health, I'm afraid. These northern winters."

The soldier's gaze traveled respectfully in my direction. I tried to look wan, as befit an invalid. Henrik whimpered and shimmied down my lap to rest at my feet.

"Frau Dommerich?"

"My wife is ill," said Johann sharply.

"Let her speak. I am required to verify her identity."

"Her identity is obvious."

So much natural authority, packed into so bass a voice. The young soldier actually hesitated. "Herr Dommerich, you've surely heard — that is, because of the demonstrations last night —"

"I have no knowledge of these so-called demonstrations," said Johann, "and what is more, I don't care. I am concerned for my wife's welfare. We have hotel reservations in Lyon, and it's already late."

The guard peered inside again, at this mysterious invalid who inspired such passionate devotion in her husband. "Yes, sir. I quite understand. I'll just —"

"Papa," Florian said suddenly, "where is Stefan?"

Else looked up from the map, which she held upside-down on her lap. "Stefan's in the boot, silly."

The air froze. There was no sound at all, except for the slight crackle of the map between Else's small fingers and the knock of my pulse in my throat.

The guard looked at the children, and then at Johann. "What did the child say?"

"Nothing."

"She said something about someone in the

616

boot, sir."

Johann knocked the ash from his cigarette into the dust outside the car. "Soldier, I assure you, the only thing in the boot of my car is my wife's baggage."

"But the girl said —"

I lifted my head and spoke in my best German. "Do you mean Stefan?"

"Yes. The girl said someone named Stefan is in the boot of the car."

I smiled. "Stefan is my son's teddy bear."

Florian opened his mouth, and I moved my hand over his lips in a gesture that looked like a caress.

"His teddy bear?"

"Yes. Doesn't your son have a teddy bear?" I looked at the soldier with my most enormous round eyes, and he began to stammer.

"I — I don't — that is —"

"What's this? Your wife hasn't given you a big strapping son?"

"No, she — that is, I'm not married —"

"Well." I looked tenderly at Johann and reached out to stroke his arm. "A fine handsome young soldier like that. I think every soldier deserves a pretty German girl to marry."

The guard's face had turned the color of a radish.

"I quite agree, my dear," said Johann, "and now I'm afraid we must be off. Are we through here, soldier?"

"Y-Yes, sir! Heil Hitler, sir!" The guard stepped back and waved us on.

"Heil Hitler, soldier. I shall be sure to write a letter to your commanding officer, praising your efficiency."

6.

On the other side of the river, the French guard was half drunk, and hardly even glanced at our passports before he stamped them at a sloppy angle. We drove on down the darkened road for perhaps fifteen minutes, watching the beams of the headlamps as they swept over the pavement, until Johann seemed to spot something on the side of the road and pulled over. A barn, made of crumbling yellow stone. I nudged the children off my lap and opened the door almost before we had fully stopped.

Under the lid of the boot, Stefan made a little groan. Johann grabbed him under the shoulders and helped him out, and he knelt into the grass and vomited. I had no handkerchief left. I waited anxiously until he had finished, and then I sat on the ground and pulled him against my chest.

"We will stop here tonight, then," said Johann. "I'll sleep in the car, you can have the barn. You can leave in the morning. Here are the keys." He handed them to me.

I stared dumbly at the metal in my palm. "You're giving us the car?"

He shrugged. "You can leave it in Monte Carlo. I will pick it up later. You *are* leaving from Monte Carlo, aren't you?"

"Yes. Help me get him up."

But Stefan shrugged us both off. The children had spilled out of the car and stood there, blinking, as he rose to his feet. "Let us have a little dinner," he said, "and then we will rest for the night."

7.

The straw was old and musty, but I had never known anything more comfortable. I settled the children a few yards away and covered them with my coat, and then I collapsed next to Stefan.

"I'm sorry," he whispered. "I smell like the devil."

"I don't care. We've done it, we're safe, we're free. We're in France."

His arm closed around me. "Yes, by God's grace."

"We'll telephone my father from Monte Carlo and let them know we're safe. They'll be worried."

"Yes, of course."

"And your troubles will be over. You will rest and recover."

"I am very fortunate, Mademoiselle, to have you watching over me."

"Yes, you are. And I was just thinking, in the car, that maybe this horrible night will

619

wake up the world to what's going on. Maybe Johann can speak to the embassy in Paris, and the whole nightmare will be over, and Wilhelmine won't have died in vain."

He kissed my hair. "My dauntless American girl. Go to sleep. We will save the fucking world in the morning."

"I can't sleep."

"Try."

I closed my eyes and pulled him closer, until his breath was warm in my hair, and that was all I remembered until I woke up some unknown hour later, and he was gone.

"Stefan?" I whispered, into the dusty silence of the barn.

"Over here."

I lifted my head and saw his shadow, sitting by the hollow in the straw where the children lay sleeping. What lucky children, I thought, to have Stefan for a father, and then I pictured Johann, bent uncomfortably on the seat of the Mercedes outside, covered by his gray uniform jacket, and for an instant my heart hurt.

But I will thank him one day, I thought. I will return to him and thank him for the gift he has given to me tonight, to Florian and me. That he loved us both so much, he gave us back to his immortal enemy.

I settled back in the musty straw and closed my eyes again. In a moment, Stefan would come back to bed and put his arms around

me, the way he always did, and in the morning we would drive down with the children to the sunshine of Monte Carlo, to the life we had dreamed together.

"Thank God," I said softly. "I thought you'd gone away."

■ ■ ■ ■

CODA

■ ■ ■ ■

"The sea does not reward those who are
too anxious, too greedy, or too impatient.
One should lie empty, open, choiceless as
a beach — waiting for a gift from the sea."
ANNE MORROW LINDBERGH

STEFAN

CUMBERLAND ISLAND 1966

1.

The knock arrives at sunset, half an hour after he stomped back, damp and chilled, from feeding the horses. He has showered and shaved and put on the teakettle, and at first he thinks the telephone wire has come loose again in the November wind, and is now flapping against the roof.

He pauses, fingers still wrapped around the handle of the kettle, and turns his cheek to the ceiling, listening. The sound comes again, three imperative knocks, knuckles against wood.

He doesn't have many visitors, and they usually mean trouble of some kind: horses loose or fences down or hurricanes on the way. That's surely why his pulse crashes against his neck, as the knock echoes about the empty rooms. Why his blood turns buoyant in his veins. Because there might be trouble.

He wipes his hands on the dishcloth and heads for the front door.

625

He doesn't have far to walk. The house is small and simple: living room, dining room, and kitchen on the ground floor, along with a small office and plenty of bookshelves. (He has too many books to count, the natural consequence of solitude.) Upstairs, two roomy bedrooms and a bathroom. One of the bedrooms has a sleeping porch, and he really does sleep there in the summer, when the heat billows up from the tall marsh grasses to merge with the smoldering sky, and you almost can't breathe the air, it's so wet. He puts up the screens with the netting to keep the mosquitoes away, and he sleeps in a pair of cotton pajamas with no blanket. In the morning, he's covered in dew.

He walks across the living room to the entry hall, past the signs of his recent visitor. If he stands still and closes his eyes, he can still smell her in the air: a hint of perfume, the soap she uses. He can almost hear the trace of her laughter, like an echo trapped in the furniture she has touched. Right there, in the corner of the living room, just two days ago, he showed her how to waltz to the "Blue Danube." Something every woman should do with a man who loves her.

When he reaches the entry hall, he pauses, because he hasn't heard the knock again, and maybe he was mistaken. Maybe he'll open the door and there will be nobody there. It's happened before, usually after his visitor

leaves. He'll think he hears something, some sign of human love and habitation — maybe she's turned back after all, maybe she'll stay this time — but when he opens his eyes, he knows he's alone again. That this promising sound was just a delusion, after all.

Knock, knock.

Well, not a delusion this time.

He draws the cool air deep into his lungs, reaches for the knob, and opens the door, and there in the light from the porch stands a dark-haired woman in a coat of soft aubergine wool, full and delicate both at once, whose eyes open wide at the sight of his face.

"Stefan," she whispers.

His hand sticks to the knob. His chest fills up with quicksilver and runs over. He thinks, Hell, I remembered her face all wrong, I forgot the shade of her eyes, I forgot her cheekbones and her pointed chin, I forgot how beautiful she is. How could I forget that? When she lives inside my skin.

"May I come in?" she asks, and it seems he forgot that, too, the sound of her voice.

Somehow, he steps back and opens the door, just wide enough.

"Would you like some tea?" he asks.

2.

The next morning, it's so much easier. He opens his eyes from a velvet sleep, and for a moment he thinks he's in Monte Carlo, at

the scorching end of August, and a tantalizing future still beckons outside his window. He can almost smell the lemon trees in the courtyard, and then he remembers it's Annabelle's skin. Her skin smells like lemons. What kind of miracle is that?

The light is still gray and hushed through the shutters. Annabelle is deeply asleep. It seems to him that he'll wake her if he stays in bed — wake her with the force of loving her — so he untangles her from his arms instead and slips downstairs to make coffee, the way she likes it.

The teacups still sit on the kitchen table, half full, and the sight makes him smile. The way they talked awkwardly — *How are you?* Fine, fine. *How do you like Cumberland Island?* It is marvelous, except for the terrible heat in July — and took their tea in tiny nervous sips.

The way Annabelle had crashed down her cup into the middle of another calcified sentence and said, *Don't look at me like that,* and he had said, *Like what?* and she said, *Like you want to kiss me.*

The way he had stared at her, hammering heart, thinking, God in heaven, what does she mean, can it be true, and then thinking, Of course it's true, it's Annabelle, Stefan, it's your own fucking *Annabelle* walking in your front door three decades later, out of the clear blue sky, wanting you to break the ice and everything else, and you are just going to sit

there with your cock in your hand while the clock ticks and the house groans and the minutes bleed irretrievably away, the dwindling minutes remaining to you both?

The way she had risen from her chair like a princess and said, *Unless you don't want to kiss me, after all,* and he said, *But of course I want to kiss you,* and she had given him a look both defiant and vulnerable and turned to climb the stairs, and he had thought how very like Annabelle this was, like no one else in the world.

The way he had then run after her and hoisted her over his shoulder and taken her up the rest of the stairs before he could doubt himself. The way she had laughed and put her soft palms on his skin and kissed him, and somehow it had all worked perfectly, being inside Annabelle again, losing himself inside Annabelle, drenching himself in the purity of her heart, his skin inside her skin, her skin inside his, in a thoroughly imperfect way.

The way it had worked again, even more perfectly imperfect, an hour later.

And Annabelle was right, as always: the awkwardness dissolved at the first touch, poof, like magic. You know where you stand with a woman, when you have just made love to her after a long absence. She knows where she stands with you. You can go to sleep

629

happy, listening to each other's heartbeats, because you know her again and she knows you, because you are no longer strangers, and you will work everything out in the morning, over hot coffee and a good smoke.

3.

When he returns with the coffee, she's awake, propped up against his pillow. Her breasts are heavier than before, darker at the tips, a woman's breasts. Just looking at them makes his ribs hurt.

She takes the coffee and sips. "So who's the woman?"

He's busy lighting a cigarette, and nearly spits it out of his mouth. "What woman?"

"The woman you were dancing with the other night. I saw you through the window." She gives him a challenging look. "Does your heart beat for her, too?"

He resumes lighting the cigarette, takes a good drag, and blows the smoke out slowly and with profound enjoyment. Then he crawls up the bed and starts kissing her breasts. "Yes, as a matter of fact. My heart beats for her, too. The two of you beauties, you are the great loves of my life."

She pushes his head away. "Bastard."

He's laughing and kissing her. He's so full of relief — that quicksilver in his chest last night, it turned out to be relief, of an elite and highly distilled grade — and so full of

Annabelle. He takes the coffee from her hand and puts it on the bedside table. He sticks the cigarette in the corner of his mouth and grasps her two hands, so she will the hell stop hitting him with them. "That was Else," he said. "Else visits me here."

As if her limbs have turned to butter. "Else?" she whispers.

"Yes. Didn't you get a good look, when you spied on the two of us through my window? She tracked me down a few years ago. I made her promise not to tell you." He removes the cigarette and resumes kissing her. "Johann was still alive."

"I see." She lies against his pillow without moving, accepting the kisses. "And when he died?"

"I thought I would wait for you to come to me. I didn't know if you wanted me, after everything. After so many years."

"Oh, Stefan. Don't be stupid." She moves finally, threading her hands in his hair.

He stops kissing her then, just lies on her soft body with his lips in her neck, smelling her lemon smell, letting the shock settle in his bones, letting her skin become his skin. He is in bed with Annabelle, and it's not a dream. He opened the door last night, and she was there, genuine hot cross Annabelle bun, warm and round in his arms.

"I brought your cello," she whispers.

"My cello?"

"The Amati you gave me. I played it everywhere for you. I played it in Carnegie Hall and the Boston Pops, I played it on every single recording I ever made. Did you hear any of them?"

He wants to say *Every one,* but his lips won't move.

"So I thought I would bring it back to you. That was my excuse, that the instrument really belonged to you, and I was just playing it for you, all these years. That was how I worked up the courage to come here."

Holy shit, he is going to cry.

"I mean, I couldn't just walk through the front door and throw myself at you," she adds, very reasonable, as if she hadn't done just that in the kitchen last night, over two cups of anemic Lipton.

So he starts to laugh instead, helpless gusts of laughter. He loses the cigarette in the pillows and has to go scrabbling for it, still laughing, shaking with goddamned unstoppable amusement, until at last he puts the cigarette in the ashtray and springs from the bed and opens up every single shutter over every single window, filling the room with a salmon-pink sunrise.

She looks at him like he's crazy. "What are you doing?"

"I am admiring your breasts in the sunshine," he says.

"Oh." She settles back in the pillows and

spreads her arms. "If that's all."

And that is one of the things he loves most about Annabelle, what has not changed about her in all these years: her joy. Like the first time he made love to her, on the cliffs at Antibes, the delight that seeped from her pores, the transparent love with which she drenched him, the wanton absence of any shame, even though she was a virgin who had been kissed only once. That was why he couldn't resist her then, and he can't resist her now. She turns his sorrow into joy.

4.

When he's finished making love to her a third time — and it takes a while, make no mistake, he's not the young man he was, not that she seems to mind the additional effort one bit — they lie boneless on the bed, drunk and sated as a pair of new lovers, surrounded by twenty-eight years of questions.

He tells her about the war, and working for the French Resistance, the bullet in his chest that nearly brought him to a bad end. He shows her the scar. Thank God for penicillin, he says. He talks about wandering aimlessly through Europe after the war — the worst years, he says, because there was no purpose anymore, no friends left alive, nothing to do but despair over the six million lives he had failed to save — until he crashed into some sort of bottom (wasn't that the phrase?) and

moved to America. He says, I thought I could at least be on the same continent as you, the same continent as our children. I could see what they were up to, what fine young people they were becoming. She says, in a breaking voice, You said *our* children, and he strokes her hair and says, Yes, I was their father and you are their mother, and you cannot possibly know how I left my heart on the floor of that barn for you to keep for me, how much my heart was in your hands.

Then why did you do it? she says. Why did you leave us like that?

Because I had no choice, my Annabelle. Because I had a profound debt to repay, a fucking world to save. Because he was the better man. Because he loved you so well.

So she tells him about the early years, how they waited in Monte Carlo until the boys arrived from England, until Margaret reached them with the girls; how she and Johann and all the children sailed to America in the *Isolde,* how they left the Mercedes in a shed at her aunt's house in Cape Cod, so no one would connect the Dommerich brood with the Nazi general who committed subversion and treason and then disappeared. How she couldn't bear him at first, because he wasn't Stefan, and then gradually the shared parenthood brought them together — he was such a good father, she had to love him for that alone — and the shared secrets, too. And then

634

Henrik started nursery school, and she wanted another baby so badly, she would have slept with Stalin if she had to. So we finally went to bed together, she says, and I got pregnant with the twins two seconds later, let that be a lesson. He laughs and says it was no more than she deserved, sleeping with someone else, and then she goes quiet and he knows what she's thinking.

He says, I came close a few times, I admit. I came damned close.

But you never?

No.

Ever?

(He sighs.)

Not even once, Annabelle, though I thought sometimes it would kill me, I was so lonely.

(There is a long silence, laden with awe.)

Why not?

Because we had a covenant, remember? And because you were raising the children for me, all the way across the ocean, and I had nothing else to give you in return. I had nothing but that.

The wind is picking up again. A shutter bangs against the side of the house, because he forgot to latch it, in his haste to see the sunshine on Annabelle's skin.

He says, And there is another reason.

What was that?

Because there was a time when this fidelity was the only virtue I had left. The only vow I

hadn't broken.

(She lies quietly in his arms, until he thinks that maybe she's gone to sleep.)

Then:

Do you know what I think?

What do you think, Annabelle? (And isn't that the best part of all? Just saying her name aloud.)

I think you're just like your son.

5.

They watch the sun sink from the shelter of the porch, curled up in the old rocking chair Stefan repaired himself, covered by a thick plaid horse blanket. There's a cold snap coming. It's maybe even going to freeze tonight, he can smell it in the air. A good night to share a bed with the woman you love.

"Two more questions," he whispers in her hair.

"What's that?"

"The first one. How did you find me?"

She laughs. "It took months. I hired an investigator. I figured you would have a new name of some kind. I gave him a list of possibilities. And a couple of weeks ago he sent me an article about Cumberland Island, and a man named Stefan Himmelfarb who was caring for the wild horses who were injured or sick, and I knew it had to be you. I read that article and I could feel you behind the ink. But when I arrived at the hotel in Saint

Mary's, I lost my nerve."

"*You,* Annabelle?"

"Yes, me. I'm not the nubile young maiden I once was, in case you hadn't noticed."

"This is nonsense. You are still the most beautiful woman I have ever met, despite the immense crookedness of your toes."

She snorts her very practical American disbelief. "And besides, you had three decades to fall out of love with me and find some other woman to warm your heart."

"Don't be stupid." He tucks the blanket around her shoulder.

"Well, that's my answer, like it or not. So what's your second question?"

"In fact, since you ask, I have a great many questions, and we will have to spend long weeks answering them all. This may take until the new year at least. But the most important question is this."

He pauses, for effect. The sun drops another millimeter, just touching the tips of the marsh grass, illuminating the backs of the horses as they saunter habitually across the meadow to the lean-to he built with his own hands, and the hay he has just laid out for them, with Annabelle's help.

And wasn't that almost as good as saying her name aloud? Sharing the evening chores, side by side, in the manner of a couple married for years. Maybe she will stay until the new year. Maybe she will stay all winter, and

they will share this routine every night. He hardly dares to think about the spring. There is such a thing as too much joy, and the perils of tempting fate.

"Well?" she says.

He turns her face toward him and fixes her sternly.

"What in the hell did the two of you do with my yacht?"

HISTORICAL NOTE

A few years ago, I came across a short article in the newspaper, concerning a vintage automobile — a rare 1936 Mercedes 540K Special Roadster — that had been discovered in a shed at an inn in Greenwich, Connecticut, where I then lived. According to the article, a German baroness had driven this extraordinary car around Europe in the years before the Second World War, having various affairs (including one with a Jewish Englishman) and generally making herself unpopular with the ruling party in Germany. Eventually, she fled to America with her Mercedes, and at the time of the car's rediscovery in 1989, it hadn't been touched in two decades. A cigarette stub still rested in the ashtray, stained with lipstick, and a single leather glove inhabited the glove compartment. Fully restored, the car sold at auction in 2012 for nearly twelve million dollars. I couldn't resist.

But I'm a writer of novels, not biographies, so I wanted to make up a story of my own

and weave it into the overall narrative of my fictional Schuyler family, which now stretches over several books. I also felt I had something more to say about the journey — physical and moral — undertaken by the people of Europe between the two world wars, and the discovery of a rare 1936 Mercedes in a Cape Cod shed seemed like the perfect springboard into this world.

Most of the characters in this book — and all of the principal ones — never existed in real life, no matter how vibrantly they live in my imagination. There was no Johann von Kleist in the German high command, and no Jewish nemesis by the name of Stefan Silverman. While the Himmelfarbs did not exist, nor did they die on the night of 9–10 November 1938, millions of German Jews were not so lucky. Kristallnacht saw the destruction of a thousand synagogues and seven thousand businesses; over thirty thousand were sent to camps like that at Dachau, and the number of dead and injured will never be known exactly. Despite the horror expressed in the foreign press in the days following the pogrom, the world — "weary of everything" — responded more or less as Stefan imagined it would. Only the quiet heroism of individual Germans emerged to redeem humanity that night.

As a writer of historical fiction, however, I try to keep the history as my background,

and my characters at the center of the stage. This novel isn't intended as a textbook on Nazi Germany and the politics of prewar Europe; for those interested in learning more about this crucial year in Hitler's consolidation of power, I highly recommend Giles MacDonogh's engaging and exhaustive *1938: Hitler's Gamble,* to which I referred again and again.

As for the identity of the father of Pepper's baby, I have no comment.

ACKNOWLEDGMENTS

The book you hold in your hands is not the original version of *Along the Infinite Sea.* Writing swiftly on a tight deadline, I tried to open the file one evening — the night before April Fool's Day, ahem — and had no luck. Neither did the assembled geniuses at the Apple Store. I sent the file to Putnam, where it was referred to the ominously titled Forensics Department. The cadaver could not be dissected, and neither could any of the copies I had saved earlier.

So I started over. I rewrote those first 250 pages — the writers among you will now proceed to throw up — and the story took an entirely different turn. Go figure. I could not, however, have decided exactly how the love triangle of Stefan, Johann, and Annabelle would play out without the emergency help of my immensely talented friend Karen White, who took my phone call and walked me through my very complicated plot until I realized what I had to do. In her own wonder-

ful novels, Karen is an expert at moments of emotional impact, and I might not have had the courage for that final resolution on the German border without her clear vision and her assurance. I hope she enjoys reading the result.

Beyond Karen and her creative assistance, I have many more wonderful people to thank for their help in putting the finished book into your hands. Alexandra Machinist, my irreplaceable literary agent, has held my hand and walked me through a fireworks year, and I am deeply grateful to her and to her hardworking colleagues at ICM for all their support. As for the talented and enthusiastic team at Putnam — my wonderful editor, Laura Perciasepe (whose name alone gives me joy); my publicist, Katie McKee; my whiz-girl marketing mavens, Lydia Hirt and Mary Stone; the ridiculously talented art department that delivers me cover after stunning cover; and a host of other superb professionals — I simply can't say enough. You have taken me on a marvelous journey, and I can only hope it's been as much fun for you as it's been for me.

I have so many people to thank in the book world — writers, bloggers, booksellers, readers — I can't even begin to list them here, but you know who you are. Your bookish enthusiasm keeps me writing, even on those days when I'm in a muddle, and I thank you

with all my heart for your kind words, your emails and tweets and Facebook posts, and your energetic company when we meet at book events.

I owe special thanks to my lovely friends at the Putnam Restaurant on Greenwich Avenue — my diner of choice, and that's saying something — who fry my bacon just so and keep the coffee coming generously while I frown and stab at my laptop all morning. It's amazing how much you can write when someone keeps stopping by to refill your coffee cup.

And finally, as always, to my family — friends, in-laws, outlaws — and most especially my beloved husband, Sydney, and our four crazy kids. I love you all.

ABOUT THE AUTHOR

Beatriz Williams is the *New York Times-*bestselling author of *Tiny Little Thing, The Secret Life of Violet Grant, A Hundred Summers,* and *Overseas.* She lives with her husband and children in Connecticut.

The employees of Thorndike Press hope you have enjoyed this Large Print book. All our Thorndike, Wheeler, and Kennebec Large Print titles are designed for easy reading, and all our books are made to last. Other Thorndike Press Large Print books are available at your library, through selected bookstores, or directly from us.

For information about titles, please call:
　(800) 223-1244

or visit our Web site at:
　http://gale.cengage.com/thorndike

To share your comments, please write:
Publisher
Thorndike Press
10 Water St., Suite 310
Waterville, ME 04901

LARGE TYPE
Williams, Beatriz
Along the infinite sea

Contents

List of Symbols

c	velocity of light, m/sec
e	particle charge, coulombs
f	frequency, cycles/sec
h	harmonic order in synchrotrons (p. 302)
i	total current, amp
k	constant in water-flow formulas (p. 261)
m	particle mass, kg
m_0	particle rest mass, kg
p	particle momentum, kg-m/sec
p_0	momentum of equilibrium particle, kg-m/sec (p. 290)
p^*	$p_0/(m_0 c)$ (p. 296)
r	radius in cylindrical coordinates (goes with θ and z)
s	position coordinate along an orbit, m
t	time, sec
u	scalar potential for magnetic field (p. 251)
v	velocity, m/sec
v_g	group velocity (p. 321)
A	vector potential (p. 252)
	atomic weight
B	magnetic flux density, webers/m² (p. 118)
	build-up factor (p. 521)
C	capacitance, farads
E	electric field, volts/m
F	force, newtons
G	gradient of a field (p. 112)

H	magnetic field, amp/m
I	current density, amp/m^2
J_n	Bessel function of order n
K	abbreviation used in phase-stability theory (p. 298)
	abbreviation used in synchrotron theory (p. 304)
L	inductance, henry
N	Avogadro's number
N_n	Neumann function of order n
P	pressure
Q	quantity of charge, coulombs
R	resistance, ohms
T	kinetic energy, joules or ev
	temperature
U	power, watts
V	potential difference, volts
W	total particle energy, joules or ev
W_0	rest energy, joules or ev
Z	atomic number
α	first Townsend coefficient (p. 75)
β	$= v/c$
γ	second Townsend coefficient (p. 77)
ϵ (or ϵ_0)	dielectric constant of free space, farads/m
η	$= (\mu_0/E_0)^{1/2} = 377$ ohms
	wavelength, m
μ (or μ_0)	permeability of free space, henrys/m
μ	microns: a parameter in AG theory; X-ray absorption coefficient
ρ	resistivity, ohms/m
	radius of curvature
σ	charge density
	collision cross section
ϕ	phase angle
ϕ_0	equilibrium phase (p. 297)
ω	$2\pi f$

1

Introduction

1-1. THE ROLE OF ACCELERATORS IN NUCLEAR SCIENCE

Particle accelerators have undergone a tremendously rapid development during the past 30 years. In few fields of science has progress been so spectacular. During this relatively short time, particle energies available for research have increased from a few hundred kilovolts to many billions of volts. Research in nuclear physics and on the properties of fundamental particles owes much of its progress to the continuously increasing energy achieved by a series of electronuclear machines, each larger and more effective than its predecessor. Also, much of the public awareness and support of the field of nuclear physics rests on popular interest in these gigantic atom smashers.

The purpose of this book is to present a description of the several particle accelerators. Fundamental principles will be discussed, and as much of the theoretical analysis of particle motion will be developed as is necessary to understand the operation of these principles in focusing and accelerating particle beams. The historical development will be outlined for each accelerator, and original contributions credited as fairly as possible. The over-all purpose is to show by comparison of their relative advantages and characteristics how the various accelerators supplement each other as tools for the study of nuclear physics and high-energy particle physics.

The record of accelerators in research is impressive. The complexity of nuclear processes has been demonstrated by hundreds of different reactions coming from artificial disintegration of nuclei by protons, deuterons, neutrons, alpha particles, gamma rays, and electrons, and by several

1

heavy ions. Induced radioactivities produced in targets bombarded by ion beams have been studied in detail to measure the lifetimes and analyze the decay schemes. New modes of disintegration and new complexities in the properties of nuclei have been discovered. Precise measurements of reaction thresholds and studies of the emergent radiations have led to an ever-increasing knowledge of atomic mass values and nuclear energy levels.

Radioactive elements have been used as tracers in many fields of scientific research: physics, chemistry, biology, medicine, metallurgy, and agriculture, to mention a few. A start has been made in the application of the radiations to medical therapy, notably for hyperthyroidism and leukemia. Neutrons from the cyclotron have been used in many fields of research, including cancer therapy. The properties of neutrons have been widely explored, and high-energy neutrons have themselves been utilized for disintegration. More recently the synchroaccelerators have succeeded in producing mesons, previously available only in cosmic rays, and studies of meson production and interactions are leading to important new knowledge about the fundamental nuclear force. New particles have been discovered, such as the neutral meson, the negative proton, and the antineutron, and it is clear that still more new knowledge is awaiting discovery. The record shows that particle accelerators have been most productive tools in exploring the nucleus of the atom.

Accelerators have found a permanent place in the science laboratories of the world. Every modern nuclear research laboratory must have some form of accelerator capable of disintegrating nuclei and producing induced activities; most of the larger laboratories have several machines to cover a wider range of phenomena. Direct-voltage accelerators, such as the electrostatic generator, are most useful in precise studies at low energy, such as the measurement of reaction thresholds or nuclear energy levels. The cyclotron is more powerful and produces particles of higher energy; it has been used as a high-intensity source of neutrons in the production of induced activities and for the study of high-energy disintegration processes. The betatron and electron linear accelerators produce high-energy electrons, and the resulting X rays are uniquely adapted to the study of photonuclear processes. Now the synchroaccelerators are rapidly taking over from cosmic rays the field of high-energy particle physics.

Each type of accelerator has made significant contributions. Because of their different capabilities, they supplement each other in covering the energy range needed for nuclear studies. Each accelerator fills a unique role, and all of them are needed. For example, the Nuclear Science Laboratory at the Massachusetts Institute of Technology has several electrostatic generators, a cyclotron, a linear accelerator, and a synchrotron, and all are being used effectively for research.

By 1940 much of the accumulated knowledge of nuclear physics had come from research using particle accelerators. However, radium-beryllium neutron sources were also in wide use and led in fact to the discovery of fission in 1939. Immediately following the first announcement, accelerators all over the world were applied to studies of this new phenomenon and rapidly exploited the field. Shortly thereafter a voluntary censorship was applied to reports of fission experiments in this country, and work was channeled into secret laboratories where accelerators were teamed with other scientific tools to produce the atomic pile and the atomic bomb. The speed with which accelerators were put to work is indicated by the transfer to Los Alamos of a working electrostatic generator from the University of Wisconsin and a cyclotron from Harvard University; both of these machines were in operation a few weeks after arrival at Los Alamos.

At the end of World War II, when physicists returned to their laboratories, the enhanced status of nuclear physics was immediately evident. The exciting and dangerous development of atomic energy, with its tremendous implications for national security, stimulated strong popular support for spending government funds on building still larger and higher-energy accelerators. With such impetus the new synchroaccelerators were rapidly developed.

Atomic reactors are finding many uses in research laboratories, but they have in no sense displaced accelerators for nuclear studies. The very high neutron intensities available from large reactors have made them the natural source of supply of induced radioactivities, which are distributed to the scientific world through the Isotope Distribution Division of the Atomic Energy Commission laboratory at Oak Ridge, Tennessee, and similar laboratories in other countries. This has relieved cyclotron laboratories of the tedious chore of production of long-lived isotopes. However, the accelerator is still essential for the radioactivity research laboratory. Positron emitters resulting from proton or alpha-particle bombardment of targets in an accelerator cannot be produced by neutrons. The very-short-lived neutron-induced activities cannot be shipped from the reactor to a distant laboratory and are best produced locally in an accelerator. Special research problems may require higher specific activities than are available from a reactor, but which can be obtained in the high concentration of neutrons in targets mounted directly behind the particle target in a cyclotron.

1-2. PROGRESS IN ACCELERATOR DEVELOPMENT

When Rutherford demonstrated in 1919 that the nitrogen nucleus could be disintegrated by the naturally occurring alpha particles from radium and thorium, a new era was opened in physics. For the first time man was able to modify the structure of the atomic nucleus. The alpha particles used had energies of 5 to 8 million electron volts (Mev), far in excess of the energies available in the laboratory. During the 1920s X-ray techniques were developed so machines could be built for 100 to 200 kev. Development to still higher voltages was limited by corona discharge and insulation breakdown, and the multi-million-volt range seemed out of reach.

Physicists recognized the need for artificial sources of accelerated particles. In a speech before the Royal Society in 1927 Rutherford[1] expressed his hope that accelerators of sufficient energy to disintegrate nuclei could be built. Then in 1928 Gamow[2] and also Condon and Gurney[3] showed how wave mechanics could be used to describe the penetration of nuclear potential barriers by charged particles and made it seem probable that energies of 500 kev or less would be sufficient to observe the disintegration of light nuclei. This more modest goal seemed feasible. Experimentation started around 1929 in several laboratories to develop the necessary accelerating devices. Details of this race for higher voltages are given in the chapters to follow. Urged on by Rutherford, the first to succeed were Cockcroft and Walton[4] in the Cavendish laboratory at Cambridge. They reported the successful disintegration of lithium by protons of about 400 kev energy in 1932. The date of this first artificial transmutation can be taken as the starting point in accelerator history.

Four successive waves of development have swept the accelerator field, characterized by four different concepts in the acceleration of particles. The first stage was the application of direct-voltage techniques in which the particles were accelerated through a single large potential drop. The magnitude of the potential drop was increased to its practical limit by using electrode terminals of large radius of curvature and by improving insulation. Voltage breakdown of the accelerating tube was minimized by subdividing the potential along the length of the column.

The second concept was the application of resonance acceleration, in which the particles were constrained to pass and repass many times through a low potential drop in resonance with an oscillating electric field, until their final energy was many times greater than the maximum potential difference in the apparatus. The chief examples of resonance accelerators are the cyclotron and the early linear accelerators.

The third stage was the application of the principle of phase-stable acceleration to resonance accelerators, from which developed the family of synchroaccelerators. Here, with an exact knowledge of the forces producing stable orbits, it has been possible to keep particles in resonance for an indefinitely large number of accelerations to attain ultimate energies up to 10 billion electron volts (Bev).*

* The symbol "Gev" is used in England and in most European countries to represent 1000 Mev, rather than the symbol "Bev" used in the United States.

The fourth stage is in its preliminary phase of development. This is the new category of superenergy accelerators utilizing the alternating-gradient (AG) principle of magnetic focusing, which reduces the size and cost of magnets for circular machines so that a much higher energy range becomes economically feasible. In 1959 an AG proton synchrotron which produces 28-Bev protons was completed at the CERN laboratory in Geneva; a similar machine which produces protons of 33 Bev energy was completed in 1960 at Brookhaven National Laboratory.

Progress of accelerator development can be followed in more detail by noting the dates at which new machines entered the race, or at which they made new voltage records. The Cockcroft-Walton voltage multiplier was soon able to operate up to 750 kv. Later a 1.25-Mv installation was built by the Philips Company (Eindhoven) for the Cavendish laboratory, following the same design principles. This has proved to be about the practical limit for the voltage-multiplier type of accelerator when operated at atmospheric pressure.

Meanwhile, the magnetic resonance accelerator now known as the cyclotron was under development by Lawrence and Livingston at the University of California. Following a proposal by Lawrence, the principle of resonance acceleration was proved by Livingston in 1931 in a laboratory model experiment. The first practical cyclotron produced protons of 1.2 Mev in 1932. These were immediately put to use for nuclear studies. Deuterons of 5 Mev were obtained in a larger machine (the "27-inch") in 1934. Other laboratories joined in the development; 10 Mev was attained by 1936 and 20 Mev by 1940. However, the energy range of 20 to 25 Mev has proved to be a practical limit for the fixed-frequency cyclotron.

The betatron went through a similar development, starting with the first small model in 1940, with which Kerst produced 2.3-Mev electrons. A rapid development at the General Electric Research Laboratory produced 20 Mev by 1942 and 100 Mev by 1945. Kerst's 300-Mev betatron at the University of Illinois is the largest, and it will probably be the last of the big betatrons; before it was completed, the synchrotron came on the scene with a more efficient principle of acceleration.

Each new instrument has had a similar history; some of them have approached the practical ceilings even more rapidly. And just as one type of accelerator was approaching its upper limit, a new invention arrived to maintain the steady increase in energy. The cyclotron, betatron, synchrocyclotron, electron synchrotron, and proton synchrotron have each held the voltage record temporarily and have raised the energy scale still higher. Finally in 1952 the principle of AG focusing was published, allowing the latest extension of the energy scale.

This development of accelerators to higher and higher energy is illustrated graphically in Fig. 1-1. In this graph the energies achieved with

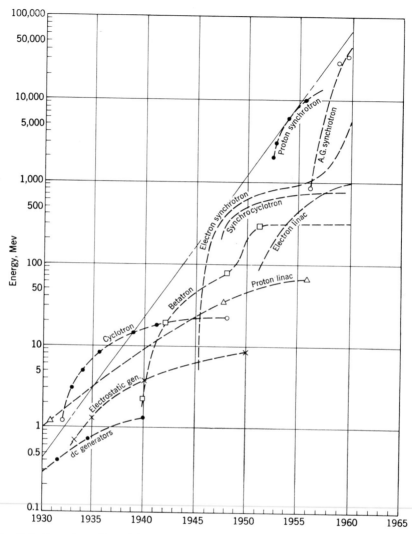

Fig. 1-1. Energies achieved by accelerators from 1930 to 1960. The linear envelope of the individual curves shows an average tenfold increase in energy every six years.

the several accelerators are plotted against the date of publication of the first announcement (which may lag many months behind the actual date of operation). When energy is plotted on a logarithmic scale, the envelope of the points is remarkably close to a straight line, indicating an increase in energy by a factor of 10 every six years. The progress of the individual machines in reaching their respective ceilings is indicated by the labeled curves below the linear envelope. The exponential increase of energy indicated by this record is impressive. The plot also serves a useful purpose in orienting the various accelerators on the energy scale. An extrapolation beyond the highest points on the curve is intriguing. It is interesting to note that the principle of strong focusing (see Chap. 15) has offered a new opportunity of extending the energy range of accelerators and has come close to fulfilling the extrapolation.

1-3. COLLABORATION BETWEEN PHYSICS AND ENGINEERING

The development of accelerators has paralleled and sometimes paced progress in the electronics industry and in several branches of electrical and mechanical engineering. In few scientific developments has there been such effective and happy collaboration with the engineering profession as in the accelerator field. These machines were conceived by physicists who saw the need for high-energy particles in research, and the physical principles are based on fundamental scientific laws. However, the physicist who continued in the field ultimately metamorphosed into a practical engineer in order to produce a reliable, working machine. Of necessity he became accomplished in wide areas of electrical and mechanical engineering and utilized fully the advice and services of professionally trained engineers. On the other hand, many men trained in engineering have found in the accelerator field a challenge and opportunity to apply their training to new problems, frequently more exciting than the problems available in engineering practice. So the design staff of the modern accelerator laboratory is composed in almost equal numbers of experimental physicists and professionally trained engineers.

The first ion accelerators were simple applications of direct high voltage to evacuated discharge tubes. Nuclear physicists leaned on experience in the X-ray industry, and as the accelerator art progressed, it stimulated further development of higher-energy X-ray machines. Focusing requirements forced intensive studies and improvements in the field of ion and electron optics. Some of the developments have since been applied in the electronics industry. New techniques for the production of X rays, such as the resonance transformer, were stimulated by accelerator developments. The electrostatic generator has found almost equal application to positive-ion acceleration for nuclear physics and to electron acceleration for the production of X rays for medical therapy and radiography. The betatron has also found an important application as a source of very-high-energy X rays.

Magnetic accelerators, of which the cyclotron was the first, employed high-frequency electric fields for acceleration and drew heavily on experience in short-wave radio transmission at the start. It is significant that many of the early cyclotronists and their technician helpers were "ham" radio operators. However, as numbers and experience grew, cyclo-tronists were able to make important contributions to the radio and radar fields. For example, the original roster of the Massachusetts Institute of Technology Radiation Laboratory, which developed microwave radar for the military services during World War II, consisted largely of nuclear physicists many of whom were cyclotronists. Cyclotron experience in magnetics and in high-frequency electronics was of real value in the early days of radar in such areas as the development of the magnetron.

We can follow this cross-linkage between accelerators and electronics still further. At the end of the war the accumulated experience in the electronics of high frequencies and pulsed circuits coming from the radar field fed back new techniques and concepts into accelerator design. The modern linear accelerator would have been impossible to conceive or build before the radar field reached its present high stage of development. The synchroaccelerators with their pulsed operation are also dependent on radar techniques. But it should be noted that the modern high-powered klystron tube with all its radar applications was originally developed in the Stanford accelerator laboratory. Modern accelerators are progress-ing further in adapting and utilizing the more sophisticated implications in the equations of motion and have already shown that they can offer new techniques and concepts to the engineering field. The principle of AG focusing appears to have a variety of applications, to traveling-wave vacuum tubes and to ion and electron optics.

Vacuum engineering is another technical field in which accelerator development contributed directly to engineering advances. The first all-metal vacuum systems were developed for accelerators such as the cyclotron, and techniques for making tight seals and high-speed pumps grew with the increasing size and energy of accelerators. The early metal pumps produced by commercial firms were based largely on this experience. As the field of vacuum engineering grew to meet the needs in vacuum distillation and isotope-separation problems, metal pumps were developed to still larger sizes. The well-known Westinghouse "30-in." fractionating oil-diffusion pump was developed for the isotope-separation plant at Oak Ridge. Even larger sizes with higher pumping speeds have since become available. These pumps have been applied directly to the recent synchroaccelerators and are a satisfactory answer to the vacuum-pump problems in these large metal-chamber machines. The most recent contribution to vacuum engineering from accelerator laboratories is the titanium-vapor pump, now in commercial production.

This healthy interchange of ideas and experience between accelerator scientists and practical engineers has been one of the most important factors leading to the rapid development in this field. Once the physical phenomena have been analyzed and understood, the remaining problems in accelerators are primarily those of engineering development. Ultimately, as in any new application of basic principles, the engineer takes over to perfect techniques and produce a reliable product. Many of the machines conceived and designed by scientists are now ready for this detailed application of engineering, and some, such as the electrostatic generator, the cyclotron, the betatron, and the linear accelerator, are already being built by commercial engineering firms. In the construction of the new supervoltage accelerators the engineering profession is also making major contributions. The variety and scope of the engineering problems involved in the accelerator field will become evident in the chapters to follow.

1-4. THE MODERN RESEARCH LABORATORY

The modern research laboratory is far different from the "ivory tower" of the traditional individual scientist who pored over his books and retorts for years before announcing precedent-making discoveries. Neither does progress in scientific research depend solely on the inventions or flashes of genius of a few outstanding wizards, as conceived by many of the lay public. Rather, the modern laboratory is an organized cooperative team of specialists, each supreme in his own field but depending on others to supplement him in the attack on the complicated problem. Usually one or more senior scientists of wide experience and ability act as advisers and critics for the younger members and coordinate their efforts.

In no field are these characteristics more evident than in the modern accelerator laboratory. Here physicists with the insight to appreciate the new knowledge available from experiments with high-energy particles and the urge to create the necessary instruments are teamed with engineers who take pride and delight in invention of the unique devices, with theoretical scientists eagerly grasping the new experimental evidence to expand our knowledge of fundamentals, with young students just beginning to see the significance of their training and trying their wings on their first flights into the unknown, and with a group of loyal technical helpers each interested in doing his best for the project but only vaguely seeing the whole outline. Such a team constitutes the modern research laboratory, and each member plays a part. The morale and spirit of the team is of great importance, and much depends on the personality of the leaders to stimulate and maintain the proper spirit.

The thrill of discovery is the reward of exploration. The exploration of the unknown in science is just as rewarding as the discovery of a new river or mountain range, and nowhere in the field of science are the rewards more dramatic than in the accelerator field. The pleasure and excitement of the working crew when a new accelerator is first tuned in to set a new voltage record is something to be remembered for a lifetime.

The senior author (MSL) well remembers the sparkling eyes and dramatic gestures of his professor and supervisor, the late Ernest O. Lawrence, when the small cyclotron at the University of California produced 1-Mev protons for the first time in scientific history.   An equal thrill comes to the experimentalist when, for example, a new ion source produces a beam current of ions greater than had been previously achieved.   But even greater is the thrill of a significant scientific discovery or the observation of a new physical phenomenon.   An equally dramatic moment at the University of California was the first observation of artificially induced radioactivity using 3-Mev deuterons.   It is easy to understand why young scientists have been willing to labor for years to build and tune up a big accelerator in order to participate in these thrills of discovery when it is completed and brought into operation.

Wholehearted cooperation is essential for the members of a laboratory team if an instrument as complicated as the modern accelerator is to run smoothly.   Each man has his special skill and is depended on to keep his component in good condition.   The experienced operator, who knows just how to manipulate the controls to get the maximum beam intensity, comes to have a pride in his machine that admits no criticism.   Pride in the machine and mutual respect for the other members of the group bring a team spirit frequently reminiscent of school days, and to a significant extent this team spirit improves the effectiveness and output of the laboratory.

A real insight into the spirit of such a laboratory is revealed by the spontaneous humor and intralaboratory jokes.   A few samples have come into public view, notably the songs composed by Arthur Roberts. Some of these songs have been recorded for the phonograph, and the lyrics and scores of a few have been published.[5]

Large accelerators need large laboratories as well as large financial support.   It is a paradox of science that the study of the smallest particles in nature requires the use of the largest and most expensive instruments.   In the early days particle accelerators were built on a shoestring in academic laboratories, using or modifying old laboratory apparatus and depending on students for the labor of construction.   There was a time when designers took pride in the low cost of their accelerators, but as the scientific results justified expansion to higher energies, the chief scientists or laboratory directors had to locate larger sources of funds. A new qualification became important in science—the ability to raise money.   Some of the more colorful personalities in the nuclear field owe their reputations as much to their promotional and organizational abilities as to their scientific contributions.

In recent years financing has come increasingly from government sources, primarily the Office of Naval Research and the Atomic Energy Commission in the United States.   Most of the large accelerators built in this country since World War II have been financed by governmental grants-in-aid. Perhaps only in a government laboratory, or one supported by government funds, is it possible to undertake a development such as the cosmotron or the bevatron which costs many millions of dollars.

Costs increase with size of machines and with energy, as would be expected. Some machines are more efficient as power transformers than others, but power is not so important for research as the equivalent beam energy. The cost per unit of beam energy has actually decreased with the increasing energy of accelerators. On this basis, a dry cell costs about 50 cents per volt; the electrostatic generator produces ions of a few Mev energy at a cost of roughly 5 cents per volt. With the cyclotron, the cost at 15 Mev is below 1 cent a volt, and with the largest synchro-accelerators the cost approaches 0.1 cent per volt. It is well to recognize this steady improvement in cost efficiency when considering the magnitude of the investments in the larger accelerators.

1-5. REFERENCES AND BIBLIOGRAPHIES

Exchange of information between accelerator laboratories has done much to speed the rate of development. In addition to the formal publications of designs and results, many of the more detailed techniques have been written up in the form of reports circulated to other laboratories. This practice has been expanded considerably in recent years by the requirement of periodic progress reports to the sponsoring governmental agencies. The chief criticisms of this technique of reporting results are that the circulation of such reports is far too limited and that it tends to decrease the detail in regular publications. Only the larger laboratories in this country and a few foreign laboratories, for example, are supplied with copies of the progress reports handled by the Office of Naval Research or the Atomic Energy Commission.

Personal visits still remain the most effective means of acquiring information on recent developments. The practice is widespread among accelerator designers. Through such visits and occasional discussions at Physical Society meetings, news of developments travels rapidly across the country. Unfortunately this avenue of communication is limited to a relative few in the field, and others must depend on rumors or second-hand information. The accelerator field is still in many respects an art, and its practitioners are often unable to describe their techniques adequately in writing.

In the chapters to follow, references will be made to many publications and laboratory reports, listed at the end of each chapter. A serious attempt has been made to identify and credit the originator of each important new concept or technique. References are given, where known to the authors, in justification of most of the arguable statements and conclusions. Specific references are made to papers summarizing the technical features or performance of individual accelerators which can be taken as typical of the species.

No attempt has been made to cover all publications in the accelerator field. This very valuable chore has been performed by others, resulting in a series of bibliographies which list and index essentially every significant publication. The first compilation was a Brookhaven National Laboratory report[6] published July 1, 1948. It was followed by University of California Radiation Laboratory reports in 1951,[7] 1952,[8] 1954,[9] and 1958.[10] In each case the new bibliography started from the date of the previous report and included only the new publications in the interim; so the entire series of bibliographies is needed to obtain a complete listing. The total number of publications listed is over 1500.

Others have listed the locations of high-energy installations in the United States and abroad, with dimensions, particle energies, and other parameters. The first listing was in the BNL report;[6] the most detailed listing is in the latest UCRL report,[10] which is reproduced in the "American Institute of Physics Handbook,"[11] 1957. The most recent compilation is an Oak Ridge laboratory report.[12] The total number of accelerators in this latest (but not up-to-date) listing is 525 throughout the world. Of these, about half are in the United States and half abroad; also about half are relatively low-voltage dc generators, and the others are resonance and synchronous accelerators.

We go now into a discussion of the early days of accelerator development to trace the evolution of the modern accelerator from the crude electric machines at the turn of the century to the present highly efficient sources of beams of accelerated particles. As we follow the story, we shall see how invention followed invention so rapidly at times that it was difficult to keep informed about the latest energy record. Each of the modern accelerators will be treated in a separate chapter in approximate order of development, which is also the approximate order of particle energy. The relationships between the several accelerators will become apparent, as will the way in which they supplement each other to cover the wide range of energies and phenomena in nuclear physics. The equations of motion of particles in electric and magnetic fields will be developed and applied to each machine. The principles of energy generation and particle acceleration will be described. Basic components will be identified and described in detail, and a few components will be discussed more thoroughly in separate chapters. So the story starts with the low-voltage generators of the early 1930s, the first of the series of particle accelerators.

REFERENCES

1. E. Rutherford, *Proc. Roy. Soc. (London)*, **117**:300 (1927).
2. G. Gamow, *Z. Physik*, **52**:510 (1928).
3. E. U. Condon and R. W. Gurney, *Phys. Rev.*, **33**:127 (1929).
4. J. D. Cockcroft and E. T. S. Walton, *Proc. Roy. Soc. (London)*, **A137**:229 (1932).
5. A. Roberts, *Phys. Today*, **1**:17 (1948).
6. E. Thomas, P. Mittelman, and H. H. Goldsmith, BNL-L-101 (July 1, 1948); AECU-31 (July 1, 1948).
7. B. E. Cushman, UCRL-1238 (March, 1951).
8. S. Shewchuck, UCRL-1951 (September, 1952).
9. F. E. Frost and J. M. Putnam, UCRL-2672 (Nov. 16, 1954).
10. G. A. Behman, UCRL-8050 (Jan. 1, 1958).
11. "American Institute of Physics Handbook," pp. 8–182, McGraw-Hill (1957).
12. F. T. Howard, ORNL Report-2644 (Nov. 17, 1958).

cylinders rotating in a hydrogen atmosphere. These compact, reliable machines are finding application in many European laboratories, wherever power supplies are required for dc currents up to a few milliamperes at voltages between 50 kv and 1 Mv.

Electrostatic generators which depend on separation of charge also have a long history in static electricity. In the early machines, positive and negative charges were separated by friction and then transported mechanically to charge a capacitor, which was often a metal sphere of large radius. Lord Kelvin is reputed to be the originator of the "charged water drop" generator; water drops electrified by friction on issuing from a nozzle fell into an insulated metal container which became charged to high potential. Others experimented on modifications of this method of conveying charge to an insulated terminal, including falling charged metal spheres. In about 1890, Righi improved the method by using a belt formed of alternate links of insulating and conducting material to carry charge to a hollow spherical terminal. Then for many years there was no activity in this field. A more recent revival was the development in the SAMES laboratory in France of an electrostatic generator which used air blasts of electrified dust to transfer the charge.

R. J. Van de Graaff[4] started the modern development of the belt-charged electrostatic generator in 1930. Charges sprayed from corona points onto a moving silk belt were transported to charge a 2-ft-diam aluminum sphere mounted on a glass rod. The immediate success of the belt-charged machine showed it to be superior to all other forms of static generators. It has become so important a tool in nuclear physics that it deserves detailed treatment and is therefore described and discussed fully in Chap. 3.

2-2. TESLA COIL

The Tesla coil utilizes electromagnetic induction to generate oscillatory pulses of high potential. In its usual form two resonant oscillatory circuits are coupled magnetically; the primary circuit has large capacitance and low inductance, while the secondary has a small distributed capacitance and large inductance owing to its being wound of many turns of fine wire. Figure 2-1 illustrates the traditional circuit for a spark-excited Tesla coil of the double-ended type. The capacitor in the primary circuit is charged to sufficiently high potential to cause breakdown of a spark gap in series with the primary windings, which produces an oscillatory discharge at the frequency determined by the inductance and capacitance in the circuit. The oscillatory current of high frequency in the primary coil induces bursts of high-potential oscillations in the coupled secondary, which are repeated at the sparking frequency. Voltage amplitude is a maximum when the two circuits are tuned to resonance.

This device was one of the first to be investigated in the search for a potential source for particle acceleration. A research team at the Department of Terrestrial Magnetism of the Carnegie Institution of Washington, consisting of Breit, Tuve, Hafstad, and Dahl, were among the first to attempt this application. They reported their results in a series of publications[5-9] in 1930 covering the Tesla coil, its voltage calibration, and the discharge tubes for accelerating particles. They used an oil-insulated secondary coil closely wound on a glass tube ending in spherical electrodes with a resonant frequency of 100 kc/sec, and reported peak potentials of 3 Mv at 1 atm oil pressure and 5 Mv when the

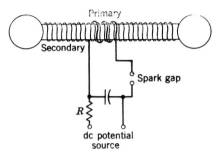

Fig. 2-1. Circuit diagram for a double-ended Tesla coil.

oil was under high pressure. Their voltage calibrations, based on sphere-gap measurements, are now believed to be in serious error. The potentials attained were probably considerably lower than the values reported.

The most significant result of the early Carnegie experiments was not the voltage source but the development of the accelerating tubes. The first attempt, using long, evacuated glass tubes with an electrode at each end, showed a limiting voltage for breakdown at about 300 kv. The next step was to divide the potential between multiple electrodes, following the concept of the Coolidge "cascade" type of X-ray tube. This type of tube had been perfected for the acceleration of electrons in high-voltage X-ray installations, primarily at the General Electric Company. It used a column of tubular electrodes in line, with relatively short gaps between the rounded ends of the electrodes. Electrons were accelerated in a sequence or cascade of several potential drops uniformly spaced along the length of the tube. This distributed the potential drop along the accelerating tube and prevented high local field concentrations; also the tubular electrodes shielded the insulating walls and prevented charging of the walls by stray electrons from the beam. Figure 2-2a is a sketch of a two-stage Coolidge-type X-ray tube. In the Carnegie laboratory the early designs used many glass bulb sections sealed together in line with concentric cylindrical electrodes supported at the seals; tubes of 15 or more sections were developed. Figure 2-2b illustrates one of the early Carnegie tubes.

The accelerating tubes were immersed in an oil bath with the Tesla coil. Breakdown potentials of up to 1.9 Mv were reported, but were probably overestimated in view of later corrections to the spark-gap voltage calibrations. In any case, the oscillatory character of the potential obtained from the Tesla coil made it unsuitable for particle acceleration.   The Carnegie group abandoned it in about 1932 in favor of the belt-charged electrostatic generator developed by Van de Graaff.   But they were able to utilize the accelerating tubes, which have proved to be forerunners of the modern tubes.

Modifications of the Tesla coil have taken several forms.   In 1933 D. H. Sloan[10] at the University of California developed a continuous-wave radiofrequency type called the "resonance transformer" (Fig. 2-3). The secondary coil was made of heavy, internally cooled copper tubing of 10 to 15 turns, supported from one end in a vacuum chamber for voltage insulation, resonant at frequencies of about 6 megacycles/sec.   The primary was a one-turn coil coupling with the secondary at the grounded

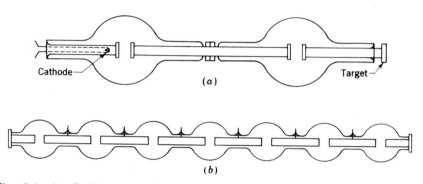

Cathode

Target

(a)

(b)

Fig. 2-2. (a) Coolidge cascade X-ray tube.   (b) Carnegie Institute multisection accelerating tube.

end and driven by a vacuum-tube oscillator circuit at the resonant frequency.

The resonance transformer has been used successfully for production of X rays; a thermionic cathode in the side of the vacuum chamber provides electrons which are accelerated toward and strike a gold-surfaced target on the high-voltage end of the coil.   An installation of this type was built in 1933 at the University of California Hospital in San Francisco by Livingston and Chaffee following Sloan's designs; it has given many years of service for X-ray therapy at voltages up to 1.25 Mv.

An experimental unit at the physics laboratories of the University of California, developed by Sloan and J. J. Livingood, had a hot cathode in place of the target on the end of the coil and a thin-foil window in the side of the vacuum chamber through which a beam of 1-Mev electrons emerged.   Sloan had hoped to use the resonance transformer for producing positive ions of twice the nominal energy by providing two accelerations.   In this arrangement ions would be injected from a source at ground potential on the chamber wall and those of proper phase would be accelerated toward and enter a hollow cylindrical tube supported on the end of the resonant coil; ions which traversed the tube in one half-period of the oscillation would emerge when the tube had a reversed polarity and would be accelerated toward the opposite chamber wall, where they could be used for experiments. This principle of energy-doubling is a modification of the resonance principle used in the linear

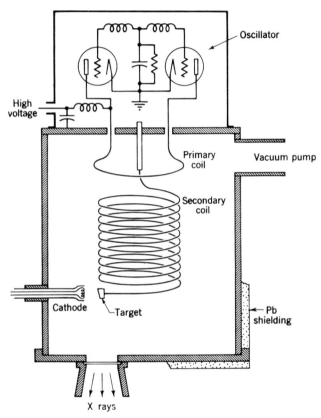

Fig. 2-3. Radiofrequency resonance transformer for 1-Mv X rays, University of California Hospital in San Francisco.[10]

accelerator. However, many technical difficulties were encountered, and this device was not sufficiently attractive to compete with the cyclotron or other positive-ion accelerators.

Another modification of the induction coil is the low-frequency resonance transformer developed before 1934 by Charlton, Westendorp, Dempster, and Hotaling[11] at the General Electric Company. Figure 2-4 is a schematic diagram of the apparatus.   In this instrument the secondary coil was made of very many turns of fine wire, wound in compact coils. It had a laminated iron core and was resonant at 180 cps.   The coil was mounted in a housing containing gas at high pressure for insulation.   The primary coil was made to resonate at the same frequency by using a large

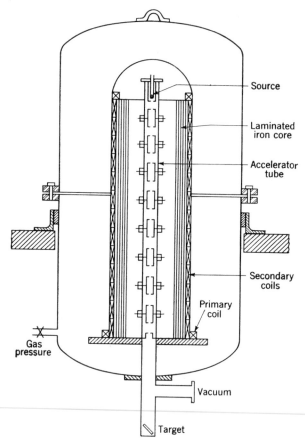

Fig. 2-4. 180-cycle resonance transformer for 1-Mv X rays, General Electric Company.[11]

capacitor and was supplied by a frequency-tripling circuit from a 60-cycle power supply.   An evacuated accelerating tube installed along the axis of the coil was used to accelerate electrons.   The cathode was heated by current from a low-voltage secondary winding at the high-potential end of the main coil, and the target was at the grounded end.   This machine has been produced commercially as an X-ray generator operating at 1 Mv and 3 ma electron current.

2-3. SURGE GENERATOR

The "Marx" circuit has been widely used by electrical engineers to produce surges of high voltage for testing electric equipment. A stack of capacitors is charged in parallel from a dc potential supply and then

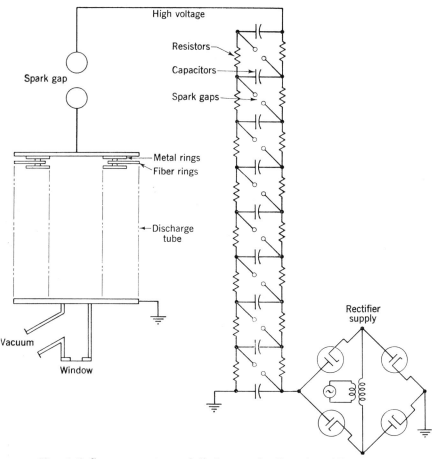

Fig. 2-5. Surge generator and discharge tube, Brasch and Lange.[13]

discharged through cross-connected spark gaps (Fig. 2-5). The potential difference developed momentarily across the stack of capacitors can be extremely high and can cause sparks many feet long in air—miniature lightning—but the duration of the voltage pulse is only of the order of a few microseconds, and it is oscillatory in character. The highest-energy surge generator was built at the General Electric plant at Pittsfield, Massachusetts, in about 1932; it was capable of producing voltage surges of over 6 Mv.[12]

Surge generators have been used primarily to test the flashover and breakdown characteristics of insulators and electric equipment and have seldom been used for the acceleration of particles. However, in 1930 Brasch and Lange[13] in Germany developed a crude vacuum tube made of alternate rings of metal and fiber tightly compressed between end plates, to which they applied a 2.4-Mv voltage surge from a stack of capacitors. The peak surge current was of the order of 1000 amp; the discharge tube practically exploded on each surge and had to be cleaned and reassembled frequently. A metal-foil window at the grounded end of the tube allowed a beam of high-energy electrons and gas ions to emerge into the air. The emergent beam has been described as having an intensely brilliant blue color, brightest near the tube window but still visible at a distance of over a meter. Presumably this discharge was attended by some nuclear disintegration and also by considerable dangerous radiation; however, at that time the former was not suspected and the latter was not appreciated. Figure 2-5 is a schematic drawing of such a generator arranged to apply a surge to a discharge tube.

The surge generator has excited considerable enthusiasm as a demonstration of electric power. The tremendous sparks and the loud reports are very impressive. However, the short-pulse character of the surge and the irregular voltage obtained are not suitable for studies of accelerated particles, and the surge generator has not been significantly useful in nuclear research.

An interesting attempt to convert a surge generator into a steady source of dc potential difference was reported by W. C. Anderson[14] in 1936. He used a number of capacitors connected permanently in series and charged successively by motor-driven rotating brushes which were supplied with a dc voltage. The capacitors were arranged around a circular commutator, and the high series potential difference was developed between the final pair of unconnected capacitors. The model was qualitatively successful in magnifying 110 volts to over 5000 volts, but has not found further application.

At this point it may be of interest to mention an attempt to utilize the high potentials developed in the atmosphere during electrical storms. In 1932 Brasch and Lange[13] stretched an insulated cable across a valley between two peaks in the Alps; from this cable a conducting cable supporting a terminal was suspended. During thunderstorms high potentials would develop between this terminal and a grounded terminal on the valley floor; sparks several hundred feet long were obtained. Plans had been made to install a discharge tube for the acceleration of particles, but experiments were abandoned when Lange was killed.

2-4. CASCADE TRANSFORMER

The requirements of high-voltage power transmission in the western United States, where 220-kv lines at 50-cycle frequency were used for long-distance transmission, led to the establishment of a high-voltage laboratory at the California Institute of Technology in the early 1920s, sponsored by the Southern California Edison Company. In this laboratory Sorensen[15] built the first cascade-transformer unit to reach 1 Mv from line to ground. A schematic diagram is shown in Fig. 2-6. Three 250-kv 50-cycle Westinghouse transformers were arranged in series. In addition to the usual low-voltage primary and high-voltage secondary windings, a third "exciter" winding at the high-potential end of the secondary was used to supply the next transformer. The transformers

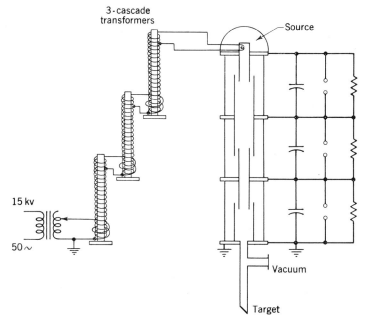

Fig. 2-6. Cascade transformer and discharge tube for 0.75 Mv, California Institute of Technology.[15]

were mounted on insulating platforms. The root-mean-square (rms) ac potential of the terminal of the last transformer was 750 kv, and peak voltage exceeded 1 Mv above ground. This installation was used for many years for the study of high-voltage breakdown of insulators, corona losses, and calibration of sphere-gap voltmeters.

After some years of service as a high-voltage test equipment for electrical engineering, the cascade transformer was taken over by C. C. Lauritsen about 1928 as a voltage source for the acceleration of particles. X-ray tubes were developed first,[16] operating at potentials up to 750 kv. Crane and Lauritsen[17] started with a simple type of X-ray tube built of a single porcelain bushing. In 1934 Crane, Lauritsen, and Soltan[18] installed a single-step positive-ion accelerating tube which would operate at potentials up to 1 Mv and initiated a program of nuclear research, using H$^+$ and He^{++} ions to produce neutrons from Li and Be targets. Another tube, developed by Stephens and Lauritsen,[19] was characterized by having an extremely short path for the acceleration of ions. Positive-ion optics were not yet understood in those days, and the beams obtained had poor focal properties.

The "Caltech" nuclear research laboratory under Lauritsen has had a long period of productivity and has trained a notable succession of research students. Eventually the superior properties of the belt-charged electrostatic generator as a steady dc potential source were recognized, and the cascade transformer was replaced. However, the transformer served an important purpose at the start and made possible a great deal of valuable research.

2-5. TRANSFORMER-RECTIFIER

The X-ray unit, using a high-voltage transformer to produce alternating voltage for an X-ray tube which also acts as a rectifier, has been developed to a high stage of perfection by many engineering laboratories. Coolidge, at the General Electric Company, introduced the thermionic cathode and perfected the high-voltage sealed-off X-ray tube. Others have developed the necessary high-potential ac transformers. The classically simple circuit of a transformer, a sealed-off X-ray tube with a thermionic cathode, and a capacitor is shown in Fig. 2-7a. Years of intensive engineering effort have failed to improve significantly on the performance of this simple circuit.

For positive-ion acceleration it is necessary to insert a rectifier tube in the circuit (see Fig. 2-7b) to maintain direct voltage across the accelerating tube, since the gas evolved from the ion source becomes ionized and would otherwise support a large electron current during the negative half-cycle.

In a strict sense the X-ray tube was the first particle accelerator, although possibly the emergent cathode-ray beams obtained by Lenard in 1894 also fit the modern definition. In 1926 Coolidge[20] produced an emergent beam of electrons at 350 kev from a sealed-off tube with a thin metal-foil window. These electron beams were never used for nuclear investigations and will not be considered further here.

However, after the early successes by Cockcroft and Walton and others in producing nuclear disintegrations by positive ions of modest energy, the simple transformer-rectifier voltage supply came into use as a positive-ion accelerator. The low-voltage accelerator has several definite advantages. Neutrons coming from exoergic reactions, such as Li(p,n), have a precisely determined minimum energy (1.89 Mev), and the lower the bombarding energy, the better the uniformity of the neutrons. The yield of neutrons from the D(d,n) reaction is large, and the energy depends on the angle of observation relative to the deuteron beam; a precisely controlled, low bombarding energy makes this reaction unique as a source of neutrons of known energy below 1 Mev. Several other reactions have resonances for bombarding energies below 200 kev.

Many descriptions of low-voltage accelerators have been published. As illustrations we shall cite three references. Zinn[21,22] started in 1936 with an extremely low-potential supply (60 kv) and then extended it to 200 kv as a source of neutrons from the D(d,n) reaction. Beam currents of over 1 ma of deuterons were obtained. In 1937 Slack and Ehrke[23]

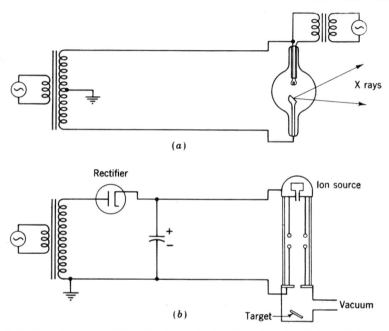

X rays

(a)

Rectifier

Ion source

+
−

Vacuum

(b)   *Target*

Fig. 2-7. Transformer-rectifier circuit producing high dc potential. (*a*) X-ray tube acts as a self-rectifier. (*b*) Rectifier required for positive-ion acceleration.

described a similar 200-kv unit used as a neutron generator. A more recently developed 200-kv accelerator (1950) is reported by Almqvist, Allen, Dewan, Pepper, and Sanders[24] and includes a voltage stabilizer.

For precise work the voltage must be stabilized by a regulating circuit such as that reported by Dewan,[25] which reduces fluctuations to 0.1 per cent. This corresponds to only 25 volts variation at the lowest energy used (25 kv).

The primary problem with this low-voltage accelerator has been to obtain sufficiently high intensities from an ion source. Many types have been tried, and several have been successful in producing beams of over 1 ma. These will be described more fully in Chap. 4, in the general discussion of ion sources. Large beam intensities are required to compensate for the low yields owing to the small probability of potential barrier penetration at less than 200 kv. The lowest energy at which such an accelerator has produced observable intensities of nuclear disintegrations, observed as neutrons from the $D(d,n)$ reaction, is about 30 kv.

2-6. VOLTAGE MULTIPLIER

The first successful disintegration of nuclei by electrically accelerated particles was achieved in 1932 by Cockcroft and Walton[26] using about 400-kev protons accelerated by a capacitor-rectifier circuit which multiplied the available potential by 4. Voltage-doubling or voltage-multiplying circuits had been developed as early as 1920[27,28] and were adapted by Cockcroft and Walton to meet their needs, but the accelerating apparatus utilizing this principle is usually called a Cockcroft-Walton machine.

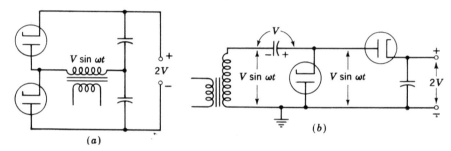

Fig. 2-8. Voltage-doubling circuits. (a) Symmetrical circuit. (b) Circuit which allows the negative terminal to be grounded.

The voltage multiplier is in principle a circuit for charging capacitors in parallel and discharging them in series. It differs from the surge generator in that it operates on alternating current, using rectifiers to charge capacitors during one half-cycle and other rectifiers to transfer the charge during the other half-cycle, so a steady direct voltage results.

The elementary voltage-doubling circuit is shown in Fig. 2-8. In the circuit shown in Fig. 2-8a the two capacitors are charged on successive half-cycles and a doubled voltage appears across the capacitors in series. Since neither end of the output is at the potential of one end of the transformer secondary, this circuit has some disadvantages in making ground connections. For this reason the circuit of Fig. 2-8b is usually preferred. Here the voltage applied to the output capacitor includes the transformer output ac voltage plus the dc charge of the first capacitor. This circuit is appropriate for addition of further stages of multiplication (Fig. 2-9a). By adding units to a total of N capacitors and N rectifiers one can obtain voltage multiplication by a factor of N. The circuit shown in Fig. 2-9a to give a fourfold voltage multiplication was the one used by Cockcroft and Walton.

The other half of the accelerator is the ion-accelerating tube, which Cockcroft and Walton had spent some years in perfecting. The two-stage tube used is illustrated in Fig. 2-9b. The papers describing their early results are classics in nuclear physics and give full details of the technical development, voltage calibrations, and experimental observations. The series of papers describing the first disintegrations[26] has earned enduring fame for the authors, who shared the Nobel Prize in physics for 1951. Their apparatus deserves recognition as the first successful particle accelerator for nuclear research.

Later Cockcroft and Walton installed a 1.25-Mv voltage multiplier of the same type in the Cavendish laboratory, engineered and constructed

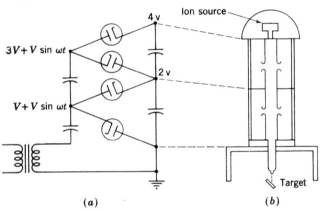

Fig. 2-9. (a) Cockcroft-Walton voltage-multiplying circuit.[26]   (b) Accelerating tube for 0.7-Mev positive ions.[26]

by the Philips Company of Eindhoven, Holland. Similar potential supplies have been used in several English and European laboratories. A photograph of the 700-kev generator at the Cavendish laboratory is shown as the chapter headpiece, page 14. The arrangement of components has become standard in most installations. Capacitors are stacked in two vertical columns capped by a large rounded terminal. The rectifiers are located in a zig-zag pattern between the capacitor stacks. A stack of filter capacitors to reduce voltage ripple is frequently added as an extra vertical array, as can be seen in the photograph. The accelerating tube is also a vertical assembly with ion beam brought down through the floor to an experimental room beneath. Shielding for the X rays produced in the tube is necessary, and the floor is usually built up to provide this shielding.

The voltage multiplier has been so successful as a potential supply for energies of around 1 Mev that it has been widely copied and modified in other laboratories. One of the first laboratories in this country to build such a unit was the University of Illinois. In 1937 Haworth, King,

Zahn, and Heydenburg[29] described such an apparatus operating at 300 kv, chiefly characterized by the economy of construction. Capacitors of glass plates and metal foil were built in the laboratory; rectifiers were constructed of glass and metal cylinders and continuously pumped. The result of a continuous development of accelerating tubes was reported by Haworth, Manley, and Luebke.[30]

The circuit operates as described above, with an output-voltage multiplication factor N equal to the total number of capacitors (or the number of rectifier tubes) with no current drain. With finite current drain the voltage is reduced below this optimum, and ripple appears in the output. Bouwers and Kuntke[31] in Germany analyzed the circuit on the assumption of perfect rectifiers and capacitors. The theory has been extended and checked experimentally by Arnold,[32] Peck,[33] and Lorrain.[34] Lorrain gives the results in the following form, in which the output voltage V is given in terms of the peak input voltage V_i, frequency f, capacitance C of an individual capacitor, and load current I:

$$V = NV_i^- - \frac{I}{12fC} \left(N^3 + \tfrac{9}{4}N^2 + \tfrac{1}{2}N\right) \tag{2-1}$$

The ripple voltage is given by

$$\pm V = \frac{I}{16fC} N(N + 2) \tag{2-2}$$

It is clear that high frequency is an advantage, both to minimize ripple voltage and to reduce size of capacitors. The optimum number of stages can be obtained by differentiation of Eq. (2-2).

Arnold[32] used selenium rectifiers instead of vacuum tubes in the design of a 500-kv generator operating at 750 cps. In his paper he checked the performance of his circuit against the theory and found it in good agreement. Lorrain[34] reports on a 500-kv generator using 24 stages and operating at 32 kc/sec; he was able to utilize available low-cost radio and television equipment. The problem of insulation against corona breakdown was solved by housing the generator in a pressure vessel with 30 psi pressure of CO_2 and Freon gas.

This type of generator is now available commercially from several suppliers, using selenium rectifiers and providing output voltages up to more than 1 Mv.

REFERENCES

1. A. W. Simon, *Rev. Sci. Instr.*, **4**:67 (1933).
2. O. Dahl, *Rev. Sci. Instr.*, **7**:254 (1936).
3. J. M. Malpica, *Rev. Sci. Instr.*, **22**:364 (1951).
4. R. J. Van de Graaff, *Phys. Rev.*, **38**:1919A (1931).

5. G. Breit and M. A. Tuve, *Nature*, **121**:535 (1928).
6. G. Breit, M. A. Tuve, and O. Dahl, *Phys. Rev.*, **35**:51 (1930).
7. M. A. Tuve, G. Breit, and L. R. Hafstad, *Phys. Rev.*, **35**:66 (1930).
8. M. A. Tuve, L. R. Hafstad, and O. Dahl, *Phys. Rev.*, **35**:1406 (1930).
9. M. A. Tuve, L. R. Hafstad, and O. Dahl, *Phys. Rev.*, **36**:1261 (1930).
10. D. H. Sloan, *Phys. Rev.*, **47**:62 (1935).
11. E. E. Charlton, W. F. Westendorp, L. E. Dempster, and G. Hotaling, *J. Appl. Phys.*, **10**:374 (1934).
12. Bellaschi, *Trans. AIEE*, **51**:936 (1932).
13. A. Brasch and F. Lange, *Naturwiss.*, **18**:769 (1930); *Z. Physik*, **70**:10 (1931).
14. W. C. Anderson, *Rev. Sci. Instr.*, **7**:243 (1936).
15. R. W. Sorensen, *JAIEE*, **44**:373 (1925).
16. C. C. Lauritsen and R. D. Bennett, *Phys. Rev.*, **32**:850 (1928).
17. R. Crane and C. C. Lauritsen, *Rev. Sci. Instr.*, **4**:118 (1933).
18. H. R. Crane, C. C. Lauritsen, and A. Soltan, *Phys. Rev.*, **45**:507 (1934).
19. W. C. Stephens and C. C. Lauritsen, *Rev. Sci. Instr.*, **9**:51 (1938).
20. W. D. Coolidge, *J. Franklin Inst.*, **202**:693 (1926).
21. W. H. Zinn and S. Seely, *Phys. Rev.*, **50**:1101 (1936).
22. W. H. Zinn and S. Seely, *Phys. Rev.*, **52**:919 (1937).
23. C. N. Slack and L. F. Ehrke, *Rev. Sci. Instr.*, **8**:193 (1937).
24. E. Almqvist, K. W. Allen, J. T. Dewan, T. P. Pepper, and J. H. Sanders, *Phys. Rev.*, **79**:209 (1950).
25. J. T. Dewan, *Rev. Sci. Instr.*, **21**:771 (1950).
26. J. D. Cockcroft and E. T. S. Walton, *Proc. Roy. Soc. (London)*, **A136**:619 (1932); **A137**:229 (1932); **A144**:704 (1934).
27. Schenkel, *Elektrotech. Z.*, **40**:333 (1919).
28. H. Greinacher, *Z. Physik*, **4**:195 (1921).
29. L. J. Haworth, L. D. P. King, C. T. Zahn, and N. P. Heydenburg, *Rev. Sci. Instr.*, **8**:486 (1937).
30. L. J. Haworth, J. H. Manley, and E. A. Luebke, *Rev. Sci. Instr.*, **12**:591 (1941).
31. A. Bouwers and A. Kuntke, *Z. tech. Physik*, **18**:209 (1937).
32. W. R. Arnold, *Rev. Sci. Instr.*, **21**:796 (1950).
33. R. A. Peck, *Rev. Sci. Instr.*, **26**:441 (1955); R. A. Peck and H. P. Eubank, *Rev. Sci. Instr.*, **26**:444 (1955).
34. P. Lorrain, R. Beique, P. Gilmore, P. E. Girard, A. Breton, and P. Piché, *Can. J. Phys.*, **35**:299 (1957).

3

The Electrostatic Generator*

The belt-charged electrostatic generator has been so successful as a voltage source for particle acceleration that it has displaced all other static machines and most of the other types of direct-voltage generators. The use of high-pressure gas insulation has freed the generator from atmospheric disturbances, and has resulted in a relatively compact design. In the energy range up to 4 or even 6 Mev to which it has been developed, it can deliver a steady, parallel beam of particles free from stray radia-

---

*The name "statitron" has also been applied to the belt-charged electrostatic generator. In an informal poll conducted some years ago by the editor of *The Review of Scientific Instruments* among most of the users of these machines in the United States, the name "statitron" received majority but not unanimous approval. It has not been generally accepted, however. Some people prefer to call the belt generator the "Van de Graaff," as it has been known to many in the past. However, in recent years the High Voltage Engineering Corporation has used the name "Van de Graaff" as a trademark for its products. In this chapter the writers have felt it more appropriate to retain the full title "electrostatic generator."

tion, which makes it ideal as a source for nuclear studies in this energy range.

The most important property of this accelerator is the unusually homogeneous beam energy. In modern electrostatic generators equipped with a beam analyzer, the energy spread of the beam and the stability with which it can be maintained are of the order of 1 to 2 kv, and experimental measurements can be made to this accuracy. The beam can be focused to small cross section at the target, and intensities have proved adequate for most purposes. Furthermore, the voltage can be varied at will, so nuclear processes can be studied as a function of bombarding energy. The electrostatic generator is supreme in the precise measurement of nuclear energy levels, and for the study of excitation functions. A large fraction of our quantitative data on nuclear properties has come from these machines. They have also been very successful as sources of X rays for medical and industrial uses. The most complete survey article was published in 1948 in an English journal by Van de Graaff, Trump, and Buechner.[1]

3-1. HISTORICAL DEVELOPMENT

The original suggestion of a belt-charged electrostatic generator seems to have come from Righi about 1890 as a modification of the "charged-water-drop" generator of Lord Kelvin. The significant principles were all known in the late nineteenth century, but the method was not developed as a source of potential for particle acceleration until the 1930s. As a Rhodes scholar in Oxford in 1927 and 1928, R. J. Van de Graaff became interested in the need for high-voltage machines to develop the field of nuclear physics, then in its infancy. He decided to experiment with the belt-charged electrostatic generator as a potential source, and on his return to Princeton University as a National Research Fellow in 1929, he built his first model.

Van de Graaff[2] described his first generator before the American Physical Society in 1931. It was simply conceived and built of inexpensive parts. Two 24-in.-diam spherical aluminum electrodes were mounted on 7-ft glass rods, each with a motor-driven silk belt to transport the charge. One sphere was given a positive charge; the other, a negative charge. An estimated 1.5 Mv potential difference was developed between terminals, limited only by corona from the terminals. The simple construction and the steady, direct voltage made the machine attractive as

At the head of the facing page is an illustration of the original air-insulated electrostatic generator at MIT designed by Van de Graaff and his collaborators,[5] now at the Boston Museum of Science. Shown in the photograph are C. M. Van Atta, D. L. Northrup, and L. C. Van Atta. (Courtesy of R. J. Van de Graaff.)

a voltage source for positive-ion acceleration.   The possibility of extending the method to higher voltages was evident, and groups in several other laboratories became interested and joined in the development.

In 1932 Van de Graaff went to the Massachusetts Institute of Technology, where, with the support of President K. T. Compton, he started on design and development tests for a really large generator.   A preliminary design study by Van de Graaff, Compton, and L. C. Van Atta[3] described the installation, which was later built in an airship hangar at the Round Hill estate of Col. E. H. R. Greene near South Dartmouth, Massachusetts.   Two 15-ft-diam spherical metal terminals mounted on vertical hollow Textolite cylinders were charged, one positively and one negatively, by two 4-ft-wide belts within the cylinders.   A discharge tube for accelerating ions was to be supported horizontally between the terminals, and the laboratory for observing nuclear experiments was to be within one of the 15-ft shells.   The concept of the project was exciting and the scale tremendous for that time.   It was essentially complete by 1936 and was described in detail by L. C. Van Atta, Northrup, C. M. Van Atta, and Van de Graaff.[4]   It developed 2.4 Mv on the positive terminal and 2.7 Mv on the negative one, with a possible total of 5.1-Mv potential drop.   However, the difficulties of mounting an evacuated discharge tube between terminals were extreme, and the machine never performed satisfactorily as a particle accelerator.   Furthermore, voltage limitations caused by the high humidity and unclean conditions within the hangar near the ocean made it evident that this location was unsuitable.

The installation was moved to MIT in 1937 and installed in a tight metal-domed building in which dust and humidity could be controlled. In this reassembly the two columns and terminals were mounted adjacent to each other; one column was used for the belts of the electrostatic generator and the other for a vertical discharge tube, so experiments could be performed in a basement room below the floor.   With this modified assembly, the machine was completed as an accelerator by 1940, accelerating electrons or positive ions to 2.75 Mev energy.[5]   It was developed to be a reliable and steady source, and gave many years of valuable service as a research tool under the direction of Professors Van de Graaff and Buechner.   However, this original MIT "Van de Graaff" has become obsolete as a scientific instrument and has been replaced by others of more modern design.   The original dual-terminal generator is now located as a permanent exhibit in the Museum of Science in Boston.

The popular appeal of this gigantic generator has been tremendous. It was an awe-inspiring experience to stand beneath the huge spheres and feel the hair rise as potential increased, and then to see the long, jagged strokes of man-made lightning as the terminal discharged to the roof or down the column.   An even more exciting experience was to ascend by a ladder, stand within the hollow terminal by an open port as it was charged, and watch the sparks striking (or more exactly, originating) a few inches away on the port rim.   Photographs of this Van de Graaff generator have been used as illustrations for many scientific articles. To many people it typifies the atom smasher of the nuclear physicist. Largely for its historical interest a photograph of the Massachusetts Institute of Technology 15-ft dual-terminal generator is shown in the chapter headpiece, page 30.

Soon after Van de Graaff had demonstrated the potentialities of the electrostatic generator in his first model, and while he was engaged in studies and designs for the large dual-terminal machine, a group headed by M. A. Tuve at the Carnegie Institution of Washington decided to abandon its previous attempts to build a Tesla-coil voltage source and to adopt instead the electrostatic generator.   A project was started with the cooperation of Van de Graaff to study the technical possibility of applying an electrostatic generator to the high-voltage discharge tubes already developed in the Carnegie laboratory.   Spherical shells of 1 and 2 m diam were mounted on Textolite columns in air, and tests were made establishing the prediction that terminal voltage is proportional to radius of curvature.   The problems of corona formation, of destructive sparks down the insulating columns, and of the measurement of potential with spark gaps and generating voltmeters were studied with the aim of developing a reliable, steady source for nuclear experiments.

The Carnegie Institution group built first a 1-m-diam generator which supplied 600-kv ions by 1933.   Then they developed a concentric-shell generator with a 1-m inner shell and a 2-m outer shell, mounted on a tripod arrangement of three Textolite columns.   Two charging belts crossed the room horizontally, and a vertical discharge tube led through the floor, so that the beam of ions could be analyzed magnetically and experiments performed in a basement room.   Potentials of up to 1.3 Mv could be maintained with the terminal positive (for accelerating positive ions to ground).   These two machines have been fully described by Tuve, Hafstad, and Dahl.[6]   They were put to immediate use in accelerating protons and deuterons for nuclear experiments.   These were the first practical electrostatic accelerators, and an important series of research papers followed the completion of the 2-m generator in 1935, starting with measurements of excitation functions which showed sharp nuclear resonances.[7]   A sketch of the 2-m generator is shown in Fig. 3-1.

One of the most important technical developments of the Carnegie Institution group was the study of voltage calibration for such air-insulated generators.   It was found that sphere-gap calibrations could not be extended to this voltage range with any confidence, but were a function of the meteorological and surface conditions of the gap electrodes. The generating voltmeter, which measures field intensity, was also found to be unreliable at potentials where corona discharge occurred. A high-energy proton beam could be brought through a thin vacuum window and the range measured, but the inherent errors in range straggling and the imperfectly known range-energy relations made this calibration also suspect. The first satisfactory calibration was obtained by deflecting

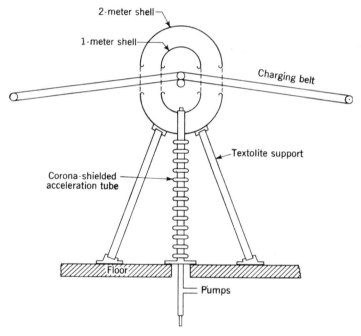

Fig. 3-1. Schematic diagram of 2-m electrostatic generator at Carnegie Institution,[6] showing the arrangement of supports, charging belts, and accelerator tube.

the emergent beam of protons by a magnetic field through a system of slits. This result was used to establish proton range-energy relations and to calibrate the generating voltmeter. The limit of accuracy was the measurement of magnetic field including the fringing effects.

The most accurate calibrations were based on the use of a column of precision resistors paralleling the discharge tube.[8] Accurate current measurements with this 10,000-megohm resistor column gave an absolute calibration which was of tremendous value to the scientific world at that time. Nuclear resonances, such as the $C(p,\gamma)$ resonances at 400 and 480 kv, the $Li(p,\gamma)$ at 440 kv, and the three $F(p,\gamma)$ levels at 328, 892, and

942 kv,[7,8] were observed and measured using extremely thin targets. These and other nuclear resonances have since been determined with such precision that they are used as substandards for calibrating instruments in other laboratories and in providing a cross-calibration of results from the different laboratories.

Meanwhile a parallel development started in other laboratories, based on the use of high gas pressure to insulate the terminal and increase the potential. Barton, Mueller, and L. C. Van Atta[9] at Princeton were the first to experiment with this modification. They used a cylindrical electrode supported by two Textolite cylinders along the axis of a horizontal pressure tank. Their first small machine developed 1-Mv potential at 7 atm air pressure, showing an almost linear increase in breakdown potential with increasing pressure. The chief advantages were the smaller size of the installation and the positive control of humidity within the pressure tank.

This principle was utilized by Herb, Parkinson, and Kerst[10] at the University of Wisconsin in the design of a series of pressure-insulated generators. The first model reached 0.75 Mv. The second, described in 1937 and again after further development and operational experience[11] in 1938, operated at 2.4 Mv and was equipped with an electronic voltage stabilizer to maintain the steady potentials needed for nuclear research. The third model, reported by Herb, Turner, Hudson, and Warren[12] in 1940, introduced the use of three concentric high-potential electrodes to distribute the potential drop and reached a potential of 4.0 Mv.

The Herb design, utilizing pressure insulation and having concentric terminal shields, has been adopted in most modern accelerators. The horizontal arrangement—with the terminal cantilevered on insulators from a grounded face plate, enclosed within a pressure housing which rolls on rails to open the chamber for servicing, and employing a horizontal discharge tube—has also found many converts. The practical limit seems to have been reached, however, at about the 4-Mev machine,[13] owing primarily to the difficulties of supporting the terminal and horizontal discharge tube as the size is increased.

During the early years other laboratories exploited the vertical mounting, with its apparent advantage in mechanical stability. In this arrangement, the insulation column sustains only compressional forces, and a large number of designs have been developed using insulation in the form of ceramic standoff insulators or short disk-shaped buttons separating metal-plate equipotential electrodes. Large pressurized generators were built at the Westinghouse Research Laboratory,[14,15] at the Carnegie Institution, and at the University of Minnesota.[16] These were designed to operate at relatively low (60 to 120 psi) gas pressure, in the hope that higher voltages could be most readily obtained by increasing the gap and the radius of curvature of the terminal. Recognition of the adverse effect of large terminal area, of the importance of polished surfaces, and of the value of multiple-shell terminals came later. As a consequence, all have been restricted to less than their theoretical limits, operating at about 3 Mv.

Another line of development has been the small, inexpensive generator for low voltage. A good description has been published of such a small machine (rated at 1 Mv) at Johns Hopkins University.[17,18]

Meanwhile, at the Massachusetts Institute of Technology a new series of developments in which J. G. Trump was prominent was started in about 1938 in the Electrical Engineering Department. Trump and Van de Graaff[19] reported on the first of a series of generators for electrons intended for use as a source of X rays for medical and industrial purposes. Years of comprehensive study of the engineering problems of high dc potential made this group acknowledged leaders in the technical field. Their studies have included such problems as the flashover potentials for solid dielectrics in vacuum and in compressed gases, the influence of electrode material on breakdown potential, the relative dielectric strengths of various gases such as Freon, CCl_4, and SF_6, and ionization as a function of depth in tissuelike material for high-voltage X rays and electrons. The use of compressed gases as insulating media was investigated experimentally at an early date, and test equipment was set up to study the problems and determine the limitations. A large share of our technical knowledge of high-voltage engineering has come from this continuous and comprehensive program.

During the war the MIT High-Voltage Laboratory developed and built several X-ray generators of 2-Mv rating for the United States Navy and in the process studied and solved many technical problems. The results are reported by Buechner, Van de Graaff, Sperduto, McIntosh, and Burrill.[20]

The next step in the development of the electrostatic generator at MIT was a large, vertical, pressurized proton accelerator designed by Buechner, Trump, Van de Graaff, and others but not described in the published literature. This machine was financed by a grant from the Rockefeller Foundation and is duplicated at the Atomic Energy Research Establishment in Harwell, England. Results of the years of comprehensive study on electrostatic problems at MIT are incorporated in the design, and the wide experience of the staff has gone into its construction. It was completed in 1950. Beams of 10 to 20 μa of resolved protons at 4 Mev are obtained[21] with occasional operation at still higher energy. This beautifully built instrument is in full operation as a research tool.

The latest step in electrostatic-generator development at MIT is the "12-Mv" generator now operating at voltages up to 9 Mv. This will be described more fully at the end of this chapter. It is a fitting climax to the story of the development of these machines at the MIT laboratories.

In 1947 Trump, Van de Graaff, Denis Robinson, and others formed the High Voltage Engineering Corporation (HVEC) in Cambridge, Massachusetts, for commercial production of Van de Graaff generators. As the first commercial firm engaged solely in the business of designing and building accelerators, HVEC holds a unique position in the field. This company has produced several compact models of the pressure-insulated electron accelerator using sealed-off accelerating tubes and operating in the 1- to 2-Mv range. It has also developed a 5.5-Mv vertical-mount pressurized proton accelerator based on the design of the MIT research machine, a 4-Mv horizontal proton accelerator of the Herb type first built for the Brookhaven National Laboratory,[22] and a variety of other sizes and types.

The most recent HVEC development (1958) is a double-ended horizontal generator,[23] called a "tandem," in which negative hydrogen ions produced in a special source at ground potential are accelerated to the positively charged high-voltage terminal in the center of the machine. Here, they traverse a gas jet in which they are stripped of their electrons to become protons. Then they are repelled by the positive terminal and are accelerated back to ground potential to emerge with an energy corresponding to twice the potential of the high-voltage terminal. The first of these units, installed at the Chalk River Laboratory in Canada, gives 1-μa beams of H^+ or D^+ ions with energies up to 9 Mev.

Since there are several hundred electrostatic machines in laboratories around the world, it is impossible here to mention any but a few outstanding historical examples. Impressive electrostatic machines have been built and important contributions to the art have also been made in many other centers: Los Alamos National Laboratory, Brookhaven National Laboratory, University of California at Los Angeles, British Atomic Energy Research Establishment, Saclay Centre d'Études Nucléaires in France, Christian Michelsens Institut in Bergen, Norway, and many other places.

3-2. PRINCIPLES OF OPERATION

The electrostatic machine is simple in concept, but the techniques and designs needed to obtain engineering perfection are complicated with details and are bounded by fundamental limitations, such as the electrical breakdown of insulation. The principle of operation is readily understood by reference to Fig. 3-2, which is a schematic diagram of a vertically mounted belt generator. The structure consists of a rounded high-voltage terminal supported on an insulating column and a moving belt to carry charge to the terminal. Charge of one polarity is sprayed on the belt at the grounded end, is carried up into the terminal by a moving belt, and is removed by a collecting device within the terminal where there are no high electric fields to disturb the collecting process. This steady current, $i = dQ/dt$, produces an electrostatic potential on the terminal.   If C is the capacitance of the terminal to ground, the terminal will be raised to a potential V by a charge $Q = CV$, and the rate of increase of potential with time is given by

$$\frac{dV}{dt} = \frac{i}{C} \qquad (3\text{-}1)$$

The capacitance of a spherical shell, if insulated and a long distance from ground, is given by

$$C = 4\pi\epsilon_0 r = 1.11 \times 10^{-10} r$$
$$\text{farads} \qquad (3\text{-}2)$$

where r is the radius in meters and ϵ_0 is the dielectric permittivity of free space in mks units.   If a terminal of radius r_1 is enclosed within a grounded concentric shell of radius r_2, the capacitance is given by

$$C = 1.11 \times 10^{-10}\, \frac{r_1 r_2}{r_2 - r_1}$$
$$\text{farads} \qquad (3\text{-}2a)$$

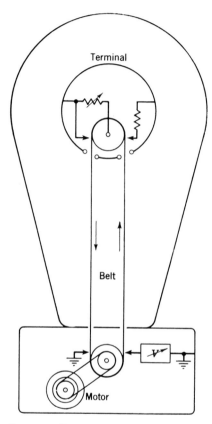

Fig. 3-2. Schematic diagram of generator enclosed in a grounded pressure tank.   Circuits are shown for spraying charge on both the ascending and descending faces of the belt.

For a typical large accelerator in which the inner terminal has a radius of 1 m and the outer pressure housing a radius of 2 m, the capacitance is about 220 $\mu\mu$f.   Such an outer grounded shell is indicated in Fig. 3-2 to represent the wall of a pressure-containing vessel such as is used in most generators.   This grounded shell is not necessary to the operation of the machine and is in fact missing in some of the earlier designs using air at atmospheric pressure.

Another common geometry is a cylindrical terminal with spherical end caps.   The capacitance per unit length of coaxial cylinders having radii r_1 and r_2 is

$$\frac{C}{l} = \frac{2\pi\epsilon_0}{\ln\,(r_2/r_1)} = \frac{0.55 \times 10^{-10}}{(\ln\,r_2/r_1)} \qquad \text{farads} \qquad (3\text{-}2b)$$

For a 1-m-long cylindrical section with 1-m-radius hemispherical caps enclosed in a 2-m cylinder, the total capacitance is about 300 $\mu\mu$f.   Capacitances for other shapes used in accelerator designs are of the same order. The dielectric constant of the gas between terminal and housing makes a small but usually negligible change in capacitance.   Additional capacitance to ground is introduced by the metallic equipotential electrodes used in the supporting column and by the equipotential concentric shells used in most modern installations.   Measured values of capacitance are, therefore, usually somewhat higher than those illustrated above.

Maximum charging currents used in modern generators are a few milliamperes.   The time rate of increase of potential given by Eq. (3-1) is of the order of 10^6 volts/sec.   At 2 ma a 500-$\mu\mu$f terminal would reach 4 Mv in 1.0 sec.   After a spark breakdown or discharge, the generator requires a finite time of this order to regain its charge.

The belt runs between a motor-driven pulley at ground potential and a pulley in the terminal.   Electric charge is sprayed on the belt at the grounded end from a fine wire or from a row of corona points (phonograph needles have been used) extended across the width of the belt and directed at the pulley or at a grounded plate behind the belt.   A corona discharge maintained between these points and ground produces gaseous ionization in the air, and charge is deposited on the moving belt.   If the terminal is to be charged positively, the points must have a positive potential relative to ground, so that positive ions will go toward the grounded pulley or plate and will be intercepted by the belt.   If the terminal is to have a negative charge (for accelerating electrons), the corona points are made negative.

The charge is removed from the ascending belt within the terminal by a similar corona-point collector connected electrically to the terminal. If the pulley within the terminal is insulated, it will rise to a potential sufficiently above that of the terminal to maintain the necessary corona discharge.   The charge appears on the outer surface of the terminal, so that (except for the effect due to the pulley potential) the inside of the terminal is field-free.   Thus the charging process occurs within the grounded base, and the discharging of the belt takes place within the equipotential terminal; both operations are separately controllable and independent of terminal voltage.

The electric-power supply used to produce the corona discharge from the needle points is indicated schematically in Fig. 3-2.   Potentials of 20 to 30 kv are sufficient, and a current capacity of several milliamperes is required.   Almost any rectifier which meets these ratings is satisfactory.   A half-wave, hard-vacuum-tube rectifier is common, using 60-cycle power.   Filtering to reduce the ac ripple is useful in giving more uniform belt charge, but not essential.   The magnitude of the corona spray current is usually controlled by varying the primary ac voltage.

This corona current determines the potential to which the terminal will rise, as will be described later.

It is also possible to spray charge of the opposite sign on the descending belt run within the terminal and to take it off at the grounded end. In this way the belt carries charge both ascending and descending, and the charging current is doubled. A charging circuit to achieve this result is also shown in Fig. 3-2. The resistor placed between the insulated upper pulley and the terminal can be adjusted to control the upper spray potential and arranged to make the charge densities equal on the upward and downward runs.

The power required to charge the terminal is calculable from charging current and terminal potential. For example, the necessary motor power (above that required for friction and windage) at 2 ma and 4 Mv is 8 kw. This assumes that belt speed is constant and that the 2-ma current returns to ground through some other path such as the discharge tube accelerating ions or electrons.

Current returns to ground from the high-voltage terminal in many ways. In a positive-ion accelerator the useful current is the beam of positive ions being accelerated down the accelerator tube. However, stray ions may strike the tube walls and may release secondary electrons, which are accelerated up the column to produce X rays on striking the ion source. Frequently a resistive load is built into the insulator column to serve as a potential divider. This may be of the order of 1000 to 10,000 megohms, uniformly distributed along the length of the accelerator tube and connected to appropriate electrodes along the column. The ultimate limit to terminal potential in the absence of an accelerator tube is corona discharge from the terminal. This is caused by the breakdown of insulation (either gas or solid) due to excessive fields at the surface of the terminal. In most installations adjustable corona-point units are installed opposite one point on the terminal surface to increase or decrease total load current and so to maintain a constant terminal potential. Occasionally a corona streamer in the gas will develop into a spark which discharges the terminal completely.

The required charging current is the sum of these several components, which behave differently with terminal voltage:

1. Positive-ion current is generally constant, determined by ion-source conditions rather than by total voltage.

2. Current in the resistive potential divider or leakage down the column is directly proportional to terminal potential.

3. Secondary electron current in the tube will be described in more detail in a later section, where it is shown to increase rapidly with voltage above an apparent threshold.

4. Corona current behaves similarly, being zero at low voltages and rising rapidly above a threshold value.

The charging-current versus terminal-voltage characteristic is illustrated qualitatively in Fig. 3-3, which shows the way in which the components listed above vary with potential.   The equilibrium potential V_e to which the terminal will rise is determined by the maximum charging current available.   Terminal voltage can be controlled by regulating the charging current or by varying the amount of corona load current with adjustable needle points.   The extremely rapid change of corona current with voltage tends to stabilize voltage at the equilibrium value, as can be observed in the graph.

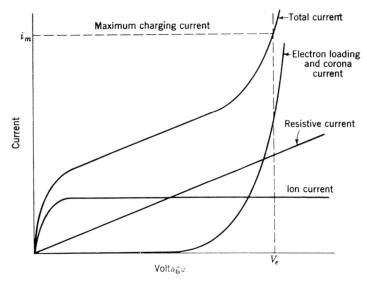

Fig. 3-3. Typical current-versus-voltage functions for the several components of the total charging current in an electrostatic generator.   Terminal potential V_e is determined by the available charging current i_m.

After a spark has discharged the terminal and while the total load current is small, the excess charging current causes terminal voltage to rise rapidly.   However, as terminal voltage approaches its equilibrium value again, the excess current becomes smaller and the rate of charging decreases.   In principle the terminal voltage will approach the equilibrium value asymptotically, but in practice the corona-control system for voltage stabilization allows an overshoot.   The time constant of this control system varies inversely with the magnitude of the corona-current variation used in the control.

The operation of the generator is simple to describe.   First the belt motors are started; then the belt-spray charging unit is turned on and the rate adjusted to bring the terminal up to the working voltage, balancing the currents on the ascending and descending belt runs.   Next the ion source is turned on and its potentials adjusted to bring the ion current up to normal.   This extra current load will decrease terminal voltage, which is trimmed back to the desired operating value by increasing the charging current.   The corona-control circuit can now be locked in to maintain this voltage.   Adjustments of ion-source or focusing-electrode voltages to improve beam focusing may require still further trimming of the control circuit.

It is well to avoid excess potential on the terminal in order to reduce the chance of destructive sparks.   Such sparks will occur frequently on first tuning up a generator, and many days of operation with slowly increasing voltage are usually required to condition the generator to hold its rated voltage.   A well-designed generator will eventually stabilize at that voltage set by the maximum allowed charging rate, i.e., when the total load current equals the charging current.   Further increase in potential can only be obtained by decreasing the electron loading, which generally improves with time if the vacuum system is tight and the discharge tube clean.   These problems will be described in more detail later.

3-3. ELECTRICAL BREAKDOWN IN COMPRESSED GASES

The breakdown potential of an insulated electrode in gas depends on several factors, which can be discussed separately:

1. Radius of curvature, area, and surface smoothness of the terminal
2. Electrode material and surface contaminations
3. Composition and pressure of the gas
4. Shape, material, and surface conditions of the insulating supports
5. Potential distribution along the insulator

Many of these factors are interrelated.   The designer of an electrostatic generator must consider the limitations of each component and eliminate weak points.

Elementary theory of electrical breakdown predicts that breakdown potential should be directly proportional to the radius of curvature of the terminal.   This is based on the assumption that ionization in the gas occurs and corona leakage develops at a fixed maximum potential gradient at the surface.   The breakdown potential gradient in air at atmospheric pressure is of the order of 3×10^6 volts/m.   This limit would be reached at a potential of 3 Mv for a spherical terminal of 1 m radius if corona did not distort the field.   The early studies by Van de Graaff and by Tuve and his associates at the Carnegie laboratory showed that this relationship was approximately correct for 1- and 2-m spheres, although practical limitations on maintaining ideal surface conditions led to lower potential limits.   Under stable conditions, however, the linear relationship between breakdown potential and radius was verified.

Paschen first formalized the relationship between breakdown potential V_m for plane-parallel electrodes, gas pressure, and interelectrode spacing as

$$V_m \text{ (in volts)} = k \text{ (pressure in atmospheres}$$
$$\times \text{ interelectrode spacing in cm)} \quad (3\text{-}3)$$

where k is a coefficient called the specific breakdown strength, which is a function of the composition of the gas and of the electrode materials. This coefficient was originally measured and found to be 30,000 for dry air at atmospheric pressure and with a 1-cm gap. It was this figure which led to the maximum field limit quoted for air of 3×10^6 volts/m. However, it was soon found that the coefficient was not a constant but varied with pressure, gap length, and electrode composition.

The type of discharge that results from breakdown depends on the shape of the electrodes, gap length, pressure, and the constants of the external circuit. The most common type of discharge is a spark. Between plane-parallel electrodes, the initial spark normally develops into an arc discharge with the current limited only by the external circuit resistance. Between small spheres spaced far apart, a corona or brush discharge may be visible near the surfaces, with the center of the gap appearing dark. With a large spherical terminal such as is used with the electrostatic generator, corona discharge usually occurs first at the surface, with the rest of the space dark.

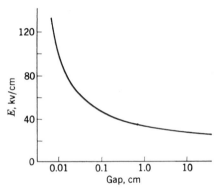

Fig. 3-4. Electric field for spark breakdown between plane-parallel electrodes in air at atmospheric pressure.

Then, occasionally, a corona streamer will develop into a spark to ground, discharging the terminal completely.

Experimental studies of spark breakdown show strong dependence on geometric arrangements, and the electric field intensity for breakdown is by no means constant. Figure 3-4 shows the electric field for spark breakdown between plane-parallel electrodes in air at atmospheric pressure as a function of gap length. Figure 3-5 shows the breakdown voltage between 25-cm-diam spherical terminals at atmospheric pressure as a function of spacing; grounding one of the terminals changes the results, an indication of the complicated influence of geometry on the fields. Sphere-gap measurements of voltage are subject to considerable error, owing to variations in corona discharge and in surface conditions. The presence of oxide films, oil, fingerprints, or even adsorbed gases will make marked changes in the sparking limit. Dust particles or surface roughness may increase fields locally, and spheres must be carefully polished and cleaned. It has also been observed that a change of relative humidity from 0 to 100 per cent increases sparking potential in air by about 3.5 per cent.

In applying these considerations to a generator terminal, we can understand why such large-radius surfaces do not reach the predicted maximum

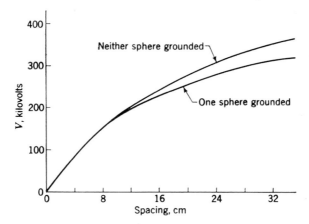

Fig. 3-5. Spark-breakdown voltage between metal spheres of 25 cm diam in air at atmospheric pressure, with and without one sphere grounded.

potentials. The charge on a spherical terminal of radius r required to produce the breakdown field of 3×10^6 volts/m at the surface is given by

$$Q = 4\pi\epsilon_0 E r^2 = 3.33 \times 10^{-4} r^2 \qquad \text{coulombs} \qquad (3\text{-}4)$$

The corresponding terminal potential would be

$$V = \frac{E}{r} = \frac{3 \times 10^6}{r} \qquad \text{volts} \qquad (3\text{-}5)$$

A 1-m-radius terminal at atmospheric pressure should have a charge of 333 microcoulombs and should rise to a potential of 3 Mv. The best value obtained consistently at the Carnegie laboratory was 1.3 Mv. The 15-ft-diam terminals of the Round Hill installation had a theoretical limit of 6.8 Mv each. The actual potential attained was 2.4 Mv on the positive and 2.7 Mv on the negative terminal.

Surface irregularities can reduce the potential limit by decreasing radius of curvature and increasing electric field locally. It was early observed that breakdown potential was reduced for terminals exposed to dust. One of the worst limitations at Van de Graaff's Round Hill installation was sparking due to droppings from birds roosting within the hangar. An insulating oil film will also reduce breakdown voltage by allowing large local fields to build up across the film. The contamination problem is largely solved in modern generators by enclosing the terminal in a pressure housing and by filtering and purifying the gas. However, great care must be taken in construction to polish the terminal and, after exposure to air, to wipe and clean the surface.

It is an experimental fact that even with polished surfaces the field cannot be pushed much above 50 per cent of the theoretical limit. Total gap length to the outer grounded walls is not a significant factor. Breakdown occurs at about the same terminal potential for all gaps longer than a practical limit. The practical minimum gap is about 1 m for a 1-m-radius terminal and is roughly proportional for other sizes.

The surface field at the terminal can be reduced by using one or more concentric terminal shells. If the potential drop between each set of shells is to be equal and the electric field at the surface of each shell is to be the same, the radii of concentric spherical shells must be in the ratio

$$\frac{r_1}{r_2} = \frac{r_2}{r_3} = \frac{r_3}{r_4} = \cdots \tag{3-6}$$

With a terminal constructed of several such shells replacing a single terminal within a given size of outer housing, the total breakdown potential can be increased about 50 per cent. The inner shell can be reduced to a size sufficient to house the ion source and power supplies essential to accelerator operation. The chief disadvantage is loss of accessibility to the terminal apparatus, causing increased complexity of maintenance. The shells are mounted on equipotential rings suitably spaced along the column to obtain the desired potential distribution. This requires that the column be designed with steps of decreasing diameter to accommodate the several shields. Figure 3-6 illustrates an arrangement for mounting such shields.

Experience with the use of concentric shells has exposed certain limitations. With increased terminal area (required for many shells) it is found that the reliable operating-potential gradient is reduced. The most recent designs use one or, at the most, two shells inside the outer terminal.

The metal used for terminals also has an effect on breakdown potential. Aluminum is commonly used because it can be spun to the desired spherical shapes and has a low density. Stainless steel is known to have a higher breakdown limit but is more difficult to form. Measurements[24] of the breakdown-potential gradients for the two metals, in the form of flat disks formed with rounded edges and buffed to a mirror finish, showed stainless steel to be much superior, especially at high gas pressure. The maximum fields obtained in these tests, at 400 psi pressure of air, were 800 kv/in. for aluminum and 1200 kv/in. for stainless steel. These values are representative of the ultimate limit for short gaps and high pressures; they are not directly applicable to the long gaps and nonuniform fields of the generator terminal. Other comparisons of electrode materials were made in vacuum, to simulate the accelerating-tube electrodes. It was found that highly polished aluminum had breakdown-potential gradients equivalent to stainless steel under high vacuum.

The use of compressed gases around the terminal to increase the breakdown potential is based on Paschen's law [Eq. (3-3)], which predicts a

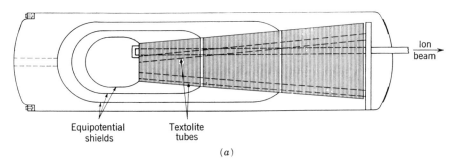

Equipotential   Textolite
shields   tubes

Ion
beam

(a)

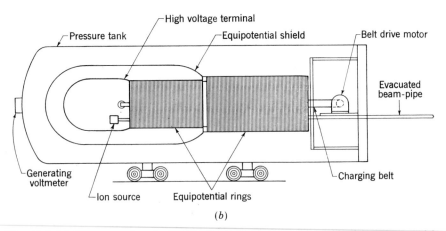

High voltage terminal

Pressure tank   Equipotential shield   Belt drive motor

Evacuated
beam-pipe

Generating
voltmeter

Ion source   Equipotential rings

Charging belt

(b)

Fig. 3-6. (a) Diagram of early University of Wisconsin pressurized generator with concentric equipotential shields, supported at the grounded end by three Textolite tubes. (b) Horizontal Van de Graaff generator for 4-Mev protons.

linear increase of sparking potential with pressure. This is found to hold over a considerable range of pressure but to fail at high pressures. An early curve of breakdown potential as a function of air pressure, by Herb and Bernet,[25] shows a considerable deviation from linearity (see Fig. 3-7). Such deviations are found to depend on the geometry and material of the electrode, the gas composition, and the surface conditions. Under controlled laboratory conditions using plane electrodes and short gaps, Trump and his collaborators found that a useful increase can be extended up to 20 atm. With the nonuniform fields of large terminals in accelerators, the sparking-potential curves always deviate from linearity above some value of pressure, which varies from one installation to another. No single curve can be cited to predict results, but sufficient data are now available for typical geometries to estimate the effect of pressure variation with reasonable accuracy. An example of the data available is the curve taken with a modern accelerator at MIT[20] (Fig. 3-7b).

Breakdown potential depends strongly on gas composition, particularly at high pressures. Air, nitrogen, and carbon dioxide were used in early pressure generators. Air has the advantage of availability but the disadvantage of supporting combustion; Textolite insulators and charging

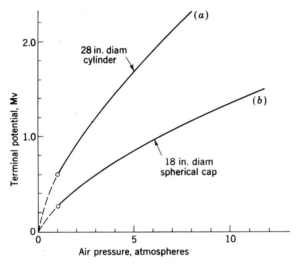

Fig. 3-7. Typical curves of terminal potential versus air pressure for electrostatic generators. (a) University of Wisconsin,[25] 28-in.-diam cylinder. (b) MIT,[19] 18-in. hemispherical cap.

belts were occasionally ignited by sparks in the compressed air. Herb et al.[12] discuss the problem of the fire hazard in compressed air in some detail and show that it can be minimized by suitable choice of nonflammable materials. Largely for this reason N_2 and CO_2 were tried in several generators, but in general gave lower spark-breakdown limits. Trump, Cloud, Mann, and Hanson[24] studied the relative sparkover limits for these gases and for mixtures of N_2 and CO_2, finding air to be superior in all cases.

It has been known since the work of Natterer (1889) that certain gaseous compounds containing chlorine, fluorine, or other "electronegative" gases gave a higher insulating strength than air. The dielectric strength of air is increased by the addition of any gas whose atoms or molecules have an electron affinity, i.e., can capture electrons and suppress discharges until the electron concentration becomes materially higher than

if the electronegative gas were not present.   However, the advantages of
these gases are somewhat offset by the formation of corrosive products
when discharges do occur, or even when heavy corona discharge is
permitted.

Several laboratories[26,27] have studied the increase in dielectric strength
of air by the addition of a saturated vapor of CCl_4 (2 psi at room temperature) and have found that the increase is maintained at approximately

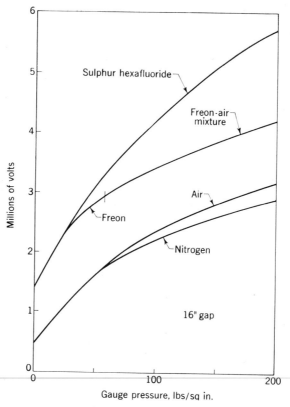

Fig. 3-8. Spark-breakdown voltage versus gas pressure for several gases in the MIT
experimental generator.[20]

the same ratio at higher pressures.   Others[28,29] investigated the characteristics of Freon (CCl_2F_2) and sulfur hexafluoride (SF_6) and found them
to be particularly promising as insulating media.   Freon, developed primarily as a refrigerant, was readily available and was studied by Trump,
Safford, and Cloud[30] both in the pure state and when mixed with air at
pressures above its vapor-pressure limit.   Schumb[31] first developed techniques for producing SF_6 in a quantity sufficient to make tests at the
Massachusetts Institute of Technology laboratory.[20]

A summary of the properties of these gases is given in the curves in Fig. 3-8, taken from MIT publications. The best gas tested was SF_6, up to a pressure of 200 psi, which almost doubled the maximum potential obtained with air at the same pressure. It has a vapor pressure of 330 psi at 25°C and can be run to even higher pressure by warming the generator housing. It can now be obtained commercially at reasonable prices and so affords a method of improving compactness and raising voltage limits of electrostatic generators. Freon, which has a vapor pressure at room temperature of only 85 psi, gives similar sparking potentials up to its vapor-pressure limit, but it is not quite so good as SF_6 at higher pressures, when air or another gas must be mixed with the Freon.

Despite the obvious advantages of the electronegative gases for high-voltage insulation, most laboratories have concluded that the corrosive products of dissociation make their use undesirable. The gases used in most installations are mixtures of nitrogen and carbon dioxide.

For all gases other than air, it is necessary to provide gas-storage reservoirs into which the gas can be pumped when the generator is to be opened for maintenance or repair. Such reservoirs are now common in new installations. The reservoir is usually made about equal in volume to the generator, and valves are arranged so that gas can be pumped either way. In a typical installation at Brookhaven, the pump-up or pump-down time is of the order of 30 min.

3-4. THE INSULATING COLUMN

Solid insulators are used to support the terminals in both vertical- and horizontal-type accelerators. The most common form of insulator is a hollow cylinder of fiber laminate. Textolite was used in the MIT 15-ft air-pressure generator, in the form of cylinders 6 ft in diameter, 22 ft in length, and $\frac{5}{8}$ in. in wall thickness. In the horizontal pressure generators designed by Herb and his associates, a truss structure of three or four smaller Textolite tubes, of 4 to 6 in. diam, is used to support the terminal.

The flashover voltage for Textolite columns depends more on the design of the connection at the terminal than on any other single factor. With a flush mounting (Fig. 3-9a) the concentration of field in the dielectric material of the column initiates corona discharge at the surface of the Textolite at lower potentials than those producing corona in the air. If the column is led through a hole in the terminal with internal edges well rounded (Fig. 3-9b), the situation is improved, but this is still the weak point. Without some form of shielding, sparks initiating at this point will flash down the surface of the column. The 6-ft-diam columns of the 15-ft MIT generator are scored with many such spark tracks. The voltage limit is dependent not so much on length of column as on the initial breakdown at the connection to the terminal. With such an unprotected single insulating column, the limit is less than 3 Mv.

In all modern generators the supporting insulators are surrounded by closely spaced equipotential rings (Fig. 3-9c), so arranged that the electric field is approximately constant along the length of the column and the weak point at the terminal connection is shielded from high fields. Such rings surround the Textolite tube truss of the Herb-type horizontal generator and are equipped with corona-point gaps between rings to equalize the potential drops. The rings are also connected internally to corresponding accelerating-tube electrodes and to "field control" bars near the belt. A 10-ft column with such equipotential rings will insulate well

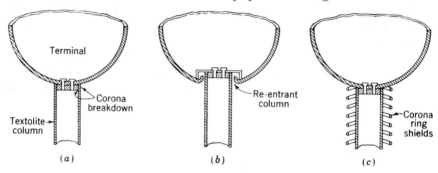

Fig. 3-9. Steps in the development of the connection between terminal and supporting column: (a) flush mounting results in corona breakdown of the insulating column; (b) reentrant column reduces but does not eliminate corona; (c) spaced ring shields along the column give a uniform potential gradient and eliminate corona.

over 4 Mv at 200 psi pressure of air, and such sparkovers as do occur go down the line of corona points without damage to the insulators inside.

The MIT vertical pressure generators use stacks of short glass or ceramic insulators, located between flat equipotential metal plates. Small bushing-type disk insulators are adequate to support a compressional load but are impractical for horizontal mounting. The use of modern adhesives has recently allowed this electrically superior construction to be applied to a horizontal mounting for short stacks capable of insulating over 2 Mv. The bushings can be corrugated to increase surface-path length. Flashover voltage for short solid insulators of this type in compressed nitrogen was studied by Trump and Andrias.[32] They used plain and corrugated cylinders of Lucite, Textolite, and Isolantite and found the limit to be set by surface flashover rather than by volume breakdown, and to be markedly improved by increased surface-path length, particularly for high gas pressures. The results of such studies have led to the design of compact generators with very short insulating columns, reaching a gradient of 1 Mv/ft without breakdown.

Despite the mechanical differences between vertical and horizontal mounting and the radically different type of column insulation, the over-all outline of the terminal, column, shields, and pressure housing is surprisingly similar. This is illustrated by comparison of Fig. 3-10, which shows the MIT vertical 4-Mev "Rockefeller" generator, and Fig. 3-6b, the

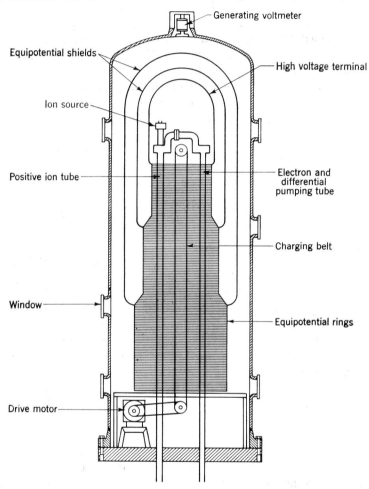

Fig. 3-10. Vertical electrostatic generator for 4 Mv at MIT.[1] Two accelerating tubes are shown, one for positive ions and the other for an electron beam with reversed terminal potential.

Herb-type horizontal 4.0-Mev generator built by the High Voltage Engineering Corporation for the Brookhaven National Laboratory. The similarity in outline is an indication of present agreement on fundamental design principles, since the two machines are culminations of experience in two separate laboratories.

3-5. CHARGE-CARRYING BELT

Flat, endless belts of insulating material have thus far proved to be the most effective charge conveyors for both air-insulated and compressed-gas electrostatic generators.   Many kinds of materials have been used for belting, and opinions differ in the several laboratories as to the best material.   The belt must have high mechanical strength, high surface and volume resistivity, and high dielectric strength, and it should be fire-resistant if air is to be used as the insulating medium.   Another important requirement is that the belt should not absorb moisture when the housing is opened to the atmosphere for maintenance or repair, or else that the time required for dehumidifying the belt be short.

Two belts of electrical insulation paper 0.017 in. thick and 47 in. wide were originally used in the large Round Hill generator.   The seams were made on a 45° bias and tapered to preserve a uniform belt thickness. Nevertheless, later experience showed that such belt joints produced a small but measurable pulsation in terminal voltage, and endless belts are now common.

The belts used and recommended at the MIT laboratory are made by the Fabreeka Products Company.   They are endless woven cotton belts which are neoprene or rubber impregnated and vulcanized.   The belts are oven-dried before being placed in the generator and are further dried during operation by recirculating the compressed gas in the tank through a dry-ice cooling coil until the dew point has reached $-35°C$ or lower. It is necessary to have this low air-moisture content (0.1 grain of water per cubic foot) to obtain the maximum voltage gradient on the belt.   In using gases other than air, which are stored and reused, such a gas dehumidifier and circulator is also essential to remove the moisture absorbed on the various insulators when the tank is opened.

The belting used by Herb and his associates is a rubberized balloon fabric made by the Goodyear Rubber Company.   These belts also must be thoroughly dried to prevent sparks along the belt which might rip the fabric.

Belts tend to stretch slightly during initial operation and must be readjusted to preserve proper tension.   Pulleys are flat cylinders slightly crowned to make the belt ride true.   A 2° taper over a short distance at each end of the pulley is usually sufficient.   Pulley alignment is critical, and bearing supports must be capable of delicate adjustment.

Belt speeds are commonly between 3000 and 5000 ft/min, and windage losses are significant.   An empirical formula for windage losses in air, relating the speed of the belt, its surface area, and the air pressure, was given in one publication[19] as

$$\text{Windage loss (hp)} = \text{pressure (atm)} \times \text{belt area (ft}^2)$$
$$\times \frac{[\text{velocity (1000 ft/min)}]^3}{6000} \qquad (3\text{-}7)$$

For a typical belt of 20 in. width, 20 ft total length, and a speed of 4000 ft/ min at 200 psi pressure, the power required to overcome windage is about 5 hp.

In pressure-insulated generators, belts are driven by motors installed within the pressure housing below a false floor at ground potential and connected by short power-drive V belts to the lower pulley. The motor must be of the fireproof, glass-insulated type manufactured by several reputable firms.

Belt charge density is limited by gas breakdown, and the same limiting field applies as for terminal potential; in air at atmospheric pressure, this field E_m is about 3×10^6 volts/m. If the electric field due to belt charge is uniform and directed normal to the belt surface in both directions, the maximum charge density σ_m is given by

$$\sigma_m = 2\epsilon_0 E_m \simeq 5.3 \times 10^{-5} \text{ coulomb/m}^2 \qquad (3\text{-}8)$$

In practice about 50 per cent of this maximum charge density is commonly attained. It is controlled by the rate of charging indicated by the corona spray current and the belt speed. If it is exceeded and the air becomes ionized at the belt surface, sparks can occur which might burn or rip the belt.

Higher gas pressure increases the permissible belt charge density by the same factor that terminal potential is increased. In fact, the higher charging rates possible in compressed gases constitute one of the primary advantages of the pressure generator. To obtain the necessary charging rate at atmospheric pressure, the belt area and speed must be large, but at high gas pressures a single belt of reasonable dimensions and speed is adequate to provide the charging current. The current delivered by a belt of width w (in meters) and speed v (meters per second) is given by

$$i = \sigma w v \qquad \text{amp} \qquad (3\text{-}9)$$

To give an example: At 10 atm pressure where belt charge density can be 2×10^{-4} coulomb/m^2, a 50-cm-wide belt carrying charge both ways at a speed of 4000 ft/min will provide a charging current of 4.5 ma.

In the operation of the MIT vertical pressure generator, it was observed that a large fraction of the variation in terminal potential was due to static charge on the inside of the belt surface, caused by friction on the pulley. It was found, furthermore, that these variations could be reduced by spraying the main charge on the inside rather than the outside of the belt surface, which was the accepted procedure previously. This change improved the voltage regulation of the generator by about a factor of 3.

Another development at MIT is the use of a layer of slightly conducting rubber on the inside surface of the belt. Such a conducting layer can be charged by induction rather than by corona spray, thus eliminating the ionization near the belt, which is believed to be the cause of much of the observed belt damage and of some of the voltage fluctuation. The method was first tested with conducting paints, which were found to wear off after a time; the conducting-rubber layer is a more permanent surface. The conductivity must be sufficient to obtain a suitable charge by induction, but not so large as to carry an appreciable current down the belt; the surface resistivity found suitable is about 10^7 ohm-m.

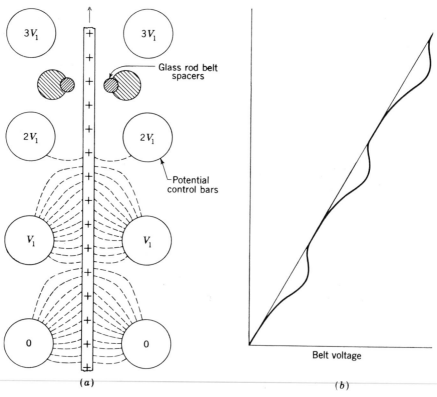

Fig. 3-11. (a) Computed electric-field pattern near belt and control bars with belt charged and moving.[1]   A set of glass rods used as belt spacers is also shown.   (b) Potential distribution along the belt due to the electric-field pattern shown in (a).

To maintain the necessary uniform transverse fields at the belt, a set of closely spaced field-control rods is located close to the belt.   These rods are located in the planes of the equipotential rings and are electrically connected.   A resistance voltage divider or suitable corona gaps maintain the uniform potential distribution along the column and the belt.   Each belt run (up and down) rides between these parallel rods, so the electric field is closely confined to a region adjacent to the belt surface.   With uniform belt charge and closely spaced equipotential planes, the gradient along the belt is very nearly uniform, and the chance of breakdown is reduced. Figure 3-11 shows the fields around the belt and field-control rods as computed and plotted at the MIT laboratory.

The electrical force of attraction between the charged belt and the control bars is so large that the belt may rub against the bars and transfer charge irregularly if it is not precisely centered. The method developed by Trump and his group to prevent such contact is to use at intervals along the column small glass rod or bead spacers which have a narrower spacing than the bars and so keep the belt centered. These belt spacers or guides are supported on additional metal bars which parallel the belt surface (Fig. 3-11).

3-6. THE ACCELERATING TUBE

The evacuated tube for accelerating ions is one of the most critical components. After long development in many laboratories, it is still the ultimate limiting factor in total potential. The tube must be constructed of insulating material, commonly porcelain or glass cylinders several inches long and of large diameter, with vacuumtight seals to metal-plate electrodes between sections. These electrodes are connected to corresponding equipotential rings in the column to maintain a uniform distribution of potential along the tube. The metal electrodes have large-diameter holes or tubular electrodes aligned along the axis of the tube, through which the particle beam passes as it is accelerated. The electrodes produce an accelerating and focusing field for the charged particles and also are arranged to protect the walls of the tube from the beam to reduce the possibility of flashover and to shield the beam from the effects of static surface charges on the insulator wall.

Flashover limits are usually lower on the vacuum side of the insulator wall than on the gaseous insulator side, probably owing to local fields developed by surface charges. Studies at MIT[1] on the flashover of solid dielectrics in high vacuum have shown that hard glasses have a higher limit than electrical porcelains; Corning Vicor (96 per cent silica glass) and Corning 7070 (a high-resistivity borosilicate glass) were reported to have the best properties. It was found, for example, that six 1-cm sections of Vicor in a total gap length of $2\frac{1}{2}$ in. can insulate 500 kv.

The vacuum seals at the joints are extremely critical, especially when operating with external gas pressures which may be as high as 300 psi. Gasket-bolted joints have largely been displaced by cementing techniques. Vinylseal (a plasticized polyvinyl acetate) has been found to have excellent properties for this purpose, being remarkably strong and vacuumtight and having a negligible vapor pressure after baking at 200°C in an oven.

The tube is run through a series of aligned holes in the equipotential planes, which produce a uniform gradient along the tube.   An important consideration in horizontally mounted tubes is the support of the heavy tube structure.   It can be hung on slings at frequent intervals along the column, carefully adjusted to eliminate bending torques.

The early accelerating tubes were constructed of rather long sections of insulator, and "drift tube" tubular electrodes were mounted along the axis, so the charged particles experienced their acceleration in a series of discrete steps as they passed across the gaps between the drift tubes. This is illustrated in Fig. 2-2b showing the first Carnegie accelerator. These gaps represent a set of electric lenses for the particles, with most of the focusing occurring in the first few gaps at the source end of the tube where the charged particles move slowly.

Progress in design to higher voltage gradients along the tube has resulted in successively decreasing the spacing between electrodes and increasing the number of gaps.   This development reached its ultimate

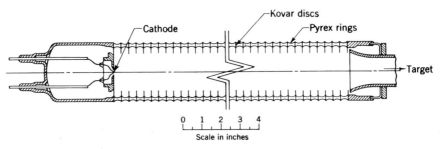

Fig. 3-12. Cross section of uniform-field accelerating tube for an electron beam.[1]

limit in the "uniform field" tube produced by the Machlett Laboratories for electron acceleration in the MIT X-ray generators built for the military services.   This was a permanently sealed tube built of large numbers of Kovar disks and short Pyrex rings, with the thermionic cathode at one end.   Figure 3-12 illustrates such an electron-accelerating tube.   The present X-ray tubes used for medical and industrial applications are assembled from short glass or porcelain rings with intervening polished aluminum electrodes, sealed with Vinylseal and baked to form a mechanically strong tubular structure.

Modern designs for positive-ion tubes use much larger diameters, owing to the necessity of providing adequate pumping speeds to accommodate the gas flow from the source.   Herb and others have developed 10-in.-diam tubes, which allow the vacuum pumps to be placed at the grounded end.   Other laboratories use smaller tubes, with a pumping outlet near the source and a second insulating tube running the length of the column to provide a gas pump-out.   This technique is known as "differential" pumping.   In one case (Berkeley) the second tube was not used and the gas discharged from the differential pump outlet at the source was pumped into a storage tank in the terminal, which had to be discharged occasionally.   A typical positive-ion tube developed by the High Voltage Engineering Corporation for the Brookhaven electrostatic generator is shown in Fig. 3-13.

Vacuum pumps for the accelerator tubes must have pumping speeds compatible with the tube diameter or with the electrode aperture diameter, if that is the limitation.   The required speed is relatively low as compared with pumps for cyclotrons or other large-volume vacuum chambers.   The requirements for ultimate vacuum and low vapor pressure are more severe, however, primarily because of the problem of electron loading, to be discussed in the section to follow.   A typical figure for ultimate vacuum demanded by most experimenters is 2×10^{-6} mm Hg.

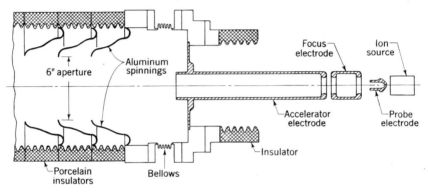

Fig. 3-13. Positive-ion source, focusing electrodes, and accelerating-tube structure for the Brookhaven 4-Mv generator.[22]

Vapor traps and baffles are essential, and these are almost universally refrigerated to low temperatures.   The practice at the MIT laboratory has been to use only mercury-vapor pumps, with refrigerated baffles. The elimination of organic vapors originating from oil-vapor pumps seems to have reduced the electron-loading problem and to justify the practice. Other laboratories have used oil-vapor pumps successfully when suitable baffling has been provided, but an occasional burst of oil vapor into the tube has sometimes caused serious trouble from electron loading, and tubes must be cleaned more often.

3-7. ELECTRON LOADING

One of the most serious problems of the positive-ion electrostatic generator is the limitation on terminal potential due to electron loading.[33] The loading is caused by electrons, usually released by secondary emission processes from the electrodes or walls of the accelerating-tube structure, which traverse the tube in the opposite direction and increase the tube current so as to limit terminal potential at constant charging rate. This beam of electrons is focused by the electric fields within the tube and strikes the ion source at the terminal end, producing X rays with an energy distribution extending up to the maximum tube potential. Such X rays are observed from the terminals in all positive-ion accelerators and, in fact, constitute one of the chief radiation hazards of the electrostatic generator. Shielding around the ion source within the terminal is difficult because of the weight of material required; shielding of the entire high-pressure shell or of the room in which the generator is housed is expensive. Nevertheless, most modern high-voltage generators have such shielding built into the walls of the room. Intensities equivalent to the gamma-ray output of several kilograms of radium have been observed occasionally in some generators.

This limitation of the accelerator tube has resulted in positive-ion energies well below the practical operating limit of the generator without the tube. Installations confidently designed for potentials of, say, 5 Mv have frequently been found to have a practical limit for positive ions of only 3 to 4 Mev. The practical voltage limit has been so difficult to estimate in advance that many generators have never reached their designed voltage when used with positive ions. The electrostatic generator has accordingly suffered from a rather bad reputation of seldom performing to specifications.

Electron loading is most conspicuous in tubes whose inner surfaces have become contaminated. One of the chief contaminants is the oil vapor or the discharge decomposition products of the vapor, when oil-diffusion pumps are used in the vacuum system without adequate baffling. The significance of oil vapor in the electron-loading problem has only been recognized in recent years. For many years experimenters had ascribed the phenomenon to other causes, such as improperly cleaned or polished electrode surfaces, gas pressure in the vacuum tube, or lack of adequate pumping speed. At the MIT laboratories early difficulties with oil-vapor pumps led to insistence on mercury-vapor pumps or on extremely cold baffles when oil was used. Nevertheless, they also have had difficulties and limitations due to electron loading, which can probably be ascribed to other contaminants such as vapor from gaskets or sealing compounds. There has been a running argument between two schools of thought for many years, in which one group argued for mercury-vapor pumps with the associated requirements of low gas flow and small-volume chambers, and the other group exploited large-diameter chambers, fast pumping speeds, and oil-vapor pumps. With the present understanding of the phenomenon the two lines of development have merged, and all agree on the importance of the minimum possible vapor pressures and surface contaminations.

The phenomenon was known in the early days of accelerator development. The first study of secondary-electron emission by positive ions, by Hill, Buechner, Clark, and Fisk[34] in 1939, was based on the urge to solve the loading problem. They measured electron yields from metallic surfaces placed in the beam of positive ions of several Mev energy, observing 4 electrons per positive ion for protons, 6 for hydrogen molecular ions, and 13 for helium ions, from molybdenum targets. The effect was nearly independent of the target metal and no method was discovered for reducing or controlling it.

The magnitude of the loading phenomenon in an operating generator will usually decrease slowly with continued operation. It can definitely be reduced by using faster pumps, better baffles, or refrigerated traps. It is a function of the gas pressure in the vacuum tube; the threshold for incidence of loading is raised by increasing gas pressure to about 10^{-5} mm Hg, and heavy gases like nitrogen or argon are more effective than hydrogen or helium in suppressing the effect. It is believed by some operators to be a function of tube diameter, in that large-diameter tubes seem to have a lower potential threshold than smaller tubes in the same generator; however, this may be associated with the relative pumping speeds. The effect is altered by surface conditions inside the tube; a tube which is subject to loading can be improved by careful cleaning.

In the past few years the problem of electron loading has been more widely recognized and studied. Experimental tests have been run at several laboratories to attempt an analysis of the mechanism of the phenomenon. Blewett[33] has suggested that it may be a consequence of the large local fields developed across thin layers of insulating contamination on electrode surfaces, such as pump oil or oxide layers, first studied by Malter[35] in 1936 at much lower energies. Malter observed large yields of secondary electrons from such surface layers when bombarded by electrons in the presence of high electric fields. He interpreted this as field emission due to extremely high local fields across an insulating surface layer.

Turner[36] showed that a large fraction of the secondary electrons came from the final slit at the grounded end of the tube in the Brookhaven proton accelerator and that they could be trapped by electric retarding fields between the last electrode and ground; reduction in electron loading current was observed as a decrease in X-ray intensity from the terminal. McKibben and Boyer[37] used magnetic fields at the base of the tube of the Los Alamos generator to deflect the secondary electrons, and from the results they concluded that negative-ion emission was also partially responsible for the effect.

New light was thrown on the effects of electron loading by Turner in some unpublished work performed during 1957. He made careful measurements of the locations of all currents which left the high-voltage terminal of one of the Brookhaven electrostatic generators and established the fact that a large fraction of the loading current returned to ground through the high-pressure insulating gas. This current he attributed to ionization of the high-pressure gas by the X rays emanating from the region around the ion source. This secondary effect was found to be contributing a large fraction of the load current. By careful shielding of the ion-source structure with sheets of lead he was able to reduce the loading current by a significant factor and so to push the terminal potential to materially higher voltages than had been previously attained.

There is reason to hope that a combination of clean techniques, low vapor pressures, and fast pumping speeds can control contaminations, that electric or magnetic clearing fields can be designed and located to reduce the magnitude of the residual effect, and that X-ray ionization can be controlled by shielding. The recent successes in this direction suggest that with this problem under control the electrostatic generator can be extended to considerably higher energies than have been available in the past.

3-8. VOLTAGE MEASUREMENT AND CONTROL

The problem of voltage calibration is fundamental, since the primary usefulness of the electrostatic generator has been for studies of reaction energies and nuclear energy levels. Our present precise knowledge of nuclear energy constants rests to a large extent on the measurements made with these machines.

In the historical summary at the beginning of this chapter, the early calibrations in the Carnegie Institution laboratory were described. Techniques for measurement of particle energy have advanced steadily in the years of development. At present, in most laboratories using electrostatic generators, particle energy is known to within 1 or 2 kev in 4 Mev, and techniques for controlling the potential to this accuracy are available. Many laboratories and individuals were concerned in the development, and the techniques are generally known and used. The ones to be described here are representative of the latest methods leading to the highest accuracy.

The "generating voltmeter" has been for years the basic instrument for observing terminal potential with single-terminal machines.[12,38] Its operation depends on the static charge induced on an insulated metal plate or vane near the outer pressure housing surrounding the terminal. The magnitude of the induced charge is determined by the electric field established by the charged terminal at the location of the vane. In the usual form an insulated vane rotates at constant speed behind a grounded shield shaped so the vane is covered during half its travel and exposed to the electric field during the other half (see Fig. 3-14). The alternating electrostatic voltage induced on the vane is amplified and rectified, and its magnitude is displayed on a dc meter at the control panel as a measure of terminal potential.   The geometry of the system limits the precision of calibration from calculations of the capacitance and the electric field. The voltage scale is usually calibrated against other standards of potential.   The most serious limitation is the distortion of electric fields due to corona discharge from the terminal, as discussed earlier.   In most installations the generating voltmeter is used as a qualitative instrument for monitoring operations, such as in tuning up the generator or in observing spark discharges.   With the advent of multiple-terminal shields its

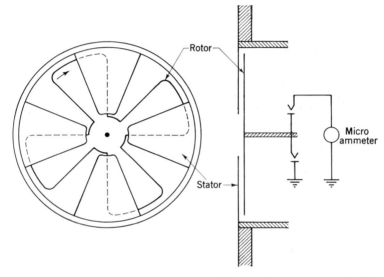

Fig. 3-14. Schematic diagram of generating voltmeter for measurement of terminal potential.[12]

usefulness is somewhat reduced, since it reads only the potential of the outer shield and its calibration depends on a constant ratio of potential drops between shields.

Another method of measuring terminal potential is to observe the current in a string of calibrated high resistors running from terminal to ground.   To give a valid reading these resistors must be free from corona losses, not an easy matter unless they are carefully shielded.   However, the resistor string can also be utilized to provide a uniform potential distribution of many small steps by connecting the resistors between successive equipotential rings.   If this is done, corona loss can be made negligible, and the resistors serve a dual purpose.   The total resistance is high, so the current drain down the stack is a small fraction of the charging current.   A typical value is 10,000 megohms per million volts, or a current of 100 μa.   A microammeter is inserted at the grounded end of the resistor column.   When used to calibrate terminal potential, the individual resistors must be measured to high precision.   If other more accurate voltage calibrations are used, this current can still be displayed on the control panel as a visible check on terminal potential.

Most modern accelerator installations use magnetic or electric deflection of the particle beam to calibrate voltage.   In some cases the instrument is itself calibrated by using natural alpha-particle groups whose energy is precisely known from measurements made at the Cavendish laboratory.   An illustration is the MIT laboratory, where Buechner uses a calibrated 180° magnet to focus and measure the energy of protons scattered from the accelerated beam.   The precision attained in absolute energy calibration is of the order of 0.1 per cent.

An important means of cross-calibrating the proton-energy scales in the several laboratories is provided by nuclear resonances.   Certain reactions are found to have extremely sharp resonances at definite proton energies when thin targets are used, and the yields from such reactions show sharp peaks.   Several resonances at energies useful for voltage calibration were measured at an early stage by the Carnegie Institution group,[7] using their precision resistance voltmeter.   Others at higher energy values have been added as the energy scale increased.   The most precise measurements in the 1- to 2-Mev range came from the Wisconsin group, reported by Herb, Snowden, and Sala.[39]   The results of their proton-energy calibration are given in the form of exact values for the thresholds of three nuclear reactions, as follows:

$$\mathrm{Li}^7(p,n)\mathrm{Be}^7 \; - \; 1.882 \pm 0.1\% \text{ Mev}$$
$$\mathrm{A}^{27}(p,\gamma)\mathrm{Si}^{28} \; - \; 0.9933 \pm 0.1\% \text{ Mev} \qquad (3\text{-}10)$$
$$\mathrm{F}^{19}(p,\alpha\gamma)\mathrm{O}^{16} \; - \; 0.8735 \pm 0.1\% \text{ Mev}$$

The energy calibration used by Herb, Snowden, and Sala came from the use of a large electrostatic analyzer, in which the protons were deflected through 90° between curved plates by an electric field which could be determined from the dimensions, and from potentiometer measurements of the applied voltage.   The analyzer was accurately constructed and end effects were calculated carefully.   Protons were passed through very narrow slits by the focusing inherent in the 90° electrostatic deflection.   Uncertainties are reported to be 0.1 per cent, or about 1 kv/Mv, including the error in the e/m value for the proton taken from latest measurements of the physical constants.   This energy scale is independent of alpha-particle energies and represents an absolute and independent calibration.

At Rice Institute in Texas, Bonner has also used magnetic deflection, using alpha-particle calibration for energy measurement.   However, he has developed a new absolute method for calibration of the magnetic field based on nuclear resonance with the proton magnetic moment.

This "proton moment" method of calibrating a magnetic field is described in more detail in Chap. 8 in the section on magnetic measurements. The value of the proton moment is known to extremely high precision, even better than alpha-particle energies. The chief source of error in the method comes from uncertainties in the geometry and in calculating the end effects in the analyzing magnet. The precision attained is equivalent to that in the two laboratories mentioned previously.

It is of interest to note that the three independent techniques of calibration outlined above are in excellent agreement, well within the experimental errors. Each laboratory has provided cross-checks by measuring the thresholds or resonance energies for several nuclear reactions, and these results agree. As an additional check, Herb and his group have measured the energy of the polonium alpha-particle group with their electrostatic analyzer and find agreement with the accepted value to within the experimental limits of error. So it is now possible to rely on energy calibrations in those laboratories to within 0.1 per cent. Other laboratories have in general relied on the energy scale given by the most accurately measured values of nuclear resonances, and calibrate their deflecting magnets and energy scales by using the resonances as substandards.

The techniques for voltage control are similar in the several laboratories. All depend on error signals from a slit system at the exit of the magnetic or electrostatic analyzer. In the magnetic analyzer, for example, the beam traverses narrow slits at the entrance and exit. If the magnetic field is constant, a variation of terminal potential will cause the beam to strike one side or the other of the exit slit. The slit edges can be insulated and currents to the edges measured and compared. A lack of balance indicates a variation of particle energy, and the sense of the difference gives the direction of deviation.

In most installations using protons for target bombardment, the mass-2 ions from the source (singly charged hydrogen molecular ions) are used for the voltage control. In a magnetic field these ions are deflected through an angle which is $1/\sqrt{2}$ that for the protons in the analyzer, and this beam is allowed to fall on the double-edged slit used for control. In this way the proton beam can be kept free from confining slits and allowed to pass through the analyzer to the target.

An amplified error current from the control slit is used to correct terminal potential. Several methods of applying this control are available. The error signal can be used to modulate the voltage of the belt-corona-spray power supply. This may be done either by controlling primary voltage of the high-voltage transformer or by varying grid potential of a vacuum tube placed in the grounded lead of the rectifier set. In the latter case the potential drop across the tube is in series with the spray points and the lower grounded pulley and hence can control the corona voltage and current.   This system is limited to a speed of response corresponding to the belt travel time.   The load current is assumed to remain essentially constant.

Another control method depends on maintaining constant charging current and varying a component of the load current.   Corona points are located at the wall of the pressure housing opposite the terminal, and the current in this steady corona discharge is varied by the error signal from the energy analyzer.   The corona-control points are usually arranged in a package of 6 to 12 points, each sticking through a hole in a grid plate. This grid plate may be grounded and the control voltage applied to vary the negative potential on the points, or the control voltage may be applied to this grid plate to vary the electric field at the points.   The corona package as a whole can be moved close to the terminal for low terminal potentials and back to the wall for maximum potentials.   Corona currents from such a negative point are very sensitive to variation of point potential.

An alternate method of controlling load current is to modulate a beam of electrons going up to the terminal from the grounded end in a second accelerating tube, which may also be used for differential pumping at the ion source.   A thermionic cathode and control grid similar to those in a standard triode are used to produce and control electron-beam current. A disadvantage of this system is the X rays produced at the terminal end of the electron-accelerating tube.

Any such control scheme depends on varying the potential of the terminal, which is of large capacitance and has a relatively long time constant.   The variation in corona load current or electron loading current must be large to keep the time of response short.   Current variations as great as 1 ma have been used, although the usual range is a few hundred microamperes.   To give a numerical example: Consider a generator operating at 4 Mv, with a capacitance of 300 $\mu\mu$f, and a control-current variation of 100 μa.   Equation (3-1) can be used to calculate the rate of change of potential.   The time required to change terminal potential by 1 per cent (40 kv) is about 0.1 sec.

The control systems described above can usually be adjusted to maintain terminal potential constant to within 0.1 per cent over long periods. The limit of precision is frequently not the control circuit but the magnet current stabilization circuit in the magnetic analyzer.

Practical techniques for switching and adjusting ion-source controls within the high-voltage terminal range from the extremely simple to the highly ingenious.   The classic method is to use strings as insulating belts extending from the base up within the shielded column to the terminal; these strings give direct mechanical coupling to the potentiometers and other controls within the terminal.   At the other extreme, beams of light are projected up the column and activate photocells in the terminal.

Modulation of light intensity is used to regulate photocell current for control. In most installations the simplicity and direct mechanical control of the system of strings have proved to be most satisfactory.

3-9. THE 12-MV GENERATORS

The last word in electrostatic-generator development is in the form of two supergenerators both originally rated for 12 Mv. One, at MIT, represents the culmination of years of research and engineering on the problems of high-voltage insulation by Professors J. G. Trump, W. W. Buechner, and their associates. The other, at the Los Alamos Scientific Laboratory, has been designed and built by Dr. J. L. McKibben, a graduate of the Herb school of accelerator design at the University of Wisconsin. Both machines are in operation, but at considerably less than the expected maximum voltage. It is still uncertain whether they can be tuned up to their original rating as proton accelerators.

The two machines are similar in general outline, but differ in many features of structural design and in many details. Both are mounted vertically and pressure-insulated. The most obvious difference is in the structure of the pressure vessel and the buildings to house the instruments. The Los Alamos machine is an enlargement of the removable-housing design. The pressure vessel can be lifted bodily off the terminal column, so the building to house it is five stories high. The MIT pressure housing is permanently installed in the laboratory building, with a removable cap at the top through which the terminal column can be assembled. The general designs are illustrated in Figs. 3-15 and 3-16.

A complete description of the MIT generator has not been published, but many technical details are available in the form of laboratory reports of the MIT Laboratory of Nuclear Science and Engineering. The following description has been made available by courtesy of Professor Trump (see Fig. 3-15).

The pressure tank is 12 feet in diameter and 32 feet high. It is rated for 400 lb/in.² pressure. The removable tank cover can be lifted by overhead crane and moved aside for the assembly of the column. A movable working platform fits inside the tank and around the column. The filling gas used is 80% N_2 and 20% CO_2. This can be pumped into storage cylinders outside the building when the tank is to be opened. The insulating column is 18 ft long, of which the upper 6 ft is 8-inch diameter, and supports a 38-inch diameter terminal, and the lower 12 ft is 60-inch diameter and supports a 68-inch equipotential shield. In operation at 12 Mv the voltage distribution will apply 4 Mv between the inner shells and 8 Mv across the outer gap. One belt 18 inches wide is driven by two 5 hp, 1800 rpm motors. Space is available for two accelerating tubes, one for positive ion acceleration and one for differential pumping. Mercury diffusion pumps are located below the baseplate. An analyzing magnet on a swivel base

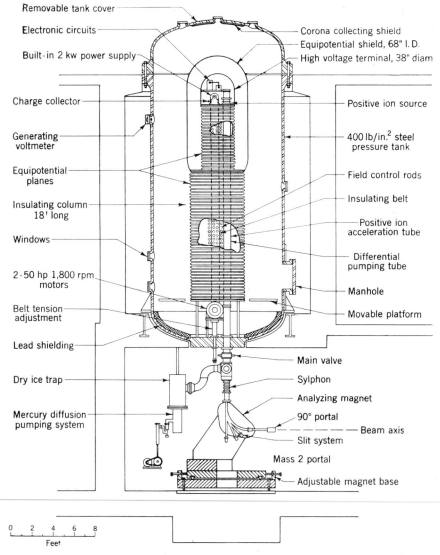

Removable tank cover

Electronic circuits

Built-in 2 kw power supply

Charge collector

Generating voltmeter

Equipotential planes

Insulating column 18' long

Windows

2-50 hp 1,800 rpm motors

Belt tension adjustment

Lead shielding

Dry ice trap

Mercury diffusion pumping system

Corona collecting shield

Equipotential shield, 68" I.D.

High voltage terminal, 38" diam

Positive ion source

400 lb/in.^{2} steel pressure tank

Field control rods

Insulating belt

Positive ion acceleration tube

Differential pumping tube

Manhole

Movable platform

Main valve

Sylphon

Analyzing magnet

90° portal

Beam axis

Slit system

Mass 2 portal

Adjustable magnet base

0 2 4 6 8
Feet

Fig. 3-15. 9-Mv electrostatic generator at MIT.   (Courtesy of J. G. Trump.)

allows the beam to be swung to alternate experimental stations within the large well-shielded laboratory room.

Under the direction of Professor Buechner, this MIT generator is now operating as a research instrument, normally at 7 to 8 Mv, but with maximum proton energies of 9 Mev.   It is the highest-energy single-stage electrostatic generator in operation.

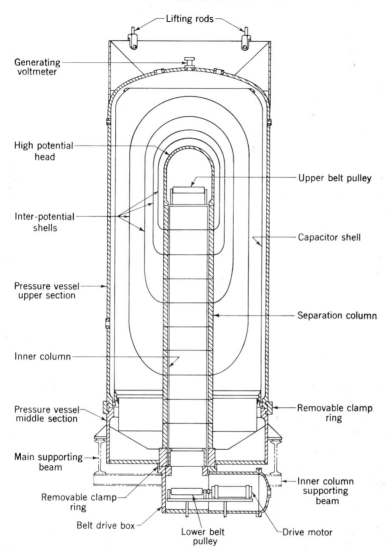

Fig. 3-16. 8-Mv electrostatic generator at Los Alamos. (Courtesy of J. L. McKibben.)

3-10. ELECTRON ACCELERATORS

Electrostatic electron accelerators have found a large field of usefulness as sources of high-voltage X rays. The 1- to 2-Mev X rays obtained have been used with good results in the field of medical therapy and in radiography of metal castings and forgings.

The electron accelerator differs from the positive-ion accelerator only in that the terminal is charged to negative potential and a thermionic cathode replaces the ion source.   However, the cathode does not evolve gas, as do positive-ion sources, so the vacuum pumping problem is much simpler and the accelerator tube can be of smaller diameter.   Furthermore, voltage stabilization is not so important, since the X rays are distributed in a continuous energy spectrum having a maximum equal to the electron energy.   Manual control of terminal potential through adjustment of charging current is usually sufficient.   Because of the smaller tube and simpler construction, an electron accelerator can be more compact for the same voltage rating.

A number of X-ray generators developed by Trump[19,40] and later by the High Voltage Engineering Corporation have been installed in hospitals and sold to industrial firms.   The most popular model is rated at 2 Mv and accelerates a beam of about 250 μa of electrons, producing an X-ray beam of quality and intensity equivalent to the gamma-ray output of 5000 g of radium.   Accelerator tubes with permanent cathodes and water-cooled gold targets are of the uniform-field type developed by Trump and his associates.   The entire instrument is only 3 ft in diameter and 6 ft in over-all length.   It is mounted in gimbals, so it can be swung into any position to direct the X-ray beam.

The most detailed description of an X-ray generator is by Buechner, Van de Graaff, Sperduto, McIntosh, and Burrill.[20]   This reports the results of a design contract with the United States Navy for a group of 2.0-Mv generators for radiographic purposes.   The schematic diagram of this generator (Fig. 3-17) shows the assembly within the pressure tank.

The most successful medical application has been to cancer therapy. The high skin tolerance for 2-Mev radiation and the great depth of penetration in tissue make it particularly effective for the irradiation of deep tumors.   Exposure from different angles can provide a cross fire of radiation on a deep-seated tumor many times as intense as the skin dose. Study of therapeutic problems has resulted in a full understanding of the dosage, the filtering techniques, and the physiological limits.   The sharp beam due to the small focal spot on the target, the freedom from side scattering at these energies, and the uniform intensity over the radiation field make this type of X-ray therapy an ideal alternate to radium therapy.

A recent summary of the medical applications and the experimental techniques is given by Trump in Glasser's[41] "Medical Physics," vol. 2.

These same properties are advantageous in radiography.   In particular, the small focal spot on the target gives a sharpness of definition much to be desired in studying flaws in metal castings or in any other of the uses of X-ray radiography.   The low absorption coefficient in metals for this radiation provides deep penetration.

An alternative use of the electron accelerator is to obtain an emergent electron beam through a thin metal vacuum window. This beam can be used to produce ionization directly in target materials. Since the beam is essentially monoenergetic, it can be deflected in magnetic fields or focused to an extremely small focal spot, of the order of 0.5 mm. The

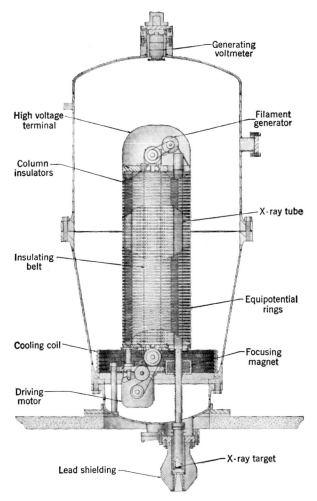

Fig. 3.17. 2-Mv electron accelerator for generation of X rays, developed at MIT.[20]

electron beam can be used for many purposes, such as sterilization of packaged goods or direct irradiation of shallow tumors, with a remarkable concentration of ionization at the end of the range of the beam. Such electron beams of controlled energy have also been used in the study of photonuclear disintegration processes.

3-11. TANDEM ELECTROSTATIC GENERATORS

The most recent development in the electrostatic-generator field is a technique for utilizing the terminal potential several times in sequence, to obtain output energies of two or more times that available in a single acceleration.   The technique involves reversing the charge of the accelerated ions in successive accelerations.   Such charge-exchange processes result in a significant reduction in beam intensity.   However, for a wide range of experiments in nuclear research a few microamperes of accelerated ions are adequate, and the higher energy is greatly to be desired.

The concept of the tandem generator has been discussed for many years and has been specifically proposed by W. H. Bennett[42] and by L. W. Alvarez.[43]   However, the first practical application was made by the High Voltage Engineering Corporation in a machine constructed for the

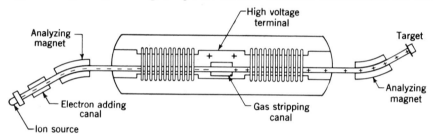

Fig. 3-18. Two-stage tandem electrostatic generator.[23]

Chalk River Laboratory of the Canadian Atomic Energy Agency and reported by Van de Graaff.[23]   Figure 3-18 shows a schematic diagram of the "two-stage" tandem principle as used in this machine.   The arrangement includes a horizontal pressure tank with the high-voltage terminal supported from both ends on insulating mounts; an evacuated accelerating tube extends for the full length.   When a hydrogen-ion beam traverses a region containing hydrogen gas at low pressure, the emerging beam consists of a mixture of protons, neutral hydrogen atoms, and negative hydrogen ions, in relative amounts depending on ion velocity and gas pressure.   Protons produced in a high-intensity radiofrequency ion source at one end of the accelerator traverse an "electron-adding" canal with hydrogen gas at sufficient pressure so that about 1 per cent of the protons emerge as negatively charged atomic hydrogen ions.   These negative ions are accelerated up the accelerating tube to the positively charged terminal; there they traverse a "stripping" canal with hydrogen gas where most of them are stripped of their electronic charges and emerge as protons to be accelerated down the other accelerating tube to ground potential; the final energy is twice the terminal potential.   In initial tests 1.5 μa of protons was obtained at 13.4 Mev energy, with a terminal potential of 6.7 Mv.

The technical features which make the tandem generator practical are themselves the consequence of long development in several laboratories. Ion sources capable of delivering several milliamperes of positive ions through a small canal with uniform velocities have become practical only in the late 1950s (see Chap. 4). Electrode alignment and beam focusing in the electrostatic generator have progressed over the years to produce extremely small-diameter, well-collimated beams. For example, the stripping canal in the terminal of the Chalk River generator is only 0.18 in. diam; the mechanical and technical perfection of the accelerating column which allows the beam to be passed through this small canal is itself the result of many years of development and is primarily responsible for the success of this machine.

The tandem principle can be extended to more than two stages of acceleration, but at the cost of inserting additional stages of charge exchange and further reduction in intensity. Van de Graaff has proposed a three-stage tandem which would use two double-ended horizontal electrostatic generators in line. Positive ions from an external source would first be neutralized in a gas-filled canal and would then coast through to the first negative terminal where they would traverse an electron-adding canal, accelerate down to ground potential and up to the positive terminal of the second generator, be stripped to positive ions in the second terminal, and be accelerated down to ground potential again with a total energy of three times the terminal voltage. Another technique is to use 180° bending magnets to return the beam externally to the ion-source end of the system and reuse the initial potential differences; with this scheme the energy could be raised to four times the terminal potential, but the target would be inside the first terminal.

REFERENCES

1. R. J. Van de Graaff, J. G. Trump, and W. W. Buechner, *Repts. Progr. in Phys.*, **11**:1 (1948).
2. R. J. Van de Graaff, *Phys. Rev.*, **38**:1919A (1931).
3. R. J. Van de Graaff, K. T. Compton, and L. C. Van Atta, *Phys. Rev.*, **43**:149 (1933).
4. L. C. Van Atta, D. L. Northrup, C. M. Van Atta, and R. J. Van de Graaff, *Phys. Rev.*, **49**:761 (1936).
5. L. C. Van Atta, D. L. Northrup, R. J. Van de Graaff, and C. M. Van Atta, *Rev. Sci. Instr.*, **12**:534 (1941).
6. M. A. Tuve, L. R. Hafstad, and O. Dahl, *Phys. Rev.*, **48**:315 (1935).
7. L. R. Hafstad and M. A. Tuve, *Phys. Rev.*, **47**:506 (1935); **48**:306 (1935).
8. L. R. Hafstad, N. P. Heydenburg, and M. A. Tuve, *Phys. Rev.*, **50**:504 (1936).
9. H. A. Barton, D. W. Mueller, and L. C. Van Atta, *Phys. Rev.*, **42**:901A (1932).
10. R. G. Herb, D. B. Parkinson, and D. W. Kerst, *Rev. Sci. Instr.*, **6**:261 (1935).
11. D. B. Parkinson, R. G. Herb, E. J. Bernet, and J. L. McKibben, *Phys. Rev.*, **53**:642 (1938).

12. R. G. Herb, C. M. Turner, C. M. Hudson, and R. E. Warren, *Phys. Rev.*, **58**:579 (1940).
13. I. Michael, E. D. Berners, F. P. Eppling, D. J. Knecht, L. C. Northcliffe, and R. G. Herb, *Rev. Sci. Instr.*, **30**:855 (1959).
14. W. H. Wells, *J. Appl. Phys.*, **9**:677 (1938).
15. W. H. Wells, R. O. Haxby, W. E. Stephens, and W. E. Shoupp, *Phys. Rev.*, **58**:162 (1940).
16. J. H. Williams, L. H. Rumbaugh, and J. T. Tate, *Rev. Sci. Instr.*, **13**:202 (1942).
17. B. Jennings, C. D. Swartz, and H. H. Rossi, *Rev. Sci. Instr.*, **15**:64 (1944).
18. D. R. Inglis, R. W. Krone, and S. S. Hanna, *Rev. Sci. Instr.*, **20**:834 (1949).
19. J. G. Trump and R. J. Van de Graaff, *Phys. Rev.*, **55**:1160 (1939).
20. W. W. Buechner, R. J. Van de Graaff, A. Sperduto, L. R. McIntosh, and E. A. Burrill, *Rev. Sci. Instr.*, **18**:754 (1947).
21. W. M. Preston and C. Goodman, *Phys. Rev.*, **82**:316A (1951).
22. E. L. Rogers and C. Turner, *Rev. Sci. Instr.*, **21**:805 (1955).
23. R. J. Van de Graaff, *Nuclear Instr. and Methods*, **8**:195 (1960).
24. J. G. Trump, R. W. Cloud, J. G. Mann, and E. P. Hanson, *Trans. AIEE* (November, 1950).
25. R. G. Herb and E. J. Bernet, *Phys. Rev.*, **52**:379 (1937).
26. F. Joliet, M. Feldenkrais, and A. Lazard, *Compt. rend. acad. sci. Paris*, **202**:291 (1936).
27. M. T. Rodine and R. G. Herb, *Phys. Rev.*, **51**:508 (1937).
28. E. E. Charlton and F. S. Cooper, *Gen. Elec. Rev.*, **40**:438 (1937).
29. H. C. Pollock and F. S. Cooper, *Phys. Rev.*, **56**:170 (1939).
30. J. G. Trump, F. J. Safford, and R. W. Cloud, *Trans. AIEE*, **60**:132 (1941).
31. W. C. Schumb, *Ind. Eng. Chem.*, **39**:42 (1947).
32. J. G. Trump and J. Andrias, *Trans. AIEE*, **60**:986 (July, 1941).
33. J. P. Blewett, *Phys. Rev.*, **81**:305A (1951).
34. A. G. Hill, W. W. Buechner, J. S. Clark, and J. B. Fisk, *Phys. Rev.*, **55**:463 (1939).
35. L. Malter, *Phys. Rev.*, **49**:478 (1936).
36. C. M. Turner, *Phys. Rev.*, **81**:305A (1951).
37. J. L. McKibben and K. Boyer, *Phys. Rev.*, **82**:315A (1951).
38. G. P. Harnwell and S. N. Van Voorhis, *Rev. Sci. Instr.*, **4**:540 (1933).
39. R. G. Herb, S. C. Snowden, and O. Sala, *Phys. Rev.*, **75**:246 (1949).
40. J. G. Trump and R. W. Cloud, *Am. J. Roentgenol. Radium Therapy*, **49**:531 (1943).
41. O. Glasser (ed.), "Medical Physics," vol. 2, Year Book Publishers (1950).
42. W. H. Bennett and P. F. Darby, *Phys. Rev.*, **49**:97, 422, 881 (1936).
43. L. W. Alvarez, *Rev. Sci. Instr.*, **22**:705 (1951).

At the head of the facing page is an assembly photograph of a duo-plasmatron ion source developed at the Oak Ridge National Laboratory. (Courtesy of Dr. C. D. Moak.)

Ion Sources

Ion sources for low-voltage dc accelerators and for the electrostatic generator have similar requirements and characteristics. The basic requirement is a parallel beam of protons, deuterons, or other light positive ions, aimed along the axis of the accelerating electrodes. There are few space limitations except that ions should emerge from the source through a small, round hole on the axis, to maintain cylindrical symmetry. Plenty of space is generally available for the electrodes and discharge chamber. Cyclotron ion sources, on the other hand, have severe restrictions on dimensions and must operate in the intense magnetic field at the center of the cyclotron chamber. They are of a special type and will be described in Chap 6. The purpose of this chapter is to discuss the problems of positive-ion formation and the several ion sources used in producing a linear beam of ions.

All ion sources utilize the ionization produced in a gaseous discharge, but the mechanisms for producing this ionization and for concentrating the discharge into a small, parallel beam vary considerably. Several classes or types of source can be recognized, grouped according to the nature of the discharge phenomena or the different physical arrangements used to produce the ionization:

1. Cold-cathode canal-ray tube
2. Spark discharge

3. Hot-cathode arc
4. Low-voltage capillary arc
5. Discharge in an axial magnetic field
6. Radiofrequency electrodeless discharge
7. Electron oscillation (P.I.G.) discharge

These sources will be described and discussed individually. However, it is possible to identify several features of an ion source which are common to all types.

4-1. PROPERTIES OF A GASEOUS DISCHARGE

In all ion sources the ionization is produced by electron impact in a gaseous discharge. The general requirements are a source of electrons, a small region of relatively high gas pressure separated from the accelerating tube, an electric field to accelerate electrons and maintain the discharge, and some mechanism for concentrating the discharge and for

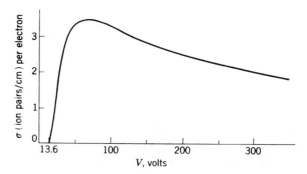

Fig. 4-1. Ionization efficiency for hydrogen at 1 mm Hg pressure and 0°C, as a function of electron energy in volts.

pulling positive ions out in a parallel beam. Usually the high-pressure discharge region is separated from the accelerating tube by a diaphragm with a small hole. This is frequently combined with differential pumping between the diaphragm and the accelerating tube to eliminate the gas. The adjustable parameters of an ion source are electron emission, gas pressure, voltage across the discharge, magnetic field, size of exit hole, geometry and surface properties of the electrodes, and the general shape and dimensions of the enclosing discharge chamber.

Ionization occurs in gases when the electron energy equals or exceeds the ionization potential of the gas. The ionization potential of the hydrogen molecule, forming H_2^+, is 15.6 volts; that for the formation of atomic ions H^+ from H atoms is 13.6 volts; the ionization potential of helium to form He^+ is 24.5 volts; and for He^{++} it is 54 volts. Ionization probability increases with electron energy, having a maximum for hydrogen at about 75 volts. This function is shown in Fig. 4-1. Electrons make collisions in the gas; their average energy depends on the energy acquired in a mean free path between collisions and so varies inversely with pressure. The potential drop across the discharge is usually considerably greater than 75 volts in hydrogen and depends strongly on the pressure.

Many texts[1] are available which present the theory and observations on gaseous ionization. It is sufficient here to note only a few of the pertinent conclusions.

Townsend studied the non-self-maintaining or dark discharges observed at fields below the spark breakdown limit and developed the theory known by his name which explains this phenomenon. Suppose a number of electrons N per second traverse the gas at a distance x from the cathode. The number of new electrons dN released per second in a distance dx owing to ionization is proportional to N and to dx:

$$dN = \alpha N \, dx \qquad (4\text{-}1)$$

The proportionality constant α is known as the "first Townsend coefficient." This leads, upon integration, to

$$N = N_0 e^{\alpha x} \qquad (4\text{-}2)$$

where N_0 is the number emitted from the cathode ($x = 0$) per second. This can be expressed in terms of the current density in the gas I and the emitted current density I_0 as

$$\frac{I}{I_0} = e^{\alpha x} \qquad (4\text{-}3)$$

The ratio I/I_0 is the gas multiplication factor.

In nonuniform fields, such as may exist in ion sources with nonplanar geometry, the electric field varies from point to point. Since α is a function of the field, a correct calculation requires summation over varying values of α, described by the relation

$$\frac{I}{I_0} = e^{\int_0^\alpha \alpha \, dx} \qquad (4\text{-}4)$$

The value of the first Townsend coefficient will depend on pressure, which determines the number of collisions in a given length of path, and also on the energy of the electron at the time of collision. This energy depends on the mean free path (an inverse function of pressure) and on electric field intensity E. Thus α is proportional to pressure P and also to some function of E/P. The customary expression is

$$\frac{\alpha}{P} = f\left(\frac{E}{P}\right) \tag{4-5}$$

The value of this function can in principle be computed from the ionization probability curve (Fig. 4-1). Usually, however, it is determined
directly from experimental observations. Values of α/P for hydrogen

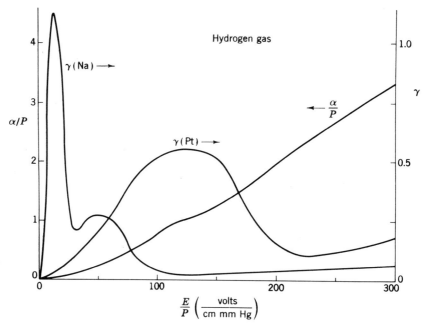

Fig. 4-2. Coefficients of ionization by electrons and positive ions in hydrogen gas, as a
function of E/P [volts/(cm) (mm Hg)]. The electron coefficient α/P is in units of
ion pairs/cm at 1 mm Hg and 0°C. The positive-ion coefficient γ is the number of
secondary electrons produced at the cathode per positive ion in the discharge.

gas are shown in Fig. 4-2 as a function of E/P. More accurate and more
extensive data can be obtained from the standard texts on gaseous
discharge.

In his early theory Townsend assumed a "second Townsend coefficient," which was the ionization per centimeter per positive ion in the gas.
From this assumption Townsend developed his theory of cumulative
breakdown of the gas and expressed the result in terms of his two coefficients. Direct gaseous ionization is not now believed to be the dominant
mechanism by which positive ions affect the discharge. Other phenomena are more important. Positive ions produce secondary electrons
on striking the cathode surface, with a probability which is a function of

ion energy and also varies widely for different surfaces. Another important mechanism is production of photons in the gas by positive ions through excitation of molecules, formation of metastable molecular states, etc. These photons, on striking the cathode, also produce secondary electrons, with a probability primarily dependent on the nature of the surface. The sum of all these effects can be lumped into a coefficient γ, which is the number of secondary electrons entering the discharge per positive ion. Using this modern form of the second Townsend coefficient, we find that the current density in the discharge becomes

$$\frac{I}{I_0} = \frac{e^{\alpha d}}{1 - \gamma(e^{\alpha d} - 1)} \tag{4-6}$$

where d is the electrode spacing.

The expression above reduces to Eq. (4-3) for $\gamma = 0$. For finite values of γ it leads to a prediction of cumulative ionization or breakdown when the denominator goes to zero. This Townsend sparking criterion is for

$$\gamma(e^{\alpha d} - 1) = 1 \tag{4-7}$$

Experimentally measured values of the secondary-electron coefficient γ for positive ions are also available for most gases and many cathode materials, usually presented as a function of E/P. Illustrative curves for γ for two surfaces Na and Pt in H_2 gas are also plotted in Fig. 4-2.

Under the conditions applying at breakdown, it can be shown[1] that the quantity $e^{\alpha d}$ is very much greater than unity. So the criterion of Eq. (4-7) can be simplified to

$$\gamma e^{\alpha d} = 1 \tag{4-7a}$$

Using values of α/P and γ as functions of E/P (Fig. 4-2), it is possible to compute the electric fields required for breakdown under various conditions. For example, Hale[2] has computed the values of breakdown

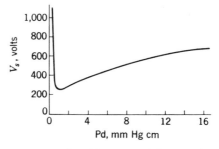

Fig. 4-3. Sparking-potential curve for nickel cathode in hydrogen gas.[2]

or sparking voltage for an Ni cathode in H_2 gas as a function of Pd (pressure times electrode spacing) and compares these computed values with the measured sparking voltages. The measured and computed values were in excellent agreement over a wide range of conditions. Figure 4-3 shows the curve of sparking potential obtained by Hale. It has a minimum value (about 230 volts) at about 1 mm Hg gas pressure for 1 cm spacing (or 0.1 mm Hg pressure for 10 cm). Dimensions of ion sources are in the range between 1 and 10 cm, so we can expect H_2 gas breakdown at minimum voltage to be obtained with pressures between 0.1 and 1.0 mm Hg.

Some ion sources operate at this gas breakdown limit, where the discharge is self-maintained and limited only by the constants in the external power-supply circuit. These are the plasma-type sources. The discharge becomes stabilized at that balance of electrons and positive ions in the gas which leads to the equilibrium condition expressed by Eq. (4-7).

Other ion sources are operated below the breakdown limit and depend on electron emission from a heated cathode to maintain the discharge. With a hot cathode the arc current can be controlled and the voltage drop adjusted to give average electron energies near the optimum shown in Fig. 4-1.

Gas pressure in the discharge must be relatively high in order to reduce the required potential to a practical value. Ionization density is directly proportional to pressure for the same discharge current, so high pressure is an advantage when ions are to be brought through small exit holes. In most ion sources the pressure is between 10^{-1} and 10^{-3} mm Hg. However, gas pressure in the accelerating tube outside the hole must be much smaller (10^{-5} mm Hg or less) to prevent electrical breakdown. Therefore, small holes are used in the walls of the chamber and also in the probe electrodes employed to pull ions out of the discharge; frequently differential pumping is applied to this region between exit hole and probe to remove the gas flowing out of the hole. Rather wide variations in the chosen conditions are noticeable in the several types of sources. Some have quite low pressures and very large holes. Others use concentrated discharges at high gas pressure and depend on differential pumping to remove the gas. Still others are designed for minimum gas flow with very small exit holes, to economize on the use of rare gases such as H^3_2 (tritium) or He^3 when these are used for source gases. No general conclusions can be derived, since each type has been considered best for some application.

Within an arc discharge a high density of ionization exists. Electrons (and some negative ions) move toward the anode. Because of their low mass the mobility of electrons is high, and they move rapidly through the gas. Positive ions go to the cathode, but because of their larger mass and lower mobility they take a longer time. An equilibrium is established with approximately equal numbers of positive ions and electrons, in which a slight excess of ions produces a positive space charge and a radial electric field. The potential of the central region, or plasma, becomes 5 to 10 volts positive relative to the walls, so positive ions are forced outward. In addition, a longitudinal potential gradient develops along the discharge column just sufficient to maintain cumulative ionization. Under equilibrium conditions the plasma is an almost uniform mixture of gas, drifting ions, and electrons, with very low internal potential gradient. In such a plasma most of the current is carried by electrons because of their much higher mobility.

Another feature of the discharge is the sheath which develops near the walls—a sharp, visible boundary of the region of ionization associated with the potential drop caused by the difference between the mobilities of electrons and ions. The outward field for positive ions exists largely across a narrow dark layer between the plasma sheath and the walls. Positive ions which originate in the plasma drift to the sheath and are directed outward, where they can emerge through an exit hole cut in the wall of the discharge chamber. Other positive ions are attracted toward the cathode and will emerge through a canal cut in the cathode.

In a molecular gas such as H_2 the formation of atomic ions (H_1^+) is believed to be a complex process involving the intermediate step of formation of atomic gas (H_1) followed by ionization of this atomic gas. Evidence for this is the observed threshold of ionization at the 13.6-volt ionization potential of atomic hydrogen gas. The molecules can be either dissociated directly or, more probably, ionized first to H_2^+, which then dissociates on collision with another molecule to form $H_1 + H_1^+$. Wall material is important in this process, since one of the limitations is the recombination of atomic gas to form molecules at the wall. Another effect is the recombination of atomic ions with electrons to form atomic gas, which tends to increase atomic-gas concentration. In the design of proton sources precautions are frequently taken to control the recombination processes by such techniques as the use of special coatings or by maintaining the walls at high temperature.

Positive ions which emerge from the side of the discharge column have low velocities, equivalent to the 5- to 10-volt potential difference between plasma and walls. They also have random directions because of thermal impacts with gas atoms. It is usually necessary to locate a probe electrode outside the exit hole in the wall of the discharge chamber, with a somewhat larger hole through which ions pass, and to maintain the probe electrode at a high potential relative to the walls. The electric field due to this probe potential will penetrate the exit hole and may distort the electric fields within the discharge. This accelerating field is the first and most important of the ion lenses used in focusing the beam of emergent ions. The physical shapes of exit hole and probe tip become very important in determining the focal properties. These problems are discussed in more detail in the following chapter, but our understanding of the focusing problem is far from complete. Much is left to the inspiration and ingenuity of the experimenter, and we observe wide differences in designs and techniques for bringing out an emergent beam.

Ions which strike the cathode have much higher energies. The cathode fall of potential between the plasma and the cathode may be a large fraction of the total arc voltage. In most arcs the ions emerging through a canal in the cathode have maximum energies of 100 to 200 volts, and they have a rather large variation in energy. On the other hand, these ions are more sharply collimated in direction than those discussed above, coming through the side sheath of the plasma. The probe electrode described above may not be needed, but an accelerating field is required, and this first accelerating lens serves the same purpose of focusing the beam. Geometry again is all-important.

A general characteristic of all ion sources is that they behave best on bench tests and almost universally fail to reach test performance when applied to an accelerator. A variety of factors are responsible. In testing a source, the usual method is to measure the emergent ion current

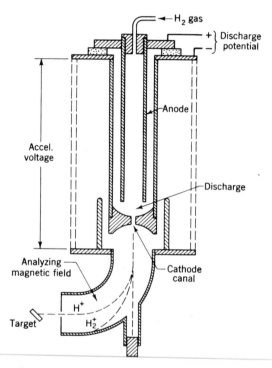

Fig. 4-4. Canal-ray ion source used by Oliphant and Rutherford.[3]

after it has been accelerated by a few kilovolts potential applied to a probe electrode. The beam observed may be strongly divergent, and only a fraction would be acceptable in an accelerator. Or gas flow may be excessive, owing to the use of large exit holes. When applied to an accelerator tube under high voltage, this gas flow might result in breakdown or in excessive electron loading currents. For accelerator use a source must have small exit holes or differential pumping arrangements to prevent loading with gas. Furthermore, the total ion beam from a source is a mixture of singly and multiply charged ions and molecular ions, while that desired for an accelerator is a single type of ion. As a consequence, reports of new high-intensity sources have frequently raised hopes, but the sources have failed to demonstrate their superiority in service.   Publications describing only bench tests are often misleading.   The final test of a source is the level of stable operation in service, with the beam focused, accelerated, and analyzed.   In the descriptions to follow it is well to remember that most publications cite beam intensities obtained in bench tests.

4-2. COLD-CATHODE CANAL-RAY TUBE

The ion source used by Cockcroft and Walton in their earliest experiments on artificial transmutation was a high-voltage cold-cathode canal-ray tube.   A potential of about 20 kv was required to maintain suitable discharge currents.   A typical design is described by Oliphant and Rutherford.[3]   The cathode and anode were long coaxial cylinders with the anode inside and having a sufficiently close spacing to the cathode to prevent discharges between the walls.   The discharge was restricted to the space around the end of the anode cylinder, just opposite a small hole in the cathode end plate through which ions emerged.   The arrangements are shown in Fig. 4-4.   The discharge was operated at 20 kv and between 10 and 100 ma current.   The source was oil-cooled at the base, and the tip of the cathode could be run at red heat.   Gas was admitted through the base into the interior of the anode.   Gas pressure was not specified but, by comparison with other high-potential discharges, must have been of the order of 10^{-2} mm Hg.   Magnetic deflection of the accelerated ions allowed measurements of separated ions.   At first the emission was largely hydrogen molecular ions, but after some hours of operation the proton component increased to about 20 per cent.   Beams of about 1 μa of protons were normally obtained.

The disadvantage of this source is the wide spread in energy of the emergent ions.   A spread of 20 kv would not be acceptable in modern accelerators.

4-3. SPARK DISCHARGE SOURCE

Experimentalists in the field of mass spectroscopy have been faced with the problem of producing ions of essentially every element in order to complete mass-spectra and mass-defect tables.   Intensities required were extremely low in comparison with present demands for accelerators, but sensitive detectors were available and exposures of several hours could be used if necessary to obtain adequate data for analysis.   One of the techniques which was most successful for a wide range of atomic and molecular ions was the spark source, in which high-voltage sparks were developed between electrodes of the chosen material. Typical of such spark sources are those described by Dempster.

Several of the high-energy accelerators, such as the linac and the proton synchrotron (see Chaps. 11 and 13), accelerate short pulses of particles to high energy so the source duty cycle may be as small as 1 part in 10,000. For example, the proton synchrotron requires a pulse of injected ions of about 100 μsec length at about 5-sec intervals. A continuously operating ion source is inefficient for such service, and considerable effort has gone into developing pulsed sources with high peak pulse currents but low average current.

One of the more intriguing pulsed sources is an "occluded gas" spark source reported by Ehlers, Gow, Ruby, and Wilcox[4] for use with the pulsed high-intensity linacs at the University of California Radiation Laboratory. The technique uses electrodes of titanium metal which have been heated and cooled in a hydrogen or deuterium atmosphere until the metal is saturated with interstitial hydrogen. Under optimum conditions about 400 cm³ of hydrogen gas can be occluded per gram of titanium. The titanium is formed in washers stacked with mica spacers to form the electrode of a spark discharge chamber. An electrical "delay line" of capacitors and inductors develops a voltage pulse of 10 to 20 kv for a pulse length of up to 500 μsec, which is applied across the discharge chamber. Auxiliary electrodes and fields are arranged to pull out and focus a beam of atomic-gas ions produced in the spark. Ion currents as large as 300 ma are observed during the pulse; the intensity decays slowly with time as the gas occluded in the electrodes is exhausted. With this source the pulsing rate was limited to one per second to avoid overheating the Ti electrode. The disadvantages are relatively short life and inclusion in the beam of a large titanium ion component.

4-4. HOT-CATHODE ARC

A common feature of many modern ion sources is the use of a heated cathode to supply electrons by thermionic emission. Copious emission can be obtained from heavy tungsten or tantalum filaments or from oxide-coated cathodes. This source of electrons makes it possible to operate the arc at considerably lower potentials than required for the canal-ray discharge. A typical value is 200 volts. As a consequence, the energy of ions emitted from the source is much more uniform. It is also possible to maintain the necessary ionization density at somewhat lower pressures and so to reduce gas flow. A wide variety of designs has been used with different arrangements for the cathode, anode, and exit hole. In general the volume allowed for the discharge is reduced considerably below that used in the high-potential cold-cathode discharge tubes. Many ingenious devices have been invented to mount the electrodes and cool them and to concentrate the discharge; a wide variety of cathode shapes has been employed.

The use of a hot cathode in a gaseous discharge as a method of increasing positive-ion density was proposed by Langmuir and Jones[5] in 1928. One of the first research teams to apply it to proton sources was Lamar and Luhr[6] at the Massachusetts Institute of Technology. In these early designs the cathode served the simple purpose of maintaining the discharge and was located inside a rather large anode cylinder. Ions were pulled out of the discharge through a canal in a probe electrode which could be biased with a negative potential. The physical arrangement of electrodes was not efficient in concentrating the discharge, and ion currents were low.

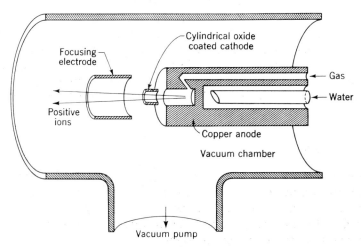

Fig. 4-5. Hot-cathode "focused beam" positive-ion source developed by Scott.[9]   A hollow cylindrical cathode is used, through which the ions emerge.

The next step in the development of the hot-cathode source was the result of a more deliberate study of the properties of the discharge, as well as the physical arrangement of electrodes to favor positive-ion emission. Fowler and Gibson[7] used a circular-loop filament close to and surrounding the exit canal through which positive ions produced in the discharge could emerge. Beams of several milliamperes of positive ions were produced in bench tests, but with a large-diameter canal and with a small atomic-ion fraction.

A thorough empirical study of the hot-cathode arc was reported by Tuve, Dahl, and Hafstad[8] using a variety of arrangements for the electrodes and the probe. The best arrangements gave about 25 μa of resolved protons after acceleration. This report came after the Carnegie Institution group had found that they could obtain higher intensities from a capillary arc, but the simpler hot-cathode source was satisfactory for several years of operation with the Carnegie electrostatic generator.

One of the most impressive bench tests of a hot-cathode hydrogen-ion source was reported by Scott.[9] The design was based on the conclusions reached in a theoretical analysis of ion sources by Smith and Scott;[10] the test apparatus is shown in Fig. 4-5. The most significant feature was a cylindrical cathode of large area to give high electron emission, aligned along the axis of the arc so that the positive ions emerged in a parallel beam through the cathode cylinder. The cathode was formed of nickel strip, oxide-coated for emission and heated by a low-voltage supply. The anode was water-cooled and located close behind the cathode, with a cup in the surface into which the gas was admitted and into which the electrons plunged from the cathode. With a cathode-anode potential difference of about 800 volts, positive-ion beams as large as 4 ma were obtained on bench tests, including nearly 50 per cent protons. The chief advantage of the source is in the high beam densities obtained because of the focusing action of the accelerating fields. However, the experiments reported did not use a canal to provide a pressure differential, and the gas flow from this source was too high to apply directly to an accelerating tube.

4-5. CAPILLARY ARC

The ionization density in the plasma of a low-voltage hot-cathode arc can be increased by concentrating the discharge in a constriction between cathode and anode. This constriction, or capillary, not only increases current density in the arc, but makes it possible to choose the wall surface to improve the atomic-ion concentration. In the constriction the high ion density forces the plasma sheath close to the walls. Positive ions are ejected radially through the sheath and can emerge through a small aperture in the wall of the capillary with only 5 to 10 volts variation in energy. Furthermore, if the wall material has a large coefficient of recombination, positive ions will rebound as neutral atoms, releasing thermal energy and heating the gas as well as increasing the atomic-gas component. Ionization in this atom-rich gas will yield a higher proportion of protons. A double advantage is gained: increased beam intensities and increased atomic-ion percentage.

The first report of such a capillary arc was by Tuve, Dahl, and Van Atta,[11] in which they credited Dr. F. L. Mohler of the National Bureau of Standards with the suggestion. They first used a quartz capillary, but then found that a metal capillary, the potential of which could be adjusted, gave equivalent results and had longer life. A later report by Tuve, Dahl, and Hafstad[12] gave a good diagram of the source (Fig. 4-6). The capillary was transverse to the direction of the emitted ion beam, with anode and cathode in separate enlarged chambers on the two sides. A probe with a small-diameter hole was located outside the 1-mm canal in the side of the capillary. Potentials of up to 7 kv were applied to extract and focus the ions. Beams of over 1 ma of ions were obtained on bench tests, with over 30 per cent protons.

Experience in other laboratories brought recognition of the advantages of the capillary-arc source and extended the development. Lamar, Samson, and Compton[13] started on similar studies at the Massachusetts Institute of Technology. Lamar, Buechner, and Van de Graaff[14,15] described a series of sources. In some they revived the use of quartz or Pyrex capillaries to increase the atomic-ion output. The MIT sources were characterized by very short capillaries and small exit holes. Ions

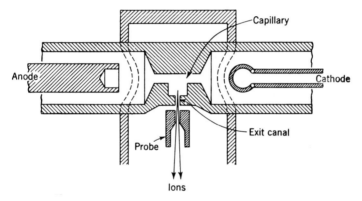

Fig. 4-6. Metal-walled capillary arc, by Tuve, Dahl, and Hafstad.[12]

diffused out of the hole at low velocity, and no high-voltage probe was used. Ion beams of several milliamperes were obtained with atomic-ion percentages up to 40. A differential pumping outlet was usually located just outside the exit hole. However, when applied to the electrostatic generators for which they were designed, the sources have in almost all instances so loaded the accelerating tube with gas that it would not hold voltage. Lower gas pressures and lower beam currents were found necessary in order to maintain voltage on the accelerator. As a consequence the available ion intensities have not proved to be practical, and in operation the sources were run below maximum yield.

Zinn[16] developed a capillary arc with an interesting axial geometry which still maintains the constriction but pulls ions out of the capillary along the axis (Fig. 4-7). This source is one of the most highly developed and has resulted in beam currents up to 500 μa when used with a low-voltage accelerator. Total ion currents up to 4.3 ma were reported, using a canal 1 mm in diameter and 6 mm long through a probe electrode maintained at 10 kv potential. Magnetic analysis showed that the beam included 15 to 20 per cent protons.   The potential drop used for the arc was about 100 volts, although higher potentials were required to start it; the maximum arc current was about 2 amp.   Pressure in the arc was estimated at 3×10^{-2} mm Hg, and gas consumption was measured as 15 cm³ of hydrogen or deuterium at atmospheric pressure per hour.

Allison[17] reported on a rugged capillary-arc source which has given good service for 8 years in a 400-kv accelerator.   It operates on an arc current of 0.75 amp and consumes 25 cm³ of gas per hour, producing a total beam current of 1.1 ma with a probe potential of 3500 volts.   About 50 μa of resolved atomic ions are magnetically analyzed and focused on the target.

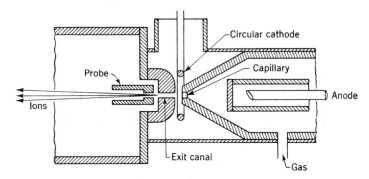

Fig. 4-7. Axially concentric capillary arc developed by Zinn.[16]

Timoshenko,[18] following the MIT development, built a high-intensity source using argon gas which produced 400 μa of singly charged argon ions through a 1-mm-diam exit hole.

4-6. MAGNETIC ION SOURCE

Axial magnetic fields can be used to concentrate the discharge in a hot-cathode arc in the region near the exit hole where a high density of ionization is needed.   Several functions are served by the magnetic field.   The electron beam is tightly collimated (see Sec. 5-5), so the discharge is limited to a cross-sectional area essentially equal to the area of the emitting surface of the cathode.   The yield is also increased because the field keeps positive ions from diffusing to the walls of the chamber and being lost.   The ratio of ion density to arc pressure is thus higher in the presence of the magnetic field.   To reach maximum effectiveness the average radius of curvature of ion paths in the field should be about the size of the exit hole.   The magnetic field required can be computed from typical ion velocities to be of the order of 1000 gauss.   In practice, an optimum field of about this magnitude is observed.

The use of a magnetic field does not make the magnetic ion source a unique type. This technique of concentrating the discharge can be superimposed on other types such as the capillary arc or the rf source to increase ionization density in the discharge. It is also useful in concentrating the electron oscillation discharge to be described later.

One of the early ion sources which employed an axial magnetic field to concentrate the discharge in a hot-cathode arc was reported by Bailey, Drukey, and Oppenheimer.[19] Figure 4-8 shows the location of the field coil around the arc chamber, designed to produce a field of 1000 gauss within the chamber. The arc itself uses a tight spiral tungsten filament to maintain the discharge. The magnetic field collimates the emission from this cathode, so a beam of electrons is projected into the field-free region in which ionization occurs. Ions emerge from $\frac{1}{16}$-in.-diam exit hole on the axis and are accelerated and focused by the potential of 3 to 5 kv on a probe

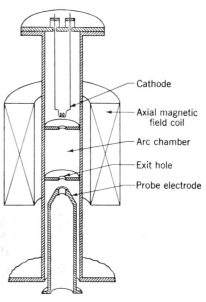

Cathode

Axial magnetic field coil

Arc chamber

Exit hole

Probe electrode

Fig. 4-8. Magnetic ion source using a hot-cathode arc, by Bailey, Drukey, and Oppenheimer.[19]

electrode. The report describes a beam of 500 μa of resolved atomic ions after acceleration to 200 kv.

Setlow[20] described a source which is similar in principle but was not equipped with the necessary probe canal and differential pumping to use with a high-voltage accelerator. It was intended as the source for a single-stage resonant-cavity radiofrequency accelerator in which gas pressure and breakdown of insulation were not limiting factors. Because of these unusual opportunities, larger apertures could be used, resulting in extraordinarily high beam intensities. When pulsed with a duty cycle of 250 μsec 60 times a second, peak ion currents of 100 ma were obtained, with 30 to 40 per cent protons.

The most intense ion source of the low-voltage, hot-cathode, magnetic-field-concentrated type described in the published literature was reported by Lamb and Lofgren[21] of the University of California Radiation Laboratory (UCRL). It represents the culmination of many years of development of high-intensity sources for the large-aperture, high-current linear accelerators developed in the UCRL and in the Livermore laboratory of the Atomic Energy Commission. It was used as an injector for the

"A-48" proton linac at Livermore (see Chap. 10).   It is literally a monster source in all respects—in size, power requirements, and cost, as well as in the phenomenal beam intensity obtained.   The output beam current of ions was 750 ma (95 per cent atomic ions) at 85 to 100 kv energy; the beam was very broad and could be focused only to a 3-in.-diam spot with $\pm 5°$ angular spread.   A very large and powerful solenoid magnet around the discharge region of the source supplied 7000 gauss at the location of the arc aperture, and a second solenoid provided magnetic focusing for

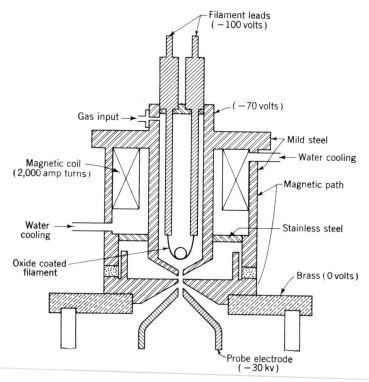

Fig. 4-9. Duo-plasmatron ion source.[23]

the emergent beam.   The aperture was a ¾-in.-diam circle of twelve ⅛-in. holes, and two 20-in. mercury-diffusion pumps were used to evacuate the blast of gas emerging through the holes.   This tremendous source should make practical the dream of accelerator designers for a really high-intensity accelerator.

A somewhat more elegant development of the hot-cathode magnetic ion source is due to von Ardenne.[22]   This device, christened the "duo plasmatron" by its inventor, was evolved in the U.S.S.R. and in East Germany.   The most important innovation in this source is concentration of the magnetic field at the exit hole by an ingenious combination of electromagnet and electrodes in a structure where the plasma-forming electrodes are also the poles of a small electromagnet (Fig. 4-9). Thus the plasma is formed only in the region where it is useful. In his original publication von Ardenne claimed output currents as high as 500 ma through a 1-mm-diam hole. He claimed further that almost all the escaping gas is ionized and that almost all ions are protons. The current and exit-hole diameter mentioned indicate ion current densities of the order of 100 amp/cm². Later studies of this ion source substantiate this figure, although developments have been in the direction of 10- to 100-ma sources with smaller exit holes. Analysis of the ion beam indicates that at least two-thirds of the emitted ions are protons. The source has been studied extensively at Oak Ridge[23] and elsewhere in the United States. It is now available commercially from the High Voltage Engineering Corporation of Burlington, Massachusetts, and from the VEB Vakutronik Corporation of Dresden, East Germany.

4-7. RADIOFREQUENCY DISCHARGE

The electrodeless discharge which can be produced in gases by radiofrequency fields is a well-known phenomenon. An axial magnetic field is often used to enhance the ion yield. One advantage of the electrodeless discharge is that cathode life is not a limitation. Another is that the electrons circulate in orbits through the gas, multiplying the probability of collision and increasing the atomic-ion concentration. The ions are removed through a canal in a probe electrode inserted into the discharge chamber along the axis of the discharge and of the magnetic field; probe potentials of a few kilovolts are required. The chief technical problems have been to concentrate the discharge in a small volume and to feed the rf energy into the discharge. The application of this type of discharge to the production of positive ions has been investigated by several experimenters in England[24,25] and in Canada.[26] Frequencies of 100 to 200 megacycles were used, developed in resonant circuits with a coil of a few turns surrounding the discharge chamber. The rf power required was quite low, of the order of 100 watts. On bench tests the ion output looked encouraging, and the large atomic-ion percentage (about 50) was favorable.

A radiofrequency source of advanced type which combines most of the advantageous features has been described by Hall.[27] He used very high frequencies (450 megacycles) and a small barrel-shaped quartz discharge chamber about ½ in. in diameter and ¾ in. long placed at the open end of a resonant quarter-wave coaxial transmission line. An axial magnetic field of 1000 gauss was produced by a coil surrounding the discharge tube and was found to increase the ion yield greatly. The physical arrangement is shown in Fig. 4-10. A 1-mm hole in the end of the chamber allowed the ions to emerge into the first accelerating gap, to which a differential pumping outlet was connected. The pressure in the quartz discharge chamber was roughly 0.1 mm Hg, and the gas flow was about 30 cm³/hr at atmospheric pressure. This source was applied to a 120-kv accelerator, and the results reported are for focused and accelerated ions at the target. Hall reports obtaining 400-μa beams containing 60 per cent protons, with an oscillator power of 60 watts.

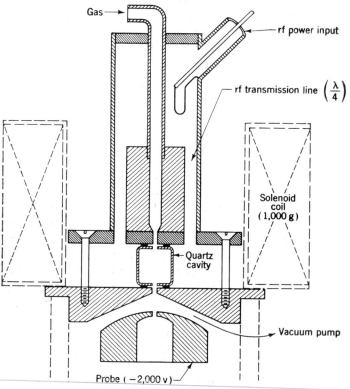

Fig. 4-10. Radiofrequency discharge ion source developed by Hall.[27]   An electrodeless discharge within a quartz cavity is concentrated by an axial magnetic field.

The radiofrequency source is capable of much higher emission when operated under pulsed conditions. At the CERN laboratory in Genèva, Switzerland, a radiofrequency source yields currents of the order of 100 ma in pulses 10 μsec long.[28]   This source requires about 7 kw of radiofrequency power at 139 megacycles.

4-8. ELECTRON OSCILLATION (P.I.G.) ION SOURCE

One of the most recently developed high-intensity ion sources utilizes electron oscillations to increase the density of ionization in the discharge.

This principle was first utilized in the Philips laboratories ionization gauge, and ion sources of this type are frequently known as P.I.G. sources. The principle was presented by Penning[29] in 1937 and was incorporated in the Philips gauge immediately. The first practical ion source of this type was reported by Finkelstein[30] in 1939, but it received relatively little attention for some years. With the developing need for high-intensity pulsed sources, the technique was revived by a group at the University of California as a pulsed source for an electrostatic generator feeding a proton linear accelerator. A detailed discussion is given by Backus[31] in the National Nuclear Energy Series, and a description of a revised source is given by Gow and Foster.[32]

The mechanism of the discharge can be described by reference to Fig. 4-11, which shows the Gow and Foster source. The discharge occurs between a cylindrical anode and two disk-shaped, secondary-emission cathodes at the ends of the anode cylinder. Hydrogen gas pressure of about 2×10^{-2} mm Hg, an axial magnetic field of about 1000 gauss, and a potential difference of a few hundred volts between anode and cathodes provide the necessary conditions for the discharge. An electron released from either cathode will be accelerated into the anode, its radial motion constrained by the magnetic field. As it coasts through the field-free region inside the anode, it loses some energy to the gas and produces some ion pairs, so it emerges from the anode with less energy than on entering and is retarded and reflected by the negative potential of the other cathode. The electron then reenters the anode and continues the axial oscillation until its energy is reduced below that required for ionization. Eventually it drifts to the anode to become part of the external-circuit current. The average energy required to form an ion pair in hydrogen is about 35 ev, so each primary electron can form 5 to 10 ion pairs. The secondary electrons formed by ionization also oscillate axially, but since their energy is low, they are less effective in ionization.

Positive ions formed in the discharge are also constrained by the magnetic field to motion in the axial direction. When the ions approach the cathode, they are accelerated toward it and strike with several hundred electron volts energy. With suitable cathode surfaces each positive ion releases several secondary electrons on impact. If more secondaries are produced than the number of ions formed per primary electron, the discharge will become cumulative and the current will increase until it is ultimately limited by the external circuit. The discharge will stabilize as a self-maintaining phenomenon at that balance of current and potential drop which results in equal numbers of ions per electron and electrons per ion. A plasma column forms through the center of the anode, terminating in a thin cathode sheath at the surface of each cathode. This sheath is estimated to be about 0.01 cm thick from considerations of the space-charge limitation of emission of secondary electrons from the cathode surface. Most of the potential drop in the discharge occurs across this cathode sheath, and it is here that the oscillating electrons are turned back. The diameter of the plasma column is small, with a suitable constraining magnetic field; in the source illustrated in Fig. 4-11 it was observed to be about $\frac{3}{16}$ in. diam.

The primary advantage of this source over the hot-cathode type is in the large ratio of ion current to electron current in the discharge. With the hot-cathode type, this ratio depends on the ratio of velocities (the mobility) of ions to electrons and is of the order of $(m_e/m_p)^{\frac{1}{2}}$, which for

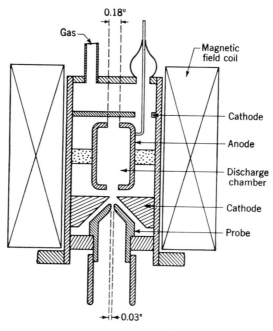

Fig. 4-11. Electron oscillation ion source by Gow and Foster,[32] based on the P.I.G. principle.

hydrogen is about 0.03. With the oscillation source the number of ions formed per electron from the cathode is increased by a factor of 5 to 10, and up to 0.3 of the current is carried by positive ions. This concentrated blast of positive ions striking the cathodes allows a relatively large number to emerge through a canal cut through one cathode. For example, if the arc current is 2 amp, about 400 ma of positive ions will strike a $\frac{3}{16}$-in.-diam spot on one cathode, and as much as 1.5 ma can emerge through a 0.030-in.-diam canal. This estimate is in good agreement with the observed emergent beam intensities. The ratio of atomic to molecular ions improves with current density, as would be expected from such a concentrated discharge, and the atomic component is observed to be about 60 per cent of the total ion output in practical sources.

Cathodes must have large secondary-electron-emission coefficients under positive-ion bombardment. An oxide film on the cathode surface plays a key role. The mechanism of secondary emission is believed to involve a layer of positive charge built up on the surface of the oxide layer by the positive ions. This provides extremely high electric fields across the layer, pulls electrons from the base metal by field emission, and releases them into the discharge. The base metals which have been found most satisfactory on tests are aluminum and beryllium. Others, such as magnesium and duralumin, are subject to loss of the oxide film and erosion by sputtering of the metal. The oxide layer on aluminum or beryllium cathodes wears away after some period of operation and must be replaced. Oxidation can be accomplished by heating and decomposing silver oxide in a side tube with the discharge running. Such conditioning takes about $\frac{1}{2}$ hr and must be repeated after about 100 hr of normal operation of the source.

The positive-ion beam emerging from the cathode canal is accelerated and focused by potentials on a probe electrode and by successive accelerating electrodes which act as ion lenses. The potential on the probe, of 5 to 15 kv, determines the beam current. This probe lens is divergent by itself, but the conical shaping is arranged to give a beam as nearly parallel as possible. Focusing is accomplished primarily by the lens between the probe and a following accelerating electrode. In continuous operation the source will produce over 100 μa of resolved protons, limited by heating of the source and by discharges in the accelerating tube.

The P.I.G. source has been very successful when applied to pulsed operation. With a pulse duty cycle of $\frac{1}{100}$ or smaller, the heating in the discharge can be readily controlled, and high current densities are used. Proton beams of 5 to 50 ma peak current during the pulse have been obtained after acceleration to several Mev in linear accelerators and electrostatic generators. A real advantage of this source over others offering equivalent beam intensities is the low gas flow through the small cathode canal, of the order of 25 cm^3/hr at standard conditions. This allows the source to be used without differential pumping at the probe canal.

A modification of this electron-oscillation source has been highly successful as a cyclotron ion source[33] (see Chap. 6). The secondary-emission cathodes avoid the cathode life limitations of hot-cathode sources, and the strong axial magnetic field in the cyclotron is helpful in collimating the discharge. In the cyclotron application, instead of ions being pulled out through an aperture in one of the cathodes, they emerge through a slit along the side of the discharge column, which can extend over much of the internal aperture of the cyclotron electrodes. As a result, very high intensities can be obtained, roughly proportional to the aperture of the slit.

The advantages of the cyclotron modification of the P.I.G. source, with its long-slit geometry, are retained in a source described by Anderson and Ehlers,[34] which is intended for use with a linear accelerator. They use a transverse magnetic field to deflect and analyze the emergent beam from the slit, so as to obtain a momentum-analyzed beam of ions. On emerging from the deflecting magnet, the beam is broad in the direction of the slit and has angular divergence in the other coordinate, so it must be further focused to provide a beam of suitable geometry to be used in linear acceleration. Such a diffuse beam is suitable for a linac of large aperture, but not for small-aperture accelerating structures.

REFERENCES

1. J. M. Meek and J. D. Craggs, "Electrical Breakdown of Gases," Oxford (1953); L. B. Loeb, "Basic Properties of Gaseous Electronics," University of California Press (1955); J. D. Cobine, "Gaseous Conductors," McGraw-Hill (1941).
2. D. H. Hale, *Phys. Rev.*, **56**:1199 (1939).
3. M. L. E. Oliphant and E. Rutherford, *Proc. Roy. Soc. (London)*, **A141**:259 (1933).
4. K. W. Ehlers, J. D. Gow, L. Ruby, and J. M. Wilcox, *Rev. Sci. Instr.*, **29**:614 (1958).
5. I. Langmuir and H. A. Jones, *Phys. Rev.*, **31**:357 (1928).
6. E. S. Lamar and O. Luhr, *Phys. Rev.*, **44**:948 (1933); **46**:87 (1934).
7. R. D. Fowler and G. E. Gibson, *Phys. Rev.*, **46**:1074 (1934).
8. M. A. Tuve, O. Dahl, and L. R. Hafstad, *Phys. Rev.*, **48**:315 (1985).
9. G. W. Scott, Jr., *Phys. Rev.*, **55**:954 (1939).
10. L. P. Smith and G. W. Scott, Jr., *Phys. Rev.*, **55**:946 (1939).
11. M. A. Tuve, O. Dahl, and C. M. Van Atta, *Phys. Rev.*, **46**:1027 (1934).
12. M. A. Tuve, O. Dahl, and L. R. Hafstad, *Phys. Rev.*, **48**:241 (1935).
13. E. S. Lamar, E. W. Samson, and K. T. Compton, *Phys. Rev.*, **48**:886 (1935).
14. E. S. Lamar, W. W. Buechner, and R. J. Van de Graaff, *J. Appl. Phys.*, **12**:132 (1941).
15. E. S. Lamar, W. W. Buechner, and R. J. Van de Graaff, *J. Appl. Phys.*, **12**:141 (1941).
16. W. H. Zinn, *Phys. Rev.*, **52**:655 (1937).
17. S. K. Allison, *Rev. Sci. Instr.*, **19**:291 (1948).
18. G. Timoshenko, *Rev. Sci. Instr.*, **9**:187 (1938).
19. C. Bailey, D. L. Drukey, and F. Oppenheimer, *Rev. Sci. Instr.*, **20**:189 (1949).
20. R. B. Setlow, *Rev. Sci. Instr.*, **20**:558 (1949).
21. W. A. S. Lamb and E. J. Lofgren, *Rev. Sci. Instr.*, **27**:907 (1956).
22. M. von Ardenne, "Tabellen der Elektronenphysik und Übermikroskopie," Deutscher Verlag der Wissenschaften (1956).
23. C. D. Moak, H. E. Banta, J. N. Thurston, J. W. Johnson, and R. F. King, *Rev. Sci. Instr.*, **30**:694 (1959).

24. P. C. Thoneman, *Nature,* **158**:61 (1946).
25. J. C. Rutherglen and J. F. I. Cole, *Nature,* **160**:545 (1947).
26. A. J. Bayly and A. G. Ward, *Can. J. Research,* **A26**:69 (1948).
27. R. N. Hall, *Rev. Sci. Instr.,* **19**:905 (1948).
28. E. Regenstreif, "Le Synchrotron à Protons du CERN," chap. 5, p. 22, CERN, Geneva (1959).
29. F. M. Penning, *Physica,* **4**:71 (1937).
30. A. T. Finkelstein, *Rev. Sci. Instr.,* **11**:94 (1940).
31. J. Backus, National Nuclear Energy Series, div. I, vol. 5, McGraw-Hill (1949).
32. J. D. Gow and J. S. Foster, Jr., *Rev. Sci. Instr.,* **24**:606 (1953).
33. C. B. Nulls, C. F. Barrett, and R. S. Livingston, Oak Ridge National Laboratory Report Y-542 (Nov. 8, 1949).
34. C. E. Anderson and K. W. Ehlers, *Rev. Sci. Instr.,* **27**:809 (1956).

5

Particle Motion in Electric and Magnetic Fields

The accelerator designer depends heavily on two mathematical tools. The first is Maxwell's statement of the interrelation of the components of electric and magnetic fields, and the second is the formulation of Newton's second law of motion for charged particles in these fields. In this chapter these relations will be tabulated and presented in the coordinate systems most useful for application to accelerators. They will then be applied to two general classes of problems.

The first class of problems relates to the accelerating systems of direct-voltage accelerators described in the preceding chapters, including the problems of focusing particle beams which travel in straight lines. Focusing analysis is required in the design of systems for extraction of beams from ion sources. Furthermore, in many high-energy accelerators the attainable electric accelerating fields are not strong enough to reach high energies in short accelerating chambers, so focusing systems are necessary which will maintain beams of small cross section over long distances. Four focusing systems will be discussed: the electrostatic lens,

96

the axial-magnetic-field lens, the alternating-gradient lens, and the magnetic edge-focusing lens.

The second class of problems relates to the orbits of charged particles in static or slowly varying magnetic fields. A foundation will be laid for the discussion in chapters to follow on the circular magnetic accelerators such as the cyclotron, the betatron, and the synchrotron. Superficially these machines are radically different. But the basic arrangement of fields is the same in all three: a magnetic field restrains the motion to a roughly circular orbit, and tangential electric fields provide the acceleration.

5-1. MAXWELL'S EQUATIONS

For the derivation of Maxwell's equations from the results of experimental physics the reader is referred to any text on electromagnetic theory. Here we shall merely tabulate these equations in the forms most useful to the accelerator designer. In vectorial form they are as follows (in rationalized mks units):

$$\text{div } \mathbf{E} = \frac{\rho}{\epsilon}$$
$$\text{div } \mathbf{B} = 0$$
$$\text{curl } \mathbf{E} = -\frac{\partial \mathbf{B}}{\partial t} \tag{5-1}$$
$$\text{curl } \mathbf{B} = \mu \mathbf{I} + \mu\epsilon \frac{\partial \mathbf{E}}{\partial t}$$

where $\mathbf{E}$ = electric field strength, volts/m
$\mathbf{B}$ = magnetic flux density, webers/m^2
ρ = charge density, coulombs/m^3
$\mathbf{I}$ = current density, amp/m^2
μ = permeability of the medium, henrys/m
ϵ = dielectric constant of the medium, farads/m

In free space

$$\mu = \mu_0 = 4\pi \times 10^{-7}$$
$$\epsilon = \epsilon_0 = \frac{1}{36\pi} \times 10^{-9}$$

so that $\mu_0\epsilon_0 = 1/c^2$, where c is the velocity of light in free space.

In rectangular coordinates Maxwell's equations are as follows:

$$\frac{\partial E_x}{\partial x} + \frac{\partial E_y}{\partial y} + \frac{\partial E_z}{\partial z} = \frac{\rho}{\epsilon} \tag{5-2}$$

At the head of the facing page are pictures of the three men who laid the foundations for the study of particle dynamics: Isaac Newton, James Clerk Maxwell, and Albert Einstein.

$$\frac{\partial B_x}{\partial x} + \frac{\partial B_y}{\partial y} + \frac{\partial B_z}{\partial z} = 0 \tag{5-3}$$

$$\frac{\partial E_z}{\partial y} - \frac{\partial E_y}{\partial z} = -\frac{\partial B_x}{\partial t}$$

$$\frac{\partial E_x}{\partial z} - \frac{\partial E_z}{\partial x} = -\frac{\partial B_y}{\partial t} \tag{5-4}$$

$$\frac{\partial E_y}{\partial x} - \frac{\partial E_x}{\partial y} = -\frac{\partial B_z}{\partial t}$$

$$\frac{\partial B_z}{\partial y} - \frac{\partial B_y}{\partial z} = \mu I_x + \mu\epsilon \frac{\partial E_x}{\partial t}$$

$$\frac{\partial B_x}{\partial z} - \frac{\partial B_z}{\partial x} = \mu I_y + \mu\epsilon \frac{\partial E_y}{\partial t} \tag{5-5}$$

$$\frac{\partial B_y}{\partial x} - \frac{\partial B_x}{\partial y} = \mu I_z + \mu\epsilon \frac{\partial E_z}{\partial t}$$

In accelerator design the cylindrical coordinate system is probably the most useful. In cylindrical coordinates Maxwell's equations are

$$\frac{1}{r}\frac{\partial}{\partial r}(rE_r) + \frac{1}{r}\frac{\partial E_\theta}{\partial \theta} + \frac{\partial E_z}{\partial z} = \frac{\rho}{\epsilon} \tag{5-6}$$

$$\frac{1}{r}\frac{\partial}{\partial r}(rB_r) + \frac{1}{r}\frac{\partial B_\theta}{\partial \theta} + \frac{\partial B_z}{\partial z} = 0 \tag{5-7}$$

$$\frac{1}{r}\frac{\partial E_z}{\partial \theta} - \frac{\partial E_\theta}{\partial z} = -\frac{\partial B_r}{\partial t}$$

$$\frac{\partial E_r}{\partial z} - \frac{\partial E_z}{\partial r} = -\frac{\partial B_\theta}{\partial t} \tag{5-8}$$

$$\frac{1}{r}\frac{\partial}{\partial r}(rE_\theta) - \frac{1}{r}\frac{\partial E_r}{\partial \theta} = -\frac{\partial B_z}{\partial t}$$

$$\frac{1}{r}\frac{\partial B_z}{\partial \theta} - \frac{\partial B_\theta}{\partial z} = \mu I_r + \mu\epsilon \frac{\partial E_r}{\partial t}$$

$$\frac{\partial B_r}{\partial z} - \frac{\partial B_z}{\partial r} = \mu I_\theta + \mu\epsilon \frac{\partial E_\theta}{\partial t} \tag{5-9}$$

$$\frac{1}{r}\frac{\partial}{\partial r}(rB_\theta) - \frac{1}{r}\frac{\partial B_r}{\partial \theta} = \mu I_z + \mu\epsilon \frac{\partial E_z}{\partial t}$$

In a static electric field the field components can be derived from a potential function V by the vector relation $\mathbf{E} = -\operatorname{grad} V$. In rectangular coordinates

$$E_x = -\frac{\partial V}{\partial x} \qquad E_y = -\frac{\partial V}{\partial y} \qquad E_z = -\frac{\partial V}{\partial z} \tag{5-10}$$

In cylindrical coordinates

$$E_r = -\frac{\partial V}{\partial r} \qquad E_\theta = -\frac{1}{r}\frac{\partial V}{\partial \theta} \qquad E_z = -\frac{\partial V}{\partial z} \tag{5-11}$$

In dynamic fields a more sophisticated representation in terms of scalar and vector potentials is necessary. Since no use will be made in this book of this representation, it will not be included here.

When the first Maxwell relation is written in terms of the potential function V it becomes

$$\text{div grad } V = \frac{-\rho}{\epsilon}$$

In this form it is known as Poisson's equation. If the charge density ρ is zero, the same equation is referred to as Laplace's equation.

5-2. EQUATIONS OF MOTION

Charged particles are accelerated in the direction of motion only by electric fields. Magnetic fields exert forces at right angles to the direction of particle motion and to the direction of the magnetic field. In vector notation the equation of motion of a particle of charge e and mass m in a combined electric and magnetic field is

$$\frac{d}{dt}(m\mathbf{v}) = e\mathbf{E} + e\mathbf{v} \times \mathbf{B} \tag{5-12}$$

In rectangular coordinates Eq. (5-12) becomes

$$\frac{d}{dt}(m\dot{x}) = eE_x + e\dot{y}B_z - e\dot{z}B_y$$

$$\frac{d}{dt}(m\dot{y}) = eE_y + e\dot{z}B_x - e\dot{x}B_z \tag{5-13}$$

$$\frac{d}{dt}(m\dot{z}) = eE_z + e\dot{x}B_y - e\dot{y}B_x$$

where the dots indicate differentiation with respect to time. In cylindrical coordinates Eq. (5-12) is

$$\frac{d}{dt}(m\dot{r}) - mr\dot{\theta}^2 = eE_r + er\dot{\theta}B_z - e\dot{z}B_\theta$$

$$\frac{1}{r}\frac{d}{dt}(mr^2\dot{\theta}) = eE_\theta + e\dot{z}B_r - e\dot{r}B_z \tag{5-14}$$

$$\frac{d}{dt}(m\dot{z}) = eE_z + e\dot{r}B_\theta - er\dot{\theta}B_r$$

All particle motions in accelerators follow from special cases of these equations. For nonrelativistic motion the mass m is a constant. For relativistic motion $m = m_0(1 - v^2/c^2)^{-\frac{1}{2}}$, where m_0 is the rest mass of the particle.

5-3. THE ELECTROSTATIC LENS

From early work on the formation of electron beams in X-ray tubes and other electronic devices it was well known that a sequence of accelerating electrodes with cylindrical symmetry had lens-like properties. This is a consequence of the radial components of the fields around and between the accelerating electrodes; these field components will act either to focus or to defocus deviant particles in the accelerated beam.

Early studies of ion-beam focusing by Tuve, Dahl, and Hafstad[1] were largely empirical and consisted of observations of the focal properties of a variety of electrode arrangements. The first accelerating gap between ion source and accelerating column was found to be the dominant lens. Studies were made with various sizes of cones, cylinders, and planes, and with one and two gaps. The properties of such electrostatic lenses were determined qualitatively as a function of electrode potentials and ion-beam energy. It was found that almost any arrangement of electrodes could give reasonably good focal properties if electrode potentials were properly adjusted. The results were used chiefly to design electrodes so that inconveniently high voltages were not required.

Buechner, Lamar, and Van de Graaff[2] investigated focusing by electrostatic lenses using photographic detection of the focused beam. They were able to show that beam divergence due to space-charge forces could be compensated by appropriate lens design. Eventually the group at the Massachusetts Institute of Technology was able to report focal spots as small as 1 mm in diameter at distances as great as 10 ft from the ion source. Important to this success were precise construction and alignment, large lens apertures, and carefully regulated electrode potentials.

In all this early work the results were largely empirical and applied only to the particular electrode configuration tested. It was difficult to separate the optical properties of the source and its electrodes from those of the accelerating tube.

The first attempts at theoretical analysis of electrostatic lenses came in the field of electron optics, stimulated by the requirements of electronic devices such as the cathode-ray tube and the electron microscope. Electron optics is now a mature field and its results are to be found in many textbooks, such as those written by Zworykin,[3] Pierce,[4] Cosslett,[5] and Terman.[6] We present here the basic treatment of electrostatic lenses with cylindrical symmetry around the beam axis.

We assume that, whatever is the particular electrode configuration, it yields a potential distribution along the z axis which we represent by

$$V(r = 0) = V_0(z) \tag{5-15}$$

Also we assume that this potential is referred to a zero at a point where the particle energy is zero so that V is a measure of particle energy. The particle energy T in electron volts is given by $T = -V$. We now can satisfy Laplace's equation if we write for the potential in the region where r is not zero

$$V = V_0 - \frac{r^2}{4}\frac{d^2V_0}{dz^2} + \frac{r^4}{64}\frac{d^4V_0}{dz^4} - \cdots \qquad (5\text{-}16)$$

From this potential function we can derive the axial and radial field components. For most lens systems it is necessary to retain only the leading terms in the expansions, so we shall use

$$E_z = -\frac{dV_0}{dz}$$
$$E_r = \frac{r}{2}\frac{d^2V_0}{dz^2} \qquad (5\text{-}17)$$

The radial equation of motion ($m\ddot{r} = eE_r$) can be written

$$m\ddot{z}\frac{dr}{dz} + m\dot{z}^2\frac{d^2r}{dz^2} = eE_r \qquad (5\text{-}18)$$

But $\qquad m\ddot{z} = eE_z = -e\frac{dV_0}{dz} \qquad$ and $\qquad m\dot{z}^2 = -2eV$

so Eq. (5-18) can be rewritten

$$Vr'' + \frac{V'r'}{2} + \frac{V''r}{4} = 0 \qquad (5\text{-}19)$$

where the primes indicate differentiation with respect to z. This "paraxial ray equation" is well known in electron optics. It does not lend

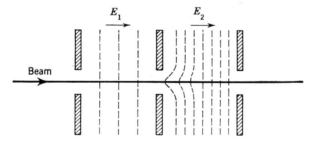

Fig. 5-1. Convergent aperture lens showing equipotentials for $E_2 > E_1$.

itself to precise solution, but it has been solved numerically for a variety of cases. The results can be found in great detail in Terman's Handbook.[6]

For weak lenses some of the properties of the electrostatic lens can be derived from approximate solutions of Eq. (5-19). Two types of lenses are of primary interest. The first type is the aperture lens shown in Fig. 5-1. In this lens the ray travels from a region of constant $E_z = E_1$ through an aperture into another region of constant $E_z = E_2$. Focusing occurs in the region around the central aperture.   The focusing region is short and the radial displacement of the particle does not change appreciably as it passes through this region.   In this case it is appropriate to write Eq. (5-19) in the form

$$\frac{d}{dz} r'V + \frac{r^3}{4} \frac{d}{dz}\left(\frac{V'}{r^2}\right) = 0$$

In view of the approximate constancy of r, we can integrate this relation to give

$$\left(r'V + \frac{rV'}{4}\right)_{\text{final}} = \left(r'V + \frac{rV'}{4}\right)_{\text{initial}}$$

If, initially, the beam was traveling parallel to the axis so that the initial value of r' is zero and if we note that $(-r/r')_{\text{final}}$ is equal to the distance the beam will travel before it crosses the axis, we can rewrite the integrated equation in the form

$$\frac{1}{f} = -\left(\frac{r'}{r}\right)_{\text{final}} = \frac{V'_{\text{final}} - V'_{\text{initial}}}{4V} = \frac{E_2 - E_1}{4T} \tag{5-20}$$

where V is the potential of the central diaphragm and f is the focal length of the system.   We have thus shown that (for accelerating fields) if the second field is the stronger, the lens is converging; if the first field is stronger, the lens is diverging.   If the fields are decelerating, the converse will be true.

A second type of electrostatic lens is that produced by the field between the ends of two coaxial cylinders.   In Fig. 5-2 we show the case where the two cylinders have the same diameter.   In the lower half of the figure, plots are included of V, V', and V'' along the axis of the system. Equally useful as lenses are other examples of this configuration in which the cylinders have different diameters.   This lens class differs from the class described in the last paragraph in that the particle travels from a region of zero field, traverses the lens, and enters another region of zero field.   Consequently, a different mathematical approach is appropriate. In this case we rewrite the paraxial ray equation (5-19) in the form

$$\frac{d}{dz} r'V^{1/4} + \frac{d}{dz} rV^{-3/4}V' + \tfrac{3}{16} rV'^2 V^{-1/4} = 0$$

When this equation is integrated between entrance and exit points through the lens, the second term disappears since V' is zero initially and finally.   In its integrated form the equation becomes

$$(r'V^{1/4})_{\text{final}} - (r'V^{1/4})_{\text{initial}} = -\frac{3}{16} \int_{\text{entrance}}^{\text{exit}} rV'^2 V^{-1/4} \, dz$$

As in the previous case, the radial displacement r will not change appreciably during passage through the focusing region. Also, if the lens is weak, the difference in potential between the cylinders will be small compared with the absolute value of V. If the initial value of r' is zero (ray

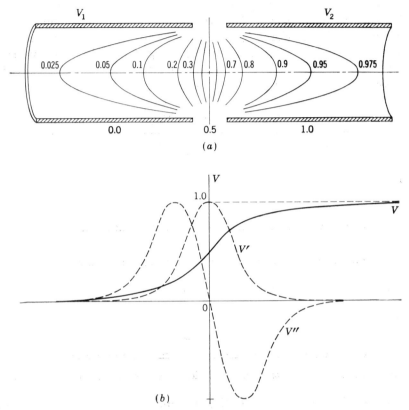

Fig. 5-2. (a) Two-cylinder lens showing equipotentials. (b) Variation of axial potential V and of its first (V') and second (V'') derivatives in the two-cylinder lens.

parallel to the axis), we can write the integrated equation in the approximate form

$$\frac{1}{f} = \frac{-r'_{\text{final}}}{r_{\text{initial}}}$$

$$\cong + \frac{3}{16}\left(\text{avg value of } \frac{V'^2}{V^2}\right) \tag{5-21}$$

Since the right-hand side of this equation is always positive, lenses of this type are always converging lenses regardless of which cylinder has the higher potential.

This result could have been predicted on qualitative grounds. The character of the particle path through an accelerating and a decelerating lens of this sort is shown in Fig. 5-3.   In the accelerating lens the fields around the gap force the particle inward as it approaches the gap.   At the gap it is accelerated, and it proceeds through slightly weaker radial fields pushing it outward.   Its velocity is higher, so these weaker fields have even less effect and it is pushed outward less than it was originally deflected inward and leaves the lens with an inward component of radial velocity.   In the decelerating lens the particle is pulled away from the axis as it approaches the gap.   Leaving the gap with decreased velocity, it enters a focusing field stronger than it felt before, and it also leaves the lens with an inward velocity component.

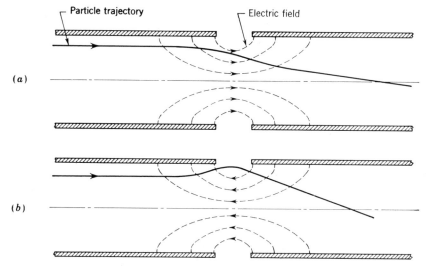

Fig. 5-3. Particle trajectories in (a) accelerating lens and (b) decelerating lens.

The focal lengths for accelerating and decelerating lenses of this type will differ slightly because of the somewhat different orbits traversed. In Fig. 5-4 focal lengths are plotted for lenses having cylinders of the same diameter for the two cases.   The coordinates used are the ratio of focal length to cylinder diameter and the ratio of the cylinder voltages; with these units the plot is independent of units or dimensions.   These graphs were obtained by numerical integration of the paraxial ray equation through fields computed for this particular geometry.

The theoretical approach presented above is somewhat naive; more sophisticated discussions will be found in the references cited.   Detailed studies of electrostatic lenses show many analogies with optical lenses. A more precise treatment can be made to show the presence of principal planes and focal points similar in every way to the cardinal points of optical systems.   Aberrations of the sorts observed in optical systems are also present.   This is particularly true if the beam diameter is a large fraction of the diameter of the focusing electrodes since, in this case, many of the assumptions made in the derivation of the paraxial ray equation are no longer valid.

The properties of a two-cylinder electrostatic lens are profoundly modified if a conducting grid is placed across the end of one of the cylinders. With a dense grid the field approaches that between a cylinder and a plane, effectively removing either the focusing or the defocusing half of the two-cylinder lens field. A grid across the second cylinder of an accelerating lens makes the lens strongly focusing; one across the end of

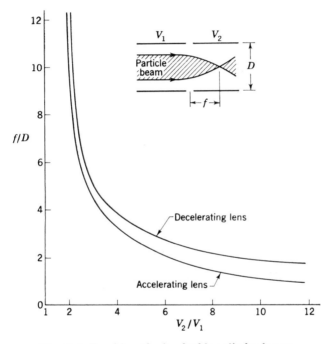

Fig. 5-4. Focal lengths for double-cylinder lenses.

the first cylinder makes it defocusing. The grid will obstruct a portion of the aperture and reduce beam transmission. Yet if the grid is made too transparent, field penetration through it will reduce its effectiveness. A practical compromise which does not reduce beam intensity unduly has made the grid lens useful for some linear-accelerator applications (see Chap. 10). Grids are used also in lens systems for focusing beams from accelerator ion sources.

Also of interest to the accelerator designer is the ion optical behavior of a uniform accelerating field with no radial components. In this system the particle trajectory is modified because the paraxial velocity is continually increasing although the radial velocity component is unaffected. Consequently a diverging beam tends to be slightly converged during acceleration and a converging beam has its convergence slightly decreased. The general tendency during acceleration is to bring the beam closer to parallelism.

Many combinations of focusing fields have been used with the various direct-voltage accelerators. A typical system used in the Van de Graaff preaccelerator for the cosmotron (see Fig. 3-13) includes a probe electrode maintained at a potential of the order of -20 kv with respect to the ion source, a focus electrode maintained at about -10 kv, and an accelerate electrode at about -60 kv with respect to the ion source. The potential difference between source and probe is kept high to extract as large an ion current as possible. The diverging beam is decelerated in the focus electrode so that it can more easily be focused; then the beam (reduced in diameter and more nearly parallel) is carried through the accelerate electrode into the uniform field of the accelerating column. Electrode potentials are computed and adjusted to give the desired beam properties at the output of the accelerator. Usually this emergent beam will be approximately parallel and will be reduced in diameter from more than 1 cm at the probe electrode to 1 or 2 mm at full energy.

5-4. SPACE-CHARGE EFFECTS

If the density of charge is high in a beam to be focused by an electrostatic lens, it may be necessary to take the space-charge field into account in designing the lens. Since like charges repel each other, this is always a defocusing field; its effect can be included in the paraxial ray equation. We assume streamline flow in the beam so that, inside the radius defined by a particular particle path, the total current i is constant. To simplify the problem, we assume that the charge density is uniform as a function of radius, although it will vary as a function of z. With these assumptions the charge density is given in terms of the current by

$$\rho = \frac{i}{\pi r^2 v} \tag{5-22}$$

where v is the particle velocity and is given by $v = (-2eV/m)^{1/2}$. The potential pattern in the beam must now satisfy Poisson's equation rather than Laplace's equation. Poisson's equation states that

$$\frac{1}{r} \frac{\partial}{\partial r} r E_r + \frac{\partial E_z}{\partial z} = \frac{\rho}{\epsilon}$$

which indicates that E_r now has the value

$$E_r = \frac{rV''}{2} + \frac{i}{2\pi\epsilon r(-2eV/m)^{1/2}}$$

instead of the value $rV''/2$ given by Eq. (5-17). When the new radial field is inserted in the derivation of the paraxial ray equation, we obtain

$$Vr'' + \frac{V'r'}{2} + \frac{1}{4}\left[r\,V'' + \frac{i}{\pi \epsilon r(-2eV/m)^{1/2}} \right] = 0 \qquad (5\text{-}23)$$

The new term introduces severe limits because it indicates a defocusing radial field that goes to infinity as r tends to zero. Thus it would appear that a beam of appreciable density can never be brought to a focus. This is not strictly true, since our simplifying assumptions are not usually justified to this degree. However, it is good practice not to attempt to include beam crossovers in lens systems for intense beams. For weak lenses in which the beam is not strongly concentrated and in which r and V do not change drastically during passage through the focusing region, it is quite possible to include the space-charge term as a correction term in computing the lens optics.

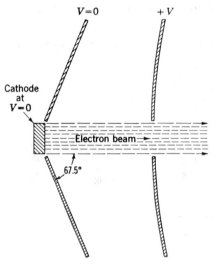

Fig. 5-5. Pierce electron gun with electrodes shaped to make $V \propto z^{4/3}$ along the edges of the electron beam.[4]

The special case of a lens system to keep a beam parallel in the presence of space charge follows from setting $r'' = r' = 0$ in Eq. (5-23). The equation is satisfied if, along the boundary of the beam, V is proportional to $i^{2/3}z^{4/3}$. Electrode structures which satisfy this criterion have been worked out by Pierce (see Fig. 5-5).[4] An electron gun designed in this

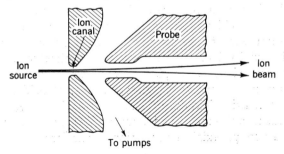

Fig. 5-6. Pierce lens for extracting ions from an ion source.

fashion is usually known as a "Pierce gun." Many variations of Pierce's electrode geometries have been evolved for maintaining desired convergence or divergence in dense charged-particle beams. The problem of space-charge limitation is most frequently encountered in accelerators at the exit of the ion source where high currents of low-velocity ions are to be extracted through small apertures. Here the Pierce electrode shape is usually modified to a reentrant cone (Fig. 5-6). The tip of the probe or first accelerating electrode is then formed as shown as a reentrant coaxial cone with a somewhat larger aperture at its tip. If desired, the space between source and probe can then be connected to a vacuum pump to evacuate the gas coming from the source.

5-5. FOCUSING BY AXIAL MAGNETIC FIELDS

Although the mathematical method for treating the magnetic lens is analogous to that just used for the electrostatic lens, the mechanism of the magnetic lens is quite different. This lens usually takes the form

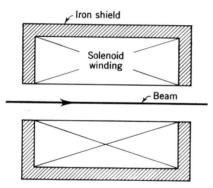

shown in Fig. 5-7. A solenoid coaxial with the beam, and usually sheathed in iron to decrease stray magnetic fields, provides a magnetic field generally parallel to the axis but having radial components at its ends. We assume that the entering beam has only axial and radial components of velocity. As the beam crosses the radial-magnetic-field components at the entrance to the lens, the cross-product interaction between these field components and the particle velocity [Eq. (5-12)] introduces a

Fig. 5-7. Cross section of a cylindrical magnetic lens for focusing by an axial magnetic field.

corkscrew motion into the beam. Inside the solenoid both the angular and the radial velocity components of this corkscrew motion interact with the axial magnetic field to give further spiral motion around the axis. Finally the radial field at the exit introduces further cross-product interaction with the axial velocity. This sounds complicated, but the mathematical treatment yields a simple result. Just as in the electrostatic case, we set up expansions of the radial and axial field components in terms of a general axial field distribution $B_z(r = 0) = B_0(z)$. We introduce these fields into the radial and azimuthal equations of motion (5-14) and arrive at a new paraxial ray equation of the form

$$r'' + \frac{eB_0{}^2 r}{8mT} = 0 \qquad (5\text{-}24)$$

If the magnetic field is approximately uniform throughout the length of the lens, the solution to the ray equation is a sinusoidal oscillation in radius and it will be possible to choose the lens length so that the system is either focusing or defocusing.

Because of the focusing mechanism, the beam will be rotated around its axis as it passes through the lens. If the beam was not originally symmetrical around the axis, the asymmetry will be rotated during the focusing process. With initially symmetrical beams this effect will be observable only through rotational velocity components left in the beam after it has been focused. The amount of the rotation can be derived from the relations used in the derivation of Eq. (5-24).

If very strong magnetic fields are used, the restoring forces indicated by Eq. (5-24) become very strong and the radial extent of the beam is small. Even in the presence of dense space charge a beam can be restrained from expanding by such an axial magnetic field. This is the mechanism (see Chap. 4) used in many ion sources to keep the ionizing electrons in the discharge from escaping.

Short magnetic solenoid lenses are also used where it is desirable to minimize the physical extent of the lens system. The field is confined to a short axial gap between the end plates of the iron sheath. The length of the uniform-field region is greatly reduced relative to the nonuniform end fields. The focal length of a short magnetic lens can be derived approximately if it is assumed that the magnetic flux density $B = B_0$, a constant, for a distance d in the middle of the lens and is zero elsewhere. The paraxial ray equation (5-24) can now be integrated and the focal length f of the lens can be derived. The result is

$$f = \frac{8mT}{eB_0^2 d} \tag{5-25}$$

where T is the kinetic energy of the particles in electron volts. If the exciting winding includes NI amp-turns, then, since $B_0 d = \mu_0 NI$,

$$f = \frac{8mTd}{e\mu_0^2 N^2 I^2} \tag{5-26}$$

For electrons $f \cong 30Td/(NI)^2$; for protons $f \cong 53{,}000Td/(NI)^2$. As an example we consider a magnetic lens to have a focal length of 1 m. Magnetic field will be maintained over a distance of 3 cm along the axis, and the particles to be focused will have an energy of 1 Mev. From the above relations, a lens for electrons will require about 900 amp-turns to maintain a flux density of about 4×10^{-2} weber/m^2 (400 gauss). For protons the lens will require 40,000 amp-turns and will have a flux density of about 1.6 webers/m^2 (16,000 gauss).

5-6. EDGE FOCUSING

Wherever particle beams enter or leave magnetic fields, the fringing fields and pole geometry will affect the beam optics. Under certain conditions the magnet may act as a lens that can be converging in both planes.

First we consider the beam optics in the plane normal to the direction of the magnetic field. A parallel beam will be assumed to enter normally

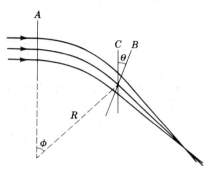

a region of field bounded by the lines A and B of Fig. 5-8. As the beam enters the field, its direction is unaltered. Had the other boundary been the line C parallel to A, the beam would also emerge as a parallel beam, though somewhat reduced in cross section. But, since the line B is inclined at an angle θ with respect to C (or A), the upper part of the beam has been deflected through a larger angle than has the lower part and the beam will emerge

Fig. 5-8. Passage of initially parallel beam through an edge-focusing lens.

converging. By some rather simple geometric construction the reader will easily discover that the distance f_1 from the boundary B to the focal or crossover point of the beam is given by

$$f_1 = \rho \, \frac{\cos (\phi - \theta)}{\sin \theta} \tag{5-27}$$

where ρ is the radius of the curvature of the beam in the magnetic field and ϕ is the angle through which the axial ray of the beam is bent in the magnetic field.

In the other plane the focal properties of the field are not so evident. In this plane the field well inside the magnet has no appreciable effect; here only the fringing field is important. We assume a coordinate system whose origin of coordinates is at the point where the axial ray crosses the boundary B. The y axis is parallel to B, the x axis is normal to B in the plane of the diagram, and the z axis is normal to the plane of the diagram. The fringing field will now have x and z components; from symmetry there will be no y component. Focusing effects will follow from interactions of the beam with the x component of the fringing field B_x. From Eqs. (5-13)

$$\frac{d}{dt} (m\dot{z}) = -e\dot{y}B_x \tag{5-28}$$

We now need some clue as to the form of B_x. From experience we know that the z component B_z will have in the xy plane the general character shown in Fig. 5-9. Above and below this plane it will decrease gradually and symmetrically around the median xy plane. We can represent this behavior by the expression

$$B_z = f(x) - \frac{z^2}{2!} f''(x) + \frac{z^4}{4!} f''''(x) \cdots$$

To satisfy Maxwell's equations, B_x must now have the form

$$B_x = zf'(x) - \frac{z^3}{3!} f'''(x) + \cdots$$

To a first approximation, good enough for the present purpose, we can say, so long as z is small,

$$\begin{align}
B_z &= f(x) \\
B_x &= zf'(x)
\end{align} \quad (5\text{-}29)$$

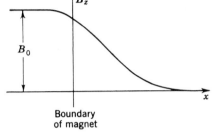

When this is substituted in Eq. (5-28), it becomes

$$\frac{d}{dt}(m\dot{z}) = -e\dot{y}zf'(x)$$

$$= -ez\left(\frac{\dot{y}}{\dot{x}}\right)\frac{d}{dt}[f(x)] \quad (5\text{-}30)$$

Fig. 5-9. Distribution of magnetic field around the edge of a magnet gap.

During passage through the fringing field, $\dot{x}$, $\dot{y}$, and z of the beam are sensibly unchanged.   Moreover, if v is the velocity of the particles in the beam, $\dot{x} = v \cos(\phi - \theta)$ and $\dot{y} = v \sin(\phi - \theta)$.   Hence Eq. (5-30) can be integrated to give

$$\begin{align}
m\dot{z}_{\text{final}} - m\dot{z}_{\text{initial}} &= ez \tan(\phi - \theta)[f(x)_{\text{final}} - f(x)_{\text{initial}}] \\
&= ez \tan(\phi - \theta)(0 - B_0)
\end{align}$$

where B_0 is the field strength well inside the magnet.   The beam has thus been deflected by an angle

$$\frac{\dot{z}}{v} = -\frac{eB_0}{mv} z \tan(\phi - \theta)$$

$$= -\frac{z}{\rho} \tan(\phi - \theta)$$

and the focal distance f_2 in the vertical plane is given by

$$f_2 = \frac{zv}{\dot{z}} = \rho \cot(\phi - \theta) \quad (5\text{-}31)$$

A range of the angles ϕ and θ exists over which Eqs. (5-27) and (5-31) indicate focusing in both planes.   By inclining the entrance plane of the magnet to the beam, similar focusing can be attained as the beam enters the magnet.

Focusing of this sort is used to restrain the excursions of the circulating beam in the zero-gradient synchrotron (ZGS) of the Argonne National Laboratory.   Edge-focusing effects are included also in the fixed-field alternating-gradient (FFAG) designs presented in Sec. 15-10.   In many other cases where beams pass through analyzing magnets this effect must be included in analysis of the beam optics.

5-7. FOCUSING BY ALTERNATING GRADIENTS

The most recently discovered technique for restraining the radial motions in beams of charged particles is that of alternating-gradient (AG) focusing.   Since it gives much stronger restraining forces than most of the other available methods, it has often been described as "strong focusing."   The basic principle as it applied to magnetic-gradient focusing in the synchrotron was first proposed by Christofilos in Athens, Greece, in 1950, in a manuscript which was not published.   The principle was independently discovered in 1952 by Courant, Livingston, and Snyder[7] at Brookhaven National Laboratory and expanded to cover the application of magnetic gradients to the focusing of linear beams. Blewett,[8] also at Brookhaven, presented the basic formulation for focusing with electrostatic gradient fields.   When Christofilos became aware of the Brookhaven publications and visited the laboratory to compare notes, his priority was immediately evident and was acknowledged by the Brookhaven group early in 1953.[9]   He later joined the Brookhaven laboratory and has been active in the further development of accelerators using this principle.   The theoretical formulations and techniques have been improved and generalized for the magnetic-field application[10] (see Chap. 15).   It seems more appropriate in this chapter to start with the specialized application to the focusing of linear beams in electrostatic gradient fields.

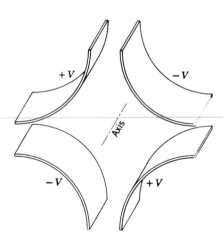

Fig. 5-10. Electrostatic quadrupole lens for use in AG focusing.

If a beam of charged particles whose axis is the z axis passes through a region where the transverse field E_x has the form $E_x = -Gx$, G being a constant, the beam will be focused in the xz plane.

But, since div **E** must be zero, it follows that E_y must have the form $E_y = +Gy$ and the beam will be equally strongly defocused in the y plane.   The discovery of AG focusing revealed the fact that if the beam now passes through a second region of reversed gradients in which $E_x = +Gx$ and $E_y = -Gy$, the net effect of the combination will be focusing in both planes. As was pointed out by the Brookhaven group, the system has its analogy in optics, where it has long been known that a beam of light passing in succession through focusing and defocusing lenses of equal but opposite strength will be focused no matter which lens comes first.

The field pattern just described is derivable from a potential function having the form

$$V = \frac{G}{2}(x^2 - y^2) \tag{5-32}$$

The equipotentials are rectangular hyperbolas, so such a field pattern can be set up by a quadrupole system of electrodes having the shape shown in Fig. 5-10.

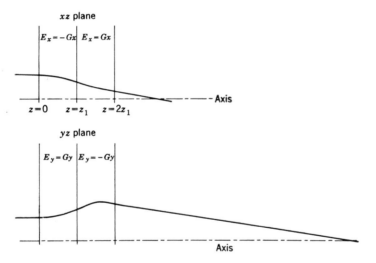

Fig. 5-11. Focusing in a two-element AG lens having $k = 0.5$ and $kz_1 = 45°$.

The precise behavior of the system can be derived by tracing a particle through the system geometry (see Fig. 5-11). In the xz plane the equation of motion in the first region is

$$m\ddot{x} = -eGx \tag{5-33}$$

whose solution is

$$x = x_0 \cos\left(\frac{eGt^2}{m}\right)^{\frac{1}{2}} + \dot{x}_0 \left(\frac{eG}{m}\right)^{-\frac{1}{2}} \sin\left(\frac{eGt^2}{m}\right)^{\frac{1}{2}}$$

$$= x_0 \cos\left(\frac{eGz^2}{mv^2}\right)^{\frac{1}{2}} + \dot{x}_0 \left(\frac{eG}{m}\right)^{-\frac{1}{2}} \sin\left(\frac{eGz^2}{mv^2}\right)^{\frac{1}{2}} \tag{5-34}$$

where the zero subscripts indicate the initial conditions.

At $z = z_1$ the position and velocity of the particle are given by

$$x = x_0 \cos kz_1 + \frac{\dot{x}_0}{kv} \sin kz_1$$

$$\frac{\dot{x}}{v} = -kx_0 \sin kz_1 + \frac{\dot{x}_0}{v} \cos kz_1 \qquad (5\text{-}35)$$

where $k = (eG/mv^2)^{1/2}$. Equations (5-35) can be written in the form of a matrix transformation:

$$\begin{vmatrix} x \\ \dot{x}/v \end{vmatrix} = \begin{vmatrix} \cos kz_1 & (1/k)\sin kz_1 \\ -k \sin kz_1 & \cos kz_1 \end{vmatrix} \begin{vmatrix} x_0 \\ \dot{x}_0/v \end{vmatrix} \qquad (5\text{-}36)$$

If the sign of the gradient G is reversed, the transformation matrix becomes

$$\begin{vmatrix} \cosh kz_1 & (1/k)\sinh kz_1 \\ k \sinh kz_1 & \cosh kz_1 \end{vmatrix} \qquad (5\text{-}37)$$

The displacement and velocity of the particle after passage through the two successive field regions can now be written

$$\begin{vmatrix} x \\ \dot{x}/v \end{vmatrix} = \begin{vmatrix} \cosh kz_1 & (1/k)\sinh kz_1 \\ k \sinh kz_1 & \cosh kz_1 \end{vmatrix} \begin{vmatrix} \cos kz_1 & (1/k)\sin kz_1 \\ -k \sin kz_1 & \cos kz_1 \end{vmatrix} \begin{vmatrix} x_0 \\ \dot{x}_0/v \end{vmatrix}$$

$$= \begin{vmatrix} x_0(\cosh kz_1 \cos kz_1 - \sinh kz_1 \sin kz_1) + \dfrac{\dot{x}_0}{kv}(\cosh kz_1 \sin kz_1 + \sinh kz_1 \cos kz_1) \\ kx_0(\sinh kz_1 \cos kz_1 - \cosh kz_1 \sin kz_1) + \dfrac{\dot{x}_0}{v}(\cosh kz_1 \cos kz_1 + \sinh kz_1 \sin kz_1) \end{vmatrix}$$

$$(5\text{-}38)$$

In the yz plane the particle position and velocity are obtained by applying the transformation matrices in the reverse order to obtain

$$\begin{vmatrix} y \\ \dot{y}/v \end{vmatrix}$$

$$= \begin{vmatrix} y_0(\cosh kz_1 \cos kz_1 + \sinh kz_1 \sin kz_1) + \dfrac{\dot{y}_0}{kv}(\cosh kz_1 \sin kz_1 + \sinh kz_1 \cos kz_1) \\ ky_0(\sinh kz_1 \cos kz_1 - \cosh kz_1 \sin kz_1) + \dfrac{\dot{y}_0}{v}(\cosh kz_1 \cos kz_1 - \sinh kz_1 \sin kz_1) \end{vmatrix}$$

$$(5\text{-}39)$$

It is not immediately evident from these rather complex expressions that we have achieved focusing in both planes. This fact can be made clear if we make the simplifying assumption that kz_1 is small enough that we can use the approximate substitutions

$$\cosh kz_1 = 1 + \frac{(kz_1)^2}{2}$$

$$\cos kz_1 = 1 - \frac{(kz_1)^2}{2}$$

$$\sinh kz_1 = kz_1\left[1 + \frac{(kz_1)^2}{6}\right]$$

$$\sin kz_1 = kz_1\left[1 - \frac{(kz_1)^2}{6}\right]$$

We consider a beam that is initially parallel so $\dot{x}_0 = \dot{y}_0 = 0$. Now, to the order of the approximation

$$x = x_0(1 - k^2 z_1^2)$$

$$\frac{\dot{x}}{v} = -\tfrac{2}{3} x_0 k^4 z_1^3$$

$$y = y_0(1 + k^2 z_1^2) \tag{5-40}$$

$$\frac{\dot{y}}{v} = -\tfrac{2}{3} y_0 k^4 z_1^3$$

The two velocities are equal for the same initial displacements and both are directed toward the axis.

In Fig. 5-11 we have traced the orbits in the two planes for the particular case $k = 0.5$ and $kz_1 = 45°$. From the figure it can be seen that the greatest displacement occurs in the focusing sector in both planes; the

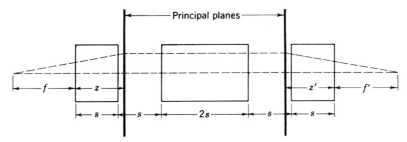

Fig. 5-12. Triplet AG lens.   Principal planes and focal distances are indicated.

particle thus experiences the strongest force when it is in the sector where the force is directed toward the axis.

The same focusing effects can be obtained if a field-free space is included between the two sectors, as is necessary in the physical arrangement of electrodes or quadrupole magnets. Analysis of the system becomes a little more complicated but is still manageable, and the applied fields are somewhat reduced.

As can be seen from Fig. 5-11, the two-element AG lens is highly astigmatic; the focal points in the two planes are at very different locations. This means that a beam initially circular in cross section will pass through a focal line in the yz plane and somewhat later will pass through a focal line in the xz plane. When better optical properties are desired, it is preferable to use triplet lenses. A favorite triplet-lens arrangement is illustrated in Fig. 5-12; the three elements of the lens can be equal in length or, as in the case illustrated, the central element can be longer; here it is twice as long as the two other elements.

Alternating-gradient lenses can be analyzed by the methods of geometric optics in terms of focal lengths and principal planes. If focal distances f and f' are defined as distances of focal points from the extreme ends of the lens array and the distances of the principal planes from the ends of the array are represented by z and z' (Fig. 5-12), it will be found that these parameters satisfy the relation

$$\frac{1}{f' + z'} + \frac{1}{f + z} = \frac{1}{F}$$

where F, z, and z' are constants for all values of f and f'. Thus the parameters F, z, and z' are constants for the lens system. Moreover, if the fields in the first and last lens element are equal, it will be found that $z = z'$.

Tabulations of F, z, and z' have been assembled at the Brookhaven National Laboratory for a variety of AG lenses with two and three elements and with various spacings between elements. Typical figures for the lens illustrated in Fig. 5-12 are collected in Table 5-1.

TABLE 5-1

PARAMETERS FOR THE TRIPLET LENS OF FIG. 5-12

$k_1{}^2 = eG_1/(mv^2)$ and refers to the first and third lens element
$k_2{}^2 = eG_2/(mv^2)$ and refers to the central lens element

		Initially focusing plane			
$k_1 s$	$2k_2 s =$	0.4	0.8	1.2	1.6
0.4	$F/s =$	6.258	17.56	−6.259	−1.753
	$z/s =$	4.584	4.486	4.344	4.181
0.8	$F/s =$	−1.904	−1.825	−1.704	−1.555
	$z/s =$	−5.143	−5.340	−5.672	−6.143
1.2	$F/s =$	−0.2250	−0.1908	−0.1487	−0.1092
	$z/s =$	−0.8047	−0.8157	−0.8328	−0.8548
1.6	$F/s =$	−0.0901	−0.0736	−0.0547	−0.0384
	$z/s =$	−0.1767	−0.1804	−0.1861	−0.1933
		Initially defocusing plane			
$k_1 s$	$2k_2 s =$	0.4	0.8	1.2	1.6
0.4	$F/s =$	−3.240	8.968	1.477	0.8207
	$z/s =$	2.269	2.291	2.332	2.402
0.8	$F/s =$	−0.2997	−0.5783	1.973	0.3561
	$z/s =$	1.374	1.380	1.390	1.407
1.2	$F/s =$	−0.0573	−0.0888	−0.3976	0.1476
	$z/s =$	0.8985	0.8999	0.9025	0.9069
1.6	$F/s =$	−0.0144	−0.0208	−0.0579	0.0629
	$z/s =$	0.6524	0.6528	0.6536	0.6548

If the expressions (5-38) and (5-39) are examined for higher values of kz_1 than those which are suitable for the approximation applied to yield the results of Eqs. (5-40), it will be discovered that the AG system discussed above is not always a focusing system.   When kz_1 passes the value of π, the system suddenly becomes strongly defocusing.   For still higher values of kz_1 the combination can again become focusing, but these higher-order systems have no advantage over the systems which keep kz_1 below π.

The AG method is a powerful means for maintaining beams over long distances.   Quadrupole lenses can be arranged in an AG sequence involving many quadrupoles.   When this is done, it can be shown by the methods of matrix analysis[10] that the condition for continuous focusing is that $\cosh kz_1 \cos kz_1$ must lie between -1 and $+1$.   If the gradients in successive lens elements are different, the condition becomes more complicated but will also be found in the reference cited.

The method is equally powerful if magnetic quadrupoles are used. The theoretical treatment is essentially the same as that given above except that the electric-field gradient must be replaced by the product of particle velocity and magnetic-field gradient.

The most spectacular application of AG focusing is in the AG synchrotron (Chap. 15).   The method is also applicable to the linear accelerator (Chap. 10).   It would appear also to be promising for beam focusing in direct-voltage accelerators.   A practical technique might result from the use of permanent-magnet quadrupoles along the accelerating column. Permanent-magnet quadrupoles of Ferroxdur or Index (nonconducting permanent-magnet ceramics) have been produced at Brookhaven.[11]   A theoretical study of AG focusing in accelerating tubes has been made at the University of California Radiation Laboratory.   Since both studies have given encouraging results, it would appear that it is only a matter of time until the permanent-magnet-quadrupole technique becomes practical.

5-8. THE CONCEPT OF EMITTANCE AND LIOUVILLE'S THEOREM

Particle beams in general are not the idealized assemblies of parallel rays thus far represented.   They do not come to perfect focal points, but because of imperfections in the methods of beam generation, they can be focused only into regions of finite size.   When every attempt has been made to make a beam parallel, the particles will still have a finite angular distribution.   Generally it will be found that, if the individual particles are plotted as points in a region where, say, the x component of velocity is plotted against the x coordinate, the particles will all lie in a region like that illustrated in Fig. 5-13, having, for most beams, a generally elliptical shape.   A similar plot will be found in the other plane, although the shape and orientation of the region will probably be different. If the beam is passed through lenses or is otherwise affected by fields, or if it is merely allowed to drift, the shape of the region enclosing the particles will change.

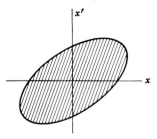

But it will be found, in linear systems, that the area of the region is constant. This constant area is a characteristic of the beam and is known as the "emittance" of the beam. So long as the energy of the beam is not changed, the emittance will be constant.

A lens system whose defining apertures are such that it can barely accept a beam of a given emittance is said to have an "admittance" equal to the emittance of the beam that it can accept.

Fig. 5-13. Emittance plot in x-x' phase space.

The constancy of the emittance of a beam is a consequence of Liouville's theorem, which says that the area in phase space occupied by an assembly of particles whose properties p_k and q_k are derivable from a Hamiltonian H by the relations

$$\frac{dp_k}{dt} = -\frac{\partial H}{\partial q_k} \quad \text{and} \quad \frac{dq_k}{dt} = +\frac{\partial H}{\partial p_k}$$

will remain constant throughout the motion. For the proof of this theorem the reader is referred to texts on the classical statistics. Here the application is evident since positions and momenta of particles are derivable from a Hamiltonian representing the total energy, kinetic and potential, of the system. Strictly speaking the phase space is a six-dimensional space for particle beams. But if the motions in the three planes are not coupled, two-dimensional plots like that in Fig. 5-13 are useful and represent areas that remain constant through systems of lenses and deflecting fields.

Other cases will emerge later in which other pairs of conjugate variables will yield constant areas in "phase space" plots. Energy and time are often found to be such variables.

5-9. ORBITS IN UNIFORM MAGNETIC FIELDS

In a uniform magnetic field the simplest form of motion of a charged particle which satisfies the equation of motion (5-12) is circular motion at constant velocity in a plane normal to the magnetic field. The equation of motion in cylindrical coordinates simplifies to

$$m r \dot{\theta} = e r B \tag{5-41}$$

where $B = -B_z = $ a constant. Since $r\dot{\theta} = v$, the particle velocity, Eq. (5-41) represents the linear momentum of the particle, which is proportional to the product Br. The motion can be visualized by reference to Fig. 5-14, in which the cylindrical coordinates of circular motion (r, θ, and z) represent the radius of the circular orbit, the angular location, and the distance from the central orbit plane of a particle between the poles of an electromagnet which produces an axial field B_z.

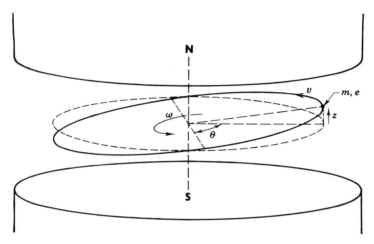

Fig. 5-14. Cylindrical coordinates for orbital motion in a magnetic field.   A particle of mass m, charge e, and velocity v in a magnetic field B moves in a circle of radius r. The angular position θ and the axial displacement z are shown.

The frequency of revolution of the particle can be obtained from the momentum relation as

$$f = \frac{\dot{\theta}}{2\pi} = \frac{eB}{2\pi m} \tag{5-42}$$

This linear relation between frequency of particle revolution and magnetic field shows that frequency is constant in a uniform and steady magnetic field if the mass of the particle remains constant, i.e., for nonrelativistic velocities.   This relation determines the applied frequency of the accelerating electric field in the cyclotron and is known as the cyclotron resonance relation.

For light positive ions having energies less than about 20 Mev, the non-relativistic expression for kinetic energy can be used, from which we have

$$T = \tfrac{1}{2}mv^2 = \frac{e^2 r^2 B^2}{2m} \tag{5-43}$$

In this energy range the kinetic energy increases with the square of magnetic field and the square of the orbit radius.   In the mks system of units, kinetic energy is measured in joules.   We shall more often have occasion to define kinetic energy as

$$\frac{T}{e} = \frac{\frac{1}{2}mv^2}{e} = \frac{er^2B^2}{2m}. \tag{5-44}$$

In this form the kinetic energy is measured in electron volts or, if we wish to include the appropriate factor, in millions of electron volts. This definition assumes the charge to be that of a single electron. If multiply charged ions are involved (such as He++), the numerical value of T/e in Mev units must be divided by the multiplicity of charge to obtain the kinetic energy.

The radii of orbits can be obtained from a rearrangement of the above relation:

$$r = \frac{10^3}{B}\left(2\,\frac{m}{e}\,\frac{T}{e}\right)^{\frac{1}{2}} \tag{5-45}$$

where B is in webers/m², e/m is in coulombs/kg, and T/e is in Mev units for a singly charged particle. Orbit radii obtained from this relation for H+, D+, H₂+, and He++ ions in a magnetic field of 1 weber/m² are plotted in Fig. 5-15 to illustrate the dimensional requirements for accelerators in

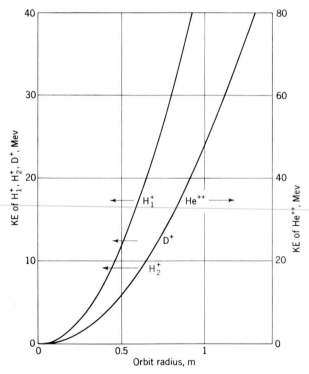

Fig. 5-15. Orbit radii (meters) for light ions in a magnetic field $B = 1.0$ weber/m² as a function of energy in Mev.

the nonrelativistic energy region. The influence of multiple charge is illustrated by the curve for He^{++}, which is essentially identical with that for H$_1^+$, although the charge-to-mass ratio e/m has a value approximately the same as that of the H$_2^+$ or D$^+$ ions.

5-10. RELATIVISTIC EQUATIONS OF MOTION

The motion of particles at high energies is also described by Eq. (5-41), but in this case the momentum must be expressed in its relativistic form. The relativistic expression for total energy W of a particle is

$$W = mc^2 = \frac{m_0 c^2}{(1 - v^2/c^2)^{1/2}} = W_0 + T = m_0 c^2 + T \qquad (5\text{-}46)$$

whence

$$\frac{v}{c} = \left(1 - \frac{W_0^2}{W^2}\right)^{1/2} \qquad (5\text{-}47)$$

The momentum p of a relativistic particle is given by

$$p = mv = \frac{m_0 v}{(1 - v^2/c^2)^{1/2}} = \frac{1}{c}(W^2 - W_0^2)^{1/2} = \frac{1}{c}[T(T + 2W_0)]^{1/2} \quad (5\text{-}48)$$

where m_0 = rest mass of particle
c = velocity of light
W_0 ($= m_0 c^2$) = rest energy of particle
T = kinetic energy of particle

Values of rest energy W_0 in Mev units are given in Table 5-2 for the particles used in accelerators.

TABLE 5-2

Particle	Rest energy, Mev
Electron.....................................	0.511
Hydrogen atomic ion (proton)................	938
Heavy hydrogen atomic ion (deuteron)........	1877
Hydrogen molecular ion......................	1876
Doubly ionized helium (alpha particle)........	3733

From Eq. (5-41) the orbit radius is now (in meters)

$$r = \frac{mv}{eB} = \frac{[T(T + 2W_0)]^{1/2}}{ceB} \qquad (5\text{-}49)$$

When T and W_0 are expressed in Mev units and B is in webers/m^2, this becomes

$$r = \frac{[T(T + 2W_0)]^{1/2}}{300B} \qquad (5\text{-}50)$$

The relationship given in Eq. (5-50) between orbit radius, magnetic field, and kinetic energy is plotted in Fig. 5-16 for electrons, protons, deuterons, and alpha particles.   Three coordinates are used: B, r, and T; as an aid to using the plot, the product Br is also introduced.   Logarithmic scales are used to encompass a wide range in the variables.   Orbit radius extends from 1 cm to 100 m, magnetic field from 0.01 weber/m² (100 gauss) to 10 webers/m² (100,000 gauss), and kinetic energy from 1 to 10,000 Mev (10 Bev).

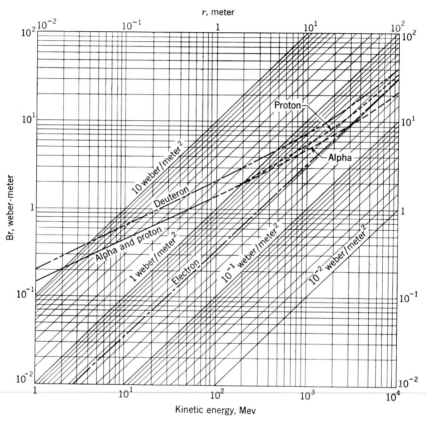

Fig. 5-16. Orbit radius as a function of energy and magnetic field.   First find the Br value for the desired particle and particle energy; follow this Br value to the intersection with the chosen value of field B; read orbit radius on the upper scale.

In Table 5-3 a few typical values are listed to show the dimensional requirements of magnetic accelerators.   Note the approach to a linear relation between radius and energy for relativistic energies where $T \gg W_0$. Note also the converging dimensions for electron and positive-ion accelerators at very high energies.

When rearranged to solve for kinetic energy, Eq. (5-49) becomes

$$T = (W_0{}^2 + c^2 e^2 B^2 r^2)^{1/2} - W_0 \qquad (5\text{-}51)$$

T can be read from the plot of Fig. 5-16 by reversing the procedure in the legend. This equation illustrates one feature characteristic of very high energies: when T becomes very large compared with W_0, the relation simplifies to

$$T \simeq ceBr \qquad \text{(high energies)} \qquad (5\text{-}52)$$

At high energies, energy and momentum become linearly proportional and as a result the particle energy becomes linearly proportional to the product Br. To give an easily remembered example, the relation is

TABLE 5-3
ORBIT RADIUS IN METERS
(At 1 weber/m²)

T, Mev	Electrons	Protons	Deuterons	He^{++} ions
1	0.00485	0.143	0.206	0.144
10	0.0347	0.454	0.643	0.454
100	0.330	1.47	2.05	1.45
1,000	3.30	5.60	7.22	4.85
10,000	33.0	36.0	38.7	21.8

evaluated for a magnetic field of 1.0 weber/m² (10 kilogauss), which is representative of fields obtained with iron-cored magnets:

$$T \text{ (in Mev)} \simeq 300r \text{ (in meters) at } B = 1.0 \text{ weber/m}^2 \qquad (5\text{-}53)$$

For example, an electron moving in an orbit of 1 m radius in a 10-kilogauss field must have an energy of 300 Mev.

The relativistic expression for orbital frequency follows from Eqs. (5-46) and (5-49):

$$f = \frac{v}{2\pi r} = \frac{eB}{2\pi m} = \frac{eB}{2\pi m_0} \frac{W_0}{W} = \frac{eB}{2\pi m_0 (1 + T/W_0)} = \frac{f_0}{1 + T/W_0} \qquad (5\text{-}54)$$

Here f_0 is the nonrelativistic "cyclotron frequency." The frequency is constant only as long as $T \ll W_0$. This same relation will be used later to show the magnitude of frequency variation involved in the acceleration of positive ions to high energies in the synchrocyclotron; as particle energy increases, with B constant, the frequency of the electric field applied to the accelerating electrodes must decrease.

Orbital frequency can also be expressed in terms of orbit radius by using the relativistic relation for velocity:

$$f = \frac{v}{2\pi r} = \frac{c}{2\pi r} \left[1 - \left(\frac{W_0}{W_0 + T} \right)^2 \right]^{\frac{1}{2}} \qquad (5\text{-}55)$$

The numerical constant is readily evaluated; as long as T and W_0 are expressed in the same units and r is in meters, we have

$$f = \frac{47.8}{r}\left[1 - \left(\frac{W_0}{W_0 + T}\right)^2\right]^{1/2} \quad \text{megacycles/sec} \quad (5\text{-}56)$$

As an example, consider a high-energy electron in an orbit of 1 m radius (the magnetic field must have the proper value). For energies above a

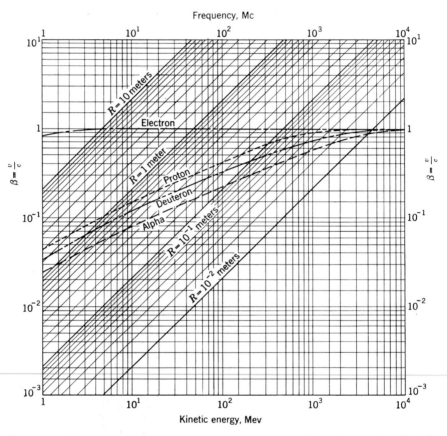

Fig. 5-17. Orbital frequency as a function of energy and orbit radius. First find the β value for the desired particle and particle energy; follow this value of β to the intersection with the chosen orbit radius; read orbital frequency on the upper scale.

few Mev, the second term involving the energies becomes negligible and the frequency approaches a constant value of 47.8 megacycles/sec.

The frequency relation of Eq. (5-55) is plotted in Fig. 5-17 over a wide range in energy and radius for electrons, protons, deuterons, and He^{++} ions. In this plot logarithmic coordinate scales are used, and the parameter $\beta = v/c$ is used as an intermediate step.

A few typical values of ion-revolution frequency are listed for the several particles in Table 5-4.   The magnetic field is 1 weber/m², and the orbit radii are those given in Table 5-3.   Note the converging values of frequency for all particles at very high energies.   The revolution frequencies for different magnetic fields are inversely proportional to the flux density.

TABLE 5-4
ORBITAL FREQUENCY
(In megacycles/sec at 1 weber/m²)

T, Mev	Electrons	Protons	Deuterons	He^{++} ions
1	9,120	15.2	7.60	7.61
10	1,380	15.2	7.60	7.61
100	145	13.8	7.34	7.40
1,000	14.5	7.46	5.00	6.05
10,000	1.45	1.32	1.22	2.11

The equations developed above give all the necessary information to determine the orbital motion of particles in a uniform magnetic field which is normal to the plane of their orbits.   This special symmetry

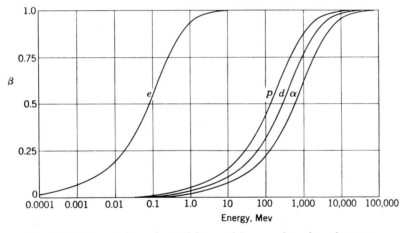

Fig. 5-18. Plot of $\beta = v/c$ for light particles as a function of energy.

has been chosen in all existing magnetic accelerators.   Basic parameters can be determined by using Figs. 5-16 and 5-17.   The transition from nonrelativistic to relativistic regions is evident.   For electrons the relativistic region is reached at a few Mev ($v = 0.98c$ at 2 Mev); protons and other positive ions reach the equivalent region at energies of several Bev ($v = 0.98c$ at 4 Bev for protons).   This result points out the essential difference between the acceleration of electrons and of positive ions, yet it shows that the problems become essentially identical at extremely high energies.

Another method of plotting the velocity of particles as a function of energy is shown in Fig. 5-18. Here the ratio $\beta = v/c$ obtained from Eq. (5-47) is plotted against energy T on a logarithmic scale for the several particles. This presentation shows the relativistic approach to constant velocity and serves to identify the energy range which requires the use of the relativistic equations for the different particles.

5-11. ORBITAL STABILITY

An additional requirement for accelerators is that they provide restoring forces for particles which deviate in direction from the orbit plane. This is a necessary requirement, as can readily be noted by considering the effect of a small, angular deviation from the plane for a particle which is traversing hundreds or thousands of revolutions. In an absolutely uniform magnetic field the orbit would be a helical spiral of small pitch,

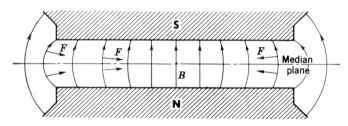

Fig. 5-19. Radially decreasing magnetic field in the cyclotron, showing the concave shape of the lines of flux and the direction of the magnetic forces acting on orbiting particles to restore deviant particles to the median plane.

and the axial displacement from the plane would increase linearly with the number of revolutions. In a magnetic field or vacuum chamber of finite extent most of the particles would be lost against the poles or the walls. It is essential that the magnetic field provide restoring forces to focus the particles about the central orbit plane.

Such restoring forces can exist in a *magnetic field which decreases in magnitude with increasing radius.* In this field the lines of magnetic flux are concave inward. Figure 5-19 is a diagram of the magnetic field between cyclotron pole faces and shows the direction of the forces on charged particles moving in orbits above or below the median plane. The direction of the force on the moving particle is normal to the local direction of the magnetic flux. It will have a downward component for particles above the median plane and an upward component for particles below the median plane. It is evident that field shaping of this sort will provide the desired restoring forces to prevent the particles from wandering off in the vertical or axial direction.

The considerations leading to appropriate field shaping to prevent particle loss in the radial direction are best seen through a study of the general equations of motion (5-14).   For our present purpose these equations simplify materially.   There is no electric field involved and there is no azimuthal component of B.   Also we shall assume that the radial and vertical excursions are so small that they do not affect the velocity in the θ direction; we can then write $r\dot{\theta} = v$ and assume that v does not change materially during the period under consideration.

We know that the field must decrease in the radial direction for vertical restoration of the particles to the orbit.   To give this statement a mathematical form we shall write

$$B_z = B_0 \left(\frac{r_0}{r}\right)^n \tag{5-57}$$

where n = positive constant
r_0 = radius of "equilibrium orbit"
B_0 = value of B_z at equilibrium orbit

Since we assume that r makes only small excursions from r_0, we can write Eq. (5-57) in the approximate form

$$B_z = B_0 \left(1 - \frac{n\,\Delta r}{r_0}\right) \tag{5-58}$$

where $\Delta r = r - r_0$.   The other magnetic-field component B_r follows from Maxwell's equations (5-1), which state that for this case curl $\mathbf{B} = 0$ and

$$\frac{\partial B_z}{\partial r} = \frac{\partial B_r}{\partial z} \tag{5-59}$$

From Eqs. (5-58) and (5-59)

$$B_r = -\frac{nB_0 z}{r_0} \tag{5-60}$$

We are interested only in the radial and axial components of the equations of motion (5-14).   With the substitutions just outlined, they become

$$\frac{d}{dt}(m\,\Delta\dot{r}) - \frac{mv^2}{r_0}\left(1 - \frac{\Delta r}{r_0}\right) = evB_0\left(1 - \frac{n\,\Delta r}{r_0}\right) \tag{5-61}$$

and

$$\frac{d}{dt}(m\dot{z}) = \frac{evBn_0 z}{r_0} \tag{5-62}$$

But we define the equilibrium orbit as that orbit for which both $\Delta\dot{r}$ and Δr are always zero.   For this case Eq. (5-61) simplifies to

$$\frac{mv^2}{r_0} = -evB_0 \tag{5-63}$$

This equation is identical with Eq. (5-41), which was presented in connection with pure circular motion; the circular orbit discussed then has now become the equilibrium orbit for the more general motion under study.

Equations (5-61) and (5-62) become still simpler when Eq. (5-63) is used as a substitution for all terms including B_0. We make the further substitution of the symbol ω for the angular velocity v/r_0 and obtain finally

$$\frac{d}{dt}\,(m\,\Delta\dot{r}) = -m\omega^2(1-n)\,\Delta r \qquad (5\text{-}64)$$

and

$$\frac{d}{dt}\,(m\dot{z}) = -m\omega^2 nz \qquad (5\text{-}65)$$

These two equations have the general form of equations of motion. On the right-hand side of each equation is the term that represents the force which restores the particle to the orbit or repels it from the orbit. So long as the sign of the term is negative for positive displacements and positive for negative displacements, the particle will continually be forced back to the equilibrium orbit whenever it becomes displaced from that orbit. Evidently this can be true only if n and $(1-n)$ are both positive, in other words, if n lies between 0 and unity.

From the qualitative discussion of the vertical motion presented earlier it seemed essential that n should be positive so that the field would decrease with increasing radius. The reason for radial restoring forces existing only when $(1-n)$ is positive is not so easily seen but may become clearer from the following argument: In the coordinate system of the particle the centrifugal force term mv^2/r must be balanced by the magnetic force evB_z. If these two terms are plotted as a function of radius (Fig. 5-20), it becomes evident that, so long as B_z does not fall off faster than $1/r$ [with $(1-n)$ remaining positive], there will be a radius at which the curves cross and the two forces are balanced. This will be the radius of the equilibrium orbit. Outside of this radius the inward magnetic force will be greater; inside of this radius the outward centrifugal force will be greater; thus there will always be a net force restoring the particle to the equilibrium orbit.

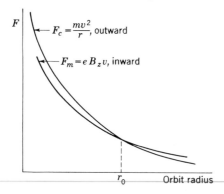

Fig. 5-20. Forces acting on a particle in a circular orbit in a radially decreasing magnetic field, showing a net force acting to restore a deviant particle to the equilibrium orbit r_0.

These restoring forces are sufficiently strong to restore a deviant particle fairly rapidly to its orbit. In the case of a 300-Mev electron traveling in an orbit of 1 m radius in a field whose n value is 0.5, the restoring force on a particle which strays 1 cm from the orbit is the same as that which would be exerted by an electric field of about 1.5 Mv/m.

5-12. THE FREE OSCILLATIONS

Equations (5-64) and (5-65) not only show that restoring forces can exist for a proper field shape, but also give the character of the motion under these forces. The general form of these equations is similar to that for simple harmonic motion, which can have the form

$$\frac{d}{dt} (\dot{x}) = -\omega_0^2 x \tag{5-66}$$

where x = displacement

$\dot{x}$ = velocity

ω_0 = angular frequency of oscillatory motion

[For example, in an oscillatory system of mass and spring, the angular frequency $\omega_0 = (K/m)^{1/2}$, where K is the spring constant and m the mass, and the motion is described by $x = x_m \cos \omega_0 t$.]

In order for Eqs. (5-64) and (5-65) to represent harmonic motion, the quantities m and ω must be essentially constant over the period of motion. We shall assume this to be the case in order to estimate the frequency of oscillations about the equilibrium orbit. Referring to Eq. (5-66) we find

$$f_r = \frac{\omega}{2\pi} (1 - n)^{1/2} \qquad \text{(for radial motion)} \tag{5-67}$$

$$f_z = \frac{\omega}{2\pi} n^{1/2} \qquad \text{(for axial motion)} \tag{5-68}$$

But $\omega/2\pi$ is the frequency of revolution f_0 of the particle in the equilibrium orbit. Evidently the oscillations about the orbit take place with a frequency only slightly lower than the particle frequency of revolution, since n must lie between 0 and 1. For example, if $n = 0.5$, both oscillations have a frequency of $0.707f_0$ and would complete one period during 1.41 revolutions. This oscillation is sufficiently rapid to justify the assumption above that no important changes will take place in m or ω during an oscillation period.

These oscillations in radius and in vertical position are known as the "free oscillations" since they continue, once started, without the action of any but the guiding field. Since the free oscillations were first studied in connection with the betatron,[12] they are also known as "betatron oscillations" in spite of the fact that they are observed in many other accelerator species.

The free oscillations usually are initiated early in the accelerating cycle. They may be due to errors in the injection system or to the finite size of the injector, or they may be initiated by small-angle scattering by the residual gas in the vacuum chamber. Gas scattering rapidly decreases in importance as particle energy increases, and the free oscillations which remain as acceleration proceeds are merely a continuation of those generated at or shortly after injection.

It is now important to assure ourselves that the amplitude of these oscillations will not grow with time. Since both the mass of the particle and the restoring force (proportional to $m\omega^2$) increase during the acceleration, we should expect that the oscillation amplitude would decrease, and this is indeed the case. Since we are now considering a long time relative to one free oscillation period, it is no longer legitimate to make the assumptions which led to the simple harmonic solution of Eqs. (5-64) and (5-65). We must now make a more precise solution of these equations. The next higher approximation to the solution of the equations of motion takes the form

$$\Delta r = C_1(m\omega \sqrt{1-n})^{-\frac{1}{2}} \sin (\int \omega \sqrt{1-n} \, dt) \qquad (5\text{-}69)$$
$$z = C_2(m\omega \sqrt{n})^{-\frac{1}{2}} \sin (\int \omega \sqrt{n} \, dt) \qquad (5\text{-}70)$$

These solutions are valid to a high order of accuracy and are sufficient for application in almost all practical cases. They show that the oscillation amplitudes damp like $(m\omega)^{-\frac{1}{2}}$. From Eq. (5-41) this is equivalent to damping like $B_0^{-\frac{1}{2}}$. At low, nonrelativistic energies, kinetic energy is proportional to B_0^2, so in this range the free-oscillation amplitude is proportional to the inverse one-quarter power of the kinetic energy $T^{-\frac{1}{4}}$. At high relativistic energies the kinetic energy becomes proportional to B_0, and the rate of damping of the free oscillations increases to the point where the amplitude is proportional to the inverse one-half power of the kinetic energy $T^{-\frac{1}{2}}$.

The assumptions used in the derivation of the damping equations (5-69) and (5-70) are valid unless one of the quantities m, ω, $1-n$, or n approaches zero. In actual accelerators m and ω are always finite. Only in the case of the cyclotron do we run into difficulty with n, which is approximately zero at the beginning of acceleration. Since this problem relates only to the cyclotron, we postpone its consideration to the next chapter.

5-13. CONSIDERATIONS AFFECTING ACCELERATOR DESIGN

In the design of a particle accelerator one of the most important decisions is the choice of aperture dimensions. The costs of the most expensive components usually depend strongly on the size of the aperture. Since the aperture must be large enough to contain the free oscillations of particles around their equilibrium orbit, the probable amplitudes must be estimated at an early stage of design.

In the cyclotron, where an approximately uniform magnetic field must be maintained over a large radial extent, it is not possible to use a large value of n. The n value chosen is that which is just sufficient to provide the necessary axial focusing and usually varies from less than 0.01 near the center to slightly higher values as the outer periphery is approached.

In ring-shaped accelerators with iron-cored magnets, such as the betatron and the synchrotron, it is usually more economical to widen the region of useful magnetic field in the radial direction than it is to enlarge the gap between poles and provide space for axial oscillations. Consequently the n value chosen is as high as possible to provide strong restoring forces in the axial direction. The usual choice is an n value of about 0.7. In the few ring-shaped accelerators which have used air-cored fields without iron magnetic circuits, on the other hand, axial extension of the field is easier and cheaper than radial extension, so n values of the order of 0.3 are appropriate.

The damping of free-oscillation amplitudes is of major significance in accelerator design and operation. Amplitudes have been shown to decrease with increasing particle energy, varying with $T^{-1/4}$ at low energies and with $T^{-1/2}$ at relativistic energies. This means that the available aperture of useful field at the start of acceleration determines initial amplitudes and is the limiting factor on the intensity of the accepted beam. The damping causes the beam to decrease in cross section during acceleration, so the high-energy beam is much smaller. Beam dimensions have a direct bearing on the design of targets or of ejection systems for emergent beams. In an electron synchrotron, for example, an initial beam width of more than 10 cm will be reduced to a few millimeters at high energy.

If a mechanism for coupling exists between the radial and axial free oscillations and if the frequencies are in fundamental or harmonic resonance, oscillation energy can be transferred from one mode to the other. Small imperfections in the uniformity of the magnetic field are sufficient to provide significant coupling. The frequencies of the two modes are identical for $n = 0.5$, so this value of n is usually avoided in design. This is not a serious limitation if the available apertures in the two coordinate directions are similar in size, but it becomes important when the axial dimension is reduced significantly below the radial dimension. Harmonic resonances can occur for n values of 0.2 and 0.8, for which the ratios of frequencies are 1:2 or 2:1; these values also are avoided in design. In the standard cyclotron the number of revolutions required to cross the $n = 0.2$ resonance is small, so effective coupling is not observed and the particle beam can remain in orbit out to larger n values. In the synchrocyclotron, however, the rate of acceleration is much slower and the beam is observed to "blow up" axially at the radial location where $n = 0.2$. These points will be discussed in more detail in the following chapters on magnetic accelerators.

REFERENCES

1. M. A. Tuve, O. Dahl, and L. R. Hafstad, *Phys. Rev.*, **48**:241 (1935).
2. W. W. Buechner, E. S. Lamar, and R. J. Van de Graaff, *J. Appl. Phys.*, **12**:141 (1941).
3. V. K. Zworykin et al., "Electron Optics and the Electron Microscope," Wiley (1945).
4. J. R. Pierce, "Theory and Design of Electron Beams," Van Nostrand (1949).
5. V. E. Cosslett, "Introduction to Electron Optics," Oxford (1950).
6. F. Terman, "Radio Engineers' Handbook," McGraw-Hill (1943).
7. E. D. Courant, M. S. Livingston, and H. S. Snyder, *Phys. Rev.*, **88**:1190 (1952).
8. J. P. Blewett, *Phys. Rev.*, **88**:1197 (1952).
9. E. D. Courant, M. S. Livingston, H. S. Snyder, and J. P. Blewett, *Phys. Rev.*, **91**:202 (1953).
10. E. D. Courant and H. S. Snyder, *Ann. Phys.*, **3**:1 (1958).
11. J. P. Blewett, N. C. Christofilos, and A. M. Vash, *Phys. Rev.*, **99**:652 (1955).
12. D. W. Kerst and R. Serber, *Phys. Rev.*, **60**:53 (1941).

At the head of the facing page is an illustration of the 16-Mev cyclotron at the Massachusetts Institute of Technology.

6

The Cyclotron
Magnetic Resonance Accelerator

The cyclotron accelerates light positive ions to high energy without the use of high voltage, thereby avoiding the limitations of insulation break-down. Ions move in widening semicircular paths in a uniform magnetic field, crossing back and forth between two electrodes in resonance with an oscillatory electric field. The ions are accelerated at each traversal of the electric field, attaining a final energy hundreds of times greater than that available from the impressed voltage on the electrodes. A simple analogy is the garden swing which can be urged to large amplitude by successive small pushes, each push timed with the natural period of the swing.

This is the principle of resonance acceleration, and the technical name for the machine is the "magnetic resonance accelerator." However, the more concise term "cyclotron," which developed as laboratory slang, has become the popular name for the instrument. The name is so well known, in fact, that it is often loosely applied to designate any type of particle accelerator, and is essentially synonymous with "atom smasher." The cyclotron was the first of the resonance accelerators. It supplied the principle and the basic concepts for the development of the modern high-energy accelerators. The simplicity of the concepts and their prompt success stimulated a rapid development which can scarcely be matched in any other field of science.

133

6-1. HISTORICAL DEVELOPMENT

The cyclotron principle was proposed in 1930 by the late Ernest O. Lawrence[1] of the University of California. It was suggested by the experiment of Wideröe[2] in 1928 in which ions of sodium and potassium were accelerated to twice the applied voltage in traversing two tubular electrodes in line between which an oscillatory electric field was applied—an elementary linear accelerator (see Chap. 10).

The conception* of the idea occurred in the library of the University of California in the summer of 1929, when Lawrence was browsing through the current journals and read Wideröe's paper in the *Archiv für Electrotechnik*. Lawrence speculated on possible variations of this resonance principle, including the use of a magnetic field to deflect the particles in circular paths so they would return to the first electrode and thus reuse the electrical field in the gap. He discovered that the equations of motion predicted a constant period of revolution, so the particles could be accelerated in resonance with an oscillatory electric field.

The principle of acceleration was announced in a short article in *Science* by Lawrence and Edlefsen[1] in 1930. Edlefsen was a graduate student who had just completed a thesis in another field; on Lawrence's request he attempted a brief preliminary experimental test of the principle. The experiment was not successful in demonstrating resonance, and no experimental results were reported. However, the basic soundness of the principle was evident and justified the public announcement in advance of experimental proof.

The senior author (MSL) was a graduate student at Berkeley at that time; this problem was suggested by Professor Lawrence as the subject for an experimental research investigation to demonstrate the validity of the resonance principle. A doctorate thesis by Livingston[3] dated April 14, 1931, reporting the results of the study, is on file in the University of California library. This was the first experimental verification of the principle of cyclotron resonance.

For this preliminary study only small-size laboratory equipment was available, including an electromagnet of 4 in. pole diameter. An illustration from this thesis (Fig. 6-1) shows the arrangement of components which is still a basic feature of all cyclotrons. A vacuum-tube oscillator provided 2000 volts radiofrequency potential to the electrode, with a frequency which could be varied by adjusting the number of turns in the resonant inductance. Hydrogen ions (H^+ and H_2^+) were produced by ionization of hydrogen gas in the chamber by electrons emitted from a tungsten-wire cathode near the center. Resonant ions which reached the edge of the chamber were observed in a shielded collector cup. Sharp peaks were observed in the collected current at the magnetic field of resonance for H_2^+ ions (and later for H^+ ions), as illustrated in Fig. 6-2, which

---

* As told to the senior author (MSL) by Professor Lawrence.

shows a typical resonance curve taken from the thesis.   At the collector radius and for the highest field used, the expected energy of the H_2^+ ions was 80,000 ev, confirmed by electric-field deflection measurements.   By varying frequency of the rf accelerating fields (reported as wavelength), resonance was observed over a broad range of frequencies and magnetic fields (Fig. 6-3), proving conclusively the validity of the resonance principle.

The next step in the development, the first practical cyclotron, used a magnet with pole faces 10 in. in diameter and produced protons of over

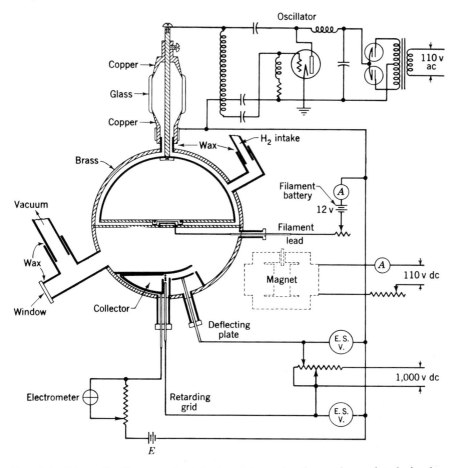

Fig. 6-1. Schematic diagram of original cyclotron chamber and associated circuits. (Livingston.[3])

1 Mev energy, the first time that controlled particles of this energy had been obtained in scientific history.   The development is described in a paper by Lawrence and Livingston[4] in 1932.

A few months before this instrument was completed, Cockcroft and Walton[5] at the Cavendish laboratory had observed for the first time the

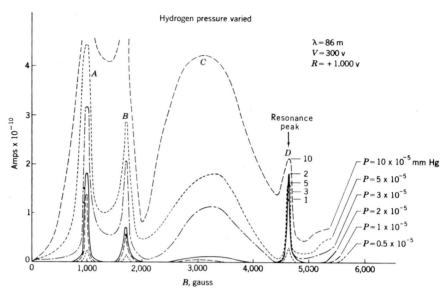

Fig. 6-2. Typical resonance curve of beam current versus magnetic field.   (Livingston.[3])

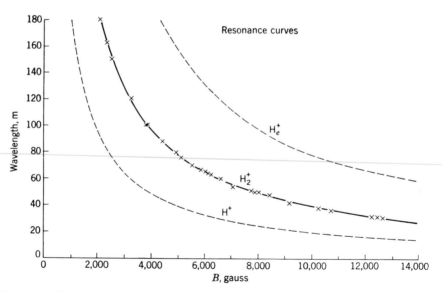

Fig. 6-3. Experimental verification of cyclotron resonance relation.   (Livingston.[3])

disintegration of Li nuclei by artificially accelerated particles, using protons of 400 kev energy (see Chap. 2).   The 1-Mev protons from the first cyclotron were promptly used to confirm and extend the British results. Disintegrations were observed in Li and in several new targets, as reported in 1932 by Lawrence, Livingston, and White.[6]

These early successes stimulated interest in many laboratories.   In Berkeley, plans were made for higher energies, and Professor Lawrence obtained financial support from the Research Corporation, which led to the design and construction of a much larger cyclotron, the "27-inch." The iron core for this large electromagnet was taken from a dismantled Poulson-arc radio transmitter donated by the Federal Telegraph Company. By the time the cyclotron was completed in 1933, ions of the newly discovered and separated heavy-hydrogen isotope (deuterons) were available, obtained from heavy-water samples supplied by the late Prof. G. N. Lewis of the chemistry department of the university.   The machine was rapidly tuned up (primarily by "shimming" of the magnetic field) to produce 3-Mev and then 5-Mev deuterons.   A team of young, enthusiastic scientists explored the new fields of deuteron reactions, induced radioactivity, and neutron production; a dozen or more short papers were published describing the progress.   The 5-Mev deuteron cyclotron was described by Lawrence and Livingston[7] in 1934.   At this time Livingston left Berkeley to join the physics department at Cornell University and to build another research cyclotron.   A later stage, after expansion of the pole faces to 37 in. diam and further development to 8 Mev energy, was reported by Lawrence and Cooksey[8] in 1936.

Potential medical applications of high-energy neutrons, available in adequate intensity for the first time, justified the design and construction of the 60-in. "Crocker" cyclotron and the development of an associated medical laboratory on the University of California campus.   This machine was completed in 1939, first operating at 16 Mev and later producing 20-Mev deuterons or 40-Mev helium ions.   It is the prototype of the modern standard cyclotron and was described by Lawrence, Alvarez, Brobeck, Cooksey, Corson, McMillan, Salisbury, and Thornton.[9]

In 1939 Professor Lawrence was awarded the Nobel Prize in physics in recognition of his achievements in the conception and development of the cyclotron.   His untimely death in 1958 terminated an impressive career as Director of the University of California Radiation Laboratory and in many positions of scientific responsibility for the United States government.

Meanwhile cyclotrons were constructed in many other laboratories, at first largely designed by graduates of the Berkeley school.   Soon these laboratories were able to make important contributions to the development.   Among the laboratories contributing significantly to the progress of cyclotronics in the early years were those at the University of Michigan,

Cornell University,[10] Columbia University, Princeton University,[11] University of Rochester, Washington University at St. Louis, Bartol Research Laboratory,[12] University of Illinois,[13] University of Indiana, Purdue University, Carnegie Institution of Washington, Harvard University, and the Massachusetts Institute of Technology.[14] A monograph by W. B. Mann[15] (1940) describes the fundamental principles and tells some of the story of cyclotron development in the Berkeley laboratory.

As a result of widespread effort, closely coordinated by publications, correspondence, visits, and exchange of personnel, the modern cyclotron is the composite product of many laboratories and scores of individual contributions. A large number of the technical developments have not been published, but after alteration and improvement as they passed from one laboratory to another, they have become part of the general store of technical information. One of the more detailed publications, by Livingston[14] in 1944, describes some of these features, illustrated by the design and performance of the MIT cyclotron, which operates at 16 Mev for deuterons or 32 Mev for helium ions.

Several commercial firms have joined in the development of the fixed-frequency cyclotron. The Collins Radio Company designed and constructed two 60-in. machines, for the Brookhaven National Laboratory and the Argonne National Laboratory, under the direction of W. W. Salisbury. The General Electric Company has built a machine of the same size for the National Committee of Aeronautics Laboratory in Cleveland. The Philips Laboratory at Eindhoven and Brown-Boveri in Switzerland have built several cyclotrons for European laboratories.

Theoretical analysis of the principles of operation and of focusing was developed by Rose[16] at Cornell University and by Wilson[17,18] at the University of California in 1938. A much more comprehensive theoretical treatment by Cohen[19] of the Oak Ridge National Laboratory gives a sound basis for the design of the modern high-energy, high-intensity cyclotrons.

The cyclotron has become a symbol of nuclear physics, and its simple principles are taught in most high-school and college physics courses. Small working models have been built by students in several high schools, and a report of one such installation has been published.[20]

A new field of special scientific interest has been opened with the development of ion sources for multiple-charge heavy ions for acceleration in a cyclotron. The Oak Ridge National Laboratory[21] has been a leader in this field of ion-source development. Ions such as C_{12}^{++}, C_{12}^{3+}, N_{14}^{3+}, and N_{14}^{4+} have been produced in adequate intensities to be accelerated in the cyclotron[22] and have been used for many research studies. An ion such as C_{12}^{3+} has almost the same e/m value as He^+ and can be accelerated at similar values of frequency and magnetic field.

However, because of its triple charge, the energy is three times that of an He$^+$ ion under these conditions.   Ions with other e/m values can be tuned for resonant acceleration by adjusting the applied frequency of the cyclotron.   Machines in other laboratories have been adapted to heavy-ion acceleration; an example is the 225-cm cyclotron at the Nobel Institute in Stockholm.[23]   Interest in the field, notably at Oak Ridge, has resulted in designs for cyclotrons specifically planned for this purpose.

6-2. THE RESONANCE PRINCIPLE

In the cyclotron an electromagnet is used to provide a nearly uniform magnetic field between the flat faces of cylindrical poles of large radius. A vacuum chamber fits between the pole faces, and two hollow copper

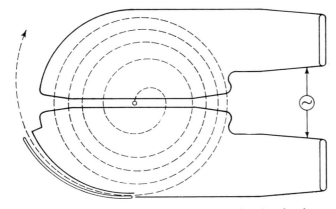

Fig. 6-4. Schematic diagram of cyclotron electrodes showing ion paths.

electrodes (Fig. 6-4) are mounted inside the vacuum chamber.   These electrodes were originally semicircular in shape, as though a flat, hollow pillbox had been cut through a diameter.   Because of their shape, the electrodes are frequently referred to in laboratory slang as D's or dees. A radiofrequency power supply provides an alternating electric field between the diametral faces of the two D's.   Ions are accelerated in this region of crossed electric and magnetic fields.

Positive ions are produced near the center of the chamber between the D's by an ion source and are accelerated toward and into the electrode, which is negatively charged at the instant.   In the electric-field-free region inside the D the ions are acted upon only by the uniform magnetic field and travel in circular orbits in a plane normal to the field.   After traversing a semicircular path, each ion returns to the diametral gap between electrodes and comes again under the influence of the electric field.   For the condition of resonance, the magnetic field is adjusted so the time required for an ion to complete a half-circle is equal to the time for reversal of the oscillatory electric field.   So, after completing the first half-circle the ion experiences another acceleration, acquires higher velocity, and traverses a path of larger radius within the other electrode. As long as this resonance is maintained, the ions are accelerated each time they cross the gap, traveling in ever-widening semicircles until they reach the periphery of the electrodes.

As was shown in Chap. 5, the force on an ion of mass m, charge e, and velocity v moving at right angles to a uniform magnetic field B has the magnitude evB and is exerted in a direction normal to the magnetic field and to the direction of motion of the ion.   This force causes the ion to travel in a circular path of radius r whose value is obtained by balancing the centrifugal force and the magnetic force thus [cf. Eq. (5-41)]:

$$\frac{mv^2}{r} = evB \tag{6-1}$$

The frequency of revolution in the circular path is [cf. Eq. (5-42)]

$$f = \frac{v}{2\pi r} = \frac{eB}{2\pi m} \tag{6-2}$$

This frequency is constant in a uniform magnetic field so long as the mass m is constant.

For acceleration in the cyclotron the frequency of the alternating electric field applied to the electrodes is set equal to the ion revolution frequency.   The linear relation between applied frequency and magnetic field is the fundamental equation of cyclotron resonance.   When evaluated for the e/m values characteristic of light ions, it gives

Protons: f (megacycles) $= 1.52B$ (kilogauss)
Deuterons: f $= 0.76B$
He^{++}: f $= 0.76B$

These relations are plotted in Fig. 6-5 to illustrate the range of frequencies required to produce resonant acceleration in magnetic fields up to 20 kilogauss.

A voltage-time graph of the potential between the electrodes of a cyclotron is shown in Fig. 6-6.   On each traversal of the gap between electrodes the particle will acquire an increment of kinetic energy $\Delta T = eV$ of magnitude determined by the phase of crossing the gap.   Particles will be moving in opposite directions in successive passages, so the energy increments are cumulative.   A resonant particle crossing at the phase of peak field (point 1) will continue to cross the gap at the same phase and will reach maximum energy in the minimum number of turns.   Particles crossing at other phases, such as points 2 and 3, will acquire smaller increments but will remain in resonance for a larger number of turns to reach

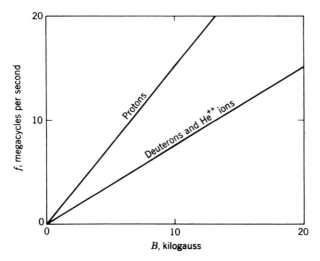

Fig. 6-5. Plot of cyclotron resonance relation for H$^+$, D$^+$, and He^{++}.

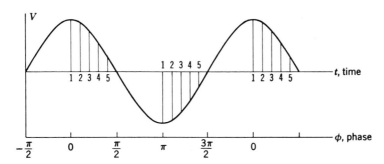

Fig. 6-6. Voltage-time graph of the alternating electric potential between D's of a cyclotron. Resonant ions which cross the gap at the phases 1, 2, 3, . . . are accelerated on each traversal.

maximum energy. If there are N accelerations and the average potential difference between D's each time the ions cross the gap is V, the final energy will be

$$T = NVe = \frac{1}{2} mv_m{}^2 \qquad (6\text{-}3)$$

Kinetic energy can also be written in terms of magnetic field B and final orbit radius R by use of Eq. (6-1):

$$\frac{T}{e} = \frac{1}{2}\frac{e}{m} B^2R^2 \qquad (6\text{-}4)$$

Here the kinetic energy per unit charge is shown to be proportional to the square of the momentum in units of BR. It is evaluated for the light ions in Mev units, with B in kilogauss and R in inches (units established by long usage in the cyclotron field), as

Protons: $T \text{ (Mev)} = 3.12 \times 10^{-4} B^2 R^2$
Deuterons: $T \qquad\quad = 1.56 \times 10^{-4} B^2 R^2$
He^{++}: $T \qquad\quad = 3.12 \times 10^{-4} B^2 R^2$

Note that although He^{++} has essentially the same e/m value as the deuteron, its double charge gives it twice the kinetic energy of the deuteron.

In using these relations to determine the dimensions of a cyclotron magnet we must remember that the radius R applies to the extent of the uniform magnetic field; the physical radius of pole faces must be larger by about one-half the gap length. Since the saturation limit of iron prescribes a maximum magnetic field in iron-cored magnets of about 18 kilogauss (depending somewhat on quality of iron and on the specific design), the maximum energy is roughly determined by the square of the pole-face radius or diameter. With a chosen magnet size, the ion energy obtainable at radius R increases with the square of the magnetic field.

An informative expression for orbit radius can be obtained by eliminating T from Eqs. (6-3) and (6-4):

$$r = \frac{1}{B}\left(2\,\frac{m}{e}\,V\right)^{1/2} N^{1/2} \tag{6-5}$$

We note that the radii of successive paths increase with a sequence of square roots of integral numbers $N^{1/2}$, getting closer together as N becomes large. This relation was used to draw the schematic ion path of Fig. 6-4, in which N is an impractically small number, but which illustrates the expanding paths.

These basic relations can be illustrated by data representative of the MIT 42-in. cyclotron. At the maximum magnetic field used (17.7 kilogauss), the useful region of uniformity extends to a radius of 18.75 in. The resonant frequency for deuterons, from Eq. (6-2), is 13.5 megacycles/sec. The maximum kinetic energy, from Eq. (6-4), is 16.0 Mev. The peak radiofrequency voltage between D's when operating at full beam intensity is measured to be 140 kv (70-kv peak between each D and ground). Ions experience phase shifts as they are accelerated, as will be shown later, so a representative ion might make 100 revolutions or receive 200 accelerations of an average value of 80 kv before attaining the final energy of 16.0 Mev. Successive ion path radii, computed from Eq. (6-5) and assuming an initial 40-kv and subsequent 80-kv accelerations, would be 0.9, 1.5, 2.0, 2.3, . . . in. Actually the first few paths will be distorted spirals rather than semicircles, as shown later. The difference in radius between the ninety-ninth and one-hundredth revolutions, Δr, is found to be about 0.1 in.

After acceleration to the maximum practical energy and orbit radius R the ions enter a deflection channel defined by a septum of somewhat larger radius of curvature. An electric field is maintained across this channel by a negative dc potential on an insulated electrode paralleling the septum. The difference in radius Δr between the last two orbits is sufficient for a useful fraction of the beam to pass behind the septum, where it is deflected outward in an opening spiral path as an emergent beam.

6-3. MAGNETIC AND ELECTRIC FOCUSING

An understanding of the detailed motion of the particles in their orbits is important, in order to appreciate the reasons for the specialized techniques which have evolved. The basic resonance principle applies to an idealized particle moving in an orbit located on the median plane of the cyclotron chamber and crossing the accelerating gaps in perfect synchronism with the electric field. However, essentially all ions being accelerated deviate from these ideal conditions; they perform oscillations about the median plane and they migrate in phase of crossing the gap. Those which remain in resonance are enclosed within an envelope inside the D's which is limited both in the transverse spread about the median plane and in an azimuthal sector enclosing the accepted phase band. During each radiofrequency cycle such a loose bunch of ions starts from the source, and the center of the bunch follows the idealized expanding orbit described previously. In each subsequent cycle another bunch is emitted and follows in the same track. We shall see that the bunches are discrete only for the first few revolutions; eventually they overlap and merge into an almost continuous radial distribution of all possible energies, contained within the limiting envelope in the transverse dimension but bounded in phase to an azimuthal sector which is probably not greater than one-quarter of the chamber. Our purpose in this section is to describe the magnetic and electric forces acting on the individual ions and holding the ions within the enclosing envelope.

The feature which makes the method of multiple acceleration practical is the focusing resulting from the shape of the magnetic field. Ions making 100 or more revolutions in a cyclotron traverse a path hundreds of meters in total length. In a uniform magnetic field, in which field lines are strictly parallel, there would be no vertical deflections and no focusing. Ions traveling at a small angle to the median plane would follow a helical path and would strike against the top or bottom surfaces of the D's; the probability of an ion reaching the collector at the periphery would be vanishingly small.

Magnetic focusing results from a small decrease in magnetic field with increasing radius, so that lines of magnetic flux are concave inward.

This shape of field exists naturally near the periphery of cylindrical poles as a result of "fringing." In the central region an adequately decreasing field can be obtained by shaping the pole faces so that the gap widens slightly with increasing radius, or the effective gap length in the center can be shortened by inserting disk-shaped iron shims in gaps between the vacuum chamber and the magnet poles. At any point off the median plane in such a concave field the field has a radial as well as an axial component (see Fig. 6-7). Deviant particles traversing such a field experience restoring forces due to the radial field component tending to return them to the median plane. The direction of forces acting on orbiting particles is also illustrated in Fig. 6-7. The magnitude of the radial component of magnetic field, and thus of the restoring force, is proportional to the displacement from the equilibrium orbit.

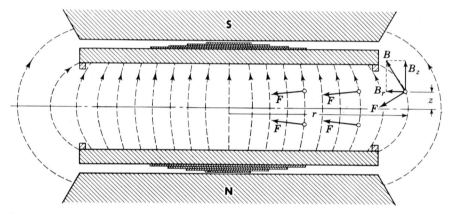

Fig. 6-7. Radially decreasing magnetic field between poles of a cyclotron magnet, showing shims for field correction.

Motion of any system under a restoring force which is proportional to the displacement is oscillatory in nature. In Chap. 5 the equations of motion were analyzed and general solutions were obtained of the resulting oscillatory motion. The results, as they apply to the type of field used in the cyclotron, can be summarized briefly. It was found useful to express the radial rate of decrease of field in terms of a radial exponent or index n defined by the relation [cf. Eq. (5-57)]

$$B = B_0 \left(\frac{r_0}{r}\right)^n \tag{6-6}$$

where B_0 is the field at some fixed radius r_0 and B is the field at a different radius r. The index n is obtained by differentiation to be $n = -\dfrac{r}{B}\dfrac{dB}{dr}$. In applying this concept to the cyclotron we determine the n value at any radius r from the field B and the local radial field gradient dB/dr at r.

Numerical n values will range from 0 at the center to values larger than 2 in the fringing field at the edge of the poles.   In Chap. 5 it was shown that for particle oscillations about an equilibrium orbit to be stable for both axial and radial coordinates, the value of n must be in the range $0 < n < 1$.

The requirement of a radially decreasing field for axial focusing limits the range of validity of the basic resonance relation, in which a uniform field is required for resonance at constant applied frequency.   The compromise which makes the cyclotron a practical accelerator is that the radial decrease in field be kept small so that resonance can be maintained over a sufficient number of accelerations for the ions to reach maximum energy.   Experience is the best guide to the optimum magnitude of this radial decrease and the shape of the field.   Those cyclotrons which have achieved high efficiency in acceleration of ions and a high-intensity beam show a consistent shape of magnetic field.   This is an approximately linear decrease over most of the pole face out to the region where peripheral fringing sets in and where the decrease becomes more rapid.   For medium-energy cyclotrons (15 to 20 Mev) the total decrease below the value of the central field out to the exit slit is about 2 per cent.   The radial decrease can be larger (3 to 4 per cent) in small machines in which D voltage is relatively high and the number of revolutions small.   It should be smaller ($\sim$1 per cent) for very large cyclotrons which approach the relativistic limit of ion energy (see Sec. 6-12) where maintenance of resonance over the maximum number of revolutions is a prime requisite.

A typical radial field distribution is that of the MIT cyclotron (Fig. 6-8).   This field gave the highest beam intensities and was the culmination of an exhaustive empirical program of field shaping.   This program used thin disk shims of various radii inserted in the two shimming gaps outside the pole faces as well as ring shims of several sizes mounted on the inner periphery of the pole faces.   The values of the index n computed from this curve are also indicated in Fig. 6-8.   The n value rises almost linearly from zero at the center to 0.02 at 15 in. (where fringing effects start), then increases rapidly to 0.40 at 18.75 in. (exit-slit location) and to 1.0 at 19.25 in.

Returning to the discussion of particle oscillations, we found in Chap. 5 that a particle displaced from the median plane in such a radially decreasing field experiences restoring forces which produce transverse oscillations about the median plane.   The frequency of these axial oscillations is

$$f_z = n^{1/2} f_0 \qquad (6\text{-}7)$$

where f_0 is the cyclotron resonance frequency given by Eq. (6-2).   The initial amplitude z_0 of these oscillations will be determined by the internal aperture of the D's near the ion source.   For the radial field distribution described above, the frequency of axial oscillations is small compared with the orbital frequency over most of the pole face. At $r = 15$ in., where $n = 0.02$, for instance, $f_z = 0.14f_0$, so seven or more revolutions are required to complete a vertical oscillation cycle. Frequency increases to a maximum of about $0.6f_0$ at the maximum practical exit-slit location.

The amplitude of the vertical oscillations decreases with acceleration to higher energy and to larger orbit radii. This can be seen qualitatively as a consequence of the increase in strength of the restoring forces while the energy of transverse oscillations remains essentially constant. The

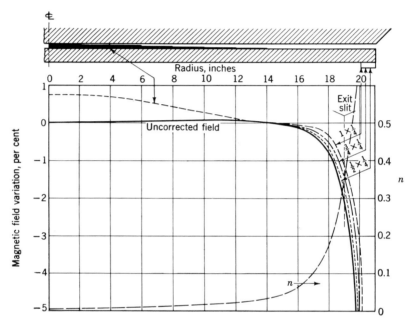

Fig. 6-8. Measured values of magnetic field as a function of pole-face radius for the MIT cyclotron.[14] The curves show the uncorrected field and the field obtained with disk shims and three sizes of ring shims at the edge of the poles.

damping relation of Eq. (5-70) shows that the amplitude is a function of the quantity $\omega n^{1/2}$, but it is not valid when the n value is extremely small, such as near the center of a cyclotron. For this special case in which the motion is nonrelativistic, we return to a study of the equation of this oscillatory motion [Eq. (5-65)], which can be written

$$\ddot{z} + \omega^2 n z = 0 \qquad (6\text{-}8)$$

The optimum shape of magnetic field in a cyclotron was found to be one in which the n value rises approximately linearly with radius. The angular frequency is nearly constant, and in Eq. (6-5) it was shown that the orbit radius varies with the square root of the number of revolutions and hence with the square root of the time of acceleration. Consequently, n is proportional to $t^{1/2}$, and Eq. (6-8) can be rewritten

$$\ddot{z} + (\text{const}) \, t^{1/2} z = 0 \qquad (6\text{-}9)$$

This constant is an arithmetic combination of machine parameters, which for the MIT cyclotron has the value 4.3×10^{16}. Equation (6-9) has an analytic solution involving fractional-order Bessel functions. It will not be quoted here since it is valid only in the case where n is proportional to r; in other cases it is necessary to integrate the equation of motion numerically. In the particular case of the MIT cyclotron the solution indicates a weak damping in the region in which n varies linearly with r, with a value $(z/z_0)_1 = 0.53$ at $r = 15$ in., where $n = 0.02$.

At larger radii the n value rises sharply, and Eq. (5-70) can be used to estimate the additional damping. Amplitudes vary approximately with $n^{-1/2}$, so the damping factor is given roughly by $\dfrac{z}{z_0} = \left(\dfrac{n_1}{n_2}\right)^{1/2}$. For the special case of the MIT cyclotron between $r = 15$ in. and $r = 18.75$ in. (exit slit) the n value rises from 0.02 to 0.4, and the additional damping factor $(z/z_0)_2 = 0.22$.

Combining the damping factors for these two regions of acceleration, we estimate the over-all damping from center to exit slit to be 0.12 for the MIT machine. The internal aperture of the D's in the central region is 1.6 in., so a possible initial amplitude is 0.8 in. and the final amplitude should be about 0.1 in. The observed height of the emergent beam (double amplitude) is about $\frac{1}{4}$ in., in reasonable agreement with this estimate.

A more detailed calculation of damping of axial-oscillation amplitudes would require numerical solution of the equations of motion and should also include the electrostatic focusing effects at the accelerating gaps, which will be discussed later in this chapter.

A practical consequence of this compaction in axial width of the envelope enclosing the ion oscillations is to make the problem of deflection of an emergent beam considerably simpler. Beam width is a basic parameter in the design of the exit-slit septum. On the other hand, the narrow beam width is a disadvantage when targets are used in the circulating beam, causing a serious problem in target cooling.

Radial oscillations also occur, about the ideal or concentric equilibrium orbit location, with a frequency given by

$$f_r = (1 - n)^{1/2} f_0 \qquad (6\text{-}10)$$

Such oscillations can be induced at the start of acceleration by off-center location of the ion source, which produces a lack of concentricity of ion orbits with the magnetic field. At the start, where n is so small as to be negligible relative to unity, the frequency of these radial oscillations is essentially equal to the ion orbital frequency. An orbit which is displaced relative to the center of the magnetic field will continue to expand in widening semicircles about the location of the displaced center. However, as the ions approach the radius of the exit slit, where the n value rises to about 0.40, the radial-oscillation frequency decreases to

$$f_r = 0.78 f_0$$

The decrease in f_r causes the orbits to precess, so the azimuth of maximum amplitude moves forward around the circumference, first by small steps and ultimately by large angular jumps in each turn. For the above example of $f_r = 0.78 f_0$ the angle of precession per turn is about 80°. The precessional motions of the individual particles are not coherent, so particles of all possible phases of precession exist within the resonant bunch. Particles of essentially the same energy will have a radial spread given by their residual double amplitude of radial oscillation and will also have an angular deviation from the equilibrium orbit. To illustrate with a practical case, a radial-oscillation amplitude of 0.50 in., at an orbit radius of 18.75 in. and an n value of 0.40, would result in an angular divergence of 0.019 radian.

Precession of orbit centers during acceleration can occur as a consequence of the unequal voltages between D's along the D faces. Since the D's are the terminating capacitances of quarter-wave resonant circuits and have a physical extension along their faces which is a significant fraction of the quarter wavelength, there will be a somewhat lower potential at the ends of the D faces nearest the lines relative to that at the extreme ends of the lines. This difference has been measured in some cyclotrons to be as great as 5 per cent. The resonant ions will receive an average smaller acceleration when crossing in one direction across D faces than in the other direction. This will cause the orbit centers to precess. The result is similar to that of a "bump" in the magnetic field at one azimuth. The effect of such a precession is to increase radial-oscillation amplitude. It can be partially compensated, under steady conditions, by displacing the ion source away from the geometric center. In some cyclotrons a displacement of the ion source of over 2 in. has been necessary to give maximum emergent beam intensities.

The radiofrequency electric field between D's also produces forces on deviant particles, depending on the shape of the electric field and on the phase of the rf cycle when particles cross the accelerating gap. The gap between D faces can be considered a cylindrical electric lens. In Fig. 6-9 a schematic cross section of the D gap is shown, indicating the lines of electric field and the direction of the forces on a particle crossing the gap. We note that there are convergent forces on entering the gap and divergent forces on leaving.

The first effect noted is a net displacement toward the median plane. This is equivalent to the "thick-lens" displacement of off-axis rays in an optical lens system.   As for the optical case, it can be shown to be proportional to the displacement z from the median plane.   It is also proportional to the ratio of energy acquired in a single crossing to particle energy.   It will be most significant for the first few gap crossings when ions are at low energy.

The effect of the electric fields in a cyclotron was first analyzed and published independently by Rose[16] and Wilson[17,18] in 1938.   Both authors considered the combined effect of the electric and magnetic fields, focusing at various stages of the acceleration, the phase shifts occurring during acceleration, and the significance in terms of the theoretical maximum

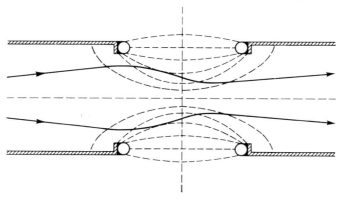

Fig. 6-9. Cross section of the electric-field pattern between the D's of a cyclotron. A typical ion path (exaggerated) illustrates the mechanism of electric focusing.

energy obtainable with a cyclotron.   Their terminology and points of view were different, but the conclusions were essentially identical.   Both described the vertical oscillations, and both showed that under certain conditions the electric field is defocusing.   A recent and more complete analysis of the effects of the cyclotron fields by Cohen[19] has corrected a few errors and has also identified some additional defocusing terms in the equations of motion.   We shall not attempt here to duplicate the detailed analysis, but shall describe the effects qualitatively.

Two mechanisms in electric focusing can be isolated and discussed. First, since the ion is being accelerated to higher velocity during its passage across the gap, the time spent in the convergent field on entering is longer than that in the divergent field.   This "energy change" effect is most pronounced in early accelerations when ion energy is low and the change in velocity is most significant.   Wilson has shown that it is most effective for a narrow gap between D's with wide D aperture.

Second, particles crossing the gap will experience an electric field which changes during the time of transit.   In that portion of the rf cycle when the rf field is decreasing in magnitude, the convergent force on entering the gap will be larger in magnitude than the divergent force on leaving, so the net result is convergence. During the other quadrant of the accelerating half-cycle, the effects will be reversed and the result will be divergence. The magnitude of this "field variation" effect also decreases with increasing particle energy and orbit radius, since the time spent in crossing the gap, and hence the magnitude of the potential change, becomes smaller.

The net result of these two major effects is an effective focusing only during early stages of acceleration and for particles within a rather limited phase band. The focal length of the equivalent electric lens is relatively short for low-energy ions of the proper phase, but becomes very long for high-energy particles. Each ion traverses the lens about 200 times. If we visualize the spiral path of the ions as unrolled into a straight line, the successive lenses of increasing focal length would be spaced at increasing intervals proportional to the square roots of a series of integers [see Eq. (6-5)]. The paths of ions through such a combination of converging lenses has been analyzed by Rose. He finds them to have long-period oscillations about the median plane, with an envelope which diverges slowly, with $T^{1/4}$. We note that with electric-field focusing only, the ion beam would diverge at large radii.

Electric focusing is strong enough to be significant only in the first few accelerations; it is maximum during the initial quarter-cycle as the ions are pulled out of the ion source and into the D. Such focusing can be observed visually under conditions of high gas pressure in the chamber when the beam of ions pulled from the source produces a faint blue glow. This glow is observed to converge as it leaves the column of ionization at the source and enters the D. Extensions on the D faces opposite the source, called "feelers" or "auspullers," have been used to improve beam intensity; they decrease the physical spacings and increase the electric field at the source. They also change the dimensions and focal properties of this first electric lens.

Quantitative experimental evidence on the effect of electric focusing or defocusing is lacking, since it is difficult to isolate this feature from the other factors which affect beam intensity. The long-period oscillations due to electric forces have not been observed, since they are submerged beneath the higher-frequency damped oscillations caused by the radially decreasing magnetic field. The few empirical studies which have been made with different shapes of feeler electrodes and ion sources have not been sufficient to show the full effect of geometry on ion-beam intensity.

The combined effects of electric and magnetic fields would predict an envelope which first increases in transverse thickness until it is limited by the internal D aperture, followed by a steadily decreasing amplitude with increasing ion energy and orbit radius due to the decreasing magnetic field. A few experimental studies have been made of the size of this beam envelope. One technique has been to measure the width of the region of induced radioactivity on the leading edge of probes inserted to different radial locations. In one such test reported by Wilson the beam width was found to be limited by the internal aperture of the D's out to about one-third of the final radius and then to narrow in a nearly linear fashion out to the exit slit. The envelope calculated by Cohen[19] for the Oak Ridge cyclotron reaches its maximum at about one-half of the final radius. In some cyclotrons the D's have been shaped to conform roughly to such a beam envelope, having wide inner vertical aperture in the central region and tapering to a narrower width at the outer edge. In several cyclotrons holes have been melted in the D's in the inner region where beam amplitude is large. Good design practice uses closely spaced water-cooling tubes on the D's in the central region to absorb the heat produced by ions of excessive amplitude. A general conclusion is that all cyclotrons experience a considerable loss in intensity during the early stages of acceleration. In this situation a more detailed analysis of fields, forces, and particle orbits during the initial accelerations might yet yield useful and significant results.

6-4. PHASE RELATIONS DURING ACCELERATION

An ion crosses the gap between electrodes twice in each revolution, each time gaining energy from the electric field. Since the rf potential between electrodes varies harmonically with time, particles can be accelerated only during half of the cycle; during the other half they would be decelerated. Those crossing the gap when the field is maximum will require the smallest number of turns to reach maximum energy; those crossing at other phases gain energy at a slower rate and make more revolutions to attain maximum energy. We can express the time variation of electric field as

$$E = E_0 \cos \omega(t + t_0) \qquad (6\text{-}11)$$

where the phase $t_0 = 0$ for maximum accelerating field. At the start of acceleration $(t = 0)$ ions released from the source, which is midway between electrode faces, will gain maximum energy when the phase $\omega t_0 = 0$. The ion current pulled from the source by the rf field is greatest at the instant of maximum field, since it seems certain from experimental observations that the emission of ions is space-charge-limited.

We shall show that the ions which constitute the resonant beam start their acceleration near zero phase but experience phase shifts during acceleration. At all times, however, the ions of the resonant beam must remain within the accelerating half-cycle. The phase relationships at the start of acceleration can be understood by analyzing the initial ion paths in the region of essentially uniform electric field between the electrode faces.

Consider a positive ion of charge-to-mass ratio e/m formed in a region in which there is an electric field E [given by Eq. (6-11)] along the x coordinate and a constant magnetic field B in the z direction. Motion will be confined to the xy plane, and the equations of motion in cartesian coordinates are

$$m \frac{d^2x}{dt^2} = eE + Be \frac{dy}{dt} \qquad (6\text{-}12a)$$

$$m \frac{d^2y}{dt^2} = \qquad - Be \frac{dx}{dt} \qquad (6\text{-}12b)$$

For cyclotron resonance the frequency of the applied electric field will be equal to the ion revolution frequency:

$$\omega = 2\pi f = \frac{Be}{m} \qquad (6\text{-}13)$$

Using the accepted symbols for time derivatives the equations of motion become

$$\ddot{x} = \frac{eE_0}{m} \cos \omega(t + t_0) + \omega \dot{y} \qquad (6\text{-}14a)$$

$$\ddot{y} = \qquad\qquad - \omega \dot{x} \qquad (6\text{-}14b)$$

We consider the ion to start from rest ($\dot{x} = \dot{y} = 0$) at $t = 0$ from the origin. Solutions of the equations of motion above give the position of the ion at any subsequent time:

$$x = \frac{eE_0}{2m\omega^2} [\sin \omega t_0 \sin \omega t - t \sin \omega(t + t_0)] \qquad (6\text{-}15a)$$

$$y = \frac{eE_0}{2m\omega^2} [\cos \omega t_0 \sin \omega t - t \cos \omega(t + t_0) - 2 \sin \omega t_0(1 - \cos \omega t)]$$

$$(6\text{-}15b)$$

Initial ion paths have been computed from these equations for deuterons at a frequency $f = 13.5$ megacycles (for which $B = 17.7$ kilogauss) and an electric field $E_0 = 25,000$ volts/cm, for several phase conditions. The paths are plotted in Fig. 6-10. In this diagram the electric field is in the x direction (D faces parallel to the y axis).

Several interesting results become apparent from the paths plotted in Fig. 6-10. The central orbit is for zero initial phase, the optimum cyclotron resonance condition, in which ions leave the source when voltage between D's is a maximum. The opening spiral path is in exact resonance with the electric field, crossing the y axis at intervals of π, 2π, 3π, etc. One limiting phase condition ($\omega t_0 = -\pi/2$) is for D-voltage zero and increasing at the start; this particle travels in a wider orbit than the

resonant particle. The other limiting phase is not shown ($\omega t_0 = \pi/2$),
but would be a mirror image of the $-\pi/2$ case. Intermediate orbits are
shown, for phases of $\pm\pi/6$ and $\pm\pi/3$. As stated earlier, the bulk of the
emission from the ion source will be concentrated in the interval when
electric fields at the source are high, roughly between the phase curves

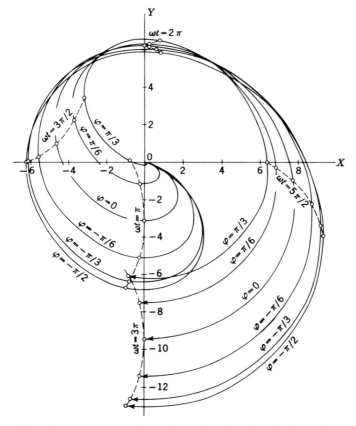

Fig. 6-10. Initial ion paths in a uniform sinusoidal electric field along the x axis and a
magnetic field along the z axis. Orbits are shown for particles starting at the center at
several phases of the electric field.

for $\omega t_0 = \pi/3$ and $-\pi/3$. This family of curves represents ions starting
toward the right D.

The most interesting result is the phase focusing for off-phase ions.
Small circled points on each curve in Fig. 6-10 show the positions of
particles at $t = t_0$, when D voltage is a maximum. These points cluster
closely around the y axis, even after only one half-cycle, and approach
zero phase asymptotically in subsequent passages. This means that all
ions from the source are bunched near zero phase, regardless of their
initial phase.

It may also be noted here that cyclotron resonance exists even without having electric-field-free regions within the D's as was assumed in the simple theory. The paths are opening spirals, rather than semicircles, but the resonance condition is still satisfied.

Another significant feature of these initial orbits is the spatial concentration for ions of all possible phases. With the exception of a narrow band near $\omega t_0 = \pi/2$, all orbits swing clear of the ion-source location, allowing the use of a tubular jacket around the column of ionization if desired, or a support for a hooded source (see Sec. 6-6). Furthermore, the whole family of orbits come to an approximate focus near the second crossing of the y axis. This physical separation of successive orbits will be sharper the narrower is the phase band being accelerated. Experimental evidence for such separation of orbits near the ion source has been reported by several experimenters. The most obvious evidence is the observation of blackened circular bands on the interior surfaces of the D's after long operation. Presumably, these bands are due to dissociation and deposition of contaminant vapors in the chamber by those ions of the resonant beams which have large vertical oscillations and so approach or strike the inner D surfaces.

The above calculation and the plot of Fig. 6-10 were made on the simplifying assumption that the electric field was uniform. However, in practice the D faces are closely spaced and the electric fields do not penetrate far into the D's, so the larger orbits are shaped solely by the magnetic field. A better approximation is to assume that the electric field goes to zero at planes $x = \pm x_D$, which are typical of the D spacing in cyclotrons. Another set of orbits have been computed for this case, in which $x_D = 2$ cm, and in which the orbits become segments of circles outside x_D (Fig. 6-11). The phase focusing and spatial focusing are less complete than in the uniform-field plot, but are still observable. After a relatively few turns the orbits approach the pattern of connected semicircles assumed in the elementary cyclotron theory.

As the acceleration continues, a phase shift will result if the ion frequency differs from the applied frequency of the electric field. A decrease in ion frequency does occur as a result of the small radial decrease in magnetic field required for focusing, of about 2 per cent as described in the preceding section. At high ion energies the relativistic increase in mass will cause an additional drop in ion frequency, of about 2 per cent for 20-Mev protons or 1 per cent for 20-Mev deuterons (see Sec. 6-12). If the applied frequency were maintained at the initial ion frequency, this would cause the ions to lag behind the voltage maximum so the phase would shift into the decelerating part of the cycle and the beam would be lost.

The method used in practice to avoid loss of resonance is to use an applied frequency intermediate between the initial and final ion frequencies.   The ions will first lead the voltage maximum causing a phase shift toward, but not exceeding, the phase of zero voltage.   Then, when ions reach a radius at which the magnetic field corresponds to an ion frequency equal to the applied frequency, the phase shift stops, and for further acceleration the shift reverses and approaches again the phase of

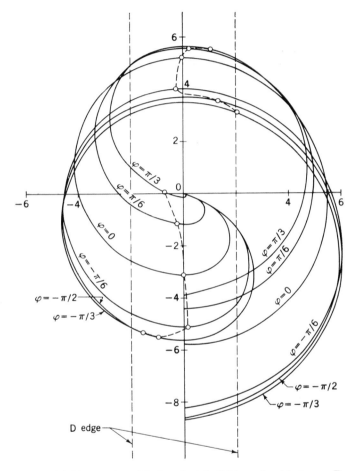

Fig. 6-11. Initial ion paths with the electric field confined between D edges.

maximum field.   When the ions reach the radius of the exit slit and enter the deflector channel (see Sec. 6-7), they should again be close to zero phase.   This is necessary so the difference in radius of successive paths, Δr, is large enough for them to pass behind the septum and enter the channel.   So the practical maximum migration in phase will be from zero to $-\pi/2$ and back to zero, a total phase migration of π radians or one half-cycle.

The actual technique used to control resonance in a cyclotron is to vary the magnetic field, with the applied frequency held constant. The result is the same as discussed above. At the start of acceleration the central field is higher than that specified by the applied frequency, so the ions lead the voltage wave and the phase shifts toward $-\pi/2$; at large radii the field is lower and phase shifts in the opposite direction.

The shift in phase during acceleration is illustrated in Fig. 6-12, in which three half-cycles of the radiofrequency are shown. The initial electric acceleration will produce focusing for particles within the shaded quarter-cycle (while potential is decreasing in magnitude during passage of the particle across the gap), but intensities are a maximum and acceleration greatest for a band (labeled A) at near maximum voltage or near zero phase. An intermediate acceleration shows this group of ions

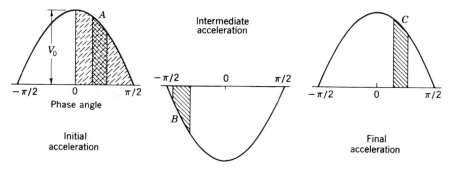

Fig. 6-12. Phase shift during acceleration of a preferred band of ions, labeled A at the start, B at an intermediate time, and C at the final acceleration.

(labeled B) at the extreme phase shift almost to $-\pi/2$. In the final acceleration the band (labeled C) is again near zero phase to provide sufficient change in radius per turn to emerge through the deflector channel.

Tuning of a cyclotron to obtain the highest energy and highest-intensity emergent beam depends on keeping the total phase shift within the limits described above. The location of the exit slit is extremely critical in this respect, since the magnetic field is falling steeply in this region and increasing the radius causes the phase shift to increase rapidly. Increasing the D voltage requires fewer turns for acceleration to maximum energy and will compensate for a larger phase shift. However, D voltage is usually limited by technical considerations of power and spark breakdown and cannot easily be pushed above a practical maximum operating value for a given cyclotron chamber and D assembly. D voltage can also be raised by decreasing the loading current to the D's, for example, by decreasing gas flow to the source, but the yield of ions is also reduced. In each cyclotron a practical compromise is reached between these several factors, which usually results in accepting a smaller exit radius and lower beam energy than the maximum obtainable value in order to maintain the desired beam intensity.

When internal targets are used to intercept the resonant beam, the Δr limitation applying to an emergent beam is removed. The practical phase shift will be from zero to $-\pi/2$ and back to π radians, a considerable increase in total phase shift. As a consequence, the resonant beam intensities on such a target will be considerably higher than the emergent beam, and target location can be at a somewhat larger radius, resulting in higher ion energy.

6-5. VACUUM CHAMBER AND ELECTRODES

The chamber which fits between the poles of the electromagnet and contains the D's, the ion source, and the deflecting electrode is arranged to serve many purposes. It must be vacuum-tight, mechanically designed with adequate structural strength to resist distortion when under vacuum, constructed of nonmagnetic materials to prevent any disturbance of the symmetrical magnetic field, of high electrical conductivity to provide low resistance for the radiofrequency currents, and equipped with a large number of ports and apertures for inserting the many electrodes and controls. The design that has evolved is a framework of thick walls with many ports through the sides and with large circular apertures top and bottom filled by iron chamber lids which are extensions of the magnet poles. A photograph of the Massachusetts Institute of Technology chamber which is typical of present design is shown in Fig. 6-13. Its design features will be described below.

The structural frame of the chamber has been formed successfully in several laboratories from rolled brass hoops; others have used welded structures of thick plates of nonmagnetic stainless steel. Still others have used soldered or brazed assemblies of copper-alloy plates. A few have been successful in obtaining vacuum-tight bronze castings. Improved metallurgical techniques now make it possible to obtain large castings free from porosity. The MIT chamber is such a casting. All surfaces are machined, and many tapped screw holes are provided to bolt ports over the apertures and retain vacuum seals.

The soft-iron chamber lids rest on ledges machined in the chamber walls, with faces accurately parallel. The circular edge is sealed by a gasket joint under pressure of a packing ring held by a ring of bolts. Most cyclotrons use water-cooled copper sheet liners on the inner faces of the lids to provide a high-conductivity surface for rf currents. However, at MIT the inner surface of the lid is copper-plated to allow maximum clearance to the D's.

The D's are inserted through a large rectangular port in the rear of the chamber. Rectangular ports on the side faces are used to mount the movable trimmer capacitor plates, the probe target, and the emergent beam port. A circular window allows inspection or insertion of probes along the diametral line between D's. The ion source is mounted opposite the window between D stems, with the cathode and anode leads paralleling the D faces.

Fig. 6-13. Shop assembly photograph of the MIT cyclotron chamber.

The D's are supported on large-diameter (8-in.) stems within even larger (24-in.) cylinders which form a resonant circuit for the radio-frequency electric oscillations used for acceleration. The electrical properties of the rf system are described in a later section.

The coaxial D lines are connected to the chamber through tapered cones with oval cross section at the chamber wall. The inner stem which supports the D is formed from heavy copper tubing of 8 in. diam flattened into an oval shape where it enters the chamber, and the D structure is built onto and supported by this flattened tubing.   This oval shape of D lines at the throat improves mechanical rigidity, increases surface area, lowers rf resistance, and results in higher electrical efficiency.   Many water-cooling tubes are soldered internally to the D's and D lines.   In fact, it has been found necessary to have these tubes spaced as closely as 2 to 3 in. to prevent local heating and warping of the D's under power. Approximately 10 kw of heat is dissipated in each D and D line during operation.   Other water-cooling circuits are distributed liberally around the coaxial lines, cones, and chamber walls, where experience shows the need.

The D's in the MIT cyclotron have a maximum outer width of $2\frac{1}{2}$ in. in the central region and are tapered over the outer half of their radius to a rounded edge having a 2-in. diam.   The gap between chamber lids was chosen to be 5 in., leaving $1\frac{1}{4}$-in. clearance between D's and lids.   This relatively short gap and small clearance are just adequate for maximum energy operation of this machine, resulting in a D-voltage limit of about 70 kv due to breakdown.   Larger clearances are required for the higher D voltages needed in larger cyclotrons.

The deflector electrode and ejection septum are mounted within one D; the high-voltage electrode is supported coaxially along the center of the D stem on suitable insulators.   The design of this deflector system is described in more detail in a later section of this chapter, as are the other components such as ion source and targets.

6-6. THE ION SOURCE

The source of ions used in most modern cyclotrons is a low-voltage, hot-cathode arc discharge.   The discharge produces a dense column of ionization which is collimated by the strong magnetic field and crosses the center of the cyclotron chamber between D's.   Positive ions formed in this region of ionization are pulled out and accelerated by the radio-frequency electric field of the D's.

The arc discharge itself is produced in a small metal-walled cavity located on the floor of the chamber against one pole face; it encloses a hot cathode which maintains a discharge current of 2 to 3 amp at relatively low potential, commonly 100 to 150 volts.   In a typical ion source an intense beam of electrons of 1 to 2 amp emerges from the cavity through an exit hole in a truncated cone, aligned with its axis along the direction of the magnetic field.   Gas is admitted to the discharge cavity from an external supply and flows out the exit hole with the electrons.   This exit hole also permits a pressure differential to maintain an adequate gas pressure for the discharge within the cavity (estimated to be 10^{-2} mm Hg).   The beam of electrons ionizes gas emerging from the exit hole, so ions are formed in place between the D's.

In the earliest cyclotrons an exposed cathode was used, located against one pole face near the center of the chamber.   Ions were formed in the gas at low pressure which filled the entire chamber, and very low beam intensities were obtained (1-μa resonant beam).   Such an exposed cathode can be seen in Fig. 6-1, which shows the first model-sized cyclotron.

The use of an arc source was first reported by Livingston, Holloway, and Baker[24] at Cornell University in 1939.   It was an adaptation of the metal-capillary arc (Chap. 4).   This first installation was in a small cyclotron with low-speed pumps.   The discharge column was contained within a $\frac{1}{8}$-in. copper tube extended across the chamber, with a small

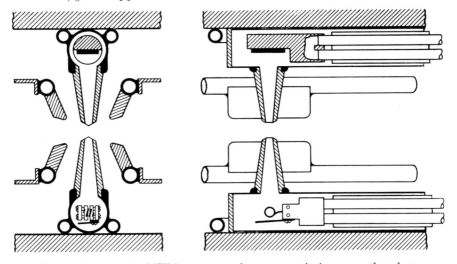

Fig. 6-14. An early MIT ion source using symmetrical cones and probes.

exit hole in the side opposite one D.   The ion paths were large enough to clear the tube in their first accelerations.

With the development of high-speed pumps for larger cyclotrons the exit hole has enlarged so the capillary can be removed and the surface of the discharge column can be exposed to the electric fields of the D's. The shape of the arc-discharge cavity and of the cones for the exit hole has been the subject of competitive development in several laboratories, and many rather distinct types have proved successful.   A review article on cyclotron ion sources[25] described the several designs and techniques developed by 1946.

Three stages of the development to higher-intensity sources are shown in Figs. 6-14 to 6-16.   An early MIT source[14] used a symmetrical, double-cone structure in which the second cavity housed a test anode which was useful in aligning the cathode with the exit hole and in monitoring ion-source operation.   Others used a single cone which terminated short of the median plane and a water-cooled plate on the opposite side of the chamber to absorb heat from the electron beam.   An improved version of the single-cone source is the "hooded arc"[26] (Fig. 6-15).   The hood limits the length of the exposed column of ionization and avoids loading of the rf power supply for the D's with currents due to nonuseful ions coming from a more extended source.   A more recent development, by

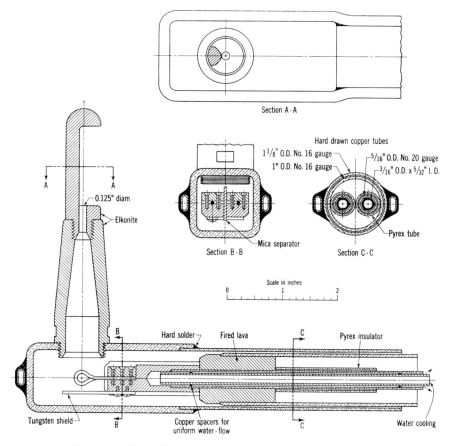

Fig. 6-15. Hooded-arc ion source.   (Carnegie Institution.[26])

R. S. Livingston and R. J. Jones[27] of Oak Ridge, is designed for a cyclotron of wide D aperture and has an arc-discharge cavity extended across the D face with a long, narrow slit facing a slotted accelerating electrode mounted on one D.

Techniques have steadily improved with years of development.   The cathode is now formed of heavy tungsten or tantalum rod, formed as a short-stemmed "V" or "U," clamped in terminating lugs and using large-diameter water-cooled leads.   The largest cathode reported is the

0.170-in.-diam tantalum rod used in the Oak Ridge source; it requires 500 amp at 4 volts dc for heating. The heating power is either dc or high-frequency ac ($\sim$100 kc) to avoid damage from vibration in the magnetic field at low frequencies. Cathode life is a function of gas composition and is materially shortened by traces of oxygen. Lifetimes in service of 100 to 200 hr have been reported. The limit is due to erosion of a small area the size of the exit hole on the cathode surface, which represents the effective emitting surface.

Erosion of cone tips or arc-cavity slits is another limit to ion-source operation. Metals such as copper-tungsten alloy have been used, and water cooling of the arc body is common. Graphite is coming into wide use for cones, arc bodies, and also for D feelers or accelerating electrodes; it operates at high temperatures with a minimum of sputtering or evaporation. Many variations on cone-and-slit design have been used, and no one design has yet gained general acceptance.

The length of the exposed column of ionization seems to determine beam intensity. It is limited by the vertical aperture of the D's or the space between D feelers. If the column is too long, off-focus ions tend to load the D circuit and increase rf power requirements; if power is limited, D voltage is reduced. At various times this optimum length has been studied for a particular cyclotron. At MIT, with an internal D aperture of 1.6 in. the optimum length of ionization column was $\frac{5}{8}$ in. For 4-in.-wide D's in the Carnegie Institution 60-in. machine it was $1\frac{3}{8}$-in. The Oak Ridge cyclotrons have been designed for very high intensities, and the source described above has a slit $2\frac{1}{2}$ in. long. For each cyclotron there will be an optimum length depending on the D aperture, the shape of the ion source and accelerating structures, the available rf power, and the available pumping speed for evacuating gas from the source.

Typical operating characteristics of a hot-cathode arc of modest power and beam output would be: arc current, 3 amp; arc voltage drop, 100 volts; electron beam from exit hole, 2 amp; gas flow, 2 cm^3/min at atmospheric pressure. The resonant ion beam pulled from such a source by the rf fields of the D's might be about 0.5 ma. The beam intensity is limited by space charge in the column of ionization and can be improved by careful design of the electrode structures or by the use of feelers on the D edges to increase the electric field.

Another development of the Oak Ridge group is the "hollow-anode ion source,"[28] used for both light and multiply charged heavy ions (Fig. 6-16). It is a modification to cyclotron conditions of the electron oscillation source known as a P.I.G. (see Sec. 4-8). It was specifically developed for large cyclotrons with wide D faces and high rf power. In this source electrons are emitted from two secondary-emission cathodes at the ends of a hollow graphite anode with quartz sleeves. A long, narrow slit in the anode allows ions to emerge, where they are pulled into the D's by the field on a slotted accelerator electrode.   A potential of about 5 kv is required to strike the arc, dropping to about 600 volts in operation.   Gas is introduced into the anode cavity from an external supply, and the narrow slit acts as a flow resistance.   Resonant beam intensities of up to 3 ma of H^+ ions have been obtained from such a source.

Even higher-intensity sources are possible if adequate power is available for acceleration.   There seems to be no practical limit to intensity if sufficient effort is spent on development of other components of the cyclotron to control heat and prevent damage.

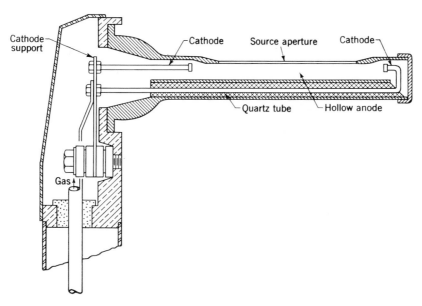

Fig. 6-16. Hollow-anode (P.I.G.) ion source, Oak Ridge National Laboratory.[28]

6-7. DEFLECTOR

The purpose of the deflecting electrode is to pull the resonant ion beam out of its circular path and direct it against an external target.   At a chosen maximum radius R a thin septum is inserted having a larger radius of curvature $R + \Delta R$ which splits the resonant beam and allows a fraction of the ions to pass into a channel behind the septum.   This is shown schematically in Fig. 6-17.   An insulated electrode mounted behind and parallel to the septum is maintained at high negative dc potential, which provides an electric field to deflect the ions outward. The deflected beam traverses an opening spiral as the ions cross the weakening magnetic field at the pole edges and passes out of the chamber through a suitable port, beyond which external targets can be located.

Voltage needed for deflection depends on ion energy T, the width of channel to contain the ion beam d, and the deflected orbit radius $R + \Delta R$.

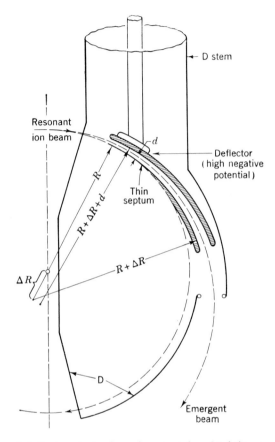

Fig. 6-17. Internal deflector electrode and septum for obtaining an emergent beam.

An estimate can be obtained by combining the relations for orbit radius with or without the deflecting potential V_d:

$$\left.\begin{array}{r}\dfrac{mv^2}{R} = Bev \\[2mm] \dfrac{mv^2}{R + \Delta R} = Bev - \dfrac{V_d e}{d}\end{array}\right\} \qquad \frac{V_d}{d} = \frac{2T}{R}\frac{\Delta R}{R + \Delta R} \tag{6-16}$$

Evaluating for the 18.75-in. radius and 16-Mev deuterons of the MIT cyclotron, with an average deflector spacing $d = 0.3$ in., we find

For $\Delta R = 0.1R$: $V_d = 47,000$ volts
For $\Delta R = 0.2R$: $V_d = 87,000$ volts

A small value of ΔR means that the deflector channel diverges from the particle orbit slowly, so a long channel is required to pull the beam out through the fringing magnetic field. A large ΔR requires high potential on the deflector, which may exceed the breakdown limit. Under operating conditions an intense beam of ions traverses the channel and divergent ions bombard the electrodes; this produces ionization in the residual gas and limits the gap breakdown potential. The optimum choice depends on the individual characteristics and physical dimensions of the cyclotron. A typical figure, used in the MIT cyclotron, is a ΔR of $0.15R$.

The deflector gap is usually tapered to accommodate the diverging beam. Spacings as small as $\frac{1}{8}$ in. can be used at the entry slit, opening to $\frac{1}{2}$ in. or greater at the exit. The limit at the entry is set by the Δr between successive turns at this radius, which can be obtained from Eq. (6-5) in the form

$$\frac{\Delta r}{R} = \frac{1}{2}\frac{\Delta T}{T} = \frac{V_{rf}}{T} \tag{6-17}$$

since $\Delta T = 2V_{rf}$ (two accelerations). For $V_{rf} = 80$ kv, $T = 16$ Mev, and $R = 18.74$ in., we find $\Delta r = 0.1$ in.

The beam entering the exit slit has a finite energy spread and also an angular divergence associated with the residual radial oscillations of the resonant beam. In Sec. 6-4 the properties of these radial oscillations were discussed. It was shown that they lead to precessional motion of the individual particle orbits and an angular divergence of the particles entering the exit slit of up to 0.019 radian, for a radial-oscillation amplitude of 0.5 in. In a deflector channel of 20 in. length this would cause a beam spread of about 0.4 in. The deflector channel is tapered from $\frac{1}{8}$ to $\frac{1}{2}$ in. along its length so as to accept particles with this radial-oscillation amplitude. Amplitudes are apparently considerably larger than this for a considerable fraction of the resonant beam, so we expect that the channel dimensions will limit emergent beam intensity to a fraction of the available intensity in the resonant beam. Again, the designer and experimenter attempt to achieve a practical compromise based on channel dimensions and the voltage breakdown limit for deflecting potential. The reduction of radial amplitudes by careful shaping of the magnetic field becomes an important feature in achieving the best emergent beam intensities.

With such an initial angular divergence and radial width of the deflected beam, it will diverge even more rapidly as it passes through the rapidly decreasing magnetic fringing field. At the location of the emergent beam port it will have a wide radial spread. The observed radial width of the emergent beam in the MIT cyclotron is over 2 in., at a distance of about 60 in. measured along the spiral path. Emergent beam intensities up to 25 per cent of the resonant beam intensity have been obtained under optimum conditions; for example, deuteron emergent beams of up to 150 μa have been obtained with a resonant beam of about 600 μa. However, such perfection in tuning and alignment is difficult to maintain, and practical operating intensities would in this case be limited to 80 or 100 μa.

The maximum orbit radius R, at which the deflector septum is located, is determined primarily by the radial decrease of magnetic field. Techniques for shaping of magnetic fields by shimming will be described in a

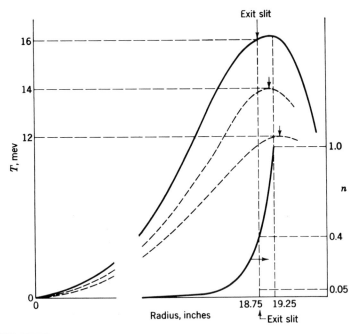

Fig. 6-18. Computed energy of deuterons as a function of orbit radius in the MIT cyclotron, showing location of exit slit. The n value computed from the magnetic field is also shown.

following section. A typical plot of magnetic field as a function of radius, obtained after suitable field shaping of the MIT cyclotron, was shown in Fig. 6-8. The maximum energy obtainable with a particular cyclotron is determined by the maximum value of the product $B^2 R^2$, following Eq. (6-4). Using the measured values of field, the energy in the MIT cyclotron has been computed for each radius, and the result is plotted in Fig. 6-18.

The plot of energy as a function of radius falls below the theoretical curve for constant field, first slowly because of the small radial decrease required for focusing and then more rapidly because of fringing fields at the pole edge.   It reaches a maximum value at a point well inside the pole edge and then decreases for larger radii.   This point represents the maximum energy obtainable with a given central field.   The septum defining the exit slit for the deflector should be located as close to this maximum energy radius as is compatible with maintenance of resonance and of a high-intensity emergent beam.   In the plot of Fig. 6-18 for the MIT cyclotron the radius of maximum energy is 19.25 in. and the experimentally determined location of the septum is at 18.75 in.   On this same figure a curve is plotted of the computed values of the index $n = \dfrac{r_0}{B_0}\dfrac{dB}{dr}$, also shown in the field plot of Fig. 6-8.   The n value is observed to rise steeply in the fringing field, reaching 0.40 at the location of the septum and 1.0 at the point of maximum energy.

Also shown as dashed curves on Fig. 6-18 are the computed values of energy versus radius for two lower values of magnetic field (with different shimming) used earlier in the process of tuning the cyclotron to higher energy.   The maximum energy radius is not a definitely established position, but is actually larger at lower fields.   This is associated with saturation of the corners of the pole edges at high flux densities.   The locations of the deflector septum for these lower-field conditions were found to be at correspondingly larger radii, shown in the figure.

In order to adjust the location of the deflector septum to optimum in the MIT cyclotron, the deflector was designed to have an adjustable radial location.   This was accomplished by pivoting the septum bar at the exit end of the channel; the water-cooling tubes which pass out of the D stem were used as levers to swing the entry end across a short arc so that R could be varied between 18 and 19 in.

Designing the correct, curved shape for the deflector septum and its paralleling deflector electrode is a straightforward but laborious process. The ion trajectory can be plotted step by step through the decreasing magnetic field and the decreasing electric field in the tapered channel, choosing appropriate values for deflecting potential, ion energy, and exit radius R.   A set of such plots can be used to pick a set of diverging orbits which will emerge at the desired place on the chamber wall and for which the required deflecting potentials are acceptable.   It will be found that the opening spiral can be fitted adequately by a septum which is a circular arc of radius $R + \Delta R$, where ΔR is about $0.1R$ or $0.2R$, as discussed above. Nevertheless, such calculations and designs can only be approximate, and it is desirable to have adjustable controls on deflector spacing and location which can be trimmed empirically for maximum beam intensity in operation.

A septum made of a thin solid-metal sheet will be bombarded by a considerable fraction of the resonant ion beam and will be damaged unless carefully designed and cooled.   The energy in the resonant beam can be greater than 10 kw for medium and large cyclotrons. Tungsten sheet was one of the earliest materials to be used successfully for a solid septum, but even tungsten is melted in a 10-kw beam. One technique used to prevent melting is to form the septum with a narrow slot on the median plane, of about the width of the resonant-ion beam. This narrow slot does not decrease the deflecting field seriously and allows most of the resonant beam to pass into the deflector channel without striking the channel walls. In the MIT cyclotron the septum is formed of two strips of tungsten, 0.020 in. thick and 12 in. long and with the edges spaced $\frac{1}{8}$ in. apart. Each strip is silver-soldered to a copper bar bent to the correct curvature, with copper tubing also soldered to the bar for cooling. Other designers use a long V slot in a tungsten-strip septum, so the heat is distributed over an extended surface area.

In the modern cyclotron with large-diameter D stems, the deflecting electrode is mounted on the end of a long supporting rod along the axis of one D stem, and the electrode itself is totally enclosed within the D. The electrode must be insulated for the 50 to 100 kv required, and the positioning adjustments work through insulators. It can be noted that no rf potential is transmitted to the deflector power supply with this mounting. The dc potential for the deflector is provided by a high-voltage rectifier unit equivalent to the power supply for an X-ray tube, and offers no unusual problems.

Some cyclotrons have been designed with deflector electrodes mounted through the chamber wall outside of the D, shaped to form the deflecting channel and extending around the outside of the D for 60 to 70° of arc. The rf field between D and deflector adds to the dc field in varying amount along the length of the channel, depending on the rf phase as a function of the angular position of the ions. This reduces somewhat the dc potentials required. In this position large rf potentials are induced on the electrode, and rf bypass capacitors are required to prevent the radio-frequency from damaging the deflector voltage supply; these are normally located just outside the chamber wall and enclosed within a metal shield to prevent rf power radiation into the laboratory. The control of discharges in the narrow channel between D and deflector has been a serious problem with this design. Nevertheless, some laboratories have been successful in obtaining very-high-intensity emergent beams.

6-8. RADIOFREQUENCY OSCILLATOR

The design of the radiofrequency power supply for the D's of a cyclotron should be a straightforward radio engineering problem. Many of the features of the rf power unit have in fact been taken bodily from experience in transmitter engineering for radio broadcast systems. However, the cyclotron system has an unusual property associated with the variable ion loading and electrical discharges in the chamber which affects load impedance, so that the impedance is not constant as it is for a transmitting antenna. As a consequence, most transmitter experience and much of the advice from radio engineers have proved inapplicable. Physicists and their helpers in the cyclotron field have, of necessity, become specialists in high-frequency electronic engineering. In early cyclotrons the oscillator required a great deal of effort in the form of improvisation and rebuilding to keep pace with the growing need for higher D voltage. The accumulated experience has led to a variety of answers to the special problems of the cyclotron, several of which have proved satisfactory.

The problem is to produce a high-frequency potential difference of 100 to 200 kv in the frequency range between 10 and 20 megacycles/sec, between the opposing faces of the D's. Resonant circuits are required to transform from the potentials available with conventional high-frequency circuits using vacuum power tubes. These resonant circuits must be mechanically rigid to maintain a stable frequency and must have high electrical efficiency (high Q) to keep power requirements reasonable. The oscillator circuit must maintain suitable D voltage under all conditions of ion loading, recover automatically from extreme load conditions such as sparks or gas discharges, and protect the power tubes from damage.

The resonant circuit is electrically equivalent to a pair of quarter-wave coaxial transmission lines with the D's supported on the ends of the inner conductors. In large modern cyclotrons these coaxial lines are of large diameter and solidly constructed so the inner electrodes and D's are self-supporting and no solid insulators are required. D lines are made of copper and are water-cooled by tubes soldered to the inner surfaces, to obtain low resistances and high Q. The outer conductors provide shielding against radiative losses and can also be incorporated as part of the cyclotron chamber vacuum system, where they can serve as large-diameter pump leads. Inner and outer conductors are connected at the electrical node by a copper disk which is movable, so the electrical length of line can be varied to cover the desired range of frequency; clamps to make positive electrical contact are essential. Usually the inner electrode support is brought out through a vacuum seal beyond the node, with screw adjustments which are used to position the D's.

The coaxial lines and D's for the MIT cyclotron, which is typical of modern design, are illustrated in Fig. 6-19. In this machine the outer conductor is formed of 24-in.-diam copper pipe and the inner conductor of 8-in.-diam copper pipe. Even larger coaxial lines are used in higher-energy cyclotrons, up to 48 in. outer and 12 in. inner diameters in some cases. In the MIT design the inner conductor is flattened into an oval shape at the edge of the chamber, and the D is a smoothly shaped extension of the oval pipe. The tapering and the smooth, rounded shape of the D are intended to provide maximum mechanical strength and to minimize electric fields at the surfaces.

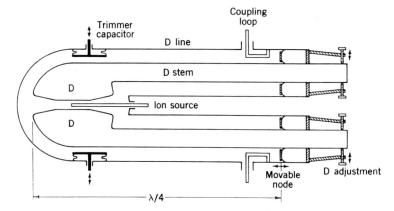

Fig. 6-19. Schematic diagram of the coaxial quarter-wave D-line circuit of the MIT cyclotron.

The equivalent circuit of the cyclotron is shown in Fig. 6-20, in which the distributed inductance, capacitance, and rf resistance of the lines and D's are represented by the lumped constants L_1, C_1, R_1, and L_2, C_2, R_2 for the two similar circuits, and C' is the D-to-D capacitance between the diametral faces which couples the two circuits. The resonant-ion load

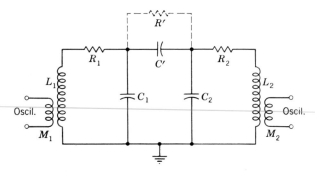

Fig. 6-20. Equivalent electric circuit for the D's and D lines of a cyclotron. The two quarter-wave resonant circuits L_1, R_1, C_1, and L_2, R_2, C_2 are coupled by the D-to-D capacitance C' and loaded by the ion beam load R'.

might be represented as an additional resistance R' paralleling C'. The two circuits are precisely tuned to resonance at the same frequency. If the two coupled circuits are mistuned, two shunt resonant frequencies will result, and the D voltages will be unequal.

Input power can be coupled most conveniently to the D circuits at the outer end of the coaxial line. This is near the voltage node, where cur-

rent is a maximum, and magnetic coupling is the obvious method. This
is accomplished by a loop coupling the magnetic field inside the coaxial
line, inserted through holes in the outer conductor through vacuum seals.
The area of the loop determines the linkage and can be varied by raising
or lowering the loop to match the impedance of the load. In principle a
single loop driving one D line is sufficient, with the other D being coupled
through the D-to-D capacitance. In practice a symmetrical system
using two power tubes in push-pull and two coupling loops is the more
common arrangement. In the equivalent circuit (Fig. 6-20) these loops
are shown, with schematic connections to the oscillator circuit and with
the mutual coupling inductances indicated as M_1 and M_2.

The circuit illustrated has several modes of oscillation. The normal
push-pull mode, in which the two D's operate with phases opposed, provides maximum D-to-D voltage for ion acceleration. In a simplified
case where the constants of the two circuits are identical ($L_1 = L_2$,
$C_1 = C_2$, etc.) and coupling to the oscillator is neglected, the frequency of
the push-pull mode is given by

$$f_{pp} = \frac{1}{2\pi[L(C + 2C')]^{1/2}} \qquad (6\text{-}18)$$

Another fundamental mode of oscillation is the push-push or parallel
resonance mode, in which the D's are in the same phase. Since in this
mode there is no voltage between D's, the coupling capacitance C' is not
effective, and the frequency is given by

$$f_{\text{par}} = \frac{1}{2\pi(LC)^{1/2}} \qquad (6\text{-}19)$$

The resonant-ion load is zero when there is no voltage between D's, so
the circuit has a higher Q and will tend to oscillate in this mode unless
suppressed.

Other modes are possible when the coupled circuits in the oscillator are
considered; these can be lumped together as parasitic oscillations. They
are generally of higher frequency than the normal mode, and D voltages
are much smaller or zero. These depend strongly on the physical dimensions of the external oscillator circuit and so are dependent on the particular design. They can be identified by an expert and suppressed by
the addition of suitable grounding straps, bypass capacitors, etc. The
only general rule is: The simpler the physical structure and the shorter
the leads and connections, the less subject is the oscillator to parasitics.

A satisfactory alternative to two coaxial lines is a single shielded-pair
arrangement, with similar large dimensions for the conductors. Although
the mechanical construction is more complicated, it has certain advantages as an electric circuit. The D-to-D capacitance is increased by the
paralleling line-to-line capacitance, separating mode frequencies and

making the circuit more stable in the desired push-pull mode of oscillation. The location of the node of zero radiofrequency potential is more readily available for tapping or adjustment, and the loop coupling the power oscillator to the resonant circuit can be designed more efficiently. This arrangement has been adopted in several of the larger cyclotrons, notably those built by the Collins Radio Company for the Brookhaven National Laboratory and for the Argonne National Laboratory. The most serious fault was found to be the mechanical problem of the movable node. Original designs did not provide adequate contact in the brushes to carry the high rf currents, and solid clamps had to be installed. The physical shaping of the node plate to carry the large rf currents has required detailed study. The node plate must also have large holes or apertures if pumps are located behind the node.

A technique frequently used to adjust or trim the relative resonant frequencies of the two D-line circuits is to use one or more trimmer capacitors which can be adjusted by remote control under full power operation. Such a variable capacitance can be provided by a movable plate on the side wall of the chamber facing one edge of the D. It must have excellent electrical contact to the walls for the radiofrequency currents and a range of motion sufficient to tune over about 1 per cent in frequency. The availability of such a tuning device makes it possible to adjust relative D voltage as desired for optimum operation.

The large amount of gas ionization produced between the D's when voltage is applied to the electrodes usually sets up a low-voltage, high-current discharge which is self-maintaining. This is the familiar "blue-glow" plasma discharge, maintained by secondary emission or electron "multipactoring"; this discharge causes gaseous ionization at high pressures. In the cyclotron the heat generated in the discharge liberates large quantities of gas from the metal surfaces and maintains the high pressure. This is particularly true at the start of operation after the chamber has been opened to air. Continuous operation under vacuum outgasses the surfaces, and the rate of gas evolution is eventually reduced. Fast pumps are required to evacuate this gas as it is produced and to keep the pressure as low as possible. Even the fastest pumps employed to date in any cyclotron are insufficient to keep the pressure below the threshold for blue-glow discharge during initial operation, but after some conditioning of the surfaces, fast pumps can maintain a low enough pressure to reduce the occurrence of such discharges significantly. This loading of the D circuit by discharge currents holds the D potentials down to a few hundred volts, too low to be effective in accelerating resonant ions. The radiofrequency D potential is also too low to provide adequate excitation for a self-excited oscillator. Unless the loading is removed, the chamber will continue to operate in the low-voltage, blue-glow discharge condition indefinitely.

When the circuit is operating at high D potentials, a different kind of discharge occurs frequently during conditioning. This is high-voltage sparking between a D and the grounded chamber lids, collimated by the magnetic field and sharply localized in position. It is apparently caused by secondary-electron emission from points, dust particles, or hot spots on the surfaces and is most frequent in regions where spacing is short or where curvature is sharpest, such as along D faces. In conditioning a fresh chamber these spark discharges occur like rain above and below the D's, until the whole surface is speckled with small discolored spots. This sparking will gradually decrease under high-voltage operation, but it sets the ultimate limit on D voltage for a cyclotron. The voltage limit can be raised by designing for greater clearance between D's and chamber lids and by providing round, smooth contours and clean, polished surfaces. It is common experience, however, that no amount of smoothing or polishing will eliminate the necessity of some high-voltage conditioning under vacuum. Clean laboratory techniques in preparing a chamber for reassembly after opening are essential; dust should be controlled and all grease removed (even fingerprints), and under no circumstances should steel wool or coarse abrasives be used in cleaning.

The oscillator circuit must be capable of driving the cyclotron through these varied conditions of sparking and discharge, without the necessity of tuning or of manual resetting of overload relays. Operation should be independent of minor frequency variations caused by ion loading or by vibrations or warping of the D's. The circuit must provide an electric field to sweep ions and electrons out of the chamber rapidly enough to prevent cumulative ionization and must be able to pull out of the blue-glow discharge condition automatically.

A variety of oscillator circuits have been developed, with varying success. Competing philosophies of circuit design have led to many friendly arguments between cyclotronists. Since each system has ultimately succeeded in its prime purpose of powering a cyclotron, it is difficult to assess the relative merits of the widely different systems. These circuits can be classified in two major divisions: (1) the master-oscillator, power-amplifier (MO-PA) circuits and (2) the self-excited oscillator circuits. In addition an intermediate form might be called the booster-oscillator circuit. The self-excited oscillator has the greatest number of variations and is used in the largest number of cyclotrons. The master oscillator has proved satisfactory for the high-power requirements of some large cyclotrons.

The MO-PA circuit follows most closely traditional radio engineering practice. Frequency is determined and excitation power is provided by a low-power self-excited master oscillator. This is used to drive the power-amplifier stage which supplies the D circuit. The MO-PA circuit has the advantage of maintaining D voltage during gas discharge conditions, if properly coupled to the D circuit, and provides at all times the electric fields to sweep out ions. However, the circuits and coupling systems required to drive the variable-impedance load of the cyclotron efficiently prove to be complex and subject to parasitic modes of oscillation. The circuit will not follow changes in D-circuit frequency due to vibrations or warping under heat, so some method of controlling frequency from the D circuit is necessary. This can be provided by a feedback from the D circuit to the frequency-determining master oscillator, sometimes called a "rubber crystal." In some installations radio engineers have solved these special problems and have developed a satisfactory power supply.

The "booster oscillator" is basically a self-excited power supply similar to those described in the following paragraphs, but is also equipped with a low-power, master-oscillator exciter stage for the main oscillator which provides excitation when the self-excitation of the main oscillator is too small. So, during blue-glow discharges when the D circuit has low impedance, the booster provides sufficient excitation to develop enough voltage across the D's to sweep out the ions. Then, when the rf D potential is high enough to provide proper excitation, the main oscillator takes over as a self-excited system and the master oscillator is no longer needed. In one or two cyclotrons it has provided a method of controlling the blue-glow discharge condition.

The self-excited oscillator is basically a tuned-plate, tuned-grid system, so closely coupled to the D circuit that frequency is determined by and excitation is taken from the high-Q resonant D circuit. In its simplest form the tuned-plate circuit is the resonant D circuit of the cyclotron; grid excitation is derived from this same circuit. This oscillator will follow changes of frequency without retuning, has a minimum number of components, and has the advantage of circuit simplicity. However, special arrangements are required to obtain sufficient excitation to quench blue-glow discharges; this problem has been the subject of much development and has led to several variations in the design.

The power-oscillator tubes can be operated either with grounded cathode, grounded grid, or grounded anode, and examples of each type exist in cyclotron laboratories. The traditional circuit is with the cathode grounded, using grid excitation and insulating the high dc anode potential from the coupling loops in the D lines with capacitors. In this circuit the grid-plate capacitance of the power tube allows possible excitation of parasitic modes of oscillation.

The grounded-grid self-excited oscillator uses cathode excitation of the power tube from a loop coupling one D circuit and feeds power from the plate (using isolating capacitors) through another loop coupling the other D circuit. In this circuit the grounded grid serves as an electrostatic shield between tube cathode and anode, so the effect of interelectrode capacitance is negligible. With power fed to one D line and grid excitation taken from the other D line, excitation occurs in the desired push-pull mode and other modes are suppressed.

A successful grounded-grid system, reported by Backus,[29] was developed for the Berkeley 60-in. cyclotron. Figure 6-21 is a schematic diagram of the circuit. Transmission lines are used to transmit power from the oscillator to the D-line coupling loop and from the other loop to the oscillator cathode. These lines must be properly terminated to avoid reflections and power loss, illustrated by the tuned stub lines shown in the figure. Power tubes can be used in parallel if required to increase power

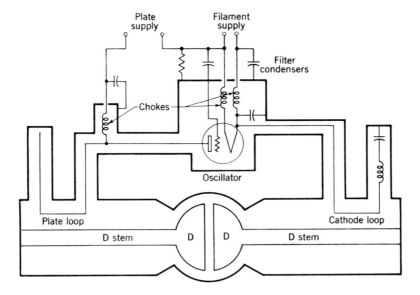

Fig. 6-21. Grounded-grid self-excited oscillator circuit for the University of California 60-in. cyclotron. (Backus.[29])

output. Cathode heating current is supplied through a choke-capacitor filter, in order to allow rf excitation of the cathode. The anode dc voltage supply must be insulated and filtered on both terminals, a slight additional complication. Blue-glow discharge reduces excitation severely and prevents high-voltage operation unless circuits are carefully tuned; in one installation (Brookhaven) a booster oscillator was installed to provide sufficient cathode excitation. In summary, it appears that in the hands of experts this grounded-grid system can be a reliable and efficient oscillator; but it is so large and complicated, so difficult to design and tune, and so subject to parasitics, that it has given considerable maintenance trouble to less experienced operators.

The grounded-anode type of self-excited oscillator has been used in several of the medium-size cyclotrons. It has some unique properties

for designer's choice, so we find cyclotrons with and without tapering and with all degrees of sophistication in magnet design.

The length of magnetic gap inside the chamber is also a designer's choice, depending on the evaluation of several other design problems. Internal dimensions of the D's are chosen on the basis of the anticipated amplitude of ion oscillations, the physical size of the ion source, and the importance of high intensities. The D's are often tapered to a narrower width at the periphery to conform to the ion beam envelope; this decreases capacitance to the chamber lids and reduces rf power requirements. The structural rigidity of the D's must also be considered in choosing their thickness. Once D dimensions are chosen, the clearance between D's and chamber surfaces can be considered. This clearance depends on the designed maximum energy and the corresponding maximum D voltage, and to a smaller extent on the smoothness of surfaces. Water-cooled copper plates are used as chamber liners by some designers, and these occupy space in the pole gap. This space was saved in the MIT chamber by copper-plating the surfaces of the iron pole faces; no serious heating due to rf currents was observed. Naturally, the longer the magnet gap the larger is the power required for excitation, varying approximately with the square of gap length. Furthermore, a wider gap reduces the maximum useful radius for acceleration due to fringing field penetration and so reduces maximum energy. Experience in evaluating these problems has led to the use of 5- to 6-in. gaps for 42-in. poles and 8- to 9-in. gaps for 60-in. poles for most cyclotrons in which maximum energy was the primary consideration. Wider gaps have been used when high intensity was considered more important.

Another engineering decision is the balance between magnet power and magnet cost. Excitation coils can be made with a large cross section of conductor, so the power for excitation is small. However, the larger physical dimensions and weights of both coil and iron yoke increase initial construction cost. A rough balance is frequently made by minimizing total cost of construction plus cost of power for 10 years.

The power source commonly used for excitation is a dc generator driven by an ac three-phase motor, usually with a smaller dc generator on the same shaft to supply the excitation current for the main generator. The magnet field must be accurately regulated to maintain a steady beam and be subject to delicate adjustment by the operator. A constant-current regulator is needed, capable of reducing fluctuations to better than 1/1000. A typical current-regulating circuit takes an input signal from the potential drop across a standard temperature-controlled resistor in series with the magnet coils and compares it against a standard potential obtained from a constant-potential battery. The difference voltage is amplified electronically and used to provide excitation for the exciter generator. A feedback control circuit maintains constant magnet cur-

rent automatically.   Controls are also provided for adjusting the magnitude of the regulated current manually and are used in tuning for peak
beam current.   In some laboratories a further control circuit senses the
beam current and automatically tunes the magnet current to maintain
peak beam intensity.   Techniques for magnet control vary widely, and
several systems have been developed which will maintain a steady cyclotron beam for hours.

One of the more serious problems in tuning up a cyclotron is the shaping
of the magnetic field to preserve resonance and maintain beam intensity.
The shimming of a cyclotron has been a mysterious blockade to efficient
operation in many laboratories and has required many weeks of cut-and-
try experimenting in almost every machine built to date.   In the early
days, practitioners of the art of shimming devised many empirical techniques for bringing in a beam, but individual differences between cyclotrons usually made these formulas unsuccessful on other machines.   However, with accumulated experience and with the modern techniques of
field measurement, it is now possible to anticipate the proper magnetic-
field shape for a cyclotron and to design the optimum shimming.

Although all cyclotron magnets are designed to give an ideally perfect
uniform field, they all require special pole-face machining or shimming to
develop the necessary radial decrease, and they all show imperfections
and inhomogeneities which require correction.   The magnetic inhomogeneities which must be measured and corrected can be identified separately
as:

1. Radial decrease required for focusing
2. Radial decrease at the periphery due to fringing
3. Azimuthal variations of field, at all radii
4. Deviations of the magnetic median plane
5. Local variations due to machining errors, blowholes, etc.

The optimum radial decrease in field was described in Sec. 6-3 as one
which decreased almost linearly from the center out to the region where
peripheral fringing sets in, with a magnitude of decrease out to this point
of about 2 per cent of the central field.   Although this field shape can be
achieved by machining of the surfaces of the pole faces, it is usually
obtained by inserting a flat pyramidal stack of thin iron shims in shimming gaps outside the pole-face plates.   Figure 6-8 shows the field shape
in the MIT cyclotron obtained by the use of such stacks in the two
shimming gaps, each consisting of four disks of 0.020-in. soft iron sheet of
6, 14, 18, and 22 in. diam.   The instrument used to measure this radial
decrease consisted of a small search coil and an integrating electronic
fluxmeter (see Chap. 8).   The coil was slid smoothly on a radial arm out
from the center, in several azimuthal locations, to observe the radial

decrease.   A series of measurements with different sets of shims led to the final choice.

Peripheral fringing causes the field to drop sharply at large radii, faster than is desirable for focusing.   Rings of soft iron fastened to the extreme edge of the poles will limit this sharp drop and extend the region of slow decrease to larger radii.   They are limited in physical size because they reduce clearance to the D stems where the stems go out of the chamber. At MIT the optimum ring section was $\frac{3}{4}$ by $\frac{1}{4}$ in.; the measured shape of field with and without this shim is shown in Fig. 6-8.   Shims which are too large produce a minimum in the radial field plot which would cause defocusing.   Also, a set of shims which are correct at high fields will be too strong and produce a defocusing minimum in the plot at lower fields, so the use of ring shims restricts the flexibility of varying the output energy of a cyclotron.

The modern technique for adjusting the radial decrease in magnetic field is to use corrective windings or shimming coils in place of the edge ring shims and the stacks of thin iron shims.   These are flat-wound coils of many concentric turns with individual leads brought out radially from the inner turns.   They can be located in the shimming gaps outside the pole-face cover plates or inside the vacuum chamber on the inner surface of the pole faces, where they must be covered with copper-plate liners for the rf circuit.   Currents can be adjusted individually in the concentric turns to provide any desired radial decrease in field.   For most of the central area of the pole face the excitation required is less than 1 per cent that of the main excitation coils of the magnet, so small currents can provide the desired radial decrease for focusing.   Near the edge the currents must be considerably greater to offset the fringing fields.   Although the technical problems are severe, especially those associated with the mechanical clamping structures, control of heating, and the many seals for bringing electric leads out of the vacuum chamber, the advantages of such an electric shimming system are obvious.   One of the more important advantages is that the electrical corrections can be varied to provide optimum shimming at any magnetic field, allowing the cyclotron to be developed into a variable-energy machine.

Azimuthal variations of field can cause serious perturbations of the particle orbits, primarily through inducing radial oscillations.   The figure of merit used to describe azimuthal uniformity is the maximum per cent variation around a circle of constant radius, and the most critical region is near the exit-slit location.   Experience, again, is the only guide to the necessary uniformity.   Most operators agree that a variation of less than 0.1 to 0.2 per cent is desirable in large cyclotrons.

Instruments for measuring azimuthal variation are described in Chap. 8.   The same type of search coil with integrating electronic fluxmeter can be used as for the radial measurements, with the coil mounted on a radial arm which is pivoted at the center and can be swung around a full circle. Before corrections, measurements of the MIT magnet showed variations as large as 2 per cent of the average field. These were due to inhomogeneities in the iron of the cast poles and to the asymmetric shape of the yokes. After careful correction by use of sector-shaped and wedge-shaped shims, the errors were reduced to less than 0.1 per cent for all radii out to the exit slit.

The magnetic median plane may deviate from the geometric median plane; the ion beam will follow the magnetic plane. A special search coil can be used to observe the median plane in the radially decreasing field, using two opposed identical coils equally spaced about the center and with the axis precisely aligned normal to the pole surfaces. At MIT the uncorrected field showed a median plane displaced $\frac{1}{2}$ in. below the central plane on which targets were located. This was adequately corrected by reducing excitation in the upper magnet windings relative to the lower ones, after which the beam emerged on the geometric median plane.

Still other inhomogeneities can be observed in a thorough program of magnetic-field measurements. A local weak spot in the field (0.5 per cent low) was observed in the MIT magnet which was presumed to be due to a blowhole in the pole casting; it was corrected by a local spot shim.

The techniques described above make it possible to design a cyclotron field which will be satisfactory without relying on the cut-and-try empirical shimming of early days. The experience at MIT is typical. After several years of empirical shimming, with continual difficulties in maintaining high-intensity operation, a careful program of measurement and correction was carried out as indicated in the illustrations above. When this program was completed, the cyclotron was reassembled and on the first operation gave the highest beam intensities ever obtained, with no further empirical shimming.

6-10. VACUUM PUMPS AND SEALS

The large-volume vacuum chambers resulting from the coaxial D-line design and the high rate of gas evolution in discharges require high-speed pumps. A good rule of thumb is to provide a pumping speed of at least 1 liter/sec at 10^{-5} mm Hg per liter of volume. Oil-diffusion pumps of large diameter which have two or three pumping stages and automatic fractionation of the oil are best suited to this purpose. The pumps must be equipped with adequate baffles to prevent back streaming of the oil vapor, so there is minimum deposition of oil within the vacuum chamber. The mechanical pumps must have sufficient displacement to pump down the chamber volume from atmospheric to the backing-pressure limit of the diffusion pumps in a relatively short time; 15 to 20 min is considered a good design figure. They must also maintain backing pressure under the high gas-evolution conditions of discharge, so the chamber will recover quickly from the bursts of gas pressure produced.

The techniques for evacuating large metal chambers have undergone steady improvement, speeded in recent years by the developments for the large synchroaccelerators. Most of these techniques originated in cyclotron laboratories and have been enlarged and extended for application to the larger machines. Concepts are radically different from those used for high-vacuum glass systems, in which surfaces are outgassed by heating under vacuum and vapors are condensed in refrigerated traps. Outgassing of the large metal surfaces in a cyclotron is impractical, and vapor evolution is small compared with gas flow, so refrigeration is less important with cyclotrons. Reliance is placed in such high pumping speeds that evolved gas and vapors are evacuated as rapidly as they are formed.

The MIT cyclotron vacuum-pumping system is typical and illustrates the techniques, although it does not contain all the features used in other installations. Two oil-diffusion pumps are used, bolted to 15-in. apertures on the bottom of the two D lines. Figure 6-23 is a diagram of the 12-in., three-stage, fractionating oil-diffusion pump. Various oils have been used successfully. A silicone-base oil has been most satisfactory and has given the longest service. The water-cooled baffle at the top of the pump is designed to intercept back-streaming oil vapor, yet to give maximum transmission for gas diffusing in the forward direction. It consists of a conical spiral of narrow, overlapping half-rings of thin copper with water-cooling tubing soldered along one edge of the rings. No refrigerant other than this water-cooled baffle is used.

The heating units at the base of the pump are formed of three 1-kw Calrod elements, cast into an aluminum block. Power can be adjusted separately on the three units to give maximum pumping speed. In operation the total power requirement for each pump is 1.8 kw.

In test runs with a calibrated air leak, the diffusion pumps developed a speed through the baffle of 1200 liters/sec each at 10^{-5} mm Hg. The total effective pumping speed for the two pumps of 2400 liters/sec is adequate for the 2000-liter volume. With no gas flow, chamber pressures of better than 1×10^{-6} mm Hg are obtained. With the deuterium gas flow from the ion source, the operating pressure is about 2×10^{-5} mm Hg, and pumping speed is materially increased by substitution of deuterium for air.

In the MIT installation no high-vacuum valves are used between D lines and pumps. Diffusion pumps are allowed to cool for a half-hour before admitting air. Valves were considered unnecessary in view of the infrequent need for opening the chamber to atmospheric pressure. Valves are commonly employed, however, in other installations.

Two mechanical pumps are connected to the low-pressure manifolds of the diffusion pumps, cross-connected so they can be operated in parallel for pump-down; a single pump can be used for normal operation. These pumps are two-stage units with a displacement of 7 liters/sec. The pair

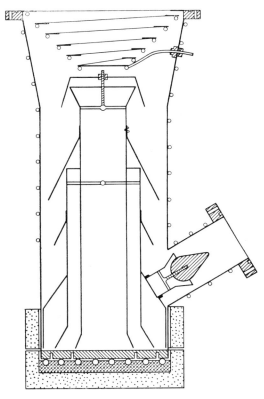

Fig. 6-23. Fractionating oil-diffusion pump of 12 in. diam developed for the MIT cyclotron. Two pumps are used.

will pump down the 2000-liter-volume chamber to the backing-pressure limit of the diffusion pumps in 20 min, about the time needed for the diffusion-pump heaters to rise to operating temperature.

The design and technique of vacuum seals have made steady progress through years of development. Simple, reliable seals are available for most of the special types of joints needed in an all-metal vacuum system. A basic design for a seal between parallel surfaces or flanges consists of a groove machined in one surface to hold a strip gasket in position, with suitable bolts between flanges to compress the gasket. The gasket may be a rectangular strip of rubber, taper-lapped at the joint and about 50 per cent thicker than the depth of the groove to allow for compression, or it may be an endless rubber ring of square cross section cut from a sheet, or it may be a continuous band of round cross section. This latter form is available commercially in a variety of sizes and materials and is known as an O-Ring. A double-gasket seal is frequently used with a pump-out connection to the space between gaskets. This arrangement makes it possible to test the seal for vacuum-tightness quickly and with certainty or to provide a pump-out port in case of a leak. Small grooves and gaskets can be used for small apertures where bolt pressure is small. On the other hand, ¼-in. gaskets have proved adequate for even the largest seals, if surfaces are machined and bolt pressure is uniform.

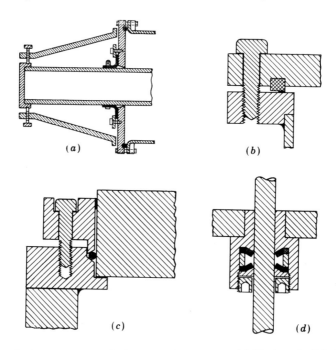

Fig. 6-24. Gasket vacuum seals for several purposes: (a) D-stem flexible joint and D-line ring-gasket seal; (b) detail of ring-gasket seal; (c) chamber lid seal using O-Ring and packing gland; (d) shaft seal allowing lateral and rotary motion.

Conductivity for rf currents through such a seal can be assured by half-covering the gasket with a thin copper-foil strip. Conversely, it can be adapted as an insulator with thick gaskets and fiber insulation around the bolts. For semipermanent seals soft fuse-wire or aluminum-wire gaskets have been successfully used.

Many movable joints are required for adjustments of the cyclotron D's, ion source, deflector, trimmer capacitors, etc. Figure 6-24 illustrates several of the seals developed for special purposes: a flexible diaphragm seal used for the adjusting motions of the large D stem (Fig. 6-24a); a square gasket in a groove for cover-plate seals (Fig. 6-24b); a typical pack-

ing-gland seal used for the chamber lids (Fig. 6-24c); and a seal which utilizes atmospheric pressure and the elasticity of rubber to make a movable
vacuumtight joint which allows in-out and rotary motion of a shaft
(Fig. 6-24d). Similar results can be obtained with O-Ring seals available
commercially.

Several grades of rubber and of synthetics are available as gasket
material. Low vapor pressure is the primary requirement; physical
strength and resilience come next. Most natural or artificial rubbers
have unacceptable vapor pressures and also deteriorate when used with
lubricating greases. Neoprene is free of these faults and is widely used
in cyclotrons. Myvaseal has even lower vapor pressures.

With the steady growth of a commercial vacuum industry, it is now
possible to buy all the essential parts of the vacuum pumping system,
including pumps, baffles, valves, and gauges. This eliminates much of
the design and development effort which went into the vacuum systems
of early cyclotrons.

6-11. TARGET ARRANGEMENTS

Targets for the cyclotron are of many types, depending on the needs of
the particular experiment. For some purposes probe targets are used to
intercept the resonant beam; these are mounted on stems with sliding
vacuum seals at the chamber wall. In this location the targets are
bombarded by the full intensity of the resonant beam, which may be
from 0.5 to 1.0 ma at energies between 10 and 20 Mev, giving a beam
power between 5 and 20 kw. Because of the small axial width of the
beam in the fringing field and the small radial spread which is desirable
when operating with an emergent beam, the cross section of the beam
may be less than 1 cm². Experience has shown that it is almost impossible to cool targets with such high power densities. Any target would
be destroyed by melting except those formed of metals of very high
thermal conductivity and high melting point. A variety of techniques
have been used to reduce power density by increasing surface area of the
target.

An oscillating probe target developed at MIT was able to dissipate up
to 10 kw of beam energy for certain target materials. The target was
formed of flattened copper tubing, in which the water-flow channel was
about 0.020 in. thick and 0.5 in. wide; water pressures of 40 psi resulted
in flows of about 1 gpm. The face of the target was also tilted relative to
the direction of the beam to increase surface area. This unit was
arranged with a flexible vacuum seal at the chamber wall so that it could
be oscillated transversely at 10 to 20 oscillations per second by external
motor drive, moving the face of the target across the beam and extending
the effective surface area to 1 in. length by ½ in. width. Thin plates of

beryllium and other metallic targets were silver-soldered to the face of this target for bombardment.

Still other techniques have been developed to utilize the resonant beam, such as deliberate detuning of the cyclotron to expand the transverse dimensions of the beam and decrease beam power density. However, in most high-intensity cyclotrons the beam intensity must be reduced below the available maximum because of this limitation on target cooling, and only the most refractory of target materials can be bombarded successfully. Nevertheless, probe targets are still used for special experiments in which the high current density is advantageous. When suitable target materials are available, the high beam density results in a high specific intensity of induced radioactivity and minimizes the inactive residue. With a Be target the concentration of fast neutrons beyond the target exceeds the neutron density in nuclear reactors by several orders of magnitude, so fast-neutron-induced activities can be produced efficiently in small target samples behind the Be target. The largest total yields of neutrons from a cyclotron are usually obtained with a water-cooled Be probe target in the resonant beam, through the $Be(d,n)$ reaction; so probe targets are used whenever the cyclotron is used as a neutron source. The yield of neutrons from this reaction is about 1 neutron per 200 deuterons at 15 Mev energy.

Targets for the emergent beam of deflected particles are located in a target box at the chamber wall where the beam emerges. This box can be separated from the cyclotron vacuum by a thin-foil window to allow rapid interchange of targets and to allow bombardment in a gaseous atmosphere if desired. For many target materials such a gaseous atmosphere (usually He) is essential for surface cooling and to limit evaporation and sputtering. With high-intensity emergent beams the thin-foil window is a limit to beam intensity; double-foil windows have been developed with gas cooling (He gas) of the foil surfaces by a gas jet introduced between the two foils. Occasionally, thin targets are used in the target box to limit bombardment energy to a narrow range, so the beam channel extends beyond the target box to a well-shielded "catcher" target at a distance. For the production of induced radioactivities in target materials which cannot readily be obtained in thin plate or foil form, a more extended target can be used which is tilted to present a large surface area to the beam; powder targets have been used in the emergent beam with this technique. Thin targets of special materials can be supported in polyethylene films.[30]

The radiation hazard to personnel from induced radioactivity in targets is a serious problem. Quick-acting valves and gates are essential to keep handling time a minimum; protective gloves and shields and long-handled tongs are important. A fully automatic target-handling mechanism would reduce the danger, but few practical systems have been devised and no system will eliminate all exposure for the maintenance staff. Cyclotron laboratories should adopt the best handling techniques from those developed for reactors.

Research studies of the primary processes of disintegration or scattering do not require high beam intensity but do require good energy resolution and low background radiation intensities. Many cyclotrons are now used primarily for the production of such low-intensity, well-focused emergent beams. These beams are brought out of the cyclotron vault through a narrow channel in the shielding wall into an external observation room in which the experimental apparatus is located, in some installations at distances of 20 to 40 ft from the cyclotron. A few such installations have been described in publications.[31,32] Usually a carefully designed set of focusing magnets is located near the cyclotron, and an analyzing magnet is used to select a narrow momentum band from the emergent beam. A typical result would be a 1-μa beam on a target of 1 cm^2 area at a distance of 20 ft, with an energy resolution of ± 0.5 per cent.

6-12. MAXIMUM ENERGY AND OPTIMUM SIZE

The relativistic increase in mass of the ions at high energies would need a magnetic field increasing radially outward to maintain resonance. This is forbidden by focusing requirements; in fact, a field which decreases with radius is essential. This conflict between the requirements for focusing and for ion resonance results in a theoretical and practical upper limit to the energy obtainable with a fixed-frequency cyclotron.

To evaluate this limit the resonance relation of Eq. (6-2) must be modified to the relativistic expression developed in Sec. 5-10, which expresses the mass in terms of particle rest energy W_0 and kinetic energy T using the relation $mc^2 = W_0 + T$:

$$f_i = \frac{c^2 eB}{2\pi(W_0 + T)} \tag{6-20}$$

Both decreasing magnetic field and increasing kinetic energy cause the resonant-ion frequency to decrease. The frequency of the electric field applied to the D's is fixed and has a magnitude intermediate between the initial and final values of ion frequency. As discussed in Sec. 6-4, this situation produces a phase shift, first toward a phase $\omega t_0 = -\pi/2$ and then back toward or beyond $\omega t_0 = 0$, with a total phase migration of about π radians. The applied rf voltage on the D's must be large enough that the number of accelerations is sufficiently small for the total phase migration to be within the above limit. Otherwise the ions move into a decelerating phase and go out of resonance.

Although this energy limit was recognized at an early date in cyclotron development, it was first analyzed in a publication by Bethe and Rose[33] in 1937. This was followed by a more detailed paper by Rose[16] in 1938. The energy limit was found to depend on the phase shift discussed in Sec. 6-4 and on the peak radiofrequency voltage applied to the D's. Rose gives the relation for the limiting energy in the form

$$T_m = KV^{1/2}(\cos \omega t_0)^{1/2} \qquad (6\text{-}21)$$

where V = peak voltage between D's

ωt_0 = initial phase

K = a constant involving the e/m of the ion and numerical conversion factors

The numerical estimates were based on the low D voltages obtained in small cyclotrons up to that time and on a theoretical shape of magnetic field for focusing. Assuming a D-to-D voltage of 50 kv, the predicted energy limits were 15 Mev for protons, 21 Mev for deuterons, and 42 Mev for He^{++} ions.

As might be expected, this theoretical threat to the future of the cyclotron was not taken seriously by experimentalists, who were convinced that technical improvements would raise the limits almost indefinitely. In fact, much larger cyclotrons have been built than were originally contemplated and much higher D voltages have been obtained. For large cyclotrons (60-in. or larger), continuous development of the rf power supplies to higher power and higher efficiency has resulted in D-to-D voltages well over 200 kv. When Rose's energy limit expression is reevaluated for this higher D voltage, it gives 30-Mev protons and 42-Mev deuterons.

A more complete analysis by Cohen[19] expresses the energy limit in terms of the minimum D voltage required to obtain a given proton energy. Figure 6-25 illustrates the D-voltage requirements to attain a given proton energy for various (linear) magnetic-field fall-off rates given in terms of the fractional decrease δ from center to edge of the field. The maximum energy limits indicated are in reasonable agreement with those cited above.

The limiting energy for a given cyclotron depends on the useful radius of magnetic field, the D spacing from the chamber lids, and the rf power available. A machine designed for high D voltage will require a long magnetic gap and high magnet power, as well as large rf power. So the cost of the magnet and rf components increases steeply, for a relatively small gain in ion energy as the limiting energy condition is approached. As a consequence, few of the existing cyclotrons approach the theoretical limits. The two largest fixed-frequency cyclotrons are the 86-in. machine at the Oak Ridge National Laboratory and the 88½-in. machine at the Nobel Institute in Stockholm. Both machines have produced protons of 22 Mev energy and deuterons of 24 Mev. Practical limitations on rf power and on the perfection of magnetic shimming have restricted the energies to values considerably below the theoretical limits.   Still larger and more powerful fixed-frequency cyclotrons could be built, but present installations appear to have come close to the practical economic limit for ion energy.

There is no longer any great pressure to push the standard cyclotron to its ultimate energy limit, since much higher energies can be attained with the frequency-modulated synchrocyclotron (see Chap. 11).   This is obtained, however, at the cost of a considerable decrease in beam intensity due to the pulsed duty cycle of the synchrocyclotron.   When the

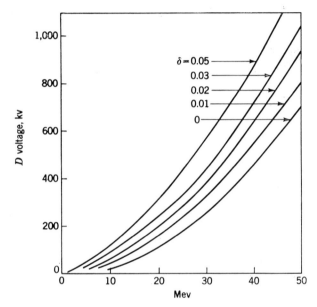

Fig. 6-25. Minimum D voltage required to obtain a given proton energy.   Curves for various (linear) magnetic-field fall-off rates, δ.   (Cohen.[19])

need arises for much higher beam intensities at energies above those available at present, the probable direction of development will be the strong-focusing cyclotron which is a variant of the alternating-gradient synchrotron described in Chap. 15.   The principle of the strong-focusing cyclotron was proposed by Thomas[34] in 1938, long before the more general theoretical development of alternating-gradient focusing came along in 1952, but it was neglected in favor of the synchroaccelerators in the intervening years (cf. Sec. 15-11).

The optimum size for a cyclotron depends on the planned use and is not necessarily the largest size.   Cyclotrons have had their greatest application in research laboratories, as sources of high-energy particles for studies of nuclear disintegration at energies surpassing nuclear potential barriers.   They have served as high-intensity sources of neutrons and for the production of a wide spectrum of induced radioactivities. A large fraction of research problems in these fields can be handled adequately with energies of less than 20 Mev.

Other accelerators supplement the cyclotron and help define its useful energy range. Electrostatic generators excel in the energy range below about 5 Mev to which they have been developed. The proton linear accelerator is the most direct competitor, producing protons of 60 Mev, and still higher-energy models are under construction. However, its short duty cycle results in considerably lower beam intensity than the cyclotron. For much higher energies, above 100 Mev, the synchro-accelerators take over. We can conclude that the cyclotron is the only instrument which accelerates light ions in the energy range from 5 to 25 Mev at high beam intensity. This energy range covers a wide variation in type of research program and in cost.

An estimate of the present cost of a 5-Mev cyclotron would be $20,000. The MIT 16-Mev cyclotron might be reproduced for about $120,000 exclusive of buildings or shielding. A modern 60-in. machine built by a commercial firm would cost at least $800,000, again exclusive of buildings. Magnet costs vary roughly with weight and so are proportional to (pole diameter)^3 or to $T^{3/2}$. However, total costs rise more steeply at larger sizes because of the additional requirements for high-power rf supplies and the surcharges on apparatus of a size approaching the limit of commercial availability. Most small cyclotrons were built 10 to 15 years ago and in academic laboratories where student help and surplus apparatus were available; they could be housed in existing buildings and operated by the existing staff. Large, modern installations require new laboratories, heavy shielding, and a staff of technical personnel for maintenance; most of the equipment must be purchased commercially and requires skilled labor for installation. So total costs rise far more rapidly than with $T^{3/2}$ in the high-energy range.

The productivity of a cyclotron, on the other hand, does not vary by such a large factor. Consider the production of neutrons or of a typical radioactivity. Yield increases exponentially at low energies where nuclear barrier penetration is the determining factor, then increases further only with target penetration as energy increases (roughly with $T^{3/2}$), and even falls below this rate of increase at high energies when target cooling is a limitation. Unit costs in the production of neutrons or radioactivity are considerably less for the medium-energy installations (15 Mev) than for larger machines (20 Mev and higher).

Other factors may be more important than cost comparisons. Research laboratories may experience a point of diminishing returns if the size and the complexity of the accelerator overburden the available staff. If the effort required for supervision, administration, and maintenance involves too large a fraction of the time of the research staff, productivity decreases. The size of the installation should not be disproportionate to the resources of the laboratory.

All sizes of cyclotron have their special areas of usefulness. A small institution with a limited budget will find that a small and inexpensive cyclotron in the 5- to 10-Mev range will be useful in providing student training and experience in nuclear physics. One in the 15-Mev range will provide a source of continuing scientific usefulness for research at minimum cost. For laboratories which have sufficient resources to take a leading role in exploring new research fields, the highest energies and highest intensities become important.

REFERENCES

1. E. O. Lawrence and N. E. Edlefsen, *Science*, **72**:376 (1930).
2. R. Wideröe, *Arch. Elektrotech.*, **21**:387 (1928).
3. M. S. Livingston, "The Production of High-velocity Hydrogen Ions without the Use of High Voltages," Ph.D. thesis, University of California, Apr. 14, 1931.
4. E. O. Lawrence and M. S. Livingston, *Phys. Rev.*, **37**:1707 (1931); **38**:136 (1931); **40**:19 (1932).
5. J. D. Cockcroft and E. T. S. Walton, *Proc. Roy. Soc. (London)*, **136A**:619 (1932); **137A**:229 (1932).
6. E. O. Lawrence, M. S. Livingston, and M. G. White, *Phys. Rev.*, **42**:1950 (1932).
7. M. S. Livingston, *Phys. Rev.*, **42**:441 (1932); M. S. Livingston and E. O. Lawrence, *Phys. Rev.*, **43**:212 (1933); E. O. Lawrence and M. S. Livingston, *Phys. Rev.*, **45**:608 (1934).
8. E. O. Lawrence and D. Cooksey, *Phys. Rev.*, **50**:1131 (1936).
9. E. O. Lawrence, L. W. Alvarez, W. M. Brobeck, D. Cooksey, D. R. Corson, E. M. McMillan, W. W. Salisbury, and R. L. Thornton, *Phys. Rev.*, **56**:124 (1939).
10. M. S. Livingston, *Rev. Sci. Instr.*, **7**:55 (1936).
11. M. C. Henderson and M. G. White, *Rev. Sci. Instr.*, **9**:19 (1938).
12. A. Allen, M. B. Sampson, and R. G. Franklin, *J. Franklin Inst.*, **228**:543 (1939).
13. P. G. Kruger et al., *Rev. Sci. Instr.*, **15**:333 (1944).
14. M. S. Livingston, *J. Appl. Phys.*, **15**:2 (1944); **15**:128 (1944).
15. W. B. Mann, "The Cyclotron," rev. ed., Methuen's Monographs, Wiley (1953).
16. M. E. Rose, *Phys. Rev.*, **53**:392 (1938).
17. R. R. Wilson, *Phys. Rev.*, **53**:408 (1938).
18. R. R. Wilson, *Am. J. Phys.*, **11**:781 (1940).
19. B. L. Cohen, *Rev. Sci. Instr.*, **24**:589 (1953).
20. El Cerrito Cyclotron, *Phys. Today*, **1**:10 (1948).
21. R. J. Jones and A. Zucker, *Rev. Sci. Instr.*, **25**:562 (1954).
22. R. J. Jones, *Phys. Rev.*, **91**:223 (1953).
23. H. Atterling, *Arkiv Fysik*, **7**:503 (1954).

24. M. S. Livingston, M. G. Holloway, and C. P. Baker, *Rev. Sci. Instr.*, **10**:63 (1939).

25. M. S. Livingston, *Rev. Mod. Phys.*, **18**:293 (1946).

26. D. B. Cowie and C. J. Ksanda, *Rev. Sci. Instr.*, **16**:224 (1945).

27. R. S. Livingston and R. J. Jones, *Rev. Sci. Instr.*, **25**:552 (1954).

28. R. J. Jones and A. Zucker, *Rev. Sci. Instr.*, **25**:562 (1954).

29. J. Backus, *Rev. Sci. Instr.*, **22**:84 (1951).

30. N. S. Wall and J. W. Irvine, Jr., *Rev. Sci. Instr.*, **24**:1146 (1953).

31. B. R. Curtis, J. L. Fowler, and L. Rosen, *Rev. Sci. Instr.*, **20**:388 (1949).

32. K. Boyer, H. E. Gove, J. A. Harvey, M. Deutsch, and M. S. Livingston, *Rev. Sci. Instr.*, **22**:310 (1951).

33. H. A. Bethe and M. E. Rose, *Phys. Rev.*, **52**:1254 (1937).

34. L. H. Thomas, *Phys. Rev.*, **54**:580, 588 (1938).

At the head of the facing page is an illustration of the University of Illinois 300-Mev betatron.[8]

7

The Betatron—Magnetic Induction Accelerator

In the betatron, electrons are accelerated by the electric field induced by a changing magnetic flux linking the electron orbit. The magnetic field at the orbit provides the central force (which produces circular motion) and increases with increasing electron energy so the orbit is of essentially constant radius. A basic arrangement is a doughnut-shaped vacuum chamber in the gap between ring-shaped poles of an electromagnet, with a shorter gap and higher fields in the central region to provide the flux linkage required for induction. Figure 7-1 is a schematic cross section of such a magnet and vacuum chamber.

The concept of using a time-varying magnetic field to provide an electric field for the acceleration of electrons to high energy has been considered by physicists for many years. It has the advantage of avoiding the limitations of insulation breakdown characteristic of direct-voltage generators, and the magnetic guide field retains the electrons in circular orbits of small dimensions so the size of the accelerator can be small. The energy gained by an electron in one revolution is equivalent to the induced voltage in a one-turn coil, if it were located at the orbit. The magnitude of this induced voltage is given, as for the transformer, by the time rate of change of magnetic flux linking the orbit, $d\Phi/dt$. Since electron velocities are large, approaching the velocity of light at a few Mev, the electrons can make many revolutions in a short time and acquire high energy.

7-1. HISTORICAL DEVELOPMENT

Among the many investigators who have attempted to accelerate electrons by magnetic induction, none were successful until D. W. Kerst[1,2] of the University of Illinois produced 2.3-Mev electrons in 1940. His success depended on careful magnet design based on the detailed orbit stability calculations of Kerst and Serber.[3] This first model was amazingly successful, producing X rays with an intensity in the forward direction equivalent to the γ-ray intensity from 1 gm of radium. It was immediately evident that much higher energies could be produced in this way. Kerst next transferred his base of operations to the General Electric Company Research Laboratory, where with the collaboration of this

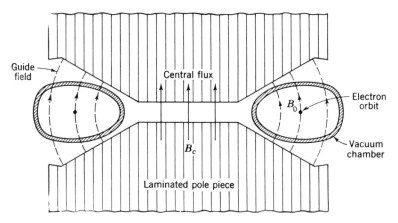

Fig. 7-1. Schematic diagram of a betatron magnet and vacuum chamber, showing the orbit field B_0 and the central core supplying the linkage flux B_c for acceleration.

experienced laboratory staff, a 20-Mev betatron was completed in 1942.[4] Westendorp and Charlton[5] of the General Electric Company continued the development with a 100-Mev machine in 1945. Commercial production was started at GE and also at Westinghouse and Allis-Chalmers companies, primarily in the 20-Mev energy range, to meet the rising demands from research laboratories, hospitals, and industrial plants. In Europe electrical manufacturing companies have also entered the field. The chief developments have come from the Philips Laboratory at Eindhoven, where Bierman[6] has built small betatrons both with and without iron yokes, and at Brown-Boveri in Switzerland, directed by Wideröe.

Meanwhile Kerst returned to the University of Illinois to build first an 80-Mev model[7] and ultimately a 300-Mev machine[8] which represents the largest and possibly the ultimate betatron.

It is of some interest, however, to look back at the early years before 1940 to see how the concepts gradually developed. Kerst[9] has made a careful survey of published and unpublished work to find the origins of the induction accelerator.

The significance of the magnetic term curl $\mathbf{E} = -\dfrac{d\mathbf{B}}{dt}$ in the equations of the electromagnetic field had been recognized by many scientists, and the formulation $\oint E\,ds = -\dfrac{d\Phi}{dt}$ for the induced voltage per turn due to a changing flux Φ is taught in all elementary courses in electricity. That this electric field would accelerate free charges as well as the conduction electrons in a wire coil of a transformer was obvious. However, the first proposal to apply this principle to the acceleration of electrons seems to have come in 1922, in J. Slepian's U.S. Patent 1,645,304. Kerst has shown that this first proposal was impractical because of the lack of suitable focusing fields. In 1927 Breit and Tuve[10] studied the possibility of using the induction principle to develop a source for nuclear studies. In their apparatus a rapidly increasing magnetic field was produced by spark discharge of a large capacitor through a coil; electrons started at the outside would spiral inward in this field and would increase in energy. However, they failed to appreciate the need for a radially decreasing field to give focusing. If the focusing feature had been added, the apparatus might have worked as an X-ray source of low efficiency, but it was abandoned in favor of the more controllable electrostatic generator for the projected nuclear studies.

Wideröe[11] in 1928 came closer to a practical accelerator. He made a major advance in recognizing the requirements for acceleration at constant radius and developed the 2:1 rule (see Sec. 7-2). However, he did not at first recognize the necessity for magnetic-field shaping to produce axial and radial focusing, and his method of injection using an external cathode gun was cumbersome and unsuitable for the relatively slow rise in magnetic field. Walton[12] built an apparatus based on the electrodeless ring discharge principle, which can be considered a forerunner of the modern betatron without iron yoke. Although he was unsuccessful experimentally, Walton made an important contribution in solving the theoretical problem of radial focusing forces (see Chap. 5). Jassinsky[13] extended the calculations of orbit stability, considering a magnetron-like situation with an axial magnetic field and radial electrostatic field. M. Steenbeck developed an idea based on the Wideröe accelerator and in 1937 took out U.S. Patent 2,103,303 on an experimental apparatus; however, the patent does not indicate that it was based on an operating machine. This was followed by unpublished work on an operating model, and Steenbeck has since claimed[14] to have obtained high-energy X rays.

Several other workers are known to have made attempts to accelerate electrons by induction; apparently all of these were unsuccessful and unpublished. However, the concept was discussed and speculations

exchanged over a period of several years by many others.   It seems clear
that the complete stability theory of Kerst and Serber and the careful
and thorough magnet design calculations of Kerst were a prerequisite to
a practical accelerator.   The major credit for the development of the
betatron justifiably goes to D. W. Kerst.

7-2. THE ACCELERATION PRINCIPLE

The fundamental problem in the design of an induction accelerator is
to maintain the necessary proportionality between magnetic field at the
orbit, B, and electron momentum $p = mv$, so that orbit radius remains
constant.

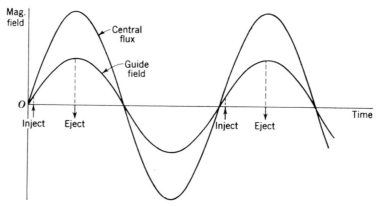

Fig. 7-2. Time cycle for acceleration of electrons in a betatron with sinusoidal magnet
excitation; the guide field and central flux are in phase.

The magnetic field at the orbit must increase with time to maintain
constant radius for electrons of increasing energy.   This is usually
accomplished by powering the magnet cyclically from an ac supply.
Acceleration occurs during the quarter-cycle when the field is increasing
from zero to its maximum.   The time cycle for acceleration is illustrated
in Fig. 7-2, on a sinusoidally varying magnetic-field plot.   Electrons are
injected at low energy when the guiding field at the orbit is small; they
reach maximum energy at the peak of the field cycle.   As the electrons
approach maximum energy, they can be diverted against a target, producing X rays.   The X rays occur in a sequence of short pulses at the
frequency of the power supply.   In order to avoid losses due to eddy
currents, the iron is laminated as in a transformer.

The magnetic field required to produce circular motion depends on the
energy of the electron.   It is given in mks units by [see Eq. (5-49)]

$$B = \frac{mv}{er} = \frac{(T^2 + 2TW_0)^{1/2}}{cer} \tag{7-1}$$

where T = kinetic energy
$\quad W_0$ = rest energy (m_0c^2)
$\quad\quad r$ = orbit radius
$\quad\quad e$ = charge
$\quad\quad m$ = relativistic mass of electron

Evaluating this relation for a numerical example where $r = 0.5m$ and $T = 100$ Mev, we find

$$B = 0.67 \text{ weber/m}^2 \text{ or } 6700 \text{ gauss}$$

This shows that high-energy electrons can be retained in reasonably small orbits by readily available magnetic fields.

The time rate of increase of momentum is a measure of the electrical accelerating force acting on the electron and can be expressed in terms of the time rate of change of flux linking the orbit. In rationalized mks units this is given by

$$\frac{dp}{dt} = \frac{e}{2\pi r} \frac{\partial \Phi}{\partial t} \tag{7-2}$$

Integrating to find the momentum acquired owing to a finite flux change, we have

$$p = \frac{e(\Phi_2 - \Phi_1)}{2\pi r} \tag{7-3}$$

But from Eq. (7-1) we have for momentum $p = eBr$, where B is in the same direction as $(\Phi_2 - \Phi_1)$, so

$$\Phi_2 - \Phi_1 = 2(\pi r^2)B \tag{7-4}$$

Thus the flux change within the orbit must be *twice* the value obtaining if flux density were uniform and equal to the field at the orbit. This is the now-famous 2:1 rule. To satisfy the requirement there must be a strong central field linking the orbit and a weaker field at the orbit. Both fields must increase proportionately with time, the central field to provide the acceleration and the field at the orbit to retain the particle of increasing energy in an orbit of constant radius. The particular orbit for which this 2:1 ratio applies can be called the equilibrium orbit. We use the symbols r_0 for the radius and B_0 for the magnetic field at this orbit, so the equilibrium momentum p_0 is given by

$$p_0 = eB_0r_0 \tag{7-5}$$

An electron having momentum $p_0 + \delta p$ differing from that of the equilibrium electron will describe an orbit of radius $r_0 + \delta r$ given by

$$p_0 + \delta p = eB(r_0 + \delta r) \tag{7-6}$$

where B represents the field strength at the new radius.   The new orbit will enclose a total flux whose rate of change is

$$\frac{\partial \Phi}{\partial t} = 2\pi r_0{}^2 \frac{\partial B_0}{\partial t} + \int_{r_0}^{r_0 + \delta r} 2\pi r \frac{\partial B}{\partial t} \, dr$$

Since B will not change materially in the neighborhood of the equilibrium orbit, we can rewrite this relation as

$$\frac{\partial \Phi}{\partial t} = 2\pi r_0 (r_0 + \delta r) \frac{\partial B_0}{\partial t} = 2\pi r r_0 \frac{\partial B_0}{\partial t}$$

Consequently, for this nonequilibrium particle, Eq. (7-2) gives

$$\frac{dp}{dt} = \frac{e}{2\pi r} \frac{\partial \Phi}{\partial t} = e r_0 \frac{\partial B_0}{\partial t} \tag{7-7}$$

But this is the same rate of change of momentum as obtains for the equilibrium particle.   Consequently, this particle will gradually tend to have the same momentum as does the equilibrium particle, since its total momentum will eventually become so large that the initial momentum error will become negligible.

The fact that the rate of change of momentum is independent of radius leads to the conclusion that [from Eq. (7-6)]

$$d[B(r_0 + \delta r)] = r_0 \, dB_0$$

whence, since B will not differ appreciably from B_0,

$$\frac{d(\delta r)}{\delta r} = -\frac{dB_0}{B_0} \left(= -\frac{dT}{2T} \text{ for nonrelativistic particles} \right) \tag{7-8}$$

We conclude that a particle released on an instantaneous orbit such that its momentum corresponds to its radial distance from the center according to Eq. (7-6) will spiral asymptotically toward the radius at which the $2:1$ rule is satisfied.   If the momentum and radius do not correspond to this relation, the particle will oscillate around the instantaneous orbit given by Eq. (7-6) in the fashion already discussed in Secs. 5-9 and 5-10.   The path of this particle will gradually tend toward the equilibrium orbit as just shown, but it will now include an oscillation around the instantaneous orbit whose radius is tending asymptotically toward the equilibrium radius.

To summarize, we have shown that a particle injected at any point in the neighborhood of the equilibrium orbit will gradually tend toward an orbit satisfying the $2:1$ rule.   This concept, first developed by Kerst and Serber, is fundamental to the demonstration of the soundness of the betatron design.

The shift in orbit radius toward the equilibrium orbit described above led Kerst to the concept of an injection system which proved successful. He reasoned that electrons released from a cathode or injection gun outside of the equilibrium orbit would have subsequent orbits of smaller radius and some of the electrons could miss the back of the injector and be accelerated. With an electron gun displaced 1.5 cm from the equilibrium orbit injecting 200-volt electrons, he noted that Eq. (7-8) indicates a decrease in orbit radius of 1 mm per revolution provided only that the rate of increase of energy is about 25 volts per turn. The gun was to emit electrons continuously at the indicated energy. As the magnetic field increased, there would be a short period when the orbits would satisy the correct relations and a fraction of the injected electrons could be captured and accelerated.

The injection scheme was successful but, as is now known, not for the reasons given. As the injection energy was increased through the range where all electrons should have been lost on the back of the injector, the intensity of the accelerated beam continued to increase. The present interpretation of this discrepancy will be discussed in Sec. 7-8, Electron Injection.

7-3. ORBITAL STABILITY

An additional requirement for acceleration is that there be spatial focusing for particles which deviate in direction from the equilibrium orbit. During acceleration the electrons must make many revolutions and so have very long total paths. In the first Illinois betatron it was estimated that the electrons made about 200,000 revolutions and traveled a total distance of 100 km during a quarter-cycle of the 60-cycle applied magnetic field. In order that the electrons do not wander to the walls of the chamber during these many revolutions, it is essential that the magnetic field provide strong focusing forces restoring the particles to the median plane and the equilibrium orbit. (It is also necessary that the gas pressure be small so beam intensity will not be drastically reduced by gas scattering.) As has been shown in Chap. 5, such focusing forces can exist in a magnetic field which decreases with increasing radius. Here we present a qualitative review of the stability conditions; the detailed equations of motion were presented in Chap. 5.

In a radially decreasing field specified by the relation

$$B_z = B_0 \left(\frac{r_0}{r}\right)^n \tag{7-9}$$

a particle will experience restoring forces both toward the median plane and toward the equilibrium orbit provided only that n lies between zero and unity. The radial restoring force will be proportional to $(1 - n)$

and the vertical restoring force will be proportional to n. The frequencies of oscillation around the equilibrium orbit were given by Eqs. (5-67) and (5-68); both are slightly lower than the frequency of revolution of the electrons in their orbits. Specifically, the frequency of the radial oscillation is

$$f_r = (1 - n)^{\frac{1}{2}}f_0 \qquad (7\text{-}10)$$

and the frequency of the vertical oscillation is

$$f_z = n^{\frac{1}{2}}f_0 \qquad (7\text{-}11)$$

where f_0 is the frequency of revolution of the electrons and is given by

$$f_0 = \frac{eB_0}{2\pi m} \qquad (7\text{-}12)$$

As was shown in Eqs. (5-69) and (5-70), the amplitude of these oscillations is damped as the electron energy increases. While the electrons are in the low, nonrelativistic range, the amplitude decreases in proportion to $T^{-\frac{1}{4}}$; in the high-energy, relativistic range the amplitude damps more rapidly in proportion to $T^{-\frac{1}{2}}$.

So long as no perturbations are introduced, the amplitude of these free or betatron oscillations will be determined by the injection conditions. The relative amplitudes of the radial and vertical oscillations will also be affected by the relative restoring forces; for n values close to unity the radial oscillations will tend to be large and the vertical oscillations will be more strongly restored. If n is close to zero, the vertical amplitudes will tend to be large and the radial oscillations will be more strongly focused. Since vertical space in an electromagnet is usually more costly than radial space, n values are usually nearer to unity than to zero; preferred values have been between 0.6 and 0.75.

Thus we see that the equations of motion of an electron in such a radially decreasing magnetic field lead to stable oscillations about the particle orbit. During the early stages of acceleration these oscillations will be centered on the instantaneous orbit, which itself will approach the equilibrium orbit asymptotically. Oscillation amplitudes are damped by the increasing magnetic field so the cross section of the circulating beam of electrons will decrease with increasing energy. Figure 7-3b illustrates a radial oscillation about the equilibrium orbit; Fig. 7-3c combines this oscillation with the asymptotic damping of the instantaneous orbit (Fig. 7-3a) to illustrate a more general case. Axial oscillations, not shown in the figure, give the true orbit a three-dimensional envelope shaped like a thin, flattened doughnut.

The location of the equilibrium orbit can be changed by changing the proportionality in the betatron relation during the progress of the cycle. It is possible to make the equilibrium orbit drift inward or outward to

strike a target on the wall of the chamber.   For example, if the central
flux change is made more rapid than indicated by Eq. (7-4) as the particle
approaches maximum energy, the momentum will increase and the
equilibrium orbit will expand.   This motion is slow enough to be essentially adiabatic, and the spatial focusing is not disturbed.   Electrons will

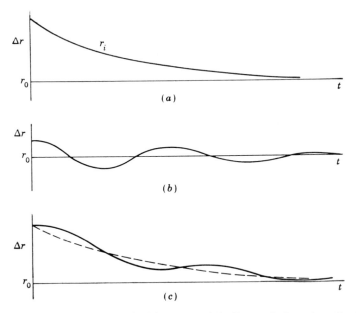

Fig. 7-3. Paths of electrons unrolled into a straight line and plotted as the displacement Δr from the equilibrium orbit r_0: (a) tangential injection on the instantaneous
circle r_i; (b) damped oscillation around the equilibrium orbit; (c) damped oscillation
around the instantaneous circle which contracts toward the equilibrium orbit.

peel off against the edge of a target, requiring hundreds of revolutions for
all the electrons to reach this radius.

7-4. MAGNET DESIGN

The magnet of a betatron provides two components, the field at the
orbit and the central flux required for acceleration.   These components
are linked through the requirement of the betatron relation: The central
flux must change at a rate *twice* that obtaining if the central field were
uniform and equal to the field at the orbit.   Two basically different magnet structures have been employed.   In the smaller betatrons a single
magnetic circuit carries the return flux for both the guide field at the
orbit and the central flux; the central flux density is increased by use of a
shorter air gap to establish the betatron condition.   For the larger
machines, separate magnetic circuits are used and the central flux core is

biased to allow a larger flux change for induction; in this case the exciting coils for the separate circuits are powered in parallel to maintain the proportionality of field and flux.

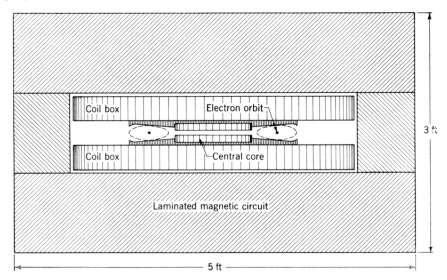

Fig. 7-4. Diagram of the magnetic circuit for the 20-Mev betatron designed by Kerst.[4]

A good example of the simple single-circuit type is the magnet for the 20-Mev betatron[4] (Fig. 7-4). This magnet has a 19-in.-diam pole face with an 11-in.-diam central core. It is constructed of stacks of 0.014-in.

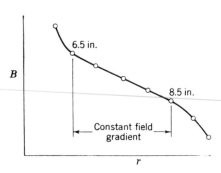

Fig. 7-5. Magnetic field versus radial position in the 20-Mev betatron, showing the region of constant magnetic gradient.[4]

silicon steel transformer laminations. Laminations of different lengths are grouped into tapered radial sectors to form the cylindrical poles. The return for the magnetic circuit consists of packages of laminations assembled as an external yoke as in transformer design, but with the packages separated by spacers to provide ducts for air-blast cooling. The total weight of iron is about 3.5 tons. The assembly is clamped together by maple planks and long bolts.

Laminations forming the pole face between the 5.5-in. and 9.5-in. radii are shaped to provide a radially decreasing field with a value of $n = 0.75$; measurements on a small dc model were used to obtain the correct shape. A plot of the field shape near the orbit location (at a radius of 7.5 in.) is shown in Fig. 7-5; here B

is plotted against r and the straight-line portion between 6.5 and 8.5 in. indicates a constant value of n.   This rate of variation of field with radius is approximately 10 per cent per inch; at 6.5 in. the required field is $1.11B_0$ and at 8.5 in. it is $0.91B_0$, which specifies dimensions for the tapered gap.

The shorter air gap in the central core is obtained by inserting two disks of laminated iron bonded into a rigid structure by a thermosetting resin. The thickness of the disks determines the residual gap length and the flux density through the core and thus establishes the orbit radius for which

Fig. 7-6. The 20-Mev betatron with magnet coils and vacuum chamber in place.   The top pole is removed.

the betatron condition holds.   This was predetermined by model measurements to give an equilibrium orbit radius of 19 cm (7.5 in.).   The vertical location of the two disks within the central gap can be varied to modify the shape of the field in the adjacent region enclosing the vacuum chamber and is adjusted to extend the region of uniform n to the smallest possible radius.   Figure 7-4 illustrates the arrangement of poles and vacuum chamber of the 20-Mev machine; Fig. 7-6 is a photograph of the magnet and chamber assembly showing the excitation coils, with the upper pole removed.

Exciting windings for the 20-Mev magnet consist of 81 turns of stranded wire about each pole, firmly clamped and contained in Textolite coil boxes.   At the chosen operating frequency of 180 cps, and with the

coils in series, an external capacitor bank of 5.5 μf is required for resonance.   A resonant circuit is desirable in order to relieve the generator of
the otherwise large reactive current.   With the resonant capacitor in
series, the current and voltage in the exciting winding are almost 90°
apart in phase and the generator has to supply only the resistive and
eddy-current losses.   The circulating power required to excite the magnet
for the 20-Mev betatron is 1750 kva; losses in the windings, the capacitors,
and the iron total only 26 kw.   One of the most expensive components of
the betatron is the capacitor bank to handle the large circulating currents;
power ratings for the capacitors must be adequate for 1750 kva in this
case.

The 180-cps power is obtained from a 3-phase 60-cycle line by means
of a frequency-tripling circuit (Fig. 7-7).   Three separate transformers
are run at very high flux density so that saturation effects, which
develop third harmonics in voltage, become noticeable.   Primaries

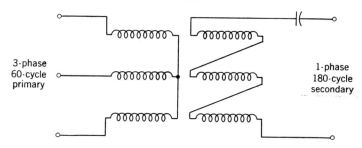

Fig. 7-7. Frequency-tripling circuit with resonant capacitor for 180 cps.

are connected in Y so the tripled-frequency voltage cancels out at the
primary terminals, and the secondaries are connected in series so
that the 60-cycle voltage cancels at the secondary terminals.   This output is connected in series with a six-turn primary winding coupling the
magnet coils and a smaller resonant capacitor bank capable of handling
the 26-kw load.

The magnetic field at the orbit for 20-Mev electrons can be computed
from Eq. (7-1) to be

$$B_0 = \frac{(T^2 + 2TW_0)^{1/2}}{cer_0} = 0.36 \text{ weber/m}^2 = 3600 \text{ gauss}$$

To maintain the betatron flux condition, the total change in flux within
the orbit given by Eq. (7-4) would be

$$\Delta\Phi = 2\pi r_0^2 B_0 = 0.082 \text{ weber}$$

We shall consider the simple case where central flux and orbit field are
proportional, and compute the magnitude of the central flux density, B_c.
If we assume this central core field to be uniform inside the 5.5-in. radius

and to have an average value of $1.11B_0$ between 5.5 and 7.5 in. (the value at 6.5), and if we compute the areas of these two regions, we obtain as an estimate of the central field

$$B_c \sim 1.0 \text{ weber/m}^2 = 10,000 \text{ gauss}$$

This illustrates the high central flux density required for such a single-circuit magnet.

Precise calculations of the flux linking the orbit, from the peak ampere-turns in the winding and the dimensions of the magnetic circuit, can be used to compute electron energy and predict the equilibrium orbit radius. An experimental method available in model studies is to use a one-turn coil at the orbit location in series with an integrating capacitor and a high resistance. The voltage developed on the capacitor at the time of ejection can be measured with a vacuum-tube voltmeter; it is proportional to the flux change within the orbit and so gives the equivalent electron energy. Both methods were used for the 20-Mev betatron, and the results agreed within 1 per cent. This indicates that the location of the equilibrium orbit was known to good precision.

The magnets for the 300-Mev betatron[8] and the 80-Mev model[7] for this machine utilize separated magnetic circuits. A sketch of the assembly of the 80-Mev magnet is given in Fig. 7-8. The flux magnet is a continuous iron core with dual return legs similar to a transformer core. The excitation windings are distributed in four symmetrical coils about the top and bottom yokes. The field magnets consist of six C-shaped cores which fit between the yokes of the flux magnet so as to produce the orbit field in an annular region surrounding the core. Laminations for these six segments are bent and stacked to form a radial array and thus produce the most uniform field possible at the orbit. This bundling into six packages leaves six V-shaped notches of sufficient dimensions to allow the passage of an X-ray beam or to insert leads for the electron injector or for measuring instruments. The careful design of this field magnet resulted in an extremely uniform magnetic field at the orbit, described as being "two orders of magnitude smoother than the fields of earlier conventional betatrons." Copper shielding is provided between the two magnetic circuits to eliminate flux leakage which might distort the fields. Excitation windings are circular and located close to the magnet gap. They consist of two equal coils—one split between top and bottom, which provides the field excitation, and one backwound coil in the gap between pole tips, which confines the field to the region between pole faces and eliminates fringing flux.

The reason for this extreme care in magnet design and the strenuous efforts to obtain uniform fields is that injection must occur at very low fields. Known techniques of injection make it possible to produce electron beams of between 50 and 100 kv, but not much higher. At 60 kv, for example, the field at the orbit at injection is 22 gauss for the 80-Mev model, but injection occurs at only 7 gauss for the 300-Mev betatron. It is obvious that small asymmetries in the field such as might result from physical irregularities or variations in remanent field would be much more serious for the large machine. Separation of the flux and field magnets was essential to obtain the field uniformity needed.

The magnetic-field shape chosen for the 80- and 300-Mev machines does not have a constant value of n, but varies from $n = 1$ at injection

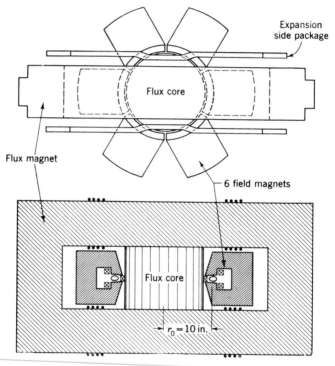

Fig. 7-8. Assembly sketch of magnetic circuits for the 80-Mev betatron, showing the separation of flux and field magnets.[7]

radius to $n = 0.2$ at the inner wall of the chamber. The value at the computed equilibrium orbit radius is $n = 0.5$; this orbit radius is 26.5 cm for the 80-Mev model and 122 cm for the 300-Mev betatron. In such a field with n a function of radius, the radial and axial oscillations are much more complicated functions than for constant n, and the shape of the orbits cannot be described simply. One advantage is that orbit position can be set for any desired n value by varying the betatron balance, and the optimum orbit location can then be determined experimentally. Also injection and ejection are both facilitated near $n = 1$ because of the spiral-shaped paths and wide spacing between turns. However, the most important reason for choosing a small value of n over most of the orbit region is that it minimizes the shrinkage in orbit radius caused by radiation loss as the electrons reach high energy. This conclusion comes from a more detailed study of the equations of motion. The problem of energy loss by radiation is described in Sec. 7-7.

7-5. BIASED BETATRONS AND FLUX FORCING

Probably the most significant improvement in betatron design occurred with the introduction of the concept of field biasing, which forces the flux to change through a larger numerical value of $d\Phi/dt$. This concept makes use of the relation found in Eq. (7-4), that the flux *change* ($\Phi_2 - \Phi_1$) is the quantity proportional to maximum orbit field B_0. In early betatrons both orbit field and central flux passed through zero ($\Phi_1 \simeq 0$) at the same instant, and the resulting acceleration was limited by saturation of the core at the peak central flux Φ_2; furthermore, to satisfy the proportionality of Eq. (7-4), orbit field is limited to a much smaller value than can readily be obtained with iron magnetic circuits. For larger betatrons this single magnetic circuit is inefficient, and it is advantageous to excite the two field components separately so both central flux and orbit field can approach the limits set by saturation of the iron. An increase in orbit field by almost a factor of 2 can be achieved by having the flux in the central core reverse direction while orbit field rises from zero to maximum. This can be accomplished by suitably biasing either of the two magnetic circuits with a direct current in the winding.

This feature was appreciated by several workers in the field. Independent publications by Kerst[15] and Westendorp[16] first described the principle of biasing and flux forcing, but it appears that other workers in Italy[17] and Germany had arrived at the same conclusions by that time and were also designing betatrons to take advantage of flux forcing.

The power required to produce a given central flux can be greatly reduced by eliminating the air gap in the central core. This follows from the fact that the energy stored in the field in iron is small compared with that in even a short air gap. With no air gap the inductance of the exciting winding is increased and the size and power rating of the resonant capacitor bank is greatly reduced. The size and cost of the capacitor can be reduced to about one-third that for a conventional betatron of the same electron energy. This saving is significant in the design of high-energy betatrons.

One way to eliminate the air gap is to have two separate magnetic circuits powered with separate exciting windings. If these windings have the correct number of turns to satisfy the betatron relation of Eq. (7-4), and if they are powered in parallel from the same resonant capacitor bank, the fields in the two circuits will rise proportionately. This arrangement for parallel powering of the two magnetic circuits is called "flux forcing." An elementary circuit showing the parallel connections for field and flux coils is illustrated in Fig. 7-9. A fine adjustment of the induced voltage and hence of orbit radius can be made by moving taps of a small autotransformer connected to one of the coils.

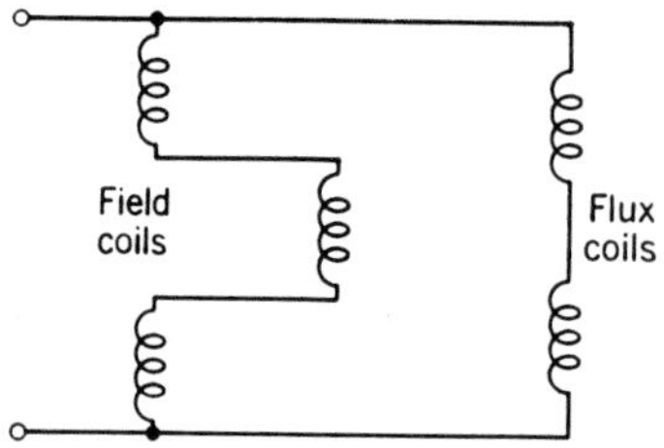

Field coils

Flux coils

Fig. 7-9. Elementary flux-forcing circuit.

The advantages of flux forcing can be obtained in another way by isolating the two magnetic circuits of a single magnet core electrically and magnetically, even though they are not physically separated. This was in fact the first proposal and was applied to the first betatron single-circuit magnets to increase the energy output. This separation can be achieved by the use of another coil in the magnet windings. Kerst called it a "backwound" coil and located it in the magnet gap just inside the doughnut-shaped vacuum chamber; Westendorp proposed a split coil having two components located in grooves in the pole faces at the same location; he called these "groove" coils. The effect of this backwound

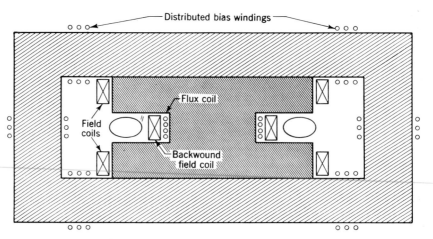

Fig. 7-10. Location of exciting and bias coils in a flux-biased betatron having a single magnetic circuit.[7]

coil is to cancel out the flux in the central core produced by the main windings, thereby confining the guide flux to the annular region near the orbit. The number of turns and the geometry of the coils can be adjusted so the central flux is completely canceled; if so, another separate flux winding is required to produce the central flux. Or the ampere-turns in the backwound coil can be smaller than for the main coil, leaving an excess to provide the central flux for acceleration.   The location of such a backwound coil is illustrated in Fig. 7-10.

A disturbing feature of the use of flux forcing in a closed flux core is introduced by the variable reluctance of the iron.   The air gap in the orbit field has essentially constant reluctance, but as the flux-core iron approaches saturation its permeability drops and its reluctance increases. This effect causes a distortion of the proportionality of flux to field, and the radius of the equilibrium orbit shifts.   Since increased core reluctance reduces central flux, the result is a slower acceleration than required for the betatron balance, and the orbit contracts.   In a betatron economically designed to have a small region of stability around the orbit this effect can be serious and requires correction.

Small changes in radius of equilibrium orbit can be corrected by adding more flux in a separate magnetic circuit; such a compensating circuit is needed also to correct for radiation losses (see Sec. 7-7) and is used in the 300-Mev betatron.

Kerst has suggested another method of maintaining the flux-field proportionality.   Two auxiliary coils can be used, one linking the central flux and one the orbit-field flux; the turns ratio can be adjusted so induced voltage is the same across the coils for the desired flux-field relation, and when the coils are connected in opposition, there will be no current in them.   Then if this relation is disturbed by the iron-saturation effect, a current will circulate in this pair of coils and will set up fields to oppose the change.   The residual error in the flux forcing system with such correcting coils will be determined by the resistive voltage drops in the auxiliary coils and can be held to any desired value.   Such techniques make it possible to use flux densities in the core as large as 14 to 16 kilogauss.

Two methods are available for biasing a betatron to provide the advantage gained by flux forcing.   These depend on whether the dc bias is applied to the orbit field or to the central flux.

In *field biasing*, the magnetic field at the orbit is arranged to have a steady component by a dc component in the windings.   If this steady field is approximately half the maximum set by saturation of the poles and if the ac component has the same magnitude, the field will vary from zero to maximum during a half-cycle of the applied ac current.   During this half-cycle the central flux will vary from its maximum negative to its maximum positive value, a total flux change approaching twice that available without biasing.   Electrons can be accelerated to nearly twice the energy at the same orbit radius.   Figure 7-11a illustrates the field and flux waveforms for such a field-biased betatron.

Injection of electrons occurs at low electron energy when the orbit field is just starting to rise from zero.   However, the rate of change of field should be fairly large at injection to obtain a fast build-up of energy and provide good focusing forces at the start, so in practice the bias is made somewhat smaller than the amplitude of the ac component. Ejection also occurs slightly before the peak of the cycle, before magnetic field has reached its maximum. The total variation of field and flux that

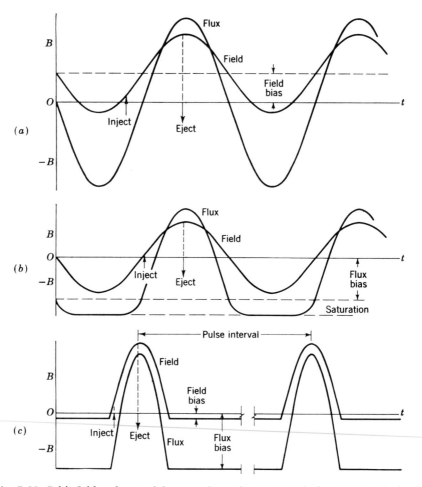

Fig. 7-11. Orbit field and central flux waveforms for (*a*) field biasing, (*b*) flux biasing—continuous operation, and (*c*) flux biasing—pulsed operation.

can be utilized, as chosen by designers, is about 86 per cent of the maximum possible.

Figure 7-12 is a simple schematic circuit for supplying dc bias current to the orbit field. The direct current is supplied in series to the groove coils and the main coils. The groove coils are used here merely to cancel the dc component in the central flux core; the main coils provide ac components for both orbit field and core flux.   An ac filter is placed in series with the dc generator in this circuit to limit the ac current in the windings of this machine.

Flux biasing utilizes a dc magnetic component in the central flux field, which nearly saturates the iron in the negative sense.   The ac component superimposed on this bias carries the flux density through zero and to a positive maximum during the quarter-cycle when orbit field is going from zero to maximum.   The orbit field can now be powered to approach its maximum practical value, and the doubled electron energy comes from the doubled change in central flux, from $-\Phi_c$ to $+\Phi_c$ during the quarter-cycle.   The waveforms for continuous operation are shown in Fig. 7-11b; here the negative half of the ac flux cycle is shown lopped off by the saturation of the iron.   It should be noted that flux biasing oversaturates

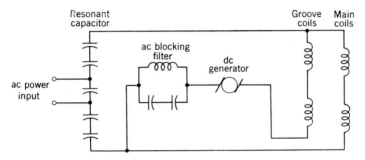

Fig. 7-12. Powering circuit for a field-biased betatron, showing the dc generator and a filter to reduce ac current in the groove coils.[16]

the central core during the negative half-cycle.   In a large magnet this results in such large and undesirable magnetic losses due to hysteresis that it is impractical to operate continuously.   However, pulsed operation is possible, and the duty cycle can be adjusted to reduce losses and heating to a satisfactory level and to hold input power to a practical value.   Figure 7-11c illustrates the waveform for unidirectional pulsing which can be used with flux biasing.

Flux biasing was chosen for the 300-Mev betatron for several reasons. First, fewer bias ampere-turns are required to saturate the central core, which has no air gap, than to half-saturate the field magnet, which does. Second, the choke coil needed in the ac filter to limit the magnitude of current induced in the bias coil during the flux change is smaller by one-tenth than for field biasing.   Third, flux biasing lends itself to unidirectional pulsing rather than continuous operation.   For the large magnet used in the 300-Mev betatron, the power consumption would have been excessive for continuous operation.   Unidirectional pulsing allows a design for lower power input, smaller coils, and reduced coil heating; magnet design is more compact, leakage flux is minimized, and capacitor ratings and costs are reduced. The smaller duty cycle due to pulsing results, however, in lower average beam intensity.

The flux bias supply for the 300-Mev betatron is not described in detail in the publications. However, that for the 80-Mev model[7] can be cited to illustrate the design. Separated bias windings are distributed about the flux core to give maximum magnetic efficiency and minimum leakage flux. Power comes from a high-capacity 4.8-volt battery, supplying 97 amp to the windings. During the flux pulse large voltages and high currents would be induced in this winding, which would oppose the flux change and essentially short-circuit the voltage pulse. A simple but clever arrangement is used to prevent this short-circuiting. A choke coil which has its secondary winding installed in series with the bias supply has a primary winding connected to the betatron terminals. As the voltage pulse builds up on the terminals, a secondary voltage is produced

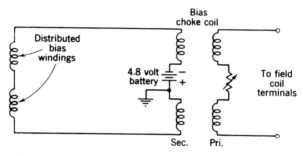

Fig. 7-13. Flux bias circuit for the 80-Mev betatron, with a choke coil to oppose the induced voltage.[7]

in the choke coil which just bucks out the induced voltage in the bias windings. The circuit for the dc-bias-coil connections, including the choke coil, is shown in Fig. 7-13. Note the center-tapped coils used for both magnet winding and choke coil; this allows mid-points to be grounded to give a balanced circuit and reduce capacitance effects.

7-6. PULSE POWERING

Continuous operation of a betatron magnet on an ac power supply is limited by heating of the iron due to hysteresis and eddy currents. As electron energy is increased, all considerations tend to increase this heating. The time of acceleration must be short to reduce losses due to gas scattering and radiation; this requires high-frequency operation, which increases the eddy-current heating. Magnetic-field intensity in the iron approaches saturation at the peak of the cycle and actually exceeds saturation in the negative cycle for flux biasing; this also increases heating. Furthermore, heating is proportional to volume and increases with the third power of a linear dimension of the magnet, while surface area, through which it can be cooled, increases only with the second power.

Oil-immersion cooling of the laminations, which is common for power transformers, is impractical for the betatron. The efficiency of air-blast cooling is limited to a fraction of that obtainable with oil cooling, and air ducts are difficult to install in a betatron magnet without seriously crippling accessibility to the vacuum chamber.

In the design of the 300-Mev betatron it was found that heating of the iron limited the duty cycle during which the magnet could be powered to about one-twentieth of the total time. Pulsed operation was chosen, with a unidirectional pulse of $\frac{1}{120}$-sec duration (essentially a half sine wave at 60-cycle frequency) repeated at a maximum rate of 6 pulses/sec. In the 80-Mev model, which was operated at the same flux densities, the limitation imposed by the scaled-down current-carrying capacity of the windings reduced the duty cycle to 1 pulse every 3 sec. As a consequence, the 80-Mev machine was not so flexible and did not produce as high intensities as could have been attained had the windings been designed efficiently for that energy.

Pulsed operation does not reduce the size or cost of the capacitor bank, which is one of the most expensive components. The size of the capacitor bank is determined by the fact that it must be able to store all the energy required to power the magnet a quarter-cycle later. Once the magnet is designed and its maximum stored energy determined, the requirements of the capacitor bank are fixed. Frequency can be adjusted by changing the series-parallel connection of the capacitor bank. In higher-frequency operation the capacitor losses will be higher and their kva rating lower, so the costs may be increased somewhat.

The pulse power supply for the 80-Mev betatron is shown in Fig. 7-14a, producing the sequence of operations indicated in Fig. 7-14b. A three-phase full-wave rectifier using six thyratrons, which has a dc output of 1100 volts, provides a charging current of 30 amp to the 5000-μf capacitor bank. The charge-discharge cycle is controlled by a pair of solenoid-type contactors, arranged as a reversing switch. The main pulse is triggered by a mercury-pool ignitron. Voltage on the capacitor bank reverses during the discharge through the exciting coils, and the final voltage is about 25 per cent less than the initial voltage owing to dissipation in the coil windings and the ignitron. This loss is made up by recharging the capacitors from the rectifiers.

The flux-forcing circuit is also indicated in Fig. 7-14a. It involves a fairly intricate balance between induced voltages in the several coils and resistive voltage drops. Field windings are represented by coils A (back-wound) and coils B (main winding) in series; the flux windings are the distributed C coils. The location of these coils in the magnet is shown in Fig. 7-8. A variable series resistor R_T in the flux circuit is used to obtain a first-order balance between the resistive voltage drops in the two wind-ings; since this is alternating current, the resistance must be measured and balanced for the fundamental frequency of the exciting pulse. Higher harmonics in the flux windings, which are due to the effect on

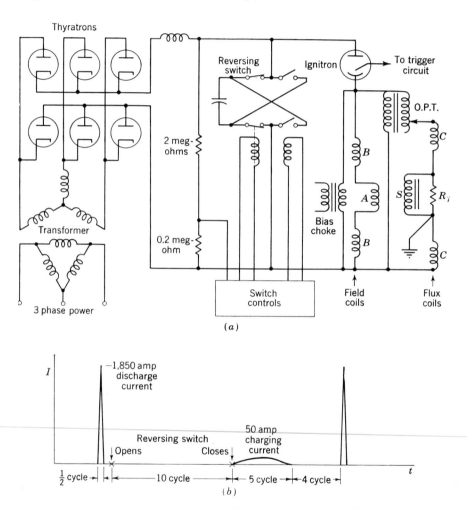

Fig. 7-14. (*a*) Pulse power supply for the 80-Mev betatron.[7]　(*b*) Sequence of power-supply operations at 3 pulses/sec.

inductance of the varying reluctance of the iron flux core, are corrected by a saturating reactor (*S*) placed in parallel with R_T.　An orbit positioning transformer (labeled O.P.T.) varies the potential applied to the flux wind-ings by a small amount, to change the field-flux ratio and position the orbit as desired.　The exciting coils are grounded at their mid-points to provide symmetrical circuits and equalize the effects of capacitance in the windings.

The large and steep rise of current at the start of a pulse induces eddy-current transients in the iron which take a finite time to become established. This is the time required for the magnetic field to penetrate the iron and depends on the thickness and condition of saturation of the laminations. This flux penetration time is given by[7]

$$t = \frac{\pi\mu d^2}{3 \times 10^9 \rho}$$

for the rise time to 95 per cent of full value for the eddy currents; ρ is resistivity in ohm-cm, d is the thickness in centimeters, and μ is the differential permeability. For the heavily biased 0.014-in. silicon-steel laminations used in the 300-Mev magnet, this time is 7.5 μsec.

During the time required to establish the eddy currents the proportionality between field and flux will be changing, so the equilibrium orbit will not have constant radius. This time may be longer than the time for the field to rise to the injection value, which depends on injection voltage. The technique used to correct for this starting transient with the 300-Mev magnet was to apply a small negative field bias (about 28 gauss) to allow time for eddy currents to become established (see Fig. 7-11c).

The only published description of the 300-Mev betatron[8] is very brief. It can be summarized by the dimensions and constants given in Table 7-1. The best photographic illustrations are published in *Life* magazine.[18] The primary purpose in building the 300-Mev machine was to attain energies at which mesons could be produced. This result has been achieved, and present activity in the Illinois laboratory centers on scientific studies of meson properties and interactions.

TABLE 7-1
CONSTANTS OF THE 300-MEV BETATRON

Maximum electron energy	315 Mev
Orbit radius	122 cm
Maximum orbit field	9.2 kilogauss
Initial flux density	−14 kilogauss
Final flux density	16 kilogauss
Weight of flux magnet	275 tons
Weight of six field magnets	66 tons
Energy stored in capacitor bank (field magnet, 85 per cent; flux magnet, 15 per cent)	170,000 joules
Flux-core bias winding	2,600 amp-turns
Injection energy	80–135 kv
Peak injection current	1–3 amp
Pulse repetition rate	6 pulses/sec
X-ray output at 1 m, ⅛ in. Pb	14,000 r/min

7-7. RADIATION LOSS

A charged particle constrained to move in a circular orbit by a central accelerating force radiates energy because of this acceleration. The magnitude of this radiation loss can be computed from the classical theory of the electromagnetic field. Iwanenko and Pomeranchuk[19] first pointed out that this effect would disturb the betatron relation and would ultimately set an upper limit on the energy that could be attained by this machine. Blewett[20] analyzed the problem as applied to betatrons, and Schwinger[21] has presented a complete study of classical radiation by accelerated electrons. A valuable analysis of radiation by accelerated relativistic electrons is available also in chap. 7 of "Electrodynamics," by Page and Adams.

These various authors have shown that an electron having velocity v and acceleration a in a direction normal to the velocity vector will lose energy by radiation at a rate given by

$$U = \frac{2 \times 10^{-7} e^2 a^2}{3c(1 - v^2/c^2)^2} \qquad \text{watts} \qquad (7\text{-}13)$$

It is worthy of note that application of a Lorentz transformation to modify this relation to a reference frame in which the electron is instantaneously at rest changes the formula to

$$U = \frac{2 \times 10^{-7} e^2 a^2}{3c} \qquad \text{watts} \qquad (7\text{-}14)$$

which is the classical formula first derived by Larmor for radiation from a slowly moving electron.

For an electron constrained to travel in a circular path of radius r, a is v^2/r; since the radiation effects are appreciable only in the extremely relativistic range, we can replace a by c^2/r. The quantity $(1 - v^2/c^2)$ can be replaced by $\left[\dfrac{m_0 c^2}{e(W/e)}\right]^2$, where W/e represents the energy of the electron in electron volts. With these substitutions Eq. (7-13) becomes

$$U = \frac{2 \times 10^{-7} e^6 (W/e)^4}{3 m_0^4 c^5 r^2} \qquad \text{watts} \qquad (7\text{-}15)$$

After substitution in this formula for the fundamental constants we obtain

$$U = 6.76 \times 10^{-43} \frac{(W/e)^4}{r^2} \qquad \text{watts} \qquad (7\text{-}16)$$

or

$$U = 4.22 \times 10^{-24} \frac{(W/e)^4}{r^2} \qquad \text{ev/sec} \qquad (7\text{-}17)$$

But one revolution takes $2\pi r/c$ sec and therefore

$$U = 8.85 \times 10^{-32} \frac{(W/e)^4}{r} \qquad \text{ev/revolution} \qquad (7\text{-}18)$$

From this relation it is evident that appreciable energy loss will not be experienced until W is of the order of 100 Mev. Above this energy the loss will increase very rapidly until, for example, a 1-Bev electron in a betatron with a radius of 10 m would lose 8850 ev of energy per revolution, an amount that would be difficult to supply by betatron techniques.

A useful concept in the mathematical treatment of radiation effects is that of an effective retarding electric field E'. The radiation loss has the same slowing-down effect on the electron as would be experienced in a continually retarding field E', which can be obtained from Eq. (7-18) as

$$E' = 1.408 \times 10^{-32} \frac{(W/e)^4}{r^2} \qquad \text{volts/m} \qquad (7\text{-}19)$$

Two other features of the radiation are derived in the references cited; the derivations are beyond the scope of this book, but the results can be stated. The radiation is generally emitted in the forward direction, and the higher the particle energy the more sharply is the radiation collimated. The half-intensity contour is a rough cone whose internal half-angle is approximately equal to $m_0 c^2 / W$ radians. For 100-Mev electrons this angle is about 0.3°. The second feature of interest is the spectral distribution of the radiation. It is spread over 10^7 or more harmonics of the fundamental revolution frequency with an energy distribution whose maximum is usually in the visible spectrum. As a consequence of these phenomena it is easy to see the radiation by looking along a tangent to the orbit (with a mirror) at the side where the electrons are approaching the observer. A bright spot of light is clearly visible; its intensity can be used as a measure of beam intensity. In Chap. 12, The Electron Synchrotron, observations will be discussed which give experimental checks of all of the predictions of the theory.

The total energy loss during acceleration can be obtained by integration of Eq. (7-17) over the acceleration cycle. For the 300-Mev betatron the total loss is about 13 per cent of the total energy. If no compensating means were included, the orbit would shrink about 20 per cent and the beam would be lost by collision with the inside wall of the vacuum chamber.

To correct for this loss the relation between orbit and flux change must be modified; central flux must rise at a faster rate than for strict proportionality. Or, alternatively, the orbit field can increase less rapidly, which can be accomplished by designing the magnet so that saturation sets in and reluctance increases in the orbit-field circuit faster than for the central flux.

A betatron with flux forcing can be arranged to have more flux added at the peak of the flux cycle to compensate for this radiation loss, at least up to some practical limit. In the 300- and 80-Mev magnets a section of the central pulse-transformer core was reserved for the dual purpose of adding flux to correct for radiation loss and for expanding the orbit against a target at ejection time. This section has about 7 per cent of the cross section of the central core and is supplied by a magnetic return circuit which does not link the exciting coils for the central core (see Fig. 7-8). Separate windings on these "expansion side packages" are excited late in the cycle by a separate power supply, with a voltage rise time designed to give the correct rate of flux increase and orbit expansion.

It is necessary to shield the side packages of laminations from the main flux in the core to prevent partial saturation by leakage flux. This is done by copper shields wrapped around the core, with an insulated, over-lapped split to prevent short-circuiting currents in the shield. Eddy currents developed in the copper sheet by the leakage flux set up reverse fields which cancel the leakage flux. This also results in a lower inductance of the side-package circuit, making it possible to pulse it with a sharply rising voltage pulse.

In the design of the 300-Mev betatron the radiation loss has been carefully considered and corrected for. Both methods are used: modifying the field-flux proportionality in the windings and forcing additional flux through the core. The fractional radiation loss is held to about 8 per cent by allowing electrons to remain in the machine for only 75° of the magnetic excitation cycle, which means that ejection occurs at 3.5 per cent below peak magnetic field. The corrections are sufficient to maintain essentially constant orbit radius up to the ejection pulse and to have an excess adequate to expand the orbit out to the target radius. This required very delicate balancing of many factors entering in the design.

The fourth-power increase of energy loss by radiation suggests that it will be impractical to attempt to push betatron designs to much higher energy. Most designers feel that the present 300-Mev machine represents the practical maximum energy for a uniform-n betatron. With the introduction of the synchrotron principle of electron acceleration it is possible to add energy electrically through use of an accelerating gap; the necessary volts per turn can be added more economically this way than through magnetic induction. So it seems probable that synchrotrons will provide a more satisfactory method of attaining higher energies. However, in practice, higher beam intensities have been attained with betatrons than with synchrotrons, and in the lower energy range, where magnet cost is not a limitation, the betatron has a distinct advantage.

7-8. ELECTRON INJECTION

Electrons are injected into the betatron tangentially at an instantaneous orbit located just inside the radial position where the magnetic field becomes defocusing. The injector gun consists of a heated cathode, a focusing electrode, and an outer shield. A typical structure is shown in Fig. 7-15, taken from the description of the 20-Mev betatron. A tight helical spiral of tungsten wire is used for the cathode, giving a line source some 0.5 to 1.0 cm long. The focusing electrode is a curved reflector behind the cathode, having a potential slightly negative relative to the cathode and shaped to produce a focused beam of electrons. The outer shield, constructed of molybdenum or tungsten sheet with a slot for the beam to emerge, is at ground potential. The cathode is operated at high negative potential, so the electrons have high injection energy. Potentials of 600 volts for the first 2.3-Mev accelerator, 20 kv for the 20-Mev machine, 60 kv for the 80-Mev model, and up to 135 kv for the 300-Mev machine have been reported, indicating a steady development to higher injection energy.

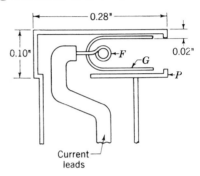

Fig. 7-15. Electron injector gun, showing filament F, focusing electrode G, and outer shield P, which is grounded. Peak beam current pulses of 1 to 3 amp are produced.

Peak injection currents of several amperes can be obtained from such a source. The beam emerging from the injector gun is not sharply focused but diverges at an angle of 5 or 10°. A large fraction of the beam is lost to the walls within the first turn.

The success of this injection scheme depends on the chance that an electron will miss hitting the back of the injector on subsequent turns. Calculations of the rate of decrease of instantaneous orbit radius as it spirals into the equilibrium orbit show the change per turn to be extremely small. The contraction will follow Eq. (7-8):

$$\frac{d(\delta r)}{\delta r} = - \frac{dB_0}{B_0} = - \frac{1}{2}\frac{dT}{T}$$

where δr = displacement from the equilibrium orbit

  B_0 = magnetic field

  T = kinetic energy

A sample calculation of the magnitude of this contraction per turn will be informative.

Consider injection of 20-kev electrons into an orbit at 8.5 in. radius in the 20-Mev betatron, in which the equilibrium orbit is at 7.5 in. To calculate the increase in energy per turn we must find the flux change or the energy change per turn at the start of the acceleration cycle. In a previous section we showed that the total flux change corresponding to 20-Mev electrons at peak orbit field was 0.082 weber. The total acceleration time is a quarter-cycle at 180 cps, or 0.0014 sec, and the slope of a sine wave at the start of the cycle is $\pi/2$ times the average slope. So the initial induced voltage per turn is

$$V_i = \frac{(\pi/2) \, \Delta\Phi}{\Delta t} = \frac{1.57 \times 0.082}{0.0014} = 92 \text{ volts/turn} \tag{7-20}$$

At the injection energy of 20 kev this represents a change in energy of 1 part in 460; from Eq. (7-5) this is equivalent to a change in displacement ($\delta r = 1$ in.) of 1 part in 920, which is roughly 0.001 in. This is much smaller than the dimensions of the injector; if it were necessary to depend on this effect alone, essentially all electrons would strike the back of the injector and be lost.

Another feature which must be considered in injection is the radial and axial oscillation of the electrons about their instantaneous orbits. For the value of $n = 0.75$ chosen for the 20-Mev betatron magnet these oscillation frequencies are $f_r = 0.50f_0$ and $f_z = 0.864f_0$. Particle orbits will be complicated three-dimensional curves which cross the equilibrium orbit once each revolution and which cross the median plane once each 208° in azimuth. A plot of the path of a typical electron projected on the median plane (which shows only the radial variations) is shown in Fig. 7-16. The damping motion is exaggerated in the illustration to show successive circles, which are numbered in order. The plot shows that the electron will miss the injector in the first, third, fifth, etc., passages and will be closest to the injector on the second revolution. However, the axial oscillations will be out of phase after two turns (720° of azimuth) and will have approximately maximum amplitude at this point, so the electron has a good chance of missing the injector vertically. Such considerations suggest that on the average an electron will traverse 5 to 10 revolutions before again having large positive radial amplitude and small axial amplitude at the location of the injector. The orbit contraction will be five to ten times greater by this time, and it might be supposed that some of the electrons would miss the back of the injector and be captured in stable orbits. The injector unit in modern betatrons is made as narrow as possible in the axial dimension in order to increase the chance of missing the injector through the vertical oscillations.

The analysis of orbit contraction above predicts the largest radial displacement at low injection energy. Early designers assumed this to be valid; note the 600-volt maximum designed for the 2.3-Mev machine. Nevertheless it was found experimentally from the start that beam intensity increased with increasing injection energy, approximately with

$V^{3/2}$. It was a mystery to all concerned how electrons could miss the injector in early betatrons. Designers accepted the experimental fact and used the highest practical injection energy.

Kerst[22] has proposed a theory of self-contraction to explain the high injection efficiencies. It offers a specific mechanism and Kerst cites some evidence to support it, but other workers feel that self-contraction is not the most important factor.

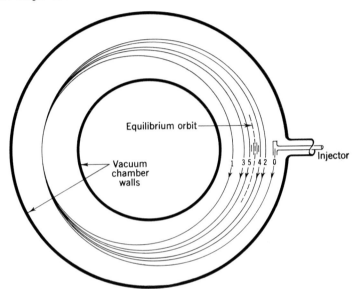

Fig. 7-16. Successive electron paths in a magnetic field for which $n = 0.75$ ($f_r = \frac{1}{2}f_0$). Damping is exaggerated to show contraction toward the equilibrium orbit following injection.

Self-contraction is due to energy withdrawn from the kinetic energy of the beam in setting up an electromagnetic field. It can be visualized most simply in terms of current in a wire loop at the location of the beam. Consider that a current is established in this loop in a time comparable with one revolution; it will produce a magnetic field within the loop which opposes the flux already threading the loop. Kerst has computed the inductance L of such a loop in the 20-Mev betatron to be about 4×10^{-6} henry, mainly because of the large central flux present. The voltage drop around this loop is given by $L(di/dt)$; if 1 amp were to be set up in one revolution, approximately 10^{-8} sec, the voltage would be

$$V = -L\frac{di}{dt} = -4 \times \frac{10^{-6}}{10^{-8}} = -400 \text{ volts} \qquad (7\text{-}21)$$

So the electron beam might be reduced in energy by 400 ev in one revolution owing to this effect alone. If several revolutions are required to establish the circulating beam, the loss might be spread out over these several revolutions.

The existence of the beam of electrons at the orbit location also means that a concentration of space charge has been set up which produces an electrostatic field. The energy in the electrostatic field due to this charge can also be estimated. Kerst has computed that the energy required to set up this electrostatic field subtracts from the beam 150 ev energy per electron in each turn. Others believe that space-charge effects can be even more important and that a detailed and precise analysis would justify this opinion.

It is clear that the complete interpretation must include the effect of magnetic-field inhomogeneities, electrostatic repulsion within the beam, build-up of electrostatic charges on the walls, damping of oscillations due to these various factors, and possibly other unrecognized influences. For example, Heyman[23] has found that it is possible to increase injection efficiency and beam intensity by applying a negative bias to the metallic coating of the chamber relative to the injector shield.

One useful improvement in experimental technique has resulted from studies of orbit contraction. This is the orbit contractor reported by Adams.[24] Adams uses a wire loop on each pole face above and below the orbit location; these loops are connected to a pulsed power supply which produces a rising current pulse during injection. The direction of current in the loops is such as to retard the rate of rise of flux within the orbit. This causes electrons in orbits outside the equilibrium orbit to be suddenly drawn in toward this orbit. The action is similar to the action of the beam on itself in self-contraction and provides a practical method of controlling this phenomenon. The increasing current in these loops reduces magnetic field inside the orbit radius relative to that outside. This change of field shape represents a decrease in n value near the orbit. Radial-oscillation frequency will be increased, as will the damping of these oscillations, by this change in n value. The complete theory of the orbit contractor is obviously complicated. Experimentally it has resulted in a considerable increase in X-ray yield from all betatrons to which it has been applied, indicating an increase in the percentage of electrons trapped at injection.

Orbit contraction is a consequence of the increase of circulating current in the beam. Consequently electrons which are injected after the time when they can be trapped, but which can circulate for a few revolutions before striking the walls, will also retard the rate of rise of central flux and hence serve to contract orbits for the useful electrons injected earlier. It was noted at a very early stage that beam intensity could be increased by continuing injection for a short time past the acceptance interval, but that there was a drop in yield if injection was continued through the full cycle. This optimum length for the total injection pulse was reported[4] to be about one-twelfth the full quarter-cycle for the small betatrons. Only a fraction of the injected electrons are actually accelerated; one author estimates[25] a final peak beam current of 0.2 amp, although the injection beam was of the order of 1 amp.   It has been observed that a low-intensity beam from a very short pulse can be increased in intensity by a larger factor than that from a long pulse when the orbit contractor circuit is utilized.   We can conclude that the postinjected beam is useful chiefly in supplying orbit contraction to the trapped beam.   Modern betatrons such as the 80-Mev machine, which is equipped with orbit contractor coils, do not require as long an injection pulse; the optimum pulse for this machine was found to be 5 μsec.

Continuous injection results in lower intensities than pulsed injection. The decrease seems to be due to the disturbing magnetic and electrostatic fields set up by the delayed electrons.   Late in the cycle, at high magnetic fields, the orbits of electrons injected at the constant injection energy will be small spirals.   These asymmetric circulating currents can set up distorting magnetic fields near the injector.   Also the electrostatic charge collected on the walls may become large enough to deflect and defocus the trapped beam.   So pulsed injection is now standard procedure, with a variable pulse length which is adjusted experimentally to give maximum beam intensity.

A rising voltage pulse on the injector is found to give higher intensities than a flat-topped pulse.   This is understandable from the simple concept of matching injection energy to magnetic field over a longer time interval. Other effects may be involved, such as the rising emission current from the injector, which aids in orbit contraction.   The optimum pulse shape also is obtained by experimental manipulation.

Azimuthal inhomogeneities in the orbit field at injection time can have a serious effect on beam intensity.   This problem was studied in detail by Adams, Kerst, and Scag[26] for four similar 22-Mev betatrons built for commercial sale; the azimuthal fields were measured using the peaking strip technique (see Sec. 7-9, Magnetic Measurements).   Fluctuations as large as ±5 gauss were observed at different azimuths, and all four magnets were different.   Such bumps in the field can produce electron oscillations of sufficient magnitude to reduce intensity significantly.   They are due to phase differences in the field at different portions of the magnetic circuit, caused by variations in lamination thickness, hysteresis and eddy-current losses, or by accidental short circuits between laminations.   The out-of-phase components can be corrected by coils located beneath the orbit at the indicated locations, powered with out-of-phase currents to correct the phase angle.   The use of such correcting coils increased yield in all betatrons to which they were applied by from 20 to 50 per cent. When the field variations were reduced to about 3 per cent of injection field (1 to 2 gauss at 45 gauss), no further improvement could be obtained.

This criterion for "smoothness" of the magnetic field applies to the geometric aperture of the 22-Mev machines; other betatrons with relatively smaller vacuum chambers would require proportionately smaller fluctuations in field.

It should be noted that the injector could be located alternatively inside the equilibrium orbit, if desired, rather than outside. The instantaneous orbit would spiral outward toward the equilibrium orbit in this case. Focusing forces for deviant electrons exist as before. The orbit contractor could be arranged as an orbit expander by reversing the direction of the current pulse. This injector location is particularly useful when an emergent beam is to be extracted from the betatron, in which case it would be advantageous to have the outer region of the chamber free from obstructions except for the extractor device. Similarly, the injector could be located above or below the orbit, in which case vertical injection oscillations would be the limiting factor.

The most complete theoretical analysis of the injection problem in the betatron was published by Schwartz[27] in a German journal. He has considered the problem of a divergent electron beam and has determined the envelope of particle paths in the first few revolutions after injection. With this more detailed analysis most of the phenomena observed at injection are explained. The time interval of acceptance into stable orbits is found to increase with injection voltage. The effect of field inhomogeneities is studied and the necessary uniformity computed. The angle of divergence at the source which can be accepted into the available aperture is found to be independent of injection voltage and to improve with improved field uniformity. During the acceptance time interval the allowed angle of divergence increases from zero to a maximum and falls back to zero. So injection efficiencies can now be fairly well computed if all constants are known.

7-9. MAGNETIC MEASUREMENTS

Probably the most significant contribution to electrical science and practice coming from the development of the betatron has been the improved knowledge of principles, methods, and techniques for magnetic measurements and magnet design, largely as a result of the design study of the 80-Mev model by Kerst and his associates. The emphasis placed by Kerst on perfection paid off in a striking way in the 300-Mev betatron, which operated at full designed energy almost from the start. It is a noteworthy example of the importance of careful design. An excellent description of these design studies and model measurements has been published.[8] We shall summarize here some of the more significant results.

The criterion for producing an azimuthally uniform magnetic field is that the reluctance be the same through any section of the magnetic circuit. The bundles of C-shaped laminations used for the orbit-field circuit were designed to have essentially equal length of iron through each path. The radial tapering at the pole face was obtained by chopping laminations of different lengths and assembling the long and short ones symmetrically, with the short ones distributed so that the magnetic inhomogeneities introduced were "fine-grained." The assembly technique was aimed at preventing any magnetic flux from having to cross from one lamination to another.

The radial variation of field across the pole face was chosen to have the index n vary from 0.2 at the inside wall to 0.5 at the orbit radius and to 1.0 at the location of the injector. The contour to provide this field shape was determined by successive trials with a dc model of one-tenth scale of the 300-Mev machine, constructed with $\frac{1}{8}$-in. laminations. Measurements were taken with a search coil and ballistic galvanometer actuated by the reversal of field in the dc model.

Excitation windings must be installed in such locations that the lines of field H are everywhere parallel to the laminations in which the induction B is to be established. This was accomplished for the orbit-field circuit by using simple circular windings, axially symmetrical with the poles. It would not have been sufficient to distribute these windings over the six back-legs of the C's.

Distortions can exist in the field because of different thicknesses of iron or imperfections in the geometry of assembly. Other distortions are observable primarily near zero field or the low fields at injection. Leakage flux from the pulsed excitation of the core can be eliminated by suitable copper shielding. Residual magnetism can vary in different samples of iron because of variations in manufacturing or handling procedures. The magnitude of the remanent field observed in the model was about 3.5 gauss, and the variations were less than 0.1 gauss. Eddy-current fields can be inhomogeneous, depending on the presence of short circuits between laminations. This was sufficiently corrected by inserting paper insulation between laminations at $\frac{1}{4}$-in. intervals. Phase lags at the pole tips caused by the distribution of eddy-current electromotive forces about the circuit may also be important; they have the effect of increasing the value of n at injection time. Although correction was not necessary in this case, it was found that such phase lags can be corrected by distributed windings about the circuit sufficient to compensate for the distributed losses in the circuit.

Several instruments have been devised for measuring small field variations at or near zero field. The "peaking-strip"[26,28] method uses narrow strips of permalloy or Hypernik, which saturate at very low fields, wound with a small solenoidal coil of many turns. Use of the peaking strip for magnetic measurements is discussed in Sec. 8-8.

A "zero-field detector" has been developed[8] which is essentially a cathode-ray gun which shoots a beam of 100-volt electrons through fine slits and against a collector. As the field passes zero, an electron pulse is collected. A bias coil can be used and pulses from two detectors can be observed in coincidence, to measure the field difference. Much shorter pulses can be obtained with this detector than with the peaking strips, and the method is free from possible errors due to variable magnetic properties of the strips. When this detector was used, no variation of orbit field with azimuth was observed as great as 0.1 gauss in the 80-Mev model.

A small milligaussmeter reported by Adams, Dressel, and Towsley[29] is capable of high precision and is a novel application of magnetic amplifier technique. The method consists in measuring the second-harmonic content of the exciting current for a ferromagnetic peaking strip which is normally excited to partial saturation. The second-harmonic component appears when the strip is biased by an external magnetic field, and the amount is directly proportional to this field. The magnitude of the sharp pulses induced in the peaking strip increases significantly with very small applied fields. The instrument has been used to measure magnetic fields from 1 milligauss to 100 gauss in flux density, using a probe of the order of $\frac{1}{4}$-in. dimensions.

Another careful study of the azimuthal variations of field in a betatron magnet is reported by Lasich, Muirhead, and Wright.[30] They claim to be able to separate the contributions to the azimuthal variations due to iron inhomogeneities, eddy currents between laminations, and eddy currents in the laminations themselves.

The rate of rise of magnetic field in the 80-Mev betatron is 4 gauss/μsec at injection, so it is necessary to be able to estimate the time of zero field within one-twentieth of a microsecond to observe field errors of 0.1 gauss. The tolerance limits of 0.1 gauss for both axial and azimuthal components of field at the orbit were set by the computed orbit displacements which they would produce. If half the field were 0.1 gauss too high and the other half 0.1 gauss too low at injection time, a radial orbit oscillation would be set up which would remove about 6 per cent of the usable radial space. If the radial field component were to vary similarly by 0.1 gauss, it would set up vertical oscillations of equivalent amplitude. A radial component at the orbit which is either inward or outward around the full azimuth can result from a phase shift caused by an asymmetry between top and bottom poles. Another way of describing this situation is to say that it results in a median plane which is not at the geometric center of the gap. The orbit will locate itself at the magnetic median plane automatically, and a radial component at the orbit averaging 0.1 gauss is capable of shifting the orbit location vertically by 1.5 in.

Instruments had to be devised to measure the radial component of field at the orbit. The best results were obtained by using the zero-field detector placed against the top and bottom poles and computing the radial component from the difference in the time of zero at the two locations.

7-10. VACUUM CHAMBER AND GAS SCATTERING

The toroid-shaped vacuum chamber enclosing the annular space between poles has undergone steady development. A glass-walled chamber was used for the first 2.3-Mev betatron, blown to a shape which fitted snugly between magnet poles and with tubulations on the outer rim for the pumping port and the injector assembly. The inside was coated with chemical silvering to shield the beam from electrostatic fields and prevent charges from building up on the walls. A resistance of the order of 100 ohms between test probes put in the side arms was used. The coating must be thin to prevent the development of excessive eddy currents which would distort the magnetic field.

The first 20-Mev chamber was assembled from flat glass washers and short glass cylinders cut from large-diameter tubing, waxed together in a rectangular cross section. Holes drilled in the outer cylinder were used for attaching the injector structure and the vacuum pump. A silver coating was applied on a sandblasted interior finish. Later developments for the GE 20-Mev chambers were of blown glass with a transparent conducting coating of tin chloride which made it possible to observe the internal components and the acceleration radiation at all azimuths. The glass chamber for the 100-Mev betatron in Schenectady, one of the largest glass doughnuts ever built, is impressive in its mechanical features and its careful design.

Other developments of betatron chambers have used ceramic materials, molded in sectors having the desired cross section and sealed end to end in place. This development has largely been the work of Almy and his associates at the University of Illinois; it is described in detail in laboratory reports. A good description of the 80-Mev chamber is published.[7] The six glazed porcelain sections have inner walls coated with Hanovia liquid bright palladium No. 62 for shielding. They are joined together by wrapping Scotch electrical tape around the joints and painting the overlap with Glyptal. Mica spacers are inserted at three of the joints; the acceleration voltage appears principally at these insulated joints. Resistors are connected between sections, and one section is left insulated to use for observing an injected beam pulse, found to be useful in tuning up the machine.

The vacuum chamber for the 300-Mev betatron is also made of molded porcelain sections, each of 20° extent. Groups of three are joined together by soldering to the metal coatings. The six 60° sections are manipulated into place in the pole gap, and final seals are made by the atmospheric compression of neoprene gaskets.   This tube, built for an orbit radius of 122 cm, has an approximately elliptical cross section with minimum inside dimensions of $4\frac{7}{8}$ and $9\frac{1}{8}$ in.

Scattering of electrons due to residual gas in the vacuum chamber has not proved to be a serious problem.   Ordinary good vacuum techniques are capable of maintaining gas pressures of the order of 2×10^{-6} mm Hg, with the usual requirements that the container be clean and nonporous and that all leaks be stopped.   The glazed porcelain chambers developed by Almy and his associates have proved to be quite satisfactory.   Fast pumps, large-diameter pumping leads, and refrigerated traps or baffles to remove vapors are required if the chamber is to be continuously pumped. Sealed-off porcelain chambers of this type have been produced commercially for the 22-Mev betatrons, using standard vacuum-tube manufacturing techniques.   The electron injector guns are permanently sealed into such chambers.

Gas scattering is a maximum at the start when electron energy is low, but it becomes less significant at high energies as the mean free path between collisions lengthens.   Collision cross sections are known or computable, and the effect of gas scattering on beam intensity has been estimated.[31]   This includes the fact that some electrons which are scattered through very small angles are refocused by the magnetic field and are not lost.   Results of such calculations show that a significant loss of beam intensity due to gas scattering will be noticeable at pressures of the order of 2×10^{-5} mm Hg.   Experimental observations of low-energy X rays produced by scattered electrons hitting the walls of the tube in the early part of the cycle are in agreement with the calculations.

7-11. INTERNAL TARGETS AND EMERGENT BEAMS

As the electrons approach maximum energy, their orbits can be expanded so they spiral outward and strike a target at the periphery. This can be done by pulsing a set of orbit expansion coils located above and below the orbit.   This sudden rise in the rate of increase of central flux upsets the betatron balance so that equilibrium orbit radius increases. In principle the same coils can be used as were described for orbit contraction during injection; the method of operation is identical but reversed in sense.   If desired, separate ejection coils can be installed to simplify switching and controls.

If the orbit expanding circuit is not used to eject the high-energy electron beam while the accelerator is in operation, electrons will follow the magnetic-field decrease and will be decelerated down to low energies again.   In this case X radiation observed coming from the walls occurs mainly after the energy has been reduced to a few Mev, when oscillations have again built up to large amplitudes.

The rate of orbit expansion depends on the rise time of the voltage pulse. This is limited by the inductance of the orbit expander coils. Kerst has proposed a method using two sets of coils which reduces inductance to a minimum and increases the rate of expansion. In this scheme a one-turn coil at the orbit radius is in series with an oppositely wound two-turn coil at a larger radius, so chosen that the reluctance of the magnetic circuit linking the two-turn coil is double that of the one-turn at the orbit. This means that the net induced voltage across the two coils is zero. As a consequence of the difference in ampere-turns, the central flux change is equivalent to that for a single-turn coil. Yet the magnetic flux through the external field return circuit is zero. This has the effect of introducing a radial field gradient across the orbit region, essentially increasing n and causing the electrons to spiral out more rapidly.

The oscillations will have been damped to small amplitude by the time the electrons reach maximum energy. The cross section of the beam is estimated to be of the order of 1 to 2 mm². This narrow beam will be swept across the target by orbit expansion in a short time, producing a burst of X rays; X-ray pulses as short as 0.6 μsec have been observed. This is the equivalent of some 200 revolutions and indicates an orbit expansion rate of about 0.0002 in. per revolution. Only an extremely thin surface of the target is struck by the electrons. The target is usually the molybdenum or tungsten surface of the injector shield, which is the first obstacle that the electrons encounter.

The X rays have a strongly forward distribution, required by momentum conservation in the interaction which is almost entirely due to electron-electron impacts. The angle between half-intensity points has been measured as 9° for 20-Mev and 3° for 100-Mev electrons. The X rays have the continuous spectrum characteristic of bremsstrahlung or deceleration radiation, with a maximum energy equal to the energy of the electrons. They penetrate the porcelain tube wall with ease, but for some applications it is desirable to have a tangential spout with a thin window to transmit the X-ray beam in order to reduce scattering by the wall. A bremsstrahlung spectrum for 330-Mev electrons from a synchrotron is shown in Fig. 12-11.

A review of nuclear experiments with high-voltage X rays by Bosley and Craggs[32] describes experimental techniques, some experimental results on such processes as photofission, nuclear photoeffect, (γ,p) reactions, and a measurement of the X-ray spectrum from betatrons.

A beam of electrons can be extracted from the betatron by using a magnetic shield or "peeler" located at the outer edge of the chamber. The first adaptation to the Illinois 20-Mev betatron was reported by Skaggs, Almy, Kerst, and Lanzl[33] in a brief note; it has been improved and developed in later applications to other betatrons. The shield is a small laminated iron bar with a channel tangent to and facing the beam. As the equilibrium orbit is expanded by the injection pulse, the beam enters the shielded channel, where magnetic field is reduced, and moves outward. Usually the peeler is located at a radius outside the $n = 1$ point. When the orbit has expanded into the region where the field falls off faster than $1/r$ $(n > 1)$, the radial focusing disappears and orbits spiral outward. Electrons can enter the channel by this spiraling action after being forced out to this radius by the orbit expander.

Those electrons which traverse the peeler channel itself emerge as a well-defined beam. Those which first experience the effect of the weakened field caused by the peeler before reaching the radius of the channel are deflected less, so the beam is fanned out radially. Figure 7-17 is a sketch of such a peeler with electron orbits indicated to show the production of such an emergent beam, which can be brought out of the vacuum chamber through a thin-foil window.

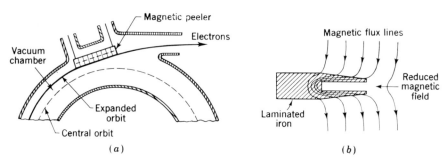

Fig. 7-17. (*a*) Location of magnetic peeler for removal of an electron beam. (*b*) Cross section of laminated iron peeler, with flux lines sketched to illustrate the magnetic shielding.

The emergent beam obtained at 20 Mev was observed to have a height of about 2 mm and a width of about 6 mm. In air outside the chamber it expands to a much larger cross section because of scattering; or it can be piped further in an evacuated spout if desired, in which case the beam remains fairly sharp. Time-average currents obtained have been of the order of 10^{-8} amp. They are emitted in pulses with a duration of less than 1 μsec, repeated 180 times per second, so the peak current during the pulse is of the order of 50 μa.

Another method of displacing the electron beam to make it available for ejection was proposed by Clark, Getting, and Thomas[34] of MIT as a mechanism for obtaining a short pulse on the target in a synchrotron. Wideröe[35] has adapted this to the betatron. The principle is that of generating radial oscillations of large amplitude by increasing magnetic field on one-half of the orbit and decreasing it on the other. If the n value is near 0.75, the frequency of radial oscillations is $0.5f_0$ and forced oscillations can be built up with maximum amplitudes at a fixed azimuth.

The method uses two coils, wound oppositely on symmetrical halves of the magnetic circuit for the orbit field, which are powered by pulsing from a resonant capacitor at ejection time.   If the two coils are balanced, they have zero coupling with the main exciting coil and a correspondingly low inductance, so the resonant frequency of the pulse circuit can be high and the beam can be expanded entirely past the target in times of the order of 2 μsec.   Calculations of oscillation amplitude build-up predict a displacement of 1.7 per cent of the radius in this time.

The ejection technique described above has been installed on the 300-Mev betatron and is used whenever pulses of microsecond duration are desired.

The resonant build-up of oscillations depends on a uniform value of n, of about 0.75.   If electrons move out into a region where n approaches 1, the radial-oscillation frequency decreases toward zero and the orbits precess rapidly.   This would result in the electrons "spilling out" around the full periphery.   The amplitude build-up must proceed rapidly enough to take only a few turns if the unidirectional character of ejection is to be retained.

An alternative device for spilling electrons out in a fairly well-defined beam was proposed by Crittenden and Parkins;[36] it uses a distorted magnetic field over a short sector of the orbit.   This technique could serve as an alternative method of getting the beam out to the location of a magnetic peeler.   Kerst and Koch[37] have discussed the relative merits of the different methods of displacing the beam, and they conclude that the orbit expansion procedure is most satisfactory for betatrons.

Still another method of extracting an electron beam is based on scattering by a thin foil.   If the foil is thin enough, the energy loss by ionization is small; an undeviated particle traverses an orbit of smaller radius but still within the focusing region of the field, so that it is reaccelerated and can traverse the foil a second and third time.   Small-angle scattering induces oscillations, and these are damped to smaller amplitudes during reacceleration.   In the process some electrons are scattered through rather large outward angles, sufficient to enter an electrostatic deflection channel as in the cyclotron, and are deflected as an emergent beam. Gund and Reich[38] have described experiments with such a scattering ejector using a 4.6-Mev betatron.   They report extraction of up to 70 per cent of the circulating electrons in an emergent beam of narrow solid angle.   However, this high efficiency could not be expected at higher energies.   The scattering foil used was 0.015-in. aluminum for this beam energy, thin enough that 95 per cent of the electrons were scattered through an angle of less than 1.15°.   The foil is made narrow vertically so that it does not interfere seriously with vertical particle oscillations as they are being reaccelerated.   An electrostatic deflector follows the foil; it uses 30 kv across a 2-mm gap and deflects the beam out of the chamber through a thin-foil window.   Just outside the window the ionization was measured to be 3×10^5 r/min, an extremely high ionization density.

An instrument for measuring betatron magnetic fields during ejection has been described by Gregg.[39]   It uses a cathode-ray-oscilloscope presentation of the field, on which the ejection pulse is observed.   Such measurements are useful in designing peelers or electrostatic deflectors for an emergent beam.

7-12. MEDICAL AND INDUSTRIAL APPLICATIONS

Ever since X rays were first used for the treatment of cancer, there has been a demand for higher energy and deeper penetration.   Early experiments in the 1- to 2-Mev energy range showed a much lower skin reaction than had been anticipated.   This was found to be due to the fact that the X rays at the skin surface carried a smaller complement of secondary electrons than at a greater depth where X rays and secondaries were in equilibrium.   This reduced skin dose and the deep penetration of high-energy X rays has made it possible to use a cross fire on a deep-seated tumor and to build up dosage at the tumor to successful levels without skin damage.   With the first successful operation of the betatron, it was clear that higher energies could be obtained than from any previous X-ray sources, and development of the 20-Mev betatrons at the General Electric Company was greatly stimulated by the known application to medical problems.

The 20- to 22-Mev betatrons give a beam of X rays from an internal target with a yield of up to 100 r/min at 1 m in the forward direction, as measured by the accepted Victoreen thimble chamber.   The beam is primarily forward, with an angle of 9° between half-maximum intensity points.   Intensity in the backward direction is 0.1 per cent of the forward maximum, making shielding problems simple.   Kerst and Skaggs[40] have published an excellent review of the use of betatrons for medical therapy. This paper describes the instrument and the properties of the radiations, as well as the biological and medical applications.

The opportunity of using a beam of electrons directly for therapy became possible at adequate energies with the emergent beams from the betatron.   Skaggs, Almy, Kerst, and Lanzl[41] have discussed the problem of electron therapy and have described the application of betatron beams for this purpose.

The betatron has also proved itself a valuable tool in industrial radiography.   The X-ray beam from a high-energy betatron can be used in showing the internal structure of steel sheets or mechanisms several inches thick.   A particularly ingenious application of the betatron to radiography is due to Wideröe.[42]   Working at the Brown-Boveri Company in Switzerland, he has developed a betatron in which beams are accelerated in opposite directions on successive half-cycles of the magnetic field wave. Two injectors are necessary and two targets are located on opposite sides of the orbit but displaced slightly so the two X-ray beams converge toward each other. With this device it is possible to make stereo-radiographs; with a suitable viewer of the X-ray pictures the structure viewed stands out in an apparent three-dimensional display.

7-13. AIR-CORE BETATRON

Bierman[6][43] of the Philips Laboratory at Eindhoven, Holland, has perfected a small betatron (9 Mev) in which the iron in the yoke and return circuit is dispensed with. He claims the advantage of a much lighter machine (110 lb) and of simpler construction. The magnetic fields required are produced with properly dimensioned air coils. Much larger currents are required to obtain the same magnetic induction as with the use of iron, but the magnetic stored energy is not excessive for small sizes, and capacitors of reasonable cost can supply the high current for pulsed operation.

The field is produced by two coils, each having 25 turns of heavy high-tension cable, mounted in sturdy coil frames to resist the strong expansive forces between turns. The doughnut-shaped vacuum chamber fits between the coils and is of much larger relative cross section than chambers for iron-cored betatrons, allowing a larger amplitude for ion oscillations. The size and spacing of the coils produce a radially decreasing field with a value of $n = 0.5$ at the orbit. The central flux is brought up to that necessary for the betatron balance by the insertion of two laminated iron bars as a core, but with an air return circuit. The separation of the bars at the center can be adjusted to obtain the correct flux balance and to aid in shaping the field near the orbit. The bars are of such diameter that they saturate at the peak of the magnetic cycle, causing orbits to contract toward a target located at a smaller radius. Figure 7-18 shows the design of this air-core betatron.

The power supply is a high-potential rectifier charging a 6.5-μf capacitor to 50 kv. A spark-gap breakdown discharges the capacitor through the coils. The discharge is oscillatory with a frequency of about 2500 cps and is highly damped, so acceleration occurs in a decreasing sequence of pulses. The injection potential for the electron gun is obtained from a small coil linking the field of the large ones, in which maximum potential is induced at the start of acceleration when the magnetic field passes through zero. The peak pulse intensity from the machine is larger than from conventional betatrons. With a pulse repetition rate limited by heating of the coils and capacitors to one per second, the average output is low.

The designer's claims for simplicity and light weight are valid. This is a much simpler and cheaper instrument than any iron-cored machine of the same electron energy. It would be ideal as a demonstration model for university lecture halls or for use in a research laboratory as a pulsed source for cloud chambers or other instruments utilizing high peak intensity. However, the pulsed operation results in a short duty cycle and

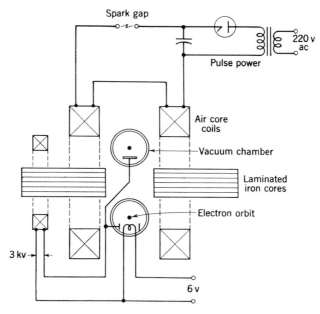

Fig. 7-18. Schematic diagram for an air-core betatron.[41]

low average intensities, so it is not so useful as a continuously operating betatron for medical therapy.

REFERENCES

1. D. W. Kerst, *Phys. Rev.*, **58**:841 (1940).
2. D. W. Kerst, *Phys. Rev.*, **60**:47 (1941).
3. D. W. Kerst and R. Serber, *Phys. Rev.*, **60**:53 (1941).
4. D. W. Kerst, *Rev. Sci. Instr.*, **13**:387 (1942).
5. W. F. Westendorp and E. E. Charlton, *J. Appl. Phys.*, **16**:581 (1945).
6. A. Bierman, *Nature*, **163**:649 (1949).
7. D. W. Kerst, G. D. Adams, H. W. Koch, and C. S. Robinson, *Rev. Sci. Instr.*, **21**:462 (1950).
8. D. W. Kerst, G. D. Adams, H. W. Koch, and C. S. Robinson, *Phys. Rev.*, **78**:297 (1950).
9. D. W. Kerst, *Nature*, **157**:90 (1946).
10. G. Breit and M. A. Tuve, *Carnegie Inst. Year Book*, **27**:209 (1927–1928).
11. R. Wideröe, *Arch. Electrotech.*, **21**:400 (1928).

12. E. T. S. Walton, *Proc. Cambridge Phil. Soc.*, **25**:569 (1929).
13. W. W. Jassinsky, *Arch. Electrotech.*, **30**:500 (1936).
14. M. Steenbeck, *Z. Physik* (February, 1943).
15. D. W. Kerst, *Phys. Rev.*, **68**:233 (1945).
16. W. F. Westendorp, *J. Appl. Phys.*, **16**:657 (1945).
17. E. Amaldi and B. Ferretti, *Rev. Sci. Instr.*, **17**:389 (1946).
18. *Life*, Mar. 20, 1950, pp. 129–132.
19. D. Iwanenko and I. Pomeranchuk, *Phys. Rev.*, **65**:343 (1944).
20. J. P. Blewett, *Phys. Rev.*, **69**:87 (1946).
21. J. Schwinger, *Phys. Rev.*, **75**:1912 (1949).
22. D. W. Kerst, *Phys. Rev.*, **74**:503 (1948).
23. F. F. Heyman, *Phys. Rev.*, **75**:1951 (1949).
24. G. D. Adams, *Rev. Sci. Instr.*, **19**:607 (1948).
25. L. Bess and A. O. Hanson, *Rev. Sci. Instr.*, **19**:108 (1948).
26. G. D. Adams, D. W. Kerst, and D. T. Scag, *Rev. Sci. Instr.*, **18**:799 (1947).
27. E. Schwartz, *Z. Naturforsch.*, **4a**:198 (1949).
28. A. F. Clark, *Phys. Rev.*, **70**:444 (1946).
29. G. D. Adams, R. W. Dressel, and F. E. Towsley, *Rev. Sci. Instr.*, **21**:69 (1950).
30. W. B. Lasich, E. G. Muirhead, and I. F. Wright, *J. Sci. Instr. Phys. Ind.*, **26**:91 (1949).
31. J. M. Greenberg and T. H. Berlin, *Phys. Rev.*, **74**:1243 (1948).
32. W. Bosley and J. D. Craggs, *Repts. Progr. in Phys.*, **12**:82 (1948–1949).
33. L. S. Skaggs, G. M. Almy, D. W. Kerst, and L. H. Lanzl, *Phys. Rev.*, **70**:95 (1946).
34. J. S. Clark, I. A. Getting, and J. E. Thomas, Jr., *Phys. Rev.*, **70**:562 (1946).
35. R. Wideröe, *Rev. Sci. Instr.*, **19**:401 (1948).
36. E. C. Crittenden and W. E. Parkins, *J. Appl. Phys.*, **17**:444 (1946).
37. E. W. Kerst and H. W. Koch, *Rev. Sci. Instr.*, **18**:681 (1947).
38. K. Gund and H. Reich, *Z. Phys.*, **126**:383 (1949).
39. E. C. Gregg, Jr., *Rev. Sci. Instr.*, **20**:841 (1949).
40. D. W. Kerst and L. S. Skaggs in O. Glasser (ed.), "Medical Physics," vol. 2, p. 11, Year Book Publishers (1950).
41. L. S. Skaggs, G. M. Almy, D. W. Kerst, and L. H. Lanzl, *Radiology*, **50**:167 (1948).
42. R. Wideröe, *Stahl u. Eisen*, **73**:706 (1953).
43. A. Bierman and H. A. Ĉele, *Philips Tech. Rev.*, **11**:65 (1949).

8

Magnet Design and Measurement

The design of iron-cored magnets calls upon the resources of the physicist, the electrical engineer, and the mechanical engineer. The fundamental principles of magnet design were established by the physicists of the nineteenth century. These principles then found application in the apparatus of electrical engineering—transformers, motors, generators, and other electrical machinery. With the development of the accelerator art, new requirements were set up which went beyond normal engineering practice; higher precision was needed in structures involving magnetic forces far beyond those usually experienced. New physical methods were evolved and new electrical and mechanical techniques were developed to meet these requirements. These procedures, in turn, have stimulated the engineering profession to make improvements in the industrial applications of electromagnets.

Theoretical knowledge of magnet design is precise in principle but has been considered inadequate in application to design problems. Until quite recently magnet designers have solved their problems by very approximate theoretical procedures and by cut-and-try magnet modeling. Although these methods are powerful and are still in vogue, a change in approach is now in process. The difficulties of the past have been introduced by the nonlinear characteristics of iron, whose permeability is a strong function of flux density; because of this, design of magnetic circuits is extremely complicated, and it has been easier to make the final steps using models which served, so to speak, as analogue computers. With

236

the advent of the modern electronic computer these problems are becoming soluble in reasonable times, and in 1961 the time appears not far off when a complete magnet design can be done rapidly without recourse to the laboratory.

At present, methods for formulation of the problems are at hand; procedures for solution of the problems using computers are in the process of evolution. Some of the methods have been tested by hand computation with completely satisfactory results. For example, the shape of the magnet for the Brookhaven AG synchrotron was deduced theoretically by methods to be discussed below. The final magnets were found to agree completely with the theoretical predictions.

In this chapter the physical principles of magnet design will be presented. Classical design techniques will be discussed, and new developments will be mentioned where they appear to be adequately established. Detailed design problems relating to individual accelerators will be reserved for discussion in the separate chapters on those machines.

The instruments and techniques employed in magnetic measurement will also be described. Different methods are used in studying the various properties of the magnetic field, and techniques differ according to whether the field is to be steady or time-varying; the two categories will receive separate treatment.

Although air-cored coils have found many applications in the accelerator field—Helmholtz coils, for example, are generally used in search-coil calibration—they will not be discussed here since methods necessary for their design and construction are fully covered in standard works on electricity and magnetism.

8-1. SPECIAL REQUIREMENTS FOR ACCELERATOR MAGNETS

Accelerator magnets depart from engineering experience primarily in the need for precise shaping of the fields in the air gap, which sets rigorous requirements on pole-face shape. This feature has been of less concern in engineering applications, where the detailed shape of the field is seldom important and gaps in the iron circuit are deliberately minimized. The accelerator scientist has had to design new types of precise instruments for measuring fields in order to determine the special shapes needed for the poles. In return the engineering field has supplied machine practice of the highest order to produce the necessary contours and has also provided magnetic materials of improved quality which have been of great value in accelerator magnets.

The desire for engineering perfection and electrical economy of the magnetic circuit is limited by other factors in the design of accelerator magnets. In general, the advantages of simple structures and precision

---

At the head of the facing page is an illustration of magnets for the Brookhaven AG synchrotron.

in manufacture, as well as the need for space around the poles to provide
access to the vacuum chamber and other components, outweigh the
importance of compact shapes or perfection in magnetic design.   The
exact field shape required to control particle orbits cannot always be
determined in advance, so magnets are frequently equipped with removable pole faces or provided with arrangements for installation of shims or
corrective windings during experimental manipulations.   In other cases
the uncertainties in planning research experiments justify considerable
flexibility in the physical arrangements; magnets are needed which can
be dismounted and reassembled by a laboratory crew.   Most magnets
represent compromises with such other requirements.

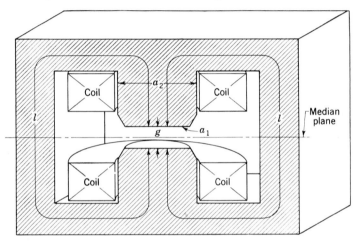

Fig. 8-1. Cross section of magnetic circuit for steady-field magnets used for cyclotrons.

Two basic magnet shapes cover most accelerator applications.   First
is the cylindrical-pole magnet used for cyclotrons to produce an approximately uniform field of high flux density across a cylindrical volume of
large area.   The field in a cyclotron magnet is constant in time.   The
magnetic circuit is assembled in large blocks, formed of solid iron forgings,
castings, or plate.   Pole faces are nearly flat and parallel, and gap spacing
is small compared with the pole diameter.   The excitation coils are
formed in two units which are equally spaced about the magnetic median
plane, to preserve symmetry about this plane.   The coils are wound in
layers with many turns of solid (or hollow) conductors and are arranged
for oil or water cooling.   Figure 8-1 is an illustration of a typical dc
magnet for a cyclotron.

Ring-shaped magnets are used to accelerate particles in orbits of
approximately constant radius, as in the betatron and the several types
of synchrotron.   A doughnut-shaped vacuum chamber fits in the gap
between pole faces, which are not quite parallel but slightly tilted to pro-

duce a field which decreases with increasing radius for focusing.   Since the particles must stay in orbits of nearly constant radius, the magnetic field must increase in magnitude during acceleration.   The magnet is excited cyclically from low to high fields, either pulsed unidirectionally or powered by alternating current.   The iron must be laminated, as in a transformer, to minimize eddy-current losses, and the material must have low magnetic hysteresis losses.   The magnetic circuit is formed of blocks of iron laminations, which require clamping structures or resin-bonding procedures.   Again, excitation coils are formed in two units, above and below the magnetic gap.   They must have a small number of turns (of large cross section) to keep the applied voltage within reasonable limits

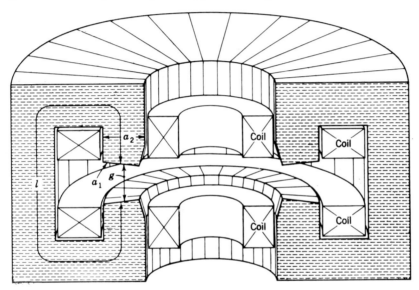

Fig. 8-2. Cross section of the C-type ring magnet with external return circuit used for some electron synchrotrons.

and are often formed of stranded cable to reduce eddy currents in the conductors.   The cross section of such a ring magnet, which is typical of those used for electron synchrotrons, is illustrated in Fig. 8-2.

   The magnet shown in Fig. 8-2 has the iron return circuit located outside the orbit.   This is called a C magnet and has the advantage that one side of the magnet gap is readily available for installation and maintenance of the vacuum chamber.   With larger orbits the return leg can be located inside the orbit, as in the Brookhaven cosmotron (a proton synchrotron), which simplifies the injection or ejection of particle beams.   Still other ring magnets, such as the Berkeley bevatron, have return legs both inside and outside the orbit; these are known as H magnets.   Such a magnet is usually formed in quadrants or octants with open field-free straight runs between sectors to provide access for pumping ports, power systems, and beam ejection.

One significant difference between dc and ac magnets is in the quality of iron and the maximum flux densities possible. The soft iron used for dc magnets has a much higher permeability than the silicon steel with low hysteresis loss used for laminations in ac magnets. This, with the looser packing of a laminated structure, makes maximum fields lower in ac magnets. Few betatron or electron synchrotron magnets exceed 14 kilogauss flux density, but most modern cyclotron magnets are designed for over 18 kilogauss. Other differences have to do with the effect on the shape of the magnetic field of eddy currents in the iron under ac or pulsed operation; detailed measurements of the dynamic properties of the field are required, particularly at low flux densities.

Another category of magnets used in accelerator laboratories includes the auxiliaries employed for beam focusing and analysis. With the larger accelerators these auxiliaries are so large and heavy as to be equivalent to cyclotron magnets, and they deserve detailed study and design. They are normally excited with dc power for steady fields and are formed of blocks of soft iron as for cyclotron magnets. The most common pole-face shape is rectangular, to provide a linear extent of magnetic field. Frequently the pole faces are wedge-shaped or tilted to provide a gradient field for focusing. An example is a magnet to deflect and analyze particle beams of 1 Bev energy, which might have pole faces of 12 in. width and 4 ft length which are spaced to form a 6-in. gap. The magnetic circuit in such a unit would be formed of rectangular iron blocks machined from forgings, with a few bolts to hold the assembly. A common shape is the H-type frame with dual magnetic return legs for which a cross section would look much like that shown in Fig. 8-1. The excitation coils would be rectangular in cross section and rectangular in plan, arranged to fit closely around the poles. Usually the poles are fitted with pole-face plates which can be removed and replaced to obtain different gap lengths, modify the taper, or change the shape for focusing.

8-2. THE MAGNETIC CIRCUIT

All the magnet types described in the preceding section serve a single purpose, that of producing a high-flux-density field between nearly flat and parallel poles. The useful region is the approximately uniform field between the pole faces; the flux outside the poles is generally of no value and is called the leakage flux or fringing flux. For this type of magnetic circuit a primary consideration in design is to make the useful flux as large a fraction of the total as practical and to reduce the energy stored in the fringing flux. Since the iron return circuit must carry the total flux, it must be larger in cross section as the fringing increases.

The two magnetic circuits illustrated in Figs. 8-1 and 8-2 will serve to illustrate our analysis.   Each circuit can be considered as an air gap of length g and area a_1 and an iron return path of length l and area a_2 (divided in two legs each of area $\frac{1}{2}a_2$ for the H-type circuit).   For present purposes the flux density can be assumed constant throughout the circuit, obtained by suitable tapering and shaping of the iron return circuit. The excitation coils fit closely around the poles and are arranged in two identical units, so the magnet is symmetrical about the median plane through the air gap.

The first relation describing the properties of a closed magnetic circuit is the fourth Maxwell equation (5-1), in which the time variation has been set equal to zero.   It can be expressed in the integral form as

$$\oint \left(\frac{\mathbf{B}}{\mu}\right) \cdot d\mathbf{l} = \iint I \, da \qquad (8\text{-}1)$$

where the line integral is around a closed loop and the surface integral is bounded by the loop.   The right-hand side of Eq. (8-1) thus represents the total number of ampere-turns linked by the loop of integration.

The second relation of importance in analyzing magnetic circuits follows from the second Maxwell equation (5-1).   Since div $\mathbf{B} = 0$, Gauss' theorem yields the relation

$$\iint B_n \, da = 0 \qquad (8\text{-}2)$$

where B_n is the component of B normal to the surface of integration. From this equation it follows that the total magnetic flux crossing any plane through the magnetic circuit is constant.   For most purposes we shall be able to assume that the magnetic flux density across any plane throughout the circuit is reasonably uniform; hence the total flux $\Phi = Ba$ (where a is the area of cross section of the circuit) will be a constant.

Where the magnetic circuit consists of an iron path of length l and an air gap of length g (as in the circuits shown in Figs. 8-1 and 8-2), the simplified forms of Eqs. (8-1) and (8-2) lead to the relation

$$\Phi = Ba = \frac{Ni}{g/(\mu_0 a_1) + l/(\mu a_2)} \qquad (8\text{-}3)$$

where Ni = number of ampere-turns in exciting windings
   a_1 = area of magnet pole face
   a_2 = cross-sectional area of iron magnetic return circuit

Equation (8-3) is extremely useful in making the first approximation to a magnet design since, for a prescribed field and air-gap geometry, it gives the number of ampere-turns necessary for magnet excitation and indicates the effect to be expected at high fields when iron permeability begins to decrease.   This equation also suggests the traditional analogy between magnetic and electric circuits.   If an electric circuit includes two resistors having resistances $g/(\mu_0 a_1)$ and $l/(\mu a_2)$, if the emf in the circuit is Ni, and if the current in the circuit is Φ, then Ohm's law for the circuit has exactly the form of Eq. (8-3).   For this reason, Ni is called the "magnetomotive force" of the circuit, and the quantities $g/(\mu_0 a_1)$ and $l/(\mu a_2)$ are called the "reluctances" of the air gap and the iron circuit, respectively.   In these terms Eq. (8-3) is equivalent to

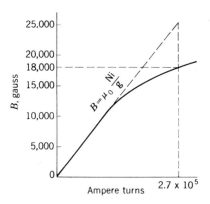

Fig. 8-3. Flux density in the gap versus excitation for the MIT cyclotron magnet.

$$\text{Flux} = \frac{\text{magnetomotive force}}{\text{total reluctance}} \quad (8\text{-}4)$$

For soft iron at flux densities up to about 10 kilogauss the permeability μ is more than 1000 times greater than that for air or vacuum μ_0, and the reluctance of the iron portion of the circuit can be neglected.   If so, the flux density in the air gap is a linear function of current.   Figure 8-3 is a plot of B versus i for a typical cyclotron magnet (MIT), showing the linear portion of the curve extending up to a field of about 10 kilogauss in the gap.   In this region of excitation the flux density is given quite accurately by

$$B = \frac{\mu_0 Ni}{g} \quad \text{webers/m}^2 \quad (8\text{-}5)$$

where $\mu_0 = 4\pi \times 10^{-7}$
Ni = ampere-turns
g = air gap in meters

To produce a field B of 1 weber/m² (10 kilogauss) in a gap of 10 cm length, the number of ampere-turns required is 7.95×10^4; with a 1000-turn coil the current would be 79.5 amp.

The permeability of iron varies with flux density, rising rapidly to a maximum value at low fields and falling off at high fields.   Figure 8-4a is a plot of magnetic flux density B against magnetic field H (in amperes per meter).   In this plot we show curves for a typical silicon steel used in transformers and for a low-carbon steel of the type used in dc magnets. For explanations of the form of the characteristic hysteresis loop shown here the reader is referred to standard texts on electricity and magnetism. In Fig. 8-4b the permeability μ is plotted against flux density B for the same two steels.   Although the silicon-steel permeability rises rapidly to much higher values than those for the soft iron, the latter displays higher permeability at the high fields used in cyclotron magnets.

At high flux densities the linear relation of Eq. (8-5) must be replaced by the more complete Eq. (8-3), because of the increasing reluctance of the iron.   This is observable in Fig. 8-3, where the plot of observed field falls below the straight line extrapolated from low-field values.   The point where this deviation starts and the magnitude of the deviation are

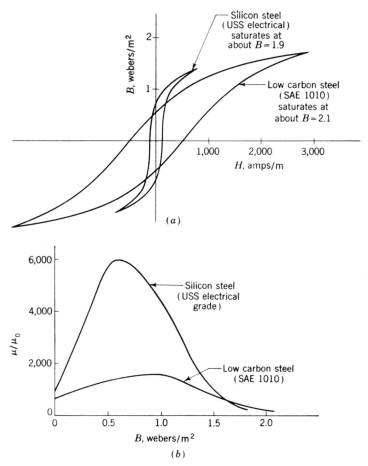

Fig. 8-4. Magnetic properties of soft low-carbon steel and silicon steel: (a) B versus H; (b) μ versus B.

affected by other features of the design.   As iron permeability decreases, the pattern of fringing flux changes, with a larger fraction of flux being forced outside the geometrical boundaries of the poles.   The degree of tapering of the poles depends on the chosen flux density and is character-ized by the ratio of areas a_2/a_1.   The shape of the tapering contour near the pole tip is the most important factor in determining the flux pattern in this fringing region; the sharp corner at the pole boundary is usually the first portion of the iron to become saturated.   The leakage flux pattern is also affected by the location of the exciting windings.   In a qualitative sense the exciting coils tend to "compress" the leakage flux between them, so the total leakage flux is a minimum when the coils are closest to the air gap.   In the iron circuit the "base" of the poles away from the air gap is the location of maximum total flux, and since it is limited in cross section by the coil dimensions, it is usually a region of high flux density and saturates before the rest of the iron circuit.

As a consequence of this complex situation at high flux densities, no simple relation is valid for computing excitation requirements.   However, useful design estimates can be obtained from observations with circuits similar to the one being considered.   A great deal of empirical information is available as the result of experience with a wide variety of magnetic-circuit shapes and for different magnetic materials.   For example, consider a circuit similar to that shown in Fig. 8-1, for which an excitation curve like that in Fig. 8-3 is typical.   Excitation requirements can be represented by the empirical relation

$$B = \frac{KNi\mu_0}{g} \tag{8-6}$$

where K is an "efficiency" factor which decreases with increasing excitation.   At 18 kilogauss, for example, the observed value of B is 0.73 of that predicted by the straight-line extrapolation of the air-gap relation of Eq. (8-5), so $K = 0.73$.   In a circuit under design which is reasonably similar to the shape and arrangement of the circuit just discussed, a judicious guess of the factor K will usually be sufficient to obtain adequate preliminary design estimates of the excitation requirements.

The dimension of pole-face diameter or width must be determined at an early stage of design, to provide the desired area of uniform field.   Since fringing flux extends outside the pole boundaries, the flux just inside the boundaries is weakened and the region of uniform field is reduced.   Experience shows that the edge of the usable region is inside the pole boundaries by about one-half the gap length.   For example, with the MIT cyclotron magnet the region useful for acceleration (see Chap. 7), which is roughly defined as a point where the field is reduced to about 0.98 that of the central field, was observed with and without any special shaping of the pole face.   Without shims the useful region was inside the pole edge by $0.6g$; with the chosen ring-shaped shims it was inside by $0.45g$.   It should be noted that this boundary of useful field is closer to the pole boundary at low fields and is forced inward at higher fields, because of saturation of the outer corners of the pole tips.

Another general design problem is the degree of tapering of the poles and the optimum shape of tapering.   The leakage flux enters or leaves the poles on the sides and at the tapered sections and adds to the total flux in the return circuit. A simple explanation of the need for tapering the poles is that the return circuit should, at each transverse section, have sufficient area to carry the total flux (including the leakage flux) without exceeding the saturation limit of the iron at any point. The area ratio a_2/a_1 can be determined if the fringing-flux distribution is known, from which an estimate can be made of the total fringing flux. The graphical technique of flux plotting, described in a following section, provides a useful method of obtaining an approximate flux plot. However, the flux pattern depends on the degree of excitation as well as on the shape of the magnetic circuit and the location of the coils. So, for excitations approaching the limit of saturation in the iron or exceeding the flux density used in earlier experience, it is usually necessary to measure the field pattern directly with scaled models employing the same quality of iron.

The shape of the taper can be estimated theoretically for low flux densities where simplifying assumptions are allowable, such as the assumption that the iron surfaces are magnetic equipotentials or that the iron has infinite permeability. An analysis developed by Bethe was used to design the tapering for the Purdue University cyclotron magnet, reported by Howe and Walerstein.[1] The criterion applied in determining the shape of taper was to secure the highest value of BR (a measure of particle momentum) between flat poles, for a given central field. The results were given in terms of the radius of pole, $r = r(z)$, at a distance z from the median plane:

$$r^2(z) = r_0^2 \left[1 + \left(\frac{2}{\pi} \frac{g}{r} \right) \ln \left(\frac{2z}{g} \right) \right] \Big/ \left[1 - \left(\frac{2}{\pi} \frac{g}{r} \right) \ln \left(\frac{2z_0}{g} \right) \right] \quad (8\text{-}7)$$

Here r_0 is the pole-base radius at a distance z_0 from the median plane, and g is the gap width. The values of BR in the gap are also given:

$$BR = B_i r_0 \Big/ \left[1 + \left(\frac{2g}{\pi r} \right) \ln \left(\frac{2z_0}{g} \right) \right]^{\frac{1}{2}} \quad (8\text{-}8)$$

where B_i is the chosen maximum flux density in the iron pole (at its base). The tapering profile of the magnet pole resulting from this calculation is shown in Fig. 8-5, along with the relative shapes and spacings of the lines of flux in the fringing field.

Another criterion for shape of taper was used in the scaled-model studies at the Carnegie Institute of Technology.[2] This was essentially to obtain the highest value of uniform field in the gap for a given magnitude of excitation in ampere-turns. The result is shown in Fig. 8-6. We note that the shape of the taper is convex in the Purdue design and concave in the Carnegie design.

This difference illustrates one of the problems in magnet design, which is the determination of the essential criteria on which decisions are to be

based. There is no unique answer. Individual designers attach importance to different properties of the field, based on the evaluation of other
aspects of the accelerator as a system. For example, the Carnegie design
gives the sharpest fall-off of field in the fringing region, which simplifies
beam deflection and in principle would provide a more concentrated

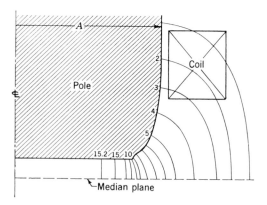

Fig. 8-5. Tapering profile of the Purdue University cyclotron magnet pole, showing
the fringing-flux pattern.

emergent beam. The Purdue design, on the other hand, is less affected
by saturation at the pole edges and allows shimming to obtain the maximum orbit radius and so the highest energy of internal resonant beam.

During past years the trend in design has been toward higher fields,
using better-quality magnetic materials and more electric power. In this

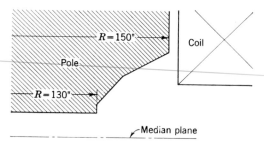

Fig. 8-6. Pole taper for the Carnegie Institute of Technology synchrocyclotron
magnet[2] which resulted in the best excitation efficiency.

development the simple magnet-circuit shapes of the early accelerators
have evolved into more compact structures which are more efficient at
higher flux densities. Improved techniques have been found for coil
cooling, allowing for more efficient coil designs. To illustrate this change
in structural shape, Fig. 8-7 shows schematic representations of three

typical magnetic circuits, all of the H-type frame; for comparison the three magnets are scaled to the same pole-face diameter and gap length. One shape is representative of early low-energy cyclotron magnets using cylindrical poles for which the maximum field would be about 12 kilogauss. The second is typical of high-flux synchrocyclotrons, with tapered poles and large-diameter coils, which might operate at 18 kilogauss. The third is an example of a "poleless" circuit in which the excitation coils are fitted closely around the gap, and which can produce uniform fields

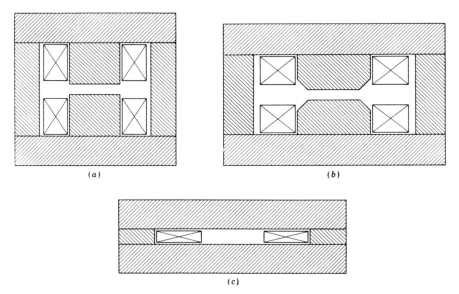

Fig. 8-7. Trend of steady-field magnet design: (*a*) early cyclotron magnet, $B_m = 12,000$ gauss; (*b*) synchrocyclotron magnet, $B_m = 18,000$ gauss; (*c*) poleless magnet, $B_m = 22,000$ gauss.

of between 20 and 22 kilogauss; this very compact circuit is being used in some modern synchrotrons and for high-flux analyzing magnets.

8-3. FIELD MAPPING AND FLUX PLOTTING

In the design and use of electromagnets it is frequently desirable to obtain a map of the magnetic field in part or all of the air gap, around corners of the pole or, perhaps, in and around the exciting coils. This map can be used to indicate the onset of local saturation, to show necessary changes in pole contour, or to evaluate forces on poles or conductors. The desired maps are almost always two-dimensional because symmetry in the structure makes the third dimension unnecessary.

The field properties used in field mapping follow from Maxwell's equations div **B** = 0 and curl **B** = μ**I**. If I is zero, these equations indicate that B can be derived from a potential function u defined in two dimensions by

$$B_x = -\frac{\partial u}{\partial x} \qquad B_y = -\frac{\partial u}{\partial y} \tag{8-9}$$

Since div $\mathbf{B} = 0$, it follows that $\nabla^2 u = 0$.   Whether or not I is zero, B can also be derived from another potential function A defined by

$$B_x = \frac{\partial A}{\partial y} \qquad B_y = -\frac{\partial A}{\partial x} \tag{8-10}$$

Since curl $\mathbf{B} = \mu \mathbf{I}$, it follows that $\nabla^2 A = \mu I$.   This A is the z component of the vector potential which, in a three-dimensional problem, would also have x and y components.

Lines of constant A are defined as "lines of force," while lines of constant u are known as "equipotentials."   In a field where I is zero, both equipotentials and lines of force can be drawn.   The equation of a line of force is obtained by writing

$$dA = \frac{\partial A}{\partial x}\, dx + \frac{\partial A}{\partial y}\, dy = 0$$

whence
$$\frac{dy}{dx} = -\frac{\partial A}{\partial x} \Big/ \frac{\partial A}{\partial y} = \frac{B_y}{B_x} \tag{8-11}$$

Similarly the equation of an equipotential is

$$\frac{dy}{dx} = -\frac{B_x}{B_y} \tag{8-12}$$

Since
$$\left(\frac{dy}{dx}\right)_{A=\text{const}} \left(\frac{dy}{dx}\right)_{u=\text{const}} = -1 \tag{8-13}$$

it follows that the line of force through a given point is always normal to the equipotential through that point.

The "Electrolytic Tank" Method

The equations for lines of force and equipotentials in an electric field are exactly analogous to those in a current-free magnetic field.   Accordingly, experimental methods used for mapping electric fields between conductors can be adapted to the magnetic-field problem.   Iron surfaces in the magnetic field will be equipotentials for flux densities below the saturation limit and so can be modeled by metallic electrodes shaped like the poles. Electric potential differences between these electrodes and points in the electric field simulate the corresponding magnetic potential differences. Several methods have been used for exploiting this analogy.

The best-known electrical analogue is the electrolytic tank—usually a flat tank of glass or other insulating material filled with a shallow layer of a slightly conducting liquid such as a weak solution of copper sulfate. The magnetic poles and the iron return circuit are simulated by shaped metallic electrodes, and between them a dc or audiofrequency ac potential difference is maintained. A probe is used to determine the local potential, usually a short piece of Ni or Pt wire of small diameter. The probe potential is set by connecting it to a potentiometer whose fixed terminals are connected to the electrodes in the tank. The probe is then moved in the electrolyte until a detector (a galvanometer for dc signals, or earphones for ac signals) indicates a null. The position of the probe is read from a cross-section plot underlying the electrolyte and can be transcribed or transmitted by a pantograph to an external plot. Usually 10 or more equally spaced equipotentials are plotted; intermediate equipotentials are included in regions where the field is highly divergent.

The lines of force are now sketched in normal to the equipotentials. It is customary in drawing plots of lines of force to make the density of lines proportional to the field strength; thus the space between adjacent pairs of lines of force will include a constant quantity of flux. Since the separation of the equipotentials is also a measure of the field strength, this means that the ratio $\dfrac{\text{separation of adjacent lines of force}}{\text{separation of adjacent equipotentials}}$ must be kept constant for all the little rectangles enclosed by lines of force and equipotentials.

An example of contour maps obtainable by this technique is the map of flux density in the fringing field, which can be used to determine the flux entering the sides of a tapered pole (see Fig. 8-5). Another useful plot gives the flux density on the median plane as a function of radial position similar to that shown in Fig. 6-8 for the MIT cyclotron.

Other methods for utilizing the electrical analogy involve the use of "conducting paper," a paper sheet coated with a uniform layer of high-resistance material. Sheets of metal of high resistivity have also been used. In both cases the technique is the same as that already described; the conducting material merely replaces the sheet of electrolyte in the electrolytic tank.

The electrical analogy suffers from several faults. The surface of a magnet pole is a true equipotential only if the permeability of the iron is effectively infinite. At high flux densities, as local saturation occurs, the equipotential no longer coincides with the iron surface and the electrical analogy gives erroneous answers. Another difficulty lies in the breakdown of the analogy when current-bearing coils lie in the region of interest. Other electrical analogues have been developed for this case, but their application is limited and they are in the process of being super-

seded by the more sophisticated numerical techniques to be described
later.

Conformal Mapping

Freehand flux plotting as a technique for magnet design has been highly
developed by the engineering profession and is described fully in several
engineering texts.[3,4]   This has become an art and requires considerable
practice for proficiency.   It can give results correct to about 10 per cent,

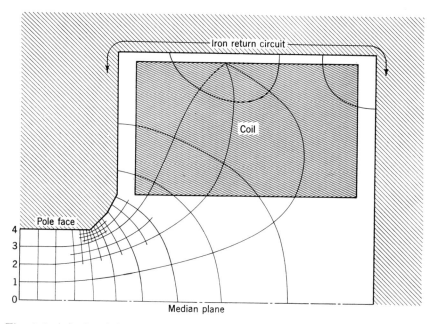

Fig. 8-8. A freehand flux plot for a cyclotron magnet with tapered poles.   The lines
of flux and the equipotentials intersect orthogonally and form curvilinear squares.

but in inexperienced hands it can also lead to gross errors.   The amateur
is advised to stick to the numerical methods described below.

The freehand flux plotter usually chooses to make the rectangles
between adjacent equipotentials and lines of force into squares by appropriate choice of spacing between lines of force.   He makes a freehand
guess at the equipotential pattern, fits in a set of normal lines of force,
and then, by liberal use of the eraser, corrects the first guess until a complete pattern of squares emerges.   Figure 8-8 is an example of such a
freehand plot of the field in the MIT cyclotron magnet.   Values of flux
density determined from the spacing of flux lines are in adequate agreement with measured values.   Further refinements in the freehand tech-

nique are described by Dwight and Abt,[5] who used the method to design a continuously curving shape for the pole tip of a cyclotron magnet.

Numerical Methods for Flux Plotting

Several iterative numerical processes have been developed for establishing field patterns. In these methods one or other of the potential functions is obtained by numerical solution of the second-order equation which describes it. We shall consider first the methods used with the scalar potential u, which satisfies the relation $\nabla^2 u = 0$. First, a large-scale plot is drawn with the known potential boundaries, and a square net of points separated by a distance δ is laid out to fill the region between the boundaries. Figure 8-9 represents a small region of this net. If the potential at the various numbered points is u_1, u_2, etc., we can

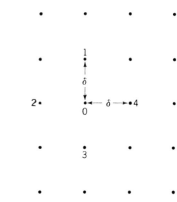

Fig. 8-9. Form of net used in relaxation flux plotting.

rewrite the equation for u at the point 0 in the form of a finite difference equation thus:

$$\nabla^2 u = \frac{\partial^2 u}{\partial x^2} + \frac{\partial^2 u}{\partial y^2} = \frac{u_1 + u_2 + u_3 + u_4 - 4u_0}{\delta^2} = 0 \qquad (8\text{-}14)$$

The most powerful method for obtaining a solution to this equation for all net points is the Southwell "relaxation" method[6] in which the errors in an assumed potential distribution are relaxed by consecutive revisions. The errors are expressed in the form of residuals, the residual at a given point being given by

$$\text{Residual at point } 0 = u_1 + u_2 + u_3 + u_4 - 4u_0 \qquad (8\text{-}15)$$

When, for the assumed distribution, the residuals have been determined for each net point, they are used to modify the potential at that point. The process converges rapidly, and a final solution is obtained when all of the residuals have been reduced below some previously accepted limit of error. Thus the solution can be carried to any desired accuracy.

The relaxation procedure in its simplest form involves reduction of the potential at the points of large residuals by one-quarter of the residual at that point. This reduces the residual at these points to zero and modifies the residuals at the neighboring points. By concentrating on the points of high residuals, the distribution is corrected step by step until it satisfies the field equations. Procedures of block relaxation are described in the references cited for correcting large regions that have residuals of the same sign. Many other techniques are available for speeding up the correction process. But the primary virtue of the method is that it converges in a positive fashion even in the hands of a relatively unskilled operator.

Figure 8-10 shows a plot of a quadrant of the fringing field around a cyclotron pole, with the magnetic potential at the median plane assumed to be zero and to have the relative value 100 at the iron pole-face boundary. Values of potential indicated at each point in the square grid were

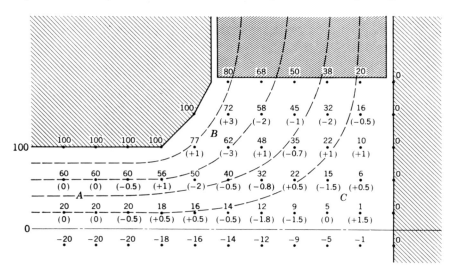

Fig. 8-10. Numerical flux plot showing the value of magnetic potential at each net point, with residual errors below in parentheses.

interpolated from the freehand potential plot which is sketched in dashed lines. The residuals for each point are shown in parentheses beneath the value of potential. It can be noted that the worst errors occur in the regions in which the divergence of field is the greatest, such as points B and C.

If the region of interest includes current-bearing conductors, the scalar potential can no longer be used. Solutions can be obtained for these cases by using the vector potential A, which must satisfy $\nabla^2 A = \mu I$. For this case the residuals take the form

$$\text{Residual at point } 0 = A_1 + A_2 + A_3 + A_4 - 4A_0 - \mu Ia \quad (8\text{-}16)$$

where a is the area of a net mesh.

The relaxation process is the same as that used for the scalar potential. When the vector potential is used, the situation at the iron boundaries is more complicated than in the case of the scalar potential. In the latter case the potential at the boundaries was specified, and no residuals appear at net points on a boundary. With the vector potential the boundary condition of normal incidence of the lines of force on an iron surface results in a zero normal derivative of A. This is taken into account by inclusion in the net of "virtual net points" just inside the iron surface. The vector potential at these points is set equal to that at the point in the air gap, which is a mirror image in the iron surface of the virtual point.

For dealing with complicated and curved boundary surfaces a composite potential function has been evolved and used by M. H. Blewett of Brookhaven National Laboratory. Her work is unpublished, and the authors are indebted to her for the following description of her procedure:

When computing magnetic fields in a region with nonrectangular boundaries, a major disadvantage in using the vector potential in relaxation calculations arises from the necessary condition at the iron-air boundary that the normal derivative of the vector potential be zero. Thus, the virtual points used for this type of boundary condition are no longer on true net points, and a considerable amount of auxiliary computation must be carried out. Another difficulty arises when computing fields in C-shaped magnets where all boundaries but one have this normal-derivative type of boundary condition. In this case, the relaxation calculations become very tedious since all of the residuals, to use the Southwell terminology, must be "swept out" through quite a narrow region and dissipated in the infinite region beyond the area of interest to the computation.

To overcome these disadvantages, a modified potential function ψ may be derived as follows: If A is the usual vector potential, then let

$$-\frac{\partial \psi}{\partial y} = B_y = -\frac{\partial A}{\partial x} \tag{8-17}$$

and so

$$-\frac{\partial^2 \psi}{\partial x\,\partial y} = -\frac{\partial^2 A}{\partial x^2} = \mu I + \frac{\partial^2 A}{\partial y^2} \tag{8-18}$$

Integrating with respect to y gives

$$-\frac{\partial \psi}{\partial x} = \int_0^y \mu I\,dy + \frac{\partial A}{\partial y} + \text{integration constant} \tag{8-19}$$

But $\dfrac{\partial A}{\partial y} = B_x$ and the integration constant is zero if the problem has the usual symmetry about the x axis. Thus

$$-\frac{\partial \psi}{\partial x} = B_x + \int_0^y \mu I\,dy \tag{8-20}$$

We see that, in the non-current-bearing regions, ψ is like a scalar potential, and in the current-bearing regions it is related to the total current enclosed at a given point.

The Laplacian of ψ can then be found and is given by

$$\Delta^2\psi = -\frac{\partial}{\partial x}\int_0^y \mu I \, dy \tag{8-21}$$

It is noteworthy that the Laplacian of ψ is zero, not only in the current-free regions, but also throughout the coils except at each vertical boundary.

If a given problem makes it more convenient, it is, of course, also easy to find another potential-like function ψ' whose Laplacian will be given by

$$-\frac{\partial}{\partial y}\int_0^x \mu I \, dx$$

From the above, and particularly from Eq. (8-20), it can also be seen that the function ψ will have fixed values on an iron-air boundary. In regions enclosing a coil, it will vary with x as $\int_0^y \mu I \, dy$ varies. In regions between coils, it will have a value proportional to the total ampere-turns enclosed.

Figure 8-11 shows a plot of the lines of force in the Brookhaven alternating-gradient synchrotron (AGS) magnet (see Chap. 15) by the method

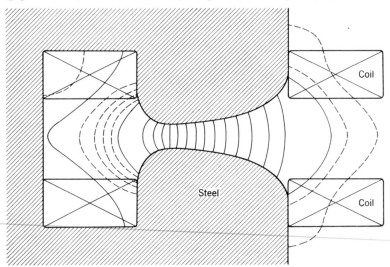

Fig. 8-11. Lines of force in the Brookhaven AGS magnet obtained by the relaxation method of M. H. Blewett. The spacing between the solid lines is a measure of the field strength. The dashed lines are interpolated in regions of weaker field; their separation indicates a field strength one-fifth as strong as would be indicated by an equal separation between solid lines.

just described. The potential function was determined to about 1 part in 100,000 at each net point, and by this means it was possible to define the pole shape, to give the desired field, to an accuracy of about 0.002 in.

Recent developments in the fields of numerical flux plotting have been in the direction of preparing programs for electronic computers that will permit rapid solutions by the methods just described.

The relaxation method can be used equally effectively to derive the field pattern in the iron of an electromagnet. With iron of uniform permeability the problem can easily be solved by hand. Although the solution is not valid as the iron saturates, it can be used to indicate the regions where saturation will first take place. When the variation of iron properties with flux density is taken into account, the problem becomes too complex for rapid hand solution but can still be handled by an electronic computer. Development of this method is now in its early stages but is progressing rapidly. The day appears not far distant when a magnet design can be completed without approximation by purely computational techniques.

8-4. USE OF MODELS IN MAGNET DESIGN

At present, most designers still find that experimental measurements with scaled models provide the most useful and exact information. Almost without exception, models have been used in determining final construction details and pole-face shape for the sequence of larger and larger magnets needed for accelerators.

Linear scale factors are used to provide the same magnetic flux pattern as in the full-scale unit, and models must be operated at the same flux density. The scale factor used depends on the kind of information desired from the model, on the accuracy demanded of the measurements, and on the dimensions of the measuring instruments available. Frequently the effort expended in developing small and precise measuring instruments is comparable to that required for the model itself. Small models are cheaper to build and modify, but measurements are more difficult and extreme precision is required in machining and instrumentation. For the Brookhaven cosmotron a scale of 1:4 was used to study the properties of a laminated magnet with 36-in.-wide poles to be excited with pulsed power; since eddy-current effects vary with the square of lamination thickness, the pulse length was also scaled to provide equivalent magnetic response. With the Cambridge electron accelerator the laminated magnet with AG pole faces of $6\frac{1}{2}$ in. width had a sufficiently small iron circuit to allow the use of full-scale (but short-length) models. At the other extreme, the 130-in.-diam steady-field magnet for the Carnegie Institute of Technology synchrocyclotron was studied with a model of 2-in. pole face, a scale factor of 1:65. The scale factor used in any case is the designer's choice.

In model studies the fixed parameters are usually pole-face diameter (or cross section) and gap length. These quantities are essentially determined by the choice of particle energy, calculations of particle orbits, and the necessary aperture for the accelerating chamber between poles. The spacing between coils may also be limited by the physical space requirements for auxiliary apparatus such as the vacuum chamber or the D lines of a cyclotron. The general structural shape of the circuit is also usually conceived at an early stage of design.

Other physical parameters which may be studied in a model are the shape of pole taper, the length of pole and area of the pole base, the dimensions of the iron return circuit, and the size and location of the exciting coils. Electrical measurements are needed to predict full-scale power requirements, such as the ampere-turns in the coils and power losses in coils and core. The most significant results, however, come from precise measurements of the field in the gap and outside the gap, in order to determine pole-face shape and the leakage flux pattern. Removable pole-face disks or plates are normally built into the model; these can be remachined or replaced to study the effects of small changes in shape on the field distribution in the pole gap.

The most serious technical problem in small-scale models is that of coil cooling, since power requirements do not scale linearly. If the same magnetic flux density is to be maintained in the model as in the final magnet, the magnetomotive force, i.e., the total number of ampere-turns in the coil, will be proportional to the scale factor [cf. Eq. (8-3)]. For example, a quarter-scale model will require only one-quarter as many ampere-turns as does the full-scale magnet. But the cross-sectional area of the coil decreases like the square of the scale factor. Consequently, the current density in the coil will be inversely proportional to the scale factor. The power dissipation per unit volume in the coil is proportional to the square of the current density and hence to the inverse square of the scale factor. In a quarter-scale model the dissipation per unit volume of the coil is increased by a factor of 16!

Cooling of small-scale models of water-cooled coils is further complicated by the reduced water flow in the smaller cooling channels, since water flow rate is proportional to a high power of tube diameter. Consequently, it is often not possible to operate small models continuously; data must be taken during short pulses to avoid overheating. Special model coils using a small number of turns and very high water pressure have been used to obtain adequate cooling efficiency. Occasionally the model-coil cooling problems have been so severe as to require the use of larger-scale models than would otherwise have been required.

One of the most detailed reports of a model study is that of Foss, Fox, Sutton, and Creutz,[2] used in the design of the 130-in.-diam synchrocyclotron magnet at the Carnegie Institute of Technology. This study represents an extreme case in that the scale factor used was 1:65. Using a technique already tested in betatron magnet design, the group constructed only half of the model; the other half was mirrored in an effectively infinite half-space of iron plate located at the midplane of the air gap. This reduced gap length and ampere-turns to half those of a full model and saved on machining of the pole shape.   The permeability of the reflecting iron must be essentially infinite for field patterns and flux densities to be undisturbed; the authors estimate that a maximum error of less than 1 per cent was caused by the finite permeability for fields up to 20 kilogauss.   In their model studies the Carnegie Tech group used a wide variety of shapes and sizes of iron for the poles and return circuits as well as many different shapes and sizes of copper exciting coils.   The design was optimized for minimum excitation (ampere-turns) to obtain the designed peak flux density of 20 kilogauss in the gap.   The final result (see Fig. 8-6) was a magnet with a flux efficiency of 86 per cent at 20 kilogauss, defined as the fraction of the total magnetic flux enclosed within the physical boundaries of the pole faces.   It might be noted that the model was too small to show the detailed shape of the field between poles with sufficient accuracy.   The necessary shimming to give the correct radial decrease needed for focusing was determined later with the full-scale magnet.

With pulsed or ac magnets, models have been an absolute necessity. In the development of the 300-Mev betatron Kerst used several stages of model studies.   The first step was a solid-core small-scale model to ascertain the gross flux and field patterns in order to determine efficient shapes and sizes for the iron cores.   He next built the 80-Mev machine, which was a scaled model of the projected 300-Mev betatron, with laminated cores and stranded cable coils, and used it with pulse powering to determine magnetic losses, field distributions, and the transient effects on the field distribution due to pulsed operation.   Because it was a scaled model, the 80-Mev machine could not be cooled adequately and was operated at reduced pulsing rates.

A series of models of increasing scale factor was used in developing the magnets for the Brookhaven cosmotron, starting with $\frac{1}{12}$-scale solid-iron cores and culminating in a $\frac{1}{4}$-scale laminated-core model section of short length which was used for detailed pulsed-power measurements to determine the full-scale pole-face profile.

In many laboratories the development of accelerator magnets has justified the humorous quotation in one of the accelerator songs written by A. Roberts: "This machine is just a model for a bigger one, of course!"

8-5. COIL DESIGN

The excitation coils provide the magnetomotive force or the ampere-turns Ni used in the circuit equations of Sec. 8-2.   In dc magnets the first parameter to be determined is the power to be dissipated in the resistance of the excitation windings.   As will be shown below, power varies inversely with volume of conductor, so to a first approximation it can be chosen at will.

Consider a coil of N turns (usually arranged in two identical units) of total cross-sectional area a so that the area of one turn is a/N. Let the average length of a turn be l. If the conductors are formed of a material of resistivity ρ (evaluated for the average temperature expected in the windings), then the total resistance of the coil will be

$$R = \frac{Nl\rho}{a/N} = \frac{N^2\rho l}{a} \tag{8-22}$$

The maximum current i is specified by the chosen peak excitation Ni. At this current the power dissipated U is

$$U = i^2R = \frac{\rho(Ni)^2l}{a} = \frac{\rho(Ni)^2l^2}{\text{coil volume}} \tag{8-23}$$

from which the coil conductor volume can be obtained once power is chosen. To be sure, the average length of turn is not independent of conductor volume but is related through the dimensions of the coil units and the distribution of the insulation material. However, a well-designed coil will have a "packing ratio" greater than 0.5, meaning that the conductor area is more than half of the total cross section of the coil or that the space for insulation, cooling, and clamps occupies less than half of the total volume. The average length per turn l can be taken as that for a turn halfway between outer and inner dimensions of the coil.

The number of turns N, which then determines the conductor size, can be adjusted to match the current-voltage ratings of the power supply. Frequently the availability of machines of standard ratings will influence the choice of voltage V. Direct-current generators are commonly produced in standard voltage ratings of 115, 230, 500, etc., volts and for a sequence of power ratings determined by the size of the machine. With voltage V, power U, and ampere-turns chosen, the number of turns is given by

$$N = \frac{NiV}{U}$$

The number of turns must be even if two identical coil units are planned. Furthermore, the number is usually taken to be divisible by the number of coil layers chosen in design (i.e., with two coil units of four layers each, the number N must be a multiple of 8). Other conditions may enter, such as possible alternate series-parallel connections of the coil layers, which would modify the choice of number of layers. If coil design departs from the normal rectangular cross section, in which all layers have equal numbers of turns, still further modifications are involved. A simple rectangular cross section is usually found to be the most economical, since it simplifies the structures of the cooling system and mechanical supports as well as the process of coil winding. With the above restriction on number of turns, limited to a multiple of some large number such as 8 or 16, the choice of voltage is also restricted to a set of values. The common decision is to choose a value of N for which the corresponding required voltage V is somewhat less than that available from the power supply, allowing a margin for surplus excitation.

The conductor shape which provides the desired cross section is heavily influenced by the technique chosen for cooling. Several alternative methods of providing the cooling will be described below.

Air cooling is standard for the windings of rotating dc machinery and is provided by the motion of the armature. With static magnets air-blast cooling is less attractive. Air ducts are bulky and interfere with other components of the accelerator; the efficiency of thermal transfer is low unless air speed is high, in which case the noise may be objectionable. Air cooling has been used in several cyclotrons and in the Berkeley bevatron and has the advantage of eliminating the problems of water cooling. However, more recent developments have made other techniques preferable, and air cooling is no longer in favor.

Oil-immersion cooling has been used for many cyclotrons, with multi-layer coils enclosed in oil tanks and with forced circulation of the oil through a heat exchanger. Sturdy mechanical brackets are required to support the tanks and hold the coils in place against magnetic forces. The most serious problem is the fire hazard, since most oils used for this purpose are inflammable. At least two damaging fires have occurred in cyclotrons with oil-immersion cooling, and insurance underwriters' rates have reflected the hazard. For this reason oil-immersion cooling is no longer considered suitable for large magnets.

Water-cooling techniques have been developed largely for accelerator applications. One successful design employs alternate layers of con-ductor and water-cooled metal, with thermal conduction through thin intermediate layers of insulation. The metal cooling layer may be formed as a spiral-wound flat plate of rectangular hollow tubing through which cooling water circulates. This "dry-wound" water-cooled coil is compact and easy to mount and clamp. Its limitations are the relatively high conductor temperatures and the possibility of water leaks. Figure 8-12 is an illustration of cyclotron coils which employ this technique of cooling.

In each of the three methods described above, the conductor edge or face is exposed to the cooling medium. The conductors are usually formed as thin strips of bar copper, wound in a flat helical spiral with interleaved ribbons of insulation between turns; the edges of the strips are bare and in contact with the cooling medium. Typical dimensions are those for the MIT coil (see Fig. 8-12) in which the copper conductor has a rectangular cross section of $\frac{1}{8}$ by $\frac{3}{4}$ in. The most useful feature of such strip-wound layer coils is that the coils can be designed for a large number of turns and can use a high-voltage power supply.

Internal cooling through hollow conductors is possible only with conductors of relatively large cross section.   In a small magnet this means a small number of turns and an undesirably low-voltage power supply. In large magnets the conductor cross section is large enough to use hollow conductors.   Extruded copper (or aluminum) bars have been used which have a rectangular external shape and a water channel along the center. This design excels in cooling efficiency and allows the use of high current densities.   Small-size copper tubing has occasionally been used for model coils; for these, high water pressures are needed.   In large magnets the

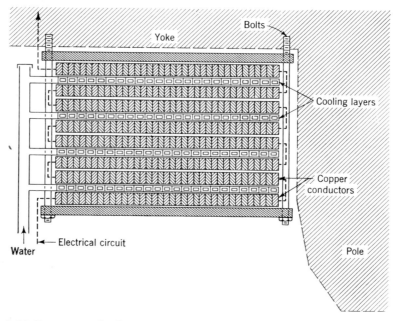

Fig. 8-12. Layer-wound coils with layers of water tubing inserted for cooling (similar to those in MIT cyclotron magnet).

chief disadvantage has been the large number of brazed or welded joints in the conductor and the consequent risk of water leaks.   This is not a serious problem for dc cyclotron magnets in which magnetic forces are steady, but has been seriously objectionable in pulsed magnets as in the cosmotron, which has had several conductor-joint failures requiring major coil repairs.

The size of the cooling channel is the most critical dimension in the design of internally cooled coils, since the water pressure required to produce a given flow is a steep function of the size and shape of the channel. The water flow required to dissipate the heat generated in the coil can be determined from the known power losses and the allowed temperature rise in the water.   In engineering units, the flow q (in gallons per minute) required to dissipate an amount of power U (kilowatts) for a temperature rise ΔT (degrees Fahrenheit) is

$$q = \frac{6.82U}{\Delta T} \quad \text{gpm}$$

Water velocity and tube diameter determine whether the flow is stream-lined or turbulent; in most cases it will be found that accelerator cooling systems are in the turbulent-flow range.

To compute the pressure drop required it is necessary first to derive the Reynolds number for the case in question. In terms of the flow q (in gallons per minute) and the tube diameter d (measured in inches) the Reynolds number is given for water at temperature $T°F$ by

$$\text{Reynolds number} = \frac{3400q}{d} \frac{\text{viscosity of water at } 75°F}{\text{viscosity of water at } T°F}$$

The viscosity ratio necessary for substitution here can be derived from the following table:

Temperature T,°F	32	40	60	80	100	140	212
$\dfrac{\text{Viscosity at } 75°F}{\text{Viscosity at } T°F}$	0.52	0.59	0.82	1.07	1.35	1.95	3.13

The necessary pressure drop ΔP (measured in pounds per square inch) can now be obtained from the formula

$$\Delta P = \frac{kq^2l}{d^5} \quad \text{psi}$$

where q = flow, gpm

d = tube diameter, in.

l = tube length, ft

k = friction constant given as function of Reynolds number in Table 8-1

TABLE 8-1

Reynolds number	k	
100	0.0086	
300	0.0028	
1,000	0.00081	Streamline flow
2,000	0.00044	
3,000 (rate of flow increasing)	0.00032	
3,000 (rate of flow decreasing)	0.00059	
5,000	0.00049	
10,000	0.00042	
30,000	0.00032	Turbulent flow
100,000	0.00024	
1,000,000	0.00015	
10,000,000	0.00011	

The above formula and tables suffice to make approximate estimates of pressure drop for circular pipes without too many sharp bends. More refined calculations can be made with the assistance of methods to be found in such texts as "Heat Transmission," by McAdams,[7] or "Hydraulics," by Daugherty.[8]

The casting of preformed coils with epoxy or polyester resins to form solid mechanical structures is now a well-developed technique. Several competent commercial firms in the United States and Europe offer this type of coil as a standard product. The coils for several of the accelerators now under construction, and for many auxiliary magnets used in the research laboratory, incorporate this feature. Resins which are either thermosetting or room-temperature-setting are commercially available and have a wide range in their mechanical and electrical properties. When glass-fiber cloth or cotton mesh is used as a base and impregnated with such a resin, the tensile strength is in the range 1000 to 3000 psi. Individual conductors are tightly bound so as to prevent any motion under magnetic forces, and the coil is rigid enough to be self-supporting with the minimum number of clamps or brackets. This technique is a completely satisfactory answer to the problems of coil distortion and motion under magnetic forces and provides a coil having a long life expectancy against failures.

Special insulating techniques are required to obtain the necessary quality and uniformity in the insulation properties of resin-impregnated coils. The mechanical and electrical properties of resin-bonded material are so interrelated that it is in general not possible to choose resins for optimum mechanical strength and at the same time obtain reliable electrical insulation. The voltage breakdown strength of a resin-impregnated layer of glass cloth or cotton mesh is usually over 100 volts/mil thickness for thin layers (10 to 30 mils) when used for low potentials, such as for turn-to-turn insulation. However, it has usually been found necessary to utilize mica-sheet or mica-flake insulation to obtain the higher voltage-to-ground insulation.

A basic technique in making resin-bonded coils is to wrap individual conductors with a porous insulation tape made of glass cloth or cotton mesh after bending and forming these conductors into the desired shapes. The coil is enclosed within an airtight form from which the air is evacuated, and the fluid (hot) resin is flowed into the form to permeate the entire coil and fill the porous insulation with the resin dielectric. After setting, the coil unit is normally baked in an oven for a final cure and the entire coil is wrapped with an outer layer of special high-voltage insulation. The technique can be used with hollow conductors, in which case the water-channel connections are brought out of the casting with the conductor terminations. Figure 8-13a shows a cross section of the coil for the Brookhaven AGS magnet (see Chap. 15), which is pulsed at 3-sec intervals, and for which a large hollow conductor is acceptable.

A special problem in coils for fast-pulsed or ac excitation is the requirement for low inductance, which means that the number of turns must be small and therefore of large cross section. Solid conductors lead to excessive eddy-current losses; stranded cables require complex clamping and insulating structures to resist magnetic forces and are difficult to cool. Although this problem exists in the electrical industry, it has

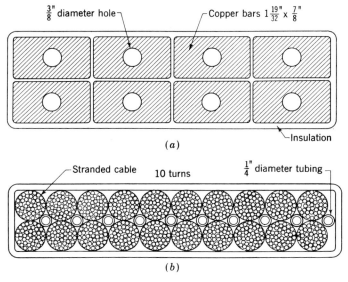

Fig. 8-13. (a) Resin-bonded hollow-conductor coil for the Brookhaven AGS magnet (see Sec. 15-8), designed for pulsing 20 times per minute.   (b) Resin-bonded stranded-cable coil with internal water-cooling tubing for the Cambridge electron accelerator (see Sec. 15-9) designed for 60-cps pulsing.

become more acute in accelerator applications in which the coils are located near air gaps where fringing fields and magnetic forces are much greater. In the Cambridge electron accelerator, which operates at 60 cps, this problem is met by utilizing the resin-casting technique. Figure 8-13b shows a cross section of the stranded-cable coil used for the conductor, as well as the thin-walled tubing which is also embedded in the casting for removing the heat.

The forces on coils in electromagnets are often very large. For example, the coil in the magnet gap of the Brookhaven cosmotron experiences a peak magnetic pressure of about 1000 lb/in. of its length. These forces are generally in such a direction as to push the coil away from the region of high magnetic field. Their magnitude and direction can be established from flux plots of the sort described in Sec. 8-3. Clamps must then be designed to prevent excessive motion under these forces, since coil motions will result in abrasion of insulation and in fatigue of the copper coil components.

8-6. METHODS OF MAGNETIC MEASUREMENT

Although magnetic fields are just as important to an understanding of natural phenomena as are electric fields, they have not reached the degree of practical importance that ensures the availability of commercial measuring equipment such as is readily available for the measurement of voltage and electric current. Until quite recent years the accelerator physicist has been faced with the necessity of building all his own magnetic measuring gear. For accurate measurement of magnetic fields it is still, in 1961, necessary to build almost all magnetic measuring equipment with the exception of a few types of approximate survey instruments which now are commercially available.

A number of magnetic-field-dependent phenomena are available for use in measurement of magnetic fields. Those whose applications will be discussed below are as follows:

1. A conductor-bearing current in a magnetic field will experience a force normal to the current and to the direction of the field.

2. A loop of wire which links a changing magnetic flux will exhibit an induced voltage.

3. Nuclear magnetic moments precess in a magnetic field at a measurable frequency whose value is a measure of the field.

4. Certain materials, notably bismuth, show a strong dependence of electrical resistance on magnetic field.

5. A potential difference appears across a current-bearing strip in a magnetic field (the Hall effect).

6. Some materials of high permeability (such as permalloy) saturate at very low magnetic fields.

7. A magnetized needle of ferromagnetic material will align itself with a magnetic field (as every sailor knows).

Varying degrees of accuracy are achievable using these phenomena. For convenience, linearity, and precision the induction of voltage in a conducting loop or search coil has always been the favorite effect, and a great variety of measuring equipment has been designed around it. Even higher precision is attainable using nuclear resonance, but the signal obtained is weak and easily lost in the presence of electrical noise. Saturation of permalloy strips can give accurate measurement of low fields in the 100-gauss range. The other effects are also capable of precision but usually only with very careful control of temperature, mechanical construction, or other pitfalls for the unwary.

We shall consider the various measuring techniques under three headings: dc measurements, measurements in pulsed fields, and measurements in high-gradient fields. The arrangement of material under these headings will be, to some extent, arbitrary and historical since, in principle, many of the methods are applicable in two or three of these categories. The dc-field section will include several methods for locating magnetic median planes.

A useful review of the techniques of magnetic measurement will be found in the paper of Symonds[9] of the Birmingham (England) proton synchrotron group.

8-7. MAGNETIC MEASUREMENTS IN DC FIELDS

Measurements Using the Force on Current-bearing Conductors

Magnetic field intensity is defined in terms of the force exerted on a wire carrying a current, following the vector cross-product relation of Eq. (5-12). The force is a maximum when the wire is normal to the field, and it is directed at right angles to the plane established by the wire and the field. The magnitude of this maximum force is given by

$$F_m = ilB \tag{8-24}$$

where l is the length of the wire.   In the mks system of units the force is in newtons (1/9.8 of the weight of 1 kg) if current is in amperes, length in meters, and magnetic field intensity in webers/m^2. One method for observing the magnetic force is to measure the torque on a pivoted loop of wire.   The torque on a loop of area A and N turns, carrying current i in a magnetic field B and located with the axis of the loop normal to the field, is

$$\tau = NiAB \sin \alpha \tag{8-25}$$

where α is the angle between the field and the normal to the loop.

Instruments have been developed for measuring uniform fields based on these fundamental definitions.   One which is typical of the precision required for high-quality accelerator applications (about 1 part in 10,000) is that of Chang and Rosenblum.[10]   They describe two techniques for measuring uniform fields, using large rectangular coils having precisely known dimensions, in which the magnetic torques are balanced by gravitational weight torques.   The large size of the coils makes this method impractical for direct measurement of accelerator magnet fields.   However, it finds a useful application in the measurement of calibrating fields such as Helmholtz coils.

Measurements Using EMFs Induced by Changing Flux

A more useful definition of magnetic field intensity comes from another basic relation, given in Eq. (5-1), for the electromotive force induced in a closed circuit by a change in the magnetic flux linking the circuit.   For our present purpose we consider a coil of N turns of area a located in a magnetic field B.   If the flux density linking the coil changes at the rate dB/dt, the instantaneous induced voltage V is

$$V = Na \frac{dB}{dt} \tag{8-26}$$

The induced current $i = V/R$, where R is the resistance of the coil and circuit.   During any finite change ΔB in time Δt the accumulated charge Q is

$$Q = \int_{t}^{t+\Delta t} i \, dt = \frac{Na}{R} \Delta B \tag{8-27}$$

In a uniform field such a flux change can be produced by "snatching" the coil from a position at rest in the field to a position removed from the field; in this case the change ΔB is numerically equal to the field intensity B.   The instrument to measure the charge (such as a ballistic galvanometer) must have a time constant long compared with the time Δt, so the accuracy of measurement will be independent of the rate of change. Magnetic field intensity is given by

$$B = \frac{Q(R_{\text{coil}} + R_{\text{gal}})}{Na} \tag{8-28}$$

Note that R includes the resistance of the coil and the galvanometer. Precision of measurement depends on the accuracy of knowledge of the dimensions and constants of the coil and on the galvanometer calibration. Or the coil can be calibrated for the coil constant Na in a standard magnetic field produced by a Helmholtz coil of precise dimensions.

The "snatch coil," or "search coil," is one of the earliest and most common of the instruments for measuring dc fields.   Small coils of many turns can be used to study the details of a field pattern.   In this case the coil is usually calibrated (with the galvanometer) by observing the charge induced using a known or standard magnetic field.

A modification called a "flip coil" uses a mechanical device such as a spring to flip the coil rapidly through 180°, while the coil remains in place. The 0° position must be accurately normal to the field, and the angle of flip exactly 180°.   The reversal in direction of flux through the coil doubles the magnitude of the current pulse and the charge passing through the galvanometer, relative to the simple snatch coil described above. Flip coils capable of an accuracy better than 0.1 per cent have been built.

Another modification is the rotating coil equipped with brushes to transmit the ac output to an ac amplifier. Rotation speed must be constant and the brushes must be of high quality. The accuracy obtained with commercial instruments is about 0.5 per cent. Such an instrument can serve a useful purpose in obtaining relative values at weak fields, but is not suitable for absolute calibration.

With very small magnets (such as models) having a short-time-constant circuit in the power supply and excitation coils, the magnet excitation current can be reversed suddenly to obtain a doubled induced pulse in the measuring coil, leaving the search coil fixed. This is also the basic technique for measuring permeability of small iron samples, in which case the measuring coil is wrapped around the (ellipsoidal) specimen, which is placed inside a solenoidal excitation coil. Magnetization curves and values of permeability which are essential in magnet design can be obtained from such small-specimen measurements.

The Integrating Fluxmeter

The integrating coil fluxmeter used in most laboratories for measuring steady or dc fields is the modern application of the search coil and is the most generally useful instrument in the laboratory. Similar developments have occurred in several magnet design laboratories, with varying sensitivity and precision, but only a few have been described in detail. Usually there are three components to the fluxmeter: a coil, an integrating dc amplifier circuit, and a recording meter. Many coil shapes have been used, from tiny coils a few millimeters in diameter wound with extremely fine wire for detailed mapping of fields in small models, to large flat coils of a few turns of heavy wire to measure average fields. A typical "exploring" coil for a cyclotron magnet would have about 1000 turns of fine wire wound on a core $\frac{1}{2}$ in. inside and 1 in. outside diameter and about $\frac{1}{2}$ in. long; it might have a resistance of the order of 100 ohms.

Circuits for dc integrating amplifiers have been developed successfully in several laboratories. The primary problem is to maintain stability of the zero or base-line reading with time. A typical method is to use a dc-ac electronic converter or "chopper," which provides an ac signal which is readily amplified, and then to reconvert the amplified signal to direct current with a second phased converter. The integrating feature is provided by a feedback from the output to the input through a capacitor and a high resistance. Charge is stored in the capacitor proportional to the amplified input, and the potential across the capacitor is a measure of the integrated current. The circuit is essentially an RC integrator with an amplifier across the capacitor; the result is equivalent to increasing the magnitude of C without decreasing the output signal level, so that high integrating precision is achieved at high output level. Gains of

Measurements Using Nuclear Resonance

The proton magnetic moment will precess about an applied external magnetic field with a Larmor frequency which is directly proportional to field intensity. The methods of nuclear absorption or nuclear induction[12,13] can be used to observe this resonant frequency and so to measure magnetic field. This is an absolute method of calibration, dependent only on the magnitude of the proton magnetic moment, which is known to a precision of 0.03 per cent. Relative measurements can be made to even greater accuracy, limited only by the precision of measuring radio-frequencies or the homogeneity of the field.

The earliest suggestion for using this property for the measurement of magnetic fields was by Roberts,[14] although others working independently have reported similar devices. Packard[15] describes a magnetic-field regulator using the nuclear induction signal from a water sample in the field. Hopkins[16] reports a portable instrument using nuclear absorption of protons in a distilled-water sample which has a precision of better than 0.2 per cent at fields up to 19 kilogauss.

The fluxmeter developed by Hopkins uses an oscillating regenerative detector with an audioamplifier whose output is presented on an oscilloscope. The proton sample can be a thin-walled glass vial holding about 0.5 gm of distilled water, located in a small coil which is a part of the resonant circuit and can be moved about in the field. The coil is set with its axis at right angles to the field, and rf oscillations are set up in the coil at a frequency determined by a tuning capacitor. When this frequency corresponds with the Larmor precessional frequency of protons, transitions occur which result in an absorption of energy from the rf field. With the regenerative detector this energy drop appears as a sharp dip in an oscilloscope trace. The technique used to locate and identify the nuclear resonance is to apply a small 60-cycle component to "wobble" the magnetic field back and forth through its resonant value, using small auxiliary coils around the sample. The frequency for resonance can be measured and reduced to magnetic field through the relation

$$B = (234.82 \pm 0.13)f$$

where B is in gauss (10^{-4} weber/m^2) and f is in megacycles per second. The width of the resonance dip depends on the homogeneity of the field and also on the material used in the proton-moment sample holder. The radial decrease built into cyclotron magnets gives a resonance width of several gauss across the sample and is found to be the limit to precision.

The Bismuth Spiral

The resistance of bismuth wire increases in a magnetic field by as much as 50 per cent for fields of the order of 20 kilogauss. At low fields the resistance-versus-field characteristic is nonlinear, but over the range from about 3 to 25 kilogauss the characteristic becomes roughly linear. This effect has been known for a long time, and bismuth resistors have often been used for magnetic-field measurements. Usually these resistors are in the form of cast spirals. The method suffers from the fact that the resistance of bismuth is also strongly temperature-dependent and is, moreover, sensitive to mechanical deformations. With adequate mechanical protection and temperature control the bismuth resistor can be very useful for survey measurements. A refined bismuth resistor probe was used by Dols, Skiff, and Watson[17] in magnetic measurements during the 1956 modification of the 184-in. synchrocyclotron at the University of California. The precautions necessary are discussed in detail in the paper describing these measurements.

The Hall Effect

The Hall effect (discovered by E. H. Hall in 1879) is the name given to the appearance of a potential difference across a strip of metal carrying a current in an external magnetic field. This is a relatively small but roughly linear effect which can be used fairly easily for measurement of magnetic fields to accuracies of the order of 1 per cent. It also suffers from sensitivity to temperature variations, but alloys can be found which are relatively temperature-insensitive over limited temperature ranges. A simple field-strength meter using the Hall effect was described by Pearson[18] in 1948, and since that time a great deal of unpublished work has been done in various laboratories, notably the CERN laboratory in Geneva, Switzerland. Commercial field-strength meters using the Hall effect and useful over the range of fields up to and above 20 kilogauss are now (1961) available. Plates of indium arsenide are available from the German firm of Siemens for use in such Hall-effect fluxmeters. With a current of 0.2 amp these plates give about 20 mv per thousand gauss.

Cyclotron Resonance

A simple method of determining the average magnetic field in a cyclotron magnet is to use the cyclotron resonance condition

$$f = \frac{1}{2\pi} \frac{e}{m} B$$

When the cyclotron is in operation, in resonance with an ion of known e/m value at a frequency f, the magnetic field can be determined with high precision, since e/m is known and the frequency of the resonant circuit can be measured to high accuracy. This is a useful method of obtaining points on the magnetization curve of the magnet. But the field in a cyclotron is always slightly tapered, decreasing with increasing radius, so this resonance frequency represents an average value of the magnetic field from the center out to the exit radius. It cannot even be identified with a particular radial location, since phase migrations of ions are a consequence of this decreasing field and the details of such phase migrations are difficult to analyze. In attempting to evaluate the central field from this average value an error of the order of 0.5 per cent is possible.

Median-plane Location by the Tilt Needle

Several methods have been developed to locate the position of the magnetic median plane in cyclotron-like magnets. Some laboratories have used variations of the pivoted steel tilt needle with a mirror on the needle and a long light beam to indicate deflections. The needle aligns itself in the magnetic field quite accurately if bearing friction is small and the needle is exactly balanced. The needle mount can be raised and lowered in the field between poles to locate that level where the light beam indicates a vertical needle position. In the slightly convex field between cyclotron poles this position can be located within a few millimeters. The unit must be placed at many points over the pole surface to obtain a plot of median-plane location.

A common phenomenon in such magnets is to find the median plane dished into a shallow saucer shape caused by asymmetries in the magnet iron or of the reinforcing iron in the foundations. A similar shape will result if the coils are not located symmetrically or if there is a shorted turn. This property can be used to compensate and correct this type of deviation in median plane. At MIT such a "dished" median plane was corrected by connecting an external resistor in parallel with one of the coil layers, which reduced the current in this layer and in this case had the effect of flattening the median plane.

In using the magnetic needle for median-plane studies, an improved technique is to superimpose a small high-frequency transverse magnetic field on the needle (using a pair of small ac coils) to set it into vibration and cancel out bearing-friction effects. The frequency can be chosen to resonate with the mechanical oscillation frequency of the needle; this resonant frequency is itself a good measure of the axial component of magnetic field.

Median-plane Location Using Balanced Coils

Another technique for observing the median-plane location is the use of two small identical coils connected in series opposition and observed with the integrating fluxmeter.   The coils are located one above the other and arranged so the pair can be moved transversely across the median plane, keeping exact alignment.   A net current pulse results if one coil moves through a stronger field than the other, which will occur in the convex field if the pair of coils is not balanced about the median plane.   The magnitude and sense of the pulse can be observed for equal displacements with the center of the pair at different locations relative to the geometric central plane.   The location of the magnetic median plane will be halfway between positions where the current pulses (of opposite sign) are equal in magnitude.

Median planes can also be located by very carefully designed search coils set on edge so that they measure only the radial component of the magnetic field.   Such coils and their mechanical supports must be made and located with very high precision.   The small residual errors in location can be eliminated by precise reversals of the coil around horizontal and vertical axes.

The Wire Orbit

One of the more ingenious devices for locating the median plane, and at the same time finding the magnetic center of the field between poles, involves the use of a current-carrying loop of wire.   The technique is described in the third University of Chicago *Synchrocyclotron Progress Report*.[11]

A flexible wire carrying a current in a uniform magnetic field is acted upon by a force normal to the wire and to the field, so it will be stretched into a circular loop.   The magnetic force per unit length of wire, which is given by the vector cross product $i \times B$, is balanced by the radial component of tension F in the wire:

$$Bi = \frac{F}{r} \qquad \text{or} \qquad Br = \frac{F}{i} \qquad (8\text{-}29)$$

A charged particle in the magnetic field traverses a path of radius of curvature r if

$$\frac{mv^2}{r} = Bev \qquad \text{or} \qquad Br = \frac{mv}{e} \qquad (8\text{-}30)$$

where mv is the momentum of the particle and e is its charge.   If the weight of the wire is neglected, it will take up a position in the field in which

$$\frac{F}{i} = \frac{mv}{e} \qquad (8\text{-}31)$$

So current and tension in a wire loop can be observed and used to obtain a measure of particle momentum at that radial position.

Actually the wire will have a finite weight. In the vertical field of a cyclotron magnet the loop will lie in the horizontal plane, and its weight will cause it to fall below the magnetic median plane in which the particle orbit is located. If the wire is supported at one point, where the leads adjoin, it will sag in the form of a catenary. Such a flat catenary can be approximated by a parabola, and the center of mass will be at one-third the height from the bottom to the top of the curve.

The method used to observe the median plane at Chicago was to support the current-carrying loop at one point, where flexible current leads were brought out, by a hydrometer float which allowed the loop to seek its own position of stability in the field. The outward forces stretch the loop into a circle, with the tension becoming greater as the current increases. The loop tends to move horizontally on the float until it

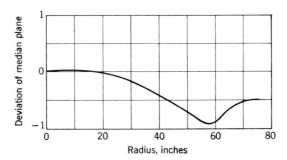

Fig. 8-15. Vertical location of magnetic median plane, before correction, in the University of Chicago synchrocyclotron magnet.[11]

encloses the maximum number of flux lines, so it picks the magnetic center of the field. The hydrometer stand can be varied in height, and the level of the float can be used to measure the combined weight of the loop plus any vertical unbalance in magnetic forces. If the magnetic forces are zero, the position of the float will not change with increase in current and tension. So the height of the stand is varied until loop position does not change with change in current. At this level the float supports just the weight of the wire loop. Heights at which this balance occurs can be measured for different loop radii. A correction must be applied for the catenary curve followed by the wire because of its distributed weight. The results of such a measurement for the Chicago synchrocyclotron magnet (Fig. 8-15) show a deviation of the median plane from the center of the geometrical gap by nearly 1 in. This deviation was corrected by suitably placed shims of iron.

The location of the center of the stretched wire loop is a measure of the displacement of the magnetic center. In the uncorrected Chicago magnet the mean center for large loops was 2 in. away from the geometrical center of the 130-in.-diam pole faces. To correct this deviation, iron shims were added to the pole faces on the side away from the displacement. The magnitude of the correction needed (shim thickness) was estimated from the force required to displace the floating wire loop sideward. The final shim pattern obtained after experimental studies was spot-welded to the pole faces, resulting in an essentially constant center for orbits at all radii.

Another good discussion of the wire-orbit method is a report by Cranberg[19] at Los Alamos, available through the United States Atomic Energy Commission.

8-8. MEASUREMENTS IN TIME-VARYING FIELDS

The measurement of alternating or pulsed magnetic fields involves techniques entirely different from those used for steady fields. Snatch coils, balanced loops, and pivoted needles are all useless. The wire orbit is stable only under very restrictive conditions. On the other hand, a varying field has the inherent property of inducing emfs in stationary coils, so a useful measure of the rate of change of flux is readily available. Instruments which can integrate this rate of change from zero field up to some higher field point in the cycle will record the magnitude of this higher field. The most critical problem is the timing of the integrating instrument, so as to obtain an instantaneous measure of the field.

The kinds of measurements required for pulsed fields also differ from those needed for dc fields. One of the most important properties is the time rate of change. This is readily obtained from the output of a fixed coil if the coil has been suitably calibrated. Absolute values of field as a function of time measured from the start of the cycle are also important, to determine orbit radius, particle energy, and frequency of rotation. A more difficult problem is to observe the variation with time of the field distribution across the pole face, due to the varying permeability of the iron circuit or to the varying magnitude of eddy-current fields in the poles or conductors. So special techniques have been developed to study the dynamic properties of the fields in pulsed accelerators.

The Integrating Fluxmeter

The integrating fluxmeter, already discussed in connection with measurements of dc fields, is equally applicable to measurements of pulsed fields. The principle is the same, but the flux change through the search coil is achieved not by moving the coil to a different field, but by leaving the search coil fixed in the changing field. Since the measurement takes place fairly rapidly, problems of zero drift in amplifiers are not so serious and often can be neglected.

The integrating fluxmeter measures only the total change in flux through the search coil; the "integration constant," which may correspond to an appreciable initial remanent field, does not register. Consequently a measurement of total field as a function of time must include a preliminary measurement of the initial field by dc techniques.

To determine the flux density at a particular instant a variety of techniques have been employed. The integrator output can be displayed on an oscilloscope with a sweep circuit giving a time base, and time markers from an electronic clock can be superimposed on the trace; the output can be observed visually and measured at any desired instant. Or the scope trace can be photographed on a moving-film camera, providing a permanent record for study and measurement. Or an electronic technique can apply the output potential to the grid of a trigger tube such as a thyratron; when the potential reaches a predetermined value, the tube fires, giving a time mark representing a given value of magnetic field which can be compared with time signals from an electronic clock. Experimenters will be able to invent other devices for displaying the signal as a function of time.

A detailed description of the application of the integrating fluxmeter to a pulsed field will be found in the paper of Green, Kassner, Moore, and Smith[20] describing magnetic measurements on the magnet of the Brookhaven cosmotron.

The Peaking Strip

An instrument which gives a precise measure of field at low field intensities is the magnetic peaking strip. The effect is based on the voltage pulse induced in a coil surrounding a sample of magnetic material when the direction of magnetization is reversed. The sample should have the highest possible permeability and the steepest or most "rectangular" B-versus-H hysteresis loop, in order that the induced voltage pulse should be a maximum. The sample should also have a large ratio of length to diameter, to minimize the "demagnetization coefficient" associated with the poles induced in the sample. The principle has been employed in magnetics laboratories for many years; a good published description of such an instrument is that by Kelly[21] as part of the program of measurement in the Brookhaven cosmotron laboratory.

A typical peaking strip would use a molybdenum-permalloy wire as a sample; the one used by Kelly was 0.002 in. diam and 2 in. length, sealed inside a small-bore quartz tube and carefully annealed. A small pickup coil of fine wire is wrapped around the center of the sample, and the unit is enclosed in a bias coil of solenoidal shape with which known bias fields can be imposed on the sample. Figure 8-16 is a schematic illustration of a peaking strip within a bias coil. The applied field on the sample can be made to traverse the hysteresis loop by applying a small-amplitude

60-cycle excitation to the bias coil, which induces voltage pulses in the pickup coil when the sample passes through zero excitation. Two pulses of opposite polarity are induced as the sample traverses the hysteresis loop. Figure 8-17 illustrates the hysteresis loop and the induced pulses of emf which are developed in the pickup coil.

For the measurement of steady magnetic fields a dc bias current is applied to the bias coil; this current produces a field on the sample equal

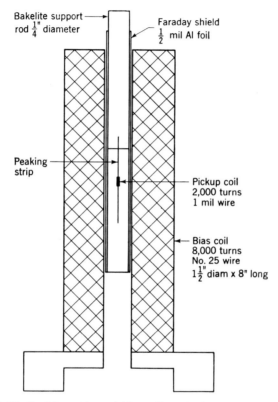

Fig. 8-16. Peaking strip and bias coil used with the cosmotron.[21]

and opposite to the one to be measured, so the net field will be zero. The small-amplitude 60-cycle excitation will result in a double-peak signal (Fig. 8-17) which can be presented on an oscilloscope with a phased 60-cycle sweep circuit to form a stabilized pattern. A balance is obtained when the two peaks of the output signal are equalized. The bias current which gives this result is a measure of the dc field.

Another useful application of the peaking strip is to the measurement of ac or pulsed fields. Since the field to be observed develops the necessary dB/dt, the 60-cycle oscillating component of field is not required, but the dc-bias measuring field is retained. With a pulsed magnet, one output peak is observed when the rising field passes through the value imposed by the bias coil; the other output peak occurs on the falling side of the magnet cycle at the same flux density. The output peaks are quite narrow compared with the excitation pulse, so they provide time signals indicating the instant when the pulse traverses the value set by the bias coil. For comparative measurements, such as the radial flux distribution across a pole face, one peaking strip can be in a fixed location to give a time signal and another can be moved from point to point across the field. If the two pulses, displayed on the same oscilloscope, coincide in time, the fields in the two locations are equal; if they differ, the bias on one coil can be adjusted to bring them into coincidence, and the bias current difference is a measure of the difference in fields at the two locations.

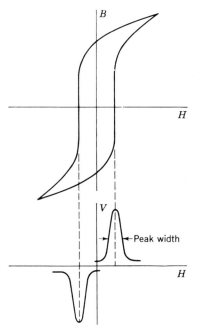

Fig. 8-17. Hysteresis loop for a peaking strip and induced voltage pulses in a pickup coil.

Pulses from such a peaking strip can be used to give a precise time signal for operation of other devices in a pulsed accelerator installation, such as the beam-injection circuits and other phased operations.

The sensitivity of the peaking strip depends on the width of the output peak, which is a function of the rate of change of field (dB/dt) and of the uniformity of the field over the length of the wire. The time width of the peak as observed on an oscilloscope can be translated into the width in gauss if the rate of change of field is known. In the Brookhaven studies[21] a rate of 10^6 gauss/sec gave an output peak with a half-power width of about 0.02 gauss; at a slower rate of 10^4 gauss/sec the observed width was 0.2 gauss.

The output peak is also broadened if the field is not uniform over the length of the wire sample. Again at Brookhaven it was found that a variation in field of 1 gauss/in. along the length of wire led to an undesirable increase in output peak width. This means that a long peaking strip is restricted in use to relatively uniform fields. A shorter strip can be used to measure fields with a finite gradient, but it suffers from a reduced effective permeability due to the demagnetization effects of the induced poles, which reduces the amplitude of the output peak and also widens the peak.

A serious limitation on the use of the instrument is the physical length of the bias coil; it can be used only in magnets with widely spaced poles. The useful range is limited to a few hundred gauss, set by the field which can be produced in the bias coil. Although larger coils could produce higher field, the larger size is a handicap. A strong bias-coil field can also distort the field distribution to be measured by changing the flux distribution in the iron pole faces, which will disturb the results.

Nuclear Resonance Fluxmeter

The fluxmeter described in the previous section, which utilizes the precessional frequency of the proton magnetic moment as a measure of magnetic field, can also be adapted to measurements in pulsed or alternating fields. The calibrating relation between magnetic field and the resonance frequency was given in Sec. 8-7. In the application to a varying field a predetermined microwave frequency is applied to the coil surrounding the sample; when the magnetic field passes through the value which is in resonance with this frequency, the oscillating power in the coil will drop. The output of the regenerative detector supplying the coil can be displayed on an oscilloscope with a calibrated time base; when the magnetic field traverses the nuclear resonance, the output will show a sharp dip which can be located to good precision with any one of the several techniques mentioned previously.

Nuclear resonance frequencies are in the 100-megacycle range at high magnetic fields (86 megacycles/sec at 20 kilogauss, for example) but are well within the range of modern techniques. The high frequency is an advantage in measurement of pulsed fields, increasing the sharpness of the resonance. The sharp pulse output can be used, like a peaking-strip pulse, to trigger other circuits in the accelerator; it has the advantage that it can be used near the maximum in the magnet excitation cycle for such purposes as triggering beam ejection systems or target-moving devices.

The chief difficulty in the use of this instrument is the electronic problem of electrical "noise" generated in the magnet pulsing circuits. The highest quality of electronic design practice is required in the construction, filtering, and shielding of the regenerative detector and the display circuits.

8-9. MEASUREMENTS IN HIGH-GRADIENT FIELDS

The ratio of magnetic gradient to field, $\frac{1}{B}\frac{dB}{dr}$, used in AG synchrotrons (Chap. 15) is a quantity which should be independent of the magnitude of field B if AG focusing is to be maintained throughout the accelerating cycle in the pulsed magnet.   A typical problem in AG-magnet pole-face design is to observe the gradient directly at different flux densities without depending on computations from field plots.

Gradient-to-field ratios used in AG accelerators are about 0.1/in., which means that the flux density varies by about 10 per cent across a 1-in. radial extent of pole face.   So the magnitude of the field changes significantly across the width of even very small search coils.   Fortunately, the most useful form of gradient field is one which has a constant gradient across the pole faces, so the errors introduced by using search coils of finite size compensate and measured values of gradient are not seriously perturbed.   However, measurements in a region where gradient is changing rapidly may be in serious error if large coils are used.   These errors can be removed to any desired order by special coil designs discussed by Garrett.[22]   By the use of correct dimensions of search coils and by inclusion of auxiliary coils, higher-order terms in the field can be canceled out to any desired point so that the emf induced in the search coil is a true measure of the field at its center.

Measurements on AG magnets are further complicated by the fact that the nonuniform field is usually changing rapidly with time.   The field pattern must be known at all times in order that the perturbing effects of eddy currents in the magnet poles and in vacuum-chamber structures can be evaluated.

A detailed discussion of the problems of measurement of fields of AG magnets will be found in the published thesis of B. De Raad,[23] which describes the methods used and considered by the CERN group.

In each magnet design program the first steps have been taken by a combination of computational methods and measurements on rough models.   These establish the gross shape of the field and the magnitude of gradient between pole faces.   Instruments and techniques described in Sec. 8-6 have been employed.   Laminated models are then built and excited with pulsed or ac power to study the electrical properties such as inductance, magnetic and eddy-current losses, and power consumption.

The "Grad-coil"

Magnetic-field and gradient measurements at high flux densities, at or near the peak of the excitation cycle, can be obtained with fixed coils, using the integrating fluxmeter described in the last section.   In order to integrate from zero to the maximum field being measured, time-trigger pulses are required.   These can be obtained from peaking strips at low field or from a nuclear-resonance fluxmeter at high fields.

A typical gradient coil (grad-coil) used with the integrating fluxmeter consists of a pair of coils of identical size and shape spaced a short distance apart radially and located with the geometric center of the two coils at the chosen position in the field.   When properly calibrated and balanced, the gradient $\dfrac{1}{B}\dfrac{\Delta B}{\Delta r}$ is given by the ratio of the difference in output of the two coils to the sum of the outputs.   With two coils of $\frac{1}{4}$ in. diam spaced $\frac{1}{2}$ in. between centers, the gradient can be measured to 0.5 per cent accuracy.   Such coils are used to survey the field between poles and to study the radial distribution.   Even smaller coils can be used to observe the details in the fringing field at the ends of the magnet sectors.   Long coils which span the full length of a magnet sector can also be used to obtain average values of gradient including the fields outside the ends of the sector.

The "Vibrating Coil"

The vibrating coil is an instrument which has been developed[24] to measure field gradients directly.   A small coil is made to vibrate at constant frequency and constant amplitude across the nonuniform field; the voltage output is proportional to the difference in field ΔB from one end to the other of the stroke.   The output of the coil is a sinusoidal voltage of maximum amplitude given by

$$V_m = 2\pi f \, \Delta x \, Na \, \frac{\Delta B}{\Delta x} \tag{8-32}$$

where f = frequency of vibration
$\quad \Delta x$ = amplitude
$\quad Na$ = coil constant (number of turns times area)
$\quad \dfrac{\Delta B}{\Delta x}$ = magnetic gradient

The instrument can best be calibrated in a known field with known gradient; computing the gradient from dimensions and vibration amplitudes is inexact.   The instrument referred to above used a very small, light coil of several hundred turns mounted on a soda straw attached to the diaphragm of an audio speaker which was driven by an audio amplifier at frequencies up to 200 cps and for which the amplitude was about 0.02 in.   It was used primarily for measuring gradients in dc models of strong-focusing magnets.

Remanent-field Measurements

Most synchrotron magnets are pulse-powered unidirectionally, with the field varying from zero (or close to zero) to maximum and back to zero cyclically.   The magnitude of the remanent field is strongly affected by the detailed shape of the preceding cycle during which the field is decreasing to zero.   The flux distribution and field gradient between pole faces due to the remanent field is not necessarily the same as that for a powered field. At low flux densities (injection conditions) the remanent field adds to the powered field to produce the total field between poles, and the resulting gradient may differ from that at higher excitations. A technique of measurement is needed which measures total field, not just that fraction due to the applied excitation. Unfortunately, the output of induced current in coils measures only the component due to the rate of change dB/dt. This measurement problem is most severe at the low-field portion of the excitation cycle, so the instruments required must be able to detect small fields with adequate precision during early times in the cycle without being disturbed by the high fields during the remainder of the cycle.

One technique which has proved successful[25] utilizes the peaking strip discussed in Sec. 8-8. Two peaking strips are used, separated by a short distance and with axes parallel, so as to obtain two readings in the gradient field. Each peaking strip is enclosed in a bias coil and also has a pickup coil to generate signal peaks when the net field through the strip passes through zero. The two output signals are displayed on an oscilloscope. With equal bias fields applied to the two strips, the two signal peaks will be displaced in time in a gradient field. Then if the bias currents are adjusted to make the pulses coincide in time, the difference in field in the two locations can be measured directly by the currents in the bias coils. If the spacing is accurately known, the field gradient can be determined. The accuracy of the results, in terms of gradient in a field of 25 gauss, is about 0.5 per cent. Note that this technique is a measure of total field including the remanent field and will also include any distortions in field due to eddy currents.

Measurements of very high precision have been made on the magnets for the 30-Bev AG synchrotron at Brookhaven by comparing the outputs of search coils in two identical magnets. One magnet is used as a permanent reference. The output of a fixed search coil in its field is compared with the output of a search coil in the magnet undergoing test by balancing the outputs in a resistance bridge. By careful attention to the calibration and precision of the resistors used in the bridge, field measurements have been obtained which, over most of the range from 100 to 13,000 gauss, are precise to 2 or 3 parts in 10,000.

In making measurements of this order of precision the final limit to accuracy may be set, not by the magnetic measuring equipment, but by the mechanical devices used to locate the equipment. The search coil used in the Brookhaven measurements was a very carefully constructed 11-turn coil with a turn area of 1 cm by 3 m. Although the coil was made of 0.002-in. tungsten wire stretched around precisely constructed supports and was shielded from air currents by enclosure in a glass tube, and although the coil supports were constructed with the highest mechanical precision attainable, still a large fraction of the final error in the measurements was due to inability to determine the exact location of the coil with respect to the magnet structure.

REFERENCES

1. J. D. Howe and I. Walerstein, *Rev. Sci. Instr.*, **9**:53 (1938).
2. M. Foss, J. G. Fox, R. B. Sutton, and E. C. Creutz, *Rev. Sci. Instr.*, **22**:469 (1951).
3. L. V. Bewley, "Two-dimensional Fields in Electrical Engineering," Macmillan (1948).
4. Ernst Weber, "Electromagnetic Fields," vol. I, "Mapping of Fields," Wiley (1940).
5. H. B. Dwight and C. F. Abt, *Rev. Sci. Instr.*, **7**:144 (1936).
6. R. V. Southwell, "Relaxation Methods in Theoretical Physics," Oxford (1946).
7. William H. McAdams, "Heat Transmission," 3d ed., McGraw-Hill (1954).
8. R. L. Daugherty, "Hydraulics," McGraw-Hill (1937).
9. J. Symonds, *Repts. Progr. in Phys.*, **18**:83 (1955).
10. W. Y. Chang and S. Rosenblum, *Rev. Sci. Instr.*, **16**:75 (1945).
11. H. L. Anderson and J. Marshall, University of Chicago, *Synchrocyclotron Progress Report*, I (July, 1947–July, 1948); II (July, 1948–July, 1949); III (July, 1949–July, 1950).
12. E. R. Andrew, "Nuclear Magnetic Resonance," Cambridge (1955).
13. P. Grivet, "La Resonance paramagnétique nucléaire," *Centre natl. recherche sci.*, Paris (1955).
14. A. Roberts, *Rev. Sci. Instr.*, **18**:845 (1947).
15. M. Packard, *Rev. Sci. Instr.*, **19**:435 (1948).
16. N. J. Hopkins, *Rev. Sci. Instr.*, **20**:401 (1949).
17. C. G. Dols, E. W. Skiff, and P. G. Watson, *Rev. Sci. Instr.*, **29**:349 (1958).
18. G. L. Pearson, *Rev. Sci. Instr.*, **19**:263 (1948).
19. L. Cranberg, "Magnetic Calibration by the Floating-wire Method," Los Alamos Report AECU-1670 (Nov. 23, 1951).
20. G. K. Green, R. R. Kassner, W. H. Moore, and L. W. Smith, *Rev. Sci. Instr.*, **24**:743 (1951).
21. J. M. Kelly, *Rev. Sci. Instr.*, **22**:256 (1951).
22. M. W. Garrett, *J. Appl. Phys.*, **22**:1091 (1951).
23. B. De Raad, "Dynamic and Static Measurements of Strongly Inhomogeneous Magnetic Fields," Uitgeverij Excelsior, 's-Gravenhage, Holland (1958).
24. J. F. Frazer, J. A. Hofmann, M. S. Livingston, and A. M. Vash, *Rev. Sci. Instr.*, **26**:475 (1955).
25. H. Nysater, *J. Nuclear Instr.*, **4**:44 (1959).

9

The Principle of Phase Stability

The discussion up to this point represents, in large measure, the status of the accelerator field in 1945. Although accelerator development continued during World War II, it was largely within closed laboratories, and very little was published. The prewar accelerators which have been described are all limited in maximum energy. Some, such as the electrostatic generators, are bounded by physical limitations such as the breakdown of insulation at high electric fields. In the cyclotron the relativistic increase in mass destroys the validity of the resonance principle at high energies. The betatron, although operating in the 100-Mev range, is limited by radiation loss. None of these machines can maintain acceleration to indefinitely high energies.

Postwar development of accelerators follows primarily from a new principle—the principle of phase stability. This principle was discovered independently and almost simultaneously in two countries; once again parallel developments in science led to an apparent coincidence. In 1944 Veksler[1] in the U.S.S.R. published a presentation of the new

284

principle. Early in 1945, before Veksler's paper reached the United States, the same principle was published by McMillan[2] of the University of California.

9-1. BASIC CONCEPTS

The new principle can be stated as follows: In a phase-stable accelerator, particles will be accelerated at a series of gaps by an alternating electric field. The gap separation and the frequency and strength of the field are adjusted so that a particle of a specified energy arriving at a particular gap at a specified equilibrium phase of the accelerating field will arrive at the next gap at the same phase. Now it can be shown that particles of the correct energy arriving at the gap at incorrect phases in the neighborhood of the equilibrium phase will experience an automatic correction toward the correct phase at succeeding gaps. In general, particles with slight phase or energy errors will continue to be accelerated with minor oscillations in energy and phase around the correct energy and the equilibrium phase. A mathematical demonstration of this principle will be given in the following sections.

This principle has found its most important applications in three accelerator types: the linear accelerator, the synchrotron, and the synchrocyclotron. Machines using this principle are known as synchronous or phase-stable accelerators as distinguished from the earlier resonance accelerators such as the cyclotron. The differences between the several types of synchronous accelerators come from different combinations of the geometric arrangements of magnetic and electric fields. They have the common feature that stable oscillations are set up in the phase at which the accelerating gap is crossed; particles remain in synchronism with the oscillating fields until they reach the physical limits of guiding and accelerating fields. In principle, acceleration can be continued to indefinitely high energies in synchronous accelerators. At present, upper limits for acceleration are set only by economic considerations.

In the linear accelerator, particles are accelerated in a linear path by a field of constant frequency. Separations between accelerating gaps increase as particle energy increases in such a fashion that the time taken by a particle to travel from any gap to the next gap is a constant, usually a full period of the accelerating field. The equilibrium phase in the linear accelerator is a phase on the rising side of the field wave across the gap. If a particle arrives too soon, it will receive too little additional energy at the gap; since now it travels too slowly, it will arrive at the next gap at a slightly later phase, which is closer to the correct equilibrium

---

At the head of the facing page are photographs of the discoverers of the principle of phase stability. On the left is E. M. McMillan; on the right is V. I. Veksler.

phase. If it arrives at the first gap too late, it will gain too much energy and will make the transit to the next gap faster than it should; again its phase at the second gap will be moved toward the correct phase. Thus the phase-correction mechanism becomes evident, at least for this particular case. If both phase of arrival and energy are incorrect, the situation becomes more complicated; we shall see later that phase stability is still effective.

The synchrotron was the machine whose invention by Veksler and by McMillan yielded the first understanding of phase stability. This is a machine in which particles are maintained in generally circular orbits by a magnetic field. As particle energy increases, the magnetic field is increased at such a rate that the radius of the particle orbit remains constant. Acceleration takes place at one or more gaps around the orbit. As the particle velocity increases, the frequency of the field must be increased to maintain a constant phase shift as the particle goes from gap to gap. Here the equilibrium phase is on the falling side of the field wave. Particles arriving too soon gain too much energy and travel on orbits of larger radius and hence larger circumference; they take longer to arrive at the next gap and so arrive nearer the equilibrium phase. Particles arriving too late gain too little energy, travel on a smaller orbit, and make too rapid a transit; they arrive, as before, nearer to the equilibrium phase.

The synchrocyclotron is a cyclotron in which the accelerating frequency is decreased as particles become relativistic. Stability of phase is maintained by essentially the same mechanism as exists in the synchrotron. This procedure was proposed by prewar cyclotronists, but its eventual success was not appreciated until the enunciation of the principle of phase stability.

The characteristics of these three machines may be summarized as follows:

Accelerator type	Frequency	Radius of particle orbit	Magnetic field
Linear accelerator	Constant	Infinite	Zero
Synchrotron	Increasing	Constant	Increasing
Synchrocyclotron	Decreasing	Increasing	Constant

In the sections which follow we shall enunciate the principle of phase stability for these various machines and examine the consequences for each case. First, however, we shall present a traveling-wave concept of the accelerating field; this concept will simplify the mathematical treatment and should clarify the description of the mechanisms which result in phase stability.

9-2. FIELD PATTERNS IN SYNCHRONOUS ACCELERATORS

The mechanism of acceleration in the synchrotron, the synchrocyclo-tron, and the linear accelerator can be described in rather simple, yet general terms. The particle to be accelerated crosses a gap across which is applied a radiofrequency field. If the particle is the equilibrium particle, it will traverse the gap at a prescribed phase of the accelerating field such that it gains a prescribed increment of energy. It now coasts through a region where it experiences no accelerating field and finally arrives at another gap (which may be the same gap as before), again at the prescribed accelerating phase. The sequence of acceleration and drift is repeated until the particle has gained the total energy for which the machine is designed.

For a mathematical representation of the accelerating field we shall consider the simplest case in which the gap is infinitesimal in length and in which the particle drifts from one gap to the next in one full period of the radiofrequency signal. If s represents distance along the particle path and s_n is the distance from the nth gap to the $(n + 1)$st gap, this means that

$$s_n = \frac{2\pi v}{\omega} \tag{9-1}$$

where v is the particle velocity and $\omega/2\pi$ is the radiofrequency.

The field configuration in the accelerator now consists of a high field for the infinitesimal distance across the gap and zero field over the distance to the next gap. This pattern can be represented by a Fourier series. If $V \sin(\omega t)$ is the gap voltage, the field along the particle orbit will be

$$E_s = \sum_n 2 \frac{V}{s_n} \sin(\omega t) \cos \frac{n\omega s}{v} \tag{9-2}$$

which can be rewritten in the form

$$E_s = \sum_n \frac{V}{s_n} \left[\sin\left(\omega t + \frac{n\omega s}{v}\right) + \sin\left(\omega t - \frac{n\omega s}{v}\right) \right] \tag{9-3}$$

Equation (9-2) represents a standing-wave field pattern; Eq. (9-3) represents a traveling-wave pattern. Both representations are valid, but the traveling-wave picture is by far the most useful. In Eq. (9-3) only one term is significant. The wave represented by the term $\sin(\omega t - \omega s/v)$ is a wave which travels in the same direction as the particle and at the same velocity as the particle velocity. The particle may be considered to be riding on this wave at an accelerating phase such that it continually gains energy from its electric field. All the other waves are traveling either at very different velocities or in the opposite direction to the particle motion. As a result these waves alternately accelerate and decelerate the particle, and their over-all effect after traversal of many gaps becomes completely negligible. The particle motion can, accordingly, be deduced from consideration of the effects of only the one significant traveling-wave component.

The traveling-wave concept has a further significance in accelerator design. Many other gap configurations and methods of gap excitation can be devised which, on analysis into traveling waves, yield a component with the same velocity and direction as those of the particle. These configurations are just as useful for acceleration of particles as the simple one described above. For example, the gaps can be separated by the distance traveled by a particle in one half-period of the radiofrequency. If the gap voltages alternate in polarity, the field pattern will include the same significant traveling-wave component. This system is the one used in the cyclotron and the synchrocyclotron.

Before we proceed to utilize this field component in analysis of particle motions, it is necessary to take into account the fact that the particle velocity is changing during acceleration. Also it may be necessary to vary the radiofrequency during acceleration so that the particle always arrives at the gap at the correct phase. The gap voltage may also vary along the complete particle orbit. We therefore represent the significant field component as follows:

$$E_s = E(s) \sin \left(\int \omega \, dt - \int \frac{\omega \, ds}{v} + \phi_0 \right) \qquad (9\text{-}4)$$

If the field E and the frequency are made to vary in the correct fashion, the first two terms in the argument of the sine will cancel and the particle will continually see an apparent accelerating field whose magnitude is $E \sin \phi_0$.

In the applications of these fields in the sections which follow, it will continually be necessary to remember that s and $\dot{s}$ are the position and velocity of the general particle, while v is the velocity of the accelerating wave.

9-3. THE PRINCIPLE OF PHASE STABILITY

We must now investigate the behavior of a particle which has fallen behind or has reached a phase ahead of the correct equilibrium phase on the traveling wave. First we consider the simplest case of the non-relativistic linear accelerator in which the particle is traveling in a straight line with approximately the same velocity as the significant traveling-

wave field component.   There will be two phases at which the particle
can continue to gain energy at the correct rate.   One of these phases will
correspond to a point on the rising side of the wave; the other will correspond to a point on the falling side of the wave.   A particle near the
correct point on the rising side of the wave but delayed a little in phase
will continually gain too little energy and so will slip farther and farther
behind; another particle a little ahead of the correct point on the rising
side will continually gain too much energy and also will move farther and
farther away from the correct phase.   Evidently particles on the rising
side of the traveling wave are not stable in phase.   On the falling side of
the wave, however, the opposite is true.   A particle lagging in phase will
gain more energy and will tend toward the correct phase, and a particle
leading in phase will gain less energy and will slip backward toward the
correct phase.   Stable oscillations will be set up around the correct phase;
it will thus be possible to accelerate a group of particles which have the
correct range of initial phases grouped around the stable phase on the
falling side of the accelerating wave.   The particle is behaving like a
surf rider who continues to be accelerated so long as he rides ahead of the
wave but is thrown back into the sea if he slips behind the wave crest.

Some confusion may arise in the reader's mind if he attempts to trace
the particle orbit through the standing-wave pattern described by Eq.
(9-2).   In this case he will find that the stable phase in the linear accelerator is on the rising side of the standing wave observed when he maintains
a fixed position in space and watches the particles go by.   Since the
traveling-wave concept is mathematically much more fruitful and conceptually clearer, we shall adopt the procedure of traveling with the
equilibrium particle and observing only the significant traveling-wave
component.

In the synchrotron and the synchrocyclotron the particle behavior is
more complicated.   A particle which has too much energy travels on a
circle of too great radius and actually takes a longer time to return to the
accelerating gap than does a particle of the correct energy.   In other
words, the faster the particle travels the farther it will lag behind the
traveling wave.   This "Alice through the Looking Glass" process
reverses the arguments just outlined for the linear accelerator.   In the
circular machines the particle has phase stability around an accelerating
phase on the rising side of the accelerating traveling wave.

The mathematical formulation of these qualitative ideas can proceed
to some extent with such generality that it relates to all phase-stable
machines.   In our analysis we shall use time as the independent variable.
Parameters describing the equilibrium particle will be distinguished by
zero subscripts.   The nonequilibrium particle will be assumed to have
parameters which deviate from the equilibrium parameters by relatively
small amounts.   For example, the momentum p of a general nonequi-

librium particle will be written

$$p = p_0 + \Delta p$$

where Δp is assumed to be small compared with p_0. The particle which is not at the correct phase of the accelerating wave will have a position error Δs.

We shall write the equation of motion for the nonequilibrium particle for the most general case, in which the particle is bent on a circular arc of radius r by a magnetic field $-B_z$. The equation of motion will be the azimuthal component of the general equation of motion (5-14) in cylindrical coordinates:

$$\frac{1}{r}\frac{d}{dt}(rp) = \dot{p} + \frac{\dot{r}p}{r} = eE \sin\left(\int \omega\, dt - \int \frac{\omega\, ds}{v} + \phi_0\right) + eE' + e\dot{r}B_z$$

(9-5)

where the first term on the right is the traveling-wave component of the accelerating field and the second term eE' represents all other possible accelerating or decelerating fields such as those corresponding to betatron acceleration by a changing magnetic flux linking the orbit, or decelerating fields corresponding to energy loss due to electromagnetic radiation. But the momentum of a particle on an orbit of radius r in a field B_z is given by

$$p = erB_z \qquad\qquad (9\text{-}6)$$

whence

$$\frac{\dot{r}p}{r} = e\dot{r}B_z \qquad\qquad (9\text{-}7)$$

and Eq. (9-5) simplifies to

$$\dot{p} = eE \sin\left(\int \omega\, dt - \int \frac{\omega\, ds}{v} + \phi_0\right) + eE' \qquad\qquad (9\text{-}8)$$

The radius r has disappeared from this equation except for its possible entry through E' or v. Since there is no E' term in the linear-accelerator case, Eq. (9-8) is a general equation describing the motion in all synchronous accelerators. It is valid for both relativistic and nonrelativistic motions.

We shall find it simplest to discuss the behavior of the nonequilibrium particle in terms of its phase. The particle phase ϕ is defined by

$$\phi = \phi_0 + \Delta\phi = \int \omega\, dt - \int \frac{\omega\, ds}{v} + \phi_0 \qquad\qquad (9\text{-}9)$$

where $\Delta\phi$ is the phase error or deviation from the equilibrium phase ϕ_0. The precise evaluation of the phase error from this equation is rather tedious; it is much easier to deduce its value from the sketch of the traveling wave shown in Fig. 9-1.   A full wavelength of the traveling wave is v/c times the free-space wavelength corresponding to the radiofrequency field because the particle must cover one wavelength in one period of the accelerating field.   Hence, in terms of the position error Δs of the non-equilibrium particle, the phase error is given by

$$\frac{\Delta \phi}{2\pi} = \frac{-\Delta s}{(v/c) \times \text{free-space wavelength}} = -\frac{\Delta s}{v/f}$$

where f is the frequency of the accelerating field.   Hence

$$\phi = \phi_0 + \Delta \phi = \phi_0 - \frac{\omega\, \Delta s}{v} \tag{9-10}$$

In this notation Eq. (9-8) becomes

$$\dot{p} = eE \sin \phi + eE' = eE \sin (\phi_0 + \Delta \phi) + eE' \tag{9-11}$$

The general procedure for solution of the phase motion is now evident. Equations (9-10) and (9-11) must be combined and reduced to involve a

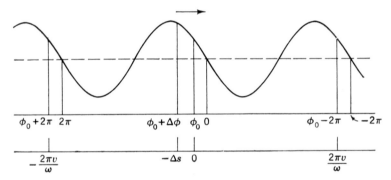

Fig. 9-1. Phase and distance scales for a wave traveling to the right.   When $\Delta \phi = 2\pi$, $\Delta s = -2\pi v/\omega$; hence, in general, $\Delta \phi = -\omega\, \Delta s/v$.

single variable.   The best procedures differ for the various accelerator types and will be treated separately in the sections that follow.   Generally we shall derive a relation between the momentum error and the rate of change of the position error and so eliminate the momentum or position error between the two fundamental relations.   This will leave us with a second-order differential equation for the phase error.   If ϕ_0 has been chosen correctly, this equation will be found to describe a stable, usually damped, oscillation in phase around the equilibrium phase.   It will be shown that, for a fairly wide range of initial phases, particles will continue to be accelerated without large deviations in energy from the design energy of the accelerator.   Particles which fall outside of the "acceptance phase range" will be lost early in the acceleration cycle. Particles which are accepted will undergo stable phase oscillations around the equilibrium phase during the acceleration cycle. This is a general statement of the principle of phase stability.

9-4. APPROXIMATE TREATMENT OF THE PHASE MOTION— THE PENDULUM ANALOGY

The general character of the phase oscillation can be shown by an approximate, nonrelativistic treatment in which the steady variations of frequency and equilibrium momentum are neglected in comparison with the more rapid periodic variations of the phase and momentum errors. We shall assume further that the electric field E is constant and that the term E' is negligible. Reminding the reader that v represents the wave velocity and p_0 represents the momentum of the equilibrium particle which is traveling at the wave velocity, we can now rewrite Eqs. (9-10) and (9-11) in the form

$$\frac{d\phi}{dt} = -\frac{\omega \, \Delta \dot{s}}{v} = -\frac{\omega \, \Delta p}{p_0} \tag{9-12}$$

and

$$\frac{d \, \Delta p}{dt} = eE(\sin \phi - \sin \phi_0) \tag{9-13}$$

We now differentiate Eq. (9-12) with respect to time, neglecting the relatively slow variation of ω and p_0. In the resulting expression we substitute from Eq. (9-13) to obtain

$$\frac{d^2\phi}{dt^2} + \frac{\omega e E}{p_0} (\sin \phi - \sin \phi_0) = 0 \tag{9-14}$$

This obviously represents an oscillation of ϕ about ϕ_0. For small deviations $\Delta \phi$ from the equilibrium phase ϕ_0 we can substitute $\Delta \phi \cos \phi_0$ for the quantity (sin ϕ — sin ϕ_0) and Eq. (9-14) becomes the equation of simple harmonic motion provided that, as before, we neglect the slow variations of $\omega e E / p_0$. In this case we can write the solution of Eq. (9-14):

$$\Delta \phi = \Delta \phi_i \cos \left[\left(\frac{\omega e E}{p_0} \right)^{1/2} t \right] \tag{9-15}$$

where the subscript i indicates the initial value of the variable. The momentum error follows from Eq. (9-12); it is

$$\Delta p = \Delta \phi_i \left(\frac{p_0 e E}{\omega} \right)^{1/2} \sin \left[\left(\frac{\omega e E}{p_0} \right)^{1/2} t \right] \tag{9-16}$$

Generally it will be found that the values of E and ω in accelerators are such that the momentum error Δp is a small fraction of the equilibrium momentum p_0.

For oscillations of larger amplitude we must return to a study of Eq. (9-14). This is the equation of motion of a rather simple mechanical system. In one of its forms this system is a simple pendulum to which a constant torque is applied. A physical model of such a pendulum is illustrated in Fig. 9-2. It consists of a rigid pendulum mounted on a good bearing and having a cord carrying a weight wrapped around the hub. If the angle between the pendulum and the vertical is represented by ϕ, the angle at which it hangs at rest by ϕ_0, and if the length of the pendulum is chosen so that the ratio $\dfrac{\text{acceleration of gravity}}{\text{length of pendulum}}$ is equal to $\omega e E/p_0$, then the equation of motion of the pendulum will be identical with Eq. (9-14). Evidently the motion of this pendulum will be a stable oscillation around the rest position so long as displacements are small. If the displacements of the pendulum become so large, however, that it swings past the point where its mass is above the point of support, it will go into continuous rotation. The torque will continue to accelerate this motion, and the rotation will become continually more rapid so that never again can it stabilize itself. The particle-phase motion described by Eq. (9-14) is similar. If the phase oscillation carries the phase past certain safe limits, it will slip backward in phase with ever-increasing phase velocity. It will immediately be lost from the pattern of steady acceleration and will probably finish its career as a charged particle by drifting to one of the walls of the acceleration chamber.

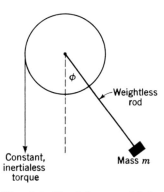

Fig. 9-2. Pendulum model for phase oscillations.

9-5. THE LIMITS OF PHASE STABILITY

A first integration of Eq. (9-14) is made possible by rewriting it in the form

$$\frac{d^2\phi}{dt^2} = \frac{1}{2}\frac{d}{d\phi}(\dot{\phi}^2) = \frac{\omega e E}{p_0}(\sin\phi - \sin\phi_0) \qquad (9\text{-}17)$$

Integration of Eq. (9-17) yields

$$\dot{\phi}^2 = \frac{2\omega e E}{p_0}(\cos\phi + \phi\sin\phi_0 + \text{integration const}) \qquad (9\text{-}18)$$

One of the limits of the stable phase oscillation is immediately evident. As ϕ increases through a range greater than ϕ_0, we see from Eq. (9-17) that the second derivative of ϕ first increases, then decreases to pass through zero when ϕ reaches the value $(\pi - \phi_0)$. For larger values of ϕ the sign reverses and the phase oscillation is no longer stable. Consequently the limit of the oscillation in this direction is $(\pi - \phi_0)$ and the integration constant in Eq. (9-18) can be evaluated by setting $\dot\phi$ equal to zero for this value of ϕ. Equation (9-18) then becomes

$$\dot\phi^2 = \frac{2eE_0\omega}{p_0} [\cos \phi + \cos \phi_0 + (\phi + \phi_0 - \pi) \sin \phi_0] \qquad (9\text{-}19)$$

The other limit of the oscillation is given by the other value of ϕ for which the quantity in the square brackets in Eq. (9-19) vanishes. The phase-acceptance ranges for various values of the equilibrium phase and the accepted fraction of a continuous injected beam are given in Table 9-1.

TABLE 9-1

Equilibrium phase ϕ_0, deg	Limits of phase acceptance, deg	Accepted fraction of injected beam
0	−180 to 180	1.000
10	−99.6 to 170	0.749
20	−65.9 to 160	0.627
30	−38.7 to 150	0.524
40	−14.6 to 140	0.429
50	7.8 to 130	0.339
60	29.1 to 120	0.252
70	49.7 to 110	0.167
80	70.0 to 100	0.083
90	90.0 to 90	0.000

From this table it is clear that phase acceptance increases markedly as the equilibrium phase moves away from the peak of the accelerating wave. In other words, the higher the electric field relative to the minimum necessary field, the more particles will be accepted.

The discussion thus far has related only to the acceptance for particles with no momentum error. When particles have been accepted into phase-stable acceleration, momentum errors will develop, and the particles will move on "orbits" in a plot of momentum error against phase error. The shape of these orbits can be established from Eqs. (9-12) and (9-13). For large errors linear approximations are not adequate, and numerical integration is necessary. The result is shown in Fig. 9-3. Here a parameter proportional to energy error rather than momentum error has been plotted against phase error for various equilibrium phases. Energy error has been chosen because energy and phase prove to be Hamiltonian conjugates. From the arguments presented in Sec. 5-8, areas plotted in this manner will be preserved throughout the motion.

A group of particles plotted in this pattern will occupy a space whose area will not change with time, although the shape of the area may go through marked variations.

The Hamiltonian describing the phase motion has the form

$$H = eE \cos \phi - eE'\phi + \frac{\omega}{c}(W^2 - W_0^2)^{1/2} - \frac{\omega W}{v}$$

where W is the particle energy, W_0 is the rest energy of the particle, and the other symbols are as used earlier in these sections.   It is not

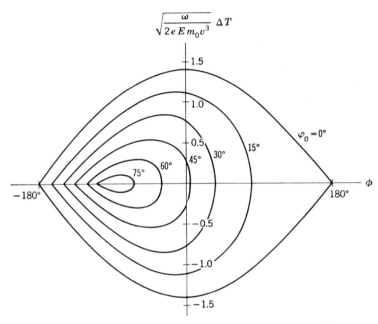

Fig. 9-3. Region of phase stability for various equilibrium phases ϕ_0.

difficult to show that Eqs. (9-10) and (9-11) can be derived from this function.

In spite of the approximate nature of the discussion in the two preceding sections, Table 9-1 is reasonably accurate for the initial phase of the acceleration cycle and gives a true picture of the amount of a continuous beam which will be captured in stable acceleration.   As a precise description of the subsequent behavior of the particle phase and momentum error, the above discussion is entirely inadequate—its value is qualitative in showing the character of the oscillation.   For a more detailed study we now consider the various accelerators in which phase stability is essential to operation.   Fortunately the phase oscillations are damped in all cases, and it will be possible to make an adequate study of the phase oscillations without consideration of oscillations of large amplitude.

9-6. PHASE STABILITY IN THE LINEAR ACCELERATOR

In the linear accelerator the frequency of the accelerating field remains constant and the wave velocity increases along the accelerator to match the increasing velocity of the equilibrium particle. There are no extra fields to produce a term of the form E' of Eq. (9-11). We shall restrict ourselves to small phase excursions around the equilibrium phase. Consequently we can write the fundamental equations (9-10) and (9-11) thus:

$$\Delta\phi = -\frac{\omega\,\Delta s}{v} \tag{9-20}$$

$$\Delta\dot{p} = eE\,\Delta\phi\,\cos\,\phi_0 \tag{9-21}$$

On differentiation with respect to time, Eq. (9-20) yields

$$\Delta\dot{s} = -\frac{1}{\omega}\frac{d}{dt}\,(v\,\Delta\phi) \tag{9-22}$$

To combine these equations into an expression in terms of $\Delta\phi$ we need to express Δp in terms of $\Delta\dot{s}$. For this purpose we use the relativistic expression for momentum discussed in Chap. 5:

$$p = \frac{m_0\dot{s}}{(1 - \dot{s}^2/c^2)^{\frac{1}{2}}} \quad\text{and}\quad p_0 = \frac{m_0 v}{(1 - v^2/c^2)^{\frac{1}{2}}} \tag{9-23}$$

where m_0 represents the rest mass of the particle, p_0 and v are the momentum and velocity of the equilibrium particle, and p and $\dot{s}$ are the momentum and velocity of the nonequilibrium particle. The expressions (9-23) can be inverted into the forms

$$m_0\dot{s} = \frac{p}{(1 + p^2/m_0^2c^2)^{\frac{1}{2}}} \quad\text{and}\quad m_0 v = \frac{p_0}{(1 + p_0^2/m_0^2c^2)^{\frac{1}{2}}} \tag{9-24}$$

whence it follows that

$$\frac{\Delta p}{p_0} = \frac{\Delta\dot{s}}{v}\left(1 + \frac{p_0^2}{m_0^2c^2}\right) \tag{9-25}$$

For abbreviation and simplification of the expressions which follow we now introduce the dimensionless variable p^* defined by

$$p^* = \frac{p_0}{m_0 c} \tag{9-26}$$

We note in passing that the ratio between p^* and unity is a measure of whether or not the treatment of the problem must be relativistic. So long as p^* is small compared with unity, nonrelativistic treatments will be adequate. For electrons $p^* = 1$ if the electron energy is 212 kev. For protons $p^* = 1$ when the proton energy is 389 Mev.

We are now able to combine Eqs. (9-22), (9-24), and (9-25) to give a relation between Δp and $\Delta \phi$:

$$\Delta p = -\frac{m_0 c}{\omega} \left[p^*(1 + p^{*2}) \frac{d\Delta\phi}{dt} + \dot{p}^* \, \Delta\phi \right] \qquad (9\text{-}27)$$

The value of $\dot{p}^*$ we know directly from the equation of motion of the equilibrium particle:

$$\dot{p}_0 = m_0 c \dot{p}^* = eE \sin \phi_0 \qquad (9\text{-}28)$$

Throughout this treatment we shall make the simplifying assumption that E is constant along the accelerator. Although solutions can be obtained for the more general case where E varies as some power of distance along the axis, these solutions are complicated and they do not correspond to the situation in any operating linear accelerator. If E is constant, Eq. (9-28) can be integrated to give

$$p^* = \frac{eEt \sin \phi_0}{m_0 c} \qquad (9\text{-}29)$$

The phase equation can now be obtained by differentiation of Eq. (9-27) and substitution of the result in Eq. (9-21):

$$\frac{d}{dt}\left[p^*(1 + p^{*2}) \frac{d\Delta\phi}{dt} \right] + \frac{eE \sin \phi_0}{m_0 c}\frac{d\Delta\phi}{dt} + \frac{\omega eE \cos \phi_0 \, \Delta\phi}{m_0 c} = 0 \qquad (9\text{-}30)$$

This is the general expression which describes the phase oscillations in the linear accelerator for both the relativistic and the nonrelativistic condition. In this form it is not easy to write an explicit analytical solution, although it is fairly evident that, if $\cos \phi_0$ is positive, the solution will have a generally periodic character with damping introduced by the second term.

The significance of the phase equation is much clearer if a change of variables is made. First we rewrite the equation in terms of the variable $p^* \, \Delta\phi$ instead of $\Delta\phi$ alone. We then introduce a new independent variable u defined by

$$u = \sinh^{-1} p^* = \sinh^{-1} \frac{eEt \sin \phi_0}{m_0 c} \qquad (9\text{-}31)$$

The new variable is a monotonic function of p^* and so of t. For low values of p^*, u is approximately equal to p^* and so is proportional to t. For very large values of p^*, u increases more slowly and becomes approximately equal to $\ln (2p^*)$.

When the algebra attending these changes of variable has been carried through, we emerge with the new phase equation

$$\frac{d^2(p^* \, \Delta\phi)}{du^2} + \left(\frac{K}{p^*} - 1\right) p^* \, \Delta\phi = 0 \tag{9-32}$$

where the dimensionless constant K is given by

$$K = \frac{\omega m_0 c \, \cos \, \phi_0}{eE \, \sin^2 \, \phi_0} \tag{9-33}$$

The character of the phase oscillation in the linear accelerator is clear from Eq. (9-32). If K is positive, a stable oscillation will be maintained up to the point where p^* becomes equal to K. Although $p^* \, \Delta\phi$ will increase in amplitude, $\Delta\phi$ itself will be damped, as we shall show later. As p^* increases to such large values that K/p^* becomes negligible compared with unity and the variable u becomes equal to ln $(2p^*)$, then the phase equation (9-32) degenerates to

$$\frac{d}{dp^*}\left(p^{*3} \frac{d\Delta\phi}{dp^*}\right) = 0 \tag{9-34}$$

whose solution is

$$\Delta\phi = \text{a constant} + \frac{\text{another constant}}{p^{*2}} \tag{9-35}$$

Although the phase is no longer oscillating around a stable equilibrium value, it is now approaching a constant value; in other words, the particle continues to be "locked" to the accelerating wave.

A knowledge of the sign and value of the constant K is now essential to any further understanding of the phase oscillation. The phase oscillation is stable only if K is positive. From Eq. (9-33) this will be true only if cos ϕ_0 is positive; since sin ϕ_0 must also be positive for acceleration to take place, ϕ_0 must lie between 0 and 90°. For the traveling wave described by Eq. (9-4), this value lies on the falling side of the wave as we expected. [This fact may be verified by differentiating Eq. (9-4) with respect to distance s.]

The value of K for most operating electron linear accelerators is about 2. The phase oscillation, accordingly, ceases to be periodic when $p^* \simeq 2$ or when the kinetic energy of the electron is about 0.37 Mev. This energy occurs near the beginning of most electron machines; hence almost the whole electron accelerator is operating above the region where phase oscillations are observed. In most operating proton linear accelerators, on the other hand, K is of the order of 1000. But protons reach momenta given by $p^* = 1000$ only when the proton energy approaches 1000 Bev. Evidently all proton linear accelerators, operating or contemplated, will enjoy stable phase oscillations.

In the proton linear accelerator, up to the highest energies yet achieved, p^* is so small compared with unity that the variable u is effectively equal to p^* and a solution of the phase equation becomes possible. When u is replaced by p^* and the unity term is neglected in comparison with K/p^*, Eq. (9-32) becomes

$$\frac{d^2}{dp^{*2}} (p^* \, \Delta\phi) + K \, \Delta\phi = 0 \qquad (9\text{-}36)$$

This is a modified form of Bessel's equation and has the solution

$$\Delta\phi = p^{*-\frac{1}{2}} \{ C_1 J_1[2(Kp^*)^{\frac{1}{2}}] + C_2 N_1[2(Kp^*)^{\frac{1}{2}}] \} \qquad (9\text{-}37)$$

where J_1 and N_1 are the Bessel and Neumann functions of the first order and C_1 and C_2 are constants determined by the initial conditions. When p^* reaches sufficiently high values, the asymptotic forms of the Bessel and Neumann functions can be used. For x large

$$J_1(x) \simeq \left(\frac{2}{\pi x}\right)^{\frac{1}{2}} \cos\left(x - \frac{3\pi}{4}\right)$$

$$N_1(x) \simeq \left(\frac{2}{\pi x}\right)^{\frac{1}{2}} \sin\left(x - \frac{3\pi}{4}\right)$$

and Eq. (9-37) can be rewritten in the form

$$\Delta\phi = \Delta\phi_i \left(\frac{p_i^*}{p^*}\right)^{\frac{3}{4}} \cos\,[2(Kp^*)^{\frac{1}{2}} - 2(Kp_i^*)^{\frac{1}{2}}] \qquad (9\text{-}38)$$

where the subscript i indicates the initial value of the parameter in question. We see that the phase oscillation is damped and decreases in amplitude proportional to $p^{*-\frac{3}{4}}$.

Over the low-energy range of most proton linear accelerators the approximation involved in using the asymptotic form of the Bessel function is not a very good one; the qualitative conclusions are, however, valid over the whole energy range.

Associated with the phase oscillation of the nonequilibrium particle will be an oscillating momentum and energy error. This error can be evaluated from Eq. (9-22), which relates the velocity error to the phase error. If T_0 is the kinetic energy of the equilibrium particle and ΔT is the energy error of the nonequilibrium particle, the fractional energy error will be (for nonrelativistic particles)

$$\frac{\Delta T}{T_0} = \frac{2 \, \Delta \dot{s}}{v} = -\frac{2}{\omega v} \frac{d(v \, \Delta\phi)}{dt} = -\frac{2 \cot \, \phi_0}{Kp^*} \frac{d(p^* \, \Delta\phi)}{dp^*} \qquad (9\text{-}39)$$

$\Delta\phi$ is given by Eq. (9-38). In taking the derivative we neglect the term derived from differentiation of the coefficient of the cosine term; this term will be found to make a negligible contribution compared with the term derived from differentiation of the cosine itself.   The result of this operation is

$$\frac{\Delta T}{T_0} = 2K^{-\frac{1}{2}} \cot \phi_0 p_i^{*\frac{3}{4}} p^{*-\frac{5}{4}} \Delta\phi_i \sin [2(Kp^*)^{\frac{1}{2}} - 2(Kp_i^*)^{\frac{1}{2}}] \quad (9\text{-}40)$$

This expression satisfies the usual initial condition of negligible energy error at the input end of the linear accelerator.   The energy error builds up to a maximum in the first quarter of the phase oscillation and then oscillates with an amplitude which damps like $p^{*-\frac{5}{4}}$.   Since, in the non-relativistic range, the kinetic energy of the equilibrium particle is proportional to p^{*2}, the fractional energy error damps like $T_0^{-\frac{5}{8}}$.

In the intermediate energy range where relativistic effects become appreciable, it is necessary to solve Eq. (9-32) without approximation. This equation has not yet been given an analytic solution, but it can rather easily be solved numerically for any particular choice of parameters.   It will be found that the damping of the phase oscillation becomes weaker as p^* approaches K but the oscillation never becomes unstable. As the oscillation finally becomes aperiodic, it is found that the fractional energy error approaches a constant value as does the phase error.

9-7. PHASE STABILITY IN THE LINEAR ACCELERATOR IF $v = c$

In the high-energy electron linear accelerator, the velocity of the electrons over most of the range of acceleration is very nearly equal to the velocity of light.   It is therefore of interest to explore the possibility of setting the phase velocity v of the accelerating wave equal to the velocity of light throughout the whole machine; this will simplify the construction since the machine will now consist of a sequence of identical accelerating sections.   This expedient proves to be quite satisfactory and is now used in all high-energy electron linear accelerators.   A detailed analysis of this system is presented by Slater[3] and by Chodorow et al.[4]

The phase behavior for this case is rather simpler to diagnose than that in the nonrelativistic machines; in fact, the analysis can proceed without restricting the phase excursions to small amplitudes.   If v is set equal to c, the two fundamental relations (9-9) and (9-11) become

$$\phi = \omega \left(t - \frac{s}{c} \right) + \phi_0 \quad (9\text{-}41)$$

and

$$\frac{dp}{dt} = eE \sin \phi \quad (9\text{-}42)$$

We differentiate Eq. (9-41) to obtain

$$\dot{\phi} = \omega \left(1 - \frac{\dot{s}}{c} \right) = \omega \left[1 - \frac{p}{(p^2 + m_0^2 c^2)^{\frac{1}{2}}} \right] \quad (9\text{-}43)$$

Equations (9-42) and (9-43) are satisfied by the following relation between ϕ and p:

$$\cos \phi = \cos \phi_i + \frac{\omega}{eE}[p - (p^2 + m_0{}^2c^2)^{1/2} - p_i + (p_i{}^2 + m_0{}^2c^2)^{1/2}] \quad (9\text{-}44)$$

where the subscript i indicates initial values of the quantities concerned. As p becomes very large, ϕ approaches an asymptotic value ϕ_f given by

$$\cos \phi_f = \cos \phi_i + \frac{\omega}{eE}[(p_i{}^2 + m_0{}^2c^2)^{1/2} - p_i] \quad (9\text{-}45)$$

For any given injection momentum p_i this equation can be satisfied provided the accelerating field E is high enough that the cosine of the asymptotic phase is never greater than unity. In practice the value of E to satisfy this requirement is of the order of millions of volts per meter. When E is sufficiently high, we have a sort of phase stability because the phase continually approaches the asymptotic value given by Eq. (9-45). In other words, the electrons are bound to the accelerating wave and will continue to be accelerated indefinitely without falling out of step with the accelerating field.

9-8. PHASE STABILITY IN THE SYNCHROTRON

The synchrotron will be described in Chaps. 12 and 13. For the present discussion it will be sufficient to summarize its characteristics.

The equilibrium particle in the synchrotron has an orbit of constant radius r_0 given by

$$p_0 = B_0 e r_0 \quad (9\text{-}46)$$

where p_0 is the particle momentum and B_0 is the magnetic field at the orbit. Since r_0 is fixed, the field B_0 must increase with time as the particle momentum increases. Focusing forces are provided just as in the betatron by shaping the magnetic field so that

$$B = B_0 r^{-n} r_0{}^n \quad (9\text{-}47)$$

where n must lie between 0 and 1. Acceleration takes place at one or more gaps around the orbit and is accomplished by application of a radio-frequency field. As the particle is accelerated and its period of revolution decreases, the frequency of the accelerating signal must be increased. Consequently, in contrast to the linear-accelerator situation, the frequency of the accelerating signal is not constant but increases during the acceleration cycle.

Particles which arrive at the accelerating gaps at incorrect phases will vary in momentum from the equilibrium value and so will travel on orbits with radii given by

$$p = Ber = B_0 er^{1-n} r_0^n \qquad (9\text{-}48)$$

The frequency of the accelerating signal is equal to the frequency of revolution $\omega/2\pi$ of the equilibrium particle or may be an integral multiple of that frequency. For generality we shall consider acceleration by the hth harmonic of the revolution frequency. The phase error now follows from Eq. (9-10):

$$\Delta\phi = \frac{-h\omega \, \Delta s}{v} \qquad (9\text{-}49)$$

In the cylindrical coordinate system having the axis of the orbit as the axis of coordinates $\Delta s = r \, \Delta\theta$ and $v = r\omega$. Hence

$$\Delta\phi = -h \, \Delta\theta$$
and
$$\Delta\dot\phi = -h \, \Delta\dot\theta \qquad (9\text{-}50)$$
but
$$\Delta\dot s = \Delta(r\dot\theta) = \frac{v}{r_0} \, \Delta r + r_0 \, \Delta\dot\theta$$

(We are assuming, as will subsequently be evident, that the radial velocity of the particle is negligible in comparison with its azimuthal velocity.) Therefore Eq. (9-50) can be written

$$\Delta\dot\phi = \frac{hv}{r_0} \left(\frac{\Delta r}{r_0} - \frac{\Delta\dot s}{v} \right) \qquad (9\text{-}51)$$

The purpose of these manipulations is to express the phase error in terms of the momentum error so that the equation of motion (9-11) can be reduced to an equation describing only the phase error. Accordingly we transform the two terms on the right of Eq. (9-51) to terms proportional to the momentum error. From Eq. (9-48)

$$\frac{\Delta r}{r_0} = \frac{\Delta p}{p_0(1 - n)} \qquad (9\text{-}52)$$

The second term on the right-hand side of Eq. (9-51) has already been discussed in connection with the linear accelerator. From Eqs. (9-25) and (9-26)

$$\frac{\Delta\dot s}{v} = \frac{\Delta p}{p_0(1 + p^{*2})}$$

The quantity v is expressible in terms of p^* by using Eqs. (9-24) and (9-26). With these substitutions Eq. (9-51) becomes

$$\Delta\dot\phi = \frac{h(n + p^{*2}) \, \Delta p}{m_0 r_0 (1 - n)(1 + p^{*2})^{3/2}} \qquad (9\text{-}53)$$

We now return to the equation of motion (9-11).   Before substituting from Eq. (9-53) in this relation, we must first make the appropriate substitution for the term E'.   In the synchrotron the term E' represents two effects, first the accelerating or decelerating effect of the changing magnetic flux linked by the particle orbit and second, significant only in electron machines, the decelerating effect of the energy loss due to electromagnetic radiation by the accelerated electrons.   For the present we consider only the first effect, the betatron effect of the flux within the orbit.   Just as was done in discussing the betatron, we write this term

$$E' = \frac{1}{2\pi r} \int \frac{\partial B}{\partial t} 2\pi r \, dr$$

The accelerating field E in Eq. (9-11) is given by

$$E = \frac{V}{2\pi r}$$

where V is the sum of the peak voltages applied across all of the accelerating gaps.   With these substitutions Eq. (9-11) can be written in the form

$$r\dot{p} = \frac{eV}{2\pi} \sin (\phi_0 + \Delta\phi) + e \int \frac{\partial B}{\partial t} r \, dr \qquad (9\text{-}54)$$

In terms of momentum, radius, and phase errors this becomes

$$\dot{p}_0 \, \Delta r + r_0 \, \Delta\dot{p} = \frac{eV}{2\pi} \Delta\phi \cos \phi_0 + e \frac{\partial B_0}{\partial t} r_0 \, \Delta r \qquad (9\text{-}55)$$

From Eq. (9-46) the first and last terms of this equation cancel each other, and we are left with

$$\Delta\dot{p} = \frac{eV}{2\pi r_0} \Delta\phi \cos \phi_0 \qquad (9\text{-}56)$$

We have now only to combine Eqs. (9-53) and (9-56) to obtain a second-order differential equation in $\Delta\phi$.   The result is

$$\frac{d}{dt} \left[\frac{(1 + p^{*2})^{3/2} \, \Delta\phi}{n + p^{*2}} \right] = \frac{heV \cos \phi_0 \, \Delta\phi}{2\pi r_0^2 m_0 (1 - n)} \qquad (9\text{-}57)$$

If $\dot{B}$ and the accelerating field remain constant, p^* will be proportional to time.   Explicitly,

$$p^* = \frac{eVt \sin \phi_0}{2\pi r_0 m_0 c} \qquad (9\text{-}58)$$

and p^* can be used as the independent variable in Eq. (9-57), which becomes

$$\frac{d}{dp^*}\left[\frac{(1 + p^{*2})^{3/2}}{n + p^{*2}}\frac{d\Delta\phi}{ap^*}\right] = \frac{hK\,\Delta\phi}{1 - n} \quad (9\text{-}59)$$

where

$$K = \frac{2\pi m_0 c^2 \cos\,\phi_0}{eV\,\sin^2\,\phi_0} \quad (9\text{-}60)$$

K is a dimensionless constant of the same character as the K that was used in analysis of the linear accelerator. In electron synchrotrons K is of the order of 1000; in proton synchrotrons K is of the order of 10^6.

Equation (9-59) describes the phase oscillations of the nonequilibrium particles. Since n must lie between 0 and 1 for radial and vertical focusing (as in the betatron), this equation can represent a stable oscillation only if $\cos\,\phi_0$ is negative. For acceleration to take place $\sin\,\phi_0$ must be positive. Accordingly the stable phase must lie between 90 and 180° on the standing wave and so must lie on the rising side of the traveling wave.

The frequency of the oscillation described by Eq. (9-59) is sufficiently high that the change of p^* during a complete phase oscillation is relatively small. For this reason an approximate solution of Eq. (9-59) will be sufficiently precise for our purposes. This solution takes the form

$$\Delta\phi = \Delta\phi_i\left(\frac{1 + p^{*2}}{1 + p_i^{*2}}\right)^{-3/8}\left(\frac{n + p^{*2}}{n + p_i^{*2}}\right)^{1/4}$$
$$\cos\int\left[\frac{hK(n + p^{*2})}{(1 - n)(1 + p^{*2})^{3/2}}\right]^{1/2}dp^* \quad (9\text{-}61)$$

where the subscript i refers to the initial value of the parameter indicated. At nonrelativistic energies

$$\Delta\phi \propto \left(1 - \frac{3n - 2}{8n}p^{*2}\right)\cos\left[\left(\frac{hKn}{1 - n}\right)^{1/2}p^*\right] \quad (9\text{-}62)$$

and we see that the phase oscillation is constant in frequency and is very weakly damped or undamped, depending on whether or not n is greater than $2/3$. In the extreme relativistic range where p^* is much greater than unity

$$\Delta\phi \propto p^{*-1/4}\cos\left(\frac{2hK}{1 - n}p^*\right)^{1/2} \quad (9\text{-}63)$$

Equation (9-63) indicates that the frequency of the phase oscillation is decreasing as energy or momentum increases and that the oscillation damps like $p^{*-1/4}$.

Associated with the phase oscillation will be an oscillation in the momentum error; the amplitude of this oscillation is given by Eq. (9-53).

The momentum error will be reflected in a radial oscillation whose amplitude will be [cf. Eq. (9-52)]

$$\frac{\Delta r}{r_0} = \frac{\cot \phi_0}{hK} \frac{(1 + p^{*2})^{3/2}}{p^*(n + p^{*2})} \frac{d\Delta\phi}{dp^*} \qquad (9\text{-}64)$$

In the nonrelativistic range it follows from Eq. (9-62) that, approximately,

$$\frac{\Delta r}{r_0} = \cot \phi_0 \, [hKn(1 - n)]^{-1/2} \frac{\Delta\phi_{max}}{p^*} \qquad (9\text{-}65)$$

where $\Delta\phi_{max}$ represents the amplitude of the phase excursion. Since the damping or undamping of the phase oscillation is very weak, Eq. (9-65) indicates that the associated oscillation in radius falls off like $1/p^*$. When the particles reach extreme relativistic energies, Eqs. (9-64) and (9-63) give for the radial excursion the approximate result

$$\frac{\Delta r}{r_0} = \cot \phi_0 \, [2hK(1 - n)p^*]^{-1/2} \, \Delta\phi_{max} \qquad (9\text{-}66)$$

Since the phase oscillation is damping like $p^{*-1/4}$ in this range, the radial-oscillation amplitude will decrease like $p^{*-3/4}$.

It should be remembered in applying the above conclusions that $\ddot{p}^*$, V, and ϕ_0 have been assumed to remain constant during the acceleration. If this assumption is not correct for a particular accelerator, it will be necessary to take this fact into account in solving Eq. (9-57). The more sophisticated treatments necessary in such cases will be found in the papers of Bohm and Foldy[5] or Twiss and Frank.[6]

A question may be raised as to the legitimacy of treating the betatron oscillations and the radial motions associated with the phase oscillations as though they were independent. In principle the general motion should be derived taking both effects into account. But it is always found that the phase oscillation is lower in frequency by a factor of 50 or more than the radial betatron oscillation. The mathematical consequence of this fact is that the oscillations are effectively decoupled and can be analyzed independently.

In electron synchrotrons the term E' of Eq. (9-11) must include a radiation-loss term. As was shown in Sec. 7-7 for the betatron, the radiation contribution to E' can be written

$$E' \text{ (due to radiation)} = -1.408 \times 10^{-32} \frac{W^4}{r^2} \qquad \text{volts/m} \quad (9\text{-}67)$$

where W is expressed in electron volts. Radiation losses are important only in the extreme relativistic range where

$$W \text{ (in electron volts)} = \frac{pc}{e} \qquad (9\text{-}68)$$

From Eq. (9-48)

$$r = r_0 \left(\frac{p}{p_0}\right)^{1/(1-n)}$$

Using these substitutions Eq. (9-67) can be rewritten in the form

$$rE' = -1.408 \times 10^{-32} \frac{1}{r_0} \left(\frac{p_0 c}{e}\right)^4 \left(\frac{p}{p_0}\right)^{(3-4n)/(1-n)} \tag{9-69}$$

Following the same reasoning that led from Eq. (9-54) to Eq. (9-57), we see that the radiation contribution to Eq. (9-56) is of the form $(e/r_0)\,\Delta(rE')$. From Eq. (9-69) and the extreme relativistic form of Eq. (9-53) this term is

$$\frac{e}{r_0} \Delta(rE') = -1.408 \times 10^{-32} \frac{(3-4n)e}{hcr_0} \frac{m_0 c^2 p^{*4}}{e} \Delta\phi \tag{9-70}$$

When this term is included in the derivation of the extreme relativistic form of Eq. (9-57) and the change is made to p^* as the independent variable, Eq. (9-59) becomes

$$\frac{d^2\Delta\phi}{dp^{*2}} + \frac{1}{p^*}\frac{d\Delta\phi}{dp^*}\left(1 + 6.03 \times 10^{-9} \frac{3-4n}{1-n} \frac{p^{*4}}{Vr_0 \sin\phi_0}\right)$$
$$= \frac{hK}{(1-n)p^*}\Delta\phi \tag{9-71}$$

This is the complete relativistic equation for phase oscillations in the electron synchrotron. Since V will be of the order of 1000 volts and r_0 will be of the order of 1 m in most electron synchrotrons, it follows that the radiation term (the second term in the square brackets) will not become appreciable until p^* is of the order of 200 or until the electron energy is of the order of 100 Mev. The radiation term will be a damping or an undamping term, depending on whether or not n is less than $\frac{3}{4}$. As energy is increased above 100 Mev, the radiation effect will become more important very rapidly. Eventually, when the energy loss per turn becomes equal to or greater than the energy supplied by the accelerating system, the approximate method used in deriving Eq. (9-71) will no longer be valid. Obviously no further acceleration can take place unless V is increased.

9-9. PHASE STABILITY IN THE SYNCHROCYCLOTRON

The synchrocyclotron differs from the classical cyclotron primarily in the fact that the frequency of the electric field is varied during acceleration so that charged particles can be accelerated past the relativistic upper limit of the classical cyclotron (cf. Sec. 6-12). Just as in the ordinary cyclotron, the path of the equilibrium particle is a spiral of ever-increasing radius r_0 given by

$$p_0 = B_0 e r_0 \qquad (9\text{-}72)$$

where p_0 is the particle momentum and B_0 is the magnetic field at the orbit. Unlike the field in the synchrotron, B_0 does not vary with time, but it does decrease slightly with increasing radius to give focusing of the betatron type. Since this weak variation has very little effect on the phase oscillation, we shall neglect it in this section and shall assume that the magnetic field is constant in both time and space. This assumption will permit us to observe the general character of the phase oscillation; for a more precise treatment the reader is referred to the paper of Bohm and Foldy.[5]

Particles which arrive at the accelerating gap at incorrect phases will vary in momentum from the equilibrium value. They will then travel on orbits whose radii are given by

$$p = B_0 e r \qquad (9\text{-}73)$$

The argument relating the phase error to the momentum error is identical with that presented in the preceding section on the synchrotron and gives the same result except that h is usually chosen to be unity in the synchrocyclotron and n has been assumed to be zero. Consequently, instead of Eq. (9-53), we obtain

$$\Delta \dot\phi = \frac{p^{*2}\,\Delta p}{m_0 r_0 (1 + p^{*2})^{3/2}} \qquad (9\text{-}74)$$

where, as before,

$$p^* = \frac{p_0}{m_0 c}$$

Since r_0 is not constant in the synchrocyclotron, we express it in terms of p^* from Eq. (9-72) to obtain

$$\Delta \dot\phi = \frac{B_0 e}{m_0^2 c} \frac{p^* \, \Delta p}{(1 + p^{*2})^{3/2}} \qquad (9\text{-}75)$$

The equation of motion (9-11) is simplified by the fact that there are no perturbing E' terms, since the magnetic field does not change with time and since radiation effects are negligible for the nuclear particles accelerated in synchrocyclotrons. The accelerating field in Eq. (9-11) is given by

$$E = \frac{V}{\pi r} \qquad (9\text{-}76)$$

where V is the D-to-D voltage.   Equation (9-11) then becomes

$$r\dot{p} = \frac{p\dot{p}}{B_0 e} = \frac{eV}{\pi} \sin \phi \qquad (9\text{-}77)$$

whence

$$\frac{d}{dt}(p^* \, \Delta p) = \frac{e^2 V B_0}{\pi m_0 c} \Delta\phi \cos \phi_0 \qquad (9\text{-}78)$$

As usual, Eqs. (9-75) and (9-78) in combination yield the phase-oscillation relation

$$\frac{d}{dt}[(1 + p^{*2})^{3/2} \, \Delta\phi] = \frac{(e/m_0)^3 V B_0^2}{\pi c^2} \Delta\phi \cos \phi_0 \qquad (9\text{-}79)$$

Once again we have derived a phase-oscillation equation that describes a stable damped oscillation provided only that $\cos \phi_0$ is negative.

Approximate solutions of this equation valid only in the nonrelativistic or extreme relativistic ranges are of very little value here because a large part of the operating range of the synchrocyclotron is in the intermediate region where p^* is of the order of unity.   Consequently detailed solutions must be obtained numerically for the particular set of machine parameters in question.   For most cases of interest it will be found that the frequencies of phase oscillation are some tens of kilocycles per second.   The energy spread after acceleration is derivable from Eq. (9-75) and the solution of Eq. (9-79) and will be found to be a fraction of 1 per cent—much narrower than the energy spreads encountered with conventional cyclotrons.   These matters will receive further attention in Chap. 11.

9-10. PHASE STABILITY IN THE MICROTRON

The microtron is an electron accelerator originally proposed by Veksler[1] and discussed at length by Henderson,[7] Schmelzer,[8] Kaiser,[9] and others referred to in the references cited. It is designed for use with completely relativistic electrons and has a cyclotron-like structure.   Since relativistic electrons have approximately constant velocity, the cyclotron principle cannot be used; instead the particles are made to arrive in the correct phase at the single accelerating gap by permitting them to slip one cycle in phase with each revolution in the magnetic field. The principle can best be understood by reference to the diagram of Fig. 9-4.   A small radiofrequency accelerating cavity is located near

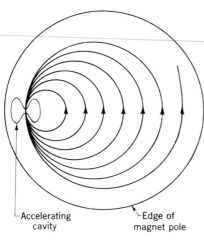

Accelerating cavity

Edge of magnet pole

Fig. 9-4. Orbits in the microtron.

the edge of a cylindrical vacuum chamber. Particles traverse the resonator and are accelerated by the radiofrequency field. They then travel on a circular orbit in the magnetic field and return to the resonator in approximately an integral number of radiofrequency cycles so that they are again accelerated. The orbit is thus a sequence of circles of ever-increasing radius, all tangent at the resonator. This device is primarily useful for acceleration of electrons to a few tens of Mev. It has the advantage over the betatron that its accelerated beam is rather easily extracted for use outside the machine. If extracted beams are not required as, for example, in the case where the machine is used for generation of X rays, the microtron has no important advantage.

The particles in the microtron experience a variety of phase stability similar in general to that found in the synchrotron. Since the steps in energy at the accelerating unit are a large fraction of the total energy, it is no longer reasonable to describe the phase oscillation by a differential equation. The correct formulation of this problem is in a finite-difference equation whose solution must be numerical. For this treatment and its results the reader is referred to the paper of Henderson, Heymann, and Jennings.[7]

REFERENCES

1. V. Veksler, *Compt. rend. acad. sci. U.S.S.R.*, **43**:444 (1944); **44**:393 (1944); *J. Phys. (U.S.S.R.)*, **9**:153 (1945).
2. E. M. McMillan, *Phys. Rev.*, **68**:143 (1945).
3. J. C. Slater, *Rev. Mod. Phys.*, **20**:473 (1948).
4. M. Chodorow et al., *Rev. Sci. Instr.*, **26**:134 (1955).
5. D. Bohm and L. Foldy, *Phys. Rev.*, **70**:249 (1946); **72**:649 (1947).
6. R. Q. Twiss and N. H. Frank, *Rev. Sci. Instr.*, **20**:1 (1949).
7. C. Henderson, F. F. Heymann, and R. E. Jennings, *Proc. Phys. Soc. (London)*. **66B**:41 (1953).
8. C. Schmelzer, *Z. Naturforsch.*, **7a**:808 (1952).
9. H. F. Kaiser and W. T. Mayes, *Rev. Sci. Instr.*, **26**:565 (1955).

10

The Linear Accelerator

In the linear accelerator, as the name implies, particles are accelerated in a straight line by an oscillating electric field. Many different electrode structures have been devised and tested, but all have the common feature that their field pattern includes a traveling-wave component whose phase velocity is the same as that of the accelerated particles. Since the particle velocity is supposed to increase as the particle travels through the accelerator, the phase velocity of the accelerating wave must also increase with distance along the accelerating structure. At extreme relativistic energies when the particle velocity approaches very closely the velocity of light, it becomes possible to equate the phase velocity to the velocity of light, so the design of high-energy electron linear accelerators can be somewhat simpler than that of nonrelativistic accelerators used for heavier particles.

The chief advantage of the linear accelerator lies in the excellent collimation of the emergent beam, as compared with the spreading emergent beams from circular accelerators. The small size of the target spot and the high beam density improve and simplify experimental techniques for studies of small-angle scattering, angular distributions, and many other problems. Shielding is simplified because small beam channels can be used in the shields; background intensity due to scattered radiation is more easily controlled.

For energies of a few Mev the chief disadvantage of the linear acceler-

310

ator lies in the energy spread of the accelerated beam. This spread is of the order of 1 per cent or so. Direct-voltage machines such as the electrostatic generator yield much better energy uniformity. At higher energies linear accelerators are physically long. It is difficult to achieve energy gains of more than 3 to 5 Mev/ft of length, and the maintenance of the associated high electric fields requires enormous quantities of radio-frequency power derived from a multiplicity of power sources. For energies in the Bev range the limit appears to be economic.

Accelerator designers have hoped that, in addition to its technical advantages, the linear accelerator might eventually present an economic advantage for very high energies. This hope has been based on the approximately direct proportionality between cost and energy of the linear accelerator. Circular accelerators, on the other hand, require magnets whose cost increases roughly as the third power of the energy for relativistic particles. This difference in the cost equations suggests that linear accelerators should have an economic advantage for sufficiently high energies. However, the sequential developments of magnetic accelerators—from the cyclotron with its solid-core magnet, to the synchrotron with its much lighter ring magnet, to the AG synchrotron which still further reduces magnet dimensions and costs—have retained the economic advantage of the magnetic accelerators.

The linear accelerator has specific and sometimes definitive advantages over other machines when a compact, well-focused beam of accelerated particles is essential. It has found a useful application as an injector for high-energy machines such as proton synchrotrons (see Chap. 13). For this purpose the proton energy required lies between 10 and 50 Mev. Most of the development of proton linear accelerators has been in this range—by 1961 no proton linear accelerator had been built for energies higher than 70 Mev.

For acceleration of electrons into the Bev range the linear accelerator is a very strong contender. Circular electron accelerators are limited to energies of a few Bev by the rapid increase in energy loss by radiation of relativistic electrons traveling in curved paths. The electron linear accelerator has no such limitation and may become the most practical choice for accelerating electrons to energies above about 10 Bev.

Design problems for proton accelerators differ from those for electron accelerators. The slower velocities of protons in the range of interest dictate the use of radiofrequencies in the range between 100 and 200 megacycles. For ions heavier than protons still lower frequencies are used. However, the higher velocities of electrons and their approach to relativistic speeds at relatively low energies have made it possible to design simpler accelerating chambers for which the accelerating electric field has

At the head of the facing page is an illustration of the Stanford Mark III accelerator with the shielding removed.

frequencies in the microwave range, commonly around 3000 megacycles.

Among the fraternity of accelerator builders the rather cumbersome term "linear accelerator" is often abbreviated to "linac." This name has found its way into the literature and is now considered acceptable. It was originally applied to the proton linear accelerator, but the appeal of the abbreviation has caused it to be used for electrons also. Specialists occasionally argue for distinguishing titles, but thus far no suitable terms have become generally accepted. In the recently developing field of heavy-ion linear accelerators the identifying title "hilac" is used in several laboratories and appears to be gaining acceptance.

10-1. EARLY DESIGNS

The first proposal for a radiofrequency linear accelerator was made by Ising[1] in Sweden in 1925. He suggested the concept of resonance acceleration and proposed using a spark-gap oscillator and transmission lines to supply radiofrequency fields to accelerating electrodes. There is no record of any experimental test of the proposal. The first report of a working accelerator was that by Wideröe[2] in 1928, and his apparatus was the direct ancestor of all resonance accelerators. It consisted of three coaxial cylindrical electrodes; an alternating electric field was applied between the central electrode and the two electrodes on either side. The frequency of alternation was such that the electrode potentials were reversed during the time required for the injected ions (K^+ and Na^+ ions) to traverse the central electrode; the ions experienced two accelerations and attained a final energy twice that available from a single traversal of the field.

The report of Wideröe's experiment was noted by Lawrence at the University of California in Berkeley, and it provided the initial idea from which the concept of the cyclotron was developed (see Chap. 6). D. H. Sloan, then a student at Berkeley, extended the linear accelerator to include 10 or more accelerating electrodes. By 1931 Sloan and Lawrence[3] had accelerated mercury ions to 1.25 Mev, and by 1934 Sloan and Coates[4] reported 2.8 Mev. These fast mercury ions, incident on a target, were found to produce soft X rays characteristic of mercury and of the target element, but no nuclear effects were observed. Lithium ions were also used by Kinsey[5] at energies up to 1 Mev, at first with no evidence of nuclear disintegrations; later unpublished work by Kinsey showed that the well-known $Li(p,\alpha)$ alpha particles were produced from hydrogenous targets. Since these early accelerators could operate only at relatively low frequencies and so could accelerate only relatively heavy ions, their usefulness in nuclear research was insignificant.

A description of these early resonance accelerators will show the simplicity of the concepts. An array of coaxial cylindrical electrodes of increasing length (Fig. 10-1) was aligned along the axis of a long glass vacuum chamber.   The electrodes were connected alternately to two bus bars extending along the length of the chamber and supplied by the radio-frequency power source.   The separation L between accelerating gaps is the distance traversed by the particles during one half-cycle of the applied electric field, whence

$$L = \frac{1}{2}\frac{v}{f} \qquad (10\text{-}1)$$

where v is the particle velocity and f is the frequency.   Each time a particle of charge e crosses a gap, it sees a field which gives it an energy increment $eV \sin \phi$, where V is the maximum gap voltage and ϕ is the phase at which the particle crosses the gap.   The early machines were designed to accelerate only the particles which arrived at a phase close to 90°, so the energy gain at each gap was about eV.

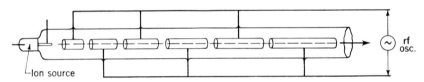

Fig. 10-1. Early linear accelerator for heavy ions with accelerating electrode lengths increasing with the square roots of a series of integers.

At low particle energies velocity increases with the square root of the energy, so successive gap separations were made to increase in a sequence proportional to the square roots of a series of integers.   The gaps between the tubular electrodes were short and the positive ions spent most of their time in the field-free regions inside the electrodes or drift tubes.   Relatively few electrodes were used (10 to 30), so the precision of spacing was not severe.   Resonance was maintained by an experimental balance of the applied voltage V to the value required by the electrode spacing.

In a typical installation (Sloan and Lawrence[3]) 30 drift tubes were used.   The first tube had an effective length of 1 cm, and the over-all length was 1.14 m.   The radiofrequency power source operated at 10 megacycles (30 m wavelength), and a peak voltage of 42,000 volts was required for resonant acceleration of singly charged mercury ions, to give a final energy of 1.26 Mev.   The beam of high-energy ions emerging from the accelerator was passed through slits and deflected by an electrostatic field through a small angle to direct it into a collector cup or against a target; this deflecting field served also to measure the energy of the emergent beam.

During this same period J. W. Beams[6,7] and his collaborators at the University of Virginia attempted the acceleration of electrons by traveling waves along a transmission line.   The wave velocity of an artificial transmission line was designed to match the electron velocity, and a sequence of potential surges was applied at one end of the line from a capacitor–spark-gap circuit. A linear array of short tubular electrodes with uniform separation was supported within a long, evacuated glass tube; the electrodes were electrically connected to the transmission line. Using 300,000-volt spark discharges, bursts of electrons were accelerated to 1.3 Mev. Although this early experiment was not successful in developing a reliable source of high-energy particles, it did presage the traveling-wave accelerator which became practical when suitable radiofrequency power sources became available.

10-2. MODERN LINEAR ACCELERATORS

The modern linear accelerators are founded on the work of two groups, one at Stanford University and one at the University of California. In the Stanford laboratory W. W. Hansen initiated a program in the 1930s for the development of high-frequency accelerators and power sources, with primary interest in the acceleration of electrons. One of the early concepts was a high-Q cavity resonator for single-stage acceleration of electrons. To excite this cavity, large quantities of radiofrequency power were required; accordingly a power-tube development program was initiated. Hansen collaborated with the Varian brothers in the invention and initial development of the klystron, which was destined to play an important role in the radar field. At the end of World War II a double-headed development was started on the iris-loaded waveguide as an accelerating structure for electrons and on the 3000-megacycle klystron to provide adequate power; in this program Hansen had the able assistance of E. L. Ginzton, M. Chodorow, and others. After Hansen's death in 1949 the program was continued and expanded by the Stanford group, utilizing radar techniques developed during the war. It has resulted in a sequence of electron linear accelerators of increasing length, power, and output energy, culminating in the present 1000-Mev linac which is described in Sec. 10-9.

Proton accelerator development started at the end of the war in the Radiation Laboratory of the University of California under the direction of L. Alvarez and with the important assistance of W. K. H. Panofsky. In this case also, radar developments made it possible to build practical accelerators with energies sufficient to be useful in nuclear physics.

The history of both of these fundamental design studies and a full description of the step-by-step developments are recorded in the Linear Accelerator Issue of *The Review of Scientific Instruments*[8] (February, 1955). A somewhat more concise discussion of modern linear accelerator design is available in the article by Lloyd Smith[9] in vol. 44 of the "Encyclopedia of Physics."

The two linear-accelerator types differ materially in appearance for a rather simple reason. As was shown in Sec. 9-2, the axial field component used in acceleration is a wave which travels with the particles and has the form

$$E_z = E_0 \sin \left(\omega t - \omega \int \frac{dz}{v} + \phi_0 \right) \qquad (10\text{-}2)$$

where z represents distance along the particle path and v is the particle velocity. Now in any real field pattern which satisfies Maxwell's equations E_0 must vary with radial distance from the axis of the particle beam. The exact solution will involve Bessel functions, but to a first approximation E_0 will have the form

$$E_0 = (\text{const}) \left[1 + \left(\frac{\pi r}{\lambda} \right)^2 \left(\frac{c^2}{v^2} - 1 \right) \right] \qquad (10\text{-}3)$$

where r = distance from axis

λ = free-space wavelength of accelerating field

c = velocity of light

The correctness of this relation can be checked by substitution in Maxwell's equations [(5-6) to (5-9)]. The variation of accelerating field across the useful aperture should be small for several reasons. Variations will lead to increased phase oscillations and to an energy spread in the accelerated beam. Also, since the field increases with radius, higher applied fields are required at the aperture boundary to provide the desired axial field; this results in higher power input to the accelerator for a desired rate of energy gain. This phenomenon is often presented in terms of a "gap coefficient" between accelerating electrodes. A system having a large radial variation of field is said to have poor gap coefficients.

The maximum desirable operating frequency can be derived from the above argument. Suppose, for example, that the field variation is not to be greater than 10 per cent across the aperture. Then Eq. (10-3) states that the minimum permissible value of wavelength is given approximately by

$$\lambda_{\min} = 10 r_{\max} \left(\frac{c^2}{v^2} - 1 \right)^{\frac{1}{2}} \qquad (10\text{-}4)$$

where $r_{\max}$ is the half-aperture. This equation indicates that, for electrons whose velocity is close to the velocity of light throughout most of the accelerator, there is no real limitation on wavelength. For protons, however, for which the velocities at the low-energy end of the accelerator will be of the order of one-tenth of the velocity of light, the minimum permissible wavelength is severely restricted. If we consider 3 cm to be a reasonable dimension for the aperture, we see from Eq. (10-4) that the wavelength must be greater than 1.5 m and hence the highest permissible

frequency is 200 megacycles.   This is the frequency actually chosen for
most proton linear accelerators.   For electron machines, on the other
hand, it is possible to raise the operating frequency to 3000 to 10,000
megacycles before serious aperture limitations arise for other reasons.
This permits the designer to use waveguide structures of a small and
more convenient size.   The result of this argument is that proton linear
accelerators are housed in large tanks (of the order of 3 ft in diameter)
resonant at 200 megacycles.   Electron linear accelerators are sections of
3000-megacycle waveguides only a few inches in diameter.

TABLE 10-1
LINEAR-ACCELERATOR PARAMETERS

	Proton linear accelerator (Berkeley)	High-intensity proton linear accelerator (A-48, Livermore)	Heavy-ion linear accelerator (Berkeley, Yale)	Electron linear accelerator (Stanford)
Injection energy	4 Mev	85 kev	500 kev	80 kev
Final energy	32 Mev	3.7 Mev	10 Mev/nucleon	1 Bev
Length	40 ft	68 ft	105 ft	300 ft
Diameter	39 in.	About 12 ft	About 10 ft	3.25 in.
Frequency, megacycles/sec	202.5	48.6	70	2856
Axial field, Mv/m	3	0.5	1.9	9.6
Stable phase	64°	45–55°	Depends on e/m of particles	90°
Max beam current	60 μa	75 ma	1 ma	8 ma
Energy spread, %	0.5	8	1	3
Focusing	Grids	Solenoids	Grids + quadrupoles	None
Beam pulse length	400 μsec	Continuous	3 msec	1 μsec
Repetition rate	15/sec	Continuous	10/sec	60/sec
Peak power	2.1 megawatts	215 kw	3 megawatts	300 megawatts
Detailed description, see Sec	10–12	10–15	10–14	10–9

For reasons to be discussed in Sec. 10-5, all high-energy linear accelerators require enormous amounts of radiofrequency power.   The development of the necessary power sources has been the most difficult problem
in the design of the modern linear accelerator, and an array of high-
powered radiofrequency equipment is one of the more salient characteristics of a linear-accelerator installation.

Two other linear-accelerator types have been developed during the
last decade.   Although both are outgrowths of the proton linear accelerator they differ sufficiently to merit mention.   The first is a linear
accelerator for proton beams of high intensity.   Here it has been necessary to increase aperture to accommodate the intense beams and, as we
have seen, this has led to materially lower frequencies.   These machines,
accordingly, involve extremely large tanks and much lower frequencies.
The second type is designed to accelerate heavier ions than protons.

Since heavy ions travel more slowly than protons of the same energy, we see from Eq. (10-4) that lower frequencies are required for heavy-ion linear accelerators than for proton machines operating over the same energy range. For this reason the resonant tanks used in heavy-ion machines are of the order of 10 ft in diameter.

The accelerating fields in linear accelerators vary from 1 to 3 Mv/m for proton machines to more than 20 Mv/m for electron machines. The 32-Mev proton linear accelerator built at the University of California (and later moved to the University of Southern California) is about 40 ft long. The 1-Bev electron linear accelerator at Stanford is 300 ft long.

In Table 10-1 we have collected some of the more important parameters of typical linear accelerators of the four types just discussed.

10-3. PARTICLE DYNAMICS IN THE LINEAR ACCELERATOR

The particles undergoing acceleration in the linear accelerator are subject to axial and radial forces. The axial field pattern and the particle motions in the axial direction have already been discussed in Chap. 9. In Secs. 9-6 and 9-7 we presented a general treatment of phase stability for all linear accelerators. The consequences of this treatment for particular accelerator types will be discussed further in the sections which follow.

The pattern of the fields which introduce radial forces is generally very complicated in an actual accelerating structure. Fortunately, this problem can be simplified by the same device as was used to simplify the problem of the axial motions. Any field pattern can be broken down by Fourier analysis into traveling-wave components traveling in the same direction as the particles and in the opposite direction. The one component which travels with the particles at the same velocity as that of the equilibrium particle will exert a continuous radial force on the particle stream. All other components will produce alternating deflections of small amplitude whose net effect will be negligible. Consequently we have to study only the field pattern which travels with the particles. The axial component of this pattern is the field [cf. Eqs. (9-4) and (10-2)]

$$E_z = E_0 \sin \left(\omega t - \omega \int \frac{dz}{v} + \phi_0 \right) \tag{10-5}$$

already discussed in Sec. 9-2. The other field components associated with this one are derivable from Maxwell's equations. To a first approximation they are a radial electric-field component

$$E_r = \frac{\omega r E_0}{2v} \cos \left(\omega t - \omega \int \frac{dz}{v} + \phi_0 \right) \tag{10-6}$$

and a circumferential magnetic-field component

$$B_\theta = \frac{rE_0}{2c^2} \cos\left(\omega t - \omega \int \frac{dz}{v} + \phi_0\right) \qquad (10\text{-}7)$$

A more precise analysis of the field pattern would show that E_0 must depend on r; its exact form is a Bessel function of zero order, and the other field components also involve Bessel functions. The pattern is, in fact, the familiar TM_{01} field pattern found in cylindrical waveguides. For the present purpose, however, the approximate forms presented above are quite adequate.

Particle motion in the r direction follows from solution of the force equation

$$\frac{d}{dt}(m\dot{r}) = eE_r - e\dot{s}B_\theta$$

$$= \frac{er\omega E_0}{2v}\left(1 - \frac{\dot{s}v}{c^2}\right)\cos\left(\omega t - \omega \int \frac{dz}{v} + \phi_0\right) \qquad (10\text{-}8)$$

For simplicity we consider only the radial force on the equilibrium particle for which $\omega t = \omega \int dz/v$ and $\dot{s} = v$, so that

$$\frac{d}{dt}(m\dot{r}) = \frac{er\omega E_0}{2v}\left(1 - \frac{v^2}{c^2}\right)\cos\phi_0 \qquad (10\text{-}9)$$

For low energies such that m does not vary appreciably from the rest mass and v is small compared with c, this equation indicates that the radial force is so strong that the particle will leave its orbit rapidly and will be lost in the radial direction. For higher energies the radial force decreases as v approaches c and finally becomes negligibly small. Some intriguing conclusions can be drawn from Eq. (10-9) if it is rewritten in the form

$$\frac{v}{(1 - v^2/c^2)^{1/2}}\frac{d}{dz}\left[\frac{m_0 v}{(1 - v^2/c^2)^{1/2}}\frac{dr}{dz}\right] = \frac{er\omega E_0}{2v}\left(1 - \frac{v^2}{c^2}\right)^{1/2}\cos\phi_0 \qquad (10\text{-}10)$$

If v is approximately equal to c and if we make the substitution

$$dz' = \left(1 - \frac{v^2}{c^2}\right)^{1/2} dz \qquad (10\text{-}11)$$

then our radial equation of motion reduces to the approximate form

$$\frac{d^2r}{dz'^2} = 0 \qquad (10\text{-}12)$$

whose solution is

$$r = r_i + \left(\frac{dr}{dz'}\right)_i z' \qquad (10\text{-}13)$$

where the subscript i indicates initial values of the parameters. The significance of this result emerges from a second glance at Eq. (10-11); dz' is the element of length in the frame of reference of the traveling particle. It has been shortened by the Lorentz contraction expressed by the equation defining it. (Proof of this statement will be found in standard references on the special theory of relativity.)

To acquire a feeling for the frame of reference of the traveling particle we assume that the accelerating field in the linear accelerator is independent of distance so that the kinetic energy $W - W_0$ of the particle is proportional to z. Let us say that

$$W - W_0 \left[= W_0 \left(1 - \frac{v^2}{c^2} \right)^{-\frac{1}{2}} - W_0 \right] = kz \qquad (10\text{-}14)$$

Using Eqs. (10-11) and (10-14) an integration can be performed with respect to z and z' from which

$$z' = \frac{W_0 z}{W - W_0} \ln \frac{W}{W_0} \qquad (10\text{-}15)$$

This seemingly simple relation has some startling connotations. The Stanford linear accelerator, designed for acceleration of electrons to 1000 Mev, is about 300 ft long. But in the frame of reference of the electrons, Eq. (10-15) indicates that the apparent length of the accelerator is only 35.3 cm. If the accelerator had been extended to twice its length to yield 2000-Mev electrons, its length in the electrons' frame of reference would have increased only to 38.5 cm. The consequence of these revelations is that the radial drift of relativistic particles is relatively very slow —so slow, in fact, that high-energy electron linear accelerators have little need of radial focusing mechanisms.

The results of these studies of radial motions will be seen in the discussions of specific designs for proton and electron linear accelerators.

10-4. THE TRANSVERSE-MAGNETIC FIELD PATTERN

In all conventional linear accelerators the field pattern is basically the transverse-magnetic field configuration well known to students of wave-guides and resonant cavities. In every case tricks are used to modify the pattern so that the particles see an apparent traveling wave whose velocity is continually that of the equilibrium particle. These various devices do not alter the fact that the field pattern must have an axial electric field as one of its major components. Each linear-accelerator system can be understood as a combination of those modes known as transverse magnetic in which an axial electric field is always present. The field pattern follows directly from a solution of Maxwell's equations in cylindrical coordinates. It has radial and axial electric-field components and an azimuthal magnetic-field component as follows:

$$E_r = \frac{\omega E_0}{v k_c} J_1(k_c r) \sin \frac{\omega z}{v} \sin \omega t \qquad \text{volts/m}$$

$$E_z = E_0 J_0(k_c r) \cos \frac{\omega z}{v} \sin \omega t \qquad \text{volts/m} \qquad (10\text{-}16)$$

$$H_\theta = \frac{\omega E_0}{c k_c \sqrt{\mu_0/\epsilon_0}} J_1(k_c r) \cos \frac{\omega z}{v} \cos \omega t \qquad \text{amp/m}$$

where r and z = usual cylindrical coordinates
E_0 = axial field amplitude on axis
v = phase velocity of wave
$\sqrt{\mu_0/\epsilon_0}$ = so-called impedance of free space = 377 ohms
$k_c^2 = \dfrac{\omega^2}{c^2} - \dfrac{\omega^2}{v^2}$
J_0 and J_1 = Bessel functions which have the following properties:

$$\text{For } x \text{ small:} \qquad J_0(x) \cong 1 - \frac{x^2}{4}$$

$$J_1(x) \cong \frac{x}{2} \qquad (10\text{-}17)$$

$$\text{For } x = 2.405: \qquad J_0(x) = 0$$
$$J_1(x) = 0.519$$

In a resonant cylindrical cavity of radius b the frequency must be such that, for $r = b$, $E_z = 0$. The field pattern of Eq. (10-16) becomes

$$E_r = 0.416 \frac{\omega b}{v} E_0 J_1\left(\frac{2.405r}{b}\right) \sin \frac{\omega z}{v} \sin \omega t \qquad \text{volts/m}$$

$$E_z = E_0 J_0\left(\frac{2.405r}{b}\right) \cos \frac{\omega z}{v} \sin \omega t \qquad \text{volts/m} \qquad (10\text{-}18)$$

$$H_\theta = 3.68 \times 10^{-12} \omega b E_0 J_1\left(\frac{2.405r}{b}\right) \cos \frac{\omega z}{v} \cos \omega t \qquad \text{amp/m}$$

In this case the ratio of the phase velocity v to the velocity of light is

$$\frac{v}{c} = \left[1 - \left(\frac{2.405c}{\omega b}\right)^2\right]^{-\frac{1}{2}} \qquad (10\text{-}19)$$

This transverse-magnetic field pattern is usually designated by the symbol TM$_{01}$. Several of its features are worthy of particular note. First, although the pattern has been expressed here as a standing-wave pattern, it can be expressed equally well in terms of traveling waves. Maxwell's equations are satisfied just as well if we change the

"$\sin \dfrac{\omega z}{v} \sin \omega t$" part of E_r to "$\cos \omega \left(t - \dfrac{z}{v} \right)$" and make the corresponding appropriate changes in E_z and H_θ.

We note also from Eq. (10-19) that the phase velocity must always be greater than the velocity of light. On the other hand, the group velocity v_g (the velocity at which information or power can be propagated) whose value for this mode is given by

$$v v_g = c^2$$

must always be less than the velocity of light. Since we wish to match the particle velocity in a linear accelerator with the phase velocity of the accelerating wave, it is obvious that we cannot use this wave without

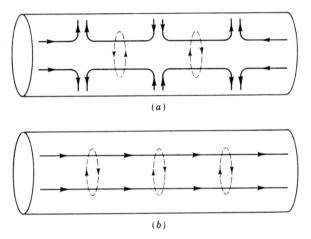

(a)

(b)

Fig. 10-2. Transverse-magnetic field patterns. Electric-flux lines are solid lines; magnetic-flux lines are broken. (a) The TM_{01} mode; (b) the TM_{010} mode.

modification because all particles have velocities less than the velocity of light.

A special case known as the TM_{010} mode arises when the phase velocity becomes infinite. In the resonant cavity this is achieved by setting $b = 2.405c/\omega$. In this case the radial field component and the group velocity disappear and the field pattern simplifies to

$$E_z = E_0 J_0 \left(\frac{\omega r}{c} \right) \sin \omega t \qquad \text{volts/m}$$
$$H_\theta = 0.00265 E_0 J_1 \left(\frac{\omega r}{c} \right) \cos \omega t \qquad \text{amp/m} \tag{10-20}$$

As we shall see, this mode is used in all linear accelerators.

Figure 10-2 shows the field patterns in cavities supporting the TM_{01}

and the TM_{010} modes.   Electric-field lines are shown as solid lines and magnetic-flux lines are shown as broken lines in this figure.

Further discussion of field patterns in waveguides can be found in standard electrical engineering texts.[10]

10-5. POWER REQUIREMENTS FOR LINEAR ACCELERATORS

In the previous section the transverse-magnetic field pattern used for acceleration in linear accelerators was shown to have an azimuthal magnetic-field component whose value is maximum at the wall of the cavity. Because of this magnetic field, paraxial currents flow in the cavity wall. From Eqs. (10-20) the amplitude of the total wall current is

$$I = 8.65 \times 10^{-3}bE_z \qquad \text{amp} \qquad (10\text{-}21)$$

where b is the radius of the waveguide and E_z is the amplitude of the axial electric field on the axis of the cavity.   The resistive losses in the walls due to these currents are the major power losses in the machine.   Since linear accelerators are always lined with copper, we can evaluate these losses numerically.   The resistance of the copper wall of a waveguide of radius b follows from the usual skin-effect formulas; it is

$$R = \frac{7.36 \times 10^{-4}}{b \sqrt{\lambda}} \qquad \text{ohms/m} \qquad (10\text{-}22)$$

where λ is the free-space wavelength of the accelerating field.   From the two relations above, the total loss in a machine of length l can now be estimated to be

$$P = \frac{2.8 \times 10^{-8}bE_z^2l}{\sqrt{\lambda}} \qquad (10\text{-}23)$$

But for the TM_{010} mode the radius of a waveguide is given by

$$b = \frac{2.405c}{\omega} = 0.383\lambda$$

Also, for singly charged particles, the maximum possible particle energy T emerging from the accelerator is given by $T = lE_z$.   Consequently, we can rewrite Eq. (10-23) in the form

$$P = \frac{1.1 \times 10^{-8}T^2 \sqrt{\lambda}}{l} \qquad (10\text{-}24)$$

This relation is not very accurate because in its derivation we have neglected the losses in all the auxiliary structures necessary to change the standard waveguide field pattern so that it will include the traveling-wave component essential for acceleration.   It does, however, establish the order of magnitude of power necessary. For example, suppose we wish to accelerate protons to 50 Mev in a machine 25 m long with a field whose free-space wavelength is 1.5 m. The power necessary, as given by Eq. (10-24), is 1.3 megawatts! To reach energies in the hundreds of Mev in a machine of reasonable length requires enormous quantities of power. It was this fact that held back the development of the linear accelerator until radar developments yielded sources of pulsed power in this range. The very high power requirements still make the linear accelerator a costly machine and have been a strong deterrent in its development even in the face of its several advantages as a research tool.

A more sophisticated derivation of Eq. (10-24) does not change its form but results in the expression

$$P = \frac{CT^2 \sqrt{\lambda}}{l} \tag{10-25}$$

where C is a constant depending only on the geometric structure of the accelerating system. So long as the pattern is unchanged, it is possible to use this formula in scaling to different energies, wavelengths, and lengths. Its most interesting consequence is that power is inversely proportional to accelerator length; in designing a linear accelerator, power can be decreased by increasing length, and the designer can choose an optimum length for which the total cost of power plus cost of the accelerator is a minimum. But when the structure is changed, the constant C changes so much that the theorem is no longer very useful. For most proton linear accelerators C is about 2.5×10^{-8}, while for most electron linear accelerators it has values of the order of 10^{-7}.

10-6. THE CONCEPT OF SHUNT IMPEDANCE

A useful figure of merit for a linear-accelerator structure is one that provides an answer to the question: How much power is needed to provide a given accelerating field? Since, as we have seen in the preceding section, the power is proportional to the square of the accelerating field, a useful ratio should be that of the square of the maximum electric field on the axis to the power dissipated per meter of length. This ratio is called the shunt impedance and has the dimensions of ohms per meter. Usually it is expressed in megohms per meter thus:

$$Z = \frac{10^{-6}E_z^2}{P} \quad \text{megohms/m} \tag{10-26}$$

For almost all operating linear accelerators the shunt impedance Z lies between 25 and 50 megohms/m. This good agreement is, at least partly, a chance agreement. The possibility certainly exists that some ingenious designer will invent a structure with a much higher shunt impedance. If this is achieved, the linear accelerator may become a much more popular device than it now is.

10-7. CAVITIES FOR ELECTRON LINEAR ACCELERATORS

The accelerating system for an electron linear accelerator consists of a sequence of small cavities (see Fig. 10-3). Each of these cavities operates in the TM_{010} mode, modified slightly by the fact that the end walls of the cavities are not solid but have openings into the adjacent cavities. These apertures have the dual function of permitting passage of the electron beam and of providing coupling from cavity to cavity so that many cavities can be excited from one power input. The size of the hole determines the degree of coupling and so determines the relative phase shift from one cavity to the next. When the dimensions have been

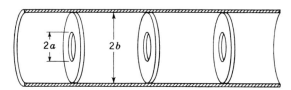

Fig. 10-3. Cutaway sketch of iris-loaded accelerating system for an electron linear accelerator.

tailored correctly, the phase changes from cavity to cavity along the accelerator to give an over-all phase velocity corresponding to the desired particle velocity. As was stated in Sec. 9-7, it is sufficient over most of the length of the accelerator to set this effective velocity equal to the velocity of light. This is true for electrons since, for energies above a few hundreds of kev, electron velocities are very close to the velocity of light.

The reason that this apparently complicated structure cannot be replaced by a simple waveguide is that the phase velocity in a simple waveguide cannot be reduced to the velocity of light. Consequently, the introduction of irises to subdivide the waveguide into separated cavities is often considered as slowing down the wave by iris loading. This picture is just as valid as the one presented in the preceding paragraph.

The arguments leading to the precise choices of the parameters of iris-loaded waveguides for electron linear accelerators have been presented by several groups. Outstanding among these studies are those of Slater,[11] of the Stanford group,[12] and of the British group at Harwell.[13] Five parameters must be determined: the wavelength of the accelerating signal, the iris thickness, the iris spacing, the diameter $2a$ of the hole in the iris (cf. Fig. 10-3), and the diameter $2b$ of the guide proper. We shall discuss these choices in that order.

As has been shown in Sec. 10-5, the power required for a given final electron energy is proportional to $(\text{wavelength})^{1/2}$. Consequently it would appear desirable to choose as short a wavelength as possible consistent with power sources and construction techniques available and yet not so small as to result in a very small waveguide with too restricted an aperture. These considerations have usually resulted in the choice of a wavelength of about 10 cm, which gives an over-all guide diameter of about 8 cm. It was a happy coincidence that power sources and other equipment at this frequency had been developed for S-band radar, and were available to scientists when they returned to their laboratories after World War II.

Iris thickness proves to have very little influence provided only that it is much less than the iris spacing. A thickness of about 0.5 cm provides adequate mechanical strength and can be contoured to prevent high field concentration and breakdown at sharp corners.

Iris separation has a fairly strong effect on shunt impedance. If too few irises are included, the desired traveling-wave amplitude for a given power input begins to decrease. When iris spacing is reduced too far, excessive power losses are introduced by currents flowing on the surfaces of the iris plates. The optimum shunt impedance occurs for 3.5 irises per wavelength, but for convenience in testing it is more usual to introduce 4 irises per wavelength, giving a shunt impedance lower than the optimum by only a few per cent.

The radii of the hole in the iris a and the guide radius b are not independent. For any choice of a there exists a value of b that will give an over-all phase velocity equal to the velocity of light. As a is increased, b also increases rather slowly. The precise relation is determined by a complex analysis, but for relatively small values of a, b is represented rather approximately by the relation

$$\frac{b}{\lambda} = 0.383 \left[1 + 20 \left(\frac{a}{\lambda} \right)^3 \right] \tag{10-27}$$

It remains only to make a choice of a. For reasons to be discussed in the next section, most modern linear electron accelerators utilize traveling-wave field patterns. The flow of energy is strongly influenced by the size of the apertures; also, as we shall now demonstrate, there is an optimum rate of energy flow. The distribution of energy along the waveguide follows from two definitions and one self-evident relation as follows. The group velocity v_g is defined by the relation

$$v_g = \frac{\text{energy flow}}{\text{energy density}} \tag{10-28}$$

The self-evident relation is

$$\frac{d}{dz} \text{ (rate of energy flow)} = \text{energy dissipated} \qquad (10\text{-}29)$$

The Q factor of the waveguide system is defined by

$$Q = \frac{\omega(\text{energy stored})}{\text{rate of energy dissipation}} \qquad (10\text{-}30)$$

From these three relations it follows that

$$\text{Rate of energy dissipation} \propto e^{-(\omega z/v_g Q)}$$

Since the energy dissipation is proportional to the square of the electric field, the electric field can be written

$$E_z = E_{z0}e^{-(\omega z/2v_g Q)} \qquad (10\text{-}31)$$

It is usual to introduce energy at equally spaced points along the accelerator. The energy enters through a directional system such that energy flow is only in the direction of motion of the particle beam. The energy that remains at the next feed point is either reflected to become a useless backward wave or dissipated in an external load. If the distance between feed points is l, the total energy gain of a particle riding on the crest of the wave from one feed point to the next will be

$$e \int_0^l E_z \, dz = \frac{2ev_g Q E_{z0}}{\omega} \left(1 - e^{-(\omega l/2v_g Q)}\right) \qquad (10\text{-}32)$$

The total power dissipation will be proportional to E_{z0}^2. Hence, if the amount of power available is constant, E_{z0} will be a constant. Q also will not change markedly with v_g; consequently the maximum acceleration will occur when the quantity $v_g(1 - e^{-(\omega l/2v_g Q)})$ has its maximum value. This occurs when v_g is chosen to give

$$\frac{\omega l}{2v_g Q} = 1.26 \qquad (10\text{-}33)$$

(If electron beam loading is appreciable, this figure will decrease.) In other words, optimum operation is attained when the distance between feed points and the group velocity result in an attenuation of the wave between feed points to a little less than $1/e$ of its initial value.

It is now necessary to establish the relation between v_g and the iris aperture radius a. The rate of energy flow through the aperture is given by the integral of Poynting's vector over the aperture. For the TM waves here in question this integral is

$$\text{Energy flow} = \int_0^a E_r H_\theta 2\pi r \, dr \qquad (10\text{-}34)$$

But from Eqs. (10-16) and (10-17), E_r and H_θ are proportional to r for r small.   Hence, so long as a/b is a relatively small ratio, the energy flow given by Eq. (10-34) is approximately proportional to a^4.   The constant of proportionality can be established either by a complicated analysis or by experiment.   For a distribution of four irises per wavelength and for a/b in the neighborhood of 0.25, the value of v_g is given approximately by

$$\frac{v_g}{c} = 2.4 \left(\frac{a}{b}\right)^4 \qquad\qquad (10\text{-}35)$$

The choice of the aperture radius a is now clearly defined.   When the distance l between feed points has been chosen and when the Q of the proposed structure has been measured or calculated, v_g is determined from Eq. (10-33).   The two radii a and b are now defined by Eqs. (10-27) and (10-35).

Once these choices of parameters have been made, the dimensions must be maintained very precisely so that the phase velocity does not deviate from the chosen value.   This is particularly important in electron linear accelerators, since these lack the self-compensating features of true phase stability.   If the phase velocity is incorrect, the electrons will drift away from the acceleration phase and will not reach the design energy.   If the phase velocity is wrong by as much as 1 per cent, the electrons will drift to a phase at which they lose energy instead of gaining energy before they have traveled more than 10 m.   Consequently the accelerating system must be constructed very precisely.   Mechanical tolerances in dimensions and locations are usually of the order of 0.0002 in., and temperatures must be precisely controlled in order that thermal expansions do not exceed these tolerances.

10-8. TRAVELING WAVES VERSUS STANDING WAVES

In the early days of the development of the modern electron linear accelerator it was not clear whether or not traveling-wave excitation of the cavity is preferable to standing-wave excitation.   At first glance it would appear that traveling-wave excitation is preferable because the standing-wave mode is made up of a combination of a useful traveling wave going in the same direction as the electron beam and a useless traveling wave going in the opposite direction; thus half of the input power is wasted.   But, as was shown in the previous section, traveling waves must be allowed to travel far enough that they are attenuated to about $1/e$ of their input amplitude.   For this condition, the power required for the traveling-wave system is exactly the same as for the standing-wave system.   The choice of system must thus be based on considerations other than power.

The choice of excitation is more strongly influenced by the type of power source available.   After the World War II development of magnetrons for radar applications, several attempts were made to use magnetron oscillators to drive electron linear accelerators.   No single magnetron was available with enough power to drive a machine of appreciable output energy; this left the accelerator designers with the two problems of keeping the magnetron frequency on the resonant frequency of the waveguide and synchronizing several magnetrons in phase.   The first problem could be solved only by using a standing wave in the accelerator so that information from the backward component of the standing wave could be used in keeping the magnetron on frequency.   The second problem was solved by the MIT accelerator group by light coupling between the various magnetrons and by a small amount of preexcitation.   But by 1950 the Stanford group had developed klystron amplifiers to the point where they yielded several times as much power as could be derived from a magnetron.   Many klystron amplifiers could be driven by a single power source, and by this means their relative phases were automatically maintained in the correct relation.

To the designer of the radiofrequency power supply for a linear accelerator, the accelerator cavity should look as much as possible like a pure resistive load.   With a traveling-wave system this is rather easy since no reflected wave appears at the driving point to give reactive components of impedance.   With the high-Q standing-wave system, on the other hand, difficulties of this sort are always experienced.   If the system is matched at full load, bad mismatches of impedance are experienced during the build-up period.

A theoretical improvement in efficiency of the traveling-wave system is possible if the power left at the end of the section driven by one power source is not dissipated externally but is returned externally to the driving point and returned to the accelerator through systems of directional couplers.   This technique has been worked out by Harvie and Mullett[14] of the Harwell group.   It can give an appreciable increase in efficiency, but it adds complexity and changes the driven impedance to one characteristic of a standing-wave system.   Consequently the technique has not become popular and is not used in modern electron linear accelerators.

10-9. THE STANFORD MARK III LINEAR ELECTRON ACCELERATOR

We begin a presentation of electron linear accelerators with the Stanford Mark III machine for several reasons.   First, it has reached the highest energy yet achieved in any linear accelerator.   Partly because of this fact and partly because it was built by an exceptionally gifted team, it is now accepted as the prototype for many other machines now under construction. It will probably be some time before new developments change this situation. Finally, it has been completely described in the literature; the reader will be able to supplement the sketchy description possible here by reference to a number of publications; most outstanding is the Linear Accelerator Issue of *The Review of Scientific Instruments*.[8]

First we shall satisfy the reader's curiosity about the expression "Mark III" with a few historical comments. Ever since the mid-1930s the high-energy electron linear accelerator had been a dream of the late W. W. Hansen. Before World War II he was frustrated by the lack of radiofrequency generators with sufficient power output. The first device to fill this requirement was the magnetron, developed during the war for radar applications, and in 1947 Hansen and his associates built a 12-ft machine powered by a magnetron in which they accelerated electrons to 6 Mev. This was the Stanford Mark I.[15] Although this machine was reasonably successful, the magnetron left much to be desired as a power source and the Stanford group set about the development of the klystron for megawatt operation in the 3000-megacycle range. In the minds of most of their contemporaries the klystron was basically a milliwatt device useful only as a local oscillator or signal generator, and the Stanford project seemed fantastic. The klystron development proved, however, to be a brilliant success, and in 1950 the Stanford group brought into operation a new accelerator, the Stanford Mark II, also 12 ft long but yielding 35-Mev electrons. It was powered by a klystron amplifier which delivered between 10 and 20 megawatts at 2855 megacycles. The amplifier was powered by a 390-kv pulser delivering currents up to 250 amp. This machine was the prototype for the Mark III, designed for electron energies up to 1 Bev and consisting essentially of thirty 10-ft Mark II accelerators arranged in a line. After some years of operation at 700 Mev this machine was brought to its design energy in 1960. In the hands of W. K. H. Panofsky and R. Hofstadter it has proved itself a very powerful tool for explorations of nuclear structure. The Mark III machine is now a prototype for machines of still higher energies. For example, at the Orsay Laboratory in France a group is engaged in construction of a 2-Bev machine like the Mark III but roughly twice as long. The most ambitious proposal for the future comes from the Stanford group, which began in 1955 a design study for a machine 10,000 ft long aimed at eventual operation at 45 Bev.

A visitor to the W. W. Hansen Laboratories of Physics at Stanford will find the 300-ft machine buried under a tunnel of concrete shielding. If the concrete were removed, he would see a 300-ft tube supported above a row of 20-ft I beams. Along one side of the accelerator is packed the radiofrequency gear in a sequence of oil tanks and shielded high-voltage houses. The output end of the accelerator delivers the high-energy beam through a concrete shielding wall into an experimental hall full of analyz-

ing and deflecting magnets and experimental electronic equipment.
Behind another shielding wall near the injection end of the accelerator
is the main control panel, an impressive array of controls, safety devices,
and trouble indicators.

The basic parameters of the Mark III machine are as follows:

Total length = 300 ft = 90 m
Length per section = 10 ft = 3.05 m
Frequency of rf power sources = 2856 megacycles
$\qquad\qquad\qquad\qquad\qquad\qquad$(wavelength = 10.5 cm)
Phase velocity $v = c$; velocity of light = 2.998×10^8 m/sec
Group velocity $v_g = 0.01c = 2.998 \times 10^6$ m/sec
Inside diameter of accelerating tube $2b = 8.247$ cm
Diameter of iris apertures $2a = 2.089$ cm
Thickness of irises = 0.584 cm
Iris spacing (center to center) = one quarter-wave = 2.625 cm
Q of cavity = 10,000
Time required to build up accelerating field = 1 μsec
Duration of acceleration = 1 μsec
Pulse repetition rate = 60 per second
Shunt impedance = 47.3 megohms/m

Figure 10-4 is a block diagram of the Mark III machine, and the
chapter headpiece is a photograph of the accelerator with the shielding
removed.

The machine was constructed in 2-ft sections, each assembled with
extreme care and with techniques especially developed for the occasion
to make possible the high precision essential to the success of the machine.
The 2-ft sections were then clamped together to form the 10-ft acceleration units. Each 10-ft section is now effectively a continuous piece of
iris-loaded waveguide, with one special section at the low-energy end.
The end of this section is closed by a disk of the usual inside diameter
but of much greater thickness than the other disks. To the high-frequency field this looks like a waveguide beyond cutoff and prevents the
high-frequency energy from passing through the accelerator in the direction opposite to the electron beam. In the outer wall of this special section is an aperture opening into a waveguide which connects the radiofrequency power source to the accelerator. This aperture serves also as
a pumping port for evacuation of the accelerator.

The 10-ft sections are arranged end to end on especially designed supports with which over-all alignment can be achieved. In the course of
this assembly, numerous mechanical and rf tests are performed to ensure
the precision of the machining and assembly.

The temperature of the machine must be controlled precisely. An
over-all temperature change is not serious since it can be compensated by

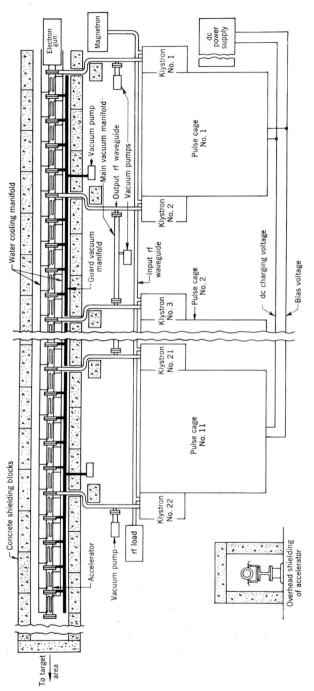

Fig. 10-4. Block diagram of Stanford Mark III accelerator.[8]

a change in operating frequency, but the relative temperatures of the sections of the machine must be maintained to better than 2°C. This is done by water cooling; copper cooling pipes are soldered along the outside walls of the 2-ft subsections.

After the accelerator itself the most spectacular Stanford achievement is the klystron development, in which the Stanford group has pioneered and which has laid the foundations for a now flourishing industry. This development involved extrapolation of klystron operation to power levels higher by a factor of 1000 than those previously achieved. Three-cavity klystrons of conventional design were reengineered to operate with 400-kv electron beams of 250 amp. Cathode problems, breakdown problems, problems of the behavior of relativistic electrons, and many other problems had to be solved. Solution of some of these problems still was not quite complete by 1961, but operation of klystrons at the 20-megawatt output level seems now to be quite predictable and reliable. Fortunately, in the relativistic electron accelerator, failure of one power source does not stop operation but merely decreases the final electron energy by about 5 per cent (for the Mark III).

A detailed description of the klystron amplifiers will not be included here since klystrons of this type are becoming shelf items with transmitting-tube manufacturers. Here we shall mention only one of the most troublesome problems encountered at Stanford. The klystrons on the Mark III machine were continuously pumped rather than sealed-off tubes, so that repairs could more easily be made on tubes which failed. The vacuum maintained in the accelerator was not good enough for the klystrons, however, since the oxide cathodes in the klystrons are very easily poisoned by traces of air. Consequently, the two vacuum systems were separated by an insulating ceramic window across the waveguide leading from the klystron to the accelerator. During the early days of operation many klystrons failed because of puncturing of this window by electrical discharges. It was thought that this was due to bombardment of the window by stray electrons from the klystrons, and a "dog-leg" bend was included in the waveguide so there was no direct path from klystron to window. This cured most of the difficulty, but residual difficulties still exist. Model tests indicate that these can be controlled by use of a double window with an evacuated space between.

The klystron development has now reached the point where 2000 hr is a conservative estimate of tube life. For some time a sealed-off-klystron development has been under way at Stanford, and it would appear that before long the continuously pumped klystron will be a thing of the past.

Injection into an electron linear accelerator can be a very simple process. In the Mark II machine the injector consisted of very little more than a hot tungsten spiral cathode biased to a negative potential of about 80 kv. Although 80-kev electrons have a velocity of only half the velocity of light, it still proved possible to inject into a section of waveguide in which the phase velocity was equal to the velocity of light. This does not seem so mysterious when it is realized that the high accelerating fields bring the electrons very rapidly to almost the velocity of light. But in the process many electrons which did not enter the first section at exactly the correct phase are lost.   So in the Mark III a "bunching section" is included which pregroups the electrons around the correct phase. This can be done in either of two ways.   The simplest method is that used in the klystron; the electrons pass through a gap at which they experience a relatively weak rf field, so some are accelerated and some are decelerated.   They are then allowed to drift for a certain distance so the accelerated electrons catch up with the decelerated electrons of the previous bunch.   With the correct drift distance the beam will be bunched around a particular phase.   The bunching is, however, somewhat nonlinear and incomplete.   For really tight bunching it is better to accelerate and bunch at the same time.   The buncher used for this purpose is merely a section of accelerator in which the phase velocity is matched to the particle velocity.   Still better bunching is achieved if the accelerating field increases along the buncher.   In the Stanford buncher the field rises by a factor of 10 in its 0.8-m length.   These variations of field strength and phase velocity are made automatic in the buncher (which is also an iris-loaded waveguide) by correct choices of the dimensions of the tapered pipe and the loading disks.

Two vacuum systems are required for evacuation of the klystrons and of the accelerator proper.   Each klystron has its own pump which maintains a pressure in the klystron of 10^{-7} mm Hg with the cathode cold and about 10^{-6} mm Hg with the cathode hot.   The vacuum requirements in the accelerator are not so stringent, and the pressure is reduced to about 2×10^{-6} before application of rf power; under full power the pressure rises to about 2×10^{-5} mm Hg.   The accelerator is evacuated by 11 oil-diffusion pumps, each of which is connected to two 10-ft sections through a manifold.   Although the ultimate pressure is not very critical, it is important for reasons to be discussed in Sec. 10-16 that oil from the pumps be prevented from migrating onto the surfaces of the accelerating cavity.   For this reason each pump is equipped with a water baffle and a liquid-nitrogen cold trap.   Addition of the cold traps was found to make a material improvement in the time required initially to bring the rf power to full operating levels.

In operation the Mark III accelerator yields an average current of about 1 μa in a beam about $\frac{1}{4}$ in. in diameter (this corresponds to an average power of almost 1 kw in the beam).   Most of the output current is included in an energy spread of about 2 per cent.   By magnetic analysis the energy homogeneity can be improved to be within any desired limits, with associated reduction of intensity.

After leaving the machine the accelerated beam passes into a beam-switching area where it can be displaced to right or left by deflecting magnets or allowed to proceed undeflected. It then enters the experimental area through holes in a wall of heavy (iron oxide–loaded) concrete 5 ft thick. On the other side of the experimental area is a large earth mound which serves as a "backstop" to reduce the radiation level in the surrounding (university campus) area.

10-10. OTHER ELECTRON LINEAR ACCELERATORS

Dozens of electron linear accelerators in the energy range of a few tens of Mev are now scattered throughout the world, serving a variety of applications. Such machines are valuable implements in radiography and in medical applications and are commercially produced by several manufacturers. In design these machines follow the Stanford lead and it appears that, for some time, the Mark III accelerator will serve as a pattern for production. Four rather different electron linear accelerators are worthy of mention; three are of historical interest, and the other may indicate a future trend.

The first machine in the former category is the electron linear accelerator at MIT. It was constructed before the klystron development and was designed to be powered by magnetron oscillators. This machine is described in the 1952 paper of Demos, Kip, and Slater.[16] It also uses an iris-loaded waveguide structure, but to match the output requirements of the magnetron drivers it is a standing-wave machine. It is formed of 20 sections each about 1 ft long and each powered by a 2800-megacycle 500-kw magnetron. The final electron energy available is about 16 Mev. The difficult problem of keeping 20 magnetrons operating at the same frequency and at the correct relative phase was solved with less difficulty than had been generally expected. The problem of injection was simplified by use of a 2-Mev electrostatic injector so that injection energies were high enough to permit injection directly into a guide having its phase velocity equal to the velocity of light. Operation of this machine was quite successful and verified the predictions of its designers. Although it was constructed with the primary objective of advancing the linear-accelerator art, it has proved itself over a period of years to be a valuable research tool, and it was still in operation in 1961 some nine years after its completion.

During about the same period a traveling-wave linear accelerator for 4 Mev was designed at the British Atomic Energy Research Establishment at Harwell.[17] This machine was powered by a single 3000-megacycle 2-megawatt magnetron; energy was introduced at the injection end of the accelerator, and the energy which emerged at the high-energy end was dissipated in a waveguide load. Later Harwell studies showed that this energy could be returned to the input and added by a directional coupling system to the magnetron output.

The third approach in the historical category was radically different from those already described.   At Yale an electron linear accelerator was built under the direction of H. L. Schultz[18] in which the operating frequency was reduced to the 600-megacycle range where triode power amplifiers were available in the 500-kw range.   Instead of the iris-loaded waveguide, the Yale group chose to employ a series of uncoupled TM_{010} cavities.   The holes through which the beam passed were made small enough that there was no appreciable coupling between cavities.   Then each cavity was driven by its own power amplifier, relative phases of the cavities were adjusted for optimum performance, and finally the eight-cavity machine was brought into operation, delivering a current of the order of 0.2 μa average at 10 Mev.   Although this approach has much to recommend it in the simplicity of the design and tune-up procedure, its relatively low efficiency compared with the 3000-megacycle machines makes it improbable that it will be duplicated.

Before passing on from these various machines, it should be emphasized that each has made its important contribution to the advancement of the accelerator art by adding to the store of experience of what can and what cannot be done.   In the use of high rf fields and high power levels there have been and still are mysterious phenomena which plague the linear-accelerator designer.   Some of these effects will be mentioned in Sec. 10-16.

The latest and most exciting modern development in the electron-linear-accelerator field is the result of many years of work at Harwell on dielectric loading of accelerator cavities.   The most promising approach has been to load the accelerating waveguide with dielectric disks instead of metal irises.   Disks of titanium oxide are used because they have high dielectric constants (of the order of 90 times that of free space) and low rf losses.   To the rf field these present many of the same characteristics as do metal disks, but they do not show the resistive losses that are found with metal disks.   Consequently the machine becomes much more efficient.   In 1957 the Harwell group reported[19] on a 1.5-Mev dielectric-loaded machine which displayed a shunt impedance of 180 megohms/m. The possibilities of this system had been realized for some years, but model machines could not be made to hold the necessary high fields. Finally the trouble was cured by a thorough cleanup of the system and a change from oil pumps to mercury pumps.   Apparently the troubles all were due to invisible oil films on the dielectric surfaces.

10-11. CAVITIES FOR PROTON AND HEAVY-ION LINEAR ACCELERATORS

The iris-loaded waveguide does not lend itself to the low phase velocities which must be used to accelerate protons or heavy ions.   If such a system is forced to low phase velocities and low frequencies, the efficiency becomes very low. Consequently a totally different approach has been made to this problem. The standard ion accelerator is a single standing-wave cavity operating in the TM_{010} mode. The electric-field lines are parallel to the axis of the cavity and terminate on the end walls of the cavity. In a 30-Mev ion linear accelerator the rf potential difference between the two ends of the cavity must be at least 30 Mev. But since an ion takes many periods of the rf field to travel from one end of the cavity to the other, some device must be introduced to shield it from the field while the field direction is such as to decelerate rather than to accelerate. This can be done rather simply by introducing a series of tubes along the axis through which the beam passes. The tube length is cut

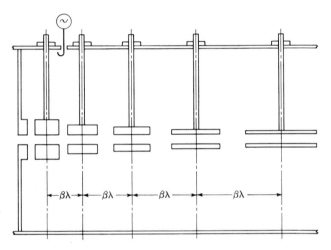

Fig. 10-5. Basic structure of positive-ion linear accelerator. As the drift-tube length increases, the diameter must decrease to maintain resonance.

so the ion takes exactly one full period to pass from the entrance of one tube to the entrance of the next. An ion which has the correct phase will see only accelerating fields; while the field is in the reverse direction, the ions are shielded by the tubes. These tubes are known as drift tubes since the ions experience no forces while they travel through them. Their length increases along the accelerator as the ion velocity increases. The over-all system presents the appearance shown schematically in Fig. 10-5. Fortunately the introduction of these drift tubes makes only local variations in the TM_{010} mode. The diameter of the cavity must be changed slightly from that of the empty TM_{010} guide, but the appropriate changes can be determined either by computation or by model studies. To the moving ion, however, all similarity to the TM_{010} mode has disappeared. The ion sees a complicated square-wave pattern whose important component is the traveling-wave component having the same velocity as that of the ion at the equilibrium phase.

The use of drift tubes in a high-Q cavity as an accelerator structure was originated by a group at the Berkeley Radiation Laboratory under the direction of L. W. Alvarez and W. K. H. Panofsky. Shortly after World War II this group constructed a 32-Mev proton linear accelerator which serves as the prototype for all ion linear accelerators now under construction. Although many mechanical improvements have been made in the original structure, the basic principles have been preserved without appreciable modification. In the next section we present the design features of the Berkeley machine.

10-12. THE BERKELEY 32-MEV PROTON LINEAR ACCELERATOR

With the evolution of the cavity concepts just mentioned, the Berkeley group undertook, shortly after the end of World War II, to construct a 32-Mev proton linear accelerator. The details of construction and operation of this machine are presented in detail in the Linear Accelerator Issue of *The Review of Scientific Instruments*.[8]

Two additional factors entered the consideration of the Berkeley group. One was the discovery of phase stability with its obvious application to the linear machine. The other was the availability of a large amount of surplus radar equipment from the armed services. The radar tubes and power supplies were to be used to excite the accelerating cavity. In operation the performance of the radar equipment proved to be unsatisfactory, but by that time better rf sources were available.

The accelerating cavity was designed for operation at 200 megacycles and so was about 1 m in diameter. Average accelerating fields of about 2.5 Mv/m were believed to be achievable, so the machine length was made 40 ft or about 12 m. It was also felt desirable to separate the rf cavity from the vacuum tank so that distortions of the tank under evacuation would not detune the cavity. Therefore the rf cavity was built of copper sheets, using a light but rigid construction; the cavity was built by an aircraft company using standard aircraft production techniques. This cavity was then supported inside a large steel vacuum tank. Both the tank and the rf liner were split in a horizontal plane so both could be opened for installation of the drift tubes. The details of construction can be seen in Fig. 10-6. The drift tubes were hung from a supporting rail at the top of the liner by thin stems; these stems are normal to and make negligible perturbations in the rf field.

The drift tubes were basically cylinders with rounded ends and varied in diameter from 4.75 in. at the low-energy end to 2.75 in. at the high-energy end. Their precise shapes were determined by modeling. Since the radial planes through the center of the drift tube and midway between drift tubes are planes of symmetry, the model cell could include only one-half drift tube; the planes of symmetry were replaced by copper sheets. In this unit cell the drift-tube shape was modified until the cell resonated at the correct over-all frequency. When the complete structure of all the unit cells was assembled, its over-all resonant frequency was the same as that of each cell. Both drift-tube diameter and relative gap spacing were modified to achieve this resonance. At the low-energy end the gap length was about 0.28 times the drift-tube length. This was gradually increased to about 0.33 at the 8.4-Mev point, and the ratio was held constant at 0.33 throughout the rest of the accelerator.

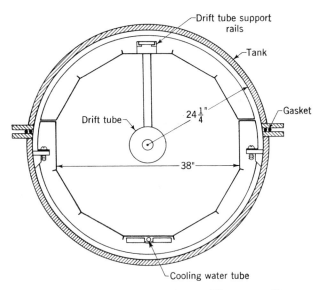

Fig. 10-6. Cross section through the Berkeley 32-Mev proton linear accelerator.[8]

One of the difficult problems facing the Berkeley group was rf defocusing of the beam. At velocities low compared with the velocity of light a phase-stable particle will be lost very rapidly by the radial components of the rf accelerating field (see Sec. 10-3). This is obviously the case because the phase-stable particle is riding at such a phase that the field is increasing as it crosses the accelerating gap. From the field pattern in the gap (Fig. 10-7a) we see that the inward force experienced by the particle as it leaves one drift tube will be more than counterbalanced by the outward force of the higher field present as it enters the next drift tube. It was realized by the Berkeley group that the radial field at the entrance to the drift tube could be largely removed if the upstream end was closed by a metal foil thin enough to permit passage of the proton beam without serious energy loss. The revised field situation can be visualized from

Fig. 10-7b. So beryllium foils 0.00003 in. thick were included in each drift tube. Unfortunately, after a few of the rf discharges inevitable in bringing the rf to full power, the foils evaporated and disappeared. They were then replaced by tungsten grids, which eventually were reduced to a few bent strips of tungsten strip located edge on to the beam. The grids solved the problem, although their optical properties were not so good as those of the foils and the rather poor focusing resulted in considerable beam loss. The structure of a typical drift tube in the Berkeley linac is shown in Fig. 10-8.

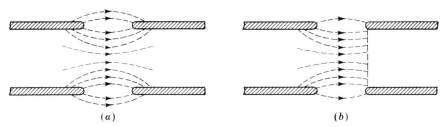

(a)   (b)

Fig. 10-7. Electric-field patterns between drift tubes: (a) normal defocusing-field pattern; (b) focusing-field pattern using grids or foils.

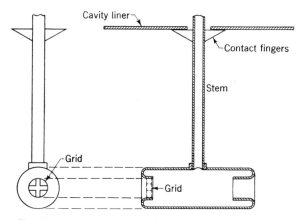

Fig. 10-8. Sketch of a typical drift tube in the Berkeley linear accelerator.

The rf power necessary to excite the tank to the desired level is about 2.1 megawatts. The Q of the tank is very high—about 70,000—consequently a period of about 200 μsec is required to bring the power up to the operating level. For good over-all efficiency a beam pulse length of 400 μsec was chosen to make the total pulse length 600 μsec, repeated 15 times per second. The power is supplied by nine self-excited power oscillators using Eimac 3W10,000A3 triodes and distributed at intervals along the tank. Coupling is such that the oscillator frequency is determined by the resonant frequency of the tank. This system will not rise by itself to full power because of multipactoring (see Sec. 10-16), and it is necessary to start the rising field cycle by a single power amplifier used as a preexciter.

The injector for the 32-Mev machine is a 4-Mev electrostatic generator built by C. M. Turner. The high injection energy was chosen primarily because of the planned use of focusing foils which would cause serious beam scattering at lower energies. With the introduction of grids much lower injection energies are now possible, and in newer machines 500-kev injectors are common.

In operation the Berkeley machine yields an average beam current of about 0.4 μa about 3 mm in diameter. The energy spread in the beam is only about 0.3 per cent. This sharply focused and homogeneous beam is a very powerful research tool; it is more intense than any external cyclotron beam yet available.

In 1958 this historic machine was dismantled and moved to the University of Southern California, where it should continue its career as a valuable tool for research in nuclear physics.

10-13. OTHER PROTON LINEAR ACCELERATORS

Because the cost per Mev of proton linear accelerators is considerably higher than that for cyclotrons, the number constructed is smaller than for electron linear accelerators. Several noteworthy machines have been constructed, however, and others are in the process of construction.

At the University of Minnesota a group under the direction of J. H. Williams has built a 70-Mev machine[20] which is now in satisfactory operation and is shown in the artist's sketch of Fig. 10-9. This machine is subdivided into three tanks, each similar in construction to the Berkeley 32-Mev machine. Protons are injected at 500 kev into the first tank and are accelerated to 10 Mev in a distance of 18 ft. They leave the first tank to pass through a short section of pipe into the second tank, where their energy is increased to 40 Mev; in the final tank the energy is increased to 68 Mev; both the second and the final tanks are 40 ft in length. Deflecting stations are included at the exit of each tank so that 10-, 40-, and 68-Mev proton beams are available. The rf power for the three tanks is supplied by a power-amplifier system whose output consists of three tetrodes operating in parallel to power the three tanks. The tetrodes are of a spectacular size and of an unusual design with built-in resonant cavities. Tetrodes of this particular design are known as "resnatrons." They are not commercially available but were built specially by the Minnesota group.

At the British Atomic Energy Research Establishment at Harwell an ambitious proton-linear-accelerator project was initiated several years ago when plans were drawn up for a 600-Mev proton machine. Detailed

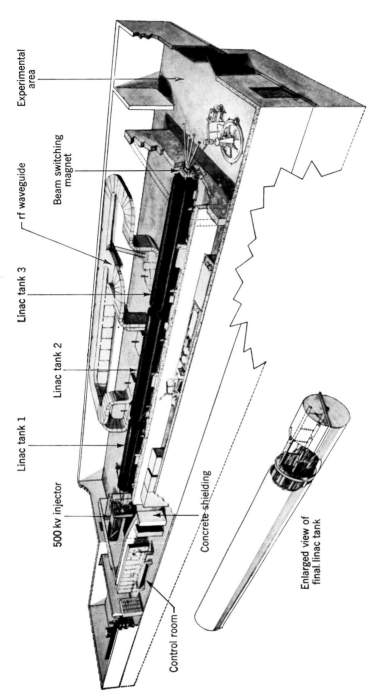

Experimental area

rf waveguide

Beam switching magnet

Linac tank 3

Linac tank 2

Linac tank 1

500 kv injector

Concrete shielding

Control room

Enlarged view of final linac tank

Fig. 10-9. 70-Mev proton linear accelerator at the University of Minnesota.[20]

341

design studies were made for the different types of accelerating cavities appropriate at the various energy ranges, and construction was started on the first 50-Mev part of the machine.   Up to 50 Mev the design was for a three-tank machine similar to the Minnesota accelerator except that it was to be powered by laboratory-built triodes.   In 1960 the 50-Mev machine was complete.   Present plans call for extension to 70 Mev; work on still higher energies has been postponed.

Grid focusing in linear accelerators is now being superseded by AG focusing (see Chap. 5) using quadrupole magnets located in the drift tubes.   Theoretical treatments of the old and new focusing methods will be found in the papers of Blewett[21] and of Smith and Gluckstern.[8]

Linear accelerators are used as injectors for large proton synchrotrons. For example, 10-Mev linacs are used as injectors for the 6-Bev Berkeley bevatron and for the Moscow 10-Bev "synchrophasotron."   The 25-Bev AG proton synchrotrons at Brookhaven and CERN (Geneva, Switzerland)[22] use 50-Mev proton linacs as injectors.   The CERN linac is similar to the Harwell machine.   The Brookhaven linac is a single-tank machine and combines the rf liner and the vacuum tank by building the vacuum tank of copper-clad steel.   Both of these linacs are powered by TH-470 triodes made by the French Thomson-Houston Company of Paris.   Both machines use magnetic quadrupole focusing with quadrupoles embedded in the drift-tube structure.   The CERN drift-tube configurations are similar to those used in the first Berkeley design.   The Brookhaven drift-tube shapes were computed using a method due to N. C. Christofilos.   Cross sections through a Brookhaven drift tube are shown in Fig. 10-10.

A discussion of linear-accelerator design would not be complete without a mention of another design for the accelerating system which has been much discussed but never tried.   This system is well presented in the review by Johnsen;[23] it consists of a helical spiral enclosed in a conducting pipe.   The technique has been used in traveling-wave tubes, which can be considered to be linear accelerators operated in reverse to deliver energy from a beam to a circuit.   Consequently there seems no reason to doubt that it would work.   It has not yet been developed, primarily because no one has devised a solution for the problem of focusing the beam in such a structure.

Extension of the proton linear accelerator to the billion-volt range has been proposed and discussed in many laboratories.   It would not be difficult to build a conventional drift-tube accelerator in several sections to reach 200 Mev.   At this energy the proton velocity has reached almost 60 per cent of the velocity of light, and it is quite possible to make a microwave cavity of the electron-linear-accelerator type for phase velocities in this range.   Consequently the accelerator would change at this point to a microwave system.   The phase velocity in the microwave system would not equal the velocity of light but would of necessity be tapered along the accelerator to match the proton velocity. Since the cost per Mev of a drift-tube accelerator is much higher than that for a microwave system, the over-all cost of the machine per Mev will become lower as the ultimate energy increases. The 600-Mev Harwell proposal did not aim at an energy high enough to realize these economic advantages. In the U.S.S.R. a proposal has been studied for construction of a proton linear accelerator in the 1-Bev range. At Brookhaven a preliminary study has been made of a 10-Bev proton linear accelerator. The cost would be more than twice that of a proton synchrotron for the

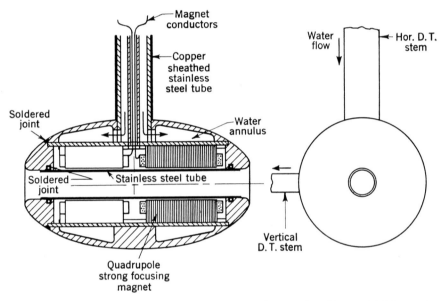

Fig. 10-10. Cross sections through a drift tube used in the Brookhaven 50-Mev proton linac, showing a focusing quadrupole.

same energy, but the beam intensity would be higher by a factor of 10^4 than that available from the proton synchrotron. Further study of the relative importance of cost, beam intensity, and beam characteristics will be necessary before such a project can be attempted.

10-14. HEAVY-ION LINEAR ACCELERATORS

Production of intense beams of ions heavier than protons is desirable for many experiments in nuclear physics and nuclear chemistry. For example, bombardment of uranium by carbon nuclei may give much information about formation of transuranic elements. Energies and intensities of heavy-ion beams produced in cyclotrons are too low for these experiments.   The linear accelerator seems ideal for this application, and a joint project was set up between Yale University and the Berkeley Radiation Laboratory for design of heavy-ion linear accelerators.[24]   Groups directed by Beringer of Yale and Van Atta of the Radiation Laboratory completed a joint design, and in 1954 construction was started on two essentially identical machines in the two cooperating centers.   Both machines are in operation and appear to justify the predictions of their designers.

Doubly charged He or C ions, triply charged N, O, or Ne ions, or several other possible ions of about the same charge-to-mass ratio are produced in special ion sources[25] and preaccelerated to 500 kev in a Cockcroft-Walton generator.   The particles are then injected into a drift-tube accelerator 15 ft long and accelerated to energies of about 1 Mev per nucleon.   The frequency of operation is 70 megacycles, and the tank diameter is about 10 ft.   The tank is constructed of copper-clad steel.

The ion beam then passes through a "stripper," which is a gas jet in which the ions lose enough electrons so their charge-to-mass ratio is doubled.   After stripping, electric accelerating fields will give twice the acceleration; the ion beam now enters the poststripper accelerator, which is 90 ft long and 9 ft in diameter.   When the beam emerges from the poststripper, its energy has been raised to 10 Mev per nucleon.   Focusing in the prestripper is accomplished by grids of the Berkeley type.   In the poststripper AG focusing is achieved by inclusion of quadrupole magnets in the drift tubes.   Radiofrequency power for both tanks is supplied at 70 megacycles by a power-amplifier system culminating in several RCA A2332 triodes.

10-15. LINEAR ACCELERATORS FOR HIGH CURRENTS

At the Livermore Laboratory of the University of California several linear accelerators have been built for acceleration of high currents of protons or deuterons.   The authors are indebted to Prof. C. M. Van Atta for the following description of these developments.

At the Livermore site of the University of California Lawrence Radiation Laboratory several linear accelerators have been built for acceleration of proton and deuteron beam currents in the range of tenths of an ampere.   This development was initially based upon use of the highest radio frequency for which high-powered, continuously operating oscillator tubes were then available, which was about 12 megacycles/second.   The Mark I Accelerator, based upon this design limitation, consisted of a cylindrical cavity 60 feet in diameter and 60 feet in length and a high-powered injector capable of injecting beam currents of about $\frac{3}{4}$ ampere of protons (or deuterons) at 125 kev.   Optimum performance of the Mark I Accelerator under continuous operation was an average beam current of about 50 milliamperes of protons at about 10 Mev.   During pulse operation a maximum peak beam current of 225 ma was attained and at a lower peak current and higher duty cycle (0.55) the maximum average beam output was 59 ma.

During construction and operation of the Mark I Accelerator improved oscillator tubes capable of continuous operation at frequencies as high as 50 megacycles/second at an output of 400 kilowatts became available. Using these new tubes and taking advantage of what had been learned from the Mark I Accelerator experience the A-48 Accelerator was designed and constructed. An improved injector system incorporating intense solenoidal magnetic focusing proved capable of injecting $\frac{3}{4}$ ampere of deuterons into a 3-inch diameter aperture at energies up to 130 kev with an angular divergence of about four degrees. With an injected beam of this quality it was feasible to design the rf accelerator with bore diameter of only 3 inches. The first stage of rf acceleration was accomplished by a two-stage, quarter-wave, resonant stem accelerator similar to a straightened out cyclotron operating at about 24 megacycles/second. Strong solenoidal focusing magnets were built into the drift tubes at the ends of the two quarter-wave stems and were also placed before, between and beyond the drift tubes to ensure that the intense beam would be kept under control. With rf pre-bunching of the injected beam the quarter-wave accelerator was capable of producing continuously 0.3 ampere of protons at 0.5 Mev, or of deuterons at 1.0 Mev. This section of the A-48 Accelerator was constructed and tested during the period April through December, 1954.

The remainder of the A-48 Accelerator consisted of two cylindrical cavities each twenty feet in length and resonant at about 48 megacycles/second. The two 20-ft cavities were completed and the A-48 Accelerator put into operation by December, 1955. The drift tubes of both cavities contained strong solenoidal focusing magnets. The output energy was 3.75 Mev for protons and 7.5 Mev for deuterons. Although the A-48 Accelerator was originally designed for a continuous output of 0.25 ampere of deuterons at 7.5 Mev, the actual currents attained during 1956 and 1957 were about 75 milliamperes of protons and 30 milliamperes of deuterons limited by the rf power input since the full design rf power was never installed. On the basis of experience with the A-48 Accelerator, those engaged in the project are confident that ion beam currents of $\frac{1}{4}$ ampere or more can be accelerated to any desired energy since the low-energy stages of acceleration are the most difficult. However, this development is not now being pursued. The A-48 Accelerator was shut down early in 1958 and has since been dismantled.

10-16. THE MULTIPACTOR EFFECT AND ELECTRON LOADING

Operators of accelerators which employ high electric fields have continually been plagued by the mysterious appearance of streams of electrons which load the power supply, induce emission of intense X radiation, and occasionally destroy parts of the machine. Such effects have already been mentioned in connection with the electrostatic generator and the cyclotron. When the fields alternate at high frequency, not only are the same effects present but also new effects appear. Most troublesome of these is the multipactor effect. This is an electron multiplication phe-

nomenon.   If an rf electric field is set up between parallel metal surfaces
and the field strength is such that an electron originating on one metal
surface can take exactly one half-period of the radiofrequency to cross to
the other surface, it can then knock out several secondary electrons which
will return in exactly a half-period to the first surface.   Secondaries from
the first surface will now repeat the process with continual multiplication
until the discharge becomes limited by space charge.   In the linear
accelerator multipactoring sets in at rather low levels between the closely
spaced drift tubes at the low-energy end of the machine.   If the machine
is powered by self-excited oscillators, the build-up of the oscillator excitation will be stopped at this point.   Consequently it is necessary to drive
rapidly through the multipactor region with an externally excited power
amplifier.

The important features of the multipactor effect can be established by
the following derivation.   We assume parallel plates in the yz plane, one
at $x = 0$ and one at $x = x_0$.   Between these plates exists an electric field
$E_x = E \sin (\omega t + \phi)$.   An electron leaving the $x = 0$ plane at time $t = 0$
with initial velocity $x = 0$ will have the equation of motion

$$m\ddot{x} = eE \sin (\omega t + \phi) \tag{10-36}$$

whence
$$\dot{x} = \frac{eE}{m\omega} [\cos \phi - \cos (\omega t + \phi)] \tag{10-37}$$

and
$$x = \frac{eE}{m\omega^2} [\omega t \cos \phi + \sin \phi - \sin (\omega t + \phi)] \tag{10-38}$$

If multipactoring is to occur, the time to travel from 0 to x_0 must be an
integral number of half-periods, so $\omega t = (2n + 1)\pi$ and

$$x_0 = \frac{eE}{m\omega^2} [(2n + 1)\pi \cos \phi + 2 \sin \phi] \tag{10-39}$$

$$\dot{x} \text{ (at } x = x_0) = \frac{2eE}{m\omega} \cos \phi \tag{10-40}$$

In order for this mathematical picture to be physically realizable we must
have $\ddot{x}$ positive at $x = 0$ and $\dot{x}$ positive at $x = x_0$.   To satisfy these conditions [from Eqs. (10-36) and (10-40)] ϕ must lie between 0 and $\pi/2$.
It can be shown by differentiation of Eq. (10-39) that the minimum
possible value of E occurs when $\cot \phi = (2n + 1)\pi/2$.   The maximum
allowable value of E occurs when $\phi = \pi/2$.   At $\phi = 0$, the value of E is
intermediate between these limits.   The values of the peak potential
difference Ex_0 between the plates are

$$V_{\max} = \frac{m}{e} \frac{\omega^2 x_0^2}{2} \qquad \text{at } \phi = \frac{\pi}{2} \tag{10-41}$$

$$V_{\min} = \frac{m}{e} \omega^2 x_0^2 [(2n + 1)^2 \pi^2 + 4]^{-\frac{1}{2}} \qquad \text{at } \phi = \cot^{-1} \frac{(2n + 1)\pi}{2} \tag{10-42}$$

In Fig. 10-11 V/f^2 is plotted against x_0. From this figure, as from the above equations, the fact emerges that for a given electrode spacing there is a maximum field at which multipactoring can occur but there is no minimum field. Conversely, for a given field there is a maximum permissible electrode spacing for no multipactoring.

The case just discussed is the simplest possible situation in an rf cavity. In most regions of the cavity rf magnetic fields are present as well as rf electric fields. In many cases the magnetic fields make multipactor-

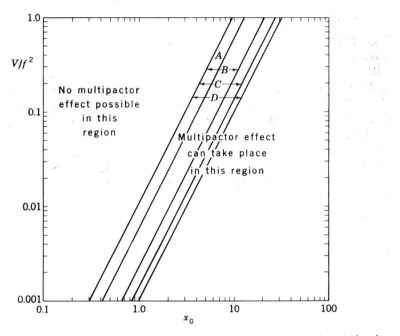

Fig. 10-11. The multipactor effect between parallel plates. In the region A the electrons require one half-period to cross from plate to plate; in region B the time required is three half-periods; in region C, five half-periods; and in region D, seven half-periods. Regions for still higher-order multipactoring are not shown but will extend indefinitely into the right-hand area of the graph. In this plot V is given in volts, f in megacycles, and x_0 in centimeters.

ing impossible. Sometimes, however, multipactoring occurs in and is dependent on the presence of rf magnetic fields. One such case is commonly found in proton linear accelerators. For many years the operators of these machines have been mystified by the appearance, after operation for some time, of discolored rings around the centers of the drift tubes. These rings appear in pairs separated by a few centimeters and symmetrically located on both sides of the vertical plane through the center of the drift tube. In the Brookhaven linac, where the drift-tube shapes are computed and all of the surrounding fields are known, it was possible to compute electron orbits in this region. The rings were found to correspond to possible points of origin of multipactor electrons. Probably the continuous electron bombardment results in deposition and polymerization of the residual gas in the vacuum tank and so leads to visible discoloration. Fortunately, this effect is sharply dependent on voltage, so it takes place for very short periods and does not involve the dissipation of much rf power.

Other spurious electrons in linear accelerators originate from the thin insulating films which have been shown (Chap. 3) to be so troublesome in the electrostatic accelerator. These electron currents are easily distinguishable from multipactor discharges by the fact that they appear at a threshold voltage as the field is increased and then increase in intensity with a high power (usually about the sixth) of the electric field. If the metal surfaces in a proton linear accelerator are not kept scrupulously clean, these currents will rise to levels where the X-ray emission reaches dangerous levels and the electron currents begin to use up an appreciable fraction of the rf power. As an example of the difficulties experienced, it was found that the 32-Mev linac at Berkeley, which is pumped by oil-diffusion pumps, must be dismantled and cleaned every six months because the X-ray output of the loading electrons reaches intolerable levels. In the bevatron injector linac, which is pumped by mercury pumps, no such effect is observed.

10-17. TECHNIQUES FOR MEASUREMENT OF RF FIELDS

During the design and construction of the accelerating cavities for linear accelerators it is frequently necessary to make experimental studies of the rf field patterns set up throughout the cavity structure. It is difficult to use conventional probe techniques without distorting the field to the extent that the measurements are meaningless. Two special and unobjectionable methods are available. The first is fairly well known to microwave engineers. It involves the introduction of a small dielectric or metal bead into the region where the field strength is to be measured.[26] This bead produces a small perturbation in the resonant frequency of the cavity; this perturbation is proportional to the square of the field strength at the bead location. Since measurement of resonant frequency can be very precise, this is a powerful method and can give accurate results. If a spherical metal bead of volume δ is used, the fractional change in resonant frequency is given by

$$\frac{\Delta f}{f} = -\frac{3}{4}\frac{\delta}{W}\left(\epsilon_0 E^2 - \tfrac{1}{2}\mu_0 H^2\right) \tag{10-43}$$

where W is stored energy.

If a spherical dielectric bead of dielectric constant E is employed, the fractional frequency perturbation will be

$$\frac{\Delta f}{f} = -\frac{3}{4}\frac{\delta}{W}\frac{\epsilon - 1}{\epsilon + 2}\epsilon_0 E^2 \qquad (10\text{-}44)$$

These two relations show that two measurements, one with a metal bead and one with a dielectric bead, can be combined to give both the electric field and the magnetic field at any given point. Only the absolute value of the field is determined; if field directions are desired, they can be deduced from measurements at several neighboring points.

The second method was developed by the linear-accelerator group at Berkeley; it is suitable for determination of electric-field strengths at higher levels. A small gas-filled spherical shell of glass or quartz is introduced into the field region and is observed by a photocell. If the size, gas filling, and pressure are adjusted correctly, the gas will break down and glow at a sharply defined field. These spheres are known to their inventors as "glo-balls."[27] Best results are obtained with Pyrex spheres about $\frac{1}{2}$ in. in diameter filled with helium at a pressure of about 10 mm Hg. A $\frac{1}{2}$-in. glo-ball prepared in this fashion breaks down at an electric field of about 120 volts/cm.

REFERENCES

1. G. Ising, *Ark. Math. Astron. Phys.*, **18**, Nr. 30, Heft 4, p. 45 (1925).
2. R. Wideröe, *Arch. Elektrotech.*, **21**:387 (1928).
3. D. H. Sloan and E. O. Lawrence, *Phys. Rev.*, **38**:2021 (1931).
4. D. H. Sloan and W. M. Coates, *Phys. Rev.*, **46**:539 (1934).
5. B. B. Kinsey, *Phys. Rev.*, **50**:386 (1936).
6. J. W. Beams and L. B. Snoddy, *Phys. Rev.*, **44**:784 (1933).
7. J. W. Beams and H. Trotter, Jr., *Phys. Rev.*, **45**:849 (1934).
8. Linear Accelerator Issue, *Rev. Sci. Instr.*, **26** (February, 1955).
9. Lloyd Smith, "Linear Accelerators," Encyclopedia of Physics, vol. XLIV, pp. 341–388, Springer (1959).
10. S. Ramo and J. R. Whinnery, "Fields and Waves in Modern Radio," Wiley (1944).
11. J. C. Slater, *Rev. Mod. Phys.*, **20**:473 (1948).
12. E. L. Ginzton, W. W. Hansen, and W. R. Kennedy, *Rev. Sci. Instr.*, **19**:89 (1948).
13. W. Walkinshaw, *Proc. Phys. Soc. (London)*, **61**:246 (1948); R. B. R.-Shersby-Harvie, *ibid.*, p. 255; L. B. Mullett and B. G. Loach, *ibid.*, p. 271.
14. R. B. R.-Shersby-Harvie and L. B. Mullett, *Proc. Phys. Soc. (London)*, **62**:270 (1949).
15. G. E. Becker and D. E. Caswell, *Rev. Sci. Instr.*, **22**:402 (1951).
16. P. T. Demos, A. F. Kip, and J. C. Slater, *J. Appl. Phys.*, **23**:53 (1952).
17. D. W. Fry, R. B. R.-Shersby-Harvie, L. B. Mullett, and W. Walkinshaw, *Nature*, **162**:859 (1948).

18. H. L. Schultz and W. G. Wadey, *Rev. Sci. Instr.*, **22:**383 (1951).
19. R. B. R.-Shersby-Harvie, L. B. Mullett, W. Walkinshaw, J. S. Bell, and B. G. Loach, *J. Inst. Elec. Engrs. (London)*, **104B:**273 (1957).
20. E. A. Day, R. P. Featherstone, L. H. Johnston, E. E. Lampi, E. B. Tucker, and J. H. Williams, *Rev. Sci. Instr.*, **29:**457 (1958).
21. J. P. Blewett, *Phys. Rev.*, **88:**1197 (1952).
22. Proceedings of CERN Symposium of 1956 (Geneva).
23. K. Johnsen, "On the Theory of the Linear Accelerator," A. S. John Griegs Boktrykker, Bergen, Norway (1954).
24. E. L. Hubbard, W. R. Baker, K. W. Ehlers, H. S. Gordon, R. M. Main, N. J. Norris, R. Peters, L. Smith, C. M. Van Atta, F. Voelker, C. E. Anderson, R. Beringer, R. L. Gluckstern, W. J. Knox, M. S. Malkin, A. R. Quinton, L. Schwarcz, and G. W. Wheeler, *Rev. Sci. Instr.*, **32:**621 (1961).
25. C. E. Anderson and K. W. Ehlers, *Rev. Sci. Instr.*, **27:**809 (1956).
26. S. W. Kitchen and A. D. Schelberg, *J. Appl. Phys.*, **26:**618 (1955).
27. J. F. Steinhaus, *Rev. Sci. Instr.*, **27:**575 (1956).

At the head of the facing page is an illustration of the University of California 184-in. synchrocyclotron, before the installation of shielding.

11

*The Synchrocyclotron**

The relativistic limitation on energy for fixed-frequency cyclotrons has restricted the useful size of magnets to about 60 in. pole-face diameter and the proton or deuteron energy to about 25 Mev. This limit is set by the relativistic increase in mass of the ions, which causes ion revolution frequency to decrease, so the ions fall out of resonance with the fixed-frequency applied electric field.

This maximum-energy limitation can be removed and the ions can be accelerated indefinitely if the applied frequency is varied to match exactly the ion revolution frequency. In Chap. 9 it was shown that particles in phase-stable orbits in a cyclotron-like accelerator will follow a slow change in applied frequency. The phase of crossing the accelerating gap oscillates about a mean value which allows just sufficient energy increase per turn to maintain resonance with the changing frequency.

When frequency is varied cyclically, a short bunch of ions will be accelerated to high energy in each frequency sweep, resulting in a sequence of such bursts occurring at the modulation frequency. The reduced effective duty cycle results in a much lower average ion output than in the conventional cyclotron (about 1 per cent), but it avoids the resonance limitation due to the fixed frequency and allows acceleration to much higher energies.

* Also known as the "frequency-modulated cyclotron."

11-1. EARLY DEVELOPMENT

The use of frequency modulation as a remedy for the relativistic limitations of the cyclotron was suggested as a consequence of the discovery of phase stability in 1945 by McMillan[1] of the University of California and independently by Veksler[2] of the U.S.S.R. The 184-in. magnet at the University of California had originally been conceived as a giant standard cyclotron by Prof. E. O. Lawrence and his coworkers. It was assembled and used for experimental purposes in the Manhattan District during World War II but was not completed as a cyclotron. At the end of the war, when McMillan proposed the use of frequency modulation, it became obvious that this method would result in higher energies, and plans were made to convert the machine into a synchrocyclotron.

The first test of the principle, at Berkeley, was made on the older 37-in. cyclotron magnet by an ingenious method of simulating the expected relativistic mass change with an exaggerated radial decrease in the magnetic field. Ion revolution frequency will decrease at very high energies because of the relativistic increase in mass; it can also be made to decrease with increasing energy in a small cyclotron if the magnetic field at large radii is reduced below the central field. The test was modeled on the anticipated operation of the 184-in. cyclotron. Deuterons of 200 Mev would experience an 11 per cent increase in mass during acceleration; the associated change in frequency, plus an additional 2 per cent for the radial decrease in field required for focusing, would require a total frequency change of 13 per cent during acceleration. To simulate this frequency change the field of the 37-in. magnet was equipped with radially tapered pole faces, requiring a 13 per cent modulation in frequency to maintain resonance with the low-energy (7-Mev) deuterons produced. With this arrangement the techniques of frequency modulation could be studied and the principle of phase-stable synchronous acceleration could be tested.

The results of the 37-in.-model test were reported by Richardson, MacKenzie, Lofgren, and Wright.[3] The test was completely successful. Very low D voltages were required, as compared with conventional cyclotron operation, and the deuterons remained in resonance for many thousands of revolutions. The frequency modulation was achieved with a rotating variable capacitor in the D circuit, using modulation frequencies up to 600 cps. The average deuteron current increased with modulation frequency as expected, to a maximum value of 0.2 μa. The results were in excellent agreement with those predicted from a theoretical analysis of phase-stable acceleration, and the success of the model experiment justified the modification of the 184-in. cyclotron to utilize this principle.

The 184-in. synchrocyclotron was brought into operation in November, 1946; it was immediately successful in producing good intensities of deuterons of 190 Mev and He^{++} ions of 380 Mev. The author list of the first report is a roster of the many members of the laboratory staff involved: Brobeck, Lawrence, MacKenzie, McMillan, Serber, Sewell, Simpson, and Thornton.[4] This impressive array of scientific and engineering talent makes it possible to understand how such a tremendous job could be completed in little more than a year. Yet another factor also entered. The fundamental soundness of the principle of phase stability and the simplicity of the basic techniques have impressed all observers. Equivalent success and speed in tuning up a synchrocyclotron have been achieved subsequently in other laboratories. In almost every installation to date, as soon as all components were completed and operable, resonant-ion beams have been obtained with a minimum of further experimentation. The synchrocyclotron has proved to be one of the simplest and most rewarding of all accelerators.

The immediate success of the Berkeley laboratory led others to build similar accelerators. The large size of this first machine stimulated others to plan for large sizes and high energies. Within a few years synchrocyclotrons were completed and in research operation in five university laboratories in the United States: at Rochester, Harvard, Columbia, Chicago, and Carnegie Tech. This rapid development was supported in large measure by government funds supplied by the Office of Naval Research and later by the Atomic Energy Commission, and it set a precedent in the United States for government support of university research laboratories.

Table 11-1 lists the larger machines in the United States and in other countries, with a few basic characteristics. They fall in two energy ranges. Those below 200 Mev energy are used for nuclear studies and single-particle scattering interactions. Those in the 400- to 700-Mev range have found their chief usefulness for the production of mesons and in the study of meson interactions.

Three machines in the 600- to 700-Mev range are the largest at present. At the University of California the rebuilt and repowered 184-in. cyclotron operates at 720-Mev protons; the U.S.S.R. Academy of Sciences has sponsored in the Joint Institute for Nuclear Research at Dubna a 6-m pole-face machine which operates at 680 Mev; and a 196-in. machine which produces 600-Mev protons was completed in 1958 at the CERN Laboratory, Geneva.

In addition to the large machines listed, small standard cyclotrons have been converted by a few laboratories (Princeton and University of California at Los Angeles) to the synchro principle to obtain higher energies than can be obtained with fixed-frequency operation.

TABLE 11-1

THE LARGER SYNCHROCYCLOTRONS

	Pole diam, in.	Magnet weight, tons	Magnetic field, kilogauss	Proton energy, Mev	Date first operated
United States:					
Univ. Calif...............	184	4300	15.0	350	1946
			23.0	720	1957
Univ. Rochester...........	130	1000	17.0	240	1948
Harvard Univ.............	95	700	20.0	150	1949
Columbia Univ............	164	2400	18.0	400	1950
Univ. Chicago............	170	2200	18.6	450	1951
Carnegie Inst. Tech........	142	1500	20.7	450	1952
Foreign:					
Univ. Amsterdam..........	71	210	13.7	28(d)*	1949
AERE, Harwell...........	110	670	16.8	175	1949
McGill Univ..............	82	260	16.4	100	1950
Werner Inst., Upsala.......	90	720	22.0	200	1953
Univ. Liverpool...........	156	1640	18.0	400	1954
Dubna, U.S.S.R...........	236	7200	16.8	680	1954
CERN, Geneva............	196	2500	20.5	600	1958

* (d) Deuteron energy.

11-2. PRINCIPLE OF OPERATION

In the synchrocyclotron light positive ions (protons, deuterons, He^{++}) are accelerated to energies significant relative to the rest energy of the particle. The ions traverse circular orbits in an approximately uniform and steady magnetic field, starting with small orbits at the center and increasing to larger radii as energy increases. In their circular motion they pass many times through the rf electric field of a large semicircular hollow electrode called a D. The frequency applied to the electrode is made identical with the ion revolution frequency, so that particles experience an acceleration on each traversal of the accelerating gap.

The steady magnetic field is produced by a solid-core electromagnet with dc excitation. For each value of particle energy in this field there is a particular equilibrium orbit radius and a specific frequency of revolution. Equations describing the orbital motion were developed in Chap. 5. Orbit radius is given by the relativistic relation (in mks units)

$$r = \frac{[T(T + 2W_0)]^{1/2}}{ceB} = \frac{[T(T + 2W_0)]^{1/2}}{300B} \qquad \text{meters} \qquad (11\text{-}1)$$

The numerical constant above applies when kinetic energy T and rest energy W_0 are given in Mev units and magnetic flux density B is in units of webers/m^2 (1 weber/m^2 = 10,000 gauss). Ion revolution frequency is given by

$$f = \frac{c^2 eB}{2\pi(W_0 + T)} = 14{,}320 \frac{B}{W_0 + T} \qquad \text{megacycles/sec} \quad (11\text{-}2)$$

Units are the same as for Eq. (11-1).

The decrease in ion revolution frequency is caused primarily by the increasing kinetic energy of the ions but is also affected by the slight decrease in magnetic field with increasing radius required for orbit stability.   The relations above are plotted in Figs. 11-1 and 11-2 to show

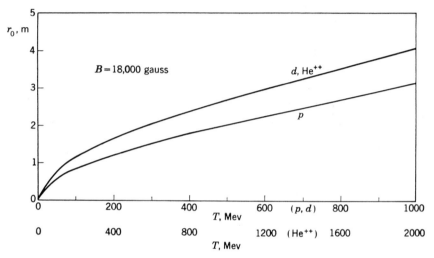

Fig. 11-1. Orbit radius versus energy for light positive ions in a magnetic field of 18 kilogauss.

the dimensional requirements and the orbital frequencies for the several light ions as a function of their kinetic energy, for a magnetic field of 18 kilogauss, which is typical of the fields used in synchrocyclotrons.

The D-shaped electrode is similar to the electrodes used in the standard cyclotron, but since the required acceleration voltage is low relative to that used in the standard cyclotron, a single D is used rather than the two D's customary in standard cyclotrons.   Particles cross the acceleration gap, between the diametral face of the D and a dummy D at ground potential, twice in each revolution.   The magnitude of the acceleration at each crossing depends on the instantaneous rf voltage, and so on the phase of crossing the gap relative to the rf wave.   As the ions gain in energy on each traversal of the gap, they travel in circles of larger radii, ultimately reaching the maximum practical radius (see Fig. 11-3).   The problem is to keep the ions in precise resonance with the applied rf field for a very large number of revolutions.   Resonance is maintained auto-

matically in the synchrocyclotron through the principle of phase stability
(see Sec. 9-9).   A brief review of this principle as it applies to the synchrocyclotron will be useful at this point.

Consider a particle which crosses the gaps at zero phase ϕ_0 when the rf
voltage is zero; its energy will not change, and it will continue to rotate
in a circular orbit of constant radius.   This orbit was defined as an
equilibrium orbit.   As long as the applied frequency is constant, a particle
which deviates from equilibrium energy will oscillate around this value of
energy and this location of the orbit.   For example, consider a particle

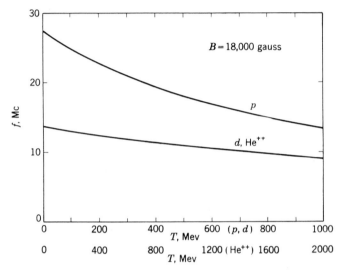

Fig. 11-2. Ion revolution frequency versus energy for light ions in a magnetic field
of 18 kilogauss.

which is not in exact resonance but crosses the gap at a phase ϕ when the
field is accelerating.   Such a particle will acquire excess energy, will
traverse an orbit of larger radius which requires a time longer than the
rf period, and so will shift in phase toward the zero-phase position.   This
motion was shown to lead to an oscillation in phase about the equilibrium
phase and to an associated oscillation in orbit radius about the position
of the equilibrium orbit.

Consider next the effect on a particle in such an equilibrium orbit of a
small decrease in the frequency applied to the electrodes.   This change in
frequency results in a phase shift, so the particle crosses the gap at a time
when the voltage is accelerating.   The particle will gain energy until it is
in resonance with the new frequency; its equilibrium orbit radius will
increase correspondingly.   Furthermore, if the frequency is decreased
slowly and continuously, the particles will follow this change, increasing

steadily in energy and orbit radius; phase oscillations will occur around that phase at which the particles acquire the average energy per turn which corresponds to the rate of change in frequency. This is the principle of the synchrocyclotron.

Because of the relatively slow decrease in accelerating frequency, the ions in the synchrocyclotron make many thousands of revolutions. For the accelerating fields ordinarily used, each phase oscillation takes several hundred revolutions. The ions, which are initially spread widely in azimuth, are slowly bunched as they are accelerated. As in the other

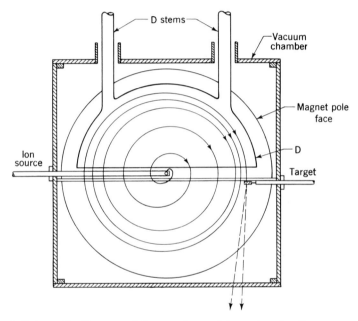

Fig. 11-3. Schematic diagram of the synchrocyclotron showing the arrangement of components within a vacuum chamber. Particle orbits shown are also schematic; in practice the particles traverse thousands of revolutions.

synchronous accelerators, a small radial oscillation around the expanding orbit is associated with the oscillation in phase.

Other motions, both in radius and in the vertical direction, are associated with initial errors in ion injection and with minor defects in the guiding magnetic field. These are oscillations of the same nature as those occurring in the betatron and have already been discussed in Secs. 5-9 and 5-10. The field index n required for adequate stability of these free oscillations is usually of the order of 0.05 in the synchrocyclotron. From Eqs. (5-67) and (5-68) it follows that the frequency of radial betatron oscillation is about 0.98 times the revolution frequency, while the frequency of vertical betatron oscillation is about 0.2 times the revolution frequency. These rapid oscillations are superimposed on the much slower phase oscillations.

The existence of such stable orbits in which ions can be trapped was demonstrated at an early date by some unpublished observations with the 37-in. model at Berkeley. When the ion source was pulsed a single time and the capacitor was rotating continuously, an initial burst of high-energy ions was observed on a target at the periphery (using a cathode-ray tube with a sweep circuit to display the instantaneous current), followed by a sequence of bursts of decreasing intensity at the modulation frequency. The interpretation is that ions which were not trapped and accelerated in the first frequency sweep were captured on successive sweeps. In another test the capacitor was rotated slowly by hand, so that the frequency sweep required several seconds. A small burst of ions was still observed at the end of the sweep, indicating that the orbits are truly stable. Ions will stay in resonance indefinitely, limited only by losses from gas scattering.

For continuous operation the frequency is modulated cyclically by a variable capacitor in the resonant D circuit. The frequency change as a function of time for such a typical circuit is illustrated in Fig. 11-4. During each sweep a bunch of ions is accelerated, so in continuous operation a sequence of pulses of high-energy ions reaches the periphery at the modulation frequency. This pulsed character of the beam can be described in terms of the duty cycle (the ratio of the pulse length to the cyclic period of modulation), which is of the order of 1 per cent. A more meaningful description is stated in terms of the capture efficiency. Since ions are accelerated intermittently, there is only a limited time interval in which ions emitted from the source can be accepted into stable orbits. Capture efficiency is the ratio of the number of ions accepted to the total number available during one frequency-modulation cycle. The calculation of efficiency is one of the principal objects of theoretical studies, and the primary problem in design is that of maximizing the capture efficiency, or the effective duty cycle.

The ion source is quite similar to that used for the standard cyclotron. A more complete discussion is given in Sec. 11-11. Some intensity gain will usually result from pulsing the source at the modulation frequency, so that ions are emitted in bursts during the acceptance time intervals.

To summarize, we can describe the general motion of the ions in terms of the superposition of three components of motion:

1. Expansion of the equilibrium orbit at a steady rate determined by the rate of frequency modulation
2. Radial phase oscillations about the equilibrium orbit and azimuthal oscillations about the position of equilibrium phase, of all amplitudes up to a maximum value set by the stable phase limits

3. Free radial and axial oscillations about the instantaneous orbits, with frequencies determined by the radial gradient of the magnetic field and amplitudes set by initial conditions and physical limitations

The rotating ions are enclosed within a curved, sausage-shaped envelope; the center of this envelope rotates at the applied frequency about the magnetic center and traverses a slowly expanding spiral path.   The angle in azimuth subtended by the envelope is determined by the extreme limits of phase oscillation.   The radial width is made up of two components, since the radial free oscillation is superimposed on the radial synchronous orbits.   The vertical or axial thickness of the envelope is given by the maximum amplitude of the axial free oscillations.   Any single particle migrates around within the envelope, making a complete

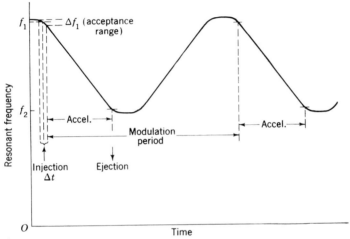

Fig. 11-4. Typical frequency-modulation cycle obtained with a variable capacitor in the D circuit.

circuit in its location within the envelope during a phase-oscillation cycle, which requires several hundred revolutions.

11-3. CAPTURE EFFICIENCY

A detailed theoretical analysis of phase-stable synchronous acceleration and of the phase oscillations was reported in two papers by Bohm and Foldy[5,6] of the University of California.   The first is on the theory of synchronous oscillations in general, but with primary reference to the electron synchrotron; the second discusses capture efficiency for a synchrocyclotron and compares results with experimental observations from the Berkeley machine.   A more detailed comparison of the operation of the 184-in. synchrocyclotron with theoretical predictions was reported later by Henrich, Sewell, and Vale.[7]   A brief derivation of the theory of synchronous oscillations has also been given in Chap. 9, with a unified terminology applying to all machines.   However, in Chap. 9 the details of the cyclotron application were bypassed to emphasize the generality of the derivation.   Some additional discussion of a qualitative nature is in order to describe the more pertinent details such as the factors affecting capture efficiency, the effects of orbit precession, and the loss of ions through coupling between the several types of oscillations at large n values.

Capture efficiency deals with conditions at the start of acceleration and during the first few phase oscillations.   The process of acceleration starts at the ion source, when the cloud of ions formed during the ion-source pulse is drawn toward the D by the applied rf voltage.   D voltage is relatively low, as compared with that of a fixed-frequency cyclotron, so the first accelerations and initial orbit radii are small.   These first spiral orbits do not penetrate the interior, field-free region of the D, but are located in the D gap where the electric field is approximately uniform. Under these conditions it can be shown that the ions are rapidly bunched, or phase-focused, around the phase of maximum voltage, $\phi = \pi/2$.   This phenomenon was described in Sec. 6-4 for the standard cyclotron and was illustrated by orbit plots showing the phase focusing and the concentration into radial bunches.   Bohm and Foldy[6] have given the theory of this prebunching in some detail in an appendix.   So, at the start of their motion the ions are closely bunched in phase around the phase of peak voltage.

During further acceleration the orbits grow larger and enter the D; the prebunching is distorted and spread into a wider phase band.   Then, as the applied frequency decreases, the phase shifts to smaller values. Those ions within the stable phase limits are captured and set into phase oscillations.   The fraction captured depends on the initial applied frequency and varies in magnitude as the frequency sweeps over an "allowed" range.

In Sec. 9-5 a general treatment of the limits of phase stability led to the conclusion that the range of initial ion phases that can be accepted in a synchronous accelerator depends on the value of the equilibrium phase; for low values of the equilibrium phase large fractions of the injected beam are accepted; for an equilibrium phase of about 30° about half of the beam is accepted; as the equilibrium phase approaches 90°, the accepted fraction becomes very small.   Particles that arrive at phases different from the equilibrium phase, but within the acceptance range, will undergo oscillations in phase in the course of which their energy will change and they will move to paths of different radius.   Thus we can draw an area in a plot of radius versus phase within which particles can be accepted and outside of which they will be rejected.   Figure 11-5 is such a plot derived for the Chicago synchrocyclotron.[8]   In this plot the areas of stability are shown for several equilibrium phases.   The direction of migration around the plot during the phase oscillation is indicated by arrows.   The areas shown in this graph do not remain fixed in space but move out in radius as the particle energy increases and as the applied frequency decreases.   Consequently, at least some of the particles will move clear of the injector before the oscillation returns them to their original azimuth and relative radial position.   The problem of how many such particles will escape has been discussed by Bohm and Foldy.[6]

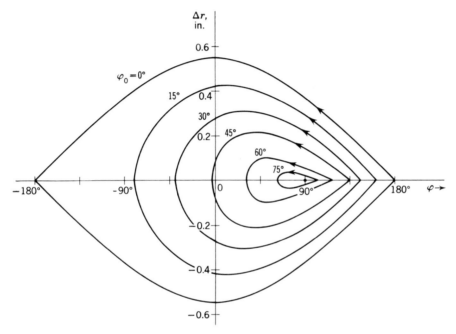

Fig. 11-5. Amplitude of radial phase oscillation Δr as a function of particle phase,[6] for several equilibrium phase angles ϕ_0 (cf. Fig. 9-3).

The results of Bohm and Foldy are presented in Fig. 11-6, taken from their paper.   A particle circulating at the wrong radius will have a frequency of revolution that differs from the applied frequency, so the radial position error shown in Fig. 11-5 could just as well be presented as a frequency error.   The ordinate in Fig. 11-6 is a function $f(\omega_0 - \omega)$ which is proportional to the difference between ion revolution frequency and applied frequency.   The abscissa is the sine of the equilibrium phase angle.   The double-branched curve labeled I gives the boundaries of the phase region in which ions would be captured into phase-stable orbits if there were no questions of interception by the injector.   This curve could have been drawn from the data presented in Fig. 11-5.   Curve II is the boundary beyond which particles will be returned to the origin. The area to the right of curve II is the acceptance area. The vertical arrows indicate the magnitude of the allowable frequency error (or radial displacement).

From the data used in plotting these graphs it is possible to compute the capture efficiency as a function of the equilibrium phase angle. The results differ slightly, depending on whether the machine is tuned by changing the rate of frequency modulation or by changing the D voltage (either will have the effect of changing the equilibrium phase). In both

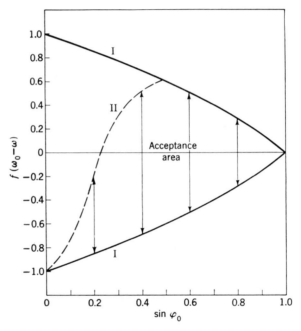

Fig. 11-6. Stable phase limits in terms of the difference between ion frequency and applied frequency, used to compute capture efficiency.[6]

cases, however, the efficiency as a function of equilibrium phase angle rises from zero at 0° to a peak between 20 and 30° and falls again to zero at 90°. Since the equilibrium phase angle should be between 20 and 30° for maximum capture efficiency, the peak applied voltage V should be between two and three times the equilibrium value of volts per turn $V \sin \phi_0$.

Experimental observations are in good agreement with the theoretical predictions. Bohm and Foldy show a plot (Fig. 11-7) of the way average beam current should vary with modulation frequency. When the experimental observations were matched in intensity to the theoretical curve at one point, they were found to be quite similar in general shape, except for a tail on the experimental curve extending to higher modulation frequencies. This is explained as due to ions which fall out of synchronism but are picked up and accelerated in a subsequent modulation cycle. The absolute magnitude of the average beam current is also in reasonable agreement with the calculated intensities based on the known peak current from the ion source and the computed capture efficiency. More details on the agreement between operational results and computed capture efficiency are given by Henrich, Sewell, and Vale.[7] They show that

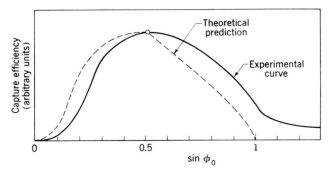

Fig. 11-7. Comparison of capture efficiency, calculated and observed, as a function of phase angle on the 37-in.-model synchrocyclotron,[6] obtained by varying the rate of frequency modulation.

the theoretical efficiency curve is valid over a wide range of D voltage and beam current.

11-4. ORBIT PRECESSION

Free radial oscillations are superimposed on the longer-period phase oscillations. The frequency is given by Eq. (5-67), and over most of the acceleration it is only slightly smaller than the resonant or orbital frequency. We would expect the azimuthal location of maximum outward amplitude of these free oscillations to precess around the chamber, with a precessional frequency given by

$$f_{pr} = [1 - (1 - n)^{1/2}]f_0 \qquad (11\text{-}3)$$

For example, the precessional frequency at a radial location where $n = 0.04$ would be $0.02f_0$, and the period of precession would be fifty times the period of revolution. When such precession occurs, the ions would reach their maximum radial amplitude at the azimuth of a probe target at intervals of about 50 ion revolutions.

Evidence for such orbit precession is reported by Henrich, Sewell, and Vale[7] from the 184-in. machine. Oscilloscope pictures of the beam current striking a probe target show a series of pulses with an average time separation of 10 μsec (see Fig. 11-8). When the probe was moved to different radii, the period was observed to vary, giving results in agreement with the precessional periods computed for the respective n values at the different locations. For this effect to be observed it is necessary for the ions to be sharply bunched in the phase of their radial oscillations and not continuously distributed in phase. We have indicated earlier how such bunching occurs during the first accelerations.

An envelope over the pulses illustrated on the oscillographic records in Fig. 11-8 shows a structure with two broad maxima separated by a longer time interval, of the order of 45 μsec. This separation agrees well with the computed period of phase oscillations and illustrates the "breathing" motion of the orbit. The fact that more than one phase-oscillation period is observable on the records means that the amplitude of free radial oscillations was larger than the radial increase during a phase period. In fact, this technique offers a method of estimating the ampli-

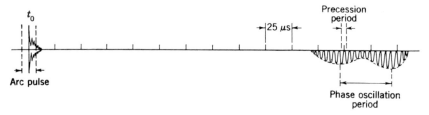

Fig. 11-8. Sketch of an oscilloscope pattern of beam intensity versus time with the 184-in. synchrocyclotron,[77] showing evidence for orbit precession and phase oscillations.

tude of the free oscillations, which in this case appears to be of the order of 3 in. and is roughly constant during acceleration.

Another experimental method of estimating the radial-oscillation amplitude of the beam is observation of the spread of the induced radioactivity on probe targets. Although the mean increase in beam energy per turn is very small (a few thousand electron volts) and the corresponding increase in orbit radius is almost undetectable, the combined effect of radial oscillations and precession of orbits spreads the beam over a finite radial width on the probe. The radioactivity observed in such tests at Berkeley was confined within 0.16 in. from the leading edge. Approximate calculations were made[7] of the spread expected for various radial-oscillation amplitudes at different radii, and the results suggest again that the free radial-oscillation amplitude was of the order of 3 in.

11-5. COUPLING BETWEEN OSCILLATIONS

A severe limitation on all synchronous accelerators is coupling between the several modes of oscillation. Under certain conditions excess energy may be fed into one type, such as the axial free oscillations, so that particles are lost to the beam through striking the D. This phenomenon was first observed experimentally in the 184-in. machine as a complete loss of the beam at about the 81-in. radius ($n = 0.2$), even though it was originally expected that the beam would persist out to the limit of radial stability at $n = 1.0$. To study the effect, copper probes in the shape of a U—with the open side of the U toward the center—were placed in the beam; they were then removed and radioautographs were made which showed that most of the beam hit the top or bottom of the U-shaped probe at about the 81-in. radius. This blowing up of the beam was explained as due to a coupling between free radial and vertical oscillations at $n = 0.2$.

At $n = 0.2$ the frequency of the radial oscillation is a second harmonic of the axial frequency, as can be shown by applying Eqs. (5-67) and (5-68).

$$\frac{f_r}{f_z} = \frac{(1 - n)^{1/2} f_0}{n^{1/2} f_0} = \frac{(1 - 0.2)^{1/2}}{0.2^{1/2}} = \frac{2}{1} \tag{11-4}$$

The probability of transferring energy from the radial to the axial mode depends on the duration of the coupling interval. This interval can be computed from the time required for the particle to pass through the resonance value of $n = 0.2$. The amplitude and so the energy of the radial oscillations must be known, as well as the physical limits of axial oscillations set by the D aperture.

The theory of coupled oscillations is given in many studies, and it was applied to this problem by Henrich, Sewell, and Vale.[7] For an assumed radial amplitude of 1 in. in the 184-in. cyclotron, the time required to transfer sufficient energy into the other mode to exceed the vertical aperture limits was found to be about 10 revolutions, with even shorter times for larger initial amplitudes. These results show that most of the beam would be lost near the $n = 0.2$ radius because of striking the D. Some ions should have very small amplitude radial free oscillations, however, and so should not exceed the vertical aperture even though the entire oscillation energy is transferred to the axial mode. Yet it was observed that essentially all the beam was lost in the 184-in. machine before it reached the radius at which $n = 1.0$. This suggested the possibility of coupling between other types of oscillations or for other harmonics.

At $n = 0.25$, coupling could occur between the vertical free oscillation and the fundamental circular motion, if azimuthal inhomogeneities in the magnetic field exist to provide a mechanism for energy transfer. The frequency of vertical oscillation would be $0.5f_0$ for this value of n. It is known that a radial component of magnetic field can affect the vertical motion of the ions and provide coupling. A radial component B_r will exist at the particle orbit if the median plane varies in location around the orbit. Even if the median plane is flat, the radial component at a small distance from the plane may vary with angle if the vertical component of field has azimuthal inhomogeneities. In the 184-in. machine the magnetic field was carefully measured as a function of angle and found to have inhomogeneities of the order of a few per cent. Henrich, Sewell, and Vale showed that this inhomogeneity was sufficient to account for the loss of essentially all ions at $n = 0.25$, even if they had survived the $n = 0.2$ resonance.

Detailed analysis of the coupling problem in the Chicago synchrocyclotron[8] showed that the $n = 0.2$ resonance is so tightly coupled as to predict almost total loss of the beam at this radius for this machine. On the other hand, the extreme care used in correcting the magnetic field for azimuthal variations led to a relatively weak coupling at $n = 0.25$. Operational experience has confirmed the predictions.

Other possible resonances can be analyzed similarly. Coupling can occur between vertical and radial oscillations, with $f_r = 3f_z$ at $n = 0.1$. Analysis of the coupling terms in the energy equation shows that for this second harmonic the coupling is insufficient to produce significant vertical amplitudes within the time interval available for resonance. The same is true for higher harmonics and for all other types of coupling which have been investigated.

At $n = 1.0$ the motion becomes radially unstable and particles enter orbits which are rapidly opening spirals. This feature might be used to advantage in ejecting an emergent beam in the simple manner used for the fixed-frequency cyclotron, if the ions could be brought out to this radius. However, the resonances at $n = 0.2$ and 0.25 effectively eliminate this possibility of obtaining a high-intensity emergent beam with the synchrocyclotron. Despite the strong coupling at the $n = 0.2$ and 0.25 resonances, some ions may survive to reach the $n = 1.0$ limit. This effect has been observed at the University of Rochester, where an oscillographic record of the secondary radiation from the chamber showed three peaks at times corresponding to the beam reaching successively the regions of $n = 0.2, 0.25,$ and 1.0.

11-6. THE MAGNETIC FIELD

The largest and most costly component of the synchrocyclotron is the solid-core magnet of large pole-face area. The magnetic field must be steady and approximately uniform over the pole face, decreasing slightly with increasing radius to provide focusing forces. So poles are roughly parallel, with a suitable contour provided on the pole faces to give a radial drop of a few per cent from center to edge.

Magnet weight and cost of iron increase roughly with the cube of the pole diameter. In the low-energy nonrelativistic range, particle energy varies with the square of the orbit radius; so magnet weight for small cyclotrons is given roughly by the $3/2$ power of the energy: $Wt \propto T^{3/2}$. But for high energies particle energy approaches a linear proportionality with orbit radius; so magnet weight increases more rapidly, approaching the relation $Wt \propto T^3$. This rapid increase in weight and cost is the chief limitation on the practical maximum energy for synchrocyclotrons. No insurmountable technical problems have been encountered up to the present largest sizes, capable of producing protons of 600 to 700 Mev. Designs for even larger machines seem practical. But the excessive cost of solid-core magnets for higher energies has transferred interest to the type of accelerator using constant orbit radius and a ring-shaped magnet (see Chap. 13), which is called a proton synchrotron.

The weight of iron is partially offset by the relatively simple design and structure of such a dc magnet. Cheap iron can be used in the form of thick plates or forgings, exciting coils are simple even though heavy, and power requirements are not excessive if a sufficient weight of conductor is used in the coils. The pole-gap length does not need to increase as fast as the pole-face diameter, since field shaping can be used to focus the resonant ions about the median plane; this results in relatively lower power requirements and smaller fringing-flux losses for large magnets and makes some reduction in weight of iron below the T^3 variation. Magnetic circuit dimensions tend toward broad, squat structures as size increases, and the magnetic efficiency is higher. These principles are discussed in more detail in Chap. 8 in the section on magnet design.

Maximum magnetic flux density is severely restricted by the permeability limits of iron, at around 18 to 20 kilogauss for soft iron forgings or rolled plates. Power requirements increase sharply above this limit, and most designers plan for fields in the gap of this magnitude. Once the maximum practical field has been established, the orbit radius can be determined for the type of ion and the ion energy desired. To illustrate the dimensions needed, Table 11-2 shows rough estimates of dimensions and magnet weight for several values of proton energy at an assumed magnetic field of 18 kilogauss at the maximum ion radius.

TABLE 11-2
ESTIMATED MAGNET WEIGHTS

Proton energy, Mev	Orbit radius at 18 kg (m)	Pole diam, ft (approx.)	Magnet weight, tons
100	0.83	6	200
300	1.50	11	1,200
600	2.26	16	4,000
1,000	3.16	22	11,000
2,000	5.18	36	40,000

The basic structure adopted by almost all designers of modern synchro-cyclotron magnets is illustrated in Fig. 11-9. It is a straightforward extension of the classic H frame used for smaller cyclotrons to the larger dimensions required here. Machined low-carbon steel forgings are used for the major components, in unit sizes as large as are practical for production and assembly. The frame consists of six elements: two poles, two yokes, and two uprights. The yokes and uprights for the H frame are rectangular machined forgings arranged to carry the load of the structure and to have a magnetic flux path as short as is practical. The poles are cylinders, machined to a good finish and usually tapered to smaller diameter at the gap. The poles terminate in pole-face disks which form the

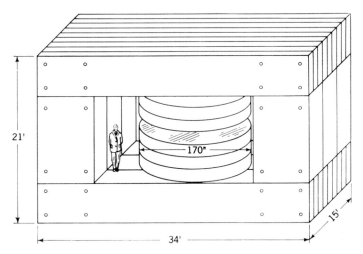

Fig. 11-9. Magnetic circuit for the University of Chicago synchrocyclotron,[8] showing the use of large rectangular forgings to form the structure.

lids of the vacuum chamber; these disks are contoured to give the radially decreasing field required for focusing.

In the smaller magnets at Harvard and at Rochester a single forging is used for each upright, and two parallel bars make up each yoke. The arrangement illustrated in Fig. 11-9 is for the 2200-ton magnet at the University of Chicago; here the maximum weight of each piece was chosen to be less than 100 tons, so the assembly could be handled with a 100-ton crane. For this large magnet three rectangular forgings are used in each upright and eight long slabs in each yoke.

Precision in machining is important to minimize air gaps at surfaces in contact, to give a mechanically stable structure, and to maintain accurately parallel pole faces. Specifications usually call for better than ± 0.010 in. precision in flatness and parallelism. After assembly the rectangular forgings are frequently welded together along the edges in contact to prevent shifting under magnetic stresses and to make the structure mechanically more stable.   In most machines the magnet poles also support the atmospheric load on the vacuum chamber, and the frame must be sufficiently rigid to prevent distortion under the combined load of atmospheric pressure and the magnetic force between poles. Very few bolts are needed in the assembly except those to support the upper pole.   The pole assemblies are held together with long bolts through the yokes or occasionally are welded in place.   In most cases, however, the pole-face disks are solid plates with blind-tapped holes in the face away from the gap, into which long bolts can be inserted to hold the disks in place.

Some few designers have used assemblies of thinner plates (bolted and welded together) such as in the original Berkeley 184-in. magnet, which uses 2-in. mild-steel rolled plate.   However, with increased experience and new techniques in steel manufacturing plants it is now possible to obtain forgings at equivalently low prices.   The structure assembled from large forgings described above has proved to be magnetically more efficient and structurally stronger, and the total cost including assembly is no greater than for an assembly of thinner plates.

Exciting coils for the magnet have also been developed into a nearly standardized design.   Two stacks of flat layer-wound coils are used for the two windings, fitting snugly around the poles.   Variations in design are chiefly in the method of cooling the conductors.   Some designers use oil-bath cooling, with the coils stacked inside an oiltight tank and with the oil recirculated through a heat exchanger for cooling.   Others prefer dry-wound coils, with the cooling fluid contained in separate layers in thermal contact with the conductors.   One satisfactory arrangement is to interweave layers of conductor with layers of water-cooled plate or tubing and to depend on the thermal conduction through an intermediate thin layer of insulation to cool the conductors.   Another method, popular in recent years with the development of new skills in the nonferrous-metals industry, is to use hollow conductors, with cooling water or oil flowing through the channel in the conductor and with electrical insulation provided for the cooling-fluid leads.   The designers' choice of number of turns and of the current-voltage rating of the winding determines the conductor dimensions in each case.

Azimuthal asymmetry of the magnetic field can cause a shift in the center of the orbit and so might reduce the maximum ion energy obtainable at a fixed radius.   Asymmetry can also induce radial oscillations, as described earlier.   Although the presence of such oscillations would not cripple the operation of the accelerator seriously, it is advantageous to keep them to a minimum.   Large radial oscillations, with the associated orbit precession, can add to the difficulty of extracting an emergent beam. An estimate of a reasonable radial amplitude is that it should be no larger than the orbit increase during a phase-oscillation cycle. The maximum amplitude is of the order of 1 to 2 in. for most of the larger accelerators. When this is translated into the maximum allowable magnetic asymmetry, it is about 0.05 per cent, or 1 part in 2000. Pole faces must be flat and parallel to this same precision, a severe criterion in such a large machining operation.

In the Chicago report[8] of magnetic-field measurements azimuthal deviations were observed ten times greater than could be expected from the dimensional discrepancies in the gap between poles. The asymmetry was ascribed to variations in magnetic permeability of the iron in the poles. Empirical shimming was required to correct for these deviations, which was done by welding thin soft-iron plates to the pole tips where indicated. A figure showing these measurements was included in Chap. 8, with a discussion of the techniques used to correct the variations.

The radial tapering of the field needed for magnetic focusing is obtained by contouring the pole faces. This is normally determined by model tests on small-scale magnets using the same quality of iron and the same maximum flux density; in these tests the contour shape is determined by empirical machining of the model pole faces. Experience with smaller cyclotrons shows that a drop of 2 to 3 per cent from center to edge of the uniformly tapered region is adequate to establish a median plane and to provide vertical restoring forces. A larger decrease is acceptable in the synchrocyclotron from the point of view of phase stability, but it increases the range of frequency modulation required and decreases final energy. So the smallest magnetic decrease compatible with focusing is usually used to keep the frequency sweep to a minimum and seldom exceeds 5 or 6 per cent.

Electric focusing due to the accelerating voltage across the D gap is negligible for the synchrocyclotron, because of the relatively low D voltage used. It is essential to extend the region of magnetic focusing in to as small radii as possible, to preserve the beam during the first few hundred revolutions at low energy. To this end the radial decrease of field is sometimes maintained by severe contouring near the center, in the form of a sharp protuberance at the center on each pole face, which reduces the gap length.

Figure 11-10 is a plot of magnetic field versus radius for the Chicago 170-in. synchrocyclotron magnet, for several values of exciting current in the windings and several corresponding values of field. The pole faces are contoured to produce an approximately linear radial decrease from the maximum central field of 19 kilogauss at a rate of about 16 gauss/in., or a total drop over the linear region of about 6 per cent. The contour required to give this shape was obtained from model measurements at the same flux density. At lower flux densities this contour results in lower values of the slope dB/dr, and for central fields below 18 kilogauss a minimum develops in the B-versus-r curve.   If the accelerator were operated at fields below this limit, the ion beam would be lost through nonstable axial oscillations at the location of the $n = 0$ minimum.   So the range of maximum central magnetic fields for which the slope is monotonic with this contouring is restricted to between 18 and 20 kilogauss.

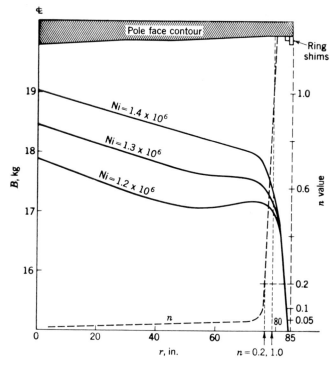

Fig. 11-10. Magnetic field versus orbit radius for the Chicago synchrocyclotron magnet.[8]   The pole-face contour used to produce the radially decreasing field is shown, along with the variation of n value.

The numerical value of n in the region of acceleration varies smoothly from zero at the center to about 0.05 at large radii.   Then, as the field falls off near the pole edge because of fringing effects, the value of n rises sharply.   The extent of the region of small n value is also illustrated in Fig. 11-10, where the rise starts at about 75 in. radius.   At $n = 0.2$ (76.5 in. in the Chicago magnet) the beam blows up because of resonance, as described previously.   This point represents the maximum practical orbit radius and defines the maximum energy.

The magnetic field should also be symmetrical about a median plane, and this plane should be flat and at the geometrical center of the gap. During acceleration the beam will follow the median plane, so deviations should be small compared with the vertical clearance inside the D to allow adequate clearance for vertical oscillations. In practice the median plane is frequently found to vary with radius; a variation of about 1 in. was observed with the Chicago magnet. This was not considered sufficient to require correction, but the relative currents in the two exciting coils were adjusted to shift the average vertical location of the median plane. An azimuthal variation of the median plane would be more serious, since it might set up vertical oscillations. Such a deviation would be observed in the azimuthal uniformity measurements described earlier and would require corrective shims.

11-7. VARIABLE-FREQUENCY OSCILLATOR

The radiofrequency system for powering the D in a synchrocyclotron depends for its frequency variation on the mechanical modulation of the resonant D circuit by a variable capacitor. A capacitor rather than a variable inductance is chosen largely for practical, mechanical reasons. The single-D system is simpler than the double-D used in the standard cyclotron, and it is adequate for the relatively low applied voltage. Electronic methods of frequency modulation were seriously considered in the early planning stages. However, the wide range of frequency modulation and the considerable change in energy stored in a large D and D-stem system make electronic modulation impractical. The mechanical system, on the other hand, acts as a reservoir to store and release electrical energy as required. The electrical efficiency or Q of a tuned mechanical system can be high, so power requirements are a minimum, while that of a broadly tuned electronic system must necessarily be low.

The rf oscillator and modulation system developed for the 37-in. model of the Berkeley synchrocyclotron was the first practical design and pointed the way for future developments. Schmidt[9] described the system in detail, discussing the several possible methods of coupling a variable capacitor to the D circuit. The system was intended to model and approximate the conditions required for the 184-in. machine. The arrangement adopted for the 37-in. model is shown in Fig. 11-11a. In this arrangement the capacitor is located at the far end of the D stem, forming a half-wavelength resonant line. The coupling loop to the oscillator is located along the stem near the rf node of the half-wavelength line.

The half-wave resonant circuit operates in the mode in which the D at one end and the floating plates of the capacitor at the other end have opposite phases or potentials. As the capacitance is varied, the resonant frequency of the circuit changes, and the location of the rf node shifts along the stem. For a frequency change of 10 to 20 per cent the physical shift in location of the node is not large, and a fixed coupling loop which is optimum for some intermediate frequency can be used to feed power into the circuit from an external oscillator over the entire frequency range. The coupling must be tight, with large mutual inductance, so the oscillator frequency will be determined by the resonant frequency of the circuit. Other components of the oscillator must have high rf imped-

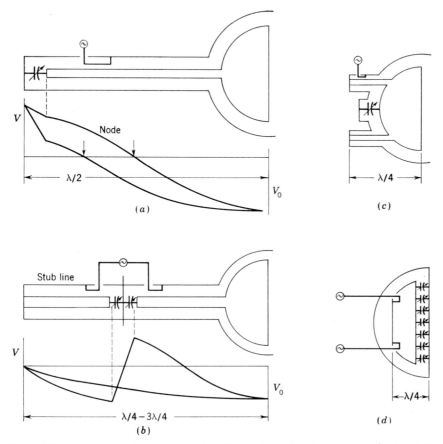

Fig. 11-11. Alternative frequency-modulation systems for the resonant D circuit in a synchrocyclotron: (a) λ/2 circuit; (b) ¾λ circuit; (c) λ/4 circuit for low energies; (d) λ/4 circuit for high energies.

ance or low Q, so they do not affect the frequency. The simplest circuit for this purpose is a grounded-grid self-excited system with cathode excitation supplied through a broadly resonant, fixed-frequency grid circuit. An alternative is a modified Hartley self-excited oscillator in which the excitation comes from a feedback connection from the plate circuit.

A more detailed description of the 37-in. oscillator system was published by MacKenzie and Waithman,[10] after some experience with the earlier circuit. In this modification a wider range of frequency was provided. The grounded-grid oscillator is described and illustrated, and its coupling to the half-wave circuit is analyzed.

With this experience the 184-in. rf system was successful from the start. After two years of operation the results were reported by MacKenzie, Schmidt, Woodyard, and Wouters,[11] describing the acceleration of deuterons to 190 Mev and He^{++} ions to 380 Mev. They give the considerations involved in this initial choice as:

1. The rotary capacitor could operate outside the magnetic field.

2. Design and construction of the D and of the capacitor could proceed independently.

3. Many of the problems involved in the design of the capacitor had been worked out on the 37-in. model.

4. Vacuum systems for the cyclotron D and the capacitor could be independent.

5. The D could be insulated to provide a D bias to control discharges.

6. The oscillator could be coupled to the rf system in air near the nodal point of the transmission lines.

7. The system is readily adjustable to give the desired shape of the D-voltage-versus-frequency characteristics.

Many technical problems were studied and solved during the construction and testing phase. Suitable water cooling had to be installed on the D transmission lines, coupling loops, and the rotary capacitor. All steel surfaces exposed to rf fields were copper-plated to reduce rf resistance. The D was mounted on vacuumtight insulators mechanically arranged to support the extended structure. The capacitor was built with seven rotor disks having 24 teeth each, rotating between stator rings with matching blades and located in a large vacuum chamber with separate high-speed pumps. Scale-model tests were used to determine the capacitance and frequency range in advance of construction. The 100-kw grounded-grid oscillator was copied from the successful design used with the 37-in. magnet.

Operational experience showed a few weak points, which were corrected. Chief of these was the low-voltage glow discharge developed in the large spaces around the D because of electron oscillations in the electric and magnetic fields. The discharge tends to load the D circuit with nonuseful ion currents and so to reduce D voltage undesirably. The discharges were eliminated by adding grounded shields around the D to reduce the volume for electric discharge and by application of a negative bias to the D to sweep out the ions formed in the adjacent region. Another general problem was the elimination of spurious resonances or parasitics. These would show up at some intermediate frequency and cause a wiggle or kink in the frequency characteristic. Methods of identifying the source of such parasitics and eliminating them by use of suitable grounding straps or other techniques call for a high level of experience and ingenuity in the designer, and they are individually characteristic of the particular oscillator circuit.

Later a revised rf system for the Berkeley 184-in. synchrocyclotron was substituted to enable the machine to be tuned for proton acceleration as well. This required a wider frequency range than for deuterons alone, and the entire system was rebuilt. The proton-deuteron system is described by MacKenzie[12] in considerable detail; Fig. 11-11b is a schematic illustration. The primary change was the addition of a stub line behind the capacitor, with a grounded node at the end of the stub line. This is equivalent to making the D circuit a three-quarter-wavelength resonant line, and the system is called a three-quarter-wave circuit. In tuning over the broad frequency range the circuit shifts gradually from a three-quarter-wave resonance at high frequencies to a quarter-wave resonance at low frequencies; the location of the two coupling loops was chosen to feed power over the entire range. The rotating capacitor was built with a sufficiently large change in capacitance to enable operation over the full frequency range required for both proton and deuteron resonance, from 23.2 to 9.5 megacycles. The mechanical details are well described in this article, as also is the electrical problem of suppressing parasitic modes of oscillation. The oscillator was built around two 9C21 tubes in parallel, in a grounded-grid circuit. The physical dimensions of the tubes and oscillator components restricted the tube location and required the use of transmission lines about three-eighths wavelength long to the coupling loop. With this arrangement the oscillator tubes could be located in the region of minimum magnetic field outside the magnet, where the reversed leakage flux cancels the useful flux; the tubes were also shielded magnetically. This new rf system was a complete success and has had a good record of steady operation.

At the University of Chicago[8] the arrangement chosen for the 170-in. machine is essentially the same as the one described above for the proton-deuteron system in the Berkeley 184-inch. It also uses a series capacitor and a quarter-wave stub to form a three-quarter-wavelength line. However, no attempt is made to cover the entire frequency range with a single capacitor, but a proton-deuteron switch system is used which shifts the range of frequency covered by the capacitor to operate with either kind of ion. The stub line is arranged with adjustable shorting bars so its electrical length can be adjusted from outside the vacuum; the lengths of the coupling lines are also adjusted to obtain optimum coupling for the two conditions; metal plates around the rotating capacitor are shifted to alter its series inductance. All these changes are arranged to be made quickly and without disturbing the vacuum when frequency is switched from proton to deuteron resonance. A rather simplified sketch of the rf system is shown in Fig. 11-12. The oscillator power tube is housed in a metal shielded cabinet with transmission lines coupling to the cathode and the plate. The tube is an RCA 5770 triode with water-cooled anode. It is surrounded by a ½-in.-thick iron tube to shield it from the fringing magnetic field of the cyclotron magnet, estimated to be 300 gauss in this region.

Other laboratories have used different arrangements for the rotating capacitor and the rf resonant circuit. Smaller synchrocyclotrons such as the one at Harvard[13] (150-Mev protons) require a smaller range of frequency modulation, and the mechanical and electrical problems are considerably simplified. An elementary quarter-wave resonant circuit can be used, with the D mounted on short stubs supported at the rf node. At Harvard the frequency range is between 25 and 18 megacycles and is obtained with a relatively simple rotating capacitor mounted at the back of the D just outside the magnet poles. The eddy currents induced in the rotor by operation in the fringing magnetic field are not serious; the heating effect is not sufficient to require water cooling. The D is supported on two coaxial quarter-wave stub lines which are large and sturdy and have high electrical efficiency. A schematic diagram of the λ/4 circuit and oscillator is shown in Fig. 11-11c. In principle no insulators would be required in this type of support, since the shorted end of the λ/4 stub line is an electrical node. In practice, however, it is desirable to impress an electrical bias on the D to suppress discharges, so a ring of vacuumtight isolation capacitors is located around the node of each stub line so the D can be electrically insulated. The oscillator circuit uses a pair of 880 tubes in a grounded-plate circuit in which the power is fed directly from the plate to a coupling loop in one D stem through a transmission line, and excitation is taken from another transmission line leading to the cathode.

A similar arrangement of capacitor and D-support stems was chosen for the 240-Mev accelerator at the University of Rochester.[14] With large D size the capacitance is increased and the lengths of the quarter-wave stub supports are shorter. The variable capacitor must also tune over a wider frequency range.

The rf system for the Columbia University[15] 400-Mev synchrocyclotron at the Nevis Laboratory at Irvington, New York, is radically different from the other large machines. It is based on the use of a variable capacitor located along the leading edge of the D in the strong magnetic field between poles. The D is a quarter-wave cavity resonator, entirely enclosed within the main vacuum chamber. Figure 11-11d shows a schematic view of such a cavity-resonator D with the variable capacitor on the leading edge. The sketch illustrates the problem of using a λ/4 stub-line circuit for the D in such large-diameter magnets—the physical length of the oscillating circuit is shorter than the distance from center to

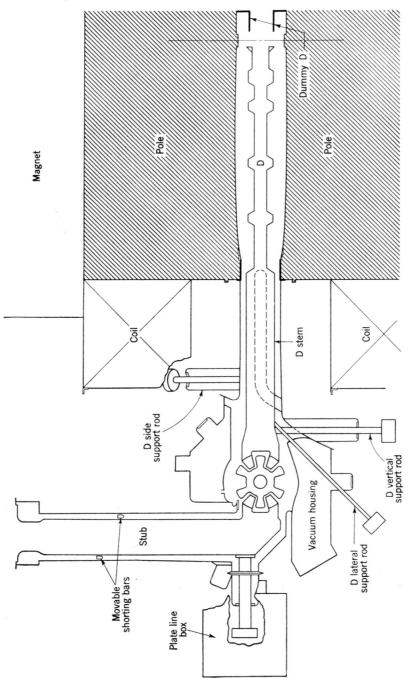

Fig. 11-12. Radiofrequency system for the University of Chicago synchrocyclotron.[8] The oscillator circuit is not shown.

edge of the cyclotron chamber. The capacitor is used to maximum effectiveness when located at the open end of the quarter-wave resonator, where voltage is a maximum, so its capacitance can be a minimum. This system has the advantage that it is essentially free from parasitic oscillations, and the energy is entirely in the fundamental mode. The only serious parasitic encountered was that associated with standing transverse waves from side to side of the flat, hollow cavity. It was eliminated by feeding the cavity symmetrically from two oscillator tubes in parallel with coupling loops located at opposite corners of the cavity. The oscillator circuit and coupling lines are of simple design.

The quarter-wavelength cavity resonator is the only existing type of circuit which could, in principle, be extended to indefinitely large pole-face diameters. However, the mechanical and technical problems of operating the rotating capacitor in the strong magnetic field are severe. Eddy currents generate heat in the rotating blades, and the rotor shaft must be water-cooled. Other problems were met in the maintenance of the insulating supports and bearings of the rotor to prevent frictional heating in vacuum. They have been solved by the development of non-lubricated Teflon bearings. A series of modifications were required before all the problems were solved. Nevertheless, the circuit has performed satisfactorily in operation, and the designers have confidence in the soundness of the principle.

11-8. VARIABLE CAPACITOR

The design of the variable capacitor depends on the range of frequency variation required, the type of circuit in which it is to be operated, and the physical location. As used in the half-wave and three-quarter-wave circuits, the capacitor is located at the outer end of the D stem and can have its own separate vacuum system. The primary problems with a rotating capacitor are the technical ones of structural strength in rotation and electrical insulation of the rotor. Electrical leads must be designed for low rf resistance. Maximum capacitance requires close spacing of the blades, and spark breakdown between blades is a limitation; smooth rounded corners, highly polished surfaces, and fast pumps which result in a good vacuum are essential. A cross section of the Chicago capacitor showing the shape of rotor and stator blades is illustrated in Fig. 11-12. A typical frequency-versus-time characteristic was shown in Fig. 11-4. An approximately linear frequency dependence on time is considered desirable over the operating frequency range, although the phase stability of particle motion holds for any decreasing function. The usual design uses rectangular blades; blade shaping to tailor the shape of the time variation is considered unnecessary.

Capacitors for quarter-wave circuits must operate in the fringing mag-

netic field at the back of the D.   The same basic design of multiple
parallel-plate capacitor is employed, with the plates rotating in the plane
of the field.   Thick metal plates have large eddy currents induced when
rotated at high speeds in the magnetic field.   The designs tend toward
thin plates having high rf conductivity, and the shaft is usually water-
cooled to remove the heat generated by the eddy currents.   In a typical
installation (Rochester) fixed stator blades are mounted on the back of
the D, and the teeth of the rotor blades mesh accurately with 0.10 in.
clearance (Fig. 11-13).   The capacitor is in the main cyclotron vacuum
chamber, and some sparking is observed when discharges occur in the
chamber and raise the gas pressure.

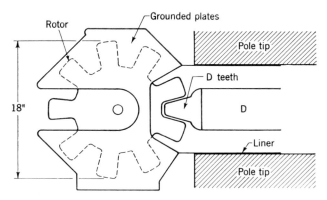

Fig. 11-13. Schematic cross sction of rotating capacitor for the University of
Rochester synchrocyclotron.[14]

The rotating capacitor in the Columbia machine is of even more special
design, since it must operate in the high central magnetic field and must
also be physically small in diameter to fit in the regions between the
outer D surfaces and the pole faces.   A double capacitor is used for symmetry, one above and another below the D.   Each consists of a long row
of small-diameter blades having four teeth mounted on a shaft which
goes across the vacuum chamber.   Maintenance problems have led to
the development of sectional units, each about 2 ft long, which can be
readily replaced.   The chief disadvantage of this system is the radiation
exposure of personnel in maintenance operations, which is partially controlled by using graphite "beam catchers" on the lips of the D to reduce
the intensity of induced radioactivity.
   A new concept for the variable capacitor was developed at Berkeley in
1956 during the rebuilding of the 184-in. machine to produce 720-Mev
protons.   The principle of the vibrating reed or plate has been adopted;
it allows a higher rate of frequency modulation than the rotating capacitor
and results in a correspondingly higher average beam intensity.   In the

Berkeley application a set of four stainless-steel plates are used, each about 4 ft long, 12 in. wide, and tapered in thickness from 2 in. at the fixed end to $\frac{1}{2}$ in. at the vibrating end. These plates are tuned to identical mechanical vibration frequencies of 64/sec and driven by electromagnetic coils in a manner entirely similar to an electrically driven tuning fork. Vibration amplitudes of over 1 in. have been obtained. The vibrating plates provide a variable capacitance to the fixed and insulated D structure, modulating the frequency as desired. This system may well replace rotating capacitors in future synchrocyclotrons. It was also incorporated in the 600-Mev CERN synchrocyclotron.

11-9. ELECTRICAL DISCHARGES

Electrical discharges between the D and ground have caused considerable trouble in the development of synchrocyclotrons. The mechanism of the discharge is a combination of several processes. It closely resembles the cumulative type of blue-glow discharge common in standard cyclotrons, but in the large volumes surrounding the D in synchrocyclotrons it is incident at considerably lower D voltage. One phenomenon which is involved is secondary-electron emission at the surfaces of the D and the liner; another is the collimation of the discharge by the magnetic field, which localizes it around sharp points or surfaces of high electron emissivity and leads to spark breakdown. However, to obtain the ordinary type of dc plasma discharge with the available potentials, the gas pressure would have to be many times larger than the pressure normally used in the vacuum chamber. It is now recognized that electron oscillations in the radiofrequency electric fields are involved, and possibly also large positive-ion orbits, both of which would increase the probability of ionization.

Electron oscillation discharges are caused by oscillatory motion of electrons in the rf fields; the electrons make many traversals of the available space, and ionization in the residual gas is greatly increased. In the stray magnetic field between poles electron paths are restricted to tight helical spirals about the lines of magnetic flux, and the electric-field component effective in producing oscillations is that which parallels the flux lines. This means that the physical distance involved is usually the spacing between the D and the grounded pole faces. In the fringing region at the edge of the poles, however, these path lengths can be considerably greater.

Large amplitude oscillation of electrons with the radiofrequency field occurs over a narrow range of applied voltage and is a function of the frequency. We consider an electron of charge-to-mass ratio e/m in a field $E = V/d$, where d is the available gap length for electron motion and the electron is in an oscillating field of angular frequency ω. The mathematical analysis is identical with that used in Sec. 10-16 in connection with the multipactoring effect. The conclusion is that there is a maximum voltage at which resonance can occur. From Eq. (10-41) this maximum voltage is given by

$$V_{max} = \frac{\omega^2 d^2}{2e/m} \tag{11-5}$$

As an example, consider a synchrocyclotron operating at a frequency of 20 megacycles, and assume a typical gap 10 cm long. We find for the maximum resonant voltage: $V_{max} = 450$ volts. This is sufficient to impart a maximum energy of 225 ev to the electrons, at which energy the probability of ionization is near optimum. As long as the peak voltage across the gap is below this limit, electrons will stay in the gap and oscillate in resonance with the field, causing a cumulative build-up of ionization which culminates in a blue-glow discharge. This heavy loading of the oscillator holds D voltage low, so the chamber continues in the discharge condition indefinitely. However, if the voltage can be made to exceed this resonant value, the amplitude will exceed the physical dimensions of the gap; electrons will impinge on the metal of the D or the chamber wall, and the cumulative ionization will be reduced. The discharge can be avoided if D voltage can be "jumped" through this resonance region rapidly, or if the free electrons in the region can be removed by some additional agency.

We note from Eq. (11-5) that the combination of high frequency and long gaps used in the synchrocyclotron raises the resonant voltage to a value at which ionization becomes efficient. If either the frequency or the gap spacing could be reduced, the voltage limit would be lowered and cumulative ionization would not be so probable. Yet frequency is fixed by the proton resonance relation, and the relatively wide spacings are necessary to keep capacitance low so as to have an efficient resonant D circuit at this frequency. So the problem of electron oscillations is inherent in the design parameters required for the larger proton synchrocyclotrons.

The electron multipactor effect, which has been a severe problem in proton linacs, was discussed in Sec. 10-16. It is probable that multipactoring is a factor in the synchrocyclotron discharge problem, although conditions are more complicated and it is difficult to identify multipactoring experimentally. In this effect the electron oscillations in resonance with the applied rf field would result in the production of secondary electrons at the electrodes on impact. Secondary emission would increase the electron density and so would aggravate the discharge.

Several mechanisms are available to control this type of discharge, once its nature is understood. The simplest and most practical technique is to impose a dc bias field between the D and ground. This requires that the D be insulated. Such a field sweeps out electrons as they are formed, holding the electron density below that critical value required to initiate the cumulative blue-glow-type discharge. This technique was readily available in the Berkeley synchrocyclotron, since the design of the oscillator circuit required that the D be mounted on insulators. The application of a dc bias of several thousand volts was found to control the discharges. The opportunity to use dc biasing is one of the considerable advantages of the half-wave and three-quarter-wave resonant systems. It has been applied to all synchrocyclotrons of this design.

Circuits utilizing the quarter-wave resonant system do not have the advantage of an insulated D, since the simplest mechanical technique would be to support it on short stub lines attached to the chamber wall. At Harvard the designers inserted a ring of isolation capacitors in each stub line at the rf node in order to insulate the D and allow dc biasing to be used. At Rochester a set of small electrodes ("spot grids") was installed on the copper liners surrounding the D; these electrodes could be biased to provide a clearing field. Considerable development was required to find the proper number and location of such grids.

Another technique which might be useful in suppressing discharge would be to use a power amplifier rather than a self-excited oscillator to drive the D circuit, and to drive the circuit through the critical voltage region fast enough to avoid initiating the discharge. The electron-oscillation effect is a resonance phenomenon which is effective only over a certain range of applied voltage. If the voltage can be increased rapidly enough, the time during which it will be in the resonance range will be too short to allow a cumulative build-up of oscillations, and the discharge cannot start. This may be practical with the resonant circuits used in cyclotrons which have a relatively low Q. If driven by a power amplifier which is sharply pulsed, the sensitive voltage region could be traversed rapidly. Some designers believe that this technique might eliminate the need for D biasing.

11-10. VACUUM CHAMBER

The main vacuum chamber houses the accelerating electrode or D and provides an evacuated region between pole tips in which ions are accelerated. Designers of large synchrocyclotrons have found it desirable to support the atmospheric pressure load on the pole tips. The top and bottom surfaces of the chamber have large holes equipped with ring vacuum seals to accommodate the iron pole tips, which form the faces of the chamber. Large side ports are also required for inserting the D and for mounting pumps and probes. The chamber itself is little more than a structural framework, supporting the atmospheric load only on the

side surfaces.   A typical and simple chamber is that for the Rochester[14]
machine (see Fig. 11-14).

The most successful designs use nonmagnetic stainless-steel plate,
welded to form the chamber shell and having machined pads around the
port apertures to provide good gasket surfaces.   The techniques of welding vacuumtight seals in nonmagnetic metals have been highly perfected
during the past 10 years.   It is now possible to obtain reliable welding
jobs from many fabricating plants.

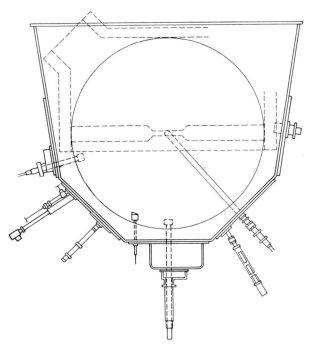

Fig. 11-14. Welded stainless-steel vacuum chamber of the Rochester synchrocyclotron,[14] showing ports for insertion of the D electrode, ion source, and various probe
targets.

Vacuum-seal designs have been discussed in earlier chapters.   The
accumulated experience in vacuum engineering has led to a wide variety
of excellent designs for all types of seals.   In the synchrocyclotron chambers with their large volumes and many ports this experience has been
put to good use.   The number of satisfactory designs is so great that
detailed description is impractical.

The inner surfaces of the chamber, including the pole tips, are usually
lined with water-cooled copper sheet to provide a low-resistance return
path for the rf currents in the D circuit.   Good electrical contact must
be maintained across any gasket joints, such as at port cover plates.   A

variety of ingenious techniques have been developed to solve such technical problems, and these are adequately described in the several laboratory progress reports referenced earlier.

Vacuum techniques have also been described in some detail in earlier chapters. The pumps and the vacuum techniques needed for the synchrocyclotron differ only in scale from those successful in smaller vacuum chambers. Many competent designs showing great individuality are evidence of the high state of perfection to which the field of vacuum engineering has now progressed. The variety and scope of such designs and their many details cannot be reported here, but they are available in the form of blueprints and technical data in the several laboratories.

11-11. ION SOURCE

Many laboratories have engaged in independent development studies of the ion source, since it is a straightforward problem in gaseous discharge and electronics. In most cases the result has been a relatively minor modification of the hot-cathode arc common in standard cyclotrons (see Chap. 6). The chief problems encountered involve cathode life, erosion of the cone tip, cooling for high-current operation, and the mechanical manipulation of the source and cathode stems. A typical source is that developed at the University of California and copied in principle in several other laboratories. The source head is illustrated in Fig. 11-15. It uses a "hairpin" of large-diameter tungsten as a cathode and a graphite cone to condense the arc and limit gas evolution. In normal operation a potential of about 200 volts will produce a total discharge current of several amperes with a hydrogen gas flow of about 0.1 liter/hr. The useful ions are formed in the emergent stream of gas just outside the cone tip by the electron beam issuing from the discharge and collimated by the magnetic field. The ions are pulled from this region by the rf fields on the D; usually extensions or feelers are attached to the D near the center to increase the electric field near the source. The limiting factor is the chamber pressure due to the emergent gas, controlled by the size of the cone-tip aperture and the pumping speed. In each installation this balance is achieved by experiment, usually resulting in a chamber pressure of about 2×10^{-5} mm Hg. Beam intensities obtained with such a source are of the order of 200 μa peak during the acceptance pulse.

The mechanical features of ion sources also have much in common. In essentially all installations the source is installed through a side port on the end of a long tube, with an internal cathode stem. A vacuum lock is normally installed to enable replacement of the cathode without loss of chamber vacuum. Because of the length of the stem this involves a mechanism to retract the cathode many feet. Mechanical devices are also needed to locate the source tip both horizontally and vertically;

these usually include a flexible joint such as a metal bellows at the chamber wall and mechanical screws or adjustments

The source stem must be at ground potential, and special spring contacts have been developed to make contact with the adjacent copper liner in order to prevent rf potentials from building up along the length of the stem. Without this precaution an rf arc which may release gas and cause discharges can develop between stem and ground.

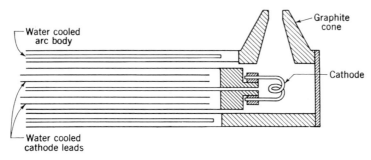

Fig. 11-15. Typical synchrocyclotron ion source.

11-12. BEAM INTENSITY AND PROBE TARGETS

Resonant-ion beam intensity is reduced below that obtained from fixed-frequency cyclotrons by the effective duty cycle or the capture efficiency, which is about 0.01, so the time-average intensities are about 1 per cent of those possible with the standard cyclotron. At Berkeley, where the development has proceeded for the longest time, resonant-ion beams up to 2.0 μa are obtained. Other laboratories report beams of between 0.1 and 1.0 μa.

The beam occurs in bursts at the modulation frequency, which for a typical installation is about 100 per second. Each burst extends over a time interval determined by the rate of expansion of orbits against a fixed target. This time interval represents 500 to 1000 ion revolutions, depending on conditions. If the amplitude of radial free oscillations is smaller than the radial phase amplitude, the time interval for the beam to clean up against the probe would be about a half-period of phase oscillations, or about 500 revolutions in a typical case. If the free oscillations have larger amplitude, the burst length may be extended to several phase oscillations. An example of the beam observed with the Berkeley machine was shown in Fig. 11-8, covering several phase periods and illustrating the effects of orbit precession. The total burst time observed, about 75 μsec, represents about 800 orbit revolutions.

Higher cycling repetition rates will increase average beam intensity and will also increase the efficiency of taking data with electronic detection equipment, which is frequently limited in the number of counts per pulse which can be recorded. The present trend toward using the vibrating-reed type of variable capacitor should result in higher intensities in future machines.

Many experiments with the synchrocyclotron can be conducted using targets mounted on probes inserted to various radial positions through a sliding seal in the chamber wall. The radial location of the probe is a measure of the ion-beam energy, and excitation functions or other experiments requiring variation of beam energy are readily performed by inserting the probe to different radii. Certain properties of the beam must be considered. For example, as ion-beam energy increases at large radii, the range of the ions in the target also increases, and ions may penetrate a thin target. If this happens, the ions of reduced energy will revolve in the magnetic field in smaller orbits; some will be reaccelerated and may again strike the probe. A given target may be a "thick" target when used at small radii and a "thin" target at the periphery. For some experiments a very thin target is desired, in order to study a narrow energy range. The ions will penetrate such a target many times. Scattering will occur, as well as absorption of energy, and many of the ions will be deflected by small angles. Such deflected ions will perform free oscillations and may strike the target in the next revolution over a wide surface area. This spreading of the beam can be observed by removing the target and scanning the surface for induced radioactivity. Any conclusions inferred from such observations regarding the size of the beam must take into account the possibility of penetration and scattering.

The radial oscillations of the beam, both synchronous and free, will affect the distribution of the beam over the leading edge of the target. The precession of orbits caused by the mismatch of radial-oscillation frequency with the circular motion has been described in an earlier section. Precession will cause the beam to strike the target at a finite distance back from the leading edge of the target. To observe it a thick target is required, in order to prevent penetration and scattering, which would also diffuse the beam. The spread in ion energy for particles striking the target is also affected by the magnitude of the radial phase oscillations; this effect has also been described in the earlier discussion of operational results with the Berkeley machine.

When deuterons strike a probe target, they can disintegrate into protons and neutrons. The neutrons emerge in the forward direction in a narrow cone; they have an energy distribution which is sharply peaked about a mean value of half the deuteron energy. The energy spread depends on momentum transfer in the interaction, including the effect of the distribution of internal momentum between the components of the deuteron. This beam of roughly monoenergetic neutrons is of considerable value for certain special experiments. Protons from the splitting of the deuteron have a similar energy and angular distribution, but they are deflected by the magnetic field in circular orbits of roughly half that for the deuterons, so they return to about the center of the chamber after a half-revolution. Detection instruments such as photographic plates placed near the center of the chamber, located above or below the plane of the beam, have been used to observe such secondaries. The cyclotron magnetic field provides energy analysis of the protons.

When the synchrocyclotron is accelerating protons and they are allowed to strike a probe target, a beam of neutrons emerges in the forward direction with energies ranging up to the maximum proton energy.

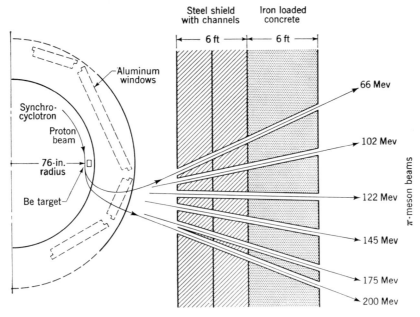

Fig. 11-16. Target and shielding arrangements for emergent meson beams in the Chicago synchrocyclotron.[8]

This is interpreted as an "exchange of charge" process between the protons and neutrons in the target nuclei. Maximum neutron energies are much higher than those from the deuteron split-up.

Mesons are produced above some threshold energy in targets by all particles. This threshold is about 150 Mev for protons, 190 Mev for deuterons, and 250 Mev for He++ ions. The "pi" mesons are produced directly in nuclear reactions and have the highest intensity; "mu" mesons are observed primarily as decay products of the pi's; neutral π mesons produce high-energy photons, a process investigated in detail for the first time in the Berkeley laboratory.

Mesons originating at a probe target can emerge from the cyclotron and will be analyzed and partially focused by the cyclotron field.   Beams of π mesons of a narrow energy spread can traverse channels in the shield and emerge to be used for experiments.   At Chicago, for example, the intensity of mesons produced by 1 μa of 450-Mev protons on the probe target is about 4×10^{10} mesons/sec.   In the most favorable energy channel about 10^3 π mesons/(cm²)(sec) are available in an energy range of 122 ± 3 Mev.   Figure 11-16 shows the arrangements in the Chicago installation to provide such analyzed beams of mesons for experiments.

11-13. EMERGENT BEAM

The deflection of resonant ions in the synchrocyclotron to produce an emergent beam is complicated by the fact that the change in orbit radius per turn is small.   The method which was successful in the standard cyclotron cannot be applied directly for several reasons.   A solid septum, even if accurately shaped and located, would intercept practically the entire beam.   Furthermore, deflection must start inside the $n = 0.2$ point where the beam blows up into vertical oscillations, and it must extend at least as far as the $n = 1.0$ radius where radial stability ceases and the beam enters opening spiral orbits.   So the deflector must pull the beam through a large radial distance.   The electric field required to bring the beam out of the magnetic field within a reasonable length of arc is very high for the high-energy particles, and voltage insulation for the deflecting potential becomes a serious problem.   Finally, because of their phase oscillations, the ions are not so tightly bunched in phase while crossing the accelerating gap as the resonant ions in the standard cyclotron.   The energy gain in the last turn (and the equivalent change in orbit radius) varies widely over the range of phase oscillation, and it may be zero.

The rate of expansion per turn ΔR depends on the maximum accelerating voltage V, the phase of crossing the gap ϕ, particle energy and velocity, and the radial gradient of the magnetic field given by the index n.   Bohm and Foldy[5] give this rate as

$$\frac{\Delta R}{R} \simeq \frac{1}{(1 - n)\beta^2} \frac{2eV \sin \phi}{W} \tag{11-6}$$

where W is total energy (including rest energy) and β is the relativistic parameter v/c.   A simpler form of this relation was used in Sec. 6-7 to describe the rate of expansion for the nonrelativistic particles in the standard cyclotron; it led to ΔR's of the order of 3 mm, quite adequate to pass behind the thin septum used to form the inner face of the deflector channel.   However, for the synchrocyclotron the calculated ΔR is less than 0.1 mm in practical cases; an example is given in the reference above.

Such a beam would be entirely lost against a septum if the orbits were concentric.

On the other hand, certain characteristics of particle motion in the synchrocyclotron can be utilized for ejection of a beam. The stability of free oscillations in the radially decreasing magnetic field makes it possible to excite wide-amplitude radial oscillations and throw the particles out locally beyond their equilibrium orbit location. At the maximum radius where $n = 0.2$ the frequency of such radial oscillations is about $0.9f_0$, so the location of maximum radial amplitude precesses about the cyclotron, moving about one-tenth of a cycle or 36° per turn. The combination of precession and large radial amplitude can spread the beam by a much greater amount than the ΔR calculated from the energy increase per turn. Phase oscillations produce a breathing motion of the equilibrium orbit and also affect the radial motion. A superposition of the maxima of radial phase oscillations and radial free oscillations gives the largest radial displacement. Vertical free oscillations can also be induced locally to deflect the resonant ions and may be utilized to pull a beam of emergent ions from the stable orbits.

The method used to eject an emergent beam in the Berkeley 184-in. machine was to set up large-amplitude radial oscillations with a pulsed electric deflector; the deflected ions then entered a magnetic shielding channel where the weakened field allowed them to fly out on an opening spiral path. A full description is given by Powell, Henrich, Kerns, Sewell, and Thornton.[16] A schematic view of the arrangement is shown in Fig. 11-17. The deflector system consists of four 1-in.-square bars spaced about the median plane, with the two inner bars pulsed negative and the two outer bars positive, extending around 120° in arc. Particles are deflected inward to set up radial oscillations, and the channel is curved to follow the trajectory. The next outward maximum of the radial oscillations comes at about one full turn from the location of the deflector, and the entry of the magnetic shield is at this point, placed about 2 in. radially outside the location of the deflector.

The pulsed voltage comes from a pulse transformer described by Kerns, Baker, Edwards, and Farly.[17] It produces a potential difference of ± 100 kv and has a pulse rise time of about 0.1 μsec. The electric deflector is pulsed by a timing system at the instant the expanding beam reaches the radius of the deflector entry. The vertical spacing between bars ($1\frac{3}{8}$ in.) allows about half the ions to reach orbits of this radius. The 0.1-μsec pulse rise is about equal to the period of one revolution of the ions, so a phasing circuit designed to time the pulse to the angular position of the ion bunch gave only a minor improvement. Measurements showed that about 10 per cent of the resonant beam which reached the deflector entry was deflected into sufficiently large oscillations to reach the entry to the magnetic shield.

The magnetic shield has undergone considerable development, starting with a structure of two concentric iron tubes, which were modified to a set of vertical bars designed to weaken the field on the median plane and finally to a tube of elliptic cross section.   The presence of these shields affects the field inside the region where resonant ions circulate and must be corrected by still other shims in the form of bars which are carefully designed and located close to the pole faces.   The magnetic channel is curved to follow the opening spiral path out through the fringing field of the magnet.   About 10 per cent of the ions entering the magnetic

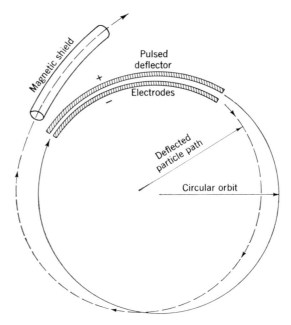

Fig. 11-17. Schematic arrangement of the pulsed electrostatic deflector and magnetic channel for the 184-in. synchrocyclotron at the University of California.

channel emerge in a reasonably well-collimated beam.   The over-all efficiency of the Berkeley ejection system is about 1 per cent.

A more efficient system for ejecting an emergent beam is the "regenerative" deflector first proposed by Tuck and Teng[8] of the University of Chicago synchrocyclotron group and first successfully applied by A. V. Crewe at the University of Liverpool.   In this system one of two magnetic anomalies is located in the vicinity of the $n = 0.20$ orbit radius to set up radial free oscillations of increasing magnitude.   The primary advantage is that this "static" deflector operates on each particle in the resonant beam as it approaches the maximum radius.

The mechanism of the regenerative deflector can be explained most readily by reference to the two-unit system proposed by Tuck and Teng. The first magnetic anomaly, called a peeler following the betatron usage, weakens the magnetic field over a short arc (about 8 in. long). The cross section of such a peeler is illustrated in the sketch of Fig. 7-17; magnetic flux is bypassed through the iron back-leg of the peeler, weakening the field between the jaws. In this weak field ions acquire an outward radial displacement relative to a circular orbit; this represents a radial free oscillation, which reaches its maximum outward amplitude after traveling about 90°. The second magnetic anomaly is a regenerator which strengthens the magnetic field locally, placed about 90° beyond the

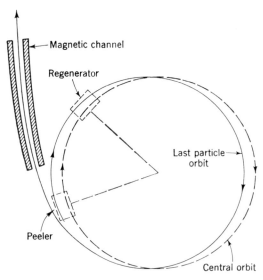

Fig. 11-18. Regenerative deflector system for ejecting an emergent beam, proposed by Tuck and Teng.[8]

peeler. It consists of iron bars above and below the central plane which concentrate magnetic flux and increase intensity at the center. The regenerator gives a second impulse, inward, which causes a further increase in radial amplitude. The increased amplitude causes the ion to swing first inward and then outward again, where it reaches the azimuthal location of the peeler with a net outward displacement. The increased penetration into still weaker fields produces larger amplitudes, so it penetrates more deeply into the regenerator field, etc. Since the process is regenerative, the displacement grows exponentially. Ultimately the amplitudes become sufficient for the change in radial location in a single turn ΔR to become large enough for the ion to pass behind the peeler and enter a magnetic shielding channel, which allows the beam to emerge from the field.

In the Liverpool application the peeler was used as described above, and the regenerator was located about 45° beyond. Analysis of the motion showed the importance of a linear (constant-n-value) decrease of field in the peeler and a linear increase in the regenerator, in order to have a constant coefficient in the exponential term describing the increase in amplitude. Magnetic measurements were made of the fields around the peeler, regenerator, and shield, and correcting shims were designed to preserve the uniformity of field on the central plane inside these magnetic anomalies. The ΔR obtained in the last turn, after exponential growth of amplitude, was about 3 in. About 20 per cent of the resonant beam entered the channel of the magnetic shield; with the initial shield about 5 per cent emerged as a collimated beam which formed a spot about 1 in. in diameter at a distance of 20 ft from the cyclotron.

A later revision of the Chicago deflector system, utilizing the experience and improved analysis of the Liverpool group, has resulted in an intensity of about 10 per cent in an emergent beam. In this revision the regenerator is used as before, but the peeler is eliminated. The property of the peeler of providing a radially decreasing magnetic field is not essential, since the fringing field of the magnet provides such a decrease around the entire orbit. New analyses showed the optimum location and strength of the regenerator unit relative to the opening of the magnetic channel. The back-leg of the peeler, formerly responsible for some intensity loss, is removed, so the final intensities are higher.

The most significant advantage of the magnetic deflector is that it acts on all particles of the beam sequentially as they expand progressively past some fixed radius and so spreads the deflection pulse over hundreds of cycles at the resonant frequency. Such a long ejection pulse is highly desirable for electronic detection instruments. The emergent beam can be focused to small diameter and passed through channels in a shield. Its monoenergetic character and its small size, which allows the use of small targets, make the emergent beam far more valuable for research than the resonant beam, which required the use of probe targets.

11-14. CONTROLS

An important part of the technical development of all accelerators is the design of circuits for supplying power to the several electrodes and other auxiliary equipment, along with the system of adjustments and controls. The most obvious component of the control system is the operator's console, on which are mounted all the switches, meters, and control devices. It is such a necessary feature in any accelerator installation that it is usually taken for granted; since it is considered to be primarily the product of electronic and electrical engineering, it is seldom featured in any physical design study. However, much experience has gone into the design of control systems and the operator's console, and many technical improvements have been incorporated. This experience has followed the radio and electronics fields, and many of the improvements have been taken from these engineering developments. But the particular needs of accelerators have made each control system unique, and many special devices have been developed by the designers. This is particularly true in the synchroaccelerators, where the pulsed duty cycle requires special instrumentation to display and control the operation of the accelerator. For this reason an exception is made in this chapter by describing the control system in some detail, as representative of the special problems for synchronous accelerators.

The more recent development of control consoles has tended toward simplification, with the minimum of starting switches, meters, control knobs, pilot lights, etc., in order not to confuse the eye and hand of the operator. Small wires and low power levels at the console are the rule. Power-switching relays and adjustable controls used for more permanent settings are relegated to auxiliary relay racks which do not require continuous maintenance or attention. The usual layout of a synchrocyclotron control room includes a relatively compact console desk, with the necessary indicators closely grouped and available to an operator in a swivel chair, and rows of relay racks along the sides of the room in which the power controls are located.

The typical console is arranged in a three-sided arc like the mirrors on a dressing table. A flat table surface for keeping records, at the proper height for a seated operator, extends around the arc. Sloping panels within easy arm's reach have all necessary control buttons and switches. The important switches and controls are prominently located in the center, usually with a beam current indicator directly in front of the operator. Auxiliary switches are grouped on the sides according to function. Pilot lights and other indicators are displayed near the appropriate switches and controls, and banks of indicators for circuits such as cooling-water flow and pump heaters are located where the operator can keep them in view without strain.

The control room must be located behind suitable radiation shields, but should be as close as possible to the accelerator, so the operator or his assistants can move readily between the control console and the machine for maintenance and test operations. In some cases observation windows have been built into the shielding wall; an example is a water-filled tank equipped with glass windows. This is probably undesirable in modern high-intensity machines, but is a relic of the days when the operator's eye and ear were important instruments for observing spark breakdowns or other phenomena. A modern equivalent is a television camera, with a display at the console.

Cathode-ray tubes with time sweeps are prominently featured on the consoles of all pulsed synchronous accelerators and are arranged to super-pose successive pulses.   Multiple-channel switches allow the operator to display any one of several variables on the scope.   The time of sweep can be varied to expand the early stages for detailed study of injection phe-nomena or to observe the output beam at the end of the acceleration. Or, the frequency-modulation cycle in the resonant circuit can be dis-played to observe any distortion of wave shape.   A superimposed pulse from the ion-source pulser will show the frequency at the start of acceler-ation, and the effect of pulse-delay circuits can be studied.   Another technique is to display the rf waveform and study the phase timing of the deflector pulse applied to the emergent beam.

Starting switches and adjustment controls for many circuits are needed on the console.   The magnet current supply customarily is a dc generator connected permanently to the magnet coils and driven by an ac induction or synchronous motor.   Excitation for the generator may come from a smaller dc generator which is itself excited by an electronically regulated field supply.   Starting switches will operate power relays in the ac power lines.   A reading of magnet current can be obtained from a shunt in series with the coils, and it is usually displayed on a panel meter.   Fine variations in current are best observed through the magnitude of the electronically regulated exciter field current, often by use of a potentiom-eter which displays a small difference between the field current and a constant bias.   The magnet current regulator should be capable of setting any value of magnet current and of maintaining constancy to within about 1 part in 1000 over the normal operating range.   Controls for turning on and adjusting the regulator are also installed on the panels at the console.

Suitable overload relays, temperature indicators, pilot lights to indicate successive stages of the operation of starting, and other monitoring sys-tems will also be grouped on the console.   Vacuum systems require many control switches and indicators.   Mechanical fore-vacuum pumps, rough-vacuum pressure gauges, cutoff valves, diffusion-pump heaters, water thermocouples, water-flow indicators, high-vacuum valves, valve-position indicators, and high-vacuum ionization gauges—these are the essential elements which require switches, interlock circuits, or pilot lights on the operator's console.   Automatic interlocks of many types are helpful in such a complicated system.   A high reading on a rough-vacuum pressure gauge or failure of the cooling-water flow can be used to close valves or turn off pump heaters.   A common arrangement on the panel display is a compact group of associated display elements with the pilot lights, position indicators, and meters disposed in vertical columns above the appropriate starting switches.

A complete set of controls for the rf oscillator and a set for the motor driving the rotary capacitor are also needed.   These must include all the necessary indicating instruments for monitoring, such as grid-current, plate-current, grid-bias, and plate-voltage meters. Pulsed operation of the oscillator may be desirable, and it is used in some installations to reduce the average power requirements. If it is used, controls for these pulsing circuits are required. The variable speed drive of the rotary capacitor should be controllable from the console, as should the starting switches. Another item associated with the rf oscillator is the power supply to provide the dc field used for suppression of discharges in the chamber.

The ion source requires cathode heating power, arc voltage supply, and gas flow. Each of these requires controls at the console. The ion source is often sensitive to discharges and must be readjusted to maintain a steady output; this may require voltage and current regulator circuits as well. The mechanical adjustments for the location of the source should also be made by remote control from the console; directional drive controls and position indicators should be located at the operator's bench. Other mechanical adjustments, such as those which determine the location of the probe target, require similar controls. Servosystems are frequently used for such purposes.

For such complex systems a well-designed set of protective mechanisms and interlocks is essential. Water-supply circuits for cooling are generally equipped with flow indicators which are interlocked to turn off power circuits in event of water failure. High-voltage equipment is protected by screens or shields with hinged doors or removable panels for maintenance; electrical interlocks on such doors will turn off power supplies when the doors are opened. Operation sequences should also be interlocked; ion source, water-cooling circuits, cathode heaters, etc., should all be on and their interlocks open before rf power switches can operate. Doors or gates in the radiation shielding must also be interlocked to prevent personnel from entering a region of high radiation intensity accidentally.

The over-all problem of circuit design, controls, cabling, and protective equipment is highly involved in a large accelerator installation. The efficient operation of the machine requires that this problem be solved in such a manner that the controls actually handled by the operator are few and simple. The trend in design is toward increasing use of automation, so the operators can concentrate on operating problems which require human intelligence for their solution.

REFERENCES

1. E. M. McMillan, *Phys. Rev.*, **68**:143 (1945).
2. V. Veksler, *J. Phys. (U.S.S.R.)*, **9**:153 (1945).
3. J. R. Richardson, K. R. MacKenzie, E. J. Lofgren, and B. T. Wright, *Phys. Rev.*, **69**:669 (1946).

4. W. M. Brobeck, E. O. Lawrence, K. R. MacKenzie, E. M. McMillan, R. Serber, D. C. Sewell, K. M. Simpson, and R. L. Thornton, *Phys. Rev.*, **71**:449 (1947).
5. D. Bohm and L. L. Foldy, *Phys. Rev.*, **70**:249 (1946).
6. D. Bohm and L. L. Foldy, *Phys. Rev.*, **72**:649 (1947).
7. L. R. Henrich, D. C. Sewell, and J. Vale, *Rev. Sci. Instr.*, **20**:887 (1949).
8. "170 Inch Synchrocyclotron," Institute for Nuclear Studies, University of Chicago, I (July, 1948); II (July, 1949); III (July, 1950); IV (July, 1951).
9. F. H. Schmidt, *Rev. Sci. Instr.*, **17**:301 (1946).
10. K. R. MacKenzie and V. B. Waithman, *Rev. Sci. Instr.*, **18**:900 (1947).
11. K. R. MacKenzie, F. H. Schmidt, J. R. Woodyard, and L. F. Wouters, *Rev. Sci. Instr.*, **20**:126 (1948).
12. K. R. MacKenzie, *Rev. Sci. Instr.*, **22**:302 (1951).
13. "Harvard 95 Inch Cyclotron," Office of Naval Research Report NR-026-012 (July, 1950).
14. "130 inch Rochester Cyclotron," Office of Naval Research Report N6-ori-126, II (July, 1946–July, 1949).
15. E. T. Booth (ed.), Columbia Cyclotron Report (Mar. 30, 1950).
16. W. M. Powell, L. R. Henrich, Q. A. Kerns, D. C. Sewell, and R. L. Thornton, *Rev. Sci. Instr.*, **19**:506 (1948).
17. Q. A. Kerns, W. R. Baker, R. F. Edwards, and G. M. Farly, *Rev. Sci. Instr.*, **19**:899 (1948).

At the head of the facing page is an illustration of the 350-Mev electron synchrotron at the University of Glasgow.   (Courtesy of P. I. Dee.)

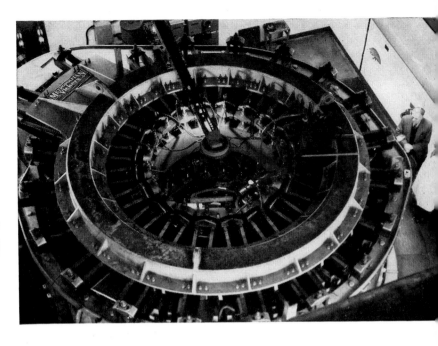

12

The Electron Synchrotron

In the synchrotron particles are accelerated to high energies in an orbit of roughly constant radius. Energy is supplied to the particles by a radiofrequency field provided at one or more points around the orbit. As particle energy increases, the magnetic guide field in the circular orbit also increases, at a rate which matches the increasing momentum of the particles. The magnet is operated cyclically from low to high magnetic fields as the particles are accelerated, resulting in a pulsed output of high-energy particles at the cycling frequency. Because of the varying magnetic field, the magnet cores are laminated as in a transformer.

Phase stability exists in the synchrotron (see Sec. 9-8) and provides a mechanism by which the particle energy is made to keep pace with the rising magnetic field. When electrons are accelerated, the phase-stable acceleration automatically follows any reasonable rate of rise of magnetic field and maintains constant orbit radius. This is due to the fact that electrons reach relativistic velocities at quite low energies ($v = 0.98c$ at 2 Mev), so the angular velocity at fixed orbit radius approaches a fixed value and the electrons can be accelerated by a constant-frequency radio-frequency supply which is basically simple in design and for which power requirements are modest.

At low energies the frequency of particle motion in a magnetic field depends strongly on energy, which means that the frequency of the accelerating field must be varied to match the particle frequency. This is a major problem in the acceleration of protons, and it requires a wide range of frequency modulation during the acceleration cycle (see Sec. 13-7). With electrons the need for frequency modulation is minimal and can be removed by using an alternative system for acceleration up to a few Mev energy.

The synchrotron has to a large extent displaced the betatron as a source of high-energy electrons. The much lighter ring-magnet structure which provides the guide field in the synchrotron is simpler and less costly than the laminated-core magnet needed to supply induced voltage for acceleration in a betatron. In the synchrotron one or more compact cavity resonators provide radiofrequency electric fields for acceleration. Furthermore, the radiative losses by electrons at high energies are corrected automatically in the synchrotron by phase shifts which increase the accelerating fields; the complicated compensating devices necessary to achieve high energies in the betatron are not required. Even in the 20- to-50 Mev energy range, in which there are many medical and industrial applications, smaller synchrotrons are competing effectively with betatrons as sources of X rays.

12-1. STORY OF THE DEVELOPMENT

Unlike earlier accelerators, most of which required slow and tedious development starting with small sizes at low energies, the electron synchrotron was conceived in its full stature as a high-energy accelerator. The first installation (by McMillan at the University of California) was designed for 320 Mev, at which energy the radiations are capable of producing mesons. Within a few years a half-dozen machines of about this energy were started in the United States, with others abroad. Seldom has a new accelerator been exploited with such promptness. The reason is that the principle was announced in 1945, just at the end of World War II when scientists had returned to their universities and were eager to engage in the new field of high-energy physics.

The development started suddenly in 1945 with independent publications describing the principle of phase-stable acceleration by McMillan[1] at the University of California and by Veksler[2] in the U.S.S.R. In his first publication McMillan discussed the application of the principle to an electron accelerator and named it the synchrotron. Readers immediately recognized the soundness, simplicity, and completeness of this new proposal. No better method can be used to illustrate the features described above than to quote directly from McMillan's brief paper, which stands as a classic in accelerator history:

One of the most successful methods for accelerating charged particles to very high energies involves the repeated application of an oscillating electric field, as in the cyclotron. If a very large number of individual accelerations is required, there may be difficulty in keeping the particles in step with the electric field.   In the case of the cyclotron this difficulty appears when the relativistic mass change causes an appreciable variation in the angular velocity of the particles.

The device proposed here makes use of a "phase stability" possessed by certain orbits in a cyclotron.   Consider, for example, a particle whose energy is such that its angular velocity is just right to match the frequency of the electric field. This will be called the equilibrium energy.   Suppose further that the particle crosses the accelerating gaps just as the electric field passes through zero, changing in such a sense that an earlier arrival of the particle would result in an acceleration.   This orbit is obviously stationary.   To show that it is stable, suppose that a displacement in phase is made such that the particle arrives at the gaps too early.   It is then accelerated; the increase in energy causes a decrease in angular velocity, which makes the time of arrival tend to become later.   A similar argument shows that a change of energy from the equilibrium value tends to correct itself.   These displaced orbits will continue to oscillate, with both phase and energy varying about their equilibrium values.

In order to accelerate the particles it is now necessary to change the value of the equilibrium energy, which can be done by varying either the magnetic field or the frequency.   While the equilibrium energy is changing, the phase of the motion will shift ahead just enough to provide the necessary accelerating force; the similarity of this behavior to that of a synchronous motor suggested the name of the device. . . .

The paper goes on to give the equations describing the phase and energy variations.   These have been derived in Chap. 9 and are analyzed further in the sections to follow.   The design parameters for a 300-Mev electron synchrotron were also presented; this is basically the same machine on which construction was started shortly afterward at the University of California.   McMillan also recognized the limitations imposed by radiation from the orbiting electrons, and in a companion paper[3] he discussed the magnitude of this loss for 300-Mev electrons, concluding that it would not seriously affect the operation of the synchrotron.   He was fortunate in finding immediate support for his proposal through the United States Atomic Energy Commission, which subsidized the Radiation Laboratory at the University of California.

The University of California machine came into full energy operation in January, 1949, with a maximum electron energy of 320 Mev.   At a pulse rate of six per second, with a 0.02-in.-thick platinum target, the time-average X-ray output observed with a Victoreen thimble chamber inside ⅛ in. of lead was 1000 r/min.

Meanwhile, before the large California synchrotron could be completed, Goward and Barnes[4] in England were able to demonstrate the validity of the principle with a much smaller machine (8 Mev) utilizing an old betatron magnet.   A quarter-wave resonator in the form of a cage of wires was installed outside the vacuum chamber.   Then the magnet excitation was increased so the flux core became saturated and the betatron phase was overrun.   When the radiofrequency was turned on, the electrons were accelerated in resonance with the applied rf electric field up to an energy twice the maximum betatron energy.

The next to succeed was a group at the General Electric Research Laboratory[5] with a 70-Mev synchrotron based on their previous experience in betatron design. A series of experiments with these early machines demonstrated the range of validity of the stability principle, worked out the necessary conditions for injecting electrons so they would be captured in synchronous orbits, and explored some of the properties of the high-energy beam of X rays. In the 70-Mev machine the forward-directed beam of visible light due to radiation by the radially accelerated electrons was observed for the first time.

The simplicity of the basic concept is reflected in the relatively few competing techniques which have been reported and in the comparatively small number of publications. A few theoretical papers have added detail to the original articles by McMillan and Veksler. Dennison and Berlin[6] analyzed the stability of the synchronous orbits and found that the amplitude of synchronous oscillations decreases with increasing particle energy. They also recognized the need for frequency modulation for electron energies below about 2 Mev, plus the fact that radiation losses at high energies would require increased accelerating potentials. Bohm and Foldy[7] at the University of California extended McMillan's calculations to describe the free oscillations in some detail; they also computed the radiation damping effects and exploited McMillan's proposal of using betatron operation at the start to avoid the difficulties of frequency modulation. Frank[8] and Blewett[9] examined in detail the process of transition from betatron to synchrotron action. All these studies are in basic agreement, varying only in the type of approximations used in the calculations and in the emphasis placed on the several aspects of the motion. Theoretical understanding of the synchrotron thus became quite adequate at an early stage.

The first wave of construction in this country was in the 300-to-350 Mev energy range. In addition to the machine at the University of California, synchrotrons of this energy were started at Cornell University,[10] Massachusetts Institute of Technology,[11] the University of Michigan,[12] and Purdue University. Most of these projects were supported by grants from the Office of Naval Research or the Atomic Energy Commission. During this early phase a 140-Mev machine was built at Oxford University, England. In general, these machines were put to immediate use for research studies, primarily in the production of mesons. An unusual design which developed the magnetic fields required without the use of iron magnets was started in the General Electric Company Research Laboratory by J. P. Blewett[13] and was carried on by J. L. Lawson[14] and his associates. Development in this energy range was climaxed by the completion in 1954 of a 350-Mev synchrotron at the

University of Glasgow; this machine was most carefully designed and engineered and incorporates all the best features of the earlier machines.

During this first phase of construction a series of papers was published giving more details on orbit theory, betatron injection, capture efficiency, magnetic properties, and other features. Others have been written following completion and testing of the machines, giving operational experience and results. These contributions will be referred to in the following sections, as they apply to specific problems or components.

More recently, the urge for still higher energies started another wave of construction in the 1000-Mev energy range. At the California Institute of Technology the magnet of the quarter-scale model of the bevatron (see Chap. 13), originally built at the University of California in Berkeley, was rebuilt and adapted for electron acceleration. In 1954 this Caltech machine came into operation at electron energies of 500 Mev; by 1958 power supplies were increased to allow operation up to 1.1 Bev. In 1959 a 1.2-Bev constant-gradient synchrotron was brought into operation at the Istituto Nazionale di Fisica Nucleare at Frascati near Rome.

Another group of large electron synchrotrons has incorporated the AG principle for the ring magnets. First of these was at Cornell University,[15] which had previously gained experience with a 300-Mev constant-gradient machine; by 1959 the larger Cornell synchrotron was in research use at 1.2 Bev energy. Three other electron synchrotrons using AG magnets reached essential completion in 1959, one at the Royal

TABLE 12-1
OPERATING ELECTRON SYNCHROTRONS

Location	Type	Orbit radius, m	Repetition rate, cps	Energy, Mev
United States:				
Univ. of Calif.*	H-type magnet	1.3	6	320
MIT	Constant-gradient	1.3	2	300
Univ. of Mich.*	Racetrack	1.2	...	300
Gen. Elec. Co., Schenectady	Air-cored	1.0	60	300
Purdue Univ	Constant-gradient	1.2	...	300
Cornell Univ	Alternating-gradient	5.0	30	1200
Calif. Inst. Tech	Quadrant	4.9	1	1100
Abroad:				
Univ. of Glasgow	Constant-gradient	1.4	...	350
Bonn Univ., Germany	Alternating-gradient	1.7	50	500
Royal Inst., Stockholm	Alternating-gradient	3.7	12	1200
Inst. Nucl. Phys. Frascati, Rome	Constant-gradient	3.6	20	1200
Univ. of Tokyo	Alternating-gradient	4.0	21	1300

* These machines were dismantled in 1959.

Institute of Technology in Stockholm with an energy of 1.0 Bev, one at the University of Bonn, Germany, at 0.5 Bev, and a 1.3-Bev machine at the University of Tokyo. The use of the strong-focusing property of AG magnets to reduce apertures in vacuum chambers and the physical size of the magnets are discussed in Chap. 15, along with other applications of the AG principle. However, for the purposes of this chapter we can restrict ourselves to the basic principles of the synchrotron as they are applied in the simpler magnets using the weak focusing of constant-gradient fields.

The larger electron synchrotrons which have been completed and are in operation for research are listed in Table 12-1.

12-2. PRINCIPLE OF OPERATION

The synchrotron accelerates electrons in an orbit of essentially constant radius by means of a radiofrequency electric field applied across a gap at one point in the orbit. The electrons are constrained to move in their circular path by a magnetic field which increases with time, from a low field which is just adequate to capture low-energy electrons at injection, to a maximum value permitted by the permeability of iron. A ring-shaped magnet provides the magnetic field over the doughnut-shaped vacuum chamber which encloses the electron orbits. The pole faces are accurately shaped to provide a field which decreases with increasing radius, with an n value of about 0.6, to supply focusing forces for the electrons; this feature is identical with the focusing principle in the betatron. During each rising pulse of the magnetic field a bunch of electrons is accelerated to high energy. Pulses are repeated at the repetition rate provided by the magnet power supply. Pulsed operation would result in eddy currents which would distort the carefully shaped magnetic field if the magnet core were of solid iron, so the core is laminated as in a betatron. The cyclic operation results in a sequence of pulses of high-energy electrons at the pulse repetition frequency.

Maximum energy of the electrons depends on orbit radius and on the maximum value of the magnetic field, following Eqs. (5-51) to (5-53):

$$T = ceBr_0 = 300Br_0 \quad \text{Mev} \tag{12-1}$$

The constant on the right applies when B is in units of webers/m² and r_0 is in meters, to give energy in Mev units. For example, an orbit radius of 1 m and a field of 10 kilogauss (1 weber/m²) will retain an electron energy of 300 Mev.

Synchronous acceleration normally starts when the electrons reach approximately the velocity of light, which in practice means an energy of 2 to 4 Mev. At this constant velocity the orbital frequency is given by

$$f = \frac{c}{2\pi r_0} = \frac{47.8 \times 10^6}{r_0} \quad \text{cps} \tag{12-2}$$

where r_0 is in meters.   The applied rf accelerating field must have a frequency equal to this electron orbital frequency, or to some harmonic of it. A 1-m-radius orbit, for example, requires an applied frequency of 47.8 megacycles (or 95.6 megacycles, etc.).   If the injection velocity is materially less than the velocity of light, the equilibrium orbit for resonance at this frequency will be smaller.   For example, at 2 Mev energy the velocity is $0.98r_0$, displaced 2 cm in the example above.   Such a small displacement is acceptable if the radial aperture is adequate.

The applied rf voltage is developed in a resonant-cavity circuit built into the vacuum chamber and driven by a vacuum-tube oscillator-amplifier.   The voltage amplitude is normally about twice the required acceleration in volts per turn, to provide an equilibrium phase angle near 30° (see Sec. 9-5).

The volts-per-turn requirement comes from the rate of rise of magnetic field and other constants of the motion including the radiation loss.   By differentiating Eq. (5-52) with respect to time we obtain

$$V_e = 2\pi r_0{}^2 \frac{dB}{dt} \tag{12-3}$$

As an example, consider the field to rise from zero as a sine wave to a maximum value of 10 kilogauss, for an orbit radius of 1 m in a time of $\frac{1}{240}$ sec, which is one quarter-cycle at 60 cps.   The initial rate of rise of field dB/dt (twice the average value for a sine wave) would be 480 webers/(m²)(sec).   We obtain for the required initial acceleration

$$V_e = 3000 \text{ volts per turn}$$

Since the time per revolution $\tau = 1/f = 2.05 \times 10^{-8}$ sec and the total time of acceleration t is $\frac{1}{240}$ sec, the number of revolutions is given by $t/\tau = 2.0 \times 10^5$.   The average value of acceleration per turn to attain a final energy of 300 Mev would be 1500 ev.   With a sinusoidal magnetic-field cycle the required volts per turn would be twice this average value at the start and would decrease to zero at the end of the acceleration interval.

In order to obtain a more efficient use of the rf power supply, the magnetic-field pulse is usually arranged to rise in a more nearly linear manner. This is achieved by discharging a bank of capacitors through the inductance of the magnet coils.   If the iron is pushed into saturation, the normal half-sine-wave pulse will be sharply peaked because of the decrease in inductance at high current.   This type of pulse is illustrated in Fig. 12-1. With such a linear rise, for the same pulse length as used in the example above, the acceleration required at the start would be slightly over 1500 volts per turn and would remain constant until the iron approached saturation.

During acceleration the electrons are kept in step with the accelerating field by phase stability in the fashion already discussed in Chap. 9, particularly Sec. 9-8.   The equilibrium electrons continue to return to the accelerating point at the correct phase; other electrons in the phase-stable range oscillate in phase around this equilibrium phase.   The phase oscillations are accompanied by oscillations in energy and so in orbit radius.   Hence the electrons are accelerated in a packet or bunch, as are the protons in the synchrocyclotron.   The aspect of this bunch as it passes the accelerating gap is shown in Fig. 12-2.   It is roughly banana-shaped; the electrons of correct phase near the center have maximum radial displacement, and the electrons of correct radius at the ends have maximum phase (or azimuthal) displacement.

The limits of phase stability were presented in Sec. 9-5.   Figure 12-3 shows the region of radial displacement and phase error in which phase stability exists for an electron synchrotron for various values of the equi-

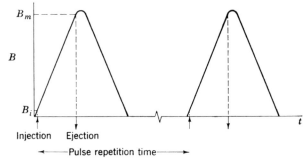

Fig. 12-1. Pulse-powering cycle of a synchrotron magnet.   Electrons are injected at low energy at low magnetic field and are ejected when the field approaches a maximum value.

librium phase angle.   This figure, redrawn from the work of Bohm and Foldy,[7] shows how much radial displacement is to be expected at various energies as a result of the phase oscillation.   At high energies the function $f(W)$ simplifies to $[\pi(1 - n)W/eV]^{1/2}$.   For example, in a synchrotron having an accelerating voltage of 1500 volts and an n value of 0.6, $f(W)$ at 300 Mev will be about 500.   For an equilibrium phase angle of 30° the maximum radial excursion at this energy is given by the graph to be 0.16 per cent of the orbit radius.   At 3 Mev the radial excursion is roughly ten times higher.   For example, in a machine of 1 m radius the oscillations at 3 Mev cover a range of ± 1.6 cm.

The instantaneous frequency of the phase oscillation follows from Eq. (9-57).   By a little manipulation of this equation it can be shown that, provided the electron energy is higher than 2 or 3 Mev, the ratio

$$\frac{\text{Frequency of phase oscillation}}{\text{Frequency of revolution}} = \left[\frac{heV \cos \phi_0}{2\pi(1 - n)W}\right]^{1/2} \qquad (12\text{-}4)$$

where the parameters are as defined in Chap. 9.

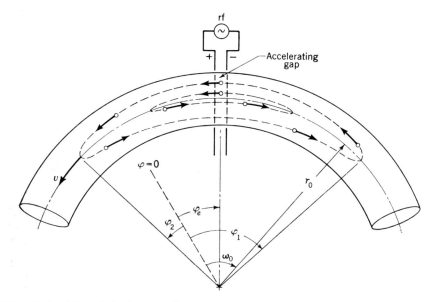

Fig. 12-2. Azimuthal phase oscillations around the equilibrium phase ϕ_0 between arbitrary limits. Electrons migrate in phase, as illustrated by the small arrows, resulting in oscillations in energy and orbit radius.

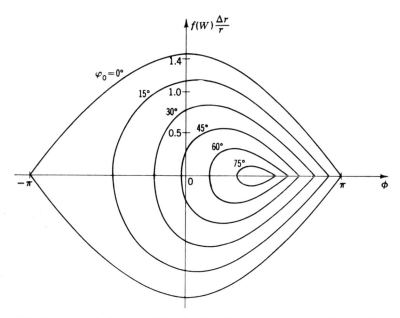

Fig. 12-3. Regions of phase stability in the electron synchrotron for various equilibrium phases. See text for discussion of the function $f(W)$.

For an electron synchrotron having an accelerating voltage of 1500 volts, a harmonic order h of 1, and an n value of 0.6, this formula indicates that at 3 Mev the phase-oscillation frequency is about 0.014 times the frequency of revolution. At 300 Mev this ratio has been decreased by another factor of 10 to 0.0014. This means that a single phase oscillation requires about 70 turns at 3 Mev or 700 turns at 300 Mev.

The usual method of bringing electrons up to the energy at which the synchronous drive can be started is to accelerate by induction, as in the betatron. The techniques in this "betatron start" will be described in Sec. 12-6, Injection. The flux linking the orbit is provided by high-permeability flux bars installed on the pole tips at the inner periphery of the magnet gap. This flux increases with time as in the betatron, providing a steady azimuthal accelerating field. Faraday's law of magnetic induction says that the induced voltage, in this case specified by the required volts per turn V_e given in Eq. (12-3), is supplied by the time rate of change of flux linking the orbit, $d\Phi/dt$. So the necessary rate of change of flux to provide betatron acceleration at constant radius is given by [cf. Eq. (7-4)]

$$\frac{d\Phi}{dt} = 2(\pi r_0{}^2)\frac{dB}{dt} \tag{12-5}$$

This equation is the betatron flux relation. It can be simply interpreted to read that the flux contained within the orbit must increase at a rate which is *twice* the value resulting from a uniform field of magnitude B_0 (the field at the orbit) if it were uniformly extended across the orbit, which is the betatron "2-to-1" rule.

The electrons supplied by the source are accelerated by this field and are distributed uniformly around the orbit. When they approach the constant-velocity condition, the rf accelerator unit is turned on at the chosen constant frequency. Further acceleration comes from this radio-frequency field, after the betatron flux condition is destroyed by saturation of the flux bars. The maximum limits of stable phase-oscillation amplitude mentioned above define the fraction of the uniformly distributed electrons in the orbit which will have the proper phase to be accepted into stable synchronous orbits. Others will gain or lose energy at too great a rate to remain within the aperture. When we consider an instantaneous transition from betatron to synchrotron drive, we find that about half of the betatron beam is accepted and bunched within the phase limits which allow synchronous acceleration. The transition from betatron to synchrotron drive is described in more detail in a later section, in which it is shown that under certain conditions nearly 100 per cent of the electrons can be captured in synchronous orbits.

During this initial betatron operation, free oscillations are set up about the equilibrium orbit in both radial and axial coordinates, because of physical deviations of the instantaneous particle paths, exactly as in the betatron. The frequencies of these free oscillations, described in earlier chapters, are between 0.3 and 0.9f_0, where f_0 is the orbital frequency, depending upon the n value of the magnetic field. These free oscillations are superimposed on the slower synchronous oscillations.

Since the free oscillations are of much higher frequency than the radial synchronous oscillation, they distort the instantaneous orbits, increase the radial extent, and also produce an axial width to the bunch. So the resonant bunch of electrons takes the form of a long thin sausage bent around the orbit. In a typical case at the start of synchronous acceleration (for the numerical example cited above) the bunch might extend around 180° in angle, have a radial width of about ±5 cm (the sum of the two radial amplitudes), and have an axial thickness of about ±2 cm.

As the magnetic field continues to increase with time, the amplitudes of both the synchronous and radial oscillations decrease (see Secs. 5-12 and 9-8). By the time electrons attain high energy, the transverse dimensions of the synchronous bunch are reduced by damping of both the phase oscillations and the free oscillations. The region occupied by the beam is now much smaller than at injection, so the area over which the magnetic field must be maintained at constant n value can become narrower. This is fortunate, since saturation of the iron sets in first at the pole edges, and fields are distorted in such a way that the central region of uniform n value narrows with increasing field.

An interesting and useful modification of the circular electron synchrotron was first suggested by H. R. Crane,[12] who proposed breaking the circular orbit into two semicircular sectors or four quadrants separated by field-free straight sections. The purpose of this change was to simplify the problems of introduction of rf cavities, injectors, and targets by inserting them into the open straight sections. The proposal was analyzed by Dennison and Berlin[16] and later by Blachman and Courant,[17] who showed that straight sections of moderate length would not destroy the stability of the particle orbits. Slightly more aperture is needed in such a machine, and the equations of particle motion are somewhat modified. The limits of stability are not so wide as in the circular machine, but the general character of both the betatron and the phase oscillations is essentially the same as that already discussed for the circular machines.

When the electrons approach their maximum energy, they can be made to strike a target on either the outer or the inner surface of the vacuum chamber. This can be accomplished in several ways. One method is to extend the magnet cycle past the point of saturation of the iron, where the condition of uniform n value is destroyed. The radial free oscillations become unstable if the n value exceeds 1, and the electrons will be spilled out of the orbit around the periphery. A reentrant target which intercepts these particles before they can hit the walls will be a source of high-energy X rays which will emerge in a tangential direction.

Note that as long as the magnetic field retains a uniform n value less than 1, the focusing properties are retained. If the field is allowed to go over its peak and down the decreasing side of the pulse, the synchronous oscillations would follow this change to a negative value of dB/dt, the equilibrium phase would shift automatically into the decelerating region of the rf cycle, and the particles would be decelerated synchronously down to low energy. During this deceleration the oscillation amplitudes would increase, so the electrons would eventually strike the walls at approximately their injection energy; a burst of low-energy X rays would be the final result. This phenomenon has been observed.

Several other procedures are available to deflect electrons against targets, either inside or outside the orbit, when they have reached high energy. It is also possible to eject a reasonably concentrated beam of electrons, so experiments can be performed outside the chamber. These techniques will be discussed in Sec. 12-11.

12-3. APERTURE REQUIREMENTS

The intensity of the beam accepted into stable orbits is dependent on the dimensions of the aperture available for particle oscillations, as well as on any constructional errors or physical deviations from the ideal theoretical conditions. Oscillation amplitudes can be computed, and estimates can be made of the increase in amplitude expected from known deviations. The probability of obtaining the maximum possible intensity can be increased by using a large factor of safety in dimensions above those computed from oscillation amplitudes. On the other hand, as the size and weight of the magnet increase, costs go up approximately with the square of a magnet gap dimension. This sets an economic upper limit on aperture dimensions. The design choice for aperture is based on judgment of the proper balance between these limitations.

Other factors affect the choice of aperture dimensions. In the gap between poles of an iron-cored magnet the leakage flux from the pole edges weakens the field between poles for a distance which is approximately half the length of the magnet gap in from the edge. This means that the radial extent of the region in which the field will have a uniform n value is considerably narrower than the radial width of the poles. Furthermore, the number of ampere-turns required for excitation is directly proportional to gap length, and the power required to excite the magnet varies with the square of the gap length. As a consequence, most designers choose a short gap and a wide radial extent of pole. However, the practical problem of providing a thin-walled, mechanically sound vacuum chamber to fit between pole faces imposes a limit on such radial extension.   In an extreme case the vacuum-chamber wall thickness would occupy an undesirably large portion of the magnet gap.   Here, a factor influencing the final choice is the success in obtaining a practical design for the vacuum chamber.

The limitations on magnet design discussed above determine the shape of the magnet gap.   Since magnet economy favors a relatively short gap with wide radial extent, the n value is chosen to make the vertical (or axial) free oscillation amplitudes smaller than the radial amplitudes. This requires higher frequencies of oscillation in the vertical mode and is accomplished by choosing the n value larger than 0.5.   Most designers have used n values in the range between 0.6 and 0.75.   A consequence of the use of these rather large n values is that the magnet pole faces must be tapered and the vacuum chamber must fit in a wedge-shaped gap.

At the start of synchronous acceleration the aperture dimensions are determined in part by the initial phase conditions.   There must be sufficient radial width to accommodate the radial phase oscillations.   An example was used in the previous section of initial phase conditions which led to a radial synchronous amplitude of ± 1.6 cm at the assumed starting energy of 3 Mev.   However, in design it might be desirable to allow more flexibility for choice of operating parameters.   To extend the example above, if we chose to use a phase angle of 15°, requiring an applied voltage of nearly 6,000 volts, and assumed a starting energy of 2 Mev to reduce the duration of the betatron phase, the anticipated radial amplitude would be ± 2.7 cm.   So a rather wide range of oscillation amplitudes occurs as a result of variations in choice of initial operating conditions. Or, put the other way around, a choice in aperture dimensions does not necessarily limit intensity but may restrict initial operating parameters. This conclusion holds only when the radial synchronous oscillations are the primary consideration, such as when particles are injected from an external source directly into the synchronous phase of acceleration.

When the betatron start is used to accelerate the electrons up to relativistic velocities before starting synchronous acceleration, the accepted intensities and so the aperture requirements are determined by the initial conditions for the betatron phase.   The intensity-aperture problems of the betatron have been discussed at some length in Chap. 7.   The primary problem is to prevent the injected electrons from striking the back of the electron gun on subsequent revolutions.   Experience in betatron operation has shown that mechanisms exist which contract the orbits sufficiently to allow an adequate fraction of the injected beam to miss the gun and to be captured in stable betatron orbits.   The trapping efficiency can be increased by the use of "contractor" coils located above and below the orbit, which are pulsed with large currents during the injection interval.   It was shown in Chap. 7 that such current pulses distort the magnetic field and particle orbits contract rapidly.

During the betatron phase the energy increases from about 100 kev at the start to, say, 3 Mev. Magnetic field meanwhile increases from about 10 gauss at the start to 100 gauss. This increase in magnetic field causes a decrease in betatron amplitudes proportional to $B^{-\frac{1}{2}}$, to about 0.3 of the original values. We can assume that the original amplitudes were limited by the vacuum-chamber aperture (usually designed to enclose the useful magnetic-field region), so the betatron amplitudes are reduced to dimensions occupying about 0.3 of the chamber dimensions. With the start of synchronous acceleration the radial spread is increased by the magnitude of the radial synchronous amplitude. We must also allow surplus radial aperture to accommodate the reduced-radius equilibrium orbit at 3 Mev energy, estimated to be about 1.2 cm less than r_0 for a 300-Mev machine of 1 m radius.

To summarize, the radial aperture must be sufficient to accept a beam having the designed value of radial synchronous amplitude plus a radial betatron amplitude of approximately 0.3 of the half-width of the chamber, temporarily located at the radius of the initial central orbit. The vertical aperture should be balanced with the radial aperture to provide acceptance of the same angular spread of electrons from the source in the initial betatron condition; this balance comes from the chosen n value of the magnetic field.

In practice the early designs allowed quite large apertures, with a radial width of 10 to 15 per cent of the orbit radius. This is now believed to be unnecessarily conservative and costly. Later designs provide a radial width of about 5 per cent of r_0. However, as discussed above, the essential function of the aperture is to accept adequate intensity during the initial betatron phase from electron guns which cannot at present produce a sufficiently collimated beam to use the minimum aperture defined by the synchrotron requirements. As a consequence, choice of aperture is really determined by the designer's judgment as to the balance between beam intensity and initial cost of the machine.

12-4. MAGNET

In some early synchrotrons magnets were used which had H-type frames similar to those used for betatrons but without the large central laminated core, illustrated by the magnet for the 320-Mev synchrotron built by McMillan at the University of California. Accumulated experience in analyzing and applying field corrections has shown this H-type magnet to have several disadvantages besides the obvious one of making the beam inaccessible. The two external return yokes produce magnetic anomalies with measurable differences in the magnitude and the phase of the field in those portions of the orbit shadowed by the yokes. Such azimuthal inhomogeneities can introduce perturbing effects on the particle oscillations and require correction, accomplished by installing special coils. The total weight of laminated iron required for the H-type frame exceeds that of the more compact designs described below, but construction is simpler. Costs of the two types are closely comparable.

Modern synchrotron magnets are formed of a ring of identical C-type units, each providing the field over a short section of the orbit. The purpose is to distribute the flux return path uniformly around the orbit, in order to reduce the magnitude of azimuthal inhomogeneities to a minimum. It is not necessary that the magnetic field be absolutely uniform in azimuth, but only that the periodicity of the irregularities be of a sufficiently high order that there are several units within each betatron oscillation wavelength. It is more important that the length and physical arrangement of return-path laminations be identical, so the eddy-current patterns are similar and the phase of the field the same in all units.

The basic arrangement of a ring magnet is shown in Fig. 12-4, representing the Massachusetts Institute of Technology synchrotron. This machine has 24 magnet units, each about 10 in. thick, assembled around an orbit of 40 in. nominal radius. The return legs of the C-type magnet frames are outside the orbit. Laminations are of 0.014-in. transformer steel and are assembled in blocks which are held together by external clamps. The pole tips are removable and especially shaped to give the desired radial field gradient; they are clamped in place with thin layers of insulation to prevent eddy-current short circuits.

The exciting coils are continuous circular windings threading all the sectors; these coils are installed after the iron units are in place. These are formed of stranded copper cable, similar to the cable used for winding transformers, and held in place by insulated brackets to restrict motion and abrasion. The requirement of low inductance, to allow pulsing with a large rate of rise of field, results in a coil having conductors of relatively large cross section and few turns. In the MIT machine the coil has 18 turns, and the peak current required to reach maximum excitation is 3800 amp.

The field index chosen in the MIT magnet was $n = 0.7$. The gap length between pole faces at the orbit is 2.9 in., and the width of the region of useful field is 3.5 in. (see Fig. 12-5). This is considered to be a relatively small aperture; most designers have chosen larger dimensions for the pole gap for orbits of this size.

A difficult technical problem in the design of such magnets is the mechanical clamping arrangement for holding the blocks of laminations, to avoid mechanical distortion under magnetic forces and to keep gap length constant. This is much more serious for laminated iron than for the solid block structures used in cyclotrons, since metal bolts cannot be used without insulating sleeves, and clamping brackets and bolts must be insulated to prevent continuous metallic loops in which eddy currents could be established. In several installations the original brackets have not been completely satisfactory, but have allowed some slight vibration under magnetic forces which erodes the insulation and cuts laminations. One method of avoiding such faults has been to use preformed blocks of laminations bonded into solid structural units with thermosetting resin.

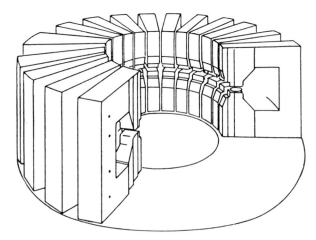

Fig. 12-4. C-type magnet of the MIT synchrotron.

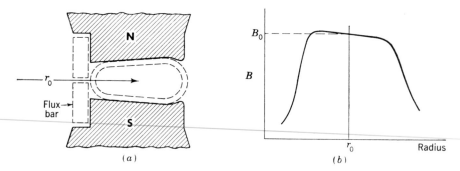

Fig. 12-5. (a) Sketch of pole face and vacuum chamber for the MIT synchrotron. (b) Plot of magnetic field across the pole face, showing a region of linear decrease with radius where $n = 0.75$.

The smaller machines use an external flux return path, since there is insufficient area within the orbit circle to accommodate the return legs. For larger machines, or for those with very small aperture and hence return circuits of small cross section, the flux return legs can be located inside the orbit. In this event the return flux threading the orbit is in the opposite direction to that required for betatron acceleration; specially designed betatron flux bars carrying flux which parallels the orbit field are required to produce the betatron condition.

Another design problem is the contouring of the pole face to provide the radially decreasing field needed for focusing. A simple flat taper is usually sufficient to provide the desired n value of 0.6 or 0.7 over the central portion of the gap. However, the field is weakened at the edges because of fringing, similar to the effect at the periphery of cyclotron magnets (see Sec. 8-2). This can be partially compensated and the region of uniform-n field extended somewhat by adding shims or shaped protuberances on the pole faces near the edges. Such shaping is needed on both inner and outer pole edges.

The desired pole-face taper and the optimum shape of the edge shims are usually determined by model measurements. These measurements are made at the injection field, when oscillation amplitudes will be a maximum and the maximum aperture should be available. At higher field intensities the pole-edge shims saturate first, and the width of the useful region of magnetic field contracts. However, by this time oscillation amplitudes have been damped to smaller dimensions, so the narrowing of the uniform-n region is not a limiting factor. The maximum practical value of magnetic field is reached when the width of the useful field band becomes narrower than the space required by the beam. With the type of steel used for laminations, and for the density allowed in packing the laminations, this limit is about 12 kilogauss.

Eddy-current effects can be seriously disturbing, especially if they occur with an azimuthal variation. They cause the magnetic field in different portions of the gap to differ in time by small amounts. The magnetic field at any point can be considered as having a component in phase with the exciting current and another component 90° out of phase. At injection time, when the average field is very small, the out-of-phase component can become dominant. A radial variation of field such as is caused by eddy currents tends to change the n value. If there is an azimuthal variation in the eddy currents, the n value will also vary around the orbit.

Many laboratories have experienced difficulties due to eddy-current effects, and much time and effort have been required to find suitable corrections. Careful design is of first importance, particularly in making each lamination which carries guide flux have the same length and dimensions. Close packing of laminations at the orbit and elimination of gaps between laminations in which fringing fields can occur will reduce the risk of trouble. If variations still exist, they can be corrected by appropriately placed windings which carry small currents 90° out of phase with the magnet excitation current. Several laboratories have designed such correcting coils. Those used with the 300-Mev Cornell machine were arranged to correct for the first and second Fourier components of the azimuthal field, with four controls to apply corrections proportional to sin θ, cos θ, sin 2θ, and cos 2θ.

Variations in the remanent magnetic field (the value at zero excitation) can occur for different portions of the iron in the magnet because of variations in the physical handling or the past magnetic history of the material. These differences can be quite significant at the low injection fields. Some experts advise a degaussing procedure for the blocks before assembly. Special care must be used in handling the blocks of laminations to prevent mechanical jars during assembly. Even when all possible precautions have been taken, the residual magnetism of structural steel in the foundations or in the building may induce an undesirable remanent field in the magnet after assembly. If the remanent field is nonuniform in azimuth, it can cause significant perturbations of the particle orbits. Such remanent fields can be corrected by dc currents in suitably located coils. Most designers try to keep the azimuthal variations below 1 part in 1000 at injection fields.

Another common magnetic fault is the displacement of the magnetic median plane from the geometric center plane of the gap. Since particle orbits follow the magnetic median plane, any displacement will shift the orbit plane. An azimuthal variation in the location of the median plane is even more disturbing, since it can feed energy into the vertical betatron oscillations. This type of fault is fairly common, since the sloping earth's field acts differently around the orbit. When such an anomaly is detected, it can be remedied by currents in correcting coils located appropriately.

12-5. MAGNET EXCITATION

Several methods are available for powering a synchrotron magnet. Alternating current can be obtained from the power lines or an ac generator to provide continuous full-wave excitation. However, the reactive current required for excitation is extremely large relative to the current needed to supply losses in the iron and copper. A simple arrangement for providing the large excitation current is to resonate the inductance of the magnet with a capacitor bank at the desired repetition frequency and to drive this resonant circuit and supply the losses from an ac generator at this frequency. This technique was used for the early synchrotrons and is still satisfactory for relatively small magnets. The limitation for the larger machines is the heat loss under continuous excitation, due to eddy currents in the iron and the resistance of the coil. Removal of the heat developed in the iron and copper because of these losses requires special cooling techniques, which are difficult to apply. The usual oil-immersion cooling used in transformers is impractical for the synchrotron magnet; air-blast cooling is noisy, bulky, and of much lower efficiency; no other schemes of equivalent effectiveness have been developed. In the absence of practical designs for a high-capacity cooling system the only alternative has been to reduce heat losses by reduction of the duty cycle of operation. Most synchrotrons of the 300-Mev size or larger are pulse-powered, with a duty cycle chosen to keep the heat evolution within the capacity of the cooling system.

The requirement of pulse powering described above applies to the compact heavy magnets which use uniform n values and have relatively wide apertures and wide poles. The introduction of AG focusing (see Sec. 5-7 and Chap. 15) allows the use of much narrower apertures and smaller magnets. With such lightweight magnets it again becomes possible to use continuous full-wave excitation without exceeding the cooling capacity.

The power supply for a pulse-powering system uses capacitors to store energy for the magnet. The capacitance must be adequate to supply the full stored energy required for the magnet at maximum excitation. In operation, the capacitor is charged from a dc source and then discharged into the magnet. If one full cycle of oscillation is allowed per pulse, at the frequency determined by the inductance and capacitance in the series circuit, the capacitor will be returned to nearly its initial voltage. Between pulses the dc source supplies the system losses. It is also possible to operate on only one half-cycle per pulse. The average power consumption is only half that of full-cycle operation, but each pulse reverses the polarity of the capacitor voltage. In recharging the capacitor between pulses the capacitor polarity must be reversed by a mechanical or electronic switch. Grid-controlled rectifier tubes can be used to charge the capacitor or act as reversing switches.

In pulse operation it is customary to use ignitrons to control the capacitor discharge. A typical ignitron is the mercury-vapor GL-506, which will carry 2000 amp peak and withstand 20 kv peak inverse voltage. Such an ignitron can carry much higher currents than the rated value on low-duty-cycle pulsed operation, if properly protected by magnetic shielding from adjacent current-carrying bus bars (which might deflect the arc from the mercury pool to the wall of the tube with possibly damaging effects).

A typical pulse-powering system, for the MIT synchrotron, has a capacitor bank of 960 μf which resonates with the inductance of the magnet at a frequency of 45 cps. The total energy stored in the magnet or in the capacitors is 15,000 joules. The peak voltage applied to the capacitors is 15 kv, and the peak current 3,800 amp. The synchrotron operates at a pulse repetition frequency of two per second, limited by the power supply.

A simplified circuit diagram of the pulse-powering system for the MIT synchrotron is given in Fig. 12-6. The rectifier for charging the capacitor bank is a full-wave, three-phase system using transformers and six rectifier tubes, delivering 15 kv.   Four GL-506 ignitrons in parallel are used as switching tubes to connect the capacitor to the coil during the pulse and to disconnect at the end of the pulse.

Electrical problems in pulse-powered systems arise chiefly from transient voltage surges which occur during the switching and can lead to breakdown of tubes or other components.   One serious transient occurs when the ignitrons first begin to conduct, applying voltage suddenly to the magnet terminals.   This transient is associated with resonance of the stray capacitance of the magnet with the inductance of the leads from

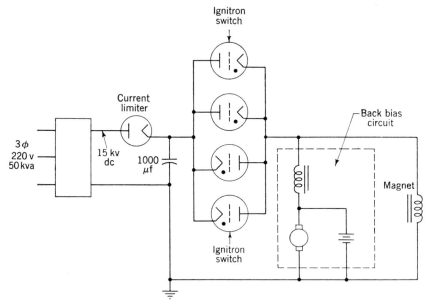

Fig. 12-6. Simplified circuit diagram for the pulse-powering system of the MIT synchrotron magnet.

the ignitrons and capacitor bank.   It can be damped out by a series capacitor and resistor across the magnet terminals, in which the capacitor is several times the stray capacitance and the resistor is chosen to provide critical damping with the lead inductance.   Another transient arises at the end of the conduction interval, when the inverse voltage builds up across the ignitrons.   This transient is caused by resonance of the full inductance of the magnet with the stray capacitance of the leads.   Again, it can be damped by a series resistance and capacitance, this time across the ignitrons.

The chief limitation of the system described above is its low repetition rate, which reduces the frequency of pulses for experimental work to an undesirably low value. Operators are now convinced that a higher repetition rate is essential, even though it increases the power requirements and the cooling problems. Other installations have been powered for higher repetition rates, of up to 60 pulses/sec.

12-6. INJECTION

A betatron start is commonly used to accelerate electrons from their initial injection energy of less than 100 kev to 2 or 3 Mev energy at which they have a velocity of over $0.98c$ and so travel in an orbit of radius not significantly smaller than the geometric central orbit. This requires that the flux linking the orbit have a time rate of change proportional to the rate of change of the guide field flux at the orbit, following the betatron relation given by Eq. (12-5). The linkage flux is provided by flux bars on the inside of the orbit, attached to the poles of the guide field magnet. They are effective only during the early stage of acceleration while the guide field is still small, and for only a very short time interval, after which they become saturated and have no further effect. Since the guide field for 2- to 4-Mev electrons is low (<100 gauss in the example used in Sec. 9-12), while the flux density in the flux bars can approach saturation, the cross-sectional area of the flux bars needed to satisfy the betatron relation can be quite small. In order to obtain this high flux density in the bars, the air gap in the flux-bar circuit is made short relative to the gap between pole faces. So these flux bars are of negligible size compared with the heavy central core required in the betatron to provide acceleration to top energy.

One arrangement for installing flux bars on the magnet poles is illustrated in Fig. 12-7. This long flux bar is clamped in place with short spaces between the bar and the poles which can be adjusted to provide the correct total flux in the bars to satisfy the betatron condition, so the equilibrium orbit is at the center of the chamber. Another arrangement (see Fig. 12-5a) uses two short flux bars fastened against the inside edge of the pole with a short gap between the two bars on the central plane. This gap can likewise be adjusted, by loosening the clamping brackets and sliding the bars, to modify the reluctance of the circuit and vary the relative amount of flux in the bars.

Several authors have analyzed the betatron-flux condition and have shown how to compute the dimensions and properties of the flux bars. Goward[18] discussed the requirements from the point of view of providing adequate flux for betatron acceleration, but made simplifying assumptions regarding the transition from betatron to synchrotron operation. Wilkins[19] discussed the magnetic aspects of flux-bar design, including a more thorough analysis of the transition problem. He described the use of flux-biasing techniques to adjust the location of orbit radius in the betatron phase and to provide a more efficient transition to the synchronous phase.

The rate of rise of flux density in the flux bars is much higher than in the iron of the magnet, so eddy currents are also greater. During the first few microseconds of the betatron phase such eddy currents have the effect of reducing the effective permeability of the bars. During this same interval the guide-field flux in the magnet depends almost solely on the pole-gap reluctance and is not much affected by eddy currents in the poles. So the betatron-flux condition is disturbed during the time

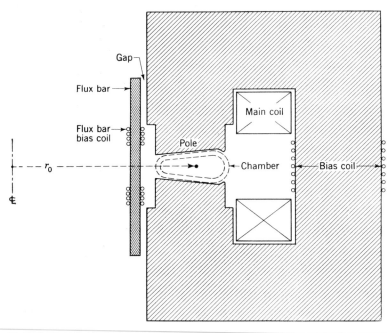

Fig. 12-7. One method of installing flux bars on the inside of the orbit of a synchrotron used for initial acceleration during the betatron start.

required for eddy-current equilibrium to be reached; this can delay the time when orbit stability becomes established beyond the normal time for injection. The difficulty can be avoided by applying a suitable negative bias to the main magnetic field, so there is adequate time for the eddy currents in the bars to reach equilibrium before the guide field reaches the injection value. A special winding of a few turns can be used for this purpose. Or direct current can be applied to the main magnet windings, using a suitable series inductor or choke in the dc leads to eliminate induced voltage surges in the dc source.

The high rate of rise of field in the flux bars requires that these bars be formed of extremely thin laminations in order to reduce the eddy-current time lag. In some installations stacks of laminations are cemented together to form solid bars for ease in clamping and mechanical adjustment. Thin foils of high-permeability material such as permalloy can be used to reduce the dimensions of the flux bars. Another possibility is to use blocks of ferrite, which has a very high resistivity and so reduces eddy-current effects. The properties of ferrite as applied to the radio-frequency system of the cosmotron are discussed in some detail in Chap. 13. The disadvantage of ferrite is that it has a lower saturation limit than iron laminations and the dimensions must be correspondingly larger.

Another problem to be considered in designing flux bars is their effect on the guide field. If they are located too close to the main gap, they may shield the guide-field flux crossing the chamber and produce local areas of weak field. A further consideration is the mechanical mounting arrangement for the flux bars on the inside of the orbit. In this location they can obstruct access to the vacuum chamber. Simple mechanical mountings which can readily be removed for maintenance are quite important.

Several physical and electrical adjustments are available to control the betatron flux during the acceleration interval. Flux-bar cross section can be changed if needed; gap spacing in the flux-bar circuit can be adjusted; dc bias can be applied to either the main magnet or the flux bars to regulate the injection time phase and the rate of rise of flux in the bars. The significant times are at the start and at the transition to synchrotron drive. Experience with betatrons is directly applicable in obtaining maximum capture efficiency at the start. A problem unique to synchrotrons, however, is the transition to synchronous drive. This will be discussed in the section to follow.

The electron gun used for injection into the synchrotron is similar to those used in betatrons. The basic design is illustrated in Fig. 7-15. The function of the gun is to inject a very intense beam (several amperes) of electrons confined in a narrow cone and at high energy (50 to 100 kev). It is also essential that the gun have a narrow radial dimension, to improve the chance of electrons missing the back of the gun on subsequent revolutions. This requires small radial spacings and limits the voltage which can be applied to the gun. In order to focus the electrons into a narrow cone a third electrode, located between the cathode and the outer jacket which serves as an anode, is used as a control electrode. The outer jacket is normally grounded, so the cathode must be maintained at high negative potential. The focusing electrode is usually a rectangular plate with a rectangular slot, approximately the size of the cathode, located close to the cathode and having a potential applied which is positive by a few kilovolts relative to the cathode. A sequence of experimental modifications has resulted in a standard gun design which produces a beam having an angular spread of 5 to 10° under operating conditions.

At the MIT laboratory Stone[20] has developed a special cathode formed of sintered molybdenum-thoria which is cut from a hollow cylinder of $\frac{5}{8}$ in. inner diameter. The sliver is about $\frac{3}{8}$ in. long and $\frac{1}{16}$ in. wide, mounted with the concave side of the cylinder facing the direction of emission. This shape seems to improve the focus to some extent over the usual tungsten spiral cathode and provides a copious current of several amperes. When installed in a conventional gun with a control electrode and an anode potential of 80 kv, it projects a beam with half the total emission concentrated within ±2° of the axis.

The radial location of the electron gun is quite critical. It is usually mounted on an adjustable stem to allow this position to be determined experimentally. The normal position is with the leading edge of the gun located at the outer periphery of the uniform-n field where the n value is approximately unity.

Experience with betatrons shows that the intensity accepted into stable orbits increases with injection voltage, varying approximately with $V^{1.5}$. However, because of the narrow radial spacings required and technical limitations on insulation, the maximum practical voltage on such an electron source is found to be between 80 and 100 kv.

The rather wide angle of emission from the gun means that a large fraction of the beam is outside the limits of stability of the radially tapered field and is not accepted into stable orbits. This unfocused portion of the beam strikes the wall of the chamber within the first turn. One consequence is that static charges can be accumulated on the inner wall of the chamber, which would distort the electric fields and reduce intensity of the captured beam. So the inner surface of the chamber is coated with a grounded conducting layer to prevent the accumulation of charge. This layer must be sufficiently thin to prevent the development of eddy currents which would distort the magnetic field. A resistivity of about 100 ohms per square has been found satisfactory.

Accepted beam intensity is determined by the fraction of the injected beam contained within the narrow cone which is focused and set into stable oscillations about the equilibrium orbit in the radially decreasing magnetic field. It is further limited by the fraction which misses the back of the injector gun on subsequent revolutions, until such time as the damping of amplitudes due to the increasing field removes the beam from this obstruction.

Several mechanisms are involved in the injection process, which have been analyzed in Sec. 7-8 in their application to the betatron. Kerst[21] first pointed out the effect of self-contraction due to the injected electron beam. The electron-beam current is in a direction to oppose the increasing magnetic flux in the flux core (or the flux bars in the synchrotron). It reduces the induced voltage below that required to satisfy the betatron relation so the electrons acquire too small an amount of energy per turn and their orbits contract, allowing them to miss the gun.   The unfocused beam intensity which strikes the walls in the first turn thus serves a useful purpose in providing a large self-contraction effect.   Further advantage of this mechanism is taken by pulsing large currents in contractor coils during the injection interval; such coils are located on the pole faces above and below the beam-orbit location in the chamber.

A second mechanism proposed by Kerst is the space-charge self-repulsion of the beam.   Space charge in the beam gives forces opposite in direction to the normal guide-field restoring forces.   This reduction in the effective restoring forces tends to decrease both the radial and vertical free-oscillation frequencies.   At injection, when space-charge density is greatest, the band of oscillation amplitudes is determined by aperture dimensions.   Then, as space charge is removed by losses to the walls and to the back of the electron gun, the free-oscillation frequencies increase and their amplitudes decrease.   This is equivalent to a forced damping of the betatron oscillations, and the reduction in amplitude allows a considerable fraction of the beam to miss the injector gun.

Other methods have been proposed to improve acceptance.   Davis and Langmuir[22] suggested a mechanism for producing a resonant distortion of the equilibrium orbit away from the injector by means of coils which are pulsed during the period of injection, to distort the azimuthal uniformity of the magnetic field.   Resonance with the radial oscillations is possible when $n = 0.75$, and this value has been adopted by the group at the General Electric Company Research Laboratory[24] to increase intensity in their air-cored synchrotron.

For very large accelerators, where the voltage gained per revolution is a significant fraction of the injection voltage, the rate of contraction of the instantaneous orbits toward the equilibrium (betatron) orbit is also large.   If the deviation of the instantaneous orbit is Δr, the contraction per turn δ is given by $\dfrac{\delta}{\Delta r} = \dfrac{\Delta E}{2E}$, where ΔE is the energy gain per turn. This may provide sufficient damping in a few turns to give a large increase in acceptance.   Whenever possible, then, the magnitude of ΔE should be made large by using techniques which maximize the rate of rise of flux in the flux bars.

Although many of these techniques are empirical, a sufficient body of experience is now available, in both betatron and synchrotron operations, to provide useful suggestions.   Adequate intensities have been obtained in most synchrotron laboratories.

12-7. RADIOFREQUENCY ACCELERATION

The accelerating system in a synchrotron is usually a quarter-wave resonant cavity, resonant at the electron orbital frequency determined by orbit radius as given in Eq. (12-2), and driven by a radiofrequency oscillator-amplifier. It is located between magnet poles and forms an arc extending part way around the orbit. If cavity wavelength were the same as in vacuum, it would extend around one quadrant of the circumference. However, it can be made physically shorter by loading it with material of high dielectric constant which has adequately low losses at the applied frequency. A practical method of forming the resonator is to make it a section of the vacuum chamber, with the same aperture and dimensions. The electrodes are plated surfaces on the inside and outside of the sector, joined electrically at the node end and with an insulated gap at the open end of the quarter-wave cavity across which the rf voltage is developed. Particles which traverse this gap are accelerated by different amounts depending on the phase of the rf field at the instant.

Ceramics are available having dielectric constants of up to 80, which can be slip-cast into the structural shape needed for the vacuum chamber. Glass and fused silica have also been used. In most cases a sector of the material chosen for the vacuum chamber itself is adapted to be the resonant cavity. The voltages required are modest, and the electric fields in the body of the material are not excessive. So heating due to the rf fields has not been a serious problem for materials with reasonably low rf loss factors. One of the best materials from this point of view is fused silica,[5] which can be blown or cast in the proper shapes, has excellent mechanical properties so walls can be kept thin, and has a dielectric constant of 4. Wavelength is reduced by the square root of the dielectric constant, so the length of a quarter-wave resonator is half a quadrant or 45° in arc.

A good description of a fused-silica resonator used in the Berkeley synchrotron has been published.[25] An important technique in its construction is the application of the conducting coating to inner and outer surfaces. The surfaces were first etched with hydrofluoric acid to remove the glaze and were thoroughly cleaned. Then Liquid Bright platinum was painted on and fired in a furnace, in two or three successive coats. This surface was then sufficiently conducting to allow a copper electroplated surface of about 0.003 in. thickness to be applied.

The plated surfaces of the cavity are scribed longitudinally with closely spaced parallel cuts to insulate against eddy currents, which otherwise would be developed in the conducting surfaces and which might distort the magnetic field in this sector. When these cuts are approximately parallel to the direction of the rf currents, they have a negligible effect on the resonant efficiency or rf resistance of the cavity. The highest electric fields are developed across the short insulating gap at the open end of the quarter-wave line. It has been found useful in some laboratories to terminate the coating in small rounded electrodes which

cover the sharp edges of the gap.   Use of such electrodes increased the
breakdown voltage by as much as a factor of 3 at MIT.

The rf amplifier or oscillator is coupled to the resonant cavity by
capacitative coupling near the rf node of the quarter-wave line.   A sketch
of the 50-megacycle resonator developed for the 330-Mev synchrotron at
the Massachusetts Institute of Technology[20] is shown in Fig. 12-8.

The radiofrequency oscillator used to excite the cavity can be located
at some distance from the magnet, with power transmitted through
coaxial cable matched to the impedance of the cavity.   The MIT oscillator operates at 46.5 megacycles and uses a WL530 triode as a power tube
in a class-C self-excited oscillator circuit.   With an input power of 7 kw,
a peak voltage of 3.5 kv is developed across the gap at the open end of the
resonator.   Several other tubes have been equally satisfactory, such as
the Eimac 3X2500A3 or the 7C24.   In general, the radiofrequency

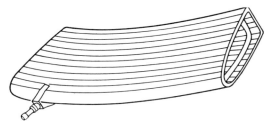

Fig. 12-8. Quarter-wave resonant cavity used for the rf accelerator in the MIT
synchrotron.   The cavity forms one sector of the vacuum chamber.

problems of the synchrotron have been minor and have been easily solved.

In such a radiofrequency system the quarter-wave resonator, the transmission line from the oscillator tube, and the tube with its associated
circuit components form a single resonant circuit.   The length of the
transmission line must be adjusted to give the proper phase; one standard
procedure is to make this line electrically one half-wavelength long.   A
schematic diagram of the Berkeley oscillator circuit[25] (Fig. 12-9) illustrates the physical arrangements and also shows the several supple-
mentary circuits for suppressing parasitic oscillations, for supplying the
triggering pulse to start the oscillator, and for "tickling" the circuit with
an auxiliary oscillator which helps to initiate oscillations and reduce the
"jitter" or uncertainty in the starting time.   The oscillator is pulsed for
about 8 msec, which is sufficient to overlap the acceleration interval.
The pulse is initiated at an adjustable instant in time determined by the
magnet excitation cycle, representing the end of the betatron acceleration
period.   It is terminated as soon as acceleration is completed.   In the
Berkeley machine this pulse length represents a duty cycle of one-
twentieth at the repetition rate of 6 pulses/sec.

The resonant efficiency or Q of the resonant-cavity circuit is of the order of 500, largely determined by the losses in the dielectric core of the cavity and in the iron pole faces of the magnet.   In a high-Q system the radiofrequency voltage build-up time will be of the order of Q cycles. So when the rf oscillator is turned on, it takes a time of about 10 μsec to reach full voltage.   During this build-up time the energy acquired from betatron acceleration is decreasing.   An analysis of the phase relations during this transition by Kaiser[26] shows that the initial phase at which the electron crosses the accelerating gap is not so critical in determining whether the particle will be accepted in a stable synchronous orbit as would be inferred from the simple theory of phase acceptance described

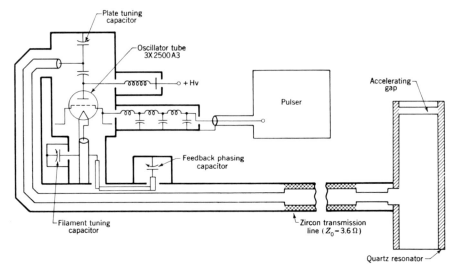

Fig. 12-9. Schematic circuit diagram of the rf oscillator for the Berkeley synchrotron.[25]

earlier.   Rather, the critical parameter is the phase velocity, that is, the difference between the angular frequency of the particle and the angular frequency of the oscillator.   Since the angular frequency of the particle at this time depends primarily on the orbit radius, in a machine of small aperture the spread in phase velocities can be kept small.

From the analysis described above, Kaiser verified previous predictions[9] that essentially all the uniformly distributed electrons in the orbit would be accepted into stable synchronous orbits, with the long build-up time expected from a high-Q resonator.   This is in contrast to the simple theory of acceptance given by Bohm and Foldy,[7] Goward,[18] and others in which it was assumed that the transition between betatron and synchrotron drive was instantaneous.   Kaiser and Tuck[27] tested this theory of electron capture in their 14-Mev synchrotron by turning off the rf accelerating voltage for a period long enough to allow the electrons to become uniformly distributed in phase. Then, when the rf oscillator was again turned on, all the electrons were recaptured except those whose phase velocities were too great, as predicted.

DePackh and Birnbaum[28] have also studied the capture process, considering all possible initial phases and phase velocities at the transition between betatron and synchrotron phases. They find that a moderately slow increase of the rf voltage from zero to its final value will minimize oscillation amplitudes, and that an asymptotic approach to the final value is an advantage. With synchrotron chambers of relatively small aperture it is now generally agreed that the capture efficiency can approach 100 per cent by using such long rf build-up times.

During the early stages of operation of the University of California synchrotron a half-wave drift tube or C electrode was used as a resonator. By analogy with the D in a cyclotron in which the resonant particles experience two accelerations per turn, on entering and on leaving the D, a C-shaped electrode in the synchrotron extending around half the orbit will also provide two accelerations. It can be considered to be a half-wave resonant circuit. This type of electrode was originally built and installed in the Berkeley machine, formed as a hollow laminated tube supported in a concentric position inside the vacuum chamber by several short stub lines through the walls. The length was somewhat shorter than 180° in arc, and somewhat higher potentials were applied to compensate. The chief problem was the mechanical difficulty of supporting such a long hollow structure weakened by the longitudinal laminations. With the development of the quarter-wave cavity resonator, which involves fewer technical problems, the original C electrode was replaced. But in principle any electrode system which provides a phased radiofrequency voltage of proper magnitude and frequency would be satisfactory.

12-8. VACUUM CHAMBER

The vacuum chambers used in the electron synchrotron are doughnut-shaped rings of ceramic, glass, or quartz. For the smaller machines (up to 70 Mev) they can be cast in single units. A photograph of such a single-unit cast ceramic chamber has been used by the General Electric Company in its advertisements (Fig. 12-10a).

In the large machines the chamber is made up of segments cemented or clamped together with sealing gaskets. A description of the University of California chamber has been published,[25] including a photograph of one sector (Fig. 12-10b). It consists of eight 45° sectors of fused silica, assembled in the form of a toroid with an elliptical cross section of $3\frac{1}{2}$ by $6\frac{1}{4}$ in. and a wall thickness of $\frac{5}{16}$ in. The sectors are joined and vacuum-sealed by covering the eight joints with wide rubber bands and using Lubriseal grease to ensure a good seal.   Sector ends were separated and insulated by thin Teflon gaskets.   A conducting coating on the inside was obtained by painting with Du Pont No. 4817 air-drying silver; this coating was grounded through a network of eight 1000-ohm resistors to avoid the accumulation of static charge.   Such a resistor network is needed to allow the betatron accelerating voltage to develop

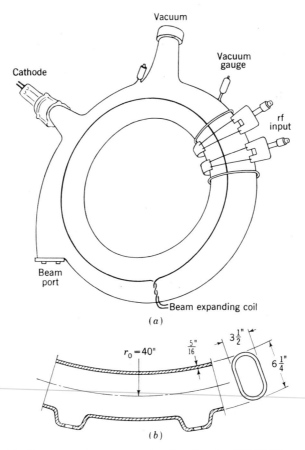

Fig. 12-10. (*a*) Cast ceramic vacuum chamber for the GE 70-Mev synchrotron.[5] (*b*) Sector of fused-silica vacuum chamber for the Berkeley 320-Mev synchrotron.[20]

between sectors.   One of the sectors was specially plated and scribed to form the quarter-wave resonator for radiofrequency acceleration.

An operating pressure of better than 10^{-5} mm Hg is required to prevent loss of beam through gas scattering.   Vacuum-pumping speeds are not large for this small chamber, and straightforward vacuum techniques are satisfactory.   The pump used in a typical 300-Mev installation is a

6-in. oil-diffusion pump with an efficient refrigerated baffle cooled to $-40°C$.

12-9. FREQUENCY-MODULATED START

In a few installations the designers have chosen to avoid some of the difficulties and possible loss of intensity in the betatron start by injecting a prefocused beam of electrons from a low-voltage dc generator directly into the synchronous acceleration phase of operation. In one synchrotron a Cockcroft-Walton machine of 400 kv is used; in another the source is an electrostatic generator producing 1-Mev electrons. The well-collimated beam is directed toward the orbit at a shallow angle and is "inflected" into the orbit by an auxiliary dc electric field maintained between two curved plates. The inflector is located at the outer edge of the aperture, near the position where $n = 1$. If the energy is less than the 2 to 4 Mev at which electrons attain relativistic velocities, their orbital frequency at the desired orbit radius r_0 is lower than the constant frequency which they attain at higher energies. In order to provide synchronous acceleration at constant radius during this early phase, the frequency of the rf cavity must be modulated to match the orbital frequency.

Crane[12,29] at the University of Michigan was the original proponent of this technique. In his synchrotron the magnet is separated into four quadrant sectors spaced by straight field-free sections, one of which is used for installation of a large resonant cavity which can be frequency-modulated; another is used for the inflecting system for the beam from the external source. This has been called a "racetrack" orbit.

Several methods are available for producing the necessary frequency modulation. The accelerating-cavity unit can be broadly resonant, having a low Q, and can be driven at the desired frequency by a power amplifier which is controlled to follow the chosen cycle. The power requirement for such a system is undesirably large. Another method would be to have a mechanically modulated resonant cavity of high Q, for which power needs would be small. However, a mechanically tuned system which uses a variable capacitor or inductor has an inherent lack of flexibility in modifying the frequency cycle, and the precision of timing at the start of the cycle is poor. A more efficient technique, adequate for a rather small range of frequencies, is to use electronic modulation of a high-Q resonant-cavity resonator.

Crane used a resonant cavity in which part of the capacitance of the circuit was a symmetrically arranged circle of barium titanate capacitors. This material has the property of having its dielectric constant vary with the magnitude of the impressed electric field. The capacitors were arranged so that a dc bias field could be applied across the barium titanate, and this dc field varied through a time cycle to control the capacitance and change the resonant frequency of the circuit.

Although the frequency-modulated start does avoid some of the difficulties associated with betatron operation, it introduces other difficulties. Injection of a narrow well-focused beam reduces the amount of space charge and eliminates the large loss of beam to the walls in the first turn, which is characteristic of injection from an electron gun. However, it is not clear that this is an advantage, since high beam intensities and space-charge effects seem to be useful in contracting orbits in betatron operation. The narrow inflected beam must also miss the back of the inflector plates on subsequent revolutions. The mismatch of free-oscillation frequencies with the orbital frequency at $0 < n < 1$ allows the electrons to make several turns before they again approach maximum outward radial amplitude at the azimuth of the inflector. During this time the increasing magnetic field will contract the equilibrium orbit radius and damp the oscillations. With careful adjustment, these effects are sufficient to allow a large fraction of the beam to miss the inflector and to be captured in stable orbits. Since injection continues for a time interval representing many turns, the beam is uniformly distributed in azimuth. Only about half these electrons have a phase relative to the rf phase which will allow them to be captured in stable synchronous orbits, as discussed in earlier sections.

As a consequence of the several limitations, beam intensity from the frequency-modulated synchrotron is lower than that normally obtained with a betatron start. Furthermore, the difficulties in the electrical problems of frequency modulation are significant. As a result, the method has not been widely used.

At Cornell University[15] the magnet for the 1.2-Bev synchrotron is of the AG type, with the return leg of the C on the inside of the orbit and with a very compact arrangement of iron and coils. There is not sufficient space on the inside of the orbit for flux bars, so betatron preacceleration is not used. Rather, a 1-Mev electrostatic generator was used to supply a focused beam of electrons, which were injected into the synchronous phase of acceleration. The frequency modulation required for a start at 1 Mev is only 6 per cent, and it was supplied by a separate radio-frequency cavity tunable over this range. The tunable power source was operated for only a short time at the start of each pulse; then the main rf constant-frequency cavity was turned on and provided acceleration to top energy. In 1961 the electrostatic generator was replaced by a 10-Mev linear accelerator, removing the need for frequency modulation. Beam intensities were greatly increased, reaching a level where radiation damage to the glass chamber became a serious hazard.

It seems probable that future development of higher-energy synchrotrons will tend toward the use of strong-focusing magnets and small apertures and that injection energy will be increased to 3 Mev or higher, at which frequency modulation is unnecessary.

12-10. RADIATION LOSS

Since the electrons in the synchrotron experience a continuous central acceleration, they must radiate energy, in accordance with the classical theory. This effect has been discussed in Chap. 7 relative to the betatron and in Sec. 9-8, where the theoretical equations were presented. The total energy lost because of radiation increases with the fourth power of the electron energy, for fixed orbit radius, following Eq. (7-18). This electromagnetic radiation extends from very long wavelengths through the optical spectrum and into the ultraviolet and soft X-ray region. The peak for 300-Mev electrons in an orbit of 1 m radius occurs at about 70 A, or in the ultraviolet. In the visible region this radiation becomes noticeable, as a reddish light, at about 60 Mev. The peak is in the center of the visible spectrum for an energy of about 200 Mev and is observed as a brilliant white light.

The direction of propagation is normal to the acceleration vector, which is radial, and so the light is emitted in the forward or tangential direction in a narrow cone. With a transparent chamber wall it can be observed by eye when looking directly at the oncoming electrons. However, this radiation is highly dangerous to the eyes and should be observed only with mirrors. During a synchronous pulse it appears as a short flash when the electrons attain sufficient energy; frequently this spot appears as a line with a radial spread due to orbit contraction as the beam moves across the chamber.

The energy loss per turn due to radiation, for electrons in a 1-m orbit, is about 150 ev at 200 Mev and 800 ev at 300 Mev. If plotted on a time axis the loss is a sharply increasing spike occurring near the end of the acceleration interval. For this radius of curvature the energy loss is small compared with the applied rf accelerating voltage. When the particles lose energy, they tend to shift to a smaller orbit radius; this causes a change in phase of crossing the accelerating gap; the phase shift increases the amount of acceleration; so the particles remain in synchronism and at the synchronous orbit radius. This feature of the synchrotron, of providing automatic compensation for radiation loss, is one of the most attractive characteristics of the machine.

It would seem that this rapid increase of radiation loss with energy would set a practical limit to the size and energy which could be obtained with an electron synchrotron. Such a limit will depend on the volts per turn supplied by the radiofrequency accelerating system. For the type of machine described in this chapter, using a single accelerating cavity and limited by the breakdown of dielectric in the cavity, the practical limit to energy would appear to be about 2 Bev.   However, modern designs are utilizing field-free straight sections in the particle orbit, in which highly resonant cavities with vacuum insulation can be mounted.   It is also possible to use two or more cavities, driven in phase.   So the volts per turn can be increased by a large factor if desired, and the energy limit can be pushed much higher.   In Sec. 15-9 is described a design for an AG synchrotron which uses 16 cavities each producing 500 kv; with this emphasis on the radiofrequency system, it is possible to design for 6 Bev, and higher.   The limit in this case seems to be an economic one, when the cost of the rf component becomes excessive relative to other components of the machine.

12-11. TARGETS AND BEAMS

The simplest method of utilizing the synchrotron beam is to deflect it against a target at the edge of the chamber at the end of the acceleration interval, to produce a beam of high-energy X rays.   The X rays are caused by deceleration of the electrons in the target and have the typical bremsstrahlung spectrum with a maximum energy equal to that of the electron beam, but with the intensity distributed over lower-energy quanta.   The spectrum computed for 330-Mev electrons[30] is illustrated in Fig. 12-11.   When a solid target is used, or if the X-ray beam must penetrate the chamber wall to emerge, the low-energy portion of the spectrum is absorbed and a peak is observed which shifts to higher energy with increased absorber.

The angular spread of the X-ray beam is small, with a half-angle in the forward direction which includes all but $1/e$ of the intensity given by

$$\theta_{1/2} = k\left(\frac{W_0}{W}\right)\ln\frac{W}{W_0} \tag{12-6}$$

where $k = 0.65 \pm 0.15$ over a wide range of electron energy, photon energy, and target material.   The detailed variation of k is given in a paper by Stearns.[30]   When evaluated for an electron energy of 330 Mev, the half-angle defined above is found to be less than 0.4°.   Experimental measurements confirm these calculations and show that the X-ray beam emerges in a very narrow forward cone.

When the electrons approach maximum energy, they can be made to strike a target at either the inner or outer edge of the chamber.   One simple method is to turn off the rf voltage while magnetic field is still rising.   The beam spirals in to smaller radii, owing to both the increase in field and the energy loss by radiation, and will strike a target located on the inner wall.   It might be noted here that the final maximum energy is lower for this smaller final orbit radius than if the beam were expanded outward against a target on the outer periphery.

Another method, which brings the beam outward, is to excite the magnet past saturation so the shape of the field exceeds the stable limit of $n = 1$ and radial oscillations become unstable.   As radial amplitudes increase, the electrons usually strike first on the back surface of the injector gun, which serves as a target.

The duration of the beam pulse on the target can be varied over a wide range.   Some experiments require a very short pulse, and others a long one.   The normal rate of contraction per turn when rf voltage is turned

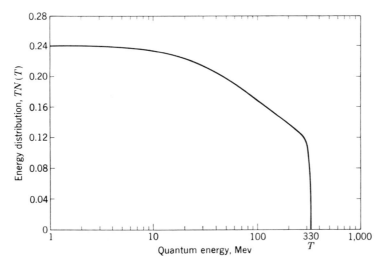

Fig. 12-11. Calculated bremsstrahlung spectrum from electrons of 330 Mev incident normally on a Pt target 0.02 in. thick.[30]

off rapidly is quite small.   This rate of contraction has been variously estimated in different machines to be less than 0.001 in. per turn by the time it strikes the target.   So only the extreme inner tip of the target is struck by the electrons.   A time which is equivalent to many turns is required for all the electrons to be cleaned up against the target.   Under normal conditions the resultant X-ray pulse lasts about 10 μsec.

Pulses of shorter duration can be obtained by setting up radial beam oscillations.   The synchrotron group at the Massachusetts Institute of Technology[31] first proposed the use of a "figure 8" coil, wound in opposite directions about the two halves of the magnet, which has the effect of increasing field in one half and decreasing it in the other.   A switch shorting this coil is timed to follow closely the turn-off of the rf voltage, before the beam has contracted into the target.   If the n value is maintained at 0.75, the frequency of radial oscillations is

$$f_r = (1 - n)^{1/2} f_0 = 0.50 f_0$$

and the electrons traverse two revolutions in one radial-oscillation cycle. Weakening the magnetic field on one half of the orbit and strengthening it on the other induces a rapid increase in amplitude.

Ejection by induced oscillations can be accomplished with a variety of systems for inducing the oscillations. It is not necessary that the distortion of the field be symmetrical, but smaller exciting coils can be used. Davis[23] proposed the use of a transient pulse in a coil around a small arc. This is illustrated in Fig. 12-12, which portrays schematically the particle paths during the last few revolutions, showing how the beam can be made to strike a target. At Berkeley, a coil around one-eighth of the pole face

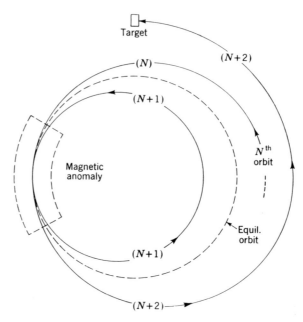

Fig. 12-12. Radial oscillations about the equilibrium orbit induced by a magnetic anomaly at one point in the orbit, useful in expanding the beam against a target.

gave a considerably increased output from the target. At Iowa State College[32] coils supported by the vacuum chamber are pulsed to change the n value over different portions of the orbit. Several of these methods have been successful in obtaining output X-ray pulses as short as 0.1 to 0.2 μsec, representing less than 10 revolutions of the electrons.

Long pulses can be obtained by decreasing rf voltage gradually. Electrons having the largest phase oscillations are first lost from synchronous stability and strike the target; others are kept in resonance until the rf voltage drops below the equilibrium value. This method has been used to stretch the target pulse length to over 2500 μsec. Such a long pulse is frequently desirable when electronic coincidence instruments are used for measurement, in order to increase the time extent of the beam and the duration of observation.

It is also possible to eject a beam of electrons from a synchrotron, although not much use had been made of such an emergent beam up to 1961. The techniques described above for producing radial oscillations can bring a beam out to the edge of the magnetic field. The injector gun should be on the inside of the orbit, if an external emergent beam is to be obtained. The emergent beam is concentrated in a fairly narrow cone and can be brought through a tangential evacuated tube to a thin window. It is also possible to use the magnetic peeler (see Chap. 7), used for the betatron, to deflect the electron beam further and to obtain a more collimated beam.

12-12. X-RAY BEAM INTENSITY

The X rays produced by the synchrotron have much higher energy than those normally used for medical or industrial purposes, for which measuring instruments have been highly developed. At a peak energy of several hundred Mev the processes of energy loss are quite different, so different instruments are required. At these energies electron showers are produced, similar to those observed in cosmic rays. Shower production is the cumulative effect of electron-pair formation and bremsstrahlung radiation by the electrons. The phenomenon of pair formation is well understood theoretically, and the cross section can be computed with some precision. The problem of intensity measurement involves knowledge of the bremsstrahlung spectrum and the integration of the pair-production process over this wavelength spectrum.

The pair-production and bremsstrahlung calculations and calibration of the X-ray beam intensity have been done at Berkeley by Blocker, Kenny, and Panofsky.[33] Thin ionization chambers are used, behind absorbers or converters of different atomic number Z, in which the electron density N_e is known. The ionization due to Compton-effect electrons is a function only of N_e and can be subtracted to find the pair-production effect. By measuring the ionization behind converters of widely different Z and comparing with the theoretical cross section for pair production, the intensity in terms of number of quanta per unit area per unit time (the flux) can be determined. Detailed equations are given, as well as tables of averaged pair-production cross sections for bremsstrahlung of different energies and for absorbers of different Z.

A cruder method of measuring intensity, also described by the Berkeley group,[33] is to use the mean energy loss of an electron per unit path in an absorber of known Z, as a function of absorber thickness. Thin ionization chambers are located at varying positions in the absorber, and the total intensity decrease is observed. Reasonably good data exist on the mean energy loss as a function of maximum energy for shower electrons. So the observed ionization absorption coefficient can be used to obtain a value for beam intensity. However, this method does not distinguish between X-ray and electron intensity in the beam.

Occasionally it has been desirable to express intensity in terms of the roentgen (r) familiar in radiation-therapy measurements. This unit is defined in terms of the ionization in air produced by a beam of photons in equilibrium with its secondary electrons. At normal X-ray energies equilibrium cannot be established in an air-filled chamber, so the practice has been to resort to "air-wall" ionization chambers. It is even more difficult to obtain equilibrium at 300 Mev, so the number of electrons associated with the X-ray beam is quite uncertain. It is for this reason that the pair-production intensity calibration is used, which is independent of the electron "contamination" of the X-ray beam. However, in order to have a practical standard of comparison, McMillan, Blocker, and Kenny[34] have proposed a standardized roentgen measurement for synchrotrons, using a Victoreen thimble chamber inside a lead cylinder of $\frac{1}{8}$ in. wall thickness, located transverse to the beam at a considerable distance. Table 12-2 gives the calibrations for the Berkeley synchrotron at two energies, expressed in units of ergs/(cm²)(r), Mev/(cm²)(r), and in "effective quanta," defined as the energy flux divided by the maximum energy, which is proposed as a more meaningful unit for high-energy radiation (see Sec. 14-4).

TABLE 12-2
VICTOREEN THIMBLE-CHAMBER CALIBRATION FOR BERKELEY SYNCHROTRON
(In $\frac{1}{8}$ in. Pb)

X-ray energy, Mev	Ergs/(cm²)(r)	Mev/(cm²)(r)	Effective quanta/(cm²)(r)
320	5.3×10^3	3.3×10^9	1.04×10^7
160	3.5×10^3	2.2×10^9	1.38×10^7

The average output of the Berkeley synchrotron[34] with the above definitions for intensity is 1,000 r/min at 1 m. This is at full energy and with a pulse rate of six per second. This can be compared with the output of the Illinois 320-Mev betatron, which is 14,000 r/min at 1 m. The higher intensities from the betatron are a result of the higher repetition rate, larger aperture, and higher input beam intensity, obtained at considerably higher cost. There is reason to believe that synchrotrons can be designed and developed to give equivalent intensities if such higher intensities are found to be worth the increased cost.

12-13. IRONLESS SYNCHROTRONS

The magnetic fields required to deflect and focus electrons can be produced by air-cored coils, without the use of iron. Several proposals for such a machine have been published, such as that by Kaiser and Tuck.[35] The individual primarily responsible for the development of such machines is J. L. Lawson of the General Electric Company Research Laboratory.[24] Lawson's synchrotron, designed for 300-Mev electrons, has undergone a long period of development and is now in operation for research. It is difficult to assess the relative merits of this kind of machine. It does have some advantages, such as the absence of eddy-current distortions in the magnetic field and freedom from the flux-density limits set by the permeability of iron. However, it also has several disadvantages, of which the primary one is the distortion of field caused by the extremely large forces on the current-carrying conductors which produce the magnetic field. Since one of the opportunities of an air-cored magnet is the possibility of using very high magnetic fields, in order to reduce orbit dimensions, the currents in these conductors are very large. Furthermore, energy dissipation is a problem, since for practical reasons it is desirable to have the conductors located within the vacuum envelope. Practical limitations seem to restrict the size to about 500 Mev, and it is possible that the most economical range is around 100 Mev.

REFERENCES

1. E. M. McMillan, *Phys. Rev.*, **68**:143 (1945).
2. V. Veksler, *J. Phys. (U.S.S.R)*, **9**:153 (1945).
3. E. M. McMillan, *Phys. Rev.*, **68**:144 (1945).
4. F. K. Goward and D. E. Barnes, *Nature*, **158**:413 (1946).
5. F. R. Elder, A. M. Gurewitsch, R. V. Langmuir, and H. C. Pollock, *J. Appl. Phys.*, **18**:810 (1947).
6. D. M. Dennison and T. Berlin, *Phys. Rev.*, **70**:58 (1946).
7. D. Bohm and L. Foldy, *Phys. Rev.*, **70**:249 (1946).
8. N. H. Frank, *Phys. Rev.*, **70**:177 (1946).
9. J. P. Blewett, *Phys. Rev.*, **70**:798 (1946).
10. Cornell University Laboratory of Nuclear Studies, *Synchrotron Progress Report* (Nov. 1, 1949).
11. I. A. Getting, J. S. Clark, J. E. Thomas, Jr., and I. G. Swope, *Phys. Rev.*, **79**:208A (1950); *Engineer*, Apr. 6, 1951, p. 440.
12. H. R. Crane, *Phys. Rev.*, **69**:542 (1946).
13. J. P. Blewett, *J. Appl. Phys.*, **18**:976 (1947).
14. W. B. Jones, H. R. Kratz, J. L. Lawson, D. H. Miller, R. D. Miller, G. L. Ragan, J. Rouvina, and H. G. Voorhies, *Rev. Sci. Instr.*, **26**:809 (1955).
15. "The Cornell Bev Synchrotron," Cornell University, Floyd Newman Laboratory of Nuclear Studies (December, 1956).

16. D. M. Dennison and T. Berlin, *Phys. Rev.*, **69**:542 (1946).
17. N. M. Blachman and E. D. Courant, *Rev. Sci. Instr.*, **20**:596 (1949).
18. F. K. Goward, *Proc. Phys. Soc. (London)*, **62A**:617 (1949).
19. J. J. Wilkins, *Phil. Mag.*, **41**:34 (1950).
20. J. E. Thomas, Synchrotrons, *Ann. Rev. Nuclear Sci.* (1952).
21. D. W. Kerst, *Phys. Rev.*, **74**:503 (1948).
22. L. Davis and R. V. Langmuir, *Phys. Rev.*, **75**:1457 (1949).
23. L. Davis, *Rev. Sci. Instr.*, **21**:971 (1950).
24. W. B. Jones, H. R. Kratz, J. L. Lawson, G. L. Ragan, and H. G. Voorhies, *Phys. Rev.*, **78**:60 (1950).
25. M. H. Dazey, J. V. Franck, A. C. Helmholz, C. S. Nunan, and J. M. Peterson, *Rev. Sci. Instr.*, **21**:436 (1950).
26. T. R. Kaiser, *Proc. Phys. Soc. (London)*, **63A**:52 (1950).
27. T. R. Kaiser and J. L. Tuck, *Proc. Phys. Soc. (London)*, **63A**:67 (1950).
28. D. C. DePackh and M. Birnbaum, *Rev. Sci. Instr.*, **21**:451 (1950).
29. H. R. Crane, *Phys. Rev.*, **70**:800 (1946).
30. M. Stearns, *Phys. Rev.*, **76**:836 (1949).
31. J. S. Clark, I. A. Getting, and J. E. Thomas, Jr., *Phys. Rev.*, **70**:562 (1946).
32. C. L. Hammer and A. J. Bureau, *Rev. Sci. Instr.*, **26**:594 (1955).
33. W. Blocker, R. W. Kenny, and W. K. H. Panofsky, *Phys. Rev.*, **79**:419 (1950).
34. E. M. McMillan, W. Blocker, and R. W. Kenny, *Phys. Rev.*, **81**:455 (1951).
35. T. R. Kaiser and J. L. Tuck, *Nature*, **162**:616 (1948).

At the head of the facing page is a photograph of the cosmotron at the Brookhaven National Laboratory, before shielding was installed.

13

The Proton Synchrotron

The proton synchrotron is the culmination of the phase-stable accelerators and yields the highest energies yet achieved. By 1961 four proton synchrotrons were operating in the energy range between 3 and 10 Bev, and three more were under construction. It represents the ultimate development of the accelerator art, involving such complicated techniques that all the skills of mechanical and electrical engineering are taxed to provide the wide variety of complex components and to assure that they function as a unit. Advanced techniques of theoretical computation are required in design, and the electronic computer has become an essential tool.

The AG modification is the most recent development, which has resulted in the production of energies of over 30 Bev. In this form the proton synchrotron has no foreseeable limitation in energy except the practical considerations of size and cost. Although the AG proton synchrotron utilizes the same principle of acceleration, the unusually large step upward in energy and the unique physical characteristics of the AG synchrotron justify a separate category; it is described in some detail in Chap. 15.

In this chapter we limit the discussion to the original concept of the proton synchrotron utilizing the low, constant magnetic gradients which are just sufficient to produce orbit stability. As the first multi-Bev accelerators, they opened up the new research field of particle physics.

Costs of accelerators in the Bev energy range are outside the limits of university budgets. Essentially all proton synchrotrons have been built with funds supplied by the governments of the countries concerned. Nevertheless, the cost efficiency in terms of the beam energy achieved per dollar of construction cost is better than for earlier types of accelerators. Costs are 2 million dollars per Bev, or 0.2 cent per volt.

For the first time there are available in the laboratory particle energies larger than the rest mass of nucleons (0.938 Bev) or of the heaviest of the "strange" particles which have been observed in cosmic-ray studies. Cosmic-ray processes can be studied under controlled conditions with directed and focused beams having intensities millions of times higher than are available in nature. The processes of meson formation and the properties of the several types of mesons can be studied at energies extending well into the cosmic-ray region. Basic forces between nucleons and mesons are directly measurable. The scientific results obtained with the new multi-Bev accelerators have been impressive. Essentially all types of strange and unstable particles observed in cosmic-ray studies have been produced in the laboratory, and many new ones have been observed and identified. At the Brookhaven laboratory the cosmotron was used to produce and study the neutral Λ^0 particle, which is heavier than a nucleon and which decays into a nucleon and a meson. The bevatron at the University of California produced antiprotons and antineutrons for the first time, created directly from energy. The Nobel Prize in physics for 1959 was awarded to Drs. Emilio Segrè and Owen Chamberlain for the discovery of the antiproton. The search for more knowledge and new phenomena goes on. Scientists are having an exciting time in the early years of research with these great accelerators.

13-1. THE MULTI-BEV ACCELERATOR

Magnetic accelerators for electrons, such as the betatron and the constant-gradient synchrotron, have been shown to have practical energy limits because of the rapid onset of radiation losses by the orbiting electrons. As we have seen, this energy loss varies with $(W/W_0)^3$, a very steeply rising function, and the practical limit is reached when the radiation loss per turn approaches the maximum practical voltage per turn. However, protons have a much larger rest mass, and the equivalent limit for protons will not be reached until much higher energies are attempted, of the order of 10,000 Bev.

The synchrocyclotron, which has been so successful as a proton accelerator in the 100- to 700-Mev range, requires a solid-core magnet. At relativistic energies magnet weights and costs increase roughly with the cube of a magnet dimension such as pole-face diameter; power cost also increases with the volume of the magnetic field between poles, or with at least the square of a pole dimension. If the synchrocyclotron were to be enlarged to produce protons of several Bev energy, the magnet would become exorbitant in weight and cost.   The obvious method of reducing magnet cost is to use a ring magnet covering only a narrow annular band. Such a fixed orbit radius requires the synchrotron principle of acceleration, using a pulsed magnetic field.   With a ring magnet the cost is very much smaller for the same particle energy, although it still increases with the cube of the radius if aperture dimensions are assumed to increase proportionally.

The only alternative principle of acceleration known is that of linear acceleration.   The present stage of development is described in Chap. 10. Although plans are progressing for higher energies, practical experience with proton linacs is still (1961) in the range below 70 Mev; many problems must be solved to extend the proton linac into the multi-Bev range. Much higher energies have been obtained with electron linacs.   The nominal advantage of a linear accelerator is that construction and power costs should be approximately proportional to energy.   However, under present conditions the circular magnetic accelerators appear to be more economical and more practical for the multi-Bev energy range.

Qualitative reasoning such as the above suggests that, to attain energies of several Bev, it is preferable to use a ring magnet to reduce magnet cost and to operate on the principle of synchronous acceleration at constant radius.   This extension of the principle was appreciated by machine designers in several laboratories.   Several groups independently calculated the basic requirements and developed designs for proton synchrotrons.

The principle of operation is basically the same as for the electron synchrotron.   A fixed orbit radius is chosen, and a ring-shaped magnet produces a magnetic field normal to the doughnut-shaped vacuum chamber enclosing the orbit.   The magnetic field increases with time as the protons gain energy, to maintain constant orbit radius.   Ions are injected into the orbit at low energy when the magnetic field is small, and energy is supplied by an accelerating electric field applied across a gap at one or more points in the orbit.   But unlike electrons which approach the velocity of light at relatively low energies ($v = 0.98c$ at 2 Mev) and so have an essentially constant frequency of revolution during acceleration to higher energies, protons do not reach the equivalent limit until they have acquired about 4 Bev energy; so the velocity and the frequency of revolution increase during the entire acceleration interval.   The applied electric field must synchronize with the changing orbital frequency of the particle, requiring frequency modulation over a wide range during acceleration, determined by the ion frequencies of revolution at injection and at maximum energy.   This feature introduces new and complicated technical problems in the design of the accelerating electrodes and of the high-frequency oscillator.

The same type of phase focusing exists to bunch the particles about an equilibrium phase of the accelerating field as for the electron synchrotron, and if the applied frequency is correct, the protons maintain a constant average orbit radius.   But an error in frequency could cause the particles to gain energy at a rate not compatible with the increasing magnetic field and to spiral inward or outward, where they would be lost against the walls of the chamber.   The required schedule of frequency modulation does not follow any simple law, but depends on the rate of increase of magnetic field, which is itself a function of the constants of the power supply and the properties of the magnet iron.   So new problems of frequency control are encountered, which are unique to the proton synchrotron.

On the other hand, the design of proton synchrotrons is based upon a considerable body of experience acquired in the development of synchrocyclotrons and electron synchrotrons.   Some of the techniques are directly applicable and can be expanded to accommodate the larger physical dimensions.   An adequate theoretical analysis of the motions of particles is available to guide designers, checked by experience in earlier synchronous accelerators.   Designers can anticipate many problems and compute quite precisely the magnitude of fields, the necessary uniformity, the effect of inhomogeneities, etc.   Because of the larger investment much effort has been applied to model tests and engineering development.   Commercial engineering firms, with their wide experience and large facilities, have been attracted by the challenge and by the opportunity to develop new and specialized equipment; they have supplied their best engineers for advice and assistance in the design of the major components.   So the physical problems of design and construction have not been so formidable as might have been expected from the size of the machines.

13-2. HISTORICAL DEVELOPMENT

The first proposal of a proton accelerator using a ring magnet, in which both magnetic field and frequency of the accelerating electric field are varied, was made in 1943 by Prof. M. L. Oliphant of the University of Birmingham, England, to the British Directorate of Atomic Energy. Because of wartime security restrictions the proposal was not published at that time.   It is reported in a detailed design study by Oliphant, Gooden, and Hide,[1] published in 1947 and accompanied by a theoretical analysis of orbit stability by Gooden, Jensen, and Symonds.[2]   It will be noted that Oliphant's original proposal antedates the discovery of phase stability by two years.   At the time of the first proposal there was no assurance that the principle was sound or technically practical.   Perhaps, had it not been for the distractions of wartime work in Great Britain, analysis of this proposal might have revealed the principle of phase stability two years earlier.

An accelerator for protons following these designs was built at the University of Birmingham, and it has been in operation at 1.0 Bev since 1953. Professor Oliphant's return to his native Australia and the untimely death of Dr. Gooden, the chief scientist on the project, slowed progress toward completion of this machine, which was the first proton synchrotron to be started. This early start resulted in freezing the basic magnet design and starting construction before other components had been analyzed and designed in detail, and also before certain improved design concepts were developed in the United States. As a result the Birmingham machine lacks some of the advantageous features of the later machines and operates at rather low intensity. Despite the early difficulties and the small number of staff engaged, it has been brought into satisfactory operation for research.

Meanwhile the principle of phase stability in synchronous accelerators was announced independently in 1945 by McMillan[3] at the University of California and by Veksler[4] in the U.S.S.R. Both papers describe two techniques for synchronous acceleration, which have been described in earlier chapters. The use of frequency modulation of the applied accelerating electric field led to the development of the synchrocyclotron. The concept of constant frequency and constant orbit radius with an increasing magnetic field has been applied to the electron synchrotron. Both papers also include implicitly the possibility of acceleration of protons in a synchrotron by also varying the frequency of the accelerating field, but neither paper was primarily concerned with this more complicated application of the principle. By this combination of techniques the limitations of the two simpler machines are side-stepped and a new range of energies has been made available.

Design studies for proton synchrotrons in the United States started early in 1947 in two laboratories supported by the United States Atomic Energy Commission. Dr. W. M. Brobeck,[5] of the University of California Radiation Laboratory, made a preliminary report of a possible design for 10-Bev protons in 1948, which was primarily a study of the practicability of a pulsed power supply for the large ring magnet required. The name bevatron was given to this billion-electron-volt accelerator.

At the same time, preliminary designs for a similar accelerator were started at the Brookhaven National Laboratory under the direction of the senior author, on leave from the Massachusetts Institute of Technology, as chairman of the Accelerator Project. The stimulus for this development came from Prof. I. I. Rabi of Columbia University. The early Brookhaven plans were reported in papers by Livingston[6] and others before the American Physical Society in 1948. As the design approached completion, a description was published by M. S. Livingston, J. P. Blewett, G. K. Green, and L. J. Haworth[7] in January, 1950. This machine was soon given the laboratory name of cosmotron.

Both the Berkeley Radiation Laboratory and Brookhaven were

encouraged in these design studies by the AEC officials responsible for research and development of instruments. When preliminary designs and cost estimates became available in 1948, a decision was made by representatives of the two laboratories and of the AEC for the construction of two machines, a 2.5- to 3.0-Bev cosmotron at Brookhaven and a 5- to 6-Bev bevatron at the University of California. In both laboratories teams of scientists and engineers were assembled to complete designs and proceed with construction. Many of the members of these teams have contributed importantly to the designs, and the results are the product of the joint efforts of a large number of individuals.

The Brookhaven cosmotron was the first proton synchrotron to be completed (in May, 1952), and it was rapidly tuned up to 2.3 Bev, the maximum energy possible with the available power supply. A period of engineering consolidation and "bug-picking" brought it back into operation at the date of the dedication ceremonies on December 15, 1952. A year of research at this energy allowed the completion of the power supply. Operation at the maximum design energy of 3.0 Bev with a beam intensity of 2×10^{10} protons/pulse repeated at 5-sec intervals was announced in early 1954.

During the period of design and construction some of the progress was recorded in publications. R. Q. Twiss and N. H. Frank[8] of MIT made a theoretical study of orbital stability in the proton synchrotron, taking design parameters compatible with those being considered at Brookhaven. Some of the components have been described in a sequence of abstracts of papers presented to the American Physical Society[9] by members of the team. N. M. Blachman and E. D. Courant[10] analyzed the gas-scattering problem; A. I. Pressman and J. P. Blewett[11] described the electrically tuned variable-frequency oscillator. An over-all description of the accelerator by Livingston, Blewett, Green, and Haworth[7] has been mentioned earlier. Finally, after completion of the machine the entire staff collaborated in presenting a complete description of all components of the operating machine, which occupies a full issue of *The Review of Scientific Instruments*, edited by M. H. Blewett.[12]

At the University of California the designers of the bevatron chose to build first a working quarter-scale model to determine requirements for the full-scale machine. With this model they demonstrated the resonance principle and showed that the structure formed of four magnet quadrants and four straight sections did not disturb the stability of the orbits. Particle oscillation amplitudes were measured in the model, but the results were inconclusive (found later to be due to magnetic inhomogeneities and alignment errors). As a consequence the design proceeded with alternative pole-tip arrangements: a large-aperture design which would allow a maximum energy of 3.5 Bev, and a smaller aperture capable of reaching 6.4 Bev. This question was resolved by the report of the initial performance of the Brookhaven machine, which showed that the smaller aperture was adequate. Accordingly, plans were quickly modified to use the small-aperture, high-energy arrangement. Initial operation at about 5 Bev at low intensity was reported in early 1954. Further development resulted in reaching full-power operation at 5.7 Bev in October, 1954, with a beam intensity of about 1×10^{10} protons/pulse repeated 11 times per minute. Maximum energy operation at 6.4 Bev is possible at a slower cycling rate. Since that date the research staff of the Berkeley laboratory has been engaged in a broad research program utilizing this high-energy beam.

Publications by the Berkeley group have been largely through laboratory memorandums and AEC progress reports, which have had a limited, although unclassified, distribution. Papers before the American Physical Society[13] have described the quarter-scale model and some of the components and include in the author list the major contributors to the design of the machine. Lofgren[14] published a brief description of the design parameters and the performance of the model in 1950. The most recent and inclusive survey is an internal laboratory report in 1957 by Brobeck.[15]

During the late 1950s several other proton synchrotrons were built, patterned to a large extent on the cosmotron or the bevatron. The largest is the 10-Bev synchrophasotron of the U.S.S.R. Joint Institute for Nuclear Research at Dubna (near Moscow), which was completed and reached its design energy in 1957. Difficulties with the magnet correcting systems and with the injector held beam intensity to low values in early operations; these difficulties appear to be solved, and the machine is now (1961) in active use for research. This machine is, for the most part, a scaled-up version of the bevatron. It is described in numerous papers in the Russian technical literature which can be traced through the papers of Veksler and others in the U.S.S.R. *Journal of Nuclear Energy*[16] and in the CERN (Geneva) symposium proceedings of 1956.[17]

Three machines are based on cosmotron design and experience. A 3-Bev proton synchrotron nicknamed "Saturne" was completed in 1958 at the Saclay laboratory of the French Commissariat a l'Énergie Atomique.[18] At Princeton University (collaborating with the University of Pennsylvania) a small-aperture rapid-cycling machine for 3 Bev energy and high beam intensity is nearing completion (1961), under the direction of M. G. White, G. K. O'Neill, and F. C. Shoemaker. At the Rutherford Laboratory at the British Atomic Energy Research Establishment at Harwell, a machine modeled on the cosmotron but scaled up to an energy of 7 Bev is under construction, directed by T. G. Pickavance.

At the Argonne Laboratory of the AEC near Chicago a proton synchrotron for 12.5 Bev energy of a somewhat different type is under construction. It is a "zero-gradient synchrotron" (ZGS) which uses a magnet of the bevatron type but with a uniform field in the magnet proper; focusing is obtained by shaping the end faces of the eight magnet sectors to give the same effect as though a field gradient of $n = 0.6$ had been included (cf. Sec. 5-6). The magnet structure is of the poleless type with minimum-size aperture and will operate at fields up to 21.5 kilogauss. Because of the compact design the magnet weight is considerably smaller than for the bevatron-type magnet. The project was initiated by a group under J. J. Livingood and is now under the direction of A. V. Crewe. It is scheduled for completion in 1962.

The most unusual machine under construction is at the Australia National University under the leadership of M. L. Oliphant. This is to use an air-cored magnetic field in four quadrants, with fields of up to 80 kilogauss produced in a shaped coil structure which does not have an iron core. The coils are to be excited by a massive homopolar generator which can store a great amount of rotational energy but will operate at a very slow repetition rate of about one pulse every 10 minutes. Many challenging engineering problems are involved, in such features as the brushes to handle the extremely large currents and the structures for supporting the large magnetic forces on the coils. The injector will be an 8-Mev cyclotron placed inside the circular coils.

In Table 13-1 are collected some of the parameters of the nine proton synchrotrons operating or under construction in 1961, which use conventional constant-gradient magnetic focusing.

Some general reviews other than those already mentioned describe the design and applications of proton synchrotrons. Blewett[19] has written a survey article for the 1956 *Reports on Progress in Physics*, and Green and Courant[20] have authored a review article in the 1959 *Handbuch der Physik*. The CERN (Geneva) Symposium on High Energy Accelerators[17] in 1956 included many papers devoted to the technical design of proton synchrotrons, along with other accelerator types, which were published in the proceedings of the symposium. Another conference on high-energy accelerators and instrumentation was sponsored by the CERN laboratory in Geneva in September, 1959, and included brief papers on the construction status and special features of several machines; these papers are published in the conference report.[21] The latest conference in this series on accelerators was held at Brookhaven in 1961; its proceedings are scheduled for publication early in 1962.

In the following sections the problems of development of the special components of a proton synchrotron will be illustrated by a rather detailed presentation of the Brookhaven cosmotron. This emphasis recognizes the much closer association of the writers with the design and development of the cosmotron than with other proton synchrotrons. It is not intended to slight the design virtues of other machines, and the authors ask indulgence for this somewhat unbalanced presentation. In partial justification it can be argued that the cosmotron was the first proton

TABLE 13-1
PARAMETERS OF CONVENTIONAL PROTON SYNCHROTRONS

	In operation, 1961						Under construction		
Location	Birmingham, U.K.	Brookhaven, U.S.A.	Saclay, France	Berkeley, U.S.A.	Dubna, U.S.S.R.	Princeton, U.S.A.	Harwell, U.K.	Argonne, U.S.A.	Canberra, Australia
Accelerator nickname		Cosmotron	Saturne	Bevatron	Synchro-phasotron	P.P.A.*	Nimrod	ZGS	
Maximum energy, Bev	1.0	3.0	2.5	6.4	10	3.0	7.0	12.5	10.6
Mean orbit radius, m	4.5	10.7	11	18.2	30.5	12.2	23.6	27.4	6.4
Number of magnet sectors	1	4	4	4	4	16	8	8	4
Peak magnetic field, kg	12.6	13.8	15	16	13	13.8	14	21.5	80
Magnet weight, tons	810	1,650	1,080	10,000	35,000	350	7,000	4,000	0
Aperture: Width, cm	50	91	60	122	150	18	91	81	22
Height, cm	21	22	10	30	40	7	24	15	22
Pulse rate, pulses/min	6	12	19	10	5	1,140	28	15	0.1
Injector	t.r.†	e.a.‡	e.a.‡	Linac	Linac	e.a.‡	Linac	Linac	Cyclotron
Injection energy, Mev	0.46	3.7	3.6	9.8	9	3.0	15	50	8
Number of accelerating stations	1	1	1	1	2	4	1	2	1
Harmonic order	1	1	2	1	1	8	4	8	1
Date of completion	1953	1952	1958	1954	1957	1962	1962	1962	1962–1963

* Princeton-Pennsylvania Accelerator.
† transformer-rectifier set.
‡ electrostatic accelerator.

synchrotron to be completed, has had a reasonably successful record of operations, and is thoroughly documented in the literature.

The discussion in this chapter is also confined to the conventional machine using constant-gradient magnetic fields. Although such magnets are large and costly compared with the more recently developed AG magnets, they have served their basic purpose well and illustrate all the essential properties of the proton synchrotron.

13-3. BASIC PARAMETERS

The largest and most costly component of a proton synchrotron is its magnet; to a considerable degree the choice of magnet parameters determines the characteristics of the other components. Consequently, the first step in design is a decision on magnet dimensions and properties. The designer's choice is based on minimizing the cost and complexity for a given value of BR, which is a measure of particle energy. Magnets for proton synchrotrons cover a wide range in their design features, which will be discussed further in a following section. This range includes a spread in orbit fields from 14 to over 21 kilogauss and wide variations in the structural shape of the magnetic circuit.

In the cosmotron, which was among the first to be started, the design involved the use of parallel bundles of iron laminations arranged in a radial array around a circle, leaving wedge-shaped spaces between bundles at the orbit. The magnetic circuit has a C-shaped cross section, so the vacuum chamber between poles is accessible around the entire outer periphery. With this arrangement the maximum magnetic field at the orbit, up to the point where saturation effects become significant, is about 14 kilogauss. At the other extreme, the magnet for the Argonne machine uses a very compact design of poles and coils, with iron return circuits both inside and outside the orbit. Maximum fields of over 21 kilogauss can be used; this results in a minimum orbit radius for the chosen energy. But the structure severely restricts accessibility to the vacuum chamber and may prove to have objectionable limitations in research operations.

The choice of magnet structure and maximum field determines the orbit radius for a chosen particle energy. The relativistic relation between particle kinetic energy T, magnetic field B, and orbit radius R is given [see Eq. (5-49)] by

$$T(T + 2W_0) = c^2 e^2 B^2 R^2 \qquad (13\text{-}1)$$

When T and W_0 are expressed in Bev units and B is in webers/m^2 (units of 10,000 gauss), the radius is given by

$$R = \frac{3.33[T(T + 2W_0)]^{\frac{1}{2}}}{B} \qquad \text{meters} \qquad (13\text{-}1a)$$

In the cosmotron, with a chosen proton energy of 3.0 Bev and with a maximum field of 14 kilogauss, the required orbit radius is 9.10 m. The mean orbit radius taken as the basic dimensional parameter was 30.0 ft (9.15 m).

The choice of orbit aperture depends primarily on the estimated amplitudes of the several types of particle oscillations at and shortly following injection. This problem will be discussed in more detail in Sec. 13-6, Injection. The choice also depends on the space allocated for the top and bottom walls of the vacuum chamber, and so on the structural design of the chamber. The most uncertain element in this decision is the geometric "factor of safety" in excess of the calculated aperture requirements to allow for the effect of magnetic inhomogeneities, scattering of particles in the beam by residual gas in the chamber, and alignment errors. Early designers tended to choose a large safety factor, which resulted in unnecessarily large aperture dimensions and increased the cost of the magnet and power supply. With experience it is now possible to compute the effects of such errors with some confidence and to reduce the safety factor to a more reasonable value. The decision on aperture balances the importance of maximum possible beam intensity against the costs for initial construction and for power during operations.

In the cosmotron the decision on aperture dimensions had to be made early, before designs were complete for the vacuum chamber and also before any model experiments could be carried out. Oscillation amplitudes were computed theoretically and estimates were made of the effect of inhomogeneities, gas scattering, and alignment errors. The gross aperture chosen was a 36-in. pole-face width and a 9-in. gap, planned to accommodate a vacuum chamber with a net internal clearance of 30 by 6 in. As will be shown in the discussion to follow, this allows a geometric factor of safety of about 1.5 times the calculated maximum oscillation amplitudes in both the radial and vertical dimensions. Operating experience shows that a large fraction of the ion beam initially captured in resonant orbits is retained within this aperture.

As indicated earlier, the bevatron designers were more conservative in their early planning and chose basic magnet dimensions which would allow alternative use of either a large-aperture chamber for low particle energy or a smaller-aperture chamber for higher energies. Their final decision was for an internal aperture of 10 by 40 in., resulting in proton energies up to 6.4 Bev.

As the design studies developed at Brookhaven and at Berkeley, it became evident that there were several reasons for providing sectors in the ion orbit free from magnetic field. An electron-synchrotron magnet with straight sections between two semicircular halves of a ring magnet, called a racetrack, had been proposed by Crane[22] for the University of Michigan synchrotron and had been shown theoretically by Dennison and Berlin[23] not to cause defocusing or to set up excessive ion oscillations. A design was chosen, at Brookhaven and also at Berkeley, in which the circular magnet was spaced into four quadrants joined by four straight sections free of magnetic field. Later, Blachman and Courant[10] published the Brookhaven calculations justifying the quadrant design and showing that the four symmetrical straight sections do not disturb orbit stability; they do modify the calculations on oscillation amplitude and frequency slightly and require a slightly larger aperture within the quadrants. Finer-grained angular asymmetries in the field, such as those caused by spaced bundles of magnet laminations, were found to have an almost insignificant effect on ion oscillations; amplitudes can be computed by using the average field around the quadrant.

A field-free region is essential to accommodate the type of induction accelerator used for ion acceleration in the cosmotron or the drift tube used in the bevatron. Another field-free region is assigned to injection of the beam of protons from the preaccelerator. Still others can be used effectively for targets or for the ejection mechanisms needed to produce an emergent beam of high-energy protons. In the bevatron the four straight sections are used for vacuum-pump manifolds as well. The absence of such straight sections in the Birmingham machine has made it necessary to mount the inflector, radiofrequency accelerator, and targets between the magnet poles.

The magnetic field must decrease with increasing radius across the pole face to provide the necessary focusing for particles in the orbit. The significance of this decrease in field (specified by the n value) in providing stability for particle orbits is discussed in Chap. 5. It is shown there that in a gap having a vertical dimension small relative to the radial extent the n value should be between 0.5 and 1.0, for a circular orbit. In the quadrant-type magnet with straight sections these limits become 0.5 to 0.8.[10] In both the cosmotron and bevatron the n value for the magnetic field at injection was chosen as 0.6, obtained by sloping the pole faces so the gap on the outside of the orbit is longer than on the inside. In both cases also, the final detailed shape of the pole faces was obtained by analysis of the magnetic circuit and checked by model measurements.

Power for magnet excitation is another basic parameter. It is closely associated with the choice of pulse repetition rate and so with the time-average beam intensity. In pulse powering, the stored energy in the magnetic field must be removed at the end of each cycle. In the large magnets required for multi-Bev synchrotrons the stored energy between poles is in the range of 10^7 to 10^8 joules. If it were to be supplied at a repetition rate of one per second and dissipated in each cycle, it would require 10 to 100 megawatts of power. Some method of storing and of reusing the energy in the magnetic field is essential. Cyclic operation is indicated, with a system which transfers the stored energy of the magnetic field to some other storage element in the circuit and returns it to the magnet in the following cycle.

Brobeck[5] first discussed the alternative possibilities of energy storage, using the preliminary conceptual design for a 10-Bev bevatron as illustration. Capacitors, while ideal for small installations using higher repetition rates, would be far too costly for such a large magnet with the long time constant inherent in the basic design. At an early stage of the cosmotron planning an estimate of the cost for the necessary capacitors was about 3 million dollars. Storage batteries can store adequate power, but they involve formidable control and switching problems as well as serious maintenance and charging problems. It was estimated at Berkeley that maintenance and charging of a battery storage system would require three shifts of 6 to 10 electricians each.

The choice of an energy storage system, at Berkeley and at Brookhaven, was a flywheel. A large flywheel can readily store ten or twenty times the magnetic stored energy in rotational kinetic energy, and 5 to 10 per cent of this energy can be delivered to the magnet during the excitation cycle by means of a generator and suitable high-current rectifiers. Furthermore, grid-controlled rectifiers can be used which act as inverters to drive the generator as a motor during the return half of the powering cycle and transfer the stored energy back to the flywheel. Losses due to heating in the magnet windings and friction in the rotating machines can be made up by a low-power motor which drives the flywheel back to full speed between pulses. The average power dissipated will be just that due to losses during the pulses and can be specified to supply any desired pulse repetition rate.

The electrical properties of the magnet windings, such as the inductance, resistance, and number of turns to provide the desired excitation, are chosen for optimum performance of the pulse powering system. Further details of the cosmotron magnet and power supply will be given in following sections.

Magnetic field increases with time during the pulse; the rate of this increase is determined by the characteristics of the power supply and the magnet windings. The time to reach maximum field, and so the time rate of increase in field, is influenced by several factors. A short rise time increases the peak value of kilovolt-amperes required to excite the magnet and so increases the cost of the power supply. However, it reduces the average power demand (at a fixed repetition rate) by reducing the heat in the windings. A short rise time also means a large dB/dt and so requires higher rf potentials from the radiofrequency accelerating system to provide the necessary volts per turn. A short accelerating time also decreases the interval at the start of acceleration during which particles can be lost from the beam because of gas scattering. Practical considerations also enter, such as the properties and ratings of commercial electric equipment and the cost of this equipment.

The magnetic-field rise time at the cosmotron was chosen to be 1 sec, although an allowable range would have been between 0.5 and 2.0 sec. The interval for returning the stored energy to the flywheel, while the pulse is decreasing, is associated with the rise time and is also about 1 sec. An independent parameter is the pulse repetition rate, which determines average power requirements. This was taken to be 12 per minute for the cosmotron. So the magnet cycle is 1 sec rise, 1 sec fall, and 3 sec for the drive motor to bring the flywheel back to speed.

At the bevatron the rise time was also taken to be 1 sec and the repetition rate at full power was set at 10 per minute.

Another basic parameter is the injection energy. Protons are pre-accelerated to injection energy in a separate accelerator usually located outside the ring of synchrotron magnets and are directed through a vacuum pipe to the injection straight section. In this location they pass through an inflecting field between shaped electrodes, which bends the particle beam into the direction of the synchrotron orbit at the chosen injection orbit radius.

Many considerations point to the desirability of high injection energy. The most significant of these is that the magnetic field at the orbit is most uniform and least subject to errors due to remanent fields and eddy currents for high injection fields. Another is that the initial orbital frequency of the particles increases with field, so a high field reduces the range over which the applied accelerating radiofrequency must be modulated. Still another is that gas scattering is minimized at high injection energy.

However, practical limits existed on the energies which could be obtained from the existing types of low-energy accelerators which were adaptable to this purpose. The types considered were the Cockcroft-Walton voltage multiplier, the electrostatic generator, the proton linear accelerator, and the cyclotron. Each type had its own limitations on energy, beam collimation, or reliability.

The physical dimensions and the general arrangements for the cosmotron are illustrated in Fig. 13-1. This shows the four magnet quadrants of 30 ft orbit radius spaced by straight sections of 10 ft length. It also shows the electrostatic generator used as a preaccelerator, which feeds pulses of protons to the inflecting plate system in one straight section; another straight section is used for the radiofrequency accelerator, a third for control electrodes and internal targets, and the fourth for the devices used to produce an emergent beam. The chapter headpiece, page 437, is a photograph of the assembled cosmotron before the surrounding shielding was added.

With the basic dimensions known, other parameters can be established, such as the ion revolution frequencies at injection and at high energy which determine the range of frequencies required in the radiofrequency system.   Equation (5-54) gives the frequency of revolution in a circular orbit as

$$f_c = \frac{c^2 eB}{2\pi(W_0 + T)} \tag{13-2}$$

In the orbit with four quadrants of radius R and straight sections of length L the orbital frequency is decreased by the path-length ratio

$$\frac{f_0}{f_c} = \frac{2\pi R}{2\pi R + 4L} = 0.824 \text{ (cosmotron)} \tag{13-3}$$

The frequency of revolution f_0 for the cosmotron is plotted as a function of the magnetic field in Fig. 13-2 and shows a range of frequencies from

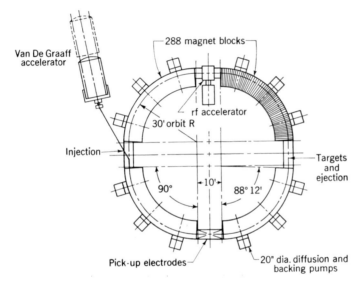

Fig. 13-1. Sketch of the cosmotron assembly showing the four quadrants and four straight sections.

0.40 megacycle/sec at 4-Mev injection where $B = 311$ gauss (or 0.35 megacycle at 3 Mev and 271 gauss) to 4.2 megacycles at the maximum energy of 3 Bev.

Ions must be accelerated on each turn by an average energy increment determined by the instantaneous rate of change of field, dB/dt, in order to maintain constant radius.   The average value of dB/dt is given by the maximum field and the rise time, but is modified by the varying inductance of the magnet windings as magnetic permeability changes during the cycle, and also by the falling voltage characteristic of the generator

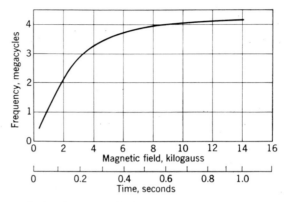

Fig. 13-2. Ion revolution frequency during the acceleration cycle for the cosmotron.

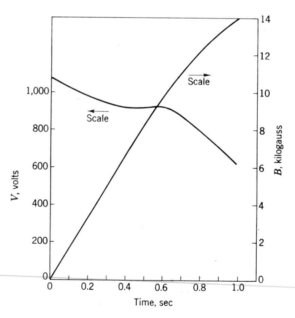

Fig. 13-3. Variation of magnetic field B and the volts per turn V required for acceleration during the cosmotron acceleration cycle.

as magnet current increases. These variations can be computed from the physical properties of the system or can be observed from scale-model studies using a time scale in proper ratio.

The measured value of B as a function of time during the 1-sec rise time of the cosmotron magnet is shown in Fig. 13-3. The values of dB/dt determined from this function start at over 16 kg/sec and drop to about 10 kg/sec near maximum field.

The rate of increase of particle energy with time is directly related to the rate of magnetic-field increase. By differentiation of Eq. (13-1) we find

$$\frac{dT}{dt} = \frac{c^2 e^2 R^2 B}{T + W_0} \frac{dB}{dt} \tag{13-4}$$

A more useful quantity is the energy increase per turn. This can be obtained by dividing the above relation by the orbital frequency f_0 given in Eqs. (13-2) and (13-3):

$$\frac{\Delta T}{\text{Turn}} = \frac{2\pi e R^2}{0.824} \frac{dB}{dt} \tag{13-5}$$

The constant in the denominator of Eq. (13-5) is the value for the orbit radius and straight section length of the cosmotron. When evaluated for an average value of dB/dt of 14 kilogauss/sec, this relation gives ΔT/turn (average) = 880 ev/turn.

The volts-per-turn function for the cosmotron is also shown in Fig. 13-3, in units of electron volts. The maximum value occurs at injection and is about 1000 ev, decreasing to about 600 ev at maximum energy. The applied radiofrequency voltage across the accelerating gap must be higher, by about a factor of 2, to maintain phase stability in synchronous oscillations. This determines the voltage requirements for the rf accelerator. The frequency variation of the accelerator during the cycle is illustrated in Fig. 13-2.

The analysis above covers the basic interrelated parameters which must be determined at an early stage of design. From these, the other constants and design requirements can be obtained. We go now into a more detailed discussion of the characteristics of the several major components.

13-4. COSMOTRON MAGNET

The magnet design chosen for the cosmotron after a careful study of alternative structures involves several unusual features. It is basically a C section with minimum-size window for the windings. Choice of the C shape was influenced by the desire to provide ready access for pumping and for beam ejection on the outside of the magnet gap along the entire periphery. Pump leads can be located as frequently as desired along the length of the vacuum chamber, a valuable feature when vacuum requirements are severe and chamber cross section is small. Access to the chamber for inspection and maintenance is also simplified. When the slot opening of the C is on the outer face of the ring, high-energy particles can emerge tangentially from the accelerator around the entire circumference, with only thin windows in the chamber wall for absorption and scattering of the radiations.   To be sure, every effort is made to eject a concentrated beam in a narrow angle; however, the external C opening is good insurance that the high-energy particles can be utilized to the maximum for experiments.

The poleless C-shaped magnetic circuit has minimal dimensions and weight and requires only two accurately machined surfaces (the pole faces).   The octagonal shape is a compromise between a square and the ideal circular shape; it is achieved by cutting off the corners of square plates in manufacture.   The magnet cross section is shown in Fig. 13-4.

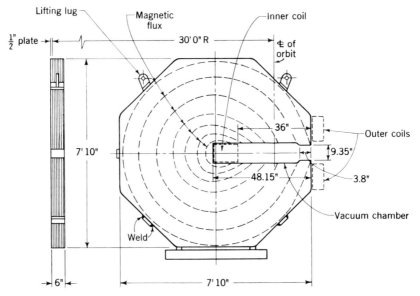

Fig. 13-4. Iron magnetic circuit for the cosmotron, showing assembly in bundles of 12 half-inch plates.

Since magnetic field increases at a rate up to 16 kilogauss/sec during the acceleration, eddy currents will be induced in the iron and it must be laminated.   A detailed analysis of the eddy currents, checked by model measurements, justified the choice of ½-in. plate, which has the advantage of being readily available in large sheets and at a low base price. The material chosen was equivalent to SAE 1010 mild steel, having a low carbon content and magnetic properties closely approaching those for soft iron.   The octagonal plates were sheared from 8-ft-wide strips and were supplied and fabricated by the Bethlehem Steel Company.

In order to simplify the problems of machining and handling the thousands of ½-in. steel plates, a procedure was devised for assembling the plates into blocks of 12, with interleaved insulation.   The 12 plates in each bundle are welded together by tie bars at the outer edges.   These tie bars are outside the magnetic circuit and do not link any appreciable flux, so they do not produce significant eddy currents.   The pole-face contours were machined in the block as a unit after assembly and welding; care was taken to remove all metal chips and burrs.   Lifting lugs on the welded tie bars allow the blocks to be handled; the weight of each block of 12 laminations is about 5.7 tons.

Short circuits between laminations might produce serious eddy-current distortions if they occurred near the magnet gap.   To test for such shorts, the insulation between laminations consisted of a sandwich of two layers of 0.007-in. insulation paper separated by a 0.001-in. aluminum-foil sheet. After processing and machining the blocks, these aluminum sheets were used to test for short circuits.

A total of 288 bundles, each about 6 in. thick, are arranged in four quadrants to form the complete magnetic circuit.   Each quadrant occupies an angle of 88.4°, which was the angle found necessary from magnetic-field measurements to produce 90° deflection of particles, because of the fringing field which extends into the straight sections.   The bundles were assembled on base plates and carefully leveled by accurate surveying techniques during assembly to keep the median plane of the gap flat. The inner edges of the bundles are in contact, and the center line of each bundle was located accurately on a surveyed radial line.   After alignment the bundles were welded together at the tie bars to form the entire quadrant structure into a rigid unit.   Settling of the foundation under the load of 2000 tons of steel was anticipated and provided for by elevation adjustments beneath the base plates.   The precision attained in assembly was within 0.005 in. in the horizontal level and 0.015 in. radially, with additional precautions to maintain vertical alignment.

The pole-face contour was shaped to produce the widest possible region with a radially decreasing field of the correct slope to provide focusing. The n value chosen was 0.6, and the acceptable range is 0.5 to 0.8. Maximum aperture is most necessary during and immediately following injection, when ion oscillations have their largest amplitudes.   So the pole was shaped to give the widest possible extent of the $n = 0.6$ slope at the injection flux density of about 300 gauss.

Measurements with a short section of a quarter-scale model were used to study the properties of the magnet and to obtain the pole-face shape. The model was in true physical scale, using $\frac{1}{8}$-in. laminations of equivalent iron plate, and consisted of seven blocks of laminations, formed around an arc of the scaled-down radius.   Effects due to the quadrant ends were observed to extend in no further than two lamination blocks, so the three blocks at the center of the model were available for typical magnetic measurements.   The exciting coils were also modeled to scale and were pulsed at the planned duty cycle.   Certain physical problems were encountered, such as the spreading or fanning of the laminations due to the repulsive forces between parallel laminations.   These indicated similar problems in the full-scale magnet and were solved by installing bolts and clamps of nonmagnetic stainless steel to restrict the spreading.

Many types of measurements were taken with the models.   In fact, the program of magnetic measurements continued in more and more detail for a period of over 2 years.   These measurements included:

1. Average field at the orbit radius as a function of time during the pulse and of the current in the windings

2. Time rate of change of magnetic field, dB/dt, as a function of time

3. Radial decrease in field at injection time and at several higher fields extending up to the maximum, for a series of pole-face shapes

4. Eddy-current effects at short times, extended past injection until they became negligible

5. Remanent magnetic fields in the gap, as a function of previous excitation history

6. Effect of corrective pole-face windings, to extend the desired n value to high fields and over as large a gap area as possible

7. Fringing fields in the quadrant end region, at various fields

8. Fringing fields at large radii on the median plane off the front of the magnet gap, to compute trajectories for emergent particles

9. Location of the magnetic median plane

Average flux densities at a particular radius were obtained with a rectangular coil located on the median plane, narrow enough to give the desired resolution in radial measurements and of a length sufficient to extend from the center of one block to the center of the next and so to overlap the wedge-shaped space between.   This coil was located at different radii to observe the radial decrease from which the n value could be computed.   As an alternative, two such coils located at different radii were used to obtain a value for dB/dr directly, and the pair could be moved radially to survey the field.

The time rate of change came directly from the induced electromotive force (emf) in a coil.   The emf was displayed on a cathode-ray tube with a time sweep, and photographs of the pulse were taken.   Calibrations were obtained from several standards.   A large precisely built Helmholtz coil was used to obtain known magnetic fields up to 1000 gauss in air, and the test coils were calibrated in this field.   Calibrated voltage amplifiers were used for the measurement of emfs.

Eddy-current effects appeared in the dynamic measurements during the first 30 μsec of the pulse.   Qualitatively the effect of eddy currents in the pole faces is to reduce the magnetic field at the midportion of the gap as compared with the field near the exciting windings.   As a result, the rate of field decrease with radius, or the n value, is increased.   If the time rate of increase of field were constant, this increase in n could be compensated by a slightly different shape of pole contour. But the initial sharp change of dB/dt at the start of the pulse induces a transient which takes a finite time to die out and extends up to injection times. The magnitude of this increase in n value over steady-state conditions, Δn, was measured by observing the difference in induced voltage in two coils spaced a short distance apart radially and located at various positions across the gap. Photographic recordings of the integrated difference voltage displayed on a cathode-ray tube were analyzed to obtain a measure of Δn as a function of time. The results are shown by the dashed curve of Fig. 13-5. The effect was large at very short times, but had dropped to a value of $\Delta n = 0.3$ at the time corresponding to injection at 3 Mev, when the magnetic field is 271 gauss.

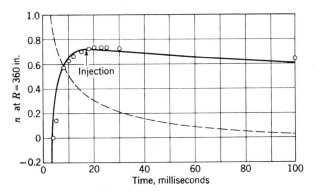

Fig. 13-5. Variation of the n value of magnetic field in the cosmotron at short times. The dashed curve is the calculated effect of eddy currents alone.

The remanent field in the iron resulting from unidirectional operation is significant and adds to the dynamic field at low flux densities. It is determined by the past history of excitation and can be removed by applying a reversed field after the main pulse, if needed. It was found to have an average value of about 25 gauss at the central orbit radius after a typical cycle of operation to maximum field and reduction to zero current. It was also observed to increase almost linearly by about 25 per cent from the inner to the outer radius of the aperture; this is due to the larger integrated coercive force in the long flux paths around the outer portions of the magnetic circuit. The radial increase due to the remanent field produced a negative Δn at injection time, which almost completely compensated for the positive Δn due to eddy currents. This was a fortunate coincidence associated with the shape of the magnetic circuit. The maximum resultant Δn, measured as the sum of both effects at injection time and over the useful width of the pole face, was of the order of ± 0.1. It was considered to be sufficiently small to make further corrections for eddy currents unnecessary. The variation of n after correction for remanent field effects is shown by the solid curve of Fig. 13-5.

The machined taper needed to attain a value of $n = 0.6$ at injection time, after including the effects of eddy currents and of the remanent field, was derived from model experiments (see Fig. 13-6). The taper starts at the inner radius of the aperture (outside the magnet slot windings) at a gap length of 9.00 in. and is a straight taper cut on each face to a position about 4 in. inside the front face of the magnet where the gap length is 9.35 in. A 4-in.-wide lip of iron is retained at the periphery with the basic 9.00-in. gap to extend the region of uniform field to the maximum possible radius. The resulting magnetic field at injection time during a normal pulse decreases about 3 per cent from the inner to the outer extent of the useful field. Figure 13-7 is a plot of the n value as a

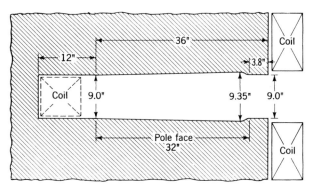

Fig. 13-6. Pole-face shape to produce an n value of 0.6 at injection fields in the cosmotron.

function of radius. The useful field region at injection is found to extend from a radius of 344 to 372 in., defined as the region in which n lies between the limits 0.5 and 0.8. No significant difference in the shape of this field was observed up to fields of about 6000 gauss.

At high fields the permeability of the magnet iron decreases and an appreciable fraction of the magnetomotive force appears in the iron. Because of the C shape of the magnetic circuit and the large difference in iron-path length for flux crossing at the two ends of the gap, the effect of decreasing permeability is to cause an increase in n value at high fields. This effect becomes significant at about 9000 gauss; it increases the value of n above the 0.8 limit over the entire pole face by the time the field reaches 12,000 gauss.

Such a large change in n value cannot be permitted, and must be compensated by auxiliary windings. Such windings need only be powered during the later part of the acceleration interval and need only change the slope or shape of the field.   An excessive n value means that the field at large radii is too small relative to that at small radii.   A method of correction is to add magnetic flux at large radii, tapering off to zero at the center of the aperture and subtracting flux at smaller radii.   This can be achieved most simply with a layer of windings distributed uniformly across the pole face, with suitably located return windings.

Before being assembled, each of the 288 blocks was checked in a detailed testing program, to determine its properties and the best order of assembly in the final magnet.   A full-scale three-block sector was set up in which the block under test was placed between two fixed guard blocks.   The unit was magnetized to full field using a 1-sec cycle to duplicate the operating condition.   Measurements were made of the maximum field in the

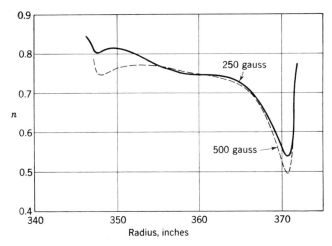

Fig. 13-7. Radial variation of n value across the pole face of the cosmotron, at injection fields.

gap, the initial dB/dt to check for shorts between laminations, the n value at injection fields, the location of the magnetic median plane, and the remanent field after a pulse.   The variations observed in the dynamic field were negligible.   Appreciable differences were observed in remanent field, however.   A statistical analysis of the results led to a preferred order of assembly which gave a fine-grained azimuthal variation in remanent field and compensated for the blocks having extreme properties.   The uniformity of average field attained in this way was much better than would have resulted from random stacking and gave the maximum possible useful area of magnetic field at injection.

The excitation windings for the magnet were designed to be compact and located as close as possible to the magnet gap.   In principle a single circular winding located in the slot of the C magnet would provide excitation. However, such a coil of large diameter would produce magnetic fields in the air both inside and outside the circular magnet. External fields well beyond the iron would be of the order of hundreds of gauss when the field in the gap was 14 kilogauss and would represent a large amount of stored energy. In early calculations and model studies with a single-slot coil the external stored energy was observed to be about 40 per cent of the stored energy in the gap itself. Return windings, split symmetrically above and below the slot on the outer face of the magnet, confine the magnetic fields more closely to the gap. Further studies with such return windings showed the external stored energy to be reduced to 13 per cent of the energy in the gap.

The slot windings were made as compact as possible to minimize the size of the coil window in the C structure and thereby to reduce magnet weight, stored energy, and power requirements. They consisted of 48 turns arranged in four layers. Each conductor was an extruded rectangular copper bar with a $\frac{3}{8}$-in.-diam hole down the center for water cooling. The bars were double-wrapped with insulation, formed to the proper circular shape, and clamped into the slot between fiber shields to prevent contact with the iron and to provide insulation.

The return windings do not have so severe a space limitation; they were designed with a 50 per cent larger cross section to reduce resistance. These are also rectangular, with a $\frac{3}{8}$-in. water-cooling channel. They are arranged in two bundles of 24 turns each, one above and one below the gap, clamped to the magnet face with many stainless-steel brackets.

Connectors joining the inner and outer windings at the quadrant ends are made of the same stock as the outer return windings, also water-cooled. Silver brazing was used to form the corner joints in the connectors, and the connectors were gasket-bolted firmly to the ends of the magnet windings. Thermal expansion was anticipated for the copper windings relative to the iron quadrant structure, and it was allowed for in the design of spring clamps to support the connectors. In the completed unit (Fig. 13-8) the windings form a continuous coil of 48 turns around each quadrant pole face, with two terminals brought out at one quadrant end.

Water-cooling leads for the 96 separate conductors in each quadrant are brought out in parallel to water manifolds located at the quadrant ends. Insulation of the $\frac{3}{8}$-in. cooling-water lines is provided by 5-ft lengths of plastic hose in each line. Water flow through the 384 parallel cooling tubes is about 500 gpm at 20 psi pressure. The water is purified to control conductivity and is recirculated through a heat exchanger.

After the assembly was completed, tests were made gradually increasing the length of pulse up to the full 1 sec and the peak current up to its maximum of 7000 amp. Small physical displacements of the connector bars at quadrant ends were observed due to the magnetic forces; the maximum displacement observed was 0.060 in. Additional steel brackets ("spreader bars") were installed between quadrant ends to brace the connector-bar assembly, and the displacement was reduced to 0.020 in. under maximum power. A systematic routine of tightening all clamp bolts and the insertion of block spacers between magnet blocks resulted in a more rigid structure in which physical motions of the iron laminations and coil conductors were reduced to even smaller values. The compact assembly resulted in very little audible creaking when the magnet was pulsed. Some was observed at the start when the magnet was first excited, but was almost completely eliminated by the tightening program.

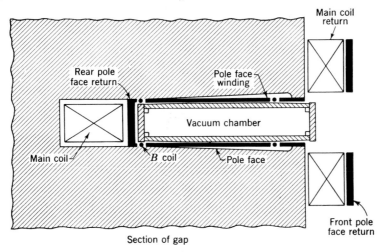

Section of gap

Fig. 13-8. Assembly sketch of water-cooled conductors forming the excitation coil of the cosmotron magnet. Correction windings on the pole face and return circuits are also shown.

After 2 years of operation (in November, 1954), a fault developed which led to an insulation breakdown between conductor bars near one of the quadrant end connections. The cause of the failure appears to have been a small water leak from a defective bar. Moisture seepage from this leak saturated the insulation and caused a destructive short circuit between adjacent conductors. This bar and adjacent bars were replaced and satisfactory operation was resumed.

In November of 1957 a more serious failure occurred when one of the coil conductors broke near the sharp bend at the end of the quadrant. Inspection of similar bars on other quadrants revealed the fact that the bars were suffering from metal fatigue due to their small motions in the fringing fields around the quadrant ends. Although these motions were very small, the magnet had, by this time, been pulsed more than 7 million times. It was evident that a local repair would no longer be adequate, and the whole magnet coil was removed and redesigned. In the new coil the conductors extend past the quadrant end and are joined to the front coil by connectors which are spaced vertically 3 ft away from the gap. These connecting bars experience negligible forces due to stray fields, and no further fatigue failures are expected. This repair involved a shutdown of more than a year; fortunately this provided an opportunity for long-overdue modifications in other components and in the experimental laboratory.

The faults and limitations of the early designs for the cosmotron magnet and coils have been described in some detail to illustrate a typical development problem in the accelerator field. As a result of this experience new concepts and techniques have been developed and widely applied in subsequent designs. The physical motions of laminations and coils in the magnetic fields can now be essentially eliminated by bonding techniques using modern adhesives and resins. The laminated cores of pulsed magnets are now bonded into solid mechanical blocks with suitable adhesives. The most successful type is an air-drying, thermosetting artificial rubber; laminations are coated with a thin layer of liquid adhesive, air-dried, stacked, and clamped into bundles and baked in an oven with a carefully controlled temperature cycle. The resulting bundles of laminations can then be assembled, aligned, and clamped in place on suitable structural bases to form the magnet. Similarly, the conductors for magnet windings are bonded into solid units. The preferred technique is to wrap the individual conductors with porous cotton or glass-fiber cloth, wind or assemble the conductors into coil units in a vacuumtight housing or mold, and vacuum-impregnate the entire coil with an epoxy resin which has good electrical insulation properties. This technique for making solid resin-bonded coils is now standard throughout the electrical industry. Most accelerator laboratories are taking advantage of these new developments in the design of magnets and coils for new accelerators or auxiliary apparatus.

The pole-face windings used to correct the field at high flux densities consist of a single layer of 20 turns of $\frac{1}{4}$- by $\frac{1}{4}$-in. copper conductor spaced across each pole face. Each conductor is an arc of constant radius extending along the length of a quadrant. The 20 conductors are spaced at $\frac{1}{2}$-in. intervals and grouped near the center of the pole face, since it is necessary to correct the fields only over a radial-aperture width of about 10 in. at high magnetic fields when radial beam oscillation amplitudes have been damped to small dimensions. The correction windings were embedded in a $\frac{3}{8}$-in. layer of polyester with glass-cloth reinforcement, cast from a liquid thermosetting resin. The resin has good insulation properties and forms a strong and rigid unit for mounting on the pole faces. The return circuits for the pole-face windings are located partly

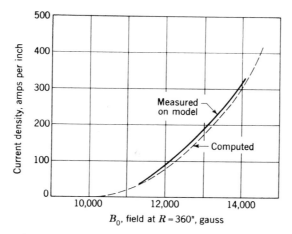

Fig. 13-9. Correction current pulse applied to pole-face windings used on the cosmotron to maintain uniform n values to high magnetic fields.

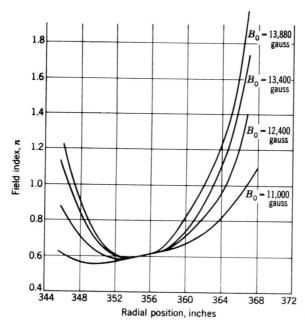

Fig. 13-10. Radial variation of n value at high magnetic fields using pole-face windings in the cosmotron.

outside and partly inside the main magnet gap.   With a proper division of these turns there can be almost zero coupling between the pole-face windings and the main field pattern, so it is possible to power the correcting windings with an independent power supply.   The pole-face return windings are also formed in a rigid arc and bonded with glass-cloth-reinforced resin.

The physical arrangements of the pole-face windings and return circuits are also shown in Fig. 13-8.   The current-time pulse used to power

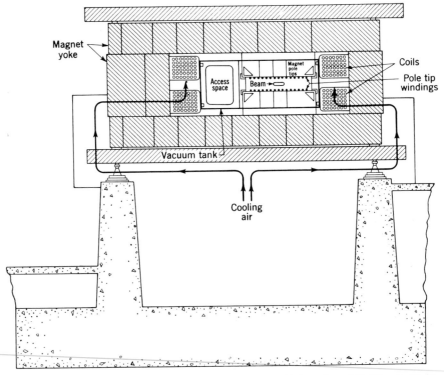

Fig. 13-11. Cross section of bevatron magnet at the University of California Radiation Laboratory.

the windings is illustrated in Fig. 13-9, and a plot showing the radial variation of n value after correction by currents in the pole-face windings is shown in Fig. 13-10.   This plot shows that the region of useful n value contracts at high magnetic fields; fortunately the damping in amplitude of particle oscillations during acceleration reduces the width of the beam so the contracted region of focusing field is quite adequate.

The magnet for the Berkeley bevatron has iron return circuits both inside and outside the orbit (Fig. 13-11).   This symmetrical structure is more efficient magnetically, in that saturation effects do not destroy the useful field region until the field reaches about 16 kilogauss.   This advantage is offset to some extent by the relative inaccessibility of the vacuum chamber; magnet yokes must be removed to install or to make significant modifications to the chamber.   As mentioned earlier, the bevatron magnet was designed to allow the use of a large pole gap and wide aperture, because of concern over the possible effect of orbit inaccuracies and gas scattering in developing large-amplitude oscillations.   Following the success at the cosmotron with a smaller relative aperture, the poles and vacuum chamber were redesigned for a 12-in. gap with pole faces of 5 ft width, a much smaller vacuum chamber than originally conceived. This arrangement is shown in Fig. 13-11, which also shows the access tunnel through which a man can crawl to service the chamber, if necessary.

A new principle of pole-face design has been developed by H. Bruck and his associates[24] for the 3-Bev accelerator at Saclay.   The pole tips are bonded units of thin laminations of two or more different pole-face shapes, stacked in a sequence to give a fine-grained alternation in profile.   These "crenelated" pole tips display the magnetic-field pattern at low fields established by the profile of the protruding laminations; at high fields when the protruding edges saturate, the field pattern is determined by the shape of the underlying base laminations.   This technique allows the magnet to be operated much closer to saturation limits without requiring pulse-powered correcting coils.   The Saclay machine has removable pole pieces to allow the use of such crenelated poles when desired.   The same principle has been adopted to determine pole-face shape for the Princeton-Pennsylvania proton synchrotron.

13-5. PULSE POWER SUPPLY

The systems for providing pulse power to the magnet, at the cosmotron and also the bevatron, use large flywheels for energy storage.   They consist of a motor, a flywheel, and a 12-phase ac generator on the same shaft, with the generator supplying a rectifier-inverter circuit connected to the magnet coils.   The motor drives the flywheel up to speed; the flywheel supplies energy to the ac generator; the rectifier converts the multiphase ac output of the generator to direct current to supply the magnet.   As energy is removed from the flywheel, it drops in speed.   Then at the peak of the cycle the grids of the rectifier-inverters (Hg vapor ignitrons) are controlled to switch to inverter action; the inverter drives the generator as a motor, fed by the stored energy in the magnetic field; the stored energy (less heat losses) is returned to the flywheel, increasing its speed. During the remainder of the pulsing cycle the motor brings the flywheel back to the original speed.

The design of this power supply was worked out in collaboration with the makers, the Westinghouse Electric and Manufacturing Company.

The ratings of the power supply had to be coordinated with the properties of the magnet and its exciting coil. Peak current was chosen to supply the necessary ampere-turns for full excitation of the magnet, and voltage was designed to bring the magnet up to full excitation in the chosen 1-sec rise time.

In the cosmotron, scaled-model measurements showed that the excitation required to produce 14 kilogauss in the gap was

$$Ni = 3.36 \times 10^5 \text{ amp-turns}$$

The total flux in the magnetic circuit including stray field was

$$\phi = 88 \text{ webers}$$

and the initial rate of change to reach peak field in 1 sec was

$$\frac{d\phi}{dt} = 58 \text{ webers/sec}$$

The total stored energy in the magnetic field at peak excitation was found to be $W = 1.2 \times 10^7$ joules, and the peak power transfer was

$$\frac{dW}{dt} = 26{,}000 \text{ kva}$$

Generator output V is related to the number of turns N and the resistance R of the coil as

$$V = N\frac{d\Phi}{dt} + Ri \tag{13-6}$$

For practical engineering reasons the manufacturers recommended a peak voltage of 5 to 6 kv for the generator and rectifier system. The cosmotron designers desired a coil with an even number of turns which could be compacted into two identical rectangular bundles fitting inside the 9-in.-high window in the magnet; this required a number of turns divisible by 2, 4, 6, or other simple integers in order to assemble the bundles from rectangular copper conductors. The external dimensions of the space allocated to the coil were known, and good estimates were available of the total copper cross section A which could be packed into this space with suitable insulation.

The resistance of a coil can be expressed as a function of the number of turns N, the average conductor length per turn L, and the copper cross section A:

$$R = \frac{\rho L}{A} N^2 \tag{13-7}$$

where ρ is the resistivity of the conductor at operating temperature. For the cosmotron dimensions this becomes $R = 4.95 \times 10^{-5}N^2$ ohms. The quantity Ri for use in Eq. (13-6) can now be obtained as

$$Ri = 4.95 \times 10^{-5} N(Ni) = 17.0N$$

The relation between voltage and number of turns can now be expressed as $V = 58N + 17.0N = 75N$. The choice of the cosmotron designers was for a coil of 48 turns, for which the applied potential at 14 kilogauss excitation is 3700 volts. Peak current is then found to be

$$i = \frac{Ni}{N} = 7000 \text{ amp}$$

This is the voltage and current required at full excitation, after the flywheel and generator have been reduced to minimum speed. At full speed at the start of the cycle, and with no load, the generator characteristics provide a potential of 5400 volts.

The inductance of the magnet changes during the cycle with the varying permeability of the iron core. Model measurements showed the inductance to have an initial value of 0.47 henry, rising to a maximum of 0.80 henry at about 1000 gauss and dropping to a final value of 0.25 henry as the iron saturates. When combined with the falling voltage characteristic of the power supply, this leads to a nonlinear increase in current (or magnetic field) with time. The measured curve of B versus t was given in Fig. 13-3.

The cosmotron power supply in service is an impressive installation. The motor is rated at 1750 hp and is of the standard wound-rotor induction type operating at 950 rpm. It is directly connected to the large flywheel, which is 9 ft in diameter and weighs 42 tons, and to the 12-phase, 60-cycle generator. This alternator has a nominal continuous-service rating of 20,000 kva, specially designed to withstand rectifier service; it will deliver 6000 volts at no load and a peak of 7000 amp at 4200 volts under full load. The power supply has taps for 50, 75, 87, and 100 per cent voltage output, with the 87 per cent tap corresponding to standard operation at 14 kilogauss field in the magnet. The rectifier inverter bank uses 24 ignitrons in a 12-phase circuit, with grids and igniters controlled to rectify the alternator output during the 1-sec acceleration interval, and then to switch to inverter action. The flywheel is reduced in speed by about 6 per cent at the peak of the cycle, representing a 12 per cent decrease in the rotational stored energy. The heat loss per cycle in the magnet windings represents an average power drain of about 800 kw; windage and thermal losses in the machines and losses in the ignitron rectifier add to make the total average power demand under full load about 1100 kw. A control system for the motor limits the line-surge demands to 2000 kva peak; it can be adjusted to make the power demand nearly constant over the 5-sec cycle.

Protection against failures in the power circuit is provided by a short-circuiting switch across the magnet terminals and by spark gaps between power leads to the magnet at each quadrant. Any voltage surge which raises voltage by 50 per cent above the designed maximum will cause the gaps to discharge, shorting the circuit. Simultaneously the ignitron excitation is removed. Under such a short circuit the magnet windings have adequate thermal capacity and cooling to discharge the peak stored energy.

The complete time cycle for the applied voltage and current is shown in Fig. 13-12. The dc voltage on the coil terminals starts at 5400 volts and decreases to 3700 volts during the 1-sec powering interval; it is

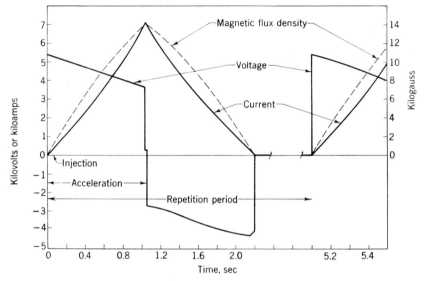

Fig. 13-12. Time cycle for applied voltage and current from the cosmotron magnet power supply. The magnetic flux density is also shown.

reversed by the ignitrons to -2800 volts and then increases in magnitude to about -4300 volts, by which time the current in the windings is reduced to zero; then the voltage is brought sharply to zero. The current cycle is also indicated, rising to 7000 amp at 1 sec and falling to zero in another 1.15 sec. The cycle is repeated at 5-sec intervals. Magnetic field varies with time in a slightly different manner than exciting current, because of the varying permeability. The remanent field of about 25 gauss is too small to be observable on the plot.

It is also possible to shorten the rise time and the time cycle if desired. For example, voltage can be reversed after 0.5 sec, at which time the current and magnetic field are approximately half their maximum values. With such reduced power demand the repetition rate can be increased.

This procedure can be used to eject protons at less than their maximum energy, in order to study nuclear processes at lower bombarding energies.

Another technique of completing the cycle after the magnet has been brought to full excitation is to short-circuit the magnet coils, removing ignitron excitation simultaneously. This technique is called "crashing" in laboratory parlance. When the coils are shorted in this way, all the energy stored in the magnetic field is dissipated in heat in the windings; the current circulating in the magnet decreases slowly, with a time constant given by the inductance and resistance of the windings. Or the coils can be shorted at any chosen time after the normal reversal of voltage has started to decrease the current. Such variations in the shape of the cycle are observed to affect the remanent fields strongly, and so may possibly have a useful function.

An auxiliary power supply is provided for the pole-face windings. This supply consists of four 40-kva dc generators on the same shaft, each supplying one quadrant. The excitation for each generator is separately controllable to adjust the time schedule of the corrective currents to optimum in each quadrant. The unit is capable of supplying a 0.3-sec pulse with a maximum current of 800 amp, sufficient to correct the field up to 14 kilogauss. When the main winding voltage reverses, induced voltages in the pole-face windings would produce large currents in the pole-face windings. This is controlled by reversing the voltage applied to the pole-face windings simultaneously with that of the main winding, and allowing current to fall to zero before opening the circuit.

The power supply for the Berkeley bevatron magnet is quite similar to that for the cosmotron, but has about twice the output capacity. This was obtained by using two generators and by paralleling twice as many ignitrons in the rectifier circuit. One major fault occurred during the early testing, because of failure of ignitrons in the pulsing circuit, which caused damage to one of the generators. The rate of ignitron "flashbacks" is higher at Berkeley than at Brookhaven, possibly because of operation closer to the power limits of the tubes.

13-6. INJECTION

The general requirements for the injection of particles into the orbit have been described in an earlier section. Protons are produced in an auxiliary accelerator, of an energy sufficient to give a high capture efficiency in the synchrotron orbit. A high-intensity, pulsed beam of particles is needed, with small energy spread, and delivered in a well-collimated beam of small cross section. The ion source for this preaccelerator is pulsed at the start of each magnet cycle, for a short time interval during which the magnetic field is in the range to accept the particles in stable orbits.

The preaccelerator chosen for the cosmotron was a Van de Graaff electrostatic generator rated for 4 Mev, built by the High Voltage Engineering Corporation. At the bevatron a 0.5-Mev Cockcroft-Walton source supplies a 10-Mev proton linac which was designed and developed at the Berkeley laboratory. Both machines give well-focused beams suitable for injection, and both have been copied in other installations.

The obvious method of directing the beam into the orbit is to deflect it between a pair of curved "inflector" electrodes which provide an electrostatic field and which are located in the field-free region at a straight section. These electrodes direct the beam into the synchrotron in a direction paralleling the equilibrium orbit and located at the outer edge of the useful aperture of the synchrotron. A basic requirement of the inflector system is that the injected particles should not strike the back of the inflector electrodes, or the chamber walls, in subsequent revolutions. The contraction in orbit radius due to the increasing magnetic field can be computed from Eq. (13-1a). For cosmotron parameters this is found to be 0.17 in. per turn at 4 Mev energy. In itself this orbit contraction would be insufficient to clear a practical injection electrode assembly, if the successive orbits were concentric.

The principle of injection utilizes the mismatch in frequency between the orbital motion of the particles and their betatron oscillations about the equilibrium orbit. Because of this mismatch the particles traverse many turns before their oscillations bring them again into the location of the inflecting electrodes. During this time the rising magnetic field causes the equilibrium orbits to contract sufficiently that the particle orbits can miss the electrodes completely.

The amplitude of the betatron oscillations depends on the spacing between the injected beam and the instantaneous location of the equilibrium orbit for a particle of injection energy. The acceptance interval starts when the equilibrium orbit is just inside the injection radius, when the oscillations are of small amplitude. As the equilibrium orbit contracts, the amplitudes increase to a maximum value which just fills the useful aperture when the equilibrium orbit reaches the center of the chamber. In the cosmotron this time interval is about 200 μsec, during which the ions make about 70 revolutions.

The parameters associated with injection into the cosmotron, at two injection energies, are listed in the following table:

Injection energy	3.0	Mev	4.0	Mev
Magnetic field at central orbit	271	gauss	311	gauss
Ion revolution frequency	0.35	megacycle	0.40	megacycle
Volts per turn for acceleration	1040	volts	1040	volts
Orbit contraction per turn	0.18	in.	0.17	in.
Time after $B = 0$	0.014 sec		0.017 sec	

A charged particle directed into the synchrotron field on a path parallel to its equilibrium orbit but at a larger radius will oscillate in the radial plane about the equilibrium orbit. The frequency f_r of this radial oscillation is given by[10]

$$f_r = \left(1 + \frac{L}{\pi R}\right)(1 - n)^{1/2} f_0 \qquad (13\text{-}8)$$

where f_0 is the orbital frequency in the quadrant and straight-section orbit given by Eqs. (13-2) and (13-3). When evaluated for cosmotron dimensions and n value, this gives $f_r = 0.70 f_0$. A full cycle of radial oscillation would require $360°/0.7 = 510°$ of azimuth, which is $150°$ beyond the angular location of the injector. Subsequent maximum outward amplitudes would be displaced from the injector position by $300°$, $90°$, $240°$, etc. So the average particle will make 5 to 10 revolutions before the maximum outward amplitude again occurs at the location of the injector. During this time (15 to 30 μsec) the equilibrium orbit will contract by 1 to 2 in., sufficient for a large fraction of the beam to miss the inflector plates.

Angular divergence of the injected beam will cause a spread in the amplitudes of radial oscillations and will also result in a spread in the initial phase of the oscillations. An angular deviation on injection is equivalent to a radial oscillation of different amplitude with the phase shifted. The effect of angular divergence is to increase the chance of striking the back of the inflector electrodes for some particles and to decrease it for others. The average probability can be computed from the physical dimensions and the properties of the oscillations. It is not significantly changed by an angular spread of $\pm 0.5 \times 10^{-3}$ radian, which is typical of the beams coming from either a well-focused electrostatic generator or a proton linac.

Angular divergence also introduces vertical oscillations about the median plane, with a frequency

$$f_z = \left(1 + \frac{L}{\pi R}\right) n^{1/2} f_0 \qquad (13\text{-}9)$$

For the cosmotron parameters this frequency is $f_z = 0.86 f_0$. These vertical oscillations are also mismatched to the orbital frequency; if amplitudes are sufficiently large and the beam is narrow, particles can pass above or below the inflector plates, even though the radial location of the particle orbit might be unfavorable. Such oscillations can be used to advantage by injecting the beam at a level above (or below) the median plane, to increase vertical amplitudes and improve the chance of missing the inflector plates. The number of free revolutions for the average ion can be increased in this way, improving the probability of capture in stable orbits.

The injection scheme described above is most efficient if ions are not being accelerated during injection. The radiofrequency accelerator can be turned on when the equilibrium orbit approaches the center of the chamber and can be brought up to full voltage within a few cycles if desired. By this time the entire chamber will be filled with oscillating particles, having a wide spread in amplitude and in phase.

In the cosmotron an unexpected perturbation of the remanent magnetic field simplified the injection problem and led to another technique for maximizing injection efficiency. It was found that the remanent median surface was not a plane in the region of the injection orbit, but was tilted upward. This distortion provides a mechanism for coupling between the vertical and horizontal betatron oscillations. In the cosmotron it was found that energy was removed from the radial oscillations at just the critical times to decrease the number of ions striking the inflector when the beam returned to its neighborhood. The magnitude of the remanent field perturbation was not exactly correct to obtain the optimum effect, so a few turns of the pole-face windings in this region of the orbit were powered and adjusted to give the desired degree of coupling. As a result, injection into the cosmotron results in almost no loss on the back of the inflector plate structure.

The 4-Mev Van de Graaff generator is a horizontal pressure-insulated electrostatic generator specifically designed and developed for operation at high pulse intensity (see Chap. 3). It produces a beam of about $\frac{3}{16}$ in. diam with an angular spread of $\pm 0.5 \times 10^{-3}$ radian. The ion source is the P.I.G. type developed at Berkeley (see Sec. 4-8) and produces pulses of up to 50 ma of hydrogen ions for about 100 μsec. Focusing of the high-intensity pulse is a problem differing considerably from the focusing of steady beams. The large positive space charge developed near the source aperture requires focusing fields different from those suitable for low-intensity operation. Voltage-stability problems also enter. Pulse-to-pulse voltages must be reproduced to a precision of about 0.2 per cent to stabilize injection conditions. This is done by operating with a low-intensity steady beam between pulses and using the analyzed "mass-2" beam of molecular hydrogen ions to control the voltage (see Sec. 3-8).

The potential of the generator terminal drops during the pulse because the ion current in the accelerating tube exceeds the charging current delivered by the belt, which is limited to about 300 μa. During a 100-μsec pulse of, say, 10 ma the 300-$\mu\mu$f capacitance of the terminal is lowered in potential by about 3000 volts, a 0.1 per cent drop. Furthermore, electron loading in the accelerating tube increases with operating voltage; at 4 Mev it can increase terminal current and cause a further drop in terminal potential. This decrease in injection energy during the pulse is opposite in sense to the rising magnetic field in the cosmotron orbit.

It results in shortening the effective injection interval and so in reducing the intensity of the injected pulse. In 1958 a pulsed capacitative liner was installed in the Van de Graaff generator to compensate for this effect. This liner is pulse-charged by a separate supply to maintain a steady terminal potential or can produce a rising voltage during the pulse, if desired.

The electrostatic inflector plates are located in a vacuum housing in a straight section. The beam from the Van de Graaff generator enters at a 30° angle to the equilibrium orbit and is deflected by this angle between electrodes which have a radius of curvature of 10 ft and an arc length of 5.2 ft. The two plates are spaced about 0.5 in. apart, and a dc potential difference of 20 to 30 kv is required to deflect the 3- to 4-Mev protons.

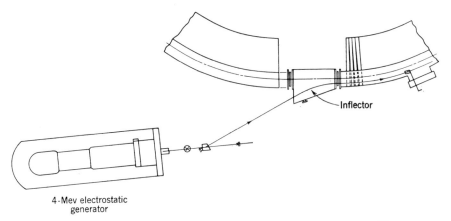

4-Mev electrostatic
generator

Fig. 13-13. Electrostatic inflector system for the cosmotron, using 4-Mev protons from an electrostatic generator.

The beam emerging from the inflector can be made accurately parallel to the equilibrium orbit by slight adjustments in the deflecting potential. The radial position of the exit end of the curved inflector channel can be varied by moving the inflector plate assembly on slides along the line of the entering proton beam from the Van de Graaff. This motion and other adjustments for elevation and alignment are controlled by mechanical devices with motors located outside the vacuum housing. Figure 13-13 shows a schematic view of the inflector system.

The energy spread of the 4-Mev proton beam from the electrostatic generator is of the order of ± 10 kv. This spread is equivalent to a band of equilibrium orbits in the magnet about 1.5 in. wide, centered on the mean orbit. The time required for an orbit to contract by this radial distance is about 25 μsec. For each value of energy the acceptance time interval is that required for the equilibrium orbit to contract from just inside the injector radius to the center of the chamber. This time is about 200 μsec in the cosmotron, representing about 70 revolutions of the particles. The effect of the energy spread is to round off the beginning and end of the acceptance time interval over times of the order of 25 μsec.

The oscillations produced by angular divergence and beam width, along with the overlap resulting from the energy spread, reduce the effective acceptance interval. The capture probability will be a maximum at the center of this interval, decreasing to zero at the practical limits. With a long pulse overlapping this entire acceptance interval, the average capture probability is estimated to be about 10 per cent. A short pulse lasting for only a few revolutions and timed for the optimum location of the equilibrium orbit would have a higher probability of capture but lower total intensity. The need to start the rf acceleration slightly before equilibrium orbits pass the center of the chamber also reduces the length of the acceptance interval. The experimental optimum obtained by varying the pulse length and timing was found to be about 100 μsec, equivalent to about 30 turns. A current pulse of 1 ma would deliver 6×10^{11} particles into the orbit in this time.

When the rf field is applied to the accelerating gap, the particles will be set into synchronous phase oscillations, centered around that phase for which the energy gain per turn is correct to match the rise rate of the magnetic field. Since the particles will be uniformly distributed around the orbit after injection, only a small portion will have the azimuthal location which matches the synchronous phase. Most of the particles will be set into synchronous energy oscillations which will cause wide oscillations in the radial location of their equilibrium orbits. The equilibrium phase angle of 30° chosen for the cosmotron results in a range of acceptance into synchronous orbits of about 180° in azimuth, so only half the circulating particles could be captured. However, it has been shown that the particles injected in the orbit already have a wide spread in the initial amplitude and phase of their betatron oscillations, such that they essentially fill the available aperture. So the fraction captured in stable synchronous orbits within the useful aperture will be smaller than half. On the other hand, the frequency of synchronous oscillations is relatively low, such that the average particle takes about 1000 revolutions to complete a phase cycle. During this time some damping occurs, so some particles are salvaged. An over-all estimate is that about 20 per cent of the injected protons should be captured in synchronous orbits. If the number of protons injected is 6×10^{11} per pulse, as estimated above for a 1-ma source pulse, the number captured in synchronous orbits would be about 10^{11} protons/pulse. Beam intensities observed in operations are in good agreement with this estimate, but do not increase linearly with higher injection current. The reason for this is not yet understood.

As magnetic field rises and particle energy increases, the amplitudes of the oscillations decrease. In Chap. 5 it was shown that the betatron amplitudes vary with $B^{-\frac{1}{2}}$. Amplitudes will have decreased to half by the time the field has increased to four times the injection value. Amplitudes may be increased temporarily by angular deviations due to gas scattering in the chamber, but will be continuously damped; gas-scattering losses should be negligible for energies above about 100 Mev. Synchronous amplitudes are also damped by the rising magnetic field, but at a slower rate, varying with $B^{-\frac{1}{4}}$ for these low energies. With further increase in field and in beam energy the intensity should remain, in principle, essentially constant.

To summarize, beam injection starts by filling the orbit with particles having a wide spread in oscillation amplitudes. Those particles which do not fall within the acceptance limits are lost against the chamber walls within the first betatron period, or within one to two turns. Then when the radiofrequency is applied, about 20 per cent are captured in stable synchronous orbits and the rest are lost to the walls during the first half of the first synchronous cycle or within about 500 turns. Further small losses can be anticipated during the next few synchronous cycles, and by gas scattering, up to an energy of about 100 Mev. Cathode-ray-tube displays of beam intensity in the orbit obtained from the pickup electrodes show that the intensity does, in fact, have the characteristics described above.

13-7. RADIOFREQUENCY ACCELERATOR

Performance requirements for the particle acceleration system were described in the earlier section on basic parameters. The particles must be supplied an energy increment on each turn determined by the rate of rise of magnetic field. The customary technique in synchronous acceleration is to apply a radiofrequency potential across a short insulated section in the metal vacuum chamber, located in a straight section. The applied frequency is either the fundamental orbital frequency of the particles or some preferred harmonic; in most proton synchrotrons the fundamental orbital frequency is used. This frequency increases during the 1-sec accelerating cycle, with increasing particle energy. In the cosmotron it extends from about 0.40 megacycle for injection at 4 Mev to 4.20 megacycles at maximum energy, following the schedule shown in Fig. 13-2.

In synchronous acceleration the voltage applied to the accelerating gap must exceed the average requirement of volts per turn to provide for a wide range in phase and energy oscillations. The choice of equilibrium phase angle, at which particles acquire the necessary volts per turn, determines the peak applied rf voltage. This choice in phase angle is a balance between the radial-aperture requirements and beam intensity.

In the cosmotron, it was taken as about 30°, for which the peak applied voltage is twice the volts per turn. This leads to energy oscillations during the synchronous cycle which have associated radial amplitudes of about ± 8 in. at 4 Mev injection energy. In Chap. 9 it was shown that a synchronous phase angle of 30° led to a range of acceptance into synchronous orbits of about 180° in phase, which means that about half the particles distributed uniformly around the orbit could be accepted, if the radial aperture were sufficient to accept the radial oscillations. The applied voltage requirements change during the accelerating cycle, following the rate of rise of magnetic field. The volts per turn needed in the cosmotron were shown in Fig. 13-3. So the peak applied voltage must start at about 2000 volts (at 0.40 megacycle) and drop to about 1400 volts (at 4.20 megacycles) at high energy.

These accelerating potentials are modest, as compared with those used in cyclotrons or other resonance accelerators in which the time for acceleration is shorter and the number of accelerations is much smaller. This is one of the primary advantages of the synchronous acceleration principle. However, the wide range of frequency variation required and the need for the frequency to follow a predetermined schedule are unique to the proton synchrotron and pose some of the most difficult problems.

If the accelerating system is to be resonant, it must be tuned over the entire frequency sweep. A resonant-cavity circuit such as is used for the electron synchrotron would require excessive power to produce the necessary potentials when off resonance. A mechanically tuned system, similar to the circuit of a synchrocyclotron which uses a rotating variable capacitor, would have to cover a frequency range of about 12 to 1, a difficult design problem. Furthermore, the variable-capacitor plates would have to be precisely shaped to fit the predetermined time schedule. If such a system were broad-banded, however, the correct frequency schedule could be impressed on it by an external oscillator, although the efficiency of such a system is low. Broad-banding involves the use of a sufficiently high impedance system that it can operate untuned over the entire frequency range. An electronically tuned oscillator can then be used to impress the correct frequency schedule on the accelerating system. The primary problem is the design of the high-impedance circuit. This is the approach used for the cosmotron, and the method has been to use ferromagnetic loading materials to give the desired high impedance.

The accelerating system for the cosmotron is essentially a radiofrequency transformer. A ferromagnetic core surrounds the particle orbit at one of the straight sections. The core material is chosen to have a useful magnetic permeability at frequencies up to the maximum 4.20 megacycles. Power is fed to a primary winding from a radiofrequency power supply electrically tuned over the frequency range. The particle orbits can be visualized as one-turn secondaries linking the transformer core. Each time a particle traverses the core it experiences an electro-motive force equivalent to that which would obtain in a one-turn second-ary winding of the transformer.

Another description of the accelerating system is that it is an induction accelerator depending on the time rate of change of flux linking the particle orbit, as in the betatron. During most of its path the proton is within a grounded metal vacuum chamber; the only time it can experi-ence the electromotive force induced by the changing flux is while it is traversing the insulating gap at the location of the flux core. The rate of change of flux, $d\phi/dt$, within the magnetic core linking the orbit while the particle is crossing the gap determines the emf and so the energy acquired by the particle. In this sense the ferromagnetic core linking the orbit is equivalent to the flux core in a betatron.

A third way of describing the operation of the accelerating system is to say that it is a cavity resonator heavily loaded with material of high magnetic permeability and high dielectric constant. The cavity reso-nator is the copper shield around the core, and the potential is developed across the insulated gap in the vacuum chamber. If it were air-filled, this cavity would be resonant at an extremely high frequency because of its small dimensions. If loaded with low-loss high-dielectric material, as for the quarter-wave resonators used in the electron synchrotron, the resonant frequency would be lower but the impedance would also be low at resonance. When loaded with ferromagnetic material, the resonant frequency lies in the band of impressed frequencies; but the cavity is so broadly resonant and has such high impedance that it can be driven efficiently at frequencies far off its resonance.

The basic problem is the choice of ferromagnetic loading material. Iron cores, even if laminated, are subject to eddy-current effects which restrict their use to frequencies of less than 100 kc. Powdered iron and permalloy foil cores can be made to extend the frequency range to about 1 megacycle. But for higher frequencies even finely laminated metallic cores are impractical because of high costs and inefficient power transformation.

The core material chosen is a ferromagnetic ferrite, which is a semi-conductor with conductivity about 10^{-7} times that for metals, so that eddy-current limitations are extended to much higher frequencies, and with an effective magnetic permeability of 500 to 1000 in the frequency range desired. This type of ferromagnetic material has been developed in several industrial laboratories within the past few years for use in pulse transformers, high-frequency chokes, and magnetic deflection yokes for television tubes. It is available under several trade names such as Ferroxcube and Ferramic. The electrical and magnetic properties of such ferrites have been studied in some detail in the various commercial laboratories. A study by Blewett, Plotkin, and Blewett[12] of the Brook-

haven staff discusses the properties of ferrites with particular regard to
their application to the cosmotron. Since its publication innumerable
studies of various ferrites have been printed in the engineering and scientific literature. The cosmotron application was, however, one of the
first in the United States and was influential in bringing these interesting
materials to public attention.

The material of the core is a synthetic manganese-zinc-ferrite, formed
by the replacement of two of the FeO groups in Fe_3O_4 by the other
metallic oxides. The oxides of iron and of the other metals are finely
powdered in a ball mill, mixed in the correct proportions with an organic
binder, and extruded or pressed to the desired shape, making due allowance for 15 to 20 per cent shrinkage which takes place on firing. The
material at this stage has the appearance of molding clay, is reddish in
color, and is not yet ferromagnetic. The shapes are then fired in a controlled oxygen atmosphere at temperatures below the melting point, so
recrystallization occurs. The final product is a hard, black ceramic
similar to porcelain. Electrically it is a semiconductor, and magnetically
it is now ferromagnetic. It can be ground like glass or porcelain to obtain
precise dimensions.

Different properties can be achieved by varying the proportions and
the firing cycle. A typical ferrite has a saturation flux density of 2000 to
3000 gauss, a Curie point at about 400°K, a permeability of about 1000 at
low frequencies (decreasing to about 500 at 5 megacycles), and a very
high dielectric constant. In general, ferrites which have high permeability have a lower frequency cutoff, and those with good high-frequency
properties have lower permeability. The losses in the material can be
described by the Q of a coil wound on a toroid-shaped sample. For the
material used in the cosmotron the Q varies from over 10 at 0.35 megacycle to 1.6 at 4.2 megacycles.

The 2800 lb of ferrite needed for the core was obtained from two
sources, because of uncertainties in the production schedules and properties. The North American Philips Company supplied Ferroxcube III
in the form of rectangular blocks 2 cm thick, surface-ground to a smooth
finish. These blocks were assembled and cemented together in the shape
of a "picture frame" with a total air gap of less than 0.001 in. The
General Ceramics and Steatite Corporation supplied a similar material,
Ferramic, in the form of extruded rods about 1 cm in diameter. These
rods were supported in frames, the ends bevel-ground, and also cemented
to form picture-frame units. Figure 13-14 shows the assembly of the
two types of ferrite material. Although the amount of ferrite ordered
from each supplier was sufficient by itself, both lots were included in the
final assembly to increase the efficiency of the accelerator.

The primary winding, of ¼-in. copper rod, is distributed about the core
for electrical efficiency, but is equivalent to a one-turn coil. The entire

core, except for the insulating gap in the straight-section vacuum chamber, is enclosed by a copper shield.   Because of the high dielectric constants, such a large assembly might develop standing waves in the transverse dimensions unless care is taken to detune such modes by shielding or by physical spacing.   The picture-frame core sections are separated by air spaces which serve the dual purpose of permitting forced-air cooling and of suppressing undesired modes of oscillation.

The amplifier which supplies the frequency-modulated excitation to the ferrite accelerator unit is a broad-banded system with an output power level of about 100 kw.   The high-level amplifier itself has four stages of push-pull amplifiers, with two Machlett 5681 triodes rated at

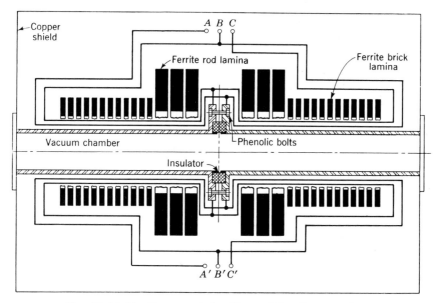

Fig. 13-14. Ferrite-core accelerating unit for the cosmotron.

75 kw plate dissipation each, in the final stage.   It takes its excitation from the output of an intermediate amplifier which delivers a signal of about 15 volts through 70-ohm transmission-line cable from the central circuit room to the location of the accelerator unit.   The intermediate amplifier is driven by a low-level (2-volt) signal developed by the frequency control system and master oscillator to be described in the following section.   Full details are given in the report by the cosmotron staff.[12]

Continuous measurement of the gap voltage is used to observe waveform and amplitude during the cycle.   For this purpose diodes are connected across the gap, or from one side of the gap to ground.   One is used as a peak-reading voltmeter, another with a voltage divider is used for amplitude control, and a third with a short-time-constant circuit is used to provide oscilloscope presentation of the gap voltage to check the waveform.

The accelerating unit in the bevatron at the University of California is a drift tube—a section of hollow rectangular conductor surrounding the beam aperture—located in one of the straight sections. If such a drift tube were extended around half of a synchronous wavelength (half of the circumference when the harmonic order $h = 1$, as in the bevatron), the full rf potential would be effective on both entry and exit, as in a cyclotron D. Space limitations in the bevatron prevent this configuration, so the drift tube is limited to a shorter length which can be contained in the straight-section vacuum chamber. Consequently the drift-tube voltage must be higher (by about a factor of 5) than the energy gain required per revolution. As the particles enter the drift tube, they are accelerated; as they leave the other end, they are decelerated. Because of the phase shift during the passage through the drift tube, the deceleration is less than the acceleration, and a net energy gain results.

The drift tube forms a resonant circuit with a ferrite-loaded inductor, and the circuit is driven by a power amplifier at the frequency of revolution of the protons. The inductor is tuned by varying a bias current in a primary winding which partially saturates the ferrite core, and the bias current is controlled to produce a variable-frequency cycle exactly matching the increasing frequency of particle motion.

13-8. FREQUENCY CONTROL IN THE COSMOTRON

The frequency of the accelerating electric field must be held to within about 0.2 per cent of the scheduled value during the cycle in order to limit the radial excursions of the equilibrium orbit and to prevent loss of particles to the walls of the chamber. The cycle must be triggered by a signal derived from the magnetic field and must start at the frequency which is compatible with the field at injection. The precision required is highest at the start of the cycle when oscillation amplitudes are greatest.

The allowed frequency error can be estimated from the magnitude of the allowable radial excursion. Equation (13-2) gives the simple form for orbital frequency. When this is modified for the effect of straight sections [Eq. (13-3)] and for the variation of magnetic field with radius, we have

$$f = \frac{c^2 e B_0}{2\pi (W_0 + T)} \frac{2\pi R_0}{2\pi R_0 + 4L} \left(\frac{R_0}{r}\right)^n \qquad (13\text{-}10)$$

By differentiation and substitution, we find the frequency error associated with a given allowed radial deviation:

$$\frac{df}{f} = -\left[n + \frac{T(T + 2W_0)}{(W_0 + T)^2}\right] \frac{dr}{R_0} \qquad (13\text{-}11)$$

Evaluation for a change in radius of 1 in., in the cosmotron, at injection, shows a frequency shift of 0.17 per cent; at maximum energy the shift is 0.60 per cent. In a similar manner the frequency error can be analyzed in terms of the deviation from ideal injection timing. It is found that a frequency error of 0.1 per cent corresponds to an error in timing of 16 μsec.

The variable-frequency signal is generated by an electronically tuned oscillator in which the tuning is accomplished by saturation of a small ferrite core in the inductance of the tank circuit.[12] The varying inductance changes the resonant frequency of this low-level oscillator, depending on the magnitude of the dc current in a winding used to saturate the core. The saturable inductance is a toroid of small radial thickness (to minimize eddy-current effects at high frequencies) ground from blocks of Ferroxcube and enclosed in a doughnut-shaped metallic jacket. The jacket serves as an oil container to maintain constant temperature and is made in two sections separated by a gasket to prevent circulating currents. The two windings, one for the dc saturating current and one for the radiofrequency signal, are wound to have minimum coupling. The rf winding is threaded through a rectangular hole cut in the side of the toroid, with a figure-8 winding which cancels out the dc flux. The dc winding is wound around the enclosing doughnut-shaped jacket, threaded through the toroid to produce the saturating flux in the core. Calibration studies have shown that the permeability varies from about 1000 to less than 10 as the magnetizing field is raised from zero to 20 amp-turns/cm in the dc windings. So the toroid inductance can be varied over a factor of 100.

The dc current in the saturating winding is controlled by a signal from a pickup in the magnetic field to produce the correct frequency-field function (see Fig. 13-2). A diode network with 28 parallel circuits of different biases is used to produce a signal having the proper output-current-versus-field function. This output current is used to saturate the core. By tuning the bias voltages and amplitudes of these parallel diode circuits, a cycle can be produced which is within 0.1 per cent of the calculated frequency cycle over the full 1-sec interval. Furthermore, the controls can be used to trim the shape of the cycle at will.

The "precut" frequency cycle established by the diode network described above is found to be extremely stable. Negative feedback in the amplifier is used to produce an amplitude control which is within 4 per cent over the cycle. This type of frequency control for the cosmotron accelerator unit depends only on the observed magnetic field during each cycle and so is independent of field variations from cycle to cycle.

The method used to start the frequency cycle on the correct frequency and at the correct time to match injection conditions is to obtain a short-pulse trigger signal from a peaking strip in the magnetic field (see Sec.

8-8). The time can be varied by varying the peaking-strip bias, which is calibrated in terms of the magnetic field. The frequency cycle is started at a magnetic field and at a frequency well below the usual injection energy, so the cycle is initiated and any transients have decayed before the protons are injected. This makes the frequency cycle independent of the precise value of injection energy or injection timing.

An alternative frequency monitoring system has also been developed, which takes its information from the radial position of the proton orbit. After the ions have been bunched and oscillations have damped out, which requires about 50 msec, the radial location of the mean orbit can be observed and used as a measure of the frequency error. A pair of hollow pickup electrodes, mounted radially inside and outside the chamber at one of the straight sections, have voltage pulses induced on them by the electrostatic charge of the bunched beam as it passes through the electrodes. The relative magnitudes of the pulses on the two electrodes will be different, depending on the radial location of the orbit. An error signal which can be used to correct the frequency cycle can be derived from this difference. At first glance it would appear simplest to apply the radial pickup electrode signal directly to the diode network system controlling the frequency cycle. A more sophisticated analysis reveals the fact that such a double-element system is subject to instability and loss of particles.

It is now agreed that it is preferable to combine the radial information with a system that does not use a programmed oscillator but derives the initial rf signal from the beam itself. If the beam is initially bunched by a frequency program shortly after injection, the master oscillator can be turned off and replaced by the induced signal from an electrode through which the bunched beam passes. Stability is obtained by controlling the phase of the accelerating signal by a phase shifter which, in turn, is controlled by the signal from the radial pickup electrodes. This system was tested on the cosmotron in 1953 by G. K. Green and E. C. Raka; its operation was quite stable and satisfactory. A short description is available in the *Handbuch* article of Green and Courant.[20]

Coherent phase oscillations in the cosmotron excited by noise in the frequency-control system were responsible for loss of some 50 per cent of the beam during acceleration until a phase-oscillation damping system, invented by E. J. Rogers,[25] was incorporated. In this system, phase differences between the rf accelerating field and the signal induced in the beam pickup electrodes are detected and fed back to the frequency control of the master oscillator in the required sense to oppose sudden phase shifts. This system improved the rf stability to the point where no detectable beam loss takes place after the initial capture process is complete.

The beam pickup electrodes just mentioned are mounted in one of the straight sections.   Electrodes are located inside and outside the orbit and yield induced signals which give a measure of the radial position of the beam and which thus enable the operator to apply necessary corrections manually to the frequency-determining network to keep the beam centered.   Other electrodes above and below the orbit give an indication of vertical beam position during the accelerating cycle.   The pickup electrode shapes are shown in Fig. 13-15.

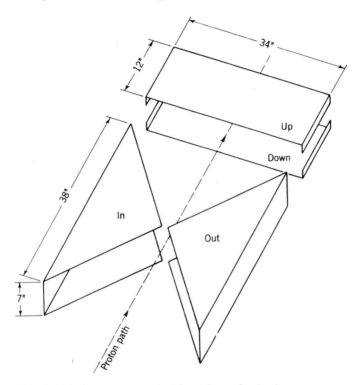

Fig. 13-15. Arrangement of pickup electrodes in the cosmotron.

13-9. COSMOTRON VACUUM CHAMBER

The vacuum chamber to contain the ion orbits during acceleration is subject to very stringent physical requirements.   It must be entirely nonmagnetic so as not to disturb the carefully designed magnetic fields. It must also be constructed in such a way that eddy currents induced in metallic components of the chamber do not disturb the field; this limitation applies primarily to the field at injection.   Not only must it be vacuumtight in the ordinary sense of having no air leaks, but all joints should be readily accessible for leak testing and gaskets should be made of materials having low vapor pressure.   The physical dimensions are also severely restricted to maintain the largest possible internal aperture for ion oscillations. So top and bottom walls, at least, must be physically thin and mechanically strong.

A natural division of the vacuum chamber is into four quadrants fitting between magnet pole faces, with four connecting straight sections. The internal aperture required in the cosmotron pole gap is about 6 by 30 in., so small that flow resistance limits the pumping speed. Pump stations must be distributed around the periphery to provide the necessary pumping speed to attain the desired ultimate pressure within the chamber. These considerations led to the choice of 12 pumping stations for the cosmotron chamber, 3 in each quadrant. Pump-out apertures of 6 by 40 in. are located in the outer wall of the chamber, connecting to the pump manifolds. Incidentally, the straight sections are free of pumps and available for other apparatus.

The quadrant vacuum chambers are constructed of bars and laminations of nonmagnetic stainless steel; rubber sheets form the vacuum wall. The steel structure supplies mechanical strength to support the atmospheric pressure load, and a rubber diaphragm bridges the narrow gaps between the steel lamination bars. The structure is assembled on two 1- by 8-in. bars on edge, preformed in 90° arcs of 342 and 378 in. radius, spaced with rectangular frames at the quadrant ends (where magnetic field is small). Bridged across the 36-in. chamber width are several hundred taper-shaped steel bars which form the top and bottom surfaces of the quadrant box structure. The 2-in. width of the bars limits eddy currents in the surface. Calculations of the eddy currents induced in the chosen high-resistivity stainless steel justify this choice of lamination thickness; model tests and operational experience bear out the calculations. The bars are attached by insulated pins at each end, and the conductivity of the rubber sheet is adequate to maintain dc ground potential to prevent accumulation of static charge.

The $\frac{1}{8}$-in. sheet material covering the top and bottom surfaces is Myvaseal rubber, produced by the Distillation Products Company. It is an artificial rubber having a vapor pressure of less than 1×10^{-7} mm Hg, considerably better in this respect than rubbers or plastics previously used in vacuum seals. Clamp bars are located around the periphery of the quadrant surfaces, and they press the sheet against the steel walls with an intermediate gasket.

Figure 13-16 is a schematic cross section of the quadrant chamber. Under atmospheric pressure the tapered bars deflect about $\frac{1}{4}$ in. The structure is mechanically designed so that no unit exceeds 50 per cent of the yield stress of the steel, but also arranged to approach this 50 per cent limit at every critical point in order to keep the thickness of metal to a minimum. The net internal clearance between bars under vacuum is about 6 in.

The gaskets used for sealing this box structure have a "dumbbell" cross section forming a double seal with a pump-out channel between seals to use for vacuum tests. The material used is also Myvaseal, extruded into the dumbbell shape. The triple joints at the box corners are sealed with molded sections of the same gasket. Many pump-out leads are provided to test the region between gaskets; all of these leads are made available at the quadrant ends or along the front wall of the chamber.

The same gasket design and technique is used to seal the ends and face-plate apertures of the straight-section vacuum boxes. In addition, flap valves located in the straight-section boxes can be closed to isolate each quadrant for independent vacuum testing or measurements.

Scattering by the residual gas in the vacuum chamber will result in some loss of ions from the beam. A series of theoretical studies of this problem was initiated by Blachman and Courant[10] as applied to the

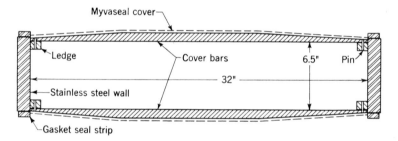

Fig. 13-16. Cross section of quadrant vacuum chamber for the cosmotron.

cosmotron conditions. Most of the scattering occurs within the first thousand revolutions, when ion energy is small and oscillation amplitudes are large. In each single-scattering process the proton is deviated from its orbit by a small angle. For most particles this angle is small enough to be within the aperture of the vacuum chamber. A small fraction have single-scattering angles sufficient to cause the particles to strike the chamber walls. Multiple scattering is also considered, and results in further loss of particles. Damping of the oscillation amplitudes in the increasing magnetic field, and the decreasing probability of scattering with increasing energy, eventually reduce scattering amplitudes so that no significant loss occurs after the protons reach an energy of about 100 Mev. The magnitude of scattering losses decreases with increased injection energy, and this is one of the chief reasons for using the maximum practical energy at injection.

The most significant factors in the calculation are the gas pressure and composition of this residual gas, proton energy and the rate of accelera-tion per turn, and the n value and physical dimensions which define the effective aperture of the chamber. The results of the calculation are expressed in terms of the pressure for 10 per cent loss or for 50 per cent loss of protons. For cosmotron injection conditions these results are[12]

$$P \text{ (10 per cent loss)} = 0.8 \times 10^{-5} \text{ mm Hg}$$
$$P \text{ (50 per cent loss)} = 1.4 \times 10^{-5} \text{ mm Hg}$$

The vacuum pumping system consists of 12 identical high-vacuum pump stations, distributed around the chamber with three on each quadrant, located in the trench that surrounds the magnet ring. Each station

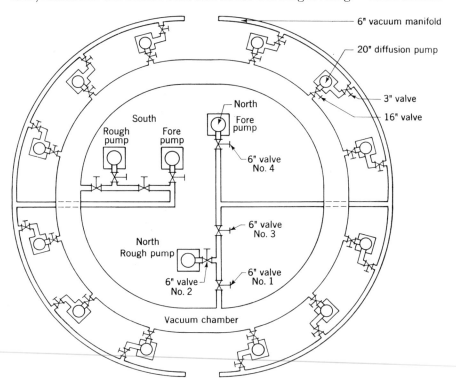

Fig. 13-17. Schematic diagram of the vacuum pumping system for the cosmotron.

is located at a manifold or plenum chamber attached to the quadrant vacuum chamber, and each manifold is equipped with a high-vacuum close-off valve, so pump units can be removed or interchanged without losing vacuum in the main chamber. A pump unit consists of a Westinghouse 20-in. oil-diffusion pump, an 8-in. booster diffusion pump, a cooled baffle and refrigeration compressor, and all associated electric equipment including pump heaters and vacuum gauges. A 6-in.-diam fore-vacuum manifold in the trench connects to four mechanical pumps located in the center of the magnet ring. Figure 13-17 is a schematic drawing of the pumping system. A circular bank of pilot lights on the control panel, which looks much like the figure, shows which valves are open or closed so the operator can monitor pumping operations.

The 20-in. diffusion pumps are rated at 7000 liters/sec speed at 1×10^{-5} mm Hg air pressure and are equipped with three-stage fractionating jets. The oils used have been Lytton-C or Myvane-20, petroleum-base oils which have similar properties. A specially designed baffle for the large oil-diffusion pump prevents oil vapor from diffusing back into the manifold and chamber; it can be cooled by the mechanical refrigerator to $-40°C$. Minimum pressures observed in the cosmotron vacuum chamber are 0.6×10^{-5} mm Hg without refrigeration and 0.4×10^{-5} mm when the baffles were cooled, after several months of continuous pumping. As a consequence, very little loss of beam intensity due to gas scattering is observed.

Vacuum leak testing and sealing is a major problem in all accelerators. Techniques for reducing the time lost on leak hunting are essential in such a large and complicated system as the cosmotron. As a start, all joints and seals were designed to be mechanically sound and trustworthy. Furthermore, all major assembly joints and port closures have a double gasket seal, using the dumbbell-shaped extruded gasket described above. The space between gasket seals is tapped to allow circulation of helium in this space or connection to a rough-vacuum pump. The helium-flow leak-detector technique, using a mass spectrograph, covers essentially every inch of gasket closure in the chamber. Leaks are readily detected, even those so small that when sealed, no improvement in chamber pressure is noticeable. For larger leaks, if the maintenance problem of opening and resealing is too time-consuming, a rough-vacuum pump on the helium channel will suffice until repairs can be made. Alarm-type vacuum gauges are located at each pump station and can be set to call the attention of the operator to any failure in the pumping system. In the event of electrical power failure, air-operated valves will close, supplied from compressed-air storage bottles. If faults develop in one of the pumping units, valves can be closed and a spare unit inserted without loss of vacuum. The vacuum controls system is made fully automatic by a complete system of interlocks which provide suitable time delays for the sequential scheduling required when pumps are turned on.

13-10. INTERNAL TARGETS USED IN THE COSMOTRON

The basic design of a C magnet with the vacuum chamber available around the entire periphery provides a favorable situation for performing experiments within the chamber, using internal targets. This advantage was recognized from the start and was one of the primary reasons for the choice of magnet structure. Another advantage of the cosmotron over electron synchrotrons is the long acceleration interval after injection, although this feature also reduces average beam intensity. With the 1-sec interval it is possible to insert electrodes, magnetic fields, or probe targets needed for observations, without having them in place to distort the fields or interrupt the beam at injection. By 0.1 sec the ions reach an energy of 300 Mev and the radial oscillations are damped to small amplitude around the central orbit. In the time remaining, targets and other devices can be inserted.

When the protons reach maximum energy, they are bunched tightly about the equilibrium orbit. Final beam dimensions are observed to be $\frac{1}{4}$ in. high by 2 in. wide, and the beam can be located wherever desired across the radial width of the uniform-field region by adjustments of the frequency cycle. The bundle of ions includes a synchronous phase spread occupying about 90° in azimuth.

The orbit can be expanded or contracted by a small variation in applied frequency. The maximum rate of expansion or contraction depends on the magnitude of the accelerating volts per turn. With an average value of 600 volts per turn required for resonance, and a peak rf potential of, say, 1400 volts, the maximum possible increase in energy per turn would be 800 ev. The practical value would be much smaller, because of the necessity of maintaining synchronous stability. Assuming expansion at the rate of 500 volts per turn, the increase in radius would be 0.0005 in. per turn. Thus, it would require 2000 revolutions or 0.5 msec to expand the orbit by 1 in., or about 3 msec to move the orbit 6 in. to intercept a target inserted to that location. Furthermore, it would require 4000 revolutions to sweep the 2-in. width of the beam across the target. Protons would strike the target in a sequence of some 4000 pulses at 4.2 megacycles frequency: each pulse would be about one-fourth of the cyclic period or 0.05 µsec duration.

Orbit contraction can be accomplished somewhat faster, by as much as 1000 volts per turn, or 0.001 in. per turn, by using frequency modulation. An alternative is to turn off the rf oscillator and allow the beam to contract while the magnetic field still increases. Although radial stability disappears for regions outside the $n = 0.8$ limit, vertical stability remains. So ions which have contracted inside the limit of uniform-n magnetic field are still well-focused vertically and spiral inward on the median plane. A target which is permanently mounted just inside the inner wall of the chamber will intercept the entire contracting beam. In practice, such a permanent target can be located on the back (inner) surface of one of the straight-section vacuum chambers.

A wire target has been used successfully without expanding or contracting the beam. The wire is mounted on a shaft above beam level which can be quickly rotated to turn the wire down into the center of the chamber. Only a small fraction of the particles in the diffuse beam will strike the wire in any one revolution. Those that do strike the wire will have a rather small probability of making a nuclear collision; most of them will be reduced in energy or scattered through very small angles. Except for a very small fraction scattered through angles large enough to be thrown out of the chamber, the particles will be reaccelerated through many turns before again striking the wire. In this way the ions strike the wire many times, on the average, multiplying the effective thickness of target. Eventually, the small wire will clean up the entire beam, spread over tens of thousands of revolutions. The efficiency of the wire target is estimated as about 10 per cent.

Ram-in targets have been developed which can be thrust into position well inside either the inner or outer wall of the chamber in a very short time, using pneumatic cylinders. Such targets are normally located in one of the straight-section vacuum chambers.

Experiments using electronic particle detection are best served with very long output times, representing many thousands of revolutions. The slow-clean-up type of targets described above is useful, frequently aided by very slow rates of orbit contraction. The longest output pulse obtained is about 50 msec, representing 200,000 revolutions.

When still longer beam pulses are desired, it will be necessary to "flat-top" the magnetic field, that is, to maintain the field at its peak value for an appreciable period such as 0.1 sec while the beam is brought slowly to a target. Although flat-topping the field does not appear too difficult, additional problems are introduced by the necessity for simultaneous flat topping of the pole-face-winding current. In 1961 these problems had not yet been solved, but were receiving intensive study.

For other experiments very short beam pulses are desired, such as those utilizing time-of-flight techniques to observe very short lifetime processes. The shortest pulse possible by the method of contracting the beam against a target is about 0.1 msec.

13-11. EJECTION OF AN EMERGENT BEAM

The full potentiality of the proton synchrotron can be realized only when the high-energy protons can be ejected from the magnetic field as an emergent beam. This goal was included in the earliest plans and was one of the important reasons for the arrangement of magnet quadrants and field-free straight sections. It was anticipated that the straight sections would be useful for the apparatus required to produce an external beam of protons.

Several methods were available, based on analogous beam-removal systems in other magnetic accelerators. Among those considered was the magnetic peeler, used so effectively in the synchrocyclotron. Resonant build-up of radial free oscillations is another possibility which has been equally useful, and it was considered seriously for the cosmotron. The method chosen, which has been successfully applied to the cosmotron[26] and has also been proposed for the bevatron,[27] goes back to first principles and straightforward techniques.

The basic technique proposed by Piccioni et al.[26] utilizes the energy reduction in a target to displace the proton beam so that it can traverse an auxiliary magnetic field placed just inside the usual beam aperture in a straight section. This auxiliary magnetic field then deflects the beam outward so strongly that it emerges about one quadrant later. In the original proposal, a second magnet outside the usual beam aperture was to be used to provide a further outward deflection and to focus the divergent beam. Later it was shown that a stronger deflection at the

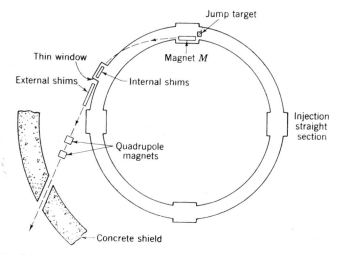

Fig. 13-18. Schematic diagram of the beam extraction system of the cosmotron. See text for description.

first magnet, together with selected field-distorting shims at the exit point, was adequate for extraction.

The "jump target" used for the original reduction in beam energy is a double structure. A beryllium "lip" 0.048 in. thick extends $\frac{1}{4}$ in. outward toward the beam from the main target, which is a beryllium block about $\frac{3}{4}$ in. thick in the azimuthal direction. By turning off the rf accelerating signal, the rising magnetic field causes the beam to contract in radius until those particles with maximum betatron oscillations strike the lip. The first effect of the lip is to reduce the amplitude of betatron oscillation, since the reduction in energy by ionization loss in the beryllium shifts the radius of the individual equilibrium orbit inward. When the betatron oscillation is effectively damped out, further energy loss causes the equilibrium orbit to contract and to pass through the thick body of the main target. This results in a much larger energy loss and, unfortunately, in some energy spread (the Landau effect).[28] The average energy loss in the $\frac{3}{4}$-in. Be target causes a decrease in equilibrium orbit radius of several inches, the precise amount depending on the n value. To make this jump as large as possible, the field shape is modified by changing pole-face winding current to give an n value as close as possible to 0.8, at which radial instability occurs. Under these conditions the beam is displaced inward about 4.5 in. one revolution later and enters the gap of the auxiliary magnet, which is located in the same straight section as the jump target.

The arrangement of components is shown in Fig. 13-18, which also indicates the beam path after leaving the deflecting magnet. The beam emerges at a point about 75° downstream from the magnet through one of the pumping manifolds. Since the normal stray field of the cosmotron magnet would induce strong nonlinear defocusing of the beam, the stray field at the point of emergence is corrected by a set of steel shims carefully tailored to avoid disturbance of the field in the main magnet gap. The beam emerges through a thin aluminum window and is finally focused by a pair of quadrupole magnets. At a distance of 35 ft from the quadrupoles most of the beam is included in a circle 2 in. in diameter. The contour of half-intensity in the beam pattern is a circle approximately 1 in. in diameter. As much as 50 per cent of the circulating beam has been extracted in this fashion.

13-12. BEAM ANALYSIS AND USE

Use of the high-energy particle beams for research in nuclear physics or in the study of particle interactions is the ultimate purpose of any accelerator. Experiments should be planned as far in advance as possible, and the design of the machine should be adapted to provide the greatest utility and flexibility in research operations. Although this volume has dealt mainly with the technical and engineering problems of accelerators as electromagnetic machines, it should be clear that the ultimate goal is the efficient use of the particle beams. The proton synchrotron provides an opportunity to illustrate the ways in which the planned experimental use influences the basic design of the machine, and also how it develops the need for major modifications.

The cosmotron was designed at a time when the production and study of the properties of mesons was considered the most immediate problem. However, plans included the study of all known types of radiation, and a thorough analysis was made of all possible particle trajectories emerging from internal targets. Trajectories were computed for mesons of a wide range in energy, scattered protons, neutrons, γ rays, etc., for various target locations. These studies strongly influenced the basic design.

They influenced the choice of proton energy and indicated the advantage of a C-shaped magnet which would allow particles to emerge around the entire periphery. The structure of quadrants and straight sections was arranged to provide the best opportunity for inserting targets and other beam-handling devices. Thin windows of aluminum foil were located by beam plots and installed in suitable locations around the chamber. Vacuum-pump manifolds were modified to provide other ports through which particles could emerge.

The radiation shield originally planned to contain the anticipated secondary intensities was a circular tier of concrete blocks 8 ft thick, located 10 ft outside the magnet and surrounding the two quadrants where beams of secondary radiations were to emerge. A 6-in.-thick layer of dense concrete and Pb bricks was provided at the beam height, through which channels could be placed for the emergent beams. A set of channels was provided for mesons of different energies coming from known target locations, analyzed by the fringing field of the cosmotron; meson channels labeled "300 Mev," "500 Mev," "1.0 Bev," etc., were available for experiments outside the shield. Fast neutrons and γ rays emerged tangentially through other channels.

Experience in operations showed that the planning was inadequate in several respects. Beam intensity was increased steadily over the early years, requiring additional shielding. The space between the magnet and shield was inadequate for the large analyzing and focusing equipment later found necessary. Furthermore, the space beyond the shield proved to be much too small for the large equipment and long beam runs needed as the field of research broadened. This space soon became overcrowded. The most serious inadequacy was the limited space originally provided in the direction of the emergent proton beams.

During 1958 and 1959 major additions were made to the buildings housing both the cosmotron and the bevatron. At Brookhaven the radiation shielding was entirely rebuilt so as to enclose the machine completely, including overhead shielding. The improved shielding is considered adequate for intensities up to 10^{12} protons/pulse, which is 1000 times larger than the intensities anticipated prior to operation. Additional experimental space was provided, with power and cooling facilities for large experimental apparatus. The arrangements allow the use of three external beams. As a result, emphasis has been shifted from experiments using internal targets to those with the external beams.

The auxiliary instruments needed for an experimental research program at these high energies have exceeded all expectations in number, size, and cost. The need for momentum analysis of the radiations has led to the development of scores of magnets of varying types. Crossed-field velocity analyzers are needed to separate different particles in the emergent beams. Cloud chambers and liquid-hydrogen bubble chambers, with their associated magnets, are large, complicated, and expensive. The development of AG magnetic lenses for focusing emergent beams offers a valuable improvement in beam density, but also requires longer beam runs. Power to supply these many magnets presents a major problem. Total power requirements exceed the power used for the cosmotron itself, and space to house the many generators has been added to the buildings. In addition, there are the steadily accumulating racks of electronic circuits for detecting and observing the radiations, lead-brick huts where photographic emulsions are exposed, and galleries of microscopes for scanning.

A general conclusion is that future planning for accelerators of this high-energy range must provide far more space, power, and facilities than had been anticipated for the cosmotron or bevatron.

REFERENCES

1. M. L. Oliphant, J. S. Gooden, and G. S. Hide, *Proc. Phys. Soc. (London)*, **59**:666 (1947).
2. J. S. Gooden, H. H. Jensen, and J. L. Symonds, *Proc. Phys. Soc. (London)*, **59**:677 (1947).
3. E. M. McMillan, *Phys. Rev.*, **68**:143 (1945).
4. V. Veksler, *J. Phys. (U.S.S.R.)*, **9**:153 (1945).
5. W. M. Brobeck, *Rev. Sci. Instr.*, **19**:545 (1948).
6. M. S. Livingston, *Phys. Rev.*, **73**:1258 (1948).
7. M. S. Livingston, J. P. Blewett, G. K. Green, and L. J. Haworth, *Rev. Sci. Instr.*, **21**:7 (1950).
8. R. Q. Twiss and N. H. Frank, *Rev. Sci. Instr.*, **20**:1 (1949).
9. J. P. Blewett; G. K. Green; W. H. Moore and J. P. Blewett; M. G. White; M. Plotkin and J. P. Blewett; J. P. Blewett; M. H. Blewett; *Phys. Rev.*, **75**:1288 (1949).
10. N. M. Blachman and E. D. Courant, *Phys. Rev.*, **74**:140 (1948); *Rev. Sci. Instr.*, **20**:596 (1959).
11. A. I. Pressman and J. P. Blewett, *Proc. IRE*, **39**:74 (1951).
12. Cosmotron Staff, *Rev. Sci. Instr.*, **24**:723–870 (1953).
13. D. C. Sewell, W. M. Brobeck, E. O. Lawrence, and E. J. Lofgren; Q. A. Kerns, W. R. Baker, G. M. Farly, and J. Riedel; E. J. Lofgren, W. M. Brobeck, E. O. Lawrence, and D. C. Sewell; L. Smith, A. A. Garren, and L. R. Henrich; *Phys. Rev.*, **78**:85 (1950).
14. E. J. Lofgren, *Science*, **111**:295 (1950).
15. W. M. Brobeck, UCRL-3912 (September, 1957).
16. V. I. Veksler et al., *J. Nuclear Energy*, **4**:333 (1957).
17. Proceedings of CERN Symposium on High Energy Accelerators of 1956 (Geneva).
18. Le Synchrotron à protons Saturne du Centre d'Études Nucléaires de Saclay, *L'Onde électrique*, **39** (1959).
19. J. P. Blewett, *Repts. Progr. in Phys.*, **19**:37 (1956).

protection. This has occurred in nearly all the early model accelerators, of all types.

With the steady development of accelerators to higher energy and higher intensity, the size and cost of machines and buildings have increased. The shielding system for a new accelerator should be planned in advance and incorporated in the building designs. Full information is needed on the properties of the radiations and on attenuation factors of shielding materials. The shield should anticipate the maximum possible energy and the ultimate beam intensity if possible. Yet the system must also allow sufficient flexibility to provide for future modifications of research experiments. In the larger accelerators, shields are massive and costly; an efficient design becomes an economic necessity.

Shielding serves two basic functions. Personnel must be protected from excessive radiation exposure, and background intensities must be minimized for experimental studies. The requirements for apparatus shielding usually exceed those for personnel protection.

In early accelerators with beams of low intensity, the scientists frequently overlooked the radiation hazard. Several have been burned by particle beams or scattered radiation, and some cyclotron operators have developed eye cataracts following overexposure to fast neutrons during tune-up. Appreciation of the hazards has grown with experience. Scientists and accelerator operators are now generally aware of the dangers, and proper precautions are taken to avoid overexposure. Government regulations limit dose rates and exposures. Laboratories are arranged to limit access to regions of high radiation intensity. "Health physicists" are employed in most large installations, with the responsibility of monitoring intensities and personnel exposures.

Shielding to minimize background radiation intensities for research experiments is a growing problem in all laboratories, with the use of more sensitive instruments and the demand for ever higher precision in measurements. Each type of instrument involves a different problem. Much can be done with electronic detectors by using multiple units in coincidence and anticoincidence circuits. However, in a typical research experiment an extensive arrangement of shielding is also required. For example, a narrow channel through a thick shielding wall is frequently used to obtain a collimated beam of the chosen radiation, lead or concrete enclosures may be needed around the detectors to reduce scattered radiation background, and the transmitted beam may be directed into radiation "traps" beyond the experimental apparatus to reduce back scattering. In such a system the shielding may be the largest and heaviest component of the experimental setup.

The radiations which are significant in the shielding of accelerators are those which have small interaction cross sections with the common materials used in shields, and so are of a penetrating character. They are also limited to those which are produced in considerable intensity. Other radiations of shorter range or of low intensity, which may be of considerable interest to nuclear scientists, are not important in this application. In each shielding situation one radiation component will usually have the maximum penetration and will determine shield composition and thickness. Frequently this dominant component is a secondary radiation produced in the material of the shield. For other components this shield thickness will usually be more than adequate. The problem is to identify the dominant component and to determine its intensity.

Another typical problem in shielding analyses is the development within the absorbers of mixtures of radiations due to secondary and tertiary processes. Two types of "showers" can be identified, those which consist primarily of electromagnetic radiations and those which consist mostly of nuclear particles. High-energy electrons produce X rays which produce secondary electrons, etc., leading to the characteristic "soft shower" observed in cosmic rays; nucleonic components are also produced, such as neutrons from photonuclear processes, but the dominant components of the shower are electromagnetic radiations. Nucleonic showers are initiated by high-energy protons or neutrons, which produce mesons and other nuclear particles and which then cause nuclear interactions with the release of still other nucleons and mesons; nuclear gamma rays also come from excited nuclei and add to the shower, but the significant radiations are nucleonic.

In this chapter the most significant of these radiations and radiation interactions will be described. The physical processes of attenuation applying to the several radiations will be presented, and appropriate interaction cross sections will be cited, in order to obtain suitable attenuation coefficients for the common materials used for shielding. It will not be possible to present a complete theoretical analysis of the complex problems involved. Rather, we shall attempt to simplify each situation and to present approximate conclusions from which qualitative estimates of the shielding requirements can be obtained. For a more thorough treatment the reader is advised to study the basic references cited.

The over-all purpose is to treat the shield as a component of the experimental system, in order to provide the maximum flexibility and usefulness for research, but with due regard to personnel protection. We start with a discussion of the biological hazards and present the accepted standards for personnel protection.

14-1. PERMISSIBLE RADIATION DOSE

Ionizing radiation causes biological damage, although the detailed mechanism is unknown. The problem of specifying the biological effects was first encountered with X rays and γ rays and led to the choice of the roentgen as the unit of radiation dosage. The ionization effects produced in tissue were found to be closely similar to those in air, for which electric instruments could be used for measurement. One roentgen is the quantity of X radiation (or γ radiation) which will release one electrostatic unit (esu) of electric charge per cubic centimeter by ionization, in an air-filled ionization chamber at standard temperature and pressure (0°C and 760 mm Hg pressure or 0.001293 gm/cm^3), in which secondary electrons are in equilibrium with the wall material.[1] (Note that 1 coulomb = 3 × 10^9 esu of charge.) Large parallel-plate ionization chambers were used with collimated beams of radiation to obtain basic calibrations. Then small "air-walled" ionization chambers were developed, with wall surfaces of plastic material which approximated air in average atomic number and in secondary-electron emission characteristics. One of the best known of the early instruments was the Victoreen thimble ionization chamber.

Radiation density decreases inversely with the square of the distance from an X-ray target and is expressed in r/cm^2. The intensity or the flux of the radiation is the amount traversing a unit area in unit time and is given in r/(cm^2)(sec) or r/(cm^2)(min). The output of a typical deep-therapy X-ray tube is about 500 r/(cm^2)(min) at 1 m distance from the target.

Absorbed Dose

Ionization in air, or in tissue, is caused primarily by the secondary electrons produced by the radiation. The average energy lost by a fast electron in liberating 1 ion pair in air is commonly taken to be 32.5 ev/ion pair (although more recent determinations[2] give the value 34.0 ev/ion pair). This energy loss per ion pair is almost independent of the energy of the ionizing electron and so holds for a wide range of X-ray and γ-ray quantum energies. Since 1 esu of charge is equivalent to 2.08 × 10^9 singly charged ions, it follows that 1 r corresponds to 5.24 × 10^{13} ev/gm air or 83.8 ergs/gm air (87.7 ergs/gm if the energy loss is 34.0 ev/ion pair).

The absorbed dose of any ionizing radiation is the energy imparted to matter by ionization and other absorptive processes. In air the absorbed dose per roentgen is the above 87.7 ergs/gm. The energy absorbed in tissue, such as within the human body, has been the subject of many calculations and also of experimental studies in "tissue-equivalent" ionization chambers. Results differ, depending on the type and energy of the radiations and the composition of the tissue, with values ranging between 90 and 150 ergs/(gm)(r). In "standard" soft human tissue (73 per cent oxygen, 12 per cent carbon, 10 per cent hydrogen, and 4 per cent nitrogen by weight) the absorbed dose is 97 ergs/gm tissue (for 34.0 ev/ion pair). Considering this variability, the Seventh International Congress of Radiology (Copenhagen, 1953) defined an international unit of absorbed dose called the "rad"[3] as one hundred ergs per gram tissue. One millirad (mrad) is equal to one-tenth erg per gram tissue.   By definition, this unit of absorbed dose can be applied to any type of tissue and to any type or energy of radiation which leads to the production of ionization.

Biological Response

Physical factors are responsible for some of the variations in biological response, although biological variability also has an important role.   One of the most important of the physical factors is the density of ionization along the track of an ionizing particle.   It is believed that the biological effect is a function of the number of ion pairs formed on the average within a single tissue cell.   For example, a cell may recover from and survive a single ionization, while it might be seriously damaged by the cumulative effects of several simultaneous ionizations.

The specific ionization in air in ion pairs per centimeter varies inversely with particle velocity, being small at high velocities and increasing by a large factor as the particle slows down.   This results in concentration of the ionization at the end of the particle range.   The specific ionization is essentially the same for singly charged particles of the same velocity and is proportional to the square of the charge for multiply charged particles. In Table 14-1 are listed the values of specific ionization in air for electrons, protons, and alpha particles of 5 Mev energy, along with the maximum values of specific ionization for each particle near the end of the range.   The same ratios apply for ionization in tissue, usually expressed in ion pairs per micron, or sometimes in ion pairs/(gm)(cm^2) of tissue.

TABLE 14-1
SPECIFIC IONIZATION IN AIR
(Ion pairs/cm)

	Energy, Mev	Specific ionization	Energy	Maximum specific ionization
Electrons	5	70	100 ev	1.0×10^4
Protons	5	2.5×10^3	25 kev	1.0×10^4
α particles	5	2.9×10^4	100 kev	4.0×10^4

The ionizing radiations produced by accelerators are of many types. X rays or γ rays release secondary electrons through three primary processes: photoelectric absorption, which is dominant for very low energies; Compton scattering, for intermediate energies; and positron-electron pair formation at high energies (the threshold energy for pair formation is 1.02 Mev).   High-energy protons are produced directly in some accelerators and may also be formed in nuclear interactions. Alpha particles occur primarily as products of radioactive decay, but may also be accelerated directly or released in nuclear disintegrations.   Fast neutrons which are produced in nuclear interactions are not in themselves ionizing because of their zero charge, but they can project high-energy protons or other charged atomic nuclei from matter by direct recoil; these will produce ionization.   Both fast neutrons and slow neutrons can cause nuclear interactions with the release of fast charged particles or gamma rays.   All these primary or secondary radiations which cause ionization are significant in varying degree in producing biological effects.

Another physical mechanism which appears to have a direct biological effect is the removal of a proton or other atomic nucleus from a chemical molecule in the cell by direct recoil from a high-energy heavy particle such as a fast neutron.   It is known that fast neutrons have an enhanced biological effectiveness compared with slow or thermal neutrons, which have insufficient energy to produce recoils.   Part of this increased effectiveness is no doubt due to ionization by the recoil protons.   It is also probable that the removal of an atomic nucleus from the molecule adds to the biological effect.

Biological and physiological studies of the effects of radiation show that the biological response varies markedly with the type of tissue or organ being irradiated.   The damage in normal soft tissue is characterized by the killing of cells, which must be eliminated through blood circulation; the magnitude of the response depends on the blood supply to the tissue and on the rate of reproduction of tissue cells.   In bones the damage is primarily associated with those tissues in the marrow which produce blood cells and is strongly influenced by chemical factors such as the selective concentration of radium or of radioactive strontium in the bones; a typical response is a reduction in the rate of production of blood cells.   Radiation can cause mutations of the lens-producing cells in the crystalline lens of the eye, which may result in opaque cataracts; fast neutrons are specifically injurious in this respect.   Harmful genetic mutations can also be produced in the gonad cells by radiation; however, most of the evidence of genetic damage has come from studies of fruit-fly or small-animal populations, and the application to the human population is inferred by calculations.   In almost every case the magnitude of the biological response is also affected by subsidiary factors such as temperature, the chemical condition of the tissue or organ, and the absorbed dose rate.

This variability in biological response has led to the concept of the "relative biological effectiveness" (RBE) as a means of comparing the effectiveness of absorbed doses of radiation delivered in different ways and producing different biological responses.   The RBE is taken as unity for the effects produced by X rays and γ rays, following the experience and practice in X-ray therapy and in the use of Co^{60} γ-ray sources.   The definition of RBE is the ratio between the dose in rads from an X-ray or Co^{60} γ-ray source to produce a biological change and the dose in rads of the radiation under comparison to produce the same biological change.[4] So by definition the RBE for X rays or γ rays is 1.00.

For most biological phenomena the factor which determines the RBE is the specific ionization of the individual charged particles. As indicated in Table 14-1, this varies from about 70 ion pairs/cm in air for fast electrons to 4×10^4 ion pairs/cm for slow α particles. In water or in tissue with density of approximately 1.0 this spread would be between 6 ion pairs/μ for fast electrons and 3500 ion pairs/μ for slow α particles. If the phenomenon concerned is one which requires only a few ion pairs per micron to produce the biological response, the alpha particle would have an RBE < 1, as compared with an RBE of 1.0 for electrons. On the other hand, if the phenomenon requires a linear density of the order of 10^3 ion pairs/μ to produce a particular response, the alpha particle would have an RBE > 1 relative to electrons. Wide variations in the experimental values for RBE are reported, but for most biological changes of interest the values of RBE are larger than 1.0 for protons, alpha particles, and other heavy charged particles. The accepted values of RBE[5,6] as a function of specific ionization, in ion pairs per micron of water, are given in Table 14-2.

TABLE 14-2
RBE AS A FUNCTION OF SPECIFIC IONIZATION

Specific ionization, ion pairs/μ water	RBE	Radiations
0–100	1.0	X rays, γ rays, electrons
100–200	2.0	
200–650	5.0	
650–1500	10.0	Fast neutrons, protons, α particles
1500–5000	20.0	Heavy recoil nuclei

The usefulness of RBE is limited by the relative inaccuracy of biological measurements of response, associated with the problem of obtaining statistical accuracy from observations with a wide variability of individual response. It is further complicated by variations in experimental factors such as the rate and duration of radiation exposure, the physical and chemical condition of the biological samples, and the type and degree of biological damage. Those phenomena for which reasonably good measurements have been obtained are either for lethal doses or for gross pathological damage such as the production of cancer, leukemia, sterility, or cataracts. It is assumed that the same RBE values apply to the much smaller dose rates which are at the level of the permissible dose for laboratory workers.

The biological unit of radiation dosage is the "roentgen equivalent man" (rem). It is the dose of radiation which has the same estimated biological effect as 1 rad of X rays or γ rays. One rem is defined[4] as RBE times one rad. One millirem (mrem) is equal to RBE times one millirad. The rem has the same inherent limitations as the RBE;

assumed or estimated values are frequently used. Its use should be restricted to the field of radiation protection involving biological response. The unique feature is that it represents the same degree of biological response for all radiations and, with suitably adjusted RBEs, to all biological phenomena.

The radiations from accelerators are mixed types and occur in different proportions, depending upon the accelerated particle, the energy, and the target material. With such mixed radiation it is seldom possible to use a single instrument to measure the energy absorption dose in rads, and even more difficult to establish a significant value of RBE. The correct procedure would be to use separate instruments to measure the rad dose of each of the radiations selectively and to measure and assign a suitable RBE for each component of the radiation. Then the rem dose would be the sum of the individual products:

$$\text{Dose (rem)} = \Sigma[\text{RBE} \times \text{dose (rads)}]$$

However, such a detailed analysis of the radiation is seldom possible. The common procedure is to determine the rem dosage only for the biologically most dangerous component of the radiation (usually fast neutrons) for which an estimated RBE is available, using an instrument which will measure the intensity of this single component either in rads or in flux of particles/$(cm^2)(sec)$. If the rem-dosage sum for the other components can be estimated to be small compared with that of the most dangerous component, the numerical value for this one component is used. In general this falls within the accepted limits of error in the definition of the rem dosage or in the definition of the maximum permissible dose.

Maximum Permissible Dose

The maximum permissible radiation dose for laboratory workers has undergone several revisions downward since the concept was initiated in about 1931, at which time the maximum permissible exposure (MPE) was set at 0.2 r/day. At first it was applied only to X-ray and γ-ray dosage, and the chief concern was the protection of radiologists and technicians. In 1934 the International Committee on X-ray Protection[1] adopted the value of 0.2 r/day as the "tolerance dose" without specifying the technique of measurement. Following the practice in X-ray technology in several countries, it was generally interpreted as the "skin dose," which includes back-scattered radiation from the surface of the body. A skin-dose rate of 0.2 r/day is roughly comparable to a rate of 0.1 r/day measured in air without back-scattered radiation. This rate of 0.1 r/day or 0.6 r/week measured in air was the generally accepted tolerance dose from 1934 to about 1946.

During the 1940s a great deal of detailed information became available on the properties of different radiations and on biological response to radiation. It was recognized that standards for exposure of sensitive tissues or organs might differ from those for whole-body exposure. For example, clinical studies of radium poisoning showed the biological significance of α-particle radiation from radium deposited in the bones. The development of chain-reacting piles and the rapid growth of the atomic-energy industry increased the number of persons exposed to radiations and made it necessary to determine the specific effects of neutrons. Fast neutrons were identified as the damaging radiation in cyclotron-induced eye-lens cataracts. The significance of the time factor was recognized in radiation exposure, and studies were made of the biological response of different organs as a function of the time duration of exposure.

In 1949 the National Committee on Radiation Protection recommended a reduction in the permissible dose rate for whole-body exposure to 0.3 rem/week. This was adopted in 1950 by the International Commission on Radiological Protection and repeated with little change in 1954. These recommendations are summarized in the *National Bureau of Standards Handbook No. 59*, September 24, 1954,[5] and also in the report of the International Commission[6] in 1955. Since the permissible limit is expressed in rem, the same value applies to neutrons and other radiations as for X rays or γ rays. Certain exceptions and interpretations are noted. The limit is set by the exposure of the more sensitive organs, which in general are sufficiently below the skin surface to represent the internal body dose. A dosimeter at the skin surface could read 0.5 to 0.6 rem/week without exceeding the internal dose limit.

The flux of fast neutrons to give a dose of 0.3 rem for a 40-hr week depends on neutron energy and on the experimentally determined conversion factor between neutron flux and biological dose. Table 14-3

TABLE 14-3
NEUTRON FLUX AND BIOLOGICAL DOSE[7]

Energy, Mev	rem/(neutron)(cm²)	Flux, neutrons/(cm²)(sec) for 0.3 rem in 40 hr
Thermal	0.104×10^{-8}	2000
0.0001	0.134	1550
0.005	0.122	1700
0.02	0.25	830
0.1	0.83	250
0.5	2.30	90
1.0	3.80	55
2.5	3.41	60
5.0	3.80	55
7.5	4.16	50
10	4.16	50

gives these conversion factors in rem/(neutron)(cm²) for a range of neutron energy; it also gives the flux in neutrons/(cm²)(sec) to give 0.3 rem in 40 hr.[7]   In the range of interest for fast neutrons from accelerators, the limiting flux is between 50 and 60 neutrons/(cm²)(sec).

By 1956 a more intensive study of radiation hazards was prompted by a growing awareness of the significance of radioactive fall-out from atomic- and hydrogen-bomb tests.   A committee on radiation hazards was established by the United States National Academy of Sciences, which published a report[8] in 1956.   A parallel study was prepared by a committee of the British Medical Council.   In 1955 the General Assembly of the United Nations authorized a Scientific Committee on the Effects of Atomic Radiation, which made a final report[9] in 1958.   Also during these years the United States Atomic Energy Commission collected and analyzed a large amount of information on radiation fall-out intensities and supported many medical and biological studies of the effects of radiation.

The principal result of these studies has been to identify the results of radiation and to estimate their effect on the genetic heritage of the race. While the risk of radiation-induced genetic mutations has been considered negligible for the relatively small number of radiation workers, the effects cannot be neglected where large populations are exposed.   Another hazard identified and studied is the incidence of leukemia and bone cancer due to ingestion of radioactive Sr^{90} from fall-out; strontium is taken up from the soil by plants which are eaten by animals and humans and is selectively concentrated in bone.   For very long-term effects the accumulation of radioactive C^{14} in the biosphere also adds to the natural radioactivity and cosmic-ray background in producing both somatic and genetic effects.

As a consequence of this increased awareness of the hazards to large populations, the National Committee on Radiation Protection has recommended[10] certain modifications in the maximum permissible doses.   A basic recommendation is that the total accumulated dose for radiation workers shall not exceed $5(N - 18)$ rem, where N is the age in years. This implies a maximum yearly permissible dose of 5 rem during the working life of the individual.   So although no change is made in the basic maximum permissible dose rate of 0.3 rem/week for occasional exposures, it is in fact reduced, for occupational workers, to 0.1 rem/week. This is required if the total accumulated dose is not to exceed the limit of 5 rem/yr.

For the general population the maximum permissible dose is based on limiting the dose to the gonads so as not to exceed 14×10^6 rem per million population over the first 30 years of life and one-third of that amount in each decade thereafter.   Of this average value of 14 rem per 30 yr for the individual, about 4 rem per 30 yr is expected from natural background radiation.   This leaves 10 rem per 30 yr for all other sources, including X-ray treatment, fall-out, or any other man-made source.   The practical equivalent is a rate for large populations which is one-tenth that for occupational workers, or 0.01 rem/week.[7]

In accelerator operations it is customary to use these latest recommendations of the maximum permissible dose as the basis for calculations of shielding requirements.   A dual standard of acceptable radiation intensities in and around accelerator installations is to be expected in the future.   Two classes of persons are involved: laboratory workers and others within the controlled area, where measurements and records of the individual accumulated dose can be maintained, and the general public residing or working in areas external to the controlled laboratory area. The permissible weekly doses (pwd) for these categories are:

1 pwd (radiation workers)
$$= 100 \text{ mrem/wk, or 20 fast neutrons}/(\text{cm}^2)(\text{sec})$$
1 pwd (general public) $= 10$ mrem/wk, or 2 fast neutrons/$(\text{cm}^2)(\text{sec})$

It might be noted that the natural background radiation at sea level and in the usual environment in inhabited areas is about 2.5 mrem/week, or about 25 per cent of the pwd for the general public.   The natural cosmic-ray background increases with altitude above sea level, and the level of natural radioactivity is higher in certain environments.   The permissible dose rates given above are considered to be conservative, and it seems unlikely that they will be reduced further in the future.

The most difficult problem in accelerator operations will be to determine the total rem dosage from the several types of radiation.   Accepted practice at present is to monitor total radiation intensity continuously with an ionization chamber calibrated in millirads and to apply a local RBE factor estimated from the high-energy neutron content of the particular installation.   This factor may be near 1.0 for low- and medium-energy accelerators, about 3 for the mixture of radiations from a cyclotron, and up to 10 for local areas near targets where the high-energy neutron component is dominant.   It is essential to provide for continuous and permanent records of accumulated exposure for the individual workers; film badges or pocket ionization chambers are commonly required in all major laboratories.   It is also desirable to have a continuous and permanent record of intensities at one or more key points within a laboratory, using ionization-chamber monitors and a recording system.   An intensity contour plot of the laboratory should be made to reveal the areas of highest radiation intensity under the more commonly used arrangements for targets and beam handling; the permanent radiation monitors can be located in these highest-intensity areas.   Such a permanent record should also be kept for monitors located outside the controlled areas, in regions where the exposure to the general public is likely to be a maximum.

14-2. RANGE-ENERGY RELATIONS FOR CHARGED PARTICLES

Primary protons, deuterons, etc., are frequently brought outside of the accelerator vacuum chamber through thin-foil windows as emergent beams.   In the energy range of cyclotrons and other low-energy and medium-energy positive-ion accelerators, beams of such monoenergetic ions have a discrete range in absorbers.

The range-energy relations for protons, deuterons, and He++ ions in several materials have been computed by Bethe[11] from basic ionization-loss theory, corrected empirically to fit the experimental results of range

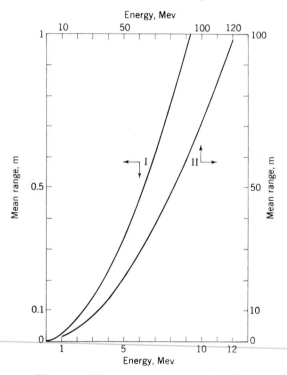

Fig. 14-1. Mean range of protons in air.[12]

measurements.   The most complete compilation is in the form of graphs of mean range as a function of particle energy, in a Brookhaven report[12] by Bethe.   A selected sample of these range-energy curves for protons in air and in several common foil materials, extending to over 100 Mev, is reproduced in Figs. 14-1 and 14-2.   The statistical nature of the energy-loss processes results in range straggling, which extends the extreme (extrapolated) range beyond the mean range.   The straggling corrections are also analyzed and presented as correction curves in the Brookhaven report; they are not reproduced here, since such precision is seldom necessary for shielding calculations. In brief summary it can be shown that straggling extends the extrapolated range beyond the mean range by about 20 per cent in most materials at low energies (<20 Mev), and this extension decreases to about 10 per cent at 200 Mev.

The range of deuteron (D^+) or He^{++} ion (α-particle) beams can be related to proton (H^+) ranges through the approximate relations

$$R_D(T) = 2R_H(\tfrac{1}{2}T) \qquad (14\text{-}1)$$
$$R_\alpha(4T) = R_H(T) + 0.2 \text{ cm} \qquad (14\text{-}2)$$

where the symbol $R(T)$ means the range of a particle of energy T. If

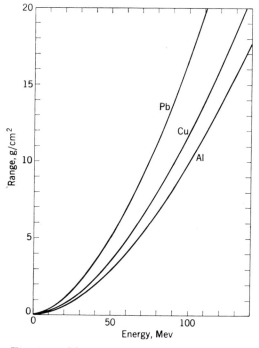

Fig. 14-2. Mean range of protons in metals.[12]

more precise values are needed, the detailed ionization-loss calculations of Bethe are available.

Beams from cyclotrons and other low-energy accelerators will be absorbed in the metal walls of the vacuum chamber. For example, 20-Mev protons have a range of 0.8 mm in Cu or 2.1 mm in Al. When brought outside the chamber through a thin-foil vacuum window, a beam of 20-Mev protons has a range of 4.0 m in air. A potentially dangerous by-product will be the radioactivities induced in the oxygen and nitrogen in the air; if such a beam is to be used in air, a suitable ventilation system must be provided. In this low-energy region laboratory practice requires careful planning to avoid exposure of personnel to either the primary beam or scattered particles from the beam. Several scientists have suffered burns of the hands or arms from such scattered beam radiation. In general, however, this is a problem in laboratory arrangements rather than shielding.

Bethe's range-energy calculations and curves extend up to 1000 Mev for protons, but for energies above about 200 Mev other processes than ionization loss are involved, and range curves are no longer accurate. In general, processes such as nuclear interactions and meson production reduce the proton energy by large steps, so the mean proton range for higher energies is reduced below the ionization-loss curves. However, the secondary radiations produced in these interactions must themselves be analyzed for their penetration and ionization, and they may extend the observed ionization well beyond the extreme range of the primary protons. At energies above 400 or 500 Mev these other processes have such large yields that they become dominant features of the absorptive process. The ionization produced by the proton becomes less important than its nuclear interactions, and it behaves much like a fast neutron at these energies. The properties of such nucleonic particles are discussed further in Sec. 14-10, Nucleonic Showers.

14-3. ELECTRON ABSORPTION

Range of Electrons

Primary electrons have a reasonably well-defined range only for energies of less than a few Mev. At these low energies, energy loss is by ionization and excitation of the atomic electrons in the atoms of the absorber. The ratio of the number of electrons to atomic weight, Z/A, is approximately 2 for all materials except hydrogen. So range can be expressed in gm/cm² for all materials (except hydrogen) without serious error.

Each electron experiences many scattering collisions and follows a tortuous path before being brought to rest, so there are wide variations in the range of individual electrons, resulting in considerable straggling. The only significant observational quantity is the "maximum range," obtained by extrapolating the number-thickness curve on a linear plot at the extreme end of the range. For monoenergetic electrons of energy T between 0.7 and 3 Mev the observed maximum range in aluminum can be conveniently expressed by the "Feather rule":

$$R = 0.542T - 0.133 \text{ gm/cm}^2 \tag{14-3}$$

The range rule holds approximately for other materials (except hydrogen). A useful rule of thumb is that the range in gm/cm² is half the energy in Mev.

For electron energies up to several Mev the range is short enough that the electrons will be absorbed by the metal walls of accelerator vacuum chambers. Thin-foil vacuum windows are frequently used to allow beams to emerge from the chamber. Such emergent beams have been used for localized irradiation for medical purposes, such as in the treatment of skin cancer, and for sterilization of packaged drugs or canned foods.

Energy loss by ionization depends on particle velocity. Electrons approach the velocity of light for energies above about 2 Mev, so the rate of ionization loss becomes essentially constant with further increase in energy. It is also nearly independent of the absorbing material. This limiting value of the rate of ionization loss is about 2 Mev/(gm)(cm²) in light absorbers, becoming smaller with denser materials to reach a value of about 1.4 Mev/(gm)(cm²) for Pb. It results in the formation of about 6.0 ion pairs/μ in material of unit density such as water or tissue. In cloud chambers or electron-sensitive photographic emulsions used for scientific observations, this minimum ionization rate results in the "thin tracks" which are characteristic of singly charged particles of "relativistic" velocities.

Radiation Loss

For electron energies above a few Mev the more important energy-loss process is the emission of radiation. This radiation is a continuous spectrum of X rays called bremsstrahlung (i.e., braking radiation) which is emitted in decelerating or deflecting impacts between the primary electrons and atoms in the target or absorber. The X rays which are produced are themselves absorbed through electromagnetic interactions such as photoelectric absorption, Compton scattering, or the production of positron-electron pairs. The attenuation of X rays due to these processes is discussed in Sec. 14-4. However, the secondary electrons which are emitted by the X rays cause further ionization and excitation of atoms, starting from the point within the absorber where they are produced, and may penetrate far beyond the range of the primary electrons. The difficulty in separating the effects of the primary and secondary electrons is the reason that range is not an appropriate measure of electron absorption above a few Mev energy.

The quantum-mechanical theory of the radiation emission process was originally developed by Bethe and Heitler;[13] simple approximations have been developed by Rossi and Greisen[14] and by Schiff.[15] Cross-section formulas and related data will be found in the article by Koch and Motz.[16] This theory predicts the spectral distribution of X rays as a function of incident electron energy and of the properties of the material in the target. A more complete description of the properties of the radiation will be given in the section to follow on X rays, where the energy distribution will be illustrated. The theory describes, and experiments confirm, a distribution in which the largest number of X rays are emitted at low photon energy, with the number-versus-energy spectrum decreasing with increasing photon energy to an upper limit which is equal to the energy of the incident electron. From the probability of emission given by the theory, the total energy loss by the electron due to radiation can be obtained.

The fractional rate of energy loss through radiation is nearly independent of electron energy. It depends on the magnitude of the electric field within the atom, since it is this field that causes the phenomenon. This atomic electric field is associated with the atomic number Z of the atoms of the absorber. In a thickness x of absorber the fractional energy loss due to radiation may be represented by

$$\frac{W}{W_0} = F(W)e^{-x/x_0} \qquad (14\text{-}4)$$

where W_0 is the initial and W the final value of the average particle energy, $F(W)$ is a slowly varying function of energy which involves the atomic number and other constants, and x_0 is a characteristic radiation length which is independent of energy.

The radiation length x_0 becomes a useful concept in the interpretation of energy-loss phenomena. Except for the modifying effect of the function $F(W)$, the radiation length can be visualized as the distance in which the electron energy is reduced to $1/e$ of its initial value. The concept has more validity when applied to a small fraction f of the radiation length; in a thickness fx_0 the particle will lose a fraction f of its energy, on the average, through radiation. The value of x_0 can be derived theoretically from the characteristics of the atoms in the absorbing material. When A is the atomic weight and Z the atomic number, the radiation length is given by[13]

$$\frac{1}{x_0} = 4.14 \times 10^{-3} \frac{Z^2}{A} (15.6 - \ln Z) \qquad \mathrm{cm}^{-1} \qquad (14\text{-}5)$$

In this relation the radiation length is given in centimeters. In practice this quantity is more conveniently measured in units of $\mathrm{gm/cm^2}$ in which the calculated values form a smooth curve as a function of Z.

Since the radiation length is independent of electron energy and the function $F(W)$ is not strongly energy-dependent, it is convenient to present the variation of energy loss with electron energy as shown in Fig. 14-3. In this figure the fractional rate of energy loss per radiation length, $-\frac{x_0}{W}\frac{dW}{dx}$, is plotted as a function of energy for a dense (Pb) and a light absorber (air). This quantity increases asymptotically with energy to the maximum rate of 1.0 at very high energies.

In contrast, the competing process of energy loss by ionization is most important at very low energies, decreasing with increasing energy to minimum limiting values at 2 Mev/(gm)(cm²) for air and 1.4 Mev/(gm)(cm²) for Pb as the electrons approach relativistic velocities. Hence the fractional energy loss due to ionization per radiation length, $\left(\dfrac{x_0}{W}\dfrac{dW}{dx}\right)_{ion}$, decreases to a negligible fraction of the total for very high energies. For comparison, this quantity is also plotted in Fig. 14-3 for Pb and air absorbers.

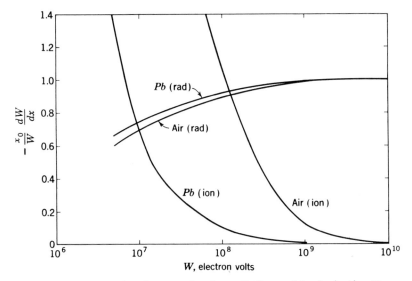

Fig. 14-3. Fractional energy loss by radiation and by ionization.[20]

Ionization loss and radiation loss are equal in magnitude at a critical energy W_c, which is given by the approximate relation[13]

$$W_c \cong \frac{800}{Z} \quad \text{Mev} \tag{14-6}$$

Theoretical computations of the magnitude of radiation loss are given in the *National Bureau of Standards Handbook No. 55*[17] and by Price, Horton, and Spinney,[18] Rossi,[20] and others. Results differ slightly, depending on the assumptions made in performing the computations, but are in general agreement as to the magnitude of radiation lengths and of critical energies. Table 14-4 gives numerical values of radiation length in gm/cm² and in centimeters for some of the common elements used in absorbers, taken from the above references, and also the critical energies

TABLE 14-4
RADIATION LENGTHS AND CRITICAL ENERGIES[20]

Substance	Z	Density, gm/cm³	Radiation lengths		Critical energy W_c, Mev
			gm/cm²	cm	
Hydrogen (liquid)..	1	0.07	58	830	(400)[18]
Carbon............	6	1.50	44.6	30.0	102
Nitrogen..........	7	......	39.4	......	88.7
Oxygen...........	8	......	35.3	......	77.7
Aluminum........	13	2.70	24.5	9.1	48.8
Iron..............	26	7.85	14.1	1.80	24.3
Copper...........	29	8.94	13.1	1.47	21.8
Tin..............	50	7.28	8.9	1.22	12.5
Lead.............	82	11.34	6.5	0.57	7.8
Air..............	(7.37)	0.0012	37.7	31,000	84.2
Water...........	(7.23)	1.00	37.1	37.1	83.8
Concrete.........	(13.2)	2.35	24	10.2	47

in Mev. Figure 14-4 is a plot of these calculated values of radiation length and critical energy as a function of atomic number Z.

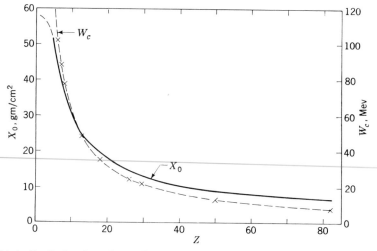

Fig. 14-4. Radiation lengths and critical energies as functions of atomic number.

For a mixture of elements, the radiation length can be obtained by summing the several individual values using the fraction of each element by weight f_i,

$$\left(\frac{1}{x_0}\right)_{mixt} = \sum \frac{f_i}{x_i} \qquad (14\text{-}7)$$

Summary

We find that electrons are degraded in energy both by ionization and by radiation. At relatively low energies and in light absorbers ionization loss predominates. The residual energy W after traversing a thickness x of absorber of density ρ is given by

$$W = W_0 - \rho x \begin{bmatrix} 1.4 \text{ (high Z)} \\ 2.0 \text{ (low Z)} \end{bmatrix} \quad \text{Mev} \qquad (14\text{-}8)$$

where ρx is in units of gm/cm^2 and the factor in brackets is the loss in $Mev/(gm)(cm^2)$.

At very high energies where ionization loss is negligible, the attenuation by radiation loss follows the simple exponential law

$$\frac{W}{W_0} = F(W)_{rad} \, e^{-(\rho x)/x_0} \qquad (14\text{-}9)$$

where ρx is the thickness of the target or absorber in gm/cm^2 and x_0 is the radiation length for this material in the same units. The factor $F(W)_{rad}$ is the fractional energy loss by radiation plotted in Fig. 14-3 and is a slowly varying function of electron energy with a magnitude between 0.6 and 1.0.

The production of X rays in the absorber follows the complementary relation

$$I = I_m(1 - e^{-(\rho x)/x_0}) \qquad (14\text{-}10)$$

where I_m represents the intensity for complete conversion to X rays. So we see that X-ray intensity is a maximum in the initial layers of the absorber and falls off exponentially with thickness. Meanwhile the X rays are being absorbed and scattered by other electromagnetic interactions which release secondary electrons and positrons. These secondary charged particles lose energy through radiation, as well as by ionization, starting from the point within the absorber where they originate. The X rays also produce neutrons through the process of photoproduction, with a cross section depending on X-ray energy and the material of the absorber.

The concept of radiation length applies only to the loss of electron energy through radiation. Its primary utility is in computing the intensity of the secondary X radiation, preliminary to determining the X-ray shielding requirements. Nevertheless, it is occasionally useful as a unit of absorber thickness in describing the production of other secondary radiations such as photoneutrons and will be used in Sec. 14-9.

Some examples will illustrate the energy attenuation of the primary electrons, without consideration of the additional problems of absorption of secondary radiations. First, consider the attenuation in Al of a beam of 20-Mev electrons, as from an electron linear accelerator. The thickness needed to reduce energy to zero by ionization alone is found from Eq. (14-8) to be 10 gm/cm² or 3.7 cm of Al.   This represents 0.4 radiation length, in which the energy would also be attenuated by radiation to $0.41W_0$, following Eq. (14-9).   Since both loss processes occur, the actual thickness needed to absorb the primary electrons is somewhat less than 10 gm/cm².   However, computation of the exact thickness is of no significance, since it is insufficient in any event to provide adequate absorption for the secondary X rays produced in the Al absorber.

As another example, consider a beam of 200-Mev electrons and a Pb absorber.   Ionization loss alone would require a thickness of 143 gm/cm² or 12.6 cm Pb.   This represents 22 radiation lengths, in which the incident energy W_0 would be reduced by radiation to about $1.7 \times 10^{-10}W_0$, which is smaller than most shielding requirements for the incident electrons.   The significant problem is again the attenuation of the secondary X rays and photoneutrons, which will be discussed in following sections.

14-4. X-RAY ATTENUATION

X rays are the principal secondary radiation from electron accelerators, emitted from all targets bombarded by the beam.   They also occur as bremsstrahlung produced in absorbers by high-energy electronic components of the secondary radiation.   Superimposed on the continuous energy spectrum of bremsstrahlung from targets or absorbers are the K, L, etc., line spectra, which are monoenergetic X rays associated with filling the inner electron energy levels in the target atoms.   The energies of these line spectra are so low as to be unimportant in most shielding problems.

X-ray absorption is a complex problem which can only be discussed properly in terms of the several energy-loss processes, which vary in relative importance as a function of photon energy, and with due regard to the changing shape of the energy distribution as the relative intensities of the secondary and tertiary products change with increasing absorber thickness.   Furthermore, the probabilities of the secondary interactions and the form of the energy distribution are also strongly dependent on the material of the absorber.

Our purpose in this section is to describe the properties of X-ray absorption for low-energy and medium-energy X rays, up to about 300 Mev, for which the interactions with matter are predominantly electromagnetic in character.   To simplify the discussion, we shall consider the following topics:

1. Attenuation of monoenergetic X rays with narrow-beam geometry
2. Attenuation in thick absorbers and with broad-beam geometry
3. Bremsstrahlung energy distribution from thin targets

4. Attenuation of continuous spectra in thick absorbers

5. Photoneutron production

The probability of any atomic or nuclear interaction is given in terms of the cross section σ, measured in square centimeters. This is the idealized, equivalent "area" of the system, comprising the incident particle or radiation and the struck atom or nucleus. The probability is assumed to be 100 per cent if the projected path of the incident ray or particle falls within this area relative to the center of the atom, and zero if it is outside this area. From this we see that σ is measured by an interaction distance r_0, such that $\sigma = \pi r_0^2$. For example, if all photons coming within a distance r_0 of 10^{-8} cm of the centers of target atoms were to cause a particular interaction, while those at greater distances would not interact, the cross section would be 3.14×10^{-16} cm^2.

Experimental determinations of cross section are obtained from the observed intensity of an interaction involving a known number of incident particles and a known number of target atoms. If a beam of incident particles of N_1/sec strikes a thin target of N_2 atoms/cm^2 and produces an interaction with a number of secondary radiations N_3/sec, the cross section is given by

$$\sigma = \frac{N_3}{N_1 N_2} \qquad \text{cm}^2$$

To be more specific, consider a beam current i in amperes ($N_1 = i/e$ electrons or protons/sec) striking a target of atomic weight A, density ρ (gm/cm^2), and thickness l (cm). The number of target atoms/cm^2, N_2, is $\dfrac{N_0 \rho l}{A}$ atoms/cm^2, where N_0 is Avogadro's number. If the rate of emission of secondary radiations is N_3/sec, the cross section is given by

$$\sigma = \frac{N_3 A e}{N_0 \rho l i} \qquad \text{cm}^2 \qquad (14\text{-}11)$$

The angular distribution of the secondary radiations is usually non-isotropic, with the emission frequently concentrated in the forward angles. In this event, the cross section per unit solid angle, specified for a particular angle, is more meaningful than the total cross section for 4π steradians. The total cross section σ_t is then 4π times the average value of the cross section per steradian.

Attenuation of Monoenergetic X Rays

The attenuation in energy of monoenergetic X rays can be computed from the theory of electromagnetic interactions. An extensive literature exists on the theoretical analyses and computations, covering a wide range in energy and for all types of absorbing materials. The results have been confirmed by many experimental measurements.

1. At very low energies "photoelectric absorption" is the dominant process; secondary electrons are emitted from the atoms in the absorber, and the full energy of the photon is absorbed. The cross section for photoelectric absorption decreases sharply with increasing energy, and it is of negligible importance for energies above 0.5 Mev. The secondary-electron energies are reduced below the incoming photon energy by amounts determined by the binding energies of the electrons in the atoms. Secondaries lose energy, by ionization of other atoms in the absorber, within a short distance because of their predominantly low energies. The angular distribution is essentially isotropic.

2. The Compton effect is an elastic collision between a photon and an atomic electron in which energy and momentum are conserved. Compton scattering refers to the secondary photons, which are reduced in energy and are scattered at a finite angle relative to the incident direction. For high-energy X rays or γ rays the scattering is largely forward, so the photon beam continues with the direction and penetrating power only slightly changed. The secondary electrons are emitted at wider angles, up to but not exceeding 90°, and with their energy dependent on the angle of scattering; for high photon energies the angles of emission of the secondary electrons are close to 90°. Again, these secondary electrons lose energy primarily through ionization in the absorber, although those of highest energy also emit tertiary X rays which are projected in the direction of the scattered electrons. The effect on a narrow beam is to degrade the energy spectrum of the forward radiation and to scatter a significant fraction of energy out of the beam as secondary electrons. The interaction cross section decreases with increasing X-ray energy, but at a much slower rate than the photoelectric interaction. This is the dominant process for most materials in the energy range above 0.5 Mev up to 10 or 20 Mev, and it is significant at even higher energies for low-Z materials.

3. Positron-electron pair formation becomes energetically possible above a threshold photon energy of 1.02 Mev ($2m_0c^2$), and the cross section rises with increasing energy. At high energies, the pairs are primarily projected forward, making small angles with the incident beam direction. For low-energy pairs the major energy loss is through ionization collisions in the absorber, at the customary rate of 2 Mev/(gm)(cm²). After the positron slows down to thermal velocities, it is usually absorbed in an annihilation process with an atomic electron, releasing the total mass energy in the form of two quanta of 0.51 Mev energy, and with an isotropic angular distribution. The higher-energy secondary positrons and electrons also lose energy through radiation of bremsstrahlung, which is projected forward.

The fact that photoelectric absorption and Compton scattering decrease in probability with increasing energy, while pair formation increases in cross section, leads to a minimum in the curve of absorption coefficient versus energy for monoenergetic X rays, with the location of the minimum a function of atomic number of the absorber. This minimum absorption coefficient μ_{min} occurs at about 3.5 Mev for Pb, 10 Mev for Cu, and 20 Mev for Al, for example. This minimum is at the energy where the cross section for pair production is approximately equal to the cross section for Compton scattering. X radiation of these energies is most penetrating in these particular absorbers. Note that these energies are considerably lower than the critical energies in these materials at which radiation loss by electrons becomes equal to ionization loss.

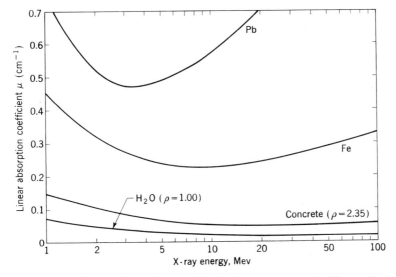

Fig. 14-5. Linear absorption coefficients for monoenergetic X rays.[17]

The ideal arrangement for computing or for measuring X-ray attenuation is with a narrow collimated beam of monoenergetic X rays traversing thin slabs of absorber composed of a single element. For this case the well-known law of exponential absorption holds:

$$\frac{I}{I_0} = e^{-\mu x} \tag{14-12}$$

where I_0 is the initial and I the final intensity after traversing a thickness x of absorber having a "linear absorption coefficient" μ. Experiments show that under ideal conditions the attenuation is exponential, as indicated by the relation above, and that the magnitudes of the observed absorption coefficients are in agreement with those computed from the interaction cross sections. Linear absorption coefficients for monoenergetic X rays in several materials are plotted as a function of energy in Fig. 14-5, taken from the *National Bureau of Standards Handbook No.*

55,[17] and each curve illustrates the minimum absorption coefficient described above.

The reciprocal of the linear absorption coefficient, $1/\mu$, is the thickness of absorber which reduces intensity to $1/e$, or to a value of $0.366 I_0$; this distance is sometimes called the "e-folding length." A more widely used unit is the "half-value thickness," which, as its name implies, is the thickness of absorber which reduces intensity to $0.5 I_0$; the half-value thickness is given by $L_{\frac{1}{2}} = (\ln_e 2)/\mu = 0.693/\mu$. Still another commonly used unit is the "10-folding length," which reduces intensity to $0.1 I_0$; it is given by $L_{\frac{1}{10}} = (\ln_e 10)/\mu = 2.306/\mu$. When used for shielding calculations, the attenuation for absorber thickness x is given alternatively by

$$\frac{I}{I_0} = 10^{-x/L_{\frac{1}{10}}} \qquad \frac{I}{I_0} = 2^{-x/L_{\frac{1}{2}}} \qquad (14\text{-}13)$$

The mass absorption coefficient $\mu_m = \mu/\rho$ has units of cm^2/g (ρ is the density in gm/cm^3), and the attenuation equation is

$$\frac{I}{I_0} = e^{-\mu_m(\rho x)} \qquad (14\text{-}14)$$

where ρx is the mass per unit area of the shield, in units of gm/cm^2. When materials such as concrete are used for shielding, the mass absorption coefficient can be computed from the known fractional densities of the several elements comprising the materials and their respective absorption coefficients. The variation of μ_m with atomic number is smooth, and values can be interpolated from a few known elements. Table 14-5 gives a limited number of values of mass absorption coefficient

TABLE 14-5

MASS ABSORPTION COEFFICIENTS, μ_m, FOR MONOENERGETIC X RAYS
AND γ RAYS
(In cm^2/gm)

Material	Z	Energy, Mev						
		0.01	0.05	0.10	0.50	1.0	5.0	10.0
Hydrogen	1	0.385	0.335	0.294	0.173	0.126	0.0502	0.0321
Carbon	6	2.13	0.178	0.149	0.087	0.0635	0.0270	0.0194
Oxygen	8	5.69	0.196	0.151	0.0871	0.0636	0.0276	0.0206
Aluminum	13	26.3	0.325	0.161	0.0840	0.0613	0.0282	0.0229
Silicon	14	34.1	0.389	0.172	0.0869	0.0635	0.0296	0.0243
Iron	26	178	1.83	0.344	0.0828	0.0595	0.0313	0.0295
Lead	82	80.1	5.19	5.29	0.145	0.0684	0.0426	0.0489
	Density:							
Air	0.00129	4.88	0.194	0.151	0.0869	0.0635	0.0274	0.0202
Water	1.00	5.09	0.212	0.167	0.0967	0.0706	0.0301	0.0219
Normal concrete	2.35	......	.....	0.15	0.087	0.063	0.029	0.023

μ_m for several elements and common materials in the energy range below 10 Mev.

Attenuation in Thick Absorbers and with Broad Beams

A monoenergetic beam of X rays undergoes Compton scattering in the absorber which degrades photon energy; the energy distribution broadens and the average photon energy is reduced with increasing absorber thickness. In general, however, the higher-energy photons persist most nearly in the incident direction, while those of reduced energy tend to be scattered out of a collimated beam. The result is a relatively slow change in the penetration of the forward beam if measured with narrow-beam geometry. Under ideal conditions the absorption coefficient is constant out to very large absorber thickness.

Secondary electrons from Compton-scattering processes are emitted mostly at angles approaching 90°, and their energy content is spread laterally away from the collimated beam. Some lower-energy scattered photons are also deflected out of the direct beam, and tertiary processes extend the transverse spread still further. The result is a steady build-up in the initial layers of absorber of the ionizing particles which accompany the X-ray beam, along with a lateral broadening of the cross-sectional area of the envelope of these ionizing particles. A large ionization chamber placed behind absorbers will read a considerably higher intensity than a small one limited to the dimensions of the collimated beam. Such broad-beam measurements detect this build-up in ionization intensity which is not observed in narrow-beam geometry. A semilog plot of intensity as a function of absorber thickness shows wide deviations from the constant slope observed with narrow beams, especially for the initial layers, so that no unique absorption coefficient can be assigned. With increasing absorber thickness the mixture of primary, secondary, and tertiary radiations approaches an equilibrium, and the slope of the semilog plot approaches a constant absorption coefficient which is a true measure of the ultimate attenuation. However, the magnitude of this broad-beam thick-absorber coefficient is in all cases considerably smaller than that for a narrow collimated beam.

Practically all shielding applications involve the total energy transmitted through absorbing walls and so require analysis in terms of broad beams. The unique absorption coefficients for narrow-beam monoenergetic X rays illustrated in Fig. 14-5 and Table 14-5 do not apply. Furthermore, there is no simple and conclusive analysis to determine the magnitude of intensity build-up or the magnitude of the broad-beam attenuation coefficient for all situations. Rather, it is necessary to analyze each separate shielding problem in terms of the geometry of the absorbing shields, the amount of incident beam collimation, and the composition of the absorbers.

As an example of the difference in attenuation between narrow-beam and broad-beam geometry, Fig. 14-6 is a semilog plot of attenuation in steel of the essentially monoenergetic 1.2-Mev gamma rays from Co^{60} when observed through plane steel slab absorbers under broad-beam geometry; this plot is given in a paper by Halmshaw and Knapp reported by Price, Horton, and Spinney.[18]   Also plotted on this figure is the attenuation curve for narrow-beam conditions using the monoenergetic absorption coefficient for this energy.   It can be noted that the observed intensity is as much as five times greater for some absorber thicknesses than that predicted by the narrow-beam absorption curve, because of an initial build-up of ionization intensity.   It may also be noted that the

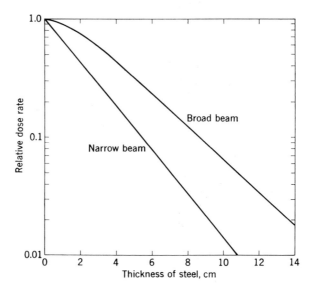

Fig. 14-6. Broad-beam and narrow-beam attenuation plots for 1.2-Mev γ rays.[18]

equilibrium value of broad-beam absorption coefficient is smaller than the narrow-beam coefficient, by about 25 per cent in this case.   This apparent "hardening" of the radiation can be understood as a consequence of the production of secondary electrons and degraded photons deep in the absorber.

It is sometimes convenient to describe the difference between the results of measurements in narrow-beam and broad-beam cases by means of build-up factors.   This problem is discussed by Price, Horton, and Spinney,[18] who present the results of build-up-factor calculations in a series of graphs and empirical relations.   We shall not reproduce a detailed analysis of the problem, but shall present only some general results and conclusions:

1. The intensity increase in the initial layers of absorber can be described by a numerical build-up factor B in the attenuation equation

$$\frac{I}{I_0} = B \frac{1}{4\pi r^2} e^{-\mu_0 x} \qquad (14\text{-}15)$$

where μ_0 is the monoenergetic X-ray linear absorption coefficient and the factor $1/(4\pi r^2)$ is the inverse-square reduction in intensity with distance r from the source.

2. The build-up factor B as defined above increases with absorber thickness, so the result is an apparent reduction in the value of μ_0.

3. The magnitude of the build-up factor is largest for low-energy radiation in low-Z shielding materials; however, this is of significance only in the shielding of very-low-energy accelerators.

4. Build-up factors depend on the geometry of the source and shield. They are largest for point isotropic sources with spherical shields (e.g., Co^{60} bomb) and smaller for plane absorbers with monodirectional sources characteristic of most accelerator shielding problems.

5. The build-up factor is of the order of 10 after 15 mean free paths (mfps) for higher-energy (10-Mev) X rays in dense absorbers. This means that additional absorber is required beyond that computed from the monoenergetic absorption coefficient, sufficient to increase the attenuation by about another factor of 10.

Bremsstrahlung Spectra from Thin Targets

The energy distribution of X rays from targets bombarded by high-energy electrons can be computed from the quantum-mechanical theory of Bethe and Heitler.[13] An expression derived by Schiff[15] gives the probability for emission of a photon of energy k in the range $d(k/W)$, where W is the incident electron energy. This expression has been used to compute the number of photons emitted in the forward direction, as a function of photon energy, for a sequence of incident electron energies between 5 and 100 Mev, given in the *National Bureau of Standards Handbook No. 55*.[17] In illustration, the spectral distribution for 16-Mev electrons is shown in Fig. 14-7, taken from the Handbook. The distribution is presented in two ways. One curve shows the relative number of photons per unit photon energy interval, which is given by the quantity $W^2\Gamma/k$, where W is total electron energy, Γ is a quantity proportional to the spectrum intensity in the forward direction, and k is photon energy. The other curve shows the X-ray intensity, which is number of photons times photon energy.

Experimental measurements of the X-ray energy distribution for a few discrete electron energies have been made with the Bureau of Standards 50-Mev betatron, and they are found to be in good agreement with the theoretical distributions.   There seems no reason to doubt that the theoretical representation is adequate for the purpose of this discussion.

The angular distribution of the radiation is a function of electron energy, photon energy, and the atomic number of the target.   Stearns[19]

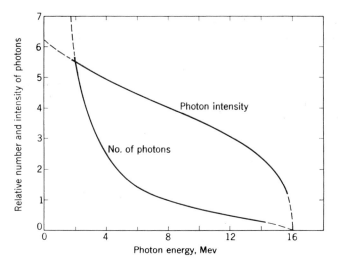

Fig. 14-7. X-ray photon spectrum and intensity spectrum for thin-target X rays from a 16-Mev betatron.[17]

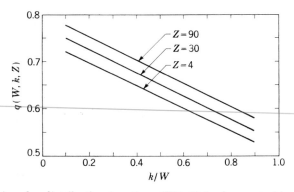

Fig. 14-8. Angular distribution function $q(W,k,Z)$ for bremsstrahlung spectra.[19]

has developed an expression for the root-mean-square (rms) angle of emission of photons, $\langle\theta^2\rangle^{1/2}$, which can be expressed as

$$\langle\theta^2\rangle^{1/2} = q(W,k,Z)\ \frac{m_0c^2}{W}\ \ln\ \frac{W}{m_0c^2} \tag{14-16}$$

where W is the total energy of the electron, $m_0c^2 = 0.51$ Mev is the electron rest energy, and $q(W,k,Z)$ is a function of electron energy, photon energy, and atomic number which is a slowly varying function of the ratio k/W and is of the order of magnitude of unity. Values of $q(W,k,Z)$ are plotted in Fig. 14-8 for several values of atomic number and for a wide range in the energy ratio k/W.[19] The radiation is strongly collimated in the forward direction, most sharply at the highest energies. For example, with 100 Mev electron energy and for a Pb absorber, the lower-energy photons have an rms angle of 2.1×10^{-2} radian ($1.2°$), and the higher-energy photons have a smaller angle of 1.5×10^{-2} radian; at 1000 Mev these angles are about 3.0×10^{-3} and 2.2×10^{-3} radian.

This sharp forward collimation of bremsstrahlung radiation is one of its most significant characteristics. The radiation from high-energy betatron and synchrotron targets is projected out of the orbit tangentially in such a self-collimated beam. Heavy shielding by dense materials is required in the forward direction, broad enough to encompass the diverging shower of secondary photons and electrons from the main beam; in other directions the shielding can be thinner, or of less dense materials.

Attenuation of Continuous Spectra in Thick Absorbers

In thick absorbers the energy spectrum of the X rays emitted from the primary target is degraded further, to a spectrum of still lower average energy. It differs from a monoenergetic beam in the sense that a continuous spectrum exists initially, so a distribution which is in equilibrium with its secondaries is reached at somewhat smaller absorber thickness. Nevertheless, scattering processes continue to broaden the beam, and the absorption coefficient observed with a broad beam is again lower than that for a collimated narrow beam. Since the magnitude of the attenuation depends in each case on the geometry and composition of the shields, on the collimation of the beam from the target, and on the thickness of the absorber, it is not possible to specify unique absorption coefficients for continuous spectra in thick absorbers.

Experimental measurements of the attenuation in concrete of the primary X-ray beam from the 50-Mev betatron at the National Bureau of Standards are reported in the *National Bureau of Standards Handbook No. 55*.[17] The results are shown in Fig. 14-9, as a semilog plot of the ionization intensity behind plane concrete barriers as a function of concrete thickness, and for electron beam energies of 6, 10, 20, 30, and 38 Mev. The density of the (normal) concrete was 147 lb/ft³ ($\rho = 2.35$ gm/cm³). On this semilog plot the attenuation curves show a small intensity build-up in the initial layers of absorber, similar to but of smaller magnitude than that for monoenergetic beams, but the curves become straight for thick absorbers, indicating a constant terminal absorption coefficient appropriate to the equilibrium mixture of radiations in each case. These terminal absorption coefficients range from 0.172/in. for 6 Mev electron energy to 0.130/in. at 38 Mev. In fact, the terminal slope is essentially the same for all energies above 20 Mev; other observations and calculations in the same laboratory show that the same value is valid up to 100 Mev.

We conclude from these measurements that for this geometry and material a single, common value of terminal absorption coefficient holds for all continuous bremsstrahlung spectra coming from electrons of all energies from 20 to 100 Mev. In concrete this terminal value of the linear absorption coefficient is

$$\mu = 0.130/\text{in.}$$
$$= 0.0513/\text{cm} \quad \text{(concrete)}$$

The equivalent mass absorption coefficient is

$$\mu_m = \mu/\rho$$
$$= 0.0218 \text{ cm}^2/\text{gm} \quad \text{(concrete)}$$

Comparison with the monoenergetic absorption coefficients of Fig. 14-5 shows this value to be only slightly larger than that at the minimum of the absorption coefficient versus energy curve for this mixture of materials.

A valid general conclusion is that the minimum absorption coefficient for monoenergetic radiation is a lower limit on, and a close approximation to, the effective terminal value of absorption coefficient for bremsstrahlung. This conclusion can be used to determine terminal absorption coefficients for other shielding materials. Figure 14-10

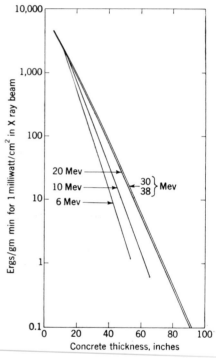

Fig. 14-9. Attenuation of X rays in concrete.[17]

is a plot of these minimum mass absorption coefficients μ_{min} as a function of Z; for each element the value of the absorption coefficient plotted is for that energy at which monoenergetic X radiation is most penetrating.

Attenuation calculations which assume a single value of minimum absorption coefficient obviously will not give accurate results for thin absorbers, since these assumptions do not adequately describe the build-up in the initial layers; it is necessary to employ a more detailed analysis to estimate the build-up factor, as described earlier for monoenergetic radiations. However, for thick absorbers the small error caused by neglecting the initial build-up in intensity is compensated by use of the minimum absorption coefficient. It is well to remember, however, that this terminal value is only an average or effective absorption coefficient which summarizes the complex effects of the broad energy distribution and of the mixture of radiations in the photon-electron shower.

As an example we shall compute the required thickness in each of several materials for shielding the X-ray beam from a 50-Mev betatron. We take the emergent X-ray beam intensity to be 500 r/min at 3 ft from the target (r_0). This is equivalent to about 5 milliwatts/cm^2 and is a

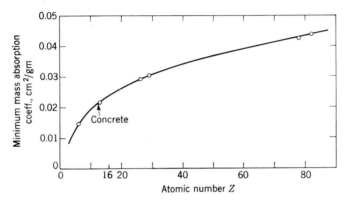

Fig. 14-10. Minimum values of mass absorption coefficients for monoenergetic X rays.

representative value of X-ray intensity from such a betatron as that reported in the *National Bureau of Standards Handbook No. 55*.[17] The intensity behind shielding walls at a distance of 30 ft (r) is to be reduced to the pwd rate of 100 mrad/week (see Sec. 14-1). We take a work week of 40 hr or 2.4×10^3 min. So the desired total attenuation is

$$\frac{I}{I_0} = \frac{0.100}{500} \times \frac{1}{2.4 \times 10^3} = 8.3 \times 10^{-9}$$

If we use the minimum mass absorption coefficient described above and include the inverse-square distance factor, the attenuation relation is

$$\frac{I}{I_0} = \left(\frac{r}{r_0}\right)^2 e^{-\mu \min (\rho x)} \qquad (14\text{-}17)$$

Values of the appropriate minimum mass absorption coefficients for concrete, iron, and lead are taken from Fig. 14-10. We obtain the following results:

Shielding material	Minimum mass absorption coefficient, cm²/gm	Shield thickness		
		gm/cm²	cm	in.
Concrete........	0.0218	536	228	90
Iron............	0.0290	403	52.5	21
Lead...........	0.0414	282	25.0	10

This concrete thickness is slightly greater than the comparable figure recommended for shielding in *National Bureau of Standards Handbook No. 55*, because of the use here of a lower value of the permissible dose. There are no equivalent experimental measurements to check the predicted thickness for iron or lead shielding.

Photoneutron Production

A word of caution is necessary with regard to drawing conclusions about X-ray shielding requirements solely from the X-ray attenuation calculations. This has to do with the production of neutrons in the absorber by the higher-energy X rays. In the foregoing analysis no attempt was made to include the special problems of neutron production or neutron shielding.

Photoneutrons from the (γ,n) process are produced in essentially all elements, with observed threshold energies varying from 2.2 Mev (deuterium) to nearly 20 Mev. Many of these processes lead to the production of radioactive isotopes, with which measurements have been made of the cross sections for production and the threshold energies. Table 14-6 lists the threshold energies of elements between $Z = 6$ and $Z = 79$, taken from the *National Bureau of Standards Handbook No. 55*.[17] Threshold energy falls irregularly with increasing Z, from 18.7 Mev for carbon to 7.7 Mev for tantalum. For the very heavy elements the threshold is at about 7.0 Mev, which is the average neutron binding energy in such elements.

Most of the measurements of photoneutron thresholds have been made with betatrons and electron linear accelerators of 20 to 50 Mev energy. At these energies the photoproduction yields are small, not exceeding a value of 10^7 neutrons/mole of radiated material for 1 r of radiation exposure (measured behind ⅛ in. Pb) except for a few of the heaviest elements. From measurements at 50 Mev, Baldwin and Elder[21] report that the yield per mole roentgen is given by the empirical relation

$$\text{No. neutrons}/(\text{mole})(\text{r}) = 1860 Z^2 \qquad (14\text{-}18)$$

The total yield does not change significantly with energy from 20 to 50 Mev in Pb. This shows that the process is a resonance interaction, in which only X rays within a rather narrow energy range are effective. The neutron yield is determined by the number of quanta within this energy band in the bremsstrahlung X-ray spectrum.

Photoneutrons are produced in the absorber, primarily in the initial layers where the major X-ray attenuation occurs. They have a roughly isotropic angular distribution (in the heavy elements), spreading out from their source within the absorber. The attenuation and absorption of these neutrons depend strongly on the material of the absorber. Low-Z, and especially hydrogenous, materials are most effective in moderating

TABLE 14-6
PHOTONEUTRON THRESHOLD ENERGIES

Element	Threshold energy, Mev
Carbon, C^{12}	18.7
Nitrogen, N^{14}	10.7
Oxygen, O^{16}	15.6
Magnesium, Mg^{24}	16.2
Aluminum, Al^{27}	14.4
Silicon, Si^{28}	16.8
Phosphorus, P^{31}	12.3
Sulfur, S^{32}	14.8
Potassium, K^{39}	13.2
Calcium, Ca^{40}	15.9
Iron, Fe^{54}	13.8
Copper, Cu^{63}	10.9
Copper, Cu^{65}	10.2
Zinc, Zn^{70}	9.2
Bromine, Br^{79}	10.7
Bromine, Br^{81}	10.2
Selenium, Se^{82}	9.8
Zirconium, Zr^{90}	11.9
Silver, Ag^{107}	9.5
Antimony, Sb^{121}	9.25
Praseodymium, Pr^{141}	9.4
Tantalum, Ta^{181}	7.7
Gold, Au^{197}	8.0

the neutrons to low energy, so they can be captured in nuclear interactions. However, the common slow-neutron capture process (n,γ), which has the largest cross section in most materials, releases gamma rays which are highly penetrating in such low-Z materials.

A general conclusion is that shielding for X rays of over 10 Mev must include some provision for attenuation of the photoneutrons. Although Pb and Fe are both highly efficient for X-ray attenuation and form compact shields, they are not suitable as neutron absorbers for neutrons of less than 1 Mev energy. For this reason concrete is preferred (it has a large fraction of hydrogen and low-Z materials), even though it makes a more bulky shield. Other alternatives are to use multiple layers of different materials, such as Pb-concrete-Pb and Pb-paraffin-concrete. The optimum design depends on the energy of the X-ray spectrum. The neutron yield must be estimated in each case, and sufficient neutron absorber must be provided. Further details of neutron attenuation are discussed in Sec. 14-6.

14-5. GAMMA-RAY ABSORPTION

Gamma rays and X rays are actually identical in so far as their observed characteristics are concerned. The two names both describe electromagnetic radiation of relatively high energy. X-ray beams consist of photons generated by slowing down of electrons; they are, in effect, bremsstrahlung. Gamma rays, on the other hand, originate in nuclear interactions. Sometimes photons described as gamma rays may have lower energies than other photons described as X rays; sometimes the inverse is the case. The two terms are used only to discriminate between the mechanisms by which the photons originate. Consequently, absorption of gamma rays will follow from the same processes already discussed in the preceding section in connection with X rays.

Gamma rays are produced by excitation of nuclear energy levels, either in a target or in residual nuclei, in essentially all nuclear interactions. The line spectra observed are characteristic of the nuclei involved, and the relative intensity of the lines varies with the type and degree of excitation. Since many different targets may be used in an accelerator, shielding estimates can be based on a composite spectrum which is an envelope of the line spectra covering a large number of possible targets, incident particles, and interactions.

A composite spectrum representative of the energy distribution of γ rays from cyclotron targets is pictured in Fig. 14-11. It has been developed from the following considerations:

1. Most targets for nuclear research have low atomic number, for which the average excitation level spacing is about 0.5 Mev.

2. A few excitation states up to 10 Mev energy exist in a few light nuclei.

3. Average spacing of energy levels in heavy targets is less than 0.1 Mev.

4. γ rays occur primarily in cascade steps between energy levels, with small probability for high-energy quantum emission.

A similar situation exists in the decay of the fission products from U fission, for which the composite γ-ray energy distribution has been measured. For comparison the γ-ray spectrum for fission is also shown in Fig. 14-11. The assumed composite spectrum for accelerator reactions has a somewhat larger fraction of high-energy photons, associated with the wider energy-level spacings in light nuclei.

The composite γ-ray spectrum described above has a shape roughly similar to the X-ray bremsstrahlung distribution for an electron energy of about 10 Mev. As described in the preceding section on X rays, the attenuation of such a continuous distribution cannot be determined from monoenergetic absorption coefficients. The same conclusions are valid as those for X rays, which showed that a "terminal" absorption coefficient exists which can be approximated by the minimum absorption coefficient for monoenergetic photons in the material. However, because of the relatively low energy of the γ-ray spectrum, the terminal coefficient

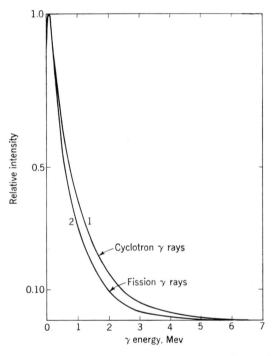

Fig. 14-11. γ-ray spectra, assumed for cyclotron (1) and observed for fission (2).[18]

will be somewhat larger than the minimum value recommended for high-energy X-ray spectra. A good approximation can be obtained from the terminal coefficient for 10-Mev bremsstrahlung (see Fig. 14-9), which is 0.155/in. concrete. The equivalent linear absorption coefficient in Pb would be about 0.55/cm, and the corresponding mass absorption coefficient is $\mu_m = 0.048$ cm^2/gm. This is somewhat larger than the minimum coefficient for Pb (0.042 cm^2/gm), which occurs at 3.5 Mev photon energy.

Photoneutron production by nuclear γ rays will be negligible, since only a small fraction have energies above the photoproduction thresholds for most materials. So, Pb absorbers of relatively small thickness are usually adequate for attenuating γ rays from an accelerator target. However, the shielding required for other radiation components, such as neutrons, will for most accelerators be considerably thicker than that required for γ rays alone. As a consequence, it is seldom necessary to analyze the γ-ray problem separately.

A more serious problem is the shielding for γ rays released in secondary reactions. Neutron capture, through the (n,γ) process, in the shielding material used for neutron attenuation releases γ rays deep in the shield. If the shield consists of low-Z materials, which are most effective for neutron attenuation, the γ-ray intensity emerging from the shield may be significant. One technique for controlling secondary γ-ray intensity is to add high-Z material to the shield. Another is to add a small amount of boron to the shielding mixture; boron has a large cross section for nonradiative capture of slow neutrons. These problems will be discussed in the section to follow.

14-6. NEUTRON SHIELDING

Neutrons are among the most penetrating of the secondary radiations from positive-ion accelerators and are potentially the greatest biological hazard. They are produced in the beam targets and also in the materials forming the defining channel for the emergent beams. They originate as fast neutrons released in nuclear disintegration reactions. Both the intensity of neutrons and their distribution in energy are determined by the particular nuclear interaction. Since a wide variety of target materials may be used in a laboratory research program and different charged particles may be accelerated, the shielding requirements for an accelerator should be based on the intensities anticipated for the highest-yield processes.

The attenuation and absorption of neutrons is a complex process involving many different kinds of interactions with atoms in the absorber, each of which has its own characteristic variability with neutron energy. The most probable interactions are elastic and inelastic collisions of the fast neutrons with nuclei in the absorber; these scattering processes involve large angular deflections and reduce neutron energy in large steps. Neutrons also produce disintegrations in which part or all of their energy is transferred to product particles or to excitation of the residual nucleus, which emits its excitation energy in the form of γ rays. After losing most of their energy through nuclear collision, the neutrons (if they survive) eventually come into thermal equilibrium with their surroundings by transferring the remaining energy by molecular excitation to the molecules of the absorber material, thereby raising the temperature of the absorber. Thermal neutrons diffuse through the absorber, making many elastic collisions before being absorbed. Their ultimate fate is to be absorbed by capture in an atomic nucleus, and the most frequent reaction is that of radiative capture, in which the binding energy of the neutron in the nucleus is released in the form of γ radiation.

The problem of moderation of neutron energy lends itself to theoretical analysis, since elastic scattering involves the conservation of energy and momentum. Statistical features of the passage of neutrons through matter are described by the "transport theory." Analyses involving the time required to slow down neutrons are developed in the "age theory." Statistical studies of the number of impacts, and the times involved, lead to concepts such as the "slowing-down length" or the "relaxation length," which is the thickness of material in which neutron energy is reduced to $1/e$ of its initial value. When neutrons attain thermal equilibrium, their further motion is analyzed by the "diffusion theory." Many theoretical articles and books have been written on these subjects. It is now possible to compute the properties of some of the simpler reactor shield systems directly from the theoretical relations. We give here only a brief survey of the more important interactions and the most pertinent data on the properties of reactor neutrons. For a more complete understanding the reader is referred to the several books on the subject, such as "Radiation Shielding" by Price, Horton, and Spinney[18] of the Harwell Atomic Energy Research Establishment, "Attenuation of Gamma Rays and Neutrons in Reactor Shields," edited by Goldstein[7] for the United States Atomic Energy Commission, as well as the individual references which will be cited.

The purpose of the present discussion is to provide information sufficient for a qualitative understanding of the problems of neutron shielding in accelerators and for rough estimates of accelerator shielding requirements. Far less information is available than in the reactor field; basic constants of accelerator neutrons are not available for the precise treatment possible with reactor neutrons. Because of this lack of data, we are forced to accept and adapt many of the conclusions and much of the data coming from reactor studies. It should be noted, however, that accelerator neutrons can be quite different in their energy distributions and in their shielding requirements.

The cross section of a neutron interaction with an atomic nucleus is commonly given in units of 10^{-24} cm^2 or "barns."* As defined previously, the atomic cross section σ is the equivalent area of the neutron-nucleus interaction. When the cross section is calculated from reaction yields (see Sec. 14-4), the resulting value in square centimeters or barns can be visualized as the area of a circle centered on the nucleus, within

* The name of this unit appears to have developed early in the atomic-energy program in the United States, based on the observation of an unexpectedly large cross section for a particular slow-neutron process which was described as being "as big as a barn."

which the center of the neutron must pass if the probability of the interaction is taken as 100 per cent inside this area and zero outside.

The geometric cross section of an interaction is calculable from the physical dimensions of the particles. If we take as the radius of a proton or neutron the accepted value when these particles are bound in nuclei, $r_0 = 1.3 \times 10^{-13}$ cm, the interaction radius of a proton-neutron interaction would be $2r_0$. The geometric cross section would then be $\sigma_{geom} = \pi(2r_0)^2 = 0.21 \times 10^{-24}$ cm^2 = 0.21 barn.

Cross sections obtained from observed yields are in some cases smaller and in other cases much larger than the geometric cross sections. A smaller cross section means either that the neutron can penetrate the nucleus without interacting or that a more probable competing process is involved. A larger cross section can be interpreted as due to a neutron wavelength or effective size which is larger than that for a bound neutron, following the concepts of the wave-mechanical theory of nuclear interactions. The neutron wavelength is given by $\lambda = h/mv$, where h is the Planck constant of action and mv is the neutron momentum. For slow or thermal neutrons, the wavelength is hundreds of times larger than nuclear dimensions.

Sources of Accelerator Neutrons

The largest interaction cross sections for neutron production are for deuteron reactions on light elements, such as D(d,n), Li(d,n), and Be(d,n). At low deuteron energy the cross section increases with energy in a roughly exponential manner, following the potential-barrier penetration function for the incident deuteron. For energies above the potential barrier the cross section rises to a peak value and then falls off slowly with still higher energy, roughly proportional to $1/v$, where v is deuteron velocity. Individual reactions may show resonance peaks at particular energies, determined by the detailed energy-level structure of the nuclei involved. However, when averaged over the individual energy levels, the cross section has the general shape described above.

Total neutron yield from a thick target increases with energy, because of the increased depth of penetration with increasing particle range. Charged-particle range increases roughly with $T^{3/2}$, so the total yield at energies much higher than the potential barrier also increases approximately with $T^{3/2}$.

Target cooling limitations may restrict the maximum yield of neutrons from accelerators. Although the highest atomic cross sections are for deuterium (in the form of heavy ice) or lithium targets, the beam power which can be absorbed and cooled without damage to these targets is small. Larger beam currents can be used with metallic beryllium targets, with which more efficient cooling techniques have been developed. The highest neutron intensities are obtained with cyclotrons, for which the beam power is greater than for other accelerators; the problems of cyclotron target cooling are described in Chap. 6.   For cyclotrons in the 5- to 20-Mev energy range, the highest neutron intensities are observed with deuterons on water-cooled Be targets, using the internal resonant beam.

The thick-target yield for 15-Mev deuterons on a Be target has been measured (University of California 60-in. cyclotron) to be 1 neutron per 200 deuterons, or 3×10^{13} neutrons/sec for a 1-ma beam.   Because of the small beam dimensions at the target, which with an internal resonant beam can seldom be made larger than a few square centimeters, there is a practical limit on the beam power which can be dissipated in the target with the present known techniques of cooling; this limit is about 5 kw for cyclotron internal targets.   At 15 Mev this means that the beam current is restricted to about 0.33 ma, and the neutron yield is about 1×10^{13} neutrons/sec.   Higher resonant-beam currents can be produced in a cyclotron, and they are used when the object is to produce a high-intensity emergent beam.   However, the useful emergent beams are seldom larger than 20 to 30 per cent of the resonant beams, and emergent beams greater than 0.33 ma are a rarity.   We conclude that a neutron yield of about 1×10^{13} neutrons/sec is a practical maximum for cyclotrons of this energy range.

Neutron output is smaller, in general, for other accelerators and for other incident particles.   With incident protons the highest-yield process is the (p,n) reaction, in which the cross sections are less than 0.2 of those for the parallel deuteron reactions.   Lower energy also reduces yield.   A 1-ma beam of protons from a 4-Mev electrostatic generator will produce only about 10^{11} neutrons/sec.   Neutron output is still smaller from electron accelerators, in which the neutrons are produced by the secondary X rays through the photoproduction or (γ,n) process, and mostly in the shielding materials used to define channels for the X-ray beam.   A 50-Mev betatron, for example, will produce about 10^7 neutrons/mole of high-Z absorbing material, per roentgen of radiation.[17]   With typical operating intensities the X-ray beam will be about 500 r/min at 3 ft from the betatron target; the total neutron yield would then be about 10^8 neutrons/mole of absorber.

Neutron energy distributions are line spectra, associated with the energy levels of the nuclei involved, and are roughly similar to the γ-ray energy distributions.   Single levels can dominate the distribution in light elements where energy levels may be widely spaced; in a few examples the neutrons are essentially monoenergetic.   In heavier targets where energy levels are more closely spaced, the intensity is distributed over a larger number of lines, which have a wide spread in energy.   In all cases the imperfect energy resolution of measuring instruments makes the observed curves take on the appearance of continuous energy distributions.

A typical neutron energy distribution is that for 16-Mev protons on a Be target in a cyclotron, observed by Gugelot and White[22] (see Fig. 14-12). Neutron energy was observed by measuring the lengths of proton recoil tracks in photographic emulsions, with suitable calculations to determine the initial neutron energies; the statistical accuracy leaves much to be desired. This distribution has a peak at about 2 Mev and a tail extending up to 9 Mev energy. Note that the distribution may have a different shape for other neutron-production interactions or for incident particles of different energy.

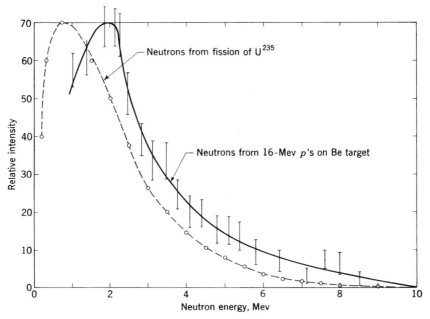

Fig. 14-12. Neutron energy distributions from 16-Mev protons on Be target[22] and from U fission.[18]

The spectrum of neutrons from the fission reaction of U^{235} is similar to the cyclotron spectrum in its basic shape. To illustrate, the U-fission spectrum[18] is also plotted in Fig. 14-12. The cyclotron spectrum observed by Gugelot and White is displaced to higher energy by about 1 Mev throughout, relative to the fission spectrum; this is a feature which may be characteristic only of this particular reaction. However, since the shapes of the neutron spectra are so similar, it is possible to utilize the extensive experimental studies and theoretical calculations of neutron attenuation in the field of nuclear reactors; these results can be applied, with slight modifications for the higher average energy, to the problems of shielding for accelerator neutrons.

The angular distribution of neutrons from a target is determined by the energy-momentum properties of the individual interaction. At low and medium bombarding energies the distribution is essentially isotropic, with a slight peaking in the forward direction. The forward peak is more prominent at higher energies. However, scattering and absorption in the physical structures of the accelerator and in the target mounting usually dominate the angular distribution as observed. For example, the magnet poles of a cyclotron absorb and reflect neutrons from an internal target, and most of the flux emerges in the plane of the accelerator chamber.

Degradation in energy by scattering in the walls of the shielding enclosure of an accelerator will also severely modify the initial energy distribution. An equilibrium mixture of radiations is developed within the enclosure which includes fast neutrons, slow neutrons, γ rays, and other components. The "source intensity" of such a mixture of radiations is difficult to define or to measure. For shielding calculations the fast-neutron component usually can be taken as the dominant one, and the quantity needed for calculations is the flux of fast neutrons/(cm²)(sec) at the shielding wall.

As an example, consider the neutron flux at the wall of a cyclotron enclosure at 10 ft from the target, with 10^{13} neutrons/sec emitted from the target. Without consideration of scattering, and assuming an isotropic distribution, the flux at the wall would be 0.85×10^7 neutrons/(cm²)(sec). Back scattering from the walls, or forward peaking of the angular distribution, might increase the flux to about 2×10^7 neutrons/(cm²)(sec). The attenuation factor required to reduce this flux to the level of the permissible dose rate, which is 20 neutrons/(cm²)(sec), would be 10^{-6}. We conclude that the attenuation factors required for fast-neutron shielding in the horizontal direction of such an accelerator source of neutrons are of the order of magnitude of 10^{-6}.

Interactions between Fast Neutrons and Nuclei

Elastic Scattering. Fast neutrons lose most of their energy through elastic scattering impacts with atoms in the shield. The energy loss is greatest in hydrogen and least for the heaviest elements. Nonrelativistic particle mechanics can be used to compute the average energy loss ΔT per collision, for neutrons of energy T_0, in material of atomic weight A (atomic units). In hydrogen the average energy loss per collision is

$$(\Delta T)_{\text{av}} \simeq T_0/e = 0.37 T_0 \qquad \text{for } A = 1, \text{ hydrogen} \qquad (14\text{-}19)$$

In heavier elements ($A > 2$) the average energy loss is given by the relation

$$\left(\ln \frac{T_0}{T_0 - \Delta T} \right)_{\text{avg}} = 1 + \frac{(A-1)^2}{2A} \ln \frac{A-1}{A+1} \simeq \frac{2}{A + \frac{2}{3}} \qquad (14\text{-}20)$$

For example, the average energy loss per collision is about 4 per cent of the incident neutron energy in Fe and 1 per cent in Pb.

The scattering cross section in hydrogen increases as neutron energy is reduced (see Fig. 14-13). It is smaller than geometric for energies above about 20 Mev and becomes larger than geometric at lower energies. Because of the large fractional energy loss per collision and the increasing cross section at low energies, elastic scattering in hydrogen is of unique significance in neutron attenuation. This process is almost the only one by which neutrons of less than 0.5 Mev energy can be degraded rapidly to very low energies. As a consequence, hydrogenous materials are almost universally used for slowing down neutrons.

At sufficiently high energies, where the associated wavelength of the neutron becomes comparable with the radius of the nucleus, another process called "diffraction scattering" contributes to the elastic scattering. As with optical scattering by an opaque disk, the consequence of this phenomenon is that most of the neutrons are scattered into a forward cone of half-angle $\sim\lambda/R$, where $\lambda = h/2\pi mv$ is the "de Broglie" wavelength of the neutron. This phenomenon affects primarily the angular distribution of recoils in the scattering process.

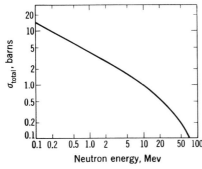

Fig. 14-13. Scattering cross section for low-energy neutrons in hydrogen.[18]

Inelastic Scattering. Inelastic scattering increases the energy loss in heavy materials. Not only is neutron energy reduced by momentum transfer, but a further amount of energy is removed through excitation of the target nuclei. The magnitude of the cross sections in different nuclei depends on neutron energy and on the nuclear excitation levels available. In the common materials used in shields there are very few energy levels below 0.5 Mev, so inelastic scattering is significant only for the more energetic neutrons. In general the excited nucleus gives off its energy in the form of nuclear γ rays. Table 14-7 gives a selected sample of measured inelastic scattering cross sections for a few elements bombarded by monoenergetic neutrons in which the maximum value of the residual neutron energy was also observed.[18] The atomic cross sections indicated by these results are in the range of 0.1 to 3 barns, which add significantly to the elastic cross sections. Figure 14-14 is a more detailed study of the inelastic scattering from Fe as a function of neutron energy, showing a threshold at 0.85 Mev which is associated with the lowest effective energy level and a fluctuating increase in cross section as higher states of excitation become available. A more detailed compilation of

TABLE 14-7
INELASTIC SCATTERING CROSS SECTIONS FOR FAST NEUTRONS[18]
(Selected sample)

Element	Initial neutron energy, Mev	Final neutron energy, Mev	Cross section, barns
Carbon	4.1	3.2	0.08
	14	11	0.52
Oxygen	14	8.8	0.52
Magnesium	2.5	2.5	0.75
Aluminum	4.1	3.2	0.7
	14	~11	1.06
Iron	1.2	0.35	0.6
	4.1	3.2	1.5
	14	~11	1.5
Copper	14	~11	0.4
Cadmium	4.1	3.2	2.1
	14	12	2.2
Lead	2.5	1	0.55
	4.1	3.2	1.9
	14	12	3.3

inelastic scattering cross sections is given in a book by Price, Horton, and Spinney.[18]

A practical consequence of this inelastic scattering phenomenon is that for iron and for several other medium or heavy nuclei the rate of energy loss is increased and neutrons are rapidly reduced to energies of less than

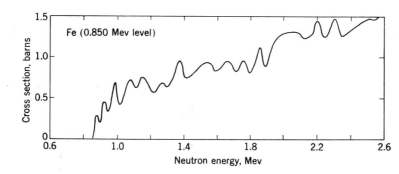

Fig. 14-14. Inelastic scattering cross section in Fe as a function of neutron energy.[18]

1 Mev. Neutrons emerging from such shielding materials have an energy spectrum with a prominent peak in the 0.5- to 1.0-Mev region. A corollary result is that iron is essentially transparent to neutrons of less than 0.85 Mev.

Nuclear Disintegration. Nuclear disintegrations which release charged particles have a smaller but finite cross section for fast neutrons and serve to absorb a small percentage of the fast-neutron flux.   In most elements the (n,p) and (n,α) reactions become energetically possible above a particular threshold energy; the probability increases with energy in excess of this threshold in a manner which is specified by the penetrability function of the charged-particle product in emerging through the coulomb potential barrier. A typical reaction is that for $O^{16}(n,p)N^{16}$, which results in a radioactive product nucleus with a half-life of 7.35 sec, for which the excitation function is illustrated in Fig. 14-15. It has a threshold at 10 Mev, and the cross section reaches its maximum value at 14 Mev. The maximum cross sections of these fast-neutron disintegrations are about 0.1 or 0.2 barn; they are significant over only a limited range in neutron energy, so they are of relatively small importance in shielding applications.

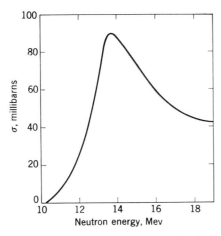

Fig. 14-15. Excitation curve for fast neutrons on oxygen, showing threshold.[18]

Some of the reactions which lead to radioactive products are useful as detectors of fast neutrons, however, where they serve to measure the intensity of neutrons in a characteristic energy band.   Table 14-8 gives a list of the more common reactions used for fast-neutron detection, with the product half-life, threshold energy, and the energy at which the penetrability factor reaches 0.5.

TABLE 14-8
THRESHOLD REACTIONS FOR FAST-NEUTRON DETECTION

Reaction	Half-life	Threshold energy, Mev	Energy for 0.5 penetrability, Mev
$Al^{27}(n,p)Mg^{27}$	10.0 min	1.96	4.5
$Al^{27}(n,\alpha)Na^{24}$	14.9 hr	2.44	9.1
$Si^{28}(n,p)Al^{28}$	2.3 min	2.7	5.4
$P^{31}(n,p)S^{31}$	2.7 hr	0.97	3.8
$P^{31}(n,\alpha)Al^{28}$	2.3 min	0.91	8.3
$S^{32}(n,p)P^{32}$	14.3 min	0.96	5.6
$Fe^{56}(n,p)Mn^{56}$	2.6 hr	3.0	7.6

The $(n,2n)$ reaction becomes energetically possible at neutron energies in excess of the binding energy of the most loosely bound neutron in the target nucleus.   At these high levels of excitation the $(n,2n)$ process competes with other possible modes of decay of the compound nucleus, such as the (n,p) and (n,γ) processes.   The low probability of an inelastic scattering collision's producing such high excitation means that the cross section for the $(n,2n)$ interaction is small, in general not exceeding 0.1 barn.   Frequently the product nucleus is itself radioactive, which provides a simple technique for observation of the reaction.   The threshold energies of fast neutrons required to produce the $(n,2n)$ reactions can be computed from the neutron binding energies.   Table 14-9 lists the neutron binding energies for some of the common elements.

TABLE 14-9
NEUTRON BINDING ENERGIES FOR COMMON ELEMENTS

Isotope	Binding energy, Mev	Isotope	Binding energy, Mev
B^{10}	8.55	Ca^{40}	15.8
B^{11}	11.5	Mn^{55}	10.1
C^{12}	19.0	Fe^{56}	11.15
N^{14}	10.7	Cu^{63}	10.65
O^{16}	15.8	Cu^{65}	9.97
Na^{23}	12.05	Zn^{67}	7.0
Mg^{24}	16.4	Cd^{113}	6.48
Mg^{25}	7.33	Pb^{206}	8.25
Mg^{26}	11.15	Pb^{207}	6.91
Al^{27}	14.0	Pb^{208}	7.38
Si^{28}	16.9	U^{238}	5.88
Si^{29}	8.5		

Removal Cross Sections.   In reactor theory the calculations of fast-neutron attenuation are simplified by utilizing the concept of a macroscopic "removal cross section"[7] which combines the atomic cross section of an interaction, in barns, and the physical properties of the absorbing material.   The removal cross section Σ_r is given by

$$\sum_r = \frac{\text{Avogadro's number} \times \text{density}}{\text{atomic weight}} \times \text{atomic cross section}$$

or

$$\sum_r = \frac{0.602 \times \rho}{A} \times \sigma \text{ (in barns)} \qquad \text{cm}^{-1} \qquad (14\text{-}21)$$

We can use the removal cross section to summarize the properties of the materials used as fast-neutron attenuators.   In comparing the relative cross sections of the different materials in the shields, the quantity Σ_r/ρ can be used; it depends only on atomic nuclear properties and is a smooth function of atomic weight.

The removal cross section gives the total of all processes tending to remove fast neutrons from the stream of neutron flux, for a slab of material embedded in a hydrogenous medium (such as water) which further attenuates and absorbs the reduced-energy neutrons coming from the slab. It is averaged over the spectrum of neutron energies coming from U fission characteristic of reactors. It is of interest to note that the neutrons responsible for the residual intensity after attenuation by large thicknesses of hydrogenous material have cross sections characteristic of monoenergetic neutrons in the 6- to 10-Mev energy range. The numerical values obtained for fission neutrons do not apply to the different energy distributions coming from accelerator targets. Nevertheless, the general trends and the relative magnitudes of absorption coefficients obtained with fission neutrons are of considerable value, because of the scarcity of data from accelerator neutrons.

TABLE 14-10
SLAB REMOVAL CROSS SECTIONS FOR COMMON ELEMENTS[7]

Element	Atomic mass	Removal cross section Σ_r, barns
Hydrogen	1	1.00 ± 0.05
Deuterium	2	0.88 ± 0.10
Lithium	7	1.01 ± 0.04
Beryllium	9	1.07 ± 0.06
Boron	11	0.97 ± 0.10
Carbon	12	0.81 ± 0.05
Oxygen	16	0.99 ± 0.10
Fluorine	19	1.29 ± 0.06
Aluminum	27	1.31 ± 0.05
Chlorine	35	1.2 ± 0.8
Iron	56	1.98 ± 0.08
Nickel	59	1.89 ± 0.10
Copper	64	2.04 ± 0.11
Tungsten	184	2.51 ± 0.55
Lead	207	3.53 ± 0.30
Bismuth	210	3.49 ± 0.35
Uranium	238	3.6 ± 0.4

A listing of slab removal cross sections for some of the common elements for fission neutrons is given in Table 14-10, taken from the study by Goldstein.[7] The results show an essentially smooth variation with atomic weight, with cross sections varying from about 1.0 barn for the lightest elements to 3.5 barns for the heaviest ones.

Slow and Thermal Neutron Interactions

Elastic scattering is almost the only slowing-down process available for neutrons of less than 0.5 Mev energy. The largest cross section is for hydrogen, where it was shown in Fig. 14-13 to rise with decreasing neutron energy, reaching a value of about 20 barns for neutrons of a few kev energy. Other elements also moderate neutron energy by elastic scattering, but in general they require more impacts, a longer time, and a greater density of material. A consequence is that the thickness of shield required to reach thermal equilibrium is shorter in hydrogenous materials than in others.

One special case is the use of graphite as a "thermal column" in reactor shielding, in which the shield thickness to reach thermal equilibrium is large but the absorption of thermal neutrons is a minimum, so the flux of emitted thermal neutrons is greater from a graphite shield than from a hydrogenous shield.

When neutrons have been slowed to a few electron volts energy, another type of inelastic scattering occurs in which energy is transferred to molecular vibrations and so is ultimately evolved as heat. Molecular energy states are mostly of lower energy than 1 ev, and the density of molecular energy levels is greatest at even lower energies. So the interaction cross sections for inelastic scattering involving molecular excitation

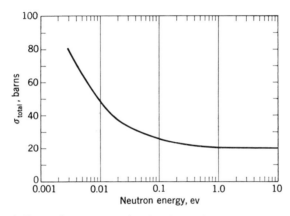

Fig. 14-16. Scattering cross section for thermal neutrons in hydrogen.[18]

rise with decreasing neutron energy for most materials. As an example, the cross section in hydrogen is shown in Fig. 14-16 for energies down to thermal equilibrium at room temperature,[18] which is about $\frac{1}{40}$ ev; the cross section in hydrogen rises to nearly 100 barns for thermal neutrons. These thermal neutrons diffuse within the material and migrate an average distance of several centimeters (depending on the material) before being absorbed.

The most probable absorptive process for thermal neutrons in most materials is the (n,γ) "radiative capture" process, in which the neutron is absorbed in a nucleus with emission of the neutron binding energy in the form of γ radiation. The capture cross section is tremendously large if neutron energy is equal to a resonance level in the nucleus formed. The magnitude of the cross section at other energies depends on how far neutron energy is from a resonance level and on the "width" of the levels.

For neutron energies which are far removed from a resonance, the cross section varies inversely with neutron velocity and is of the magnitude of a few barns for slow or thermal neutrons. At resonance, however, the radiative capture cross section can be 10^3 or 10^4 barns, for low-lying resonance levels.

A reaction of particular interest is the radiative capture in cadmium, due to a resonance level at 0.18 ev, for which the cross section at the peak is 8×10^3 barns. The level width overlaps the thermal Maxwellian distribution, and the cross section is still large ($>1 \times 10^3$ barns) for all energies below 0.3 ev. As a consequence, cadmium absorbs slow and thermal neutrons with great avidity and is commonly used in thin sheets of about 1 mm thickness as a slow-neutron capture shield. The γ rays from neutron capture in Cd are highly penetrating, having a peak emission at 3 Mev with some quantum energies up to 9 Mev. Additional shielding must be provided for these γ rays, if the slow-neutron flux is sufficiently intense.

Another absorptive process for thermal neutrons which is of significance in shielding is the $B^{10}(n,\alpha)Li^7$ reaction, in which the energy released ($Q = 2.8$ Mev) appears as the recoil energies of the product particles. These heavily ionizing charged particles have very short range and are locally absorbed. So boron is used in shielding applications to absorb slow and thermal neutrons without the production of capture γ rays. This is not a resonance-level capture process. The cross section follows the "$1/v$ law," being inversely proportional to neutron velocity. At a velocity of 2200 m/sec, which is the mean velocity of room-temperature thermal neutrons, the cross section for the B^{10} isotope is 4.0×10^3 barns. For the mixture of B^{10} and B^{11} isotopes existing in the natural element the average atomic cross section is 7.6×10^2 barns.

Other thermal-neutron absorbers of high cross section are He^3, Li^6, In, and a few rare earths. None of them are competitive, in a practical way, with Cd and B as thermal-neutron absorbers.

Measurements of Neutron Attenuation in Shields

The neutron intensity from high-yield medium-energy accelerators such as the cyclotron has been shown to require attenuation factors of about 10^{-6} for the fast-neutron component. The neutron energy spectrum is of somewhat higher average energy than for U-fission neutrons, but the general shape of the energy distribution is similar. Attenuation measurements and calculations for reactor neutron shielding give the most complete information. However, the attenuation factors needed for reactors are in the range of 10^{-8} to 10^{-10}, and the program of measurement and analysis had led to complex shielding systems which involve composite layer structures and mixtures of materials. Reactor shields are also designed to be specific for the neutron energy spectrum from fission and to provide a proper balance of attenuation for the neutron and γ-ray components of pile radiation.

In general, simpler and more flexible structural arrangements are desired for accelerator shields, to allow for modifications in research experiments. Considerably less experimental effort has been applied to the study of shielding problems, and only a few basic types of shields have been tested with accelerator neutrons. The materials which have been used are of three general categories: hydrogenous substances, concrete mixtures, and iron plate. In the following pages each of these materials will be discussed and the experimental evidence presented, both from reactor shielding studies and from the more limited observations on accelerator neutrons.

Water. As the need for shielding developed, tanks of water were used for neutron shielding in early cyclotrons, largely because the laboratories had not been designed for more adequate arrangements. Water is very effective in moderating neutron energy and in reducing fast-neutron intensity. However, water has an undesirably low absorption for γ rays, which are emitted from targets and also produced within the water shield by capture of thermal neutrons, so the emergent γ-ray intensity has been excessive in most installations. Except for a few special applications in which B is added in solution, such as for viewing ports in shielding walls, water is no longer used.

Attenuation of the fast neutrons from a U-fission source in water has been measured in the AEC Shielding Facility Laboratory,[23] using the plane-collimated geometry applicable to practical shields. Fast neutrons were detected by observing the recoil protons in a fast-neutron counter. The semilog plot of intensity versus thickness shows an initial build-up which changes into an essentially linear decrease from 20 to 150 cm.[18] This equilibrium absorption coefficient has a value of 0.092/cm or 0.234/in. of water. Calculations from basic attenuation theory suggest that this value is equivalent to that expected for monoenergetic neutrons of about 8 Mev.[7] The total attenuation of 200 cm of water for fast neutrons is about 1×10^{-8}, more than is needed for most accelerator applications.

At still greater thicknesses and larger attenuations, other phenomena enter which further reduce the neutron absorption coefficient; these are associated with the production of photoneutrons within the water shield by the γ rays. This special problem of the production of photoneutrons was discussed in Sec. 14-4 and is analyzed for still higher photon energies in Sec. 14-9.

Gamma-ray attenuation in water cannot be described by a single absorption coefficient. The soft components of the incident γ rays from the fission reaction are absorbed in the initial layers, giving an initial large absorption coefficient. Thermal-neutron production and absorption and the resultant build-up of capture γ rays in the initial layers, combined with the absorption "hardening" of the incident flux, result in an absorption coefficient which decreases steadily with thickness of water. Total attenuation after 200 cm of water is only 7.5×10^{-4}, as compared with 1×10^{-8} for fast neutrons. A thickness of over 300 cm is required to give a γ-ray attenuation factor of 10^{-6}, at which thickness the absorption coefficient is about 0.071/in. of water. This comparison illustrates the basic limitations of a water shield for such mixed radiations.

Bor-paraffin. A somewhat more compact hydrogenous shield is a mixture of paraffin and boron. Paraffin has an even higher hydrogen content than water and so is more effective for fast-neutron attenuation. By the addition of about 2 per cent of boron by weight (usually in the form of borax), the nonradiative capture process in boron absorbs most of the thermal neutrons, so the capture γ-ray intensity can be reduced to an acceptable level. However, the absorption coefficient of the mixture for the incident γ rays is still much too small to provide adequate attenuation for this component. A layer of Pb blocks can be used inside the bor-paraffin shield to absorb such incident γ rays. In a typical application a melted mixture of bor-paraffin is cast into wooden or metal forms which are shaped to fit closely around the accelerator or the experimental apparatus, with an internal layer of Pb blocks. The chief limitation of such a composite shield is leakage of radiation through cracks and unshielded apertures. This technique has been used in a few cases to provide attenuation factors of 10^{-3} to 10^{-4} for fast neutrons.

Concrete. Concrete is the most frequently used of all shielding materials, usually incorporated in the walls and roof of the accelerator housing. Ordinary concrete, of density about 2.35 gm/cm³ or 147 lb/ft³, is by far the cheapest of all shielding materials. It has high water content for slowing down neutrons, about 33 per cent by weight of Si in the sand and gravel, and small amounts of heavier elements such as Fe and Ca which help absorb γ rays.

The attenuation of the fast-neutron component of U-fission neutrons in concrete[18] is illustrated in Fig. 14-17. This curve is based on a few experimental measurements with theoretical calculations to extend the curve to large attenuation factors. The initial absorption coefficient in the first 2 to 3 ft of concrete is about 0.24/in., decreasing to a value of about 0.18/in. for thicknesses in excess of 5 ft. The corresponding values of the 10-folding length, the thickness which reduces intensity to $0.1 I_0$, are 9.7 and 12.8 in. of concrete. Because of the variable coefficient, it is necessary to compute the attenuation separately for each range of shield thickness. For example, a thickness of 3 ft will provide an attenuation factor of about 1.8×10^{-4}; a 6-ft thickness will give about 1.2×10^{-7}.

The U-fission γ-ray attenuation in concrete also has an absorption coefficient which varies with thickness.   The initial linear absorption coefficient is about 0.21/in., decreasing after 5 or 6 ft to a terminal value of 0.16/in.   The terminal value is smaller than for the fast-neutron component, probably because of the production of new γ rays within the

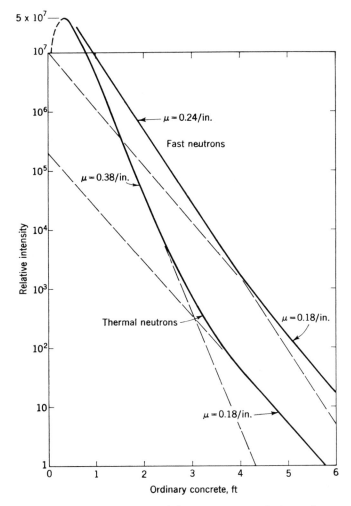

Fig. 14-17. Attenuation in concrete of fast neutrons and thermal neutrons from U fission.[18]

shield in neutron-capture processes.   The initial attenuation coefficient for γ rays is considerably smaller than for fast neutrons.   For example, 3 ft of concrete will provide an attenuation factor for γ rays of only 6.0×10^{-4}, and 6 ft will give 4.0×10^{-6}.   Both of these factors are smaller than the neutron attenuation factors in concrete.

Lower-energy neutrons have a different type of attenuation. Figure 14-17 also shows a curve for the thermal-neutron intensities in a concrete shield, for neutrons coming from a U-fission reactor.[18]   These thermal-neutron intensities were observed through the radioactivities induced in foil samples inserted in the shield. The initial build-up in intensity is greater than 50 per cent and occurs in the first 2 to 3 in. of concrete. This is followed by an initial attenuation with an absorption coefficient of about 0.38/in., changing steadily with increasing thickness to a value of about 0.18/in. after 5 ft of concrete.   This final value is essentially the same as for the fast-neutron component and can be considered to be the terminal coefficient for an equilibrium mixture of fast and slow neutrons. At even greater thicknesses, which apply for higher-energy accelerators, the production of photoneutrons by the γ rays reduces the observed slow-neutron attenuation rate still further; this will be discussed in a following section.

The steep build-up of thermal-neutron intensity just inside the surface of the shield and the rapid attenuation of the thermal-neutron component mean that the ratio of thermal to fast neutrons is a function of the thickness of the shield; it is a maximum at the peak of the thermal-neutron intensity curve.   For relatively thick shields, in which the intensity of the fast-neutron component has been reduced below the tolerance level, the surviving intensity of thermal neutrons is always well below tolerance.   A general conclusion is that the fast neutrons are the dominant radiation and that shields should be designed for fast-neutron attenuation.

Accelerator neutrons have been used for attenuation measurements in only a few laboratories.   Gugelot and White[22] studied the neutron and γ-ray attenuation in different concrete mixtures, using the radiations from the $Be^9(p,n)B^9$ reaction with 16-Mev protons from the Princeton cyclotron.   They measured thermal and resonance slow neutrons through the activities induced in Ag foil detectors, but did not observe fast-neutron intensity directly.   Furthermore, their measurements extended to only 15 in. of concrete, which is insufficient to observe the terminal values of absorption coefficients for large attenuations.   The results showed the usual build-up of thermal-neutron intensity in the initial layers and an approximately linear attenuation after 20 cm with a half-value thickness of 10.7 cm for the thermal neutrons in normal concrete, equivalent to a linear absorption coefficient of 0.065/cm or 0.17/in. of concrete.   This value is somewhat smaller at these thicknesses than that observed with fission neutrons and may be associated with the higher average energy of the neutron spectrum from this reaction.   The comparative neutron spectra were illustrated in Fig. 14-12.

The major effort in the study by Gugelot and White was in comparative measurements of the neutron and γ-ray attenuations in several types of loaded concrete, involving substitution for the sand and gravel in the ordinary concrete mixture of magnetite, limonite, scrap iron, and a composite of limonite and iron. A selected sample of their results is given in Table 14-11. The most effective mixture for neutrons and γ rays was shown to be concrete with 26.3 per cent limonite by weight, 59.4 per cent iron punchings, 4.7 per cent water, and 9.6 per cent cement; the mixture had a density of 4.41 gm/cm³. The half-value thickness for thermal neutrons in this material was 5.4 cm, giving an absorption coefficient of 0.326/in. The coefficient for γ rays in this mixture was found to be 0.22/in., averaged over an attenuation factor range of 10^{-6}.

TABLE 14-11

NEUTRON AND γ-RAY ATTENUATION IN CONCRETE MIXTURES[22]

Absorber	Density, gm/cm³	Neutron half-intensity thickness, cm	γ-ray half-intensity thickness, cm (at 20 cm)
H₂O	1.00	5.4	14.8
Concrete	2.35	10.7	13.3
Concrete + magnetite	3.78	8.5	9.0
Concrete + limonite	2.63	4.8	9.0
Concrete + limonite + iron	4.41	5.4	7.9

It is noteworthy that although the best neutron absorption (smallest half-intensity thickness) was observed with limonite concrete of density 2.63, which has the highest concentration of water, the strongest γ-ray attenuation came from the denser concrete including a large amount of scrap iron. We also note that in all cases the half-intensity thickness for γ rays exceeds that for neutrons.

Delano and Goodman[24] used neutrons from the MIT cyclotron coming from the $Be^9(d,n)B^{10}$ reaction with 15-Mev deuterons. The neutron spectrum was not measured, but is believed to have a somewhat lower average neutron energy than that used by Gugelot and White, from comparison of the results. Fast-neutron detectors were employed, by observing the induced radioactivities in samples of Al and Fe foil interspersed in the shield, as well as thermal- and resonance-neutron detectors. The fast-neutron-induced activities were the 10-min period from $Al^{27}(n,p)Mg^{27}$, the 14.9-hr period from $Al^{27}(n,\alpha)Na^{24}$, and the 2.6-hr period from $Fe^{56}(n,p)Mn^{56}$. These reactions are among those listed in Table 14-8, where they are shown to have thresholds at 1.96, 2.44, and 3.0 Mev, respectively; the energies calculated for 0.5 penetrability of the potential barriers are 4.5, 9.1, and 7.6 Mev. Despite this apparent difference in energy sensitivity, the three fast-neutron detectors showed similar attenuation curves, with an attenuation factor of 8.3/ft of concrete, equivalent to a linear absorption coefficient of 0.177/in. of concrete.

This value is essentially the same as that for the fast-neutron component of fission neutrons for equivalent concrete thicknesses.

Delano and Goodman also measured the attenuation for thermal neutrons to be a factor of 10/ft, which means an absorption coefficient of 0.19/in. of concrete. This can be compared with the Gugelot and White result of 0.17/in. and the terminal absorption coefficient for fission neutrons of 0.18/in. The attenuation of γ rays in concrete was also measured, giving 0.15/in. over the linear portion of the absorption curve, to be compared with 0.16/in. obtained for the fission γ rays.

Although the evidence is incomplete, it seems probable from the experimental studies that cyclotron neutrons are somewhat more penetrating in concrete than fission neutrons. This result must be associated with the higher energies of cyclotron neutrons. Since it can be expected that neutron energy spectra from accelerators in the several energy ranges will differ significantly, it follows that no single attenuation plot will be valid for all applications. Rather, each problem requires individual analysis to determine the specific shielding requirements. The absorption coefficients and attenuation factors described for fission and cyclotron neutrons are useful primarily in determining the order of magnitude of the shielding needed.

Another conclusion is that γ-ray attenuation is small relative to neutron attenuation in ordinary concrete. This imbalance is important in reactor shielding applications, where large attenuation factors are required. Ordinary concrete is seldom used in reactor shielding, where it is important to have similar attenuation factors for neutrons and γ rays. Accelerators require smaller attenuation factors, and space is usually not so critical, so an excessive thickness of ordinary concrete can be used to provide the necessary γ-ray attenuation.

Loading of concrete with iron ore or iron scrap increases the γ-ray attenuation and decreases the total thickness of shielding required for neutrons. Cost is materially increased, and the practical compromise is based on economic factors. Limonite or ilmenite ores can be substituted for the sand and gravel in concrete to obtain densities up to 250 lb/ft^3, and with a cost increase by about a factor of 4. These ores make strong concrete aggregates and are nonmagnetic. Magnetite has the disadvantage that the ore is magnetic and that dust from erosion of shielding blocks becomes a hazard to the magnets used in accelerator laboratories. The further addition of scrap iron (rivet punchings are common) can increase density to a maximum of about 450 lb/ft^3, but cost increases sharply. Engineering estimates[18] suggest that doubling the density by adding iron increases the cost by about ten times. For accelerator applications a shield of ordinary concrete of sufficient thickness to attenuate the γ-ray component is considerably cheaper than a thinner shield of loaded concrete which would provide a better balance of absorption coefficients.

Iron.   Iron plate or forgings have been used in a few high-energy accelerators to provide a compact and dense shield when large attenuation factors are required and space limitations exist.   At the University of Chicago synchrocyclotron laboratory concrete is used for most of the wall and overhead shielding, but iron is employed to form the channels for emergent beams in the wall facing the research laboratory.

As a neutron shielding material, iron has a fundamental limitation due to its small elastic cross section and the absence of energy levels for inelastic scattering at energies below 0.85 Mev, as discussed in the previous section.   Compared with hydrogenous materials iron is very inefficient in slowing down neutrons, and the rate of build-up of thermal neutrons is slow.   This is illustrated by the observation that the peak of thermal-neutron intensity in an iron shield is 40 cm behind the face of the shield,[6] while the peak is at about 5 cm from the face for a water shield and 10 cm for an ordinary concrete shield.   However, from this point on, the fast-neutron attenuation in iron is reasonably high, having a linear absorption coefficient of 0.6/in. at 20 in., which decreases to 0.3/in. at 60 in.   A 60-in. iron shield will provide a total neutron attenuation of about 10^{-8}.

Gamma rays are attenuated quite effectively in iron.   The initial attenuation rate following the usual wide-beam-geometry build-up in intensity is nearly 1.0/in., and the terminal mass absorption coefficient after 3 to 4 ft is 0.030 cm^2/gm or a linear coefficient of 0.24/in. of iron. A 60-in. iron shield will provide a γ-ray attenuation factor of over 10^{-8}.

Effect of Channels and Ducts through Shields

For most accelerators there is a need to bring emergent beams of particles or radiation through a shielding wall, in order to perform experiments under low-background-intensity conditions beyond the wall.   A typical problem is that of bringing a beam of charged particles through the shielding wall within an evacuated pipe.   The limitation on the use of such beam channels is the current of neutrons or γ radiation which they also transmit, which increases the background intensity beyond the wall.

The transmission of a straight cylindrical duct of radius r and length z (shielding-wall thickness) can be computed under simplifying assumptions.   If the source intensity of fast neutrons or γ rays, I_0, inside the shield is isotropic and these particles are assumed to suffer no reflections from the inner wall of the duct, the emergent intensity is given by the geometric limitations to be

$$I = I_0 \left\{ 1 - \left[1 + \left(\frac{r}{z} \right)^2 \right]^{-\frac{1}{2}} \right\} \qquad (14\text{-}22)$$

This curve is plotted in Fig. 14-18 for a range of z/r from 2 to 100.

Slow or thermal neutrons have a somewhat modified penetration through channels.   Reflection by scattering from the interior wall of the duct plus leakage into the duct from the initial portions of the shielding wall increases the transmission above the geometric value for small duct ratios (up to $z/r = 20$), while it is smaller for greater lengths.   Experimental measurements using fission neutrons from a reactor give the transmission curve for thermal neutrons in a cylindrical duct (see Fig. 14-18).

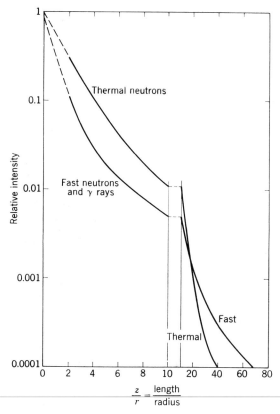

Fig. 14-18. Transmission of fast and thermal neutrons in straight cylindrical ducts of radius r and length z.

If it is possible to use an offset or bent duct, the transmission of fast neutrons and γ rays can be reduced to much smaller values.   Because of internal reflection, offsets or bends are not so effective for thermal neutrons.

The intensities transmitted through channels or ducts may nullify the large attenuation factors for which a shield has been designed.   For example, a 6-in.-diam channel through a 60-in. wall ($z/r = 20$) will transmit about 1×10^{-3} of the incident neutron flux over the area of the channel.   If several such channels are used, the flux emerging from the channels may exceed that transmitted through the body of the shield. In other words, if large channels must be used, large attenuation factors may be superfluous. In most situations, however, the limitation is on the size and number of channels which can be used with safety.

In several accelerator laboratories in which channels through the primary shields are used to bring out emergent beams, the intensity of radiation in the experimental area outside the shield has been excessive because of the total of the radiation leaking through channels or cracks in the shield plus the radiation produced by the emergent beam. In these cases the experimental area has also been provided with shielding, and the experiments have been operated by remote control.

14-7. INDUCED RADIOACTIVITY

One of the major hazards in accelerator operations is radiation exposure of personnel to induced radioactivity, both in the handling of targets and in repair operations on the machine. Remote-handling techniques and fast-acting systems are required for target changing, chemical processing of targets, and other routine operations. The intensities are in general smaller than those from reactor operations, but otherwise the problems are similar. The range of energies in the composite γ-ray and β-ray spectra from accelerators is similar to the fission-product spectrum, including in fact many of the same isotopes. Absorption coefficients in Pb and other shields are essentially the same as those for fission-product activities. Recommendations for handling techniques and shielding requirements can be taken directly from the experience and specifications available in the many studies and reports coming from reactor technology and radio chemistry. Useful summaries of the best practices are given in the "Handbook on Radiation Hygiene" edited by Blatz,[25] "Nuclear Engineering Handbook" edited by Etherington,[26] and other reference works.

The activities produced in accelerators cover a wide range in intensity and in half-life, coming from many radioactive isotopes. The many different materials used in and around an accelerator which can be bombarded by the positive ions, neutrons, and γ rays lead to a spread in half-lives nearly as great as in the fission-product spectrum from a nuclear reactor, and the composite decay curve is similar. A general observation on this composite decay is that the rate of decay measured at a time t after the machine is turned off shows a half-life of approximately t. The same is true for fission products where the apparent half-life is about $1.2t$.

The intensity of radioactivity within the shielding enclosure of an accelerator is closely proportional to the neutron intensity, which is an equilibrium mixture of fast, slow, and thermal neutrons. Most of the activities are products of the (n,γ) or neutron-capture reaction, which is most probable for thermal neutrons, with smaller intensities coming from the (n,p), (n,α), and $(n,2n)$ fast-neutron disintegrations and a few high-energy γ-ray reactions.

Highest intensities come from accelerators such as the standard cyclotrons which have high neutron yields. At the MIT cyclotron the intensity following shutdown under normal operating conditions is sufficient to give one daily permissible dose in about 10 min, which is barely sufficient for target-handling or tune-up adjustments. Repairs and other maintenance tasks are postponed whenever possible until after an overnight or weekend shutdown, when the safe time for a daily dose is extended to several hours. Individual personnel exposure is monitored, and the working time within the enclosure is limited to prevent overexposure. Fast-acting mechanical systems are necessary for opening ports and changing targets. Long-handled tongs are used for removing the active target rapidly to a Pb-shielded carrying case. In a few laboratories remote-handling facilities have been developed for target changing or other routine operations. Nevertheless, in most well-shielded accelerator laboratories personnel exposure to radioactive γ rays and β rays is the dominant radiation dosage.

Something can be done in design to minimize the intensity of the induced activities, by careful choice of the materials used for chambers, ports, and probes. For example, the half-life of the activity induced in carbon by proton, deuteron, or neutron bombardment is short relative to that in copper. The D's of a cyclotron which are subject to bombardment by off-focus ions can be provided with graphite edges and linings; the intensity decays rapidly following shutdown, so radiation exposure during repairs can be minimized. Materials used for target holders, beam channels, and other parts subject to beam bombardment can also be chosen to reduce the activity level.

When a target is being bombarded for the purpose of producing specific radioactivities in the target, the bombardment can be usefully continued for a period of two or three half-lives; beyond this the increased yield is small. For short-lived activities the bombardment is short, and for longer-lived isotopes it can be maintained for much longer times. The highest intensity produced in a single cyclotron target, to the knowledge of the authors, is about 7 curies of Na^{24} ($T = 14.9$ hr) from a sodium target bombarded for 24 hr by deuterons in the MIT cyclotron. This occurred in about 1945, before even greater intensities of induced radioactivities could be obtained from nuclear reactors, which have now taken over the production of such high-intensity samples. For most research experiments the intensity produced in a sample seldom exceeds 100 millicuries and is more frequently in the range of a fraction of a millicurie.

Many induced activities cannot be produced by the neutrons in a reactor, but can be formed only with charged-particle beams.   This is true of essentially all positron emitters.   So this large area of research is still reserved for accelerators.

Radiochemical processing of activities in targets is usually performed within shielded chemical hoods or "caves," with remote-handling facilities such as long-handled tongs or elementary master-slave manipulators, observed through thick windows in the shield or by mirrors.   Most accelerator laboratories which produce activities in significant intensity have been equipped with such elementary "hot labs."   Other technical devices may be useful, such as "ball-and-socket" tong manipulators, "glove boxes" for manual handling of β-active materials with thick gloves, and viewing periscopes.   These devices have been developed to

TABLE 14-12

Pb Shield Thicknesses for Co^{60} and Cs^{137} Sources of
Induced Radioactivity to Give Tolerance Dose,
at Surface of 7.5 mrem/hr
(Spherical shields)

Pb thickness, in.	Activity, curies	
	Co^{60}	Cs^{137}
1	1.4×10^{-5}	1.3×10^{-4}
2	1.9×10^{-4}	7.5×10^{-3}
3	1.7×10^{-3}	2.5×10^{-1}
4	1.3×10^{-2}	6.4
5	9.0×10^{-2}	1.6×10^2
6	6.0×10^{-1}	3.7×10^3
8	2.3×10^1	
10	8.0×10^2	

an advanced state in the field of nuclear chemistry, and accelerator operators would do well to adapt this experience to their needs.

The basic shielding material for γ rays is lead, in the form of bricks, sheets, or carrying cases.   Table 14-12 lists the source strengths of two common radioactive isotopes, Co^{60} and Cs^{137}, which can be shielded by given thicknesses of Pb to reduce the emergent intensity to the tolerance dose of 7.5 mrem/hr at the surface of the shield.[26]   Note that about 3 in. of Pb is required to shield 1 millicurie of Co^{60}.   Accelerator operators should be aware of the basic shielding requirements in the handling of targets and should monitor all such operations with suitable instruments.

In the energy range of cyclotrons and other low-energy or medium-energy accelerators used for production of radioactivity, an estimate of expected intensity can be obtained from the beam power, or the product of beam energy and time-average beam current.   As a rough rule of thumb, the slow-neutron intensity and so the level of induced radio-activity are proportional to beam power. In a standard cyclotron operating at 15 Mev and $\frac{1}{3}$ ma of deuterons, the beam power is 5 kw; intensities from operation at this range of beam power are potentially dangerous and require careful monitoring.

Induced radioactivity is a much smaller problem for the high-energy synchronous accelerators, because of the pulsed character of the beams and the low time-average beam current. The beam power from the Brookhaven 3-Bev cosmotron is about 10 watts, so the intensities of induced activities are proportionately lower. Furthermore, the more penetrating character of both the primary and secondary radiations from such high-energy machines means that much of the neutron attenuation occurs deep in the shields, so only a small fraction is available to produce radioactivity in the surface layers.

14-8. ELECTRONIC SHOWERS

High-energy electrons lose most of their energy in producing a cascade shower of X rays, secondary electrons, and positrons. This "soft shower," as it is called in cosmic-ray terminology, starts with a high-energy electron which loses energy by radiation. The X rays have a continuous energy distribution (see Sec. 14-4) with the maximum energy given by the energy of the incident electron, but with most of the intensity in lower-energy quanta. X rays are absorbed primarily through electromagnetic interactions which produce secondary electrons, lower-energy photons, and electron-positron pairs. This second generation of charged particles again loses energy primarily by radiation, with ionization loss becoming more important as energy decreases. The cascade process continues, with an increasing number of photons and charged particles, until the secondaries are sufficiently reduced in energy to be absorbed through ionization. The shower also grows in transverse width because of the predominantly transverse directions of the Compton secondary electrons, until the decreasing energy of the secondaries limits further transverse growth. For very-high-energy incident electrons (> 1 Bev) the shower develops a columnar shape, with a central core of the higher-energy radiations and a surrounding sheath of lower-energy secondaries.

High-energy X rays also produce photoneutrons through photodisintegration processes. Although the neutrons carry only a small fraction of the total energy of the shower, they prove to be the dominant component after large attenuation through thick absorbers, because of their considerably greater penetration. The attenuation of the neutron component of such a shower will be described in more detail in Sec. 14-9. In this section we discuss separately the properties of the soft electronic shower components.

The basic properties of the cascade shower are well described by cosmic-ray shower theory.[14,20]   The cross sections and angular distributions of the several electromagnetic interactions are known, including the variations with energy.   Statistical calculations predict the growth and spread of secondaries and the attenuation resulting from absorptive processes.   From such studies have come predictions of the number of secondaries in the shower, per incident electron, at different incident energies and as a function of absorber material and thickness.   From the resulting transverse distributions the total ionizing intensity can be computed as a function of depth in the absorber.   The validity of the results has been confirmed by experimental cosmic-ray observations.

Theory predicts an exponential build-up of ionizing radiations in the initial layers of absorber.   The magnitude of this build-up depends on the incident energy in the shower.   The energy of secondaries in low-energy showers rapidly falls below the energy at which radiation is the dominant process, and these secondaries are absorbed through ionization.   For much higher incident energies the radiation-electron cascade continues for many more generations, and the exponential build-up continues to greater thicknesses.   Eventually the mixture of radiations reaches an energy distribution in which the most penetrating component is the X rays of minimum absorption coefficient.   This results in a terminal absorption coefficient of the shower having this minimum X-ray absorption coefficient.   The "transition" curve of intensity versus absorber thickness shows an initial exponential build-up and a terminal exponential decay, with the magnitude and location of the peak-intensity point varying with incident energy and with absorber material.

As an aid to simplifying and correlating the results of calculations or measurements, absorber thickness is usually specified in units of radiation length x_0 (see Sec. 14-3).   As used in shower theory, it is essentially the mean thickness, in gm/cm^2, in which one generation of the cascade process occurs, i.e., an electron radiates a photon and the photon is absorbed, giving another electron (or pair).   Energies are also usually stated in units of the critical energy W_c at which radiation loss and ionization loss are equal and which has different values in the different materials.   Values of x_0 and W_c for the common elements were listed in Table 14-4 and plotted in Fig. 14-4.

The results of cosmic-ray calculations and measurements are not directly applicable to accelerator shielding problems, since cosmic-ray data involve a spread in energy.   Although it is possible to calculate attenuation curves for monoenergetic electrons from shower theory, it is more useful to observe the effects of accelerator electrons directly.

The best experimental evidence on the attenuation of an electronic shower comes from the Stanford linear accelerator.[27]   Kantz and Hofstadter[28] studied the attenuation of the electronic shower component from incident 185-Mev electrons, in the process of determining efficiencies and dimensions for scintillation and Cerenkov counters to be used for high-energy particles. They observed the ionization intensity with a small scintillation counter placed at various depths and transverse locations in a stack of slabs of absorber which was aligned in the direction of the electron beam. Absorbers of carbon (graphite), aluminum, copper, tin, and lead were used. These authors show that the output of the

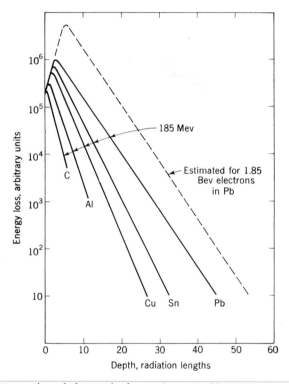

Fig. 14-19. Attenuation of electronic shower from 185-Mev electrons[28] and estimated attenuation of 1.85-Bev shower in Pb.

scintillation counter is proportional to the energy loss in this element of the stack. Intensities were observed over a wide transverse spread at each depth and summed graphically to obtain the total energy loss at this depth. Similar measurements were made over a series of depths in the absorber. Their results are shown in the semilog plot of Fig. 14-19 as the solid curves labeled with symbols for the absorbing materials.

The area under each curve (Fig. 14-19) is proportional to the total energy of the shower and so to the incident electron energy. Different fractions of the incident energy are transformed into the ionizing radiations which actuate the scintillation counter in the different materials. In each curve the initial build-up shows an approximately linear increase on the semilog plot, in agreement with the predictions of shower theory. The magnitude of the build-up and the absorber thickness for peak intensity increase with atomic number of the absorber, again in agreement with theory. Beyond the peak intensity point each curve quickly reaches an essentially linear decrease, with a slope indicating the terminal absorption coefficient for each material. These terminal coefficients are in each case very close to the values of the minimum X-ray coefficients in the several materials, which were presented in Fig. 14-10 in the earlier section on X-ray absorption.

The close agreement of the experimental observations (Fig. 14-19) with shower theory makes it possible to predict the shape of similar energy-loss curves for higher incident electron energies. In any given material a higher-energy electron would have a transition curve with the same slope in the build-up portion and the same terminal absorption coefficient. The build-up would be extended to higher intensity and greater absorber thickness, but the slopes of both portions of the curve would be identical with those for 185 Mev. For example, an incident electron of 10-times-higher energy (1.85 Bev) would have an energy loss curve shifted vertically by a factor of 10, or one decade on the semilog plot. In illustration, a dashed curve is shown in Fig. 14-19 for 1.85-Bev electrons in a Pb absorber. The same incident intensity of 1.85-Bev electrons would require additional absorber to give an attenuation factor of 10^{-1}, in order to have the same emergent intensity. If the Pb absorber required for 185-Mev electrons were 45 radiation lengths thick (26.6 cm), the 1.85-Bev electrons would require 53 radiation lengths, an increase of 18 per cent in Pb thickness for 10-times-higher energy.

The above analysis and conclusion have oversimplified the problem considerably. A more complete study would require detailed analysis of the several competing electromagnetic interactions, including the angular distributions, and the simple results above would be slightly modified. However, it does present a reasonable approximation to the attenuation of the electronic components of the electronic shower. As stated earlier, the photoneutrons produced in the shower can become dominant components for large attenuations and must be considered for a more complete understanding of the shielding requirements.

The transverse spread of the electronic shower was also studied by Kantz and Hofstadter. They plot isoenergetic profiles as a function of depth and transverse spread within the absorbers, from which it is possible to determine the dimensions of a cylindrical volume within which any chosen percentage of the total shower energy would be contained. Their results show that a cylindrical volume with a diameter of about one-fourth the length would contain the shower in light-density material such as C or Al, while a cylinder with a diameter of about one-half the length is needed in denser materials such as Cu or Pb.

The columnar shape of the electronic shower means that it can be absorbed locally in dense shields placed in the direction of the primary beam. Shielding requirements in transverse directions (for example, roof shielding) are small in comparison with those in the forward direction, as far as the electronic shower is concerned. However, it should be noted that the photoneutrons produced in the shower can have a much wider angular spread and will be the dominant components in determining the transverse shielding requirements.

14-9. PHOTONEUTRONS

The high-energy X-ray component of the electronic shower produces neutrons through the photonuclear disintegration reaction (γ, n) in essentially all elements. This process (see Sec. 14-4) was shown to have a characteristic threshold energy for each element (see Table 14-6). The cross section rises with increasing energy above threshold to a broad maximum known as the "giant resonance," at an energy of 15 to 20 Mev in most elements. This resonance represents a region of unusually high density of excitation states in the target nucleus. In the photodisintegration process the neutrons are emitted with energies in the range of 8 to 12 Mev, leaving the product nucleus in its ground state or a low-energy excited state.

X rays with energies above the giant resonance also release neutrons through the photodisintegration reaction, but with smaller cross sections; however, the neutrons emitted have proportionately higher energies and are more penetrating. In the discussion of high-energy neutron attenuation in the section to follow we shall show that the penetration of neutrons increases sharply in the 100- to 300-Mev energy range. Consequently, these high-energy neutrons become the dominant component for high-energy electron accelerators, despite the fact that photodisintegration cross sections are two orders of magnitude smaller than the electromagnetic interactions which lead to the electronic shower described in the preceding section.

We distinguish between two classes of photoneutrons in this analysis, of different energy ranges: (1) neutrons of less than 60 to 80 Mev energy which are produced at or near the giant resonance, and for which the attenuation in absorbers does not differ significantly from cyclotron or fission neutrons; (2) neutrons of more than 80 Mev energy produced by the direct photoeffect in essentially all nuclei at high energies, and for which the attenuation is much smaller than for the giant-resonance neutrons.

Giant-resonance Neutrons

The phenomenon of resonance in a nuclear interaction means that the production cross section is peaked at a particular value of photon energy k_0. Let $\sigma_r(k)$ be the atomic cross section for producing a photoneutron by a single photon of energy k in the region of resonance. The total atomic cross section, integrated over energy from threshold to well above the resonance, is determined only by the gross atomic properties of the target or absorber, such as atomic weight A, atomic number Z, and neutron number N. The magnitude of this integrated cross section has been shown[29,30] to be

$$\sigma_r(k)\,dk = 0.08\,\frac{NZ}{A} \qquad \text{Mev-barns} \qquad (14\text{-}23)$$

The constant 0.08 applies for medium or heavy elements; a smaller constant of about 0.02 holds for light elements such as carbon. The yield of photoneutrons per incident photon is given by the product of atomic cross section and the number of atoms per square centimeter in the absorber along the track of the photon, which represents a mean free path for this interaction. This distance is given by the "track-length integral."

In cosmic-ray-shower theory the track length is essentially the thickness of absorber in which one generation of the electronic cascade occurs, i.e., in which a photon produces a secondary electron (or pair) and the electron generates another photon. In photoneutron production the track length is the average distance between neutron production interactions along the path of the photon. The integrated track length, integrated over the energy distribution of the photons radiated from an incident electron of energy W_0, and for a photon energy k, has been shown[20] to be given by

$$\pi(W_0,k) = 0.6\,\frac{W_0}{k^2} \qquad (14\text{-}24)$$

Note that the integrated track length has units of (energy)$^{-1}$; the constant applies when W_0 and k are expressed in Mev. In photoneutron production the photon energy k can be taken as the value k_0 at the peak of the giant resonance.

The yield of photoneutrons per incident electron of energy W_0 can now be evaluated[20] from

$$Y(n)_r = \frac{N_0 x_0}{A} \times 10^{-24} \int \sigma_r(k)\pi(W_0,k)\,dk \qquad \text{neutrons/electron} \qquad (14\text{-}25)$$

where N_0 is Avogadro's number and x_0 is radiation length in gm/cm^2.

In illustration we evaluate for an incident electron energy W_0 of 1 Bev. The yield will be directly proportional to electron energy. Table 14-13 lists values for A, Z, N, x_0, and k_0, for three typical absorbers: concrete, iron, and lead. Estimated values of the atomic constants are used for concrete. The radiation-length values come from Table 14-4. The resonance energy k_0 for the giant resonances decreases somewhat with increasing atomic number, and the values used are averages of the appropriate ranges of atomic number.

TABLE 14-13

PHOTONEUTRON YIELDS FROM 1-BEV ELECTRONS

	Concrete	Iron	Lead
A, atomic weight	(27)	56	207
Z, atomic number	(13.2)	26	82
N, neutron number	(14)	30	125
x_0, radiation length	24	14.1	6.5 gm/cm^2
k_0, resonance energy	22	18	14 Mev
Giant-resonance neutrons ($W_0 = 1.0$ Bev):			
$\dfrac{N_0 x_0}{A} \times 10^{-24}$	0.54	0.15	0.02
$\int \sigma_r(k)\,dk$, resonance cross section	0.27	1.0	4.0 Mev-barns
$\pi(W_0, k_0)$, track length	1.2	1.9	3.1 Mev^{-1}
$Y(n)_r$, yield at 1.0 Bev	0.18	0.27	0.23 neutron/electron
Photodisintegration neutrons ($W_0 = 1.0$ Bev):			
N_D, deuteron number	6	11	25
$\int \sigma_p(k)\,dk$, cross section	0.12	0.22	0.50 Mev-barn
$\pi(W_0, k)$, track length	9.0	9.0	9.0 Mev^{-1}
$Y(n)_p$, yield at 1.0 Bev	0.58	0.30	0.09 neutron/electron

Under the heading "Giant-resonance Neutrons" in Table 14-13, the yields are computed for the three absorbers. The yields are surprisingly similar for the different materials. Within the limits of precision applicable to these calculations, and to shielding problems in general, a single value can be used for all materials:

$$Y(n)_r = 0.25 W_0 \quad \text{neutrons/electron } (W_0 \text{ in 1-Bev units}) \quad (14\text{-}26)$$

The only significant error will be an overestimate of the yield at low energies and in light elements.

The angular distribution of these relatively low-energy photoneutrons is essentially isotropic. They spread in all directions from a line source along the core of the columnar photon-electron shower within the absorber. Other components, such as the high-energy photodisintegration neutrons, are more penetrating and determine the shielding requirements in the forward direction. The resonance photoneutrons are significant mostly in determining the transverse shielding requirements. For this purpose the attenuation coefficients for cyclotron neutrons can be used without serious error (see Sec. 14-6).

Photoneutrons of More than 80 Mev

The high-energy neutrons arise from the direct photoeffect. The most successful theory is that of the "effective deuteron" model, first developed by Levinger.[31] In this model, the photon is absorbed by proton-neutron pairs within the nucleus, for which the cross section is taken to be that for the photodisintegration of the deuteron, $\sigma_p(D)$. The cross section for any element is determined by the effective number of proton-neutron pairs in the nucleus, called the deuteron number N_D. In light elements the observed cross sections lead to a value of N_D close to the theoretical value, of about $1.5NZ/A$. In heavy elements the observed cross sections are smaller than the theoretical value, because of nuclear absorption of the outgoing neutrons (and protons) and the subsequent emission of lower-energy neutrons. Since these lower-energy neutrons have smaller mean free paths and are more readily absorbed, they do not contribute so effectively to the total photoneutron flux. Measured values by Odian[32] of the cross sections in lithium and oxygen lead to deuteron numbers

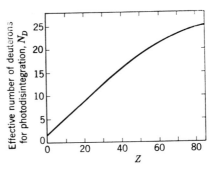

Fig. 14-20. Effective deuteron number photoneutron production as a function of Z.

$N_D(\text{Li}) = 3.0$ and $N_D(\text{O}) = 4.5$. Estimates have been made by Wilson[30] of the effective number of deuterons in iron and lead: $N_D(\text{Fe}) = 11$, and $N_D(\text{Pb}) = 25$. These values have been used to sketch the curve of N_D versus Z shown in Fig. 14-20, and appropriate values are also included in Table 14-13.

At high energies the dominant contribution to the cross section is through the emission and subsequent absorption of mesons. Those mesons which are not internally absorbed will produce nuclear reactions in other nuclei with the release of other neutrons. So the total cross section for neutron production includes the alternate production of mesons. We shall calculate the intensity of emitted mesons in Sec. 14-11. It will be shown that their intensities are in general small and that they are not significant in shielding calculations relative to the fast neutrons discussed here.

The cross section for photodisintegration of the deuteron has been measured up to 900 Mev energy at the California Institute of Technology.[33]   It is found to be essentially constant up to about 300 Mev, with a value of $\sigma_p(D) = 7 \times 10^{-5}$ barn, and to fall off with increasing energy to a value which is negligible for shielding calculations above 1 Bev.   At 900 Mev it is decreasing at a rate faster than with $1/k^2$.   Wilson[30] has shown that for the energy range between 300 Mev and 1 Bev the cross section can be approximated by

$$\sigma_p(D) = \frac{6}{k^2} \quad \text{barns} \tag{14-27}$$

where k is in Mev units.   The total cross section when integrated over the energy range from above the resonance (taken as 80 Mev) to the upper limit of electron energy W_0 is

$$\int \sigma_p(D) \, dk = 7 \times 10^{-5} \int_{80}^{300} dk + 6 \int_{300}^{W_0} \frac{dk}{k^2} \quad \text{Mev-barns} \tag{14-28}$$

This results in a value of 0.02 Mev-barn at 1 Bev, and fits the Cal Tech data up to 900 Mev.

For other elements the cross section is given by the product of deuteron number and the deuteron cross section; values for the several materials are listed in Table 14-13.   To determine the yield in neutrons per electron for thick absorbers, we again apply the principles of shower theory, using Eq. (14-25).   The track-length integral is dominated by the value at the low-energy limit, taken rather arbitrarily as 80 Mev.   For 1-Bev incident electrons the integrated track length has the value of 9.0 Mev^{-1}, and it varies directly with electron energy.   Yields in the several materials are listed in Table 14-13 under the heading "Photodisintegration Neutrons."   With these assumptions, the yield is found to decrease with increasing atomic number, having a value for medium-weight elements which is roughly equal in magnitude to the yield of low-energy resonance neutrons.

These high-energy neutrons are more penetrating than the resonance neutrons, as will be described in a following section.   They become the dominant component for shielding calculations involving large attenuations in thick absorbers.   The angular distribution is peaked in the forward direction, although not so sharply as the photon-electron shower. The high-energy neutrons which are the most penetrating are contained within a forward cone having a half-angle of about 30°.   This requires the thickest and densest shielding in the forward quadrant.

In illustration, consider the neutron intensity which can be anticipated from a 1-Bev electron accelerator with a time-average beam intensity of 0.1 μa, or 6.25×10^{11} electrons/sec.   This is characteristic of the intensities from electron linear accelerators or from high-repetition-rate electron synchrotrons. Assume that the electron beam strikes a thick shield of ordinary concrete, at a distance from the accelerator of about 30 ft, collimated so the beam is narrow compared with the transverse width of the shower developed within the absorber. The transverse spread of the high-energy components of the electronic shower, and so of the photoneutrons, is about 1 m^2, so the emergent intensity is distributed over this area. This emergent intensity is to be reduced by shielding to below the tolerance level of 20 fast neutrons/(cm^2)(sec), or to a total of 2 $\times$ 10^5 neutrons/sec over the shower cross section. The total yield of high-energy photoneutrons within the absorber is about 0.6 neutron per incident electron, or 4 $\times$ 10^{11} neutrons/sec. The attenuation factor required of the shield in the forward direction is 5.0 $\times$ 10^{-5}, for the neutron component. The attenuation for such fast neutrons is discussed in a following section, where it is found to require about 21 ft of ordinary concrete to give this attenuation.

14-10. NUCLEONIC SHOWERS

Nuclear Star Production

Very-high-energy nucleons (protons or neutrons) produce another type of shower, composed primarily of nucleonic products of high-energy interactions. A typical interaction of a multi-Bev proton, for example, on striking a medium or heavy nucleus, is the production of a nuclear star in which a number of heavy-particle fragments such as protons, neutrons, and pi mesons (pions) share the energy and momentum of the incident nucleon. Residual nuclei may also be left in a state of high excitation energy, in which case further protons and neutrons are "evaporated" as low-energy nucleons. The charged-particle products can be observed in photographic emulsions or in cloud-chamber photographs; they show some "black" prongs due to relatively low-energy protons, "gray" prongs from higher-velocity protons or mesons, and some "minimum ionization" or "thin" tracks characteristic of very-high-energy pions or mu mesons. Neutrons and neutral pions leave no visible tracks, but their numbers can be estimated from statistical considerations; they are approximately equal to the number of charged products. The number of prongs in the star increases with incident nucleon energy and is also related to the atomic number of the struck nucleus.

Experimental evidence of star-type interactions comes from cosmic-ray studies as well as from observations with 3-Bev protons from the Brookhaven cosmotron and 6-Bev protons from the Berkeley bevatron. With 6-Bev protons Moyer reports[29] the "average star" produced in concrete to have the following composition and share of the incident energy:

Bev

3 cascade or recoil protons	kinetic energy	3.0
2 cascade or recoil neutrons		
4 evaporation protons	kinetic energy	0.2
5 evaporation neutrons		
2 charged pions	kinetic plus rest energy	2.6
1 neutral pion		
14 nucleons	total binding energy	0.2
Incident energy		6.0

The product particles are attenuated in the absorber through a variety of nuclear interactions. The higher-energy particles produce tertiary stars releasing still other nucleons and pions. Both protons and neutrons undergo elastic and inelastic scattering and also exchange-of-charge interactions. The charged components also lose energy through ionization. The result is a build-up in the number of particles and a decrease in the average energy. Some of the charged pions decay into mu mesons, which can lose energy only by ionization and which ultimately decay into electrons. Neutral pi mesons decay into pairs of γ rays of about 68 Mev each; these γ rays produce electron pairs and Compton electrons as they degrade in energy. Moyer[29] has estimated the intensity of these degraded components for each 6-Bev incident nucleon surviving and emerging from a thick shield of concrete to be:

Protons (from cascade and evaporation)................. 4
Charged pions.. 3
Muons... 0.3
Neutrons (cascade, evaporation, and secondaries).......... 7
Slow neutrons.. 70
Electrons (from pion decay and nuclear γ rays)........... 10 (?)
Gamma rays (ionizing dose) .... 3×10^{-4} mr

This result is compatible with the evidence for build-up in cosmic rays.

The analysis above applies to the situation where the incident protons enter the shielding. If the primary beam impinges on a local target and does not strike the major shielding wall, the general radiation outside may not be as rich in high-energy protons or pions as indicated above.

A high-energy nucleonic shower will be strongly collimated in the forward direction. The highest-energy secondaries which carry most of the energy of the product particles will be projected forward, because of momentum conservation. Lower-energy evaporation particles will have a wider spread and may approach an isotropic distribution in angle. O'Neill[29] used a Monte Carlo calculation of the star-producing component of a nucleonic shower to predict the distribution of stars inside the face of an iron shield. He found that for incident energies over 1 Bev the rms angle from the beam direction of the stars was within ±14° up to as much as 36 in. depth in the absorber. Particles projected at wider angles are generally of lower energy and are more rapidly attenuated in the shield. In the Monte Carlo calculation described above, O'Neill found that the half-value thickness of iron was about 6.3 in. in the direction of the shower and only 4.5 in. in the transverse direction. The result was a roughly columnar shape of envelope enclosing the star-type interactions in the shower.

High-energy Neutron Attenuation

The attenuation of neutrons of up to 8 or 10 Mev energy was discussed in Sec. 14-6, where the absorption coefficient was found to approach a terminal value for thick absorbers. This terminal absorption coefficient is about 0.18/in. of concrete, for shields of more than 4 or 5 ft thickness. Equivalent coefficients for other materials can be obtained by comparisons with the data on removal cross sections for fission neutrons. Similar values are indicated for the attenuation of photoneutrons released by X rays or γ rays, although the rate of absorption of the primary photons is considerably smaller.

For neutron energies up to 50 or 60 Mev the same type of energy-loss interactions occur as for lower energies, and the absorption coefficient is believed not to decrease significantly. Above these energies the type of nucleonic cascade or shower described in the preceding paragraphs becomes energetically possible. Neutrons produce stars which release other neutrons, deep in the shield and directed primarily forward, although of lower energy. As long as the neutron energy exceeds that necessary for star formation, the neutrons tend to reproduce themselves. This multiplication of neutrons deep in the shield extends the effective range of the neutrons before they are absorbed and results in a significant decrease in the observed absorption coefficient, for sufficiently high-energy neutrons.

Experimental evidence on the attenuation of neutrons of 100 Mev energy or higher is quite incomplete. And cosmic-ray theory gives very little information on the nucleonic cascade process. Almost the only direct evidence comes from measurements of half-value thickness of concrete at two neutron energies, 100 and 300 Mev, taken by Moyer[29] and his associates at the University of California 184-in. synchrocyclotron. Concrete slabs were used in broad-beam geometry applicable to shielding walls, and the absorption of the fast-neutron component was observed directly. The half-value thicknesses obtained were 10 in. of concrete at 100 Mev and 18 in. of concrete at 300 Mev.

Panofsky[29] has summarized the available evidence in the form of a curve of half-value thickness in concrete as a function of neutron energy (see Fig. 14-21). The experimental points are supported by calculated values for other neutron energies, for the same broad-beam (poor geometry) condition. The most significant feature is the rapid increase in half-value thickness for energies between 100 and 300 Mev. This is due to the development of the nucleonic cascade, as described above. Above about 300 Mev the production of pions becomes energetically possible; this provides an additional process through which fast neutrons can lose energy, so the half-value thickness again becomes essentially constant.

The most important elementary interaction in the energy range between 100 and 300 Mev is nucleon-nucleon scattering for which the cross section per nucleon varies with energy but depends only in a minor way on atomic number of the absorber. To a first approximation the absorption coefficient is directly proportional to the density of the material, and the half-value thicknesses are inversely proportional to density.

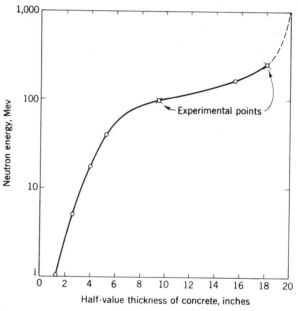

Fig. 14-21. Neutron attenuation half-value thickness as a function of neutron energy.[29]

Moyer's measurements on concrete can be used to predict the half-value thickness for other materials, in this same neutron energy region. Table 14-14, prepared by Wilson,[30] gives half-value thicknesses for several of the common materials used in shields and shows this close inverse proportionality.

An attenuation curve of total neutron intensity as a function of shield thickness can be developed from such half-value thicknesses and estimates of the number and energy distribution of neutrons within the shield. Such a curve was presented by Panofsky[29] for the attenuation in concrete of the neutron component of flux in the direction of the beam expected from a high-energy electron linac. This computed attenuation plot is

TABLE 14-14
HALF-VALUE THICKNESSES FOR HIGH-ENERGY NEUTRONS

	Earth	Concrete	Fe-loaded concrete	Iron	Lead
Density.................	1.5	2.35	4.0	7.8	11.3 gm/cm³
$L_{1/2}$ at 100 Mev..........	15	10*	7.5	4.5	4.5 in.
$L_{1/2}$ at 300 Mev..........	25	18*	13	8	8 in.

* Measured values.

shown in Fig. 14-22.   Panofsky used three ranges of neutron energy in forming the composite curve.   For $T < 80$ Mev he uses a half-value thickness of 4.8 in. equivalent to a constant absorption coefficient of

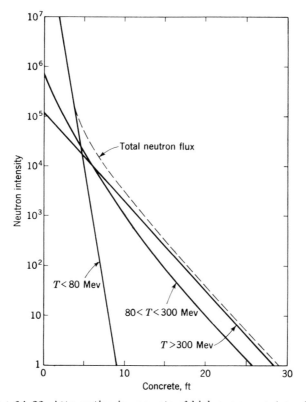

Fig. 14-22. Attenuation in concrete of high-energy neutrons.[29]

about 0.18/in. of concrete.   For $80 < T < 300$ Mev he develops an attenuation curve with a coefficient varying with thickness, ranging from 0.07/in. to 0.035/in. of concrete.   And for $T > 300$ Mev he uses a half-value thickness of 20 in. or a coefficient of 0.035/in.   This curve can be considered an extension of Fig. 14-17 to higher energies and greater thicknesses. For thicknesses greater than about 7 ft of concrete the highest-energy neutron component becomes dominant. It can be noted that this high-energy neutron absorption coefficient, of 0.035/in. of concrete, is lower by far than that for any other radiation component discussed in this chapter. Fast neutrons, in the energy range above a few hundred Mev, are the most penetrating of all radiations.

Attenuation of 3-Bev Protons

Measurements by Beebe, Cumming, Moore, and Swartz at Brookhaven, reported by Lindenbaum,[29] give the attenuation of the nucleonic shower initiated by a narrow external beam of 3.0-Bev protons in iron-loaded concrete of density 4.3 gm/cm^3. They measured both the number of penetrating particles and the ionization density at 12-in. intervals between blocks of concrete out to a total thickness of 13.5 ft. The beam was found to spread transversely to a half-intensity width of about 2 ft halfway through the stack. Build-up effects were still noticeable up to 4 ft. For larger thicknesses both the density of penetrating particles and the ionization intensity at the beam center followed a simple exponential attenuation with approximately the same half-value thickness of 8.5 in. Assuming that absorption coefficients are proportional to density, this corresponds to a half-value thickness in ordinary concrete of 15.6 in.

Ionization energy loss of the primary protons is about 200 Mev/ft in the loaded concrete, so proton energy is reduced to a few hundred Mev in penetrating the 13.5-ft shield. The average energy part way through the shield where measurements were taken would be less than 1 or 2 Bev, and nuclear interactions would produce a wide spread among the individual particles. Thus, the observed absorption coefficient cannot be assigned to any specific proton energy. Rather, this half-value thickness represents an average value applying to the mixture of radiations in a nucleonic shower initiated by 3-Bev protons. The Brookhaven workers state that geometric and other factors make their value a lower limit, and that their results are compatible with a half-value thickness for the more penetrating components of the shower of as much as 10 in., equivalent to 18.3 in. of ordinary concrete.

These results are in reasonable agreement with the half-value thicknesses observed at Berkeley with fast neutrons and show that the attenuation of a nucleonic shower is nearly independent of the type of particle which originates the shower.

Shielding for Nucleonic Showers

The dominant component of the nucleonic shower is high-energy neutrons, with energies of 300 Mev or higher. For such neutrons the thick-absorber half-value thickness is found to be about 20 in. of ordinary concrete or the equivalent linear density of other materials.   In concrete this terminal linear absorption coefficient is 0.035/in. and for other materials the mass absorption coefficient is $\mu_m = 0.0058/(\text{gm})(\text{cm}^2)$.

The intensity of these high-energy neutrons builds up in the absorber, primarily through nuclear star processes, reaching a maximum in the initial layers.   High-energy charged particles are also released in the star processes, along with a much larger number of lower-energy particles and radiations.   All these components degrade in energy at various rates through other interactions, including star production for those of sufficient energy.   The neutrons of >300 Mev have the lowest interaction cross section.   The number of these penetrating neutrons, per incident proton or neutron, reaches a maximum of 5 to 10 when the incident energy is 6 Bev.   A reasonable estimate of the number at the peak of the shower build-up is one to two such fast neutrons per Bev incident energy. We conclude that an upper limit to the number is given by

$$N_n = 2W_0 N_{\text{incid}} \ (W_0 \text{ in Bev})$$

At high incident energies the shower develops a columnar shape with a relatively restricted transverse cross section within the absorber, of the order of 1 m^2 or 10 ft^2 for the high-energy neutrons.   Shielding in the forward direction must, in general, be sufficient to reduce the high-energy neutron intensity to below the tolerance level of 20 neutrons/(cm^2)(sec), which means a total of about 2×10^5 neutrons/sec for the cross section of the penetrating core of the shower.

As an example, we use the foregoing analysis to compute the shielding required in the forward direction for a beam of 10^{10} neutrons/sec of 5 Bev energy.   The number of incident high-energy neutrons at the shower maximum is

$$N_n = 2 \times 5 \times 10^{10} = 1.0 \times 10^{11} \text{ neutrons/sec}$$

To reduce this to the tolerance value of 2×10^5 neutrons/sec beyond the shield requires an attenuation factor of 2×10^{-6} for the high-energy neutron component alone.   Using the terminal absorption mean free path of 20 in. of ordinary concrete, this requires a thickness of 22 ft of ordinary concrete or 13 ft of iron-loaded concrete of density 4.0 gm/cm^3. To this must be added the thickness required for the shower to develop to maximum intensity, which is about 2 ft in ordinary concrete.   We conclude a shielding requirement in the forward direction of 24 ft of ordinary concrete or 14 ft of iron-loaded concrete.

Obviously, much more detailed calculations are desirable in any specific shielding situation.   The transverse spread can be calculated with statistical techniques using the specific energies and absorber materials, and the source intensity of high-energy neutrons should also include estimates for those of less than 300 Mev energy.   Nevertheless, the crude estimate above is in surprisingly close agreement with more detailed calculations of the shielding needed for the assumed intensity.

This technique of computing shielding requirements only for the dominant or most penetrating component of the radiation must be used with caution. It is suitable in this case only because the attenuation for all other components is much larger, sufficient to make the emergent intensities of these other components negligible. In this case, also, the source location of fast neutrons at the shower maximum is reasonably well defined; in other situations the source of radiation might not be so easily localized.

14-11. MESON PRODUCTION AND ATTENUATION

Meson Production by Photons

The simplest mechanism by which π mesons (pions) are produced is photoproduction, through the interactions

$$\gamma + P \rightarrow N + \pi^+$$
$$\gamma + N \rightarrow P + \pi^-$$
$$\gamma + P \rightarrow P + \pi^0$$

(14-29)

It is customary to write these relations using the symbols P and N for the protons and neutrons and identifying the charged or neutral pions with superscripts. Each of these processes has a threshold γ-ray energy for which the reaction becomes energetically possible, which can be computed from the pion masses and the kinematics of the collision. At this threshold the kinetic energy of the pion in the center-of-mass system of coordinates must be zero, from which it follows that the threshold photon energy is given by

$$W_t = m_\pi \left(1 + \frac{m_\pi}{2M} \right)$$

(14-30)

where m_π is the pion mass and M is the nucleonic mass. Present experimental evidence indicates rest masses and equivalent energies for charged and neutral mesons of

$$m_\pi{}^\pm = (276.1 \pm 2.3)m_e = 141 \text{ Mev}$$
$$m_\pi{}^0 = (264.6 \pm 3.2)m_e = 135 \text{ Mev}$$
$$m_\mu{}^\pm = (209.6 \pm 2.4)m_e = 107 \text{ Mev}$$

In the laboratory system of coordinates the pion energy at threshold is a function of the angle of emission with respect to the incident photon direction. The kinematic equations are given in detail in "Meson Physics," by Marshak,[34] and in other reference texts. For our purposes the threshold γ-ray energies for photoproduction can be taken as not significantly greater than the pion mass values.

Photoproduction of pions by γ rays is analogous to photoproduction of neutrons (see Sec. 14-9), except that production thresholds and resonance energies are higher. The most intense single group of pions comes from the $(\frac{3}{2},\frac{3}{2})$ resonance level identified in the "weak coupling" theory of photomeson production, for which the energy is about 300 Mev. At the peak of this resonance the cross section is known[34] to be about 2×10^{-4} barn. A total or integrated cross section can be obtained as in Eq. (14-23), integrating over the energy spectrum of γ rays coming from the incident electrons, from threshold to above the resonance energy. A track-length integral can be evaluated from Eq. (14-24), using a value of $k_0 = 300$ Mev for the resonance energy. The yield of resonance pions can then be determined from Eq. (14-25). When this yield is evaluated for an incident electron energy $W_0 = 1.0$ Bev, using appropriate constants for the different shielding materials (Table 14-13), we find

$$Y(\pi)_r = 1 \times 10^{-3} \text{ pion/electron} \qquad \text{(earth or concrete)}$$
$$Y(\pi)_r = 2 \times 10^{-3} \text{ pion/electron} \qquad \text{(iron)}$$
$$Y(\pi)_r = 4 \times 10^{-3} \text{ pion/electron} \qquad \text{(lead)}$$

Comparison with the photoneutron yields given in Table 14-13 shows that the resonance photomeson intensities are about 1 per cent of the resonance photoneutron intensities. Most of the photomesons have energies of less than 100 Mev.

Pions are also produced by γ rays having energies above the resonance energy, through the direct photodisintegration process, again analogous to the production of high-energy photoneutrons. Measurements at the California Institute of Technology of the photodisintegration cross section in hydrogen with energies up to 1.2 Bev show it to be essentially constant for energies above 500 Mev, with a value of 6×10^{-5} barn. This can be taken as the cross section per nucleon in computing yields from other materials.

Yields can be obtained in a manner parallel to that used for photodisintegration neutrons, although the use of the track-length integral may lead to some error at these high energies. When the yield is evaluated for an incident electron energy of 1 Bev, we find

$$Y(\pi)_p = 1 \times 10^{-3} \text{ pion/electron} \qquad \text{(earth or concrete)}$$
$$Y(\pi)_p = 5 \times 10^{-4} \text{ pion/electron} \qquad \text{(iron)}$$
$$Y(\pi)_p = 2 \times 10^{-4} \text{ pion/electron} \qquad \text{(lead)}$$

The intensities are only about 1 per cent of the high-energy photoneutrons shown in Table 14-13, and the cross section for pion production is in fact included in the photoneutron cross section.

Meson Production by Nucleons

Meson production interactions by nucleons become significant for energies above 200 to 300 Mev. Single pions are produced through a number of elementary processes such as

$$
\begin{array}{ll}
P + P \rightarrow N + P + \pi^{+} & N + P \rightarrow N + N + \pi^{+} \\
P + P \rightarrow P + P + \pi^{0} & N + P \rightarrow P + P + \pi^{-} \\
& N + P \rightarrow N + P + \pi^{0}
\end{array}
\tag{14-31}
$$

The threshold kinetic energy of the incident nucleon is given by

$$
\frac{T_t}{c^2} = \frac{(m_\pi + 2M)^2 - (2M)^2}{2M}
\tag{14-32}
$$

When evaluated for a single nucleon target (hydrogen), the threshold energy is 291 Mev for producing charged pions and 281 Mev for neutral pions. In complex nuclei the internal potential energy of individual nucleons in the nucleus—the Fermi energy—lowers the threshold. It can be as low as 180 Mev in heavy elements. From considerations of charge conservation and statistical weight the number of positive pions should be about twice the number of negative pions.

Experimental measurements, analyzed by Marshak,[34] show that the cross section for single positive pion production by protons of 340 Mev on protons is about 2×10^{-4} barn/steradian.

At higher bombarding energies, and in complex nuclei, the nucleonic shower phenomena (see Sec. 14-10) become energetically possible. Pions are emitted as components of the star processes, and several can be released in a single interaction. The evidence cited in Sec. 14-10 shows that the number of high-energy pions released in a 6-Bev shower is about half the number of high-energy cascade nucleons, and that they carry something less than half of the total energy.

Meson Attenuation

Charged mesons lose energy by ionization, with the rate of loss increasing as the velocity decreases. When they have been slowed down by ionization or collisions, the negative pions are captured by nuclei, releasing their mass energy in the form of γ rays or disintegrating the nucleus with the emission of neutrons. In about one-third of the negative pion interactions a neutron of about 7.0 Mev energy is released. On the other hand, slow positive pions cannot enter nuclei, and they usually decay into muons and neutrinos, with a characteristic half-life of 2.54×10^{-8} sec. The positive muon itself decays into a positron and neutrino with a half-life of 2.15×10^{-6} sec, and the positron loses energy by ionization, radiation, and annihilation. The neutral pions (π^0) have essentially no interaction with nuclei and decay promptly (10^{-15} sec) into two γ rays of

68 Mev each.   These γ rays add to the soft component of the shower and are attenuated by pair production and other electromagnetic interactions.

High-energy charged pions have the same sort of nuclear interactions as protons of equivalent energies, and the cross section is essentially the same.   For shielding considerations, the most significant of the interaction products are the high-energy neutrons.   As was shown in a preceding section, protons in the Bev energy range develop nucleonic showers for which the attenuation is determined by the fast-neutron component. It is known that pions of these energies also produce star-type processes which are indistinguishable from those produced by nucleons.   For example, the number of high-energy neutrons produced in such star processes is estimated by Moyer[29] to be 1 from 500-Mev pions, 2 from 1-Bev pions, and 3 from 3-Bev pions.   These neutrons will be directed into a small forward angle, as is true for other high-energy neutrons in the shower.

We can conclude that charged pions are essentially equivalent to protons of the same energy in maintaining the nucleonic shower.   Like protons, the rate of ionization associated with their charge means that they are attenuated more rapidly than the fast neutrons in the shower. So we return to the results of Sec. 14-10 and the attenuation plot of Fig. 14-22 as the basic data for estimating the shielding requirements for the nucleonic shower.

Properties of μ Mesons (Muons)

The muons formed by decay in flight of high-energy π mesons represent a special problem in shielding.   Under certain conditions it is possible for the muons to penetrate shields which are otherwise adequate for attenuation of the nucleonic components.   The reason is that muons have a negligibly small cross section for nuclear interactions, so ionization is the only process by which they can lose energy.   The rate of energy loss, for singly charged particles of relativistic velocities, varies from 2 Mev/(gm)(cm²) in light absorbers to 1.4 Mev/(gm)(cm²) in Pb.   This results in a penetration of about 7.0 ft/Bev energy in concrete, 2.5 ft/Bev in iron, or 2.1 ft/Bev in Pb.   Depth of penetration is directly proportional to energy.   In most installations the installed shielding for attenuating the nucleonic shower is sufficiently thick to absorb the total energy of the muons.   However, for low-intensity multi-Bev accelerators the shielding required to reduce the emergent shower intensity to below tolerance may not be sufficient to absorb the entire energy of the muons.

The lifetime for decay of slow positive pions into muons is 2.54×10^{-8} sec.   The negative pion decays only in the absence of matter, but the half-life is presumed to be the same.   If the pion beam is allowed to traverse considerable distances in air or vacuum before entering a dense absorber, a significant fraction will decay in flight into muons.   The mean free path for decay is determined by the mean life, the velocity of the pions ($v \simeq c$), and the relativistic time-dilatation factor. In the multi-Bev energy range for which the muon component is a potential hazard, the time dilatation $W/m_\pi c^2$ is significant (W is pion energy and $m_\pi c^2$ is pion rest energy) and increases the decay mean life by this factor.

The mean free path for decay of pions is given by

$$L_m = c \left(\frac{W}{m_\pi c^2} \right) \tau \qquad (14\text{-}33)$$

where τ is the mean life at low energies. As an example, for 5-Bev pions the time-dilatation factor is 35, and the mean free path for decay is 390 m. If the first dense shielding is at a distance of, say, 25 m or 80 ft, about 6.5 per cent of the negative pions will decay into muons. If the shielding is less than 35 ft of concrete or 12.5 ft of steel, this fraction of the incident muon flux will penetrate the shield. Even though the intensity is low in terms of biological hazard, it might impose an objectionably large background of ionizing radiation on detection instruments such as liquid-hydrogen bubble chambers or electronic scintillation counters.

The most obvious technique for removing the muon background is to place a shield of high-density material near the target where the pions are formed. This shield can have a conical or cylindrical shape with relatively small transverse dimensions, because of the forward collimation of the high-energy pions, and must be of sufficient length to attenuate the pion beam through nucleonic interactions. An iron shield for a beam of 10^{10} pions/sec of 5 Bev energy would be about 10 mean free paths or 7.5 ft long.

14-12. SKYSHINE

Upward-directed radiation which is scattered back toward the surface of the earth by collisions with air nuclei is known as "skyshine." Relatively low-energy fast neutrons (1 to 10 Mev) prove to be the significant radiation component for most accelerators. This is due to the fact that the cross section for elastic or inelastic scattering is large for neutrons in this energy range, while the absorption cross section is much smaller, so such neutrons can diffuse over considerable distances. The RBE of Mev neutrons is also larger than for γ rays or electronic components, so the biological effect of skyshine is determined predominantly by the low-energy neutron content.

The mean free path for scattering interactions with the O and N nuclei in air has been variously estimated; Lindenbaum[29] used 450 ft for 1- to 5-Mev neutrons, Williams[29] chose 270 m (685 ft) for 5 to 10 Mev, and Panofsky[29] used a mean free path of 1000 ft for his calculations. On the average, each upward-directed neutron will have a scattering impact at this distance, so the source for skyshine is a diffuse hemispherical dome in the air above the accelerator with a mean radius of one mean free path. However, for purposes of calculation the source is usually presumed to be a point in air directly above the accelerator at an altitude of one mean free path.

Most accelerators are surrounded in the horizontal direction with thick barrier shields to attenuate the direct radiation to suitable intensity levels in adjacent laboratories. Skyshine radiation scattered over the barriers adds to the attenuated direct radiation intensity behind the shields. Relative intensity is determined by the distance and the geometric arrangement of the barriers. Close behind a barrier, where the solid angle of sky available for skyshine is reduced, the direct intensity may be dominant; at larger distances the skyshine frequently exceeds the transmitted intensity. We shall show that at large distances the rate of decrease of intensity due to skyshine varies roughly with the inverse first power of distance from the source, while direct radiation intensity falls off as the inverse square. So for locations well beyond the immediately adjacent laboratories or beyond project boundaries the residual intensities due to skyshine are usually dominant.

Accelerators of small physical size, such as cyclotrons, are usually housed in buildings with overhead roof shielding sufficient to reduce skyshine intensity outside the buildings to acceptable values. Larger, higher-energy machines such as the proton synchrotron are also normally placed in shielded tunnels to control the upward-directed intensity. However, the very-high-energy machines require extremely large laboratories within which experiments are performed on emergent beams. The cost of providing roof shielding for such large experimental areas sets a practical economic limit on the attenuation for upward radiation. In some cases it is more economical to shield the roofs of nearby occupied laboratory areas or to depend on huts for local shielding around the individual targets in the exposed experimental areas.

In a nonabsorbing medium of infinite extent the outward flux density at a distance r from a point source of N_0 neutrons/sec is

$$\phi(r) = \frac{N_0}{4\pi r^2} \qquad \text{neutrons}/(\text{cm}^2)(\text{sec}) \qquad (14\text{-}34)$$

The attenuation of the outward-directed flux due to scattering interactions with a scattering mean free path λ is $e^{-r/\lambda}$. So the scattered flux intensity at a distance r is given by

$$\phi_s(r) = \frac{N_0}{4\pi r^2}(1 - e^{-r/\lambda}) \qquad (14\text{-}35)$$

Panofsky first pointed out that the first term in the expansion of Eq.

(14-35) is an inverse first-power term of the form $1/4\pi r\lambda$, and that this first term becomes dominant at distances where $r > \lambda$.

A complicating factor is introduced by the effect of the ground surface on the intensity and energy distribution of the scattered neutrons. The heavier elements in earth or other solid materials have a larger absorption cross section for neutrons than oxygen or nitrogen, so the ground becomes a "sink" for neutrons, in the form of a horizontal plane bounding the hemispherical dome of skyshine. Since we are interested primarily in intensities close to the ground surface, the effect of this ground absorption is marked. However, earth is not a perfect absorber, and the "albedo" or back-scattering coefficient is estimated to be between 0.5 and 0.8 for neutrons of this energy. So the earth acts as an inelastic reflector for about half of the neutrons striking it. These reflected neutrons will then be rescattered by the air to add to the total skyshine intensity.

The general steady-state diffusion problem for neutrons under these conditions has not been solved. Partial or approximate solutions have been presented by Lindenbaum;[29] these were evaluated with constants and cross sections appropriate to incident neutrons of 1 to 5 Mev energy. The average total cross section for elastic and inelastic scattering in O and N was taken to be 1.5×10^{-24} cm² per nucleus, which is equivalent to a mean free path of about 450 ft in air. For convenience in plotting, the results are presented as the variation of the quantity $4\pi r^2\phi(r)$ as a function of radial distance r from the source in units of mean free paths. These results are shown in Fig. 14-23 for two conditions, with values of Lindenbaum's constant $C = \dfrac{\text{elastic cross section}}{\text{total cross section}}$ of 0.90 and 0.50. The value in air without any absorbing material such as the half-plane of earth is about 0.97; that adjacent to the ground plane is taken to be 0.50. The two curves in the plot represent extremes, with the upper curve more appropriate to large distances and intensities at considerable heights above the ground plane, while the lower curve is closer to that expected near the ground surface.

Lindenbaum notes that the general solution to the diffusion equation can be presented in the form of two terms, the first varying inversely with r^2, which is dominant near the source, and the second, which is the diffusion term, varying inversely with r. In drawing the curves he evaluates the two terms numerically. He also notes the differences between the low-energy and high-energy neutron components and suggests that the diffusion term could itself be expressed as two terms with different constants for low and high energies. His final result represents his own choice of approximations and simplifications, but is in reasonable agreement with the conclusions of Panofsky and of Williams, using different approximations.

Williams[29] uses a considerably simpler argument to estimate skyshine intensities, based on Eq. (14-35) and assuming that only the initially scattered radiation from the upward-directed flux is effective. From this assumption Wilson[30] has computed the skyshine flux as a function of

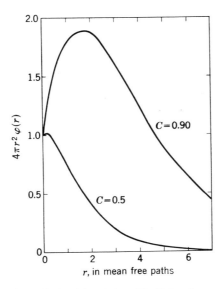

Fig. 14-23. Calculated total skyshine intensities[29] for two assumed values of the ratio $C = \dfrac{\text{elastic cross section}}{\text{total cross section}}$.

radial distance from a source of 1 neutron/sec. The results are based on an assumed mean free path of 1000 ft and are presented in Table 14-15.

TABLE 14-15

SKYSHINE INTENSITY FOR A SOURCE OF 1 NEUTRON/SEC

Distance, ft	Flux, neutrons/(cm²)(sec)
100	3.3×10^{-10}
200	1.7×10^{-10}
300	1.0×10^{-10}
400	0.7×10^{-10}
500	0.5×10^{-10}
1000	0.2×10^{-10}

Some practical examples show the magnitude of skyshine intensity. With the 3-Bev Brookhaven cosmotron and with barrier shields only (no overhead shielding) the intensity behind the barrier at 50 ft from the machine due to skyshine was observed to be 20 neutrons/(cm²)(sec) for a proton source intensity of 2×10^9 protons/sec and an estimated neutron source intensity of 10^{10} neutrons/sec. Overhead shielding was installed to provide an attenuation factor of 10^{-3} in order to allow operation at higher intensities, requiring a layer of concrete beams 2.5 ft thick.

At the University of California 184-in. cyclotron a roof shield of one-fourth the thickness of the barrier shielding was required to reduce skyshine flux to a value comparable with the direct component in the beam direction. This ratio is characteristic only of the particular energy and intensity of the 184-in. cyclotron. If intensity were to be increased, say by a factor of e, the thickness of shield would have to be increased by one radiation length, both in the beam direction and in the overhead shielding for skyshine.

A general conclusion is that some overhead shielding is required to reduce skyshine intensities for essentially all accelerators for which neutron source intensity exceeds about 10^9 neutrons/sec.

REFERENCES

1. International Committee on X-ray Protection Report (1934).
2. W. P. Jesse and J. Sadaukis, *Phys. Rev.*, **97**:1668 (1955).
3. International Recommendations on Radiological Units, *Radiology*, **62**:106 (1954).
4. "Report of International Commission on Radiological Units and Measurements," *Natl. Bur. Standards (U.S.) Handbook No.* **62** (1957).
5. "Permissible Dose from External Sources of Ionizing Radiation," *Natl. Bur. Standards (U.S.) Handbook No.* **59** (1954).
6. *Brit. J. Radiol.*, Suppl. No. 6 (1955).
7. H. Goldstein (ed.), "Attenuation of Gamma-rays and Neutrons in Reactor Shields," U.S. Atomic Energy Commission (May 1, 1957).
8. Biological Effects of Atomic Radiation, National Academy of Sciences and National Research Council Report (1956).
9. United Nations Scientific Committee on the Effects of Atomic Radiation, U.N. General Assembly Official Records, XIII Session, Suppl. No. 17, A/3838 (1958).
10. National Committee on Radiation Protection and Measurements, *Radiology*, **68**:260 (1957).
11. M. S. Livingston and H. A. Bethe, *Rev. Mod. Phys.*, **9**:245 (1937).
12. H. A. Bethe, BNL-T-7 (June 1, 1949).
13. H. A. Bethe and W. Heitler, *Proc. Roy. Soc. (London)*, **A-146**:83 (1934).
14. B. Rossi and K. Greisen, *Rev. Mod. Phys.*, **13**:240 (1941).
15. L. I. Schiff, *Phys. Rev.*, **83**:252 (1951).
16. H. W. Koch and J. W. Motz, *Rev. Mod. Phys.*, **31**: 920 (1959).
17. *Natl. Bur. Standards (U.S.) Handbook No.* **55** (Feb. 26, 1954).
18. B. T. Price, C. C. Horton, and K. T. Spinney, "Radiation Shielding," Pergamon Press (1957).
19. M. Stearns, *Phys. Rev.*, **76**:836 (1949).
20. B. Rossi, "High Energy Particles," Prentice-Hall (1952).
21. G. C. Baldwin and F. R. Elder, *Phys. Rev.*, **78**:76 (1950).

22. P. C. Gugelot and M. G. White, *J. Appl. Phys.*, **21**:369 (1950).
23. "Reactor Handbook," U.S. Atomic Energy Commission, No. AEC-D-3465 (1955).
24. V. Delano and C. Goodman, *J. Appl. Phys.*, **21**:1040 (1950).
25. Hanson Blatz (ed.), "Handbook on Radiation Hygiene," McGraw-Hill (1959).
26. Harold Etherington (ed.), "Nuclear Engineering Handbook," McGraw-Hill (1958).
27. M. Chodorow, E. L. Ginzton, W. W. Hansen, R. L. Kylh, R. B. Neal, and W. K. H. Panofsky, *Rev. Sci. Instr.*, **26**:134–204 (1955).
28. A. Kantz and R. Hofstadter, *Nucleonics*, **12**:36 (1954).
29. "Conference on Shielding of High-energy Accelerators," New York (Apr. 11–13, 1957); U.S. Atomic Energy Commission No. TID-7545 (Dec. 6, 1957).
30. Richard Wilson, "A Revision of Shielding Calculations," Cambridge Electron Accelerator Report CEA-73 (May 12, 1959).
31. J. S. Levinger, *Nucleonics*, **6**:64 (May, 1950).
32. A. C. Odian et al., *Phys. Rev.*, **102**:837 (1956).
33. A. V. Tollestrup et al., *Phys. Rev.*, **101**:360 (1956) and **121**:630 (1961).
34. R. E. Marshak, "Meson Physics," McGraw-Hill (1952).

15

Alternating-gradient Accelerators

A new principle of magnetic focusing for accelerators, called alternating-gradient (AG) or "strong" focusing, which was started in 1952, has led to a series of machines capable of much higher energies than was economically practical with earlier techniques. The most dramatic applications are the several superenergy proton synchrotrons recently completed or under construction. At the CERN laboratory in Geneva the first of these large accelerators was brought into operation at 28 Bev in late 1959. At Brookhaven National Laboratory a machine of similar dimensions was completed in 1960, with a proton energy of 33 Bev. Two developments were under way in 1961 in the U.S.S.R.—a 7-Bev machine which was nearing completion and a 60- to 70-Bev machine on which construction was starting.

The principle of AG focusing has found applications to other accelerators. The method was first used and tested at Cornell University on a 1-Bev electron synchrotron. An electron synchrotron for 6 Bev using strong-focusing magnets is scheduled for completion in 1962 in Cambridge, Massachusetts, jointly sponsored by Massachusetts Institute of Technology and Harvard University. A similar electron synchrotron is under construction at the DESY laboratory associated with the University of Hamburg in West Germany. Another 6-Bev electron accelerator is under construction at Erevan in Soviet Armenia.

A modification of the principle called "sector focusing" has been adapted to the fixed-field cyclotron; it demonstrates that the proposal by Thomas[1] for such magnetic focusing (in 1938) can be viewed as a special case of AG focusing. A series of fixed-frequency cyclotrons using this principle has been built and others are under construction, primarily for the acceleration of multiply charged heavy ions. The feasibility of extending this principle of sector focusing to proton energies up to 850 Mev has been studied, primarily at the Oak Ridge National Laboratory and in England, and offers an opportunity to attain very-high-intensity beams up to this energy range.

Gradient fields developed by magnetic (or electric) quadrupoles have found applications in proton linear accelerators and in laboratory apparatus for utilization of particle beams in linear systems. The strong-focusing quadrupole magnetic lens is now an established component in all high-energy physics laboratories and in many other laboratory applications. Still other uses have been found for quadrupole focusing, as in traveling-wave electron tubes for amplification at microwave frequencies.

An extension of the concept by the use of AG focusing in fixed-field systems has led to the design of new types called fixed-field alternating-gradient accelerators (FFAG), primarily by the Midwestern Universities Research Association (MURA) now located in Madison, Wisconsin. This group of designers has built and tested a series of models involving several different ideas, some of which have the promise of much higher beam intensities than possible with the pulsed synchrotrons discussed above.

The AG concept has added a new dimension to accelerator design, with benefits to a wide range of accelerator types and techniques. A major contribution has been an improved theoretical understanding of orbit stability. The wide application to many different problems justifies the view that AG focusing has become one of the significant forward steps in accelerator development.

15-1. ORIGINS OF THE CONCEPT

The principle of AG focusing originated at Brookhaven National Laboratory in the summer of 1952, at a time when the cosmotron was nearing completion. A report of the early concepts was published by Courant, Livingston, and Snyder[2] late in 1952; it described the possible application to a high-energy proton synchrotron and also discussed the use of magnetic quadrupole lenses in focusing linear beams of particles. In a companion paper Blewett[3] showed that alternating electric-field gradients had the same focusing properties as alternating magnetic gradients and discussed the application to linear accelerators.

At the head of the facing page is an aerial view of Brookhaven 33-Bev AG synchrotron.

A brief description will now be presented of the factors which led to the conception of this focusing principle. The anticipated completion in 1952 of the cosmotron, which was the first multi-Bev accelerator, had attracted to Brookhaven many scientists who were engaged in developing experimental apparatus for research studies. It also attracted a delegation of European scientists representing the newly established CERN laboratory in Geneva, to assess the cosmotron as a model for a 10-Bev machine. In preparation for this visit, the senior author (MSL), on summer leave from MIT, initiated a study of the problems involved in a design for higher energy than 3 Bev. It was known that magnetic saturation effects limited the useful aperture of the C-shaped magnets of the cosmotron at high fields, although this limitation was not considered to be prohibitive in view of the other significant advantages of the C shape. A possible technique which would retain the C shape and also expand the useful aperture would be to alternate the back-leg locations from inside to outside the orbit. This would result, at high fields, in a corresponding alternation in magnetic gradients from positive to negative in the successive magnets as a result of saturation. The first concern was whether this alternation in gradients would destroy orbital stability.

E. D. Courant made a preliminary study of orbital stability under these conditions. A first guess involved pole faces sloped to produce alternating gradients with successive sectors having n values of about $+0.2$ and -1.0, which would give an average value of -0.6 as used in the cosmotron. Surprisingly, this preliminary study showed that orbit stability was improved rather than damaged by the alternation in gradient. A second calculation by Courant with n values of about 10 showed even stronger focusing and still smaller particle oscillation amplitudes. At this time H. S. Snyder joined in the speculative designing and helped to develop the general principle of dynamic stability involved in this use of alternating gradients. Larger and larger gradients were assumed in further stability calculations, each time based on sketch designs of magnets and estimates of the other parameters of a possible accelerator. Stability limits were identified, leading to suitable configurations of "positive" and "negative" magnet sectors and field-free straight sections between sectors around the orbit. Mechanical configurations were conceived which would produce the desired large magnetic gradients, and the requirements for magnet excitation power were estimated. Some of these early speculations led to such large gradients and such small vacuum chambers that construction was obviously impractical. However, it became more and more obvious that the basic concept was sound, and that the use of alternating gradients would allow major reductions in the transverse dimensions and the power requirements for magnets. Such a reduction in cost of synchrotron magnets for a given orbit radius would make it possible to design machines with much larger orbits and for much higher energies.

By the time the European delegation arrived at Brookhaven th
cept had been developed sufficiently to be presented to them as
nificant improvement over the cosmotron design.   They were impre....
by the new concept, and on their return they stimulated studies of AG
orbit stability in British and European laboratories.   For example, in
England, Adams, Hine, and Lawson[4] identified and studied the problem of orbital resonances which might threaten orbit stability.   This
problem of orbital resonances will be discussed in following sections.
When first presented by the British investigators, this seemed to raise a
serious challenge to the practical use of alternating gradients.   Further
work showed that the objectionable resonances could be avoided by care
in design and by use of suitable control systems to maintain constant
gradients during the magnet excitation cycle.   Confidence in the soundness of the new principle grew in all laboratories participating in the
studies.

Several other laboratories contributed design studies of AG machines.
The senior author (MSL) supervised a "Design Study for a 15-Bev
Accelerator" at MIT, with the able assistance of R. Q. Twiss and J. A.
Hofmann, and with consulting support from about 20 members of the
MIT and Harvard Physics Departments.   The result, published as a
Report[5] of the MIT Laboratory of Nuclear Science in June, 1953, was the
first relatively complete analysis of a practical design for an AG accelerator.   The junior author (JPB) served for 6 months as a consultant to
the new CERN laboratory, then returned to Brookhaven to join in the
construction of the 33-Bev AGS.   The Brookhaven and CERN groups
moved ahead steadily in the theoretical analyses and engineering developments that culminated in the success of the large AG proton synchrotrons
at both laboratories.

As so frequently happens in scientific research and development, this
concept was developed independently elsewhere.   N. C. Christofilos, an
electrical engineer of American birth, educated and working in Athens,
had been studying accelerators as a hobby for some years; he developed
several new and unusual ideas on accelerator design in the form of private
reports and patent applications.   His unpublished report, "Focusing
Systems for Ions and Electrons and Application in Magnetic Resonance
Particle Accelerators," dated 1950, presented the concept of AG focusing
and the conceptual design of an accelerator using this principle.   He
also applied for United States and European patents on the idea.   A copy
of his report was privately transmitted to the University of California
Radiation Laboratory, but was not given serious consideration.   After
the Brookhaven publication in 1952, Christofilos came to the United
States and demonstrated his priority, which was recognized in a brief
note published by Courant, Livingston, Snyder, and Blewett[6] in 1953.
Christofilos joined the staff of the Brookhaven Laboratory for a time,
where he continued his speculative designing of accelerators and other

devices and also made contributions to the laboratory program leading toward the large AG machine. He became particularly interested in the linac injector for the synchrotron and made a number of valuable contributions to its design.

15-2. THE PRINCIPLE OF AG FOCUSING

Alternating-gradient focusing involves the use of much higher transverse gradients than those previously used in betatrons and synchrotrons. As was shown in Chap. 5, stability can be achieved by including gradients whose n values $\left(n = -\dfrac{R}{B}\dfrac{dB}{dr} \right)$ lie between zero and unity.   In this case the free or betatron oscillation frequency is somewhat less than the frequency of revolution.   This is now known as "weak focusing," in contrast to AG or "strong focusing."

In the AG system the particle passes alternately through strong focusing and defocusing lenses and is deflected alternately inward and outward.   On the average it finds itself displaced farther from its orbit in focusing lenses than in defocusing lenses because in each focusing lens the particle has just been thrown outward by the preceding defocusing lens. But the focusing force or the defocusing force, as the case may be, is proportional to the field and hence to the displacement (in a field with a gradient).   Consequently, the fact that the particle is generally further displaced in focusing sections indicates that the net force on the particle will be a focusing force.

Within rather wide limits the above conclusion is true.   The net restoring force on the particle, though not nearly so strong as the individual focusing or defocusing force, is still much stronger than could be attained in weak-focusing systems.

This fact is reflected in the frequency of the free or betatron oscillations in an AG synchrotron.   The strong restoring forces result in several betatron oscillations per revolution instead of less than one per revolution as in the weak-focusing case.   In the accepted notation, ν (or Q, in European laboratories), the number of betatron oscillations per revolution, has been increased from the weak-focusing range of 0.2 to 0.6 up to the range between 5 and 100.

The most important consequence of the stronger restoring force is a decrease in oscillation amplitude and hence in necessary aperture.   The amplitudes are decreased in approximately the same ratio that the free oscillation frequencies are increased.   Strong focusing readily gives reductions of factors of 10 in aperture over weak focusing; this means factors of 100 or more in magnet cross sections and in tonnage of magnet steel.

Another consequence of the strong restoring forces is a reduction in the radial spread of equilibrium orbits associated with momentum variations such as are introduced during synchronous oscillations. This "momentum compaction factor" is in the range of 0.05 to 0.02 for the several AG machines in being, compared with unity for a magnet with uniform field or values greater than unity for weak-focusing magnets. As a result, the transverse dimensions of the magnetic region between pole faces can be made much smaller than for weak-focusing machines, with a consequent decrease in the physical size of the magnets, the stored energy in the field, and the power required for excitation. The size of the vacuum chamber to fit between the smaller poles is materially reduced, to the extent that the conductance of the chamber for gas pumping is small and vacuum-pump ports must be closely spaced around the orbit.

As a result of this reduction in physical size of the magnets, the cost of the magnet component and the magnet power supply are reduced relative to costs of other components. It becomes practical to cycle such a magnet at higher frequency, increasing the number of beam pulses per second and so the time-average intensity of the beam. Other components become relatively more costly when cycling rate is increased, especially the radiofrequency system for accelerating particles. One parameter which cannot be reduced with increasing maximum energy is the orbit radius, which is associated with the limitation on the magnetic permeability of iron. The over-all orbit radius is larger, in fact, than for weak-focusing machines of the same energy, because of the necessity for many field-free spaces between AG magnet sectors. Thus the cost of buildings to house the machine becomes a dominating cost component for AG accelerators.

When the sequence of AG lenses is extended around an orbit to close on itself, other stability limitations enter which are associated with orbital resonances. If the frequency of the free oscillations is an exact integral harmonic of the orbital frequency, the pattern of orbit trajectories repeats identically in each turn. Any misalignment or magnetic anomaly which produces a small deviation in the trajectory at one point in the orbit is repeated at the same phase of the oscillatory motion in successive turns, which results in a rapid build-up of amplitude; the particle is quickly lost against the chamber walls. To avoid such a beam "blow-up," it is necessary to detune the free-oscillation frequencies from resonance with the orbital frequency. If they are nonresonant, the phase of the free oscillations changes in each turn at the location of the anomaly, so the effect is averaged out and excessive amplitude build-up does not occur.

The major resonance to be avoided is that for which the free oscillation is an integral harmonic of the orbital frequency. The restriction applies to both transverse coordinates, in the radial and axial directions. The integral resonances can be plotted on a "stability diagram" developed in AG theoretical analysis (see Sec. 15-5), in which the two coordinates represent the free-oscillation phase shifts per turn in the radial and vertical directions.   On this diagram the loci of points for which ν_r and ν_z have integral values show up as "integral stop bands" bounding diamond-shaped areas.   A typical stability diagram (for the Cambridge electron accelerator) is shown in Fig. 15-9.

15-3. ANALOGUES OF AG FOCUSING

The physical principles of AG focusing can be illustrated by reference to analogies in other fields of science or engineering.   In the mechanical field the rapid alternation of forces in opposite directions can produce a type of dynamic stability which has many similarities.   A simple example is the inverted pendulum, which under static forces alone would fall to one side with any small displacement from the vertical.   However, the pendulum becomes stable in the inverted position if the base is oscillated rapidly up and down through a short stroke.

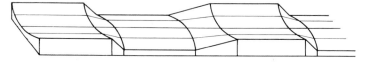

Fig. 15-1. The alternating trough.

Another mechanical system demonstrating dynamic stability, which is also useful as a model for AG focusing, is the "alternating trough" shown in Fig. 15-1.   A ball will roll along a concave-upward trough, and if displaced from the axis will describe a harmonic trajectory about the center line.   However, a ball will roll off the side of an inverted trough which is convex upward.   Now if an alternating trough is formed of successive equal-length sections of concave and convex trough, with center lines forming a straight line and smoothly molded transition sections between, a ball will perform stable oscillations as it rolls along the trough, within a limited range of velocities.   This stability range can be demonstrated by rolling the ball from different heights down an inclined plane to give it various initial velocities and directions.   The shape of a displaced trajectory is a complicated curve which repeats periodically, with the shape depending on the initial phase of the motion relative to the phase of the trough periodicity.   Within the stable range of velocities, rather wide deviations in physical displacement or angle of injection will result in trajectories which are confined to the trough. This system is useful as an analogue to AG focusing, since the trajectories of the rolling ball are quite similar in shape to the orbits of a particle in an AG ring-magnet accelerator, if the orbits were unrolled along a straight line.   A mechanical model serves to illustrate the wide variation in shape of orbits having different phases relative to the trough.

The most direct analogue to this type of magnetic focusing is in the field of lens optics.   First, consider two thin lenses, one convex and one concave, with focal lengths f_1 and f_2 (negative), separated by a distance s. The optical relation for determining the over-all focal length F is

$$\frac{1}{F} = \frac{1}{f_1} + \frac{1}{f_2} - \frac{s}{f_1 f_2}$$

If for simplicity we take $f_1 = -f_2$, we find $F = |f|^2/s$, which is positive (convergent) for any finite separation distance and independent of the order of the lenses.   If thick optical lenses are used in the example above, the focal lengths must be measured from the usual principal planes. Since the principal planes will have different locations for the converging and diverging lens surfaces, the location of the focal point depends on which lens comes first in the sequence.

Now let us extend the analogy by considering thick cylindrical lenses, for which each face has a double cylindrical curvature, such that a given lens would be converging in one transverse plane and diverging in the plane at right angles, with the two focal lengths f_1 and f_2 (negative) as before.   A pair of such thick lenses with orientations rotated by 90° and separated by a distance s between principal planes would be converging in both transverse planes, with the same focal length.   However, the image will be astigmatic, because of the different locations of principal planes in the two transverse coordinates.   To obtain a point focus, one of the focal lengths would have to be modified.

A magnetic-gradient lens pair has the same focal properties for charged particles as the thick optical lenses described above have for light.   The magnetic sectors have a physical extent, and the transverse gradients in the two perpendicular directions are equal in magnitude but opposite in their focusing properties on the particle beam.   Figure 5-11 is a schematic illustration of particle paths through two such regions of alternating magnetic gradient, showing a net convergence in both transverse coordinates.   The image is astigmatic, as with the optical lenses, but the two focal planes can be brought into coincidence by varying the excitation of one magnet sector.   A complete analysis of this quadrupole magnetic lens was given in Sec. 5-6.   Such a lens can be constructed using four symmetrical poles of alternating polarity, with pole faces shaped to a rectangular hyperbola.   A simple two-element lens system (doublet) has the astigmatic aberration described above.   A three-element system (triplet) using focusing-defocusing-focusing sectors in sequence can decrease the astigmatic and other aberrations.   Other properties of quadrupole magnetic and electric lenses were discussed in Chap. 5.

To continue the optical analogy still further: A sequence of thin positive and negative lenses of alternately positive and negative focal length can be arranged in a linear array to be continuously converging. (A modification of this principle is used in periscopes.) The sequence will be converging if spacings between lenses are arranged such that an off-axis ray never crosses the optic axis, which restricts spacings to the range $-2F < s < 2F$. Since the angular deviation is proportional to the distance from the axis in such a system, the ray trajectories will be spread most widely in the centers of the converging lenses, with minimum spread in the diverging lenses. This is an example of the general principle in lens optics that the converging lenses are the aperture stops. Magnetic-gradient lenses have the same property, in that the largest deviations in trajectory occur within the magnet sector which is converging (in that coordinate).

15-4. AG FOCUSING IN LINEAR SYSTEMS

The basic arithmetical methods used in analysis of AG focusing systems were presented in Sec. 5-6 with particular reference to lens systems consisting of a few quadrupole elements. In accelerators employing AG focusing the particles pass through many thousands of AG elements and

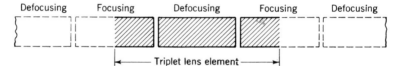

Fig. 15-2. Basic triplet lens element of an AG focusing system.

the methods of matrix analysis yield results so complicated that it is no longer easy to understand the results. In this section we shall present the basic methods of analysis together with some approximate representations that make the particle behavior more evident.

Although the single quadrupole is the basic element of the system, it becomes more profitable in thinking of AG systems to break the system down into a sequence of triplet lenses consisting (see Fig. 15-2) of the downstream half of one quadrupole, the whole next quadrupole, and the upstream half of the next one. Initially we shall assume that all quadrupoles are of length z_0 and have equal field gradients alternating in polarity from one quadrupole to the next. Since magnetic focusing is used in most accelerators, the analysis will be for quadrupole magnets rather than the electrostatic quadrupoles discussed in Chap. 5. In this case the parameter k used in Eqs. (5-35) will represent the quantity $(eB'/mv)^{1/2}$, where e, m, and v are the charge, mass, and velocity of the particles and B' is the gradient of the magnetic field. By the methods described in Sec. 5-6 we find that the exit position and transverse velocity

x and $\dot{x}$ of the particle are given in terms of the entrance position and velocity x_0 and $\dot{x}_0$ by the matrix transformation

$$\left| \begin{matrix} x \\ \dot{x}/v \end{matrix} \right| = \left| \begin{matrix} \cos kz_0 & (1/k)\sin kz_0 \\ -k\sin kz_0 & \cos kz_0 \end{matrix} \right| \left| \begin{matrix} x_0 \\ \dot{x}_0/v \end{matrix} \right| \tag{15-1}$$

for motions in the focusing plane, or

$$\left| \begin{matrix} y \\ \dot{y}/v \end{matrix} \right| = \left| \begin{matrix} \cosh kz_0 & (1/k)\sinh kz_0 \\ k\sinh kz_0 & \cosh kz_0 \end{matrix} \right| \left| \begin{matrix} x_0 \\ \dot{x}_0/v \end{matrix} \right| \tag{15-2}$$

for motions in the defocusing plane.

To trace a particle through our basic triplet, we must derive a transformation matrix by multiplication of the three matrices representing the three elements of the lens. The final position and velocity of the particle will be given, for the plane in which the first element is focusing, by the transformation matrix

$$\left| \begin{matrix} \cos\dfrac{kz_0}{2} & \dfrac{1}{k}\sin\dfrac{kz_0}{2} \\ -k\sin\dfrac{kz_0}{2} & \cos\dfrac{kz_0}{2} \end{matrix} \right| \left| \begin{matrix} \cosh kz_0 & \dfrac{1}{k}\sinh kz_0 \\ k\sinh kz_0 & \cosh kz_0 \end{matrix} \right| \left| \begin{matrix} \cos\dfrac{kz_0}{2} & \dfrac{1}{k}\sin\dfrac{kz_0}{2} \\ -k\sin\dfrac{kz_0}{2} & \cos\dfrac{kz_0}{2} \end{matrix} \right| \tag{15-3}$$

The result of this multiplication is the matrix

$$\left| \begin{matrix} \cosh kz_0 \cos kz_0 & (1/k)(\sinh kz_0 + \cosh kz_0 \sin kz_0) \\ k(\sinh kz_0 - \cosh kz_0 \sin kz_0) & \cosh kz_0 \cos kz_0 \end{matrix} \right| \tag{15-4}$$

This matrix looks remarkably like the element matrices of Eqs. (15-1) and (15-2). So long as the product $\cosh kz_0 \cos kz_0$ falls between -1 and $+1$, the matrix can be rewritten in the form

$$\left| \begin{matrix} \cos\mu & (1/K)\sin\mu \\ -K\sin\mu & \cos\mu \end{matrix} \right| \tag{15-5}$$

where

$$\cos\mu = \cosh kz_0 \cos kz_0 \tag{15-6}$$

and

$$\begin{aligned} K^2 &= \frac{-k^2(\sinh kz_0 - \cosh kz_0 \sin kz_0)}{\sinh kz_0 + \cosh kz_0 \sin kz_0} \\ &= \frac{k^2(1 - \cosh^2 kz_0 \cos^2 kz_0)}{(\sinh kz_0 + \cosh kz_0 \sin kz_0)^2} \end{aligned} \tag{15-7}$$

Evidently, for $\cosh kz_0 \cos kz_0$ between -1 and $+1$, both μ and K are real and the representation of Eq. (15-5) is legitimate. But this matrix has precisely the form of the focusing matrix equation (15-1), and hence it indicates that, for the condition stated, the triplet is a focusing lens. We can now add an indefinite sequence of identical triplets and be assured that this sequence will continue to restore a beam to the axis provided only that

$$-1 < \cosh kz_0 \cos kz_0 < +1 \tag{15-8}$$

This is known as the "criterion of stability" for an indefinite sequence of AG quadrupoles of equal length and strength. The condition given by Eq. (15-8) indicates that kz_0 must lie between 0 and 1.86 radians. Other stable regions exist for higher values of kz_0 for which low values of the cosine combined with the increasing values of the cosh still are able to satisfy the condition of Eq. (15-8); these regions are narrow and require high gradients; hence they are never used in practice.

Had we chosen as our basic element the triplet whose first element is defocusing, we should have obtained a slightly different matrix in place of Eq. (15-4), but the stability criterion would still be Eq. (15-8).

If the alternating elements in an AG system do not have the same lengths and field gradients, the analysis is a little more complicated but follows the procedures just outlined. If the quadrupoles have alternating lengths z_1 and z_2 and alternating k values of k_1 and k_2, the stability criteria prove to be, as before,

$$-1 < \cos \mu_1 < +1$$
$$-1 < \cos \mu_2 < +1$$

where

$$\cos \mu_1 = \cos k_1 z_1 \cosh k_2 z_2 + \frac{1}{2}\left(\frac{k_2}{k_1} - \frac{k_1}{k_2}\right) \sin k_1 z_1 \sinh k_2 z_2 \quad (15\text{-}9)$$

in the plane where the lenses numbered 1 are focusing and

$$\cos \mu_2 = \cosh k_1 z_1 \cos k_2 z_2 + \frac{1}{2}\left(\frac{k_1}{k_2} - \frac{k_2}{k_1}\right) \sinh k_1 z_1 \sin k_2 z_2 \quad (15\text{-}10)$$

in the other plane.

In Fig. 15-3 the region of stability is shown plotted in $k_1^2 z_1^2$ versus $k_2^2 z_2^2$ space for three different conditions: $z_1 = z_2$, $z_1 = 1.5z_2$, and $z_1 = 2z_2$. Since k^2 is proportional to the field gradient B', the two coordinates of the plot are proportional to $B_1' z_1^2$ and $B_2' z_2^2$. The shape of the stable region in this plot has led to its nickname of the "necktie diagram." It is clear from these plots that the region is decreased when the quadrupole lengths are not equal; the necktie begins to look a little wind-blown.

The particle orbit through the sequence of quadrupoles has a character that is not at all clear from the arithmetic just presented. The triplet lens whose behavior is described by the matrix equation (15-4) is not nearly so strong a lens as one of the individual focusing quadrupoles; consequently, the effect of a sequence of such triplets will be to produce an oscillation around the axis whose wavelength is much longer than the length of an individual quadrupole. But superposed on this motion will be a smaller motion away from the axis in defocusing quadrupoles and toward the axis in focusing quadrupoles. The path will, in short, be an oscillation of several quadrupole lengths in wavelength with a "wiggly motion" superposed. Moreover, the maximum of the oscillation must lie in a focusing quadrupole, since this is the only region where the curvature of the orbit is concave looking from the axis. There will not, in general, be a fixed relation between the phases of the slow oscillation and the wiggly motion; on different waves of the slow oscillation the wiggles

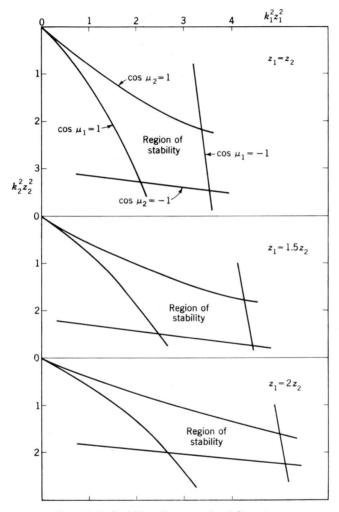

Fig. 15-3. Stability diagrams for AG systems.

will be different. But the envelope of all waves with different starting phases will always have maxima in focusing sectors. Hence focusing sectors will require somewhat larger apertures than will defocusing sectors. Sometimes advantage of this fact can be taken in design.

The only method for a precise orbit calculation appears to be an iterative application of transformation matrices; this operation can be done easily with an electronic computer.   Examples of such orbit calculations are presented in Fig. 15-4.   The two orbits shown in that figure are for initial unit displacement in a sequence of quadrupoles of equal lengths

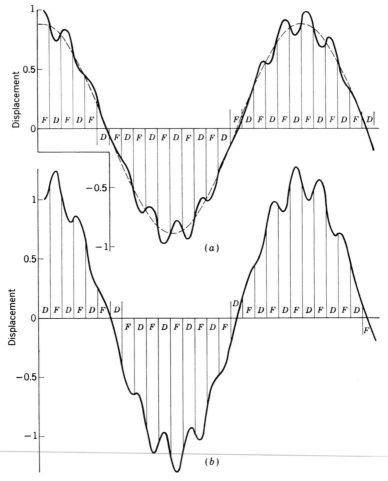

Fig. 15-4. Orbits through a 28-element linear AG focusing system having $k = 0.2$ and $z_0 = 5$.   Particles are injected with unit displacement and parallel to the axis in the center of a lens element.   (a) Orbit in the initially focusing plane; (b) orbit in the initially defocusing plane.

having $k = 0.2$ and $z_0 = 5$.   One orbit begins in the center of a focusing quadrupole, the other in the center of a defocusing quadrupole.

In most accelerators using AG focusing the wavelength of the major oscillation covers several quadrupoles.   For this case an approximate analytic solution describing the complete motion is possible and gives the important characteristics of the motion with sufficient accuracy for most purposes. The general equation of motion through the quadrupole sequence can be written (cf. Sec. 5-7)

$$\frac{d^2x}{dz^2} + fk^2x = 0 \tag{15-11}$$

where f is a function that has the value $+1$ in focusing quadrupoles and -1 in defocusing quadrupoles. This equation is a form of Hill's equation; the reader who wishes more detailed analysis of this equation is referred to Whittaker and Watson's "Modern Analysis" or to Courant and Snyder.[7] For the present purposes, guided by our observations of orbit behavior thus far, we shall guess that an approximate solution might have the form

$$x = \cos\frac{\mu z}{2z_0}\left[1 + \delta \sin\frac{\pi z}{z_0}\right] \tag{15-12}$$

where the first term represents the long-wavelength oscillation and the term in the bracket represents the wiggly motion that is superposed. The value of μ will be given by Eq. (15-6), and the value of δ will be obtained by substitution in the equation of motion. When this substitution is made, we obtain

$$\cos\frac{\mu z}{2z_0}\left[\left(fk^2 - \frac{\mu^2}{4z_0{}^2}\right)\left(1 + \delta \sin\frac{\pi z}{z_0}\right) - \frac{\pi^2\delta^2}{z_0{}^2}\sin\frac{\pi z}{z_0}\right]$$
$$- \frac{\mu\pi\delta}{z_0{}^2}\sin\frac{\mu z}{2z_0}\cos\frac{\pi z}{z_0} = 0 \tag{15-13}$$

We can obtain an approximate value of δ from this equation by averaging over the full period of the oscillation, i.e., over the length of two quadrupoles. We shall assume that, over this distance, the long-wavelength oscillation remains approximately constant so that the sine and cosine of $\mu z/2z_0$ can be considered to be constant. The average values of the function f and the sine and cosine of $\pi z/z_0$ will be zero. The quantity $f \sin (\pi z/z_0)$ will, however, have an average value of $2/\pi$. In view of these considerations Eq. (15-13) simplifies to

$$\frac{2\delta k^2}{\pi} - \frac{\mu^2}{4z_0{}^2} = 0$$

whence

$$\delta = \frac{\pi\mu^2}{8k^2z_0{}^2} \tag{15-14}$$

This rather rough and ready solution can be tested on the orbits plotted in Fig. 15-4. For these orbits, μ [from Eq. (15-6)] has the value 0.585. Hence, from Eq. (15-14), $\delta = 0.134$. The dashed curve in Fig. 15-4 is the $\cos (\mu z/2z_0)$ part of our approximate solution (15-12). The deviations of the orbit from the dashed curve do indeed follow quite closely a sinusoidal oscillation of amplitude proportional to that of the long-wave oscillation. From the curve, δ is about 0.13 as predicted.

It should be reemphasized that this approximate solution is not valid unless the major oscillation covers eight or more quadrupole lenses. Generally, accelerators do not use shorter wavelengths than this because the lens strengths become inconveniently strong and call for higher gradients than are easily produced.

The exact solution of Eq. (15-11) is usually expressed in the form

$$x = A\beta^{1/2} \cos\left(\int \frac{dz}{\beta}\right) \qquad (15\text{-}15)$$

where A is a constant. β satisfies the differential equation

$$\beta\beta'' - \frac{\beta'^2}{2} + 2fk^2\beta^2 - 2 = 0 \qquad (15\text{-}16)$$

β is a periodic function, repeating over a distance $2z_0$. Its form is shown over one period in Fig. 15-5, for the two cases $kz_0 = \pi/2$ and $kz_0 = \pi/4$.

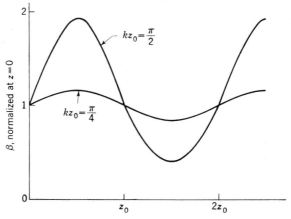

Fig. 15-5. Form of the factor β used in Eq. (15-15).

The factor $\beta^{1/2}$ in Eq. (15-15) corresponds to the factor $[1 + \delta \sin (\pi z/z_0)]$ that was introduced in the approximate solution of Eq. (15-12).

An important example of AG focusing in linear systems is the modern proton linear accelerator. Here, as was shown in Sec. 10-3, the particles are subject continually to a defocusing force of strength

$$\frac{er\omega E}{2v} z \left(1 - \frac{v^2}{c^2}\right) \cos \phi$$

This force is exactly the same as the proton would experience in a defocusing magnetic-field gradient of strength

$$B'_{\text{eff}} = \frac{\omega E}{2v^2} z \left(1 - \frac{v^2}{c^2}\right) \cos \phi \qquad (15\text{-}17)$$

To find what applied B' required for stability, it is necessary to add the effective defocusing B'_{eff} to an applied alternating B' to see whether the combination lies within the stability diagram.   We note that the defocusing problem is most severe for low values of v.   Hence, for an example, we consider the low-energy end of a proton linac into which protons are injected at 500 kev (or $v = 10^7$ m/sec approx.).   We assume that the linac is designed to operate at 200 megacycles/sec and that its average accelerating field E_z is 2 Mv/m.   This gives an effective defocusing gradient

$$B'_{eff} = 12.6 \cos \phi \text{ webers/m}^3$$
$$= 3200 \cos \phi \text{ gauss/inch}$$

$\cos \phi$ in working linacs is usually of the order of 0.5; hence the effective defocusing gradient is of the order of 1600 gauss/in.   From the stability diagram, the gradients that must be provided to overcome this defocusing are of the order of 10,000 gauss/in.

15-5. AG FOCUSING IN CLOSED ORBITS

If AG focusing is to be used in a circular machine, extra bending fields must be added to hold the particles in the circular orbit.   Conceptually the simplest method for accomplishing this would be to alternate quadrupole lenses and bending magnets.   This method has been given much

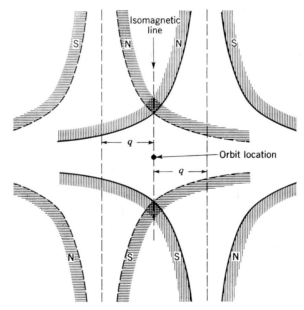

Fig. 15-6. Method of displacing successive quadrupoles to give a bending field in addition to the focusing fields.

thought but has lost out in competition with the more economical method in which quadrupole and bending fields are combined in the same unit. This is done quite simply by displacing the successive quadrupoles by a distance q in opposite directions (see Fig. 15-6) such that the particle feels a bending as well as a focusing field. Since at least half of the quadrupole is not used, it can be left out of the design. In principle it could be replaced by a sheet of iron (or "neutral pole") along the vertical plane of symmetry (see Fig. 15-7). But this refinement also has been eliminated by careful shaping of the magnetic poles to give a quadrupole plus bending field without further additions. The final shape of AG magnets used in synchrotrons is illustrated by Fig. 15-8, which is a cross section through the magnet used in the Brookhaven 33-Bev proton synchrotron.

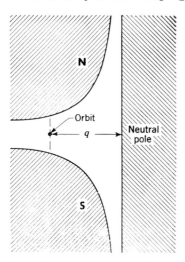

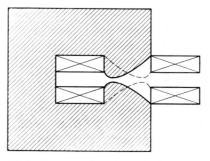

Fig. 15-7. Replacement of half a quadrupole structure by a neutral pole.

Fig. 15-8. Cross section through the magnet in the Brookhaven 33-Bev AG proton synchrotron.

In AG-focused machines having closed orbits the phenomena are essentially the same as those observed in linear AG systems, with two exceptions—one relatively unimportant and one of crucial importance.

The relatively unimportant consideration follows from the entry of the effects of centripetal force. This effect will become evident from a rederivation of the equations of motion [cf. Eqs. (5-14)]. The radial equation of motion has the form

$$m\ddot{r} - \frac{m\dot{s}^2}{r} = Be\dot{s}$$

where s represents distance along the orbit. This is easily converted to

$$\frac{d^2r}{ds^2} - \frac{1}{r} = \frac{Be}{p} \tag{15-18}$$

where p is the momentum of the particle. If we now make the substitutions

$$r = r_0 + x$$

$$B = B_0 \left(1 - \frac{nx}{r_0} \right)$$

$$p = p_0 + \Delta p$$

where x/r_0 and $\Delta p/p_0$ are assumed to be small compared with unity, then Eq. (15-18) becomes

$$\frac{d^2x}{ds^2} + (1 - n) \frac{x}{r_0^2} = \frac{1}{r_0} \frac{\Delta p}{p_0} \tag{15-19}$$

For the present we consider only particles for which $\Delta p = 0$, and the equation of motion becomes

$$\frac{d^2x}{ds^2} - (1 - n) \frac{x}{r_0^2} = 0 \tag{15-20}$$

But
$$\frac{1 - n}{r_0^2} = \frac{n - 1}{-n} \frac{n}{r_0^2} = \frac{n - 1}{-n} \frac{eB'}{m\dot{s}} = \frac{n - 1}{-n} k^2$$

where k is the parameter defined in the preceding section. Consequently the equation of motion becomes

$$\frac{d^2x}{ds^2} + \frac{n - 1}{n} k^2 x = 0 \tag{15-21}$$

In the next magnet sector n and B' will be reversed in sign, and the equation of motion will be

$$\frac{d^2x}{ds^2} - \frac{n + 1}{n} k^2 x = 0 \tag{15-22}$$

These two equations can be combined in the form

$$\frac{d^2x}{ds^2} + \left(f - \frac{1}{n} \right) k^2 x = 0 \tag{15-23}$$

where f is the quantity used in Eq. (15-11); it has the value $+1$ in focusing sectors and -1 in defocusing sectors; Eq. (15-23) is identical with Eq. (15-11) except that f has been replaced by $(f - 1/n)$. But in AG machines n is usually of the order of 100 or more, and hence the term $1/n$ is usually negligible. Therefore it will be found that orbits in circular AG machines will have essentially the same characteristics as orbits in linear machines in so far as radial deviations from the orbit are concerned.

In the vertical plane the equation of motion is identical with that derived in the linear case.

The second point of difference is much more serious. It is now very important that the orbit does not include an integral number of betatron oscillations per revolution. If the number ν of betatron oscillations per revolution is too close to an integer, the smallest orbit perturbation will build up a disastrous oscillation amplitude which, in a few revolutions, will result in complete loss of the beam. This fact was first pointed out by Adams, Hine, and Lawson[4] shortly after the first publication of Courant, Livingston, and Snyder. For a time this observation was rather depressing to the early workers on AG focusing, since some premature optimism about pencil-sized vacuum chambers proved to be invalidated by a high density of resonances. But more sober consideration indicated that, by proper design, the resonance regions, or "stop bands" as they are now called, could quite safely be avoided.

As a result of these resonances the white-necktie diagram of the linear AG system takes on a plaid appearance. The location of the resonances can rather easily be determined from the fact that μ, whose cosine is the quantity presented in Eqs. (15-9) and (15-10), is the phase shift in the betatron oscillation per quadrupole pair. If the closed orbit includes N quadrupole pairs or $2N$ AG quadrupoles, the total phase shift around the orbit will be $N\mu$. If $N\mu$ is an integral multiple of 2π, a resonance will occur. Since μ can reach values as high as π ($\cos\mu = -1$) in the stable region, a system of N quadrupole pairs will have $N/2$ possible resonances in each plane. The location of these resonances for a machine having $N = 24$ is shown in Fig. 15-9. Except for minor corrections because of the inclusion of field-free straight sections between magnet units, this figure applies to the Cambridge AG electron accelerator discussed in Sec. 15-9.

Since the integral resonances cannot be crossed, the stable operating region for a closed AG machine is limited to one of the diamond-shaped regions between resonance lines. Higher-order resonances also are possible—for example, one in which an integral number of betatron oscillations is included in two or more revolutions. The first of these, the "half-integral" resonance, can cause some beam loss but does not appear to be disastrous. Higher-order resonances can be excited in badly distorted fields but do not appear to be very dangerous.

In the case of the half-integral values of ν_r and ν_z, the width of the stop band is small. "Sum" resonances occur where $\nu_r + \nu_z$ is integral; these cross the stability diamond at its mid-point. They also are narrow and need not disturb the beam significantly. The radial-axial resonance, for which $\nu_r = \nu_z$, is of some concern in that certain magnetic anomalies called "twists" can cause a transfer of oscillation energy between these modes; in this case the oscillation frequencies are shifted apart and may move uncomfortably close to an integral resonance.

In the design of constant-gradient AG magnets, the "working point" is chosen to be within the stability diamond at a location where any motion of the point during the acceleration cycle will not cross the more serious resonances. Integral resonances must be avoided; half-integral and sum resonances can be crossed only if the working point moves across the resonance rapidly; twist resonances can be eliminated from concern by weak compensating fields. The exact location of the working point depends on the way in which magnetic properties vary during the cycle. If the magnets are to be pushed to high fields where saturation effects tend to reduce gradients and lower ν_r and ν_z, the initial location of the working point should be in the high-ν region of the stability diamond. Furthermore, low injection fields involve magnetic remanence effects

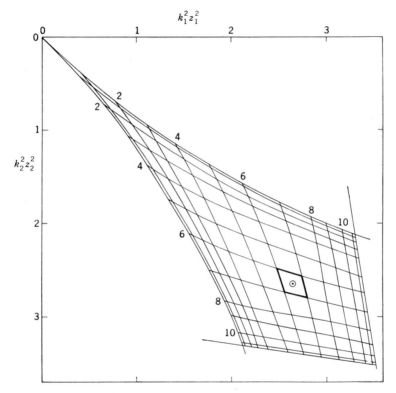

Fig. 15-9. Stability diagram for an AG synchrotron having 24 focusing and 24 defocusing sectors. Integral resonances only are indicated. A possible operating point at $\nu_r = \nu_z = 6.4$ is indicated in the diamond bounded by the sixth- and seventh-order resonances. With minor corrections because of the inclusion of field-free straight sections, this diagram applies to the CEA electron machine described in Sec. 15-9.

which tend to lower ν values; to minimize gradient corrections at and just following injection, the location should be in the high-ν region. Such design and planning considerations lead to a choice of ν either just below the center of the diamond (e.g., $\nu = 6.40$ at Cambridge) or just below the upper tip of the diamond (e.g., $\nu = 8.75$ at Brookhaven). Field correcting windings must be provided to compensate for any major change in location of the working point during the acceleration cycle.

Both linear and closed AG systems are extremely sensitive to misalignments of focusing quadrupoles because AG focusing, though relatively strong, is the net effect of focusing and defocusing forces which, separately, are several times as strong as their combined effect. For instance, it can be shown rather easily from the analysis already presented that the net focusing force in a system having the typical value of 1 for $k_0 z_0$ is lower by a factor of 12 than either of the focusing or defocusing forces that combine to give the AG focusing. This means that if one quadrupole is misaligned by a distance δ, its effects on the beam will be of the order of 12δ. Alternating-gradient focusing systems now in use generally must be aligned to between 0.1 and 0.01 of the tolerable deviation of the particle beam from its orbit. The precise figure depends on the choice of length and strength of the quadrupole focusing units.

15-6. MOMENTUM COMPACTION IN AG SYNCHROTRONS

In the preceding sections it was shown that restoring forces in circular machines with AG focusing are strong enough to reduce betatron oscillation amplitudes to values much lower than those found in machines with conventional or weak focusing. It may not be obvious, however, that particles having momenta that deviate from the equilibrium momentum will not make wide excursions from the equilibrium orbit. If this were so, the phase oscillations in an AG synchrotron would result in large radial motions, and the advantage of small betatron oscillation amplitudes would be lost. Fortunately, this is not the case—large momentum errors result in relatively small radial excursions.

The result just stated is not obvious and is not easily made obvious by qualitative arguments. It seems simplest to trace the orbit for a particle with a momentum error and establish its deviation mathematically. The equation of motion for a particle with a momentum error was established in the last section. It is

$$\frac{d^2x}{ds^2} + (1 - n)\frac{x}{r_0{}^2} = \frac{1}{r_0}\frac{\Delta p}{p_0} \tag{15-19}$$

where n alternates in sign when s increases by a distance s_0. If we set up an origin of coordinates in the center of each quadrupole element and write down the solutions of this equation, we shall obtain a trigonometric function in the radially focusing sectors and a hyperbolic function in the radially defocusing sectors. When these are matched at the boundaries in position and slope we obtain the solutions (assuming that $n \gg 1$) in the radially focusing sectors,

$$x = \frac{1}{k^2 r_0}\frac{\Delta p}{p_0}\left\{1 + \frac{2\cos ks}{\sin (ks_0/2)[\coth (ks_0/2) - \cot (ks_0/2)]}\right\} \tag{15-24}$$

and in the radially defocusing sectors,

$$x = \frac{1}{k^2 r_0} \frac{\Delta p}{p_0} \left\{ -1 + \frac{2 \cosh ks}{\sinh (ks_0/2)[\coth (ks_0/2) - \cot (ks_0/2)]} \right\} \quad (15\text{-}25)$$

The form of this orbit is illustrated in Fig. 15-10.   The average value of x over a distance $2s_0$ is obtained by integrating.   We obtain for $\bar{x}$, the average value of x,

$$\frac{\bar{x}}{r_0} = \frac{4}{k^3 r_0^2 s_0} \frac{\Delta p}{p_0} \left[\frac{1}{\coth (ks_0/2) - \cot (ks_0/2)} \right] \quad (15\text{-}26)$$

But $\coth x - \cot x = 2x/3 + 4x^5/945 +$ higher-order terms.   For x less

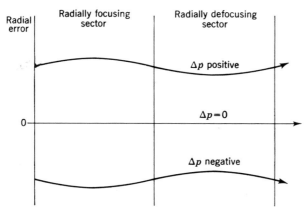

Fig. 15-10. Orbits of particles having positive, zero, and negative momentum errors in an AG synchrotron.

than about 1.1, we are correct to 1 per cent if we set

$$\coth x - \cot x = \frac{2x}{3}$$

So for all likely values of ks_0 the average value of x can be written

$$\frac{\bar{x}}{r_0} = \frac{12}{k^4 r_0^2 s_0^2} \frac{\Delta p}{p_0} \quad (15\text{-}27)$$

We now recall that μ, the phase shift in the betatron oscillation per $2s_0$, is given by

$$\cos \mu = \cos ks_0 \cosh ks_0$$

whence, if ks_0 is less than 1.1, we can write with an error of less than 2 per cent

$$\mu^2 = \frac{k^4 s_0^4}{3} \quad (15\text{-}28)$$

In terms of μ we can write for $\bar{x}$

$$\frac{\bar{x}}{r_0} = \left(\frac{2s_0}{\mu r_0}\right)^2 \frac{\Delta p}{p_0} \tag{15-29}$$

But N, the total number of pairs of quadrupoles around the ring, is $\pi r_0/s_0$, and ν, the total number of betatron oscillations in one revolution, is $N\mu/2\pi$. Hence

$$\frac{\bar{x}}{r_0} = \frac{1}{\nu^2} \frac{\Delta p}{p_0} \tag{15-30}$$

This will prove to be a very important result, since it shows that relatively large momentum errors in AG machines will not result in large displacements of the beam. For example, in the Brookhaven AG synchrotron, where $\nu = 8.75$ and $r_0 = 128.5$ m, the radial error for a 1 per cent momentum error is only about 1.6 cm. In a weak-focusing machine with an n value of 0.7 and a radius of 128.5 m, the radial excursion for a 1 per cent momentum error would be 4.1 m!

15-7. PHASE STABILITY IN AG SYNCHROTRONS

Derivation of the phase excursions in the AG synchrotron follows the same pattern as that deduced for the conventional synchrotron in Sec. 9-8. The one exception is that Eq. (9-52), which described the excursion in radius for a given momentum error, must now be replaced by the momentum compaction relation equation (15-30) derived in the preceding section. With this change the phase oscillation equation (9-57) becomes

$$\frac{d}{dt}\left[\frac{(1 + p^{*2})^{3/2}\,\Delta\phi}{1 + p^{*2} - \nu^2}\right] = \frac{heV\,\cos\,\phi_0\,\Delta\phi}{2\pi r_0{}^2 m_0\nu^2} \tag{15-31}$$

where $\Delta\phi$ = phase error
  eV = energy gain per revolution
  ϕ_0 = equilibrium phase
  p^* = mv/m_0c, whence $1 + p^{*2} = (1 - v^2/c^2)^{-1} = (W/W_0)^2$
  ν = number of betatron wavelengths per turn
  W = total energy of particle, ev
  W_0 = m_0c^2/e = rest energy of particle, ev
When $1 + p^{*2}$ is replaced by $(W/W_0)^2$, Eq. (15-31) becomes

$$\frac{d}{dt}\left[\frac{W\,\Delta\phi}{1/\nu^2 - (W_0/W)^2}\right] = \frac{hc^2V\,\cos\,\phi_0\,\Delta\phi}{2\pi r_0{}^2} \tag{15-32}$$

This equation has consequences somewhat more complicated than previous phase-stability equations since the quantity $1/\nu^2$ is usually much less than unity in AG synchrotrons. For energies W less than νW_0 the phase oscillation will be stable only if $\cos \phi_0$ is positive as in the linear accelerator. For W greater than νW_0 the phase oscillation is stable only if $\cos \phi_0$ is negative as in the conventional synchrotron. The energy νW_0 is evidently a transition energy (and will be written W_{tr}) at which the equilibrium phase shifts discontinuously from one side of the accelerating wave to the other.

The reason for this behavior is that at low energies, momentum compaction effects prevent the orbit from wandering in radius enough to permit action of the conventional synchrotron mechanism. What remains of the synchrotron mechanism is overpowered by the linear-accelerator mechanism—particles which have too much energy return more quickly to their starting point, and vice versa. Above the transition energy, however, the particles have approached so closely to the constant velocity of light that the linear-accelerator mechanism is no longer strong enough to overpower the residual synchrotron mechanism and the machine suddenly begins to operate like a conventional synchrotron.

The phase transition phenomena predicted for AG synchrotrons troubled early designers who, at that time, were not confident of their ability to make the necessary sudden shift in phase of the accelerating signal. An ingenious, though cumbersome, design that avoided the phase transition was evolved by Vladimirskij and Tarasov,[8] and work was initiated in the U.S.S.R. on a model of this design. Further theoretical analysis of orbit behavior at phase transition was made at CERN[9] and at Brookhaven[7] with encouraging results, to be outlined below. Finally an electrostatically focused AG electron synchrotron (the "electron analogue") was built at Brookhaven, and it was shown that the phase transition could be passed with relative ease.

In the neighborhood of phase transition the phase-oscillation relation equation (15-32) must be rewritten. Since v is approximately equal to c in this region, the momentum equation (9-58) can be written

$$p_0 = \frac{eW}{c} = \frac{eVt \sin \phi_0}{2\pi r_0}$$

whence

$$W - W_{tr} = \frac{cV \, \Delta t \sin \phi_0}{2\pi r_0}$$

where Δt represents the difference in time between the achievements of energies W and W_{tr}. When these simplifications are inserted in Eq. (15-32), it becomes

$$\frac{d}{dt}\left(\frac{\Delta \phi}{\Delta t}\right) + K \, \Delta \phi = 0 \qquad (15\text{-}33)$$

where

$$K = \frac{W_0^2 hc^3 V^2 \cos \phi_0 \sin \phi_0}{2\pi^2 r_0^3}$$

Equation (15-33) has a solution in Bessel functions of order $\frac{2}{3}$ which approaches finite limits as Δt approaches zero. For the details of this treatment the reader is referred to the work of K. Johnsen[9] and of Courant and Snyder.[7] It is, however, evident that Eq. (15-33) bears some resemblance to the equation of motion of a pendulum whose mass is increased without limit; at $\Delta t = 0$ the mass has become infinite and the motion is stopped momentarily. This analogy is qualitatively correct; at phase transition the amplitude of phase oscillation is momentarily reduced to a small value. At the same time the momentum errors are momentarily increased, since they are proportional to the rate of change of the phase error [cf. Eq. (9-53)]. Fortunately, in actual AG machines we find that the increase in momentum error and in radial position error does not reach, at transition, the values which have already been passed shortly after injection. For these reasons it has proved possible to pass the phase transition by the mere insertion of a discontinuous phase jump at the correct time. In the Brookhaven and CERN AG proton synchrotrons the timing of the phase jump must be correct to about 1 msec, an easily attainable precision.

15-8. AG PROTON SYNCHROTRONS

At the end of 1961 two large AG proton synchrotrons were in operation —the 28-Bev machine at CERN and the 33-Bev accelerator at Brookhaven. A third 7-Bev model in Moscow was scheduled for operation in 1962; it was to provide design information for a 50- to 70-Bev machine whose construction was beginning in the U.S.S.R. The AG proton synchrotron held undisputed sway over all other accelerator types. The Brookhaven and CERN machines achieved energies higher by a factor of 3 than any other accelerator types. The only possible competitor was the Stanford electron linac, still in the design stage. At the time of writing it appears that no particle energies higher than 33 Bev will be achieved before 1965.

Some of the history of the Brookhaven and CERN projects has already been told in the first section of this chapter. The collaboration between the two groups which began in 1952 with the discovery of AG focusing was maintained throughout the construction period, and, as a result, the two machines have striking similarities. An early debate was held in both groups about the wisdom of proceeding to construction around an untested idea. The theoretical groups in both centers were concerned about the validity of their analyses of the beam behavior at phase transition, and the interpretations of the effects of magnet misalignments were complex and subject to some question. In both centers proposals were made for construction of a low-energy AG-focused electron synchrotron as a check on the theory before the final commitment of some 30 million dollars. Finally it was decided that the electron machine should be built at Brookhaven; for CERN this was a happy solution, since the CERN group could now proceed with design without drastic commitment before results emerged from the Brookhaven electron machine.

The AG electron accelerator was in no sense a model. It was designed for electrostatic AG focusing and for a final energy of 10 Mev. It was merely to serve as a computer to solve the problems of phase transition and misalignment, and so it came to be known as the "electron analogue." At the end of 1955 this machine was brought into operation; in every respect the electron beam supported the theoretical predictions.[10] Phase transition was passed with no detectable loss of beam, and beam resonances proved to be exactly as predicted. Both CERN and Brookhaven proceeded into construction with feelings of deep relief (except for certain members who had sufficient faith in theory that they believed the model to be unnecessary). The CERN proton synchrotron (generally known as the CERN PS) was completed and brought to energy in November, 1959; the Brookhaven AG machine (known as the Brookhaven AGS) reached its design energy in July of 1960. After a tune-up period of about 3 months both machines went into operation for high-energy experiments. Initial operation was at one shift per week. Within about 2 years it is expected that both machines will operate day and night, 7 days a week. Beam intensities of 3×10^{11} protons/pulse had been achieved both at CERN and at Brookhaven with no evidence of limitation by space charge.

The CERN project was initiated under the direction of O. Dahl of Norway and F. Goward of the United Kingdom. Later, Dahl returned to Norway; soon afterward, because of Goward's sudden death, direction of the PS passed to J. B. Adams of the United Kingdom and C. Schmelzer of Germany. The Brookhaven AGS was built under the direction of L. J. Haworth, G. K. Green, and the junior author (JPB).

The differences between the CERN PS and the Brookhaven AGS are almost entirely in mechanical design. No important differences exist in basic concepts. The writers, whose acquaintance with the Brookhaven machine is much more intimate, will therefore consider it sufficient to describe the AGS with only occasional reference to points of difference between Brookhaven and CERN.

The AGS includes 240 magnet sectors in an FFDD sequence (F is a focusing and D a defocusing sector), which means that the number N of quadrupole pairs (Sec. 15-5) is 60. The circumference of the ring is about 800 m, and the distances occupied by one lens element (in this case, two magnets) is 6.7 m. The ratio of magnetic-field gradient B' to magnetic field B is about 4.2 per cent per centimeter or 4.2 per meter. Hence k^2 ($= eB'/mv$ as before $= B'/Br_0$) is 0.033. The phase shift μ of the betatron oscillation per quadrupole pair [$\mu = k^2 s_0^2/\sqrt{3}$ from Eq. (15-28)] is 0.85. Hence the total number ν of betatron oscillations per

revolution should, on this approximate analysis, be 8.1. This is somewhat oversimplified, however, because the magnets in the AGS occupy
only about two-thirds of the circumference of the ring and are separated
by field-free straight sections of various lengths. When a detailed
analysis is made of the orbits through magnets and straight sections, it is
found that the correct value of ν for the AGS is 8.75.

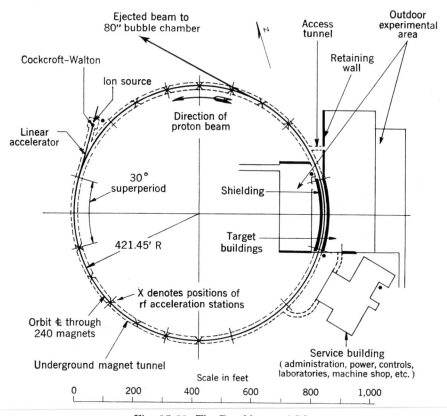

Fig. 15-11. The Brookhaven AGS.

The AGS magnets are arranged in 12 "superperiods" or identical groups
of 20 magnets each. Between superperiods and in the middle of each
superperiod is a 10-ft straight section that can be used either for one of
the 12 accelerating stations, for injection, for targets, or for other beam
ejection means. The magnets are C-shaped, and the first 10 magnets in
each superperiod have their return legs outside the orbit; the next 10
return legs lie inside the orbit. This configuration allows ejected or
scattered beams to clear magnet structures alternately inside and outside
the orbit so experiments can be set up both inside and outside the ring.

Between the magnets within the half-superperiods 12 of the straight sections are 2 ft in length and 6 are 5 ft in length.

The general configuration of the AGS is shown in Fig. 15-11.   Injection is roughly opposite the target area.   The experimental area around the target region of the ring was expanded shortly after the machine became operative to a total of about 80,000 ft^2, or about 2 acres.   This enormous area is needed because beam-handling and analyzing equipment for 30-Bev particles is inevitably massive and extensive.   At this energy a magnet maintaining a 20-kilogauss field over a distance of 10 ft bends a particle beam by less than 3°.   Counter telescopes are long and complex, bubble chambers have grown to lengths of 6 ft and more, and adjacent beams from the machine aimed at different experiments must be shielded from each other by enormous masses of concrete.   Merely to protect the experimental area from the circulating beam in the synchrotron the target building requires a tunnel made of concrete blocks weighing a total of 14,000 tons.

The major components of the machine are as follows.

The Magnet

The AGS magnet configuration was shown in cross section in Fig. 15-8. Each magnet is about 36 by 39 in. in cross section and is about 8 ft long. Total weight of the 240 magnets is about 4000 tons.   The pole contour was determined to give a constant field gradient over as wide a region as possible; it was computed by relaxation methods (see Sec. 8-3) and was verified by exhaustive model measurements.   The magnet pole is 12 in. thick and gives a satisfactory field pattern over a radial region 7 in. in extent.   This pattern is good up to about 11 kilogauss, where it begins to deteriorate, and it becomes unusable at about 13 kilogauss.   If, to the cyclotron expert, this seems rather a low field, it must be emphasized that field gradients are high and that fields of 13 kilogauss at the orbit correspond to fields of over 20 kilogauss at the minimum gap.

The field in the AGS magnet reaches its peak in about 1 sec and is restored to zero in about the same period.   At 30 Bev the cycle can be repeated every 2.4 sec.   At 20 Bev the shorter cycle can be repeated every 1.6 sec, and at 10 Bev the repetition period can be reduced still further to 0.8 sec.

To keep eddy-current effects to a minimum, the magnet is constructed of 0.030-in. laminations.   A study of the magnetic properties of steel by the Brookhaven magnet group revealed the fact that steel's most unreliable magnetic property is its coercive force and hence its remanent field. At injection field, about 120 gauss, remanent effects are very important. Accordingly, further studies were made of effects on remanence of chemical composition, heat treatment, etc., of steel.   The conclusion of the study was that no clear-cut predictions are possible at the present stage of the steelmaking art. The only solution appeared to be a thorough shuffling of magnet laminations from the complete series of production runs. Although this involved the use of a large area of a steel plant over a long period, the steel industry was very helpful, and all requirements of the magnet group were met. As a result the magnets as finally assembled were remarkably uniform in properties. All magnets were carefully measured; at intermediate fields they were found to be identical to better than 2 parts in 10,000. At injection fields they were identical to about 4 parts in 10,000, a quite acceptable figure.

The laminations were stamped by a carbide die whose precision was better than 0.001 in. They were stacked and welded into an open box structure under high pressure.

The magnet coils are in four units per magnet (see Fig. 8-13). Each unit was carefully insulated with mica and glass cloth and was cast in polyester resin; the individual units each include eight turns and are of such a thickness that they can be inserted through the gap of the assembled magnet core and moved into final position. A series-parallel connection of the coils gives the complete magnet a peak rating of 7000 amp at about 5000 volts.

In the AGS, errors in magnet location result in errors in orbit location about twenty times greater. It was agreed that orbit displacements up to 1 cm could be tolerated; thus tolerances on magnet location of about 0.5 mm or 0.020 in. were fixed. These tolerances proved, on more detailed analysis, to be valid over a limited range, specifically over a betatron wavelength. The greater the distance around the ring, the more relaxed became the tolerances. This fuzzy definition was clarified when it became evident that only misalignments which produced field errors including a harmonic close to the ν value of 8.75 were of paramount importance, and other harmonics were of lesser importance depending on their displacement from ν. Strict attention was paid to anything that could produce a seventh, eighth, ninth, or tenth harmonic in the field pattern. Correcting coils were included and connected for application of these harmonics. To date it has not been necessary to use these corrections.

A machine of $\frac{1}{2}$ mile circumference to be aligned to 0.5 mm local precision raises unusual problems of soil mechanics. It is not customary to build structures to such precision, and few precedents exist for this undertaking. Both at CERN and at Brookhaven the earth and its underpinnings were studied very carefully. At CERN a test-tunnel section was built and observed over a long period. At Brookhaven load tests on the local soil were run by piling and unpiling some 2000 tons of concrete. The problems in the two sites proved to be completely different. At CERN a thin layer of shale covered a soft bedrock (the Molasse) that was subject to earthquake tremors and to seasonal displacements with the snow load on adjacent mountains.   At Brookhaven the laboratory is built on sand that extends in a relatively homogeneous fashion to a depth of 1500 ft down to bedrock.   At CERN, accordingly, it was necessary to support the magnet on a monolithic concrete ring supported on springs, while at Brookhaven the magnet rests on concrete caps covering steel piles driven 50 ft into the sand.   (It seems that it is not always unwise to build on the shifting sand.)   Both foundations have proved stable and satisfactory.

Eddy-current effects at injection fields did not appear to be troublesome so far as the magnet was concerned.   Serious field distortions appeared, however, in auxiliaries, particularly in the Inconel vacuum chamber where thickness tolerances could not be met with sufficient precision to guarantee azimuthal uniformity of eddy-current depression of the field. It was therefore decided at Brookhaven to decrease the initial rate of rise of the magnetic field by a factor of 4 by inclusion in series of a saturating inductor whose saturation characteristic was such as to hold $\dot{B}/B$ at or below its value at injection.   This proved to be a 200-ton device whose performance was precisely as predicted.   At CERN no series inductor has been included.

For adjustment of the initial ν values and for field corrections at high fields both Brookhaven and CERN have included a number of multipole magnets.   In the AGS, 24 quadrupole magnets can be adjusted to keep the ν values constant as the magnet saturates; 36 sextupoles can be used to correct nonlinearities in the field pattern or, in other words, to keep ν constant with radius.   At CERN a number of octupoles can be used to correct second-order field disturbances.   These are not included in the AGS.   Very careful and detailed orbit studies will be necessary to prove whether or not octupoles are useful.

The power supply for the AGS magnet system is similar to that used at the Brookhaven cosmotron (see Sec. 13-5).   It includes a 35,000-kva 12-phase alternator driven by a 5000-hp motor and carrying on the same shaft a 40-ton flywheel for energy storage and equalization of load on the power line.   The output of the alternator is rectified in a bank of 24 ignitrons and then supplied directly to the magnet through an extra magnet unit which supplies field to various timing devices necessary for timing injection, rf turn-on, etc.   These are, for the most part, peaking strips or wires of high-permeability material which are located in biasing coils and which bear windings (see Sec. 8-8).   As the field plus bias passes through zero, these strips go rather suddenly from negative to positive saturation.   A peaked signal is induced in the windings and can be used for timing.   The time of appearance of the peak can be adjusted by variation of the current in the bias winding.

The various multipoles also are powered by rotating machines, in this case dc generators with programmed field control.

Injection

Both at CERN and at Brookhaven, protons are injected into the synchrotron ring at 50 Mev. At Brookhaven, ions produced in a cold-cathode ion source are preaccelerated to 750 kev in a Cockcroft-Walton set built by Philips and consisting of a cascade-transformer voltage-multiplier stack and a filter stack supported on a 0.008-μf capacitor and supplied through a 5-megohm resistor from the cascade transformer.

The Brookhaven linear accelerator[11] is electrically a single tank of copper-clad steel. Mechanically it consists of 11 pipes of copper-clad steel about 3 ft in diameter and 10 ft long, flanged at their ends and bolted together. The shapes of the 124 drift tubes were computed,[12] and they were machined out of solid copper. At the low-energy end they are pancake-shaped; as their length increases along the tank, they become first almost spherical and then football-shaped. In each drift tube is a pulsed quadrupole magnet for compensation of the defocusing effects of the accelerating field. Radiofrequency power required is about 3 megawatts at 200 megacycles—this is supplied at the center of the tank by two TH-470 (French Thomson-Houston) triodes whose outputs are combined in a waveguide hybrid junction.

From the linac output the proton beam travels (see Fig. 15-12) about 140 ft through focusing and steering arrays, viewing screens, defining slits, and an analyzing magnet which is used to deflect the beam for measurement of energy and energy spread. The path approaching the injection point is parallel to the synchrotron orbit but displaced 3 in. outward. Approaching the inflector, the beam is bent by the stray fields of three magnet sectors and enters the inflector with an inward direction of 1.5°. The inflector consists of two plates on either side of the orbit, charged to + and −80 kv. This field straightens the proton orbit and directs the protons into the desired equilibrium orbit in the synchrotron. When the synchrotron vacuum chamber is filled, the field is turned off in a fraction of a microsecond; if it is left on, the beam is lost on its second traversal through the inflector.

The injection field in the AGS is 120 gauss; in the CERN PS injection is at about 150 gauss. In both cases the injection field is several times the remanent field. Higher injection energy would move injection into still higher and more uniform fields, but construction of injectors of energies higher than 50 Mev introduces serious problems of both cost and design of the electrostatic inflector. Independent studies at Brookhaven and CERN both resulted in the choice of 50 Mev as the optimum energy for injection.

The 50-Mev linac injector for the AGS has its output beam included in an area about 1 cm in diameter and with an angular spread of about 2 milliradians. This beam is easily matched to the synchrotron's require-

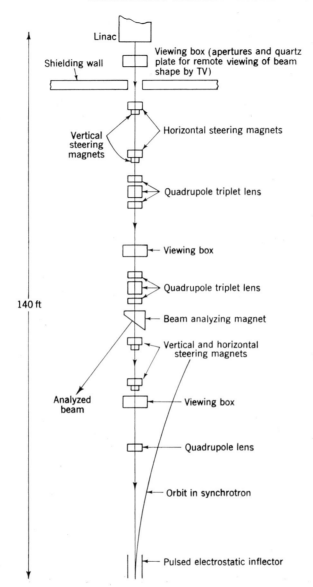

Fig. 15-12. Injection system of the Brookhaven AGS.

ments; no appreciable fraction of the beam is lost between linac output and synchrotron input.

RF Accelerating System

At 50 Mev the injected protons have about one-third of the velocity of light, while at 30 Bev the velocity has reached about 0.9995 of the velocity of light.   The frequency of the accelerating system must therefore vary over a factor of about 3.   This variation takes place very rapidly during the first fraction of the cycle.   Transition energy in the AGS is about 7 Bev and is reached in less than $\frac{1}{4}$ sec; by this time better than 99 per cent of the frequency range has been covered.

The frequency of revolution increases from its injection value of 125 kc to 375 kc at full energy.   If this frequency were used in the accelerating system, however, the radial excursions due to the phase oscillation would be large, and the various accelerating stations around the ring would have small phase shifts with respect to each other to be maintained over the whole frequency range.   To avoid these difficulties, the rf system uses the twelfth harmonic of the fundamental frequency and operates from 1.5 to 4.5 megacycles.   Stations located in twelve of the twenty-four 10-ft straight sections are supplied from a central driver by cables of equal lengths; the stations run either in phase or 180° out of phase with each other, depending on their location.

Energy gain per turn is about 100 kev, or 8 kev per accelerating station. The accelerating units are double ferrite-loaded cavities kept in tune by saturation of the ferrite.   The saturating current of about 1000 amp maximum passes through the wall of the accelerating cavity and is controlled by a bank of 100 paralleled power transistors.

The accelerating frequency in an AG synchrotron must be controlled with much higher precision than that in a classical synchrotron, particularly around transition.   This problem is met in the AGS by deriving the accelerating signal directly from the proton beam.   The beam is bunched in the first few revolutions after injection by a programmed oscillator, and the primary signal is then derived from a cylindrical electrode through which the beam passes.   This signal is amplified and brought to the accelerating stations.   It still is possible for slow phase drifts to cause the beam to drift inward or outward; this is corrected by derivation of a signal from a pair of pickup electrodes inside and outside the beam orbit and application of the signal to a controlled phase shifter in the chain to the accelerating units.   The pickup-electrode signal is proportional to beam displacement and is fed back with such a polarity as to reduce this displacement.   This system, used both at Brookhaven and at CERN, appears to hold the beam throughout acceleration with no detectable loss after the first few milliseconds.   At transition, a sudden phase shift of about 120° transfers the operating phase from one side of the accelerating wave to the other.   This phase shift must be made in a fraction of a millisecond at a time correct to better than 1 msec, tolerances that are rather easily met.

It was thought originally that losses at transition would be decreased by decreasing the amplitude of the accelerating signal as the phase is shifted, and the possibility of modulating in this fashion was incorporated in the AGS rf system.   Since, without changing amplitude, there is no apparent beam loss at transition, this modulation is not used.

Vacuum System

The vacuum chamber in the AGS is approximately elliptical in cross section, with the major axis horizontal and 7 in. in extent; vertically the maximum dimension is a little over 3 in.   It is fabricated of Inconel, a stainless metal of high resistivity (over 100 μohm-cm) and 0.078 in. thick. In almost all magnet gaps the chamber has the configuration just described, but in some places special sections are fabricated of greater width to permit injection or beam ejection.   In the straight sections are located bellows, vacuum pumps, valves, pickup-electrode stations, target boxes, beam-ejection mechanisms, and other miscellany.

The AGS is pumped entirely by Evapor-ion pumps, which operate by a combination of the gettering action of evaporated titanium and the pumping action of a glow discharge.   These pumps were chosen since they do not require refrigerated baffles or cold traps.   For the linear accelerator they seemed particularly appropriate since they would introduce no organic contamination into the high rf field regions.   After about 18 months of operation this still appears to have been a wise choice, since the intense X rays emitted by linacs with oil pumps have not yet appeared.

Targets

In both the AGS and the PS, thin targets are used through which the beam makes multiple traversals.   Scattering by atomic electrons is small enough that a proton that has not made a nuclear collision will continue to circulate, contained by the strong momentum compaction of the AG machines.   Circulation continues until the proton makes a nuclear collision; thus very high target efficiencies are achieved.

An undesirable feature of the accelerated beam from the experimental point of view is its bunching by the rf accelerating signal which, at full energy, results in the containment of all protons in bunches occupying less than 10 per cent of the azimuth.   This results in intermittent jamming and inactivity of counters used in detection of collision products. To avoid this problem the beam is debunched by turning off the rf accelerating field and allowing the beam to drift, under the influence of the still-rising magnetic field, to a target located an inch or so inside the equilibrium orbit.   This requires a period of several milliseconds, during which the beam becomes rather thoroughly debunched.

The output of both machines includes large numbers of μ mesons (muons) which are weakly interacting particles.   Consequently they appear in large numbers even after interposition of more than 15 ft of heavy (iron-loaded) concrete.   These particles seem to present the worst shielding problem and may be quite troublesome in experiments that require low background.

Operation

Both at Brookhaven and at CERN the hopes of the synchrotron designers have been exceeded by the performance of the AG machines. Reasonable care in meeting design tolerances has been rewarded by a steady beam that appears to deviate from the center of the vacuum chamber by not more than a centimeter.   Variation of parameters of the magnetic field and its gradient results in observations of beam behavior in perfect agreement with theoretical predictions.   Integral resonances are indeed impassable, but half-integral and other resonances can be crossed with impunity.

From the performance of the two large AG synchrotrons now operating it is safe to predict that the present method can be extrapolated upward in energy by at least a factor of 10 without serious technical difficulty. Cost appears to be the only visible limitation on extension of the AG art to hundreds or thousands of Bev.

15-9. AG ELECTRON SYNCHROTRONS

The principle of acceleration in the electron synchrotron is basically simpler than for the proton synchrotron, since electrons approach the limiting velocity of light at relatively low energies, and their orbital frequency becomes constant.   This allows the use of high-Q resonant cavities for acceleration, without the need for frequency modulation and requiring much lower power.   Some amount of preacceleration is required to reach constant orbital frequency.   This was accomplished in the constant-gradient synchrotrons (see Chap. 12) either by use of an external preaccelerator and an inflection system to direct the linear beam into the orbit or by initial betatron acceleration in the synchrotron field.

In AG electron synchrotrons it is easy to avoid the technical difficulties associated with the phase transition; a transition energy exists, but usually it is below the injection energy.   As was shown in Sec. 15-7, phase transition takes place at an energy of νW_0.   For most AG machines now in operation or construction ν is of the order of 10.   For electrons W_0 is about 0.5 Mev; the transition energy will thus be of the order of 5 Mev, which lies below the energy of the linac injectors planned for the AG electron machines in construction.

Alternating-gradient magnets allow considerable reduction in dimensions of the magnet and the gap between poles; at the same time they reduce the momentum compaction factor to make acceptable a much larger fractional spread in momentum than in the constant-gradient machines.   The basic principle of acceleration is unchanged, and the

advantages of constant-frequency acceleration remain.   The real significance of AG focusing is that much higher energies become economically
practical and technically feasible.   (However, the higher energies introduce new and serious design problems involving the energy loss by the
orbiting electrons due to radiation.)   Furthermore, the smaller size of
magnets and the reduction in magnetic stored energy allow the AG magnets to be pulsed at a higher repetition rate than has been customary with
constant-gradient magnets.   The faster cycling rate results in significantly higher time-average beam intensities, as well as higher energies.
The AG electron synchrotron is capable of producing beam intensities
approaching those from linear accelerators, with similar cycling rates and
with a considerably larger duty cycle for the high-energy beam; the long
duty cycle has many advantages for research using electronic detection
apparatus.

A fundamental limitation on any magnetic accelerator for electrons is
the radiation loss due to radial acceleration in the magnetic field.   The
loss per turn (see Sec. 7-7) is

$$V = 8.85 \times 10^4 \frac{W^4}{r_0} \qquad \text{ev/turn} \qquad (15\text{-}34)$$

where W is total electron energy in Bev units and r_0 is radius of curvature
in meters of the orbit in the magnetic field.

Since radiation loss varies inversely with radius, problems can be minimized by using large orbit radius and a correspondingly low magnetic
field.   However, the fourth-power increase with energy limits the maximum energy for which practical designs can be conceived to about 50
Bev.   Even at lower energies the economic advantage of the circular
machine relative to the linac decreases.   The large orbits (and low fields)
result in increasing the size of buildings to house the ring-shaped accelerator, and the buildings become the most costly components.

The first large AG electron synchrotron aimed at approaching this
practical maximum energy limit is the Cambridge electron accelerator
(CEA), sponsored by MIT and Harvard University with a design energy
of 6 Bev;[13] it is scheduled for completion in 1962.   Two similar machines
are now (1961) under construction, with the same design energy and based
to a large extent on the CEA designs; one is at the Deutsches Elektronen
Synchrotron (DESY) laboratory at Hamburg, Germany,[13] and the other
at the Institute of Physics laboratory of the Armenian Academy of
Sciences at Erevan, Armenia, U.S.S.R.[13]   Since the Cambridge machine
is further advanced and includes most of the features planned in the other
laboratories, it will be described in some detail.

Several electron synchrotrons of lower energy utilize AG focusing.   At
Cornell University an electron synchrotron originally planned as a constant-gradient machine was modified to use AG pole faces, more as an

experiment in design than because of any fundamental requirement; it was brought into operation in 1954 and has been developed to deliver 1.1-Bev electrons. The Cornell machine was the first practical AG accelerator, and its success reinforced confidence in other laboratories in the design of still-higher-energy machines. Later, a 500-Mev AG synchrotron was built at the Physikalisches Institute der Universität, Bonn, and was completed in 1959. Two other AG electron synchrotrons are approaching completion (1961), each for about 1.2 Bev energy; one is at the University of Lund and the other at the University of Tokyo.

The Cambridge electron accelerator is sponsored by MIT and Harvard University, under the direction of the senior author (MSL); it is supported by the United States Atomic Energy Commission. Detailed design started in 1956. It was conceived as a research installation for the university scientists of the area for the study of high-energy particle physics. Electrons were chosen because of their obvious value as a supplement to protons in the field of high-energy interactions. The design energy of 6 Bev is five times greater than has been reached in existing electron accelerators and is sufficient for production of all known fundamental particles (except xi pairs). At this energy it will be possible to extend electron scattering experiments into a new energy range. The energy approaches the technically practical limit possible with circular machines, within the size of the available site of Harvard University.

The limitation on maximum energy due to radiation loss, based on Eq. (15-34), requires a relatively large orbit radius and lower magnetic fields than those normally used in proton synchrotrons. The choice of an orbit radius of approximately 118 ft leads to a peak magnetic field of about 7600 gauss for 6 Bev energy. This peak flux density is well below the value where magnetic saturation effects occur, and it removes the need for magnetic correcting devices at high energy; it also results in relatively small magnetic stored energy and low power requirements. Another valuable consequence is the opportunity to use a high repetition rate (60 cps), which minimizes the growth of radiation-induced oscillations and also results in a high time-average beam intensity. The several major components will be discussed in turn.

Magnet

The design of the system of AG magnets is based upon the requirement of strong momentum compaction, the need for a simple structure which can be assembled with precision to give the best obtainable uniformity between magnets, and the desire to minimize power requirements and cost of construction. The periodicity of the magnet structure ($N = 24$ AG units) and the number of betatron oscillations per turn ($\nu = 6.40$) were chosen to obtain a small momentum compaction factor (0.03). The periodic structure is a simple alternation of 24 F (focusing) and 24

D (defocusing) magnets spaced by field-free regions O; one AG period can be represented by the symbols FODO. The 48 magnets are identical except for the alternation in shape of pole faces, and they have equal field strengths at the "isomagnetic line" at the center of the magnetic-field region. The C-shaped back-legs of the magnetic circuit are all on the inside of the orbit, so beams of radiation can emerge tangentially from the vacuum chamber at any point around the orbit.

The pole-face shape is basically hyperbolic, to give uniform gradients in both radial and vertical coordinates. The distance from the isomagnetic line to the vertical axis of this hyperbola determines pole-face shape and is a measure of the focusing strength of the magnet; it is called the "characteristic length" and has the value $q = 11.38$ in. (see Fig. 15-6). The value of q determines the magnetic gradient through the relation

$$q = \frac{B_0}{dB/dr}$$

and it is associated with the n value of AG theory by $n = r_0/q$, where r_0 is the radius of curvature of the equilibrium orbit at the isomagnetic line. One of the primary advantages of the FODO structure is that the value of q can be varied (over a small range determined by the useful width of field) by moving one class of magnets radially inward and the other class radially outward. This independent adjustment of the effective gradient allows the ν value to be varied around the design value of 6.40 for high fields.

The pole-face profile varies slightly from the ideal hyperbolic shape to provide a small variation in gradient across the pole face. This variation is designed to keep betatron oscillation frequency independent of the radial location of the equilibrium orbit, coming from the "breathing" motion of the equilibrium orbit associated with the synchronous oscillations in particle momentum. If it were not applied, the betatron frequency would change (about 2 per cent per inch) with radial location, which could result in coupling between the betatron and synchronous oscillations and the introduction of satellite stop bands due to field or gradient errors; crossing such stop bands could lead to loss of beam intensity. This variation from hyperbolic shape produces a sextupole field distortion; it takes the place of the sextupole lenses used in proton AG synchrotrons to provide similar corrections at high fields. So quadrupole or sextupole magnetic lenses are not needed in the Cambridge accelerator for magnetic corrections at high fields.

The length of magnet gap is minimized to reduce excitation requirements; it is chosen as 2 in. at the isomagnetic line. Pole width is $6\frac{1}{2}$ in., with the isomagnetic line 3 in. from the open face of the gap; this provides about 5 in. of useful width of essentially constant-gradient field. To minimize edge effects and extend the region of useful field, the "nose" at the closed-gap side is rounded, and a flat step is provided at the open-gap side. This choice of vertical and radial aperture was based on computed oscillation amplitudes just following injection, assuming certain limitations on the properties of the injected beam from the linac preaccelerator. The aperture will accept an energy spread of 2.5 per cent, an angular divergence of 1.5×10^{-3} radian, and a beam diameter of 0.5 in.; it also includes a factor of safety to allow for growth of amplitudes due to alignment errors or magnetic inhomogeneities, and space for the walls of the vacuum chamber. The pole-face shape and vacuum-chamber dimensions are illustrated in the sketch of Fig. 15-13.

Magnet cores are formed of 0.014-in. sheets of high-silicon transformer steel, to minimize losses at 60 cps excitation, and are die-cut to the chosen

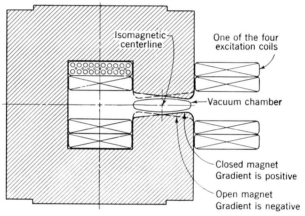

Fig. 15-13. Magnet configuration and vacuum chamber for the CEA AG electron synchrotron.

pole-face shape with 0.0005-in. precision. Sheets are sorted and preselected in sequence to randomize any nonuniformity of material or manufacture. They are bonded into blocks about 11 in. long with a rubber-base phenolic resin, utilizing an assembly and bonding jig which maintains 0.001-in. precision. The individual magnet is assembled on a heavy box girder about 12 ft long, using 12 core blocks in two straight assemblies of 6 blocks each, mounted on machined rails which make an angle of 3.75° (360°/96) to conform more closely to the circular orbit. The rails are machined flat and located with a precision of 0.002 in., and they provide the basic alignment for each magnet. Each set of six core blocks is clamped between nonmagnetic stainless-steel end plates by insulated stainless-steel tie rods. These end plates also carry a ¾-in. layer of laminations oriented normal to the ends of the magnet poles, to minimize eddy currents in the laminations due to fringing fields in the magnet ends. These "end packets" of transverse laminations reduce heating of the end laminations to the extent that lamination cooling is not required for full-power operation. A wedge-shaped space at the center of the magnet between the two straight assemblies, about 4 in. long, is used to admit coil leads, cooling water tubes, etc.

Each magnet is energized by a 40-turn winding, in the form of four flat coils which enclose the 12 core blocks and end packets and are thin enough to be inserted between the magnet pole tips ($1\frac{1}{2}$ in.). The conductor is a double layer of stranded cable, with individual strands insulated to prevent circulating eddy currents, embedded in a resin binder (see Fig. 8-13). The heat is removed by water circulating in copper tubing meshed between the conductors and also embedded in the resin

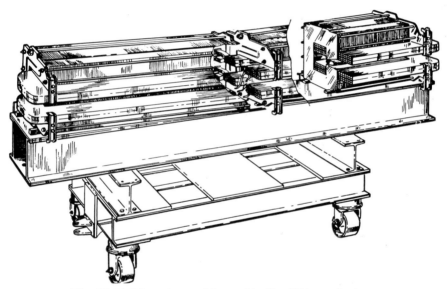

Fig. 15-14. Magnet assembly used in the CEA synchrotron.

binder of the coil. The structure and assembly of the magnet unit is illustrated in the sketch of Fig. 15-14.

Magnets are mounted on adjustable supports resting on piers which are physically separated from the floor of the circular tunnel and mounted on piles driven deep into the subsoil. These supports consist of jacks and hydraulically invoked ball bearings for transverse motion, capable of reproducible settings within 0.001 in. An optical surveying procedure is used to locate magnets with a positional accuracy of ± 0.01 in. (rms) in the radial and azimuthal coordinates and ± 0.005 in. in the vertical. This procedure uses a ring of 16 survey monuments outside the circle of magnets, along with accurately machined jigs to hold measuring instruments mounted on the machined magnet rails and the die-cut surfaces of the magnet cores. The surveying techniques are adequate to obtain satisfactory alignment for initial operations.

Magnet Power

The magnet excitation cycle is a full-biased sinusoidal waveform obtained by superposition of a 60-cycle component of current with peak amplitude $\frac{1}{2}I_m$ and a dc component with amplitude $\frac{1}{2}I_m$, following the relation

$$I(t) = \frac{1}{2}I_m(1 - \cos 2\pi ft) \tag{15-35}$$

Full-biased excitation is desirable to make the time rate of change of field at injection $(dB/dt)_i$ small, which reduces eddy-current distortion of the field at this critical time. It also minimizes power requirements by reducing magnetic losses to those in a half-cycle.

The power-supply system for the magnet of the CEA has several unique features. It is entirely electronic and uses no motor-generator equipment. The dc bias current is provided by a three-phase full-wave rectifier circuit using commercial ignitrons. This supplies all 48 magnets in series, with an output of 420 amp at 840 volts.

The ac circuit is essentially a self-excited class-C oscillator, operating at a resonant frequency of 60 cps and having a Q of over 100. This circuit involves energy storage inductors (air-gap) and capacitors, connected to separate magnets (in pairs) in such a way that there are 24 resonant subunits of the circuit. The electric circuit is shown in Fig. 15-15. The air-gap inductor has minimum excitation when the magnets are fully excited and stores the entire magnetic energy when the magnets are at zero excitation; the capacitors are arranged in banks to transfer energy from magnet to inductor and back and to provide 60-cycle resonance. To ensure that current in the magnet does not go negative, silicon rectifiers are inserted in series. These rectifiers provide zero current and zero rate of change of current at the start of each excitation cycle, to maintain uniformity from cycle to cycle at injection time. The ac component slightly exceeds the dc component of current, so a "back voltage" is developed across the rectifiers which is used in a feedback circuit to maintain the correct ratio of ac/dc currents from the two power supplies. This feature allows the use of commercial-grade regulation in the power supplies.

For reasons of economy the energy storage inductor is built as a toroidal ring of 12 cores and 12 air gaps, with 24 identical coils mounted on the cores to supply the 24 magnet power units. The ac component of current in the resonant circuit is provided by a pulser circuit supplying primary windings on the choke. This pulser consists of a multiphase rectifier, a storage capacitor, and a pulse-forming network utilizing igni-

trons as switching elements.   It develops short pulses of power synchronized with the resonant frequency and timed by a trigger signal to occur
during the decreasing-current portion of the magnet excitation cycle.
The ac power losses involved in the magnets, inductors, and capacitors

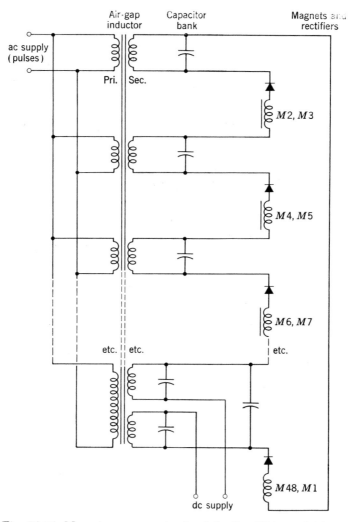

Fig. 15-15. Magnet power-supply circuit for the CEA synchrotron.

in the resonant circuit are about 700 kw.   The total power losses are
about 1100 kw.

The most important property of this power circuit is the uniformity of
current in the 24 subunits of the power supply.   The series connection
requires that current be identical in each unit, to within the limit set by

leakage through insulation or variation in stray capacitance.   Any variation in inductance or capacitance of the separate circuits results in a variation in the voltage across the unit, not in the current.

Injector

Electrons are preaccelerated to an energy of 25 Mev in a linear accelerator, directed tangentially toward the orbit from the outside, and are then inflected into the synchrotron orbit by a pulsed magnetic field located in one field-free space between magnets.   The linac was constructed by Applied Radiation Corporation; it consists of two 10-ft sections of iris-loaded waveguide operating at a frequency of 2855 megacycles.   It produces an output pulse of up to 200 ma of electrons at 25 Mev energy, in a pulse of about 0.7 μsec duration (sufficient to fill one turn in the orbit), within the energy spread and angular deviation required for injection.

The inflecting magnetic field, in the vertical direction, is located in one straight section and is developed by a shaped coil of conductors through which a pulse of current is sent from an auxiliary power supply. This power circuit is arranged to switch off the current (and inflecting field) in a time of about 0.1 μsec, which leaves most of the injected beam to circulate around the orbit.   This modulation of the circulating beam by the switch-off interval of the inflector is a useful property for sensing current and location with pickup coils in the synchrotron orbit.

Radiation Loss

Radiation loss reaches a peak value of 4.5 Mev per turn at 6 Bev energy, following the relation given in Eq. (15-34).   The radiation is emitted as discrete quanta distributed over a bremsstrahlung spectrum with a characteristic energy of 18 kv.   The quantized emission causes momentum recoil of the electrons, which disturbs their orbits and excites certain modes of oscillation.   On the other hand, the average loss of energy by radiation also provides damping for most of the modes of oscillation. This subject has been analyzed by Robinson[14] with special reference to the Cambridge accelerator conditions.

The emission of a quantum of radiation reduces the energy of the electron; this suddenly shifts the equilibrium orbit inward and initiates a radial betatron oscillation about the new equilibrium orbit.   The rate of energy loss is greatest where radius of curvature is smallest, or at the location of the maximum outward amplitude in an existing betatron oscillation.   This slight concentration also tends to increase the amplitude of the radial betatron oscillations.   In addition, the change in energy disturbs the particle from synchronism and sets up synchronous phase oscillations about the equilibrium orbit.   The effects due to individual quanta add with random phase to increase the amplitude of both phase and radial oscillations with time.

For radial betatron oscillations the net result is antidamping, or an exponential increase of amplitude with time, which could drive the electrons against the walls if it persisted. The choice of 60-cps excitation for the magnet reduces the time interval for radiation such that amplitudes will not exceed an estimated rms value of about 0.3 in. by the time they reach 6 Bev; this amplitude is acceptable within the aperture of the synchrotron. The synchronous oscillations are excited by radiation loss but also damped, so they approach an equilibrium distribution in which only a small fraction will exceed the allowable energy deviation determined by the peak radiofrequency accelerating potential. Vertical betatron oscillations are damped to small amplitudes and are not excited by radiation loss.

Radiofrequency

The radiofrequency accelerating system consists of a set of 16 high-Q resonant cavities, located in field-free gaps between magnets. They are tightly coupled by a circular ring of waveguide, fed through a radial waveguide from a power oscillator in the center of the ring, and operate as a single resonant circuit at a frequency of 475.8 megacycles. Each cavity consists of two half-wavelength resonators operating out of phase, with half-wavelength spacing between accelerating gaps; the double cavities are uniformly spaced around the ring with waveguide links which are electrically tuned to an odd half-integral number of wavelengths. Electrically, one may compare this system with a linear accelerator having 32 accelerating gaps spaced by one half-wavelength and operating in the resonant π mode.

The frequency is chosen to be a high integral harmonic (360th) of the orbital frequency (1.32 megacycles), primarily to reduce the amplitude of synchronous oscillations at injection, but also to give physical dimensions for the cavities which fit in the limited space between magnets and which have a high electrical efficiency. The frequency is also chosen to be the exact one-sixth subharmonic of the linac frequency; thus the linac can be synchronized with the rf system if desired. The physical structure is illustrated in Fig. 15-16. The two half-wave resonators are each partially loaded with reentrant drift tubes to reduce electron transit time and to provide a useful electric-field region slightly larger than the beam aperture. The two resonators are coupled by an inductive slot in the center wall, and each resonator has an inductive aperture on the side (top) surface for coupling to the waveguide with an alumina ceramic vacuum window closing the aperture. The separate components are overcoupled, which splits the mode separations sufficiently to allow each element to be tuned individually to resonance and ensures that the entire system operates in the chosen π mode. The measured Q of a prototype cavity unit is 25,000, and the shunt impedance is 7.0 megohms.

At the start of acceleration where $(dB/dt)_i$ is small, the peak rf voltage needed across each accelerating gap is about 20 kv, or about 0.6 Mv per turn.   At the end of the cycle where radiation loss must be compensated, the requirement is about 200 kv per gap, or about 6 Mv per turn.   The accelerated electrons, at an estimated maximum intensity of 10^{11} electrons per cycle, correspond to a circulating current of 20 ma.   Peak power requirements for the system of 16 cavities and waveguide, including beam loading, are about 300 kw.   Average power can be estimated from the expected schedule of rf voltage during the cycle to be about 60 kw.   This

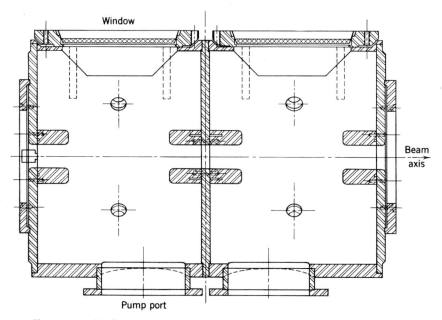

Fig. 15-16. Radiofrequency accelerating cavity for the CEA synchrotron.

power is supplied from an RCA superpower triode of the class A15040, which is the output tube in a power supply designed and constructed by RCA.

The effect of the circulating beam current on the rf system is most important when the rate of acceleration is small, just following injection. The circulating pulsed beam induces out-of-phase voltages on the cavities and will "pull" the phase of the resonant cavities away from the optimum synchronous phase angle.   To compensate for this effect, the applied radiofrequency can be slightly mistuned from the resonant frequency, and the amplitude can be rapidly increased.   It appears that beam loading will set an upper limit on the injected intensity of about 10^{11} electrons per pulse with the present radiofrequency system.

Vacuum System

The vacuum chamber fitting between magnet pole faces is formed of oval cross-section, stainless-steel tubing, deeply slotted transverse to the orbit to minimize eddy-current distortion of the field and covered with a layer of bias-wrapped glass cloth impregnated with an epoxy resin and baked to provide the vacuum surface.   The narrow slots are spaced at $\frac{1}{2}$-in. intervals, cut alternately from opposite sides, such that the stainless-steel chamber forms a continuous metallic circuit which can be electrically heated for vacuum bake-out.   The metal wall will absorb the low-energy synchrotron radiation without structural damage; a glass or ceramic chamber would probably disintegrate under bombardment of this radiation, which has a power density estimated at 10 watts/cm^2 at the chamber wall.   The chamber cross section is flat enough to allow the chamber to be assembled from the outside of the magnet ring through the pole-tip gap.

Straight sections between magnets are occupied by 16 radiofrequency cavities, 16 pickup coil housings, 1 inflector housing, and 15 other chambers for targets and beam-handling devices.   Each of these 48 cavities has a vacuum-pump port and is evacuated by a high-voltage titanium-discharge pump (Drivac) manufactured by Consolidated Electrodynamics Corporation.   Pump power supplies for the discharge pump are located in the central power building.   Fore-vacuum pumps (Cenco #25 Hyvac) connected through liquid-air traps are used for initial evacuation; they are turned off—and sealed off by closing valves—when the titanium pumps come into operation.

The pumping speed of a Drivac is over 300 liters/sec.   When tested on a radiofrequency cavity with full power, the observed pressure is less than 0.5×10^{-6} mm Hg.   The average pressure in the vacuum chambers is expected to be below 1×10^{-6} mm, at which the gas-scattering losses should be negligible.

Targets and Beams

Targets can be mounted in six or eight straight-section cavities between magnets; from those targets gamma-ray and charged-particle beams will emerge in a tangential direction.   Targets can be located at the edge of the beam aperture, where they will not intercept significant intensities at injection, and the high-energy beam will be contracted or expanded to strike the targets.   One scheme for striking the targets is to distort the equilibrium orbit locally by pulsing auxiliary magnets located in other straight sections ahead of and behind the target location.   Other schemes involve excitation of radial betatron oscillations.   Gamma rays from such targets at the edge of the orbit are sharply collimated and can traverse small-diameter channels in a thick shield to emerge into a large experimental hall. Charged particles can be analyzed for momentum in deflecting magnets and also directed through channels in the shield. Figure 15-17 shows the arrangement of target areas and shielding to provide emergent beams of radiation.

An emergent electron beam will be essential for some experiments. Such a beam can be extracted by use of a pulsed "current strip" at the edge of the aperture and parallel to the beam orbit. The pulsed magnetic

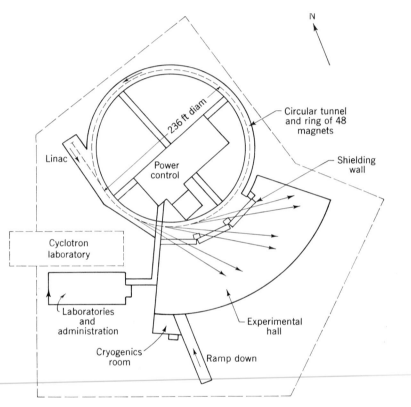

Fig. 15-17. Plan of the CEA synchrotron showing shielding and target areas.

field produced by this current strip will develop radial betatron oscillations, sufficient for a large fraction of the beam to "jump" the thin strip and be deflected out of the orbit.

Electronic control of the several orbit distorting devices will allow the beam to be directed alternately against different targets or out the emergent beam channel. When a full complement of beam-handling apparatus is developed, several experiments can be served simultaneously.

The maximum intensity anticipated with the Cambridge machine is about 10^{11} electrons/pulse, which at 60 cps is a time-average beam intensity of about 1 μa or a beam power of 6 kw at 6 Bev.   Control of the rate of orbit distortion should allow the beam to be ejected or directed against a target over a time interval of up to 1 msec; this represents a time duty cycle of the emergent beam of about 6 per cent of the total time, a feature which is highly desirable for experiments using electronic detection apparatus.

15-10. THE FIXED-FIELD ALTERNATING-GRADIENT PRINCIPLE

Shortly after the Brookhaven discovery of AG focusing in 1952 L. J. Haworth, director of the Brookhaven laboratory, realized that the strong momentum compaction in AG machines would make it possible to design an AG synchrotron with a magnet system whose field did not vary with time.   He considered the case of a sequence of magnet sectors whose fields increase with radius but in which the polarity of the field alternates from one sector to the next.   The particle beam is bent alternately inward and outward but will evidently travel on a closed orbit if the sectors which bend the beam outward are shorter or have weaker fields than the sectors which bend the beam inward.   Although all fields increase outward, the gradients alternate because the field polarities are alternating.   This idea was investigated by H. Snyder, who showed that the idea was sound but that the circumference of such a machine would be several times that of a more conventional AG synchrotron with a field that increases with time.   The idea was not pursued further at that time and was not published.   A year later the same idea was suggested by T. Ohkawa in Japan and by A. A. Kolomenskij, V. A. Petukhov, and M. S. Rabinovich in the U.S.S.R. (who called the machine a "ring phasotron").   Again the proposals did not receive general circulation.   Finally in 1954 K. R. Symon, working in a group assembled to consider a high-energy accelerator for the American Middle West, reinvented the idea and was struck by a number of its advantages that previously had not been appreciated.   The Midwest group plunged into an intensive study of FFAG (fixed-field alternating-gradient) accelerators and soon invented a number of interesting variants culminating in the so-called Mark V or "spiral-ridge" model, which was proposed by D. W. Kerst and which will be described later in this section.

True priority in this particular field of AG machines must be given to L. H. Thomas,[1] whose invention of an AG cyclotron in 1938 was so far ahead of its time that it attracted almost no attention.   The consequences of FFAG advances on the cyclotron have been so important that they will be reserved for discussion in the next section.

Enormous numbers of internal reports on FFAG methods have been written in various laboratories, but probably the best references in this field are the Proceedings of the two CERN conferences in 1956[15] and

1959,[16] where the most important conclusions are presented by the various leading workers in the field.

In September of 1954 fourteen of the major universities and colleges in the Midwest formed the Midwestern Universities Research Association (MURA), whose primary function was to be the recommendation of a high-energy accelerator design to serve the physicists of the Midwest. The area covered centered roughly on Chicago, and MURA was incorporated in the state of Illinois. An enthusiastic and talented group was assembled, supported initially by finances contributed by the universities and later by Federal government agencies, and the FFAG principle was studied intensively. Initially the members worked in their own institutions, but by 1957 the group had been assembled in a rebuilt garage in Madison, Wisconsin; here models were assembled and operated, a digital computer was set into continuous operation, a large site was acquired and developed on the outskirts of Madison, and a series of conferences was held.

The enthusiasm and initiative of the MURA group constitute a phenomenon unique in accelerator history. Although its major proposals had not been accepted by 1961, it has made major contributions to accelerator theory and technique. The spiral-ridge cyclotron, a MURA sideline, has been widely studied, and several such cyclotrons are in construction or operating. Also the MURA group has been a major catalyst in the initiation of the Argonne 12.5-Bev ZGS project,[17] which is aimed at providing the Midwest with a high-energy machine at the earliest possible date.

The betatron field has also been profoundly affected by FFAG advances. The FFAG betatron, in which the guide field remains fixed in time, is capable of much higher intensity than the conventional betatron, and FFAG betatrons may well be serious competitors in the 10- to 100-Mev X-ray field where intensities of electron linear accelerators previously were unsurpassed.

Major advantages claimed for FFAG machines are as follows:

1. Since the magnetic field does not vary through remanent and saturation ranges, it can be set up and shimmed to any desired accuracy, as can the field in a cyclotron.

2. Eddy-current distortions of field are absent, and the magnet need not be laminated.

3. A metallic vacuum chamber can be used without field distortion.

4. Switchgear for pulsing high inductive voltage drops and intermittent forces on magnet coils are avoided.

5. The frequency modulation in the rf accelerating field is less critical.

6. High intensity can be attained by frequent repetition of the rf cycle.

7. Accelerated beams can be "stacked" in a circulating beam whose intensity can be built up to such high levels that it becomes possible to

think of collisions between particle beams circulating in opposite directions. Stacking at intermediate energies can permit acceleration at high repetition rate without the use of high rf voltages, because particles can be carried away from the injector at a rapid rate, stacked, and then carried the rest of the way at a lower rate.   A third advantage of stacking lies in the increased flexibility in duty factor that becomes possible when the beam is stacked at maximum energy.

The MURA studies have shown that these advantages are offset by some serious difficulties, chief among which are those associated with the design of the large and complicated magnet structure that is necessary.

Of the several MURA schemes for utilizing the FFAG principle, two have emerged as most interesting—the so-called Mark I or radial-sector machine and the Mark V or spiral-sector accelerator.   These will be presented in somewhat more detail.

The Radial-sector FFAG Accelerator

This is the machine independently proposed by Haworth, Ohkawa, Kolomenskij et al., and by Symon.   Its general configuration is illus-

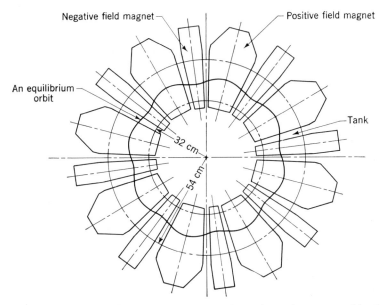

Fig. 15-18. Radial-sector FFAG accelerator.   This configuration was used in the first MURA electron model.

trated in Fig. 15-18.   On the median plane the magnetic field has only a z component, which can be written

$$B_z = B_0 \left(\frac{r}{r_0}\right)^k f(\theta) \qquad (15\text{-}36)$$

where B_0 is the field at some arbitrary radius r_0 and at a point where $f(\theta)$ has the value unity, and $f(\theta)$, the azimuthal dependence of field, can be written as a Fourier series thus:

$$f(\theta) = \sum_n (g_n \cos nN\theta + f_n \sin nN\theta) \qquad (15\text{-}37)$$

Here N represents the total number of identical sectors, each including a focusing and a defocusing magnet unit. Two more quantities must now be defined: the "flutter factor" F, which is a measure of the spatially varying part of the field, is defined by

$$F^2 = \sum_{n=1}^{\infty} (g_n{}^2 + f_n{}^2) \qquad (15\text{-}38)$$

and G, a quantity important in deriving the free or betatron oscillation frequencies, is defined by

$$G^2 = \sum_{n=1}^{\infty} \frac{g_n{}^2 + f_n{}^2}{2n^2N^2} \qquad (15\text{-}39)$$

Typical values of F and G for field patterns useful in radial-sector machines are given in the caption of Fig. 15-19. For field patterns in

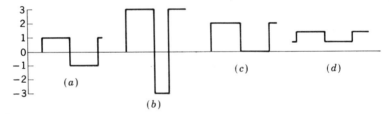

Fig. 15-19. Azimuthal field distributions possible in FFAG accelerators. (a) Sectors of equal length. Here $g_0 = 0$, $F = 1.4x$, $G = 0.9x/N$. (b) Positive curvature sector twice as long as negative curvature sector. Here $g_0 = 1$, $F = 4.0$, $G = 2.4/N$. (c) Sectors alternating with field-free regions of equal length. Here $g_0 = 1$, $F = 1.4$, $G = 0.9/N$. (d) Sectors alternating with regions of half-field strength. Here $g_0 = 1$, $F = 0.27$, $G = 0.15/N$.

which the magnet sectors are of unequal lengths and hence have g_0 not equal to zero, it is customary to normalize by choosing B_0 such that $g_0 = 1$. In these cases F will be of the order of 4 and G will be of the order of $3/N$.

Analysis of FFAG orbits is so complex that smooth approximations generally fail to give accurate results. Approximate methods are used only as a guide in preliminary design. From this point on it is necessary to make numerical computations of such complexity that a digital computer is essential. It is significant that one of the first acquisitions of the MURA group was an IBM 704 computer.

Orbit characteristics are derived in two stages. First, the wavy equilibrium orbit through the alternating fields must be derived. Then it is possible to compute the free or betatron oscillations around this orbit. For the details of this analysis the reader is referred to the paper of Symon et al.[18]

From the smooth approximation the free-oscillation frequencies or, more precisely, the number of oscillation waves per revolution are given by

$$\nu_r^2 \cong 1 + k + k^2 G^2$$
$$\nu_z^2 \cong -k + k^2 G^2 + \frac{F^2}{2} \qquad (15\text{-}40)$$

The magnet for a radial-sector FFAG machine must be designed to provide sufficient radial aperture for the whole energy range from injection to full energy and sufficient vertical aperture to accommodate the

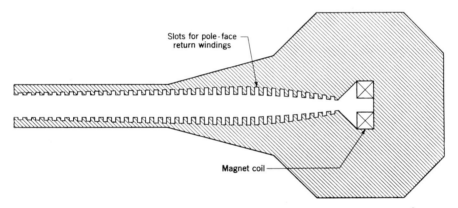

Fig. 15-20. Cross section through magnet for radial-sector FFAG accelerator.

large vertical oscillations at injection and the somewhat damped vertical oscillations at full energy. In cross section this magnet has the configuration illustrated by Fig. 15-20.

The circumference of a radial-sector FFAG synchrotron will be of the order of six times that of a conventional AG synchrotron without straight sections. When this factor is included in design, the mass of the magnet for an FFAG synchrotron becomes much larger than that of a conventional AG synchrotron.

Resonances in FFAG machines are just as important as those in conventional synchrotrons and are generally avoided by designing for "scaling" orbits—the field pattern is such that the betatron frequencies are the same at all radii. Recently the MURA group has shown that some economies are possible in nonscaling machines, but in this case analysis becomes even more complicated.

A small radial-sector FFAG electron synchrotron was built by the MURA group at the University of Michigan and later moved to the MURA laboratory in Madison, Wisconsin. This model, designed for electron acceleration to 400 kev, was brought into operation in 1956.[19] Its general configuration was that of Fig. 15-18. Table 15-1 summarizes its major parameters. The performance of the MURA model was entirely satisfactory; it came into operation immediately, with very little initial adjustment, and was used for numerous studies of resonances and effects of misalignments of magnet sectors. In all cases the results were in agreement with the theoretical predictions.

TABLE 15-1

PARAMETERS FOR RADIAL-SECTOR FFAG SYNCHROTRONS

	MURA 400-kev electron model	Possible 10-Bev proton synchrotron
Number of magnet pairs N	8	64
k	3.36	192.5
Ratio of length of orbit in positive-curvature magnets to length of orbit in negative-curvature magnets	2.5 approx.	1.6 approx.
Injection energy	25 kev	5 Mev
Injection radius	34 cm	95 m
Final radius	50 cm	97.3 m
Aperture at injection	4 cm	30 cm
Aperture at full energy	2.4 cm	6 cm
ν_r	2.8	21.7
ν_z	2.1	3.9

Table 15-1 also includes a list of parameters for a possible 10-Bev radial-sector FFAG proton synchrotron. Several salient features emerge from this table and from the magnet design of Fig. 15-20. First, the magnet is enormous; its radial aperture is 2.3 m, and its total weight will be of the order of 15,000 tons or more. Its structure is complicated and presents severe mechanical problems. Since tolerances are tight as in the conventional AG synchrotron, the magnet pole faces must be restrained to a positional precision of the order of 0.2 mm, a severe problem in the extensive and weak magnet structure illustrated. On the other hand, a rapid repetition rate for acceleration to top energy makes possible in this machine a beam intensity of the order of 10^{14} protons/sec. This intensity is higher by a factor of 100 than that of any other proton accelerator in this energy range. The associated rf problems are not severe; they will be discussed later in this section.

The Spiral-sector FFAG Accelerator

This ingenious device is, perhaps, MURA's major contribution to the accelerator art. As described by Kerst (its inventor) and shown in Fig. 15-21, the device provides AG focusing either by spiral magnet sec-
tors or by inclusion on the pole faces
of spiral ridges to give regions of
increased field over a spiraling configuration. To the novice the action of this configuration will be
relatively incomprehensible except
in terms of the mathematical results. The MURA group considers
the spiral-ridge structure to be a
case of alternating edge-focusing
effects (see Sec. 5-6). The focusing mechanism will receive more
detailed consideration in the next
section, where it again appears in
the sector-focused cyclotron. Pri-

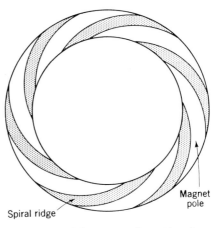

Fig. 15-21. Magnet configuration for a spiral-sector FFAG accelerator.

marily because the field need not reverse, this design results in an FFAG configuration much more economical than the radial-sector system.

In this case, on the median plane the magnetic field has only the z component

$$B_z = B_0 \left(\frac{r}{r_0}\right)^k \sum_n (g_n \cos n\phi + f_n \sin n\phi) \qquad (15\text{-}41)$$

where
$$\phi = K \ln \frac{r}{r_0} - N\theta$$

Aside from the term $K \ln (r/r_0)$, the field pattern is the same as that in the radial-sector machine. This is the term that gives the field its spiraling characteristic; the logarithmic form is such as to ensure scaling or constancy of betatron frequency with radius. K is related to the angle γ at which field spirals cut radial lines by

$$K = N \tan \gamma \qquad (15\text{-}42)$$

Again the flutter factor F and the parameter G are defined as in Eqs. (15-38) and (15-39). In this case, however, the field does not reverse, and F and G have lower values than in the radial-sector case. Here F usually lies between 0.2 and 1.5 and G lies between $0.2/N$ and $1/N$.

Free-oscillation frequencies in the spiral-sector FFAG synchrotron are given by the smooth approximation

$$\nu_r^2 \cong 1 + k + k^2 G^2 \qquad (15\text{-}43a)$$

as in the radial-sector machine, and

$$\nu_z{}^2 \cong -k + k^2 G^2 + F^2 \left(\frac{K^2}{N^2} + \frac{1}{2}\right) \tag{15-43b}$$

Since the field need not reverse in this design, the circumference factor can be reduced as low as 2. Orbit compaction is not so strong as in the radial-sector machine, however, and a larger radial aperture is required. The magnet weight for a spiral-sector machine can be about half that for a radial-sector machine. But this is still about ten times greater than the weight of a corresponding conventional AG synchrotron.

A spiral-sector FFAG electron synchrotron for about 120 kev final energy was built by the MURA group as a model on which to study orbits. This model was constructed at the University of Illinois and assembled at the MURA laboratory in Madison. Like the radial-sector model, it worked immediately and gave results in good agreement with the predictions.[20] The parameters of this model are collected in Table 15-2. Also included in this table are parameters for a possible spiral-sector 10-Bev proton accelerator.

TABLE 15-2
PARAMETERS FOR SPIRAL-SECTOR FFAG SYNCHROTRONS

	MURA 120-kev electron model	Possible 10-Bev proton synchrotron
Number of spiral sectors N	6	30
Angle of spiral with radius vector [$\tan^{-1} (K/N)$]	46°	84.3°
k	0.70	53
K	6.25	300
Injection energy	35 kev	50 Mev
Injection radius	31 cm	46 m
Final radius	52 cm	50 m
Final vertical aperture	3.8 cm	15 cm
ν_r	1.40	8.4
ν_z	1.12	7.2

It will be noted that the high-energy machine has a much larger spiral angle; the spiral is approaching much more closely to a circle. Whereas in the MURA model it was easy to make each spiral sector a separately excited magnet, for the high-energy machine it is much simpler to make the spiral sectors mere ridges on the pole face of one large magnet.

Colliding Beams and the Two-way ("Synchroclash") FFAG Accelerator

When the possibilty of beam stacking in FFAG machines was realized and analysis led to the conclusion that circulating beams of 10 to 100 amp were quite possible, the MURA group began to think actively of the possibility of experiments involving colliding beams. At relativistic energies the kinetic energy available for nuclear reactions is disappointingly small when the target particle is at rest in the laboratory system. For proton-proton collisions the kinetic energy available is given by the expression

$$W_0 \left[\left(2 + \frac{2W}{W_0} \right)^{\frac{1}{2}} - 2 \right] \tag{15-44}$$

where W is the total proton energy and W_0 is its rest energy of 938 Mev. The following table indicates the result:

Energy of accelerated proton, Bev	Kinetic energy available, Bev
6.2	2
25	5.2
100	12
540	30

With these figures in mind the MURA group reasoned that it could make two 15-Bev FFAG accelerators and study reactions in the center-of-mass system where all the energy is available; this double machine would be equivalent, in terms of nuclear reactions possible, to a single machine of 540 Bev! With the possible circulating currents there should be about 10^7 collisions per meter of beam path; this would mean about 100 resulting particles per square centimeter per second at a distance of 1 m. Although the problems of direct observation of collisions would be formidable, this seemed sufficiently promising to merit further study. A detailed design study of the double clashing-beam accelerator using the spiral-sector design was completed in 1956. In the same year, however, T. Ohkawa[21] realized that the radial-sector FFAG design would work even if the length of the orbit in the positive-curvature magnets were made the same as the orbit length in the negative-curvature magnets. In this case identical radial sectors would alternate in polarity, and it should no longer matter in which sense the beam circulates. Consequently, beams could be made to circulate simultaneously in both directions, and beam collisions could be observed at a number of orbit intersections around the machine. Ohkawa showed also that spiral sectors can be used in a two-way machine.

Beam dynamics in the two-way radial-sector machine differ somewhat in characteristics from those found in radial-sector machines, where positive-curvature magnet sectors are longer than negative-curvature sectors. From the smooth approximation the betatron-oscillation frequencies are given by

$$\nu_r^2 \cong 2k$$
$$\nu_z^2 \cong \frac{F^2}{kG^2} \tag{15-45}$$

The fact that g_0 for the two-way machine is zero and hence F and G cannot be normalized as before is rendered unimportant since only the ratio F/G appears in these equations.

The two-way radial-sector machine was now studied by the MURA group, and a possible 15-Bev design was completed. Simultaneously a 40-Mev two-way electron model was initiated;[22] it was completed early in 1960 and tested successfully. Parameters of the model and of the proposed 15-Bev proton accelerator are collected in Table 15-3.

TABLE 15-3

PARAMETERS FOR TWO-WAY FFAG SYNCHROTRONS

	MURA 40-Mev electron model	Possible 15-Bev proton synchrotron
Number of magnet pairs N......	16	66
k............................	9.3	212
Injection energy..............	100 kev	50 Mev
Injection radius..............	124 cm	175 m
Final radius..................	198 cm	180 m
Vertical aperture at injection....	7 cm	35 cm
Final vertical aperture.........	5 cm	15 cm
Circumference factor..........	8.0	5.8
ν_r............................	6.36	24.75
ν_z............................	5.34	4.30
Weight of magnet steel.........	32 tons	62,500 tons
Weight of copper in magnet coil	7 tons	3,000 tons

Detailed study of the two-way 15-Bev design led to some sobering conclusions. High-energy physicists were dubious about the possibilities of studying nuclear reactions in the inaccessible colliding-beam region. Unless the pressure in the vacuum chamber was kept to the order of 10^{-9} mm Hg, the colliding-beam reaction products would be obscured by a tremendous background because of collisions with residual gas nuclei. Finally, the cost of the machine proved to be astronomical. For these reasons, in 1960 it appeared improbable that colliding beams would receive very immediate consideration. In any case it appeared that colliding beams, if ever studied, would be produced by one accelerator and two storage rings, using the method discussed in the last section of this chapter.

RF Acceleration in FFAG Synchrotrons

The fact that stable orbits for all energies between injection and final exist continually in FFAG accelerators leads to several rather surprising conclusions with respect to methods of acceleration. It is, of course, quite possible to accelerate with a frequency modulated from initial to final revolution frequency or a harmonic thereof just as in a conventional synchrotron. A transition energy exists in FFAG machines just as in other AG machines. Its value W_t is given by

$$W_t{}^2 = (k + 1)W_0{}^2 \qquad (15\text{-}46)$$

This transition energy can be passed by making the appropriate shift in rf phase, as has been done with the CERN PS and the Brookhaven AGS.

The first point of difference with conventional practice lies in the fact that, while a frequency that is a harmonic of the revolution frequency carries the beam to high energy, it may also pick up injected particles on a different subharmonic and accelerate them to some intermediate energy. While the primary region of phase stability (cf. Fig. 9-3) is sweeping up in energy and carrying its content of particles with it, other regions of stability with different harmonic relations to the revolution frequency also are sweeping up in energy. As an example, suppose that protons are injected at one-eighth of the velocity of light (about 7.5 Mev) and are accelerated into the 10-Bev region, or virtually to the velocity of light. Suppose, further, that the accelerating frequency is the second harmonic of the revolution frequency. As the frequency increases to 1.5 times its initial value, it matches the third harmonic of the injection frequency; particles picked up on this harmonic will be accelerated to two-thirds of the final design velocity or to about $\frac{1}{3}$ Bev. When the frequency reaches twice its initial value, fourth-harmonic acceleration becomes possible with a final velocity of half the design velocity, here corresponding to about 200 Mev, etc. When the second harmonic has deposited its protons at the final radius and the rf is turned off, the groups accelerated on other harmonics will be left circulating at their respective radii until picked up by another rf signal or until eventually they are lost by scattering by the residual gas.

In the vocabulary of the MURA group (now generally accepted) the regions of stability are known as "buckets" taking part in a "bucket lift" carrying the particles to higher energies. Even more buckets can be added by simultaneous application of other frequency-modulated signals. The MURA group has shown, moreover, that successive buckets can be brought to full energy and dumped at the final radius to give a beam circulating at full energy and continually increasing in intensity until limited by the requirements of Liouville's theorem. This limit does not appear to set in until circulating currents of the order of 10 to 100 amp have been established.

One of the most disconcerting concepts of the FFAG acceleration picture follows from the conclusion from Liouville's theorem (cf. Sec. 5-8) that the phase space, of which the buckets are a part, is incompressible. Hence while the buckets are rising in energy carrying their particles with them, particles that do not lie in the buckets must be forced down in energy. Conversely, if the buckets are pushed downward, the remainder of the phase space is pushed upward. In other words, if the frequency is modulated downward, particles not in phase-stable regions will be accelerated. From the MURA experiments this indeed appears to be the case.

Another intriguing idea in a fixed-field machine is that of "stochastic acceleration." This is one of the few concepts in this field not due to MURA; it was originally proposed in the U.S.S.R. by Burshtein, Veksler, and Kolomenskij[23] and tested on a small cyclotron by Keller, Dick, and Fidecaro[24] of CERN. These authors claim that, since all orbits exist simultaneously in an FFAG accelerator, it is necessary only to modulate the accelerating frequency at random, and sooner or later some particles will be accelerated. Other particles will be returned to the injector, but it seems reasonable to expect that this will be only about half of the injected particles. Indeed the frequency of the accelerating signal need not be distinguishable; the accelerating signal can be random noise. The CERN experimental results bear out these conclusions.

It is possible that these novelties will prove to be important. In 1961 this does not appear probable.

Some technical difficulties arise in connection with rf acceleration in FFAG accelerators, partly because of the difficulties of introducing field-free sectors and partly because of the large radial aperture. In the radial-sector machine, field-free sections are rather easily introduced, but in spiral-sector machines, introduction of radial straight sections requires redesign of the magnet structure, although it appears to be quite practicable. The large radial aperture makes for difficulty in construction of an accelerating system which can be modulated over a wide frequency range and which, simultaneously, is economical of power. The latter fact becomes important if rapid frequency modulation is required to produce high average beam intensity. The difficulty is associated with the large gap capacity that goes with large aperture and with the long path for magnetic flux linking the whole aperture. Saturating dielectric or ferromagnetic materials suitable for wide-range tuning under these conditions will perforce introduce large losses that will rise very rapidly as the rate of acceleration is increased. It is to be hoped that this problem, like so many others, will be solved by the inventive ingenuity of the MURA group.

15-11. SECTOR-FOCUSED CYCLOTRONS

The first proposal for a sector-focused cyclotron was made by Thomas[1] in 1938. This came at a time when early cyclotron designers were concerned with the maximum energy limitation at about 25 Mev imposed by the relativistic increase in mass of the accelerated particles. To maintain resonance with the fixed-frequency accelerating electric field provided by the D's, as particle mass increases, the magnetic field should increase at large orbit radii. However, this requirement conflicts with the radially decreasing field needed to maintain axial stability of particle orbits. Thomas proposed the use of alternately high and low regions of magnetic field around the orbit, such as could be obtained with radial sectors of iron fastened to the pole faces to give alternately short and long gap lengths. The average field around an orbit could then increase at large radii to maintain resonance. Thomas showed that an orbiting particle in this azimuthally varying magnetic field would experience axial restoring forces which would provide the desired orbit stability.

This proposal of an azimuthally varying field (AVF) was recognized as being theoretically sound, but the computations were complex as compared with the simple relations then in use by cyclotron designers. The theory of particle orbits in magnetic fields was in its infancy, and Thomas's scheme was so far in advance of the general understanding by practitioners of the art that its virtues were not immediately accepted and put into practice. Furthermore, the cyclotron was in an early stage of development, and many practical problems of engineering development took precedence. As a result, the idea lay fallow for many years.

When the principle of synchronous acceleration was announced in 1946 and the use of frequency modulation and pulsed operation was proposed to overcome the relativistic limitation, it led to the speedy development of the synchrocyclotron and the construction of a sequence of machines of higher and higher energy. The only apparent restriction on energy was that of size and cost. Accelerator designers concentrated their efforts on such synchronous machines, and the low beam intensities which came as a consequence of pulsed operation were at that time considered acceptable.

It was not until 1949, when orbit theory was greatly advanced, that the AVF concept was revived under the stimulus of potential applications to national defense which required high beam intensities. Studies were started in 1949 at the University of California under security restrictions and became known to other laboratories only after declassification in 1955. The present sector-focused cyclotrons at the Livermore laboratory are a direct outgrowth of these studies. During this period two electron models were built at the University of California Radiation Laboratory to test the focusing principle, reported much later (1956) by Kelly, Pyle, Thornton, Richardson, and Wright.[25] Work also started in the early 1950s at the Oak Ridge National Laboratory, under the direction of R. S. Livingston and following the theoretical analyses of T. Welton.

Meanwhile, the discovery of the AG focusing principle led to the FFAG ideas discussed in the preceding section. The MURA group showed the advantages of spiral ridges on cyclotron pole faces over the radial sectors proposed by Thomas.

By the time these two lines of development merged, it became evident that Thomas's proposal of sector focusing was a special case of the general theory of AG focusing as applied to constant magnetic fields. The final result has been the development of a whole family of cyclotrons—"isochronous," or sector-focused, or AVF—some using radial and some spiral alternations in field. The common characteristic of all such machines is the use of fixed frequency for acceleration, which results in the large duty cycle and the high beam intensities characteristic of the standard cyclotron. The time-average beam current is about 100 times higher than for synchrocyclotrons, which accelerate pulsed beams by the use of frequency modulation.

The emphasis in the development of sector-focused machines has been on high beam intensity and on obtaining variable output energy. This latter feature can be obtained by using sector-shaped coils to control the magnitude of the azimuthal variation and circular coils of different radii on the pole faces to control the radial increase of average field. These coils maintain the field pattern as the main field is varied. Such coils can be powered to provide the necessary focusing fields for any chosen output energy, when combined with radiofrequency circuits which can be tuned over a suitable range in frequency. This technique solves a problem which has long been a handicap to research scientists using standard cyclotrons. The variable frequency and field property can also be used to provide the correct focusing fields for the acceleration of a variety of ions, such as H^1, D^1, H_2, D_2, He^3, or He^4.

The first practical cyclotron embodying these principles was the 42-in. standard cyclotron at Los Alamos, which was rebuilt by Boyer in 1954, using radial sectors and coils and with a variable-frequency oscillator. It has been highly successful in providing variable output energy and has been used for the acceleration of several types of ions.

A conference on sector-focused cyclotrons was held at Sea Island, Georgia, on February 2–4, 1959, at which most of the United States experts in this field were present. The published report[26] of the papers presented gives a full description of the status of the field at that date. A tabulation in an appendix to this report lists 15 sector-focused cyclotrons in various stages of design and construction; only two machines were in operation at that date, at Los Alamos and Delft, Holland, producing 16- and 12-Mev deuterons, respectively. By 1961, several machines in the 50- to 75-Mev proton energy range were approaching completion, at the University of California at Los Angeles, Oak Ridge National Laboratory, and the University of Colorado. Studies are in process for still higher energies at several laboratories; the largest is for 850 Mev, at Oak Ridge.

An AVF magnet has three or more (N) high-field regions (hills) and a corresponding number of lower-field regions (valleys) symmetrically located in azimuth. The average field around any orbit increases with radius at the calculated rate to match the increase in particle momentum and to maintain constant orbital frequency. This oscillation in flux density on the median plane distorts the particle orbit from a circle into a curved polygon, illustrated in an exaggerated form in Fig. 15-22. Orbit-stability calculations are based on the fields encountered around such a

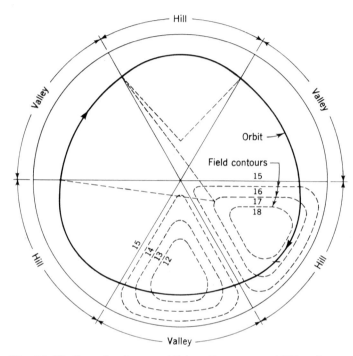

Fig. 15-22. Curved polygon orbit in a three-sector AVF cyclotron

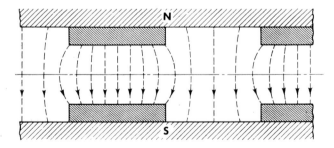

Fig. 15-23. "Unrolled" pole-face contour and flux pattern in an AVF cyclotron.

noncircular orbit and include a radial component of momentum mv_r. The field pattern off the median plane is also distorted from the parallel shape obtained in a uniform-field magnet. If the pole-face contour and flux-line pattern around an orbit were to be "unrolled" into a plane, it would appear similar to that illustrated in Fig. 15-23. The curvature of flux lines produces azimuthal components of field B_θ at locations off the median plane.

The "Thomas" force F_z, which provides vertical stability in this field, is due to the interaction of the radial component of momentum mv_r with the azimuthal component of field B_θ. The direction of this force alternates as the particle moves around the orbit, from convergence to divergence about the median plane. This rapid alternation of focusing and defocusing forces provides the same type of stability which is characteristic of the forces in AG focusing, resulting in a net convergence. The mathematical analysis of the motion follows in a manner parallel to that discussed in Sec. 15-10. In general, this net focusing about the median plane must be large enough to more than compensate for the axially defocusing effect of the radially increasing average field.

Two additional axial restoring forces arise from the field pattern produced by a spiral-shaped azimuthal variation. The spiral shape can be defined by the angle γ between the direction of the spiral ridge and the radius vector; in a spiral this angle will increase with increasing radius. Because of this angle there will be a radial component of field B_r at points off the median plane, which will be directed alternately inward and outward as the particle crosses the boundaries of the hills and valleys. The azimuthal momentum of the particle mv_θ interacts with this radial field B_r to produce an alternating force in the axial direction, similar to and in addition to the Thomas force.

A second and different axial force due to the spiral pattern comes from an imbalance in the magnitudes of the axial forces at the boundaries of hills and valleys; these are not exactly equal, but the convergent forces are slightly larger. This can be understood by considering the noncircular shape of the orbit which results in the orbit's making a small angle δ (the Thomas angle) with a true concentric circle at these boundaries. The geometry can be visualized by reference to the sketch in Fig. 15-22. The Thomas angle is outward when the particle crosses the boundary between valley and hill and inward when it crosses the boundary between hill and valley. The particle spends a longer time going through the axially focusing region in the latter case than it does in traversing the defocusing region. Since the convergent force acts over a longer time interval, the result is a net convergence.

Each of the forces discussed above enters as a separate term in the equations of motion. The sum of the Thomas force and the two forces due to the spiral shape opposes the defocusing action of the radially increasing magnetic field. The problem in design is to balance the opposing terms, each of which is quite large, to obtain a net focusing action which is relatively small but sufficient to maintain axial stability.

If the field in a conventional cyclotron were to increase with radius at such a rate as to keep the frequency of revolution of the circulating par-

ticles constant, its radial dependence would follow from the fundamental
relations

$$\frac{v}{c} = \frac{Be}{m} = \frac{Be}{m_0}\left(1 - \frac{v^2}{c^2}\right)^{\frac{1}{2}} = \text{const}$$

whence

$$B = B_0\left[1 - \left(\frac{B_0 er}{m_0 c}\right)^2\right]^{-\frac{1}{2}} \tag{15-47}$$

where B_0 is the field at zero radius.

If we define a field index k, as in the preceding section, to represent

$$\frac{r}{B}\frac{dB}{dr}$$

we obtain from Eq. (15-46)

$$k = \left[\left(\frac{m_0 c}{B_0 er}\right)^2 - 1\right]^{-1} = \left(\frac{c^2}{v^2} - 1\right)^{-1} \tag{15-48}$$

Evidently k cannot be kept constant with radius as in the spiral-sector
FFAG machines, but will change from a very small value near the center
of the machine through 0.2 at a radius where protons of 100 Mev would

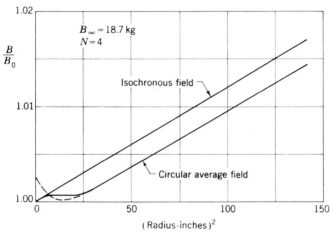

Fig. 15-24. Plots of magnetic field B and average field $\bar{B}$ for the 50-Mev AVF cyclotron
at the University of California at Los Angeles.

circulate to very high values as v approaches c.   This will result in a variation with radius of the frequency of radial oscillation—the machine
cannot be a scaling accelerator in the language of MURA.

Inclusion of spiral ridges will compensate for the vertical defocusing in
a field of the type described by Eq. (15-47), but the azimuthally averaged
field must have the same general character as given by Eq. (15-47).

The radial and vertical oscillation frequencies will be given approximately by Eqs. (15-43), with the flutter factor F and the parameter G defined as before by Eqs. (15-38) and (15-39).

Ratios of maximum field under a ridge to minimum field between ridges have been chosen in various designs with values ranging from 1.3 to 3, giving flutter factors F ranging from about 0.2 to about 1. Near the center of the magnet, where the ridges come together, the field becomes essentially constant, and this region requires special treatment to provide adequate axial focusing. One technique is to shorten gap length to provide a slightly higher field at the center, so the average field decreases with radius from the center out to the point where the AVF fields become significant.

To arrive at an isochronous design, it is necessary to trace orbits through the AVF field pattern and derive an azimuthal average $\bar{B}$ which should satisfy Eq. (15-47). Deviations from this relation indicate the trimming that must be done on the spiral ridges. Figure 15-24 shows the radial field plots for $\bar{B}$ and B for the 50-Mev machine at the University of California at Los Angeles.[26]

Because of the relatively small values of k used in AVF cyclotrons the terms involving G in Eqs. (15-43), giving the betatron oscillation frequencies, are negligible, and these equations can be written

$$\nu_r{}^2 \cong 1 + k$$
$$\nu_z{}^2 \cong -k + F^2 \left(\frac{K^2}{N^2} + \frac{1}{2} \right) \tag{15-49}$$
$$\cong -k + F^2 \left(\tan^2 \gamma + \frac{1}{2} \right)$$

where γ is the angle defined by Eq. (15-42). It is the angle at which field spirals cut radial lines.

The radial betatron frequency in a conventional cyclotron is always less than unity. Here, however, since k is positive and increases with radius, the radial frequency for an isochronous machine is always greater than unity. If it reaches the value of 1.5, a half-integral resonance can occur. For protons [from Eq. (15-48)] this occurs at about 450 Mev. It appears that this resonance can be passed, but the integral resonance that appears for $\nu_r = 2$ is regarded as an impassable barrier. This sets an upper limit of about 900 Mev on isochronous AVF cyclotrons. Above this energy it will be necessary to return to the frequency-variation methods used in the synchrocyclotron.

The vertical betatron oscillation tends to become unstable as k increases, unless the angle γ is increased. Vertical stability is improved also by increasing the flutter factor F.

The variables which can be adjusted in design to obtain a small positive value (about 0.02) for $\nu_z{}^2$ are the number of sectors, the angle of the spiral, and the angular width of the hill. Although N, the number of sectors, does not appear explicitly in the first of Eqs. (15-49), it does have an effect on the radial oscillation through the stability criterion which requires that ν_r be less than $N/2$. For radial stability it is best to have a large number of sectors and a small spiral angle; however, for axial stability a smaller number of sectors and a large spiral angle are desired, in order to obtain the largest possible flutter factor. The choice is the smallest number of sectors compatible with radial stability and the largest sector angle for which the hill angle can be adjusted to give axial stability. The higher the design energy, the more stringent these criteria become. For energies up to about 25 Mev, three sectors with zero spiral angle (radial sectors) are sufficient. For the energy range between 40 and 80 Mev the usual choice is four sectors and a maximum spiral angle at the periphery of about 45°. At still higher energies design parameters become more critical, and much more detailed analysis is required to avoid radial resonances. Design studies for the highest energies now being considered (850 Mev) involve massive programs for orbit computations and are beyond the scope of this book.

15-12. ACCELERATORS OF THE FUTURE

Scientists in the field of high-energy particle physics continue to press for accelerators of still higher energy. The scientific justification of this demand for ultra-high-energy machines goes far beyond the scope of this volume, but the evidence is impressive. Each new generation of accelerators in a new, higher energy range has brought new insights into the nature of the fundamental particles. Mesons, hyperons, and other short-lived strange particles have been discovered and their properties studied. New transitions between these excited states of matter have been observed, and new principles have been proposed such as the "conservation of strangeness." Studies of the scattering of high-energy particles have shown that the charge and mass distributions in the fundamental particles are so complex as to require new concepts in the theories of nuclear forces. Speculations are starting on the validity of some of the most basic physical laws such as those of quantum electrodynamics, and experiments have been conceived which would test the range of validity. Accelerators which started as tools for nuclear physics have progressed to be the essential instruments for this new field of particle physics, which goes as far beyond nuclear physics as nuclear physics went beyond atomic physics.

Still other scientists have conceived of new areas of research which might be opened by use of accelerators producing much higher intensities than are possible with existing machines. With an increase of several orders of magnitude in intensity and targets which could survive under the bombardment, the secondary radiations could themselves become important tools for a wide range of new experiments. Pi-meson, K-meson, or even antiproton beams, which have the intensity and beam quality of present primary beams, might prove necessary to resolve the unforeseen problems of the future. Neutrino reactions are also of tremendous theoretical interest, but the flux required for detailed study is greatly in excess of the output from existing accelerators.

In the past, higher energies have resulted partly from a sequence of new concepts for acceleration and partly from technical developments which significantly improved the simplicity or economy of the machines. We could ask whether there are new concepts which would represent a major step in basic principles or whether there are new technical ideas which could be used to extend the energy range using present principles. The answer is that several such concepts have been proposed, and of both types.

Two new principles for acceleration were presented by U.S.S.R. scientists at the CERN conference on high-energy accelerators in 1956.[27] Budker proposed a "plasma betatron" which would utilize the self-focusing properties of an extremely large electron beam in the circular orbit of a betatron-type accelerator. It is known from studies of high-density plasmas that such an intense electron beam would collapse to small transverse dimensions and develop a toroidal magnetic field of such strength that extremely high-energy electrons could be retained in relatively small orbits. However, it is also known from studies with the plasma devices used in thermonuclear experiments that such a beam develops instabilities. Experimental work by Linhard at CERN was reported in the 1959 CERN conference[28] and was generally inconclusive. Although there are still some enthusiasts, there are few who believe this principle can be exploited in a high-energy accelerator, at least within the foreseeable future.

Veksler[27] discussed some theoretical calculations on an even more speculative concept—that of "coherent impact acceleration." This would utilize "collisions" between relativistic electrons in plasma bunches and single ions, in which, if the forces acting on the ion could be made coherent over the entire plasma bunch, the ion could be accelerated to extremely high energies. In the 1959 CERN conference[28] Veksler reported no significant progress, and there is little expectation that this concept will prove practical until there have been major advances in plasma physics and in the theoretical understanding of cooperative phenomena.

Several technical improvements have been proposed which, if they become practical, could lead to important changes in the characteristics of accelerators. The "plasma guns," which are just showing promise in thermonuclear experiments, could potentially be developed into ion sources of very high intensity. The use of cryogenic cooling for the excitation windings of magnets, if developed to be economically practical, could revolutionize the field of magnet design; it might lead to air-cored coils producing extremely large magnetic fields and having correspondingly smaller dimensions. Cryogenic cooling of the radiofrequency systems used for acceleration, such as the waveguides in linacs, could also conceivably lead to greatly improved electrical efficiency in the transformation of rf power and provide faster rates of acceleration.

The synchroclash FFAG machine described in Sec. 15-10 is based on the concept of collisions between two counterrevolving beams; beam intensity must be several orders of magnitude greater than from present accelerators, but if it could be attained, the result would be a major increase in the effective energy of the interaction. For example, as shown in Sec. 15-10, protons of 100 Bev energy would be required, if directed against a fixed hydrogen target, to provide the same excitation energy available in collisions between two counterrevolving protons each of 6.0 Bev energy.

The "storage ring" utilizes the same principle. If the beam from an accelerator is diverted sequentially into two intersecting magnetic orbits, the circulating currents can be built up over reasonable times to hundreds of amperes, such that each beam becomes a target for the other and the sum of the kinetic energies is available for excitation. An electron storage-ring system has been designed and installed by G. K. O'Neill[28] for the Stanford 1-Bev linac to test the principle. Storage rings have also been proposed for proton accelerators, to provide excitation energy in the proton-proton interaction equivalent to very much higher output energies. If applied to the present 33-Bev Brookhaven AGS machine, they would provide 66 Bev of excitation energy in the center of mass, equivalent to that from a 2500-Bev proton beam against a fixed target. O'Neill estimates that a set of storage rings for a proton accelerator would cost approximately the same as the accelerator itself and would have similar dimensions. Somewhat higher estimates have been made at CERN.

The advantage of storage rings in providing high excitation energy means that they will probably be installed in some proton machines. However, the limitation to a single nucleon interaction and the unfavorable geometry for experiments on the secondary radiations make them less satisfactory as laboratory tools than existing high-energy machines. The storage ring should probably be considered as a useful but costly target arrangement rather than as a substitute for an ultrahigh-energy accelerator.

The most practical proposals for superintensity or ultra-high-energy accelerators are based on extensions of existing principles. Proposals for both types utilize AG magnetic fields to guide and focus the particles. This is not too surprising, since the development of the AG principle is still in its early stages; further elaboration and exploitation of the principle can be expected.

Accelerators for superhigh intensities must, almost by definition, be of the continuous-operation rather than the pulsed type, utilizing steady magnetic fields. We can also limit our speculations to those which produce sufficiently high energy to be in the range of interest of high-energy particle physics. Within these restrictions the most favored type is the isochronous cyclotron, discussed in Sec. 15-11. As mentioned, the fixed-field fixed-frequency cyclotron has the capability of being developed up to an energy of about 850 Mev, at which the integral resonance represents a practical limit. Intensities available from existing cyclotron ion sources will supply up to 20 ma of circulating beam, and much higher intensities could be obtained if suitable rf power sources for acceleration were available. Even if limited to 20 ma, the beam power at 850 Mev would be 17 megawatts! Engineering limitations on radiofrequency power and cooling are the most significant blockade to progress toward ultrahigh intensities, for this range of energies. Another major problem will result from the tremendous intensities of induced radioactivities produced in such a machine; remote-control devices would be required for most maintenance and repair operations, as in nuclear reactors.

With the outstanding success of the 30-Bev AG synchrotrons at CERN and Brookhaven, these high-energy pulsed machines have become strong competitors with the lower-energy continuous machines as high-intensity sources of secondary radiations. Such high energies lead to multiple production of mesons and increased output of hyperons, such that the most interesting secondary radiations have a more favorable ratio of intensity to background. The future may well show that the most intense beams of many secondary radiations will come from pulsed machines of the highest possible energies, rather than from lower-energy machines specifically designed for high-intensity primary beams.

The most practical present proposals of superenergy accelerators utilize the principle of the AG proton synchrotron. A study group at California Institute of Technology in the summer and fall of 1960, under the leadership of Prof. Matthew Sands, made a preliminary study and issued a report[29] on a proton AG synchrotron for 300 Bev. This speculative design study proposes a cascade synchrotron using two circular orbits—one of large aperture and small energy (10 Bev) for initial acceleration of a beam from an injection linac (50 Mev) and a second ring of small aperture and large radius (1300 m) for acceleration to 300 Bev. The beam would be extracted from the booster ring at 10 Bev in a single turn and injected into the larger orbit; studies of this transfer problem suggest that it is practical, using known techniques, and potentially highly efficient. Damping during acceleration in the booster accelerator will reduce the beam dimensions such that the aperture in the main ring accelerator can be made very small (2 cm by 5 cm), so the magnet is small and power requirements modest compared with the scaling factor. The AG magnet would consist of 1200 sectors of alternating gradients, using an equivalent n value of 8600 and producing 43.25 betatron wavelengths around the orbit.   In the judgment of several expert critics, the problems of orbit alignment and magnetic uniformity are within the scope of known techniques, and other parameters of the main accelerator and booster accelerator are not far outside the practical limits of present technology.   In the preliminary cost estimates it is interesting to note that the buildings, tunnels, and facilities represent about half the total cost, which is of the order of 125 million dollars.   In 1961, another design study for machines of 100 to 300 Bev was in progress at the Lawrence Radiation Laboratory of the University of California.   Still higher energies were under study at the Brookhaven National Laboratory and in the U.S.S.R.

Enthusiasts for other accelerator types have also speculated about ultimate limits and the practicality of much higher energies.   The proposed Stanford electron linear accelerator, which would be 2 miles long and initially powered to reach 15 Bev, could be extended by addition of many more rf power supplies to about 45 Bev, which would approach the technical limitations on maximum energy gain per unit length.   The cost of the initial installation is estimated as about 100 million dollars; the higher-energy modification might increase this cost by half.

Proton linacs are potential competitors for high intensities, but the costs involved in extending energies into the multi-Bev range seem excessive.   However, new technical concepts for increased efficiency of rf power transformation may change this situation.   Such developments will be spurred by the need for proton linacs as injectors into large magnetic accelerators.   Some designers conceive that a multi-Bev proton linac could be substituted for the booster synchrotron of the California Institute of Technology proposal, with significant improvement in the rate of cycling and the average beam intensity.

The electron synchrotron is limited by radiation loss caused by radial acceleration in the magnetic field used for containment.   However, this limit can be raised by use of very large orbits and very low magnetic fields. In an orbit the size of the main ring for 300-Bev protons of the California Institute of Technology study, electrons could be accelerated to 40 or 50 Bev before reaching this radiation loss limit, in a fast-pulsed magnet having very low peak magnetic fields (about 2000 gauss).   The radiofrequency power required to compensate for radiation loss would approach that needed for a linear accelerator and would be the most serious technical problem.

This speculative survey of possibilities indicates that there are no insurmountable technical limitations on the development of accelerators into the energy range of several hundred or even 1000 Bev.   However, the size and cost will be at least an order of magnitude larger than for existing machines.   Furthermore, each of these gigantic machines will require a major laboratory installation.   The complexity and cost of the apparatus and instruments required for meaningful experiments with modern high-energy accelerators have increased in recent years even more rapidly than for the accelerators themselves.   The cost of a large liquid-hydrogen bubble chamber and its associated facilities is in the range of 5 million dollars; analyzing magnets for momentum analysis of the secondary radiations are as large as cyclotron magnets; Cerenkov counters and scintillation counters are as large as washtubs; data reduction and analysis systems require full-scale computers.   The cost of the buildings, tunnels, and foundations to house and shield a large accelerator and its associated laboratories has become a dominant factor in the total cost, in some cases exceeding that for the machine and its power supplies.   Electric-power requirements have risen much faster than accelerator energy and are already taxing the available supply in some areas.   These trends will be continued in the ultra-high-energy machines of the future.   It is conceivable that the cost of the accelerators will be a small part of the total cost of such a laboratory installation.

The question to be resolved is not so much whether higher-energy or higher-intensity accelerators can be conceived and constructed, but whether the field of high-energy particle physics justifies the investment of major funds in the extensive laboratories which will be required.   One of the most significant factors is the need for a greatly expanded roster of scientists and engineers to staff the laboratories and conduct the experiments.   For example, the staff at Brookhaven for construction of the 33-Bev AGS was about 175; this is barely adequate for minimum operations and will have to be increased considerably for most efficient use. The demand for manpower to construct and operate new laboratories for superenergy machines may prove to be a basic limitation to the rate of development.

Such gigantic enterprises may well tax the resources of individual countries, but might have meaning if conceived as international laboratories.   The experiment in joint operation of a high-energy laboratory by the CERN group at Geneva, supported by 13 European countries, is an excellent illustration of the usefulness of such international cooperation.

It might be useful to summarize some of the more obvious factors involved in planning for an ultra-high-energy accelerator installation. Location of the site should be chosen for reasons better than those of political compromise.   It should be accessible to visiting scientists and so should be reasonably close to a major airport; it should have very large electric-power facilities close at hand; it should have pure water supplies for cooling; it should be within reach of heavy transportation facilities, and if possible close to a major industrial center.   The laboratory will require a large staff, and plans must include proper housing, recreational facilities, and opportunities for intellectual stimulation.   An important feature is close association with one or more major universities.

In choosing the type of accelerator and designing the system of components, several desirable features can be identified from past experience. It should be capable of providing for a wide variety of experimental uses, with multiple locations for targets and beams.   Very long beam runs are essential for experiments with high-energy particles; experimental areas should be planned to allow expansion of space and facilities.   A long duty cycle has many advantages over short pulses, for electronic detection experiments and for maximum intensity.   Yet, short beam pulses have their own special utility and should be provided by beam control systems. Reliability of operation is essential and should be designed into the system through maximum use of duplicate replaceable parts and components and by conservative design.   Simplicity, symmetry, and replaceability are good watchwords in design.

The history of accelerators is far from complete.   This glimpse of the future suggests that the opportunities for further development to still higher energies are as hopeful as at any time in the past.   As this book goes to press, the giant 30-Bev AG proton synchrotrons at CERN and Brookhaven are just coming into research operation, at an energy five times higher than that of earlier proton accelerators.   The Cambridge accelerator will shortly be completed, with electron energies also five times greater than those of existing machines.   Certainly, much will be learned in the next few years, from these and other high-energy machines and from advanced experiments in other laboratories.   Yet, in the minds of many responsible scientists the need for still higher energies is already evident. A basic justification is that the time scale for design and construction of ultra-high-energy machines is so long that design and planning must even anticipate the need, to provide a fast start when the evidence becomes clear.   As Robert Browning wrote many generations ago, "Ah, but a man's reach should exceed his grasp, or what's a heaven for?"

REFERENCES

1. L. H. Thomas, *Phys. Rev.*, **54**:580 (1938).
2. E. D. Courant, M. S. Livingston, and H. S. Snyder, *Phys. Rev.*, **88**:1190 (1952).
3. J. P. Blewett, *Phys. Rev.*, **88**:1197 (1952).
4. J. B. Adams, M. G. N. Hine, and J. D. Lawson, *Nature*, **171**:926 (1953).
5. "Design Study for a 15-Bev Accelerator," *MIT Research Lab. for Nuclear Sci. Tech. Rept. No.* **60** (June 30, 1953).
6. E. D. Courant, M. S. Livingston, H. S. Snyder, and J. P. Blewett, *Phys. Rev.*, **91**:202 (1953).
7. E. D. Courant and H. S. Snyder, *Ann. Phys.*, **3**:1 (1958).

8. V. V. Vladimirskij and E. K. Tarasov, *Z. Tekh. Fiz. (USSR)*, **26**:704 (1956).
9. "Lectures on the Theory and Design of an Alternating-gradient Proton Synchrotron" (CERN-PS Group, Geneva, 1953).
10. G. K. Green and E. D. Courant, *Handbuch der Physik*, **44**:320 (1959).
11. J. P. Blewett, Proceedings of CERN Symposium of 1956 (Geneva), p. 159.
12. N. C. Christofilos, Proceedings of CERN Symposium of 1956 (Geneva), p. 176.
13. Proceedings of International Conference on High Energy Accelerators and Instrumentation of 1959, Session 3A (Geneva).
14. K. W. Robinson, *Phys. Rev.*, **111**:373 (1958).
15. Proceedings of CERN Symposium of 1956 (Geneva), pp. 32, 36, and 44.
16. Proceedings of International Conference on High Energy Accelerators and Instrumentation of 1959, Session 2A (Geneva).
17. Proceedings of International Conference on High Energy Accelerators and Instrumentation of 1959 (Geneva), p. 359.
18. K. R. Symon, D. W. Kerst, L. W. Jones, L. J. Laslett, and K. M. Terwilliger, *Phys. Rev.*, **103**:1837 (1956).
19. F. T. Cole, R. O. Haxby, L. W. Jones, C. H. Pruett, and K. M. Terwilliger, *Rev. Sci. Instr.*, **28**:403 (1957).
20. D. W. Kerst, E. A. Day, H. J. Hausman, R. O. Haxby, L. J. Laslett, F. E. Mills, T. Ohkawa, F. L. Peterson, E. W. Rowe, A. M. Sessler, J. N. Snyder, and W. A. Wallenmeyer, *Rev. Sci. Instr.*, **31**:1076 (1960).
21. T. Ohkawa, *Rev. Sci. Instr.*, **29**:108 (1958).
22. Proceedings of International Conference on High Energy Accelerators and Instrumentation of 1959 (Geneva), p. 71.
23. E. L. Burshtein, V. I. Veksler, and A. A. Kolomenskij, USSR Acad. Sci., 1955, p. 3.
24. R. Keller, L. Dick, and M. Fidecaro, *Compt. rend. acad. sci. (Paris)*, **284**:3154 (1959).
25. E. L. Kelly, P. V. Pyle, R. L. Thornton, J. R. Richardson, and B. T. Wright, *Rev. Sci. Instr.*, **27**:493 (1956).
26. *Proc. Natl. Acad. Sci. (U.S.) Publ.* 656 (Feb. 2–4, 1959).
27. Proceedings of CERN Symposium of 1956 (Geneva), pp. 68 and 80.
28. Proceedings of International Conference on High Energy Accelerators and Instrumentation of 1959 (Geneva), pp. 139 and 160.
29. M. Sands, "A Proton Synchrotron for 300 Gev," Report No. 10, Synchrotron Laboratory, California Institute of Technology (June 30, 1960).

Name Index

Subject Index